WORLD
ENCYCLOPEDIA
OF
POLICE FORCES
AND
PENAL SYSTEMS

WORLD ENCYCLOPEDIA OF POLICE FORCES AND PENAL SYSTEMS

George Thomas Kurian

Facts On File®
New York・Oxford

World Encyclopedia of Police Forces and Penal Systems

copyright © 1989 by George Thomas Kurian

Library of Congress Cataloging-in-Publication Data

Kurian, George Thomas.
   World encyclopedia of police forces and penal systems.
   Includes index.
   1. Police—Dictionaries. 2. Corrections—Dictionar-
ies. 3. Criminal law—Dictionaries. I. Title.
HV7901.K87 1988   363.2'03   88-3553
ISBN 0-8160-1019-6

British CIP data available on request
Printed in the United States of America
10 9 8 7 6 5 4 3 2 1

CONTENTS

Introduction	ix

MAJOR COUNTRIES

Afghanistan	1
Albania	3
Algeria	4
Angola	6
Argentina	8
Australia	11
Austria	20
Bangladesh	25
Belgium	27
Bolivia	30
Botswana	33
Brazil	37
Bulgaria	40
Burma	43
Burundi	45
Cameroon	47
Canada	49
Chad	59
Chile	61
China	64
Colombia	69
Congo	79
Costa Rica	81
Cuba	85
Cyprus	89
Czechoslovakia	91
Denmark	94
Dominican Republic	97
Ecuador	99
Egypt	102
El Salvador	107
Ethiopia	109
Fiji	113
Finland	115
France	127
Germany (East)	136
Germany (West)	138
Ghana	146
Greece	152
Guatemala	155
Guinea	157
Guyana	159
Haiti	161
Honduras	162
Hong Kong	163
Hungary	168
India	171
Indonesia	179
Iran	184
Iraq	188
Ireland	190
Israel	192
Italy	197
Ivory Coast	204
Jamaica	208
Japan	211
Jordan	220
Kampuchea	224
Kenya	225
Korea (North)	230
Korea (South)	232
Kuwait	236
Laos	238
Lebanon	239
Lesotho	241
Liberia	244
Libya	247
Madagascar	249
Malawi	250
Malaysia	252
Mauritania	257
Mexico	258
Mongolia	262
Morocco	264
Mozambique	269
Nepal	270
Netherlands	272
New Zealand	282
Nicaragua	284
Nigeria	286
Norway	295
Pakistan	297
Panama	302
Papua New Guinea	305
Paraguay	307
Peru	309
Philippines	312
Poland	315
Portugal	318
Puerto Rico	322
Romania	324
Rwanda	326
Saudi Arabia	328
Senegal	331
Sierra Leone	333
Singapore	335
Somalia	339
South Africa	343

Spain	347	Falkland Islands	506
Sri Lanka	350	French Guiana	507
Sudan	352	Gabon	507
Swaziland	354	Gambia	508
Sweden	356	Gibraltar	509
Switzerland	362	Grenada	509
Syria	366	Guadeloupe	510
Taiwan	368	Guinea-Bissau	510
Tanzania	371	Iceland	511
Thailand	374	Kiribati	512
Trinidad and Tobago	378	Liechtenstein	513
Tunisia	381	Luxembourg	513
Turkey	385	Macau	515
Uganda	389	Maldives	515
Union of Soviet Socialist Republics	391	Mali	516
United Kingdom	401	Malta	517
United States	416	Mauritius	518
Uruguay	468	Monaco	519
Venezuela	470	Montserrat	521
Vietnam	473	Nauru	521
Yemen Arab Republic	477	Netherlands Antilles	522
Yemen (South)	478	Niger	522
Yugoslavia	479	Oman	523
Zaire	481	Qatar	524
Zambia	484	St. Helena	525
Zimbabwe	487	St. Kitts-Nevis	525
		St. Lucia	526
		St. Vincent and the Grenadines	527

SMALLER COUNTRIES AND MICROSTATES

		San Marino	527
		São Tomé and Príncipe	528
Andorra	491	Seychelles	528
Anguilla	491	Solomon Islands	531
Antigua and Barbuda	492	Suriname	532
Bahamas	492	Togo	532
Bahrain	494	Tonga	533
Barbados	494	Turks and Caicos	534
Belize	496	Tuvalu	534
Benin	496	United Arab Emirates	535
Bermuda	497	Vanuatu	536
Bhutan	498	Vatican	537
Brunei	499	Western Samoa	537
Burkina Faso	500		
Cape Verde	501		
Cayman Islands	501	Appendix I Interpol	539
Central African Republic	502	Appendix II World Police Directory	551
Comoros	503	Appendix III Bibliography	563
Cook Islands	503	Appendix IV Comparative Statistics on Police	
Djibouti	504	Protection	565
Dominica	505		
Equatorial Guinea	506	Index	569

INTRODUCTION

The *World Encyclopedia of Police Forces and Penal Systems* is a descriptive survey of the national law enforcement and corrections systems of 183 countries of the world. Police forces and corrections are the two ends of the criminal justice pipeline, and this encyclopedia brings them together as a continuum. Excluded from the survey is the middle segment of the pipeline, comprising the courts and the legal system, which will be fully described in my forthcoming *World Legal Encyclopedia*.

Even though criminal justice science is coming into its own as a major discipline, police and corrections remain among the least studied institutions of human society and ones on which the least information is available on a global basis to scholars and researchers. In the 19th century, economics was known as the "dismal science" because it dealt with such unpleasant things as taxes, rent, and interest. Economics has vacated this name today, and the title has fallen on criminal justice science. The reasons for this are twofold. The first is the instinctive and historical academic distrust of the more forbidding aspects of police and correctional studies, and the second is the uncommunicative nature of police and penal professionals who see little practical benefit in scholarly investigation. The attention of dogged researchers needs to be focused on police and penal institutions for a number of decades to bring available information to the level of at least that obtaining in related fields, such as military science. What is currently available in the police and corrections fields is of very poor quality and there are gaps that cannot be closed without more sustained cooperation from national governments.

Information on police forces and penal systems is not only meager and uneven, but it is heavily concentrated in certain areas of law enforcement to the exclusion of others. For example, reasonably reliable information is available for most countries on the structure and organization of the police establishment, but very little is available on education, recruitment and training, and much less on police history. The problem is particularly severe in the case of East European countries and the least-developed countries (LDCs), the former for political reasons and the latter for economic reasons. The situation is not helped by the fact that Interpol, the major international police organization representing *most* noncommunist nations of the world, does not have a competent publishing or data collection program and has never taken a strong initiative in promoting police studies. It depends on the voluntary cooperation of its members for input into its irregularly published *International Crime Statistics*. Further, this publication provides only strict crime data and does not deal with law enforcement forces.

The state of the art in law enforcement data is reflected in the organization of this work, particularly in the length of the individual chapters and the intensity of discussion on the various topics in the schema. While every effort was made to present information in a uniform and consistent manner for all countries, gaps in available information were too insurmountable in the case of the minicountries, which make up nearly one-third of the nations of the world. In order to overcome this deficiency, countries have been divided into two groups: Major Countries and Smaller Countries and Microstates. With a few exceptions, all countries with populations of over 500,000 are placed in the first group. However, the basic criterion is the availability of information and not the size of the population. Thus Seychelles appears in the first group and Benin in the second group.

Within each chapter, information is organized under four headings: History and Background; Structure and Organization; Recruitment, Education and Training; and Penal System. This basic pattern of arrangement, used in general throughout the book, has been modified in some cases to suit the needs of the particular entries. In some cases, there was no information on History and Background to warrant the inclusion of that section. Where there is no information on Recruitment, Education and Training, it is so noted under that heading. The guiding purpose in the organization of material has been to achieve the maximum consistency and clarity of presentation given the limitations of the subject matter and available information.

The primary inspiration for this work came from Edward W. Knappman, executive vice president of Facts On File. Over the long years of its gestation, his confidence in this project never wavered and his patience—perhaps the rarest of publishing virtues—never ran out. The project was fortunate in having a very supportive editor in Kate Kelly, whose competence is laced with buoyant humor. My thanks are also due to William D. Drennan, whose copy-editing skills are evidenced in the pages that follow.

During the course of collecting information, I drew heavily on the unstinted help of Philip John Stead, former dean of John Jay College of Criminal Justice in New York City, and one of the world's best known authorities on police systems. He was a pillar of strength for the project, and his unfailing kindness can be only inadequately acknowledged in this brief Introduction. I am also much indebted to Patrick Edobar Igbinovia, a Nigerian scholar, whose diligence is attested by eight chapters in this book and whose dedication to criminal justice studies is matched by few other professionals I have known. Finally, I must acknowledge the assistance of my daughter, Sarah Kurian, who helped with the organization of materials and the compilation of statistics.

George Thomas Kurian
Yorktown Heights, New York

MAJOR COUNTRIES

AFGHANISTAN

BASIC FACT SHEET

Official Name: Democratic Republic of Afghanistan
Area: 647,497 sq km
Population: 14,183,671 (1987)
Capital: Kabul
Nature of Government: Communist dictatorship
Languages: Pushtu and Dari
Currency: Afghani
GNP: $3.52 billion (1985)
Territorial Divisions: 29 provinces
Population per Police Officer: 540
Police Expenditures per 1,000: N.A.

History & Background

For centuries, until the accession of Abdur Rahman Shah in 1880, public order on a countrywide basis was nonexistent. Each tribe defined proper behavior for its members, trying and punishing offenders for violations of tribal codes. Intertribal relations were, more often than not, governed by armed force. Tribal chiefs and village leaders regarded themselves as independent rulers over their respective areas, and they treated those who traveled through their domains according to their whims. Brigands and robbers were common, preying mostly on passing caravans and travelers.

Abdur Rahman (1881–1901), a strong and forceful ruler, began early to establish order. He applied these laws universally and forcefully, although many of them conflicted with tribal customs, such as Pushtunwali, the code of conduct for Pushtuns. He organized Muslim courts and tribunals to deal with crimes against the state, property and person. Abdur Rahman personally presided over the trials of all serious cases. His decisions often reflected a crude sense of fair play, but his punishments were occasionally harsh and capricious. Common punishments included amputation of a hand or foot and blinding. The official "blinder" became a prominent member of Abdul Rahman's court. Maximum punishments were reserved for those offenses that caused misery to others and exploited the poor. The death penalty was common and included such forms of execution as death by starving and stoning and being blown from a cannon. Ordinary prisoners were required to pay for their food as well as for the use of their cells.

The amir greatly increased his police force and installed a network of informers and agents. In Kabul one of every four able-bodied adults was engaged in some form of police work.

Abdur Rahman's policies were generally continued under his successors, Habibullah Khan, Amanullah Khan, Nadir Shah and Mohammad Zahir Shah. In 1942 the gendarmerie was established and placed under the Ministry of the Interior. It took over police tasks in the rural parts of the country from the police and the military. The police was limited to urban areas. In the 1950s, a National Police Academy was established in Kabul and a number of police officers received special training in the United States under an AID agreement. The program was terminated in 1959 and replaced by a similar one with West Germany.

Structure & Organization

Police functions are performed by the Army, the National Police, and the Afghan Gendarmerie. In general, the police work in large urban areas and the gendarmerie in rural areas. The strength of these two groups is unofficially estimated at 50,000. Both agencies are under the Ministry of the Interior's Police and Gendarmerie Department. Traffic police, however, is under the Provincial Administration Department of the Ministry of the Interior.

The National Police fall into two categories: municipal and provincial. The Municipal Police maintains public order in the organized cities and towns. They also operate prisons and jails, arrest criminals, investigate criminal cases, serve summonses, guard government buildings and escort government vehicles. The Provincial Police, under the authority of the

1

provincial governor, maintain public order in rural areas and in towns that do not have a formal municipal government. All civil police forces wear the same uniform, patterned after that of the Army, but with certain distinguishing police patches. Normally, the police are posted in pairs and carry side arms. On night patrol or emergency missions provincial police usually carry a rifle as an additional weapon.

Each of the larger cities, except Kabul, has a small group of civil police under the direction of a chief of police, an official on the staff of the mayor. They function as a city police force and are paid from the municipal funds. The Kabul police is under the general supervision of the State Department of Police.

The Afghan Gendarmerie is the rural and frontier police force and operates in those areas not covered by the National Police or the Army. Its tasks include garrisoning of some of the less important frontier posts, patrolling sensitive stretches of the border, occupying important road checkpoints, and settling or suppressing disturbances in rural areas. Some of these functions have been taken over by the Army since the Soviet occupation of the country.

The gendarmes are usually mounted, but some safety patrols along the main roads employ small trucks or jeeps. In addition to these patrols, manned posts are established at various intervals in the difficult mountain pass regions. Other duties assigned to the gendarmerie include escorting government convoys, guarding vital installations, providing emergency aid, checking on military exemptions and deferments, collecting conscripts for the Army, and apprehending deserters and conscript evaders.

Recruitment, Education & Training

No information is available on recruitment and training under the present regime.

The Penal System

The penal system was originally designed to enforce punishments imposed by court sentences. Since the overthrow of the monarchy, the government has initiated certain actions directed toward the rehabilitation of prisoners. Among these are an expanded training program and the establishment of a reform school for juvenile delinquents. In addition, private associations in certain provinces have taken steps to help women prisoners through rehabilitation classes.

In past years, the government tended to use prison labor to produce wares, especially clothing, for the military. More recently stress has been laid on the teaching of trades and handicrafts, permitting inmates to retain the money earned from the sale of their products. Stonemasonry, pottery making, and rug and carpet weaving are among the most common trades and crafts taught.

Almost all cities and towns have jails, and the larger administrative and population centers have prisons. In villages where gendarmerie posts are located, a lockup room is maintained for the detention of prisoners pending their further disposition. Food for prisoners is commonly furnished by relatives or friends; otherwise the accuser is called upon to provide it. Provincial and central government officials make periodic inspections of jails and prisons.

Bail has never been a regular feature of Afghan law. In cases of common crimes involving wealthy persons or those with good connections, bail is sometimes granted. Corruption, however, is so widespread that it is possible for families of people detained for common crimes to obtain their release after paying bribes to the police or other officials.

There are no effective constitutional or legal safeguards against arbitrary arrest or detention. The principal internal security organ is KHAD (Khidamate Atilaati Daulati), which has extensive powers to detain and question suspects. Warrants are not used, nor is the right of habeas corpus respected. Formal charges are brought only after months of interrogation, and prisoners languish incommunicado during this period. Torture and physical and psychological intimidation remain standard techniques used by KHAD.

Statistics on crime are not collected or published on a national basis. Indications, based on fragmentary information, are that smuggling, pocket picking, burglary and theft rank highest in incidence. Because of revenge traditions rooted in tribal honor, homicide ranks highest among the serious crimes. Water and property rights are vital in the predominantly agricultural communities, and disputes concerning these rights frequently end in violence. Few professional thieves or burglars are involved in reported crimes. First offenders predominate, because the graduated system of punishments serves as a deterrent to recidivism. Most pocket picking is done by children, usually girls and boys between nine and 14 years of age. When arrested, these juvenile offenders are normally released on bond into the custody of their parents, in the absence of juvenile detention homes.

Death sentences are carried out by shooting by the Army or gendarmerie personnel. Convicts are sentenced to hard labor on roads, canals, or other public works projects. Flogging, common in the past, has become increasingly rare.

ALBANIA

BASIC FACT SHEET

Official Name: People's Socialist Republic of Albania
Area: 28,748 sq km
Population: 3,085,985 (1987)
Capital: Tirana
Nature of Government: Communist dictatorship
Language: Albanian
Currency: Lek
GNP: $2.9 billion (1986)
Territorial Divisions: 26 districts
Population per Police Officer: 550
Police Expenditures per 1,000: N.A.

Structure & Organization

Police and security forces are under the control of the Ministry of the Interior. They are organized into three directorates: the Directorate of State Security, Frontier Guards and the People's Police. The state security force, as is the case in Communist countries, takes precedence over all other forces and is designed as an apparatus for uncovering and destroying enemies of the regime. Frontier Guards patrol the borders. The People's Police are municipal police who perform the functions normally discharged by police forces in other countries.

The Directorate of State Security (Drejtorija e Sigurimit te Shtetit, commonly called Sigurimi) is organized into four battalions and has more plainclothes policemen than uniformed. Its stated mission is to prevent counterrevolution and to eliminate opposition to the party. The Sigurimi has seven sections: political, censorship, public records, prison camp, two sections for counterespionage, and a foreign service. There is also a foreign service section. Sigurimi is in charge of the political indoctrination of prisoners and others considered socially dangerous.

The Frontier Guards are organized into five battalions. Although organized along military lines, it is under the Ministry of the Interior. Guards are trained at the Guard School in Tirana. Guards personnel are recruited by conscription but carefully screened for political orientation.

The People's Police has five branches: the Police for Economic Objectives, Communications Police, Fire Police, Detention Police and General Police. The General Police functions overlap those of the security police to some extent, but the former operate on a purely local level. Each municipal headquarters has a political commissar in addition to an operational commander.

Recruitment, Education & Training

A 1948 law requires all able-bodied men to serve two months in an auxiliary police capacity. They serve without pay, but wear regular police uniforms with a red armband.

The Penal System

No crime statistics have ever been published in the country. Similarly, no information is available on penal institutions.

ALGERIA

BASIC FACT SHEET

Official Name: Democratic and Popular Republic of Algeria
Area: 2,381,471 sq km
Population: 23,460,614 (1987)
Capital: Algiers
Nature of Government: One-party dictatorship
Language: Arabic
Currency: Dinar
GNP: $57 billion (1985)
Territorial Divisions: 31 wilayas (provinces), 161 dairat (districts), 691 communes
Population per Police Officer: 840
Police Expenditures per 1,000: N.A.

Structure & Organization

Primary responsibility for the maintenance of law and order and for internal security is exercised jointly by Algeria's two separate police organizations: the Gendarmerie Nationale and the Sûreté Nationale. Both agencies were constituted soon after Algerian independence in 1962 and modeled on the police system of Metropolitan France. Both employ French procedures, and much of the equipment was supplied by France. In 1971, however, French assistance was suspended because of political differences between the two countries over the Western Sahara issue.

The Gendarmerie Nationale, a component of the Army (ANP, Armée Nationale Populaire), is the main rural police force. It has been described as a national guard on permanent active duty. Because of its size, training, equipment inventory and tactical deployment capability, it is highly regarded as a versatile and competent paramilitary force. Its personnel strength was estimated in the mid-1980s at 20,000.

The chief responsibilities of the Gendarmerie Nationale are to maintain law and order in rural areas, provide security surveillance of local inhabitants, and symbolize central government authority in traditionally lawless regions. Its units made major contributions to the suppression of the *wilaya* insurgency in 1963 and 1964 and of Colonel Taher Zbiri's attempted coup in 1967.

The Gendarmerie Nationale is organized into battalions, with companies and platoons stationed separately in villages along the coast, in such remote mountainous regions as the Kabylie and the Aures, and in plateau villages between the coast and the desert. A highly mobile force, the Gendarmerie Nationale uses both motor and animal transport, while a modern communications system interconnects its various units with each other, with the Army and with the Ministry of Defense. Gendarmerie Nationale equipment includes light infantry weapons and armored cars with mounted machine guns and light cannons.

Although dependent on ANP general staff for logistical assistance and for reinforcement in major disturbances, the Gendarmerie Nationale is largely autonomous as an operational force. Its commander is an Army colonel who reports directly to the Minister of Defense and the president.

The Sûreté Nationale is the principal police force in cities and urban centers. It is charged with the maintenance of law and order, the protection of life and property, the investigation of crimes and the apprehension of offenders. In addition, it performs other routine police functions, including traffic control. Total personnel strength is not revealed but is estimated at about 50,000.

Subordinated administratively to the Ministry of the Interior and commanded by a director general, the Sûreté Nationale is organized generally along the lines of its French counterpart, with operational and investigative branches and supporting services. The Judiciary Police branch, for example, is responsible for criminal investigations, working in close coordination with the office of public prosecutor in the Ministry of Justice. Police units assigned to the capitals of the *wilayyat* (provinces) are under the nominal control of the governors. In daily operations, the Sûreté Nationale is clearly distinguished as a uniformed national metropolitan force under the direct control of the

Minister of the Interior. Elements of the Sûreté Nationale also play a role in countersubversive activities, formerly carried out by the Compagnie Nationale de Sécurité.

Although the Ministry of the Interior operates a customs service, the Sûreté Nationale assigns police contingents to work with customs inspectors at all legal points of entry. Their main concern is to apprehend undesirable immigrants and traffickers in contraband. Police assigned to seaport precincts operate under the control of the National Port Office, which is responsible for security in the maritime zones.

Recruitment, Education & Training

Some French instructors continued to work with the Algerian police well into the 1980s. Initially, both the Gendarmerie Nationale and the Sûreté Nationale recruited among the former freedom fighters. Since then, pay and conditions of service have been maintained at levels sufficient to attract qualified recruits. Both organizations operate their own schools: the Gendarmerie Nationale's main training center is at Sidi Bel Abbes, the former headquarters of the French Foreign Legion. Officers are trained at Sidi Mohammed and El Harrach. Information on the locations of the Sûreté Nationale training schools is not available.

The Penal System

Little information is available regarding the country's penal system, which includes large central prisons in Algiers, Medea, Berrouaghia, Oran, Tlemcen and Constantine. There is at least one jail in each *wilaya*. Supervision and operation of the penal system are coordinated by the Ministry of Justice.

Persons convicted of civil crimes are sent to provincial civil prisons, while those found guilty of more serious crimes against the state or crimes that carry the death penalty are sent to one of three penitentiaries. Conditions in penitentiaries are reported to be much worse than those in the civil prisons. Prisoners are often crowded together, and sanitary and medical arrangements are poor. Each prison has a contract with a local doctor who visits the prison to treat ill prisoners, while seriously ill prisoners are sent to local hospitals. Prisoners are generally fed a bland and starchy diet, augmented by provisions and meals from their families. Families are allowed to visit civil prisons once a week.

The Constitution provides that no one may be prosecuted, arrested or held except as provided by law. It also limits detention for questioning in criminal investigation cases to 48 hours, after which the suspect must be charged or released. The Penal Code provides for informing detainees immediately of charges against them. Algerian law does not provide a bail system. Lawyers are allowed 24-hour access to their clients. Such meetings take place under the supervision of a guard.

Inviolability of the home is guaranteed by the Constitution and generally is honored in practice except in rare cases involving military security. Police may not enter a house without a warrant from the local prosecutor or investigating magistrate, nor may they enter a residence during night hours.

In the absence of official statistics on crime, the incidence of crime in Algeria can be deduced only from fragmentary sources. Most crime reported in the press consists of offenses against persons, property, public morals and the economic system. Since independence there has been an upswing of crime in the larger cities of Algiers, Oran, Annaba and Constantine. As in other countries, the police blame the judiciary for leniency toward criminals, while the judges cite larger caseloads and insufficient investigation by the police as contributory causes for the rise in the crime rates.

The majority of crimes against property consists of petty thefts, stolen automobiles and store break-ins. Only a small portion of these crimes is cleared by arrest. Other offenses include prostitution, vagrancy and drug abuse. Prostitution is illegal, although certain houses of prostitution are permitted to operate. Begging is also illegal, and numerous arrests on charges of vagrancy are made each year. A more serious problem is drug trafficking, especially in hashish, emanating from the Rif area of Morocco. In 1975 the government amended its penal code to mandate the death penalty for drug dealers and smugglers.

Algeria's strict gun control laws have served to keep serious-crime rates from rising even higher. The Penal Code prohibits the sale and possession by private individuals of all firearms. Only the police and the uniformed members of the ANP may possess pistols, revolvers and automatic weapons. Police also exert efforts to maintain control of concealed dangerous weapons, such as daggers and knives.

The criminal acts of greatest concern to the national government are those defined by the Penal Code as "economic offenses," which cover a broad range of activities, including corruption, misuse of public funds, strikes or work stoppages by public workers and food hoarding. Penalties for economic crimes are unusually severe, ranging from heavy fines and long prison terms to the death penalty. In contrast to other developing countries, corruption is readily and openly denounced in the semiofficial press.

ANGOLA

BASIC FACT SHEET

Official Name: People's Republic of Angola
Area: 1,246,700 sq km
Population: 7,950,244 (1987)
Capital: Luanda
Nature of Government: Marxist dictatorship
Language: Portuguese
Currency: Kwanza
GNP: $3 billion (1986)
Territorial Divisions: 18 provinces
Population per Police Officer: N.A.
Police Expenditures per 1,000: N.A.

History & Background

The national police force, known as the People's Police Corps of Angola (Corpo de Policia Popular de Angola [CPPA]), was created on February 28, 1978, at about the same time that the civil war was drawing to a close. Most of its personnel were transferred from the ranks of the Forces Armadas Populares de Libertação de Angola (FAPLA).

Structure & Organization

CPPA is lead by a commander who is also a member of the Central Committee of the MPLA Labor Party. Other CPPA officer grades are comparable to those in the military. Lower-ranking police personnel are referred to as sergeants and agents. The main headquarters is located in Luanda and is subordinate to the Ministry of Defense. Organizationally, CPPA is compartmentalized according to functions and is believed to have sections or divisions covering criminal activities, traffic, railroads, ports and harbors, and mining. Military police are frequently mentioned in news reports, but their responsibilities are not defined, nor are their functions vis-à-vis those of the regular police. The military police was one of the units reportedly purged after the May 1977 coup attempt.

There are police commands in the provincial capitals and police squadrons below the provincial level. It is not known how much of the country is under actual CPPA control because of continuing guerrilla warfare. The principal training academy is the Kapolo Martyrs Practical Police School in Luanda, where the training is both political and technical. Political indoctrination of police recruits has increased since the

MPLA Congress of December 1977, and party cells have been established in the smallest police groups. A political commissariat exists at the main police headquarters, and all CPPA officers receive FAPLA training as political teachers.

In addition to the CPPA, there is another police organization, known as the Directorate of Information and Security of Angola (Direção de Informação a Seguranca de Angola, DISA), set up by East German advisers. Little is known about this organization except that it is the national security police, combining intelligence-gathering and criminal investigation. DISA is directly subordinate to the president of the republic ratehr than to the minister of defense, as is CPPA.

In 1978 the government established the State Secretariat for Internal Order as a supervisory and advisory board within the office of the president. The secretariat was charged with the prevention of a broad range of crimes, including those involving firearms and explosives.

Recruitment, Education & Training

Since 1978 a voluntary system of recruitment has been in force. The CPPA runs a training school, staffed by Cubans, for new recruits in Luanda.

The Penal System

At the end of the civil war, MPLA took over the colonial prison system, which had been heavily damaged during the conflict. Many facilities were looted. The immediate task of the new government was to rebuild the system and to train personnel to take over its operation. The National School of Penal Technology opened in 1976, and its students were sent to Cuba for specialized training in penology.

The operation of the penal system is the responsibility of the Ministry of Justice. The system consists of maximum- and minimum-security prisons; and so-called production camps, where prisoners are sent to be rehabilitated through regular work and reeducation programs. There is less constraint at production camps, although the inmates are still under guard. The treatment of the prisoners varies according to their behavior and degree of rehabilitation. A Danish mariner, Paul Matthieson, traveling alone along the West Coast of Africa in 1977, developed engine trouble and entered an Angolan port. He was promptly imprisoned and was held for about five months until the Danish authorities demanded his release. Recuperating in a hospital, Matthieson provided the only available first-hand account of an Angolan prison, which he said was "indescribable." Mistreatment of political pris-

oners is common, including parading them in public, solitary confinement, physical intimidation and prolonged use of force. In 1984 the Angolan government was cited by the ILO for violation of ILO Convention 105, which prohibits the use of forced prison labor.

Crime statistics have not been reported by the Angolan government since it came to power, and newspaper references to crime are rare. Given the unsettled political and economic conditions in the country, violent crimes are probably on the rise. The Ministry of Justice's periodic summaries of criminal justice activities refer to assault, drug trafficking and diamond smuggling as the major problems but without giving any details. The *Jornal de Angola* occasionally reports on police sweeps through Luanda districts to counter criminal activity by "enemies of the revolution who live by plundering and exploiting the people."

CRIME STATISTICS (1984)

		Number Reported	Attempts %	Cases Solved %	Crime per 100,000	Offenders	Females %	Juveniles %	Strangers %
1.	Murder	717		89.12	10.3	339		0.98	
2.	Sex offenses, including rape	1,309		86.86	18.31	480		4.04	
3.	Rape	427		84.77	5.97	299		6.79	
4.	Serious assault	26		65.38	0.36	11		4.00	
5.	All theft	5,446		59.25	76.16	2,966		3.48	
6.	Aggravated theft	515		67.37	7.20	230		2.15	
7.	Robbery and violent theft								
8.	Breaking and entering								
9.	Auto theft								
10.	Other thefts	4,931		58.4	68.96	2,736		3.63	
11.	Fraud	631		85.89	8.82	285		0.63	
12.	Counterfeiting								
13.	Drug offenses	491		93.27	6.87	249		4.07	
14.	Total offenses	17,166		77.59	240.05	7,162		3.00	

Criteria of juveniles: aged from 7 to 15 years.
Note: Information for some categories is not available.

ARGENTINA

BASIC FACT SHEET

Official Name: Argentine Republic
Area: 2,766,889 sq km
Population: 31,144,755 (1987)
Capital: Buenos Aires
Nature of Government: Parliamentary democracy
Language: Spanish
Currency: Austral
GNP: $63.3 billion (1985)
Territorial Divisions: 22 provinces, 1 district, 1 territory
Population per Police Officer: 1,270
Police Expenditures per 1,000: $8,429

History & Background

Argentina's national police establishment consists of
two principal elements: the Federal Police and the
provincial police forces. The older agency, the Federal Police (Policia Federal) was established in 1880
and in 1943 its authority was extended to the provinces, giving it jurisdiction over all federal crimes,
including political offenses. It was reorganized in
1971 and placed under a high-ranking command officer of the armed forces. The force is directly subordinate to the Ministry of the Interior and maintains
its headquarters in the capital. In the mid-1980s it had
a strength of some 25,000

Structure & Organization

Police headquarters is organized into a number of
superintendencies and directorates charged with various functions and responsibilities. The two principal
superintendencies are Investigations (Investigaciónes)
and Federal Security (Seguridad Federal). The superintendency of investigations comprises four departments: Intelligence, Narcotics, Surveillance and Special Services, and Financial Offenses. The
superintendency of federal security comprises the Department of Presidential and Congressional Surveillance; the Aviation Department; and the Directorate
of the Interior, which is divided into Cultural and
Student Affairs, Foreign Affairs, Records and Information, and Tactical. The Records and Information
Division controls the granting of identity cards worldwide. Also subordinate to the chief of the Federal
Police are the Directorate General of Traffic; the
Directorate General of Federal Protection, in charge

of civil defense; the Directorate General of Urban
protection, which includes the superintendency of
firemen; and the Superintendency of Police Establishments, which runs the Higher School of Police, the
NCO School and the Cadet School, all in Buenos
Aires.

There are three other directorates concerned with
corollary activities of the police force apart from law
enforcement. These are Communications, Social Work
and Health, and General Secretariat. The first operates
the police telephone and radio and telegraph networks;
the second runs medical facilities for policemen and
prisoners; and the third has charge of police archives,
issues regulations and bulletins, and operates the police libraries, museum and bands.

The Federal Security and Investigations directorates
constitute the operational units. The Investigations
Directorate conducts criminal investigations and
maintains identification files. It operates most of the
police technical facilities and has charge of the crime
laboratory. Its jurisdiction, however, is limited to the
capital, and federal investigative functions in the provinces are carried out by the regional police offices.
The policemen on the beat, traffic officers and all
federal uniformed police (with the exception of women
police) are under the Federal Security Directorate,
which is divided into Burglaries and Thefts, Drug
Prevention, Fraud and Embezzlements, Harbors,
Murder, Personal Security, Police Liaison, Vehicle
Thefts, and Vice. There is also an infantry Guard
Corps, including the Mounted Police Corps.

The grade structure of the Federal Police is made
up of two categories: officers and enlisted personnel.
There is no provision for advancement from enlisted

to officer status, and a candidate must attend the two-year course at the Colonel Ramón L. Falcón Police Academy to attain officer status. Officer grades below inspector general, the highest police level, range from subadjutant officer up to senior inspector.

Basic enlisted police become patrolmen after a short period as probationary agents. Noncommissioned officer ranks start with corporal and advance through first corporal, sergeant, first sergeant, clerk noncommissioned officer, adjutant noncommissioned officer and principal noncommissioned officer. The highest enlisted rank authorized for the women police is first sergeant. Officers are periodically required to attend advanced courses at the Superior Police School. Recruitment is limited to those between 19 and 26 years of age.

Dark blue tunics and trousers are worn by all ranks, together with a cap of the same color. Blue shorts and black ties complete the uniform. Officers carry a pistol holstcr suspended from a jacket pocket, while other ranks have a Sam Browne belt for the purpose. All ranks carry a pistol, usually 9mm, while policewomen are issued .38 pistols.

The provincial police are concerned principally with crime falling within the realm of provincial jurisdiction. In cases involving federal jurisdiction, they are subordinate to the regional police office of the Federal Police in their area. In some of the border provinces there is a degree of overlapping of provincial authority because of the jurisdiction of the National Gendarmerie over international boundaries and frontier zones. The provincial police are similar in structure and operation to the Federal Police. However, the provincial police are not up to the standards of the federal or Buenos Aires force. Equipment is of lower quality, personnel are not as competent or well trained and pay scales are lower. Many of the larger provinces have their own police academies, but their facilities and programs do not meet the high standards of the federal academy.

The provincial police are under the control of the provincial governor and in most cases are commanded by an inspector general or chief. Staff structures conform closely to the federal pattern but are usually less elaborate and have fewer directorates or other subdivisions. Larger cities also have a municipal police whose operations are confined to the limits of the urban area. These provide citywide police services, including traffic control, with centralized guidance from the provincial police headquarters. In rural areas, provincial police are organized into divisions, commissariats, subcommissariats and detachments. Because of a shortage of motor vehicles, many patrols are carried out on horseback.

The Buenos Aires Police Force (Policia de la Provincia de Buenos Aires) comprises three investigation brigades—Center, North and West—and also a Commissariat for the Surveillance and Guard of the Presidential Palace. In addition, there is a Security Guard Detachment in the Avellaneda area and a Highway Patrol Division.

The paramilitary Argentine Gendarmerie is in charge of border control, with 20,000 men organized into three regional commands with headquarters at Córdoba, Bahía Blanca and Rosario, respectively. Its echelon consists of battalions, squadrons, groups and sections. The gendarmerie also includes an aviation section with several light aircraft.

In 1973 a National Intelligence Center was created to coordinate the intelligence agencies of the Federal Police and the armed forces. Its principal component was simply known as SIDE (Secretaria de Información de Estado). Under the military junta rule, it carried out antisubversive activities and channeled strategic national security intelligence to the president and the National Security Council (Consejo Nacional de Seguridad, CONASE).

Recruitment, Education, & Training

The Superintendency of Police Training Establishments runs the police schools, all of which are open to the personnel of the provincial forces: the Higher School of Police, the NCO School and the Cadet School. All the schools are in Buenos Aires.

The Penal System

Penologists consider Argentina's prison system to be one of the most outstanding in Latin America. There are both federal and provincial prisons, but not every province has both. In all, the system includes some 15 federal and 60 provincial institutions. Although federal prisons are better run, those of Santa Fe and Buenos Aires are reputedly among the best.

Federal prisons are under the jurisdiction of the General Directorate of Penal Institutions and the Ministry of the Interior. The directorate is headed by a director general, who is advised by a council composed of a professor of penal law, the director of psychiatric services, the chief of the National Prison and Criminal Registry, and the director of the Released Convicts Welfare Agency. Similar agencies are found in the provinces.

Approximately half of the total prison population is in federal prisons and the remainder in provincial institutions. The Penal Code provides for incarcerating provincial prisoners in national facilities if their sentence is over five years and if local facilities are not available. Federal offenders may also be placed in provincial institutions. Many prisoners are given an opportunity to work, for which they are paid.

The federal penal institutions are modern and well

built with adequate quarters and workshops, and their personnel are well trained and well equipped. The federal institutions include several prison farms and "open door" facilities where trustworthy prisoners are subject to minimum security restrictions. Few provincial prisons, however, meet the standards of the federal prisons, their most serious problem being overcrowding. There are also several institutions for women and facilities for minors called homes, which provide training in agriculture and various trades.

The Penal Code provides for a number of rehabilitative measures. Prisoners are permitted to work on special projects within or without the prison, and, after a trial period, may be released from prison and placed on parole. Inmates are graded on performance, and their release is dependent on a record of good conduct.

Although generally sanitary, Argentine prisons suffer from overcrowding. Although the Penal Code calls for the separation of inmates according to character and offense, shortage of space frequently makes this impossible. Despite improved prison conditions since the return of democracy in 1983, there were continuing protests, hunger strikes and riots in a few prisons in 1985 resulting from violent treatment of prisoners during cell block searches and disrespectful treatment of visiting family members. At least one prisoner committed suicide and another died during the riots.

Although the Penal Code contains strong provisions guaranteeing habeas corpus and controls on police powers, the police have the authority to detain a person incommunicado for up to eight days during investigation, even in the case of minor offenses. The right to bail is provided by law and is honored in practice. Public defenders are assigned by the courts to indigent defendants, but their caseloads are generally far in excess of what they can reasonably be expected to handle.

With the exception of politically motivated crimes, the crime rates are historically low, first because of a traditional respect for constituted authority, and second because of a large and relatively prosperous middle class. Crime rates among those of European origin are small in comparison with those of migrant workers from neighboring Latin American countries. Rape, molestation, and moral offenses are extremely rare. Crimes committed under the influence of alcohol are most numerous in rural areas. Car theft and armed bank robberies have increased in recent years. Juvenile delinquency is not as yet a serious problem, although it is frequently tied to the use of marijuana. The law provides for the imprisonment of parents guilty of gross negligence toward their children. There are over 100 establishments, both public and private, for the care and rehabilitation of minors.

AUSTRALIA

Bruce Swanton
Garry Hannigan and David Biles

BASIC FACT SHEET

Official Name: Commonwealth of Australia
Area: 7,686,848 sq km
Population: 16,072,986 (1987)
Capital: Canberra
Nature of Government: Parliamentary democracy
Language: English
Currency: Australian dollar
GNP: $171.07 billion
Territorial Divisions: 6 states, 2 territories
Population per Police Officer: 460
Police Expenditures per 1,000: $16,132

History & Background

Police in Australia have their origins in the three major British settlement initiatives in New Holland: Sydney (New South Wales), 1788; Swan River (Western Australia), 1829; and Adelaide (South Australia), 1836. In all cases, the formation of police organizations was preceded by the appointment of individual constables who were mostly subordinate to magistrates and whose duties could be described only marginally as police work in any modern sense of the term. Such appointments bore close similarity to 18th- and early-19th-century practices in England.

The most important settlement was New South Wales, which in the early days covered not only the area occupied by the present-day state of New South Wales but also that of the present day states of Tasmania, Victoria, Queensland, Northern Territory and the external Norfolk Island Territory. The colonial government permitted the creation of numerous small police bodies to meet local and special needs throughout the vast region, but the largest and most significant was always that of Sydney Town, the seat of government.

First settlement, in 1788, occurred at Sydney Cove; the great majority of settlers transported were English or Irish convicts. Thefts of precious food, several serious assaults and a generally low level of public behavior in the infant colony prompted the appointment of 10 or 12 (historical records contain conflicting accounts) convict constables in 1789. These men, who received lodging, rations and clothing only, were made subordinate to the judge advocate and other military officers until the cessation of military rule in 1796. Although these first constables were referred to as "police" by the judge advocate at the time of their appointment in 1789, it seems probable that the convicts operated initially as a night watch only.

As time went by and the areas surrounding Sydney were explored and settled, constables, many of them freemen, were appointed in the outlying regions. In the larger towns full-time constables operated 24 hours a day.

Once military government terminated in New South Wales, constables operating in Sydney Town were subordinated to the first magistrate. Though also known as superintendent of police, that official was first and foremost a justice of the peace. The first 20 years of Sydney's growth were limited and, as a result, the evolution of police function and organization was slow.

Convict constables were appointed at Norfolk Island penal settlement in 1791 and at Port Dalrymple, Van Diemen's Land (now Tasmania), in 1804.

The year 1811 saw a significant reorganization of the Sydney "police," although the various grades of constables remained subordinate to the first magistrate. It was not until 1839 that the various Sydney Town constables were headed by a full-time police official. In the rural areas of New South Wales, constables were appointed by local justices, and they remained accountable to the particular bench by which they were appointed.

As the colony's population increased in the second and third decades of the 19th century, various security

11

and administrative problems resulted in the creation of a number of discrete "police" bodies, e.g., mounted patrol, water police, border police, native police and gold police. Some of these were disbanded, some combined with others and some were absorbed by other colonies. A similar situation occurred in Australia Felix, now known as the state of Victoria.

Following wild New Year's rioting in Sydney in 1850, efforts were made to consolidate all police bodies in the area now known as the state of New South Wales. These efforts were not entirely successful, and it was not until the 1861 communal rioting at Lambing Flat goldfields that the government was able to achieve its aim fully. In 1862 the present police department of New South Wales was created.

Victoria separated from New South Wales in 1851, achieving colonial status in the process. The Victorian colonial government inherited a fragmented collection of police bodies very similar to those of New South Wales. The new government consolidated its police services in 1853.

Queensland did not separate from New South Wales until 1859. At that time New South Wales police, in particular the Native Police, had a general responsibility for policing in the area despite the presence of local town and water police constables. An inspector general of police was appointed in 1860, but fragmentation of responsibility continued until 1864. Even then the Native Police retained a separate identity until disbanded in 1900.

In Tasmania, separate police bodies existed prior to 1857, when police services were reorganized. Legislation passed in 1856 empowered municipalities to raise their own police forces. Twenty-one such forces were established over a period of years. In addition, a body known as the Colonial Police (the name was changed a few years later to Territorial Police) was created. The Territorial Police covered those areas not subject to municipal government. In 1899, the various police bodies were consolidated, thus creating the present police department of Tasmania.

Following the commencement of the first civil settlement in Western Australia, at the Swan River Colony in 1829, a number of constables were appointed by the governor. These freemen plied their normal trade, acting in their office of constable only when necessary. By 1832, however, conflict between aborigines and settlers was so fierce that many settlers left the colony. Local constables continued to be appointed in both towns and rural areas. They remained subordinate to justices of the peace. Police numbers started to increase in 1849, in anticipation of the arrival of transported British convicts. In 1853 all police were placed under the authority of a superintendent. In 1861 a thorough reorganization was effected, and the present police department of Western Australia dates from that year.

The colony of South Australia was first settled in 1836, and a number of freemen constables were appointed soon after landing. These men, who were subordinate to justices of the peace, continued to work at their normal calling, exercising their authority as constables as and when necessary. Unfortunatley, the new colony's existence quickly attracted large numbers of undesirables, many of whom were escaped convicts from areas to the east and from Van Diemen's Land. In 1838 a police force of 20 members was established, with colonywide jurisdiction. The force had a chief officer who was answerable to a four-person commission, but in 1840 a member of the police commission was appointed commissioner of police, and the board was abolished. Thus the police department of South Australia is the oldest surviving police force in Australia.

Between 1863 and 1910, Northern Territory was governed by South Australia. From 1865 to 1869 a small body of constables was employed at Escape Cliffs, the scene of the territory's first major settlement attempt. These men, who performed many other tasks, such as caring for stock and exploring, were subordinate to the government resident. Escape Cliffs was abandoned in 1869 and its personnel dispersed. A detachment of South Australian police arrived at Palmerston (now Darwin), the successor location to Escape Cliffs, in January 1870. South Australian police personnel undertook the territory's policing needs for the next 40 years. Eventually, however, the South Australian government felt it could no longer bear the administrative costs involved, so in January 1911 the federal government took over responsibility for the huge but sparsely populated region. A new 'police body, the Northern Territory Mounted Police,

AUSTRALIAN POLICE FORCES BY YEAR OF ORIGIN

Agency	Year of Origin
South Australia Police Force	1838
Victoria Police Force	1853
Western Australia Police Force	1861
New South Wales Police Force	1862
Queensland Police Force	1864
Tasmania Police Force	1899
Northern Territory Police Force	1911[1]
Australian Capital Territory Police Force	1927[2]

1. *Continuity broken, 1926–31.*
2. *Absorbed by AFP in 1979.*

was formed to replace the withdrawn South Australian police employees. In 1926 the Northern Territory Police Force (the "mounted" had by then been dropped from the title) was split into two discrete organizations, but in 1931 it was reconstituted.

The Federal (later changed to Australian) Capital Territory Police Force was formed in 1927 as a result of a decision to hold federal parliament sittings at Canberra. The Australian Capital Territory Police Force remained a separate organization until 1979, when it was absorbed by the Commonwealth Police Force, which is largely concerned with security. The resulting hybrid was retitled the Australian Federal Police, although the ACT police component provides the body's only traditional police function.

Structure & Organization

Due to the very large number of police stations scattered throughout the Australian states and territories, it is almost impossible to give a breakdown of what staff each police station has. Some police stations have only a patrol area extending 60 miles (100 kilometers) in one direction and 120 miles (200 kilometers) in another. The one-man police station is common in states such as Queensland. The officer generally spends part of his day in the police station attending to administrative work and part of the day patrolling the district. Some patrols in remote areas take days.

Within the major cities there are what are commonly called suburban police stations. These stations are usually staffed by 10 or 12 officers who attend to all administrative work, such as serving summonses and executing warrants of commitment. They also patrol their area to both prevent and detect crime. The larger cities often have a specific section of police assigned either to general patrol or special patrol, e.g., Victoria's special patrol group. These officers are assigned to patrolling city streets.

Each police force maintains a large number of police stations, patrol bases and detective offices. At some locations all three are combined in a single structure; at other locations separate functions are assigned separate buildings.

In terms of operational emphases, three categories predominate: traffic, criminal investigation and general duties. General duties is a catch-all category that includes patrol, public order and station duties. Unfortunately, detailed personnel breakdowns by function and task are not easily available in Australia.

In very broad terms, just over a quarter of all personnel in the various state police forces are directly concerned with traffic control and criminal investigation. The remainder perform all the other duties, including water police, air wing, communications, special patrols, rescue and disasters, station operation, prosecutions, youth clubs, clerical, records and research.

Police departments include both civilian and sworn employees. Generally speaking, apart from research, training and radio dispatching duties in some forces, civilians have been kept out of police work. Civilians perform clerical, cleaning and maintenance duties. The relationship of the head of the civilian component of police departments to the chief police officer varies somewhat according to state. In some departments the secretary, or director of administration, is a powerful figure rivaling the chief officer in status. In other departments the secretary tends to be subordinate. In all cases, though, the chief officer of a state police force is the operational head and has direct access to his minister.

A major feature of the Australian police service is that it is exclusively state- or territory-based, which means that single agencies provide metropolitan as well as urban and rural police services. Members normally begin their service in a metropolitan area. After a couple of years many are assigned to a smaller town. There is no clear pattern, however. Some police officers prefer country service and spend nearly all their careers at country stations, while others prefer metropolitan duty.

In those states having a metropolitan mobile patrol, e.g., South Australia and Queensland, patrol personnel operate from patrol bases. General-duty police work from traditional police stations; detectives and traffic personnel sometimes operate from special premises. The resulting reduced interaction between detectives and other police causes a reduction in the transfer of local knowledge and information. Area crime collator services are designed to overcome such disadvantages, inevitably some loss of information transfer occurs. Whether this loss is signficant is unknown.

All Australian police forces are now highly mobile, possessing large fleets of vehicles.

Defining the characteristics of the typical police officer is complicated by the lack of contemporary statistical data and by the great divergence in age grouping of police, which lends itself to considerable contrasts in education and training. There is almost an older and a younger grouping of officers within the various forces.

The typical police officer in Australia is male. Females are significantly underrepresented in Australian police forces at all levels. This underrepresentation is not entirely accidental. Until recent times there was a deliberate effort to control the intake of females to the service and confine their numbers to a preset level. There was for many years a rule that forced policewomen to resign once they got married. Some forces have prescribed tasks they consider suitable for policewomen to carry out, and such forces recruit to fill these positions only. Generally, however, women police are slowly permeating most areas of police work, although in some areas they are not permitted to work night shifts.

The typical Australian police officer is a native of Australia. Little effort is made to recruit minority or migrant groups into the service. There are very few aborigines in most state forces, and most of them are police aides.

New recruits are required to conform to strict physical requirements prior to entry and during their training period. However, once sworn in to the service, little control is maintained over the physical conditions of officers. There is no provision for a weekly physical exercise period (compulsory or otherwise) for members of the various forces, and before long many members decline in physical condition and in some instances develop the average physical condition and appearance of their counterparts outside the services.

The typical Australian police officer is male, over five feet, nine inches (173 cm) tall, between 20 and 30 years of age, married, Anglo-Saxon and generally in modest physical condition.

All police forces operate on a 24-hour-day basis the year through. Police officers are required to commence and complete duty at various times. Duty rosters are drawn up and promulgated, usually a week in advance. Generally, police officers must work an eight-hour day and a five-day week. There is great variance between general police hours of work and administrative hours of work. The administrative staff usually works office hours, from 9:00 A.M. to 5:00 P.M. The majority of general police workers—traffic patrol, criminal investigation, etc—work a variety of shifts.

There is some variety among the leave entitlements provided by individual states. This variety is due to a number of factors, such as officers doing shift work as opposed to administrative work. Officers working shifts (general police duties) are in some cases entitled to additional annual leave.

All police officers in Australia are issued uniforms. Naturally, some officers are required to work in plain clothes. Departmental designs vary somewhat, but except for tropical and subtropical areas, shades of blue predominate. Embellishments vary according to state and territory heraldry and preference.

Each police force has a winter and a summer uniform to take into account for the change in season. This is a relatively recent phenomenon, since until the 1960s, the only concession to summer heat was a lightweight uniform. Nowadays, short-sleeved and open-necked shirts are worn in summer, whereas tunics are worn in winter. Some departments, e.g., South Australia, also provide a patrol jacket.

Commissioned officers wear slightly different uniforms, taking into account rank differences. Their basic uniform is similar with badges of rank and cap braid accounting for the major differences.

All police carry batons, handcuffs, and notebooks when performing duty. In some instances the handcuffs and baton are openly displayed.

Officers of all ranks are able to wear service medals on formal occasions. When in general working uniform ribbons only are worn, displayed on the left breast. A number of police service medals are issued to police. The Long Service and Good Conduct Medal is issued after 22 years of service. The National Medal is issued after 15 years, and the Queen's Police Medal may be awarded to recommended members. The latter is the most difficult to obtain, with usually only two or three a year issued to each police force. In Victoria police may be awarded the department's own Police Medal for Gallantry. All police commissioners issue "favorable records," "commendations," and the like to officers who have performed their duty in an exemplary manner or with distinction.

The practice of a department funeral is still observed in most forces for those police officers killed in the line of duty. Some police forces have a departmental flag.

Police in Australia, like police throughout the world, suffer from substantial levels of occupational stress. Many police employee unions have argued for general wage increases before industrial courts, their arguments based on the frequency and high levels of occupational disadvantage, including stress. Generally, uniformed police can travel to and from work in their uniforms without fear of recrimination from neighbors or members of the public, yet police are occasionally assaulted in the execution of their duty. Unfortunately, comprehensive figures for all states are not available for minor assaults on police.

Each state and territory police commissioner, subject to ministerial approval, has discretion to establish the rank structure he feels appropriate for his department. Hence there are some differences among states as to nomenclature as well as the number of ranks considered necessary. There is, however, a clear distinction between commissioned and noncommissioned ranks in all agencies. Commissioned officers of state police forces are appointed by the executive council of their respective governments. Noncommissioned officers and constable ranks are appointed and promoted by the commissioner of police.

Generally, an officer is promoted to each rank after obtaining necessary promotional qualifications. However, there are exceptions to this rule. In Queensland, a senior constable, once he or she has achieved 15 years of continuous service in the force, is automatically upgraded to the rank of sergeant 3/C. Thus officers promoted in such a manner cannot strictly be regarded as supervisors. There are no promotional examinations for the various ranks of commissioned officers. These officers, once they have obtained commissioned rank, are upgraded through the various levels—inspector to superintendent—at the discretion of the commissioner of police and the minister or executive council. Each officer is evaluated by the commissioner as to his or her suitability for higher rank and responsibility.

There is no great difference in the amounts paid to officers of the same rank in the various states. Payment of increments is determined by the length of service in a particular rank. The police officers, apart from the minimum pay entitlements, are entitled to additional benefits, such as overtime.

Each state police commissioner has the authority, subject to directions from the minister, under the various police regulation acts to transfer an officer of any rank to any part of the state or territory to which the officer beongs. The criteria for assignments are based on the premise that the effective and efficient running of a police organization is paramount. For example, if a commissioner of police requires additional staff at a particular police station, he or she has thc authority to assign such additional staff as the commissioner considers necessary. It is not unusual, in the case of an officer not working well at a particular station, to assign him or her to another station. Such assignments have a punitive nature attached to them and sometimes are the subject of a labor dispute. At times, of course, the supervisor may be at fault rather than a subordinate member.

This formal system, of course, does not prevent police associations from making informal approaches to police administrations with a view to having unwanted transfers canceled or a satisfactory compromise attempted.

Compared to the armed services and many overseas police forces, the proportion of commissioned and noncommissioned officers to other ranks in Australia may seem low. Apart from questions of sufficient supervisors and executive officers, such small percentages, especially of commissioned officers, seriously affect the career prospects of police personnel. On the other hand, with the single entry system practiced in Australian police forces, increased percentage of commissioned rank positions would undoubtedly result in a drastic drop in executive quality.

In no instance are police officers formally permitted to find employment in any outside occupation or task of their choosing. To work at a second job outside their police work, police officers are required to obtain the permission of the commissioner of police or chief secretary. This permits the department to monitor the activities of the officers and restrict them from working in certain occupations. An unsuitable occupation would be the employment of a police officer in a hotel or betting shop.

All police officers in Australia are covered by superannuation schemes, which provide a certain income on retirement or a lump sum payment and/or an income. In the case of the premature death of an officer, prescribed payments are due his or her family. Some forces have their own pension scheme. In others, employees are automatically enrolled in state government superannuation funds.

Recruitment, Education & Training

Preemployment testing and standards for police entry in Australia vary slightly from state to state, although few marked differences are apparent. The various selection criteria vary from time to time.

New South Wales

Candidates for entry into the police department must visit the force recruiting office. A preliminary medical examination precedes a police entrance examination. Those candidates who pass the test are then subjected to a detailed background investigation. These procedures are followed by a personal interview. Provided all these preliminaries are satisfactory, the candidate then appears before a selection board, which takes a final assessment. Subject to Selection Board approval, candidates then begin an 11-week initial training course. At the completion of that course, the trainee is sworn in as a probationary constable.

Candidates must be at least 19 years of age and under 35 years of age at the time of appointment. They must also be Australian or British subjects by either birth or naturalization.

Those candidates who have either matriculated or passed the Higher School Certificate at a satisfactory level are excused from the police entrance examination, which consists of tests in English, mathematics, dictation, essay writing and general knowledge.

Victoria

In Victoria, police candidates are required to complete an application form. They must be either of British nationality or Australian citizens by birth or naturalization. The minimum acceptable age is 18.5 years, to a maximum of the 35th birthday. For females the lower age limit is 20 years.

A general ability test is given to all candidates. They must, in addition, pass tests in English, reading, spelling, dictation, general knowledge and mathematics.

Queensland

Police candidates in Queensland are required to be between 18 years, four months and 39 years, four months, although preference is given to applicants under 35 years. The minimum education standard is that of Queensland Junior Certificate (or equivalent), with at least 18 points in five subjects, including at least four points in English.

South Australia

Applicants for entry into the police department of South Australia must be between 19 and 29 years old.

The police department of South Australia employs a "recruit entrance test battery" comprising (1) general reasoning ability tests and (2) specific abilities test.

The police department of South Australia subjects candidates to four cognitive tests. First is the ACER word knowledge test. Second, 30 words are played to candidates by audio tape; applicants are required to write them down as a form of spelling test. Third, candidates' listening comprehension is tested by playing them a recorded taped report of an event of particular relevance to police, e.g., a break and enter; then examinees are asked a series of questions based on the audio report. Fourth is the ACER number test.

A selection panel interview subsequently assesses candidates on qualities such as motivation, adaptability, stability, social impact and physical impact.

Western Australia

Candidate prerequisites in Western Australia are enumerated in the regulations to the Police Act 1892 (as amended).

Western Australia police candidates are required to take the Otis Higher Test, Form C, for IQ testing. This form was adapted by ACER from the Otis Self-Administering Test of Mental Ability, Form C, for use by the department.

Two written tests are given to applicants to join the Western Australia police department. The first is a one-hour essay on a selected topic. The second is one-hour arithmetic paper. A 60% pass is mandatory for both papers.

Formal objective personality testing is not undertaken by the police department in Western Australia. Instead, all applicants are subjected to a personal assessment interview. This interview covers areas such as overall personality, attire, general demeanor, speech, self-expression, temperament, aggressiveness, mental alertness, attitude to discipline and maturity.

Tasmania

Police candidates in Tasmania must be not less than 19 years old nor older than 33 years, although male applicants possessing at least two years' service in a police force or one of the armed services are acceptable up to and including 35 years old.

The Tasmanian police department requires all candidates to complete two written general ability tests designed to assess verbal and numerate ability ranges and to obtain IQ range and percentile rating. The two tests are the ACER higher test, Form M, Section Q, for numeracy and the ACER higher test, Form M, Section L, for literacy.

Candidates are also required to take an internal examination in English and mathematics. Again, a pass is mandatory if a candidate is to be successful.

Candidates who pass the general ability test then must complete the personality tests.

Each police force in Australia has its own training academies, which provide recruit and in-service courses. Those agencies with cadet programs—i.e., Western Australia, South Australia, Tasmania, Victoria and Queensland—also either use academy resources for cadet training or, in the case of Victoria, operate a separate cadet academy. However, Victoria's police department is in the process of phasing out its cadet program.

Recruit courses now average 20 weeks but vary greatly among states as to duration and content. In Tasmania, for example, adult recruit training lasts 20 weeks and offers places to both males and females between 19 and 33 years of age. Generally, two such courses are run each year. On occasions fishery officers and national parks and wildlife officers also undergo the basic course for constables. The syllabus covers four core areas: police law, education, practical subject and out-station duty. The so-called police law element refers to acts and regulations, practical police duties, evidence, police regulations and standing orders. Education periods concentrate on English, arithmetic, geography and government. Practical subjects include first aid, drill, self-defense, physical training, fingerprinting and ballistics. Out-station duty refers to periods spent at police stations observing procedures in the field. Retention rate of recruit courses averages 95%. In-service training courses in the same department cover administration (for inspectors and subofficers), detective training, bomb disposal, prosecuting, first aid, traffic and diving.

The cadet course in the same agency consists of a two-year residential course. The police law element is roughly the same as that for adult recruits. Education covers English, arithmetic, geography, government, psychology, sociology and typing. Cadets spend approximately five months on practical training at out stations. Religious and moral instruction is conducted on a nondenominational basis by visiting clergy. The retention rate for cadet courses averages 70%.

Despite differing emphases on cadet and adult recruitment and in-service training, recruit training is broadly similar throughout Australia. Major differences are more reflective of style and ethos than of content. Western Australia, South Australia, Victoria, Tasmania and Queensland still rely heavily on cadet recruitment, whereas New South Wales and the Australian Capital Territory depend entirely on adult recruits.

Executive training has received greater emphasis in all Australian police forces in recent years. Victoria and Queensland have colleges in addition to their academies. A major, (although not the exclusive) role of the colleges is to prepare executive talent.

The Australian Police College runs executive and specialist courses for members of all police forces and selected law-enforcement agencies.

A small but growing number of police officers in Australia take tertiary studies. Some officers are in degree courses at universities, and a greater number are studying for police/administration of justice diplomas. Three such courses are now available in New South Wales, two in Victoria and one in South Australia. Another is due to begin in Queensland, in 1983. In addition, the Queensland Education Department operates a police arts and sciences certificate course on behalf of the police department.

At present relatively few police officers in Australia hold degrees. In the past, the tendency in Australia has been for police officers to acquire legal or accountancy qualifications and then leave the service. There has been a highly desirable swing away from legal studies, with greater interest shown in police studies, social sciences and business/commerce.

The Penal System

The principles, organization and procedures of criminal justice are British in origin. Criminal law was separately codified in Queensland, Western Australia and Tasmania, and relevant law was consolidated by the federal government and other states. As a result, legal terminology and definitions vary considerably among the states.

The death penalty was abolished in federally controlled territories in September 1973. Several states have also abolished the death penalty: Queensland in 1922, New South Wales in 1955 and Tasmania in 1968. In other states, the death penalty is generally restricted to convictions for murder, although it could be technically imposed also for rape and piracy with violence.

The Australian correctional system is entirely the responsibility of the states; no prisons are maintained by the federal government. The states operate a total of 78 prisons, of which New South Wales has the most, with 21, and Tasmania the least, with three. Imprisonment rates show striking differences among the states. Western Australia generally imposes the most prison sentences, and its prisons contain a high percentge of Aboriginals. Queensland sends Aboriginals to reserves rather than to prisons. Recidivists are most in Tansmanian prisons and least in South Australia. The percentage of open prisons also varies, with Western Australia leading with about 24% of its prisoners in such facilities.

Parole was first adopted in Victoria in 1956, and the other states have followed suit. Tasmania, however, does not have a formal parole board.

Consolidated statistics on crime have been compiled and published regularly by the federal authorities since 1964. The data cover the state police forces, which handle almost all criminal offenses. The categories of reported crime are homicide, serious assault, robbery, rape, breaking and entering, motor vehicle theft, fraud, forgery and false pretenses. Definitions of categories are generally but not entirely uniform among the reporting states and territories. The major lack of uniformity is in the definition of serious assault. Not included in the statistics are larceny and theft other than that of motor vehicles, which are more widespread than other crimes. A lack of uniformity in recording practices among states has further reduced the comparability of statistics. In some states, the conviction of a single individual for multiple offenses was treated statistically as one offender, while in other states each offense was counted separately.

Australia has experienced a considerable increase in crime since the 1960s. Based on newspaper accounts, crimes of violence against the person—murder, rape, robbery and assault—in Melbourne and Sydney surpass those of London and are approaching those of New York in per capita terms. Patterns of violence also show great similarity to those of the United States rather than Great Britain.

The two most severe crime problems—both products of the turbulent post-World War II era—are drugs and juvenile delinquency. New South Wales organized the first specialized drug squad in 1927, and during the 1960s most state police forces established similar bodies. Enforcement of drug laws is also being carried out by the Commonwealth Police Force, the Bureau of Narcotics, and the Department of Customs and Excise. Juvenile crime has registered the greatest increase in assault and malicious damage.

The collection and publication of criminal statistics is the responsibility of the Australian Bureau of Statistics, while the Australian Institute of Criminology has a statutory responsibility to advise on these matters. Other agencies at the state level, such as the New South Wales Bureau of Crime Statistics and Research and the South Australian Office of Crime Statistics, also collect and publish data for their own jurisdictions. Also, the annual reports of police, court and correctional agencies include statistics related to their own work. A national summary from most of these sources is published each year in *Year Book Australia.*

Notwithstanding the wide range of data sources, there is considerable dissatisfaction in criminal justice circles with the reliability, comprehensiveness and timeliness of the data available. As a result, the Australian Bureau of Statistics has extensive plans to improve the quality of criminal and criminal justice statistics.

Victimless crimes, such as gambling and prostitution, are of concern to police forces in Australia, although the nature of that concern seems to have changed in the past decade or two. Today there is less concern than previously with the activities of individual prostitutes or gamblers, provided they are reasonably discreet and do not cause public offense, but there is an increasing realization that many of these activities may be controlled by organized crime, and there is also suspected political corruption in some quarters. The operation of illegal casinos in Sydney has been widely acknowledged for many years, with the locations being given in the media from time to time. This blatant flaunting of the law, and its implications, are of grave concern to law-abiding citizens.

One area of victimless crime now of less concern to police relates to homosexuality. In recent years the law has been changed in South Australia, Victoria and the Australian Capital Territory to decriminalize consensual homosexual acts between adults in private and, with a more tolerant attitude being generally expressed by the public, police in other jurisdictions are also unlikely to take action in these cases. The area of victimless crime that is very vigorously debated, however, relates to the possession and use of marijuana, but none of the state governments has indicated an intent to decriminalize such behavior.

Police intervention in family crises is of continuing concern and frustration. Some estimates have suggested that over 50% of police calls for service are related to domestic disputes, but only a small proportion of these cases results in prosecutions, largely because witnesses frequently decline to give evidence. In South Australia the police burden in relation to family crises has been significantly reduced by the creation of a crisis intervention service within the local Department of Community Welfare. This service, which operates 24 hours a day and is staffed by social workers and welfare officers, visits homes at the request of police and also does follow-up work with families. Initial response is still made by police, but through this service they are often able to hand over the counseling work to specialists.

Police in all jurisdictions continue to undertake the unpleasant task of notifying relatives in cases of sudden death. They are also responsible for missing persons and for the location and return of children who run away from home.

CRIME STATISTICS (1984)

		Number Reported	Attempts %	Cases Solved %	Crime per 100,000	Offenders	Females %	Juveniles %	Strangers %
1.	Murder	534		84.83	3.42	398	10.55	5.03	
2.	Sex offenses, including rape	12,065		58.86	77.23	3,658	1.12	18.15	
3.	Rape	2,154		63.14	13.79	842	0.36	14.73	
4.	Serious assault	9,156		74.15	58.61	6,066	7.90	12.84	
5.	All theft	720,211		13.51	4,610.47	114,000	24.24	46.28	
6.	Aggravated theft	202,486		12.36	1,296.23	23,411	7.71	54.44	
7.	Robbery and violent theft	13,056		17.36	83.58	2,143	12.55	27.62	
8.	Breaking and entering	274,039		8.84	1,754.28	27,336	7.36	54.47	
9.	Auto theft	91,340		22.65	584.72	10,088	5.44	48.78	
10.	Other thefts	314,776		25.12	2,187.90	75,802	34.32	41.40	
11.	Fraud	74,006		77.12	473.75	13,175	28.78	12.46	
12.	Counterfeiting	471		66.66	3.02	104	6.73	1.92	
13.	Drug offenses	56,368		99.56	360.84	35,287	15.49	8.57	
14.	Total offenses	1,077,451		32.64	6,897.37	196,941	20.48	27.22	

Criteria of juveniles: aged from 10 to 17 years.
Note: Information for some categories is not available.

Police handling of white-collar and economic crimes is a complex area, as procedures vary from place to place. All of the larger police forces have fraud squads comprised of detectives, many of whom are qualified in accounting. These squads generally handle only relatively serious cases involving, say, over $10,000, and they pass on lesser cases to normal criminal investigation procedures. Also in the larger jurisdictions the governments have established corporate affairs commissions to regulate and explore company law. In most cases police fraud squads and corporate affairs commissions have worked closely together, even to the extent of sharing premises, but in some instances doubt has arisen as to their relevant spheres of authority. In recent years the Australian public and its political representatives have come to appreciate the enormous costs to the community of white-collar and economic crime; consequently, more vigorous and coordinated police activity in this area can be expected.

AUSTRIA

BASIC FACT SHEET

Official Name: Republic of Austria
Area: 83,835 sq km
Population: 7,569,283 (1987)
Capital: Vienna
Nature of Government: Parliamentary democracy
Language: German
Currency: Schilling
GNP: $66.26 billion (1985)
Territorial Divisions: 9 Länder
Population per Police Officer: 470
Police Expenditures per 1,000: N.A.

History & Background

The major dates in Austrian police history are 1221, when the Citizen's Watch was formed to protect life and property in Vienna; 1531, when a Day and Night Watch was formed; 1569, when the City Guard was formed as the first police force; 1754, when police officers were appointed over the City Guard under a chief of police; and 1789, when the Guard was brought under centralized command. A secret police coexisted with this force from 1713 and a military police from 1775. In 1849 the provincial police were reorganized and police directorates formed in the major cities. The secret police began to evolve into what is now the Criminal Police. Austria was also instrumental under Chief of Police Johann Strauber in holding the second Congress of Criminal Police, at which the groundwork was laid for the International Criminal Police Commission, which later become INTERPOL.

The first centralized police force, created by Emperor Francis Joseph I, followed the patern of the regional gendarmerie that existed in Lombardy and South Tyrol since Napoleonic times.

Although its role was to maintain public order and security, the Gendarmerie was organized on military lines within the regular Army. It was divided into regiments, wings, platoons, sections, corporalships and posts. Its relationship to other security forces and the citizens' militia was governed by the principle that the gendarmerie must not be hindered in the exercise of its duties and in the planning of its operations by any other armed force, and that it must be given any aid and support it needed. The direction of security operations was entirely in the hands of the gendarmerie's own military hierarchy. After 1860, however, the gendarmerie, while remaining a security force organized on a military pattern, was placed under the authority of the Ministry of the Interior in operational and financial matters, with the Army High Command retaining only military and disciplinary jurisdiction. This meant that the gendarmerie's law-and-order role was now under the control of the administrative authorities.

In the years following this change of status, the gendarmerie was reorganized on the pattern that essentially prevails to the present day: provincial commands, regional commands, district commands and stations. In 1876, the gendarmerie ceased to be part of the Army. After the breakup of the monarchy in 1918, the gendarmerie was transformed into a "civilian security force" but still retained a military-type organization. After Austria's annexation to the German Reich in 1938, the Austrian gendarmerie was merged with the German Police, to be restored to its old status as a uniform-wearing armed security force within the civil service after the breakdown of the Pan-German Empire.

Structure & Organization

Since Austria is a federal state, legislation is enacted at the federal and provincial levels, and law enforcement in respect to police matters (in the functional sense) takes place either at the federal or at the provincial, district or municipal level. Austria's administrative authorities are divided into federal, provincial and municipal authorities. But in functional terms their activities may overlap—i.e., federal authorities may take charge of provincial or municipal matters, and vice versa.

Matters pertaining to "security administration"—other than those relating to "local security police," where the municipalities are sovereign—are a federal responsibility both with regard to legislation and with respect to execution (this function is referred to as "security administration of the state"). The lowest rung in the hierarchy of these security authorities is occuped by the district administrative authorities (district "captaincies," organizationally part of the provincial administration, and municipal authorities in the larger towns), and by the federal police authorities (federal police directorates) in those places where these federal services have been established. In addition to public security, the district administrative authorities and the federal police authorities are also in charge of "administrative police (see above). The second tier in the hierarchy is formed by the security directorates—one for each province—which are exclusively concerned with public security. In Vienna, the federal police directorate is at the same time the security directorate (since Vienna ranks as a province in its own right). The Directorate-General for Public Security in the federal Ministry of the Interior is at the head of this hierarchy of the "security administration of the state."

In the Austrian legal system, only duly constituted public authorities have the right, within the limits set by the law of the land, to use force. To enable them to exercise their coercive powers, the security authorities have police forces under their command: The federal police authorities control the Federal Security Guard (uniformed police) and the Corps of Criminal Investigators (plainclothes police); the security directorates have the federal gendarmerie at their disposal.

The Federal Police Authorities (Federal Police Directorates)

The beginnings of a state-run police system in Austria date from the middle of the 18th century (i.e., the reign of Empress Maria Theresa). After the revolution of 1848, which dealt a severe blow to the old Austrian police apparatus, a new police system was introduced whose basic features remain intact today. One major novelty was that police directorates (Polizeidirektioinen) or superintendencies (Polizeikommissariate) were set up in towns where a need was felt for them on account of the large scale of policing necessary or in view of other special conditions.

Under the present Austrian federal Constitution enacted in 1920, the federal government is empowered to set up federal police authorities by decree. The federal government last made use of these powers on December 7, 1976, when it issued an ordinance concerning the geographical and substantive spheres of activity of the federal police authorities. Up to December 31, 1976, Austria had seven federal police directorates—one in Vienna, the federal capital, and one in each of six provincial capitals (Linz, Graz, Salzburg, Innsbruck, Klagenfurt, and Eisenstadt)—as well as seven federal police Kommissariate (Villach, Wiener Neustadt, St. Pölten, Wels, Steyr, Leoben and Schwechat). As of January 1, 1977, all 14 federal police authorities bear the title Bundespolizeidirektion (Federal Police Directorate). The Vienna police directorate has a police office in each of the districts of the city, known as the Bezirkspolizeikommissariat for the area concerned. The Vienna Direktion is headed by the police president. Under his command, the directorate's business is conducted by the staff division, the state security division, the criminal investigations division, the administrative police division and the Kommissariat division. Each of the divisions is headed by a chief of division and comprises several subdivisions. The heads of Vienna's district police offices bear the title "town captain." The federal police directorates outside Vienna are headed by "police directors." Given their order of magnitude, their organizational patterns differ somewhat from that of Vienna.

The senior administrative appointments in federal police authorities are held by graduates in law. They are not, however, mere administrators but executive officers as well, and as such they may wear uniforms and carry arms.

The Security Directorates

First established in 1934, the security directorates— one for each of the country's nine Bundesländer (provinces with far-reaching autonomy)—were restored after the end of World War II. As mentioned earlier, the Vienna federal police directorate doubles as security directorate, since Vienna is not only the country's capital but also a Bundesland in its own right.

The present legal status of the security directorates derives from an ordinance issued by the federal minister of the interior in 1946, which defines the geographical and substantive competence of these authorities (i.e., their functions within the framework of the "security administration of the state"). The organizational structure of the security directorates resembles that of the federal police authorities. Each directorate is headed by a director of security. Under his supervision, the tasks entrusted to the directorate are carried out by the staff division, the State security division, the criminal investigations division and the administrative police division. Again, each of these divisions functions under a chief of division. Only the staff division is commanded by the director of security himself.

The Directorate-General for Public Security in the Federal Ministry of the Interior

Supreme control of the police was first lodged in the Ministry of the Interior (as it then was) in 1850. With brief interruptions, it has remained with the home department (which was known by different names at different times) to the present day.

At the time of writing, the Directorate-General for Public Security is one of the *Sektionen* that make up the federal Ministry of the Interior. The directorate is divided into groups as follows: A (federal police), B (supreme command of the gendarmerie), C (state security), D (criminal investigation) and E (administrative police). Each group comprises a number of divisions. The head of the directorate has the title director-general for public security.

The Federal Security Guard

The Austrian Federal Security Guard developed from a civilian security force introduced in the years following the 1848 revolution to replace the previous military police force.

The Federal Security Guard is an armed police force wearing a uniform and organized on a military pattern. Its members are attached to the federal police authorities to help them with their executive tasks, and they are subordinate to these authorities in operational and organisational terms. In the territories of the federal police authorities other than Vienna the officers of the Security Guard report to the head of the Central Inspectorate, and in Vienna to the head of the Inspectorate-General of the Security Guard. The officers of the Security Guard primarily serve on guard or patrol duty, escort people detained and so on. They are assigned either to central police offices or to outlying posts. When on duty they wear their uniforms. Detailed rules on the design and composition of their uniforms and on when and where to wear them are contained in a standing order concerning the uniform and equipment of the officers of the federal police, issued in 1969.

The officers of the Federal Security Guard have the following arms and weapons at their disposal: rubber truncheons, pistols, carbines, submachine guns, automatic rifles, and tear gas. Furthermore, the Federal Security Guard is equipped with helmets, armored shields, and bulletproof and fireproof clothes for defense. Specially trained dogs are used for guarding, hunting about, tracking, finding dope or corpses and searching for avalanches. Uniform regulations governing the use of arms by all Austrian security forces were issued in 1969.

The federal police authorities have the necessary number of passenger cars, operational motor vehicles, trucks, special vehicles, motorcycles and motorboats. Aircraft are under the direct control of the federal Ministry of the Interior.

To ensure communications, the federal police authorities have a sufficient number of mobile, portable and stationary radio sets. It is intended in due course to equip every policeman on the beat with a small two-way radio.

For action in case of disasters, the Security Guard has engineering equipment, lighting units, medical supplies and equipment, various types of protective clothing, radiation protection devices, gas masks, water life-saving equipment, etc.

The Corps of Criminal Investigators

Given its specific nature, the origins of this service are rather obscure. It was after the revolutionary year of 1848 that the first official order was issued for plainclothes officers to be attached to the police authorities. From these beginnings the corps gradually developed into what it is now.

The members of the corps wear civilian clothes on duty. They carry arms and are required to identify themselves by presenting their identity card and badge. Their function within the security system is to obtain information, investigate crimes, shadow suspects and trace wanted persons.

The Federal Gendarmerie

Organized as a military-style armed and uniform-wearing force under a central command controlled by the directorate-general for public security in the federal Ministry of the Interior, the gendarmerie polices the major part of the country (i.e., all areas not coming under the jurisdiction of a federal police authority), with about two-thirds of Austria's population.

The gendarmerie comprises eight provincial gendarmerie commands (one for each *Land*, except Vienna), subdivided into 40 regional commands, 90 district commands and 1,048 gendarmerie stations.

In each province the gendarmerie is a homogeneous force in operational, economic and administrative terms.

Each provincial command, headed by the *Land* gendarmerie commandant, a colonel, is in the capital of the province concerned, which is also the seat of the provincial government. A command consists of "groups" (organization and operations, personnel, training, technical supply, economic supply) with the necessary number of "desks," plus the staff division, the specialized divisions (criminal investigations, traffic, trainee unit) and the regional commands dispersed over the province. The groups and desks as well as the staff division, the specialized divisions and the regional commands are headed by commissioned officers. The district commands and gendarmerie stations also come under the jurisdiction of the provincial command.

For each administrative district there is a district gendarmerie command at the seat of the district administrative authority. In the district towns as well as in other important localities in the district, there are gendarmerie stations that are subordinate to the district command.

Already between 1918 and 1938, a certain measure of specialization had set in among the members of the gendarmerie, a process that has had to be stepped up continually since 1945. Thus we now find specially trained gendarmerie officers conducting criminal investigations, directing traffic, policing the country's airspace, lakes, rivers and Alpine areas, and manning workshops. Besides special talents on the part of the officers concerned, these jobs require thorough training, including refresher courses, in such subjects as detective work, driving, aircraft piloting, motorboat driving, photography, police-dog handling, observation from aircraft, motorcar repair and maintenance, radio engineering, repair and maintenance of arms, mountaineering, and radiation detection. The gendarme gets his basic training in a 16-month course. Candidates for middle-level command positions attend special courses lasting for one year, and those aspiring to senior jobs take part in two-year special training programs. In addition, the gendarmerie organizes seminars on management, administration, leadership, protection against disasters, and the like for its senior officers.

Two or three district commands, with their gendarmerie stations, form a regional unit under the appropriate regional command.

In matters of public security, the provincial command takes orders from the public security directorate, and the district commands and gendarmerie stations are subordinate to the district administrative authority. The internal affairs of the gendarmerie are in the hands of its own bodies.

The gendarmerie has a central training establishment for all its units. It provides basic training as well as refresher courses and specific programs for officers marked out for senior appointments or special tasks.

As regards arms, transport and telecommunications, the gendarmerie has the same facilities as the Federal Security Guard.

Municipal Police Forces

Some Austrian municipalities still maintain their own police forces to provide local security services. Austrian constitutional law stipulates that in areas policed by a federal police authority, with its attached federal Security Guard units, provinces or municipalities shall not establish any other security forces. Hence municipal police forces exist in only a few smaller towns, excluding, of course, those where a federal police authority, and therefore a federal Security Guard contingent, exists. On the whole, the municipal police forces may be regarded as relics from the past.

The police uniform is a bottle-green, open-necked tunic with gold buttons worn with a belt over black trousers. White or blue-gray shirts and a black tie complete the uniform, which is topped by a dark green cap with a gold cord. Senior ranks wear a red band around the cap. Women police wear a similar tunic with a matching skirt and a cap that is a cross between a pillbox and a forage cap. Personnel on traffic duty wear either a white tunic or a long white overcoat with white tops to the cap (women wear a white cap with red piping). In the summer the jackets are discarded and blue-gray open-necked shirts are worn with long sleeves. Other uniforms are worn for special duty, such as ski patrols.

The major police ranks are as follows:

Polizeiprasident

Polizeiprasident Wirklicher Hofrat

Oberpolizeirat

Polizeirat

Polizeioberkommissar (three grades)

Polizeigeneral

Polizeioberst

Polizeioberstleutenant

Polizeimajor

Polizeimeister

Polizeioberleutenant

Polizeileutenant

Polizeigruppeninspektor

Polizeibezirkinspektor

Polizeirevierinspektor

Polizeirayoninspektor

Polizeioberwachman

Polizeiachmann

All police pistols, carbines, rubber truncheons, and tear gas and water cannon are issued during public disorders.

Recruitment, Education & Training

Police recruitment is directed at military personnel who have been recently demobilized. Candidates who meet the minimum requirements are trained at the local level for the Security Guards and at the central level for the gendarmerie. After three years of service, they may transfer to the Federal Criminal Investigation Corps, becoming detectives on completion of a specialist course.

University graduates with degrees in law and at least one year of legal practice may become interim police commissioners. Their appointment becomes permanent after four years and additional training. The officer corps is open to the lower ranks, and policemen often rise to commissioned status after additional training.

The Penal System

The early criminal codes merely listed crimes—their definitions were considered self-evident—and provided for extreme punishments. They did not list all possible crimes, and a judge was authorized to determine the criminality of unlisted offenses and to fix sentences at his discretion.

The first unified criminal code was enacted in 1768 during the reign of Empress Maria Theresa. The code sanctioned, although not expressly, torture or "painful interrogation." Torture was not abolished until 1776 and capital punishment until 1783. Capital punishment was reintroduced in 1795 and was abolished a second time, in 1950.

The Josefine Code of 1787, enacted by Joseph II, was the first to declare that there was no crime without a law—i.e., an act not defined as a crime in the code was not to be treated as a crime in the courts. The code was revised in 1803 and 1852 and has remained the basis of the current Penal Code. Imprisonment in chains and corporal punishment were abolished in the mid-1800s.

A commission was appointed in 1954 to work on a reform of the Penal Code that will incorporate changes in the philosophy of criminal justice brought about by two world wars. The emerging code permits greater latitude in the determination of appropriate sentences and their execution.

The Austrian codes have drawn liberally from those of other countries but have retained some peculiarly Austrian features. Among the latter is the distinction in law among three classes of lawbreakers: those who are reformable, those who commit crimes on impulse, and those who are incorrigible.

All prisons, from county jails to maximum-security institutions, are regulated by the federal Ministry of the Interior. Revisions adopted in 1967 to the Penal Code have emphasized rehabilitation, educations, work, prison wages and provisions for assisting prisoners upon their return to society. Regulations stipulate that all able-bodied prisoners will be put to useful work. If the proceeds exceed the state's expenses for the prisoner's maintenance, the prisoner is paid a wage, part of which is paid as pocket money and the remainder on release. Prisoners may be permitted to attend outside classes.

Workhouses, first established in 1932, play a role in rehabilitation. Petty criminals over 18 years of age who have never been able or willing to find employment are placed in workhouses. Sentences are usually limited to three years, except in the cases of recidivists, who may be remanded for up to five years.

CRIME STATISTICS (1984)

		Number Reported	Attempts %	Cases Solved %	Crime per 100,000	Offenders	Females %	Juveniles %	Strangers %
1.	Murder	184	45.7	97.3	2.44	180	15.6	5	13.9
2.	Sex offenses, including rape	3,316	10.7	76.8	43.91	1,815	3.5	12.2	7.9
3.	Rape	397	38.8	71.5	5.26	296		10.3	9.5
4.	Serious assault	123	8.9	96.7	1.63	128	9.4	2.3	11.7
5.	All theft	180,387	6.2	29.3	2,388.66	32,529	21.3	21.7	9.8
6.	Aggravated theft	63,100	14.1	29	835.56	9,923	6.7	25.1	8.5
7.	Robbery and violent theft	2,247	10.2	60.2	29.75	1,384	12.4	17.8	15.8
8.	Breaking and entering	60,853	14.1	27.8	805.81	8,539	5.8	26.3	7.4
9.	Auto theft	1,278	19.3	35.4	16.92	281	3.6	11.0	10.3
10.	Other thefts	116,009	1.9	29.5	1,536.18	22,325	28.0	20.3	10.3
11.	Fraud	22,742	2.0	82.7	301.15	13,984	21.1	1.7	7.9
12.	Counterfeiting	731	1.0	16.3	9.68	128	14.1	5.5	39.1
13.	Drug offenses	5,442	0.2	99.3	72.06	4,759	20.5	5.9	56.0
14.	Total offenses	391,602	3.6	54.2	5,185.55	187,019	17.5	10.0	7.4

Criteria of juveniles: aged from 14 to 17 years.

BANGLADESH

BASIC FACT SHEET

Official Name: People's Republic of Bangladesh
Area: 143,998 sq km
Population: 107,087,586 (1987)
Capital: Dhaka
Nature of Government: Civilian dictatorship
Language: Bangla
Currency: Taka
GNP: $13.9 billion (1985)
Territorial Divisions: 4 divisions, 21 regions, 64 districts, 495 thanas
Population per Police Officer: 2,560
Police Expenditures per 1,000: N.A.

History & Background

The foundation of Bangladesh police administration is the Police Act of 1861, which created a provincial police under the control of an inspector general in each of the territories ruled by the British in the Indian subcontinent. It was supplemented by the Criminal Procedure Code of 1898 and the Police Regulations of Bengal of 1943, both of which continued to remain in force after the departure of the British and the creation of Bangladesh in 1972. But it was not until 1976 that a metropolitan police force was established in Dhaka, the capital. This was followed by the introduction of a metropolitan police force at Chittagong, in 1978. A number of committees and commissions helped to broaden and streamline police functions, particularly during the 25 years that Bangladesh was under Pakistani rule. These include the Shahabuddin Committee of 1953, the Hatch Barnwell Committee of 1956, the Committee on the Increase of Force in Dhaka and Naryanganj of 1957, the Constantine Commission of 1960–61, and the Mitha Commission of 1969. The War of Independence took a heavy toll on the number and morale of the police force. As a result, the force was expanded and reconstituted and its training facilities modernized during the 1970s.

Structure & Organization

The Bangladesh Police is headed by an inspector general of police, who reports to the Ministry of Home Affairs. Below the headquarters level, the force is organized by districts and divisions. Police officers are categorized as gazetted or subordinate—roughly analogous, respectively, to commissioned and non-commissioned officers in the military services. The subordinate grades are further classified into upper and lower categories. The top four police grades, in descending order, are inspector general, deputy inspector general, superintendent and assistant superintendent. Below these gazetted ranks are the upper subordinate positions, in descending order, of inspector, subinspector and assistant subinspector. Below them are the bulk of policemen in the lower subordinate grades of head constable and constable.

The inspector general supervises staff departments concerned with criminal investigation, identification, communications, administration and supply. He is further responsible for supervision over the police ranges, divisions coterminous with the political divisions and each under a deputy inspector general. Within the ranges, the districts form the fulcrum of police operations. The district chief is a superintendent; subordinate to him are one or more assistant superintendents and a number of inspectors and those in other ranks. The senior subdivisional police officer is an assistant superintendent. The *thana*, or station house, is supervised by one of the upper subordinate grades, called the station house officer, with about 10 head constables and constables at the station. The *thana* is also the seat of the lowest court and magistrate in the legal system. Assisting the regular police are part-time village constables called *ansars*, who report violations to the nearest police station and apprehend offenders on police orders. The *ansars* are recruited locally and receive a pittance for their efforts. There are at present 486 active police stations.

At all levels the senior police officer responds to

the chain of command within the police organization, but he is also under the general direction of designated civil government officials. These multiple lines of command sometimes cause confusion and disagreement, but the principle of civilian control is fairly well established. Thus, at the national level, the inspector general reports to the home secretary; at the divisional or police range level, the deputy inspector general answers to the divisional commissioner; and at the district level, the police superintendent answers to the deputy commissioner. Although the deputy commissioner has no authority to interfere directly in the internal organization and discipline of the force, one of his important duties is to inspect the police stations of his district at regular intervals. In cases of disagreement, the deputy commissioner generally prevails over the police superintendent but is dependent on police cooperation for the success of his administration. In case of serious differences, both may refer the dispute to higher authorities for resolution.

Countrywide, the regular police are overworked. In the lower subordinate grades, which account for 90% of the force, the pay is poor, advancement slow, and educational levels and public acceptability low. Corruption is rampant at all levels.

There are no municipal forces except at Dhaka and Chittagong, where the metropolitan police forces are headed by commissioners. Both forces have efficient antiriot units. The Armed Police Reserve is primarily a riot control force. The Anti-Corruption Department, administered by a cabinet secretariat, is a special investigative unit. Internal security is the responsibility of the Department of National Security Intelligence.

Recruitment, Education & Training

There are no training facilities other than that at Sardah in Rajshahi District. Information is not available on its programs.

The Penal System

In general the criminal codes and procedures in effect in Bangladesh continue to be those inherited from the British Raj, as amended by first Pakistan and then Bangladesh. The basic documents include the Penal Code, first promulgated in 1860 as the Indian Penal Code; the Police Act of 1861, the Evidence Act of 1872, the Code of Criminal Procedure of 1898, the Criminal Law Amendment Act of 1908 and the Official Secrets Act of 1911.

The major classes of crime are listed in the Penal Code, which is the country's most important and most comprehensive penal statute. Among listed categories of more serious crimes are activities called "offenses against the state"; an offense of this nature is also defined as "war against the state." Section 121 of the Penal Code makes antinational offenses punishable by death or imprisonment for 20 years. The incitement of hatred, contempt, or disaffection toward a lawfully constituted authority is also a criminal offense, punishable by a maximum sentence of life imprisonment.

Among other categories of felonies are offenses relating to the armed forces, such as mutiny or desertion; offenses against public tranquillity; offenses against public health, safety and morals; offenses against Islam; offenses against the person; and offenses against property.

Punishments are divided into five categories: death, banishment, imprisonment, forfeiture of property and fine. Imprisonment may be simple or rigorous, ranging from a minimum of 24 hours for drunk and disorderly conduct to a maximum of 14 years at hard labor. Juvenile offenders may be sentenced to detention in reformatory schools for a period of three to seven years; for minor infractions whipping (not exceeding 15 lashes) may be prescribed as an alternative to detention. The Penal Code applies to all citizens except the president, accredited diplomats, provincial governors and justices, judges of the Supreme Court, children under seven years of age, persons of unsound mind and those who act in self-defense.

Preventive detention may be ordered under the Security of Pakistan Act of 1952, as amended, and under Section 107 of the Code of Criminal Procedure. In addition, the Disturbed Areas (Special Powers) Ordinance of 1962 empowers a magistrate or any officer in charge of a police contingent to open fire or use force against any persons breaching the peace in these areas and to arrest and search without a warrant. Persons charged with espionage are punished under the Official Secrets Act of 1911 as amended in 1923 and 1968. The statute provides death as the maximum penalty.

The penal system, under the office of an inspector general of prisons, is governed by the Penal Code of 1860, the Prisons Act of 1894 and the Prisoners Act of 1900. Bangladesh has not been able to devote much money or effort on modernizing the prison system inherited from the British. At the division or police range level, the senior official is called the director of prisons, and at the district level he is the jail superintendent. Below the district jail level are the thana and village police backups. All installations are manned by prison police. In general, prisons are overcrowded, filthy, and primitive, with few amenities.

BELGIUM

BASIC FACT SHEET

Official Name: Kingdom of Belgium
Area: 30,540 sq km
Population: 9,873,066 (1987)
Capital: Brussels
Nature of Government: Constitutional monarchy
Languages: French & Flemish
Currency: Belgian franc
GNP: $79.9 billion (1985)
Territorial Divisions: Wallonia & Flanders regions: 9 provinces
Population per Police Officer: 640
Police Expenditures per 1,000: N.A.

History & Background

Although most Belgian towns had municipal police forces during the Middle Ages, it was not until the French occupation in 1795 that a formal gendarmerie system was established. This system was retained under Dutch rule (1815–30) and after Belgium became independent in 1830.

Structure & Organization

Three kinds of police exist in Belgium: the gendarmerie, the criminal police and a number of commune police forces. There is also a parish constable system in the rural areas.

The Gendarmerie

The modern Gendarmerie is one of the armed forces but not part of the Army. On military matters it reports to the Ministry of National Defense, on matters relating to police work it reports to the Ministry of the Interior, and on matters relating to judiciary it reports to the Ministry of Justice. The command structure includes a general headquarters and a training school at the top and territorial groups, mobile groups and criminal investigation detachments in the field. Its main functions are the investigation of crimes, the escorting of prisoners, preventive police work, the restoration and maintenance of public order, the enforcement of traffic laws, and military police duties. Although the Gendarmerie's jurisdiction extends over the entire kingdom, it normally operates only in those areas outside the jurisdiction of municipal police forces. For operational purposes, the country is divided into

five regions, each of which covers two provinces, and each region is commanded by a colonel. Within each region there are two territorial groups (only one in the case of the Brabant region, which includes Brussels) plus a mobile group, each of which is commanded by a major or lieutenant colonel.

Each of the nine territorial groups covers a province and is divided into a number of districts. A traffic police section is attached to each territorial group. Each district is divided into brigades, each of which is composed of a warrant officer and at least six other officers. These brigades are scattered over the whole country, each covering one or more rural communities. A surveillance and investigation detachment is also assigned to each district. Its members work in civilian clothes.

Each mobile group is commanded by a lieutenant colonel and is divided into squadrons, each under a captain and troops, under a warrant officer. In addition to the five regional mobile groups, there is a mobile legion of two groups under the direct control of the commandant of Gendarmerie.

The highest rank in the Gendarmerie is lieutenant general, and the highest rank among noncommissioned officers is *maréchal de logis*.

The standard Gendarmerie uniform consists of a blue uniform and a cap with red piping on the trouser legs, cuffs, and caps. Red collar tabs bear the gendarmerie insignia and, in the case of officers, insignia of rank. To this uniform is added a Sam Browne belt, which carries the standard 9mm automatic pistol as well as a billy club. The uniform is similar to that worn by the municipal police except that the latter have silver, not red, embellishments. During emergencies, Lee Enfield rifles are issued to the gendarmes.

The Communal Police

Each of the 345 major towns and municipalities has a Communal Police force. They are usually under the control of the mayor, although in the larger towns the force is headed by a police commissioner who is an officer of the Judiciary Police, and in criminal matters they work under the direction of the crown prosecutor. They are responsible for all general police functions within the municipal boundaries. The larger units have special sections dealing with criminal and traffic offenses as well as uniformed patrols. Municipal detectives work strictly in accordance with their instructions from the police commissioner and the mayor.

Commune Police officers wear dark blue uniforms and a peaked cap. They are authorized to carry either a 7.65mm automatic pistol or a .38-caliber revolver. Communal Police are divided into divisions and brigades, apart from specialized services. The highest rank in the communal police is *commissaire en chef* (chief commissioner).

The Criminal Police

The Judicial (or Criminal) Police force is commanded by a general commissioner under the Ministry of Justice. Its personnel operate under the authority and control of the *procureur général* (public prosecutor) attached to each of the appeals courts as well as the *procureur de roi* (crown prosecutor). The Judicial Police deals only with the most serious crimes.

Each of the 22 Judicial Police brigades is headed by a *commissaire en chef,* who is in charge of all criminal investigations and who assists the public prosecutor in preparing evidence for the courts. The central headquarters of the force in Brussels is also the national central bureau of INTERPOL. The headquarters also houses the Central Criminal Police Records Office and the Scientific Police Laboratory. Judicial police personnel work in plain clothes but carry either a Browning 7.65 automatic pistol or a P.38 revolver.

The Rural Police are stationed in the 245 small towns and villages. Each unit may consist of one or more constables. Larger towns with large agricultural areas within their boundaries may also have a rural constable attached to their commune police force. One parish constable may look after several communities if their total population does not exceed 5,000. Parish constables are grouped into brigades, each under a supervisor, who is responsible to the mayor for general duties and the public prosecutor for criminal matters.

Parish constables are appointed by the governor of the province on the recommendation of the town or parish council and with the approval of the local commissioner of police and the public prosecutor. They are competent to deal with all police matters, although their responsibility is limited to rural crimes. They wear the same uniform as the Communal Police. The highest rank in the rural police is *chef de brigade* (brigade chief). Rural Police personnel are authorized to carry FN Browning type .22 automatic, 7.65mm or Smith & Wesson .38 special revolvers.

Recruitment, Education & Training

Officer candidates for the Gendarmerie are recruited through competitive examinations. Once accepted, they undergo a five-year course at the university level. Promotion is based on further examinations. Training and refresher courses are provided at the Royal Gendarmerie School.

Commissionaires of the Commune Police are appointed by the crown, while other officers are appointed by the town councils with the approval of the provincial governor and on the advice of the crown prosecutor. Training is provided by the Communal Police Training Center in Brussels.

Applicants for Judicial Police are selected on the basis of competitive examinations and are further trained at the School of Criminology and Scientific Police at Brussels. Additional personnel are recruited from the Gendarmerie and the Communal Police.

The Penal System

In minor cases, criminal justice is administered by justices of the peace, by the local police or by the police courts in 222 judicial cantons. Serious cases, such as misdemeanors and felonies, are tried before the 26 district courts, the tribunals of first instance. Justices of the peace and police courts have the authority to levy fines and impose short-term jail sentences. More than 99% of the convictions in any given year are for petty crimes classified as police cases—public inebriation, disorderly conduct, disturbing the peace, simple assault and minor traffic violations as well as for vagrancy, truancy and failure to vote (a legal offense in Belgium).

More than half of those sentenced to prison terms are granted a conditional sentence, under which confinement is intermittent and under which prisoners serve sentences on weekends after payment of judicial fines and penalties. Death sentences are rare; in peacetime they are usually commuted by the king to life imprisonment.

Belgian prisons have a well-deserved reputation for cleanliness, satisfactory food, efficient management and effective rehabilitation programs. However, statistics show a high degree of recidivism—about 40%. Criminal statistics are carefully compiled and published periodically.

CRIME STATISTICS (1984)

		Number Reported	Attempts %	Cases Solved %	Crime per 100,000	Offenders	Females %	Juveniles %	Strangers %
1.	Murder	322		86.0	3.27				
2.	Sex offenses, including rape	3,473		55.2	35.28				
3.	Rape	558		74.0	5.67				
4.	Serious assault	8,724		75.9	88.62				
5.	All theft	183,536		13.6	1,864.29				
6.	Aggravated theft	77,477		8.7	786.98				
7.	Robbery and violent theft	4,920		18.5	49.98				
8.	Breaking and entering								
9.	Auto theft	13,837		10.6	140.55				
10.	Other thefts	87,302		17.6	886.78				
11.	Fraud	1,433		57.1	14.56				
12.	Counterfeiting	168		24.4	1.71				
13.	Drug offenses	3,296		97.8	33.48				
14.	Total offenses	231,328		21.2	2,349.74				

Criteria of juveniles: aged from 0 to 18 years.
Note: Information for some categories is not available.

BOLIVIA

BASIC FACT SHEET

Official Name: Republic of Bolivia
Area: 1,098,581 sq km
Population: 6,309,642 (1987)
Capital: La Paz (seat of government); Sucre (legal capital)
Nature of Government: Limited democracy
Language: Spanish
Currency: Peso
GNP: $3.79 billion (1986)
Territorial Divisions: 9 departments
Population per Police Officer: N.A.
Police Expenditures per 1,000: N.A.

History & Background

Bolivia has one of the most centralized police systems in Latin America. The first significant legislation covering law enforcement agencies was enacted in 1886. The system remained basically unchanged until 1950, when it was substantially revised in the Organic Law of Police and Carabiñeros, sometimes referred to simply as Law No. 311. Together with the law of 1886, it provides the legal basis for the present-day police system.

Until the Revolution of 1952, the police force was subordinate to the regular armed forces, and most senior posts were given to Army officers. The situation changed radically in 1952 with the rise of the Movimiento Nacionalista Revolucionaria (MNR). The police sided with the revolutionaries and were rewarded by being given greater jurisdiction, and their technical competence was developed by a U.S. AID training mission.

Structure & Organization

Under the Constitution, the president of the republic is the commander in chief of the *carabiñeros* and the National Police Corps (Cuerpo de Policía Nacional). In this capacity, he names the director general of both agencies and may administer their activities directly during times of internal stress. Under the president, the direct control of the police forces is exercised by the Ministry of the Interior. In times of war, the uniformed *carabiñero* units may be transferred to the Ministry of National Defense and their activities integrated with those of the regular armed forces, as though they were reserve units.

Operational control is vested in an appointive di-rector-general, who is invariably a high-ranking career police official. The director-general is also commander of the National Police Academy, head of the National Identification Service and chief of the Bolivian section of INTERPOL. International police cooperation is significant in that Bolivia is a prime staging area for illegal narcotics trafficking.

The office of the director-general, which serves as the national headquarters for all police and *carbiñero* activities, consists of a command group and 12 numbered staff sections. Field elements are stationed in all sectors of the country, where they function without accountability to departmental, provincial or municipal governments. Subordinate headquarters known as brigades are established in the capital of each of the nine departments. Each brigade is divided into two commands, one urban and the other provincial. The urban command at the departmental capital has charge of the police stations and local jails and is divided into sections that have personnel assigned for patrol and investigative duties.

Most corps personnel and units within a department, regardless of size, composition, mission or station, are considered part of the brigade in the area they serve and are members of a single departmental unit. An exception is the city of La Paz, where two separate regiments of the police are kept under the direct control of the director-general and president. Other exceptions are made in sections of the country where dependence on regular departmental brigade forces is not deemed politically advisable. Two such areas—San Ignacio de Velasco in Santa Cruz department and Tupiza in Potosi department—have independent *carabiñero* detachments in addition to regular brigades.

Certain departmental brigade personnel of the rural command are on duty at a series of frontier posts scattered at 27 critical points along the borders and at river and lake ports of entry. They include customs police as well as uniformed *carabiñeros* engaged in combating smuggling and illegal border crossings.

In the mid-1980s the police and *carabiñeros* of Bolivia numbered about 10,000 men, including officers. Most of the corps is concentrated in the La Paz area, where about 50% of its uniformed members and 60% of its civilian personnel are stationed. Within the corps itself, approximately 80% are uniformed *carabiñeros* and 20% are civilian police investigators and minor functionaries. Both wings are undermanned. In La Paz there is a rudimentary crime detection laboratory. When funds are available, some use is made of police informers, but more often police rely on periodic massive roundups of known miscreants to keep the crime rates down.

A police career offers few attractions, other than for corruption. Pay scales are low, and opportunities for advancement are rare. Little if any, social prestige is attached to members of the police corps. Most policemen come from a relatively low economic stratum and are, in many cases, illiterate.

Personnel of the corps are classified into three distinct groups. The first is made up of uniformed personnel, known as *carabiñeros*. The second includes all auxiliary and technical personnel, such as doctors, dentists, veterinarians, chaplains, communications and transportation specialists, and social service workers, who may be either uniformed *carabiñeros* or civilians. The third is made up of police investigators and identification personnel, who are almost exclusively civilians.

Uniformed personnel are grouped into four general classifications, with a graded system of rank within each class. In descending order, the classifications are field officers *(jefes)*, company officers *(oficiales)*, noncommissioned officers *(clases)* and privates *(tropos)*. Ranks generally correspond to those in the Army.

Uniformed personnel are promoted on the basis of annual examinations given when they enter the "zone of consideration." This zone is determined by time in grade, which is usually four years for all except captains and sergeants, who must spend five years in grade before becoming eligible for promotion. Classification of civilian personnel is based on a simple nonmilitary two-category system composed of superiors *(functionarios superiores)* and subordinates *(funcionarios subalternos)*.

Recruitment, Education & Training

Cadets accepted for the National Police Academy are not subject to the age limitations for enlisted military service, and matriculation automatically exempts them from their military obligations. Entrance requirements are lax. Since the arrival of the U.S. Police Training Mission in 1956, specialized training in criminal law, personnel administration, police methods and techniques, and riot control tactics have been introduced. Upon graduation, cadets receive a bachelor of humanities certificate, a saber and a commission as second lieutenant in the *carabiñeros*.

Before 1956 police and *carabiñero* training was largely of the on-the-job type. Enlisted men received about four months' training in active units and were then assigned permanent duties, while officers received only their formal training at the National Police Academy. Since 1956, when the U.S. police training mission revamped the training programs, more of the in-service training was taken over by the National Police Academy, special unit schools are run by the brigades, and some officers are being sent abroad for training. Among the specialized courses being taught at the academy are detection, riot control, police ethics, public relations, preparation of reports, personnel relations, leadership, criminal law and procedure, and methods of interrogation and identification. Another special course, on counterinsurgency, is patterned after a similar course at the Special Warfare School at Fort Bragg in the United States.

The Penal System

The Penal Code recognizes three types or orders of punishment that may be imposed on criminals, regardless of whether the offense was a misdemeanor or a felony: corporal punishment, such as imprisonment; noncorporal punishment, such as deprivation of civil rights; and pecuniary punishment, such as fines. Capital punishment for any reason was abolished by the 1961 Constitution but was held constitutional by the Supreme Court in 1973. The second most severe punishment is 30 years of hard labor with no recourse to pardon or clemency. For serious crimes, the statute of limitations specifies 10 years from the date of commission. Judicial pardon does not exist in the Penal Code, but both the president and the National Congress have this power in certain circumstances.

The national penitentiary is in La Paz, and there is at least one in each of the nine political departments. Most provinces have jails of their own. Other facilities include a correctional farm at Caranavi; a reformatory for women at La Paz; and three reformatories for juveniles, one at La Paz and two near Cochabamba. These institutions, with the exception of the reformatories for juveniles, are under the Ministry of the Interior.

The Correctional Farm at Caranavi is a unique institution where regulations are strict, prisoners are tightly secluded in their cells at night under enforced silence, communication with the outside world is closely monitored, and families are rarely permitted to visit inmates. Nevertheless, during the day, prisoners engage in common work in the fields, and meals are better. The Women's Reformatory at La Paz is operated by a Roman Catholic order of nuns, whose charity and dedication have made it a model institution. In other institutions, corruption, malnutrition and insanitary conditions are endemic.

Bolivia does not collect or publish criminal statistics on a regular basis. Press surveys suggest that petty thievery ranks high on the list of most common crimes. Also reported with considerable frequency are disorderly conduct and attacks upon persons, including rape. The number of crimes rises substantially during holidays and festivals, when drinking in excess is common.

The national boundaries of Bolivia are among the most difficult in the world to police. Twenty-seven frontier posts are manned by *carabiñeros* at critical points, but their net restraining influence on smuggling appears to be small.

BOTSWANA

Patrick Edobor Igbinovia

BASIC FACT SHEET

Official Name: Republic of Botswana
Area: 600,372 sq km
Population: 1,149,141 (1987)
Capital: Gaborone
Nature of Government: Limited democracy
Languages: English & Setswana
Currency: Pula
GNP: $905 million
Territorial Divisions: 10 administrative districts
Population per Police Officer: 750
Police Expenditures per 1,000: $6,705

History & Background

On July 1, 1884, a force of about 100 Europeans, named the Bechuanaland Mounted Police, was organized to police the newly annexed crown colony of British Bechuanaland, which lay north of Griqualand and west and south of the Molopo River in what is now the Republic of South Africa. When the annexation took place a protectorate was also proclaimed over that part of Bechuanaland laying north of the Molopo, but the imperial authorities at that time did not intend using this police force in the protectorate.

Owing to the activities of European filibusters operating from Rooigrond, near Mafeking, the imperial government sent a military expedition under Sir Charles Warren to restore order in the colony. This military force and 4,000 men, including the Bechuanaland Mounted Police, under Warren conducted a bloodless campaign and restored peace.

The withdrawal of Warren's expedition saw the defense of the colony and protectorate entrusted to a new force, raised on August 4, 1885.

This force, the Bechuanaland Border Police, was formed in accordance with instructions from the imperial secretary in Cape Town. The recruits were required to present themselves at Barkly West (in South Africa) for attestation. For the most part they had served in Warren's field force in Bechuanaland. Enrollment began at Barkly West on August 15, 1885, and 97 mounted and fully equipped men left for Mafeking on August 18, followed by a second troop of 95 of rank and file two days afterward, absorbing the Bechuanaland Mounted Police into its ranks and,

with headquarters at Mafeking under the command of Colonel Sir F. Carrington, operated both north and south of the Molopo River. It was instrumental in safeguarding the protectorate against would-be filibusters and paved the way of the 1890 Rhodesian Pioneer Column through the protectorate. In 1893 a strong Bechuanaland Border Police column played an important part in the Matebele War.

The year 1895 saw the cession of British Bechuanaland to the Cape Colony and the transfer of a number of the Bechuanaland Border Police to the Cape Police Force. Simultaneously, the eastern border of the protectorate was transferred to the British South Africa Company's administration, to which service about 120 men of the Bechuanaland Border Police were transferred. Of the balance, about 90 men remained under the protectorate administration, the force reverting to its original designation of Bechuanaland Mounted Police.

When these transfers were effected, the high commissioner caused the formation of a native force, designated the Protectorate Native Police, whose members were recruited from Basutoland.

Almost immediately after the disbandment of the Bechuanaland Border Police the Jameson Raid took place, followed by Joseph Chamberlain's decision to deprive the British South Africa Company of control of its military forces.

As a result, the British South Africa Police Force was formed under the command of an Imperial Commandant-General, with headquarters in Salisbury, Southern Rhodesia. The Bechuanaland Mounted Police became No. 1 Division of this force, and the Protectorate Native Police remained in existence, working in cooperation with No. 1 Division. This division rendered outstanding service during the siege of Mafeking.

At the end of 1902, No. 1 Division broke away from the British South Africa police, and control of the police in the protectorate became vested in the resident commissioner. The two protectorate forces were merged and renamed the Bechuanaland Protectorate Police. The resident commissioner was appointed commandant, while the chief police officer was deputy commandant.

Since then its composition has changed periodically, and reorganizations of the force occurred in 1936 and 1947. In 1947 there were changes in the structure of the force: The title of the chief police officer, who had been known as the deputy commandant, was changed to commissioner of police, with the status of a head of department. Likewise, all the military ranks previously in use changed to police ranks—i.e., deputy commissioner, superintendent, inspector, sergeant and constable. This force was responsible for enforcement of all written laws of the country, suppression of external enemies, performing all immigration duties, and matters akin to customs and excise.

On September 30, 1966 when the Bechuanaland Protectorate became the independent, sovereign Republic of Botswana, the name of the force was changed to the Botswana Police. The strength of the force at independence was 734 men, which was quite inadequate to provide police services or to safeguard the security of the boundaries of the new republic. The immediate task facing the force at independence was therefore the rapid building up of its strength to meet existing commitments and to tackle the new responsibilities that resulted from the creation of an independent republic. The first local commissioner and deputy commissioner were appointed in 1971, and localization has proceeded to the stage where the Botswana Police may now be truly regarded as a national force.

Structure & Organization

The Botswana Police are divided into two divisions and 10 districts. The two police divisions are the North and the South, respectively. Each, under the command of an assistant commissioner of police districts, are run by either superintendents or senior superintendents of police. The police districts vary in size; the largest has up to nine stations and the smallest has four.

The Northern Division has its divisional headquarters at Francistown and the Southern Division at Gaborone.

The police force has the following operational components:

Criminal Investigation Department

Traffic Department

Diamond Squad

Serious Crime Squad

Special Support Group

Force Communications Branch

Criminal Investigation Department

The Criminal Investigation Department is under the command of a senior superintendent based at Gaborone, where he also supervises the running of the Criminal Record and Fingerprint Bureau, Photographic Section, Central Arms Registry and the training of CID details.

Completed dockets in all cases of a serious or complicated nature are required to be passed to the OC of the CID for perusal and onward transmission to the attorney general for further direction. The Criminal Record Bureau operates as a separate section of the Criminal Investigation Department under the command of a superintendent.

Special Support Group Apart from being engaged in the control of foot-and-mouth disease along the Zimbabwe border, members of this branch are deployed on night patrol duties in the towns. However, as a new branch of the force, much importance is attached to the training of personnel.

Force Communications Branch This branch is responsible for radio communication, installation, maintenance, and training of radio operators. It showed remarkable improvement in 1979 as far as communication and training are concerned. In that year, 20 officers attended and passed typing, teleprinter and telex operators courses.

The force has no separate mounted section, but recruits are still given an equitation course and instruction in animal management as part of their basic training, and mounted escorts are provided on ceremonial occasions.

Camels are used for patrolling the Kgalagadi district, and horses at other stations where the terrain is suitable. Mules and donkeys are used as pack animals.

Force headquarters is based at Gaborone, the national capital city. The following officers form the headquarters unit:

commissioner of police

deputy commissioner of police

senior assistant commissioner

assistant commissioner

2 superintendents

2 assistant superintendents

2 inspectors

2 subinspectors

3 sergeants

9 constables

The total figure is far below that approved for the headquarters.

The basic uniform consists of a khaki tunic and shorts worn with knee-length stockings and puttees. Headgear consists of a blue peaked cap or beret. Police on general duties are not normally armed.

Of the total force strength of 1,572 in 1979, two were women sergeants and 18 were women constables. For the first time since the birth of the Botswana Police, seven women were also promoted to the rank of subinspector, in 1979. They are required to exercise control over their subordinates, both male and female, and have the same responsibilities of command and discipline as their male counterparts, with whom they share equal career opportunities.

Recruitment, Education & Training

The power to appoint police officers of the rank of assistant superintendent and above (with the exception of the commissioner of police) is vested in the Public Service Commission. Subordinates—NCO's and those in other ranks—are appointed by the commissioner of police.

All members of the force who have been admitted to the permanent establishment and have passed prescribed police qualifying examinations may be considered for promotion within the force.

The Police Training Depot is at Gaborone.

A candidate for enlistment as a constable must be:

1. a citizen of Botswana

2. at least 20 years old

3. medically and physically fit for service in the force

4. not less than five feet, 8 inches tall and with an expanded chest measurement of 32 inches

5. the holder of a Standard VII education certificate

6. of exemplary character and sober habits

CRIME STATISTICS (1984)

		Number Reported	Attempts %	Cases Solved %	Crime per 100,000	Offenders	Females %	Juveniles %	Strangers %
1.	Murder	69		78.26	7.49	45	11.11		
2.	Sex offenses, including rape	514		56.80	55.81	220		5.90	
3.	Rape	412		0.50	44.73	156		6.41	
4.	Serious assault	3,324		77.34	360.90	2,369	11.10	2.57	
5.	All theft	15,202		44.52	1,650.55	7,043	12.32	8.34	
6.	Aggravated theft	4,405		70.05	478.27	1,265	5.92	16.20	
7.	Robbery and violent theft	411		27.00	44.62	111		0.90	
8.	Breaking and entering	3,994		27.89	433.65	1,154	5.71	15.85	
9.	Auto theft								
10.	Other thefts	6,201		45.37	673.27	2,728	17.08	11.21	
11.	Fraud	424		49.29	46.04	199	9.54	3.01	
12.	Counterfeiting	3		66.66	0.33	2			
13.	Drug offenses	409		89.97	44.41	378	15.60	2.64	
14.	Total offenses	46,478		72.73	5,046.33	34,354	9.65	2.83	

Criteria of juveniles: aged from 8 to 18 years.
Note: Information for some categories is not available.

It has been found necessary to have Police Depot educational tests to ensure that a recruit possesses a reasonable standard of education. Any potential recruit who fails the test is rejected whether or not he or she has an educational certificate.

Recruits in the force are locally trained at the Police College in Gaborone. Entrants have at least a junior certificate, but in some cases a good pass in Standard VII has been considered. The course for recruits lasts 22 weeks. The Police College also runs refresher courses for other ranks of the force. Some senior police officers have attended courses at Hendon Police College and Bramshill in the United Kingdom. In addition, some officers from the CID and the Traffic and Communications Branch have attended courses in the United Kingdom.

The Penal System

Urbanization and its social problems remain major contributory factors in crime increase. Young people drift from rural villages to urban centers and add to the already swelling numbers of the unemployed in towns. These unemployed young people together with refugees from neighboring countries account for the escalating crime in towns. Another matter of concern to the police is the obvious increase in the use of *dagga* (marijuana) by youths, especially those residing in towns.

Development in the mining sector has given rise to diamond smuggling, hence the formation of a diamond squad within the force. Local and international smugglers have been prosecuted time and again. Armed robberies are common. Although the force had previously handled robberies, these involved only physical force or instruments such as knives. It is strongly suggested that arms have fallen into wrong hands following intensification of the liberation war in the southern region of Africa, by renegades using cross-border tactics.

The Prison Department operates 17 prisons throughout Botswana with total approved accommodation for 1,042 inmates. The average number of inmates per day has been increasing steadily since 1972. In 1975 a large jump occurred due primarily to the large number of illegal immigrants held in the prisons and also because of long sentences for stock theft.

BRAZIL

BASIC FACT SHEET

Official Name: Federative Republic of Brazil
Area: 8,512,100 sq km
Population: 147,094,739 (1987)
Capital: Brasília
Nature of Government: Constitutional democracy
Language: Portuguese
Currency: Cruzeiro
GNP: $250 billion (1986)
Territorial Divisions: 22 states, 4 territories, 1 federal district
Population per Police Officer: N.A.
Police Expenditures per 1,000: N.A.

History & Background

Historically, the primary police agencies for maintaining law and order in Brazil have been the state civil police forces, sometimes known as the ''governors' armies,'' which also played a prominent part in the political strife of the 1920s and 1930s. The Vargas regime moved to curb them in connection with federal intervention in the states. After the collapse of the Vargas government the elected state governments resumed control over the state police forces. After the 1964 military revolution, the federal government took steps to bring the ''governors' armies'' under more effective federal control but had only varying success. The major states of São Paulo, Minas Gerais, Guanabara, and Rio Grande do Sul have generally preserved their traditional strength in the police field, although the federal Army has assumed an increasing role in police and security matters.

Structure & Organization

The federal police structure was basically reorganized by the 1967 Constitution and a decree of June 1972 that eliminated the former highly centralized Federal Department of Public Security and created the Department of Federal Police (Departmento de Polícia Federal, DPF). The new structure is based on centralization of DPF planning, coordination and control, and technical services in Brasília (known as Department A) and detailed execution in each of the state capitals of DPF functions (known as Department B). The four general areas of DPF jurisdiction include: Maritime, Air, and Frontier Police Services; the prevention and suppression of narcotics traffic; investi-

gation of penal infractions against national security; and countering international terrorism. The DPF also provides for the state police forces' technical services relating to data processing and collection and dissemination of police intelligence.

The comprehensive function relating to national security is handled by the DPF's Division of Political and Social Order (Delegacias de Ordem Politica e Social, DOPS), which collaborates closely with the military commands. Among the technical agencies under DPF are the National Institute of Identification and the National Police Academy. Also under DPF is the Federal District Police Force in Brasília, with over 9,000 members. Training for DPF cadets and officers is provided by the Federal Police Academy and the specialized Police Center, the latter handling postgraduate courses.

The Federal Highway Police is attached to the Ministry of Transport and Public Works and control traffic and inspect licenses on the major highways. Also under the same ministry are the Federal Railway Police and the Dock Police Force.

The State Military Police, sometimes referred to as the state militia, forms by far the largest law-enforcement segment in the country, with a strength over 200,000. The force is organized on a military basis; its members hold military titles and usually receive more military than police training. They are considered auxiliary military forces and can be mobilized in the event of external or civil war. Decree Law 667 of July 2, 1969, placed the State Military Force under the Ministry of the Army. As such, each State Military Police unit is an integral part of the armed forces and reports to the headquarters of the respective military region, of which there are 11: Rio de Janeiro, São Paulo, Pôrto Alegre, Belo Horizonte, Curitiba, Recife, Salvador, Belém, Cuaiba, Fortaleza and Brasília. Each State Military force normally consists of three commands: capital, state (or interior) and traffic. All activities are coordinated by an operations center.

Each State Military Police unit is commanded by active duty Army officers and is organized like an Army unit. Four or more platoons *(pelotoes)* make up a company *(companhia)*, and four or more companies a battalion *(batalhão)*. Within each force there is one maintenance battalion, a number of Military Police battalions, various police detachments, and a Surveillance and General Investigation Section divided into sectors. There are independent companies for special duties, such as dog handling, radio patrol and music. The number of battalions varies according to the size of the population.

The Civil Guards, a component of the State Military Police, is responsible for preventive policing activities such as traffic control, street policing and the staffing of precincts. They also provide general support to the civil police.

The State Civilian Police is both an urban and a state force. It is organized into districts *(delegacãos)* headed by superintendents *(superintendentes)*. Each district comprises a number of stations *(postos de polícia)* and detachments *(plantoes polícias)*. The term *delegacãos* is also applied to specialized investigative units within a district, such as units dealing with robbery, theft and homicide, narcotics, forgeries and fraud, juveniles, vehicle theft, and surveillance. The chief law-enforcement officer in each state is the secretary of public safety, appointed by the governor. There are no municipal police forces.

Another civil unit is the Forest Police. They operate under the state's secretary of agriculture to protect the vast state-owned forests and to liaise with the fishing and hunting licensing department of the state's Agriculture Ministry.

Most State Civilian Police maintain a radio patrol department having a fleet of vehicles equipped with two-way radios for general patrol services. Most state capitals and cities are divided into precincts manned by from three to 150 men. Precinct police duties include handling complaints, issuing documents for civil purposes, providing guard services for public buildings and street patrolling.

The police uniforms vary according to duty and location. The basic uniform is an olive green tunic and trousers with a dark green peaked cap. For patrols in the interior, a United States-style uniform of steel helmet, calf-length boots, shirt and olive-green trousers is worn, while for ceremonial occasions a dark blue uniform with high neck is worn with a plumed shako. On normal patrol duties, uniformed police carry a Taurus .38 revolver. Other weapons include submachine guns, tear gas grenades, armored water-cannon vehicles.

Recruitment, Education & Training

The Federal Police Academy, established in 1968 with U.S. technical assistance, provides basic and advanced training to officers in the federal and state police forces. There is also a specialized police center in Brasília for postgraduate courses.

The Penal System

The penal system is based on the Penal Code of 1940. It has two sections, the first of which is concerned with general principles, distinctions among various types of crimes, and specifying various kinds of punishments. Capital punishment and banishment were forbidden by the constitutions of 1946, 1964 and 1967 but reappeared with the promulgation of the constitutional amendment of 1969. Among the crimes punishable by death are: collusion with foreign governments against the state, sabotage against military installations, violence against visiting heads of state and governments, attempt to overthrow legally constituted government by violence or subversion, and acts of terrorism, murder or arson. The death penalty is execution by firing squad.

Decree Law 898 stipulates a maximum of 30 years in prison as equivalent to life imprisonment. Prisoners are eligible for parole after the first year. Restrictions and regulations affecting those serving sentences of detention *(detencão)* are considerably lighter. If they are first offenders, they may be paroled after serving only half of their term.

There are close to 5,000 penal institutions in the country. There are 51 correctional institutions, including 27 penitentiaries, six houses of custody and treatment, 12 agricultural colonies and six houses of correction. Of the places of detention, 12 are military prisons, 1,580 are prisons *(cadeias)*, 2,803 are jails *(xadrezes)* and five are institutions for minors. Fourteen of these institutions have an inmate capacity of over 500.

Most prisons consist of single cells. Incorrigible prisoners remain locked in their cells, while others are assigned to various work units. Roll call takes place twice a day: at 7:30 A.M. and 9:30 P.M. Prison industries include manufacture of clothing and straw mattresses, carpentry shops, and machine and welding shops. The prison chapels are used for Protestant services on Saturday and Roman Catholic Mass on Sunday. Agricultural colonies have mostly multiple cells, which hold 20 men in double-deck bunks. Most of the prisoners work on farming tasks under the supervision of armed guards. In farm colonies inmates live with their families in small houses under no custodial restraints. Clothing for both the inmate and his family and a family allowance are provided by the state. Penal institutions for women are usually operated by religious orders, such as the Sisters of the Good Shepherd, which runs the Reeducational Colony for Women in Guanabara and the Institute for Feminine Social Readaptation at Pôrto Alegre. The word "prison" is not applied to these institutions.

Prison facilities continue to be overcrowded and poorly maintained and managed. The states of São Paulo and Minas Gerais have begun a major construction program of medium- and maximum-security regional prisons.

Official crime statistics are published irregularly and are far from complete or reliable. In a typical year, more than 25% of the crimes are homicides, another 22% robberies, 10% narcotics trafficking and 5% rapes.

BULGARIA

BASIC FACT SHEET

Official Name: People's Republic of Bulgaria
Area: 110,912 sq km
Population: 8,960,749 (1987)
Capital: Sofia
Nature of Government: Communist dictatorship
Language: Bulgarian
Currency: Lev
GNP: $57.8 billion (1985)
Territorial Divisions: 27 Okrugs (districts)
Population per Police Officer: N.A.
Police Expenditures per 1,000: N.A.

Structure & Organization

The People's Militia is the principal law-enforcement agency in Bulgaria. It is assisted by part-time, voluntary paramilitary auxiliaries and, in serious situations, by a small, centrally organized, full-time internal security force that acts as a light infantry unit. The State Security Police, evolved from the secret police of the late 1940s and 1950s but much reduced in size, deals with crimes that are national in scope or pose a threat to the society or its institutions. The People's Militia, the voluntary auxiliaries and the security units are organized within the Ministry of Internal Affairs.

Bulgaria was a police state in the proper sense of the term until the period of readjustment following the death of Joseph Stalin in the Soviet Union. Until then, the police machinery was modeled on that of the Soviet Union, with over 200,000 men in uniformed and armed police forces. Although the state and security organs continue to exist, many of them have been renamed and shifted among the various ministries. They also have been shorn of much of their arbitrary powers, and their personnel have been reduced considerably in number. State security functions and so-called political crimes loom large in the Communist mind, but because of the relative stability of the regime, they no longer contribute to a general atmosphere of repression. The secret police generally operate in the background, greatly reduced in size and importance, and their main functions are the surveillance of foreigners and potentially dangerous domestic dissidents and the collection of military intelligence.

The People's Militia may be characterized as the local police. Although strictly subordinate to the Ministry of Internal Affairs, it has offices at the level of the *okrug* (district) and local police stations at the *obshtina* (urban borough or village commune) level. All militia organizations also have some degree of responsibility to the People's Councils in their jurisdictions.

The principal functions of the People's Militia are: maintenance of law and order; protection of personal and public property; regulation of traffic; execution of government resolutions, orders and instructions; monitoring of rules of residence; collection of taxes; rescue and aid to victims of accidents or natural disasters; supervision of quarantine measures; monitoring of drinking establishments; combating rowdy, irresponsible or antisocial behavior; and care of stray children.

Many People's Militia functions go beyond the commonly acknowledged limits of law enforcement. They have unusual powers in dealing with beggars and vagrants. The police may prohibit a person from visiting a specified town or area or leaving his or her residence for specified periods. Some may be prohibited from meeting certain other specified persons or from frequenting certain parts of towns. Some persons may be denied the use of common carriers or the privilege of attending sports events or of visiting certain public institutions. Prostitutes, for example, may be denied the right to become telephone subscribers. The police may also require a person to report to them on a daily or other regular basis. All individually held ammunition, weapons and explosives are registered with the People's Militia. By law there is no production of cold weapons—brass knuckles, scimitars, daggers, and the like—in the country.

The police collect and maintain a major share of local records for the *obshtina* People's Councils. These records deal with vital statistics, citizenship, identification, travel visas, registration of residences, licenses and permits, and employment data. Laws regulating the stay of foreigners in the country are administered and enforced by the People's Militia.

A branch of the People's Militia, known as the Departmental Militia, guards sensitive areas. They are assisted by Local Guard Service units, manned by volunteers who guard factories, public buildings and public utilities installations. Militiamen sign on for a minimum of three years which may be extended by increments; the retirement age is at 50 or after 20 years of service.

There are two paramilitary organizations: The People's Territorial Militia, with a nominal strength of about 150,000; and the Voluntary Organization for Cooperation in National Defense, designed to assist the police during emergencies.

Recruitment, Education & Training

No information is available on recruitment, education and training.

The Penal Code

The Penal Code's preamble states that its purpose is to protect the society and the state, the person and the rights of its citizens, the economy, the state's property and laws, and to educate the citizens in socialist conduct of life. Citizens are to be punished only when they are found guilty of crimes specified in the Penal Code by a proper court. Juveniles under 14 years are not criminally liable, and minors between 14 and 18 years have only limited liability. Punishments are divided into 11 categories and include some that are peculiar to socialist states, such as deprivation of rights to occupy certain public offices, practice certain professions and reside in certain places. The death penalty is never mandatory in peacetime, but it is optional for a number of crimes. The second most severe sentence is imprisonment for 20 years, often imposed in lieu of death. The stipulated sentences for crimes against the state tend to be more severe than sentences for crimes against individuals.

The Ministry of Justice is responsible for the overall administration, activities and security of prisons, but outside guards are provided by the Ministry of the Interior. All prisoners are required to receive "reeducation," which consists of political indoctrination, general education and vocational education. All of them are also required to perform "useful" labor.

Detention centers are classified in three categories: prisons, labor-correctional institutions and correctional homes, the last for minors. According to the seriousness of the offense, a prisoner may be confined in light, general, strict or enforced strict disciplinary regimes, as prescribed in his or her sentence. The light regime is for first offenders and the enforced strict regime for recidivists and serious offenders.

Prisoners are segregated by age, sex and disciplinary regime. Women and minors are not subject to the enforced strict regime. Repeaters are confined in separate prisons from first offenders. Because there are only a limited number of prisons, wards within the same building complex are used to meet legal requirements for the segregation of people in various categories.

All inmates are assigned the type of work they are required to do by law within seven days of their arrival at a prison. Their wages conform to the national norms for similar kinds of work. Inmates receive 20% for their needs, and the remaining 80% is paid to their families.

Prisoners have rights by law. These include the right to communicate with the prosecutors and the courts, time outdoors, exercise, visitors, correspondence, food parcels and possession of personal effects. Visitors, correspondence and parcels are subject to official scrutiny or censorship. All conversation with outsiders must be in Bulgarian, unless translators are present.

Prisoners are rewarded for good behavior and punished for bad. When a prisoner's pattern of conduct becomes apparent over a period of time, the prisoner may be moved into a lighter or more severe disciplinary regime, granted an extra privilege or denied one to which he or she ordinarily would be entitled. Commitment to solitary confinement is limited to two weeks at any one time.

A number of sentences do not involve confinement. For offenses related to poor discipline, an individual may be given a corrective labor sentence, involving harder work, longer hours or stricter supervision. The law also provides for sentences that restrict the movement of an individual, either requiring the person to remain in one area or prohibiting visits to any other area. Another such sentence involves internment without deprivation of liberty, usually in a prisoner's own place of residence. Such a sentence may last from one to five years. The prisoner may not hold a job outside his area.

Criminal authorities in Bulgaria view crime as a social phenomenon and combating it as a matter of social edification as much as law enforcement. Petty crime is viewed as an affront to society even when it does not lead to physical damage to property. Misuse of government property, including theft and pilfering, is rampant in the country. The problem is compounded by the lenient sentences handed down by the courts. More serious crimes, such as crimes of violence, political crimes, and economic crimes have been on the decline since the 1950s. Consumption of alcohol is not excessive when compared with that of other East European countries, but it has been increasing steadily and has been a major contributor to crime and antisocial behavior; nearly 90% of those charged with rowdyism or disturbing the peace act under its influence, as also increasing percentages of those apprehended on rape, assault and murder charges. Increasing tourism has resulted in special problems in resort areas, such as smuggling, black marketeering and prostitution. Also classified as a crime is the smuggling or distribution of Bibles and other Christian literature into the country.

BURMA

BASIC FACT SHEET

Official Name: Socialist Republic of the Union of Burma
Area: 676,552 sq km
Population: 38,822,484 (1987)
Capital: Rangoon
Nature of Government: One-party dictatorship
Language: Burmese
Currency: Kyat
GNP: $7.05 billion (1986)
Territorial Divisions: 7 divisions, 7 states
Population per Police Officer: 650
Police Expenditures per 1,000: N.A.

Structure & Organization

The National People's Police, organized under the Ministry of Home Affairs, consists of the Burma Civil Police and the Rangoon City Police. Although organizationally independent from the Army, the military continue to dominate the upper echelons of the police force. The general headquarters is in Rangoon under a director general, assisted by a deputy director general. The Police Council, made up of ranking police, Army and cabinet officials, is the senior policy-making body.

The Rangoon headquarters has two special departments and two principal staff sections: the Supply and Finance Section and the Administration and Training Section. There is no separate operations directorate; rather, the chain of command runs directly from the office of the director general to subordinate units in the field.

Two special units are the Criminal Investigation Department (CID) and the Special Intelligence Department (SID), the latter concerned more with intelligence-gathering and counterintelligence work. Half of the SID personnel are stationed in Rangoon, with the rest at rural outposts. The CID staff is distributed among three bureaus: Crime Bureau, the Scientific Bureau and Railway Police Bureau.

The Rangoon City Police is an autonomous metropolitan force operating exclusively within the capital city and its environs. It is headed by a director and has an estimated strength of 5,000. In addition to regular law enforcement, it is responsible for the registration of motor vehicles, the surveillance of foreigners and the security of Rangoon Harbor.

The Burma Civil Police comprises all forces stationed outside the capital and forms the bulk of the National People's Force. Its uniformed personnel are the patrolmen on the beat and the rural constables. Its members often act as guards of government buildings and assist the Army in operations against insurgents. The Civil Police is organized into 12 subordinate geographic regions corresponding to the seven administrative divisions and five constituent states. Each region is headed by a director or vice director and is subdivided into districts, stations and outposts. Much of the operational control is exercised by the Army through its direction of "Security and Administrative Committees" composed of civil and military officials at various levels.

The average city police headquarters is housed in a frame building enclosed by a fence or barbed wire, and most rural police posts are smaller versions of their city counterparts. All but the most remote outlying posts are connected to the national communications network, the hub of which is in Rangoon. Police vehicles are generally adequate for local needs. Rural patrols are conducted mostly by motor vehicles, but rivers and coastal areas are patrolled by boats.

Grades in the National People's Force conform closely to those of the colonial British police force. Ranks below the director level range from constable up to superintendent through corporal, sergeant, station officer and inspector. Successive pay increases since the mid-1960s have brought police compensation into line with equivalent Army ranks and have done much to allay police disaffection vis-à-vis the military. Police uniforms closely resemble British tropical military wear. Army khaki uniforms with distinctive insignia are worn in the field and in hot weather. For garrison or urban duty, enlisted men wear blue trousers with a bluish-gray Angora shirt. Headgear is either a beret or a wide-brimmed Gurkha hat. Noncommissioned officers wear their chevrons on the right sleeve only.

Officers have a blue or a khaki service coat and wear a peaked service cap or a beret for field duty. Noncommissioned officers are armed with a pistol, while patrolmen carry only a baton, unless issued with other weapons during emergencies. The Metropolitan Division of the Rangoon City Police has a distinctive uniform consisting of a white jacket worn with dark blue trousers or breeches. The police have their own decorations: four medals, one of which is reserved for officers, given for gallantry, distinguished service and conspicuous devotion to duty.

Counterintelligence activities are conducted by the National Intelligence Bureau (NIB) and the Bureau of Special Investigations (BSI). The NIB is made up of various intelligence and specialized security agencies, such as the Military Intelligence Service of the Ministry of Defense. Headed by a director, the NIB is a component of the Central Security and Administrative Committee. The BSI is directly under the office of the chairman of the Revolutionary Council. It was originally organized to investigate corruption among political leaders and government employees, but this aspect of its work seems to have been dropped. The agency is engaged mostly in investigating possible threats to the regime.

Recruitment, Education & Training

The most common form of instruction is on-the-job. The Police Officers Academy in Mandalay conducts annual courses for officer candidates and also has a course of advanced instruction for officers at the intermediate level.

The Penal System

Burma's prison administration, under the direction of the Ministry of Home Affairs, is regulated by the provisions of the Penal Code, which appears as Volume VIII of the Burma Code. The system is loosely organized, however, and most detention facilities receive little central guidance or supervision. There is a prison facility of some kind in most towns of any size, but most of them are old buildings in poor repair. The best available information indicates that there are about 40 detention facilities in the country, about 10 of which are central prisons, 20 district jails, and 10 subjails and guardhouses. Most consist of a frame or log enclosure surrounded by a barbed wire fence. Conditions in even the two largest prisons, those at Rangoon and Mandalay, are described as poor.

There is one reformatory for juvenile offenders, called a training school, in Rangoon. None of the country's penal institutions is known to have workshops or handicraft facilities, and none has teachers, social workers, vocational training instructors or medical personnel assigned to their permanent staff. Nevertheless, the treatment of prisoners is generally good, and Burmese jails compare favorably with those in other nations in Southeast Asia.

There is no official publication of penal statistics, and no information on the incidence of crime reaches the outside world.

BURUNDI

BASIC FACT SHEET

Official Name: Republic of Burundi
Area: 27,834 sq km
Population: 5,005,504 (1987)
Capital: Bujumbura
Nature of Government: One-party dictatorship
Languages: Kirundi & French
Currency: Burundi franc
GNP: $963 million (1983)
Territorial Divisions: 15 provinces
Population per Police Officer: N.A.
Police Expenditures per 1,000: N.A.

Structure & Organization

Burundi's police system comprises the National Police (Police Nationale), the Judicial Police (Police Judiciare des Parquets, PJP) and the Gendarmerie. The PJP was created by Decree No. 1/21 of January 24, 1967, with a central office in Bujumbura and with field offices, called Mobile Judicial Police Units (Bri-gades Mobiles de Police Judiciare). Each mobile unit is commanded by a brigade chief.

The Central Directorate is organized into four sections: administrative secretariat, general documentation, identification and professional training. The bureaus of information, publicity, statistics and central archives are divisions of the general documentation

CRIME STATISTICS (1984)

		Number Reported	Attempts %	Cases Solved %	Crime per 100,000	Offenders	Females %	Juveniles %	Strangers %
1.	Murder	166			3.67				
2.	Sex offenses, including rape	57			1.26				
3.	Rape	57			1.26				
4.	Serious assault	81			1.79				
5.	All theft	1,142			25.26				
6.	Aggravated theft	767			16.97				
7.	Robbery and violent theft	3			0.07				
8.	Breaking and entering								
9.	Auto theft								
10.	Other thefts	372			8.23				
11.	Fraud	381			8.43				
12.	Counterfeiting								
13.	Drug offenses	27			0.60				
14.	Total offenses	3,712			82.11				

Criteria of juveniles: aged from 1 to 18 years.
Note: Information for some categories is not available.

section. The mobile units represent the active arm of the PJP in the collection of evidence and the arrest of criminals. Each field office includes a secretariat, an investigations section and a regional archives section.

Recruitment, Education & Training

Officers of the PJP are recruited by the Ministry of Justice based on competitive examinations. Successful candidates are admitted to the Professional Training Center of the PJP for an 18-month training cycle, upon completion of which they are given a 12-month probationary appointment as police officers. Personnel are organized into corps of officers and auxiliaries.

Rural policing is undertaken by the Gendarmerie.

The Penal System

Several types of prisons were constructed under the German and Belgian colonial regimes. Each province had a central prison and a work camp for long-sentence prisoners. The most important prisons are at Rumonga (near Bujumbura), Gitega and Muhinga. Prison conditions apparently are severe because of overcrowding and lack of adequate hygiene, medical care and food. Prisoners are segregated according to the nature of their crimes, are allowed regular family visits and participate in rehabilitative work programs, including agricultural production. Families are expected to provide additional food and other personal items to relatives in prison. Food rations are very limited, and there have been several reports of deaths in prisons from starvation.

Since independence there has been a substantial rise in burglary, petty theft and assault. Few people use the streets after dark, and there are night patrols to ensure the safety of those who do.

CAMEROON

BASIC FACT SHEET

Official Name: Republic of Cameroon
Area: 475,439 sq km
Population: 10,255,332 (1987)
Capital: Yaounde
Nature of Government: Limited democracy
Language: French
Currency: CFA franc
GNP: $7.3 billion (1984)
Territorial Divisions: 10 provinces
Population per Police Officer: 1,170
Police Expenditures per 1,000: N.A.

History & Background

The Cameroon National Gendarmerie was officially established in 1960 by transferring members of the preindependence security forces—the French Guard and the French-led Cameroonian Guard. Members of the old Civic Guard in the Bamileke ethnic area were also brought into the new national force. The total Gendarmerie strength of 3,000 men included the new mobile gendarmes who, in addition to special vehicles, had greater firepower. Gendarmerie organizational structure and command hierarchy were similar to those of the armed forces. Officers were trained at EMIAC (École Militaire Interarmes Camerounaises) and were, in effect, military officers assigned to internal security duties. By 1965 all command and supervisory posts in the Gendarmerie were held by Cameroonians, and French personnel were withdrawn. In 1966 a separate company called Republican Guard (Garde Républicaine) was set to protect the presidential palace and as an honor guard for state occasions. Each province has one legion—nominally about 400 men—of gendarmerie, called the Provincial Gendarmerie.

Structure & Organization

Police operations at the national level are conducted by the federal Sûreté, commanded by a director. The country is divided into a number of districts, each containing general police stations, or commissariats, regional Police Judiciaire services and frontier posts. The Police Judiciaire is concerned with investigation of serious crimes. The uniform consists of khaki bush shirts with a navy blue kepi. All personnel carry an automatic pistol. Police equipment also includes antitank rocket launchers and mortars, and armored cars.

The Gendarmerie mission includes highway security and traffic control, and investigation and surveillance of suspects. It is regarded by the government as a counterbalance to the regular military establishment. It is said to be feared and disliked by much of the population.

The National Police, Cameroon's other law-enforcement agency, is commanded by a delegate-general on the presidential staff. It maintains regional offices in all parts of the country and handles routine police work in all the larger towns. It encompasses a Directorate of Judiciary Police divided into brigades for criminal investigation, a Public Security Commissariat and a General Information Commissariat. Other units are in charge of traffic and frontier duties.

Recruitment, Education & Training

No information is available.

The Penal System

The Cameroonian Penal Code, a unified code embodying principles drawn from both French and British traditions, was adopted in 1968 after more than four years of preparation by a special commission. The code prescribed extremely severe penalties, including death, for even minor forms of theft.

Supervision of the penal institutions is the responsibility of the minister of justice. Cameroonian law makes a distinction between detention and imprisonment. Detainees are not permitted to work or earn money for the support of their families, while prisoners are permitted to do so. Very poor prison conditions, including overcrowding, inadequate food and sanitation and poor medical attention are major problems. The 1985 Annual Report of Amnesty International mentioned deaths of some inmates as a result of malnutrition. In 1986 the government launched a major prison construction and renovation program.

Under Cameroonian law, a person arrested on suspicion of committing an offense may not be held for more than 48 hours without a court order. This provision is generally observed in nonpolitical cases. Citizens are sometimes stopped by the local police, who sometimes threaten to harass or detain them unless a bribe is paid, but for the most part those detained are released within 24 hours.

Press reports and official comments show concern over the increasing incidence of a variety of crimes, including theft, forgery, assault, confidence games, rape, looting and prostitution. In 1972 changes in the Penal Code authorized more stringent laws against vagrancy and offenses against public morals, an indication that these offenses were becoming more widespread.

CANADA

BASIC FACT SHEET

Official Name: Canada
Area: 9,970,610 sq km
Population: 25,857,943 (1987)
Capital: Ottawa
Nature of Government: Parliamentary democracy
Languages: English & French
Currency: Canadian dollar
GNP: $366 billion (1986)
Territorial Divisions: 10 provinces; 2 territories
Population per Police Officer: 360
Police Expenditures per 1,000: N.A.

History & Background

The first policemen in Canada appeared on the streets of Quebec in 1651. Their duties were to watch for fires and to protect the citizens at night. In 1673 Count de Frontenac, the governor of New France, drafted the first police regulations, which within three years were applied to the whole colony. Other settlements in Canada followed suit and developed their own systems of parochial security.

After the French yielded Canada to the English on the Plains of Abraham in 1759, these security systems remained intact for almost a century. It was not until 1838 that Governor-in-chief Lord Durham put into effect a new system of policing in Montreal and Quebec City. In 1840 Montreal became an incorporated city with authority to maintain its own police system. In 1843 a police force was established in the city with a chief of police, three officers and 48 men. Quebec City developed its police force along the same lines as Montreal and by 1833 had a chief of police, an office that has continued there without interruption.

Meanwhile, similar developments were taking place in English Canada. In 1793 the Parliament of Upper Canada passed a law authorizing the appointment of a high county constable for each provincial district who was, in turn, to appoint unpaid constables in every parish and township. This system worked for a while until the mid-1830s, when the "influx of criminal elements among new immigrants" made the force woefully inadequate. In 1835, six years after the Metropolitan Police was founded in London, the city of Toronto replaced its "night watch system" with a six-man police force, one of whom was the chief of police. By 1852 the force had uniforms and its strength

was increased to about 12 constables. In 1858 the government enacted the Municipal Institutions of Upper Canada Act, authorizing towns and cities to form their own police force under a board of commissioners of police. Further, in 1860, the Appointment of Constables Act authorized the Court of General Sessions of the Peace to appoint "a sufficient number" of fit and proper persons to be constables of the county. The two acts remained in force until 1949, when they were replaced by the Police Act of Ontario.

In the meantime, other towns and cities were experimenting with peacekeeping institutions, although sporadically. Because most crimes were committed under cover of darkness, these institutions were commonly known as the night watchmen. By 1825 there were uniformed and paid constables in St. John's in Newfoundland. These constables "were to perambulate the streets until the time appointed for the shutting up of the spirit shops and one hour after and were not to quit their posts until the town was quiet. The High Constable was to go through the town at least twice between ten o'clock at night and one in the morning."

In 1871, following the removal of the military garrison from St. John's, the Newfoundland Constabulary was formed with jurisdiction over the whole island. This constabulary lasted until 1935, when it was replaced by the Newfoundland Rangers.

The first constable was appointed in Halifax in 1749. Two years later, the town was divided into eight wards, each empowered to elect two constables to work under the direction of the justices of the peace. Despite the existence of a constabulary, crime continued to flourish in the city, and branding was authorized as a deterrent: M for murderer, T for thief, and so on. When even such harsh measures had little effect, the magistrates themselves started patrolling the streets. In 1817 an elaborate system of night patrols manned by volunteers was instituted; this proved effective and became permanent. In 1829 a magistrate drew up a manual of "Rules and Regulations for the Establishment and Governing of a Watch and Patrol in the Town of Halifax." The man in charge of the patrol was given a 37-inch staff as a symbol of his authority, and the second-ranking watchman an iron rattle.

In Manitoba, the Council of Assinobia authorized a part-time volunteer peacekeeping force of 60 officers in 1835. Thirteen years later, 56 military pensioners were recruited in England for this purpose and brought to the Red River Settlement. In 1870, when the province of Manitoba was formed, a small provincial force was created. In Winnipeg, a chief constable and two constables were sworn in on February 24, 1874, as the first members of the Winnipeg City Police Force.

The vast central prairie region, known first as the Northwest Territories and later as Saskatchewan and Alberta, were policed by the Northwest Mounted Police. As a result, municipal police forces here evolved more slowly. Regina had its first police force in 1903, Calgary in 1885 and Edmonton in 1893. In British Columbia, law-enforcement agencies were established soon after settlement.

The Canadian railway police have a history as old as that of the larger provinces and cities. Almost all railway companies employed from the very beginning individual constables, guards, detectives and special agents to protect their property. By 1900 the Montreal terminals alone had 40 constables in plain clothes guarding freight yards, sheds and shops, plus one or two uniformed policemen at each main passenger station. The present Canadian Pacific Railway Police, known as the Department of Investigation, came into being in 1913, and the present Canadian National Railway Police, known within the company as the Investigation Department, came into being in 1923.

The provincial police forces came into being after the provinces were formed at Confederation in 1867. However, the Royal Canadian Mounted Police has taken over police functions in eight provinces: Saskatchewan, Alberta, New Brunswick, Nova Scotia, Prince Edward Island, Newfoundland, British Columbia and Manitoba.

Federal police history begins in 1845, four years after the union of Upper and Lower Canada. In order to control disorderly work gangs employed on the widening of the Welland and St. Lawrence canals, the government passed an act in that year authorizing a "body of men not exceeding one hundred exclusive

of officers and to be called "The Mounted Police." A few years later, in 1849, rioters burned the Parliament buildings, forcing the government to raise a force of 50 men, known as the Mounted Constabulary Force. The need for protection against further disorders led to the formation of the Dominion Police by an act of Parliament in 1868. Their initial duties were to guard the Parliament buildings, but over succeeding years the force expanded and assumed additional duties, mostly in eastern Canada and British Columbia. During World War I it supervised enemy aliens and, through its secret service, combated subversion and terrorism. It survived until 1920, when it was absorbed by the Royal Canadian Mounted Police.

The Northwest Mounted Police was established in 1873 to police the Northwest Territories, the vast western plains that the Canadian government had purchased from the Hudson's Bay Company in 1869. The police was designated to protect the Indians and their buffaloes from imminent extinction, to prevent conflicts between Indians and settlers and to provide security for the contemplated transpacific railway through the area. The enabling legislation provided for a force of not more than 300 uniformed policemen under a commissioner and mounted on the "hardy horse of the country." They would patrol the frontier, collect customs, prevent whiskey trading with the Indians and maintain general law and order. The first police posts were established at Fort Edmonton and at Fort Ellice. In the Northwest Territories, the police officers acted as postmasters, health specialists and customs collectors. By 1900 the total strength of the force was about 750 men. In 1904 the title "Royal" was conferred on the force, making it the Royal Northwest Mounted Police. In 1905 the provinces of Saskatchewan and Alberta contracted with the federal government for the RNMP to do their provincial policing as well. Manitoba and British Columbia were added to their jurisdiction by the end of World War II, shortly before it was absorbed by the Royal Canadian Mounted Police.

The last major national police agency is the National Harbors Board Police. The legal basis of this police is the National Harbors Board Act of 1936. In 1953–54 an amendment to this act authorized the appointment of peace officers within the meaning of the Criminal Code for the enforcement of the act and for the protection of lives and property within a radius of 25 miles from each Harbors Board property.

Canadian police agencies, especially the RCMP, maintain close relations with their U.S. counterparts. Seven Canadian provinces border on 10 U.S. states, and Ontario is separated from three more states only by the Great Lakes. To the northwest, Yukon and British Columbia border on Alaska. Crossing the border, which is relatively open, is a simple procedure and enables criminals to move easily from one country to the other.

The closest relations are between the FBI and the RCMP. Although the RCMP is a police force and the FBI an investigative agency with police powers, the two bodies have much in common. The RCMP has a liaison office in Washington, D.C., and the FBI has one in Ottawa. Because of the movement of criminals between the two countries, a great deal of criminal information flows continually between these two agencies. A computer link between the RCMP Canadian Police Information Center and the FBI computer is maintained, giving each immediate access to the other's data. Many American criminals, including some of the "Ten Most Wanted," try to avoid arrest by fleeing to Canada, and a number of these, such as James Earl Ray, the assassin of Martin Luther King, Jr., are eventually arrested through RCMP efforts. Other areas of cooperation are narcotics, espionage, terrorism and counterfeiting.

Structure & Organization

The Federal Police (RCMP)

The federal police of Canada is the Royal Canadian Mounted Police, established in 1920 and currently operating under the Royal Canadian Mounted Police Act of 1970. The nucleus of the force was the Royal Northwest Mounted Police. Over the years the RCMP has expanded not only geographically, by adding provinces to its federal jurisdiction, but also functionally, by undertaking new tasks at the request of the federal and provincial governments. For example, its repertoire of duties now includes narcotics control, smuggling, customs and excise work, marine and aviation services, antiterrorism, and forensic science. Some acts, as the Customs and Excise acts and the Explosives Act, give the RCMP special powers of enforcement. The RCMP also enjoys broad investigative powers and capabilities and, in this sense, is comparable to the U.S. FBI. Usually the RCMP investigates with the understanding that if sufficient evidence is forthcoming, then prosecution will be launched. Although the Criminal Code is a provincial responsibility, in certain cases the RCMP can enforce its provisions in its own right, such as provisions dealing with fraud, counterfeiting and narcotics. The RCMP also assists those federal government departments that have their own special investigators, such as the Department of Justice, the Department of National Revenue, the Post Office Department and the Immigration Service. It polices international airports and national parks, guards all government buildings and provides escort for visiting dignitaries.

The RCMP is headed by a commissioner who reports to the solicitor general of Canada under the 1970 act. The commissioner has the status of a deputy minister. The headquarters at Ottawa is divided into two main segments: one for operations and the other for administration and support. Each section is identified by a letter of the alphabet. Operations sections comprise the Security Service under a director; a Criminal Operations Section under a deputy commissioner; a "C" directorate in charge of criminal investigations; and an "L" directorate, which runs the laboratories and identification service, the Canadian Police Information Center, and a Telecommunications Branch. The administrative and support sections consist of an administrative section under a deputy commissioner; an "A" directorate in charge of organization and personnel; an "S" directorate in charge of finance and supply; an "R" directorate in charge of records; an "M" directorate in charge of Marine Service; a deputy adviser on bilingualism; and a departmental security officer.

Because the RCMP is a unique police force having both federal and provincial police responsibilities, the specialized RCMP services, such as the National Criminal Intelligence Repository, the National Securities Fraud Respository, and the National Fingerprint Identification System, are available to both federal and provincial authorities.

RCMP field operations are directed from 13 divisional headquarters designated alphabetically and, with two exceptions, are located in provincial and territorial capitals. The exceptions are Montreal and Ottawa.

In Quebec and Ontario, which have their own provincial police forces, RCMP responsibilities are strictly federal. The 13 operational divisions contain 41 subdivisions, which maintain nearly 700 detachments. Each operational headquarters, like the Ottawa national headquarters, contain two divisions, one for operations and the other for administration and support. Branches and sections at divisional headquarters correspond to directorates and branches at Ottawa.

The RCMP also includes three other divisions: One is the headquarters division at Ottawa; the other two are the training divisions at Regina, Saskatchewan, and Rockliffe, Ontario. Based at the latter ("N" division) is the celebrated RCMP musical ride.

The RCMP Marine Services operates about 60 vessels of various sizes for police patrol work on the East and West coasts, the St. Lawrence Seaway and the Great Lakes. The Air Section operates some 25 aircraft to convey laboratory experts; prisoners; and dog masters with police tracking dogs. Aircraft are widely used in search and rescue work.

As a result of an official inquiry into RCMP countersubversive activities in Francophone Quebec, it was

ORGANIZATIONAL CHART

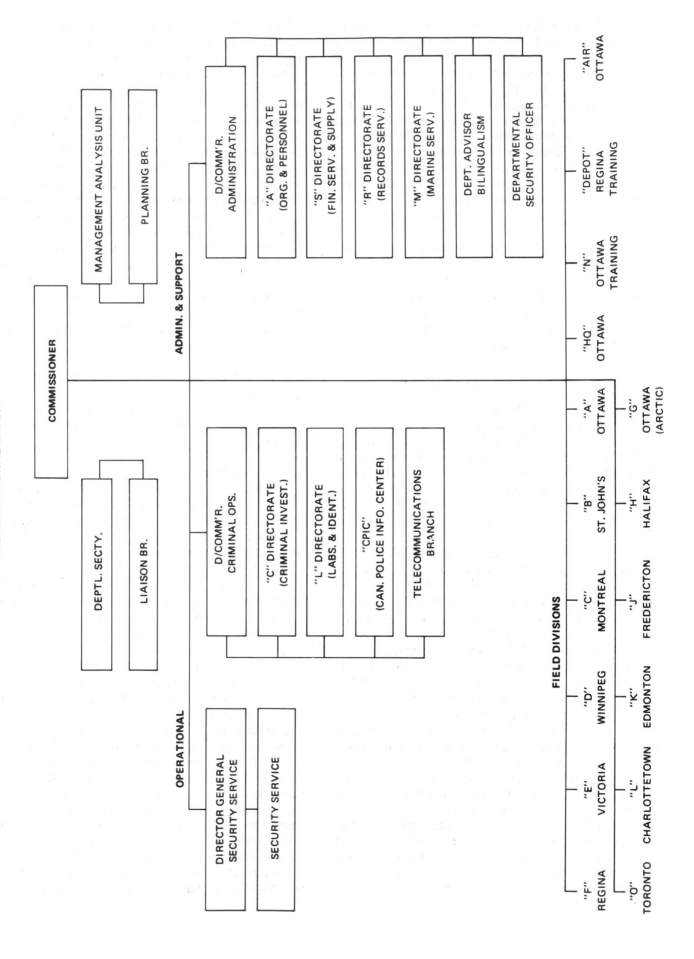

COMMISSIONER

DEPTL. SECTY.

LIAISON BR.

MANAGEMENT ANALYSIS UNIT

PLANNING BR.

OPERATIONAL

DIRECTOR GENERAL SECURITY SERVICE

SECURITY SERVICE

D/COMM'R. CRIMINAL OPS.

"C" DIRECTORATE (CRIMINAL INVEST.)

"L" DIRECTORATE (LABS. & IDENT.)

"CPIC" (CAN. POLICE INFO. CENTER)

TELECOMMUNICATIONS BRANCH

ADMIN. & SUPPORT

D/COMM'R. ADMINISTRATION

"A" DIRECTORATE (ORG. & PERSONNEL)

"S" DIRECTORATE (FIN. SERV. & SUPPLY)

"R" DIRECTORATE (RECORDS SERV.)

"M" DIRECTORATE (MARINE SERV.)

DEPT. ADVISOR BILINGUALISM

DEPARTMENTAL SECURITY OFFICER

FIELD DIVISIONS

"F" REGINA

"O" TORONTO

"E" VICTORIA

"L" CHARLOTTETOWN

"D" WINNIPEG

"K" EDMONTON

"C" MONTREAL

"J" FREDERICTON

"B" ST. JOHN'S

"H" HALIFAX

"A" OTTAWA

"G" OTTAWA (ARCTIC)

"HQ" OTTAWA

"N" OTTAWA TRAINING

"DEPOT" REGINA TRAINING

"AIR" OTTAWA

stripped of its internal security responsibilities in 1981, and these responsibilities were assigned to a special branch of the Security Service.

The RCMP maintains 27 foreign offices, in Abidjan, Bangkok, Beirut, Berne, Bogotá, Bonn, Brussels, Buenos Aires, New Delhi, The Hague, Hong Kong, Kingston, Lima, London, Manila, Mexico City, Nairobi, Paris, Port of Spain, Rome, Santiago, Stockholm, Sydney, Tel Aviv, Tokyo, Vienna and Washington, D.C.

As a paramilitary body, modeled on the Royal Irish Constabulary, the uniform of the Northwest Mounted Police followed a military style as worn by the Victorian Army. Its scarlet tunic became identified with the service in fact, fiction and media. The original pillbox hats and white cork helmets were officially replaced by the familiar broad-brimmed hat in 1901. Blue-black breeches with a wide yellow stripe and brown riding boots complete the traditional ''review order'' uniform, which is now restricted to ceremonial occasions. The working uniform now consists of brown jackets over blue trousers, worn with a peaked cap in blue with a white band. All RCMP personnel carry Smith and Wesson .38 special revolvers and .308 Winchester rifles.

The ranks and badges in the RCMP are as follows:

Rank	Badge
Commissioner	Crossed sword and baton under a crown
Deputy commissioner	Crossed sword and baton under a Bath star
Assistant commissioner	Crown over three Bath stars
Chief superintendent	Crown over two Bath stars
Superintendent	Crown over one Bath star
Inspector	Crown
Staff Sergeant	Four inverted chevrons
Sergeant	Three inverted chevrons
Corporal	Two inverted chevrons
Constable	None

Officers wear badges on epaulettes; others, on the sleeve.

The Provincial Police

The British North America Act gives provincial legislatures the exclusive authority to establish and operate police forces. The legislative basis of these police forces is found in the Police Act of each province, which specifies oaths of office; rules and regulations; and powers of the local boards of police commissioners, and of the provincial police commission where one exists. The provisions of these acts are very similar, although some are broader than others. For example, in Quebec the act empowers the director-general of the provincial police force to assume control of any municipal police force within its jurisdiction in case of an emergency.

The duties of the provincial police are usually carried out in rural and semirural areas outside the jurisdiction of municipal police forces. In certain types of law enforcement, however, provincial police have provincewide jurisdiction to ensure that laws are uniformly enforced. Such powers apply in the areas of traffic control of highways, sale and licensing of liquor, and criminal investigation. Provincial and municipal police support each other, and there is a continual flow of information across the lines of jurisdiction.

The field organization of the provincial police forces differs only in detail. Those of Ontario and Quebec are noted below. The organization of the RCMP as a provincial police is the same in all its contract provinces. For police purposes, a province is called a division and is identified by a letter: ''K'' for Alberta, ''J'' for New Brunswick, and so on. All divisions except Prince Edward Island (''L'') are divided into subdivisions, and these into detachments. British Columbia (''E'') is the largest division, with seven subdivisions and 175 detachments, of which 43 are municipal police detachments. The strength of a detachment varies from one to 30 men. The officer in charge of a division is the provincial commissioner of police, who holds the RCMP rank of assistant commissioner except in Prince Edward Island, the smallest division, which is headed by a superintendent, and the Maritime divisions, which are headed by chief superintendents.

The vastness of the provincial jurisdictions has led to the creation of an efficient means of transportation and communications. The RCMP operates its own air sections, both fixed-wing and helicopters, many of them used for traffic control. The RCMP also has a number of deep-sea vessels for policing the inland waters and the coasts.

With increasing urbanization, smaller provincial detachments have been consolidated into centralized units known as ''hub'' or ''zone'' units. Detachments are assigned to small towns and villages from these central units.

In contract provinces, the RCMP is under the direction of the provincial attorneys general and the administrative control of the Ottawa headquarters. The cost of police services in such cases is based on a percentage of the actual per capita cost calculated annually on RCMP expenditures plus a certain assessment for pension contributions minus amounts subtracted for exclusively federal expenses. These latter include such expenses as the cost of the national police services, and expenditures for the acquisition and construction of land and buildings. The contract provides for a specific number of RCMP detachments, with a further levy for additional detachments. In emergencies, such as industrial strikes, the RCMP deploys additional manpower, if necessary by seconding personnel from outside units. In many cases such additional personnel, up to 10% of the contract strength, are supplied at no further cost to the provincial government. The provincial governments have also full access to the RCMP National Police Services, including the Crime Detection Laboratories, the National Fingerprint Identification Service, the Canadian Police College and the Canadian Police Information Center.

On balance, the contract system works to the advantage of the provinces. It enables the provinces to maintain a highly efficient police system and a high standard of law and order at a subsidized cost. It eliminates possible political interference in police operations. The provinces also derive considerable savings in training, equipment and transport.

More than one-third of Canada is outside the provincial system. The Northwest Territories and the Yukon Territory, covering an area of 1,512,000 square miles, are under the direct jurisdiction of the federal government. The attorney general of Canada, who is also the minister of justice, is responsible to Parliament for the policing of these vast territories, where the RCMP is the only police force. Detachments in these areas are serviced by aircraft, and snowmobiles are used instead of the old dog teams.

The Ontario Provincial Police The Ontario Provincial Police was established in 1909 with 45 men under a superintendent and with operational headquarters in Toronto. In 1912 the force was completely reorganized and the title of superintendent was changed to commissioner. The number of divisions increased from two in 1909 to nine in 1922 and 17 in 1959. The Ontario Provincial Police Training School was opened in 1929. In 1930 it took over highway patrol from the Department of Public Highways.

Headed by a commissioner, the OPP is divided into 17 districts, each under a superintendent, supervising a total of 193 detachments. The commissioner is assisted by two deputy commissioners, one in charge of services and the other in charge of operations. Each of these two branches has three divisions, each headed by an assistant commissioner assisted by a chief superintendent.

OPERATIONS

Division	Responsibilities
Field Division	Auxiliary field administration
Special Services Division	Antirackets; auto theft; criminal investigation; intelligence; security; special investigations
Traffic Division	

SERVICES

Division	Responsibilities
Administrative Division	Finance; planning; properties; registrations; staff inspection
Personnel Division	Career management; training and development
Staff Services Division	Central records; communications; community services; quartermaster stores; transportation

The OPP conducts its own training and recruitment. Cadets are trained at the OPP Training College.

The OPP uniform is a dark blue jacket and trousers with a narrow red stripe on the legs for noncommissioned ranks up to and including staff sergeant and a similar uniform with a black maple-leaf-patterned trouser stripe for officers. All ranks wear a black Sam Browne belt. The headgear is a dark blue peaked cap with a light blue-gray band. The summer dress is a blue shirt with large shoulder patches instead of the jacket. All ranks carry a .38-caliber revolver.

Quebec Police Force The Quebec Police Force, headed by a commissioner, is divided into eight districts, each under a chief inspector or inspector. The Operations Service includes the Criminal Investigations Bureau, the antiterrorist Security Service, the Special Intelligence Service and the Scenes of Crime Service. Police activities are governed by the Quebec Police Act of 1967.

The Quebec Police Force uniform is a dark olive green tunic and trousers with matching cap and gold-colored badges. A brown leather belt with a pistol holster and pouches for handcuffs and ammunition are worn over the tunic. In winter a fur cap replaces the peaked cap, while in summer a short-sleeved shirt is worn with a tie.

Municipal Police Forces

The municipal police forces of Canada include city, town, village, county and township police forces. Collectively they constitute the largest body of police in the country, and they handle the most crimes. They vary from one-man forces in small villages to the two largest ones, of Metro Toronto and Montreal Urban Community (MUC). Police legislation requires provincial governments to make a per-capita grant to the municipalities toward the expenses of law enforcement.

Municipal police forces have the power to enforce all laws within their jurisdiction, including federal statutes, the Criminal Code, provincial statutes and municipal bylaws. Some have their own drug squads. A typical municipal police force comprises two main segments: operation and administration. In a large city, such as Ottawa, the chief of police is assisted by three deputy chiefs, the first handling field operations (patrol and traffic), the second staff operations (criminal investigations), and the third administrative and staff services.

Some municipalities choose to have the provincial police undertake municipal police duties. In eight provinces, the contracting force is the RCMP, which acts as the provincial police in these provinces. Quebec has no legal provision for such contracting.

The RCMP, which contract-polices 169 municipalities, follows the same procedures in these contracts as it does with respect to provincial contracts. The standard RCMP municipal contract calls for the performance of all regular police duties except issuing licenses, collecting taxes, impounding animals, fire prevention, and enforcement of health and sanitation laws. The cost to the municipality is based on a per capita cost, with the municipality providing office, jail and garage accommodation. Ontario is the only province where the provincial police do contract policing for municipalities. In some cases the OPP has taken over municipal police duties when municipal policing was found to be unsatisfactory.

Every police force in Canada operates under the supervision and control of civilian authorities. The highest elected law-enforcement authority in every province except Ontario, Quebec and New Brunswick is the attorney general; in Ontario it is the solicitor general, and in Quebec and New Brunswick it is the provincial minister of justice. Below this level, there are representative local bodies, variously known as Police Boards, Police Commissions or Boards of Police Commissioners. These are independent bodies composed of elected or appointed civilian members,

including at least one elected member as head. The board is responsible for the administration of the police force. It engages and dismisses personnel, deals with police associations regarding pay scales, supervises the disciplinary system and prepares the police budget. The system prevents police forces from being subject to local politicians while providing a degree of public accountability for their operations.

Quebec, Ontario and Alberta have Provincial Police Commissions that exercise oversight of all provincial and municipal police forces within those provinces. The commissions are free of political control and are answerable only to the attorney general or equivalent official. The commissions advise police forces on organization and administration. They have broad authority to inquire into any matter relating to law and order and the control of crime. They enforce standard codes of discipline and review disciplinary actions against police officers. They also run police training colleges or schools and monitor recruitment procedures. Similar commissions exist in Nova Scotia, Manitoba, Saskatchewan and British Columbia.

Recruitment, Education & Training

Applicants to the RCMP are required to pass a written test, undergo physical examination and fingerprinting, and to have completed at least secondary education. The applicant is interviewed by a personnel officer at the place of application, but the final selection and appointment are made from the headquarters in Ottawa.

To qualify for the force, a candidate must be single; be a Canadian resident with Canadian or British citizenship; be between 18 and 29 years of age; be between five feet, eight inches and six feet, five inches tall with proportionate weight; have a motor vehicle operator's license; be physically fit; have good character references; and be able to read, write and speak either English or French, preferably both. Since 1974 the RCMP has accepted women recruits, and now all major police forces accept women. Standards for them are the same as for men, except for height and weight. The starting salary is the same for women and men.

Police training starts with basic recruit training. This is followed by in-service training reinforced by periodic refresher courses and specialized training in specific technical areas.

The RCMP conducts basic training at Regina, Saskatchewan. In Ontario and Quebec, certain limited preliminary training takes place within the individual municipal and provincial police forces before the recruits undergo basic recruit training at Aylmer, Ontario, and Nicolet, Quebec, respectively. The needs of the Maritime provinces are met by the Maritimes

Police Academy at Charlottetown, Prince Edward Island. British Columbia has a school for municipal police training.

Basic training varies in duration from six months at the RCMP camp to three months at Aylmer. Training time is also divided among classroom instruction, practical work and physical training. At the completion of basic training, a recruit may be assigned to any location in Canada except the Northwest, where service is voluntary. University graduates enter the service as a first-class constable at a salary and rank equal to that of a regular member in his or her third year.

The Canadian Police College is operated by the RCMP at Rockcliffe, Ontario. The courses at the college are advertised in the RCMP *Gazette,* a monthly sent to all organized Canadian police forces. The principal courses include executive development, police administration, drug investigation, criminal investigation, counterfeit investigation, gambling investigation, and identification methods and techniques.

Service contracts in the RCMP are for an initial period of five years, renewable on the basis of performance. Nonofficer ranks receive their appointment from the commissioner, and officers from the solicitor general. Promotions are determined by the Treasury Board.

RCMP members receive an annual leave of 21 days in their first year, rising to 28 days in their 10th year. They are entitled to hospital, medical and dental care and to retirement benefits.

The Penal System

Criminal law in Canada is completely removed from common law. All criminal offenses and most criminal procedures are contained in the Criminal Code of Canada, an act of the federal Parliament. Section 8 of the code states that there are no criminal offenses except as described in it. However, common law defenses are retained, as in the criminal law of England.

There are two grades of criminal offenses in Canada. The less serious are called summary conviction offenses, which carry a maximum sentence of six months in prison and/or a fine of C$500. The more serious are called indictable offenses, for which the maximum punishment is life imprisonment. The most serious indictable offenses are within the exclusive jurisdiction of a judge of the court of Queen's Bench sitting with a jury. All other indictable offenses allow the accused an election as to mode of trial: trial by magistrate, trial by a district or county court judge sitting alone, or trial by a Queen's Bench judge and jury. Many criminal offenses are called dual offenses, which allow the prosecutor a choice whether to pros-

ecute the accused in a summary manner or by indictment. First offenses usually are prosecuted in a summary manner, and aggravated first offenses and repeated offenses by indictment.

Section 12 of the code provides that no person under age seven years shall be prosecuted for an offense, and Section 13 states that no one between seven and 14 years shall be convicted of a criminal offense unless that person is competent to realize the consequences and nature of his or her criminal conduct. Criminal offenders under 16 years are called juvenile delinquents. Juveniles are dealt with in separate courts, where the procedure is informal and they are not subject to adult punishment. A juvenile's criminal record is not considered if the person comes before an adult court after his or her 16th birthday.

Every criminal offense requires a criminal intent *(mens rea)* on the part of the accused. Where the offense requires a specific intent, that intent must be proved by the crown. There are no offenses of strict liability in the criminal code, except in the cases of violations of regulations that are not criminal offenses. The criminal intent must be proved even in cases involving criminal negligence. An attempt to commit an indictable offense is punishable equally with the substantive offense.

Certain specific defenses are expressly provided for in the code. These include insanity, self-defense, necessity, consent, drunkenness, provocation, double punishment, *res judicata,* and inconsistent verdicts. In addition to these defenses, the Canadian Bill of Rights contains guarantees of civil liberties and fair procedure that are, by and large, in favor of the accused.

Sentencing of criminal offenders is within the jurisdiction of trial judges, except in cases where the law provides for maximum and/or minimum sentences. In the latter cases, the judge's discretion is limited. Under the Criminal Code there is provision for appeal to the Provincial Court of Appeal with leave of that court in the case of indictable offenses and to a district or county court judge in the case of summary offenses. Imprisonment is the sentence of last resort because of its severity and its generally adverse effects on the accused.

The maximum term of imprisonment is six months for summary offenses and life for indictable offenses. The Criminal Code also provides for other types of custodial penal measures, such as indeterminate detention of those found to be habitual criminals or dangerous sexual offenders. A habitual criminal is defined as one who has been convicted of at least three independent indictable offenses for which he or she was liable to five years' imprisonment or more. Relative to the total imposition of penal sanctions, imprisonment has been declining in Canada in recent decades, while fines, probation and suspended sentences have increased.

Juvenile criminal offenders are dealt with separately under the Juvenile Delinquents Act of 1970. Special penal measures are specified for juveniles, such as placement in foster homes or training schools. Section 441 of the Criminal Code prohibits the publicizing of a juvenile's trial in the interests of protecting the offender and his or her family.

The National Parole Board was created in 1959 by the Federal Parliament as an independent authority. Under Section 8 of the Parole Act the board is empowered to release any offender on either full parole or day parole. Under the parole system, the board informs each offender of his or her parole eligibility date. The granting of parole is not irrevocable. Offenders sentenced to life imprisonment for treason or first-degree murder will not be eligible for parole until after 25 years, and those convicted of second-degree murder until after at least 10 years.

The criminal process is an adversarial one, with all prosecutions in the name of the Queen. Rules of evidence are based, for the most part, on common law. The accused is presumed innocent until proven guilty, and the burden of furnishing proof beyond a reasonable doubt rests with the crown.

Pretrial detention is discouraged in Canada. Arrested offenders are required to be released by the magistrate after being issued a summons, except in extraordinary circumstances. Peace officers are required to issue appearance notices rather than take the accused into custody, unless the officer believes that the detention of the accused is necessary for public safety.

Canadian penal philosophy is moving toward rehabilitation and away from retribution. Incarceration is the punishment of last resort and theoretically the most severe. The death penalty was abolished in 1976, and no criminal executions have taken place since 1962.

The penal institutions are run by both federal and provincial governments; the former operates penitentiaries and the latter provincial jails, reformatories, training schools and similar facilities. Offenders sentenced to two or more years' imprisonment serve time in federal penitentiaries, while those sentenced to two years or less are placed in provincial jails. Federal penitentiaries are administered by a commissioner under the solicitor general of Canada, and provincial jails by the corrections branch of the provincial Department of Health and Welfare or Department of Social Services. Offenders sentenced to federal penitentiaries are classified according to the gravity of their conduct. Habitual and dangerous offenders are placed in maximum-security facilities; others, in medium-security facilities. Provincial jails have industrial or farm annexes, where nondangerous offenders work under moderate supervision.

Women and juveniles are imprisoned at separate facilities under both provincial and federal systems.

CRIME STATISTICS (1984)

		Number Reported	Attempts %	Cases Solved %	Crime per 100,000	Offenders	Females %	Juveniles %	Strangers %
1.	Murder	1,590	58	83.7	6.33	1,349	10.4	5.0	
2.	Sex offenses, including rape	14,793		65.4	58.88	6,025	0.8	16.7	
3.	Rape								
4.	Serious assault	29,280		79.1	116.54	17,321	8.7	8.1	
5.	All theft	1,284,876		22.1	5,114.14	254,596	13.1	34.3	
6.	Aggravated theft	380,222		21.8	1,513.38	81,152	3.0	34.6	
7.	Robbery and violent theft	23,310		32.1	92.78	7,822	6.6	14.1	
8.	Breaking and entering	356,912		21.1	1,420.60	73,330	2.6	36.8	
9.	Auto theft	76,613		22.9	304.94	15,063	0.3	32.0	
10.	Other thefts	828,041		22.2	3,295.82	158,381	19.2	34.3	
11.	Fraud	122,775		69.7	488.68	38,500	23.9	4.6	
12.	Counterfeiting	989		21.4	3.94	119	16.0	13.4	
13.	Drug offenses	54,950		88.0	218.72	34,507	11.3	7.0	
14.	Total offenses	2,713,986		46.4	10,802.36	657,845	15.0	22.6	

Criteria of juveniles: aged from 7 to 18 years.
Note: Information for some categories is not available.

Custodial institutions for juveniles include detention homes, training schools and foster homes. The Juvenile Delinquency Act provides that no juvenile may be placed in a penitentiary, jail or police station in close proximity to adult offenders.

The most utilized noncustodial penal measures are fines, suspended sentences and probation. The Criminal Code provides that where the accused has committed an indictable offense for which he or she is liable for imprisonment for five years or less, that person may be fined in lieu of an authorized punishment. Judges are authorized to impose imprisonment in default of payment of the fine.

CHAD

BASIC FACT SHEET

Official Name: Republic of Chad
Area: 1,284,634 sq km
Population: 4,646,054 (1987)
Capital: N'Djamena
Nature of Government: Civilian dictatorship
Languages: French & Arabic
Currency: CFA franc
GNP: $405.7 million (1985)
Territorial divisions: 14 prefectures, 54 subprefectures, 27 administrative posts
Population per Police Officer: 990
Police Expenditures per 1,000: N.A.

Structure & Organization

Until 1961 the Sûreté was a unified police force for all four countries in French Equatorial Africa, and it was headquartered in Brazzaville. In 1966, the Chadian government initiated a substantial increase in the national police organization. The Sûreté serves both as the police force of the major towns and as the national police. Its duties include the maintenance of law and order, crime prevention, maintenance of criminal records and identification files, control of immigration, national security intelligence operations, and border patrol. A separate judicial police operates under the direction of the courts, with authority to investigate crimes and detain and arrest people. Other elements are a vice squad, the presidential palace guard and the National Police Academy.

The agents of the Sûreté are uniformed and carry light arms. For serious situations they call upon their own quasimilitary units—the Chadian Security Companies (Les Compagnies Tchadiens de Sécurité, CTS). These units were originally part of the Sûreté as a constabulary security force with the structure and arms of the light infantry units, including weapons such as mortars.

The National Gendarmerie was created in 1960, and the first national to head it was appointed in 1971. The force was organized into two different types of formations: 25-man mobile platoons in which were grouped the gendarmes who had been assigned primary responsibility for mob control, and brigades of four and eight gendarmes whose primary duty was regular police work in small towns and rural areas. The gendarmes are usually armed with rifles or machine guns as well as pistols. In a typical situation,

the Mongo Gendarmerie District in central Chad has nine brigades and two mobile platoons, although police work in the town of Mongo itself is performed by the urban corps of the police. Most of the National Gendarmerie is concentrated in the southern and southwestern parts of the country, although some units are located in Abeche in east-central Chad.

The major area of CTS operations is western Chad, where its troops generally perform duties outside urban areas, including border control around Lake Chad. Both there and along the southern borders, the major law-enforcement problem is cattle smuggling, and the CTS is well equipped to deal with bands of smugglers and cattle rustlers.

The National Guard, with an estimated strength of over 4,000 has no central headquarters. Instead, the companies are allocated to the various prefectures to perform guard duty or other security services as assigned by the local prefect. The National Guard also keeps several men in N'Djamena, where they provide ceremonial guards as well as protection for government buildings.

Recruitment, Education & Training

National Guard units are given light infantry weapons and internal security training to enable them to support Army operations when needed, but they are not as well trained and equipped as the other security forces. Its men have no basic police powers. The Nomad Guard (Garde Nomade) was stationed in the northern desert area until it fell to rebel forces in the late 1970s.

Police training is undertaken primarily at the National Police Academy, which provides an eight-month course for recruits, and at the officers' school at N'Djamena. High-ranking police officers sometimes are sent abroad for training in France, the United States or Israel.

The average educational level of the recruits entering the services is quite low. Training is slow and difficult. For political reasons, the ministers in control of the various security forces change frequently, reducing the effectiveness of their writ. The common Chadian retains his or her traditional distrust of all police, especially if the police are from a different ethnic group. Since the civil war, the police forces have been plagued with low morale and poor discipline.

The Penal System

A rudimentary penal system exists in areas controlled by government forces, but no information is available on it since the civil war.

CHILE

BASIC FACT SHEET

Official Name: Republic of Chile
Area: 756,945 sq km
Population: 12,448,008 (1987)
Capital: Santiago
Nature of Government: Military dictatorship
Language: Spanish
Currency: Peso
GNP: $16.1 billion (1985)
Territorial Divisions: 12 regions, 1 metropolitan district, 14 provincial subdivisions
Population per Police Officer: 470
Police Expenditures per 1,000: $6,459

History & Background

The first police organization in the country was established in Santiago in 1758. It consisted of a squadron of 50 men, called the Queen's Dragoons, quartered near the governor's palace. In 1903 it was incorporated into the army as the Regiment of Gendarmes, and in 1927 the unit was placed under the minister of the interior by presidential decree and renamed Carabiñeros de Chile.

Structure & Organization

There are two separate law-enforcement agencies in Chile, both under the Ministry of the Interior. The primary organization is known as the Carabiñeros; the second, the Investigaciónes. The total strength of the former is 30,000; that of the second, 4,000. The Carabiñeros are responsible for maintenance of public order; the Investigaciónes, for investigation and intelligence-gathering.

The Carabiñeros
The Carabiñeros are headed by a director general, whose headquarters are in Santiago. Under him are the *prefecturas* (first-rank police stations), *comisarias* (second-rank police stations), *subcomisarias* (third-rank police stations), *tenencias* (fourth-rank police stations), *retenes* (police posts) and advance guards. The senior police chief in each province is directly subordinate to the *intendente* (the provincial representative of the president of the republic), and the police chief in each department is subordinate to the governor.

The Carabiñeros are divided operationally into seven directorates, 17 departments and 10 *prefecturas*. The directorates are: Order and Security; Personnel; Planning; Technical and Professional Support; Welfare; and Training. The departments are: Analysis and Evaluation; Armaments and Munitions; Borders and Boundaries; Civic Action; Data Processing; Drug Control and Prevention of Offenses; Finance; Forest; Internal Security; Legal; Minors; Police Services; Public Relations; Social Action; Supply; Traffic Control; and Transport. The *prefecturas* are: Santiago Central; East; North; South; West; Air Police; Minors; Radio Patrol; Special Forces; and Traffic.

The Carabiñeros are also in charge of policing in Santiago. The city is divided into 35 commissariats, of which 26 are territorial and the remaining operational.

The Carabiñeros are a highly respected organization considered to be one of the most efficient police forces in South America. They patrol not only the urban and rural areas but also the most isolated sections of the country. Their operations extend to the fields of education, sanitation, and health and welfare. They conduct schools and houses for homeless boys.

The Investigaciónes
The Investigaciónes, headquartered in Santiago, is under a director general, from whom the line of command runs through the deputy director to the provincial inspectors. It is divided into a number of departments, including the Forensic Medicine Laboratory. It also includes an Air Police Brigade, and a National Bureau of Foreigners and International Police, which carries out passport control and represents Interpol. The Special Units Prefecture is divided into

six brigades: Fraud, Murder, Robberies, Vehicle Theft, Vice and Women. Substations are located in the provinces of Antofagasta, La Serena, Valparaiso, Santiago, Talca, Concepción, Temuco and Valdivia. Personnel of the Investigaciónes are located in the urban centers throughout the country. The agency supervises the National Identification Bureau, which contains registers of the fingerprints of all citizens when they reach age 21. The bureau also issues to all adult citizens identification cards, which must be carried on their persons.

The judicial police force, known as the Gendarmerie de Chile, is independent of the other police forces and reports to the Ministry of Justice. It runs probation and prison services.

The main security agency is the National Intelligence Center (Centro Nacional de Inteligencia, CNI) which replaced the National Directorate of Intelligence (Dirección Nacional de Inteligencia, DINA) in 1978. The armed forces and the Carabiñeros have their own intelligence-gathering units: the Military Information Service, the Naval Information Service, the Air Force Information Service, and the Carabiñeros Information Service.

Recruitment, Education & Training

Basic training is provided by the Escuela de Carabiñeros, while postgraduate and refresher courses are provided by the Instituto Superior de Carabiñeros. Specialists graduate from the Centro de Especialidades de Instrucción de los Carabiñeros, and NCOs from the Escuela de Suboficiales de Carabiñeros.

The Penal System

The Prison Administration was organized under the Ministry of Justice in 1930. Previously, penal institutions had functioned more or less independently and were not responsible to the central government. There are over 140 institutions designed to house approximately 15,000 people. The institutions are classified according to the length of inmate sentences: for prisoners whose sentence is less than 60 days and for those under trial or awaiting trial; for prisoners sentenced to a period from 61 days to five years; and for prisoners serving sentences longer than 5 years. There are also 23 correctional institutions for women supervised by a religious order. On Santa Maria Island, southwest of Concepción, there is an agricultural institution where prisoners are permitted to live and work with few constraints. There is also a special rehabilitation center for delinquent minors. In the provinces there are no juvenile prisons, and minors are detained in special sections of adult institutions. Of the total prison population, more than 60% are

either awaiting trial or under trial. Prison personnel receive special training in penal methods.

In certain circumstances a penalty depriving a first offender of freedom may be conditionally suspended. He or she will, however, be obliged to reside in a designated place and to submit to the supervision of the Prisoners' Aid Society.

The usual regime for the execution of a prison sentence is a progressive system comprising four stages. In the first stage, solitary confinement, which lasts a minimum of one month, imposes maximum restrictions. The second stage usually runs through four phases. The first phase puts an end to the isolation of the prisoner, allowing the prisoner to communicate with his or her family; the prisoner receives a small remuneration for work and is obliged to attend classes. During the second phase, remuneration is increased, and the prisoner may communicate with persons other than his or her family. During the third and fourth phases, living conditions and remuneration are gradually improved. The minimum duration of this stage is one year; each phase usually lasts three months but may be prolonged in the event of bad behavior. During the third stage the offender is confined to a cell only at night, and receives the maximum remuneration for work and enjoys maximum freedom of communication. The duration of the fourth stage, the period of conditional release, is half the length of the sentence for first offenders. Offenders are considered for conditional release during semiannual visits of the judges of the penal institutions. The judges' decisions are based on the information provided by the Prison Board. Conditional release is granted by decree and may be revoked if the offender does not satisfy the necessary conditions.

The Criminal Code imposes the obligation to work on offenders sentenced for a period of 61 days to five years, not necessarily as a means of rehabilitation but so they may reimburse the institution for their maintenance as well as meet the obligations of civil responsibility arising from their offenses. Moreover, their remuneration serves to provide certain items for themselves along with contributions to their savings funds.

There are four methods for the utilization of prison labor: state use, public works, contract and lease. State use denotes the manufacture of prison-made goods, which are supplied to institutions for public consumption, such as office supplies and furnishings, clothing and bedding, road signs, and automobile license plates. The public works system employs prisoners on construction and improvement of public roads, bridges, dams, buildings, parks, draining and clearing land, and preservation of forests. Under the contract system, inmates are hired out to a private contractor, who provides the necessary tools, yet the work is carried out almost entirely within prison confines. The prison administration takes no part in the operations nor in the sale of the goods produced. Contract labor is regulated by decrees that limit the duration of any one contract to five years and require the contractor to reimburse the government for its convict labor on a per capita basis as well as for the use of prison facilities. Under the lease system, the guarding, supervision and maintenance of prisoners are almost completely in the hands of private contractors, who reimburse the state at a fixed rate per prisoner and unit of time and who are authorized to employ prisoners outside prison confines. There are two varieties in the lease system: one in which the prisoners return to the prison at night, and the other in which they remain at all times under the control of the lessee.

In addition to these methods, there are shops centrally administered by the Government Directorate of Prison Workshops, where inmates work in accordance with their aptitudes as determined by the Institute of Criminology. Theoretical and practical training are given in printing, carpentry, mechanics and foundry work under the direction of a foreman. The Criminal Code also permits prisoners to do free work of their own selection, either alone or in cooperation with other prisoners, provided it conforms to prison regulations.

All prisoners are entitled to Social Security benefits under the Social Security Law of 1952. Six percent of earnings are paid by the state to the Social Security Service to ensure prisoners regarding illness, old age and invalidity, with benefits that may accrue to their families. In addition, working inmates are entitled to protection under the Family Allowance Law of 1953, by which annual payments are made to wives and children. They are also covered by workmen's compensation laws and receive wages during hospitalization.

Of the average annual arrests of over 700,000, almost one-third resulted from drunkenness, followed by assault, theft, burglary, driving while intoxicated and homicide. Of the arrests by the Investigation Section of the National Police, about half are by judicial order, with the other half on grounds of suspicion.

The term "juvenile delinquent" applies to offenders between ages 16 and 18. If the juvenile court decides that the action was committed with "discernment," the minor is sentenced to the lowest penalty applicable to an adult for the same offense and is sent to a prison for adults, where the minor is confined apart from them. Juveniles under age 16 and those between 16 and 18 who acted without "discernment" are subject to protective measures. Generally, the minor is returned to the custody of his or her parents, may be put under supervision or may placed in an institution.

CRIME STATISTICS (1984)

		Number Reported	Attempts %	Cases Solved %	Crime per 100,000	Offenders	Females %	Juveniles %	Strangers %
1.	Murder	744	8.06	85.75	6.26	620	14.20	6.61	0.16
2.	Sex offenses, including rape	4,281		76.27	36.04	1,485	40.74	17.00	0.40
3.	Rape	1,257		70.80	10.58	311	2.90	6.75	
4.	Serious assault	16,706		66.87	140.64	2,078	7.46	4.33	0.14
5.	All theft	87,709		21.90	738.39	10,185	10.30	12.43	0.19
6.	Aggravated theft	55,404		17.26	466.43	5,860	5.78	14.40	0.15
7.	Robbery and violent theft	4,324		21.74	36.40	737	4.34	12.35	0.13
8.	Breaking and entering								
9.	Auto theft	901		69.60	7.59	40	7.5	7.5	
10.	Other thefts	31,404		28.70	264.38	4,285	16.48	9.80	0.23
11.	Fraud	9,208		64.61	77.52	4,026	14.36	0.32	0.75
12.	Counterfeiting								
13.	Drug offenses	1,345		82.60	11.32	1,353	11.01	3.70	1.77
14.	Total offenses	163,059	0.04	44.88	1,372.73	35,486	14.24	7.75	0.34

Criteria of juveniles: aged from 0 to 18 years.
Note: Information for some categories is not available.

CHINA

Dorothy Bracey

BASIC FACT SHEET

Official Name: People's Republic of China
Area: 9.6 million sq km
Population: 1,064,147,038 (1987)
Capital: Beijing
Nature of Government: Communist dictatorship
Languages: Putonghua (Standard Chinese [Mandarin]), Yue, Wu, Minbei Minnan Xiang, Gan
Currency: Renminbi yuan
GNP: $262 billion (1986)
Territorial Divisions: 22 provinces, 5 autonomous regions
Population per Police Officer: 1,360
Police Expenditures per 1,000: N.A.

History & Background

Confucian China had no professional police force. Law-enforcement duties were carried out by "runners" employed by the provincial magistrate; the magistrate directed important investigations himself and combined in his person the offices of chief of police, procurator and presiding judge.

After the overthrow of the Manchu dynasty, the Republic of China was established in 1912 under the leadership of Dr. Sun Yat-sen, leader of the Nationalist Party. In 1949, the People's Republic of China, under the leadership of Mao Zedong and the Chinese Communist Party, came into being. At that time it created a Ministry of Public Security under the "State Affairs Yuan" or "State Council," headed by the premier; the first minister of public security was a former general of the People's Liberation Army, Lo Wei-chin.

From the 1960s on, the ministry in Beijing played an important part in the factional conflict of the Cultural Revolution (1966–69). Mao instructed the Red Guards to "smash Gongjiangfa [police, procuracy and courts.]" As a result, they singled out the police, attacking them for abuse of power and for taking a reactionary stand. Although the army seems to have gained control of police units in other parts of the country, in Beijing the police proved to be a strong power base for Hua Guofeng, who would be premier and party chairman after the Cultural Revolution ended.

Since the early 1980s, reform and reorganization of the police have consisted of decentralizing the police apparatus and using it to balance the power of the military. Thus, in 1983 25 divisions of the People's Liberation Army were transferred from the military to the Ministry of Public Security, where they are known as the Armed Police. At the same time, however, responsibility for prisons and most other correctional institutions was moved from the Ministry of Public Security to the Ministry of Justice. Counterespionage activities, formerly handled by the police, became the task of the newly created Ministry of State Security.

Structure & Organization

The People's Republic of China has a national police force that is headed by the minister of public security, a member of the State Council. Under the ministry, in descending order, are (1) public security departments at the level of the provinces and the three municipalities directly under the central government; (2) public security bureaus at the county and municipal levels; (3) public security subbureaus at the rural and urban district levels; and (4) public security stations at the commune and city district (neighborhood) levels. At each level there are specialized units for traffic, Social Security, census, criminal investigation, fire and foreign affairs, the latter dealing with crimes involving foreigners; these specialized units appear to report both to their jurisdictional commands and to the specialized unit at the next higher level. Also reporting to the minister of public security are the armed police, who protect government buildings, foreign embassies and consulates, power and utility centers, and frontiers.

Supplementing the work of the police are a variety of neighborhood and workplace committees composed of residents and workers who maintain security and order and help settle disputes; these were established in the 1950s and have been reaffirmed in the post-Mao period. Most relevant to law enforcement are the security defense committees, composed of between three and eleven members and subject to the direction of the local police. The committees assist the police in maintaining order, preventing criminal activities, investigating crime, and teaching the letter and the spirit of governmental laws and policies. Since all members of the committees are local residents who know their neighbors well, they are able to provide valuable information and assistance to the authorities.

The 1982 Constitution of the People's Republic of China makes several direct and indirect references to the power of the police. Article 37 states that "the freedom of person of citizens of the People's Republic of China is inviolable. No citizen may be arrested except with the approval or by decision of a people's procuratorate or by decision of a people's court, and arrests must be made by a public security organ. Unlawful deprivation or restriction of citizens' freedom of person by detention or other means is prohibited; and unlawful search of the person is prohibited." Article 39 guarantees that unlawful search of, or intrusion into, a citizen's home is prohibited, while Article 40 protects the freedom and privacy of correspondence "except in cases where, to meet the needs of state security or of investigation into criminal offenses, public security or procuratorial organs are permitted to censor correspondence in accordance with procedures prescribed by law." Article 41 deals with the right of citizens to criticize and make suggestions about any "state organ or functionary" and the duty of the state to deal with such criticisms and suggestions without suppressing them or retaliating against citizens making them. Article 41 also states that "citizens who have suffered losses through infringement of their civic rights by any state organ or functionary have the right to compensation in accordance with the law."

The Criminal Law also addresses the possible abuse of police powers. Article 136 states that "the use of torture to coerce a statement is strictly prohibited. State personnel who inflict torture on an offender to coerce a statement are to be sentenced to not more than three years of fixed-term imprisonment or criminal detention. Whoever causes a person's injury or disability through corporal punishment is to be handled under the crime of injury and given a heavier punishment." According to Amnesty International, former detainees maintain that beatings are common in detention centers and that shackles and solitary confinement still are used. Police officials deny that such abuse is common, and currently both the law and police training place importance on the protection of human rights.

Police having supervisory or command duties are increasingly graduates of Beijing's Public Security University, of another university, or of one of the public security colleges. It is the aim of the ministry to raise standards so that all other members of the police force will have a secondary school education followed by a year of training at a local police school or academy. In the past, most police recruits had served previously in the People's Liberation Army, but this appears to be less true now. Promotion has tended to be relatively slow, and even a first promotion may not take place until after fifteen or twenty years of service; Deng Xiaoping's policy of retiring older members of the military and replacing them with younger officers also appears to affect the police. At present between 20 and 30% of recruits are female; at least in theory, all positions are open to them, and at least some command positions are in fact held by women. In the autonomous regions, considerable effort is made to recruit police from the local non-Han nationalities.

Peer pressure is considered a major factor in bringing about and maintaining proper behavior by police. The organization responds to improper conduct with punishment, but also with reeducation.

Police assigned to neighborhood stations will usually begin their careers as security police or "census police," responsible for keeping track of residents and transients of a certain area. Each officer is responsible for approximately 600 residences in a particular area; anyone wishing to move to or from a particular area, or even to visit or leave it for an extended period, must get permission from the police and register with them, making it possible for the police to monitor the population closely. They work closely with committees of neighborhood residents in carrying out activities related to crime prevention, mediation of minor disputes, supervising individuals recently released from prison, and intervening in the careers of potential deviants and troublemakers. Census police are rarely transferred and may spend most of their career in one neighborhood, a practice that allows them to establish close ties with the residents. These police wear a kahki-green uniform with red piping (supplemented by fur-collared greatcoats in winter) and usually work six days a week, their eight-hour shifts interrupted by a two-hour lunch break. In contrast, traffic police work night shifts as well as day shifts. They wear white jackets and white hats with blue or brown trousers. In urban areas traffic police are assigned to police booths at intersections or on main roads. The booths are connected by telephone to district or neighborhood stations; citizens (few of whom have telephones in their homes) who wish to report incidents to the police will often go to one of these booths. With the exception of the armed police, members of the public security forces do not carry weapons on a regular basis.

Under Mao Zedong, the concept of rank in the military and government was eliminated, with individuals being identified in terms of their responsibilities; a police officer, therefore, might be referred to as an investigator, as being in charge of a neighborhood police station, or as head of a forensic laboratory. A rank structure was slowly reintroduced into the military in the late 1980s, and it is possible that a similar development will take place in the Ministry of Public Security.

There are no authoritative data concerning the total number of police personnel, although one source estimates that there are approximately 2 million full-time members of the Ministry of Public Security.

Police patrol activities take place almost entirely on foot and bicycles. Traffic police are making increased use of sidecar motorcycles. Jeeps are used for transportation and crowd control, while trucks are employed to move large numbers of personnel.

China does not have a modern communications system; this contributes to the fact that the police command and control system is not as highly developed as it is in many other countries. This means that police officers frequently work on their own and must make decisions independently, without a two-way radio or in many cases even a telephone with which to ask for instructions or assistance. However, this lack is not as great a problem as it might seem in apprehending fugitives, since the lack of mobility within the country, combined with the system of resident registration, makes it difficult for a criminal to go far from the scene of the crime.

Internal Security Operations

A Ministry of State Security was established in June, 1983, with the mandate to "ensure China's security and strengthen the struggle against espionage;" its first Minister had previously been Vice-Minister of Public Security. Although these duties had previously been the responsibility of the police, a ministry specializing in securing the state "through effective measures against enemy agents, spies, and counterrevolutionary activities designed to sabotage or overthrow China's socialist system" was seen as a necessary measure due to the increased activities of foreign intelligence agencies or secret services after China adopted its policy of "opening to the world." As a security agency, it is empowered to investigate, detain, arrest, and hold pretrial hearings.

Traffic Police

Traffic police are responsible for controlling the chaotic conditions on China's urban streets, conditions that will become even more chaotic as the endless streams of bicycles are joined by a growing number of trucks and cars. Traffic police are often stationed in booths at major intersections; from the booth the officer is in telephone contact with the neighborhood or district police station. The officer is easy to find if a citizen has an emergency or a complaint; telephoning the police station enables the traffic police officer to ask for a backup to be dispatched or to receive advice on handling the situation alone. Traffic reports are sent to the district rather than the neighborhood police station.

Criminal Identification

Major cities such as Beijing and Shanghai have adequate laboratory facilities, although others are in need of improvement. Fingerprints are not used extensively. Computers, many of them manufactured in the People's Republic of China, are slowly being introduced. It is unclear whether there is any centralized criminal record facility, although the police are helped tremendously by the detailed records maintained by the census police.

China became a member of Interpol in the mid-1980s and participates in its activities. The Ministry of Public Security has also sponsored professional delegations of police officers from other countries for mutual exchange of information. The ministry has a Research Institute that systematically scans the literature of other countries for information on police personnel policies, equipment, systems and law. The institute also does studies on the ways in which other countries handle crimes that might in time become problems for China; an example is the importation of pornographic material. Narcotics officers have been sent to the United States for training and, with the support and direction of the French police, international seminars on narcotics control have been held in Beijing.

Police officials consistently point out the need to professionalize the police of the People's Republic of China, and doing so is one of their major aims. Just what this means is not always clear, but it includes at a minimum improved training, modern management techniques and greater reliance on technology. It may also involve curtailing any tendencies of public security agencies to bypass the legal process for administrative sanctions such as Reeducation Through Labor in dealing with politically or socially deviant individuals. Committees to work with the police in applying such sanctions have been established, and the duration of Reeducation Through Labor has been set at one to three years, with a possible extension of one additional year. It certainly means greater contact with police forces in other parts of the world, both to exchange information on developments in training, management and technology and to work together to combat common problems.

Recruitment, Education & Training

Chinese young people are assigned their jobs by the government; the assignments are made on the basis of applicant choice, need for personnel in particular occupations, and performance on competitive examinations. As part of the attempt to raise the number of university-educated members of the police (approximately 10% as of 1985), university students may undertake a six-month "internship" with the public security forces. In spite of growing job opportunities in the private sector, police work still appears to be an attractive career to large numbers of qualified youths.

The pride of the police training system is Public Security University in Beijing. The university expects to enroll 3,000 students when it is fully operational. Students with no previous police experience attend the university for five years, while serving-police officers attend for a shorter period. The university is designated to educate a core of administrators for all police operations and functions. Also in Beijing is Police Officer University, which offers a more technical program; its graduates usually are assigned to first-line supervisory positions. Graduates of either institution may be assigned to any part of the country.

Each of the 29 provinces and three major cities also has a police college. Probably typical is Shanghai College of Public Security, which was established in 1949; closed during the Cultural Revolution; and reopened in 1978, when it was classified as a secondary technical school. In 1983 it received the status of a college and from then on accepted only graduates of senior middle schools; new recruits receive a three-year course, while students with police experience stay two years. The college expects to have entering classes of 200 recruits and 200 in-service students each year.

Students study either English or Japanese; Chinese literature, which includes grammar, logic and vocabulary; public speaking; police science; criminal investigation and interrogation; criminal psychology; internal security; communications; driving police vehicles; military and weapons training; boxing, drill and physical training; appropriate conduct for police officers; legal principles, constitutional law, and criminal law and procedure; and political theory, including political economy, history of the Chinese Communist Party, and the philosophies of Marx, Lenin and Mao Ze-

dong. Students are taught that "the people's police are the servants of the people" and that they must listen to the criticism of the masses and accept their supervision. This is a primary aspect of "following the mass line," an important principle of Chinese Communist government.

Recruits who do not qualify for the universities or colleges for public security are nowadays given a one-year course at a local police school or academy. An in-service training program for older police who have not received this course is now in place.

The Penal System

China's first Penal Code and Code of Criminal Procedure were promulgated in 1979, soon after the passage of the 1978 Constitution. The Penal Code defines criminal acts and establishes the statute of limitations. The death penalty was authorized for flagrant counterrevolutionary acts and for homicide, arson, criminal intent in causing explosions, and similar offenses. Both codes place certain restrictions on police powers regarding arrest, investigation and seizure. Under emergency conditions, a policeman could arrest a suspect, but a court or procuratorate is required to approve the arrest. Within 24 hours the accused has to be questioned and his or her family or work unit notified of the detention. Any premeditated arrest requires a warrant. Warrants are also required for searchers.

The majority of the prisoners are sentenced to hard labor, of which there are two kinds: criminal and administrative. The former is for a fixed number of years, while the latter is for an indeterminate period, but usually three or four years. Both categories may be found at state farms, mines and factory prisons. The people's procuratorates supervise the prisons, ensuring compliance with the law. Prisoners work eight hours a day, six days a week. They are forbidden to read anything not provided by the prison, to speak dialects not understood by the guards, or to keep cash, gold or jewelry. Mail is censored, and generally only one visitor is allowed per month.

Sentences are reduced for prisoners who show signs of repentance and render meritorious service. Any number of reductions can be earned totaling up to half the original sentence, but at least 10 years of a life sentence has to be served. Both probation and parole are granted when certain conditions are satisfied.

Crime statistics are not very reliable and vary from one source to another. Post-1984 estimates vary from four to five crimes per 10,000 population. Officials suggest that the crime rate in the early 1980s was as high as 7.5 per 10,000 and was reduced by the nationwide "anticrime campaigns" of 1983.

Drug Offenses

Chinese officials report that their problems with narcotics are minimum, but the problems are at least serious enough to warrant a recent increase in the penalties for manufacturing, selling or transporting such substances. The 1979 criminal law provided a sentence of up to five years' imprisonment, with heavier punishment only for recidivists. In 1982, the same crimes "when the circumstances are particularly serious" may result in not less than 10 years' imprisonment, life imprisonment or death. There is particular concern about the mountainous regions of Yunnan, which border on Burma, where local residents have reported a number of executions for opium trafficking. China's reputation for being free of narcotics has also attracted smugglers who attempt to bring drugs into the country and then transport them to some other nation, knowing that travelers and goods from China receive less attention from narcotics authorities than those from most other countries. Increased security measures at borders resulted in the confiscation of 24.4 kilos of opium in 1985.

Juvenile Delinquency

The Chinese believe firmly that it is important to deal with juvenile deviance before it develops into more serious adult crime. Police often explain that "young people should be treated with care, and the police should be like parents to them." This policy took on particular importance in the post-Cultural Revolution period, when juvenile crime came to be seen as a major problem. Newspaper articles indicate that China had 10 times more juvenile delinquency in the 1980s than in the 1960s and that 80% of criminals apprehended in the mid-1980s were under age 25. The most frequent offenses appear to involve fistfighting, theft, and hooliganism, while assault and murder account for only 10 to 15% of the total. Drunkenness seems to be rare.

Gambling and prostitution provide some problems for law-enforcement authorities. Both are against the law and were for a number of years almost totally eliminated, although a very small resurgence has taken place in the mid-1980s, especially in the major cities frequented by foreigners. In both cases, the policy seems to be to arrest and punish only those who organize such activities for profit and for the police to pay little attention to those who merely participate, although neighborhood or workplace committees may attempt to deal with them. Family crises are also seen as the proper jurisdiction of these semiformal organizations rather than public security officials; this attitude seems to pertain even to wife abuse and female infanticide, both of which have increased as a result of the birth control policy that allows each couple to have only one child.

White-collar and other economic crimes are a particular concern in a socialistic economy, as they can be seen as undermining the state as well as injuring individuals. Encouraging individual initiative and inviting foreign investment, among the basic principles of Deng Xiaoping's "Responsibility System," have lent themselves to corruption and other economic crimes, with which the authorities have dealt strictly.

COLOMBIA

Jorge Penen Deltieure

BASIC FACT SHEET

Official Name: Republic of Colombia
Area: 1,138,914 sq km
Population: 29,956,000 (1986)
Capital: Bogotá
Nature of Government: Representative democracy
Languages: Spanish
Currency: Peso
GNP: $37.61 billion
Territorial Divisions: 22 departments, 5 intendencies, 5 commissariats, Bogotá Special districts
Population per Police Officer: 420
Police Expenditures per Capita: N.A.

History & Background

Both in the Pre-Columbian age and during the Conquest and colonial periods, no police service existed in Colombia apart from the military. When the War of Independence ended in 1819, legal resolutions on public order were issued to set up the new nation, and for the first time an incipient police corps was created, but it was later absorbed by the army. It was not until 1858, that the penal and judiciary administration established an autonomous and functional police corps. In 1871 a frontier police force was created, and in 1880 a section in charge of investigating crimes and imposing sanctions on infringements was organized. In 1888 Law 90 was issued, to establish the National Police Corps, and in 1890, under Law 23, the government was authorized to organize it by contracting foreign technicians. French expert Marcelino Gilibert, who had served with distinction in the police services of his country, where he became police prefect of the city of Paris, was invited by the Colombian government for this purpose. Decree 1000 of 1891 reorganized the corps in accordance with Gilibert's proposals, and he was later appointed corps director to start operations with 500 units under the Ministry of Government in January 1892. The uniform design was similar to that of the French police corps. However, the Civil War of 1899–1901 forced the National Police Corps as such to disappear when it was incorporated into the armed forces. In 1903 a new effort was made to reorganize this corps under the Ministry of War, but in 1906 the National Police Corps returned to the Ministry of Government. At that time the system of anthropometric identification was introduced and the judicial police were set up. In 1914 a school to train detective agents was founded, and in 1915 a mission from the Spanish Civil Guard was invited to reorganize the corps. In 1916 the Cavalry Corps was established.

The Police Corps School was founded with the help of French technicians. This mission achieved considerable progress in setting up criminal investigation and urban vigilance systems. In 1926 a reorganization took place and three sections were structured: Vigilance Police, Judicial Police and Detectivism. The Argentinian police mission recommended the modernization of police systems and introduced the so-called Vucetich dactyloscopy identification system, useful in criminal investigation. Between 1934 and 1936 institutional modernization advanced toward achieving a professional status for the police. Thus the Dactyloscopic Identification Cabinet was established, and the handling of files, dossiers and card catalogs was improved.

Since the National Police Corps was not able to serve all the national territory then, each department, municipality and territorial political-administrative division creeated its own police corps, which was not always well accepted nor respected because it acted under political pressure. These local and regional police organizations disappeared when, by Legislative Act 1 of 1945 amending the national constitution, Congress ordained the establishment of the police service. Decree 0945 of 1940 created and organized the "General Santander" School of Officers, which constituted a milestone in police history.

The National Police Corps was reorganized as a result of serious disturbances on April 9, 1948, in Bogotá, during the IX Pan-American Conference, that resulted in the assassination of leftist political leader Jorge E. Gaitán and the looting of part of the city, as well as disturbances in the rest of the country. In 1950 it was again reorganized, with the assistance of British and Canadian police corps technicians. In the same year police schools in Manizales and Bogotá were created to train agents and carabineers. This measure was of enormous importance in the modernization and technical direction of the National Police Corps. In 1952, the year of the military coup, the National Police Corps was incorporated into the armed forces, but this situation was corrected in 1958 when the police became a civil armed corps. Since then the police have been reorganized three times: in 1966 by Decree 1667, in 1971 by Decree 2347 and in 1983 by Decree 2137.

Structure & Organization

The National Police has a total force of 61,100: officers, 2,600; sergeants major, 4,500; agents, 47,000; and civil guards, 7,000. For police service purposes, each of the departments, intendencies and commissaries in which the national territory is administratively divided has a police department, and the city of Bogotá, as a special district, and Medellín and Cali have metropolitan police corps. Each of those police departments (30 in all) is divided into police precincts; each precinct into stations; and each station into substations. The police station is the operational basic unit of the police organization. The police precincts cover the territory of several municipalities, which are political-administrative divisions of each of the departments, intendencies and commissaries. Theoretically, the percentage proportion of National Police Corps strength is one policeman per 545 inhabitants. Nevertheless, when it is noted that 60% of the population or 18 million people, are concentrated in urban areas, and that 70% of the rural population, or 8.4 million people, live in the remaining 45% of the rural areas, the real proportion is one policeman per 475 inhabitants in the most crowded areas, and one policeman per 70 persons in the least crowded ones.

The territorial jurisdiction of the Police Departments is the same for the large political-administrative divisions in which they are included. The territorial extension of the police precincts is more dependent on the need for the service than on the territorial extension or the volume of population.

For 1985, the annual police budget was 30 billion pesos ($U.S. 141.5 million).

The National Police Corps is structured as follows:

General Direction

Police Departments

Metropolitan Police

other organs

General Direction
The general director is appointed and can be removed by the president of the republic. For direction and command purposes, the National Police Corps is under the Ministry of Defense. The post of general director is held by an officer with the rank of National Police Corps general in active service, belonging to the Vigilance Service Field.

Police Departments and Metropolitan Police
The Police departments and the metropolitan police are the basic units of urban and rural vigilance services and constitute the operational core of the system. In the departments, intendencies, commissaries and municipalities, the police corps is operatively at the disposal of the governor, intendent, commissary and mayor, respectively, who, as the prime civil authority, are the police chiefs of their jurisdictions and give orders through the respective police commander. On emergency and other special occasions, those civil authorities can command directly to keep public order. The commanders of police departments, metropolitan police, precincts and stations have operational authority within their jurisdictions to distribute services and personnel in accordance with public needs. The departmental and metropolitan police commanders report to the operations director about services and personnel. In addition, they direct, supervise and control the vigilance services in their jurisdiction and report to their immediate superior about personnel discipline.

Other Organs
The General Inspection branch oversees the force's morale, regulations and functioning. The General Inspection evaluates the performance of the various police branches.

Planning Management is a technical planning and consulting organ to prepare studies, instruction projects, orders, plans and programs relating to the structure, organization and use of the police services, and it submits recommendations on the subject. Its Division of Police Services designs all activities concerned with the police services at a national level, carries out delinquency and infringement studies, and issues regulations and handbooks for application in the different fields of professional activities. Its Division of Budget and Finance prepares the yearly budget and the expense and investment project. Its Division of Human Resources submits studies, projects and programs on the selection, incorporation, formation, training and management of personnel, and collects, examines and elaborates institutional statistics to provide the General Direction with reliable information that might be useful for decision-making.

Operations Management is in charge of all police services at the national level. The Section of Expert Services of the Operations Division controls highways, mines, ports, drugs, railroads, natural resources and environment, and the air services of the National Police Corps. The Judicial Police and Investigation section headed by the general prosecutor performs the functions inherent in the Judicial Police of the National Police Corps, as an auxiliary of the Public Power's Judicial Branch, in accordance with the prescriptions of the Penal Procedures Code. The Judicial Police Division compiles and analyzes information concerning criminality at a national level. The Criminologist Division functions as a technical auxiliary of the Judicial Branch, producing opinions and expertise for submission to judges. The Information Section collects, processes, evaluates and transmits all information and data pertaining to public order. It exercises vigilant counterintelligence on the conduct of the members of the National Police Corps itself, and it controls and supervises the operations of agencies supplying private vigilance and security for the transportation of goods.

The Administrative Management section handles the control and execution of the budget as well as logistics services, acquisitions, and the administration of goods and chattels and real estate for the use of the National Police Corps. It is divided into eight branches.

The average age for a policeman in Colombia is 27 years. Nearly 97% of the force is male. A large number of policemen have an educational level no higher than elementary school. Most can hardly read and write or do basic mathematical calculations. Police agents come from the lowest-income class. Approximately 70% of them are married, a situation that favors them in a certain way, as they obtain study premiums and bonuses for their children and many other family allowances. The average physical size is five feet, five inches (1.68 m). The recruitment of women to the uniformed police began only in 1980, when policewomen appeared in the vigilance service for minors. The National Police Corps also includes female personnel assigned to the official and sergeant majors' staffs. Currently policewomen account for 3%, or 1,500 persons in the total uniformed personnel of the National Police Corps.

Police standing and image in the community is influenced by historical mistrust and suspicion, notwithstanding the fact that the corps has become more professional and less political. A large proportion of the community still does not trust policemen and consequently does not cooperate with them. To enter into the community and strengthen its relationship, the National Police Corps frequently carries out educational, sanitary and recreational programs in various communities.

For professional purposes, policemen follow the pyramidal hierarchical system of rank and authority for transmitting orders and exacting obedience. In consequence, discipline becomes a necessary element in the correct performance of the National Police Corps, and the quality of the police services depends on its observance. In accordance with police regulations, any order given by superior authorities must be accomplished by the subordinates. This procedure is defined in the National Police Corps' discipline and honor regulations of 1979.

Police "brutality" is neither systematic nor chronic. It is associated with periodic outbreaks of violence following mass protests or demonstrations. These violent demonstrations start with shouts against the establishment, followed by throwing of stones and all kinds of devices against the public force—burning automobiles, breaking windows, plundering, etc. They finally end only with the police use of tear gas and guns, leaving a number of people injured and dead. On rare occasions the "death squads" have executed their own form of vigilante justice. There are also reports of torture of suspects by the police. This practice occurs rarely and is not a fixed or official policy, but rather one applied by isolated units. In the long run, the torturers are unmasked and prosecuted. Corruption is not widespread considering the scanty salaries, which are hardly above the minimum established national salary.

Complaints about police misconduct are registered and classified at the Office of Complaints of the Police headquarters and then referred to the officer in charge, in accordance with the right-to-claim section in Article 45 of the constitution. The law fixes sanctions for those who hamper or delay the process. The Office of Inspection and Discipline of the Police Headquarters, which follows the procedures outlined in the discipline and honor regulations of the National Police Corps, handles the data corresponding to each claim. The above regulations classify faults into several categories, as follows: against morale, against Police courtesy and against the prestige of the institution; also, against the exercise of authority, command, subordination, obedience, service or function, the performance of academic duties, and professional confidence; and against fellowship, administrative responsibility and police reputation.

For uniformed personnel these disciplinary regulations contemplate minor sanctions, such as simple, formal and severe admonitions, in addition to greater punishments, such as simple or strict arrest, temporary suspension of the post or salary, and definite withdrawal from the post or the institution. For nonuniformed personnel, the disciplinary regulations contemplate simple or severe admonitions, fines of up to 20% of the salary earned, suspension from the post for up to 30 days or finally withdrawal from the post or job. These regulations also include basic conduct rules that constitute the code of police ethics to which all members of the National Police Corps must adhere. A good part of the conduct defined as faults are no more than infractions of professional ethics that usually lead to the imposition of disciplinary sanctions. On the other hand, crimes invoke penal sanctions. Verdicts on disciplinary violations are directly pronounced by the president of the hearing, or by the person presiding over the Honor Tribunal, depending on the rank of the accused and the nature and seriousness of the fault. In cases of crime and for disciplinary and penal matters, the general director of the police passes judgment.

The Constitution confers on the nation's general prosecutor the authority to supervise and impose sanctions on all official employees for irregular behavior during the performance of their duties or jobs. This authority is in addition to the power conferred by law on the superiors of officials and employees in disciplinary matters, which means that the initiation of a disciplinary investigation by the general prosecutor automatically stops the one started by the superior of the accused; the findings obtained so far by the latter must be transferred to the former. Once a sanction is imposed—either by the general prosecutor or by the superior—the principle of *non bis in idem* is applied, which means that two separate sanctions cannot be applied to the same conduct.

The Vigilance Service plays the most important role within the operational functions of the National Police Corps, and its main objective is to keep and guarantee the nation's public order and prevent and eliminate public disturbances against normal peace, health, morality, ecology and public monuments. The Vigilance Service is rendered in urban and countryside areas on a six-hour shift basis. The personnel assigned to this job must remain during every other shift on an "availability status" to return to work if public order disturbances should eventually arise. Furthermore, such personnel may be kept on alert in the event of serious disturbances. The typical office work routine is carried out on an eight-hour daily schedule, starting at eight o'clock every morning, with a 30-minute lunch break. The administrative staff does not work on Saturdays.

Before each vigilance shift, the staff of sergeants major and agents is convoked to a "relation" assembly, during which the commanding officer or his assistant admonishes personnel who have not followed the disciplines of the institution and gives instructions concerning service to be rendered and the areas to be watched. Weapons, ammunition and other working elements are handed over for each shift prior to a thorough inventory, which records the brand, caliber and number of weapons handed and the amount of ammunition. In addition to allowing control and use of police material, this practice facilitates the investigation, whenever necessary, of the number of shots made and, through ballistics tests, determines the person who shot and the weapon used.

Vigilance is performed by agents assigned to fixed locations, such as diplomatic offices, ministries, government offices and banks, and also by patrols on foot, on horseback, or in patrol cars, through streets, squares, parks and other open public places. From the motorized patrols, the agents can communicate by radio with Headquarters and other patrols. Occasionally, during strikes, public demonstrations, political meetings, etc., on-foot personnel are equipped with walkie-talkies to enable them to enlist quick help from additional public forces. During the vigilance period the personnel must note damage to street lighting, sewerage and aqueduct services, and a report is turned out by the superior to the corresponding service entity for the necessary repairs. In cases of crimes affecting the integrity of people, the vigilance personnel must request the presence of the judicial police and ambulances, and protect the site where the occurrence took place in order to keep the useful evidences untouched.

The uniform worn by the members of the National Police Corps is light olive green, differing from the dark olive green worn by members of the Army. It includes a cap with a black visor, a high-buttoned jacket with buttons in the middle, three golden buttons, loops on each shoulder, two outside pockets with flaps on the chest, and two inside pockets with outside flaps at both sides of the jacket and golden buttons. There are straight-cut trousers, a light beige shirt, a black tie, and black socks and shoes. There is a belt of like material with a buckle for officers, and a black leather belt with the metal police star for agents.

Officers promoted to general wear on the upper part of the cap the coat of arms of Colombia surrounded by half a crown of double laurel branches, and a smaller coat of arms of Colombia on each one of the collar tips; between the coat of arms and the visor, a double golden cordon is shown, and on the visor two laurel branches and a golden rib. A black baton with a golden tip serves as an authority symbol.

Colonels and lieutenant colonels display the same coat of arms of Colombia and a double golden cordon on the cap but a single laurel branch on the visor. Majors, captains, lieutenants and second lieutenants display the national coat of arms on the cap, without the laurel crown, a single golden cordon, and a golden rib on the visor. On the edges of the collar they wear the coat of arms of Colombia without the laurel branch crown. Sergeants major wear the nation's coat of arms on their caps and a black leather strap instead of the golden cordon. There are no adornments on the visor. The same coat of arms appears on the edges of the collar. They do not wear a belt, unless they carry a gun. On the left arm sleeve they display the rank insignia. Agents display on the cap the national coat of arms and a small strap between the cap and the visor. On the collar edges appear small crossed guns, the badge at the left, and at the right a whistle hanging from a chain that is fixed at the shoulder loop and crosses the right pocket.

Officers wear gala uniforms to attend special ceremonies of the institution, social celebrations such as weddings, and academic meetings. By means of bracelets fixed on the sleeves and just below the left shoulder, uniformed personnel bear the emblem of the specialty to which each belongs.

Cadets from the School of Officers wear a high-buttoned gray jacket, white trousers and black shoes. For parades and official presentations, they wear the Prussian helmet. For the performance of the Vigilance Service, officers carry .45-caliber pistols; sergeants major and agents carry .38-caliber guns. In areas where police cases are frequent, agents carry a wooden stick (commonly known as a *bolillo,* after its shape) that allows the subjugation of the delinquent without the use of fire weapons. In urban and countryside areas, night vigilance patrolling is reinforced by carbines. Motorized patrol personnel carry light Madsen-type submachine guns.

Policemen run physical hazards according to their specialty and the task they have to perform. Violence on policemen is increasingly frequent as a result of terrorists and subversives operating both in the countryside and in the cities, sometimes with political interests. The members of antiguerrilla and other special services, such as the Special Anti-Kidnapping Operating Group (GOES), are not entirely successful in counteracting such situations. On the other hand, the country's socioeconomic problems have caused a disproportionate increase in common delinquency, leading to serious criminal attempts on policemen's lives.

The use of bulletproof vests and other safety devices is restricted to the members of specialized groups, such as the GOES, and the members of personal guard services to high state officers. The budget does not allow for mass acquisition of these safety devices. The Available Force, which is devoted to counteract mutinies, riots, and mass-protest demonstrations, wears protective helmets and shields of a special design and make. For special public order situations, the police have recently acquired gum-bullet guns, antimutiny cars equipped with external protective systems, high-pressure water-spouting devices, gas-throwing guns, etc.

The ranks of officials and sergeants major comprise the following titles on a descending scale:

1. *Official generals*
   General
   Major general
   Brigadier general

2. *Superior officials*
   Colonel
   Lieutenant colonel
   Major

3. *Subordinate officials*
   Captain
   Lieutenant
   Second lieutenant

4. *Sergeants major (subofficials)*
   Sergeant major
   First sergeant
   Vice first sergeant
   Second sergeant
   First-in-command
   Second-in-command

According to their duties, officials and sergeants major are classified as vigilance officials or service officials.

Only Colombian-born citizens can be officials or sergeants major. They are entered in the roster during the second lieutenant and second-in-command stages, the former upon completion and approval of the necessary studies at the "General Santander" School of Officials and the latter on graduation from the formation schools for sergeants major.

To be promoted to the rank of lieutenant, it is necessary to remain four years as a second lieutenant, spending three years in the Vigilance Service. To attain the rank of captain, four years are needed as a lieutenant in the Vigilance Service. The rank of major is reached after five years as captain, two of which must be served as station commander, or district or station subcommander in Bogotá. The rank of lieutenant colonel requires five years in the immediately preceding category with two years' service as station commander in Bogotá, or district commander, or as subcommander of a police department or the metropolitan police, or as the director of one of the sergeant major or agent formation schools. The rank of colonel is attained after four years of service as lieutenant colonel, two of which as commander or subcommander of a police department, the metropolitan police, or director or assistant director of the police formation schools, or police station commander in Bogotá. Promotion to brigadier general follows five years as a colonel including one year as director, administrative division head, police department commander, metropolitan police, formation school director, special unit commander, or any operational position within his category. The rank of major general is reached after four years of service as brigadier general.

Within the Vigilance Service branch, the ranks of captain and major require enrollment in a special training course that covers studies on law and police techniques. All service officials must complete a three-month training course in accordance with their specialty. For the lieutenant colonel rank it is necessary to attend the superior Police Academy course. Promotion to colonel is subject to the government's free selection among lieutenant colonels who have distinguished themselves. For promotion to brigadier general, the government freely selects among colonels with a superior Police Academy diploma and who have completed the upper studies course. The government freely selects new major generals and generals.

The Second-in-command title is attained upon completion and approval with the best marks, the required studies at the formation school for sergeants major. Promotion to First-in-command and Vice first sergeant requires completion of a specialized course, attendance at which is awarded by contest. In general terms, sergeants major are promoted on account of their conduct, professional skills confirmed by the ratings obtained in the final examinations, their psychophysical attitudes and a minimum service period in the lower ranks.

The National Police Corps owns a microwave radio communications network for fixed-to-mobile and fixed-to-fixed communications with almost all police departments throughout Colombia. It also has radiotelephonic services used by department commands and its district commands. For antiguerrilla operations and during public disasters, the police use portable radio transceivers similar to those used by the Army. There is a good supply of walkie-talkies for the Vigilance Service in urban areas. Telegraphic communications are done by the national system services, which cover 85% of the towns and cities in the country. The motorized patrols for the Vigilance Service in cities are equipped with radiocommunication systems and are commonly known as radio patrols.

In rural areas with problems caused by high delinquency rates or for socioeconomic reasons, police cars are provided with communications systems connected to their respective commands. In important cities with high population densities and public order difficulties, such as Bogotá, Medellín, Cali and Barranquilla, the National Police Corps has established "Station 100," which is equipped with electronic computer systems that compile the most detailed information to facilitate police operations. The E-100 system is open to all service personnel to ensure accurate exchange of information. All calls received by telephone or radio are recorded at the E-100 dispatch center. The operation of the system is handled at the central command as well as at the stations and at district commands. In addition, the police have crime data banks that include dactyloscopic records and all information concerning penal background on sentences pronounced and on modus operandi. Every year the National Police Corps publishes statistical bulletins on crime and infractions. The bulletins appear in the magazine *Criminalidad* and contain data compiled by the Board of Judicial and Investigation Police through its Center of Crime Investigation and Statistics. People can at any time request this information, and the police must supply it.

In accordance with the National Police Code, the National Police Corps is responsible for keeping the internal public peace, and it is only when the police sources become insufficient to restrain serious disorders by themselves that military help is justified. Under such circumstances, the prime civil authority of the place may request military assistance, in writing, to the Army commander of the place in which the disturbance is taking place or where the public disaster has occurred. When the police and the Army must act simultaneously, this is known as "Operational Control," and the highest-ranked Army official assumes the command or direction of the operation, in addition to the penal responsibilities if the orders given by this authority openly violate civil rights guaranteed in the constitution. Consequently the police ordinarily assume control of civil disorders.

Some time ago the National Police Corps acquired anti-explosive units for use in the largest population areas, to detect and deactivate bombs and similar explosive devices. This job is performed by specially trained and qualified personnel using electronic detection equipment and vehicles that offer the least possible risk of danger.

The National Police Corps also has intelligence and counterintelligence units, supported by the Army, for permanent vigilance regarding activist subversive groups, with a good record of success.

The opening of private correspondence and telephone interception are possible only through legal authorization, since the national constitution guarantees their inviolability. For specific crime investigation purposes, judges can authorize interception of mail and telephone taps, but under no circumstances is the police or any other security organization allowed to do this on their own.

The Road Police, a unit of the National Police Corps, oversees highway and other road traffic and plays the role of judicial police whenever accidents occur with dead and injured people involved. The functions of the Road Police cover, among others, administration of the Land Transport Code; preparation of acts (known as "partes" in cases of infractions); patrolling; and aid to victims of accidents and those with broken-down cars; accident sketch drawing; and information to drivers and tourists. The police who perform this job are specialized and operate throughout the country, even though the number of experts is inadequate due to budget shortages.

In the event of violations of traffic regulations, the police officer writes the infraction report, which is then submitted to Headquarters and to the corresponding police official, who must follow a process in accordance with standing bylaws. The sanctions range from ordinary fines to cancellation of the driving license and confinement of the vehicle to official yards.

Criminal Identification

For criminal identification by means of fingerprints, the National Police Corps applies the ten-fingerprint system, with files and records kept since the establishment of the Security Police Groups, mainly in the Administrative Security Department (DAS). Both the police and the DAS exchange information on a permanent basis. All dossiers with penal records are carried by the latter and kept up to date according to legal reports. At present, efforts are being made to acquire computers to speed up criminal identification. Both entities also keep files that allow identification of criminals by the modus operandi. The "described portrait" system has been modernized by use of "identikits." For all legal purposes, the only laboratory opinions or other expert opinions considered valid are those of the Central Institute of Legal Medicine, an entity under the Ministry of Justice, with specialized scientists. The institute develops scientific studies to improve criminal investigation methods to help judges and police officers. The National Police Corps also owns laboratories to train its judicial police staff properly. The institute is provided with spectrographs, chromatographs, analyzers, and electronic microscopes for ballistics, toxicology, biological and all other analyses to identify criminals. Colombian law does not contemplate use of polygraph and related devices; consequently, the use of these methods by the police or other auxiliary organs is not admissible in court. For more than twenty years the National Police Corps has bred German shepherds at the School of Carabineers. There is a group of specialized policemen who initially received training in Germany, including studies on reproduction, breeding, education and training of the dogs. The dogs are used in different police actions and at present render excellent performance in antinarcotic programs, especially at airports and frontier posts. The National Police Corps owns approximately 100 trained dogs.

The police station is the basic unit of the National Police Corps. In urban centers police stations are usually under a colonel or lieutenant colonel and an assistant commander. The stations have patrol cars and motorcycles but sometimes are undermanned. They have radiotelephones, and telephone and microwave communication systems that allow them to establish contact with Main Station 100, the police department command on which they depend, with the metropolitan police, and with their patrol-car crews. A small group of judicial police officers operates in each station, and they can carry out primary criminal investigations until relieved by the judicial police (SIJIN) at the police department or metropolitan police commands. Each station also includes an office used exclusively to record offenses that are then referred to the SIJIN for investigation and, finally, to the judicial offices, criminal investigation courts, to initiate the penal process. Infractions and minor crimes are recorded at the police commissaries under the Ministry of Justice. In important cities such as Medellín, Cali and Barranquilla, there are an average of seven police stations with some 400 units among officers, sergeants major and agents in each. Furthermore, there is a group in some of the stations known as the Emergency Force, to break up mass-protest demonstrations and public order situations that require the immediate attention of the police. In small cities the police force is smaller, as public order problems are smaller. Bogotá, with an estimated population of 5 million, has 14 Police Stations and a permanent-strength group of 7,500 units. The vigilance service in the nation is organized in six-hour shifts. Married personnel ordinarily rest in their homes, while unmarried staff usually rest in their respective police station headquarters. There are cells at the Stations—usually quite uncomfortable because of their small size and poor sanitary services—where people are held after their capture for a crime; they are then put at the disposal of the corresponding judicial authority, for investigation pending indictment. The Station personnel cooperates with the Community Activity Boards of the city districts to improve community welfare, such as for street pavements, parks and houses, and with sports committees to organize and carry out events.

Recruitment, Education & Training

During the past few years the National Police Corps has promoted enrollment for officers, sergeants major and agents using attractive advertising campaigns, including newspaper ads, with special emphasis on the importance of the Police Service and its many benefits. To join as a simple recruit, it is essential to have the moral, intellectual and physical qualities required by the force. The applicant must not have a penal record, must have completed at least the fifth grade of elementary school and be in excellent physical and mental health. Applicants for sergeant major must take an additional Terman B test for mental skills.

The Superior Police Academy is at the "General Santander" Cadet School in Bogotá, where officials obtain their highest professional titles. The curricula comprise the Professional Police Study Area, which lasts 12 weeks, and is complemented by a special course at the Public Administration School (ESAP) under the control of the Ministry of Education and the presidency of the republic. The Superior Police Academy's Professional Police Study Area covers the following curricula:

1. *Police administration*

    Planning

    Unit organization

    Management techniques

    Control and evaluation

    Personnel handling

    Budget planning and execution

    Police operations

    Seminars

2. *Police supporting studies*

    Police maneuvers

    Physical culture

3. *Complementary sciences area*

    Police law

    Police law procedings

    Police philosophy

Under the Official Police Career Bylaws, it is not possible to be promoted to colonel without having completed the Superior Police Academy course. If the course cannot be taken, the interested party must submit a special study project on the subjects in the course. Furthermore, it is not possible to become a brigadier general without having a diploma from the academy. This academy also offers high police studies; upon their successful completion, one has the title of police administrator.

The "General Santander" Police Cadet School, established in 1940, is responsible for the preparation of the future National Police Corps Officials. The cadets also follow their normal high-school studies in the institution. The courses run in six terms of 16 weeks each. The training level is high, as it is designed to combine both police discipline and professional performance skills, to develop leadership abilities and service capacity. Upon completion of their studies, the students receive the Police Studies Licentiate diploma, which qualifies them to work in organizations dealing with areas such as personnel, banking and money transportation security and private security.

The Education Division of the National Police Corps develops the curriculum of the institution's schools.

With respect to the physical training of policemen, gymnastics and training in the martial arts take place at the schools during the formation stage; however, once personnel are assigned to fulfill their duties, the shortage of personnel in training units hinders the frequency of physical and training practices in self-defense methods.

The Penal System

The legal system is based on Spanish law, particularly the Spanish Code of 1822. Legislation has tended to represent idealized standards of behavior and to be highly legalistic. It regulates all social relations in detail and defines all possible types of criminal activity. The Code of Criminal Procedure was enacted in 1938 and substantially modified in 1971 and 1976.

The investigation of a reported crime is conducted by an instruction judge, who is charged with determining whether a crime has been committed. If there is at least one credible witness or other serious proof, the judge may order a provisional preventive arrest of the suspect, who cannot be held for more than 12 hours without a warrant except under the special provisions of a state of siege. The judge must notify the appropriate court and district or local attorney within 24 hours, and the accused cannot be held incommunicado for more than 72 hours.

The investigation must be completed within 30 days, during which period an accused is not under oath and may not be compelled to give testimony against himself or herself. The right to an attorney, whether engaged by the accused or appointed by the court, is guaranteed. Provisional release on bail is obligatory if requested unless the crime is very serious. The instruction judge indicts and arraigns the accused if there is evidence of guilt, and a record of the investigation is sent to the local circuit judge for referral to the proper trial court. Although provision is made in the code for a swift trial, the backlog of cases is such that the accused often has to wait for years before the trial comes before the court. Juries consisting of three persons are used only in criminal trials before superior judges.

The Colombian penal system operates under the Penal Code of 1938 and its subsequent revisions. All crimes are identified in the code, and no person can be convicted for any act not expressly prohibited.

The punishments recognized in the code are confinement in a penitentiary for from one to 24 years, which involves maximum security conditions and forced labor and always begins with a period of solitary confinement of one month to two years; imprisonment for six months to eight years, which is served in a less secure installation or an agricultural penal colony; arrest for one day to five years, an even less severe confinement in which a prisoner may choose his or her own work from that available in the prison facilities; simple confinement for three months to three years, in which the convicted person is merely confined to an area of the country at least 62 miles (100 kilometers) from his home; and fines of up to 5,000 pesos. Accessories to crimes are punished by prohibition of residence in a specific place, prohibition of public rights, loss of pensions or wages, banishment to an agricultural penal colony, loss or suspension of citizenship and, for foreigners, deportation. Capital punishment has been prohibited since 1910.

A judge is given a great deal of latitude in deciding the sentence and in having the punishment fit the criminal as well as the crime. Factors such as poverty or lack of education are considered as mitigating factors in determining the severity of the sentence.

The largest penitentiary is La Picota in Bogotá. Similar penitentiaries for adult males are in Medellín, Palmira, Ibagué, Manizales, Pamplona, Popayán, Cartagena, Pasto and Barranquilla. Each judicial district and municipality has its own jail, and some 80% of the prison population are confined in these institutions. There are two jails for women, in Tunja and Cuenca, and two agricultural penal colonies, one in Acacías and the other in the jungle near Araracuara. Two small prisons, one in Bogotá and the other on Gorgona Island, complete the prison system.

As many as 75% of prisoners are denied or are unable to produce bail, and it is not uncommon for the accused to spend several years awaiting trial. Often an inmate would serve time equal to the sentence he would have received if tried and convicted and would finally be released without the usual judicial proceedings.

Juveniles below 14 years of age, if convicted of a crime, are placed on probation and entrusted to their parents. Those between 14 and 18 years are confined

CRIME STATISTICS (1984)

		Number Reported	Attempts %	Cases Solved %	Crime per 100,000	Offenders	Females %	Juveniles %	Strangers %
1.	Murder	776			2.54	103			
2.	Sex offenses, including rape								
3.	Rape	1,338			4.39	598			
4.	Serious assault	21,539			70.63	7,746			
5.	All theft	65,019			213.21	25,249			
6.	Aggravated theft								
7.	Robbery and violent theft	10,000			32.79	2,802			
8.	Breaking and entering								
9.	Auto theft	4,324			14.18	492			
10.	Other thefts	4,627			15.17	2,460			
11.	Fraud	5,119			16.79	2,717			
12.	Counterfeiting	427			1.40	520			
13.	Drug offenses	10,292			33.75	10,621			
14.	Total offenses	209,581			687.24	88,898	7.90	3.05	

Criteria of juveniles: aged from 12 to 16 years.
Note: Information for some categories is not available.

to a reformatory, the principal ones being in Bogotá and Fagua.

Prisoners may be granted a conditional release for good conduct after they have completed two-thirds to three-fourths of their sentence. In addition, a preparatory release may be granted two to three years before this time when prisoners are permitted to work outside and return to the prison at night.

Penal reform measures initiated in 1936 accented rehabilitation through work, and many prisons were equipped with spinning and weaving shops, iron works, foundries, and carpentry, mechanical and tailoring shops. Many of these facilities have been allowed to deteriorate, and many prisoners are engaged by private contractors.

Colombia has a substantial crime problem, which reached alarming proportions in the 1970s involving 1.5% of the population. Of reported crimes, 75% occurred in urban areas and 40% was concentrated in the three major urbanized regions: Bogotá, Cali and Medellín. Males committed 92% of the crimes and persons between ages 20 and 39 committed 65%. The distribution of crimes among the six classifications of the Penal Code was: crimes against property, 58%; crimes against the person, 19.5%; crimes against individual liberties, 1.5%; sex-related crimes, 5%; crimes against public administration, 1%; and miscellaneous crimes, 15%. In rural areas cattle rustling and hijacking of trucks are reported to be growing. Bogotá is said to have the highest crime rate in the world. Of particular concern to the police are the large number of professional pickpockets. Smuggling is the nation's chief illegal activity, both in consumer goods and in narcotics. Narcotics are second only to coffee as an export item through underground channels. Cocaine is generally brought into the country in crude form from Ecuador, Peru and Bolivia and refined in laboratories for export. Marijuana is grown in the northern regions. Officials claim that narcotics operations are controlled by organized-crime elements from the United States. Some of the drugs find their way into Colombia's schools and university campuses. According to a government study, 43% of Colombian students regularly use drugs.

CONGO

BASIC FACT SHEET

Official Name: People's Republic of the Congo
Area: 342,000 sq km
Population: 2,082,154 (1987)
Capital: Brazzaville
Nature of Government: Civilian dictatorship
Language: French
Currency: CFA franc
GNP: $1.8 billion (1984)
Territorial Divisions: 9 regions
Population per Police Officer: 870
Police Expenditures per 1,000: N.A.

History & Background

The National Gendarmerie, heir to the French Gendarmerie, was organized in 1961 as in integral part of the Army and with a strength of about 500 men. Although its size has quadrupled since then, its organization, composition and disposition have remained basically the same. Before 1969, the gendarmerie headquarters in Brazzaville controlled its territorial units through three subordinate field headquarters—the Southern Command at Pointe-Noire, and the Central and Northern commands at Brazzaville. Additional mobile platoons were located at each command headquarters for use as reserve strike forces in emergency situations. In 1969 the territorial organization was modified to conform to the six military zones. The Southern, Central and Northern commands were abolished and the gendarmerie units were redistributed among the six military zones. Mobile reserve units were retained at Brazzaville, Pointe-Noire, Dolisie and Jacob. The gendarmerie command was integrated into that of the military by placing the senior gendarmerie unit commander under the authority of the military zone commander who, in turn, reported to the Army headquarters in the capital.

Structure & Organization

The police and security forces of Congo consist of the National Gendarmerie; the Sûreté Nationale; and various armed youth elements of the Congolese Labor Party, the country's sole political party. All units are controlled by the Army and are directly responsible to the president.

Recruitment, Education & Training

The gendarmerie is lightly armed, principally with French weapons, and very closely follows French techniques. Officers are trained in the National Police School in Brazzaville and in French police academies. Motorized elements are equipped with light 2½-ton trucks and jeeps.

Little information is available concerning the Sûreté Nationale, a relatively small civilian police and investigative unit that was established after independence as the counterpart of the French Sûreté Générale. Commonly known as the Security Service or the National Police, it carries out regular municipal and urban police duties, in contradistinction to the National Gendarmerie, which functions in the role of a provincial or state police. The Sûreté Nationale is also charged with immigration control, detection of fraud, suppression of black marketing and the investigation of certain crimes against the state.

Because of its broad mandate, the Sûreté Nationale exerts influence beyond its numbers. In 1966 it became part of the Directorate General of Security Services. Its control became progressively centralized under the office of the presidency. The security forces employ a number of Cuban advisers.

The police are also responsible for the operation of the civil defense organization (Protection Civile), which incorporates the Fire Department.

The Penal System

The penal system consists of institutions for both juvenile and adult offenders, administered by the keeper of the seals and the minister of justice. The principal prisons are in the major urban areas, but larger towns, such as Fort-Rousset, Ouesso, Gamboma and Mossendjo, also maintain facilities for prisoners sentenced to relatively long terms. The government publishes little information concerning rehabilitation programs. No general statistics on crime are available from official sources.

The security apparatus, under the direction of the presidency, is headed by the State Security Organization (DSGE), which is patterned after those in Eastern Europe.

CRIME STATISTICS (1984)

		Number Reported	Attempts %	Cases Solved %	Crime per 100,000	Offenders	Females %	Juveniles %	Strangers %
1.	Murder	19	15.79	100		1.06			
2.	Sex offenses, including rape								
3.	Rape	14		100		0.78			
4.	Serious assault	9		100		0.50			
5.	All theft								
6.	Aggravated theft	97		100		5.39			
7.	Robbery and violent theft								
8.	Breaking and entering								
9.	Auto theft								
10.	Other thefts								
11.	Fraud	31		100		1.72			
12.	Counterfeiting								
13.	Drug offenses	15		100		0.83			
14.	Total offenses	185	1.62	100		10.28			

Criteria of juveniles: aged from 0 to 17 years.
Note: Information for some categories is unavailable.

COSTA RICA

BASIC FACT SHEET

Official Name: Republic of Costa Rica
Area: 50,700 sq km
Population: 2,811,652 (1987)
Capital: San José
Nature of Government: Representative democracy
Language: Spanish
Currency: Colon
GNP: $3.7 billion (1985)
Territorial Divisions: 7 provinces
Population per Police Officer: 480
Police Expenditures per 1,000: N.A.

Structure & Organization

The president of Costa Rica is directed by the Constitution to maintain a "necessary public force," and it is the responsibility of each government to determine the strength and composition of this force. Since 1948 its principal components have consisted of the Civil Guard, the Fiscal Guard and the police forces. The Civil Guard, which is the major element of the police forces, has a Presidential Guard, a largely ceremonial unit. It also operates the small air and maritime force and is designed as the nucleus of any volunteer force raised in the event of an outside threat to national security. The Civil Guard performs standard law-enforcement functions in the preservation of law and order, prevention and detection of crime, patrolling streets and highways, and control of traffic.

The president of the republic is designated commander in chief of all public forces. There is no top-level supervisory staff, and operational coordination among the various agencies involved in law enforcement has generally been left to the discretion of local commanders. Five separate ministries are involved with various aspects of public order and security, each with its own functional areas.

The Civil Guard is under the control of the Ministry of Public Security through its director general of public forces. The minister is concerned primarily with policy and the director general with day-to-day operations. In addition to direct supervision of the Civil Guard, the director general has a number of staff and operational responsibilities. His staff comprises sections for plans and operations and intelligence, and in the operations section he directs the detective force, traffic force, motor maintenance, communications and the bands. The minister has a principal assistant, designated an administrative supervisor, whose responsibilities include personnel, supply, budget, medical services and immigration control. Two other ministers have jurisdiction over certain Civil Guard activities. The minister of government is in charge of budgetary allocation for supplies and equipment. The minister of the presidency has jurisdiction over the National Police School, which recruits and trains all police officers at the national level.

The Fiscal Guard, under the Ministry of Economy and Finance, is composed of two elements: the Treasury Police and the Customs Police. The Treasury Police has a wide scope of responsibilities, ranging from control of narcotics and illicit liquor to countersubversive activities. The Customs Police monitors the collection of customs fees.

The Judicial Police is a small force at the disposal of the members of the Supreme Court. It is indirectly under the aegis of the minister of justice. The Town and Village Police is the second-largest police organization under the minister of government. It serves as a rural constabulary and municipal police force in areas not covered by the Civil Guard.

The Civil Guard, the largest national law-enforcement agency, has a strength of close to 3,000 people. Made up of well-trained volunteers, its area of responsibility is limited to the national capital and six provincial capitals. Organization is essentially along military lines, using military titles and terminology and equipment designed primarily for tactical military rather than for civil police action. Most of its armament and equipment is furnished through U.S. military assistance, and many of its officers are trained in the United States.

The grade structure for both officers and noncommissioned officers parallels that of the U.S. Army but provides no rank higher than colonel, which is held by the director. Below him there is one who holds the rank of lieutenant colonel. Officers in charge of service units are designated first or second commanders. In the noncommissioned officer category, the grades of senior and chief master sergeants have not been established.

The Civil Guard is organized into companies that range from 80 to 350 people, generally averaging 100 people. Normally, about half of the Civil Guard's total strength is stationed in the capital. Two companies, with a complement of 900 people, are assigned to police duties in the city. They are augmented by a radio patrol unit, which is a permanent mobile striking force. Also permanently stationed in San José is the Presidential Guard. This is an elite corps whose sole mission is to guard the person and palace of the president. Criteria for entry into this crack company are demanding, and it is generally conceded to be the best-equipped and best-trained unit in the police forces.

A third Civil Guard company, stationed in the capital on a rotating basis, performs no standard police duties but is engaged in full-time training. At the conclusion of a training cycle its personnel are assigned to regular duty and replaced by those of another company. It is also charged with the control of the store of arms and ammunition of the entire Civil Guard. As a ready reserve, it is considered to be on call for use in case of emergency or for dispatch to any threatened area.

Each of the six provincial companies constitutes the police force of the capital of its respective province. These companies are loosely supervised on a national level by the director general of public forces in San José, but distance from the capital and dearth of supervisory personnel result in a considerable degree of autonomy and independent action. Companies are rotated periodically between mountain and coastal provinces, and each gets its turn to participate in the concerted training program.

The staff element of the Civil Guard is directly under the director general in San José. It determines policy and directs operations, and its services are available not only to the Civil Guard but also to all police agencies throughout the nation through the Plans and Operations Section and the Intelligence Section. The Civil Guard also operates police auxiliary services, such as communications, detection and investigation, traffic control, motor maintenance, and bands. The communications function is handled by the Department of Radio Communications, which operates all police radio networks linking the head-

quarters with each of the six provincial companies. The Detective Force is a plainclothes detective organization that is responsible for all criminal investigation on a nationwide basis. The Traffic Force regulated and controls traffic for the entire nation, licenses vehicles and operators, and processes the punishment of violators. A central traffic court in the capital handles all violations for the entire country. The Guard's bands provide music for ceremonies and occasional concerts. There is a School of Police Music, a 60-piece band in San José and a 30-piece band in each of the provincial capitals.

In addition to the regular Civil Guard, there is also a volunteer reserve, made up mostly of teenagers who meet weekly for drill and instruction by the regular forces. These reservists are furnished a uniform, and they have special insignia, a shoulder patch consisting of a black panther in an orange circle.

The uniforms and the insignia of the police forces are virtually indistinguishable from those of their U.S. counterparts. The garrison uniform is olive-green wool in winter and khaki cotton in summer. There is a blue dress and a white dress uniform for officers and a short white jacket for enlisted men for ceremonial occasions. All ranks are supplied with battle dress and fatigues. Headgear range from the peaked service cap to fatigue hat or steel helmet. The various police units wear the same uniforms with minor changes in insignia, and the traffic police add a seasonal uniform consisting of a white shirt and green trousers.

U.S. Army insignia of grade are used for both officers and noncommissioned officers, but there are no general officers. Insignia are worn as in the U.S. practice, one exception being the officer's dress blue, where the emblem of rank is worn on the sleeve cuff instead of the shoulder strap. Officers and men also display their insignia of rank on the front of their headgear.

The Town and Village Police is responsible for law and order in all parts of the national territory except the national capital and the seven provincial capital cities. In addition to the regular police duties, it is assigned judicial authority, conducting summary trials for violations of the Police Code and carrying out any sentences imposed. In many outlying communities, the police are the only representatives of the government, and people turn to them for public services of all kinds. A police agent becomes the arbiter of local disputes and the focal point for the dissemination of government information and mail and telegraph delivery. In many small communities with a high illegitimacy rate police often are called upon to determine fatherhood and care for abandoned children.

The organization of the Town and Village Police is along political administrative lines. Each of the seven provinces is divided into two or more cantons, which in turn are made up of two or more districts. Overall police supervision is exercised by an inspector general appointed by the minister of government, and six locally appointed provincial inspectors, but supreme authority resides in the provincial governor. It is noteworthy, however, that a governor has no police authority within his own capital, where the power rests with the Civil Guard under the centralized control of San José.

The police chief (*jefe político*) at the canton level and the principal police agent *(agente principal de policía)* in the district constitute the police executives in their respective areas. They act as a combination mayor, magistrate and chief of police. In a majority of the districts, the principal police agent also serves as the postmaster. In addition, there are about 1,500 auxiliary agents *(agentes auxiliares)* who perform basic police duties at the canton or district level, or who are scattered in one or more smaller villages or hamlets.

The Treasury Police, one of the two components of the Fiscal Guard, is the only other nationally significant police force. It is the only law-enforcement agency with legal authority to investigate political matters and to enter and search buildings. Its responsibilities include control of narcotics, intoxicants, countersubversion, cattle inspection, suppression of contraband activities, and protection and conservation of natural resources. The Treasury Police, with an authorized strength of 600 people, maintains detachments at 55 locations throughout the country, and its members patrol their areas by foot, animal transport and vehicle. New members of the force are given an initial two-week training course at the National Police School and are thereafter assigned to units.

Recruitment, Education & Training

The Civil Guard is considered to be one of the best-trained police forces in Latin America. Training programs are thorough and uniform throughout the organization. The National Police School, founded in 1963, offers a varied curriculum of professional training, and a number of Guardsmen receive advanced training in the United States.

The Penal System

The prison system consists of two national penitentiaries and a number of prisons and detention facilities distributed throughout the country. The penitentiaries are run by the Ministry of Social Welfare, while subordinate facilities are operated by local authorities. The Central Penitentiary is in San José and is used as a detention facility for persons awaiting trial and as a maximum-security prison for dangerous criminals.

The San Lucas Penitentiary, on an island in the Gulf of Nicoya, southwest of Puntarenas, is a model institution and minimum-security prison for less serious offenders. Surrounded by shark-infested waters, it was initially thought to be escapeproof until a series of successful escapes in the early 1960s led to its conversion to a prison-farm type of facility emphasizing rehabilitation rather than punishment. Families are permitted to visit inmates each week, and conjugal visits for husbands and wives are authorized.

Outside of these two penitentiaries, the prison system is loosely organized and receives little centralized guidance or direction. Few penal statistics are published, and local authorities have a free hand in methods and procedures. There are jails or detention facilities in most communities down to the canton level, and these range from simple enclosures with little security and few amenities to well-constructed prison buildings with sound protection and adequate accommodations.

The Civil Guard maintains a jail in each of the provincial capitals, and the political chief is responsible for facilities at the canton level. In all penal institutions, the rising crime rate has created growing problems of overcrowding, sanitation and security. The Penal Code includes an Organic Judicial Law that requires penal magistrates to visit prisons in their jurisdictional area at least once a week to hear complaints and confer with the wardens.

Respect for constituted authority and the traditional influence of the Church and family have worked to reduce the general incidence of crime. The existence of a sizable and prosperous middle class and the absence of extreme contrasts of wealth and poverty have also helped to eliminate many of the common incentives to crime. Although there is national concern over the increase in the crime rate in urban areas, such increases have not been of serious proportions in relation to the growth of the population.

Crimes against property, such as robbery and theft, are more prevalent than crimes against persons. The incidence of juvenile delinquency and offenses committed by women are low, and life and property are, for the most part, secure throughout the nation. The use of marijuana, however, appears to be a growing problem, and reports indicate its widespread use in schools and colleges. Of the record of arrests published by the government, a preponderant majority are misdemeanors handled by the Judicial Police. Most of the cases for theft or robbery are those involving small sums, and some of the assault cases are unaggravated offenses with no serious consequences.

Criminal statistics are published periodically by the government, presenting figures on such aspects as sex, age and geographical distribution. Of the total number of offenders, only 10% are women. Geographically, San José Province, the country's most populous, leads in number of offenders, followed by Alajuela Province; Limón Province had the least. Misdemeanors subject to the Police Code far exceed the more serious crimes. Drunkenness is the most prevalent offense, followed by disrespect for or resistance to authority. Also relatively high are disorderly conduct and traffic offenses. By occupation the largest number of violators are agricultural workers, followed by craftsmen, skilled workers and drivers of public conveyances. By age span, the highest number of offenders are among the 30-to-39-year-old group, followed by the 40-to-49 and the 20-to-24 age groups.

CUBA

Structure & Organization

Law enforcement and internal security functions are concentrated in the powerful Ministry of the Interior, organized into three vice ministries: Vice Ministry for Security, Vice Ministry for Internal Order and Crime Prevention, and Technical Vice Ministry. The Vice Ministry for Internal Order and Crime Prevention is the largest division. Its jurisdiction is purely domestic. The Vice Ministry for Security is charged with the detection and prevention of threats to national security. The Technical Vice Ministry is externally oriented toward foreign espionage, intelligence-gathering and the promotion of revolution abroad.

The predecessor of the Vice Ministry for Internal

MINISTRY OF THE INTERIOR

Vice Ministry for Security
|
State Security Department
|
General Directorate for
Immigration and Naturalization
|
Border Guard Forces

Vice Ministry for Internal
Order and Crime Prevention
|
General Directorates:
  National Revolutionary
  Police
  Fire Prevention
  Penal Establishments
|
Directories:
  Political
  Operational
|
Departments:
  Crime Prevention
  Associations Registration
|
National Section of ID Card
Systems and Population
Registry
|
Fingerprinting System
National Revolutionary Police
School

Technical Vice Ministry
|
Liberation Directorate
|
General Directorate for Intelligence
|
Directorate for Training and
Cadres
|
Directorate for General Services
|
Foreign Relations Department
|
Information Department
|
Automation Section

Order and Crime Prevention was the General Directorate of Public Order, which was created in 1961 when all the police and investigative forces were merged, although the various departments retained some autonomy. There are three general directorates under this vice ministry, the most important one being the General Directorate of the National Revolutionary Police. The police force is supplemented by the armed forces, the militia and the Committees for the Defense of the Revolution (CDR) in enforcing the country's laws. Although hard data are not available, indications are that the National Revolutionary Police is relatively small—about 15,000 officers—and maintains a fairly low profile. It is complemented by approximately 60,000 militia members assigned to police duties. All criminal investigations are handled by the Technical Investigations Office of the Vice Ministry for Internal Order and Crime Prevention. It is aided in its tasks by the Fingerprinting Section; the Department of Crime Prevention; and the Legal Advisory Office, which prepared charges against individuals. Juvenile delinquency, which receives considerable national attention, is dealt with by the special Juvenile Affairs Office. Two other noteworthy departments of the Vice Ministry for Internal Order and Crime Prevention are the Associations Registration Department, which watches potentially dangerous groups, such as religious organizations; and the National Section of Identification Card Systems and Population Registry. The latter unit is designed to cut down on labor absenteeism, work slacking, idleness and delinquency among workers by having them and their families register with the Ministry of the Interior. To be eligible for state employment, pensions or state housing, all individuals need an identification card. This card, coupled with a work record card, listing merits, demerits, crimes, residence and place of employment, and serves as a mechanism for monitoring the status and activities of the majority of the population.

The most important agency under the Vice Ministry for Security is the State Security Department (Departmento Seguridad del Estado, DSE). The DSE is, in fact, Cuba's KGB. Originally known as G-2, the DSE was until recently the zealous cerberus of the Revolution, charged with the elimination of dissidents and counterrevolutionaries. It has become less of a terror in recent years, directing its efforts against homosexuals and dissident intellectuals rather than against saboteurs, infiltrators and unrepentant capitalists. DSE agents function as part of regular patrols and conduct surveillance within assigned areas in collaboration with local CDR's and the National Revolutionary Police. These patrol agents wear uniforms and have military rank. In the past they enjoyed broad discretionary powers to interrogate, search and arrest individuals. It employs informants and covert agents to infiltrate suspect agencies, enterprises and organizations and to report suspicious activities.

The Vice Ministry for Security also administers the General Directorate for Naturalization and Immigration and the Border Guard Forces. The latter is primarily a sea operation, as Cuba does not have land frontiers.

The third vice ministry of the Ministry of the Interior is the Technical Vice Ministry, which deals with intelligence activities abroad through the Liberation Directorate and the General Directorate for Intelligence (Dirección General de Inteligencia, DGI). Although formally under the direction of the Ministry of the Interior, they appear to have considerable autonomy and report directly to the brothers Castro, Raúl and Fidel. DGI operations are mainly overseas through Cuban embassies and through infiltration of Cuban exile groups in the United States. It is primarily a counterintelligence agency, but it is also actively engaged in intelligence-gathering. Most DGI officers are KGB-trained at the Otroviskaya School of Military Counterintelligence near Moscow.

The Liberation Directorate is a covert offshoot of the DGI and is responsible for exporting the Revolution by training, supplying and providing information to pro-Castro guerrilla groups in other countries. The agency is said to be directed personally by the Castros.

If the National Revolutionary Police is a junior partner in the police system, the senior partners are the Committees for the Defense of the Revolution (Comites de Defensa de la Revolución, CDR). Created in September 1960, their major function is "fighting against the counterrevolutionary class enemy." Originally the CDR had the single purpose of serving as an adjunct to the security apparatus of the Ministry of the Interior and the Revolutionary Armed Forces (Fuerzas Armadas Revolucionarias, FAR). Their function was—and still is—to identify counterrevolutionaries at the local level, to keep track of their activities and to inform the proper government authorities. The CDR became a major civil defense force during the national emergency created by the Bay of Pigs invasion, rounding up numerous actual and suspected enemies of the regime and delivering them to the revolutionary tribunals for summary disposal. They also helped to keep the Cuban population mobilized for defense during the Cuban missile crisis of 1962 and played a key role in the rapid nationalization and confiscation of over 55,000 small businesses during the Revolutionary Offensive in 1968.

As the CDR evolved, they developed a number of roles in addition to their historic ones, including patrolling the streets and reporting robberies or unusual activities to the police or militia. They also testify about the morals and conduct of individuals brought before the popular tribunals and enforce the tribunal's sentences in case of banishment or house confinement. Other functions include reporting lazy workers and absentees, catching truants, organizing "click patrols" to check on the use of electricity, and listing the possessions of individuals who had asked to leave the country.

Beyond the criminal justice sphere, the CDR play a significant role in the indoctrination and propaganda process. This role was strengthened through the creation of combined CDR and FAR committees whose purpose was to "instill patriotic sentiment in our people." CDR memberships are also mobilized as volunteer labor in agriculture and production. They hold health drives, immunization campaigns, cleanup campaigns, savings drives and recycling drives. They watch the quality of the local services and schools.

The CDR have a reported total membership of 5.5 million citizens over 14 years of age. This is approximately 50% of the total population and over 80% of the adult population. They are organized on a geographical basis under a National Directorate. Directly subordinate to the National Directorate are six provincial directorates, who supervise 200 district directorates, who, in turn, supervised 4,500 sectional directorates. There are over 30,000 base or neighborhood committees, with an average membership of 120 to 150. Almost every work center, apartment building, people's farm or city block has a local CDR. The local CDR is headed by a president elected by the membership and is divided into a number of subcommittees (frentes) that coordinate their actions with the various governmental organs. By its very nature, such an extensive organizational structure has made it difficult if not impossible for citizens to avoide contact with the CDR, thus making their vigilance role that much more easily accomplished.

Recruitment, Education & Training

No information is available on recruitment, education and training.

The Penal System

The penal system comprises three or four types of prisons. The most common is the state work farm (granja), where prisoners serve their sentences in minimum-security institutions while engaging in productive labor and undergoing rehabilitation. There are over 100 such work farms scattered throughout the island. A different penal institution is the maximum-security prison or penitentiary, about 50 in number, where serious criminals and counterrevolutionaries are incarcerated. Prisoners in these institutions do not do productive labor and are not eligible for rehabilitation programs. Overcrowded and harshly administered, they are the scenes of much torture and brutality. The

most notorious are the Castillo del Príncipe in Havana; La Cabaña Fortress; Boniato Prison; San Serverino Castle, and America Libre, one of three women's penitentiaries. A third kind of prison is the reeducation center for minors. About 20 in number, these prisons house juvenile offenders. A fourth kind of prison, which is reportedly phased out, is the UMAP Concentration Camp, formed in 1966 for homosexuals, predelinquents, dissident intellectuals, wayward bureaucrats and political dissidents. These concentration camps were particularly odious because they existed solely to deal with nonconformists, dissidents and unenthusiastic revolutionaries and reeducate them through a harsh regimen.

From the Castro takeover of the country, until the late 1970s the majority of Cuban prisoners were what usually are known as political prisoners, a category in which were lumped not only those accused of political crimes but also antisocial activities. According to some sources as many as 100,000 persons were arrested after the Bay of Pigs invasion and imprisoned without any semblance of due process. The regime has consistently refused to provide information regarding the treatment and number of political prisoners. In the absence of official data, the estimates have varied from 1,000 (according to Fidel Castro) to 15,000 (according to Cuban exile groups). Reports by the Inter-American Human Rights Commission and Amesty International indicate that political prisoners are subject to brutality, abuse and torture. The former has charged that prisoners are not advised of charges against them, not given impartial or public hearings, not afforded an opportunity for defense, not allowed to appeal, tried on ex post facto laws, and executed during their appeal or while in prison. Major systematic abuses include: beatings by guards and officers, withholding of food and water, withholding of medical care, withholding of fresh air and exercise, withholding of family visits for years, withholding of mail for years, solitary confinement, torture by electronic devices, use of water cells where prisoners are forced to stand in a level of water so they can neither sit nor lie down, and forced participation in medical experiments. However, according to Amnesty International, conditions in prisons and the treatment of prisoners have improved since the 1970s.

Most prisoners are in some form of rehabilitation program. Everyone is eligible for such programs with the exception of felons and political prisoners. Although participation is "voluntary," prisoners often are forced into them through pressures, such as threat of starvation and denial of medical care. There are a variety of rehabilitation plans, but most follow a general pattern. From prison the prisoner goes to a work farm for reeducation while engaging in productive labor. After a while he or she becomes eligible for conditional liberties, such as passes to leave the work farm for trips home or to town. Leave is entirely unsupervised. Passes are granted once in every 45 days for a three-day period. Prisoners are eligible for release after serving 25% of their sentence or at least one year in the program. According to government spokespersons, the major purpose of reeducation in the program was not so much to create good revolutionaries as to neutralize negative attitudes toward the Revolution. To this end, they are schooled in Fidelism and Marxism-Leninism.

The country's Criminal Code has changed over the years as the socialist nature of society has developed and as the philosophy of Fidelism has infused the legal system. Most legislation has been directed against crimes that are classified as political. Between 1959 and 1963 the Cuban government passed over 1,100 laws. The most notable of these, Act 425, defined counterrevolutionary activity and authorized the use of the death penalty in such cases. Individual rights were often ignored or dealt with summarily. New procedural laws enacted by the Council of Ministers in 1973 lowered the age of penal liability from 18 to 16 and established strict penalties, including death, for such crimes as homosexuality, crimes against the family and children, and crimes against the national economy. The Cuban criminal justice philosophy is based on the collective good, and crime is defined as action against the collective. Illustrative of this point is Article 116 of the Law of Penal Procedure, which obliges citizens to inform against criminals and deviants, and states that "whoever fails to report illegal acts will incur the penal responsibility."

There is considerable evidence that conventional crimes have diminished sharply since 1959, when Fidel Castro took over; some estimate that it has been cut in half. The government has successfully banned gambling, prostitution and drug trafficking, for all of which Cuba was notorious before the Revolution. Gambling, prostitution, begging and petty corruption are virtually nonexistent. In the first 10 years of the Castro regime drug convictions declined by 90% and homicides by 80%. The decrease is attributed both to the reinstitution of the death penalty for even nonindex (minor) crimes and to the willingness of revolutionary tribunals to impose harsh penalties. Some crimes were eliminated as a result of the reordering of social and economic priorities. Drunkenness and drug traffic diminished because alcohol and drugs became scarce. Begging disappeared because of vagrancy laws and because the state provided for basic needs. Prostitution ended, but the government made houses available, for a small fee, to couples who wished to spend the night in friendly comradeship.

Since the Revolution, most crimes are of two kinds: counterrevolutionary crimes, and crimes against property. Since the state owns all property, any crime against property is also a crime against the state. During the first 10 years of the Revolution, crimes against property, especially black marketing, petty theft, manipulation of ration cards, etc., tripled, and peaked during the Revolutionary Offensive of 1968, when 55,600 small businesses and privately owned enterprises were nationalized. During 1968 over 80 acts of sabotage aimed at industries, warehouses, schools and public buildings occurred throughout the country. The government's response was to tighten control by registering workers, passing the Antiloafing Law, revitalizing the CDR as agencies for vigilance, and extending the death penalty to sabotage.

Despite numerous attempts by the government to deal with juvenile delinquency, it remains a serious problem. In the mid-1950s over half of all crimes were committed by juveniles. The most common juvenile crimes are vagrancy, sexual promiscuity and vandalism. One explanation for this phenomenon is the high-school dropout rate. A total of 12% of the school-age population are neither working nor studying, and this group was particularly susceptible to antisocial foreign influences. At the urging of Fidel Castro, who maintained that juvenile delinquency was the result of the leniency of the old Criminal Code, the age of criminal responsibility was lowered to 16 in 1973. Sanctions were made tougher against moral and economic crimes. Youths who were not in school or working were drafted into the armed forces youth column, where they were assigned to productive labor. Further, the Law of the Organization of the Judicial System of 1973 set up new procedures for dealing with juvenile offenders. Once arrested, juveniles were sent to centers for evaluation and diagnosis, and the hard-core offenders were sent to centers for reeducation. From 1968 through the early 1970s, the state also waged a campaign against long hair, jukeboxes, rock music and miniskirts, but this appears to have relaxed in the 1980s.

CYPRUS

BASIC FACT SHEET

Official Name: Republic of Cyprus
Area: 9,251 sq km
Population: 683,651 (1987)
Capitol: Nicosia
Nature of Government: Representative democracy
Language: Greek
Currency: Cyprus pound
GNP: $2.4 billion (1984)
Territorial Divisions: 6 administrative districts
Population per Police Officer: 180
Police Expenditures per 1,000: N.A.

History & Background

The police system, like the armed forces, is organized along communal lines. The 1960 Constitution called for two police organizations: an urban police, to be commanded by a Greek Cypriot; and a rural police, or Gendarmerie, to be commanded by a Turkish Cypriot. The constitutional system broke down in 1963. On the Turkish occupation of northern Cyprus, the Turkish Cypriot Police was incorporated as an arm of the 5,000-man Turkish Cypriot Security Force within the Ministry of Defense and Interior of the Turkish Cypriot Administration in the North. No further details of this sectoral force are available.

Structure & Organization

The Greek Cypriot Police is organizationally and operationally separate from the National Guard within the Ministry of the Interior and Defense of the Republic of Cyprus. The force is headed by a chief of police responsible to the Ministry of the Interior and Defense. He is aided by a deputy chief, and, below him, two assistant chiefs. Headquarters consist of four departments: Administration; Traffic; Criminal Investigation; and Planning, Training and Public Relations. Under the headquarters are seven division chiefs, each of whom supervises a police district, and under them are station chiefs. There are also five special units in the headquarters: the Police Training School, the Aliens and Immigration Service, the Fire Service, the Cyprus Information Service, and the Mobile Force. The latter two units, although administratively responsible to the chief of police, are operationally controlled elsewhere. Operational control of the Cyprus Information Service, a small intelligence unit concerned with both security matters and common crime, is held by the president of the republic. The Mobile Force, a reincarnation of the Police Tactical Reserve of the early 1970s, was established in 1978 as an elite unit to protect high-ranking officials and foreign embassies and to act as a kind of special weapons assault team in the event of terrorist attacks. Its operational control is in the hands of the National Guard, an officer of which is its commander.

The police force is armed beyond normal requirements. Its arsenal includes armored cars and light artillery acquired in the 1960s during the intercommunal struggle. The police are also armed as a counterweight to the National Guard, whose right-wing composition has proved a threat to the government on several occasions.

Recruitment, Education & Training

Training is provided at the Police Training School at Athalassa, southeast of Nicosia, for both enlisted personnel and officers. Some three-quarters of the force hold the rank of constable. Salary scales are comparable to those for other civil service positions; basic salaries are supplemented by sizable cost-of-living allowances, rent allowances, a yearly one-month bonus, and lesser allowances for special duty and merit.

The Penal System

The Penal Code divides punishments into four categories: death by hanging, imprisonment up to life, whipping and fines. The death penalty has been handed down in only a handful of cases in recent years, and in every instance it was commuted to life imprisonment by the president of the republic. The few long prison terms also have usually been shortened to lesser terms by parole or pardon. The prison population on the average never exceeds a few hundreds, most serving short terms. Whipping, although sanctioned by law, is never carried out.

The national crime rate of 3.7 serious crimes per 1,000 inhabitants is one of the lowest in Europe. A major reason cited for this low incidence is the homogeneous character of the community. Nearly three-quarters of all offenses are traffic-related, and another 15% pertain to violations of labor laws and municipal regulations. Drug abuse is low, although the island is one of the trafficking areas for hashish and heroin en route to Western Europe from the Middle East. Crime is highest among males aged 17 to 20 in urban areas and lowest among juveniles under 17 and females.

CRIME STATISTICS (1984)

		Number Reported	Attempts %	Cases Solved %	Crime per 100,000	Offenders	Females %	Juveniles %	Strangers %
1.	Murder	11	27.3	118.2	2.06	6		33.3	
2.	Sex offenses, including rape	30	3.3	113.3	5.61	25	4.0	72.0	8.0
3.	Rape	3	33.3	100	0.56	1			
4.	Serious assault	87		129.9	16.27	55	9.1	5.5	12.7
5.	All theft	2,338	2.4	76.3	437.17	636	8.5	23.6	19.5
6.	Aggravated theft	990	5.4	83.1	185.12	298	3.4	31.2	29.2
7.	Robbery and violent theft	14		78.6	2.62	7			42.9
8.	Breaking and entering	976	5.4	83.2	182.50	291	3.4	32.0	28.9
9.	Auto theft								
10.	Other thefts	1,348	0.1	71.4	252.06	338	13.0	16.9	10.9
11.	Fraud	427		125.1	79.84	149	12.1	2.0	18.1
12.	Counterfeiting								
13.	Drug offenses	54		107.4	10.10	46	10.9		54.3
14.	Total offenses	3,444		73.2	643.98	1,117	8.2	17.6	19.4

Criteria of juveniles: aged from 7 to 16 years.
Note: Information for some categories is not available.

CZECHOSLOVAKIA

BASIC FACT SHEET

Official Name: Czechoslovak Socialist Republic
Area: 127,870 sq km
Population: 15,581,993 (1987)
Capital: Prague
Nature of Government: Communist dictatorship
Languages: Czech & Slovak
Currency: Korona
GNP: $135.6 billion (1985)
Territorial Divisions: 2 republics, 10 regions
Population per Police Officer: 640
Police Expenditures per Capita: N.A.

Structure & Organization

The law enforcement forces in Czechoslovakia are not called police but rather security. The National Security Corps (Sbor Narodni Bezpecnosti, SNB) comprises Public Security (Verejna Bezpecnost, VB) and State Security (Statni Bezpecnost, SB). The former is a uniformed police that performs routine police duties throughout the country. The latter, the former Secret Police, is a plainclothes force, also nationwide, which is at once an investigative agency, an intelligence agency and a counterintelligence agency.

The SNB is an armed force organized and trained to perform police rather then military duties. Its members are subject to military discipline and are under the jurisdiction of military courts. Ranks in the SNB correspond to those in the military. It is a voluntary service, although a conscription system was used to rebuild it after considerable loss of personnel at the end of the Dubcek period.

The VB performs all routine police functions at all levels, from federal to local, with a strength, according to the best available estimates of 80,000, of which two-thirds are in the Czech Republic and the rest in Slovakia. Units are distributed throughout the *krajs, okreses* and districts. The olive drab SNB uniform is almost identical to that of the military except for red shoulder boards and red trimming on the hats. Public security vehicles are yellow and white. The initials ''VB'' appear on the sides, front and rear of police vehicles.

Another armed security force subordinate to the Ministry of the Interior is the Border Guard (Pohranicni Straz, PS), which was established in 1950 as a separate agency under the then Ministry of National Security. The strength of the PS was estimated at 14,000 in the mid-1980s. The Border Guard is an armed force subject to the same military regulations as the Army. The Border Guard is equipped with armored vehicles, antitank guns and machine guns. The bulk of the PS is stationed along the West German and Austrian borders. The basic operational unit is the battalion, divided into companies and platoons and grouped into brigades.

People's Militia units were formed in 1948 out of the Communist armed guard units that took over factories, mines and other installations during the chaotic days after World War II. Historians credit these units with paving the way for the Communist takeover of the entire country in 1948. The mission of the People's Militia is defined as the defense of the socialist society, and militiamen are given powers of arrest equal to those of the regular police. The total strength of the force is reportedly between 100,000 and 125,000.

Recruitment, Education & Training

Selection for the enlisted ranks requires completion of eight years of schooling, and for officers university-level education and a graduate degree. The Ministry of the Interior's Advanced School of the National Security Corps in Prague grants academic degrees to the SNB and the Border Guard.

The Penal System

For the first 32 years of its existence—except for the Nazi period—Czechoslovakia was governed under two different penal codes. That used in Bohemia and

Moravia was the Austrian Penal Code and that in Slovakia the Hungarian Penal Code. Both codes had been amended during the years of independence, but no distinctly Czechoslovakian code had emerged until after the 1948 Communist coup. The 1950 Penal Code, hastily improvised after the Soviet model, was harsh and repressive and was designed to protect the rulers and not the ruled. Amendments in the 1950s eliminated some of its worst aspects, but a further revision in 1961 was aborted by the Stalinist faction. The Dubcek reformers took aim at the repressive measures that had been codified since 1950, and, despite the brevity of their tenure, began a process that resulted in a new Penal Code. Published in November 1969, the new code incorporated provisions intended to safeguard further the basic rights of citizens. Most of these provisions were invalidated after the fall of Dubcek, and through a number of new retrogressive provisions, curbs were again placed on the freedoms enjoyed by the people during the Prague Spring. Under the heading "Sedition," people participating in mass demonstrations against the state could face sentences of up to 12 years in jail, and under certain circumstances, such as conspiracy, death sentences could be imposed. Even mild criticisms of the regime or the Soviet Union could lead to prison sentences . A 1973 amendment dictated punishments of a wide range of subversive activities as well as for defamation of the republic, its state organs and the president. These amendments were used to suppress the Charter 77 Movement by invoking the criminal provisions of the code to muzzle even legitimate dissent. After General Secretary Husak rose to power, the Penal Code was used to jail even puppeteers and rock musicians charged with inciting disrespect for authority.

The amendments to the Penal Code approved by the Federal Assembly in April 1973 increased the maximum allowable prison sentence from 15 to 25 years for so-called antisocialist crimes. The death sentence was extended to cover hijacking or kidnapping, and penalties were increased for fleeing the country and for disclosing state secrets. Sentences were made more severe for crimes against the state and state property than for those against the person or personal property.

The general provisions of the Criminal Procedure Code are favorable to the accused. A person may not be prosecuted for acts not established as crimes in law; an accused may select and privately consult with his or her attorney; the accused may defend himself or herself; and the trials are to be conducted in a language known to the accused and in a manner suited to his or her level of comprehension. Only evidence submitted during trial can be considered in determin-

ing verdict and sentence. The code also provides that the accused be informed of his or her rights during detention, investigation and trial. However, violations occur. For example, despite a restraint against entry into a home and seizure of property without warrant, house searches are conducted without warrants. Persons are detained before trial for more than the two months stipulated in the law and held for more than the 48 hours after arrest, as limited by law. Although the code states that trials must be open, closed ones are more often the rule. Sometimes prosecutors make changes in the case file without informing defense lawyers, and sometimes the defense is denied permission to call witnesses.

There is a corresponding dichotomy between legal precepts and actual practice in the administration of prisons. According to law, "The purpose of imprisonment is to prevent the convicted person from engaging in continued criminal activity and to educate him or her systematically toward becoming a law-abiding citizen. Imprisonment must not violate human dignity." Prison authorities are directed to treat prisoners with compassion and respect for human dignity. Prisoners are required to work, and work hours and wages are to be comparable to those outside. Prisoners may build up savings. Cultural and educational projects are provided during nonworking hours, and prison libraries are to be well stocked.

However, from firsthand accounts of released prisoners, living conditions in jails fall far short of these requirements. Beatings by guards are commonplace; food and medical attention are substandard; and family visits are curtailed or prohibited. Czechoslovakia has been the target of a number of condemnations by Amnesty International in this respect.

Details on the country's penal institutions (referred to officially as "corrective educational facilities") are not publicized and are at best pieced together from scattered accounts. The best-known prisons are at Prague-Pankrac, Bory-Plzen and Litomerice in Bohemia, Mirov and Ostrava in Moravia, and Leopoldov in Slovakia. People being held during pretrial investigations or those awaiting appeal hearings are incarcerated at Prague-Ruzyne and Brno-Bohunice. The system, including the Corps of Corrective Education (as the prison guards are euphemistically called), is administered by the governments of the Czech and Slovak republics through their ministries of justice.

The conditions in the country's 16 remand prisons are described as disastrous. Cells are tiny; facilities are primitive; and prisoners are charged for their upkeep, which they are required to pay after their release. Prisoners are often punished by having their food ration cut and by taking away the privilege of receiving one package every three months. Educational programs rarely exist, and prisoners are allowed only one book per week, more often than not a collection of dull speeches by a party functionary.

Violent crime is reported to have declined since the 1970s, although there are frequent newspaper reports of robbery. Theft of government property is particularly prevalent, to the chagrin of Communist propagandists. Official corruption is also on the rise, even in the higher echelons of power. As in many other socialist states, there is strong government concern over growing alcoholism and drug abuse and associated crimes.

DENMARK

BASIC FACT SHEET

Official Name: Kingdom of Denmark
Area: 43,070 sq km
Population: 5,121,766 (1987)
Capital: Copenhagen
Nature of Government: Constitutional monarchy
Language: Danish
Currency: Krone
GNP: $38.4 billion (1985)
Territorial Divisions: 14 countries, 275 communes
Population per Police Officer: 600
Police Expenditures per 1,000: $67,601

History & Background

The earliest reference in Danish history to a police function is in 1224:

> . . . it is ordained that the watchmen shall be at their posts and ready to begin their duties as soon as the watchmen's bell is rung in the evenings.
> [Copenhagen Town Regulations]

Around 1590 a permanent corps of policemen, with 140 men, was established in Copenhagen, and detailed instructions were issued for them in the Town Laws of 1643. In 1682 a chief constable was appointed to supervise the work of the police, and the Law of 1683 vested police powers in the Town Council and the mayor. Among the duties of the constable were the following:

> to inspect inns; enforce good behavior at public amusements; prevent loose public morals; keep the streets clean; prevent the sale of injurious foodstuffs; combat the spread of infectious diseases; supervise the quarantine services, cases of venereal diseases and the medical service; exercise a general control of the food supply; help in case of fire; and see that the regulations in regard to extravagance in dress, food and drink, as well as those affecting games of chance and usury, are properly observed.

The chief constable was authorized to appoint police constables for this purpose. In 1814 the chief constable of Copenhagen became police director, a title that remains to this day.

In 1863 the city police was reorganized, the watchmen were removed and detective bureau was established. Police representatives went to London to study the English police system, and on their return introduced many features of the London Metropolitan Police into Copenhagen.

The police were again reorganized in 1919 by an act of Parliament, which established a nationwide state police force with headquarters at Copenhagen and under an officer known as the chief of state police, who was placed in the Ministry of Justice. It was further required that the chief of state police and his four superintendents be appointed by the king and should be trained in law.

Structure & Organization

In 1938 the city police forces and the state police merged into one system, headed by a police commissioner. The system did not do away with the local autonomy of the 72 local chiefs of police. The national commissioner does not interfere with the local operations, for which the chief constable is answerable directly to the Ministry of Justice. The national commissioner is, however, responsible for appointments, training, promotion, the distribution of personnel and materiel, and finance. He also directly controls the traffic police.

The national police system is headed by the minister of justice, who is also the chief of police. He is assisted by the national commissioner, the police president in Copenhagen, and the local police directors.

The headquarters staff comprises 12 chief inspectors, who are responsible for administrative sections such as equipment, salaries, budget, personnel, maintenance, registry of motor vehicles, criminal records and registry of aliens. The national headquarters also controls the Police College, the dog corps, Interpol, the Identification Division and the Forensic Science Laboratory.

The Copenhagen Police Force is headed by a police director with seven departments, each under an assistant director. The first assistant director is head of all the uniformed police in the city and is assisted by two police commanders and 15 superintendents. The second assistant director is in charge of the Patrol Department, which is divided into nine geographical areas. He assigns police personnel to one of the following tours of duty: 7 A.M. to 3 P.M., 3 P.M. to 11 P.M., and 11 P.M. to 7 A.M. Each tour of duty is worked for a full week in rotation. The second department has three other sections: the emergency section, which is also responsible for planning royal receptions and for crowd control; the civil defense section; and the resocialization or rehabilitation section, which functions as a welfare office, assisting the homeless and the unemployed to find work, placing alcoholics and drug addicts in proper institutions, helping the down-and-out to find economic security, and locating relatives and missing persons. This section is also in charge of police youth clubs, which steer youths between eight and 17 years away from the direction of crime.

The third assistant director is in charge of the Criminal Investigation Department (CID). The CID is divided into five lettered units: A, dealing with homicide, rape, assault and blackmail; B, dealing with forgery, embezzlement, fraud, breach of trust, usury, perjury, and postal and railway crimes; C, dealing with burglary, robbery, auto theft and smuggling; D, dealing with political crimes, sabotage, espionage and explosives; and E, providing an emergency 24-hour service in any of these areas to the other units.

The remaining four assistant directors are in charge of the Traffic Department, the Prosecution Department, the Health and Sanitation Department (which also deals with sexual offenses), and the Trade and Domestic Relations Department.

Outside of Copenhagen, Denmark is divided into seven regions, each comprising six to eight police districts for a total of 53 districts. Each district is headed by a chief constable or police director (*politimester*), one of whom is nominated as the regional commander responsible for the coordination of police activities within the region. Each district has a population of between 20,000 and 100,000. A police district is composed of one more police stations staffed by uniformed and plainclothes CID police. The CID is integrated into the district police, but CID personnel are subordinate to the police directors. In the larger districts the CID is divided into several departments,

each specializing in a certain category of crime, but in the smaller ones they receive assistance from the CID emergency squad at the national headquarters. Each district also includes the rural police, who patrol isolated areas with no police stations. Whereas major criminal cases are handled by the local public prosecutor, minor offenses, known as "police cases," are handled by the chief of police. He initiates proceedings in such cases and acts as the prosecutor before the courts.

In larger districts, the special sections that handle health cases, sex offenses, etc., are referred to as the Civil Police. They are specially trained for this work, although all members of the regular police force receive basic training in these areas as well.

Specialized sections within the national police are Department D, which handles the National Criminal Records files and the national registry of motor vehicles; and Department E, which handles aliens, the Police College, the Intelligence Service and the Flying Squad. The police are also responsible for civil defense through the Civilforsvarafdeling.

The basic uniform is a dark blue jacket and trousers worn with a blue forage cap or a peaked cap with a white cover. Badges and piping on hats and epaulettes are in gold. Police are entitled to wear a firearm when on duty, but its use is strictly controlled. Before a firearm is used, a warning must be given and, if a superior is present, only on his orders. Every time a weapon is used or its use is threatened, the fact must be officially reported. The use of truncheons is also similarly controlled.

Patrol cars have two to three policemen, each armed with a Browning Automatic 7.65mm pistol. Policemen do not wear holsters, and the weapon is carried in a side pocket. Each patrol car is equipped with a siren, police frequency radio and revolving lights. Arrested persons are picked up in specially equipped enclosed vans. Dogs are used for crowd control, searches, and detection of narcotics and explosives.

The regular police workweek is 40 hours. Overtime is compensated by equal time off or by extra pay. All uniformed patrolmen are on a rotating tour of duty, working seven days on a morning assignment followed by seven days on a day assignment and seven days on a night assignment. Annual vacations are allotted according to age; those under 50 years receiving 18 days and those over 50 years, 24 days. Cost-of-living allowances are factored into the salary scales; there are other allowances for special duty. Policemen do not receive free medical treatment but are covered by officially approved insurance. The mandatory retirement age is 63 years, but senior officers are permitted to remain on the force until 70 years old.

Besides the social insurance available to all Danes

67 years old and older, there is a regular police pension paid by the department. This pension is available also to disabled officers who retire prematurely and to the widows of officers who are killed in the line of duty.

The Danish police were unionized in 1902. The Danish Federation of Police Officials is not affiliated with any political party. However, police officers are not allowed by law to go on strike.

Recruitment, Education & Training

Chief police officials are appointed by the crown on the advice of the minister of justice. Recruits who satisfy the rigorous physical standards receive a 10-week training course at the Police College in Copenhagen. They are then placed on probation for two years, on the successful completion of which they are granted permanent positions.

There are two grades in the police service. Members of the force without legal training may be promoted only as far as assistant deputy commissioner. Those with a law degree work as police directors or as assistants to police directors.

During the first three years on the force, a policeman studies in three different courses: the original basic course, and two further courses, each of 11 weeks' duration, with practical training sandwiched between courses. Before six years on the force, there is a mandatory 22-week course. After six years, a police officer may be transferred to the CID upon his or her request or to the civil police, and thereupon must attend a further 12-week course. After 14 years of service, a police officer is automatically promoted to sergeant. There is competition for promotion to posts above sergeant. All police officers above sergeant are required to attend mandatory in-service training courses every eighth year.

The Penal System

The first Danish Criminal Code was promulgated in 1866. The present code was enacted in 1930 and became effective in 1933. It has been amended a number of times, most recently in 1967. It is divided into a general part defining the general principles of liability, complicity and penalty, and a special part listing crimes. The Criminal Code is based entirely on statutes; there is no case law.

The death penalty was abolished in 1930. Petty offenses are prosecuted by the chiefs of police in lower courts. Major felonies and misdemeanors are tried in the higher courts. Persons arrested for crimes must be arraigned within 24 hours.

In addition to the Criminal Code, other laws govern the penal system, such as police regulations, municipal ordinances and traffic regulations. Failure to observe these laws may involve up to two years' imprisonment. Criminal cases that involve sentences of eight years or more must be tried by a high court formed by three judges assisted by 12 jurymen.

CRIME STATISTICS (1984)

		Number Reported	Attempts %	Cases Solved %	Crime per 100,000	Offenders	Females %	Juveniles %	Strangers %
1.	Murder	295	79.7	90.51	5.71				
2.	Sex offenses, including rape	2,191		58.06	42.86				
3.	Rape	392		56.12	7.67				
4.	Serious assault	5,909		80.01	115.59				
5.	All theft	363,487		14.94	7,110.28				
6.	Aggravated theft	115,831		15.13	2,265.81				
7.	Robbery and violent theft	1,819		47.99	35.58				
8.	Breaking and entering	114,012		14.60	2,230.22				
9.	Auto theft	24,002		23.48	469.51				
10.	Other thefts	223,654		13.92	4,374.97				
11.	Fraud	12,236		65.41	239.35				
12.	Counterfeiting	148		22.30	2.90				
13.	Drug offenses	9,812			191.94				
14.	Total offenses	451,069		21.35	8,823.50				

Criteria of juveniles: aged from 0 to 14 years.
Note: Information for some categories is not available.

DOMINICAN REPUBLIC

BASIC FACT SHEET

Official Name: Dominican Republic
Area: 48,734 sq km
Population: 6,960,743 (1987)
Capital: Santo Domingo
Nature of Government: Representative democracy
Language: Spanish
Currency: Peso
GNP: $14.9 billion (1986)
Territorial Divisions: 26 provinces
Population per Police Officer: 580
Police Expenditures per 1,000: N.A.

History & Background

The National Police (Policía Nacional Dominicana) was formed in 1936 through a merger of the municipal police of Santo Domingo and other towns.

Structure & Organization

The National Police Force is headed by a director general, who is directly subordinate to the secretary of state for interior and police. The director general is assisted by a deputy director and by two secretariats, one for internal affairs and planning and the other for public relations. Administration and operations are carried out by three sections—Administration and Support, Police Operations, and Special Operations—each headed by an assistant secretary general.

The Administration and Support Section supervises personnel, education and training and finances and is

CRIME STATISTICS (1984)

		Number Reported	Attempts %	Cases Solved %	Crime per 100,000	Offenders	Females %	Juveniles %	Strangers %
1.	Murder	582	0.96	95	9.32	538	0.43		
2.	Sex offenses, including rape	272	45	91	4.36	263			
3.	Rape	235		85	3.76	184			
4.	Serious assault	9,812		89	157.17	9,891	2		1.3
5.	All theft	4,544	6	60	72.79	2,702	6.10		
6.	Aggravated theft	1,561		68	25.01				
7.	Robbery and violent theft	250	4.2	75	4	154			
8.	Breaking and entering								
9.	Auto theft	638		86	10.22	546			
10.	Other thefts	2,095		38	33.56	802	12		
11.	Fraud	386		85	6.18	313	0.3		
12.	Counterfeiting	29		92	0.46	23	0.10		
13.	Drug offenses	547		93	8.76	768	1.3	0.4	15
14.	Total offenses	18,396		86	294.68	21,517	16	2.5	2.4

Criteria of juveniles: aged from 9 to 17 years.
Note: Information for some categories is not available.

responsible for the logistical system, communications, transportation, records and the police laboratory. The Police Operations Section carries out regular police duties, including patrolling, traffic control, criminal investigation, rural operations and prevention of civil disturbances. Patrolling is done on foot and by horseback, bicycle, motorcycle, automobile, boat and plane. The Special Operations Section supervises the training and work of the secret police.

Four regional directors report to the assistant director general of operations. The headquarters of the regions are Santo Domingo, San Pedro de Macorís, Santiago de los Caballeros and Barahona.

Recruitment, Education & Training

Cadets and officers receive training in Santo Domingo at the Police Academy, established with U.S. aid. The National Police is also active in civic projects.

The Penal System

After the Dominican Republic achieved independence, the French Criminal Code was adopted in 1845, and a Spanish translation in 1867. The present code was adopted under President Ulises Heureaux in 1884. The death penalty, which according to law was executed by a firing squad, was abolished in 1924, and a maximum penalty of 30 years' imprisonment at hard labor was substituted. The maximum penalty is applicable to homicide and arson. That for rape is six to 10 years, and for robbery five to 20 years. In 1970, Congress passed a law that denied bail in criminal cases.

The national penitentiary is La Victoria, in Santo Domingo. Twenty other towns have prisons or equivalent facilities. Of these the largest are in Santiago, La Vega, Puerto Plata, San Francisco de Macorís, Moca, San Juan, San Cristóbal and Barahona. Prisoners receive payment for their labor; 30% of the money earned goes to the family of the prisoner, 25% to the prison workshops, 25% to the prisoner's pension fund and 20% to the prisoner personally.

The government does not publish criminal statistics, but the Santo Domingo dailies report crime with great regularity. Robbery appears to be the most frequent, followed by assault, murder, rape and fraud. Rural crime is only a small proportion of the total.

ECUADOR

BASIC FACT SHEET

Official Name: Republic of Ecuador
Area: 283,561 sq km
Population: 9,954,609 (1987)
Capital: Quito
Nature of Government: Representative democracy
Language: Spanish
Currency: Sucre
GNP: $10.7 billion (1985)
Territorial Divisions: 20 provinces
Population per Police Officer: 260
Police Expenditures per 1,000: N.A.

History & Background

The Congress established by the Constitution of 1830 required municipal councils to create their own police departments and establish appropriate regulations for law enforcement. For the first 30 years of the country's existence as an independent nation, the police systems were either under the control of the municipalities or the Army. The police evolved slowly under provincial aegis until 1937, when the first national police organization was formed. Control of the police reverted to the central government, and in 1951 the name was changed from National Civil Guard to National Civil Police (Policía Civil Nacional, PCN).

Structure & Organization

The primary responsibility for the maintenance of public order in Ecuador rests with the National Civil Police under the Ministry of Government. Article 120 of the Constitution of 1945 defines the police force as a civil institution for the preservation of internal order and individual and collective security. Its members enjoy no special privileges.

In the mid-1980s the strength of the law-enforcement agencies was about 12,000, of which the National Civil Police constituted about 60%. The PCN is headed by a commander, who reports directly to the minister of government. The administration consists of four operational divisions and the National Training Institute. The four divisions are: the Urban Service, the Rural Service, the Traffic Service and the Criminal Investigative Division. The commander is assisted by a staff that includes four sections: personnel, intelligence, operations and logistics.

The country is divided into four police districts, with headquarters in Quito, Riobamba, Cuenca and Guayaquil. The first district includes the provinces of Carchi, Imbabura, Pichincha, Cotopaxi, Napo and Pastaza; the second the provinces of Los Ríos, Bolívar, Tungurahua and Chimborazo; the third the provinces of Cañar, Azuay, Loja, Morona-Santiago and Zamora-Chinchipe; and the fourth or coastal district the provinces of Esmeraldas, Manabi, Guayas and El Oro. The Galapagos Islands are included in the fourth district. The police in Guayaquil and Quito are organized in regiments of about 700 people each, while the 19 provinces have police corps varying in size according to the size of the population. The 19th corps is on Isabela Island in the Galapagos Islands.

The Urban Police is a separate force in larger towns and cities. In 1972 a Tourist Police was established in Quito as part of the Urban Police. The Tourist Police consists of people who are fluent in English and well versed in the country's art, folklore and history.

The Rural Police generally serve in scattered units throughout the nonurbanized areas of the country. The local police chief also serves as the judge in minor cases. The Petroleum Police watches over and protects oil installations in the eastern zone.

The Traffic Division of the PCN functions on all streets and highways except in Guayas Province. The division issues licenses, controls traffic signals and investigates traffic accidents. The traffic problem is confined mainly to Quito and Guayaquil, but the Pan American Highway passes through the length of the country and carries an ever-increasing number of vehicles.

The Criminal Investigation Division was a separate unit until 1964, when it was placed directly under the PCN. It is a plainclothes force that investigates all major criminal cases, regardless of the agency of arrest. Another plainclothes unit is the Ecuadorian section of Interpol, with headquarters in Quito and nine agents under a chief and deputy.

The Customs Police is under the Ministry of Finance. The officers and men of the Customs Police are often accused of corruption and collusion with smugglers.

The Guayas Traffic Police is a separate unit created by legislative decree in 1948. It is an autonomous provincial force with about 500 people.

Education & Training

Most of the PCN commissioned officers are graduates of the National Training Institute. The Police Academy is in Quito, and the course for cadets is three years. A cadet, after graduation, had to serve as an officer for at least two years or pay a fine. Lower ranks are trained at the Other Ranks' Training School (Escuela de Formación de Tropa).

The Penal System

The penal system is operated by the National Directorate of Prisons under the Ministry of Government. The two largest institutions are the Garcia Moreno Prison in Quito and the Penitenciario del Litoral in Guayaquil. There is also a municipal jail in Quito and jails in all the provincial capitals except those in the eastern part of the country. There is one agricultural penal colony, the Colonia Penal de Mera, on the bank of the Pastaza River.

Most prisons are overcrowded, and juveniles and lesser offenders are confined with hardened criminals. Living conditions are unsanitary, causing prisoners to fall prey to various diseases. Prisoners are paid for their labor in the prison workshops. One-third of the wages earned goes to the prisoner's expenses, one-third to the court to take care of the prisoner's civil obligations and one-third is paid to the prisoner upon his or her release. Prisoners become eligible for parole after serving three-fourths of their sentence. There are few special establishments for the relatively small number of women prisoners, and they are generally houses in separate sections of general prisons.

One of the most modern penal establishments in the country is that in the northern city of Tulcán, near the Colombian border. It has three sections—for males, females and minors—and also a number of classrooms and other facilities. Other prisons are unsanitary and overcrowded. In urban areas, people often express resentment over the ease with which criminals can obtain their freedom after light sentences. Newspapers have reported cases of recidivists arrested as many as 40 times.

The Penal Code was adopted in 1938. Capital

CRIME STATISTICS (1984)

		Number Reported	Attempts %	Cases Solved %	Crime per 100,000	Offenders	Females %	Juveniles %	Strangers %
1.	Murder	400		90	4.53	366	1.91	2.19	
2.	Sex offenses, including rape								
3.	Rape	520		92.12	5.89	480		3.33	
4.	Serious assault	485		94.43	5.50	462	1.30	2.16	0.22
5.	All theft								
6.	Aggravated theft								
7.	Robbery and violent theft	2,449		94	27.76	2,333	4.20	6.30	1.07
8.	Breaking and entering								
9.	Auto theft	684		86.99	7.75	628		3.34	0.32
10.	Other thefts	6,124		90.20	69.41	6,025	1.83	3.25	
11.	Fraud	602		89.87	6.82	541	1.11	1.11	1.11
12.	Counterfeiting								
13.	Drug offenses	184		75	2.09	138	2.90	1.45	1.45
14.	Total offenses	25,765		98.20	292.01	25,583	13.50	11.28	1.01

Criteria of juveniles: aged from 1 to 18 years.
Note: Information for some categories is not available.

punishment is outlawed. The maximum sentence is 16 years of hard labor.

The authorities are concerned over the rising incidence of urban crime, a problem not limited to Ecuador. The principal reported crimes are picking pockets; fraud; robbery; and murder, using knives and firearms. There are also many cases of fraud, especially involving impersonation of police officials. Juvenile crime is reported to be increasing and is related to a rise in drug trafficking and use.

EGYPT

BASIC FACT SHEET

Official Name: Arab Republic of Egypt
Area: 1,001,449 sq km
Population: 51,929,962 (1987)
Capital: Cairo
Nature of Government: Limited democracy
Language: Arabic
Currency: Egyptian pound
GNP: $21.2 billion (1985)
Territorial Divisions: 26 governorates
Population per Police Officer: 580
Police Expenditures per Capita: N.A.

History & Background

Before the 1952 Revolution, the general public's (and particularly the *fellahin*'s) attitude toward the police was one of fear, alienation and noncooperation. The concept of political identification with the government and its laws was largely absent. Contacts with officialdom, usually limited to conscription, tax collection and property transactions, were painful and to be avoided. The police existed to secure the rights of the rich and powerful. At the same time, the *fellahin* had a high propensity for individual and group violence, despite their reputation for docility.

The common Egyptian's interpersonal relations were governed by the concepts of personal and family honor, implied in which were retaliation and vengeance. Violence, although formally condemned by the Koran, was condoned when it took the accepted form of vindication of honor. Retaliation for murder, rape, adultery or crop burning was customary. Even violence against the police or government officials was acceptable if seen as a reprisal for injustice. Theft outside one's local group was not perceived as a crime but as a means of enriching oneself at the expense of an outsider. Taxes were regarded as an onerous burden, to be evaded if possible. Trials, convictions and imprisonments were seen not as the workings of a rational and necessary system of justice but as serious affronts to personal dignity and therefore justification for retaliation against whoever he thought was responsible for getting one into trouble with the police. By the same token, the *fellah* was reluctant to give testimony during investigation or trial because of fear of reprisals. In the hierarchical administrative system, each official, down to *umdah* or village headman, pressed hard on those below him to placate those above him. In these circumstances rioting was fairly common and violence was an established safety valve for expressing personal and public anger and frustration.

The new government that took over in 1952, following the free officers' coup, initiated a series of police reforms to overcome the traditional public hostility. Under the monarchy, police and internal security matters were divided among several ministries. According to James Cramer in *Uniforms of the World's Police*, "All these ministries were rife with corruption, and overlapping responsibilities caused endless chaos. There was no overall plan for organization, training and equipment, morale was poor, and public relations were at an all-time low." The new government placed all police functions under the Ministry of the Interior. Standards of selection and performance were raised, a program of training was initiated and a public-relations campaign was launched.

Although many of these objectives were not fully realized under Nasser, general progress was made toward all of them. Police organization and morale were strengthened, the standard of public security was strengthened and the incidence of serious crimes declined during the first 10 years of the Nasser regime. More importantly, some constitutional guarantees of rudimentary human rights were established that had never previously existed in 5,000 years of Egyptian history. But the society was by no means open. Political security and censorship were particularly tight under Sharawi Muhammad Guma, the minister of interior, and Sami Saharf, the chief of the secret service.

In late 1970, under President Sadat, a new series of police and law-enforcement reforms was initiated by Minister of the Interior Mamduh Salim, who later became prime minister. These included changes in the police officer training program. After the October 1973 War, Sadat proceeded to dismantle the economic, social and political controls imposed by Nasser. Censorship in the arts and the media was almost entirely lifted, some property confiscated during the previous administration was returned, a police anti-corruption campaign was launched and hundreds of political prisoners were freed. The notorious Turah prison was demolished and turned into a national cultural exhibition center. Sadat and his chief ministers still held all the reins of power but used them more judiciously—or at least less capriciously—than Nasser, and as a result the police-state atmosphere built up under Nasser substantially dissipated. The Egyptian society has become even more open and free under Mubarak.

Structure & Organization

The Police and Security Service is a national organization directed from the capital under the Ministry of the Interior, with subordinate elements parallel to and supporting the governorates and lower subdivisions of local government. In addition to criminal investigation, maintenance of law and order, and supporting the court system in enforcing the law, the police have a broad range of responsibilities that include prison administration, immigration control, suppression of smuggling, security intelligence, traffic and emergency relief. The police are also used to supervise elections and facilitate the *haj,* or pilgrimage to Mecca. In time of war or martial law, the police are subject to military direction. Military training, a major part of basic police training, enables the police to fit with relative ease into their role as a paramilitary force.

The national police is organized on military lines, with the line of command running from the minister of the interior down through sequentially lower echelons. The organization shows Turkish, French and British influences and the centralized flavor it acquired under the monarchy. The total strength of the force is estimated at over 100,000, of which some 10,000 are officers. In addition, there are some 60,000 security militia and village watchmen who as police auxiliaries performed night guard duty in rural areas.

In 1971 a presidential decree reorganized police and security affairs under eight departments of the Ministry of the Interior: State Security Investigations; Emigration and Nationality; Inspection; Criminal Investigation; Transport and Communications; Administrative Affairs; Police Support; Officers' Affairs; and Personnel Affairs. In August 1971, the minister of the interior took over three general departments and assigned the rest to four deputy ministers. Those grouped directly under the minister were State Security Investigations, Organization and Public Relations. Under the deputy minister for public security were Public Safety, Travel, Immigration and Passports, Port Security, Criminal Evidence Investigations, Emergency Police Rescue, Ministerial Guards and Central Police Reserves. Under the deputy minister for special police were Prison Administration, Militia and Civil Defense, Police Transport and Communication, Traffic and Tourism. Under the deputy minister for personnel affairs and training were the Police College, the Institute for Advanced Police Studies, the Enlisted Training Administration, Personnel, and the Policemen's Sports Association. Under the deputy minister for administrative and financial affairs were General Administration, Police supplies and Procurement, Budgets, Accounting, Construction and Legal Affairs.

The new Police Authority Law passed by the People's Assembly on February 22, 1972, identified the president of the republic as the chief of police and the minister of the interior as the superior of police. The minister is assisted by the Supreme Police Council in the formulation of policy. This new law created the new positions of first undersecretary and undersecretary, to be filled by senior police major generals. The law also reidentified all police ranks. In the officer grades these are the same as in the Army, starting with the major general and descending to first lieutenant. Below first lieutenant is the grade of lieutenant-chief police warrant officer, followed by three descending grades of police warrant officers. The municipal police patrolmen or constables have the grades of first or second assistant policemen. Enlisted police-soldiers have the usual four military grades of master sergeant, sergeant, corporal and private. The irregular part-time and other security watchmen have the grades of chief of guards, deputy chief guards and guard. Regular police insignia are the same as those of the Army. The basic uniform consists of a khaki close-neck tunic worn over matching trousers with a khaki peaked cap. A Sam Browne belt completes the uniform. There are variations of this standard uniform depending upon the type of duty and the region.

Under the same law of 1972 personal history files, dating from birth, are kept on all officers, and reports are added yearly in January before the preparation of promotion and transfer orders, which are customarily issued in July and August. Annual reports are seen by the officer concerned and approved by the Supreme Police Council before they go into the files.

Promotion through the rank of brigadier general is according to seniority and vacancy, but to major general is by selection. The mandatory retirement age is 60, but major generals could receive up to three years' extension. Police pensions are set at 80% of pay at time of retirement and 85% for disability in the line of duty.

In each governorate a director of police commands all police in the governorate. Both the governor and the director of police answer to the minister of the interior on all security matters. In the district subdivisions of the governorate, district police commandants have similar positions and functions at that level. While municipal and district police have modern facilities in larger cities and towns, this is not the case in villages with a population of 5,000 or less, where the force is poorly manned and often horse-mounted. Only about one-eighth of the rural villages have even a police station. A village or rural district station typically includes an officer in charge having the grade of captain or major, 10 to 20 policemen of lower grades and various numbers of village guards. A typical station has two floors, quarters upstairs for the commander and policemen on duty, and two or three duty rooms, two cells, and a stable for six or eight horses on the lower level.

The police assignment and transfer system, under which up to one-fourth of those of officer rank are shifted annually, was revised in 1972. The new system, the provisions of which cover all regular police, set up three appointment districts according to general desirability of assignment. District 1 includes the offices of the Ministry of the Interior and all police posts in the Cairo and Alexandria governorates, with the tour of duty set at five to 10 years; District 2 includes the governorates of Lower Egypt, the Suez Canal area, Giza, Bani Suwayf and Al Fayyum, with a tour of duty of four to five years. District 3 encompassed all remaining governorates, with a tour of duty of three years. Such inducements as extra leave are provided for voluntary extension of service in District 3. After training, initial assignments for new policemen, with some exceptions, are made in their home areas, but the transfer of policemen under probation is prohibited. Initial appointments of the Police College Graduates are made in accordance to a set priority of governorates, starting with Cairo. Similarly, the large cities have priority for the assignment of new municipal policemen of the constable grade.

Disciplinary action in the police service may be administrative or judicial; in the latter case it is regulated by the Military Justice Law of 1966, administered by the Ministry of the Interior in cooperation with military authorities.

In spite of great progress since 1952 in the status, equipment, pay, education and general morale of the police force, thousands of security police conscripts mutinied on February 25, 1986. They went on a rampage and destroyed many hotels and other build-

ings before the mutiny was put down by Army troops on February 27. In all, some 10,000 members of the 300,000-man Central Security Command participated in the rebellion. The force is made up mostly of illiterate youths from rural areas who are drafted for three-year terms and paid about $4 per month. In the initial outburst, the mutineers sacked three luxury hotels in the suburb of Giza, near the Pyramids, completely destroying two of the hotels by fire. The mutiny then spread to a number of other barracks in Ismailia, and in the southern Nile cities of Sohâg and Asyût, a Muslim fundamentalist stronghold. Rioters also stormed a prison in Tura, south of Cairo, and freed most of the convicts there. The death toll in the uprising was estimated officially at 107 and the number of wounded at 719. President Mubarak swiftly fired Interior Minister Ahmed Roushdi and transferred nine other senior police officials, including two deputy interior ministers.

Recruitment, Education & Training

With some exceptions, officers must be graduates of the Police College at Cairo, and all men entering the service must complete a three-month course conducted at the college. Particular attention is given to the training of officers in modern methods and techniques, and selected cadres are sent periodically to foreign police schools. The Police College is in the Al Abbasiyah suburb of Cairo on a 40-acre tract equipped with a laboratory, and facilities for police dogs and horses.

Officer candidates must be the offspring of Egyptian parents and are required to have a grade average of at least 55% in secondary school, except for the sons or brothers of men who were killed in active police or military duty and sons of police and military officers. The curriculum includes security administration, French and English language, military drill, civil defense, fire fighting, criminal investigation, forensic medicine, sociology, radio communication, first aid, anatomy and cryptology. Also emphasized are public relations and political orientation along with military subjects such as infantry and cavalry training, marksmanship, group leadership and field training. Graduates of the two-year program receive a degree of bachelor of police studies and are commissioned police lieutenants. The annual number of new officers varies but has been estimated as up to 700. Advanced officer training is given at the college's Institute for Advanced Police Studies, and graduation from this school is required for advancement beyond the rank of lieutenant colonel.

The three-month basic course at the Police college for enlisted ranks maintains a military environment but stresses police activities and techniques. Upon completion of the course, the students are sent to their assigned units, where they receive additional on-the-job training. Some noncommissioned officers are sent to police schools abroad.

In 1975 the college instituted a doctoral program in criminology and a two-year program to commission as first lieutenants selected applicants already holding degrees in medicine, engineering and law. Not all training is conducted at the Police College. Other centers exist, such as a criminal evidence investigation institute and a police communications institute.

The Penal System

Prison administration is under the jurisdiction of the Ministry of the Interior. Prison officials usually are graduates of police or military schools. The Higher Council of Prisons, formed after the 1952 Revolution, serves as the police body. Reforms instituted after 1952 include the installation of separate facilities for women and juveniles, provision of medical services to prisoners, and increased emphasis on rehabilitation. First offenders are not stigmatized with a criminal record for minor breaches, and in case of need provision is made for assisting a prisoner's family.

The penal institutions are divided into penitentiaries, general prisons, district jails, and reformatories for juvenile offenders. Criminals with the heaviest sentences are sent to penitentiaries, where they are subjected to hard labor under strict supervision. Sol-

itary confinement is imposed only as a disciplinary measure for bad behavior. General prisons are located in the governorates to house offenders sentenced to terms of three months or more, while district jails are used for prisoners sentenced to terms of three months or less. The village police station lockups are for temporary incarceration only and are not regarded as penal institutions. In the mid-1980s there were 30 general prisons, not counting the district jails. Three of them are penitentiaries. The nationwide average daily prison population in these prisons was 30,000, although the facilities are designed to hold less than 20,000. As a result prisons are overcrowded, insanitary and poorly maintained. According to the director general, most of the nation's prisons were built at the beginning of the century and are outmoded. Overcrowding is also true of the four juvenile rehabilitation institutions, where the total rated capacity is only 6,000 for a population double that size.

Prisons are inspected regularly by the Ministry of the Interior officials. Officials found guilty of negligence or brutality are subject to summary dismissal. Except in the penitentiaries, the work assigned to prisoners is designed to be educational and rehabilitative. Each prison operates an elementary school aimed at inculcating minimal literacy.

Toward the end of the Nasser era criminal statistics began to show a marked decrease in reported felonies for the first time in this century. In 1965 the number of felonies was only half what it was in 1939. The

CRIME STATISTICS (1984)

		Number Reported	Attempts %	Cases Solved %	Crime per 100,000	Offenders	Females %	Juveniles %	Strangers %
1.	Murder	703	35	92.0	1.53	1,279	3.0		
2.	Sex offenses, including rape	189		97.0	0.41	204	2.0		
3.	Rape								
4.	Serious assault	339		97.0	0.74	531	4.0		
5.	All theft	16,650		60.5	36.15	10,341	2.7		
6.	Aggravated theft	171	11	95.0	0.37	278	3.0		
7.	Robbery and violent theft	171	11	95.0	0.37	278	3.0		
8.	Breaking and entering								
9.	Auto theft	1,497		22.0	3.25	418	0.2		
10.	Other thefts	14,982		64.0	32.53	9,645	2.8		
11.	Fraud	1,915		46.0	4.16	1,915			
12.	Counterfeiting	1,422		93.0	3.09	1,319			
13.	Drug offenses	7,571		100.0	16.44	7,442	4.0		
14.	Total offenses	1,095,000		88.5	2,378.48	971,463	4.0		

Criteria of juveniles: aged from 0 to 18 years.
Note: Information for some categories is not available.

relative decrease was even more impressive considering the sharp growth in the national population and the rapid shift in population from rural to urban areas, both of which conditions were favorable to rising, not decreasing, crime rates.

According to police data, bandit gangs, an old problem in Egypt, have virtually disappeared, and there has been a decrease in crimes in which firearms were used. The incidences of murder, rape, burglary, forgery, cutting communication wires and endangering transportation are reported to have decreased, while arson has decreased more than any other major crime.

At the same time, there is a growth in other kinds of crime: traffic offenses, petty thievery, assaults on public servants, illicit trafficking in drugs and narcotics, kidnapping, currency smuggling, passing forged checks, and smuggling small-bulk, high-value items. The Egyptian press periodically reports increases in public sector crimes, such as embezzlement, fraud and bribery. Suicide, classed as a crime, has increased by about 25% since 1971, the most common cause being family and interpersonal disputes. The age range most affected was the 20- to 30-year old group, and the most frequent method was jumping from high places.

Serious crimes rose in the early 1980s as a result of Muslim-Coptic clashes and the rise of Islamic fundamentalists. Attacks on police stations, burning of churches, armed daylight robberies, train holdups and kidnapping of women have increased dramatically. Security officials blame the crime wave on liberal judges and laws and the general decline in the Egyptian economy.

EL SALVADOR

Structure & Organization

The security forces are made up of the National Guard, the National Police and the Treasury Police. All three are paramilitary organizations commanded by Army officers subordinate to the minister of defense. Each force, although centralized and directed by its own commander, works in close coordination with the armed forces.

The National Guard, formed in 1912, was set up by Spanish officers, who patterned the new organization after the Spanish Civil Guard (Guardia Civil). It is a constabulary-type force used primarily for rural police duties. Numbering about 3,500, it is distributed geographically throughout the country in five infantry commands comprising 14 separate companies. Each command has its headquarters in the principal city within its jurisdiction, usually a departmental capital, and assigns its companies as needed to the surrounding rural areas. The men wear Army-type uniforms and are armed with standard infantry weapons.

The National Police (Policía National) is primarily an urban force. It is a centralized force under a director general, with headquarters in San Salvador. It constitutes the Department of Public Security within the Ministry of National Defense. Although directly controlled from the capital, local detachments enjoy considerable autonomy.

The National Police, organized in its present form in 1945, is the outgrowth of a number of predecessor bodies since colonial times. Before independence, the Corps of Watchmen patrolled the towns and main highways at night. The first unified force was established in 1843 with the formation of the Corps of Police, which was charged with maintaining law and

order in the urban districts. This body eventually became the National Police. In 1868 the Civil Guard was founded to augment the Corps of Watchmen. Although at first their sphere of operations included both urban and rural areas, in time they became an exclusively rural force until 1912, when they were supplanted by the National Guard.

Police headquarters comprises three major branches: the general, the investigative and traffic. It also has the fire department under its jurisdiction. The general branch comprises all uniformed patrolmen on the beat. Investigative police are plainclothes detectives and crime laboratory technicians concerned with detection and criminal investigation. The traffic police work almost exclusively in the larger towns and cities. Except for traffic policemen who carry only a billyclub, most policemen are armed with both a billyclub and a pistol. In addition, the Cuerpo de Vigilantes Nocturnos y Bancarios ("Night and Bank Watch Corps") engage in night patrols and bank surveillance.

Officers wear olive green long- or short-sleeved shirts with matching caps. Those in other ranks wear beige shirts and coffee-colored trousers with a Sam Browne belt with a pouch and holster in black and a helmet. The traffic police wear the same uniform but with black knee boots.

The Treasury Police is a small corps organized in 1926 for customs duties and control of contraband activities. It operates primarily at airports, seaports and border areas, with headquarters in the capital. Its agents wear Army uniforms and are unarmed, but they usually work together with an armed member of the National Guard.

Officer grades of the National Police and Treasury Police start at subinspector and ascend through inspector, second commandant, first commandant and director general. Noncommissioned officer ranks are the same as in the Army, and a patrolman is called an agent. Insignia of rank consist of silver or gold bars—one and two silver bars for subinspector and inspector, respectively, and one and two gold bars for second and first commandant, respectively. The director general wears the insignia of his Army rank.

Recruitment, Education & Training

No information is available on recruitment, education and training.

The Penal System

The constitution prescribes that the penal system be designed for rehabilitation rather than punishment. Article 168 states, "The state shall organize the penitentiaries with the aim of reforming offenders, educating them, and teaching them industrious habits, looking toward their rehabilitation and the prevention of crime."

Overall direction and administration of the prison system is vested in the director general of penal and rehabilitation centers under the minister of justice. The prison system is composed of three national penitentiaries and 30 jails or preventive detention facilities distributed throughout the country. The penitentiaries are operated by the federal government, while subordinate facilities are administered by local authorities. The three penitentiaries—in Ahuachapán, Santa Ana and San Vicente—house approximately half the prison population.

Each of the country's departments has at least one jail or detention facility, and there is one in every departmental capital. The department of San Salvador, however, has no facility for men, although there is a prison for women at Lake Ilopango. There is one other institution for women, at Santa Ana. Prison facilities range from simple frame enclosures with little security and few amenities to well-constructed, professionally planned buildings with sound protection and adequate accommodations. Other than the penitentiaries, the prison system is loosely organized and receives little centralized guidance or control. Few penal statistics are published. The average annual prison population is estimated at about 5,000, but the smaller town jails house less than 100 inmates. Increasing crime rates and arrests have created problems of overcrowding and sanitation in many of the smaller jails.

The Salvadorans are noted for their ordered and disciplined behavior and respect for constituted authority. Nevertheless, they are volatile and prone to violence when aroused. This is generally borne out by national crime statistics, which show a marked preponderance of offenses against persons compared to those against property.

Although the incidence of crime has been rising for several years, the increase has not been significant in relation to the growth of population. The maintenance of law and order is still well within the control capabilities of the police forces. Subversive pressures are minimal, and there are no discernible threats to established order.

Official statistics indicate that assault and homicide are the most frequent offenses, followed by robbery and theft, and then fraud. Offenses by women constitute approximately 12% of the overall total, and those by minors some 10%. Those in the 22-to-29 age group are preponderantly the most frequent offenders. The department of San Salvador has the highest crime rate, followed by San Miguel and Santa Ana. San Sebastian has the lowest. The great majority of offenders are laborers and agricultural workers, followed by unemployed persons and skilled workers. Professional and technical personnel have the lowest rate.

Traffic violations have registered sharp increases in recent years, especially in the department of San Salvador. In a typical year there are over 50,000 traffic citations for minor infractions and 2,000 for serious breaches, including excessive speeding.

ETHIOPIA

BASIC FACT SHEET

Official Name: Socialist Ethiopia
Area: 1,221,900 sq km
Population: 46,706,229 (1987)
Capital: Addis Ababa
Nature of Government: Marxist dictatorship
Language: Amharic
Currency: Birr
GNP: $4.63 billion (1985)
Territorial Divisions: 14 provinces
Population per Police Officer: 1,100
Police Expenditures per 1,000: N.A.

History & Background

The first formal Ethiopian police force was formed in 1935 in Addis Ababa and four other cities, where it was trained by British instructors. The Imperial Ethiopian Police was organized in 1942 under British auspices as a centralized national police force with paramilitary and constabulary units. In 1956 the separate urban police forces were merged with the national police. Initially administered as a department of the Ministry of the Interior, the national police had evolved by the early 1970s into an independent agency commanded by a commissioner of police directly responsible to the emperor. Local control over the police was minimal, despite imperial proclamations that granted governors general police authority in their regions. Assistant police commissioners in each district were assigned to work in conjunction with the governors general, but in practice administration was directed from Addis Ababa. The national police force was, however, assisted by regional units of the Territorial Army commanded by the governor general and by an unpaid civilian auxiliary in areas where police were scarce. Police posts were found in all cities and larger towns and at strategic points along the main roads in the countryside. The police usually were locally recruited and were familiar with the areas they served, but they were viewed as hostile by the populace. Police operations generally emphasized a punitive rather than a preventive function. By 1974 the national police numbered approximately 28,000 in all branches, including 6,800 in a mobile emergency force, 1,200 frontier guards and a 3,200-member commando unit with rapid reaction capability. Paramilitary forces were equipped with weapons and vehicles provided by West Germany, and commandos and frontier guards were trained by Israeli counterinsurgency specialists. About 5,000 constabulary police, mostly recruited locally, and 2,500 commandos were stationed in Eritrea.

One of the first acts of the military government, known as the Provisional Military Administrative Council (PMAC), after the 1974 coup was to circumscribe the authority of the national police, which was strongly identified with the old regime and regional and "rightist" interests. In Eritrea, however, the Army took over the police functions in 1975 from local police units believed to be sympathetic to the secessionist movement in that region. The police voluntarily stayed at their posts for some time after their dismissal to protect civilians from attack by unruly soldiers.

Structure & Organization

The national police were thoroughly reorganized in 1977. Overall command was vested in a commissioner loyal to the Dergue, as PMAC was known by this time. Policy is formulated by the regime's security committee and implemented through the Ministry of the Interior. The Army assumed a larger role in criminal investigation and in maintaining public order. Local law-enforcement duties, normally carried out by the constabulary, were taken over by the People's Protection Brigades. The Army's new 8th Division, formed from police commando units and other special units, was brought together in an augmented 9,000-man paramilitary emergency mobile force for employment in counterinsurgency operations.

109

The Directorate of Police, operating under a commissioner, includes a special criminal investigation branch, which directs counterinsurgency activities through regional branch offices. Another branch of the directorate deals with the investigation of economic crimes, particularly smuggling. The Revolutionary Operations Coordinating Committee, organized at the subdistrict level, cooperates with the police in countering smuggling and other forms of economic sabotage.

The Dergue has stressed that the task of the national police is essentially political in nature—more involved with the suppression of political dissent as the local law-enforcement role has been shifted to the People's Protection Brigades. President Haile-Mariam Mengistu, chairman of the government, has described its operations as contributing to the "intensification of the class struggle."

Police constables are recruited for service usually at an early age and trained in their native regions. Training is designed to make police stations in remote areas self-sufficient. Standards of training are not uniform. In-service or specialized training is limited outside Addis Ababa. A high percentage of rural constables can neither read nor write and do not keep records of their activities. Many crimes are traditionally considered to be private matters and are often ignored by the police unless one of the interested parties files a complaint. In contrast, the Addis Ababa police are highly efficient and are organized into uniformed, detective, and traffic units; a riot squad, or flying column; a Police Air Wing with light aircraft; and a police laboratory. A small number of women are assigned to police units in large cities and generally are employed in administrative positions or in keeping custody of female prisoners. National police officers are paid uniformly according to the basic wage scale that applies to members of the armed forces.

The basic police uniform consists of stone-colored trousers and long-sleeved shirts worn with dark blue belts and blue caps. A form of windcheater is worn over the top in inclement weather.

As a rule, police in constabulary units are unarmed except for batons. Small arms usually are kept in designated armories and are issued for specific duties. Weapons used in paramilitary units include heavy machine guns, submachine guns, automatic rifles, sidearms, mortars, grenades, tear gas, light armored vehicles and other equipment designed for riot control and counterinsurgency. Larger police units, such as that in Addis Ababa, are equipped with modern Soviet-built military vehicles, which serve as both police cars and police vans. In many rural areas, however, horses and mules are often a constable's sole means of transportation.

In March 1975 the PMAC called for the formation of peasant associations for enforcing and implementing land reform measures. Proclamation 71, issued later that year, gave these associations a legal status, authorizing them to create "conditions facilitating the complete destruction of the feudal order." Elected executive committees were empowered to draft internal regulations in each peasant association territorial unit, which by 1980 numbered 23,000 with an estimated 7 million residents. Criminal and civil jurisdiction are exercised in each unit by peasant association tribunals. The PMAC also legitimized local revolutionary defense squads, already operated by individual peasant associations, granting them police powers within each designated area. Defense squads were also assigned to protect public property and to enforce land reform measures, but their original function was the essentially political one of rounding up—and often eliminating—suspected opponents of the military regime.

In August 1975 Proclamation 47 recognized the urban dwellers' associations (kebeles or neighborhoods) in Addis Ababa and five other cities. Organized along lines paralleling those of the peasant associations, Addis Ababa's 291 kebeles, with the neighborhood constituencies ranging from 3,000 to 12,000 residents, had an elected executive council, judicial tribunal, jail and defense squad. Dubbed afagne (strangling), the kebele defense units were largely responsible for carrying out the PMAC's Red Terror. During that campagn, the power of the kebeles was virtually unlimited, and the defense squads emerged as the regime's principal instruments of coercion in the capital. Defense squads usually ranged in size from 10 to 20 men on duty at any given time. In 1978 an estimated 10,000 vigilantes were selected to form the People's Protection Brigades, which were to be official local law-enforcement agencies within each association jurisdiction. Although officially described as semi-autonomous, they were placed under the direct control of the Central Committee's security chief. All routine police duties at the local level are being performed by these brigades. Members of the brigades receive training of up to five months in police and military tactics from East German instructors.

Recruitment, Education & Training

Officers usually are commissioned after completion of a cadet course at Sendafa (formerly Aba Dina) Police College near Addis Ababa. The school was opened in 1946 and staffed by Swedish instructors, but since 1960 the faculty has consisted entirely of Ethiopians. Candidates for the two-year course must have a secondary-school education or its equivalent. Enrollment was significantly increased after the 1974 coup, and the college's annual output is about 200 graduates.

Instruction at Sendafa includes general courses in police science, criminal law, tactics, traffic control, sociology, criminology, physical education and first aid, as well as political indoctrination. Practical training is given midway in the two-year program and may entail field service in troubled areas. A limited number of cadets who pass the final examinations with distinction are selected for further, specialized training. The Police College also offers short-term courses and refresher training for service officers and cooperates with the Army in the training military police in traffic control and criminal investigation techniques.

The Penal System

The *Fetha Negast* (The Law of Kings), introduced into Ethiopia sometime in the 17th century, was the penal code and the basis for criminal juridical procedure until 1930, when Emperor Haile Selassie introduced a Penal Code that, although primitive in its philosophy, strove for modernity in its application. In 1958 a revised Penal Code drafted by a Swiss legal expert became effective, and it was augmented in 1961 by a Criminal Procedures Code drafted by a prominent British jurist. Although modified after the 1974 coup, the Penal and Criminal Procedures codes have not been abrogated formally. Martial law was introduced formally in November 1974 by a decree that set up a system of military tribunals empowered to impose death penalties or long prison terms for a wide range of political offenses. The Penal Code was amended in July 1976 to institute the death penalty for "committing antirevolutionary activities." Investigation of political crimes came under the overall direction of revolutionary operations coordinating committees in every *awraja* (subregion). Search warrants were waived in political cases. Association tribunals are empowered to deal with criminal offenses, although their jurisdiction is limited to their urban neighborhood or rural area. Criminal trials are open to the public and conducted by elected magistrates without formal legal training and unrestrained by legal formalities. Procedures, precedents and punishments differ considerably from tribunal to tribunal. Torture sometimes is utilized to compel suspects and witnesses to testify. In theory sentences of death must be reviewed by the Dergue, but there is very little central interference with the administration of local justice. Decisions of the tribunals are executed through associations' public safety committees and enforced by the People's Protection Brigade. Without effective review of their actions, tribunals have ordered summary executions and indefinite jailings during which suspects sometimes disappear.

In 1976 revision of the Penal Code also opened up new categories of so-called economic crimes. The long list includes hoarding, overcharging, interfering with the distribution of consumer goods, sabotage of workplace or of agricultural production, conspiring to confuse members of the work force, and destruction of public property.

Prison administration is vested in a military official, the administrator of prisons, who is responsible to the Central Committee. Official criminal and penal data are unreliable and even misleading because they do not count political prisoners or those convicted of petty crimes or those detained in locally administered *kebele* and peasant association jails.

Each administrative unit, including 556 districts, 102 subregions and 14 regions, plus Addis Ababa and other major cities, has at least one prison facility and usually more than one. Addis Ababa's Akaki Prison, considered the country's most modern facility, is the central regional prison for Shewa. Akaki has separate quarters for female prisoners, and it is believed that the surviving members of the former imperial family are kept there. The largest number of prisoners, mainly political detainees, is believed to be housed in Alem Baqaqn (literally "the end of the world"), a prison built in Addis Ababa by Menelik II late in the 19th century. Other large political prisons in Addis Ababa are reportedly operated at 4th Division Headquarters; the 3rd Police Station, which also serves as headquarters of the National Police; and at Menelik's Palace, headquarters of the Dergue. Asmera, another center for political prisons, has penal facilities at Sembel, Hazhay and Tsezerat. Police stations and Army garrisons invariably have jails used for shorter- or longer-term detention of prisoners. Each of the 23,000 peasant associations and 291 *kebele* associations operates jails in its jurisdiction. Association headquarters in each district and subregion and the 25 higher *kebele* headquarters in Addis Ababa also have prisons.

A prison farm at Robi in the Arsi region provides accommodations for about 1,000 prisoners. A single institution oversees the rehabilitation of male juvenile criminal offenders. There is no comparable facility for girls, who usually are remanded to the custody of their parents or guardians. The number of young political offenders of both genders is reportedly large, but most are released after a period of "political rehabilitation."

Prison life is gloomy and for political prisoners extremely brutal. Rehabilitation consists of severe beatings, exhausting work and political indoctrination. A public confession is proof of rehabilitation and, in some instances, a political detainee's willingness to torture fellow prisoners is regarded as an indication of his or her penitence. Recreational facilities are virtually nonexistent, and there is no program for assistance to prisoners after they are released. Punishment of prisoners in custody is the major preoccupation of prison officials. Conditions in smaller, more remote prisons are regarded as being even more brutal than in Addis Ababa, and association jails are worse yet. As part of the program for making prisons even more forbidding, Cubans are reportedly building new prisons that will add facilities for solitary confinement of prisoners. Ethiopian prisons have hitherto lacked this refinement.

In its 1978 *Report on Human Rights Violations in Ethiopia,* Amnesty International stated that Ethiopian prisons failed to abide by the "UN" Standard Minimum Rules for Treatment of Prisoners. A large number of prisoners often share a common cell. Food and luxuries, such as tea and tobacco, brought by relatives are communalized by ad hoc committees organized in each cell for self-imposed discipline, food distribution, care of the sick and aged, and orientation of new inmates. According to the Amnesty International report:

> Cells are pest-infested, unventilated and lacking in the most basic sanitary facilities. Medical attention is inadequate and not available at all facilities. Even the seriously ill are rarely given hospital treatment and prisoners are allowed to die from natural causes. Death of a prisoner is viewed with relief by cellmates because it relieves overcrowding to that extent. At Alem Baqaqn, for example, it is estimated that at least 50 prisoners are kept in cells measuring four meters by four meters. Families are generally in-

formed of the death of relatives in prison by being told that "food is no longer necessary."

There is emphasis in the larger prisons on work as a means of production and not as rehabilitation. The largest prison industry is weaving, usually on primitive looms, to produce cotton materials used for making rugs, carpets and *shammas*. The other activities include carpentry, blacksmithing, metalworking, jewelry making, basket weaving, flour milling and baking.

The care and welfare of the prisoner rests with his or her family, not the state. Prisoners are expected to provide their own bedding and to pay "candle money" on entering prison for candles to light cells or, where electricity is available, to buy tea and tobacco. The family is expected to provide food, for which it receives a small allowance, provide fresh clothing and do laundry, if it is to be done at all.

Income from materials produced in prisons is used for maintaining penal facilities. Prisoners receive about 10% of the proceeds derived from the sale of items, but, typically, these funds are plowed back into communal projects. Work furloughs sometimes are permitted for some classes of political prisoners. Most guards are veterans of military service who receive small plots of land in exchange for temporary duty with a prison.

FIJI

BASIC FACT SHEET

Official Name: Fiji
Area: 18,376 sq km
Population: 727,902 (1987)
Capital: Suva
Nature of Government: Military dictatorship
Language: English
Currency: Fiji dollar
GNP: $1.19 billion (1985)
Territorial Divisions: 4 divisions
Population per Police Officer: 440
Police Expenditures per 1,000: $24,800

Structure & Organization

The Fiji Police Force has an authorized strength of 1,200 officers and men in addition to civilian employees. It is augmented by a police reserve, a supplementary force of 800 special constables paid on a per diem basis when on duty. There are no other local or private police forces except for a small contingent of uniformed guards at Nadi International Airport, near Suva in western Viti Levu.

Under the supervision of the prime minister, the force is commanded by a commissioner of police from headquarters at Suva. The headquarters staff consists of a deputy commissioner, a Special Branch, the Criminal Investigation Division, the Immigration

CRIME STATISTICS (1984)

		Number Reported	Attempts %	Cases Solved %	Crime per 100,000	Offenders	Females %	Juveniles %	Strangers %
1.	Murder	20		95.00	2.89	38			
2.	Sex offenses, including rape	225		80.88	32.56	210	0.95	2.38	
3.	Rape	38	19	86.84	5.50	46		10.86	
4.	Serious assault	2,022		76.55	292.62	1,908	3.09	0.15	
5.	All theft	11,348		33.77	1,642.26	4,874	3.42	1.41	
6.	Aggravated theft	2,302		33.79	333.14	929	1.07	3.33	
7.	Robbery and violent theft	229		56.33	33.14	151		1.98	
8.	Breaking and entering	2,073		31.30	300.00	778	1.28	3.85	
9.	Auto theft								
10.	Other thefts	9,046		33.77	1,309.12	3,945	3.97	0.96	
11.	Fraud	181		83.97	26.19	160	4.37		
12.	Counterfeiting								
13.	Drug offenses	38		100.00	5.50	40	2.50		
14.	Total offenses	13,834		47.44	2,002.03	7,230	4.57	1.53	

Criteria of juveniles: aged from 0 to 17 years.
Note: Information for some categories is not available.

Branch, the Training Department, the Police School and a band. Below headquarters level there are four major police districts, whose boundaries correspond to the territorial ones. These police districts are further subdivided into a variable number of provinces depending on the size of the population, and each province consists of a number of stations and posts. Because of the large numbers of Indians in the population, the police have substantial Indian representation.

Members of the Fijian Police of different racial origins wear distinctive uniforms when on duty. Fijians wear blue shirts, white *sulus* (short sarongs), red cummerbunds, black belts and sandals. They do not wear headgear of any kind, but Indian constables wear blue caps fitted with a badge, blue shorts or blue slacks and black shoes. Both groups carry truncheons but no firearms. When engaged in rural patrols, both groups wear khaki uniforms, Fijians with shorts and Indians with slacks.

Recruitment, Education & Training

Training is provided by the Police School at Nasorulevu, near Suva. No information is available about recruitment procedures.

The Penal System

Fijian prisons are administered by the commissioner of prisons. Of the eight penal institutions, the largest is in Suva, and there are three on Viti Levu. Vanua Levu, Taveuni and Rotuma have one prison each, and the eighth penal institution is a prison farm at Maboro, near Suva. All prison regimen is oriented toward rehabilitation, and recidivisim is at a low level. In addition to vocational and literacy training, prisoners are encouraged to grow food and participate in team sports.

Major violent crimes are rare, and 95% of the reported offenses are minor offenses, such as drunkenness and traffic violations.

FINLAND

Patrick Edobor Igbinovia

BASIC FACT SHEET

Official Name: Republic of Finland
Area: 337,113 sq km
Population: 4,939,880 (1987)
Capital: Helsinki
Nature of Government: Parliamentary democracy
Language: Finnish
Currency: Finnmark
GNP: $53.45 billion
Territorial Divisions: 12 provinces, 377 communes
Population per Police Officer: 640
Police Expenditures per 1,000: $44,927

History & Background

The history of the Finnish police dates to the Middle Ages, when Finland emerged as part of the Kingdom of Sweden. At that time, keeping public order in towns differed notably from maintaining order in the countryside, and it was not until new legislation was passed in the 1960s that these differences were done away with.

The towns of Sweden-Finland were at first allowed broad autonomy in keeping public order. According to a town law enacted in the 1350s, maintenance of public order and safety was the responsibility of town councils, although the king's bailiff was supposed to keep watch over it. In the 17th century, administration began to be concentrated in the crown. An indication of this development was the transfer of administration of the towns from town councils to the royally appointed provincial governors. Various types of civil servants existed for maintaining order and public safety. So-called servants of the town were closest to what are now called police officers. The Ordinance of 1776 aimed at improving the deteriorating order and public safety of Stockholm, Sweden-Finland's capital, by establishing the first master of police post.

As a result of the 1808–9 war, Finland was annexed to Imperial Russia as a grand duchy of the Russian czar. The first Chamber of Police in Finland under the czars was established in 1916 in Turku, then the capital. The duty of this chamber was to keep order, prevent crime and breaches of the peace, and act as a court for minor offenses. The Chamber of Police's judicial powers were not abolished until 1897. The fact that the state appointed the members of the Chamber of Police meant a considerable increase in the government's authority over the police. Following Turku, the other large towns in Finland received their own Chambers of Police, and the police officers were given a uniform. In 1861 the name "Police Department" was officially used for the first time. Town police at the turn of the century were divided into the law-enforcement branch and the detective or plain clothes branch. In addition, some police departments had bureaus for criminal investigation, and vice squads.

In 1903 and 1904, town police finally became part of the state administration. This, however, did not immediately result in any improvement in the handling of police affairs, as witnessed by a declaration of the Ministry of Justice in 1906 to the effect that there were shortcomings in the police and that even politics had interfered in police operations. Nonetheless, town police continued to be administered under the previously described system through the early years of independence until 1925.

Progress was slower in police affairs in the countryside but more coherent than in towns. Old provincial laws make mention of county sheriffs as some sort of "orderkeepers." In the 16th century, independent feudal lords became king's bailiffs, whose job was to oversee keeping law and order. Sheriffs were originally the people's representatives to the king, and public prosecutor was just one of the sheriff's many functions. From the 16th century onward, however, the sheriff was appointed by the king's bailiff and was the representative of the state entrusted with administrative duties and keeping law and order. The sheriff's office required a certain amount of personal expenditure in carrying out some duties; for this reason, wealthy peasants usually were selected for the post.

In 1634 and 1635, the administrative system of Sweden-Finland was overhauled. Governors became king's bailiffs, and administrative districts were known as *kihlakunta*. According to the Ordinance of 1688, the administration of the district was under the direct jurisdiction of the king's bailiff, from the supervision of law and order to prosecution. By the Royal Decree of 1675, provincial governors, who 30 years earlier had been placed in charge of larger administrative districts, were required to appoint sheriffs, who were to be loyal peasants living in the area. The duties of king's bailiff were later transferred to the sheriff.

No major changes occurred in rural police affairs in the first half of the 19th century. Sheriffs were relatively uneducated and inefficient and had neither regular deputies nor common standing operating procedures. This provided an impetus for reform of the system. In 1891 different types of low-ranking posts were abolished in the rural areas, and it was decreed that each sheriff's office was to have a sufficient number of state-hired constables.

In 1896 the rural police were given its own statutes and improved regulations. After that, during the early years of independence and until 1925, rural police operations followed the same course.

Town and rural police were brought together under the same set of regulations in the Police Act of 1925. However, towns still had the responsibility of contributing one-third of some of the costs of the police department. This financial burden was removed only in 1977.

Police affairs were also reformed in other ways. The police force has traditionally been a body of civil servants under the jurisdiction of the Ministry of the Interior, where a special Police Affairs Department was established to direct, supervise and unify the police operations of the whole country. To aid provincial governors, "inspectors of police" have been appointed in each province to handle police affairs.

In 1918 a temporary police school was established within the Helsinki Police Department. This school was transferred in 1926 to the Ministry of the Interior. A special law for police schools was enacted in 1929.

The level of crime investigation was improved in 1927 by the establishment of additional posts for detectives in the provinces. These posts were transferred to provincial criminal investigation police centers established in 1938. In 1926 a Crime Research Center was set up in Helsinki for the scientific investigation of crime. The center was also commissioned to handle affairs relating to Interpol.

Finland is one of the pioneers in the training of police dogs. The police kennels were established in 1918.

Toward the end of the 1920s and in the early 1930s, there was a great deal of unrest and civil disturbance in Finland. At this time the Mobile Command Force was established to deal with the situation. Over the years this force was given additional duties, and its staff was increased. In this way the present Mobile Police were formed.

The Second World War interrupted the active development of the police forces. During the war, the historical posts of king's bailiffs were abolished and their duties were transferred to the sheriffs' offices. When the statute regulating inspectors of police was amended, this office was given the power of prosecutor in addition to administrative and police duties.

In 1955 the Central Criminal Investigation Police was formed by combing the Crime Research Center with the Criminal Investigation Police Center of Uusimaa Province.

In 1961 new premises were built for the Police School at Otaniemi in Espoo near Helsinki, which meant improved facilities for training.

The State Police, which had possessed extensive authority, were abolished in 1949. In their place, the Security Police, with less authority than the ordinary police, were established.

The maintenance units, or "supply depots," vital to the performance of police duties, have their own history, too. The oldest of these is a gun supply depot, founded as early as 1919. In 1945, the central police stores were established to take care of police supplies. The name was changed in 1955 to supply depot. Repairs to police vehicles were made in the repair shop of the Mobile Police, which was upgraded in 1954 to a police car supply depot. Due to the long distances necessary to return to the capital for small repairs and general maintenance, regional car repair shops have since been set up. In 1938 the first radios were introduced into police service, needing a repair unit of their own. In the beginning this was only a small department within the gun supply depot, but it grew until in 1949 it was big enough to have the unofficial title of police communications supply depot. It was established officially only in 1965.

The Police Act was put in force in 1967. It is the first comprehensive law in Finland that covers all police activities. This legislation canceled all separate regulations that had been in force for the different branches of the police. In 1973, the act was amended and additions were made to the accompanying statutes. At this time, advisory committees for police administration were established, which allowed laypeople limited opportunities to participate in the development of the police force and its functions.

In 1973 the police department of the Ministry of the Interior received its present form and became the supreme command of the police. In the provincial administrative boards, a police bureau now functions as the provincial command of the police. The new legislation did not change the field organization of the police. The Central Criminal Investigation Department was reinforced by annexing the remaining provincial criminal police centers to it.

Structure & Organization

The most important law for the police in Finland is the Police Act of 1966. Included in this act are regulations governing the organization, functions, duties and rights of the police. According to Section 1 of the act, the primary duty of the police is to protect the legal constitution and social order and to maintain public order and safety. The carrying out of these duties is traditionally considered as belonging to internal affairs. Therefore, the police in Finland are organized under the supervision of the Ministry of the Interior. In the other Nordic countries, the police come under the administration of the Ministry of Justice.

The police in Finland are organized on three levels: central administration is in the Ministry of the Interior, regional administration is within the provincial administrative boards, and the province is divided into police districts for local administration. One of the departments in the Ministry of the Interior, the Police Department, acts as the central administrative body for the police. The head of the Police Department, the commander in chief of Police, is also the operational head of all the police forces in Finland. Instead of being organized as a separate, independent, central administration bureau, as in Sweden, the direction of the police forces in Finland comes under the immediate supervision of the minister of the interior. However, the Police department of the ministry is organized structurally as a central administrative bureau that functions as the supreme command of the police. A corresponding body is the Border Guard Department of the Ministry of the Interior, which acts as supreme command for the Border Guard. The Border Guard has some of the same duties as the police, namely, maintaining public order and safety along the border and in coastal areas. The police work together with the Department of Social Affairs and Health in cases concerning drug abuse, vagrants and the protection of children.

The special functions of the Police Department are handled by the Central Criminal Investigation Department, the Security Police and the Mobile Police. Regional administration of police comes within the sphere of competence of the provincial administrative boards under the governor of the province. An inspector of police in each province heads the province's police bureau, which is in charge of day-to-day police operations and local administrative duties. The inspector of police and his aide, the assistant inspector of police, also act as referendaries and are the highest-ranking prosecutors in the province. There are no police forces directly under this official at the provincial level. However, he has operational command over the local police units. In addition, the provincial sections of the Central Criminal Investigation Department and the Mobile Police are functionally subordinate to the inspector of police in the province.

The police district is the local administrative unit of the police in Finland. For historical reasons, there are two types of local police authorities: Town Police Departments, headed by police chiefs, and Rural Police Districts, headed by sheriffs. Today their internal organization is not essentially different. There are Town Police Departments in 35 of the "old towns"— towns that were established prior to Finland's independence. In addition, there are over 200 Rural Police Districts, which consist of one or more municipalities. To ensure adequate operational capability, some police districts are combined into collaborating areas where, for instance, patrolling and emergency services are carried out jointly.

Police officers belonging to local police units are also government employees. The state is responsible for all other expenditures of the local police as well as salaries. In other words, Finland has no police that are maintained by cities or towns.

Police organization in Finland is characterized by a hierarchy in which supervisors have operational authority. The local police units are referred to as *paalikkoviranomaisia* or chief authorities, which are headed by police chiefs or sheriffs. The chief of a police district handles all matters under his authority to his superiors. Police subordinates have a much stricter duty to obey their superiors than do those in other branches of the civil service. In Finland, however, one can hardly speak of "blind obedience." Because most police units have a small complement and a large area of operations, police officers in the field often must make independent decisions, especially in tight corners. This has been taken into account in the legislation, which has granted constables broad rights in undertaking urgent measures independently, e.g., when making a preliminary arrest. However, the constable must immediately report these measures to his superiors, who have the final authority in following them up.

A police chief has other duties besides regular police operations. Most prosecutors in Finland are part of the police organization. The head of the provincial administrative board's police bureau, the provincial superintendent of police, is at the same time the provincial prosecutor, whose job is to prosecute premeditated-murder cases and other serious crimes. The sheriff is at the same time the local administrative authority. He acts as a prosecutor in the lower court, as the official debt collector and as a notary public. In the "old towns" the prosecutors are in principle separated from the Police Department. In practice, however, the small-town police chief often has the job of prosecutor on the side.

The police organization is a top-heavy hierarchy. To balance this, there were attempts, beginning in the 1970s, to bring the police into closer contact with the general public. For this purpose, advisory committees were established at every level of police administration. Representatives of the general public also serve on these committees. For example, there is an advisory committee in each police district, chaired by the chief of the district, and as members those persons appointed by the town council. The advisory committee makes suggestions and states opinions, but has no real decision-making powers. The effect of these committees has been very positive.

The rights of the police are regulated by law. In its operations, the police force must respect and safeguard the basic rights of the citizens, which are listed in the second section of the Finnish Constitution Act of 1919. The police may interfere with a citizen's otherwise protected rights only in circumstances stipulated by law and legal precedents. No police operation may be based on a vague, general authorization. The Finnish constitution expresses the principle of a law-abiding administration, according to which all authorities must base their operations and jurisdiction on the regulations contained in the law.

The main regulations concerning police authority in law enforcement are contained in the second paragraph of the Police Act. This contains stipulations concerning, among other things, the removal and arrest of those causing public disorders, drunkards, persons breaching the peace, etc., and how to cordon off an area of civil disturbance. Two other laws contain stipulations about coercive methods allowable in criminal investigations. These methods are currently being revised and will be codified in one law. Section 12 of the Police Act set guidelines and limits for the application of police authority. It emphasizes the principles of necessity and fairness in police operations. This regulation states that the police should attempt to keep public order and safety primarily by means of advice, suggestions and commands and that the police must not interfere with a citizen's rights more than is necessary to obtain these goals.

The police have the right to use force when meeting resistance in carrying out their official duties. The allowable measures are the use of bodily force, a billy club, tear gas or comparable implements, the use of police dogs and, in extreme cases, the use of arms. In Finland a police officer in the field always carries an officially issued pistol. The Criminal Code contains regulations concerning the use of force; one of its defects is the lack of specifically detailed instructions as to the circumstances under which the police have the right to use shotguns or rifles. Force may be allowed only to the degree necessary for carrying out official duties, and is justifiable only when taking into account the type of official duty and the underlying circumstances involved if a person is injured, or claims to have been injured, because of police action. The police officer is required to get him or her to a doctor for examination and any treatment needed.

Local police may be divided functionally into an administrative bureau, the public safety police and the criminal investigation police. Public safety duties are those that have to do with maintaining the general public's order and safety. The rights of the public safety police are stated particularly in the second section of the Police Act, discussed above. One category of duties particular to Finnish conditions is the care and handling of drunkards and the prevention of smuggling alcoholic beverages, as the state has a monopoly on the manufacture and sale of alcohol in Finland. For the moment, there are no detoxification centers in Finland run by social service or health authorities. Instead, drunk persons who need taking care of or who are causing a public disturbance are put in the police stations for sobering up.

A very important part of police duties is the control of land traffic, and nowadays that of traffic on waterways as well. Traffic control is carried out by both the local police and the Mobile Police. Detailed regulations concerning the rights of the controlling authorities are given in the road traffic and boat traffic laws. In addition, the Police Act contains regulations concerning stopping a vehicle by force.

The officers of the public safety police also carry out questioning and other investigative measures in cases of violation of public safety or traffic rules. The fines for these violations usually are determined by a simple method, the stipulated penalty procedure. After initial questioning of the accused, the procedure is merely paperwork in most cases. The accused has the right, however, to demand that his or her case be given a hearing in the full lower court. Under the stipulated penalty procedure, the police inform the violator in writing of the violation and the size of the proposed fine. The police then inform the lower prosecutor of the violation and its fine; in turn, that person sends the papers on to the stipulated penalty judge, who usually confirms the fine, but who has been known to lower it.

The administrative offices of the local police handle

many matters, among them permits granted by the police. The chief of the police district, for instance, grants passports, drivers' licenses, permits for the possession of firearms and permits for public entertainments. If an application for a permit is rejected or later canceled, a protest can be made against the chief's decision to the provincial administrative board. The local police also oversee the registration of foreigners and makes sure they obtain residence and work permits where necessary.

The other main segment of police duties is criminal investigation. Crimes usually are first investigated by the local police. Difficult cases are handled by the Central Criminal Investigation Department, either alone or in cooperation with the local police. In a way, the criminal investigation police are part of the judicial system. Their link with the judicial system is emphasized by the arrangement (explained above) under which most chiefs of police districts are also prosecutors in the lower courts. Thus general management of the pretrial investigations and the prosecutor's duties are in the same hands. Although this arrangement has been criticized in principle, in practice it has worked reasonably well. An investigation usually is headed by an inspector or sergeant. All constables, however, have the right to carry out investigations, and in urgent cases to expedite criminal procedure by force.

Concerning coercive measures allowed in the criminal process, such as arrest, imprisonment, confiscation, home search and body search, the rules in Finland are, by international comparison, of a very high standard, closely resembling those of its neighboring country Sweden. A special feature of the Finnish judicial system is that the police chief or inspector or others of equal rank have the authority to place the most likely suspect of a crime in custody. The case against the prisoner must be brought before the court within a specified (usually short) time. There is currently under preparation a change in the law to the effect that the authority to remand imprisonment would belong solely to the courts. The amount of time a person has spent in custody prior to sentencing is taken into account and deducted from the sentence. Arrest and remand imprisonment take place in the police prisons, which are supervised by the Ministry of the Interior and the provincial administrative boards. Detailed instructions for the treatment of persons under arrest are given partly in the laws and partly as administrative directives.

In Finland, the Security Police have no right to arrest nor to detain anyone. Neither can they make house searches. The Security Police must turn over to the Central Criminal Investigation Department anyone they have apprehended and whom they suspect of having committed a crime, within 24 hours of his

or her apprehension. The Central Criminal Investigation Department must decide whether an arrest is to be made and the suspect detained.

The position of the police in the state administration has been classified as belonging to the administration of internal affairs since the time of the Kingdom of Sweden-Finland, but it became clearly evident that this was its proper place only after Finland became part of Imperial Russia. In 1918, the Civil Affairs Commission and the Internal Affairs Commission of the transition period were combined into the Ministry of the Interior. The statute for the ministry was issued in 1926, when its Administrative Department, Department for Police Affairs and Department for Border Guard Affairs were also established.

Today the ministry has seven departments, of which the Police Department naturally concerns itself with police affairs. Indirectly the Administrative Department also influences police operations. The Administrative Department's duties include economic planning for the entire ministry, preparation of the budget, and bookkeeping and accounting.

From the point of view of the coordination of the police with the other governmental agencies, the most important departments of the ministry are the Department of the Border Guard, the Rescue Department and the Department of Environmental Protection. Through the provincial administrative boards, the activities of the police are influenced by the Provincial, Communal, and Housing Administration departments. Since the Department for Police Affairs was established in 1926, it has undergone many changes. It officially became the supreme command of the police in 1973. The Police Department, and through it the entire police force, is under the tight control of the government, since the department's civil servants simultaneously report to the cabinet. This means that all far-reaching decisions are made at the ministerial level. The minister of the interior gives the basic guidelines for police operations and is therefore continually kept informed on important police matters.

The tasks of the ministry's Police Department include maintenance of public order and safety, police administration, Finnish citizenship, authorization of the right to travel abroad, supervision of foreigners traveling and residing in Finland, capture of known criminals, supervision of special trade regulations, supervision of special trade regulations, supervision of lotteries and fundraising drives, and control of arms and ammunition.

The Police Department is divided into four bureaus: Administrative Bureau, Police Bureau, Technical Bureau and Bureau of Alien Affairs. In addition, there are a planning group and a secretary for information. For the development and operation of information systems, the Department of Police has a joint unit in Hämeenlinna with the Ministry of Justice.

The supreme police command consists of a commander in chief (the head of the Police Department at the ministry), the assistant department chief (supervisor of police) and the office chief of the Police Bureau (deputy supervisor or police superintendent).

The Administrative Bureau is in charge of legislative matters, territorial division, personnel matters, the right of Finnish citizens to travel abroad, permit administration and all matters that do not come under the other bureaus.

The Police Bureau is in charge of matters concerning public order and safety, the operational direction of the police, the apprehension of criminals, police rights, training, physical education and sports, police dogs and complaints against police officers. In addition to the bureau chief (supervisor of police), there are senior inspectors and inspectors who are also part of the police organization.

The Technical Bureau is headed by a bureau chief who must have a degree in engineering. This bureau is in charge of matters relating to supply depots, the Police Dog Institute, buildings and office space, police vehicles, instruments and supplies, and the impounding of property. One of the more unusual duties of this bureau is care of graves of foreign soldiers in Finland.

The Bureau of Alien Affairs is in charge of matters relating to acquiring Finnish citizenship, passport control, border stations, foreigners' residence permits and matters relating to the supervision of foreigners in Finland.

The planning group handles economic planning, budgets, and work research and rationalization.

The civil servants of the Department of Police must have experience in police affairs, and most of them also have a degree in law or the experience behind their rank of police inspector. The majority of police officers in positions of authority also have had a great deal of experience in the field, serving as chiefs of police districts in the countryside.

The number of personnel in the Department of Police is insufficient to deal with the numerous tasks assigned to the police. This has been demonstrated on special occasions requiring extra police duties, such as the Conference on Security and Cooperation in Europe in 1975.

The 1973 amendment to the Police Act created an advisory committee system within the police administration. These committees consist primarily of laypeople. The Ministry of the Interior is assisted by the Police Affairs Advisory Committee, the provincial administrative boards by the Order and Safety Affairs Committee, and each police district by its own advisory committee. The committees do not have decision-making powers. However, they are to improve relations between the police and the general public by making recommendations and directing attention to public opinion on drawbacks in the system.

The foundation for police operations is the Police Act and its explicatory decree. According to this legislation, the duty of the police is to protect the legal constitution and social order and to maintain public order and safety. The police must pay special attention in their operations to violations of order and to the prevention of crime and accidents. Police duties also include those general services they render to the public.

Upon request, the police provide official assistance to the authorities, civil groups and private persons.

The task of maintaining public order and safety include, among other police duties, criminal investigation, crime prevention, traffic control, and the preparation of cases so that legal action can be taken and indictments made. In Finland, a police officer has the right to refrain from informing his superiors or the prosecutor of minor infractions. This is exceptional in that the police of many countries must inform their supervisors in all cases.

In the countryside, the police also function as official prosecutors, debt collectors, and collectors of unpaid government fees and taxes. It could be said that police operations in Finland touch on every public aspect of a citizen's life.

The Central Criminal Investigation Department is a separate police unit directly subordinate to the Ministry of the Interior, and its police officers have police authority in the whole country. Its duty is to give assistance to other police units by performing criminal investigations commissioned individually for each case that by nature belongs to the investigations area of the Central Criminal Investigation Department. Furthermore, the department on request assists the police with scientific and technical questions during the criminal investigation, and also prepares statements to be used in court. The Central Criminal Investigation Department also keeps the national registers of offenders and offenses in the whole country and acts as the National Central Bureau of Interpol in Finland. The Central Police radio station, which is primarily concerned with international communications, operates in connection with the Central Criminal Investigation Police.

The Central Criminal Investigation Department has its headquarters in Helsinki and a provincial department performing crime investigations in every province. The main division is divided into five bureaus: the Bureau of Administration (personnel and account matters), the Bureau of Investigation (criminal investigation), the Bureau of Identification (study of fingerprints and keeping a fingerprint register), the crim-

POLICE ORGANIZATION IN FINLAND

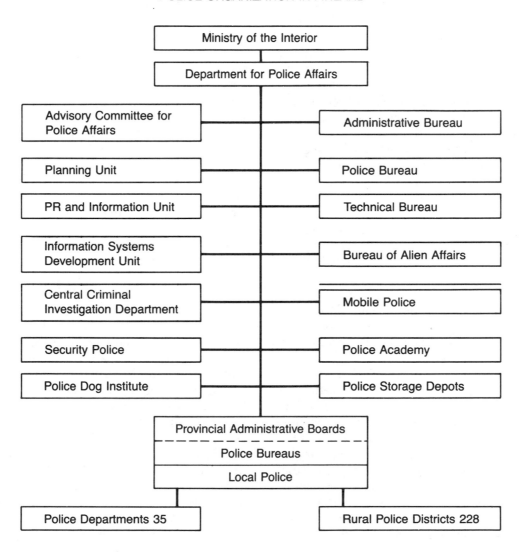

inal laboratory (investigations requested concerning traces at the scene of the crime, crime equipment, poisons, etc.) and the Bureau of Information (registers of different kinds and Interpol activities).

The total personnel of the Central Criminal Investigation Department amounts to 270 persons, of whom 151 are police officers. Due to the various duties of the department, the basic training of the personnel is remarkable. Most of the police begin their duties in the Central Criminal Investigation Department in the local police districts, having attained the rank of overconstable (detective sergeant).

Acting on a motion presented by the Ministry of the Interior in 1930, the cabinet established a special police department to be allied with the Helsinki Police Department. Called the Mobile Police Command, it was meant to operate throughout the whole country to prevent smuggling, control traffic movements, and above all quell the general civil disturbances of that time. The nickname *lentavat* (fliers), still used in the countryside, dates from that time.

At present, the Mobile Police are directly subordinate to the Ministry of the Interior and operate throughout the country. Headed by a chief and an assistant chief, the Mobile Police have in each province a department that is divided into command forces in the larger communities. Inspectors act as the heads of the provincial departments. The headquarters, in Helsinki, is also the department for Uusimaa Province and has bureaus for accounts and budgets, training and technical affairs as well as for administration.

The Police Act states that the Mobile Police must assist other police units, maintain public order and safety, aid in crime prevention and traffic control, and function as the national police reserve.

The Police Act divides the Mobile Police's primary duties into four groups: (1) control, organization and guidance of land traffic, as well as traffic education and research; (2) prevention of illegal importation of alcoholic beverages, and their unauthorized manufacture, transport or sale; (3) supervision of water traffic, hunting, fishing and nature conservation; and (4) assisting other police units in searches and investigations and in capturing fugitives from justice. In addition, the Mobile Police aid other authorities and perform other duties as specifically instructed by the Ministry of the Interior.

The special duties of the Mobile Police include the security guard for the president of the republic; passport control at the Valimaa border station on the Finno-Soviet frontier; responsibility for police operations at Helsinki-Vantaa Airport; and providing police escort for state visitors.

The Security Police, established in 1948, investigate and solves crimes against the state, offenses against the law and order of the state or the community and crimes that may endanger public safety.

The Security Police operate under the supervision of the Minister of the Interior through the Department for Police Affairs. Headed by the chief of security police and his assistant chief, the headquarters is divided into bureaus, with district offices in various parts of Finland.

The Police Dog Institute is subordinate to the Ministry of the Interior. The institute's tasks are the acquisition of dogs suitable for police work, the basic training of dogs and handlers, and the arranging of advanced courses for dogs and handlers. In addition, the institute is in charge of tactical development of the dogs and informs the other police agencies of potential uses for police dogs. Hämeenlinna, with its extensive, forested surroundings about 62 miles (100 kilometers) north of Helsinki, offers ideal conditions for training police dogs. The buildings of the institute were constructed in 1927. The new classroom and dormitory building completed in 1977 considerably improved the facility.

There has been a tendency in Finland in recent years to concentrate police dogs into groups in the operationally most important police districts. This has resulted in better emergency capabilities. It has been possible to use the special vehicles required for dog patrolling more effectively, and advanced training has been easier to organize.

The work of police dog groups, which are part of the public order and safety police, is done by cruising in special police dog patrol cars. In disturbance-prone areas, patrolling is done on foot.

With the help of police dog patrols, criminals have often been successfully caught at the scene of the crime, or tracked and caught in the forest. It is easy to become lost in a sparsely populated country with large, heavily forested areas, such as Finland. Prompt use of police dogs has saved many lives annually, locating persons lost in the forest.

At the end of 1977, Finland had 464 municipalities and 262 police districts. There were urban police departments in 35 municipalities, and 429 municipalities were grouped into 227 rural police districts. Thirty-two police districts operated on an individual basis, and 73 belonged to cooperative districts.

The urban police departments are in the oldest towns of Finland. In the nation's capital, Helsinki, there is a police department employing over 2,000 staff members. It is led by a police chief and divided into the Administrative Division; the Public Order and Safety Line (Operations Bureau, I to III zonal divisions, Emergency Squad, Traffic Division); the Criminal Investigation Line (general division, I–II investigation divisions, Social Division); and the Administrative Police Line (administrative offices, Passport Division, the civil registry); and the Planning and Economics Division.

The Turku Police Department is an example of an

organization smaller than that in Helsinki. Located in the Turku-Pori Province, this department has a total staff of 440. A police chief heads the department, assisted by the chiefs of the divisions for public order and safety, and for criminal investigation.

The Police Department is a so-called command bureau, which, however, extensively uses special task forces in planning and executing police operations.

The overall administration of the Police Department is handled by the Administrative Division, which is composed of the administrative offices and the Economics Division. The former is headed by the secretary of the Police Department and takes care of different matters concerning various permits as well. The latter is headed by a chief accountant and handles matters concerning the budget, accounts, etc.

An assistant police chief heads the Public Order and Safety Division, composed of the radio police unit, the Traffic Division, the Traffic Accident Division and the Traffic Bureau. These units are headed by police commissioners under the supervision of the assistant police chief. The radio police unit is in charge of emergencies and police dog operations. The duties of the Traffic Division include traffic control and guidance. The Traffic Accident Division investigates traffic accidents and cases of drunken driving. The Traffic Bureau is in charge of permits relating to traffic.

In addition, there is a central bureau directly under the police officer in charge of the department. This bureau controls those trades requiring special permits, and it supervises the Central Police radio station and the car maintenance workshop.

The city is divided into two precincts for carrying out duties related to public order and safety. An inspector heads each precinct. Their other duties include investigation of smaller crimes, placing drunks in sobering-up cells, and supervision of ports, railroad stations, bus terminals and airports in their jurisdiction. The mounted police are attached to one precinct.

The Criminal Investigation Division is headed by a divisional director aided by an assistant divisional director. To carry out investigations of crime, the division is broken up into groups, each headed by an inspector. Group I investigates thefts; Group II, murder cases and other crimes of violence as well as arson; Group III, fraud; and Group IV assists other authorities in carrying out official duties when required. In addition, the division has Group E, which carries out intelligence-gathering duties and has a technical bureau for investigations at the scene of crimes; it also has a lost property office.

The Social Division, headed by an inspector, investigates crimes against the Narcotics Act and violations of the Temperance Act; supervises vagrants; and assists social and welfare authorities in their duties.

The Civil Register Division is composed of two bureaus: the Population Records Bureau; and the Address, Passport and Information Bureau, whose duties include keeping the address register, granting passports and ID cards, passport control at ports of entry, alien supervision and use of a computer terminal that has access to vehicle registration and a registry of wanted criminals.

The Police Department is also assisted by an advisory committee in each police district. Its ten members are nominated by the town council.

In each police district there is also a Work Safety Committee, in which the representative of employers and employees treat together matters concerning work safety.

In addition, the Police Department has a youth police group, which does preventive police work among juveniles.

In a rural police district of medium size, there is a sheriff who serves as head, assisted by an inspector and about ten sergeants and constables. Finland's largest rural police district is Espoo, in the vicinity of Helsinki; Espoo employs over 200 staff members. The smallest district is in Pertunmaa in northern Karelia, where there are only four policemen.

The largest rural police districts have a Public Order and Safety Division; a Traffic Division; a Criminal Investigation Division; and an Administrative Division, which also handles a variety of permit and other administrative matters as well as the collection of debts. The urban police have no debt collection duties.

The majority of Finland's police districts are small (10 to 12 policemen) and thus have no divisions. In these districts, every policeman does in turn all the various police duties. However, a separate administrative unit usually exists, staffed by two to four female employees.

Police duties are performed only by men and women who have been through police training, but clerical jobs are carried out by those employees who have received general office clerks' training and a special course in police administration jobs. They are usually women.

Kouvola District in Kymi Province will be described to present a clearer picture of a rural police district. The district is fairly large for Finland. It is divided into the following divisions and bureaus for carrying out police duties and for personnel administration:

1. *Administrative Division*

   Administrative Offices

   Lost Property and Address Bureau

   Information Bureau

2. *Collection Division*

   Confiscation and Impounding Bureau

   Debt Collection and Fine Bureau

3. *Public Order and Safety Division*

   Field Bureau

   Investigation Bureau

   Police Prison

4. *Crime and Prosecution Division*

   Offices of the prosecutor

   Offices of the Criminal Investigation Department

   Investigation Bureau

The duty of Kouvola District, as well as the other districts, is to carry out police, prosecutor, executive and general administrative jobs as well as other duties assigned to the district. The operating area is the town of Kouvola and the municipality of Valkeala. Together they cover an area of over 386 square miles (1,000 square kilometers) with a population of about 41,000. The staff in Kouvola consists of a sheriff, two deputies, two inspectors, 10 sergeants, 32 constables and 28 other staff. There are always at least four policemen on duty. This is the most common staff strength during the night. During the day and evening, seven to nine public order and safety policemen are on duty, and there are five to six criminal investigation police on duty during the day, and two at night. The district has six radio-equipped cars, a support station of the police radio and a computer terminal. There are also four police dogs, one of which has been specially trained to detect bombs and other explosives.

The work of the Public Order and Safety Police (POSP) is both preventive and investigative. Patrolling takes place mainly in uniform in marked cars. Interventions are made into everything that threatens public order and safety. A police action may be advisory and guiding in nature but may also lead to lawsuits and punishments if needed. The POSP in Kouvola controls car traffic, pedestrian and bicycle traffic, and traffic on the waterways, as is the case with the corresponding POSP in other districts.

Emergency calls to the police in the evenings and at night usually involve assistance in settling family disputes (such as wife-beating) or fights in private dwellings. Also, drunk and disorderly persons create a great deal of work for Finnish police officers.

It is a police duty to organize and direct searches for lost and missing persons. In the Kouvola District, as in much of Finland, there are vast forested areas and many lakes, and each year several persons become lost. Very often searches are carried out with the assistance of local Army units and voluntary emergency service organizations.

Different types of traffic damage occur daily in Finland. Unless the damage is very minor, the police are called upon to investigate the extent of the damage, i.e., what has happened and who is guilty. The police are also called upon to investigate other accidents, such as fires and explosions. Usually the POSP is the first to be alerted and to arrive on the scene.

Most of the CID person's day is spent investigating crimes such as theft, assault and battery, embezzlement, and fraud. The criminal investigation police's crime prevention activities consist of different types of surveillance and intelligence-gathering duties in places where crimes are most often committed or that criminals are known to frequent. This activity also includes different types of duties of an educational nature, and the CID participates in many events arranged for the general public. The CID also visits educational institutions. The particular objects of the systematic education of law-biding citizens and traffic education are the students in the seventh to the ninth grades in school, i.e., 13- to 16-year-olds.

Investigation of crimes is the same in rural areas as it is in towns. In Louvola and smaller police districts, the criminal investigator is an all-round policeman whose job is to do everything connected with an investigation at the scene of a crime, including taking pictures and lifting fingerprints and other marks. In larger districts there are usually specialists available for these various tasks. Finland's rural areas are in the process of setting up a regional crime investigation system, to which end the training of detectives was begun in 1977.

Kouvola is one of Finland's main crossroads in the national road and railroad system. For this reason, a large number of "mobile criminals" move through the district. The criminal investigation police usually work during the daytime in Kouvola. In the evening there are only two police on duty. At night, the criminal investigation police work only in exceptional cases.

Kouvola's police districts and the other five surrounding districts began in 1968 an experiment in collaboration, with Kouvola acting as a central district. The objective of the collaboration was to concentrate certain services and to transfer personnel from the abolished "on call" posts to field surveillance. Joint operations included patrolling, emergency calls and guarding of prisoners, so the patrols available worked in addition to their own district, throughout the area covered by the six cooperating districts. This collaboration included public order and safety operations and preliminary investigation services. The actual investigation of crimes is handled by each district separately.

When the personnel of the rural police districts came under the Working Hours Act (40 hours per week), it became impossible to arrange police operations to cover the entire 24 hours in a day with the small number of police personnel available. The collaboration first tried in the Kouvola districts has since been extended to cover the whole of Finland. Because no overhaul of district division aiming at further concentration is expected, the development of this collaboration is the most practical way to improve the availability of police services.

Police operations in Finland have undergone considerable changes in the recent past. Urbanization and its accompanying rapid increase in population have brought about notable increases in police duties, which in turn have set in motion a process of change in the police organization itself. The police have, however, been able to adapt fairly well to these changes. There are, of course, problems, but the police everywhere in the world have problems. The keys to keeping police operations up to date in these times have been improved training, development of technical instruments and tools, and increased systematic planning. The status of the police in Finnish society clearly improved since the 1970s. The latest opinion poll indicates that over 85% of the citizens think the police are doing a good job.

Personnel of all ranks wear a dark blue uniform consisting of trousers and either a tunic or a hip-length blouse. Headgear consists of either a blue peaked cap or a blue Scandinavian-style forage cap, with a badge worn centrally in the front. In summer the tunics may be discarded in favor of a blue long-sleeve shirt worn with a black tie.

Recruitment, Education & Training

The Ministry of the Interior is responsible for training of all police personnel as well as their development and coordination of activities.

Police training is given at the Police Academy in Otaniemi, Espoo, near Helsinki (for noncommissioned officers, officers and chiefs, as well as various specialized courses) and at the Police Training Center in Tampere (for ordinary policemen and cadets).

On-the-job training is given in the provinces and in special units through liaison offices and correspondence courses.

The first police training courses in Finland were organized in association with the Helsinki Police Force in 1918. From 1918 to 1961, police training took place at the police school on Suomenlinna (an island near Helsinki). In the beginning, the curriculum consisted of a basic general education course followed by courses in either criminal police work or ordinary law inforcement. After 1926, basic education took

place in the provinces and in the field, and the specialized courses were given at Suomenlinna.

In 1961, a new building for the Police Academy was completed at Otaniemi. In the same year, the content of the police training courses underwent significant revision and renovation. From 1962 to 1973, all police training took place in the Police Academy. Since 1973 there has also been a Police Training Center, first located in Helsinki and later moved to Tampere. In the beginning, the center was only for the training of cadets, but in 1977 it was expanded to include the training of policemen as well.

Since 1976, the police training program has included special courses in professional training, including, among other subjects, planning short- and medium-term police operations; information systems; methods of operational direction; and the staff's own training expectations. The combined expertise of police teachers and personnel active in the police force are used in preparing the programs.

In addition to training, the Police Training Center also selects the new police cadets. The center carries out a preliminary screening of those who wish to become policemen, and it arranges entrance examinations with the intention of finding the best possible candidates to be trained to take up the duties of policemen.

The police statute stipulates the following requirements for male applicants to the cadet courses: He must be over 19 but not yet 30, have completed secondary school, finished military service with the rank of at least a noncommissioned officer, be certified in good health, be at least five feet, nine inches (175 centimeters) tall, be of good character, and otherwise be fit for police work. Annually there has been an average of 3,500 applicants, of whom 7 to 8% are trained.

At present the police cadet course takes five months. Training is given in nine subjects for which the cadets receive grades: police administration, police service, criminology, traffic, criminal and criminal processing law, language, psychology, state and social studies, and physical education and self-defense. In addition, training is given in first aid, typing, civil service law, gun handling and firing, civil defense, in the use of various technical instruments, and in driving a police car. Besides theoretical instruction, police cadets receive practical training from the local police. On completion of the course, the Police Training Center assigns the graduates to police duties in various districts.

Following the cadet course comes a year to a year and a half in active police work, after which all policemen are sent to a six-month course that is a continuation of instruction in the main subjects introduced in the cadet course, with the addition of criminal tactics and techniques. Mandatory courses for which no grade is given include instruction in civil law, civil defense, first aid, typing, the use of various technical instruments, and gun handling and firing. Completion of the course leads to the position of senior constable.

Training for a noncommissioned police officer includes instruction in the following subjects: police administrative law, criminal law, criminal trial law, civil law, traffic, police tactics, criminal tactics and techniques, psychology, language (Finnish or Swedish), the use of guns, physical education, first aid and civil defense, and forensic medicine. The aim of the course is to provide supervisory ability, and competence in operational planning and tactical direction. Completion of the course leads to the rank of sergeant.

The training for police officers included: administrative law, criminal law, the law of criminal process, civil law, traffic, police tactics, criminal tactics, psychology and language. In addition, instruction is given in forensic medicine, psychiatry, criminal techniques, gun handling, first aid and civil defense. The aim of the course is to prepare the student to assist the police chief as well as to act independently in field supervisory positions. Successful completion of the course leads to the rank of inspector (lieutenant).

Penal System

No information is available on the Finnish Penal System.

CRIME STATISTICS (1984)

		Number Reported	Attempts %	Cases Solved %	Crime per 100,000	Offenders	Females %	Juveniles %	Strangers %
1.	Murder	275	59.6	93.8	5.62	279	8.2	8.2	
2.	Sex offenses, including rape	1,064		79.6	21.74	919	2.1	12.9	
3.	Rape	317		70.7	6.48	271		14.0	
4.	Serious assault	1,788		83.3	36.53	1,765	7.5	19.8	
5.	All theft	93,708		29.3	1,914.42	47,697	8.3	53.2	
6.	Aggravated theft	2,92		40.6	59.80	2,392	4.8	33.7	
7.	Robbery and violent theft	1,649		57.0	33.69	1,640	8.5	38.4	
8.	Breaking and entering	37,818			772.61				
9.	Auto theft	8,402		49.3	171.65	7,664	4.7	66.0	
10.	Other thefts	80,730		26.3	1,649.28	36,001	9.3	52.5	
11.	Fraud	33,693		84.5	688.33	35,376	15.4	11.8	
12.	Counterfeiting								
13.	Drug offenses	2,273		91.7	46.44	2,389	18.6	19.7	
14.	Total offenses	654,978		82.4	13,380.94	588,306	10.0	22.6	

Criteria of juveniles: aged from 0 to 20 years.
Note: Information for some categories is not available.

FRANCE*

BASIC FACT SHEET

Official Name: French Republic
Area: 547,026 sq km
Population: 55,596,030 (1987)
Capital: Paris
Nature of Government: Parliamentary democracy
Language: French
Currency: Franc
GNP: $526.63 billion (1985)
Territorial Divisions: 22 regions, 96 metropolitan departments
Population per Police Officer: 630
Police Expenditures per 1,000: N.A.

History & Background

The earliest reference to a police force in France is in the seventh century, during the reign of Clotaire II. French police history thus spans over 14 centuries, and its major landmarks are set forth in chronological form as follows:

615	Clotaire II appoints *commissaire-enquêteurs* to maintain the peace.
803	Charlemagne issues edict on the functions and duties of watchmen.
1032	Henri I appoints prévôt de Paris.
1254	Louis IX institutes royal watch under Chevalier du Guet.
1306	A *commissaire-enquêteur* au Châtelet is appointed for each Paris quarter.
1524	Francis I appoints *enquêteurs-examinateurs* in *bailliages* and prévôts in the provinces.
1544	The Maréchaussée, the military police, is formed.
1667	Louis XIV reorganizes the Paris Police and installs a lieutenant general as commander.
1699	*Commissaires* of police are appointed in provincial centers
1789	The French Revolution overthrows the monarchy. The Prefecture of Police is abolished. Thiroux de Crosne, its last lieutenant general, hands over authority to Baily, mayor of Paris, and the Provisional Police Committee.
1790	Decree creates 48 *commissaires* of police for Paris, elected every two years.
1791	Decree authorizes creation of *commissaires* of police "wherever necessary."
1799	Joseph Fouché is appointed minister of police.
1800	The Prefecture of Police of Paris is established.
1802	Napoleon abolishes the Ministry of Police.
1804	The Ministry of Police is restored, with Fouché as minister.
1808	The Code of Criminal Procedure is enacted.
1810	The Penal Code in enacted. Fouché is dismissed.
1815	Fouché is reappointed as minister of police during the "100 Days" and is retained as such by Louis XVIII.
1811–27	E. F. Vidocq creates the Sûreté branch at the Prefecture of Police.
1829	Sergeants de Ville police are appointed as street patrol in Paris.
1832	The Sûreté is reorganized by Louis-Philippe.
1851	Lyons is given a state police.

*Portions of this chapter are based on Philip John Stead's *Police of France* (New York: Macmillan, 1983).

127

1854	Central *commissaires* instituted in cities, with several *commissaires* of police; Paris adopts the London system of beat policing.
1855	State Railway Police is established.
1856	Political Police squads are created.
1870–71	Corps of *gardiens de la paix* is instituted; Sûreté-Générale is founded.
1883	The Prefecture's Training School is founded.
1883–1914	A. Bertillon introduces scientific measurement systems at the Prefecture of Police.
1884	Prefects are given police powers in towns of 40,000 or more inhabitants.
1893	The police adopt scientific fingerprinting techniques.
1894	Renseignements Généraux (Police General Intelligence) branch is created.
1897–99	Direction de la Surveillance du Territoire (Counterespionage) branch is created.
1903	Law defining police functions of the Gendarmerie is enacted.
1907	Regional detective squads are formed by Clemenceau.
1908	Marseilles is given state police.
1910	E. Locard starts Forensic Science Laboratory in Lyon.
1935	Prefecture's Officer Training College is founded.
1941	Under the Vichy regime, the state police are given to towns with over 10,000 inhabitants; the Sûreté's Police College is founded at St.-Cyr-au-Mont d'Or, near Lyons.
1944	German garrison commander surrenders at Prefecture of Police.
1945	CRS (Republican Security Companies) are founded.
1946	Interpol moves headquarters to Paris from Vienna.
1948	Police are deprived of the right to strike.
1959	The Code of Penal Procedure is enacted.
1966	Law of July 31 integrates personnel of the Prefecture of Police and Sûreté Nationale and creates office of secretary-general of police at the Ministry of the Interior.
1969	The office of secretary-general is renamed director general of the National Police.
1982	The minister of the Ministry of the Interior and of Decentralization (as the Ministry of the Interior has been called since the accession of President François Mitterrand) delegates his control of the Police Nationale to the secretary of state in charge of public security.

Structure & Organization

The French police system is basically of a dual nature, its two major components being totally dissimilar. The older of the two, the Gendarmerie Nationale, is under the Ministry of Defense, the Police Nationale, the civil police, is under the Ministry of the Interior and of Decentralization.

The Gendarmerie, the premier regiment of the French Army, polices some 95% of the national territory, including all communes with less than 10,000 inhabitants. They work at the lowest level in small units of between five and 55, according to the size of the area. There are 4,000 such units called *brigades* (squads; not to be confused with the higher military formation of the same name), normally stationed in barracks in the main town of the canton. Organizationally, many brigades form a company, a number of companies form a group, and a number of groups form a legion. Known as the Departmental Gendarmerie, they operate from fixed points, reside in their duty area and constitute the largest component of the force.

The next largest component is the Mobile Gendarmerie, riot police who may be employed anywhere in the country. They are deployed on a regional or departmental basis and are equipped with tanks, armored vehicles and light aircraft. There are 120 squadrons of them, each of 135 officers and other ranks.

The third main formation of the Gendarmerie is the Republican Guard, consisting of a regiment of cavalry and two regiments of infantry always stationed in Paris. The Republican Guard had few rivals among the police forces of the world for color and pageantry.

The Gendarmerie operate under the control of a director general, who is a civil magistrate. An inspector general who is invariably a general is the liaison with the minister of defense.

The national civil police, the Police Nationale, operate mainly in urban centers with over 100,000 inhabitants. It is headed by a director general, who presides over a complex organization below him and reports directly to the minister of the interior and of decentralization above him. The major components of the National Police correspond to those of most other Western countries: the Urban Police, the Directorate of Criminal Investigation, and the Air and Frontier Police. However, there is one branch of the

National Police that has no obvious counterpart in either the British or the American police structure: the Republican Security Companies (Compagnies Républicaines de Sécurité, CRS). They are civil version of the Mobile Gendarmerie, approaching the latter in numbers and equipment and organized in 61 companies of between 210 and 255 officers and men. Their modus operandi is military, based on barracks, with military titles and forms of address. They are a highly trained and professional force, although lacking in the heavy armament of the Mobile Gendarmerie. The CRS may best be described as an emergency reserve force.

Since the 1960s Paris has become the breeding ground of terrorist groups of all persuasions, and this has brought to the forefront two formerly less known units of the National Police: the Directorate General of Intelligence and Gambling, and the Directorate of Counterespionage (Surveillance du Territoire, DST).

The police of metropolitan Paris are an integral part of the Police Nationale, but the city occupies such a key place in French police history that it dominates the rest of the country and is a microcosm of the Police Nationale. In addition, the prefect of police of Paris is also the prefect of the Paris Zone of Defense, the jurisdiction of which extends over Hauts-de-Seine, Seine-St.-Denis, and Val-de-Marne, the three territorial departments encircling Paris.

Although heavily centralized, police administration makes some concessions to local governments. The Code of Communal Administration endows the mayor of a commune with police powers in specified areas, such as traffic. The policing of the rural areas of the commune is also the mayor's responsibility and is normally performed through a *garde champêtre,* a cross between a rural guard and a forest ranger. There are about 30,000 of them, and their role in the life of their communities is considerable.

The French police system is sharply different from the Anglo-American model. The ratio of police to public is greater than in the United States and the United Kingdom. Police power is heavily concentrated in Paris, and this power is exercised and the police personnel are deployed solely as the central government determines. In France, the high command of the police is not in the hands of professional police officers but in those of civilians. For the French, policing is too serious a matter to be left to policemen alone. Intelligence-gathering also claims a larger share of the police pie in France than in the United States and the United Kingdom.

The Police Nationale (PN)
The three top officials of the Police Nationale are, in order, the minister of the interior and of decentrali-
zation; the secretary of state in charge of public security; and the director general, who, from his headquarters in central Paris, is the chief operating and administrative officer.

Three services are directly attached to the office of the director general. They are the Central Automobile Service, which maintains the force's vast fleet of motorized vehicles; the Security Service of the Ministry of the Interior and of Decentralization; and the Central Sports Service.

Two "external" services are also central: the Inspectorate General of Police, and the Official Travel and Security of High Personages Service. The Inspectorate General is charged with policing the police and conducts the disciplining and prosecution of errant officers. Internal punishments include cautions, reprimands, transfers, suspensions, demotions and dismissals. It is also concerned with efficiency and periodically culls out those unsuited for police service.

There are three administrative services at the PN headquarters: the Directorate of Personnel and Materiel, the Directorate of Regulations and Legal Affairs, and the Directorate of Training.

Seven operational directorates constitute the hub of the headquarters:

1. The Central Directorate of General Intelligence has three satellite subdirectorates: the Subdirectorate of General Political Information, the Subdirectorate of Social Information and the Subdirectorate of Racecourses and Gambling. The information amassed by these units reaches the *commissaire* of the republic (or, in Paris, the prefect of police), the prefect of the defense zone, the director of General Intelligence and the Minister of the Interior and of Decentralization.

2. The Central Directorate of Judicial Police conducts all detective or criminal investigation. Its director is the nation's chief detective and the head of the French section of Interpol. Directly under him are an office for liaison with the Gendarmerie; a Central Service for Judicial Identification, which oversees all police laboratories; the Subdirectorate for General Services and Liaison, in charge of legal and criminal research and statistics; the Subdirectorate of Criminal Affairs, which deals with organized crime, prostitution, subversion, narcotics and kidnapping; and the Subdirectorate of Economic and Financial Affairs, which deals with white-collar crime, counterfeiting, forgery, etc.

   The Central Directorate of Judicial Police controls the work of the Regional Crime Services (Services Régionaux de Police Judiciaire, or SRPJ, as they are commonly known). Each of the 19 SRPJ jurisdictions corresponds to that of an appeals court, to whose prosecutor general they are closely linked. A region thus contains several territorial departments. The Paris SRPJ maintains a vast archive known as the central criminal records system.

3. The Central Directorate of the Urban Police is the command headquarters for the police stationed in cities and circumscriptions. In smaller cities the urban police work under a single *commissaire*, who is responsible for both administrative and criminal investigation matters. In larger cities the chief of police is known as a central *commissaire* presiding over *commissaires* of police for each quarter, each with a small unit of uniformed and plainclothes officers. The City Detective Department is generally commanded by a *commissaire* whose grade is in proportion to the size of the department. In large cities all the major operational directorates of PN headquarters are represented.

The urban police (except in Paris, Lyon and the Rhône, Marseille and the Bouches du Rhône, and Lille and the Nord, where the prefect of police and the prefects delegated for police, respectively, have control) are under the direct jurisdiction of the *commissaire* of the republic, who has delegated much of the day-to-day operational control to the director of urban police.

4. The Central Service of the Republican Security Companies is a separate branch of the PN. The 61 CRS companies have an authorized strength of 87 *commissaires* of police, 434 commandants and *officiers de la paix* of all grades, and 15,157 *gardiens de la paix* and noncommissioned officers. The 61 companies are aggregated into 10 groups, the group commanders being responsible to the chief of the Central Service. Although the CRS is primarily a riot control force, its personnel perform many other functions, such as mountain rescue, being life guards, and airport policing.

5. The Directorate of Counterespionage is covered by the official secrets regulations, and no details of its organizational structure or personnel are released.

6. The Central Service of the Air and Frontier Police.

7. The Service of International Technical Cooperation deals with the training in France of police officers from other countries and provides advisory services to foreign police forces.

In May 1985 the PN adopted a new service uniform designed by Pierre Balmain. The traditional képi was replaced by a military-style peaked cap, and a ManuRhin revolver is carried in an open holster attached to the belt. The new uniform is dark blue (as the old one was). The képi is now worn only with ceremonial uniforms. The CRS uses battle dress in riot situations. *Commissaires* wear uniforms on special occasions only. It consists of a naval-type double-breasted jacket with silver-embroidered oak leaf symbols of rank on the cuffs and lapels.

The Gendarmerie Nationale

The Gendarmerie is France's most visible and ubiquitous police force, and most foreigners have the misconception that they are the *only* French police. At the national level, the Gendarmerie is administered by a director general who reports to the Ministry of Defense. He is assisted by an inspector general, who is invariably a ranking military officer with direct access to the minister of defense.

The Gendarmerie has a regional headquarters in each of France's six defense zones. All the gendarmes in a region make up a legion comprising both Departmental Gendarmerie and Mobile Gendarmerie. The former are stationed permanently in the region.

A region contains several territorial departments, themselves divided into *arrondissements*, each of which comprises communes (municipalities with elected councils and mayors) and cantons (electoral districts). The headquarters of Departmental Gendarmerie companies usually are in the largest commune of an *arrondissement*. At the company level, there are a criminal investigation unit, and a reserve platoon for emergency duties. All gendarmes are required to live in military quarters.

At entry level of the Gendarmerie hierarchy there are parallel civil authorities. The director general is subordinate to the civilian minister of defense, the regional commanding general is in contact with the prefect of the defense zone; the departmental commanding colonel, and the *commissaire* of the republic; the company commander with the deputy *commissaire* of the republic in the *arrondissement;* the commander of the brigade with the mayor of the commune. On the judicial side, the Gendarmerie officers come under the control of the public prosecutors and the *juges d'instruction.*

Other Gendarmerie subdivisions include the Gendarmerie d'Outre-mer (Overseas Gendarmerie), which has groups and companies in France's far-flung colonial territories. One legion is stationed in the Antilles, with groups in Guadeloupe, Martinique and Réunion, and another legion in the Pacific, with groups in New Caledonia and French Polynesia. There is also a company in St. Pierre and Miquelon and a School of Overseas Gendarmeries at Nouméa in New Caledonia.

The Gendarmerie Maritime is responsible for the security of harbors and installations. The Gendarmerie de l'Air, formed in 1943 and annexed to the Gendarmerie Nationale in 1947, is in charge of security for air force bases. Civilian airfields are guarded by the Gendarmerie des Transports Aeriens. The Gendarmerie de l'Armament protects arms depots and factories. The Gendarmerie's Helicopter Section provides communications service and rescue assistance during forest fires and other emergencies.

Two security departments within the Gendarmerie are the Special Security Group and the antiterrorist Intervention Group.

The Gendarmerie winter uniform is medium blue trousers with a wide blue stripe on the seams, worn with blue or white shirt and a black tie. The summer uniform is khaki terylene trousers and tunic, white or khaki shirt and black tie. In all seasons, a Sam Browne belt is worn along with a blue képi.

Unlike countries where all regular on-duty uniformed police officers have the same powers with regard to criminal offenses, police powers differ according to grades in France. Only those who are designated *officiers de police judiciares,* or OPJ, have the right to keep a suspect under surveillance or custody, called *garde-à-vue.* Further, those who are entitled to sign reports called *proces-verbaux* must be gendarmes, except those classified as officers of the judicial police, or inspectors of the National Police.

When a crime is discovered, the police must immediately notify the public prosecutor of the area. In most cases this is done by writing, but a serious case would be reported over the telephone. Once the prosecutor has been informed, the matter comes under his control, and thereafter the police act under his direction.

Police activity in criminal cases falls under three categories:

The first of these is the preliminary inquiry, a term that covers the whole complex of activities involving the establishment of the fact that a crime has been committed, its essential elements, the identification of the victim, witnesses, perpetrators and accomplices. During this phase the police may act on their own initiative or as directed by the public prosecutor. The judicial police may keep a suspect under *garde-à-vue.*

The second type of police activity involves flagrant offenses, where a person is caught in the commission of a crime. Here the police may arrest the perpetrator and bring him or her at once before the nearest officer of the judicial police. No warrant is required in such circumstances.

The third category of police activity in criminal cases is *en délégation judiciare* (in judicial delegation), where the police act as delegates of the public prosecutor or the *juge d'instruction,* who may give them warrants to search and seize, to arrest, or to summon witnesses, or they may issue a *commission rogatoire* (rogatory commission), empowering the police to make general or particular inquiries in a case.

Recruitment, Education & Training

As with other civil service appointments, entry into police service is by means of competitive examinations. Candidates must be French nationals or naturalized citizens of five years' standing. They must have fulfilled their obligations to national service.

Exacting physical standards and a good character are also essential. Their previous background will be scrutinized by the appropriate prefect.

Recruitment to any of the five corps of police personnel is based on a prescribed set of qualifications and requirements. The *enquêteurs* (investigators), the lowest grade, need no educational certificates but need to take a competitive examination at the high-school level and be between 19 and 28 years of age. The second grade, *gardien de la paix,* is roughly equivalent to a constable. They need no academic certification but must take a competitive examination at the upper secondary education level. There is a minimum height requirement of one meter, 68 centimeters. The age limits are from 19 to 28 years. The third grade is *officier de paix,* who corresponds to a police lieutenant. There are two ways to reach this rank: by lateral entry from outside for 50% of vacancies, and by promotion from the uniformed ranks for the other 50%. The external candidates must be between 19 and 28 years; at least one meter, 68 centimeters tall; and possess at least the equivalent of an associate degree. The fourth grade is the *inspecteur,* a plain-clothes officer. Here again external candidates are allotted 50% of the vacancies. Such candidates must have at least an associate degree and be between 21 and 30 years of age. The highest grade is that of *commissaire,* the basic command rank. Here, external candidates, who are allotted 45% of the vacancies, must hold a university degree and be between 21 and 30 years of age. The majority of in-service appointments to this category are set apart as rewards for meritorious service within the police.

Police training has a long history in France. The Prefecture of Police School, the École Pratique des Gardiens de la Paix, was founded in 1883, and the École Technique de Police in 1895. The Sûreté Nationale had no professional training institution until the founding of the École Nationale Supérieure de Police in 1941. The higher training of the Police Nationale is now concentrated there.

Because the recruitment system presorts entrants into the police service by grades, training is also based on grades. The *enquêteurs* receive the least training. A 164-hour program is designed to give them some acquaintance with penal law and procedure, with investigation and self-defense, and also give them some typewriting skills. The *gardiens de la paix* receive six months' basic training, one month of which is spent on attachment to police formations. Three centers—at Reims, Chatelguyon and Vannes—train those who will be assigned to urban police in the provinces. A center at Vincennes prepares those who will serve in the Prefecture of Police at Paris. Recruits for the Republican Security Companies are trained at the CRS school at Sens.

Gardiens de la paix are taught five groups of subjects: general, civic and ethical, specific police duties, technical, and physical education.

Officers de paix have a two-year program divided into 12 months at the École Supérieure des Officers at Nice, followed by a year of practical training.

The *inspecteurs'* program lasts 16 months, including one month's pretraining in an urban police formation followed by seven months at the École-Nationale de Police at Cannes-Écluse, after which there are three months of initiation into practical plainclothes and uniform police work in a commissariat, a city detective department and a regional crime service. Thereupon the candidates return to Cannes-Écluse for another two months of examinations, on completion of which they receive their first appointment.

The most arduous and complex training is reserved for the *commissaires* at the celebrated École Nationale Supérieure de Police at St.-Cyr-au-Mont-d'Or in Lyons. The academic program in this school covers the whole spectrum of police work. The small, permanent faculty of the school, all senior police officers, is supplemented by visiting specialists drawn from the Police Nationale. The program, which lasts for two years, is divided between academic study and examination on the one hand and practical internship on the other. The academic program focuses on human sciences, general police and criminal police, interspersed with oral and written examinations and the writing of theses. The internship is initially with an urban police formation (for three weeks at the level of a *gardien de la paix,* one week at the level of an *inspecteur* and three weeks at the level of a *commissaire;* then one week, with General Intelligence and one week with General Investigation, both at the *inspecteur* level). During the second year practical training includes two and a half months with an urban police formation, a month of criminal investigation, a month of general intelligence, a week with the Air and Frontier Police, a week with the CRS, two weeks with a private enterprise studying labor conflicts, and a week at a police training center. They then have the choice of spending a further week at a prefecture, a prosecution department, a mayor's office, a Gendarmerie formation or a prison.

Advancement within grades is based upon satisfactory performance and into higher grades on completion of special training and rank in competitive examinations.

Grades   Badges

Management Personnel
Directeur
Sous-directeur
Inspecteur-général
Controleur-général
Commissaire divisionnaire
Commissaire principal
Commissaire de police

Plainclothes Personnel
Inspecteur divisionnaire
Inspecteur principal
Inspecteur
Enquêteur

Uniformed police
Commandant de groupement

Commandant	Four silver bands
Officier de paix principal	Three silver bands
Officier de paix	Two silver bands
Brigadier-chef	One narrow gold band with red stripe
Brigadier	One narrow gold band
Sous-brigadier	One silver bar
Gardien	None

All badges are worn on the epaulettes and the headgear.

For uniformed personnel the retirement age is 55 and for higher grades between 55 and 60. A pension is granted on the basis of years in service and may range up to 80% of salary for those with 40 years' service.

Police officers have a 46½-hour workweek except in Paris, where it is 41¼ hours. Police officers working at night have a reduced workweek of 37 hours. Overtime is compensated with equal time in vacation. Vacation is 31 days per year, with additional days if the vacation is taken before May 1 and after October 31. In addition to basic pay, police officers receive local allowances, child allowances, a clothing allowance, and additional allowances for night duty and special services. Policemen also receive free public transportation, full medical coverage and disability benefits. Most policemen belong to the Fédération Autonome des Syndicats de Police, France's major police trade union.

The recruitment and training of the Gendarmerie differ from those of the National Police in being more rigorous and exacting. Applicants must have fulfilled their obligations to national service, be between 18 and 35 years of age, in good health, of impeccable character, and at least one meter, 68 centimeters tall. No academic certificate is required. Basic training is given at the Preparatory School of Gendarmerie at

Chaumont followed by additional courses at one of the Gendarmerie Training Centers, at Fontainebleau, Maison-Alfort or St.-Asear. Postgraduate courses are provided at the Preparatory High School of Gendarmerie at Montluçon. Auxiliary gendarmes are enrolled in the Training Center for Auxiliary Gendarmes at Auxerre and the Training Group for Auxiliary Gendarmes at Bergeac. Gendarmerie officer candidates usually are recruited from the Army Officer Corps (either active or reserve), but before being given commands, they are trained at the Gendarmerie Officers School at Melun. The extended training during this four-year probation is one of the most demanding in the world and accounts for the proficiency and professional conduct of the gendarme in the field. Those who opt for specialized services, such as the Republican Guard, receive further training.

The Penal System

The French criminal justice system is governed by the Penal Code of 1810 and the Code of Criminal Procedure, which was completely revised in 1959 from its earlier 1808 version. The Penal Code is divided into four books or parts: Book I identifies punishments for various offenses; Book II deals with criminal liability or responsibility; Book III defines various offenses and their sanctions; Book IV deals with violations.

The French divide criminal offenses into three classes: felonies, misdemeanors and violations. This classification determines the gravity of the offense, the nature of the sanctions and the type of court that hears the case. There is no cumulative sentencing for multiple offenses, and judges are required to impose the most severe of all available punishments. Also, offenses may not be excused or mitigated unless as provided for in law.

Under the Code of Criminal Procedure, there are only two instances where persons can be deprived of their liberty prior to the determination of guilt. One is temporary detention for 24 hours (renewable for another 24 hours by a procurator or examining magistrate) by the judicial police during preliminary investigation. The other is through the execution of a warrant by an examining magistrate. There are four kinds of such warrants, for: (1) appearance, (2) attachment, (3) confinement and (4) arrest. The powers of interrogation, search and seizure are also governed by the Code of Criminal Procedure. This code makes a distinction between two kinds of interrogation: the hearing of witnesses, and confrontation or questioning of the accused. Search and seizure can occur with or without a warrant. Legal searches and seizures without warrants involve offenses that are called flagrant offenses.

Detaining a person before trial is considered an exceptional measure, and an accused may not be detained for more than five days after his or her first appearance before an examining magistrate when the maximum penalty provided by law for the offense is less than two years' imprisonment. In other instances detention may not exceed four months. Bail may be granted before or during the course of a trial, and the manner in which it is granted is explained in Articles 145 through 148 of the code.

The French correctional system underwent a major transformation at the end of World War II, when a progressive regime was introduced. The regime was composed of five phases: The first lasted nine months, during which the inmate was kept in maximum-security isolation. The inmate was interviewed and evaluated by a correctional counselor at this stage. At the end of the period, the inmate was either advanced to the second phase or retained for further observation. Those who advanced to the second phase ate and slept in isolation but were given work assignments. This phase continued for six to 12 months. During the third phase, which lasted approximately one year, the inmate lived in a separate cell during sleeping hours but was allowed to participate in group activities. Phase four allowed the inmate to work in the private sector while living in the prison. The fifth phase was a conditional release in which the inmate worked without supervision and was placed on parole for one to three years, at the end of which he or she would be discharged.

The next significant innovation was the passage of the Code of Criminal Procedure in 1958, which introduced the position of a sentencing judge. Like the examining magistrate, this official is selected from among the ranks of the magistracy for a three-year term. Article 722 of the code explains the sentencing judge's duties:

> He shall determine for each convict the principal manner of his penitentiary treatment, according especially the placement on the outside, semi-liberty and the permission to leave; he may take the initiative to have a recommendation for parole established; in the establishments where the regime is progressive . . . he shall rule on his admission to the different phases of that regime.

The most severe punishment in French law is life imprisonment. The death penalty was abolished in 1981, but until then capital punishment was carried out by decapitation.

The correctional system is administered by a highly centralized national bureaucracy, at the top of which is the Penitentiary Administration within the Ministry of Justice. The prison service is divided into nine regions, each under a director. Prison personnel are trained at the National School for Penitentiary Administration.

There are three types of penitentiary facilities: jails, special institutions and prisons. Jails are found throughout the country close to the courts of major jurisdiction. They are used to detain both the accused before trial and for convicted offenders whose term does not exceed one year. Most French jails are small. Originally built with single cells to accommodate 40 to 50 inmates, they now hold three to four times that number. Few have proper rehabilitation or work release programs.

Special institutions are designed for offenders suffering from physical handicaps or behavioral disorders that fall short of insanity. They include health centers and psychiatric hospitals. There are also special centers, called penal guardianships, for chronic recidivists.

Prisons are classified into high-security facilities and detention centers. Whether a prisoner should be assigned to the former or the latter is determined by the classification unit in Fresnes, which conducts diagnostic testing for this purpose. Detention centers offer greater degrees of freedom and individual responsibility and have both closed and open types of facilities.

Alterations in inmate sentences and changes in prison regimes are determined by the sentencing judge. There are five principal means at the judge's disposal.

The first is the grant of parole or conditional liberty at the judge's discretion for prisoners serving a term of three years or less and with the approval of the minister of justice for inmates serving longer terms. Parole usually is granted to first-time offenders after half the term is served, to recidivists after two-thirds of the term, to chronic offenders after three-fourths of the term and to lifers after 15 years.

The second means is called sentence reduction. Each year the prisoner's record is reviewed by the sentencing judge and the sentence reduced for good behavior. The reductions average about seven days per month for sentences of less than one year and three months per year for longer sentences.

The third means is work release, a system that allows the inmate to work outside the prison during daytime and spend the rest of his or her time in a local jail or halfway house. The costs of maintaining the inmate in the institution are then deducted from the inmate's wages. Work release usually is granted to people during the last six to 12 months of their sentences.

The fourth means is leave of absence from prison for short periods of up to 10 days per year for those inmates who have served at least one-third of their sentences. The fifth and last means is temporary suspension, which has been used infrequently and has been available only since 1975. It permits the judge to suspend the sentence of a person convicted of a misdemeanor for up to three months in cases of

CRIME STATISTICS (1984)

		Number Reported	Attempts %	Cases Solved %	Crime per 100,000	Offenders	Females %	Juveniles %	Strangers %
1.	Murder	2,540		83.50	4.63	2,983	14.85	5.53	22.19
2.	Sex offenses, including rape	17,624		77.43	32.14	11,518	6.45	10.38	17.09
3.	Rape	2,859		80.83	5.21	2,600	3.65	15.12	26.19
4.	Serious assault	38,389		74.77	70.01	32,754	8.95	8.33	19.89
5.	All theft	2,254,494		15.46	4,111.64	295,766	14.84	26.54	17.06
6.	Aggravated theft	501,910		15.65	915.36	76,180	7.84	27.66	16.82
7.	Robbery and violent theft	57,907		21.57	105.61	15,018	10.75	23.51	22.63
8.	Breaking and entering	444,003		14.88	809.75	61,162	7.13	28.69	15.40
9.	Auto theft	265,030		11.42	483.35	27,517	4.11	26.56	13.60
10.	Other thefts	1,487,554		16.12	2,712.35	192,069	19.15	26.09	17.64
11.	Fraud	794,547		88.65	1,449.06	328,054	28.26	0.93	7.09
12.	Counterfeiting	15,550		100.00	28.36	2,489	22.42	3.54	13.10
13.	Drug offenses	28,794		100.00	52.51	28,794	12.28	9.12	21.90
14.	Total offenses	3,681,453		40.40	6,714.06	921,983	18.78	11.39	15.21

Criteria of juveniles: aged from 13 to 18 years.
Note: Information for some categories is not available.

serious personal emergency. An alternative is serving part of the sentence on weekends.

The sentencing judge is the president of two groups that assist the judge in his or her duties: the Commission for the Application of Sentences, in each prison, and the Committee for Assistance to Liberated Convicts, set up in each court of major jurisdiction.

The French have been slow in developing noninstitutional sanctions. The use of suspended sentences was reduced by the Security and Freedom Act of 1980 in cases of violent crimes and recidivists.

In 1945 the Ministry of Justice, when taking over administration of the correctional system from the Ministry of the Interior, embarked upon a reform of the juvenile justice system that is continuing to this day. The linchpin of this system is the judge for juveniles. In determining the age of criminal responsibility, the French take into consideration the age of the offender and the type of the offense. Full penal sanctions can be imposed on juveniles between 15 and 18 if the judge deems it appropriate and on juveniles between 13 and 14 if the offense is serious. But the Penal Code requires that in these cases the sentence be shortened by at least half. Children under age 11 are protected from any type of criminal proceedings.

There are two types of juvenile courts: the Court of Assize for Juveniles, composed of a judge from the district Court of Appeals, two judges for juveniles, and nine jurors. The second is the Juvenile Court, composed of one magistrate for juveniles and two law assessors. Unlike the Court of Assize for Juveniles, which handles felonies committed by those between 15 and 18, the Juvenile Court has both civil and criminal jurisdiction and often handles juveniles who are victims rather than offenders or those who simply are in need of help. The procedures used in the Court of Assize for Juveniles are the same as those for adults, but those used in the Juvenile Court are less formal because the task of the latter court is more protective than punitive.

There are two detention centers designed to house juveniles sentenced to incarceration, one a closed facility and the other open. That at Oermingen has a progressive three-phase regimen. Other institutions serving juvenile offenders are observation centers, resident training centers and after-care centers. Observation centers are open facilities, resident training centers closed ones, and after-care centers transitional ones. In more recent years educational action centers have been established as halfway houses. Educational guidance and open treatment centers provide training and counseling during the day but offer no residential facilities.

Germany (East)

BASIC FACT SHEET

Official Name: German Democratic Republic
Area: 108,178 sq km
Population: 16, 610, 265 (1987)
Capital: East Berlin
Nature of Government: Communist dictatorship
Language: German
Currency: Ostmark
GNP: $174.7 billion (1985)
Territorial Divisions: 14 districts, 218 counties
Population per Police Officer: 1,000
Police Expenditures per 1,000: N.A.

History & Background

The Soviet occupation authorities formed a City Police in East Berlin in 1945, and it was slowly enlarged to cover the whole Soviet Zone during the next four years. Under the Yalta and Potsdam agreements, police forces were to be local and decentralized in both Germanys. However, with the formation of the East German state on October 7, 1949, the supervision of the police forces—organized on the basis of the five existing states of the Soviet Zone—was transferred to the newly organized interior administration headed by Erich Reschke. The term Volkspolizei (People's Police) came to be applied to the new force.

Included within the structure of the People's Police was a special group called Barracked People's Police (Kaserneirte Volkspolizei, KVP). As the name indicates, KVP lived in barracks in rural areas and were organized and equipped as light infantry. The cadre comprised mostly former officers of Hitler's Wehrmacht converted to communism while prisoners in Soviet camps. They wore Soviet uniforms and carried Soviet weapons. At its peak, the KVP numbered over 45,000 men, and from among its ranks the administration formed the Frontier Police and the Railway Police (later the Transport Police). In 1949 the first police training school was established, headed by such venerable Communists as General Wilhelm Zaisser and General Heinz Hoffmann. Until 1956 the KVP functioned as the nation's armed forces (in the absence of a standing army). When the Ministry of National Defense was formed in that year, the KVP lost many of its heavily armed units to the People's Army.

Structure & Organization

The Volkspolizei is a centrally administered force headed by the deputy minister of the interior. The principal branches of the force include: Criminal Police, Traffic Police, Water Police, Factory Guards, Fire Department, Railway Police and Customs Police. The larger municipalities are covered by City Police forces and rural areas by the Special Police, staffed by civilian volunteers. Current personnel strength of the Volkspolizei si about 30,000.

In East Berlin there is a separate Police Presidium, with People's Police inspectorates in each of the city's eight administrative sectors.

The police uniform is gray-green for the general police, dark blue for Transport Police and firemen, and white for the Traffic Police.

The Ministry of Internal Affairs also controls the Border Security Force, who are trained and armed as a military unit for patrolling border areas, including the Berlin Wall. Intelligence and counterintelligence work is undertaken by the State Security Service (Staatssicherheitsdienst, SSD), and espionage work by the Chief Administration for Reconnaissance (Hauptverwaltung fur Aufklarung, HVA). The Ministry of State Security has a dedicated riot control regiment named after Felix Dzierzynski, the founder of the Soviet Cheka.

Recruitment, Education & Training

No information is available on East German Police recruitment, education and training.

The Penal System

The prevailing Penal Code is that of 1968, which replaced the German Code of 1871. It was amended in 1974 and again in 1977.

The code is divided into nine sections: crimes against the sovereignty of the regime and against peace, humanity and human rights; crimes against the regime; offenses against the individual; offenses against youth and the family; offenses against socialist property; offenses against personal and private property; offenses against general security; offenses against public order; and military offenses. As in other socialist systems, most of the code's sections—in this case, five of nine—deal with offenses against the regime and its interests.

Punishments usually consist of fines or imprisonment but involve some efforts at rehabilitation, especially in the case of juvenile offenders. Execution is not mandatory for any crime in times of peace but can be authorized for eleven crimes against the state and for murder. Execution, if adjudged, is carried out by a firing squad.

There are two distinct penal systems. One, operated by the Ministry of the Interior, is for criminal offenders convicted and sentenced by the court system. Statistics on crime and prison populations are never published.

The second system comprises penal institutions operated by the Ministry of State Security, which operates outside the jurisdiction of the courts. Political prisoners are generally subjected to harsh sentences of incarceration without any judicial remedy.

The major acts governing the criminal justice system are:

The Penal Code of 1968, as amended in 1974 and 1977

The Code of Criminal Procedure of 1968, as amended in 1974 and 1977

The Court Constitution Act of 1974

The Law on the Social Courts of 1968

The Law on the Procurator's Office of 1977

The Law on the Execution of Penalties Involving Imprisonment of 1977

The Law on the Reintegration of Citizens Released from Prison into Social Life of 1977

Since the end of World War II, crime has decreased in East Germany. There are few professional criminals, underworld gangs or rackets, counterfeiters, or crimes involving drugs or narcotics. Armed robberies are virtually unknown. Violent crimes occur rarely. The East German crime rate is seven times lower than that of West Germany per 100,000 inhabitants.

The basic principle of East German criminal law is "No punishment and no crime without law." Retroactivity and analogous application of penal laws to the disadvantage of the offender are not admissible. The only ground for criminal liability is a punishable act that either endangers society (verbrechn) or is incompatible with social conduct (vergehen).

The adoption of the 1968 Criminal Code resulted in the decriminalization of many economic offenses, sex offenses, acts of negligence, and violations or infringements of civil or labor law. Prosecution is also limited by the creation of offenses that are prosecuted only at the request of the injured party. On the other hand, several new crimes have been added to the code, such as hijacking and environmental pollution. Criminal liability is limited to persons of responsible age over 14 years and of sound mind. In the case of recidivists, legislation provides for more serious punishments, but there are no other special provisions for distinct categories of offenders.

Prison sentences are imposed in only about one-third of all punishable acts. The minimum sentence is six months and the maximum two years in minor cases and 15 years in serious cases. In the most serious cases, life imprisonment may be imposed. Minor offenses such as hooliganism are subject to imprisonment for up to six weeks. Additional punishments, such as fines, confiscation of objects, withdrawal of licenses or restriction of residence may be imposed. The court may order special therapeutic treatment for alcoholics and sex offenders. The death penalty is sanctioned only for the most serious crimes, particularly against the state and in aggravated cases of murder. In most cases death sentences are commuted to life imprisonment.

The penal system falls within the jurisdiction of several agencies: The courts are responsible for punishments not involving imprisonment; the Ministry of the Interior is responsible for prisons and jails as well as death sentences (by shooting); and other state agencies and District Councils are responsible for additional punishments. Probation is the most common noncustodial sanction.

Prison sentences are administered by the Department for the Execution of Sentences under the 1977 Law on the Execution of Sentences. All adult prisoners are required to work and are paid 18% of normal wages. A prisoner is expected to pay for his or her food and board out of earnings; what is left is partly placed in a reserve fund and partly paid as pocket money.

Prison privileges, such as visits and correspondence, are determined by the prisoner's conduct. Parole may be granted by an order of the court, again on the basis of an assessment by the prison authorities. The 1977 Law on Reintegration provides guidelines for the restoration of prisoners to useful social life.

Germany (West)

BASIC FACT SHEET

Official Name: Federal Republic of Germany
Area: 248,577 sq km
Population: 60,989,419 (1987)
Capital: Bonn
Nature of Government: Parliamentary democracy
Language: German
Currency: Deutsche mark
GNP: $667,970 billion
Territorial Divisions: 10 Länder
Population per Police Officer: N.A.
Police Expenditures per 1,000: N.A.

History & Background

The earliest police system in Germany was in Mainz, where a reference to a polizey-president appears in 1732. The title was changed to Polizei-Amt-Mainz in 1879. In 1889–90 a Kriminal-polizei branch was established. Meanwhile, police forces were established in other cities and states: in Schleswig-Holstein in 1867 and in Berlin in 1848. Following World War I, Germany was permitted a National Security Force of 150,000 men. It was disbanded in 1920 and reformed into local forces known as Schutzpolizei (Public Safety Police).

When the Nazis came into power they once again centralized the control of the police and broadened their powers. The police became a tool of the ruling party under the control of the minister of the interior. The regular police agencies included the town and city forces, motorized gendarmerie in rural areas, waterways, fire, air-raid warning and auxiliary police forces, and the administrative police bureaus that enforced welfare, health and building codes and kept police records. Much more powerful than the regular police were the security police (Sicherheitspolizei, SIPO), which incorporated the Criminal Investigation Police and the Border Police as well as the newly created Secret State Police (Geheime Staatspolizei, Gestapo).

These institutions disappeared with the end of World War II. After the establishment of the Federal Republic and until 1955 the Allied authorities permitted police forces under *Land* control. Their mission was limited to maintaining public order and safety and keeping criminal records. Some of these restrictions were lifted within two years as West Germany was perceived to be an ally rather than an enemy in the growing Cold War. The first central police agency, the Federal Border Force (Bundesgrenzschutz, BGS), was created to handle special functions that overlapped *Land* jurisdictions. A second force, the Standby Police (Bereitschaftspolizei), was designed as a paramilitary backup force to assist *Land* agencies in emergencies. Although under *Land* control, it could be moved from one *Land* to another under federal direction.

Structure & Organization

Of the nearly 180,000 police officers in the Federal Republic of Germany, about 150,000 belong to the police forces of the ten federal states and West Berlin. Of slightly under 30,000 federal police officers, 26,000 are with the Federal Border Police and about 2,500 work for the Federal Office of Criminal Investigation. These figures clearly show that the police in the Federal Republic of Germany are strictly a state matter, as laid down in the constitution, or "basic law," of 1949. Federal jurisdiction in police matters is defined by law.

Duties and powers of state police forces are determined by police codes that are for the most part uniform as far as substantive law is concerned, with the effect that anyone involved with the police would hardly notice any difference from one federal state to the other. Still greater uniformity is being sought after and is at present under discussion. The state police forces, for instance, all had different uniforms until 1976, when a standard uniform was introduced for the whole country, which is mandatory for all police officers since 1980. The only difference in them is the state emblem on the sleeve. While substantive law governing police activities is largely uniform, there are considerable differences in procedural law. The main differences are to be found in the distinction between executive and administrative police functions, and in organizational structures, especially concerning higher-level positions. Organizational structure at the regional level is, however, uniform. At the head of every state police force stands the politically responsible interior minister for that state, whose job also includes a large number of other functions. Below the ministerial level there are intermediary and local authorities who are organized and named according to region.

The executive police include the Municipal Police, the Criminal Police, the Mobile Police, the Coast and River Police and, in Bavaria, the Border Police.

The administrative police are referred to as police in only a few federal states. Otherwise the duties of the administrative police are assumed by administrative authorities whose activities are limited more to the administrative side of danger prevention. This is best shown by means of an example: When a demolition order has been issued for a dilapidated house, it is a matter for the Building Authority. Should, however, a house be on the verge of collapsing as a result of a storm or some other cause, any executive police officer aware of the situation is required to intervene and, if necessary, have the house torn down.

Duties, powers, jurisdiction and organizational structures are defined by the state police codes. Sufficient cause for police intervention is defined in all states as the presence of a danger for individuals or the general public that threatens public security and order. This nearly uniform general clause may possibly be replaced by an enumeration of functions in the course of future harmonization of police law. Beyond this general clause the extent and limits of police duties are defined by abstract, generally binding, equally applicable and published legal norms. Police officers are equally bound by civil service regulations and federal police regulations. Exact knowledge of the Code of Criminal Procedure is part of the training of every police officer since, according to this same code, the police are required to investigate and prosecute all criminal offenses. In this area they are bound by the authority of the director of public prosecutions, who is responsible for the criminal proceedings.

In view of the area to be covered in the Federal Republic of Germany (60.7 million inhabitants and 95,728 square miles [248,000 square kilometers]), close cooperation among the various state police forces is called for. This is realized through regular meetings of the interior ministers of the states (in the city-states of Hamburg, Bremen and West Berlin they are called interior senators), which are also attended by the federal minister of the interior. At these conferences all principal questions concerning the duties, organization and equipment of police are dealt with.

The Municipal Police
Of the various branches of service—Municipal Police, Criminal Police, Standby Police, and Coast and River Police—the Municipal Police has by far the largest staff, is on duty and thus visible to the citizenry 24 hours a day and has the broadest range of duties. On patrol duty, mostly in cars, they keep their respective district under surveillance. Whether for a traffic accident or a murder, the uniformed Municipal Police are, as a rule, the first to arrive at the scene of the incident; are, initially at least, responsible for everything; and should the matter fall outside their jurisdiction, they take initial measures until Criminal Police specialists take over further investigation.

With traffic increasing steadily and a present level of 22 million registered motor vehicles for 60.7 million inhabitants, the average citizen in the federal republic is most likely to be confronted with the police in a road traffic situation. Aside from a very small percentage of incorrigible reckless drivers, German motorists show understanding for the refereeing function of the police in seeing that the rules are abided by in everyday traffic on German roads and motorways. All too often it is a deadly serious matter. The annual mortality rate on the roads is about 15,000, the population of a small German town.

Although every police patrol car on duty keeps an eye on motorist compliance with traffic regulations and intervenes in case of violations, every local police force has a section devoted exclusively to monitoring motor traffic. In North Rhine-Westphalia, for instance, it is called the Traffic Service. They have radar-equipped cars that accurately register speeding violations. The radar cars automatically snap photos that are accepted as evidence in court. As in the case of other traffic violations, the police (although only if the motorist concerned agrees to it) can collect a "warning fine" of at most DM 40 on the spot. In the case of more serious violations the person concerned is charged, resulting either in a fine of up to DM 1,000 set by the responsible administrative authority, or a higher fine determined by a court.

Police work in enforcing compliance with traffic regulations does not consist only of repressive measures. It also involves an increasing amount of traffic safety training and public information, especially as concerns children and, not to be forgotten, the elderly. Many local police forces have a "traffic puppet theater," which puts on shows in kindergartens and first-year classes at primary schools. The puppeteers are police officers who often write their own sketches, designing them for small children with considerable pedagogical skill. In specially equipped youth traffic safety schools, often municipally financed, policemen teach school children of all ages how to handle bicycles or small motorbikes correctly in traffic. Older citizens also receive special attention in the effort to provide more information on traffic safety. In homes for the aged, at afternoon gatherings of senior citizens and on special bus tours (often in cooperation with the Highway Patrol, automobile clubs, municipalities and churches), police officers instruct old people on how to react correctly in traffic situations.

Besides the patrol car service directed from central command posts the police have at their disposal a number of special services equipped with horses, dogs, special vehicles and helicopters.

The Criminal Police

The Criminal Police, popularly termed "Cripo," are responsible for determining guilt in criminal offenses and reporting their findings immediately to the responsible director of public prosecutions. According to the Code of Criminal Procedure, Cripo plainclothesmen have the right of search and seizure. Every local police authority includes an office of the Criminal Police. How big and well equipped it is depends on the size of the local force. The Criminal Police manifest slight local and regional differences in organization. The local offices, called "commissariates," usually are structured according to types of offense, are sometimes regionally divided and are responsible for all criminal offenses in their district.

The main aim of criminal police work is to solve serious crimes as quickly as possible. The *Police Criminal Statistics* put out annually by the Federal Office of Criminal Investigation show that the Criminal Police are experiencing success in countering serious crimes, but the success rate is rather low with respect to thefts, where petty offenses make up a large percentage of the total.

The high percentage of successfully resolved serious and very serious crimes is due in large part to the technical means at the disposal of the Criminal Police. Every local Cripo station can, if necessary, fall back on highly qualified specialists from the State Office of Criminal Investigation. Also, there are Centers of Criminal Investigation, usually two or three to a region, which investigate certain serious offenses in the neighboring districts. They have well-equipped crime laboratories and specialists from many areas, so they are able to evaluate a large part of the evidence found themselves. Any evidence they are not able to analyze is sent to the respective State Office of Criminal Investigation. This could be anything from an entire car, wrapped in a plastic covering and shipped by rail, to a cigarette butt from which, for instance, the dried saliva residue can be taken to determine the smoker's blood type.

Backing up the local Criminal Police in almost all of the federal states are several Mobile Special Forces (MSF) units that can be employed anywhere in the country. These highly trained officials are used especially in pursuit of dangerous criminals and criminal gangs, in cases of bank robberies or kidnappings. The MSF are equipped with very fast unmarked cars having, among other things, a hidden police radio. Other special equipment includes movie and still cameras and an infrared night viewer for observation purposes.

The Criminal Police forces include women in all West German states. Their police work is variously organized. In one instance they have their own separate section, the Women's Criminal Police (WCP), and in another they are fully integrated in almost all areas of Cripo activity. Their main function is the same everywhere: combating juvenile delinquency and crimes against children such as sexual offenses or maltreatment.

Technical progress in crime-fighting is most evident in the expansion of the Criminal Police's communications and information system. Thus, for instance, teletyped messages are handled by computer in the countrywide teletype net. A computer "reads" the addresses at the top of the teletyped message and makes the necessary connections automatically. If an urgent message is typed into the computer and the required line is being used to transmit another message, it will register which of the two messages is more important and, if necessary, interrupt the transmission of the less important text.

Begun in the early 1970s, the net of police computers has grown increasingly dense. Every local Criminal Police headquarters has today at least one data terminal connecting it with the computers at the State Office of Criminal Investigation or the Federal Office of Criminal Investigation. Television receivers and transmitters are routine at all of the larger Cripo headquarters. They are used to transmit photographs, fingerprints, visible evidence from the scenes of crimes, samples of handwriting or documents in minutes via the telephone net to any given police headquarters in the federal republic. The system is used primarily to transmit information requested from the federal Office of Criminal Investigation and can, if required, transmit information to other European countries.

The State Office of Criminal Investigation

Every state has a central crime-fighting headquarters: the State Office of Criminal Investigation (SOCI). The duties of this Cripo central headquarters, with certain differences in the various federal states, are essentially the following: gathering all significant information and documents relevant to the prevention and investigation of criminal offenses; analysis of the information and constant notification of all police headquarters of the current crime situation; carrying out of complicated technical analyses in the crime laboratory and the writing of expert reports; investigating activity concerning serious offenses of more than regional import at the request of the respective interior minister or the competent justice authorities—primarily in cases of terrorism, recurrent larceny offenses, counterfeiting, narcotics or offenses involving government security.

All of the cases the State Office of Criminal Investigation works on have one thing in common: They almost always require persevering and geographically extended investigation, often going outside the territorial limits of the federal republic into other European countries or even beyond. Thus, for instance, the international operations of car racketeers are often traced to North Africa or the Near East with the cooperation of the Federal Office of Criminal Investigation.

Every State Office of Criminal Investigation represents a nodal point in the countrywide police data interchange. Every local Criminal Police headquarters can "tap" the computer belonging to the Federal Office of Criminal Investigation and find out within seconds whether any other police headquarters in the federal republic has a criminal file on a given person. As soon as a code is typed into a terminal at local Cripo headquarters, information from the central computer at the Federal Office of Criminal Investigation in Wiesbaden is flashed onto the terminal screen as to whether a court in the federal republic has issued a warrant for the arrest of the person in question. Other information relevant to police work, to be discussed later, also is stored in the FOCI computer and is accessible to the Municipal Police through the respective SOCI.

The crime laboratories at the State Offices of Criminal Investigation provide the local Cripo units with important aid. They employ the most modern scientific and technical methods to be able to analyze even the slightest traces of substances that might prove useful as evidence. Among other things, a State Office of Criminal Investigation carries out laboratory tests on firearms, spent cartridges and bullets for expert analysis and identification.

The Federal Office of Criminal Investigation

The Federal Office of Criminal Investigation (FOCI) has a considerably broader range of duties on the federal and international levels. The legal foundation was laid for this organization in 1951 with the Law Concerning the Establishment of a Federal Office of Criminal Police (Federal Office of Criminal Investi-

gation). As a subordinate higher federal authority, it is directly responsible to the Federal Ministry of the Interior.

This law at the same time imposes upon the states the obligation to provide cooperation. On the basis of several amendments to this law, the FOCI now has the following duties: It is both central headquarters for law enforcement in the Federal Republic of Germany and central headquarters for electronic data interchange between federal and state police. It maintains intelligence, identification and technical analysis services, issues police reports and statistics, carries out research and development in law-enforcement methods, backs up state police in crime prevention efforts, and holds advanced training courses in specialized areas of criminology.

The FOCI has specific terms of reference concerning internationally organized trade in drugs, arms and ammunition or the production or circulation of counterfeit money. The FOCI also is responsible for the investigation of politically motivated offenses insofar as they are directed against the constitutional bodies of the federal government, official guests of the government or diplomatic missions. The FOCI also provides personal security for members of constitutional bodies and especially endangered official visitors. In 1975 a new section was created to fight terrorism. At the request of the states, by order of the federal minister of the interior or at the request of the supreme federal prosecutor or the examining magistrates at the Federal High Court, and if the supreme federal prosecutor directs the investigations, the FOCI can be granted additional investigative powers in special cases. Finally, the FOCI also is the location of the national central headquarters of Interpol.

The Federal Border Police

The Federal Border Police (FBP) were constituted on the basis of a law of 1951. They are mainly barracks-quartered, fully motorized federal police responsible for guarding the frontiers of the federal republic, particularly those with East Germany and Czechoslovakia.

FBP officials from the Border Police Duty Guard carry out police checks at the border crossing points in close cooperation with officials from customs, the Bavarian Border Police and the Coast and River Police.

The Standby Police

The main focus of local police headquarters in every state is on everyday police functions. If a local police headquarters requires the support of entire police units for mass demonstrations, official visits or natural disasters, it can call upon the responsible state minister of the interior to send in the Standby Police,

ORGANIZATION CHART OF THE WEST GERMAN POLICE FORCE

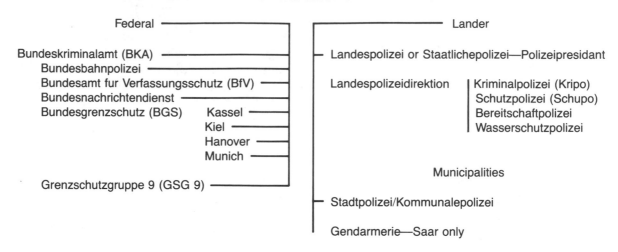

barracks-quartered and fully motorized police units in which young policemen usually receive their basic training. An administrative agreement of 1950 between the federal government and the states provided the legal basis for establishing the Standby Police. Personnel, training and accommodation expenses are paid for by the states, while the federal government finances motor vehicles, telecommunications, field hospital and other types of equipment, arms, and ammunition. This guarantees uniform equipment of Standby Police forces in the different states. This is necessary since there are occasions on which one state requires additional police forces from neighboring states. This was the case with various mass demonstrations in 1977 against the building of nuclear power plants. Another example of this kind of cooperative federalism were police operations during the official visit of Soviet Communist Party chairman Brezhnev in 1973. At that time, to ensure the safety of the official guest, the Bonn chief of police, as head of the locally competent police force, was given command of Federal Border Police and Standby Police from North Rhine-Westphalia, Lower Saxony, Rhineland-Palatinate and Hesse. They were put on round-the-clock duty with from 2000 to 4000 men involved in each shift.

All of the 11 federal states maintain a Standby Police force that is uniformly equipped and organized as to headquarters, sections, and larger and smaller operational units. The total number of Standby Police in all federal states is about 22,000, of whom a large number are still being trained and cannot yet be used in police operations. There are purely operational sections and combined sections including both active operational sections and combined sections including both active operational units and units in training. For larger operations local police forces can also be drawn upon to form rapidly complete units of 100 men each, known in North Rhine-Westphalia as alarm units.

In Baden-Württemberg permanent 100-man operational units have been organized from regular police forces. Just like regular forces, they are on duty around the clock for, say, smaller demonstrations or large-scale traffic checks. Should it suddenly be necessary to employ a large, complete unit in a manhunt, a search party or some other operation, normal duty is immediately interrupted and the whole unit is ready for rapid deployment.

The Standby Police are used for crowd control purposes at mass gatherings involving political, sports, cultural and economic questions, in emergency activities made necessary by disasters or serious accidents, for the protection of persons and property as well as in search actions involving escaped criminals or missing persons.

The personal equipment of the individual police officer and the overall technical equipment of the units as a whole are designed for these special operational purposes. Thus, for instance, the various operational units have at their disposal road-blocking vehicles with drop-down barriers or armored cars. In these vehicles police officers are protected from attacks of all kinds even if their antagonists use firearms. Such special vehicles have been used increasingly to protect property and for airport security. In addition, the Standby Police have their own telecommunications units and technical units, including frogmen or other specialists.

The Coast and River Police

The Federal Republic of Germany has 4,371 navigable waterways. German inland shipping is responsible for about 30% of goods transport in the nation and is the second-largest means of transport thereafter German railways. The heavy traffic on German rivers requires police surveillance, and the problem is augmented by increasing recreational boat traffic. In North Rhine-Westphalia, the largest federal state, over 40,000 people are actively involved in water sports, part of them members of over 100 sailing and 20 motorboat clubs. These figures alone show the necessity for police presence on the water. This function is fulfilled by the Coast and River Police, who patrol the waterways around the clock in fast, modern boats. In cases of shipwrecks involving dangerous (e.g., chemical) cargo, they are the ones who assume responsibility for warning other shipping. The Coast and River Police in North Rhine-Westphalia includes around 300 officials with a fleet of 31 patrol craft. The police officers often have inland or maritime shipping experience. The Coast and River Police School in Hamburg trains candidates from all federal states.

The Motorway Police

Heavy traffic with maximum densities of over 50 vehicles per minute and other aspects of motorway traffic led the state interior ministers to create a separate police organization for the surveillance of the federal motorways: the Motorway Police. This police force is there to facilitate and regulate the flow of traffic, to register accidents rapidly and take all necessary measures to remove the injured from wrecked vehicles and arrange their transport to hospitals, and to help motorists with break-downs, since gasoline stations or workshops are often many miles away. The Motorway police have a network of motorway police stations and faster patrol cars than the remainder of the police. In the mid-1950s the system of "overtaking traffic check" was developed. Motorists are aware that at any time a police car can appear in their rearview mirror and, via loudspeaker, ask them to pull off at the next parking lot, where they would be fined for their traffic violation.

The Railway Police

Right after opening the first railway line on German soil in 1835, its management was asked to look after questions of security and order themselves. This was the beginning of the Railway Police, a specialized force with limited terms of reference. Their many duties consist of eliminating dangers that may threaten the functioning of the railways and the prevention and investigation of criminal acts and disorders at train stations and on trains. The Railway Police are employees of the German Federal Railways and thus are part of neither the state nor the federal police forces. They are responsible to the federal minster of transport. The number of Railway Police is limited to 2,400 in all of the federal republic. Thus limited, not every situation can be dealt with. When larger police operations are necessary, as in the case of demonstrations on a station platform, political extortion and the like, the local Municipal or Criminal Police are called out to help.

Recruitment, Education & Training

Basic police training is provided at State Police schools (Landespolizeischule). There is also the Federal Police College at Hiltrup, near Münster, which serves all West German police forces.

Training for the intermediate service level of the Municipal Police, (the majority of all police officers are at this service level) takes three years altogether. After a year of basic training there is a period of training in the Standby Police followed by a period of classroom work in preparation for the first professional examination. In some federal states the basic training period is spent at a police vocational school.

Those persons who meet the requirements can transfer to the senior service level, involving lower- to middle-echelon command positions, and complete a three-year training course at a school of public administration. Should someone not have the prerequisite school credentials, these can be acquired in a one-year preliminary course.

Particularly qualified persons at the senior service level can transfer to the superior service level and thus to higher command positions in the police organization. The training period is two years, including a year at the Federal Police College. To enter the superior service a university preparatory school leaving certificate or proof of an equivalent level of education is required. In training for intermediate service importance is attached to the promotion of general knowledge as well as police-specific subjects. Trainees receive instruction in German, civics and English.

The Criminal Police accept only candidates for the senior service. The prerequisite is a university preparatory school leaving certificate *(Abitur)*. Police officials in intermediate service who show an aptitude can be transferred to the Criminal Police. Training varies from state to state. As a rule it involves a two-year preparatory service period with several classroom courses, some of them lasting several months.

The Penal System

As a civil law system, German law is primarily codified. Many of its codes date back to the German Reich—the Penal Code to 1871 and the Code of Criminal Procedure to 1879. Over the years both have undergone numerous changes and revisions.

As in other civil law systems, court decisions are not sources of law but rather only tools for interpreting the codes. The common law doctrine that precedent is binding is unknown in West Germany, although lower court judges tend to follow prior higher court decisions in many cases. As a federal state, West Germany requires all states to follow federal legislation in criminal cases, even though all courts are state courts except the highest appellate courts and the Federal Constitutional Court.

During the past 10 years West German criminal law has undergone drastic changes. On the one hand, new crimes were added to the Penal Code, such as kidnapping, hijacking, terrorism and white-collar crime. On the other hand, many other offenses were decriminalized, including moral offenses such as adultery, bestiality, and homosexuality among consenting adults. Abortion was considerably liberalized. Petty misdemeanors such as traffic violations and noncompliance with trade regulations were removed from the criminal process and placed under the jurisdiction of administrative and law-enforcement authorities.

The scope of West German criminal law is considerably different from that of common law countries. Both strict responsibility and punitive damages do not exist under West German law. However, ordinary negligence is sufficient for criminal responsibility.

The Penal Code places criminal offenses in one of two categories: felonies punishable by imprisonment for at least one year, and misdemeanors punishable by imprisonment for a shorter term or a fine. The latter category is much broader than in the United States and includes many crimes normally considered as felonies, such as larceny, fraud, extortion or negligent homicide. The classification of offenses determines the jurisdiction of the court that tries them.

Juveniles under 14 years have no criminal responsibility, and their offenses are handled by guardianship courts. Juveniles between 14 and 18 years are criminally responsible if they can discern the unlawfulness of their acts, but sanctions are limited to educational and disciplinary measures.

In the civil law tradition, West German law differentiates between substantive and procedural law. Thus, instead of defenses, the criminal code speaks of justification and excuse. An act that violates the literal terms of the criminal law is justified when it serves to protect a superior interest, as in self-defense. An act may be illegal but the offender may not deserve punishment if he or she acted under extraordinary psychological pressure, as in a case of duress. West German law also distinguishes between justifying necessity and excusing necessity. The concept for self-defense is also broader. Thus, deadly force may be applied even to defend property in case of simple theft.

The West German penal philosophy combines punishment and rehabilitation. It is guided by four main principles: The punishment should fit the crime, sentencing should be by the judge who tried the case, sanctions should not violate human dignity, and social justice should determine the execution of penal measures.

Capital punishment has been abolished by the West German constitution and may not be imposed even under military law or in time of war. Imprisonment is for a fixed term, with a maximum of 15 years or life. Life imprisonment, which is mandatory in cases of murder or genocide, calls for incarceration of between 15 and 25 years before release. According to the Penal Code a prison sentence of more than six months may be imposed only "if special circumstances concerning the offense or the personality of the offender render confinement indispensable."

The West German equivalent of a probation is suspension of a prison term for a fixed period and the placement of the defendant under a probation officer. The upper limit for sentences that may be suspended is two years.

Most short-term jail sentences have been replaced by fines, which are levied in about 83% of all cases. Fines are fixed according to a day-fine scheme borrowed from the Swedish criminal justice system. No increased sentences are provided for recidivists or habitual offenders.

A prisoner may be paroled after serving two-thirds of his or her term, although in exceptional cases parole may be granted after half the term has been served. No parole is provided for life imprisonment.

The penal system is governed by the Code on the Execution of Prison Sentences and Measures involving the Deprivation of Liberty. Penal institutions are administered by prison authorities on the state level under the supervision of the state ministries of justice. Prisons are supervised by special courts that are organized on the district court level. These courts hear complaints against prison authorities and cases dealing with the revocation of probation or parole. The prosecutor supervises the execution of penal sanctions and sets the date when the offender has to begin serving the prison term or when he or she has to pay a fine. However, the prosecutor is not authorized to interfere with prison administration.

Offenders are classified according to age, sex, type of offense, length of sentence and prior convictions before being assigned to a penal institution. Inmates convicted for a term of one year or more are first assigned to an observation unit for classification.

Penal facilities are classified as closed or half open.

Most penal institutions still are located in old-fashioned, large, star-shaped buildings built before World War II. The more modern buildings are mostly built in pavilion style and are designed to hold between 200 and 300 inmates. Institutions of social therapy are ranked as penal institutions but are managed by physicians.

Inmates are obliged to work and are paid a few marks per day. Inmates in training programs are also paid. Disciplinary measures are listed in the Code on the Execution of Prison Sentences. They include warnings, denial of entertainment such as television or sports programs, visitor limitations, and placement in solitary confinement for up to four weeks. The code also permits inmates to leave the institution for up to 21 days per year.

CRIME STATISTICS (1984)

		Number Reported	Attempts %	Cases Solved %	Crime per 100,000	Offenders	Females %	Juveniles %	Strangers %
1.	Murder	2,760	66.8	94.1	4.51	2,785	12.5	a) 4.7 b) 0.3	21.6
2.	Sex offenses, including rape	39,919	13.3	67.1	65.25	19,889	9.7	a) 9.1 b) 2.1	16.6
3.	Rape	5,954	45.5	70.1	9.73	4,302	0.9	a) 7.3 b) 1	26.3
4.	Serious assault	63,746	6.4	84.6	104.19	69,216	10.4	a) 11.9 b) 1.7	18.2
5.	All theft	2,611,647	9.7	30.7	4,268.72	534,518	30.1	a) 19.8 b) 9.8	14.5
6.	Aggravated theft	978,829	20.4	20.0	1,599.89	91,751	8.9	a) 18.3 b) 7.3	22.0
7.	Robbery and violent theft	28,012	22.9	49.9	45.79	18,691	8.4	a) 18.6 b) 4.4	18.4
8.	Breaking and entering	950,817	19.4	19.1	1,554.10	73,060	9.1	a) 18.2 b) 8	13.5
9.	Auto theft	72,170	28.7	32.0	117.96	19,501	4.6	a) 23.9 b) 1.3	8.2
10.	Other thefts	1,560,648	2.1	37.4	2,550.87	461,324	33.4	a) 21 b) 10.6	14.6
11.	Fraud	399,800	5.6	92.2	653.47	236,698	23.8	a) 5.7 b) 0.7	12.1
12.	Counterfeiting	742	7.3	96.5	1.21	659	15.3	a) 3.9 b) 0.5	41.1
13.	Drug offenses	60,588	2.1	94.7	99.03	50,398	17.2	a) 7.0 b) 0.1	17.6
14.	Total offenses	4,132,783	7.3	46.7	6,755	1,254,213	23.6	a) 12.5 b) 5.3	16.6

Criteria of juveniles: aged from 14 to 17 years; children under 14 years not responsible.

GHANA

Otwin Marenin

BASIC FACT SHEET

Official Name: Republic of Ghana
Area: 238,538 sq km
Population: 13,948,925 (1987)
Capital: Accra
Nature of Government: Military dictatorship
Languages: English, Twi, Fanti, Ga, Ewe, Dagbani
Currency: Cedi
GNP: $4.96 billion
Territorial Divisions: 8 administrative regions, 58 districts, 207 local administrative districts
Population per Police Officer: 620
Police Expenditures per 1,000: N.A.

History & Background

The origins of the police forces of the Gold Coast and Ghana lie in efforts by a committee of merchants to protect trading depots and routes. In 1830 merchants hired a number of men as guards and escorts. Following the signing of a treaty between the British and coastal leaders, the Gold Coast Militia and Police was established in 1844 and numbered about 120 men. The force was disbanded in 1860 and superseded by a corps, about 90 men, of Queen's Messengers, while the paramilitary duties that the GCMP had performed were given to regular military units. During the Ashanti wars, the Queen's Messengers were combined with Hausa Constabulary, imported from Lagos, into a Gold Coast Armed Police Force, which supported military efforts during the campaigns. At the end of the wars, in 1876, the British converted this armed force into the Gold Coast Constabulary which existed until 1901. In that year the constabulary was split into two forces with the paramilitary functions assigned to the Gold Coast Regiment and police functions placed in the Gold Coast Police Force. The British established a protectorate over the northern territories in 1901 and in 1907 created a Northern Territories Constabulary for that area. The constabulary was absorbed into the Gold Coast Police Force shortly after World War I, leaving the colony with one police force, which existed, basically unchanged, until independence.

During the 1950s the British instituted various reforms in the Gold Coast Police Force to modernize, enlarge, centralize control and better equip the force.

The main effort, though, focused on the Africanization of the force. Ghanaians had been superior police officers during the early period of colonial rule; yet, beginning around 1900–10, the British began to restrict their access to higher positions in all branches of the colonial administration. This discrimination against qualified Ghanaians, on a purely racial basis, became one of the main foci of nationalist agitation. In 1951, 64 of 80 superior officers in the Police Force were expatriates; by 1958 only 11 expatriates, out of 128 superior officers remained. President Nkrumah appointed the first Ghanaian commissioner of the force, E.R.T. Madjitey, in 1958. By the early 1960s the only expatriates still with the force were a few technical advisers and instructors.

The Ghana Police Force did not fare well under President Kwame Nkrumah, who disliked and distrusted the police, though he was not adverse to using the force when it suited his political needs. Distrust between Nkrumah and the police culminated in 1964, after an unsuccessful assassination attempt on the president's life by a police constable. The Police Force was disarmed; the commissioner and nine senior officers were sacked; eight others were detained; the Border Guards unit was removed from the Police Force and placed under the military; the size of the force was reduced from 13,247 in 1964 to 10,709 in 1965.

Two senior police officials were among the first to suggest that Nkrumah be overthrown, and they managed to gain co-coinspirators in the police and the army. The police were used extensively during and immediately after the coup, which occurred in February 1966, to round up suspected sympathizers and place the leaders of Nkrumah's party in protective custody. The involvement of the police in a coup against a civilian government was quite unusual and has not been repeated in any other African country, with the exception of the 1981 coup in Gambia, which has no military. Various police officers became regional and district administrators and seemed to have been better liked and accepted than their military counterparts. The size of the police force rose from its level in 1965 to 17,692 in 1966 and to 19,895 in 1968. The Border Guards unit was restored to police control, though taken away again and made an autonomous unit in 1972.

Resources and equipment of the police were increased. A study mission to Ghana in 1968, under the auspices of the Office of Public Safety of the United States Agency for International Development, found the communications, transport and criminalistic resources of the police force in sorry shape and the force, in its judgment, just beginning to "emerge from the trauma of the Nkrumah regime." Yet it also found that the preoccupation of higher police officials with administering the country diverted their attention from managing and running the police force properly. The mission recommended that the force receive transport and communications supplies and training for specialists and that the U.S. government "provide guidance to the Ghanaian Police . . . in police management, records management and training."

Structure and Organization

From its inception until the adoption of the republican constitution of 1960 the police were considered part of the civil service of the colonial and independent state. The 1960 constitution declared the police a separate public service and renamed the Ghana Police Force the Ghana Police Service, to be controlled by the president and the Public Service Commission. The 1969 Constitution established a Police Council to advise on administrative and disciplinary procedures regarding the service. In 1974, the National Redemption Council amended the Police Force Act 1970 (Act 350) by decree (NRCD 303) to make the Police Service an autonomous public service, responsible for its own development and accountability; the name of the police was changed back to the Ghana Police Force.

The Ghana Police Service is placed, along with immigration, prisons and the national fire service, under the Ministry of Internal Affairs.

Under Act 350, the Police Force Act, the police are charged with the "prevention and detection of crime; the apprehension of offenders; the maintenance of public order; and the safety of persons and property." The police are also responsible for the licensing of motor vehicles, the issuing of driver's licenses, the control of motor traffic, the licensing of firearms, the issuing of permits for ammunition, the inspection of weights and measures and the licensing of selected trades: goldsmiths, domestic servants.

The Ghana Police Service is organized into 10 regional commands and several groups and branches associated with the national headquarters. The Service is under the operational control of the inspector-general (a title created in 1966). The Police Council, first established in the 1969 constitution, advises the I-G on all matters of personnel and policy. The I-G is responsible for the service to the minister of internal affairs and through the ministry to the president and the political power structure of the country.

Regional commands coincide with the administrative divisions of the country, with the addition of a regional command for Ghana's main port, Tema harbor. Each region is commanded by a deputy or assistant commissioner. Each region is divided into divisions, districts, stations and posts. In 1985, there were 52 districts and 558 stations and posts.

Functionally, the service is divided into five groups: General Administration, Criminal Investigations Department, Special Branch, Police Hospital and National Ambulance Service.

General Administration is divided into the following administrative units. The Directorate is responsible for administrative matters regarding personnel and welfare, operations, planning and development, and public relations. The Paymaster-General and Controller's office deals with pay, finances and audit. The Quarter-master-General deals with supplies and stores. Recruitment and Training supervises the Police Depot (which is responsible for all recruitment into the service) and the Police College. The Licensing unit deals with the motor vehicles licensing, driving permits, and domestic servants' and goldsmiths' licenses. The Armoured Car section, stationed in Accra, was established in 1958 to serve as a mobile reserve force in cases of serious civil disorders. The Mounted Squadron, stationed in Accra and Tamale, is used for crowd control, town patrol and ceremonial occasions. The Force Mechanical Engineer unit is split into a works division, responsible for minor building projects and repairs on existing police buildings, and a mechanical division, responsible for the maintenance and repair of all police vehicles. Units of this branch are located at regional centers in addition to the main workshop at Accra. The Communications branch is charged with the planning, installation and maintenance of all police radio stations, and is also responsible for all internal communications of the Service that involve radio or teletype. The branch accepts emergency messages from the public and other governmental agencies for transmission. The police network is the most extensive and reliable means of communications in Ghana. Most of the equipment used is manufactured by Motorola.

The Women's Corps was established in 1952 with 12 recruits. By 1962 it had reached a strength of 130 and the first woman cadet officer had been enrolled at the Police College; in 1975, its strength was 702 members. The Women's Corps deals mainly with matters affecting women, children and juvenile delinquents, and does occasional probation work and traffic duties. The Motor Traffic Unit controls the highway patrol squad and runs the police driving school, its aim is to ensure greater responsibility and safety by public and police drivers.

The Criminal Investigation Department is responsible for the investigation of all serious crimes; it runs the criminal records office and fingerprint bureau; and presents and prosecutes cases in court. Members of the C.I.D. are stationed at all regional command levels. C.I.D. headquarters, in Accra, is divided into these sections: registry of correspondence relating to crime and criminals; criminal records office and fingerprint bureau; crime branch responsible for the investigation of serious crime and special matters; forensic science laboratory, established in 1959, responsible for criminalistic research and application; fraud squad; flying squad; central firearms registry; crime statistics; legal section; liasion with InterPol; and detective training school, established in 1968 with British aid, which teaches regular and refresher courses in special and technical topics.

The Special Branch collects, assesses and disseminates information concerning the security of the nation and the maintenance of law and order. The branch also provides VIP protection.

The Police Hospital was established in 1975 to provide for the medical needs of members of the Police Service and other agencies within the Ministry of Internal Affairs, and their families.

The legal powers of the police follow British precedents—police officers have few powers not possessed by each citizen, and the exercise of their powers is strictly limited by law and police statutes. Police are expected to think of themselves as servants of the public, for without information, cooperation and support from the public they would be ineffectual. Their actions toward suspects are governed by the Judges' Rules—they must treat suspects civilly and inform them of their rights when being charged with an offense. The use of force and firearms is allowed in self-defense, for the prevention of a serious indictable crime or the escape of a suspect or prisoner for such a crime, and on the command of a superior officer during emergency situations.

The Escort Police wore its own distinct uniform: khaki jacket and shorts, red fez and brown boots. It patrolled unarmed but could be equipped with staves during riot duty. About half of the Ghana Police Force during the 1950s and 1960s consisted of Escort Police.

Dissatisfaction with having illiterates in the Ghana Police Force grew as education became more widely available. Each independence government has sought to reduce the size of the Escort Police, but success has come slowly. The 1967 Mills-Odoi Commission on the Structure and Remuneration of the Public Services in Ghana recommended the "progressive cessation of recruitment of illiterates within the Service" in view of the increasingly larger number of middle-level school leavers (the minimum educational qualification for joining the General Police). The 1974 Salary Review Commission again urged that only middle school leavers should be recruited, leading to the disappearance of the positions of regional and district sergeant major, the highest post within the Escort Police. Recruitment of illiterates ceased in 1975. Escort Police members have also been urged to upgrade their educational qualification so that they can move into the General Police division.

The General Police

The General Police deal with all routine police matters. They perform station, court and clerical duties, traffic control and all technical work. They do not, normally, perform patrol duties. Their uniform is dark blue, with a peaked cap and black boots. In general, rank and salary structure of both branches are similar, but promotion opportunities for Escort Police are limited. The two groups receive different training.

Recruitment Education & Training

Recruitment into the service is at two levels: rank and file and commissioned officer levels. All recruits must be between 18 and 34 years of age; five feet eight inches tall (women must be at least five feet four inches), though this requirement may be waived if the applicant has special qualifications; be physically fit and pass a medical examination; and have no criminal record. Applicants for the Escort Police must have a minimum facility in spoken English; applicants for the General Police must possess a Middle School Leaving Certificate (about eight years of formal education); applicants for direct entry into the commissioned officer corps must have a pass degree from a recognized university.

Entry into the commissioned officer corps is also by promotion from the inspectorate level. Outstanding members of the inspectorate may be recommended by their superiors and, if they pass a written examination

Organization Chart

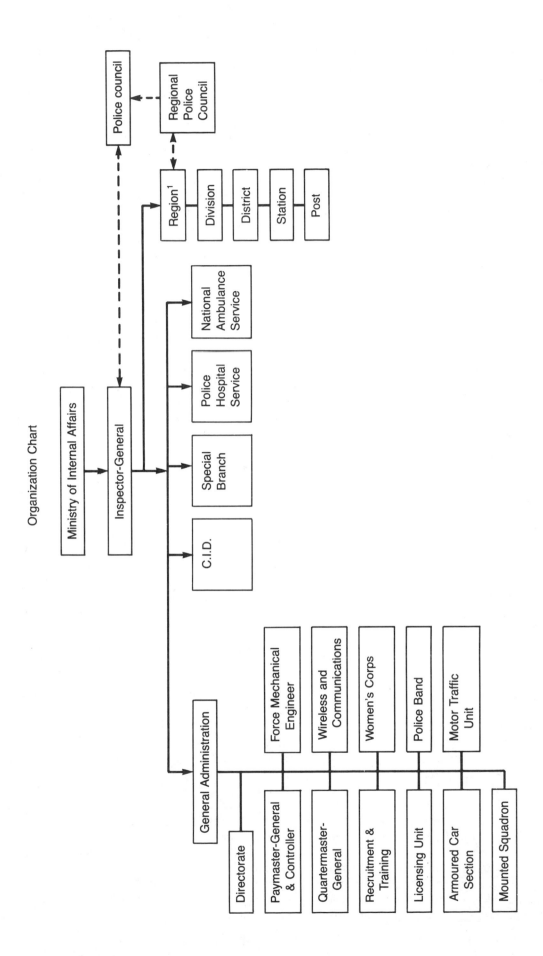

[1]Regional commands coincide with the major administrative units into which Ghana is divided, with the addition of a special regional command for the Tema harbor area. The regions are Greater Accra, Tema, Central, Western, Brong-Ahafo, Ashanti, Eastern, Volta, Northern and Upper Region.

and oral interview, are allowed to enter officer cadet training.

Most of the applicants for the Escort Police have come from the northern areas of the country, which lacks educational facilities, while most members of the General Police and officer corps have been recruited from the southern areas.

Training for rank and file, both Escort and General Police, is provided at the police depot at Elmina, a coastal town; though Escort Police have been trained at regional depots as well. Since 1975, recruits are given a nine month course of instruction in physical training and drill, unarmed combat and baton use, first aid and firearms training. Escort police receive instruction in general education and patrol and escort duties. General Police receive training in criminal law and procedures, methods of investigation, current affairs and social sciences.

The Police College, established in 1959 and located on the grounds of the police depot in Accra, gives a nine-month officer cadet course for new recruits to the officer ranks and two-to-six-week refresher courses in general and technical subjects. The college is staffed by police officers, who are supplemented by guest lecturers from the police, government agencies and universities.

The officer cadet course teaches criminal law and procedures, laws of evidence, police administration, finance practices, familiarization with police standing and service orders, practical police work, general and social science topics. There is, as well, a heavy emphasis on drill and physical fitness. Instruction is supplemented by visits to all agencies of the criminal justice system.

Upon successful completion of the course, cadets are sworn in and promoted to assistant superintendent. They may be stationed with any branch or in any area of the country, though personal preferences and capabilities are taken into account.

The Penal System

As a consequence of more than a century of legal evolution, the application of customary law to acts defined in modern courts as crimes has disappeared. Since 1961 the criminal law administered by all courts has been completely statutory and based on the criminal code. Essentially a consolidation, rearrangement and simplification of earlier colonial legislation, the code is founded on English law and introduces no innovations.

Two of the three broad categories of offenses cited in the code deal with offenses against the person. The third category defines a wide list of offenses against public order, health and morality, ranging from serious crimes against the safety of the state, piracy, perjury and riot to petty public nuisances and cruelty to animals. Some of the offenses are peculiarly Ghanain: drumming with intent to provoke disorder, smuggling of cocoa and settlement of private disputes by methods of traditional ordeal.

In additions to provisions of the Criminal Code, a number of separate enactments are aimed at strengthening public order, such as the Deportation Act, the Public Order Act, the Avoidance of Discrimination Act, and the Pharmacy and Drugs Act. Criminal Court procedure is guided by the Criminal Procedure Code enacted in 1960. As in English law, on which the code is based, habeas corpus is allowed and suspects may be released on bail. The legal system does not make use of grand juries but under the Constitution's fundamental rights, defendants charged with criminal offense are entitled to trial by jury if so desired.

A system of grading establishes five degrees of offenses and specifies maximum punishments. Capital offenses, for which the maximum penalty is death by hanging, are limited to murder, treason and piracy. First-degree felonies punishable by life imprisonment include manslaughter, rape and abetment of mutiny. Second-degree felonies, punishable by 10 years' imprisonment, include causing intentional and unlawful harm to persons, perjury and robbery. Misdemeanors punishable by varying terms of imprisonment include assault, theft, unlawful assembly, corruption by a public officer and public nuisances. Increased penalties are authorized for persons with a prior criminal record. Corporal punishment is no longer permitted.

Punishments for juvenile offenders are subject to two restrictions. No sentence of death may be passed against a juvenile and no juvenile under age 15 (or 17 in the case of district or juvenile courts) may be imprisoned.

Ministerial responsibility for the prison system has shifted from time to time since independence, but the operation is fixed by statute and is divided into two main categories of adult and juvenile correction. The penal system proper is governed by the Prisons Ordinance, which lays down basic rules for prison operation and treatment of prisoners. the Constitution of 1969 established a Prison Service, whose director is appointed by the president and is responsible to the minister of interior. Prison policies and regulations are regulated by the Prisons Services Board, consisting of a member of the Public Services Commission as chairman, the Prison Service director, a medical officer of the Ghana Medical Association, a representative of the attorney general, the principal secretary of the minister responsible for social welfare and three other persons appointed by the president, of whom one must be a woman and the other two religious functionaries. The Prisons Service Board is required to review the state of the nation's prisons every two years, hear complaints of mistreatment of prisoners and make recommendations for reform.

Prison service is a career service. Most of the prisons are greatly understaffed. Service standards require one staff member for every three prisoners, but ratios of one to five or one to eight are not uncommon. However, the quality and competence of the prison officers and guards, called warders, have improved steadily over the years. Most of them are recruited from the more literate Ewe and Ga ethnic groups. The service maintains a school and depot at Maamobi, near Accra, for the purpose of training recruit warders. The facility offers a six-month training course for senior staff members, special courses for matrons, and preparatory courses for promotion examinations.

Only a few new prisons have been built since World War II, although prison population has quadrupled during the same period. Many of the facilities are more than 100 years old—old forts converted into prisons—and have few or no modern amenities. In the mid-1980s there were 27 penal institutions. There are six central prisons for men, located in Accra (Ussher Fort and James Fort), Sekondi, Kumasi, Tamale and Nsawam. Ussher Fort is the top maximum security prison. In all institutions long-term prisoners are housed together with petty offenders. Two central prisons for women—at Ekuasi and Sekondi—handle all offenders whose sentences exceed three months. For short-term confinement of local offenders and persons under remand, the central prisons are supplemented by 15 small local prisons, six of which have annexes for women. Two open prison camps house convicts who have demonstrated good behavior. Built since independence James Camp near Accra and Ankaful near Cape Coast are the only facilities not suffering from overcrowding. Both have industrial workshops and farms where prisoners can work, and

Ankaful has an 80-bed hospital. Juveniles are incarcerated at Maamobi, near Accra.

After the overthrow of Nkrumah, the military government appointed a commission of civilian officials to investigate the prison system. Of the 29 facilities that the commission inspected, nine were found unfit for human habitation, two were found suitable only as police lockups and 13 were judged to be suitable only for short-term detainees. Few of the commission's recommendations were acted upon and prison conditions remain substandard, with poor ventilation, sanitation and kitchen facilities. Only Maamobi reformatory has sports facilities and only Ankaful has adequate medical services.

Within the correctional system, remand homes, probation homes and industrial schools are operated by the Ministry of Labor and Social Welfare. Remand homes are located in Accra, Sekondi, Cape Coast and Kumasi and probation homes in Accra and Jacobu Ashanti for boys and Kumasi for girls.

The Ghana Police Service reports violations in three separate categories: crimes, statutory offenses and traffic offenses. Crimes are violations of the criminal code and statutory offenses violations of administrative ordinances. Theft and personal violence are the principal forms of law breaking. Much of the personal violence of a criminal nature involves assault and disorderly conduct. Murder, manslaughter and rape are relatively rare. The highest growth in crime rate has been among males in the 20- to 24-age group. Juvenile delinquency and crime are mainly confined to the urban areas.

Drug addiction, smuggling and possession of firearms are among the most serious law enforcement problems. The use of marijuana, called *wee,* became widespread in the 1960s and has resisted official efforts to suppress it. A trend toward organized crime beginning in the 1970s, centered in Accra, Kumasi and Sekondi-Takoradi, has been partially checked by enlisting military cooperation.

GREECE

History & Background

The earliest municipal police forces in Greece were organized soon after liberation from Turkish rule in 1829. Large towns had police chiefs appointed by the crown, while town mayors headed the police departments of smaller towns. The Gendarmerie (Khorofylaki) were organized in 1833 as an auxiliary Army unit for policing rural areas where bandits held sway.

In 1849 police departments separate from the municipal authorities were created in Athens and nearby Piraeus under a director of police subordinate to the Ministry of the Interior. Field Guards were assigned to rural areas. In 1893 the Athens and Piraeus Police were militarized and the whole country placed under military police. City Guards were formed in key towns. In 1906 the Gendarmerie took over the policing of the entire nation. Athens, Corfu, Patras and Piraeus were allowed to reintroduce the City Police system between 1921 and 1925.

The first chief of the City Police, Frederick Holliday of Scotland Yard, patterned the force after the London Metropolitan Force. In 1929 the City Police force was given authority over regional security matters.

Structure & Organization

Civil police functions in Greece are performed by the Gendarmerie (Khorofylaki) and the City Police (Astynomia). The latter has jurisdiction in four cities (Athens, Piraeus, Patras and Corfu) and the former throughout the rest of the country. Both are national police forces under the centralized control of the Ministry of Public Order. There are no local police departments.

The police are paramilitary forces and carry side-arms and clubs while on regular duty. Heavier weapons are issued during emergencies. Special riot units are equipped with Swiss-built armored personnel carriers. The two police organizations have a total strength of about 40,000.

The Gendarmerie and the City Police furnish personnel for the Tourist Police, special units of which are stationed in Athens and other tourist resorts, where they patrol railroad depots and airports and frequently serve as guides. Members of the force have a working knowledge of at least one foreign language, usually English.

Other specialized police forces are the Customs Guards; the Forest Police, the Agrarian Police, who protect farm property and livestock; and the Harbor Corps, who act as a coast guard. Women make up only a small portion of the police, usually serving in an auxiliary capacity.

The Gendarmerie

The Gendarmerie was organized in 1833 on the model of the French police. Recruits were veterans of the War of Independence, and their original mission was to suppress banditry in the mountainous countryside. The exploits of its first commandant, French philhellene and onetime Napoleonic officer François Gragier, is now part of Greek folklore.

The modern Gendarmerie exercises a broad range of powers, including civil defense, relief operations during natural disasters, and enforcement of public health regulations. The Gendarmerie also serves as judicial police, prison guards and highway patrol.

The Gendarmerie is commanded by a lieutenant general assisted by two major generals and an inspectorate directed by a lieutenant general. The country is divided for operational purposes into a number of districts and directorates, each under a brigadier or colonel. These, in turn, are divided into Gendarmerie commands corresponding to an administrative prefecture or a city subdirectorate. The principal functional units are the Security Police, the Traffic Police, the Market Police, the Tourist Police and the Emergency Squad. The smallest rural operational unit is a subcommand, and in the towns a police department. Both are commanded by a major or captain in charge of a number of police stations.

Officers wear a dark green-gray tunic, trousers and cap, while other ranks wear similar uniforms in light green-gray.

The City Police

The City Police is headquartered in Athens, with directorates in Piraeus, Patras and Corfu, and is commanded by a lieutenant general. In each of the four cities there is a director general with the rank of brigadier. The line of command runs through subdirectorates, security police, traffic police, market police and motorized units as well as an emergency squad, each of which is commanded by a police director. These commands are further divided into precincts that, in turn, are divided into police stations, commanded by captains and lieutenants, respectively. Officers wear a dark gray tunic and trousers with a cap of the same color. Other ranks wear a similar uniform in light gray.

A special City Police unit deals with white-collar crimes and counterfeiting. In Athens the City Police maintains a riot squad with quick reaction capability. A new police unit, the Special Security Group, was formed in 1976. The unit was created by the Ministry of Public Order in response to the 1975 murder of Richard Welch, the U.S. CIA station chief in Athens. The unit is specially trained to combat politically inspired terrorist acts, such as abduction, air piracy, holding of hostages, armed robbery, and assault on public officials and foreign diplomats. Special Security personnel guard public officials, embassies, public buildings and other possible targets of terrorist attacks. They are organized in attack teams with Special Weapons and Tactics (SWAT) capability and are expert marksmen.

Recruitment, Education & Training

Both the Gendarmerie and the City Police operate training academies, which provide a three-year university-level program. Candidates must have a secondary-school diploma to qualify for admission. Upon graduation they are commissioned as second lieutenants. Noncommissioned officers qualify for promotion

CRIME STATISTICS (1984)

		Number Reported	Attempts %	Cases Solved %	Crime per 100,000	Offenders	Females %	Juveniles %	Strangers %
1.	Murder	181	45.3	87.20	1.83	204	3.90	6.30	5.03
2.	Sex offenses, including rape	504	6.0	96.40	5.10	740	12.40	8.10	6.18
3.	Rape	92	34.78	91.20	0.93	106		10.37	4.71
4.	Serious assault	363	5.4	98.90	3.67	401	6.73	4.98	7.23
5.	All theft	22,527	1.5	18.50	227.78	5,621	7.72	27.73	7.93
6.	Aggravated theft	7,424	0.3	19.60	75.07	2,396	1.09	9.28	4.62
7.	Robbery and violent theft	226	7.5	46.40	2.29	171	8.10	12.86	21.14
8.	Breaking and entering	7,198	2.93	30.30	72.78	2,225	7.90	30.01	6.30
9.	Auto theft								
10.	Other thefts	14,901	9.8	41.70	150.67	3,225	13.50	17.40	7.47
11.	Fraud	537	0.6	83.40	5.43	534	11.98	3.37	5.84
12.	Counterfeiting	62	0.0	79.03	0.63	71	19.71		60.00
13.	Drug offenses	532	0.2	98.40	5.38	1,017	8.65	1.96	9.76
14.	Total offenses	352,488	0.2	94.34	3,564.08	352,317	6.70	3.55	9.75

Criteria of juveniles: aged from 7 to 17 years.

to officer ranks through examination and a two-year course at the Policy Academy. Police recruits receive six months of basic training. Recruits under 21 years of age can satisfy their military service obligation by service in the Gendarmerie, but City Police recruits must have completed their military service. The police are considered part of the civil service in matters relating to pay.

The Penal System

The Penal Code is based on the Bavarian codes introduced into Greece by King Otto. It is based on Roman law as modified by the Napoleonic Code and has been revised and amended frequently.

The Penal Code defines three grades of crime: felonies, misdemeanors and petty offenses. The 1975 Constitution forbids unusual punishments, including long prison terms. Imprisonment for felonies ranges from five to 25 years and that for petty offenses and misdemeanors from 10 days to five years. Confinement in a reformatory may also be imposed for five to 20 years and confinement in an institution for the mentally deranged indefinitely. Confiscation of property is not permitted. Greece retains capital punishment for some categories of serious crimes, but it has not been imposed for many years.

Under certain circumstances police officers may arrest persons caught in the act of committing a crime; otherwise, no one may be arrested or imprisoned without a judicial warrant. Suspects must be arraigned before an examining magistrate within 24 hours of arrest. Within three to five days of arraignment magistrates are obliged either to release suspects or to issue a warrant for imprisonment pending trial. The maximum detention permissible before trial is nine to 18 months. Administration measures to restrict the movement of citizens are prohibited unless accompanied by a court ruling.

After an arrest, the police may conduct a preliminary investigation under the supervision of the public prosecutor. Thereafter the police turn the suspect and the documents pertinent to the case to court authorities. As a rule, the state possesses the exclusive right to prosecute criminal suspects. However, an injured party may initiate prosecution when the competent public prosecutor refuses to act.

The accused is protected by law from the use of a confession obtained by torture or other illegal means. He or she must be informed of the contents of all documents bearing on the investigation before they are transmitted to the public prosecutor and may examine and obtain copies of these documents. The accused then has up to 48 hours to decide on a plea. He or she has the right to post bail pending trial except in the case of serious crimes. Criminal and political cases are tried by panels composed of both judges and lay jurors in so-called mixed courts. The accused is present during trial and may compel the appearance in court of defense witnesses. The court must appoint legal counsel if the accused lacks a lawyer. Criminal trials are open to the adult public. The burden of proof rests with the prosecution. In imposing sentences, the presiding judge is restricted by law, and there are limitations on the size of the fine or the length of imprisonment. Magistrates in juvenile courts have considerable latitude in sentencing youthful offenders. Parents may be held accountable for the behavior of their children in certain cases.

The penal system comprises a central penitentiary and several correctional farms, as well as district prisons near each court for suspects awaiting trial and convicts serving short-term sentences. Rehabilitation is stressed through vocational training and productive labor. The law prohibits the hiring out of prison labor to private contractors. The rehabilitation of juvenile offenders is conducted through training schools that offer recreational camps and home furloughs on religious holidays. Professional probation officers are attached to all juvenile courts.

Greece has a very low crime rate by any standard. The most common offenses are simple assault, crimes against property, and commercial and traffic law violations. Violent crimes, such as rape, murder or armed robbery, are very rare and receive headline treatment in the press when they occur. The streets in Greek cities are considered safe at all hours.

Gun control regulations are strictly enforced. Possession of firearms, except by hunters, is forbidden to all private citizens. Severe penalties are also prescribed for the sale or illegal possession of narcotics. Actions regarded as assaults upon family or personal honor are considered private matters, and redress or, in some instances, revenge is handled by the parties involved without recourse to courts of law or the police.

Of persons sentenced to prison, more than 80% receive terms of less than three months, and another 10% receive terms of three months to one year. Less than 20% of those convicted are under 25 years of age, and only about 10% are women.

Juvenile crime is very insignificant as a result of the influence of the Greek Orthodox Church. Juvenile gangs are virtually nonexistent.

GUATEMALA

BASIC FACT SHEET

Official Name: Republic of Guatemala
Area: 108,780 sq km
Population: 8,622,387 (1987)
Capital: Guatemala City
Nature of Government: Representative democracy
Language: Spanish
Currency: Quetzal
GNP: $9.2 billion (1985)
Territorial Divisions: 22 departments
Population per Police Officer: 670
Police Expenditures per 1,000: N.A.

Structure & Organization

The primary law-enforcement agency is the National Police force under the minister of government. The Judicial Police (distinct from the investigative force of the judiciary), a separate entity within the same ministry, performs a police intelligence and investigative role. The Border Patrol is in charge of the collection of tariffs, taxes and other revenues. Although it performs a Treasury Department function, the Border Patrol is administratively under the Ministry of Government.

All three agencies have nationwide jurisdiction; yet the National Police and the Judicial Police operate almost exclusively in Guatemala City. Largely by default, the armed forces perform civilian law-enforcement and internal-security functions in rural areas. A special unit of the Army, the Mobile Military Police (Policía Militar Ambulante), combats rural insurgency and banditry where civilian police protection is lacking.

Some 6,200 small communities of 200 or more people have no paid police. The local mayor (alcalde,) usually the justice of the peace, selects one or more individuals from the community to serve one or two years as local constables, usually without pay. They are not recognized as police by the government but are respected as ''lawmen'' within the community. Some 4,000 of these communities are organized farms.

Since the 1970s, the law-enforcement efforts have been modernized with the establishment of a Police Academy in the capital, the Central Complaints Division, a central crime laboratory, a fingerprint system, model precincts and Rural Mobile Patrols.

The director general of the National Police, a senior active-duty officer on loan from the Defense Department, reports directly to the Ministry of Government. The police command structure is composed of a small staff in charge of operational divisions in the central headquarters and five regional zones. Authority and control are so highly centralized that even routine matters have to be approved by the director general.

The National Police, numbering over 8,000 in the mid-1980s, has about two-thirds of its strength in the national capital, with the remainder deployed largely in the 21 departmental capitals under four zonal commands, similar to the military regional areas. The remaining outlying police elements are assigned to departmental stations and substations in fewer than 100 other population centers (municipios or aldeas). There are, however, 14 mobile detachments that could be readily dispatched to trouble spots.

The major uniformed operational elements under central control in the capital and environs are the precinct enclave; a variety of patrol units (foot, motorcycle, jeep and patrol car); and a Traffic Department, with the combined functions of Traffic Division and Department of Motor Vehicles. Responsibility for accident investigation rests with still another section of the uniformed police division.

For a period of almost a year, in 1964–65, the National Policy agency operated without a criminal investigation or detective unit when the entire unit was transferred to the Judicial Police. Subsequently, an Investigative Division was reestablished within the agency with a group of graduates from the International Police Academy in Washington, D.C.

The Division of Administration and Services incorporates all the personnel and logistics support elements, such as maintenance of buildings, supplies and vehicles, communications network, licensing, and detention centers.

The principal ranks are director general, followed by deputy director general, inspector general, corps commander, deputy corps commander, section commander, deputy section commander, inspector, sub-inspector and agent. The official uniform consists of dark blue trousers with a sky-blue stripe on the legs, a matching tunic and a sky-blue shirt. Belt and tie are black. A soft, peaked cap in dark blue completes the outfit. The principal weapons are a .38 special revolver and M1 .30-caliber carbines.

The Judicial Police is the principal intelligence and investigative element, with a personnel complement of close to 1,000, all of whom are stationed in Guatemala City, with only occasional assignments in the provincial areas. Judicial Police members are more highly skilled and better paid than those of the National Police. In order of size, the three operational divisions of the Judicial Police are the Internal Division, the Transient Division and the International Division.

The Guatemalan Border Patrol (Guarda de Hacienda) was initially established in 1954 as a semimilitary law-enforcement body, uniformed and armed, to operate under the direction of the minister of the treasury. Later, the operational affiliation of the patrol passed to the Ministry of Government. The headquarters of the patrol, under a head styled the chief, is in Guatemala City.

Patrol units of varying strength are assigned to each of the 22 departmental capitals and to most border or coastal departments; one or more additional units are located at strategic sites. Departmental chiefs are subject to the intermediate zonal command of the National Police but report directly to the Border Patrol hierarchy. Nearly two-thirds of the 1,800 members of the Border Patrol are assigned to field units.

The Border Patrol has a wide range of prescribed duties, mostly relating to customs and revenue collection. It prevents smuggling, apprehends violators and seizes contraband; enforces immigration and passport laws; prevents illegal sale and manufacture of alcoholic beverages; monitors ports of entry, customs warehouses and authorized distilleries; enforces tariff laws; enforces laws against counterfeiting and narcotics; and controls exports. In addition, Border Patrol members are gaining an increasing role in counter-subversion, especially the surveillance of domestic or alien subversive elements. The training and experience gained in locating and raiding illicit stills often prove valuable in ferreting out illegal arms caches. Although described as a mobile force, the Border Patrol's transportation and communications capabilities are woefully inadequate.

Currency and banking offenses are dealt with by the Special Investigation Section of the Bank of Guatemala.

Recruitment, Education & Training

Recruitment, education and training are provided by the Police Academy in the national capital.

The Penal System

Prisons, rehabilitation and parole are administered by the director of prisons under the Ministry of Government. Three major penitentiaries for men are located on the outskirts of Guatemala City and in the departments of Quezaltenango and Escuintla. The major penitentiary for women is Santa Teresa, in the national capital. In addition, there are 19 prisons for men and 20 for women in the other departments, and a central house of correction for juveniles. The average prison population at any one time is about 7,000, although the prisons are designed to hold only two-thirds that number.

Local jails come under the jurisdiction of the police or the justice of the peace in towns and larger villages. Outlying Indian communities and many of the plantations maintain their own detention centers. Generally, those offenders who are awaiting sentencing are not held in the same cell with convicted criminals.

Penal statistics are fragmentary and unreliable, partly because of the lack of standards in reporting and recording crimes among the various agencies. The overall rate for all types of offenses ranges from 27 to 33 per 1,000 inhabitants in Guatemala City. Well over half of all offenses are crimes against public order, about 35% crimes against the person and only 6% crimes against property.

Single men in the age group from 21 to 30 years commit the greatest number of major crimes. Crime is concentrated in the months of August, October and December, when the principal religious and national holidays take place. The ends of the week and month, when workers receive their paychecks, coincide with days of maximum consumption of liquor and the highest incidence of crime.

GUINEA

BASIC FACT SHEET

Official Name: Republic of Guinea
Area: 245,957 sq km
Population: 6,737,760 (1987)
Capital: Conakry
Nature of Government: Civilian dictatorship
Language: French
Currency: Syli
GNP: $1.95 billion (1985)
Territorial Divisions: 33 provinces, 36 prefectures
Population per Police Officer: 1,140
Police Expenditures per 1,000: N.A.

Structure & Organization

The police force of Guinea consists of three major elements: the Sûreté Nationale (National Police), the Gendarmerie and the Republican Guard (Garde Républicaine). Although three distinct organizations, they are under the common control of the General Directorate of Security Services, which is attached to the Ministry of the Interior and Security.

The General Directorate of Security Services, in Conakry, consists of six bureaus responsible for criminal investigation, state security, economic-law enforcement, traffic management, public safety and technical services. This centralized police service, headed by a general director assisted by a deputy, is responsible for discipline of police personnel and supervision of police services throughout the country.

As the governor of each administrative region is responsible for law enforcement and the maintenance of peace and order in his area, there is a dual responsibility for internal security. These responsibilities are not clearly demarcated, but the ministry appears to be concerned primarily with overall command and administration of the security forces, and control of security matters of national interest, whereas the regional and local administrations are responsible for the distribution of security forces in their local areas and their deployment during local disturbances.

Sûreté Nationale (SN) is the designation given to the civil police forces in all cities and towns. Recruitment, direction, administration and training of this 2,000-man force are vested in the General Directorate of Security Services. The Sûreté functions operationally under the governors of the administrative regions to which they are assigned. Each governor has at-

tached to his staff a chief of police. The police force is further subdivided into precincts or town quarter detachments, and these, in turn, into police posts. Under the country's first president, Sékou Touré, the Sûreté had an additional function of countering subversive activities against the state and protecting the "achievements of the revolution."

A special section of the Sûreté Nationale is charged with checking the activities of foreigners in the country, including their entry and exit. SN detachments are at work at seaports and airports and at customary border crossing points.

The ranks and grades of the Sûreté Nationale resemble those of the military forces, but with different titles: police commissioner *(commissaire de police)*, deputy commissioner *(adjoint au commissaire de police)*, inspector of police *(inspecteur de police)*, sergeant major *(brigadier-chef)*, sergeant major *(adjutant)*, sergeant *(brigadier)*, corporal *(assistant de police)* and private *(agent de police)*.

The Gendarmerie is a paramilitary force with an estimated strength of 1,500 and enforces law and maintains public safety in rural areas, where 80% of the population lives. The main force is divided into brigades, at least one of which is assigned to each administrative region. A brigade is composed of six to 36 gerdarmes and ordinarily is commanded by a lieutenant who is appointed to his post by presidential decree. Besides the regular brigades assigned to administrative regions, some additional units—designated as Gendarmerie frontier brigades—are distributed among the administrative regions on the country's borders. The primary mission of the frontier brigades is to assist the Customs Service in its efforts to prevent smuggling and illegal border crossings. The Customs Service itself is a separate organization under the Ministry of Finance and has some law-enforcement units of its own.

Conakry has at least three Gendarmerie brigades—the port, the airport and the city brigades. Another Gendarmerie unit is the mobile detachment *(peloton mobile)*, operating under the direct control of the Gendarmerie commander. There are also two so-called criminal brigades, one for the Fouta Djallon area and one for Conakry. These personnel are authorized to make criminal investigations, take depositions, collect fines and make special reports.

The system of grades and ranks in the Gendarmerie corresponds to that of the Army. Lower ranks include senior sergeant major *(adjutant-chef)*, sergeant major *(adjutant)*, sergeant *(maréchal des logis chef)*, corporal *(gendarme troisième classe)*, private first class *(gendarme deuxième classe)* and private *(gendarme)*.

The Garde Républicaine is a paramilitary organization with an estimated strength of about 2,000 officers and men. It reinforces the Gendarmerie in the administrative regions. In Conakry, besides guarding the presidential palace, it provides the band and the motorcycle escort that are used for official welcoming ceremonies for visiting dignitaries. One company guards the portion of Camp Alpha Yaya, near the Conakry airport, that is used as a political prison.

Recruitment, Education & Training

The police personnel are trained at the National Police School at Kankan. This school was initially French in organization and curriculum, but the arrival of Czech and other East European instructors in 1969 served to degallicize the flavor of the training programs.

The Penal System

Little information is available on Guinea's penal system. The prison service was organized soon after independence, taking over the facilities established by the French in colonial times. From 1958 to 1960 the general responsibility of the prison service was vested in the Ministry of Justice. In 1972 it was transferred to the Ministry of the Interior and Security.

There are three kinds of penal facilities: the Camayeene Central Prison in Conakry; local prisons, of which there is at least one in each administrative region; and undefined lockups maintained at the district or *arrondissement* level. Political prisoners usually are sent to security force installations for confinement. There are three such camps in the Conakry area: Camp Mamdou Boiro, Camp Almamy Samory and Camp Alpha Yaya. Heads of penal facilities usually are former police commissioners in the same region.

The widespread use of penal labor was one of the bitter complaints against the French colonial administration; yet the practice continued under President Sékou Touré. Rehabilitation is accepted in principle but without any practical application.

Under Touré no criminal statistics were ever published, and little data have emerged since his death. The incidence of and trends in crime can be gauged only from official speeches and press reports. During the colonial period, smuggling was a flourishing activity against which law-enforcement efforts were largely ineffective. Both smuggling and black-marketing have continued unabated. This clandestine trade, which apparently is both in and out of the country, involves a wide variety of consumer goods and also diamonds from the forest region. The task of suppressing black-market operations is a difficult one, as most customers tend to protect the illicit dealers who supply goods that are often unobtainable through regular channels. Illegal currency transactions have also plagued the country since independence.

The penal system is based on the Penal Code of 1965, as amended in 1968, and the companion Code of Criminal Procedure. The Penal Code has three books: Book I defines three categories of offenses: *crimes* (felonies), *délits* (misdemeanors) and *contraventions* (violations). Book II establishes the general principles to be followed in determining criminal responsibility. Book III specifies punishments for the various crimes.

GUYANA

BASIC FACT SHEET

Official Name: Cooperative Republic of Guyana
Area: 214,970 sq km
Population: 765,844 (1987)
Capital: Georgetown
Nature of Government: Limited democracy
Language: English
Currency: Guyana dollar
GNP: $460 million (1985)
Territorial Divisions: 6 districts
Population per Police Officer: 190
Police Expenditures per 1,000: N.A.

History & Background

The Guyana Police Force (GPF) was established under Police Ordinance 10 of 1891 and has been continued under Chapter 77 of the Guyana Police Ordinance since independence in 1966. The force is an armed semimilitary unit administered by a commissioner under the control, since 1961, of the Ministry of Home Affairs. The GPF consists of the regular force together with the supernumerary, rural and special constables. Among its areas of responsibility are traffic control, national security, passports and immigration, registration of aliens, and firearms control. It includes a mounted branch trained for riot control. Members of the force are normally unarmed. The Fire Department, which was part of the GPF until 1957, is now a separate organization.

Structure & Organization

Guyana is divided into seven police divisions commanded by senior officers based at their divisional headquarters with the exception of F Division, which is at the force headquarters in Georgetown.

The two main administrative divisions are Line Operations and Staff Services. Line Operations is responsible for operational functions, while Staff Services is responsible for supply, personnel, data communications, transport and other material. The Staff Services functions are carried out mainly at GPF headquarters and Line Operations functions mainly in the territorial divisions. Line Operations duties comprise patrol and beat, traffic regulation and control, and criminal investigation. Staff Services duties en-

compass budgeting, planning and administration, police records system, purchasing, transportation, and the forensic science laboratory. In the territorial divisions, Staff Services functions are under Line Operations supervision, while in the headquarters Line Operations functions are directly controlled and supervised by Line Operations agencies.

The working uniform consists of dark blue trousers and short-sleeved, open-neck shirt, together with a dark blue cap. Senior officers wear a khaki tunic with short sleeves and an open neck with matching trousers and a dark blue cap.

Recruiting, Education & Training

No information is available.

The Penal System

The Prisons and Probation Department is also under the portfolio of the minister of home affairs. The department is administered by a director who controls the main prisons at Georgetown, Mazaruni and New Amsterdam. First offenders sentenced to short terms are sent to New Amsterdam and those serving longer sentences to Sibley Hall, Mazaruni. Repeated offenders serving over three months are jailed at Mazaruni or Georgetown.

Responsibility for the care of prisoners is that of a chief probation officer. He is also responsible for the administration of two juvenile schools: the Essequibo Boys' School and the Belfield Girls' School. The Probation Service also provides matrimonial conciliation services. In addition, it runs a remand home and probation hostel in Georgetown for probational juveniles. Rehabilitation and training are increasingly emphasized in the new prison facilities in the country.

Police statistics are published regularly, and they show significant increases in the incidence of crime. Of the reported offenses, murder, larceny and arson are the highest, but there are wide annual variations.

HAITI

BASIC FACT SHEET

Official Name: Republic of Haiti
Area: 27,749 sq km
Population: 6,187,115 (1987)
Capital: Port-au-Prince
Nature of Government: Military dictatorship
Language: French
Currency: Gourd
GNP: $1.8 billion (1986)
Territorial Divisions: 5 departments
Population per Police Officer: 400
Police Expenditures per 1,000: N.A.

Structure & Organization

The Police Department of Haiti (Département de Police) is a relatively weak and poorly organized agency, overshadowed by the military on the one hand and the National Security Volunteers (Volontaires de la Sécurité Nationale, VSN), formerly the Tontons Macoutes, on the other. Despite its name, the Port-au-Prince Police Force is an Army unit. Each of the five departments has its own regional police units. No information is available on their functions and operations.

On the other hand, many of the normal police duties are carried out by the paramilitary National Security Volunteers, organized by former President François Duvalier as a counterpoise to the Army. VSN members receive the equivalent of basic military training and are on the payroll of the communities they serve. Total strength of the VSN is estimated at 15,000. The VSN performs internal security functions and runs a nationwide informer system.

Recruitment, Education & Training

No information is available.

The Penal System

The Penal Code of Haiti was first promulgated in August 1835 and was amended nine times between 1846 and 1935. It recognizes three categories of offenses—felonies, misdemeanors and police contraventions—and defines the penalties for each. The punishments enumerated are: death, imprisonment for life with forced labor, imprisonment with forced labor for a specified number of years and jail for a specific period. Death sentences are executed by a firing squad in a public area. Men condemned to forced labor are employed on public projects and women inside the penal institutions.

There are two penitentiaries: Fort Dimanche and the National Penitentiary, both in Port-au-Prince. Prisons are in the cities of Les Cayes, Hinche, Gonaïves, Cap-Haïtien and Port-de-Paix. Prison labor is for state use only, and prisoner-made goods are made available to public agencies. Prison conditions are very primitive, although prisoners are permitted to receive visitors, food and medical treatment. Prisoners are often kept, especially in the notorious Casernes Dessalines military prison, in degrading circumstances, stripped to their underwear. The cells in the Casernes have no windows, no lights and only buckets for toilets.

No official statistics are available on crime, but based on newspaper reports, the leading categories of crime are those against property, disturbing the peace and those against persons. Crime rates are relatively low in the rural areas, perhaps because Haitians do not resort to violence unless severely threatened. The swift and brutal punishments meted out by the Tontons Macoutes during the long Duvalier years also helped to keep the crime rate down.

HONDURAS

BASIC FACT SHEET

Official Name: Republic of Honduras
Area: 112,088 sq km
Population: 4,823,818 (1987)
Capital: Tegucigalpa
Nature of Government: Limited democracy
Languages: Spanish
Currency: Lempira
GNP: $2.6 billion (1986)
Territorial Division: 18 departments
Population per Police Officer: 1,040
Police Expenditures per 1,000: N.A.

Structure & Organization

Basic police functions are the responsibility of the Public Security Force (PSF), formerly the Special Security Corps (Cupreo Especial de Seguridad, CES), created in 1963 after the military coup of that year as a replacement for the Civil Guard, which had performed police functions until then. Technically the CES commander, an Army officer, is the secretary of defense, but day-to-day operations are under the immediate control of a director general. The force employs over 3,000 men, most of them drawn from the Army. The director general is assisted by a staff consisting of a subdirector general, an inspector general, a legal adviser and a Public Relations Department. An administrative and logistics section, a personnel and statistics section, a finance office, a telecommunications service and a medical service complete the headquarters.

Below this level, CES is split between specialized branches organized on a national scale and local units performing routine tasks. The specialized branches include, the Directorate of National Investigations (DNI), the Traffic Police, and training academies for officers and enlisted men.

The DNI is composed of Intelligence, Criminal, Identification and Immigration departments, a police laboratory, and a section dealing with minors. The frontier and rural units are responsible mainly for combating contraband activities. The Traffic Department, under a general commandant, is divided into offices dealing with vehicle inspection, licenses and registration, investigation of accidents and traffic routing.

Recruitment, Education & Training.

The FUSEP training school in Tegucigalpa conducts a variety of courses for both recruits and career officers. Subjects taught include police communications, patrol, investigation, first aid, control of civil disturbances, infantry instruction, civil procedure, the Criminal Code, interrogation and control of contraband. From time to time officers are sent to the International Police Academy in Washington, D.C., for further study.

The Security and Special Investigation Department of the Central Bank of Honduras handles offenses relating to currency and banking.

The Penal System

No penal statistics are available, but violent crimes are reportedly rare and happen mostly in the two cities of Tegucigalpa and San Pedro Sula. Burglary and theft are the most common offenses.

HONG KONG

Patrick Edobor Igbinovia

BASIC FACT SHEET

Official Name: Hong Kong
Area: 1,060 sq km
Population: 5,608,610 (1987)
Capital: Victoria
Nature of Government: British dependent territory
Language: English
Currency: Hong Kong dollar
GNP: $34.2 billion (1985)
Territorial Divisions: Hong Kong, Kowloon, New Territories
Population per Police Officer: 220
Police Expenditures per 1,000: $76,780

History & Background

The history of the Royal Hong Kong Police Force dates back to the colony's beginnings when, in April 1841, a former Army officer was appointed magistrate with powers to recruit men for police duties. The majority of these early policemen were either ex-soldiers or ex-sailors and, in 1844, the first Indians were recruited. The following year a superintendent of the London Metropolitan Police arrived with two inspectors to organize a police force capable of establishing and maintaining law and order in the new colony. He started with 71 Europeans, 51 Chinese and 46 Indians.

As Hong Kong expanded over the years, so did its police force. The Water Police were increased, and the harbor was continuously patrolled. In 1867, the first contingent of 100 Sikh recruits arrived and, during 1872, forty-five Scots arrived to reinforce the British contingent. The title of captain superintendent of police was changed to inspector-general in 1936 and in 1937 it was again changed, this time to commissioner of police. The force continued to expand after World War II and, by 1950, was 4,162 strong, almost double the prewar figure. By the end of 1980, the force, which started off with a humble band of ex-servicemen, had over 21,981 disciplined and 4,272 civil posts, giving a grand total of 26,253 men and women serving, and all the specialist departments associated with a modern police force.

Structure & Organization

For policing, Hong Kong is divided into four territorial districts: Kowloon Police District, Hong Kong Island Police District, New Territories Police District and Marine Police District. Overall direction of the force is by the commissioner of police from his headquarters on Hong Kong island. Each police district is divided into divisions and subdivisions. There are eight divisions in Kowloon, six in the New Territories, four on Hong Kong Island and three in the Marine Police District. Each district has a headquarters and a Criminal Investigation Department. The three land districts also have traffic offices. Each land district is commanded by an assistant commissioner. He is assisted by two chief superintendents, one of whom is the deputy district police commander with a special responsibility for operational matters; the other oversees district administration.

Hong Kong waters lie within a 190-kilometer boundary, commonly referred to as the Square Boundary. The sea area is 1,850 square kilometers, the focal point of which is the principal port of Victoria, whose container terminal is reputed to be the third largest in terms of tonnage in the world. In addition to 15 fishing ports, the Marine Police District encompasses 244 islands, some of which are sparsely inhabited or uninhabited.

The Marine Police District is commanded by an assistant commissioner, with a senior superintendent as his deputy. A superintendent is responsible for operational matters. Administration is dealt with by a chief staff inspector and an executive officer.

The Marine Police District fleet consists of 92 vessels, ranging from 34-meter cruising launches to static pontoons.

Policing on Hong Kong, Kowloon and in the main towns of the New Territories follows a similar pattern. The outlying rural districts are policed by patrols that often go out for several days at a time and so provide regular police cover for remote villages. The Marine Police District patrols the 1,850 square kilometers of territorial waters, including harbor areas and outlying islands. There are 20,000 small craft to control, with a maritime population of about 80,000. Launch patrols vary from eight hours to three days.

Criminal Investigation Department (CID)

The Criminal Investigation Department has its headquarters on Hong Kong Island, and there are CID detachments in each of the police districts. A wide range of work is covered by the department, which is divided into the Support Group and the Operations Group.

The department is commanded by a senior assistant commissioner as director of criminal investigation; his deputy is an assistant commissioner. The director is responsible for the coordination and efficiency of the CID as a whole, and he advises the commissioner on all matters relating to crime.

The CID is organized into three levels: Headquarters, District and Division. CID Headquarters is divided into four groups, each headed by a chief superintendent, and is organized as follows:

Special Operations
   Homicide Bureau
   Organized Crime Bureau
     Triad Society Bureau
     Special Crimes Division
   Criminal Intelligence Bureau
Commercial Crime

Narcotics
Administration and Support
   Criminal Records Bureau
   Identification Bureau
   Interpol Bureau
   Ballistics and Firearms Identification Bureau
   Crime Prevention Bureau

All CID Headquarters units are available on a 24-hour basis, either in a specialist capacity or on a complementary basis to CID District and Division formations.

District CID components consist largely of crime units concentrating on specific serious crimes; they are commanded by a senior superintendent, who is responsible to the district police commander.

Divisional CID components are commanded by the senior superintendent commanding the unit concerned and comprise investigation teams, action squads, the Antitriad Section and the Intelligence Section.

At the end of 1980 the overall strength of the CID stood at 4,484 in all ranks, together with 649 civilian officers in supporting roles.

Operations and Support Services

Communications and Signals The force operates a wide range of telecommunications systems, which include computer-assisted command and control centers, microwave trunk links between centers, a personal radio system in the urban areas, and District- and territorywide VHF mobile radio systems.

In 1980 an interim scheme was designed and installed to provide a police communications system in the Mass Transit Railway. Personnel operating in the modified initial system now communicate with their control center from within trains, tunnels and station concourses and aboveground. Consultants have been engaged to design and engineer a police communications system for the full extended Mass Transit Railway.

A major project was undertaken to design alterations to the traffic networks and to compile specifications for tender for the complete replacement of all equipment on these networks. Installation commenced in 1981.

The force operates a computer-assisted teleprinter system, which was expanded in 1980 by three receiver and 16 transmitter units to give the system 115 units. It now includes all formations down to the subdivisional level, with the exception of a new remote rural subdivision. During the year the store-and-forward teleprinter system, which is interfaced with the command and control center computers, handled some 286,000 messages, many of them to multiple addressees.

Projects completed in 1980 included the provision of dedicated intercommand links between POLMIL Headquarters and higher command at district command and control centers, using microwave links and private telephone circuits; the removal of New Territories Police District Headquarters telecommunications to the new headquarters at Sha Tin; the complete remodeling and reprovision of Marine POLHIL Headquarters to provide facilities for joint command of maritime operations relating to illegal immigration; enhancement of the computers used to assist the control and command centers that provide a wanted-vehicle checklist; and additional visual display units and high-speed printers to extract instant hard copy from the VDU's and to increase the efficiency of the computer system generally.

The force operates a comprehensive telephone network comprising 63 interlinked exchanges; 10 small automatic telephone exchanges have been installed in various units to meet increasing demand.

Police Tactical Unit (PTU) This unit has an establishment of six companies and provides an immediate reserve of manpower for use in an emergency. It fills an important training role by providing up-to-date instruction in internal society and crowd control tactics, with company personnel drawn in rotation from police districts and who serve for 30 weeks with the unit.

The Police Personnel Carrier Unit also operates under the direction of the PTU and comprises 14 Saracen armored personnel carriers, which are used in emergencies ranging from natural disasters to internal security operations. Also under the command of the commandant of the Police Tactical Unit is the Special Duties Unit, a highly trained volunteer group that forms part of the force's counterterrorist capability.

Royal Hong Kong Auxiliary Police Force The Royal Hong Kong Auxiliary Police Force has an establishment of 5,176, with its commandant in the rank of senior assistant commissioner (auxiliary). He is supported by an Executive Headquarters Unit commanded by a regular chief superintendent and staffed by regular and auxiliary police officers. Each district is commanded by a chief superintendent (auxiliary).

The command structure is similar to that of the Regular Police Force, being divided into districts, divisions and special units.

The Auxiliary Police Force is an integral part of the Regular Police Force. There is a unified command at all levels; day-to-day auxiliary officers work alongside their regular counterparts and assist them in maintaining law and order.

In an emergency, when the commissioner may order mobilization of the Auxiliary Police Force, their officers provide valuable support for internal security. The partial mobilization of the Auxiliary Police Force since July 1979 helped considerably to ease the strain on regular manpower in combating the influx of refugees and illegal immigrants.

Parity of pay with the Regular Police Force for junior officers was approved in April 1980; as a result, there was healthy response to join the Auxiliary Police Force, and additional recruit training courses were organized to cope with it. The Auxiliary Police Force was brought up to its full establishment in 1981.

The efficiency of the Auxiliary Police Force is maintained by scheduled in-service training at Auxiliary Police Headquarters on Hong Kong Island and at various other unit bases. For the convenience of those auxiliary recruits residing in the New Territor-

ities, a training center was opened in Kwai Chung in 1980.

In winter a dark blue tunic and matching trousers are worn with a shirt and tie. In summer a khaki, open-neck tunic with short sleeves is worn with khaki shorts and blue knee socks. A blue cap and black Sam Browne belt are worn throughout the year.

All officers of all ranks carry a .38 Colt Police Positive revolver when on duty (a .38 Colt Detective Special for the plainclothes branch). Rifles, shotguns and submachine guns are available for special tasks, and the Marine Police District boats carry a 5.5 Browning MG.

Recruitment, Education & Training

In 1980, the minimum educational qualification for recruits joining the force as police constables was raised from Primary 6 to Form 5 (Grade 11). Consideration, however, still is given to applicants with a minimum of Form 3 education if they have relevant working experience or other attributes worthy of acceptance. The decision to raise the entry point caused a drop in applications, but the number of candidates found acceptable increased.

Basic Training
Constables The course for constables, at the Police Training School lasts 20 weeks and, like that for inspectors, covers law, police and court procedures, self-defense, first aid, life saving, weapons training and drill.

At the end of their formal training, constables undergo a period of supervised assignment to operational units. Prior to graduating from the school, both constables and inspectors receive joint internal security training.

Inspectors Following an extensive two-year review, a revised inspectorate training syllabus was implemented in October 1980. In addition to academic and practical subjects, the revised syllabus seeks to develop management and leadership skills.

After the first week of familiarization and administration, overseas officers commence an eight-week course of instruction in colloquial Cantonese. Simultaneously, local officers embark on a varied program which includes community service, adventure training, assignment to government departments, and written projects. Local and overseas officers then combine for a 27-week segment of professional training.

Continuation Training
Continuation training includes promotion courses for noncommissioned officers; refresher courses for station sergeants and sergeants after three, six, and

eleven years' service in the rank and constables after three, six, eleven and sixteen years' service in the rank; traffic courses for district and divisional traffic personnel, traffic wardens and senior traffic wardens; and command courses for inspectors and superintendents.

The expanded district continuation training scheme has continued to function effectively. Constables graduating from the Police Training School attended two consecutive days of training a month for two years in their own districts. The scheme serves as a link between the induction training and in-service training. Ten training centers are established in the four police districts and serve approximately 3,500 constables.

Specialist Training

Detective Training The main 12-week CID training courses take in an average of 20 inspectorate officers, 20 sergeants and 100 constables for each course. Inspectors from the Immigration Department, the Customs and Excise service, and Police officers from Malaysia and the Philippines also attend. Emphasis is placed on the practical aspects of criminal investigation and documentation.

New premises at Kai Tak have made it possible to commence additional courses.

There are four CID training courses a year for uniformed branch Inspectors with CID potential. Each course lasts four weeks.

Courses for speaking functional English for selected junior officers also last four weeks, are run by the government's Training Division and are designed to improve the English of officers who already have a reasonable knowledge of it.

Marine Training

Entry into the Marine Police is voluntary for both junior and inspectorate officers. The former may elect to join on recruitment to the Police Training School or may apply to transfer at any time after leaving the school. Inspectors are drawn from the general officer cadre and may join the Marine Police immediately after completing the same training as their land-based colleagues or apply later.

The school provides a number of courses, ranging from two-week refresher courses to induction courses lasting four weeks, and five-month courses for radiotelegraphists. After completing the necessary sea time, both junior officers and inspectors must take examinations for their Marine Department certificates in navigation, engineering and radiotelegraphy.

There has been a steady increase in the number of women officers joining the Marine Police. Training for women in both navigation and radiotelegraphy is exactly the same as that for men and, after completing

their initial training, women officers serve on launches with their male counterparts. In 1980, a total of 593 Regular Police officers of all ranks completed Marine Police courses. Additionally, 69 launch mechanics attended courses in Singapore to familiarize themselves with the engines in the new Damen launches.

Language Training

The need for police officers to be trained to speak both English and Cantonese is a matter of major importance. In addition, it is recognized that a knowledge of certain other languages and dialects is becoming increasingly desirable due to the influx of tourists.

All members of the force are encouraged to obtain a language qualification; indeed, it is a condition for confirmation to the permanent establishment or for the offer of a further contract for an overseas officer to attain a standard of competency in colloquial Cantonese. Officers attend full-time training courses as part of their induction training and also during their second tour of service.

Fluency in English is a requirement before an NCO or a constable may be promoted to the inspectorate or for a direct entry appointment without previous police experience. When officers lack academic or English-language qualifications on appointment, facilities exist for them to attend full- or part-time courses at the Police Education and Language Section or at the numerous educational institutions in Hong Kong.

The Police Education and Language Section, staffed by qualified teachers, is jointly managed by the Force Training Wing and the Civil Service Training Division. This section provides language training and further education for members of the force on full-time and day-release bases.

Cadet Training

During its first decade of operation, the Police Cadet School has provided an increasingly important reservoir of recruits for the force. In addition, it projects a good image by its continuous involvement in community affairs and service.

Adventure Training

The Police Adventure Training Unit (PATU) operates from the Police Cadet School and offers 11-day in-service residential courses to all officers of the force, including auxiliaries. Annually 23 courses are held, six specifically for recruit inspectors from the PTS and two for rural area patrols from the Marine Police District.

The courses are run on the "outward bound" principles of character and leadership training through physical challenge. Activities include expedition work on both land (hiking) and sea (canoeing), rock climbing, orienteering and survival exercises.

The Penal System

The 1980s saw a significant increase in crime; overall crime registered an increase of 18.4%, with upward movements of 20.7% in key crime and 20.1% in violent crime. The underlying causes encompass social and economic considerations, including a population increase (exacerbated by heavy illegal immigration) and the creation of urban communities in the form of new towns; a further factor was the redeployment of significant numbers of police officers to counter illegal immigration, which for a time weakened urban police coverage.

Juvenile crime—crime involving children from 7 to 15 years old—has reached a disturbing level. The causes of this upsurge have yet to be identified, but matters such as decreasing parental control, triad influence in high-density housing areas, violence depicted in films and television, insufficient recreational facilities, and tempting displays of luxury products in department stores are contributing factors.

Involvement by recent immigrants in crime is also a matter of considerable public interest. Of particular concern is the involvement of recent immigrants, particularly those who have arrived in Hong Kong illegally, in serious and high-value robberies, more often than not involving use of firearms.

There has also been significant growth in the incidence of crime in the New Territories. This was not unexpected, because of the rapid rate of urbanization and population growth there. However, in general the distribution of crime among districts is proportionate to population.

Throughout the 1980s "quick cash crimes," as reflected by robberies and burglaries, have remained at a high level.

CRIME STATISTICS (1984)

		Number Reported	Attempts %	Cases Solved %	Crime per 100,000	Offenders	Females %	Juveniles %	Strangers %
1.	Murder	88	4.5	67.0	1.64	86	15.1	10.5	
2.	Sex offenses, including rape	1,354		68.5	25.30	1,045	2.4	5.2	
3.	Rape	87		52.9	1.63	45	0.0	0.0	
4.	Serious assault	7,874		66.4	147.14	5,030	7.4	7.0	
5.	All theft	54,202		27.3	1,012.86	13,452	14.8	13.2	
6.	Aggravated theft	23,276		14.7	434.95	3,844	4.0	19.8	
7.	Robbery and violent theft	10,624		20.5	198.53	2,596	4.6	19.5	
8.	Breaking and entering	12,652		9.9	236.42	1,248	2.6	20.7	
9.	Auto theft								
10.	Other thefts	30,926		36.8	577.90	9,608	19.1	10.6	
11.	Fraud	2,041		39.3	38.14	711	9.8	4.2	
12.	Counterfeiting	29		65.5	0.54	25	20.0	0.0	
13.	Drug offenses	13,134		96.0	245.43	11,206	5.3	0.7	
14.	Total offenses	94,135		48.7	1,759.07	43,311	9.2	6.8	

Criteria of juveniles: aged from 7 to 15 years.
Note: Information for some categories is not available.

HUNGARY

BASIC FACT SHEET

Official Name: Hungarian People's Republic
Area: 93,030 sq km
Population: 10,609,447 (1987)
Capital: Budapest
Nature of Government: Communist dictatorship
Language: Hungarian
Currency: Forint
GNP: $20.72 billion (1985)
Territorial Divisions: 19 megyes, 5 autonomous cities
Population per Police Officer: 710
Police Expenditures per 1,000: N.A.

Structure & Organization

The Hungarian police system is composed of a number of related police establishments, including the Civil or People's Police (Rendorseg), the Workers' Militia, Internal Security Troops, Industrial Guards, Security Police and the Frontier Guard.

The Civil Police are the local law-enforcement agency, performing routine police functions, such as traffic control. Although they function in local jurisdictions, they are organized centrally under the Ministry of the Interior. Various types of special units exist within the Civil Police. The Air Police control airfields and, with the help of helicopters, assist ground police in rescue work and criminal pursuit. The Water Police patrol the major rivers, and also cooperate with Border Guards in combating smuggling and illegal border crossings. The Civil Police also issue identification cards and maintain records on all nationals and aliens. Operationally the police are divided into towns and they, in turn, into districts, boroughs and stations. Training is provided at the Police Officers' Academy, established in 1971.

The Workers' Militia or Workers' Guard (Munkas Orseg) was formed in late 1956 or early 1957 to suppress the 1956 revolutionaries. Organized along the lines of a national guard, the militia was drawn from workers who did their training after working hours and in their home areas. Over 80% of the militia are Communist Party members, and an increasing number are women. Over 65% of the militia are industrial or agricultural workers. Estimates of the militia's membership vary widely, but most observers place it at about 250,000. There are few restrictions on the quality, experience or age of new members.

Unit commanders undergo 12 weeks of training at the militia's central school in Budapest, where 65% of the time is spent in practical exercises.

The Internal Security Troops (Belso Karhatalom) have existed since the earliest days of the Communist regime. The force is most frequently referred to as interior troops and occasionally as the constabulary. They are lightly armed but have a considerable amount of mobile equipment, as they are required to be able to respond to calls from any part of the country. Career men serve on a voluntary basis, but recruits are acquired from the annual draft of 18-year-olds. The conscripted youth serve from two to three years. Interior troops are a uniformed force and operate in typical military units. Uniforms are the same as those worn by the Army personnel but are distinguished by blue backgrounds on rank shoulder boards and collar insignia.

Industrial Guards and the Government Guard Command are elements formed after the 1956 revolt. Industrial Guard units are charged not only with preventing sabotage but also with containing pilferage, which was rampant during the post revolt period. Now the men serve as full-time guards on a regular work and salary basis. The Government Guard Command (Kormanyarseg Parancsnoksag) was formed in 1972 under the Ministry of the Interior. The guards serve in the capital as an elite unit on ceremonial occasions.

The Security Police or Secret Police is modern-day Hungary's most visible Stalinist legacy. Although the State Security Authority (Allamvedelmi Hatosag, AVH) existed under that name for a few years only, the Secret Police still are generally referred to as the

AVH. Detested, hated and feared, the AVH ran a reign of terror until 1956. They earned their reputation by operating stealthily, making arrests at night and holding their victims incommunicado, and after brutal interrogation, forcing them to confess to some crime against the state, for which they were either executed or sentenced to long terms in prison or detention camps. They particularly harassed Church organizations, youth groups, mass organizations and former aristocrats. They controlled passports and monitored all movements of people into and out of the country. Two divisions conducted trials and prosecutions of individuals apprehended by the agency. Another maintained dossiers on all persons who had membership in any non-Communist group and thus were potentially dangerous.

The AVH was dissolved in 1956 after they had fired into unarmed crowds. Although they were reformed under a new name and invested with a few of the old police powers, the worst practices were virtually eliminated. The new Security Police is as much hated as the old but not nearly as feared.

The Frontier Guard is similar to the AVH in personnel strength, organization, training and equipment. They also wear Army uniforms, distinguished by green backgrounds on shoulder and collar insignia. Most of the force is deployed along the land boundaries with Yugoslavia and Austria, where the border installations include double barbed-wire fencing, strips of plowed and carefully raked earth, watchtowers, searchlights, land mines, and 24-hour patrols using trained dogs.

Recruitment, Education & Training

No information is available on recruitment, education and training.

The Penal System

Hungary's traditional legal system had been influenced by Roman law but, in contrast to it, had no real codes. An accumulation of legal custom was compiled in 1517 and modified in succeeding centuries. A Criminal Code was finally published in 1878. Its general portions were rewritten in the early 1950s, but the articles pertaining to specific crimes were permitted to remain as they were until the entire code was republished in 1961. The first formal Civil Code was also published at that time. Both codes and a decree on criminal procedure were republished in the early 1970s, aligning the legal system more closely with the Constitution as amended in 1972. Terminology is also more definitive. The revised codes reflect a decreasing emphasis on human rights and a growing emphasis on state security. Sentences authorized for antistate crimes are more severe than those for crimes against persons and personal property. The state is the paramount responsibility of the criminal justice

CRIME STATISTICS (1984)

		Number Reported	Attempts %	Cases Solved %	Crime per 100,000	Offenders	Females %	Juveniles %	Strangers %
1.	Murder	397	48.9	94.6	3.72	394			
2.	Sex offenses, including rape	2,044		75.6	19.14	1,498			
3.	Rape	653		67.0	6.11	624			
4.	Serious assault	6,016		82.7	56.34	5,249			
5.	All theft	76,887		46.6	720.00	22,821			
6.	Aggravated theft								
7.	Robbery and violent theft	1,653		62.6	15.48	1,470			
8.	Breaking and entering	22,537		45.1	211.04	5,656			
9.	Auto theft	424			3.97				
10.	Other thefts	54,350		47.1	508.95	17,165			
11.	Fraud	3,846		87.2	36.02	1,954			
12.	Counterfeiting	47			0.44	29			
13.	Drug offenses	457			4.28	119			
14.	Total offenses	157,036		67.6	1,470.54	83,493	13.5	11.6	2

Criteria of juveniles: aged from 14 to 18 years.
Note: Information for some categories is not available.

system; the individual merits protection only when he or she is a cooperating and contributing member of the state. The judiciary is not an independent branch of government but is subordinate to the Ministry of Justice.

There are four classes of prison regimes: three classes of penitentiaries and local jails. Maximum-security penitentiaries remain the core of the system. The same prison complex may include more than one class of prisons, either in separate buildings or in different sections of the same building. The courts determine the regime to which a prisoner is assigned based on the gravity of the crime and his or her criminal history. Rehabilitation programs vary widely, depending on the facilities available. However, all inmates are required to work, either within the prison complex or outside. Labor camps, a familiar phenomenon in the early years of the Communist regime and after the 1956 rebellion, no longer exist. The prison population has also declined sharply since many antisocialist activities have been decriminalized. Inmates serving time for political and economic crimes are fewer than ever before in the history of Communist Hungary.

At the same time, nonpolitical crimes have shown a steady upswing. Crimes against public order, serious and violent crimes, juvenile crimes, and crimes committed by women are the major categories that have increased sufficiently to cause official concern. Gang crimes have reached dangerous proportions. Social crimes, such as begging and prostitution, particularly vexing to the regime, which sees no place for them in a socialist society, have also increased, especially in the Budapest area.

Alcohol is a factor in about one-fourth of all crimes and in one-half or more of attempted murders, crimes against juveniles, and crimes against public order. It also leads to a large proportion of traffic accidents and drownings. Hungary's suicide rate is the highest in the world, and at least one-half of all suicides are committed after heavy bouts of drinking. On-the-job drinking has become such a problem that plant managers are required to use breath analyzers on workers before each work session.

INDIA

S. M. Diaz

BASIC FACT SHEET

Official Name: Republic of India
Area: 3,287,590 sq km
Population: 800,325,817 (1987)
Capital: New Delhi
Nature of Government: Parliamentary democracy
Languages: Hindi, English, 14 other languages
Currency: Rupee
GNP: $194.82 billion (1985)
Territorial Divisions: 22 states; 9 union territories
Population per Police Officer: 820
Police Expenditures per 1,000: N.A.

History & Background

Historically the modern state police forces evolved from the Sind model (1843), adopted by Sir Charles Napier soon after his conquest of the area. His experiment in Sind of a police organization functioning on the pattern of the Royal Irish Constabulary had succeeded, while other experiments elsewhere of trying to adopt the Metropolitan Police System and the Moghul Police pattern failed. As a result the Sind model was extended to Bombay (1853) and to Madras (1859). The Police Commission of 1860 recommended its adoption all over the country, and the Indian Police Act of 1861 followed. The principal features of the Police Act of 1861 were that policing was to be a civil function exercised by the state governments, and that the state police force was to be organized hierarchically on the lines of the Army, under an inspector general of police, who was to be responsible for the internal administration of the police and accountable to the state government. On August 15, 1947, India became independent and in 1950 it became a republic. Strangely enough independent India did not make any radical changes in the structure of the police system it inherited from the British.

Structure & Organization

The total number of police personnel in the country, uniformed and mufti, as well as armed and civil police, is estimated at one million. This includes the state police forces and the central police organizations. Police is a state subject and, therefore, the state police forces are the mainstay of the country's police system. Of the total police strength of 45,000 in Tamilnadu, a typical state, 40,000 represent the civil police, including about 2,500, who function out of uniform, in the CID at state level, covering the intelligence, investigation, antismuggling and other units as well as the Crime Branch, Special Branch and the Records Sections at the district level. The district also has armed reserves, which are counted along with the civil police strength of 40,000.

The state-level armed police units account for the remaining 5000. In Tamilnadu State, there are 873 police stations.

A rural police station normally polices a population of about 75,000 to 1,000,000. The area of the jurisdiction varies. But the strength of the jurisdiction consists usually of one subinspector, two head constables and 15 to 20 constables. They look after all the law and order, crime investigation and other work of the precinct. On the other hand, an urban police station, which covers only about 40,000 to 50,000 inhabitants living in a part of a city or large town, is functionally divided between law and order and crime and is provided with a staff of two subinspectors, six head constables and about 36 to 40 constables. This is because of the multifarious duties of policing that arise in an urban community, with a heavier rate of crime as well as other deviances of a minor nature, which are normally ignored in a rural community. Traffic regulation and action on traffic violations are dealt with by a separate unit, with detachments organized for the whole city. In an urban police area, the ratio of police to civilians is one to 600, while in a rural community it is one to about 1,100. These figures take into account police engaged in all types of duties. The average rate is one police officer per 1,000 civilians. The figure is higher in most of the states and less in some states. The all-India figure is 13.1 per 10,000 (*Crime in India,* 1981). The cost of the police organization to the state exchequer is ordinarily about 11% of the state budget.

The objective of the police in India, as in any other democratic country, is the protection of society, through effective maintenance of public peace and order and meaningful protection of the life, property and cherished rights of the citizen. The following are the resultant functions:

1. safeguarding internal security of the state

2. maintenance of public peace and order

3. enforcement of the law, through prevention of crime and detection and prosecution of offenders

4. social control through social legislations

5. social defense

6. social welfare

In India, the principal law enforcement organizations, as already stated, are the state police forces. Their structure is hierarchical. The chief of the state police is the director-general of police. He has senior aides assisting him, territorially or functionally, with the rank of inspector general or deputy inspector general. The really important functionary at the middle level is the superintendent of police in charge of the district. He in turn is assisted by sub-divisional police officers and inspectors of police. However, the station house officer in charge of a police precinct, either with the rank of subinspector of police or inspector of police, is the backbone of the police organization. He exercises all police authority under the law and has the most contacts with the people. His staff consists of the requisite number of constables and head constables and sometimes an assistant subinspector in large stations.

A police station or precinct is the base of operation for all police activities of the locality, such as patroling, inquiries, surveillance of criminals, reporting of crime and investigation, etc. All police stations have communication facilities, and transport facilities are progressively being provided. In the cities, there is coverage by patrol cars linked to a central control room, with facilities for dealing with emergencies. Because this coverage is only a fraction of what it is in advanced countries, response to calls gets delayed. There are other police agencies under the Ministry of Home Affairs of the Central Government, such as the Central Bureau of Investigation (CBI), Intelligence Bureau (IB), Central Reserve Police (CRP), Border Security Force (BSF), Central Industrial Security Force (CISF), National Police Academy (NPA), etc. The railways have a Railway Protection Force (RPF).

The state police organizations function under the provisions of the Indian Police Act of 1861. For prevention of crime and for apprehension of the offender, as well as for search and seizure, the Criminal Procedure Code of 1973 prescribes the authority. Provisions exist in the same enactment for registration and investigation of a crime report and the interrogation of a suspected offender and other witnesses. Police functionaries are answerable for their actions, through their departmental superiors, to the home minister of the state, who normally is also the chief minister. While this is true in respect to police functions, which are discretionary, their accountability for mandatory duties under the law is only to the law of the land and to the courts. It was under these circumstances that the National Police Commission (1975–81) thought it fit to recommend a New Police Act and a pattern of broadbased nonpolitical public safety committees, as in Japan and Canada. Otherwise, police authority in India operates very much on the same lines as in other democratic countries. The right to use minimum force, including firearms, accrues to a police functionary under three sets of circumstances. The first is in self-defense, which is a right available to all citizens. The second is to prevent certain offenders from escaping, themselves personally or with their loot. Third and most important, a police officer of and above the rank of station house officer may, under certain circumstances, declare an assembly as unlawful and order it to disperse. If the assembly does not, he may resort to minimum force, including shooting, to disperse it in the public interest. With the increase in crimes of violence in contemporary society, this authority had to be exercised often in recent years, putting undue strain on the police and also resulting in mounting criticism. For actions by the police in the discharge of their duties, the police receive protection subject to the findings of judicial inquiries. However, police officers who have acted illegally, are liable for prosecution and punishment, as well as disciplinary action by the department.

The typical policeman may be described in each one of the three groups corresponding to the three levels of entry: the police constable at the lowest level, the subinspector of police in the middle and the police service officer in the higher echelons. The typical police officer on the beat may be of any adult age, generally male, educationally any level between 8th standard and 10th standard, married and living with his wife and at least two children, quite often in police quarters. His height ranges from five feet six inches to six feet and he is well-built, in many cases with a prominent mustache. He normally wears a red turban, or more recently a blue peak cap, and carries a *lathi,* which is a slightly longer and rougher version of a truncheon of a British police officer. Different ranks are identifiable by their insignia. These are roughly parallel to the Army's, but in white (not yellow) metal. On the other hand, the typical sub-inspector of police directly recruited is well educated and fairly competent. He wears a khaki uniform with a peak cap of the same color but is generally unarmed. He carries a revolver in a holster only when he goes on a particular job of apprehending an offender, or on a special raid or for dealing with a violent crowd. The Indian Police service officers belong to a higher educational level and are generally competent in their administrative assignments. In recent years, women have been admitted to all ranks of the police organization, including the Indian Police Service. Public attitude towards the police continues to be one of suspicion and non-cooperation.

The normal working hours of the ordinary police officer, on patrol or other duty, are eight hours a day. But the subinspector generally has no limitation to the working day of eight hours duty. Senior officers also have to work as long as it is necessary to clear their work. A typical police officer's daily work schedule involves, in addition to substantial hours of office routine, some parade ground work, investigation duties, visits to places for inquiring into complaints and appearances in court. While the junior functionary may attend to whatever he can within eight hours, the station house officer generally has to work from early morning to late evening without compensation to get all work done. The senior officer tries to adhere to regular office hours except for interviews, inspections and special assignments. The police do not have holidays as such. Police officers are entitled to a month's leave once a year, subject to the exigencies of service. Subinspectors and senior officers take longer leave once in two or three years.

In the past the police in India did their tours of duty in the time honored way, the higher levels on horseback and the others in bullock carts. Since then, the bullocks and horses have been replaced by fleets of vehicles, with the District Armed Reserve, consisting of transport vehicles, buses and lorries, jeeps and prison wagons. All cities and big towns have control rooms linked to a certain number of wireless patrol mobiles. Compared to the resources of other cities of the western world and even cities of Southeast Asia, the number of patrol vehicles is not adequate; citizens' calls made to the control rooms are responded to in 15 to 30 minutes. In the police stations, there is a pool of bicycles for individual use by

constables. The police of coastal towns have police boats to deal with smugglers and other offenders along the coast. Helicopters and other aerial vehicles for police use are rare. A few states have made a beginning with light planes and helicopters, but it will be a long time before they are in common use. Armed reserve units have at least one transport vehicle per platoon. All senior police officers have vehicles. The system of control rooms, with linked wireless mobiles and central striking forces, is also functioning reasonably well.

The police in India took to radio communications earlier, and with much more ease, than to mechanized transportation and other aspects of modernization. In the aftermath of World War II, defense surplus high frequency (HF) radio transceiver sets were made available to the police departments. Initially it was "fixed to fixed" radio communication with HF sets, using Morse Code. Later very high frequency (VHF) sets were manufactured in India and these replaced the HF sets for short-distance communication of the radio telephonic variety. A more recent development is the linkage of the VHF system to the micro-wave, and the consequent extension of the radio-telephonic communication system to long distances through high-level repeater stations. By this method most police stations have been brought into the VHF network. And the final development is the combination of this communication facility to the modern data-bank in the police computer system. All information and intelligence relating to crime and criminals are stored in computers, ready to be extracted and used whenever required. The Indian police computers are now responding more quickly to calls for information from various police stations. The on-line processing system, however, has not yet taken shape.

Internal Security Operations

Maintenance of public peace and order is the state police's job. Since independence, riots have increased enormously as a result of an increasing consciousness of the citizen's rights. But the police have by and large managed these situations reasonably well. They have also conducted massive general elections successfully. It is only during statewide political demonstrations or terrorist activities that the police have found themselves in need of calling for the support of the special central police or the Army to maintain internal order. Most countries have developed their own anti-riot police systems. In India, the Civil Police with the support of the Reserve Police Sections perform this role. The sequence of the exercise is warning—use of gas; warning—*lathi* charge; warning—use of firearms. Then, the armed police of the state and the Central Reserve Police come in, as a second line of reserve, for maintaining public peace and order. These forces have been pressed into service quite often in recent years to deal with emerging law and other situations. Only in rare cases have the police found it necessary to call in the army in aid of the Civil Authority. The riot police normally have guns that use ammunition with staying power. They also use steel helmets, bamboo shields and sticks. They have not yet taken to wearing bulletproof vests. While dealing with students, the police in India use light canes instead of *lathis*. Student agitations ordinarily receive kid-glove treatment, which perhaps is one reason for the increasing incidence of such cases. In dealing with guerrillas and terrorists, however, the "rule of law" police methods have been found wanting even with a relatively homogeneous population. In India, with its heterogenous and pluralistic society, it is even less effective. The police are slowly learning to deal with such developments; they will also need appropriate legal and other instruments, which are being gradually provided now. There are bomb disposal squads. Other surveillance, bugging of telephones and interception of mails are done within limits and with the prior approval of the appropriate authority in the rare cases that warrant them.

Traffic Police

The traffic police form a separate wing of the police organization of every city and large town in the country. In the rural areas, the ordinary civil police themselves attend to traffic police duties. In the cities, where the traffic police are separately organized, they are under a special deputy commissioner of police, reporting directly to the commissioner of police of the city. Their functions are primarily traffic regulation, enforcement and investigation. For effective enforcement, the police do not yet have modern radar-based equipment for recording speeds but manage with flying squads and speed-trap units. The traffic police wear white shirts for better visibility. These officers at the traffic points, regulating and enforcing traffic on the roads, are obviously the most visible representatives of the police. Their good or bad performance, therefore, catches the public eye most readily, and leads to favorable or unfavorable generalizations, which make or mar the reputation of the concerned police organization. But unfortunately, the Traffic Police in India have not established a positive public image. The traffic staff in charge of enforcement and investigation performs a useful function, as a result of which traffic laws are meaningfully enforced. The accident rate is about eight per thousand vehicles in Madras City, for example. The number of traffic accidents in Madras City in 1984 was 5790; fatalities alone totaled 384. While the more serious traffic accidents are handled by the Traffic Investiga-

tion Branch, the ordinary traffic violations and parking offenses are dealt with by the Regulating Staff.

Criminal Identification

The main focus of the criminal identification programs in India, as part of the criminal justice system, is on the fingerprints of the accused. But other items of evidence, like footprints, handwriting, photographs and anthropometric measures, are admissible as corroborative material, according to the Indian Evidence Act. The Identification of Prisoners Act of 1920 authorizes photographing and taking measurements of prisoners, soon after arrest, by the police officer or magistrate. Measurements also include fingerprints and footprints. Fingerprint evidence is normally held to be conclusive if there are at least seven points of identity. Test Identification Parades are a major procedural pattern of the evidentiary structure, built up by the investigator during his inquiries, to test whether people who claim that they have seen and can identify the accused can really do so under conditions that will make the identification acceptable as evidence in court. Also other bits and pieces of physical evidence at the scene or on the persons of the victims or the accused could establish the linkage and so prove guilt. The forensic science laboratories play a prominent part in dealing with all these. Every state now has a forensic science laboratory. Some states like Tamilnadu have mobile laboratories in major centers and scientific assistants in districts, making these facilities available in remote rural areas. In the years the forensic science laboratories have been in existence, they have made a substantial contribution to the investigation of some very difficult cases of murder and road accidents by identifying traces of blood, hair, paint flakes, glass pieces and other physical clues. They have also successfully used the method of superimposition and reconstruction of a deceased person's identity from the skeletal remains of the skull and available photographs. There are also two Central Forensic Science Laboratories. The state police organizations have no identification centers as such, but the CIDs of states have special facilities for identification and interrogation. Police dog squads and kennels exist in most of the states. Polygraphs are not yet popular, but some states and central police organizations have them.

The Police Act of 1861 envisaged a hierarchy of ranks in the state police force, as in the chart.

Since then, the chief of police of a state has been upgraded to the rank of director-general of police, with a pay of Rs (rupees) 3,250 per month, plus dearness and other allowances totaling up to Rs 5,000 per month. The force now has a few inspectors general of police, heading functional areas. Their pay, in-

The Police Act of 1861 envisaged a hierarchy of ranks in the state police force, as in the chart below:

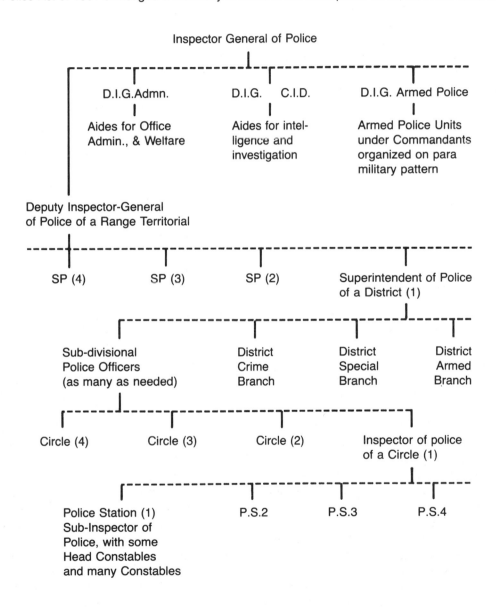

cluding dearness and other allowances and perquisites, amounts to Rs 4500 per month. The deputy inspectors general would get Rs 4,200 per month. The superintendents of police receive an average of Rs 3,500 per month. The financial compensation of a sub-divisional police officer is about Rs 2,500, an inspector of police Rs 2,000 and a subinspector of police Rs 1,500 per month. Pay of an assistant subinspector is Rs 1,200, police head constable Rs 900 and constable Rs 700 a month. All ranks of the police force get a free house or house rent in lieu. It is believed that, among policemen, individual or group practices of obtaining illegal gratification are not uncommon. As far as promotion is concerned, seniority is respected and promotion goes by a consideration of seniority and merit, at least in the higher levels, to the customary two promotions. Beyond that, promotion is beleived to be based on merit, tempered largely by the confidence of the political executive. But at the lower level, many constables continue to stay on as constables because they are not qualified for higher positions and are not outstanding enough to be considered for special promotion.

Normal retirement age is 58 years. Some put in for premature retirement after age 50 or 20 completed years of service.

Recruitment, Education and Training

Unlike in the United Kingdom and other countries, entry level into the police forces in India is normally at three levels. The first level of entry is as a police constable. Beside the basic physical requirements of five-feet, 6-inches height and 32–35 inch chest measurements, medical fitness is insisted on. The educational qualification for this recruitment level used is being increased from 8th standard to the school-leaving level of 10th standard or matriculation. Selection is done on the basis of an interview following a physical test at district level by the superintendent of police. Security clearance is necessary before appointment. For the second level of entry the qualification is a degree in any discipline. They have to sit for a written examination organized by the State Public Service Commission and later an interview. For scheduled castes and scheduled tribes, who are socially and educationally backward, marginal concessions are given in respect to educational qualifications and age. There is also a hiring quota. This ensures a reasonable distribution and representation, appropriate to the social structure. The higher level of Indian police service officers is selected by the Union Public Services Commission on the basis of a two-tier Civil Services Competitive Examination, conducted nationwide, followed by an interview. The annual number of senior positions in the country for which such a

selection is made is 2,344. Also at this level there is a marginal concession on age, a lower cutoff point as regards marks and a reservation of 15% for scheduled castes and 7.5% for scheduled tribes.

The police service is not the first preference among the Civil Services for most of the candidates. At the lower levels of subinspector of police and constable, however, a percentage of the aspirants come to the police service by choice, drawn by the glamor of a uniform and the authority that goes with it. The profile of entrants to the police force at all levels, therefore, is quite mixed. The average number of recruits annually is roughly about one-twentieth of the total strength of the force at all levels. Though there is provision for direct entry at three levels, 30% of the higher-level positions are reserved for those who rise from the lower cadres. Selection for these reserved positions is made generally on the basis of the previous record of service.

The Indian Police Service officers are trained in the Sardar Vallabbhai Patel National Police Academy, at Hyderabad. The medium of instruction is English, as foreign students also attend the academy. But all Indian officers have to learn Hindi. The one-year course for new entrants to the service covers police sciences, law, criminology, police-community relations and management, as well as parade ground drills, training in use of arms, physical fitness programs, equestrian exercises and training in martial arts. The institution also offers training for superintendents of police with six- to eight-years' service for a period of 10 weeks. This course deals with administrative, criminological and management problems at expert theoretical and practical levels. The academy conducts a two-week top-management program for deputy inspectors general.

Apart from this National Police Academy, there are police training colleges in most of the states for the training of subinspectors. Their one-year training covers roughly the same subjects, with more emphasis on investigation and day-to-day management of police work in the precincts. There is no riding and less management input and more importance is given to the local laws and language of the state. Each state has one or more police training schools for the training of police constables. In addition to training in foot drill, arms drill and use of arms, they are also instructed on law, elements of investigation and basics of police-community relations. Besides these direct-line institutions, there are central detective training schools in Calcutta, Hyderabad and Chandigarh for police investigators. The Internal Security Academy at Mount Abu, Rajasthan, conducts coordinated courses for higher-level administrators in handling problems of internal security. In addition, the Institute of Criminology and Forensic Science, New Delhi, conducts integrated training courses in criminology and forensic science for various levels of different agencies connected with the criminal justice system. An advanced course in criminology of six weeks, which this institution conducts, deserves special mention because it brings together senior police officers, district judges, senior prosecutors, prison superintendents, senior probation officers and even officers of the armed forces to discuss problems of the administration of criminal justice against a background of criminological concepts and correctional practices. In addition, all the central police organizations have their own training institutions. In the police training institutions, the medium of instruction at the lower levels is generally Hindi or the local regional language, but at the higher levels it is English. All trainees are taught Hindi and the regional language for effective communication with the public of their own areas. Dropouts are few. Once they complete the institutional training, entrants to the police at all levels have to go through a period of on-the-job training. Considerable importance is attached to this phase of the training, during which competent seniors are expected to guide, supervise and report on the candidates before they are assigned to their stations.

The Penal System

Under the Constitution, criminal jurisdiction belongs concurrently to the union and the states. The prevailing criminal laws are substantially embodied in two principal statutes: the Indian Penal Code and the Code of Criminal Procedure. These acts have precedence over any state legislation and cannot be altered or amended by the states. All legislation is subordinate to the Constitution and the fundamental rights guaranteed by it can be limited only by specific legislation enacted by Parliament.

The Indian Penal Code was drafted by an English jurist in 1837 but did not come into force until 1862.

Based mainly on English criminal law, the code defines the basic crimes and punishments in a volume of 23 chapters. Six principal categories of punishment are provided for: death, life imprisonment, rigorous imprisonment with hard labor, simple imprisonment, forfeiture of property and fine.

Because of the division of powers in the Constitution, some offenses are exclusively within union jurisdiction, some are entirely within state jurisdiction and some are joint. For example, illegal production and sale of alcoholic beverages is a state matter, but the regulation of weapons, ammunition and explosives is a union matter, under the Arms Act of 1959. Procedurally, preventive detention powers are shared by the union and the states.

Criminal procedure is governed by the Code of Criminal Procedure of 1898, a major revision of the Code of 1861. Its basic features resemble those prevailing in the United Kingdom. The accused is presumed innocent until proven guilty; juries are used only in criminal cases; no person may be compelled to give evidence incriminating himself; all accused in criminal cases are entitled to counsel; arrests and house searches usually require a warrant; officers may arrest vagrants and habitual offenders without specific cause; release on bail is permitted; private persons may arrest a person in the act of committing an offense; seditious and obscene material may be seized; searches must take place in the presence of reputable witnesses and the owner of the premises; a person under investigative arrest may not be held longer than 24 hours without authority from a magistrate, who may authorize additional detention for up to 15 days.

There are two principal kinds of trials: warrant cases, for which the punishment can extend to death or imprisonment for more than one year; and summons cases, tried before a magistrate without formal charge.

The Indian Penal Code classifies crime under nine main categories:

Category	Representative Acts
1. Against the state	Waging war; assaulting the president
2. Against the armed forces	Abetment of a mutiny; desertion
3. Against public tranquillity	Rioting
4. Election fraud	Bribing voters
5. Relating to health, safety, decency and morals	Selling pornographic literature
6. Relating to religion	Defiling a place of worship
7. Against persons	Slavery; forced labor
8. Against property	Theft
9. Relating to marriage	Varies with the community involved

Under the Penal Code crimes are categorized broadly as cognizable or noncognizable. The difference between the two is the same as between felonies and misdemeanors. The most common crime is theft. A peculiarly Indian crime is dacoity, or robbery committed by five or more persons acting together. Smuggling is a centuries-old activity virtually impervious to enforcement efforts and fueling extensive corruption among customs officials. Murders are limited by a lack of access to firearms and are primarily caused—according to an old Indian proverb—by three things, *zan, Zar* and *zamin*—lust, loot and land. Fraud, swindling and cheating occur extensively. Offenses against the Suppression of Immoral Traffic in Women and Girls Act of 1956 are most frequent in the urban areas. Gambling is widespread but, apparently, not highly organized. Drugs, an ancient problem, have assumed new and menacing forms against which law enforcement is rarely effective. The juvenile criminal rate is not yet alarming, but an interesting footnote is the fact that its most-publicized expression is "Eve-teasing," a form of girl-watching in which boys throw provocative innuendos at passing girls.

The Constitution provides that correction and the custody of prisoners are state functions. The corrections system is managed by the Prisons Act of 1894 and the Prisoners Act of 1900. The highest state official in jail administration is the inspector general of prisons, or, if there is no such separate office, the inspector general of police. At the district level, the responsible official is the superintendent of police.

Prisons are poorly staffed and usually congested and conditions of health, sanitation and food are only minimal. Daily rations might include lentils soaked in molasses for breakfast, 22 ounces of rice, and nine ounces of lentils at midday and the same for supper. There are 20 model prisons scattered in 11 states, 10 of them in Uttar Pradesh, the most populous state. These prisons have no walls. Prison life in other prisons is generally very onerous. Where solitary confinement is used, prisoners may be chained with leg irons.

Criminal statistics are recorded and assessed in each state at the statistics and research cell of the state CID. Some of the states have a police computer wing to record and process crime statistics. These computers also help in retrieval of crime information as and when required by investigating officers. At the national level, the Bureau of Police Research and Development coordinates the work of collection, collation and assessment of crime statistics for India. They publish a review every year entitled *Crime in India*. This volume contains useful information on crime typology, trends and rates. Unfortunately, however, there is considerable delay in compiling and publishing this annual review. Crime has been steadily increasing over the decade, 1971–1981. The increase in crime during the decade has been double that of the population increase during the same period. Among the states, the higher crime rates are recorded by Madhya Pradesh, Tripura and Maharashtra, but among the cities this dubious distinction is held by Bangalore, Delhi and Kanpur. However, the overall incidence of crime in India is still low compared to that in many other countries. The figures of offense under the local and special laws, such as gambling, prostitution and prohibition acts, are higher. But systematic enforcement of these laws is done only in some states, like Tamilnadu, Maharashtra, Gujarat and Madhya Pradesh. If all states did the same, the total would be much more.

The clearance rate for the year 1981 for the police was 71.4%, representing the ratio of the cases disposed of by the end of the year to the total number of cases recorded during the year, including those that were pending disposal at the beginning of the year. The corresponding clearance rate for the courts was only 23.9%. The clearance rate for offenses under the local and special laws is 83.3%. In some states police clearance of cases is delayed. But the major problem, however, is the delay in clearance by the courts.

The Indian Criminal Justice System, which has done well in the past, is presently bursting at its seams and a speedy overall review and remedial measures are necessary.

INDONESIA

History & Background

Under Dutch rule, the principal police force was the Dutch Algemeene Politie, which functioned as the federal police force. In Java and Sumatra, the police were administered by the Recomba. Other states had their own local police forces. In 1946 the Mobile Brigade was formed to disarm remnants of the Japanese soldiery. On independence in 1947 all these forces were unified into a national police system.

Structure & Organization

A number of state organs, with overlapping jurisdictions and operations, are charged with law enforcement and security in Indonesia. These include the national police, ordinary and special military units, the Command for the Restoration of Security and Order (Kommando Operasi Pemulihan Keamanan dan Ketertiban, KOPKAMTIB), and the State Intelligence Coordinating Agency. The national police and KOPKAMTIB, however, are the predominant law-enforcement agencies.

The Police of the Republic of Indonesia (Kepolisian Republik Indonesia, KRI) is a national force directed and controlled by the central government in Jakarta. There are no local police forces. Under the armed forces' reorganization of 1969, the police ranks as the fourth military service of the Armed Forces of the Republic of Indonesia (Tentera Nasional Indonesia) under the Department of Defense and Security. The strength of the police force is estimated at 140,000. In the aftermath of the 1965 aborted coup, when the police were found to have been heavily infiltrated by the members of the Indonesian Communist Party, the

police suffered a decline in influence, a decline that persisted into the 1980s.

Headquarters of the national police in Jakarta includes four main staff sections—for intelligence, personnel, logistics and plans. The commander of the police has the title of chief, as distinct from the other three military services, whose heads have the title of chief of staff. Structurally, the police are organized into 17 police districts, reduced from 21 in early 1974 under four regional groupings of Sumatra, Java and Madura, Kalimantan and Sulawesi (Celebes). Districts are subdivided at the *kabupaten* or regency level, each of which has three lower levels of subdivisions. The primary police unit is the block, which may be a single street or section of a *kampung* (urban quarter).

Each district, with its headquarters in a provincial capital, has police units assigned to it, their strength and composition varying according to the size and characteristics of the area. These units are organized as city police forces or rural police forces. Although they work in conjunction with the local government, they are operationally under the command of the district police commander, who reports directly to the national police headquarters.

Functionally, the police are organized into a number of specialized elements that include the general uniformed police, criminal investigation police and security police. Elements of these are normally assigned at every operational level. A special force, the Mobile Brigade, is maintained at the national headquarters, from which units are dispatched or assigned as needed. A small sea and air police force serves as a coast guard, although its seacraft and aircraft are woefully inadequate. Largest of the functional groups is the uniformed police, including the regular police, the traffic police, the women police and the *perintis* (special) police. These together constitute the conventional law and order forces of the republic.

In urban neighborhoods and rural areas the regular police (Samapta Bhayangkara) operate out of police stations or posts manned by squads of three to five patrolmen. They perform normal police and guard duties. The traffic police are assigned mainly in urban areas, where, in addition to controlling traffic and patrolling highways, they supervise the licensing of vehicles, educate the public in traffic safety and compile traffic statistics.

Organized in 1951, the women police are concerned mainly with the welfare of women and children. These police specialize in the prevention of crimes by or against women and children; the suppression of prostitution and traffic in women and children; the control of pornography; and the inspection of orphanages, institutions of the blind, hospitals and rest homes.

The *perintis* police are organized in units of 12 men, drawn from members of regular police willing to accept the risks involved in special high-risk assignments. Better armed and more mobile than the regular police, they live in separate barracks under rigid discipline. *Perintis* police have the same uniform as the regular police but are distinguished by special badges.

The Criminal Investigative Division is the central national crime fighting force. It plays a major part in the investigation of criminal activity of a nonlocal nature, such as kidnapping, prostitution, counterfeiting, organized thievery, and criminal activities involving foreigners. Among other things, it handles fingerprinting and criminal registration, collates and analyzes criminal statistics and maintains a crime laboratory. It is also the liaison agency with Interpol, which Indonesia joined in 1952.

The Security Division has detachments at the district and city levels, along with major units at the national headquarters. The division's activities are rarely made public but are believed to include the surveillance of political parties, known dissidents, labor unions and the mass media.

One of the oldest police units is the Mobile Brigade, formed in 1946. It was originally assigned to task of disarming remnants of the Japanese soldiery, providing for the security of the chief of state and the capital city and similar tasks. Throughout the history of the republic, elements of the Mobile Brigade have been called upon in times of grave threats to national security, as in the military confrontation with Malaysia in the early 1960s, or in times of major disturbances, as in the suppression of the 1965 Communist coup.

The Mobile Brigade is organized along military lines, and its component battalions are equipped and trained for operations in the manner of Army light infantry. It includes a parachute battalion and is supported by light armor and an efficient communications system. The Brigade is based in Jakarta, where some of its units are permanently assigned as a guard for the president and the vice president, while other units are dispatched as task forces wherever needed. Units not so engaged are assigned to assist the regular police. Reflecting the general restoration of law and order in the country in the 1970s, the military orientation of the Brigade was deemphasized in favor of a more conventional law enforcement role. Mobile Brigade personnel are also engaged in civic action tasks under the armed forces' dual function policy. The Mobile Brigade is also believed to have undergone a gradual reduction in its strength to about 12,000.

The national police headquarters are divided into four echelons: top echelon (the chief); staff echelon (assistant chief and inspectorate); service echelon (the secretariat and communications); and executive echelon (identification, personnel, stores, traffic, finance, intelligence, firearms, health, law, provost, research and development, and crime laboratory).

Throughout the armed forces, officer ranks and enlisted grades were standardized after 1969. Thus police ranks and grades were made identical at all levels to those of the other three military services, although designations differed in some respects. The exceptions are that no class of warrant officers exists, and corporals are ranked in the private rather than the noncommissioned officer class.

Rank	Badge
General	Four stars under a crest
Lieutenant general	Three stars under a crest
Major general	Two stars under a crest
Brigadier general	One star under a crest
Colonel	Three eagles
Lieutenant colonel	Two eagles
Major	One eagle
Captain	Three bars
First lieutenant	Two bars
Second lieutenant	One bar
Assistant lieutenant I	Two wavy bars
Assistant lieutenant II	One wavy bar
Sergeant major	Four gold chevrons

Chief sergeant	Three gold chevrons
Sergeant I	Two gold chevrons
Sergeant II	One gold chevron
Corporal I	Two brown chevrons
Corporal II	One brown chevron
Bhayangkara (protector)	Two brown bars
Bhayangkara II	One brown bar

Pay and emoluments are generally equivalent throughout the armed forces. Although no definitive information is available on the budget and financing of the national police, it seemed, from published reports, to face the same kind of budgetary restraints as the other branches of the military. For example, the Mobile Brigade derives part of its budget from operating a transportation company, a whitewash factory, and a variety of banking and agricultural enterprises.

The standard weapon of the conventional police is the pistol, which is carried by all personnel. A small number of machine guns are available at various headquarters and police stations, primarily for the use of the *perintis*. Jeeps and passenger cars are used by supervisory personnel, and bicycles by the lower ranks. The police uniform is a light cotton shirt with short or rolled sleeves, trousers with combat-style boots (shoes for officers), and khaki brown hats. Rank insignia are worn on shoulder boards or on the sleeve.

Police ethics and conduct are regulated by a basic police law and by unpublished police regulations and procedural statutes. As with the other armed forces, the police maintain their own military-type courts to try cases involving criminal infractions by their members. There are courts of first instance consisting of a panel of three judges, and appeals courts.

KOPKAMTIB was created in late 1965 as a special organ to deal with pressing internal security problems. Its original function was to purge from the government and the armed forces Communists suspected of complicity in the 1965 abortive coup. It was also instrumental in enforcing the integration of the armed forces after 1969. (They were formerly semi-independent services.) By 1974 KOPKAMTIB was a large and powerful organization, overshadowing all other law-enforcement agencies in the national security field.

The KOPKAMTIB organization is shrouded in secrecy. It is believed to be an autonomous organ within the Department of Defense and Security but not a formal component of the Armed Forces of the Republic. Essentially it is only a command structure with regular military officers assigned to it. Below the central headquarters level, KOPKAMTIB officers are regular military commanders appointed concurrently to KOPKAMTIB positions. KOPKAMTIB does not recruit its personnel, although it maintains its own communications channels.

In addition to its countersubversive functions, KOPKAMTIB exercises certain inquisitorial oversights with respect to corruption and economic crimes. It has special competence in such sectors of the economy as the rice distribution system, which is basic to both public order and national development plans. Furthermore, the new passport regulations issued in the early 1970s gave KOPKAMTIB authority to approve passport applications of Indonesians desiring to travel abroad for professional purposes.

KOPKAMTIB is used increasingly as an organ of political indoctrination and censorship. In 1973 it took a leading role in an official campaign against long hair in young people. KOPKAMTIB commanders also have the power to prohibit the presentation of plays and motion pictures, ban the discussion of certain subjects within universities, and impose prior censorship over the publication of pamphlets and printed material. Publishers and editors require KOPKAMTIB clearance to apply for a publishing permit from the Department of Information. Following the outbreak of disorders during the visit of Japanese prime minister Kakuei Tanaka in 1974, it banned the publication of a number of newspapers.

KOPKAMTIB has broad legal powers as well to arrest, interrogate and detain individuals, including members of the armed forces.

Although an extralegal organ of government, KOPKAMTIB is not a "supergovernment," as it often has been called. The government has made efforts to soften its awesome image and curb its potential to become an arbiter of political power. In 1976 President Suharto assumed formal command of the force while delegating operational control to its chief of staff. This move was seen as a warning to overambitious KOPKAMTIB commanders.

Recruitment, Education & Training

Police personnel are recruited on a voluntary basis from applicants between 18 and 25 years of age with at least a sixth-grade education. They are required to pass a written and oral competitive examination, be physically fit, be free from alcoholic tendencies and be of good moral character. Officer personnel enter the ranks through graduation from the Armed Forces Academy. Academy cadets receive one year of training in a common curriculum, followed by three years of additional training at the police branch of the academy.

Among police training institutions, the most important is the National Police Command and General Staff School, established in Jakarta in 1964. Attendance at this school usually is a step toward higher assignment as a police inspector or commissioner. The Mobile Brigade maintains a specialized academy at Porong in East Java. A small and select number of officers attend police academies abroad, especially in the United States. The Police School at Sukabumi in West Java provides basic training for all enlisted recruits as well as a more advanced training course to qualify promising enlisted men for higher positions.

The Penal System

Penal institutions are administered by the Office of Prisons and Jails in the Department of Justice. They include both penitentiaries for those sentenced for severe offenses and local jails for lesser offenders. Of the over 350 prisons, the largest and most important are in Java. At lease one prison and one or more local jails are in or near each major city. A penal colony with a capacity to house 6,000 inmates in a complex of nine separate prisons is on the island of Nusa Kambangan near the city of Tjilapjap in south-central Java.

Living conditions in these institutions vary considerably according to the kind and age of the facility. The newer prisons, such as those at Trenggalek and Tulungagung in East Java, are built to conform to international standards and contain modern features such as running water, electricity, separate cells, sports fields, a hospital and a library. More typical, however, are crowded barracks that house twice as many in-mates as they were designed for. Most have no electric lights or running water; have covered pit toilets; and have small windows, if any. Inmates sleep on mats spread on hard floors.

There are specialized prisons for women and youth in Java. Where it is not possible to confine them in separate institutions, which is usually the case outside Java, juveniles and women are segregated from adult males. Ordinarily prisoners are permitted visits by family members and can receive limited amounts of food and other articles. Money for inmates may be deposited with prison authorities, to be issued to the inmates for cigarettes and personal necessities. Under some circumstances, prisoners are permitted to spend nights at home.

All prisons provide some kind of medical care, although generally it is rudimentary. Some have resident doctors operating out of a small hospital. But in most cases there is no doctor, and the hospital or clinic is supervised by a medical attendant working under the direction of a district civilian doctor, who visits the prison about twice a week.

Rehabilitation programs include literacy classes, moral and religious training, and workshops to teach crafts and skills. Some prisons operate small industries or agricultural enterprises that sell their products on the local market. Proceeds are used to pay a small wage to the working inmates, to buy recreational equipment, and to maintain buildings and grounds. Most prisons operate trustee systems. Some have

CRIME STATISTICS (1984)

		Number Reported	Attempts %	Cases Solved %	Crime per 100,000	Offenders	Females %	Juveniles %	Strangers %
1.	Murder	1,456		72.46	0.90				
2.	Sex offenses, including rape	5,197		64.52	3.22				
3.	Rape	1,991		60.57	1.23				
4.	Serious assault	13,726		61.47	8.49				
5.	All theft	92,055		37.08	56.97				
6.	Aggravated theft	70,267		37.28	43.49				
7.	Robbery and violent theft	8,155		42.33	5.05				
8.	Breaking and entering	62,112		36.62	38.44				
9.	Auto theft	7,946		19.95	4.92				
10.	Other thefts	13,842		45.88	8.57				
11.	Fraud	14,874		49.59	9.21				
12.	Counterfeiting	1,025		54.34	0.63				
13.	Drug offenses	877		66.02	0.54				
14.	Total offenses	71,735		62.85	44.40				

Criteria of juveniles: aged from 14 to 17 years
Note: Information for some categories is not available.

honor systems that permit prisoners to work outside the prison confines.

In a category by itself is the penal colony on Buru Island, between Sulawesi and Irian Jaya. The colony occupies an area of 250,000 acres, divided into 18 units of 500 to 1,000 prisoners each. Families are permitted to join prisoners for permanent residence on the island. Overall administration of the colony is in the hands of a special body called the Buru Re-settlement Executive Body, headed by the attorney general and including the local KOPKAMTIB and military commanders. KOPKAMTIB maintains responsibility for the prisoners as part of its responsibility for all political prisoners associated with the 1965 coup. The physical security of the colony is in the hands of a military command that is part of the 15th Army Area Command. The official goal is to make the colony self-supporting eventually.

IRAN

<table>
<tr><td colspan="2" align="center">BASIC FACT SHEET</td></tr>
</table>

BASIC FACT SHEET

Official Name: Islamic Republic of Iran
Area: 1,648,000 sq km
Population: 50,407,763 (1987)
Capital: Tehran
Nature of Government: Theocratic dictatorship
Language: Farsi
Currency: Rial
GNP: $82.4 billion (1986)
Territorial Divisions: 24 provinces
Population per Police Officer: N.A.
Police Expenditures per 1,000: $21,088

History & Background

Since 1979, when the mullahs toppled the shah, Iranian law-enforcement agencies have undergone a major transformation. The National Police and the Gendarmerie, or the rural police, the major elements of the imperial law-enforcement establishment, still retain their identity, but in a vastly different setting. The dreaded SAVAK, the secret police organization, has been replaced by SAVAMA, an acronym for Information and Security Organization of the Nation, which performs Gestapo functions for the mullahs, as SAVAK did for the shah. The Revolutionary Guard and the Komitehs, or "block wardens," have been introduced into the system and serve as the purely Jacobin institutions for inspiring terror in the citizens, enforcing cruder forms of Islamic justice, and handling routine law-enforcement tasks with true Islamic fervor.

Gendarmerie

The Gendarmerie, the older police agency, has had an uneven record since its founding in 1911. It has been completely reorganized twice: after World War II, and after the 1979 Islamic Revolution. Originally set up under the Ministry of Finance to control rural banditry so that taxes could be collected in the lawless countryside, the Gendarmerie was organized and commanded by Swedish officers in its formative years. When Reza Pahlavi was crowned as Reza Shah in 1926, he absorbed the Gendarmerie into the Army in an effort to consolidate central government authority. The organization remained unchanged until 1943, when it was given autonomy under the Ministry of the Interior. It retained this autonomy until 1980,

when it was brought back under Army control and placed under an Army commander.

A major landmark in the history of the Gendarmerie was the U.S. Military Mission to the Imperial Gendarmerie (GENMISH), which was assigned to Tehran from 1953 to 1956. Consisting of approximately 20 U.S. "advisers," GENMISH was responsible for developing the Gendarmerie as a modern force with United States-built weapons. Gendarmerie equipment consists of light aircraft, helicopters, armored patrol cars and jeeps, trucks, and motorcycles. The mobility of the force is enhanced by a nationwide radio network linking all posts.

National Police

The National Police was founded in the early decades of the 20th century when first Italian, then Swedish advisers offered police training to Iranians and founded the first school for training police officers. It was not, however, until 1921 that Reza Khan, shortly after his assumption of power, brought the various departments under the central control of the Ministry of the Interior. In its formative years, the National Police was essentially a paramilitary force, and as late as the 1970s, its military heritage was reflected in the complexion of the force. By the mid-1970s, however, most of the military officers of the upper ranks, whose presence had been a cause of dissension among the career police officers below them, had been reassigned to the armed forces, leaving the National Police an entirely civil force.

The demilitarization of the National Police was accompanied by an upgrading of the quality of personnel, the modernization of virtually every aspect of their operations and the doubling of the size of the force. During much of this period, these efforts were aided by the Public Safety Division under the U.S. AID training mission, which worked principally in the areas of training, communications, narcotics control and traffic control. The AID training mission was terminated during the 1960s. Perhaps the greatest progress was made in the area of recruitment and training. Whereas in the past a large number of recruits were illiterate and received little training, by the end of the 1970s recruitment had become highly selective and training was required throughout a policeman's career.

Structure & Organization

Gendarmerie

The duties of the Gendarmerie have expanded considerably since the early days of suppressing rural bandits. Its mission includes, in addition to regular police functions, the apprehension of smugglers, the maintenance of border security, traffic control on highways, and acting as an adjunct to the Army in times of civil emergency or war. In a more abstract yet real sense, it represents central governmental authority to much of the Iranian population. In a country where peasant allegiances have historically been directed toward local authorities, the Gendarmerie is a constant reminder of the authority of Tehran.

In the mid-1980s, the Gendarmerie numbered approximately 100,000 men distributed over 2,000 posts in villages and towns with a population of fewer than 5,000. Such localities encompass 80% of Iran's territory and 60% of the population.

The Gendarmerie uses the same basic uniform as the Army and has the same rank structure. The largest Gendarmerie unit is the district, of which there are 14. Districts, in turn, are divided into two or more regiments, each headquartered in a provincial town. About a third of the districts operate at brigade strength. Each regiment controls about six companies, whose command posts are in the smaller municipalities. Finally, company areas are apportioned among posts— in villages, at road junctions and in strategic rural areas—which are the smallest Gendarmerie units. Gendarmerie posts are of squad size and usually are under the command of an officer and two or more noncommissioned officers. Central headquarters are in Tehran. In addition to its stationary units, the Gendarmerie contains numerous mobile units with the capability to sustain pursuit of hostile persons or groups.

National Police

In the mid-1980s, the National Police operated with about 50,000 men. Like the Gendarmerie, the National Police come under the direction of the Ministry of the Interior. Their responsibility for law enforcement covers all cities of over 5,000 in population. In addition to the usual urban police activities, the National Police are responsible for passport and immigration procedures, issuance and control of citizens' identification cards, driver and vehicle licensing and registration, railroad and airport policing, and prison management.

The National Police are organized along hierarchical lines. Routine activities are carried out by city headquarters. Functions that exceed city jurisdiction are conducted by provincial headquarters, and those that exceed provincial jurisdiction are the responsibility of the national headquarters in the capital. Organization is also horizontal: There are scores of different bureaus responsible for various police activities: prisons, selection, recruitment, traffic, communications, narcotics, passports and immigration, identification, intelligence, and welfare.

Police uniforms consist of a navy blue jacket and trousers for officers and navy blue battle dress for other ranks. A navy blue peaked cap (with a red band for officers) is worn by all ranks. All police personnel carry Walther automatic pistols.

Until the fall of the shah the best-known Iranian police organization was SAVAK (Sazeman Ettelaat va Amniyat Kashvar, National Intelligence and Security Organization), founded in 1957 and given ultimate responsibility for internal security. Under its first director, Teimur Bakhtiar, a Kurd, SAVAK acquired a reputation for brutality that it was never able to live down in later years. SAVAK was attached to the office of the prime minister, and its director had the title of deputy to the prime minister for national security affairs. Although officially a civilian agency, it had close ties to the military, and many of its senior personnel were officers of the armed forces, and its directors often close confidants or childhood friends of the shah. In addition to SAVAK, the Special Intelligence Bureau operated inside the palace, outside of SAVAK's ambit.

SAVAK was originally founded to round up the members of the outlawed Tudeh Party, but later it expanded its activities to fulfill its broader mission of gathering intelligence and neutralizing opposition to the shah. These activities included press censorship and control of publications, and surveillance of opposition breeding spots such as universities, labor unions and peasant organizations, many of which were infiltrated by SAVAK agents and paid informants. SAVAK was also active in foreign countries, where it watched for external threats to Iranian national security.

Although the name SAVAK was abolished by the Islamic regime in 1979, many of its powers and functions have devolved on an organization called SAVAMA, which pursues the enemies of the regime as ruthlessly as SAVAK ever did. In addition, the Revolutionary Guard serves as the militia, enforcing the decrees of the government without reference to procedural and legal niceties. The neighborhood Komitehs, which originally acted as block wardens, seem to be less active in the mid-1980s. There have been efforts to disband them, and many have disappeared.

Recruitment, Education & Training

Gendarmerie

Some gendarmes are conscripts who have completed their military service, or inductees selected for this duty. Many are volunteers. Most officers come from the military. In special cases, the Army lends officers to the Gendarmerie, but they retain their Army rank and eventually return to their own units. Except for inducted enlisted personnel, who serve for two years, the usual enlistment period is five years, and the reenlistment period is three years. Most gendarmes make the service a career and stay in for 20 years, the minimum period required to obtain retirement benefits. Promotion for enlisted men is based on length of service, ability and the recommendation of their immediate superior, just as in the Army and the National Police. A panel of examiners, appointed by the commanding general, must approve all promotions. The appointment of all senior officers must be approved by the cabinet.

Historically, morale among the gendarmes has been low. Low pay and poor living conditions in isolated posts combine to erode their competence and integrity. Corruption is widespread, and generally the gendarme is hated and feared as a repressive agent who lives by extortion and conducts illegal activities on the side. To counter the deterioration in the service, the shah introduced a number of reforms in the 1960s and 1970s—better pay and living conditions, improved retirement and medical benefits, new educational programs and a higher standard of recruitment. Before these reforms could bear fruit, the Revolution intervened and the Gendarmerie found itself in a diminished role in the new Islamic society.

National Police

The pride of the force is the National Police University in Tehran, which houses training facilities for officers and enlisted men. To be accepted for the officer school an applicant must have a high-school diploma and meet exacting physical and mental standards. Only about 10% of the candidates for officer training meet these requirements. Those who do spend three years studying police sciences at university level. The suc-

cessful cadet graduates as a second lieutenant with a licentiate degree. Subsequent promotions depend on length of service, quality of performance and completion of further training.

Upon reaching the rank of a lieutenant colonel, the officer again enters the university for nine-month senior officer course, which consists of training in such fields as modern police tactics, administration and planning. This course is mandatory for further promotion.

Recruit patrolmen also train for three months at the National Police University before becoming law-enforcement officers. In addition to passing this course, enlisted men must pass a literacy test, show proof of grade-school education and pass a physical and mental examination. In-service training for both officers and men consists of a series of 12-week courses in a variety of subjects, including criminal investigation, traffic regulation and control, civil disturbances control, narcotics law enforcement, prison management and radio communications.

The Penal System

The Penal Code of 1925, as amended over the years, governs the operation of the penal system. The original code classifies offenses on the French model into contraventions or minor offenses, misdemeanors, and felonies, the last of which carry sentences of more than two years' imprisonment. There are three degrees of imprisonment for felonies: the first degree carries two to 10 years, the second degree three to 15 years, and the third degree life imprisonment or execution. An important amendment in 1960 to the Penal Code authorizes the detention of the insane in asylums, of repeated recidivists in deportation camps, of vagabonds in work camps or agricultural colonies, of alcoholics and drug addicts in medical treatment centers, and of juvenile delinquents in reeducation centers. Penalties are greater for recidivists. There is no probation system, and those released early receive no supervision. Provision is made for granting amnesty to prisoners, although clemency is much more common.

The Islamic regime has revised the Penal Code to make it conform more closely to the Sharia (the Islamic legal code). In 1985 the government announced the development of a new machine for surgical amputation of four fingers of the right hand of convicted thieves. Death by stoning has been reinstituted as a punishment for moral crimes such as adultery, particularly in the so-called holy cities. There are many reports of floggings, both as a means of torture and as a punishment for sexual offenses. In its 1985 report, Amnesty International recorded an estimated 6,108 executions between February 1979 and the end of 1984, not including secret executions. Special Revolutionary Guard units check on all social activities contrary to Islamic norms. Women whose clothing does not completely cover the hair and all of the body except hands and face, or who wear makeup, are subject to arrest. If they are, in the words of the prosecutor general, "reformable," they may be lectured and released; otherwise, they go to jail. Sometimes people are arrested on trumped-up drug or other charges when their actual offenses are political. Political arrests are made by members of the Revolutionary Guard, normally without warrants. There is no judicial determination of the legality of an arrest in Iranian law. Detainees are held for long periods without being charged with a crime. For political crimes no bail is permitted, and neither is access to a lawyer. In 1982 the Ayatollah Khomeini issued an eight-point decree condemning some of the violations of human rights, such as entering private homes without warrants, tapping phones and opening mail. A Headquarters for the Enforcement of the Imam's Decree was set up in Tehran, as were a number of provincial and local offices. These offices were soon flooded with complaints about violations of rights of privacy.

The prison system is officially under the Ministry of Justice, but the Ministry of the Interior and the armed forces also play a considerable role in its operation and management. There are three categories of prisons: police jails, under Gendarmerie supervision in rural areas and under National Police supervision in urban areas, used for preventive detention and short-term prisoners; court prisons, under the criminal courts, used primarily for sentences of intermediate duration; and penitentiaries, under direct military supervision for long-term sentences. Each city and town has a prison. Tehran has two large prisons, including Qsar, the country's largest, with a capacity of 6,000 inmates but usually housing several thousand more.

During the 1960s and 1970s, during the latter half of the Reza Shah Pahlavi reign, there were intermittent attempts to reform prisons and upgrade their conditions. The emphasis was on providing gainful work to prisoners, either in crafts inside or in farming outside prison walls. Prisoners were paid for their work. Prison reform also emphasized literacy training.

The prison reform produced a large number of so-called open prisons, where inmates were allowed to work outside the prison without being subject to systematic supervision. The work usually involved road construction, forestry and agriculture. In 1969 the Qezelhesar Detention Center, a prison with some 1,200 inmates southwest of Tehran, became a model prison for the reform program. Inmates here were provided with sports facilities, and small huts were available for conjugal visits.

Conditional liberty may be granted to a prisoner who has served half his sentence in the case of misdemeanor; two-thirds in the case of a felony; or after 12 years in the case of life imprisonment. Conditional liberty is not available to recidivists. Specific conditions are fixed by the court that grants conditional liberty. The prisoner may be subject to surveillance by the National Police or Gendarmerie even in a state of conditional liberty. Prisoners convicted by military tribunals suffer the loss of all civil rights for 10 years, regardless of the length of the sentence.

After the establishment of the Islamic revolutionary government, prison conditions swiftly deteriorated, partly because of the heavy influx of political prisoners and the scant regard for public or international opinion by the new prison officials. Stories of torture are rampant and cover a wide range of inhuman practices, particularly in the notorious Evin Prison in Tehran. The more common practices include mock executions; solitary confinement; beatings on the soles of the feet; other beatings; kicking; and blindfolding for long periods. The jails are grossly overcrowded. Toilet facilities are inadequate or totally lacking. Medical treatment is rarely available. Food is full of dirt and bugs.

The Iranian government began to keep criminal statistics only recently, but since the Islamic Republic was established, has discontinued the practice. The nature of the crimes has also changed since 1979 as a whole new body of violations of the Islamic Sharia has been added to the statute books. The police, however, claim that the streets of Tehran are safe even for women and children at night. In addition to conventional crimes, arrests reported by the press include black marketing and hoarding, corruption, alcoholism and drug abuse, and disrespect toward mullahs.

IRAQ

BASIC FACT SHEET

Official Name: Republic of Iraq
Area: 434,924 sq km
Population: 16,970,948 (1987)
Capital: Baghdad
Nature of Government: Military dictatorship
Language: Arabic
Currency: Dinar
GNP: $35 billion (1986)
Territorial Divisions: 18 provinces
Population per Police Officer: 140
Police Expenditures per 1,000: N.A.

Structure & Organization

The Iraqi Police Force, formed in 1919 under British auspices, is one of six paramilitary and internal security forces: the Popular Army or the People's Militia (Al Jaysh al Shabi), the Futuwah or the Youth Vanguard, the Border Guards, the Mobile Force and the Department of General Intelligence (Al Mukhabarat) are the other five. The Police Force functions under a director general of police, who is subordinate to the Ministry of the Interior. Territorially, the Police Force is divided into 19 units—one for Baghdad and one in each of the 18 governorates. Functionally there are a number of specialized components, including traffic, narcotics and railroad. Police ranks are identical with those of the Army. Policemen wear khaki drill uniforms (white for traffic police), and all carry sidearms.

The Mobile Force is a militarized police force used to support the regular police in the event of major internal disorder. The Mobile Force is armed with infantry weapons, artillery and armored vehicles. The Border Guards are stationed principally in northern Iraq along the borders with Turkey, Iran and Syria to guard against smuggling and infiltration.

The most dreaded and possibly the most important arm of state security apparatus is the Department of General Intelligence, created in 1973 after the abortive coup attempt by Director of Internal Security Nazim Kazzar. Foreign observers believe that several separate intelligence networks are incorporated within the department.

Recruitment, Education & Training

The police operate at least two schools: the Police College for those with secondary degrees, and the Police Preparatory School for those without.

The Penal System

A new Penal Code was introduced in 1969, expanding the definition of crime to embrace acts against the political, economic and social goals of the Baath regime.

The penal system is administered by the Ministry of Social Affairs and Labor and is dominated by the central prison at Abu Ghreib near Baghdad; this prison contains some 3,000 prisoners. Three smaller, branch prisons are in Al Basrah, Babylon and Ninevah governorates. Smaller centers of detention are located throughout the country. The size of the prison population is not known, but in 1978 the government granted amnesty to 7,000 prisoners to mark the 10th anniversary of the Baath rise to power, and it may be surmised that the prison population is several times that number.

Very little is known about the conditions of the prisons. It is believed that prison conditions vary according to the category of the institution. In the central prison, untried prisoners are separated from those who are convicted, females are separated from males, and those convicted of felonies are separated from those convicted of lesser crimes. Political prisoners are kept separately from those convicted of ordinary crimes. According to reliable reports, both physical and psychological torture are used in prisons, especially to extract confessions from political prisoners.

The incidence of crime may be gauged from data periodically released by the Prisons Administration. Based on such data, theft, forgery, bribery, homosexuality, misappropriation of public funds, murder and smuggling are the most serious crimes, although not necessarily in that order. The incidence of crime is highest among urban adult males. Crime in rural areas accounts for only 22% of the total. By socioeconomic categories, the highest number of criminal offenders is found among wage earners, peasants and government officials.

IRELAND

BASIC FACT SHEET

Official Name: Ireland
Area: 70,282 sq km
Population: 3,534,553 (1987)
Capital: Dublin
Nature of Government: Parliamentary democracy
Languages: English, Gaelic
Currency: Irish pound
GNP: $14.3 billion (1985)
Territorial Divisions: 26 counties
Population per Police Officer: 490
Police Expenditures per 1,000: $58,654

History & Background

Irish police history begins in 1822 with the establishment of four provincial forces in the North, West, midlands and South, with headquarters in Armagh, Ballinrobe, Daingean and Ballincollig, respectively. These forces were consolidated in 1836 as the Irish Constabulary under an inspector general. In the same year the Dublin Metropolitan Police was established by an act of Parliament, with headquarters in Dublin Castle. It was an unarmed force unlike the provincial force, which was renamed the Royal Irish Constabulary in 1867.

On the establishment of Ireland as an independent republic in 1922, the Royal Irish Constabulary and the Dublin Metropolitan Police were merged into a new force, the Garda Síochána (Guardians of the Peace). It was a British-style unarmed force under a commissioner of police, who reported to the Ministry of Justice. The organizational structure of the force has not changed materially since then.

Structure & Organization

The headquarters of the Garda Síochána in Phoenix Park, Dublin, consists of the commissioner, two deputy commissioners and four assistant commissioners. One of the deputy commissioners is in charge of the Dublin Metropolitan Area, where one-third of the force is stationed. There are seven departments at headquarters, headed by officers of superintendent or chief superintendent rank: Administration, Crime, Operations, Personnel, Planning, Security and Training. Sections include Crime Investigation, Garda Patrol, Traffic, Drugs Squad and Aliens Office. Work in these sections is supported by a Technical Bureau, which has eight units: Investigation, Fingerprint, Ballistics, Photography, Mapping, Printing, Transport and Dog Handling.

In the cities of Dublin, Cork, Limerick and Waterford there are juvenile liaison officers who handle juvenile offenders. These officers are actively associated with boys' clubs. Women were first recruited into the force in 1959 when a female corps, the Bán Gardai, of 12 policewomen was constituted.

The Dublin Metropolitan Area is headquartered at Dublin Castle and comprises four divisions, each headed by a chief superintendent: North, North Central, South and South Central. It also controls the Communications Center and two special units within the Crime Investigations Branch: the Central Detective Unit and the Special Detective Unit. Metropolitan divisions are divided into districts, each under a superintendent. Stations (precincts) are in charge of sergeants.

Outside Dublin, the Garda has 18 regional divisions, each headed by a chief superintendent. The divisions are roughly coterminous with the counties, and the division headquarters is almost always in the county capital. Divisions are further divided into districts, each under a superintendent, and districts, in turn, into subdistricts, each under a sergeant. The strength of the stations varies according to the population of the area; in many rural areas they are one-man operations.

The Garda uniform consists of a dark blue open-necked jacket and trousers and a dark blue peaked cap. Officers wear the same uniform except that the blue is flecked by gray. Women Garda members wear a jacket with a dark blue skirt. Beat Garda personnel are equipped with walkie-talkies and two-way radios. They are unarmed except for billy clubs.

The Garda work a 40-hour week and are entitled to a 30-day annual leave. Members of the force who reach age 50 and who have served for 30 years retire on full pension. Early retirement is permitted to female Garda members who marry or to those who suffer injury or become disabled.

Advancement to the highest rank is technically available to any member of the Garda. Promotion to ranks up to inspector is by a qualifying examination. A limited number of positions are filled by special promotion or as a reward for outstanding service. Appointment to the rank of superintendent and higher is made by the Ministry of Justice on the recommendation of a special board.

Recruitment, Education & Training

Applicants for Garda service must be between 18 and 26 years and must meet exacting physical and mental standards. A successful applicant must pass an 18-month course and then undergo a full year's in-service training at the Garda Training Center, established in 1964 at Templemore. For specialized courses there are training schools at Limerick, Bishopstown and Sligo.

The Penal System

No information is available on the penal system.

CRIME STATISTICS (1984)

		Number Reported	Attempts %	Cases Solved %	Crime per 100,000	Offenders	Females %	Juveniles %	Strangers %
1.	Murder	37	21.6	83.8	1.08				
2.	Sex offenses, including rape	265		70.9	7.70				
3.	Rape	68		52.9	1.98				
4.	Serious assault	119		84.0	3.46				
5.	All theft	89,155		27.5	2,591.39				
6.	Aggravated theft	38,235		27.7	1,111.34				
7.	Robbery and violent theft	1,878		26.7	54.59				
8.	Breaking and entering	36,357		27.8	1,056.76				
9.	Auto theft	1,020		9.7	29.65				
10.	Other thefts	49,900		27.7	1,450.40				
11.	Fraud	4,986		79.6	144.92				
12.	Counterfeiting	4		75.0	0.12				
13.	Drug offenses								
14.	Total offenses	99,727		32.2	2,898.68				

Criteria of juveniles: aged from 14 to 17 years.
Note: Information for some categories is not available.

ISRAEL

BASIC FACT SHEET

Official Name: State of Israel
Area: 20,720 sq km
Population: 4,222,118 (1987)
Capital: Jerusalem
Nature of Government: Parliamentary democracy
Language: Hebrew
Currency: Shekel
GNP: $21 billion (1986)
Territorial Divisions: 6 districts
Population per Police Officer: 270
Police Expenditures per 1,000: $23,099

History & Background

The immediate forerunner of the Israeli police force was the Palestine police force, and the Police Ordinance of 1926 is still the principal law governing police operations and functions. The new national force came into being in 1948 during the War of Independence with a minimum of resources, few personnel, and little equipment from its predecessor organization.

Structure & Organization

National Police Force

The police force is a centralized organization directed and controlled from the national headquarters. The highest-ranking officer and director is the inspector general, who reports directly to the Ministry of Police. The inspector general is invariably a career officer who has worked his way through the department.

The national headquarters is divided into three major departments: Patrol and Training, Administration, and Investigation. The Patrol and Training Department exercises staff supervision over patrol and traffic operations and all police training. The functions of the Administration Department includes personnel, pay and finance, communications, supply, and buildings and property. The inspector general also has advisers for planning and operations, public relations and legal affairs.

The Investigation Department deals with all crimes not specifically dealt with by the Patrol Department. The department functions on several levels. At the national headquarters there are four divisions: The Criminal Investigation Division supervises and coor-

dinates investigation units all over the country. The Economic Investigation Division investigates crimes of an economic nature, while the Special Duties Division investigates offenses connected with the security of the state and maintains records of all persons entering or leaving the country. The Criminal Identification Division maintains the fingerprint files, criminal records, and all central files for the police force, constructs models for use in court and maintains a laboratory for polygraphic, photographic and ballistics investigation.

Operating forces are organized into four major subordinate commands, including three police districts and the frontier force. Districts are further subdivided into subdistricts, stations and posts. The Northern District, with headquarters at Nazareth, comprises the Haifa port and six subdistricts, including one for the northern sector of the West Bank, called Samaria by Israel. The Tel Aviv District has four subdistricts including one for occupied Gaza and northern Sinai. The Southern District, with headquarters at Jerusalem, comprises the Lod Airport unit and five subdistricts, including one for the occupied southern sector of the West Bank, called Judea by Israel. The chiefs of police in districts and subdistricts are called commanders. In urban subdistricts, the force is organized as a single operational unit, with various bureaus to deal with different aspects of police work. In rural subdistricts, stations and posts carry out operational functions, while the subdistrict headquarters is responsible for all staff functions. Women police are responsible for patrol and traffic duties in urban units and auxiliary functions at headquarters.

The police also function as a border patrol, guard-

Inspector General

Legal Adviser

Internal Comptroller and Public Complaints Commissioner

Police Spokesman

Court of Discipline

Assistant Inspector General ———— Data Processing

Operations Department

Research and Development Unit

Demolition Unit

Operations Division

Patrol Division

Traffic Division

Standards, Organization and Methods Division

Training Division

Investigation Department

General Investigation Division

Special Tasks Division

Fraud Investigation Division

Criminal Identification Division

Administration Department

Finance Division

Quartermaster Division

Transport Division

Communications and Electronics Division

Housing and Property Division

Purchasing and Selling Division

HQ Service Unit

Transport Division

Personnel Administration

Archives Unit

Northern District

Haifa Subdistrict

Galil Subdistrict

Amaqim Subdistrict

Sharon Subdistrict

Shomron Subdistrict

Tel Aviv District

Yarkon Subdistrict

Yafo Subdistrict

Dan Sub-district

Southern District

Jerusalem Subdistrict

Merkaz Subdistrict

Negev Subdistrict

Yehuda Subdistrict

Aza and Zfon Sinai Subdistrict

Ben Gurion Airport Unit

Border Guard

Civil Guard

ing against infiltration from neighboring countries that are in a state of war against Israel. The Marine Patrol operates as a coast guard under the supervision of the Northern District's Haifa port unit. In times of war the Marine Patrol comes under the Military Command.

In all urban subdistricts there are special juvenile units, which investigate crimes committed by children. They are distinct from the regular police and wear civilian clothes rather than uniforms. They also operate safety patrols, a student force that functions as an auxiliary traffic control force.

The police enjoy the confidence and respect of the public, and morale and discipline are considered excellent. Morale remains high despite a shortage of manpower. The relatively low pay, however, is a major problem, and many of the best-qualified personnel, especially among senior officers, are attracted by the opportunities available in the civilian economy. To remedy this situation special allowances are offered to officers serving in occupied areas and those who agree to five-year contracts. A "technical alert" bonus is also offered to those outside occupied areas. Discipline is strict and is administered in accordance with the provisions of the Police Ordinance of 1926, as amended in 1963. Personnel charged with violating rules and regulations are tried before a court of discipline appointed by the inspector general. The court is composed of three police officers senior in rank to the accused. Maximum punishments are imprisonment for not more than two years, a fine not to exceed three months' pay or both. A sentence in excess of three months' imprisonment requires confirmation by the minister of police; all other sentences must be confirmed by the inspector general.

Complaints about abuses of power by the police are handled by the commissioner for internal control and public complaints.

The uniform of the Israeli police is a navy blue jacket and trousers with a peaked cap. Weapons are not carried as a general rule, although night patrols carry .38-caliber revolvers, and the Border Guard is issued with M-16 rifles necessary for carrying out its duties. Safety patrol uniforms are light khaki.

The total strength of the police fleet is 2,080 vehicles, and over 100 vehicles are added to the fleet annually. In 1977 these vehicles covered a total of 88 million kilometers (55 million miles). All vehicles normally are replaced after three years of operational duty.

Traffic Police

Israeli traffic is notoriously disorderly, and traffic accidents take a heavy toll every year. It has been said that more Israelis have died on the roads than on the battlefields. The principal reasons seem to be (apart from lack of self-discipline among drivers) the condition of the roads and the shortage of traffic police personnel. Out of a total road network of 5,300 kilometers (3,291 miles), only 220 kilometers (137 miles) have double lanes. Because of the shortage of manpower, the traffic police have been forced to rely on women and children as well as devices such as speed monitors and electronic cameras. Particular stress is also placed on periodical testing of the roadworthiness of vehicles and elimination of mechanical defects.

Criminal Identification Division

The Criminal Identification Division operates 16 laboratories, as follows:

- Analytical Laboratory
- Ballistics Laboratory
- Biological Laboratory
- Imprints and Materials Laboratory
- Documents Laboratory
- Fingerprints Laboratory
- Photographic Laboratory
- Traffic Lights Laboratory
- Mobile Crime Laboratory
- Laboratory for Technical Means of Surveillance
- Album and Identikit Office
- Property Registration and Identification Office
- Scientific Interrogation Laboratory
- Guidance and Supervision Unit
- Training and Interrogation Section
- Institute for Forensic Medicine

Recruitment, Education & Training

Except for the Border Patrol or the Frontier Force, the police rely on a system of volunteers. Conscripts are used in the Frontier Force, where the reenlistment rate is high and where about 40% elect to remain in the service. Personnel turnover has been fairly large in the police force as a whole. Confronted with serious manpower drain through resignations, the minister of police has indicated that he would recommend that police service be made compulsory.

Police ranks are generally comparable to those in the armed forces. The inspector general (mefakeach klali) holds a rank equivalent to that of major general. The other ranks are as follows:

Police Rank	Military Equivalent
Commander (nitzav)	Brigadier general
Assistant commander (nitzav mishneh)	Colonel

Chief superintendent *(sgan nitzav)*	Lieutenant colonel
Superintendent *(rav pakad)*	Major
Chief inspector *(pakad)*	Captain
Inspector *(mafakeach)*	First lieutenant
Deputy inspector *(sgan mafakeach)*	Second lieutenant
Sergeant major *(rav samal)*	Sergeant major
Sergeant *(samal rishon)*	Sergeant
Corporal *(samal sheni)*	Corporal
Lance corporal *(rav shoter)*	Lance corporal

Training for both the border police and the regular police is conducted at the National Police Training Depot at Shefar-am, 20 kilometers (12 miles) east of Haifa. The Frontier Force course comprises a total of 12 weeks of instruction followed by two weeks of unit training. (Unit training is carried out in the regional training centers and outside the framework of courses.) Citizenship and physical conditioning are emphasized along with professional subjects. Study of the Hebrew language is mandatory. Military training is basically along infantry lines and includes small arms, scouting and patrolling, guard duty, weapons, equipment and first aid. A major portion of the military phase is conducted at night.

Recruits for the regular police undergo a five-month course of instruction. The course includes the usual citizenship and military training and specialized training in law, investigation, traffic control and other aspects of police operations. Courses are also provided for officers, noncommissioned officers and officer candidates. Officer courses vary in length and according to their purpose; they are designed mainly for refresher and specialist training. The six-month noncommissioned officers' course emphasizes the skills of leadership. Attendance, although voluntary, is a prerequisite for promotion, and trainees are selected by a board of officers. An officer candidate course lasting nine months is open to noncommissioned officers in the grade of sergeant or sergeant major. Applicants must be recommended by a district commandant, and the final selection is made by a board of officers.

Specialist training includes an investigators' course lasting 10 weeks; trainees are noncommissioned officers and other enlisted personnel with five to seven years' service. Specialist training is also provided in a wide range of other professional and technical skills, such as photography, fingerprinting, ballistics, criminal identification and recordkeeping.

Higher-ranking officers attend the Senior Officers' College, where they receive instruction in national policy, staff operations, criminology and sociology.

Senior officers are also encouraged to attend universities and other institutions in Israel and abroad with financial support from the government.

The Penal System

Israeli legal codes and judicial procedures are derived from a variety of sources—partly from the British Mandate, partly from the Ottoman Turkish codes and partly from the Napoleonic Code. The principal representative of the state in the enforcement of both civil and criminal law is the attorney general under the Ministry of Justice.

Generally warrants are required for arrests and searches except in extraordinary circumstances. An arrested person must be brought before a judge within 48 hours. The judge may order his release with or without bail, or may authorize further detention for up to 15 days. Any further detention requires the permission of the attorney general. Unless detained for an offense punishable by death or life imprisonment, an arrestee may request release on bail consisting of personal recognizance, cash deposit, surety bond or a combination of the three. A person held in custody must be released unconditionally if no charge against him or her has been filed for 90 days. Suspects in custody may be held incommunicado for a maximum of seven days upon the written authorization of the minister of defense or the inspector general of police. There are juries in Israeli courts.

Punishments for convicted criminals include suspended sentences, fines and imprisonment. The death penalty may be imposed for treason or conviction for Nazi war crimes, but Adolf Eichmann was the only person to be executed by Israel. Prison sentences are mandatory only for exceptional crimes, such as terrorism.

The penal system is administered by the Prisons Service, a branch of the Ministry of the Interior but independent of the Israeli police, and is headed by the prison service commissioner. The prison system consists of a score of prisons, most of which were built in the 1930s by British Mandate authorities. In addition, there are police lockups in every major town and in military detention centers in the occupied territories.

The growing incidence of common crime and the growing number of Arab security offenders have led to considerable overcrowding in prisons. The average living space per prisoner in Israel is 2.2 square meters, less than one-third the average in many Western countries. Some prisons, such as Ashqelon, have less than 2 square meters per prisoner. Other living conditions, such as food quality and the availability of medical care, are more favorable. Two new prisons opened in the late 1970s, at Beersheba and Atarot.

Prisoners are offered vocational training in a variety of trades. Employment is also offered, at token wages. Two hours are allotted each day for recreation, and most prisoners are allowed two visits per month. Short-term furloughs are granted for good behavior, and a temporary parole is often allowed common criminals after serving one-third of their sentence. After completing two-thirds of their sentence, non-security prisoners may receive a permanent parole for good behavior.

Criminologists are agreed that the incidence of crime in Israel is becoming a major national problem. Per capita crime has increased manyfold since 1948, and organized crime is widespread and has penetrated even the government. A variety of reasons has been offered for this rapid growth of criminal activity, including an overextended police force, growing alienation of poorer Israelis and the difficulty in enforcing bureaucratic regulations. Data annually compiled by the Central Bureau of Statistics reveal that the detection rate—the percentage of reported crimes that are solved—has been dropping steadily since 1960. This rate is 50% higher for Arabs than it is for Jews, and higher for Oriental and African Jews than for European and American Jews.

CRIME STATISTICS (1984)

		Number Reported	Attempts %	Cases Solved %	Crime per 100,000	Offenders	Females %	Juveniles %	Strangers %
1.	Murder	77		68.8	1.83	84	4.8	1.2	
2.	Sex offenses, including rape	2,052		69.6	48.86	1,201	1.4	17.8	
3.	Rape	229		83.8	5.45	211	2.4	16.1	
4.	Serious assault	803		78.6	19.12	979	5.6	14.7	
5.	All theft	172,773		14.5	4,113.64	13,920	10.4	26.4	
6.	Aggravated theft								
7.	Robbery and violent theft	1,468		27.7	34.95	436	3.1	17.6	
8.	Breaking and entering	54,599		11.4	1,299.98	3,825	3.4	38.5	
9.	Auto theft	14,055		11.9	334.64	1,216	3.3	43.7	
10.	Other thefts	102,642		10.8	2,443.86	8,176	15.1	18.6	
11.	Fraud	12,221		69.0	290.98	4,105	24.3	2.9	
12.	Counterfeiting	48		25.0	1.14	5			
13.	Drug offenses	4,415		86.7	105.12	4,350	8.5	9.3	
14.	Total offenses	252,245		27.4	6,005.83	56,946	12.9	13.0	

Criteria of juveniles: aged from 12 to 18 years.
Note: Information for some categories is not available.

ITALY

John Cammett and Mary Gibson

BASIC FACT SHEET

Official Name: Italian Republic
Area: 301,223 sq km
Population: 57,350,850 (1987)
Capital: Rome
Nature of Government: Parliamentary democracy
Languages: Italian
Currency: Lira
GNP: $371.05 billion
Territorial Divisions: 20 regions, 95 provinces, 8,081 communes
Population per Police Officer: 680
Police Expenditures per 1,000: N.A.

History & Background

Italy has two major police forces: the Carabinieri, organized within the Ministry of Defense; and the State Police (Polizia di Stato), administered by the Division of Public Security within the Ministry of the Interior and traditionally referred to as the PS. The older of the two forces, the Carabinieri, was established in 1814 in the Kingdom of Piedmont to guarantee public order and guard the king. Modeled on the French Gendarmerie, the Carabinieri's duties have focused on, but not been limited to, patrolling small villages and the countryside. As the leader of Italian unification, the Kingdom of Piedmont transferred many of its institutions, including the Carabinieri, to the new state created in 1861. With the growth of cities in the late 19th century, the duties of the Carabinieri grew to include maintenance of order and criminal investigation in urban as well as rural areas. The Carabinieri remained Italy's larger major police force at the turn of the century, numbering approximately 18,000.

The origin of the State Police also traces to the Kingdom of Piedmont but dates only from 1852. Again in imitation of the French (their Sécurité Publique), the Piedmontese king created a special unit to handle administrative matters, guarantee public order, and pursue criminal investigations exclusively in the growing cities. Needless to say, the duties of the Carabinieri and the PS sometimes overlapped, and this confusion led to tension and rivalry. At the end of the 19th century, the PS remained the less significant force, numbering only 7,000 men. The prestige of the PS increased after 1902 with the founding of the internationally recognized School of Scientific Policing (Scuola di Polizia Scientifica), which encouraged and coordinated the new techniques of fingerprinting, photography, laboratory testing, and exhaustive physical and psychological examinations of criminals. The school also taught PS administrators the theories of Cesare Lombroso, the Turinese medical founder of "positivist criminology."

Like those of most other Continental states, these police forces were highly centralized and militarized. Like those of France, Italian police are in these respects at least entirely different from the British, American and Soviet police. In England and Scotland there are respectively about 46 and 22 different local police forces. Some years ago the USSR also moved toward decentralization of its police, and the United States has no less than 40,000 different bodies of governmentally organized police.

As noted below, there are a number of other police forces on the Italian peninsula. Until quite recently, however, they have shared a substantial continuity with regard to their police functioning and action in the century and a quarter since the establishment of a united Italy. The emphasis has generally been on police action as one of political control and indeed repression of those considered dangerous.

Even the Fascist regime changed little or nothing of this continuity but merely continued to utilize the preexisting police structures.

The Carabinieri (CC) was not only the first established but also and continuously the first in prestige.

It was soon designated as the "first corps of the Army," and all its members were given special legal protection: Anyone striking or wounding a member of the *carabinieri* on duty was punished with life imprisonment or even the death penalty. Even today the per capita expenditures for the Carabinieri are higher than those for any other Italian police force.

The Polizia di Stato, founded in 1852, was intended to be more like a police organization in the usual sense of the word; however, it, too, was thoroughly militarized. The PS was supposed to operate in urban areas, whereas the CC's jurisdiction was to be the countryside and small towns. But actual lines of demarcation have always been difficult to maintain.

Both police corps under the new Italian state began their work inauspiciously. From 1860 to 1865 they were used principally to repress the widespread "brigandage" in the South, i.e., to overcome the opposition to the new Kingdom of Italy. It is said that the CC suffered more casualties in those years than in all the wars of the "Risorgimento." Worse still, the idea of the police as an organ of repression became solidly established among the people. Throughout the rest of the century, police activity in repression and even massacres of peasants and workers was frequent and well documented.

Finally, the victory of fascism in 1922 was facilitated if not ensured by a kind of complicity among the Army, the police and the Fascists. But the situation was, if anything, worsened by the mindless attacks of the Left against the police and their families. In their indignation, the socialists failed to see the potentially positive aspects of policing that under other circumstances might have helped the people. In any case there was little change in police behavior under Fascism except for a vast increase in the budget, especially for the "secret" police. The latter was set up in 1926 by Arturo Bocchini with the meaningless initials of OVRA, to round up political opponents of the regime. They were then tried under new legislation by "special tribunals" that lacked any pretense of due process. Although never as ruthless as the German police of the Nazi regime, OVRA managed to stifle most opposition, forcing its leaders into foreign exile, jail, internal exile, deportation to German concentration camps, or death.

The Fascist experience modified but did not overturn the traditional police structure. Mussolini alternated his affection between the two forces, ultimately relying more heavily on the PS to protect his regime and enforce his laws. He never purged the two forces, and many officers, including high-ranking officials, never became members of the Fascist Party. They did, however, follow orders obediently and turned against the regime only after the Allied invasion and the beginning of the resistance.

Both the Carabinieri and the PS survived the fall of fascism and continue their complementary and sometimes conflicting roles today. Of roughly equal size, they have been challenged in the postwar years by terrorism of the extreme Right and extreme Left and by Mafia violence. More change has occurred in the PS, which has successfully won the right to unionize under a new law of 1981. This law also demilitarized the PS, amalgamating the administrators and uniformed force into one civilian organization.

Structure & Organization

Italy has seen a significant growth in its police since the 19th century, when it trailed behind other European nations in the ratio of officers to population. Today, however, the situation is quite different. The following table indicates the names, size and cost (in millions of lire) in 1975 of the major Italian police forces:

MAJOR ITALIAN POLICE FORCES

Name	Size	Cost (in millions of lire)
Carabinieri	91,239	491,177
Polizia di Stato	80,156	325,811
Guardia di Finanza	41,708	107,100
Capitanerie di Porto	2,446	8,293
Guardie Forestali	7,000	30,000
Agenti di Custodia	15,049	67,000
Vigili Urbani	40,000	200,000
Polizia privata	62,000	—
Guardie Campestri	6,000	—
Guardie Zoofile	1,290	—
Total	346,888	1,229,381

The ratio of the number of police to the total population is very high in Italy, at least in comparison with other countries of Western Europe. If we include only the Carabinieri, the PS, the Finance Police and corrections officers, the ratio comes to one policeman for every 256 inhabitants. If all the groups included in the preceding table are counted, then the ratio is one policeman for every 165 citizens. Comparable figures for other European countries are as follows:

POLICE FORCES OF OTHER EUROPEAN COUNTRIES

Country	Size	Ratio to Population
Norway	4,700	1 to 840
Denmark	7,242	1 to 687

Country	Size	Ratio to Population
Holland	24,000	1 to 557
Sweden	14,991	1 to 543
Britain	110,000	1 to 489
Northern Ireland	4,000	1 to 387
West Germany	174,000	1 to 343
France	168,000	1 to 310

Hence we may conclude that there are about twice as many policeman per capita in Italy as in comparable countries of Western Europe. On the other hand, the Italian army is comparatively small and neglected. The adverse ratio is therefore not quite so extreme, since the military has at least an emergency police function in all those other countries.

As we have seen, many different groups exercise police power in Italy. In addition to the Carabinieri and the PS, the following will be briefly described: the Finance Police (Guardia di Finanza), the Municipal Police (*Vigili Urbani*), the Prison Guards (Agenti di Custodia) and the Forest Police (Corpo Forestale). The Carabinieri, Finance Police and Prison Guards are "militarized," i.e., are organized in military ranks and form part of the armed forces during wartime. As noted earlier, the PS was demilitarized under a 1981 law. Like the Municipal Police and the Forest Police, the PS is now organized along civilian lines, although its members are still uniformed and carry firearms.

All these forces, except the Municipal Police, are organized at the national level. Decisionmaking is centered in Rome, and orders are handed down through the prefects who, as the highest-ranking administrators in each province, also exercise police powers. Although in theory the prefect coordinates the various forces, in practice the division of police powers, especially between the PS and the Carabinieri has undercut efficiency. The new law of 1981 established new committees at both the national and provincial levels, composed of officers of the PS, the Carabinieri and the Finance Police, to further communication and coordinated action among the larger forces. The committees are labeled, respectively, the National Committee for Order and Public Security (Comitato Nazionale dell'Ordine e della Sicurezza Pubblica) and the Provincial Committees for Order and Public Security (Comitati Provinciali per l'Ordine e la Sicurezza Pubblica).

Polizia di Stato (PS)

The Polizia di Stato, called until 1981 the Corpo di Guardia di Pubblica Sicurezza, is under the jurisdiction of the Department of Public Security in the Ministry of the Interior. With its reorganization in 1981, the PS also absorbed the small Corps of Female Police (Corpo di Polizia Femminile). This female corps had been established in 1959 to investigate crimes involving women and children. Numbering only 500, women in this corps had been given the civilian titles of "inspector" and "assistant." As part of the PS, women and men now share the same titles, functions, pay and career opportunities.

The PS is organized in geographical units, mobile squads and special offices. Most police are organized territorially and are subordinate to the prefect and *questore*, or provincial police chief. Each province is further divided into clusters *(ragruppimenti)*, groups *(gruppi)*, nuclei *(nuclei)*, subnuclei and sections that resemble precincts in the United States. Mobile squads operate under direct orders from Rome and can be assigned anywhere in the nation to deal with major disorders or other emergencies. Finally, the special offices include highway, railway, frontier and postal police. More technical offices include the National Data Center, the crime labs and the various police schools.

Since the law of 1981, the ranks of the PS have been reformed to correspond to those in the civilian bureaucracy. Before 1981, only national and regional administrators had civilian titles, while the uniformed corps was organized in a military fashion and formed part of the armed forces. At present the major job categories, each with several levels, are (from lowest to highest) agent, assistant, superintendent, inspector, commissioner and director. Agents, assistants and superintendents correspond to the former body of uniformed guards; inspectors to the former ranks of uniformed officers; and commissioners and directors to the civilian administrators. Entrance to the force can now occur at the rank of agent, inspector or commissioner, depending on the applicant's previous schooling.

According to the law of 1981, members of the PS are to "protect the liberty and rights of citizens; enforce the laws, regulations, and measures of the state; guarantee order and public security; prevent and repress crimes; and give aid in case of emergencies or accidents." PS functions usually have been divided into three general categories. First, the PS constitutes the main administrative police, issuing licenses and permits. Second, the PS acts as a public security police, preventing disorder through neighborhood patrols and surveillance over disorderly persons and places. Third, part of the PS serves as judicial police *(polizia giudiziaria)*, pursuing criminal investigations and arresting criminals. In this capacity, the PS takes orders from the state prosecutors in the Ministry of Justice. Judicial police thus remain organizationally part of the Ministry of the Interior but become functionally subordinate to the Ministry of Justice.

Arma dei Carabinieri (CC)

The Carabinieri forms part of the Ministry of Defense and therefore hold ranks similar to those of other soldiers: inspector, sergeant, captain, major, lieutenant colonel, colonel and general. Inspectors and sergeants command stations, the smallest territorial division; captains command companies; majors and lieutenant colonels command groups of companies at the provincial level; colonels command legions; and generals command divisions and brigades. The commander of the entire corps usually is a three-star general on leave from the Regular Army. Almost every small village has at least one member of the Carabinieri to provide security, in contrast to the PS, who are stationed only in larger towns and cities.

When engaged in police duties, the Carabinieri is functionally under the supervision of the Department of Public Security in the Ministry of the Interior. Although the Carabinieri does not function as administrative police, its varied activities include public security and judicial policing. It has also developed a host of specialized branches to investigate drugs and narcotics, disarm bombs, ensure pure food and drink, and enforce safety standards in industry. The Carabinieri is known for its large information bank, and it answers requests for data from the PS, armed forces, Justice Department, prefects and national ministers. Finally, 100 men make up the Corazzieri, a squad that guards the person of the president of the republic.

Finance Police

The Finance Police traces its origins to the customs guards of the various preunification states of the Italian peninsula. In 1862 these local guards were centralized into a militarized Corps of Customs Guards, which has participated in all Italian wars. A 1958 law defines the organization and duties of its present descendant, the Finance Police. Originally entrusted with collecting customs and protecting the frontiers, the Finance Police has expanded its activities to include investigation of tax fraud, drug trafficking and contaminated food. It seeks to block contraband, especially the export of currency, and has successfully recovered stolen art and archaeological treasures. Officers stationed on the coast also carry out coast guard and rescue work. Both officers and new recruits undergo training at one of a variety of specialized schools, including the Academy for officers at Rome, the Mountain Training School at Predazzo and the Nautical School at Gaeta.

Municipal Police

Municipal Police are under local control, and their organization and duties vary from region to region. The Vigili Urbani, the most important sector of the local police, enforce local traffic laws (a special office of the PS oversees national highways). Under reform legislation passed in 1967 and 1975, most traffic violations are punished by fines and considered only administrative offenses. Serious cases go to court for criminal prosecution.

Prison Guards

Subordinate to the Minister of Justice, the Prison Guards are militarized and exercise police powers. Two-thirds of the corps is responsible for order and surveillance in Italy's prisons. The final third serves as personal guards or drivers for judges and officials in the Ministry of Justice.

Forest Police

The Forest Police form part of the Ministry of Agriculture and perform the functions of protecting the forests, reforestation and assisting mountain residents.

Italy's Central Data Center (*Centro Elaborazione Dati*) is in Rome, within the Office for Coordination and Planning of the PS. The law of 1981 that reorganized the PS also laid out strict guidelines for the collection of computerized information and access to it. Information on persons must come from public sources or result from judicially authorized investigations. The government is forbidden from collecting data on citizens simply because of their religion, race, opinions, or affiliation to a union or other organization. Access to information is limited to administrators and officers in the police, secret services and the Justice Department. A parliamentary committee oversees the functioning of the Data Center to assure its compliance with these regulations.

Italy's national central office of Interpol is in Eur, a suburb of Rome. Branch offices are in Milan, Naples, Palermo and Cagliari. Sharing the same building as the Superior Institute of Police, Interpol-Rome coordinates its activities with the PS in general and especially the mobile squads. Each year it initiates tens of thousands of investigations in other nations and pursues an equal number of cases at the request of other members of Interpol. Interpol-Rome is the world center for the investigation of art theft and draws on relevant expertise of the Carabinieri and Finance Police as well as that of the PS.

Recruitment, Education & Training

Since the late 19th century, a majority of Italy's police officers have come from the South, i.e., the regions below Rome, and the islands of Sicily and Sardinia. These areas have long been economically underdeveloped, and a career in the PS or Carabinieri offers Southerners job security and a steady, though not necessarily high, salary. The following data on the uniformed ranks of the PS confirm this geographical tendency:

GEOGRAPHICAL BACKGROUND OF PS RECRUITS, 1961–68

Campania	24.80%	Lombardy	3.29%
Puglia	13.00%	Venice	2.43%
Sicily	12.95%	Friuli VG	2.53%
Lazio	12.28%	Piedmont	2.28%
Sardinia	5.93%	Marches	2.14%
Calabria	5.14%	Umbria	1.78%
Abruzzo-Molise	5.02%	Emilia R.	1.54%
Basilicata	1.83%	Trentino-A.A.	1.49%
		Tuscany	1.30%
		Liguria	1.17%
South	80.23%	North	19.77%

Thus nearly half of the PS recruitments come from three southern regions: Campania, Puglia and Sicily. This in turn has led to a special problem in manpower allocation. Since most of these men eventually find ways to attain posts near their homes, the southern regions are habitually "overmanned" and the northern areas "undermanned."

Education for the same group of recruits of the 1960s rarely included a diploma from even the high middle school of the Italian system. A total of 48% of all recruits had finished only elementary school, 49% had graduated from lower middle school and 3% had received the high middle school diploma. These statistics do not include the civilian administrators, who have always been highly educated and who must possess a university degree in law or political science when hired.

Another problem in manpower allocation often seriously affects police morale. In the United States this is known as the problem of having too many policemen in clerical and administrative functions and too few "on the beat." To be sure, this malfunction is all but universal, yet it seems to be particularly exacerbated in Italy. It is estimated that only 7% of police personnel were employed in patrol and radio cars. That figure indicated that in the whole of Italy only 5,462 policemen were on patrol. Worse still, since they work shifting tours of duty, there were only 1,365 on the job at any given moment. By way of comparison, it is claimed that Paris has about 500 squad cars working at night, whereas Milan has no more than 40 and Turin only about 30.

Where were the others? It appears that most policemen were working in purely administrative capacities or in information-gathering and assessment. Quite a few others were employed as chauffeurs or assistants of superior officers, provincial prefects or other high governmental officials. Finally, with the rise of "terrorism," a large number of policemen are now forced to serve as bodyguards and escorts of actually or potentially threatened individuals.

The PS has traditionally been the leader in establishing schools for its recruits. Founded in 1902 in Rome, the School of Scientific Policing first provided advanced training for the civilian administrators of the PS. Salvatore Ottolenghi, a student of Lombroso, was the first director of the school and sought to revolutionize policing through the application of new scientific theories and techniques of investigation. Students took courses in "positivist criminology," which taught the Lombrosian methods of the physical measurement and categorization of criminals. Through Lombroso, Italy became a leader in the movement at the turn of the century to track the biological causes of crime. Students were also trained in the new techniques of fingerprinting, photography, blood and stain analysis, handwriting analysis, and other new tools of criminalistics. The school developed the first identification center for the PS, compiling detailed dossiers on all inmates in Regina Coeli Prison in Rome. As the century progressed, an array of other schools was eventually established for all ranks of the PS.

Today, requirements for entrance at the lowest rank of agent in the PS include Italian citizenship, physical and psychological fitness, an official certificate attesting to moral character, and proof of having completed the minimum years of schooling required by law. All recruits must be between 18 and 28 years old and successfully complete an examination of basic verbal and arithmetic skills. Once accepted as recruits, aspiring agents must attend a 12-month course at one of the Schools for Agents (Scuole per Agenti) in the major cities. These schools train recruits in four areas: general culture, professional instruction, military techniques and sports. General culture courses ensure that all agents can speak standard Italian and can do elementary mathematics. Professional instruction includes material on penal law, penal procedure and judicial policing. Military courses give instruction in the use of firearms and crowd control, while the section on sports includes health and first aid. After a final examination, the new agent receives practical training for another six months in a PS office.

The second level of recruitment occurs at the rank of inspector, which is equivalent to the former officer corps of the militarized PS. In addition to the general qualifications required of agents (such as Italian citizenship), prospective inspectors must be between 18 and 30 years of age and have a high-middle-school diploma. The public examination includes oral and written sections on general culture and math. Upon passing this examination, recruits attend an 18-month course at the Police Academy in Rome. Established in 1964, the academy is internationally renowned for its offerings, which often are at a university level.

Courses cover three types of materials: law and economics; science and culture; and technical and military training. Final oral, written and practical tests lead to a diploma. Recruits remain "on trial" for six months after being appointed as inspectors.

The highest entry level is that of commissioner, equivalent to the lowest level of the previous civilian functionary. Applicants must not be over 28 years old and should possess a university degree in law or political science. After passing a public examination, aspiring commissioners attend the Superior Institute of Police (Instituto Superiore di Polizia) in the Eur suburb of Rome. This institute is the direct successor of the School of Scientific Policing and offers a similar, although expanded, curriculum. For nine months, students pursue advanced education in constitutional law, penal law, penal procedure, laws regulating the PS, civil law, workers' rights, legal medicine, scientific policing, international police cooperation, foreign language, physical education and personal defense. Optional courses form an equally long list for specialization in the areas of finance, transportation, information and computers, etc. Successful completion of the final examinations precedes nomination to the rank of commissioner.

The Penal System

The criminal justice system is based on the Napoleonic Code, which in turn was based on the codification of Roman law under Emperor Justinian. Crimes and punishments are spelled out in great detail in the Penal Code, which has a strong moral tone and deals with matters that in other countries are left to the individual. The code attempts to be as thorough as possible and does not leave out even athletics.

The Italian system relies heavily on the investigating judge, who balances the interests of the accused with those of society. The investigating judge is charged with determining whether the suspect is to be charged with a crime. During the investigation, which sometimes runs for years, the suspect is ordinarily kept in prison.

The criminal justice system is archaic and has not had a thorough overhaul in years. The Penal Code, originally promulgated in 1931, was slightly modified in 1976. Some parts of the code have been nullified by the Constitutional Court and others have been revised by Parliament. Nevertheless, some provisions are redolent of fascism, and charges may be made under such catchalls as "subversive propaganda," "association for criminal purposes" and "instigation of class hatreds." The code makes it a crime to insult a government servant, and a verbal insult to a policeman can lead to months of imprisonment. A suspect could be imprisoned for years without his ever being brought to trial, or while investigation is proceeding to determine whether he or she should be brought to trial. A 1965 addition to the Penal Code permits the government to place anyone who is considered a danger to society in "obligatory domicile" on small islands. This provision is frequently invoked against Mafia leaders. The constitution also establishes judi-

CRIME STATISTICS (1983)

		Number Reported	Attempts %	Cases Solved %	Crime per 100,000	Offenders	Females %	Juveniles %	Strangers %
1.	Murder	2,982	59.7	65.12	5.25	1,032		4.07	
2.	Sex offenses, including rape								
3.	Rape	1,007		84.31	1.77	1,062		11.30	
4.	Serious assault								
5.	All theft	879,882		8.50	1,548.39	93,918		14.91	
6.	Aggravated theft								
7.	Robbery and violent theft	20,274		20.91	35.68	6,790		11.24	
8.	Breaking and entering								
9.	Auto theft	157,018		6.92	276.32	13,385		13.87	
10.	Other thefts								
11.	Fraud	18,247		74.63	32.11	16,975		1.38	
12.	Counterfeiting								
13.	Drug offenses	11,275		97.64	19.84	16,725		3.99	
14.	Total offenses	1,207,242		25.10	2,124.47	388,214		6.00	

Criteria of juveniles: aged from 14 to 18 years.

Note: Information for some categories is not available.

cial control over the police in criminal justice activities.

If the police apprehend a suspect in the act of committing a crime or if they have a basis to believe that a suspect in a serious crime is about to escape, they are permitted to act on their own initiative but are obliged to inform the judicial authorities within a specified time. The police are authorized in such cases to arrest and interrogate suspects and search their residences. Once arrested, suspects must be taken immediately to a judicial official, and the public prosecutor must be notified within 48 hours. A magistrate must be informed of a house search, and all seized materials must be handed over to the magistrate unopened. Prior judicial approval also is required for tapping telephones. Delays and deficiencies in the criminal justice system occur partly because of rivalries and overlapping jurisdictions among police organizations and partly because of poor cooperation between police and judicial personnel.

There is no death penalty in Italy. The maximum punishment is life imprisonment with little or no prospect of release before death. The Penal Code provides for declaring a person to be a habitual criminal, but this provision has rarely been used.

Prisons are administered by regulations drawn up in 1931, although the harshest of these have been modified by the Constitutional Court. Prison conditions vary widely. In many cities, prisons are ancient structures that were built centuries ago as monasteries or convents. Since 1969 there have been frequent prison riots and disorders, partly as a result of a rise in prison population as a result of mass arrests of radical leftists. A high proportion of the prison population consists of those awaiting trial. About half of these are eventually found innocent after spending years in jails.

The prison system is administered by the Ministry of Justice. Top officials usually are magistrates, but most of the prison guards are ill-trained.

IVORY COAST

BASIC FACT SHEET

Official Name: Republic of the Ivory Coast (Côte d'Ivoire)
Area: 322,463 sq km
Population: 10,766,632 (1987)
Capital: Abidjan
Nature of Government: Limited democracy
Language: French
Currency: CFA franc
GNP: $8.0 billion (1985)
Territorial Divisions: 34 prefectures, 161 subprefectures
Population per Police Officer: 4,640
Police Expenditures per 1,000: N.A.

History & Background

The Gendarmerie is the oldest branch of the police, dating back to 1854, when the metropolitan French service was extended to West Africa and a Senegal detachment with jurisdiction over the present Ivory Coast was formed. Initially it consisted of local militia strengthened by cadres of metropolitan Gendarmerie and officered exclusively by Frenchmen. In 1900 the militia gave way to an organized corps of professionals specifically recruited as policemen, and this integrated force became the Gendarmery of French West Africa and remained so until independence. In 1912 Africans were first admitted to office rank. Throughout its colonial existence the Gendarmerie enjoyed the status of an elite corps and was generally respected and admired. Since independence it has retained this position, and in the matter of manning, equipment and appropriations generally appears to be somewhat favored over the Sûreté.

The forerunners of the Sûreté Nationale were local police forces known as *gardes-cercles,* formed at administrative centers to supplement the Gendarmerie, who were too few in number to handle minor police matters. The local forces were not supported financially by the central administration, and the authority of each was limited to its immediate area. Some moves were made to absorb these separate units into the centrally controlled Gendarmerie but, in time, the distinct functions of local and territorial police came to be recognized, and the two branches were accepted as permanent institutions.

The metropolitan Sûreté extended its jurisdiction to the federation of French West Africa (Afrique Occidentale Française, AOF) in 1924. Under the direction of an inspector general headquartered at Dakar in Senegal, police units were designated Services Extérieurs and stationed in each colony under a single local authority. The various forces were organized into urban and rural departments (*commissariats* and *postes de police,* respectively).

On independence, the Ivory Coast took over the colonial police organization. A retired French police official was named interim director of the Sûreté, and virtually all other top positions remained in the hands of Frenchmen. In 1962 the first Ivorian was named to a top post, as police commissioner of Abidjan, followed by the appointment of another Ivorian, as director of the Sûreté. In the following years the Sûreté has been augmented with several new posts, notably at Abengourou and Adjame. By 1962 most major towns had Sûreté units, including urban stations at Beoumi, Bouafle and Divo and mobile brigades at Seguela and Korhogo. In addition, the Sûreté had been given responsibility for border control, with eight border control stations at strategic sites along the country's frontiers.

Structure & Organization

The Ivorian Police Force is composed of two separate establishments: the Gendarmerie Nationale and the Sûreté Nationale. Both were developed under the colonial regime, and both were transferred to the control of the Ivory Coast upon independence virtually without change. The forces are patterned closely after the police of metropolitan France, organized along French lines, trained to French standards, and French in doctrine and practice.

The rank and file of the police force have always been West Africans, and by 1962 Ivorians had been promoted to command both the Gendarmerie and the Sûreté, although French officers continued to hold high positions well into the 1980s. There is no dearth of applicants for entry into the force, which offered incentives lacking in other agencies. Veterans who have discharged their military obligations are given preference for enlistment.

The police are generally respected and obeyed, even in rural areas where there is traditional distrust and suspicion of official authority. Even when harsh in the discharge of their obligations, they are rarely brutal or oppressive.

For purposes of administration, the Gendarmerie is part of the country's military forces and is separate and distinct from the police. Functionally it is virtually indistinguishable from the regular police force.

Like other military services, the Gendarmerie is under the minister of defense, but it is normally administered and controlled through a chain of command distinct from the rest of the military. Its commandant is directly subordinate to the minister of defense, except in times of emergency, when he is under the command of the armed forces' chief of staff. The Gendarmerie is manned entirely by voluntary enlistment, and many of its members are Army veterans, who are encouraged to enter its ranks after completing their military service. Total strength is about 3,000.

Officially designated as the senior service, the Gendarmerie takes precedence over all other services. It furnishes ceremonial units for state occasions and provides military police for the other branches of the armed forces.

Operational command is exercised on a territorial basis through commandants assigned to each of the country's four administrative *départements*. Organization conforms to the metropolitan system and is based on the legion, one of which is assigned to each *département*. Legions have no fixed organization but are made up of a variable number of subordinate units, in accordance with the requirements of the *départments* in which they serve. In general, each legion is composed of two elements: departmental companies and mobile squadrons.

Departmental companies, comprised of a variable number of brigades, man fixed stations and carry out patrolling, investigative and special duties. Mobile squadrons, made up of a number of platoons, constitute reserve elements for quelling public disturbances.

The grade structure of the Gendarmerie closely parallels that of the Army, but following the precedent of its French predecessor, a corporal is designated a brigadier and a sergeant is *maréchal des logis*. Other ranks are the same, but privates are called *gardes;*

specialists attach their designator, such as *garde clairon* for a bugler and *garde chauffeur* for a driver.

The Gendarmerie uniforms are entirely of French design, with minor adaptation to lend national character. The basic uniform is khaki shorts and trousers, which are issued both short and long. French-type shoulder boards are worn with a trefoil braid. The headgear is a peaked garrison cap with the distinctive device of a vertical bayonet.

The Sûreté Nationale is the true police system and is directly under the Ministry of the Interior. Located at Abidjan and headed by a director appointed by the president, the headquarters of the Sûreté lays down policy and oversees operations. Although field components retain a considerable degree of autonomy, the control of the Sûreté is firm, and a close rein is maintained through periodic inspections.

In addition to subsections charged with inspection and administration, the Sûreté maintains a small Corps des Agents de la Sûreté, who work directly out of the headquarters. These agents, who operate in plain clothes, constitute a type of criminal investigation department. They are also charged with identification, public morals, and vice-squad activities, the latter operating principally in the major cities.

Directly below the Sûreté, active police forces are grouped under a central *Préfecture de Police,* headed by a director. The senior police officials, regardless of their operational station, are members of the Corps of Officers (including commissioners) or Corps of Inspectors of the Prefecture. Normally a police officer or inspector in an outlying station would have little contact with the office of the central prefecture in Abidjan unless summoned to headquarters.

The central prefecture is in effect the command element of the active police forces, which comprise the auxiliary police, the Police School and the Service de Police (see the chart). The auxiliary elements consist of small units assigned to specialist duties, such as airport police, traffic control, sanitation and boarder patrol. Most of them are assigned to the Abidjan area, with a few small groups in other cities.

The Service de Police, sometimes called Police d'État, is the principal component of the law-enforcement system and includes both urban and rural forces stationed throughout the country. Its uniformed members are the *gardiens de la paix,* or peace officers; they include the patrolmen on the beat, the country constables, defenders of the law, and protectors of people and property. They also function as *police judiciare*—that is, criminal police authorized to apprehend the lawbreaker and bring him or her before the bar of justice. Generally they are unarmed, and they are issued weapons during emergencies only. They wear a blue uniform with a blue kepi. Badges and piping are in silver.

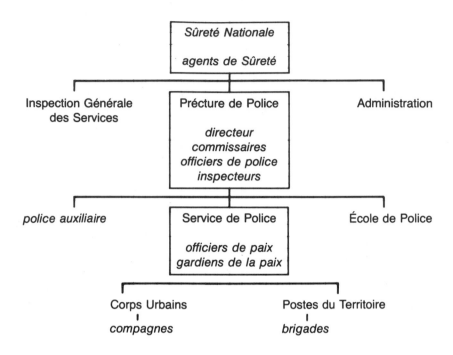

Sûreté Nationale

agents de Sûreté

Inspection Générale
des Services

Précture de Police

directeur
commissaires
officiers de police
inspecteurs

Administration

police auxiliaire

Service de Police

officiers de paix
gardiens de la paix

École de Police

Corps Urbains
compagnes

Postes du Territoire
brigades

The *gardiens de la paix* are supervised by *officiers de paix,* who rank below *officers de police,* who generally are staff officers at higher echelons. The Service de Police is made up of two major components: the Corps Urbains and the Postes du Territoire. The former are the city police departments, ranging in size from a small station commanded by an inspector to stations on the commissariat level headed by a commissioner. If size warrants, the force is organized into companies, generally commanded by an *officier de paix* or a noncommissioned officer. The company, or in the case of the rural police, the brigade, is the smallest administrative police unit.

Postes du Territoire are the headquarters of the rural police, who patrol the outlying areas. Generally the central station is in a small town centrally situated in the unit's area of responsibility. Each force is made up of mobile brigades (sometimes called mobile intelligence brigades), which conduct regular surveillance of their assigned territory and are ready to move quickly to any threatened locality in an emergency. Most brigades have some motorized equipment and can transport small groups in motorcycles or trucks.

Gardiens de la paix make up the bulk of the country's police, accounting for some 10% of the overall strength. Vacancies are filled by competitive examinations, for which a diploma indicating completion of elementary education is required.

There are five grades of *gardiens de la paix.* After a recruit has satisfactorily passed his *stagiaire,* or probationary period, he may move up to fourth-echelon status and from there move progressively to the first echelon, at which point he may be appointed a noncommissioned officer. The police noncommissioned officer structure closely parallels that of the Army, with ranks from *brigadier* (corporal) to *adjudant* (warrant officer). Within each noncommissioned grade, provision is also made for in-grade promotion, categorized as *échelons.* The highest rank a noncommissioned officer can reach is *adjudant chef de ler échelon.* From there he would have to advance to officer rank, where the system departs from the Army equivalents and adheres to police designations, from *officier de paix* through *commissaire.*

Recruitment, Education & Training

Under the colonial regime, most police training was conducted on the job, in local units. Selected noncommissioned officers and, in time, officers sometimes were sent to the police school in Dakar, or a more limited number to Paris. Generally, recruit training was undertaken at the local unit level. The training was limited to the French personnel but trickled down to the African policemen through on the job guidance.

In 1962, soon after independence, the Centre de Formation Professionelle de la Police opened in Abidjan to provide a centralized training program and speed up the Africanization of the officer corps. In 1963, the center became the official Police School.

The training facilities of the Gendarmerie are considered to be among the country's best. Its school at Camy Akouedo, near Abidjan, is a high-caliber institution with a thorough curriculum and an excellent physical plant. The officers also receive on-the-job instruction and periodic training.

The Penal System

Although extensive revisions have been made in the country's criminal law and procedures since independence, the French Penal Code is still the basis of jurisprudence, and changes effected have not altered its essentially French character.

No information is available on Ivory Coast's penal institutions.

Crime statistics are fragmentary and often outdated, but published reports indicate a relatively low incidence, with the Ivory Coast possibly slightly better than the average for West Africa. Larceny and embezzlement are the most common offenses. Assaults are fairly common, mostly in urban areas, and often result from intoxication. Murder, rape and armed robbery are rare and usually are attributed by authorities to Africans from neighboring countries. New categories of offenses, such as automobile theft and reckless driving, have become fairly commonplace. Nevertheless, overall, the Ivory Coast presents a favorable comparison with its neighbors in crime rates.

CRIME STATISTICS (1984)

		Number Reported	Attempts %	Cases Solved %	Crime per 100,000	Offenders	Females %	Juveniles %	Strangers %
1.	Murder	142	22.54	76.06	1.78	129		6.20	
2.	Sex offenses, including rape	642	25.39	73.99	8.03	536		18.47	
3.	Rape	405	29.14	81.48	5.06	375		17.87	
4.	Serious assault	4,808	2.45	58.15	60.10	3,557		5.74	
5.	All theft	12,061	6.05	46.84	150.76	6,503		8.03	
6.	Aggravated theft	3,422	7.54	38.75	42.78	1,621		7.53	
7.	Robbery and violent theft	2,101	5.28	39.08	26.20	1,085		7.74	
8.	Breaking and entering	1,321	11.13	38.23	16.51	536		7.09	
9.	Auto theft	537	8.38	38.18	6.71	158		13.29	
10.	Other thefts	8,102	5.27	50.83	101.28	4,724		8.02	
11.	Fraud	4,884	6.49	47.81	61.05	3,484		2.24	
12.	Counterfeiting	208	7.21	82.69	2.60	178		8.99	
13.	Drug offenses	839	1.31	75.80	10.49	856		10.28	
14.	Total offenses	23,584			294.80	15,243		6.66	

Criteria of juveniles: aged from 1 to 18 years.
Note: Information for some categories is not available.

JAMAICA

BASIC FACT SHEET

Official Name: Jamaica
Area: 10,991 sq km
Population: 2,455,536 (1987)
Capital: Kingston
Nature of Government: Parliamentary democracy
Language: English
Currency: Jamaican dollar
GNP: $2 billion (1986)
Territorial Divisions: 12 parishes
Population per Police Officer: 450
Police Expenditures per 1,000: $24,259

History & Background

The Jamaica Constabulary Force (JCF) was founded following the Morant Bay Rebellion of 1867, with a strength of 948 members under an inspector general. The force was modernized in 1948 under the direction of W. A. Calvert of the London Metropolitan Police Force, who introduced many changes, such as employment of women police, setting up a traffic branch and instituting a new training program. The JCF was completely Jamaicanized on independence in 1962.

Structure & Organization

The Jamaica Constabulary Force had a strength of 6,000 officers and men in 1986. Supplementing the JCF are such entities as the volunteer Island Special Constabulary, numbering 2,500, and the district constables, totaling about 1,800. The former is used as a reserve force to assist in emergency operations; the latter operate in smaller localities. In 1973 the National Home Guards was created, but information on its strength is not available. There is also an unknown number of parish special constables who serve on the regular force on special occasions and are paid only when on duty. Larger cities have municipal police forces, but their functions are restricted to enforcing municipal regulations and protecting municipal property.

Heading the JCF is the commissioner of police, assisted by six to eight deputy and assistant commissioners. For operational purposes the island is divided into five areas: Area I, Montego Bay; Area II, St. Mary; Area III, Mandeville; Area IV, Kingston; Area V, St. Thomas. These areas are further subdivided into 18 divisions, headed either by superintendents or deputy superintendents.

There are a number of special units or sections under the direct control of headquarters, although part of their personnel may be stationed outside Kingston. The Criminal Investigation Department (CID), consisting of detectives or inspectors, has men stationed in all towns. Under the CID are the Criminal Records Office, the Fingerprint Bureau, the Fraud Squad and the Forensics Laboratory. A special branch conducts police intelligence and provides physical security for visiting dignitaries. The Traffic and Transport Section provides mobile patrols throughout the island and is responsible for maintaining the police radio network. A mounted police detachment, although used mainly for ceremonial functions, helps in traffic and crowd control and in patrolling parks and wooded areas. Immigration and passport services, once under civilian control, have been carried out by the police since the end of World War II. Operating in Kingston Harbor since 1912 and in a few other seaports are the water police, who also deal with crime on the waterfront.

More than 250 specially trained men make up the Mobile Reserve, which handles riots, drug cases, and conducts house-to-house searches permitted under special laws. In 1975 a squad of men from the Mobile Reserve was formed specifically to combat the political violence that was becoming more frequent. The Dog Section, a small unit, is used to search for missing persons, to track criminals, and to aid patrols in high crime areas. The 200 or so women in the police force are under the command of a woman superintendent in the police headquarters, but each unit has some women attached to it. All police personnel receive numerous allowances in addition to their basic salary, including housing and uniform allowances.

Until the 1970s the police had a good reputation, at least among the upper and middle classes. During the 1970s, with the increase in drug trafficking and political violence, there were frequent charges in the media about police corruption and brutality. Partially in response to these criticisms, the police began an image-building program. A Citizens' Complaint Board was set up to receive complaints from the public of instances of police misconduct and to make independent investigations.

Recruitment, Education & Training

A police training school is at Fort Charles near Port Royal at the end of the Palisadoes Peninsula. New recruits, who are called cadets, take written, oral and medical tests before admission to the school. They receive an 18-week basic course in police law, self-defense, first aid and drill. Ordinarily they are sent to a rural post for 10 months of on-the-job training and return to the school for a six-week senior recruit course before becoming constables. More advanced training is provided for constables, corporals and sergeants. Completion of the advanced course is required before promotion to higher ranks.

The Penal System

In general, the Jamaican legal system, including much of its substantive and procedural criminal law, derives from that of Great Britain. The relevant statutes are those in force at the time of independence, including a number enacted by the British Parliament and those subsequently enacted by the Jamaican Parliament. As in all countries with roots in the English system, these statutes are interpreted and applied in terms of common law.

Although there is no overall penal code, the Prevention of Crime Law of 1963 established minimum penalties for certain crimes, thus limiting the sentencing discretion of judges. For example, the conviction on charge of possessing marijuana (or *ganja*) makes imprisonment mandatory, although the magistrate may vary the length of the sentence.

Some criminal acts may also involve civil wrongs. A person accused of assaulting or libeling another person, for example, may be prosecuted under criminal law by the director of public prosecutions. The injured party may, however, file an additional civil suit for compensation.

In 1975 the prisons, the Probations Department and the reform schools, all previously under the Ministry of Youth and Community Development, were moved to the newly created Ministry of National Security and Justice and consolidated into the Department of Correctional Services. That department also operates a training school for prison guards, called warders, recruited on the basis of civil service written and oral examinations.

There are five prisons and a Gun Court Rehabilitation Center with an average annual population of close to 3,000. The department's annual budget is subsidized by the sale of prisoner-made goods and the fees received from operating the Rockfort Mineral Baths using prison labor. About half the number of prisoners are under 25 years of age, and most serve sentences of less than a year.

The major prison is the General Penitentiary, in downtown Kingston near the harbor. It is a maximum-security institution with a separate section called the Female Prison. The St. Catherine District Prison, another maximum-security institution, is where death row is located. It has a separate section for young male habitual offenders. The Richmond Farm Prison is a minimum-security prison for first offenders serving long-term sentences, while the Tamarinf Farm Prison houses recidivists serving short sentences. Fort Augusta Prison, in a fortress, is a minimum-security prison for prisoners with a good behavior record. Hill Top Prison was converted in 1973 to a reform school. The Gun Court Rehabilitation Center houses those convicted by the Gun Court.

Technically, the prisons offer means of rehabilitation, although there are only token facilities in this respect. Most prisons have workshops, some have agricultural projects and bakeries, and a few conduct literacy programs for inmates. However, living conditions in the prisons are substandard, and complaints of ill treatment are not infrequent.

Generally, young offenders under age 17 are tried before a juvenile court. During trial, they are kept in what are known as "places of safety," where they receive classroom and vocational training. Generally, places of safety are charitable and religious institutions. If found guilty by the court, juveniles may be placed on probation, or sentenced either to a reform school (called an "approved school") or to a children's home.

Most of the work of the Probation Department consists of juvenile cases. Generally, about one-third of all juvenile court cases end with the offender being placed on probation; in contrast, only 20% of sentenced adults are placed on probation. Before 1948 there was no official Probation Department, and the Salvation Army performed probationary work for the government on a voluntary basis. Since then, probation officers have been assigned to every court in the country, and every parish has a Parish Probation Committee to oversee the work of probation officers.

The incidence of crime has been steadily rising, a phenomenon attributed partly to unemployment, partly to political conflicts and partly to racial animosities. About 47% of the reported crimes occur in Kingston and St. Andrew, which together contain only 25% of the national population. As a result of stricter police controls in towns, many criminals fled the cities and carried on in rural areas. Some relatively isolated areas still appear to be free of crime—for example, in Cockpit County, where the Maroons live, few serious crimes have been reported in this century.

Senseless crimes as well as assaults on the police—typical of deep-rooted sociopathological problems—are not uncommon. The government has responded with increased police patrols, and judges have handed out stiffer sentences in an effort to stem the tide of violence. The passage of the 1974 Suppression of Crimes Act was a landmark in these efforts that also included house-to-house searches without warrants, the imposition of curfews and the increased use of military patrols.

Two special features of the crime wave were the narcotics connection and the growing number of felonies committed by juveniles. Jamaica is a major link in the drug chain that extends from Bolivia to the United States. There are strict laws on the statute books against growing *ganja* as well as its consumption and sale. Juveniles are involved heavily in drugs, and they also are responsible for many other serious offenses, such as larceny.

JAPAN

BASIC FACT SHEET

Official Name: Japan
Area: 372,313 sq km
Population: 122,124,293 (1987)
Capital: Tokyo
Nature of Government: Constitutional monarchy
Language: Japanese
Currency: Yen
GNP: $1.37 trillion (1985)
Territorial Divisions: 47 prefectures
Population per Police Officer: 480
Police Expenditures per 1,000: $55,594

History & Background

There have been two formative periods in the development of the modern Japanese police: the Meiji Restoration, especially the years from 1872 to 1889, and the Allied occupation from 1945 to 1952. The first full-time professional policemen were appointed in Japan in 1871; three years later the Keihoryo (Police Bureau) was established in the Ministry of Home Affairs (Naimusho). This system remained in force until 1947, when it was totally reorganized by the occupation authorities. The principal thrust of this reorganization was to decentralize the police establishment on American lines. All large cities and towns in the country with populations over 5,000 were given an independent police force. The Public Safety Commission system (Koan Linkai Seido) was introduced at national and prefectural levels as well as a democratic system of administration and command. In rural communities with a population of less than 5,000 the National Rural Police was established. The responsibility of the police was limited to affairs strictly concerned with keeping peace and order, dealing with crime, and protecting life and property. It was soon found that decentralization had many drawbacks that considerably impaired police effectiveness and resulted in increased financial burdens for the cities, towns and villages. To correct these defects, the system was changed again in 1954. The dual system of municipal police and rural police was abolished and the two forces were integrated into a central police force under the name of Todo Fuken Keisatsu (Prefectural Police). The Public Safety Commission was established as the principal administrative agency with the right to intervene in prefectural police matters. At the same time, the political neutrality and democratic administration of the police force were clearly defined and guaranteed.

Structure & Organization

The three main law-enforcement organizations in Japan are the National Public Safety Commission (NPSC), the National Police Agency (NPA) and the prefectural police. The National Public Safety Commission (Kokka Koan Linkai), under the direct authority of the prime minister, is responsible for all police operations and activities in the nation pertaining to public safety, training, communications, criminal identification, statistics and equipment. The NPSC is composed of a chairman and five members. The chairman holds the office of a state minister, but to ensure political neutrality, he has no vote except in case of a tie. Members of the commission are appointed by the prime minister with the consent of both houses of the Diet and are selected from persons who have had no previous career as professional policemen or attorneys during the preceding five years. Not more than two members of the commission may belong to the same political party. The major responsibility of the commission is to supervise the National Police Agency and to appoint or dismiss senior ranking police officers.

The National Police Agency (Keisatsucho) is headed by a commissioner general who is appointed or dismissed by the NPSC with the approval of the prime minister. The internal divisions of the NPA are the secretariat, five bureaus and one department: The five bureaus are the Police Administration Bureau, the

Crime Control Bureau, the Traffic Bureau, the Safety Bureau and the Communications Bureau. The Safety Department functions within the Criminal Investigation Bureau. There are three agencies affiliated with the NPA: the National Police Academy, the National Research Institute of Police Science and the Imperial Guard Headquarters.

Under the NPA there are seven regional police bureaus (Kanku Keisatsu Kyoku) and two police communications divisions, in Tokyo and Hokkaido. Each of the seven bureaus supervises the activities of its subordinate departments with the exception of the Tokyo Metropolitan Police and the Hokkaido Metropolitan Police. Regional and metropolitan police forces function under the administrative supervision of metropolitan and regional Public Safety Commissions. These commissions consist of five members in the case of Tokyo and other major cities and three members in the case of other prefectures, all appointed by the prefectural governor with the consent of the prefectural assembly. The prefectural police headquarters serve as the center of operations in each prefecture and are headed by senior police officers holding the rank of senior superintendent or director (honbucho). The Tokyo Metropolitan Police Department (TMPD) enjoys a special status and is headed by a superintendent general (keishisokan).

Each prefecture is divided into several police districts, each with its own police station (kaisatsu sho) or, in the case of urban areas, city police departments (shi keisatsubu). The lowest unit of the police establishment is the police box (hashutsusho or koban), manned by two police officers, in towns and residential police box (chuzaisho), manned by a single police officer, in villages. Kobans may be found in the strangest settings: above bars, on traffic islands, beside underpasses, or in the arcade of railway stations, while chuzaishos look like ordinary homes or cottages. The only thing common to these police boxes is the red light globe hung over their front doors. Unlike the United States, where police operations are centered around the patrol car, the Japanese police depend on a fixed-post deployment system, with the koban as its hub. Only one-sixth of all patrolmen work in cars, although the ratio is changing in favor of cars as a result of an increasing emphasis on mobility. Because of the relative congestion of Japanese cities and the smaller proportion of land devoted to streets (14% in Tokyo as compared to 35% in New York), patrol cars do not possess an advantage in response time.

In addition to regular police, a number of specialized police agencies function under different ministries. These include the Railway Security Police, the Forestry Police, Inspectors of Labor Standards, Maritime Safety Officers, Narcotics Control Officers, Mining Affairs Inspectors and Fishery Inspection Officers.

The typical Japanese police officer is young, male, married and high-school-educated. About half are under the age of 35, as compared to 59% of the population in that age bracket. Only 1.5% are women in what is an almost entirely male profession. Women have been recruited only since 1946, and they are employed only in the largest 17 prefectures, where they are assigned to traffic regulation, counseling of juveniles, and plainclothes work against pickpockets and shoplifters. Other prefectures have female traffic wardens who are not sworn officers. Nowhere have women been integrated into patrol work on an equal footing with men. The educational level of policemen is higher than that of the population as a whole; 63% have graduated from high school (as compared to 32% for the nation as a whole) and about 7% have graduated from a college. Policemen are also upwardly mobile in terms of social class and generally are the sons of blue-collar workers who consider law enforcement as an avenue of professional advancement.

The proportion of local officers on the force varies from city to city—from 99% in Aomori Prefecture to 13% in Tokyo. While on patrol the demeanor of Japanese policemen is self-effacing, low-key and unauthoritarian. They do not swagger or posture and often are as inconspicuous as mailmen. In conformity with social mores they avoid eye contact with the people unless specifically obligated to do so. The average Japanese policeman is small in stature relative to the general population.

Only about 50 policemen are discharged for misbehavior annually, and departmental punishments, such as temporary suspensions, reductions in pay and formal reprimands, are given to less then 600. Complaints about police behavior are unusual and have declined in recent years to about 125 per year. Many reasons have been cited for the high standard of personal conduct among Japanese policemen, the most common being the difference in strategies pursued in Japan for generating and sustaining responsible police behavior. In many other countries responsible police behavior is predicated on external mechanisms and complaints, while in Japan emphasis is placed primarily on the police community itself and their community spirit. This is not to say that there are no institutional channels for ensuring public accountability. Civilian supervision of police activities has been provided in several ways. First, the Human Rights Bureau of the Ministry of Justice, established in 1948, hears complaints about infringements of civil rights. In addition to an official staff in every major city, the bureau uses 10,000 unpaid civilian counselors scattered throughout the country to discover violations of rights. Though the bureau does not have compulsory powers of investigation, it can ask for an accounting from the police and make recommendations concerning punishment. Second, chiefs of police are frequently summoned before prefectural legislatures to answer questions about performance or specific issues. The third mechanism is the Public Safety Commission, which functions as the ultimate civilian board of review. The fourth institution policing the police is the media, which in Japan is free and vigorous, and quick to denounce police imperfections. In addition, police officers can be sued for civil damages, although they are not liable personally, as in the United States.

Police work is not only less demanding in Japan but also less dangerous. Firearms play a negligible part in crime. Of approximately 100,000 serious offenses committed annually in Tokyo, less than 16 involve handguns. Policemen are not haunted by the fear of a sharpshooting assassin or a fiery ambush. Less than five officers are killed each year in line of duty and hardly ever by firearms. The killing of a policeman therefore causes more shock and outrage in Japan than in comparably advanced countries.

Japanese policemen are one of the hardest working groups of a hardworking people. The hours of police work are irregular as well as long. Most patrolmen are on duty for 56 hours a week, working on a so-called three-shift system under which they work one day from 9:00 A.M. to 5:30 P.M., then the next day from 8:30 A.M. to the following morning at 10:00 A.M., followed by a day of rest, then reporting on the fourth day to begin the cycle anew. (In contrast, the average workweek in Japanese industry is 45 hours.) Officers are allowed to take eight hours of rest between each 24-hour tour of duty, but only if circumstances are normal. Policemen are given 20 paid holidays each year, but few take them; taking of the full vacation is believed somehow to detract from dedication to one's duty. During working hours policemen display a great degree of punctilio. They rarely take off their hats in public or inside the precincts and invariably put on white gloves while on duty. When leaving or entering, patrolmen salute senior officers. Their uniform is extremely formal, except in summer. It consists of a four-button double-breasted coat worn over a white shirt and tie. In winter the coat and trousers are black; in spring and autumn, steel blue. A Sam Browne belt is worn over the jacket. In summer they shed their coat, strap and necktie and wear an open-necked steel-blue shirt with matching trousers. The police cap is peaked in front with a short black visor. On the front above the visor is the gold emblem of the police, a five-pointed star enclosed by pine branches. Shoes are black, but patrolmen generally wear ankle-length boots. Rank insignia are worn on coat lapels or breast pockets. There are neither identifying numbers nor name tags. Each

ORGANIZATIONAL CHART OF THE POLICE OF JAPAN (NATIONAL LEVEL)

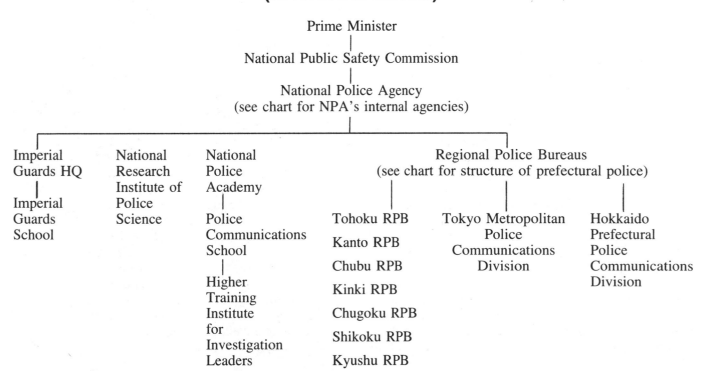

policeman carries standardized equipment: a .38-caliber revolver in a holster attached to the right shoulder by a lanyard, handcuffs in a rear-left belt pouch, a 24-inch (60-centimeter) nightstick with a leather thong down the left leg, a small radio receiver in the breast pocket, and a light rope 15 feet (4.5 meters) long in a trouser pocket, used for the ancient rope-tying art of *hojo*.

There are eleven ranks in the police force. In descending order they are commissioner general, superintendent general, superintendent supervisor, chief superintendent, senior superintendent, superintendent, police inspector, assistant police inspector, police sergeant, senior policeman and policeman.

Senior officers over the rank of chief superintendent are given the same salary and allowance as regular public service personnel, while officers below that rank are covered by a compensation system based on three factors: seniority, rank and education. All policemen receive automatic increases in salary every year, resulting in a doubling of base salary every 20 years. But the annual rate of increase declines progressively from 5% in the initial years to 1% after 20 years. University graduates receive a four-year seniority at the outset, and the differential is maintained throughout their careers. Passage of a written examination is required for promotion from patrolman to sergeant, from sergeant to assistant inspector and from assistant inspector to inspector. Beyond the rank of an inspector, promotions are made on recommendation of superior officials.

Salary figures for Japanese policemen include a base salary plus allowances. Such allowances are extensive and often amount to two-thirds of base pay. They include supplements for dependents, subsidized housing, free medical care and hospitalization, low-cost loans and consumer goods at discount prices, commuting facilities, overtime, and a bonus equal to 40% of the base wage paid in three installments annually. When computed on this basis, the average police salary is 48% above the average for all Japanese industrial workers. However, policemen are prohibited from supplementing their income through moonlighting.

The total annual pay (including allowances) for police officers of various ranks and terms of service in Tokyo are:

TOTAL ANNUAL PAY OF JAPANESE POLICE OFFICERS

(amounts in dollars)

Status	Annual Salary	Allowances	Total
Newly appointed policeman	1,050	850	1,900
Policeman with 20 years of service	2,500	1,600	4,100
Police inspector with 25 years of service	3,100	2,400	5,500
Police superintendent with 30 years of service	3,800	3,200	7,000

Opportunities for career advancement in the police are greater in Japan than in the United States. Almost one-third of Japanese policemen hold supernumerary rank—rank higher than patrolman—compared with 15% in U.S. state police. A Japanese patrolman has one chance in four of becoming a sergeant, compared with one in eight in U.S. state police. There is also a constant circulation of staff designed to prevent units from becoming ingrown. Whenever a policeman is promoted he is transferred to another post, and tenure in supervisory positions generally is no longer than two years. Such rotation prevents policemen from developing vested interests in their communities and undesirable local elements from acquiring any form of control over a station's activities.

Retirement age in the National Police Agency is between 50 and 55 and in the prefectural police between 55 and 58. Although officers are not required to retire at these ages, they are encouraged to do so through higher lump sum severance payments. After 30 years of service an officer will get 50.4 months' severance payment for voluntary retirement but only 41.25 months' for involuntary retirement.

There are three principal types of police vehicles motor vehicles, boats and helicopters. Motor vehicles are classified into five categories: police patrol cars, traffic patrol cars, white motorcycles (also known as *shirobai*), investigative cars and transportation cars. In addition, a total of about 30,000 bicycles have been provided for police officers assigned to police boxes throughout the country.

About 80 units of radio-equipped police boats, each of which ranges in tonnage from five to 25, and in length from about 24½ feet (eight meters) to 66 feet (20 meters) have been assigned to the 10 water police stations having jurisdiction over the major ports, as well as isolated islands, lakes, marshes and rivers.

A total of 22 police helicopters currently are assigned to prefectural police headquarters such as Tokyo, Kanagawa, Osaka and Hokkaido.

The operation and administration of communications are centrally supervised by the National Police Agency. The communications network extends from the NPA to the eight regional police bureaus, from the regional police bureaus to the prefectural police headquarters, and from these headquarters to the prefectural police stations, police boxes and resident police boxes. Telephone trunk lines are operated under the system of automatic nondelay service activated through multichannel microwave telephone lines. They also utilize special communication techniques such as facsimile and telephotograph for rapid exchange of documents, photographs and fingerprints. A shortwave radio telephone network is maintained as a standby service for emergency situations when telephone service has been interrupted by a disaster. Shortwave radio also is used to exchange information with Interpol. The Tokyo radio station of the NPA is the Interpol regional central radio station for Southeast Asia. Each metropolitan and prefectural police jurisdiction maintains a shortwave radiotelephone network for radio-equipped cars in patrol duties. To cope with emergency calls and to speed police response, a uniform "dial 110" system has been introduced nationwide. Individual police officers are provided with walkie-talkies. Other communication equipment and devices include mobile multichannel radiotelephone cars, wire and wireless television cars capable of transmitting video images direct to police headquarters, and airborne radio equipment mounted on police helicopters.

An electronic data processing system was introduced for the first time n 1964. Four large electronic computers have been installed at the NPA on an online batch processing system with links to metropolitan and prefectural police headquarters, The system is used primarily for inquiries about stolen goods, firearms, traffic accidents and, since 1976, juvenile runaways.

Security Police

Because Japan has no sizable racial, religious or linguistic minorities, it has been relatively free from the kinds of civil disorders that have afflicted other Asian nations. Nevertheless, it has faced serious disturbances from radical left-wing student activists or guerrillas, such as the Sekigun-Ha (Red Army Faction). There are no national riot-control police in Japan, and the mission of suppressing terrorism and riots is performed by the Kido-Tai (Riot Police Units), comprising 9,700 regular officers of prefectural police forces and 5,200 officers of the Tokyo Metropolitan Police Department. In addition, there are 4,200 officers on reserve status. These officers are mostly young and specially trained in the use of special antiriot equipment.

Traffic Police

Accidents and fatalities have steadily declined since 1970. This decline is credited to the traffic police, who function under the Traffic Bureau of the NPA. The bureau controls 22,000 traffic police officers equipped with 3,000 motorcycles and 1,000 cars, 65,000 patrol police officers, 25,000 traffic wardens and 28 computerized traffic control centers. The bureau processes about 6 million traffic violations annually, of which 71.5% were settled through payment of a fine (hansoku-kin). The bureau also issues licenses to Japan's 37.02 million drivers, holds driver aptitude test examinations and undertakes traffic safety campaigns. One of its most onerous duties is the enforcement of a law, perhaps peculiar to Japan, prohibiting the possession of motor vehicles by persons without their own or a rented garage. The computerized sophistication of traffic signals has been achieved, thus easing severe traffic jams in big cities. (Traffic jams up to about a third of a mile [500 meters] in length are reported as common in Tokyo.) Traffic policemen make constant use of built-in loudspeakers in their cars to control traffic. Large vehicles are banned from entering major cities during rush hours.

Criminal Identification

Special sections of the National Police Agency and the prefectural police conduct criminal identification work of various types, such as detection and collection of data from the scene of crimes, scientific or forensic examination, comparison tests and cross-checking. Over 5,100 officers are engaged in such activity. Centralized and computerized master files of fingerprints and photographs are maintained by the Identification Section. In addition, the National Research Institute of Police Science provides expert scientific backup, especially in high-technology areas. Two new units known as Identification Centers handle technical matters beyond the capability of the prefectural police.

As in other countries, police dogs are used extensively in Japan. Police dogs are classified into two categories: search dogs (sosaku ken), used to pursue criminals' footmarks or to sort items through the use of the sense of smell; and watch dogs (keikai ken), used to interdict criminals and to guard installations.

Recruitment, Education & Training

Entry into the police force is made at two levels: patrolman and assistant inspector. Recruitment for patrolmen is conducted separately by each prefecture. Applicants must pass physical, intellectual and voca-

ORGANIZATIONAL CHART OF THE NATIONAL POLICE AGENCY OF JAPAN

National Police Agency

Commissioner General

Deputy
Commissioner General

Secretariat	Police Administration Bureau	Criminal Investigation Bureau	Safety Department	Traffic Bureau	Security Bureau	Communications Bureau
General Affairs Division	Personnel Division	First Investigation Division	Crime Prevention Division	Traffic Planning Division	First Public Security Division	General Affairs Division
Finance Division	Education Division	Second Investigation Division	Juvenile Division	Traffic Enforcement Division	Second Public Security Division	Wireless Communications Division I
Equipment Division	Allowance and Welfare Division	International Criminal Affairs Division	Safety Division	Traffic Regulations Division	Third Public Security Division	Wireless Communications Division II
Efficiency Administration Division	Inspection officers	Identification Division	Pollution Control Division	License Division	Security Division	Communications Research Division
Legal and Planning Administration Division		Criminal Research and Statistics Division	Patrol Division	Superhighway Supervising Division	Foreign Affairs Division	
					Security Research Division	

tional aptitude tests in addition to an oral interview. Patrolmen are required to have high-school diplomas but may rise as high as their talents warrant. Recruitment to the rank of assistant inspector is done on a national basis by the National Police Agency. Applicants are required to have a four-year college education and to have passed the advanced civil service examination. However, only about 15 persons are recruited annually at this level. In Japan, as elsewhere, police work tends to attract the more conservative youth. Extensive background checks by the local police are carried out on all recruits to determine whether they are of good character. Although the constitution prohibits job discrimination on the basis of political belief or affiliation, the police reject applicants with "antisocial tendencies," particularly if the applicant or members of his family are associated with left-wing movements.

There are two types of police education and train-

ing: school education and job training. School education is designed for newly recruited police officers, newly promoted police officers and officers in need of specialized professional training. Metropolitan or prefectural police schools conduct education and training for newly recruited officers, while regional police schools conduct education for officers who are to be promoted to the rank of police sergeant or assistant police inspector. The National Police Academy trains newly appointed police inspectors. The Highest Training Institute for Investigation Leaders, attached to the Communications School, is a special institute for senior officers in command position in the investigative field.

Curriculum for police training establishments includes moral guidance, general education subjects, jurisprudence, practical subjects and technical subjects such as judo, kendo, pistol handling, shooting, arresting techniques, physical training and military

ORGANIZATION OF PREFECTURAL POLICE

Ordinary Prefectural Police	Major Prefectural Police (Osaka, Kyoto, Aichi, Kanagawa, Hyogo, Fukuoka)	Hokkaido Prefectural Police	Tokyo Metropolitan Police Department
Governor	Governor	Governor	Governor
Public Safety Commission	Public Safety Commission	Public Safety Commission	Public Safety Commission
Prefectural police headquarters	Prefectural police headquarters	Area Public Safety Commission (Asahikawa, Kushiro, Kitami, Hakodate)	Metropolitan Police Department
Police station	City police department	Hokkaido prefectural police headquarters	Superintendent general
Police school	Police station	Hokkaido Police School	Metropolitan police schools
Police box	Police school	Police station	Police stations
Residential police box	Police box	Police box	Police box
	Residential police box	Residential police box	Residential police box

drill. Training programs are thorough and tough, and 5% of the candidates sent to the Tokyo Police School fail to complete the course.

The Japanese police have also developed a unique tutoring arrangement whereby responsibility for teaching new recruits is given to experienced senior officers. Such on-the-job training is supplemented by training meetings, short study courses, distribution of training aids, and foreign assignments for study purposes. Every year approximately 10,000 policemen undergo training upon promotion, and some 40,000 do technical courses lasting from three weeks to a year. Serving patrolmen are also given monthly homework assignments.

The Penal System

Until the Meiji Restoration the criminal justice system was controlled mainly by the provincial lords. Public officials, not laws, guided the people to conform to traditional morality in accordance with Confucian ideals. Specific enforcement varied from domain to domain. No formal penal codes existed, justice was generally harsh and punishment depended upon one's status. Kin and neighbors could share blame for an offender's guilt; whole families and villages could be flogged or put to death for one member's transgression.

After 1868 the justice system underwent a rapid transformation. The first publicly promulgated codes, the Penal Code and the Code of Criminal Procedure, both of 1880, were based on a French model. Offenses were specified, and punishments were graded and set for each offense. Both codes broke with tradition in a number of their features. All citizens were dealt with as equals, punishment by *ex post facto* law was prohibited, guilt was held to be personal rather than collective, and offenses against the emperor were spelled out for the first time.

These features notwithstanding, certain provisions reflected traditional attitudes toward authority. The procurator represented the state and sat together with the judge on a raised platform, above the defendant and his counsel. Under a semi-inquisitorial system, the primary responsibility for questioning witnesses lay with the judge, and counsel for the defense was permitted to question witnesses only through the judge. Counsel for the defense was not permitted to assist the suspect during the preliminary fact-finding investigation conducted by the judge. Since in all trials available evidence had already convinced a preliminary judge of a defendant's guilt, the trial judge acted less as an independent arbiter than as a reviewer of procedures—undermining the defendant's legal presumption of innocence until proved guilty and further weakening the legal recourse open to his or her counsel.

Reflecting the growing influence of German law in Japan, the Penal Code was substantially revised in 1907. The French practice of classifying offenses into three classes was eliminated. More importantly, where the old code had allowed very limited judicial discretion as to sentencing, the new one granted the sentencing judge wide discretion. In 1923 the Code of Criminal Procedure was also revised along German lines without altering court procedures.

After World War II the occupation authorities initiated reform of the more archaic features of the Penal Code. Offenses relating to war, the imperial family and adultery were omitted, but the rest of the code was not substantially altered. The Criminal Procedure Code, however, was revised to guarantee the rights of the accused. The system became completely accusatorial, and the judge, although still able to question the witnesses, decides the case on evidence presented by both sides. The preliminary investigative procedure was abolished. Prosecutors and defense counsel sit on an equal level below the judge.

Prisons existed in feudal Japan as early as the 16th century, originally to hold people for trial or prior to execution. Life imprisonment was rare, and convicted persons were either executed or banished. However, there were a few facilities for short-term confinement. Prisoners were treated according to their status and housed in barrackslike quarters. The position of prison officer was hereditary, and staff vacancies were filled by relatives.

During the Meiji Period, Japan adopted Western-type penology. In 1888 an after-care hostel (halfway house) was opened for released prisoners. Staffed mainly by volunteers, the institution helped ex-convicts reenter society, from which they had been ostracized for the shame they had incurred. The Prison Law of 1908 provided basic rules and regulations for prison administration, stipulating separate facilities to house those confined to confinement with labor, confinement without labor and short-term prisoners.

The Juvenile Law of 1922 established administrative organs to deal with offenders under the age of 18 and officially recognized voluntary workers as the major channels of community-based treatment of juveniles. After World War II, juvenile laws were revised to extend jurisdiction to those under age 20, and a probation and parole system for adults was established. Volunteer workers were reorganized under a new law.

The Correctional Bureau of the Ministry of Justice is responsible for the administration of the adult prison system as well as the juvenile correctional system and three women's guidance homes for ex-prostitutes. The ministry's Rehabilitation Bureau operates probation and parole systems. Prison personnel are trained at an institute in Tokyo and in branch training institutes in each of the eight regional correctional headquarters under the Correctional Bureau. Professional probation officers are trained at the Research and Training Institute of the Ministry of Justice.

The prison population per capita is among the lowest in the world and is about 50,000 per year. Some 46% are repeat offenders, which results from the fact that first offenders rarely enter the penal system. Upon confinement, prisoners are classified according to sex, nationality, kind of penalty, length of sentence, degree of criminality and state of mental and physical health; then, they are placed in special programs. Under a system stressing incentives, prisoners are initially assigned to community cells, then earn better quarters and additional privileges based on their good behavior. Most convicts are put to work, for which a small stipend is paid on release. Most juvenile offenders are placed in training schools where vocational and formal education is emphasized.

Noninstitutional treatment is used to substitute or supplement prison terms. A large number of those given suspended sentences are released to the supervision of voluntary officers under the guidance of professional probation officers. Adults usually are placed on probation for a fixed period, and juveniles until they reach age 20. Volunteers are used in supervising parole for low-risk offenders and generally handle no more than five cases at a time.

The National Police Agency divides crime into six main categories: felonies, violent offenses, larceny, intellectual offenses, moral offenses and other offenses.

- Felonies: murder, conspiracy to murder, robbery, rape, arson
- Violent offenses: simple and aggravated assault, extortion, intimidation
- Larceny: burglary, vehicle theft, shoplifting
- Intellectual offenses: fraud, embezzlement, counterfeiting, forgery, bribery, breach of trust
- Moral offenses: gambling, pornography
- Other offenses: possession of stolen property, destruction of property, unauthorized entry, prostitution, customs violations, possession of narcotics

Japan has one of the lowest crime rates in the world and is in that respect the envy of the industrialized world. The rate of violent crime, for example, is 31 per 100,000—under 10% of that in the United States, under 25% of that of West Germany and 80% of that of England and Wales. Property crime also is correspondingly low. Tokyo enjoys the reputation of being the safest of the world's major cities.

The most important factor keeping crime low is the continuing dominance of traditional social values. Within his immediate social groups, a Japanese incurs rights and obligations—including the one not to bring shame—and meets powerful expectations to conform. These potent social sanctions give Japan an advantage in criminal justice that Western nations cannot claim. Other factors include the general ethnic homogeneity of the country (a fact that Prime Minister Nakasone stated in 1986 in a pejorative reference to American blacks), a prosperous economy from which no social classes are deliberately excluded and a ban on firearms.

This is not to say that Japan is free from the major criminal problems brought on by urbanization and industrialization. Fairly widespread are white-collar crimes, such as computer and credit card fraud, and false insurance claims. Drug abuse is a universal problem, especially in cities and among juveniles, and takes a heavy toll on law-enforcement resources. Juvenile crime accounts for 39% of all crimes, and its ominous manifestations are not much different from those in the West—motorcycle gangs, runaways, shoplifting and drugs.

Another criminal problem is a mixture of traditional Japanese and modern American activities: organized crime. Underworld groups are estimated to number over 2,500. Although concentrated in big prefectures, they operate in 70% of the cities. Seven large syndicates dominate underworld crime and control approximately one-third of all gangs and gangsters. The largest gang, Yamaguchigumi, is found in 34 prefectures and is affiliated with 463 other gangs.

Known generally as *yakuza* gangs, these groups are survivors of the samurai ethic, pose as defenders of traditional Japanese virtues and form the core of right-wing political parties. Underworld figures account for 10% of all arrests and approximately 50% of those arrested for drug smuggling, intimidation, extortion and gambling. They are also known to be increasingly involved in white-collar crime. They account for one-fifth of all *sokaiya* activity—a crime peculiar to Japan in which extortionists buy small shares of company stocks, then are paid by companies either to manipulate stockholder meetings or to refrain from exposing company secrets or transgressions.

Two minority groups account for a disproportionately large portion of crime: the Koreans and the *burakumin*. The latter are descendants of outcast communities of feudal Japan and, although ethnically Japanese, the objects of extreme prejudice. Because of their alienation from mainstream society, they suffer from a high degree of juvenile delinquency and are also generally uncooperative with the police.

CRIME STATISTICS (1984)

		Number Reported	Attempts %	Cases Solved %	Crime per 100,000	Offenders	Females %	Juveniles %	Strangers %
1.	Murder	1,762	46.9	97.2	1.47	1,788	18.5	4.1	2.6
2.	Sex offenses, including rape	4,295	20.1	83.9	3.57	3,083	1.3	37.1	2.1
3.	Rape	1,926	33.4	89.6	1.60	1,907	0.9	37.9	2.6
4.	Serious assault	23,540		94.5	19.58	32,358	6.8	33.6	3.8
5.	All theft	1,367,893	4.5	58.7	1,137.68	294,866	23.3	49.0	1.6
6.	Aggravated theft	304,209	14.9	69.9	253.01	30,902	7.8	46.1	1.9
7.	Robbery and violent theft	2,188	13.8	78.8	1.82	2,031	5.7	32.9	3.6
8.	Breaking and entering	302,021	14.9	69.8	251.19	28,871	7.9	47.0	1.7
9.	Auto theft	35,319		50.7	29.37	8,312		62.2	
10.	Other thefts	1,028,365		55.7	855.30	255,652		48.9	
11.	Fraud	109,070	2.1	97.7	90.71	51,698	9.8	34.2	2.0
12.	Counterfeiting	110		25.5	6.09	12	33.3	8.3	33.3
13.	Drug offenses	1,929		100.0	1.60	1,519	23.6	7.2	13.4
14.	Total offenses	1,747,410		66.5	1,453.33	591,375	18.0	38.9	2.9

Note: Information for some categories is not available.
Criteria of juveniles: aged from 14 to 19 years.

JORDAN

BASIC FACT SHEET

Official Name: Hashemite Kingdom of Jordan
Area: 90,650 sq km
Population: 2,761,695 (1987)
Capital: Amman
Nature of Government: Absolute monarchy
Language: Arabic
Currency: Dinar
GNP: $4.01 billion (1985)
Territorial Divisions: 8 governorates
Population per Police Officer: 630
Police Expenditures per 1,000: $27,536

History & Background

An outgrowth of the legendary Arab Legion, founded by Glubb Pasha, the Public Security Force (PSF) was formed by law in July 1956 when the legion was bifurcated into the police and the Army. From April 1957 to November 1958 the police were again placed under Army control, during 20 months of martial law, but the force has been an autonomous one ever since. During the 1960s the force grew from 7,000 officers and men to roughly 9,000. The relatively modest size of the force reflects the primary role the Army still plays in internal security maintenance.

Structure & Organization

The official designation of Jordan's national police establishment is the Public Security Force. Centralized in times of peace under the direction and control of the Ministry of the Interior, it becomes subject to the military governor general during periods of martial law and is subordinate to the Ministry of Defense and the army commander in the event of war.

Geographically, the police force is divided into metropolitan (Amman), rural (small towns and villages) and desert contingents. Headquarters of the force in the capital provides an array of centralized technical functions. Organizationally, the police are organized on the basis of districts that correspond to the five governorates, the capital city and its suburbs, and the desert region. Each district is organized into subdistricts and precincts. With the exception of the Amman metropolitan area, all district organizations are under the operational supervision of a director.

The Public Security Force performs routine police functions as well as special tasks, such as locating missing persons, guarding shrines, assisting customs and immigration officials, traffic control, and operating the country's penal institutions. The force is commanded by an officer with the title of director general of public security, usually an Army general, who is personally picked by King Hussein on the basis of ability as well as demonstrated loyalty to the crown. The headquarters functions are divided into four commands: Administrative Police, Provincial Police, Judicial Police and Support Police. The Administrative Police are charged with the routine maintenance of security and the prevention of crime. When criminal offenses are reported or detected, the follow-up action is under the purview of the Judicial Police, who conduct criminal investigations, apprehend suspects and prosecute offenders.

The police are armed with revolvers, nightsticks, rifles and light automatic weapons. In Amman and the large towns, crowd and riot control equipment are available to the force. In Amman the police are fully motorized, while in the desert areas the traditional camel-mounted desert patrol survives, supplemented by four-wheel-drive vehicles.

The role of women in the Public Security Force is notable, as Jordan was the first Arab country to induct women into its police force, in 1970. At first there was considerable adverse reaction from conservative elements, but through effective public relations this opposition has softened over the years. Most women are in the fingerprinting and other technical areas in the police laboratory as well as in budget and accounting, public relations, licensing, prison operations and the security of foreign visitors. Some have been as-

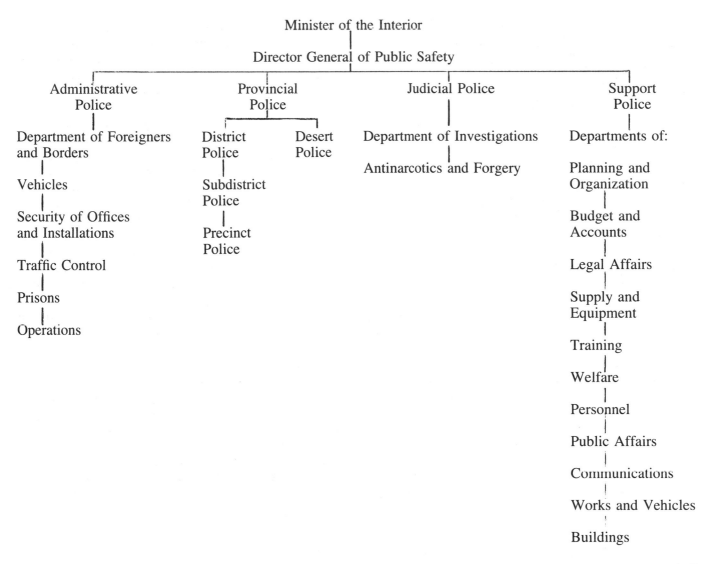

Minister of the Interior

Director General of Public Safety

Administrative Police

Department of Foreigners and Borders

Vehicles

Security of Offices and Installations

Traffic Control

Prisons

Operations

Provincial Police

District Police

Desert Police

Subdistrict Police

Precinct Police

Judicial Police

Department of Investigations

Antinarcotics and Forgery

Support Police

Departments of:

Planning and Organization

Budget and Accounts

Legal Affairs

Supply and Equipment

Training

Welfare

Personnel

Public Affairs

Communications

Works and Vehicles

Buildings

signed to street patrols in Amman and to border patrol. In 1978 women were brought into the traffic police in the capital.

Ranks and insignia are identical with those of the Army, although titles are different. Police uniforms in the Amman metropolitan area are dark blue in winter and light tan in summer. Rural police wear an olive drab uniform lighter in shade than that of the Army. The desert police retain their traditional Arab garb. Police pay scales are about the same as those of the Army but differ somewhat in special allowances. All uniformed personnel carry pistols and rifles. As a result of a public-relations campaign launched in the 1970s, the Public Security Force enjoys the respect and favorable regard of the public.

In the aftermath of the 1970–71 civil war, the influx of Palestinian activists and heavy internal security demands on the police, a new paramilitary organization, the Civil Defense Force, was established to supplement the national police in situations that exceeded police capabilities. It incorporated some of the functions and personnel of the former popular militia. Despite its outward appearance as a civil agency, its top leaders are carefully selected from high-ranking Army personnel. The unit's strength is estimated at about 10,000.

The intelligence service was established in 1973 as the Directorate of General Intelligence (DGI). It is separate from the military intelligence section of the Armed Forces General Staff. Although formally subordinate to the prime minister, the directors of this organization, all of whom have been high-ranking Army officers, have close personal access to the king. DGI is reputed to have close contacts with the U.S. CIA and is reported to have received large sums of money from that organization, some of it paid directly to the king. Not much other information is available on the structure and operations of this covert agency.

Recruitment, Education & Training

Police personnel are drawn through voluntary enlistments. Most recruits have had some military training before they enter the force. The government has encouraged the police to accept a larger number of Palestinians than is the case with the Army. Training is provided by the Royal Police Academy in Amman and the Police Training School at Az Zarqa. Both institutions have substantial enrollments from neighboring Arab countries. The Academy also conducts special refresher courses.

The Penal System

The Criminal Code, adopted in 1959, is based on the Syrian and Lebanese codes, which in turn are modeled on that of France. The code divides criminal offenses after the French fashion into felonies, délits (misdemeanors) and contraventions and specifies punishments for each. Punishments for felonies range from death by hanging to imprisonment with or without hard labor for periods ranging from life to three years. Sentences for death must be approved by the Council of Ministers. Death penalties for crimes tried before special military courts are carried out by military firing squads. A significant innovation is the provision of minimum penalties for all major infractions, leaving little room for the discretion of the courts.

When the police believe that a person has committed a crime or when someone is caught in the commission of a criminal act, the suspect is taken to the nearest police station for registration and interrogation. Usually a warrant is required for an arrest; however, in cases where delay would be harmful to justice, or when a person is apprehended in a criminal offense, the accused may be detained without a warrant of arrest for as long as 48 hours. After than time, a court order is required to cover further detention of the suspect. Arrest charges must indicate the specific charges in every case. The police magistrate first informs the accused of the charges and questions him or her and any available witnesses to determine if there is a *prima facie* case against the suspect, who has the right to counsel at this stage. If the magistrate finds evidence of guilt, the case is transmitted for further investigation to the local public prosecutor. The code grants provisional release on bail as a matter of right when the maximum penalty prescribed for the charged offense is imprisonment not exceeding one year and when the person has not been previously convicted of a felony or sentenced to more than three months in prison.

The right of habeas corpus is provided for in the Constitution, but in practice does not provide the same protection as in English common law. In most cases the police manage to establish some need to detain suspects. Law-enforcement personnel are exempt from liability for depriving a person of liberty when the arrest is made in good faith or in the interest of public order. The public prosecutor may extend the period of detention by 10-day increments up to 30 days, pending investigation. Thus a suspect may be jailed for one month before formal charges are brought.

The penal system is administered by the Prisons

CRIME STATISTICS (1984)

		Number Reported	Attempts %	Cases Solved %	Crime per 100,000	Offenders	Females %	Juveniles %	Strangers %
1.	Murder	70	0.26	90.0	2.72	64	6.25	12.5	3.12
2.	Sex offenses, including rape	497		97.5	19.31	598		20.7	12.9
3.	Rape	24		24.0	0.93	24		4.2	12.5
4.	Serious assault	437	0.46	98.2	16.98	522	13.4	39.9	4.9
5.	All theft	3,859	0.43	63.7	149.91	3,439	3.0	36.7	18.9
6.	Aggravated theft	1,208	0.24	68.2	46.93	956	1.0	15.3	2.6
7.	Robbery and violent theft	44		52.3	1.71	30		2.1	
8.	Breaking and entering	1,164	0.24	66.4	45.22	926		13.2	2.6
9.	Auto theft	178		67.9	6.91	253		6.3	
10.	Other thefts	2,473	0.19	64.3	96.07	2,230	2.0	15.1	16.3
11.	Fraud	276		77.9	10.72	226	5.3	0.9	18.6
12.	Counterfeiting	31		100.0	1.20	35			
13.	Drug offenses	65		100.0	2.53	151			36.4
14.	Total offenses	16,215	1.15	68.6	629.92	16,455	3.2	38.6	16.3

Note: Information for some categories is not available.
Criteria of juveniles: aged from 7 to 17 years.

Department of the Directorate of Public Security under the Ministry of the Interior. The penal system is composed of roughly 25 prisons and jails. All except Amman Central Prison are under the management of the district police chiefs and sometimes are referred to as police jails. In addition, area prisons are located at Irbid in the extreme northwestern section and at Al Jafr, east of Ma'an in the south-central desert region. The smaller district jails are in or near the district or subdistrict police headquarters. Generally, convicted offenders sentenced to more than one year are sent to area prisons and those sentenced to three months or less are kept in district jails. The most hardened criminals are sent to Al Jafr.

All penal institutions are used for the detention of persons awaiting trial as well as those serving sentences. Convicted offenders are, however, housed separately from those yet to be tried. The major prisons have separate sections for women prisoners, as do a few of the police jails in the larger urban centers. A juvenile detention center for minors under 19 years is in Amman. All facilities are operated in accordance with the provisions of the Prison Law of 1953, which details regulations relating to the treatment of prisoners.

Jordan was one of the first Arab countries to recognize the theory of rehabilitation as a basis for incarceration. This concept is alien to Muslim law and custom, which emphasize retribution and maximum punishment. However, rehabilitative programs are hampered by the lack of facilities and a professionally trained staff. Some effort is made to provide literacy and limited industrial training classes in Amman Central Prison, the country's largest, but in few others. Even work is not compulsory except for prisoners sentenced to hard labor.

Prison conditions are described as Spartan but not inhuman or degrading. The prisons are periodically inspected by the International Committee of the Red Cross. Crowded conditions in some prisons were relieved by a June 1985 royal amnesty releasing over 1,000 inmates. There is no evidence of torture, and there is a special office to handle public complaints of abuse by security officers.

KAMPUCHEA

History & Background

Until the Communist (and later Vietnamese) takeover of the country, law enforcement was the responsibility of the Royal Khmer Police under the direction of a secretary of state who was subordinate to the minister of the interior. It was a loosely centralized force that included the National Police, patterned after the French Sûreté; the Municipal Police in Phnom Penh; rural town police; and the paramilitary Surface Defense Force—a constabulary composed of the Provincial Guard and the Chivapul, a local volunteer militia. The police were reorganized in May 1970, when most of the component forces were transferred to the Army. After the institution of martial law in 1970, the provost marshal and the military police handled the general maintenance of law and order, including traffic control. The National Police continued to act as a bureau of investigation and surveillance under a central commissariat. Under Pol Pot the police name was changed to People's Militia.

Structure & Organization

The situation in Cambodia after the Vietnamese invasion is unclear.

Recruitment, Education & Training

No current information is available

The Penal System

Prisons are located in Phnom Penh and the provincial capitals. In addition, a prison camp is maintained on an island in the Gulf of Thailand offshore from the town of Keb in Kampot Province. The prison system is administered by a director in the Ministry of the Interior.

Physical torture is reported in Phnom Penh prisons by the Lawyers' Committee for Human Rights. The Ministry of the Interior maintains at least three prisons in which suspected supporters of the resistance have been held without charges, often for years. The provincial police maintain additional detention and interrogation centers.

The Lawyers' Committee estimates political prisoners in the thousands. T-3, the main prison in Phnom Penh, and the Prey Sar Prison together hold over 2,000 prisoners, including many political prisoners.

KENYA

History & Background

The Kenya Police is descended directly from the security guards first formed by the British in East Africa and evolved during the colonial era. The first organized security force was composed of armed guards called askaris, who were hired locally by the Imperial British East Africa Company beginning in 1887 to protect the stations along the caravan route from Mombasa to Uganda. In 1886, after the takeover of the administration in British East Africa by the British Foreign Office, the beginning of a genuine police unit under a professional police superintendent took place in Mombasa, the coastal terminus of the trade route. Another independent force, the Uganda Railway Police, was organized the following year to safeguard the construction of the railroad.

The Mombasa police formed the nucleus of what became after 1902 a reorganized and consolidated British East Africa Police, whose headquarters was moved in 1905 to the rapidly growing city of Nairobi. The Kenya element of this force was renamed the Kenya Police upon the formation of the Kenya Colony in 1920. Expanded during World Wars I and II by sizable levies of Indian and African recruits, the force took on border patrol duties and protection of installations. By the end of the 1940s, the Kenya Police possessed a good communications system, a police training school, a crime laboratory, a police kennel and an air arm.

Under the impact of the Mau Mau emergency from 1952 to 1960, in which the police bore the brunt of operational responsibility, the Kenya Police underwent unprecedented expansion and consolidation. The regular police more than doubled in size, to over 13,000 in addition to 8,000 men in the Kenya Police Reserve. The quality and capability of the force also was enhanced by the institution of a paramilitary strike force, known as GSU; a police intelligence apparatus; and a police communications system. Upon independence in 1963 the Kenya Police was transferred intact to the Kenya government, although a large contingent of British and Asian officers remained on the official payroll for a few more years.

Structure & Organization

Headquarters under the commissioner of police is in Nairobi. The organizational structure consists of centralized administrative and communications services; specialized functional branches, also centralized at the headquarters; and territorial organization.

Under the Police Act, Chapter 84 of the Laws of Kenya, revised in 1970, the Police Service Commission and the police commissioner both determine policy and supervise operations. Below the national headquarters in the chain of command are the eight provincial commands, whose jurisdictions are coterminous with the territory of each province and the capital district. Under each provincial command are a number of divisions with headquarters usually in the capital city of the corresponding civil district. Under division headquarters are the police stations and posts in cities, towns, and other localities. In practice the outlying and provincial units enjoy a good deal of operational autonomy under the general control of the provincial and district commissioners. Mobile units may be dispatched from the headquarters to the subordinate units as needed.

Major arms of the police are the general duty police, the paramilitary General Services Unit (GSU) and the Railways and Harbors Police. Specialized functional units include the Criminal Investigation Directorate (CID); the Intelligence Directorate; a stock theft unit; the Police Air Wing; and a highly rated dog unit, used mainly in urban work.

The GSU is a mobile combat force whose arms include rifles, Bren guns and light mortars. Formed in 1953 to deal with the Mau Mau uprising, the GSU has retained its role as a specially trained crack internal security force. Operating in conjunction with the Police Air Wing, GSU units are dispatched from strategically located base camps to any point in the country to deal with civil disturbances or other threats to civil order. GSU forces consist of some 3,000 men organized into constabularylike companies stationed in barracks under their own company commanders. They have their own transportation, communications and equipment and they operate in the field as self-contained units. Several units are based in the capital; and others are in Nakuru and Kisumu.

The special Railways and Harbors Police, commonly known as the "formation," is charged with all police functions relating to the prevention and detention of crimes committed on or against land or water transportation lines or installations. A waterborne marine section has units at Mombasa, Kisumu and Lake Victoria. Commanded by an assistant commissioner of police with the title of commandant, the force has about 1,000 constables and 300 officers and noncommissioned officers divided into three divisions. Its independent criminal investigation division is popularly known as the "formation crime branch."

The CID is responsible for all matters relating to criminal investigation, and it maintains all criminal files. It is a plainclothes detective force with distinct branches in the various headquarters and a functional chain of command to the national headquarters. The Intelligence Directorate is concerned with domestic intelligence-gathering and subversive criminal activity.

The Police Air Wing, organized in 1959, got its first operational experience during the *shifta* insurgency in the mid-1960s. With about 15 aircraft capable of operating from crude airstrips, it performs reconnaissance, communications, supply and evacuation services for the police.

An adjunct to the regular Kenya Police is the Administrative Police, earlier known as the Tribal Police, which serves as the agent of law and order in rural areas where there are no stations or posts manned by the regular police. Members of the Administrative Police are customarily recruited in the ethnic community where they serve. Although under the administrative control of the district commissioner, and subject to the general direction of the provincial commissioner, members of the Administrative Police are under the day-to-day operational control of the local chief or subchief. The chiefs and subchiefs play a key

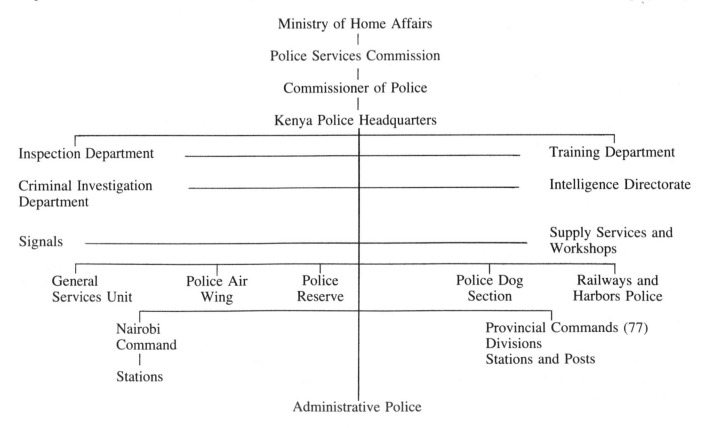

role in protecting public order and arresting suspected wrongdoers. Regular police usually are called in to handle serious crimes such as murder or other matters beyond the capability or authority of the Administrative Police.

Another auxiliary force, the Police Reserve, was formed in 1948 as a volunteer force to bolster the regular police in emergencies. Unlike the Administrative Police, which is a standing police force, police reservists serve only when called upon. The strength of this force, which peaked during the Mau Mau emergency at 9,000, has been declining over the years and now is believed to be less than half that number. Volunteers must be at least 18 years old and enlist for at least two years.

The Nairobi headquarters is the hub of a nationwide police communications system considered to be among the most advanced in Africa. It includes both radio and radiotelephone links. A self-contained bunker installation capable of withstanding armed onslaught serves as an emergency national communications and operations center. In 1975 a very high frequency (VHF) communications network was established linking patrol cars on major roads throughout the country and the Nairobi metropolitan system with a central control in police headquarters. Most of the over 2,000 police vehicles, from trucks to motorcycles, are radio-equipped. Nairobi also is the site of a regional Interpol police communications station, opened in 1973.

In the mid-1980s there were 19,000 men and women in the police force, not including administrative and reserve police personnel. Senior ranks and inspectors constitute about 8% of the force, noncommissioned officers 16%, and lower ranks 76%, a distribution that has remained basically unchanged since independence. An estimated one-third of the total police manpower is assigned to technical and support activities, a relatively high proportion compared to other developing countries.

Police grade structures have not departed from the preindependence British patterns. Appointed officers range from commissioner to cadet assistant superintendent; inspectorate officers from chief to cadet assistant inspector; and subordinate officers from sergeant to constable. The Administrative Police has a separate rank and pay scale below that of the Kenya Police and includes only noncommissioned and constable ranks. The police personnel system is part of the civil service system. Like other civil servants, police are prohibited from membership in a trade union or moonlighting. Generally, police compensation is fair by local standards.

The tropical military-style uniform consists of a short-sleeved shirt worn with long or short trousers and garrison hat, or, for lower ranks, a plastic helmet. The characteristic color is blue-gray. GSU personnel wear a green, camouflage-cloth bush jacket and deep red beret. Uniformed urban police carry only a baton in the British manner but are issued weapons during emergencies. Plainclothes police are armed with a pistol, and police in outlying posts have a rifle.

Recruitment, Education & Training

Police recruits are enlisted voluntarily on a nationwide basis by recruiting teams. National policy calls for achieving, as far as possible, an ethnically balanced force, but it is believed that the Kikuyu dominate the force, as they do the other public services. Over the years, the educational level of the recruits has improved, and more applicants possess secondary and even higher education qualifications. Policemen enjoy a reasonable degree of social status, although some of their functions, as enforcing tax collection, make them unpopular.

Police recruit and officer training and courses for reservists are conducted at the Kenya Police College, established at Kiganjo, near Nyeri, in 1948. Specialized training is provided at a number of other institutions both inside and outside the police establishment. The Criminal Investigation Directorate Training School at Nairobi conducts courses for the CID; the Kenya Polytechnic Institute, for communications personnel; refresher and other kinds of training, including part-time literacy and continuing education courses for field personnel, are offered at provincial training centers. Six-week courses in weapons familiarization and basic refresher training are provided for the Administrative Police at the Armed Forces Training College at Lanet, near Nakuru, in the Rift Valley. Personnel of the Railways and Harbors Police attend refresher and technical courses at their own training center, but some are sent for more specialized training to the Railways Training College. Supervisory and management training for senior police personnel is provided at the Kenya Institute of Administration.

The Penal System

Kenya's penal code is incorporated in Chapter 63 of the Laws of Kenya, 1962, as amended by supplementary legislation since 1962. Although considerably changed in detail, the code is substantially the colonial penal code promulgated in 1930. Enforcement of unwritten or customary law in criminal matters was abolished in 1966.

Criminal offenses fall into two categories: felonies and misdemeanors. Offenses of both kinds are listed in the code under the major categories of crime against the state, crime against public order, crime against persons or property and crime against religion or morality. Criminal responsibility takes into account extenuating and mitigating factors, such as self-defense and impairment of mental faculties. Children under seven years are not held criminally responsible, and penalties for minors between seven and 12 years are considerably less severe than for older persons. The maximum punishment for felonies is death; the minimum, three years' imprisonment. The death sentence, for which hanging is prescribed, may not be imposed on a person under 18 years or on a pregnant woman. Whipping with a rod or cane may be inflicted on males, with a maximum of 24 strokes for adults and 12 for minors.

Since independence there has been a trend toward increasing the severity of the punishments for certain offenses, such as theft and robbery with violence. The death penalty was imposed in 1973 for violent armed robbery.

Except in flagrant cases, the police may arrest a suspect only upon issuance of a warrant. The arrested person must be taken before a magistrate for charging within 24 hours. Minor offenses are prosecuted by complaint; major crimes, by indictment. Minor offenders are brought directly before a lower court magistrate, while major ones are referred to the office of the attorney general, who remands the case to the appropriate court. The magistrate decides on the basis of a hearing whether to dismiss the complaint or to draw up charges or, when a major crime in involved, a bill of indictment. The accused is entitled to counsel at the hearing. If the accused is charged, he or she may be granted bail at the discretion of the court, except when charged with a capital offense. The High Court is the only court that may issue a writ of habeas corpus.

The corrections system is administered by the Kenya Prisons Service, the Children's Department, and the Probation Department of the Ministry of Home Affairs. Corrections personnel are under the civil service system and have a grade and pay structure parallel to that of the Kenya Police. The central training institution for prison personnel, including recruits and cadet officers, is the Prisons Training School in Nairobi.

Prison institutions include regular prisons of general or special purpose, with varying degrees of security; approved schools and remand homes for juvenile offenders; and detention camps. The latter includes temporary barracks or tent compounds, work camps and prison farms. Overcrowding in all correction facilities has long been a serious problem, brought about by both a steady rise in the number of persons committed and a trend toward increased legal penalties and longer sentences imposed by the courts. More than half the number committed are classified as persons held ''for safe custody'' and includes those held in pretrial or preventive detention, vagrants, debtors and other nonconvicts.

In comparison with other developing countries, Kenya's treatment of prisoners is enlightened and modern. The emphasis in penal policy is on rehabilitation. Training programs to teach new skills to enable prisoners to make a living after release is the primary goal of the system. Prison trades include carpentry, tailoring, metalwork, shoemaking and matmaking. Official policy also calls for each prison to maintain a vegetable farm. Literacy and education courses also are available. Those who have some schooling may take correspondence courses for higher education. In a typical prison, the living quarters are austere but comfortable and clean. Inmates are permitted to watch television in the evening. Food is well prepared, allowing for four different diets, taking into account customs and religion. The prison medical officer plays an active role in prisoner management and sees prisoners regularly. Inmates have name tags with personal names rather than numbers. Incentives are given for good conduct, including permission to have books and to attend cultural events and authorization to have more frequent visits and correspondence. Special, or highest-stage, prisoners are permitted dormitory quarters and special furniture and extra bedding in their cells.

Prisoners other than those under preventive detention or life sentence may have up to one-third of their sentence remitted for good behavior. The records of inmates serving sentences of seven years or more are periodically reviewed by a board of review, which may recommend to the president that the prisoner be considered for reduction of sentence. In addition to remission of part of the sentence, the longer-term prisoner with a good record may be released three months early on parole to aid his or her adjustment to civilian life.

A probation service program provides help to released convicts during the difficult transitional period to civil life. Halfway houses, accommodating 15 probationers each, have been established at Nairobi and Mombasa. Cooperating with the probation and parole authorities in aiding discharged prisoners is the Prisoners' Aid Society, founded in the 1950s. It helps prisoners with small loans, the purchase of working implements and the temporary maintenance of their families until they are able to resume their role as breadwinners.

As in other developing societies, the rapidly escalating crime rate, especially in urban areas, is a major national concern. The upsurge in crime is, in large part, linked to the pressures of urban life on a traditional society, the loosening of the customary norms and values, the weakening of social sanctions against deviant behavior, the craving for material goods, and chronic unemployment. Nairobi's crime and delinquency rates are by far the highest in the country.

Juvenile delinquency is a distinctly urban phenomenon. Prostitution involving teen-age girls, rape and drug traffic (mostly in *bhang,* a form of cannabis) are other kinds of sharply rising crime. Many of the criminals are unemployed youth for whom crime is a means of social protest.

Urban crime is becoming increasingly sophisticated, with highly organized gang operations; daylight bank robberies; and use of guns instead of the traditional *panga,* or long-bladed bush knife. Even the theft of cattle, the most prevalent rural crime, is becoming more sophisticated. *Kondoism,* armed robbery by gangs accompanied by murder or mayhem, is becoming commonplace.

Of the crimes reported to the police, offenses against public and private property account for more than three-quarters. Much crime obviously goes unreported because of traditional taboos or attitudes. Formal legal sanctions and procedures seem irrelevant in a society imbued with the ideas of revenge and payment of blood money.

CRIME STATISTICS (1984)

		Number Reported	Attempts %	Cases Solved %	Crime per 100,000	Offenders	Females %	Juveniles %	Strangers %
1.	Murder	883	4.9	4.53		613	12.1	5.2	
2.	Sex offenses, including rape	1,513	21.1	7.77		1,386	4.6	9.8	
3.	Rape	376	28.5	1.93					
4.	Serious assault	13,435	30.9	68.96					
5.	All theft	16,679	25.9	85.61					
6.	Aggravated theft	25,005	11.5	128.35					
7.	Robbery and violent theft	7,065	14.5	36.26					
8.	Breaking and entering	17,940	10.3	92.08					
9.	Auto theft	970	4.5	4.98					
10.	Other thefts	13,414	17.7	68.85					
11.	Fraud	1,828	13.5	9.38		60	16.7		
12.	Counterfeiting	62	27.4	0.32		1,526	6.8	2.0	
13.	Drug offenses	8,749	93.9	44.91		8,749	10.6	0.9	
14.	Total offenses	93,469	28.9	479.77		72,282			

Note: Information for some categories is not available.
Criteria of juveniles: aged from 1 to 17 years.

KOREA (NORTH)

BASIC FACT SHEET

Official Name: Democratic People's Republic of Korea
Area: 121,129 sq km
Population: 21,447,977 (1987)
Capital: Pyongyang
Nature of Government: Communist dictatorship
Language: Korean
Currency: Won
GNP: $23 billion (1985)
Territorial Divisions: 9 provinces
Population per Police Officer: 460
Police Expenditures per 1,000: N.A.

Structure & Organization

The Ministry of Public Security (called the Ministry of the Interior until 1962) is a powerful ministry that oversees a constellation of functions relating to law enforcement, civil order and national security. Both conventional and secret police are subordinate to this ministry, as are traffic control, fire prevention and the penal system.

Under the minister of public security are four vice ministers, each in charge of several bureaus. Party control over the ministry is extremely close. The determination of overall policy and the coordination of party and government functions relating to security are vested in the Justice and Security Commission. Party control also is exercised directly through party cells within the various organs of the ministry itself.

Below the ministry there are public security bureaus in each province, public security sections in each city or county, and a number of substations in cities and regions bordering the DMZ. A resident policeman or constable is assigned to each village. The public security agencies at the county level are headed by a lieutenant colonel of police, and at the city and province level by a senior colonel roughly comparable to a chief of police. The usual complement of a county public security section is about 100 men.

One group of bureaus in the Ministry of Public Security includes most of the conventional functions relating to law enforcement. One of these, the Protection and Security Bureau, is the approximate equivalent of a national police force. It operates through its subunits in the county and urban public security sections and perhaps to a lesser extent through rural constables. Its agents investigate crimes; control traffic; register births, deaths and marriages; authorize passports; and check entry of foreign vessels into North Korean ports. Fire prevention also is a responsibility of this bureau.

All personnel of the Ministry of Public Security are ranked in military fashion. No firm data are available on the strength of the ministry personnel, although estimates of 50,000 seem likely. It is not clear whether this total includes the People's Guards, also under the ministry. All senior officers above the colonel rank are trained at the Central Party School.

A prominent feature of the state public security apparatus is total control over the movement and activities of all citizens. Students and all persons above 18 years carry an identification card. Changes in place of residence and employment require official permission. Travel within the country is restricted both by positive controls and practical difficulties. An employee has to secure a travel permit from his boss for a trip outside his or her regular place of work. Eating away from home entails further difficulties in the form of ration coupons. At each place of sojourn, a traveler has to deposit his or her documentation with the hotel or other accommodation for examination by the local public security authority. All these regulations have added to the operational burdens of the police force.

The Central Domestic Intelligence Agency is the equivalent of a secret service. It is a bureau in the Ministry of Public Safety under a vice minister. It is believed to control a pervasive network of spies, but no other information is available on its operations.

Recruitment, Education & Training

No current information is available.

The Penal System

The Criminal Code of March 3, 1950, along with the Code of Criminal Procedure of the same date, are the basic statutes that define the system of criminal justice. All are closely patterned after the Soviet model of the Stalin era.

The country's prisons are under the jurisdiction of the Reform Bureau of the Ministry of Public Security. The procurator general is authorized to see "that the execution of judgments and the activities of corrective institutions conform to the law."

There are no data on the prison population or the conditions of the prisons. Two prison camps are known to exist: Camp 8, which houses serious offenders, and Camp 149, where prisoners are permitted to have families with them and to grow food for their own consumption. Banishment to remote areas also is used as a form of penal servitude.

KOREA (SOUTH)

<table>
<tr><td colspan="2" align="center">BASIC FACT SHEET</td></tr>
</table>

Official Name: Republic of Korea
Area: 98,500 sq km
Population 41,986,669 (1987)
Capital: Seoul
Nature of Government: Modified democracy
Language: Korean
Currency: Won
GNP: $88.44 billion (1985)
Territorial Divisions: 9 provinces
Population per Police Officer: 800
Police Expenditures per 1,000: N.A.

History & Background

After an abortive attempt to employ the existing Japanese colonial police in South Korea to maintain public order after World War II, the U.S. occupation authorities established in October 1945 a new force under a Police Affairs Division within the military government. This force was placed under the Ministry of Home Affairs upon the establishment of the First Republic on August 15, 1948. This force was a paramilitary constabulary in which the police and military functions were combined. Even after the formal establishment of a discrete military service by the Armed Forces Organization Act of November 1948, the differentiation between the police and the military in the maintenance of domestic order remained unclear. During the Korean War the police forces were employed in military operations.

The new force was plagued from the beginning by a low degree of professionalism, the retention of Japanese-trained cadres in the higher ranks, endemic corruption, and flagrant use of police power for partisan political activity. Major reforms did not take place until the revolutionary military junta seized power in 1961. The new regime reorganized the structure of the force, placing it on a sound institutional basis; instituted recruitment by examination and merit promotion; and introduced modern concepts of management, administration and training.

Structure & Organization

The Office of National Police Affairs (ONPA, called the National Police Bureau until September 1974) is headed by a director general holding the rank of vice minister in the Ministry of Home Affairs. The director general also has jurisdiction over the National Police College, the Maritime Police, the National Police Hospital and the Scientific Crime Laboratory.

The police are broadly organized into three echelons of command. The ONPA, in Seoul, functions as the national headquarters. It is organized into 12 divisions, which, along with the four auxiliary organs, constitute the central organization of the national police. At the second echelon are the police bureaus in Seoul and Pusan and in each of the nine provinces. The third echelon consists of local police stations. Their jurisdictions coincide in general with the local administrative jurisdictions—cities *(si)* and counties *(kun)*. Each local police station has a varying number of branch stations throughout the jurisdiction. Over the years the command structure has become highly centralized, with ONPA overseeing even local police chiefs. The base of operations is made up of 175 first- and second-class police stations, 1,344 substations and almost 1,000 police boxes.

The three broad areas of functional responsibility of the National Police are public security, fire control and maritime policing. At the end of 1970 a special combat police, organized into 24 combat companies, was charged with operations against subversive infiltration. It guarded coastal and mountainous areas, and units are also stationed in Seoul, Pusan and other major cities.

Other specialized units include a small air police force, railways police, customs police, airport police, fire division and maritime police. The maritime police is the equivalent of a coast guard. Equipped with patrol ships, some high-speed boats and possibly some light aircraft, it patrols the major harbors and the coastal waterways. Its responsibilities include protection of the fishing fleet, aiding vessels in distress and enforcing maritime laws.

The judicial police is a separate force located within different government agencies operating under the general direction of the local prosecutors' offices. In addition to personnel directly associated with the judicial process it includes prison officials, forestry inspectors, sanitation and food inspectors, railroad police, and dangerous drugs and narcotics control officers. There is also a small police component of the Homeland Reserve Force.

Police manpower has shown a gradual increase since the mid-1960s but has not kept pace with overall population growth. The ratio of police to population has remained stable for a number of decades at one to 800. The nine police ranks—constable, sergeant, lieutenant, captain, inspector, superintendent, superintendent general, deputy director general and director general—were instituted in 1969. Until then there had been only six ranks. Women constitute only a small portion of the police force, employed mainly for traffic control, suppression of vice, care of abandoned infants and children, and investigation of female suspects.

The regular police uniform includes dark blue trousers and jacket worn with shirt and necktie, a peaked cap, and combat boots worn over the lower trouser legs. A light uniform is worn in summer. The usual weapons are revolvers and nightsticks. Carbines and some heavier arms are stored at central police stations. The bicycle is the principal transport in both city and country; motorcycles, jeeps, trucks and a small num-

ber of horses also are employed. The air police are equipped with light aircraft of the Cessna and Beechcraft variety.

Occupying a commanding position in the political and police power system is the Agency for National Security Planning (ANSP), formerly the Korean Central Intelligence Agency (KCIA). Unlike the U.S. CIA, the ANSP is a domestic secret police, although its enabling charter of June 1961 gives it a much broader mandate, directing it to "supervise and coordinate national security-related intelligence and criminal investigation matters, both domestic and foreign, and the intelligence matters of all elements of the government, including the military." Not subject to the jurisdiction of prosecutors, the ANSP exercises virtually unlimited powers of investigation, arrest, detention and interrogation. In its rooting out of suspected Communist subversion, the ANSP focuses particularly on such sources of dissidence as university students, the press, Christian churchmen and intellectuals. Dragnet arrests, secret police tactics, torture and kidnapping are some of the methods commonly employed by ANSP.

Little verifiable information is publicly available on the size, funding and inner workings of the ANSP below the top leadership level. ANSP headquarters is in a campuslike compound called Yimundong, popularly known as Namsan (South Mountain), on the northeastern outskirts of Seoul. The agency is believed to have substantial extrabudgetary income from hotels, resorts, casinos and such enterprises as the mammoth Walker Hill resort south of Seoul, but also from "contributions" from business concerns. No estimates of agency personnel strength can be re-

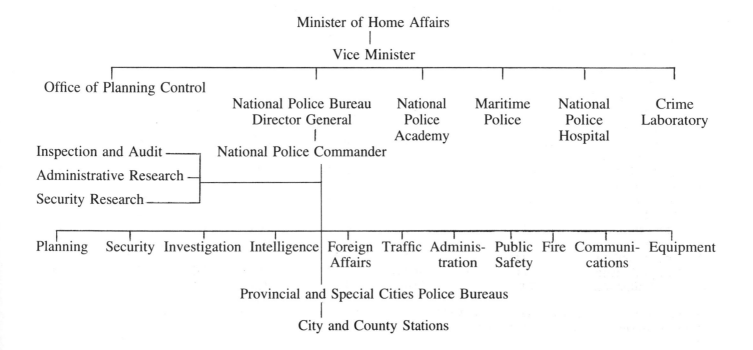

garded as accurate, but a cadre strength of 10,000, including overseas agents, is cited by knowledgeable observers.

The ANSP is believed to be divided into eight functional areas under two assistant directors, one for external affairs and one for internal affairs. The first is primarily administrative. The second, third and fifth bureaus (there is no fourth bureau because Koreans believe the number unlucky) are concerned with domestic cultural affairs, counterintelligence and internal security, respectively. The sixth is "dirty tricks" operation, the seventh is concerned with overseas intelligence-gathering and the eighth and ninth deal entirely with North Korean affairs.

Agency personnel are stationed in branch offices in each provincial capital and city. ANSP personnel are assigned to ministries, the military, banks and businesses, newspapers, labor organizations and cultural associations. Through the immigration office of the Ministry of Justice, it controls entry into the country and through the passport office of the Ministry of Foreign Affairs it controls the travel of Koreans abroad. It also keeps an eyes-and-ears watch over every element of society through a pervasive network of agents and informers.

Recruitment, Education & Training

Recruits for the entering grade of constable must have completed middle school and their military service.

They receive a 12-week basic training course at police schools in each province. Applicants for the entering officer rank of lieutenant are selected from those who hold college degrees and pass an entrance examination. The 12-month officer training course at the National Police College includes the basic recruit training course and on-the-job training in a metropolitan police department.

The National Police College, on the outskirts of Inchon, south of Seoul, is the flagship school of the force. The college provides combat police training and offers specialized courses of two to four weeks' duration in the eight fields of secret service, antiguerrilla warfare, command, intelligence, criminal investigation, traffic, public safety and fire fighting. The police schools in each of the provinces train provincial constables.

The Penal System

The Criminal Code of 1953 replaced one that had been in force under the Japanese administration for 40 years. The 1953 code combines features of Chinese, Anglo-American, Japanese and German criminal law. Confucian concepts are evident in a provision calling for more severe penalties for a high official than for an ordinary person committing the same crime and for offenses against lineal kin. German influence is evident in provisions regarding protection of the state. Anglo-American legal values are reflected in provi-

CRIME STATISTICS (1984)

		Number Reported	Attempts %	Cases Solved %	Crime per 100,000	Offenders	Females %	Juveniles %	Strangers %
1.	Murder	551	5.1	94.2	1.36	547	16.5	11.5	0.73
2.	Sex offenses, including rape	15,201		93.7	37.60	21,896	30.4	13.7	0.11
3.	Rape	4,051		99.2	10.02	5,831	0.3	47.2	0.12
4.	Serious assault	26,014		96.8	64.34	29,885	19.3	6.0	0.17
5.	All theft	111,179		55.9	274.99	66,279	9.0	49.1	0.18
6.	Aggravated theft	28,631		95.4	70.82	38,670	5.3	60.1	
7.	Robbery and violent theft	3,007		98.1	7.44	3,908	1.1	54.8	0.33
8.	Breaking and entering	25,624		95.1	63.38	34,762	5.8	60.7	
9.	Auto theft								
10.	Other thefts	82,548		42.2	204.17	27,609	14.1	33.7	0.38
11.	Fraud	83,466		89.4	206.45	84,934	19.2	1.3	0.08
12.	Counterfeiting	28		7.1	0.07	2		50.0	
13.	Drug offenses	311		100.0	0.77	486	22.2	7.6	2.88
14.	Total offenses	784,708		86.2	1,940.90	817,315	10.6	11.0	0.24

Note: Information for some categories is not available.
Criteria of juveniles: aged from 13 to 19 years.

sions concerning the protection of human rights. Native Korean values surface in concepts of evil motive as an aggravating circumstance in an offense.

There are nine degrees of punishment, led by death by hanging and penal servitude for life. Those under 14 years are not subject to the provisions of the code. Its provisions, however, apply not only to aliens within the national jurisdiction but also to offenses against the national interest committed by Korean nationals anywhere in the world. The category of crimes against the state is a distinct feature of the criminal statutes, spelled out in Chapters 1 through 8 of Part II of the Criminal Code. Also directed against acts affecting internal security are the National Security Act of 1960 and the Anticommunist Law of 1961.

The prison system is administered by the Bureau of Reformatories in the Ministry of Justice. Penal institutions include two detention facilities for those held under investigation or in pretrial detention, 21 regular prisons (officially called "reformatories"), two prisons for juveniles and one branch prison. There is also a training school for prison officials.

Some 10% of the prisoners are juveniles, and slightly over 4% are female. Separate incarceration facilities are maintained for lepers, tubercular patients, the retarded and for prisoners classified as leftists.

A program for the reconstruction and reform of the penal institutions was undertaken soon after the end of the Korean War, under the Committee for the Reconstruction of Correctional Institutions. As a result, the emphasis shifted in penal policy from punishment to rehabilitation. In the modern penal institutions an enlightened regime has been introduced, with daily activity routines, recreational facilities and frequent family visits. Physical amenities include central heating and flush toilets, which are unavailable to the poor in outside communities. Provisions for education and vocational training still are rudimentary, although a system of parole is in effect.

The greatest incidence of crime occurs in the metropolitan cities and in other cities with over 50,000 inhabitants. Crimes against property constitute the largest category of crimes. A growing incidence of crimes by women and juveniles is the most prominent problem of law enforcement. Periodically the government cracks down on "social vices" such as long hair and pornography.

KUWAIT

Structure & Organization

The Kuwait Public Security Department is the national police force and is divided into three territorial departments and 10 administrative departments. The three territorial departments correspond to the three governorates of Hawalii, Al Ahmadi and Kuwait, in each of which the police is headed by a director of security. Under him there are a number of district police commands, each headed by an area commander appointed by the governor. The director of security of the Kuwait Governorate is a full colonel, while the nine area commands under him are headed by officers having the grades of captain, major or lieutenant colonel. These officers supervise a total of 27 police stations manned in shifts by three or four officers and 10 or more policemen and police guards.

CRIME STATISTICS (1984)

		Number Reported	Attempts %	Cases Solved %	Crime per 100,000	Offenders	Females %	Juveniles %	Strangers %
1.	Murder	18			1.06	12			83.33
2.	Sex offenses, including rape	1,033			60.76	1,101	15.80	0.91	60.49
3.	Rape	9			0.53	9			44.44
4.	Serious assault	50			2.94	35	2.86	22.85	
5.	All theft	2,206			129.76				
6.	Aggravated theft								
7.	Robbery and violent theft	62			3.65	19		5.26	89.47
8.	Breaking and entering	674			39.65	658	0.91	2.13	10.18
9.	Auto theft	143			8.41	16			50.00
10.	Other thefts	159			9.35	75	1.33	9.33	73.33
11.	Fraud	132			7.76	98	2.04	1.02	64.29
12.	Counterfeiting								
13.	Drug offenses	579			34.06	789	3.42	0.38	54.12
14.	Total offenses	9,786			575.65	8,802	6.48	3.39	62.93

Note: Information for some categories is not available.
Criteria of juveniles: aged from 0 to 17 years.

The 10 administrative departments arc: Alien Registration, Communications, Crime Prevention, Criminal Investigation, Emergency, General Security, Identification, Public Relations, Prisons and Traffic. The Emergency Department includes Fire Service. The police service was opened to unmarried women in 1975.

Police officer grades are the same as in the regular armed forces, except that the highest listed police rank is that of major general. Officer base pay and social allowance scales are the same. The police do not use the rank of warrant officer, but they do have five grades of noncommissioned officers—in descending order, master sergeant, corporal, lance corporal, policeman and police guard. The pay and allowances for a master sergeant are about the same as for a chief warrant officer in the Army, and for a police guard about the same as for an Army private. The intermediate police noncommissioned grades are somewhat more highly paid than their Army counterparts.

Officers wear black uniforms in winter and khaki gabardine uniforms in summer. Other ranks wear dark blue uniforms in winter and khaki in summer, both with a high closed neck. Officers wear black caps, while other ranks wear blue caps. Patrol officers normally carry a pistol.

Recruitment, Education & Training

Training is provided at the Kuwait Police Academy and Training School.

The Penal System

Under the Law of Criminal Procedure of 1960, offenses against the law are classified as felonies or misdemeanors, with a third category of administrative violations covering minor infractions such as traffic violations. Official criminal statistics are not particularly reliable because many crimes go unreported or are dealt with in traditional tribal councils.

New prisons built in the 1950s and 1960s have an estimated capacity of 10,000 prisoners.

LAOS

BASIC FACT SHEET

Official Name: Lao People's Democratic Republic
Area: 236,804 sq km
Population (1986): 3,765,887 (1987)
Capital: Vientiane
Nature of Government: Communist dictatorship
Language: Lao
Currency: Kip
GNP: $765 million (1985)
Territorial Divisions: 16 provinces
Population per Police Officer: 280
Police Expenditures per 1,000: N.A.

History & Background

The police services of Laos were reorganized several times between initial independence in 1945 and 1975. In the process, a number of previously autonomous forces, such as the Gendarmerie and the security forces, were consolidated into a single Laotian police force. The consolidation was largely effected by 1955, when the United States began a training program for the unified service. Until 1961 the United States furnished advisers, weapons, uniforms, vehicles, and communications equipment and funds to construct precinct stations and the Laos National Police Training Center outside Vientiane. The training and assistance program was discontinued between 1961 and 1965, when the police were brought back to military control and became, in effect, a paramilitary organization known as the Directorate of National Coordination.

In 1965 the police were again reconstituted as a separate organization and were renamed the Lao National Police under civilian control in the Ministry of the Interior. After the Communist takeover, the police retained this status and continued to operate under the minister of the interior.

Structure & Organization

Headed by a director general, the directorate of the national police functions as police headquarters for the national police. Below the directorate the force is organized regionally into the metropolitan force of Vientiane and the territorial police of the provinces. The organization includes administration, logistics, communications and training services. In addition to the operating services of the regular uniformed police, three special units exist: the Special Police, the Judi-cial Police and the Immigration Police. Only officers of the judicial police have the formal power of arrest.

Although all units are under the direct authority of the directorate general in Vientiane, provincial commissioners of police report not only to their central headquarters but also to their respective provincial governors. The provincial police commissioners also participate in provincial administrative councils. At the district level, the district chief issues orders directly to the district police branch.

Grades within the police follow French nomenclature, ranging upward from probationary policemen and brigadiers in the ranks to commissioners and controller in the officer ranks. The highest rank is that of principal controller. Pay and allowances follow the military scales, making possible the transfer of personnel between the two services. The police force is considered to be quite effective and professional in the discharge of its duties and enjoys a favorable social standing.

Recruitment, Education & Training

The Lao National Police Training Center is the main police training facility. Courses are given in four categories: recruit training, cadet officer training, advanced course for senior staff and noncommissioned officers, and specialist training in such areas as fingerprints and communications.

The Penal System

The Penal Code was promulgated by the French colonial government in 1932 and has not been materially altered since then.

The prison system operates under the Ministry of Justice, but very little other information is available.

LEBANON

```
┌─────────────────────────────────────────────────────────────────────┐
│                        BASIC FACT SHEET                               │
│                                                                       │
│  Official Name: Republic of Lebanon                                   │
│  Area: 10,360 sq km                                                   │
│  Population: 3,320,522 (1987)                                         │
│  Capital: Beirut                                                      │
│  Nature of Government: Limited democracy                              │
│  Languages: Arabic and French                                        │
│  Currency: Lebanese pound                                            │
│  GNP: $5.3 billion (1985)                                            │
│  Territorial Divisions: 4 provinces                                  │
│  Population per Police Officer: 530                                  │
│  Police Expenditures per 1,000: N.A.                                │
└─────────────────────────────────────────────────────────────────────┘
```

History & Background

It is doubtful if an effective police force still exists in Lebanon, a country where near-anarchy has prevailed since 1976. The police were one of the first casualties of this civil war, although some remnants of it may still survive, at least on paper.

Before 1975 the national police were the Internal Security Forces under the command of a director general, who was responsible for its various divisions, such as the Gendarmerie, the Beirut Police, the Judiciary Police and the Joint Training Institute. The Gendarmerie was a paramilitary force, with units in all the rural areas as well as a mobile reserve. It had a strength of nearly 3,000 officers and men. The Beirut Police, with over 1,000 men of all ranks,

CRIME STATISTICS (1984)

		Number Reported	Attempts %	Cases Solved %	Crime per 100,000	Offenders	Females %	Juveniles %	Strangers %
1.	Murder	576		35.59	19.20	659	1.36	3.64	5.15
2.	Sex offenses, including rape	95		88.42	3.17	118	9.32	6.77	28.81
3.	Rape	34		73.52	1.13	41	4.87	9.75	34.14
4.	Serious assault	388		75.77	12.93	546	1.64	2.38	4.94
5.	All theft	5,185		15.93	172.83	5,308	2.09	1.92	2.84
6.	Aggravated theft	2,088		9.33	69.60	2,127	0.47	1.55	2.16
7.	Robbery and violent theft	736		6.92	24.53	745	0.13	0.26	1.34
8.	Breaking and entering	1,352		10.65	45.07	1,382	0.65	2.24	2.60
9.	Auto theft	1,627		5.22	54.23	1,645	0.18	0.54	0.60
10.	Other thefts	1,470		37.14	49.00	1,536	6.38	3.90	6.18
11.	Fraud	1,440		93.33	48.00	1,486	13.86	1.07	15.94
12.	Counterfeiting	15		86.66	0.50	18	0.00	0.00	11.11
13.	Drug offenses	184		98.91	6.13	271	4.79	1.84	21.40
14.	Total offenses	14,677		43.26	489.23	15,594	4.93	1.98	6.13

Note: Information for some categories is not available.
Criteria of juveniles: aged from 7 to 18 years.

functioned as the premier urban police. The Judicial Police handled criminal investigations.

Structure & Organization

Some police functions are being discharged, albeit unofficially, by the politico-religious militias.

Recruitment, Education & Training

No information is available since the civil war.

The Penal System

No information is available since the civil war.

LESOTHO

Itumeleng Kimane

BASIC FACT SHEET

Official Name: Kingdom of Lesotho
Area: 30,460 sq km
Population: 1,621,932 (1987)
Capital: Maseru
Nature of Government: Absolute monarchy under military auspices
Language: Sesotho
Currency: Maloti
GNP: $730 million (1985)
Territorial Divisions: 10 districts
Population per Police Officer: 1,130
Police Expenditures per 1,000: N.A.

History & Background

The Lesotho (then Basutoland) Mounted Police came into existence in 1872. Colonel Charles Griffiths, the first governor's agent and later the resident commissioner, raised the force, which at its inception was reported to have had 110 men; the officers appointed were all sons of local chiefs. The magistrates in each of the then magisterial areas recruited a quota of men in their districts as troopers. The magistrates themselves were also police officers. Each man was required to provide his own pony and was supplied with a yellow cord uniform.

In 1878 European officers were commissioned into the force with military ranks, which continued to be used until 1958, when police ranks were adopted. However, in 1972 military ranks were reintroduced into the force and are still used today. There being no territorial forces other than the police, the force is responsible for both defense and internal security.

The duties and responsibilities of the force were originally very limited, being mainly to support and protect the colonial resident magistrates and to act as interpreters and messengers. Over the years as the duties and responsibilities of police officers multiplied, the force expanded.

During the earlier days the force demonstrated its abilities in various ways. For instance, detachments of the police fought alongside the Cape (Cape Colony) Mounted Forces at Mount Moorosi (Quthing) and various other places throughout the country during the Gun Wars of 1880–81. Volunteers also joined the Allied forces and served with distinction in World War I, and in World War II in Africa and Europe. Other detachments of the police assisted the Bechuanaland (now Botswana) government to restore and keep order in 1949 and 1952.

In those days the police were, in addition, responsible for the prisons. This was changed in 1946, when the responsibility for the prisons was passed to a newly established Prisons Department.

The force has not only expanded over the years, but its responsibilities have also become diversified, and various specialized branches have developed. For example, in 1946, the old Pioneer Camp under Badge Hill became the Police Training School (now Police Training College, PTC) and in the same year the Criminal Investigation Department was formed. In 1953 the Special Branch and Signals (Radio) Section was formed. The Special Branch became known as the Intelligence Branch, and since 1978, when it assumed an autonomous command, to date has come to be called the National Security Service (NSS).

In 1964 the police mobile unit was formed and joined the Police Training College at Pioneer Camp. In 1966 the Protective Security Unit was established and became part of the Police Mobile Unit. In 1967 the Stock Theft Unit was formed to take the responsibility regarding stock theft operations full-time.

In 1974 the Police Community Relations Division and the Narcotics Squad were formed. Both officers commanding in these branches received specialist training overseas, the former under the auspices of the International Police Association of the United States and the latter under UN auspices.

The branches and units of the Lesotho Mounted Police fell under the overall command of the commissioner of police until 1977, when the command was broken up into three divisions as follows:

- the Police General Unit, which maintained the name Lesotho Mounted Police
- the Police Mobile Unit, now called the Lesotho Paramilitary Force
- the Intelligence Branch, now known as the National Security Service

Each of the three divisions is commanded by a major general. However, the three commands work in close harmony.

In 1982 the Police General Unit had a force of 1,530 men and women in police stations and outposts throughout the nation.

Structure & Organization

The headquarters of the force is in Maseru, the national capital, and comprises the following branches:

- Administration (including finance and stores)
- National Security Service
- the Criminal Investigation Department
- the Police Training College
- the Traffic Department
- the Signals Branch
- the Women Police Department
- the Stock Theft Unit

The commissioner of police is the commanding officer of the force and is responsible to the prime minister, who is the minister of defense and internal security.

For a long time, before the creation of a 10th district (Thaba-Tseka), Lesotho was divided into four district commands for policing purposes, which in turn had nine subdistricts.

The topography of Lesotho is mountainous, and in much of the country road communication, even bridle paths, are nonexistent. In many areas the only method by which a member of the force can carry out his normal police duties is either on horseback or on foot. Considerable development continues to take place throughout the country, with self-help schemes to improve existing roads and develop new ones. Such development assists the police force in their day-to-day operations, facilitating the use of mechanical transport.

Women were first recruited into the Lesotho Mounted Police in 1970 as police officers; at that time they were 12 in number. By 1987 the Women Police Department constituted 15% of the police strength.

Internal Security Operations

The special branch, now known as the National Security Service (NSS), is the intelligence organization of the force. It is responsible for the collection, assessment and dissemination of all information that may affect the security of the Kingdom of Lesotho. It is headquartered in Maseru and is under the command of the assistant commissioner of police. The branch, however, has staff in each district headquarters and other stations.

A number of experienced expatriate NSS officers have been hired, and the NSS has been reorganized, improved and expanded over the years. With the employment of a full-time training officer, NSS training has been put on an appropriate footing, and courses are held regularly at the Police Training College.

The National Security Service now forms a separate section under its own major general.

The Criminal Investigation Department

The battle against crime and the continuous work of crime prevention is undertaken by this Department. The officer commanding and his staff at police headquarters are involved with crimes of special importance, such as murders affecting several divisions. They also deal with cases where liaison is required with neighboring forces or cooperation with forces anywhere in the world. In addition, all papers relating to crime, suspected crime and administration of the department are handled at the headquarters. In every division (policing district) there is a branch of the Criminal Investigation Department.

The duties and responsibilities of this department include the following:

- investigation of all types of serious crime
- publication of instructions and advice on subjects relating to investigation of crime and crime prevention
- publication of the police gazettes in regard to wanted persons, stolen and found materials, and stolen and found property
- compilation of criminal statistics
- provision of specialized services in connection with fingerprints and photography
- initial licensing of firearms
- investigation of cases related to illicit diamond dealing
- stock theft prevention and detection

The uniform was changed in 1880, when the battle dress with riding breeches were introduced. The military uniform was used by the force, as it was also responsible for external defense. At independence in 1966, the present-day khaki uniform was introduced as summer dress and has been modified over the years. The winter dress was changed to navy blue and some black suits in 1976 during the 10th anniversary of independence.

Recruitment, Education & Training

The Lesotho Mounted Police Training School, now known as the Police Training College, is located on the outskirts of Maseru. At this site are parade grounds for both mounted and foot drill, dormitories, and canteen and other facilities such as tennis courts and a soccer field. The college library was completed in 1982.

Staffing positions were as follows: one superintendent of police, one inspector, one subinspector, two sergeants, two corporals and two troopers.

Since 1982 recruitment has been restricted to applicants with at least a secondary level of education, over and above the normal physical and health standards necessary to join the force. In that year, 161 of 302 applicants were accepted; 35 of the applicants were female, of whom 10 were accepted.

The period of initial training is eight months, during which recruits resided at the school. The training program covers general police duties at border posts, common and statutory law, criminal investigation, mounted and dismounted drill with and without arms, riot drill, musketry, animal management, first aid and sports. In 1982 the period of initial training was revised as follows:

- graduate recruits: from nine months to six months, including two months' attachment
- below graduate recruits: from nine months to 12 months, including two months' attachment

The Penal System

No current information is available.

CRIME STATISTICS (1984)

		Number Reported	Attempts %	Cases Solved %	Crime per 100,000	Offenders	Females %	Juveniles %	Strangers %
1.	Murder	726	33	42	53.19	5,013	6.3	10.6	
2.	Sex offenses, including rape	986	1.3	43.5	72.23	1,968	0.30	29.11	
3.	Rape	658	1.97	37.7	48.21	1,505		33.08	
4.	Serious assault	3,480		46.81	254.95	4,949	12.8	15.5	
5.	All theft	8,625		30.13	631.87	9,194	15.23	18.8	
6.	Aggravated theft								
7.	Robbery and violent theft	839		14.42	61.47	1,395	0.14	35.62	
8.	Breaking and entering	3,345		16.86	245.05	2,916	18.10	34	
9.	Auto theft								
10.	Other thefts	3,231		24.3	236.70	5,048	4.12	16.9	
11.	Fraud	132		30.9	9.01	330	17.87	13.4	
12.	Counterfeiting								
13.	Drug offenses	414		72.7	30.33	860	8.83	6.86	
14.	Total offenses	22,427	36.27	25.66	1,643	33,178	83.69	15.25	

Note: Information for some categories is not available.
Criteria of juveniles: aged from 10 to 14 years.

LIBERIA

BASIC FACT SHEET

Official Name: Republic of Liberia
Area: 111,370 sq km
Population: 2,384,189 (1987)
Capital: Monrovia
Nature of Government: Military dictatorship
Language: English
Currency: Liberian dollar
GNP: $1.04 billion (1985)
Territorial Divisions: 13 counties
Population per Police Officer: 1,570
Police Expenditures per 1,000: N.A.

Structure & Organization

Liberia's principal law enforcement force is the Liberian National Police Force. Until its establishment in 1924, law enforcement and internal security had been almost entirely in the hands of the Liberian Frontier Force, then the country's Regular Army. The only other agency that is directly concerned with police and criminal matters is the National Bureau of Investigation, which works closely with the police in criminal investigation.

Two other organizations have functions impinging on national security, although their responsibilities stop short of criminal justice. The Executive Action Bureau is the president's advisory group on security matters and is charged with counterintelligence and control of subversive activities. The Liberian Joint Security Commission is a policy body that coordinates the armed forces and the police services.

The National Police Force is both a local and a national police. Police personnel are recruited from all parts of the country on a voluntary basis. The Mende are strongly represented because of their special aptitude for police work. The police headquarters, in Monrovia, is under the jurisdiction of the attorney general and is commanded by a director appointed by the president. All police officials hold honorary military status, the director holding the rank of colonel. Police officers are armed with pistols, but patrolmen carry only a nightstick and a whistle.

Central headquarters is made up of two principal operating components: the Operations Office and the Technical and Administrative Services. The latter, headed by an inspector, performs all administration and services for both the headquarters and the field

units, known as regional posts. It also operates the Police Academy, located in Paynesville, outside the national capital. The Operations Office directs the active police forces. Headed by a senior inspector who is the country's third-ranking police officer, after the director and the deputy director, its centralized control ensures a firm rein on all operational field components, both municipal and rural.

The Operations Office is composed of four main staff sections. The Criminal Records and Identification Division maintains statistics on crime and criminals and serves as the national repository for all identification data. The Traffic Division directs the Traffic Police. The Patrol Division oversees the officer on the beat and the rural constable. The Criminal Investigations Department (CID) is a plainclothes detective force.

Directly under the Operations Office are the two major field elements of the force: the Monrovia Police and the County and Provincial Police. The former is headed by a deputy inspector with jurisdiction over all police operations within the capital. The latter is under the charge of an inspector who controls all the regional posts throughout the country. There are eight of these county headquarters, located in each of the county administrative capitals. Normally each regional post is headed by a deputy inspector. In practice, the outlying rural units enjoy a considerable degree of autonomy as a result of the shortage of supervisory personnel, distance from the capital and limited communications. However, the chain of command is clearly defined and implicitly followed. The largest by far of the field units is Montserrado County.

Grade structure generally conforms to the U.S.

pattern. Police ranks below director and deputy director range from patrolman up to senior inspector. Advancement follows a progressive course up through sergeant, lieutenant, captain and inspector, and there also are several specialist grades. Each regional post commander generally has a lieutenant and three or four sergeants in addition to patrolmen.

Police pay, although not high, compares favorably with equivalent professions and is considerably higher than that of the National Guard. Installations and physical facilities, however, are antiquated and jerry-built. Many police stations are converted residences, and few have security facilities for holding detainees. Most police vehicles are old and in need of replacement. The rolling stock of the regional posts are limited to one or two cars and a motorcycle, but the vehicles often are out of commission, awaiting maintenance or spare parts. There is little mobile or portable communications equipment, and local messages are sent over the telephone or by messenger. The Police Academy, however, has modern communications equipment and houses the Interpol communications center. All West African Interpol traffic passes through this station.

The National Bureau of Investigation (NBI) was organized in 1958 as the Bureau of Special Services under the guidance of U.S. consultants. In 1961 it was combined with the Executive Mansion Special Security Police, until then a component of the National Police Force, and its name was changed to its present one. In 1962 it was removed from the jurisdiction of the Department of Justice and placed directly under the chief executive. Duties assigned by law to the NBI include personal protection of the president, cases involving narcotics, counterfeiting, immigration violations, malfeasance by public officials, and political surveillance.

The NBI consists of a headquarters in Monrovia and three field offices, in Buchanan, Harper and Gbarnga. Most of its activities are concentrated in the national capital, with agents making fields trips to the interior as required. The headquarters is organized into service and operational subdivisions and has a small inspection staff and a training section.

There are two service elements, designated Administrative Services and Technical Services; there is an air wing section in the latter. In the operational area, two main subsections are concerned with investigation and security, respectively. The first conducts investigations of individuals and organizations and maintains current information on potential sources of disaffection or unrest. The Security Division, the largest NBI component, incorporates the Executive Mansion Special Security Police, which guards official residences and government buildings. Members of the Executive Mansion Special Security Police hold military rank and constitute the only uniformed element within the NBI. Their distinctive Army-type blue uniform is worn only on special occasions. While on duty they are armed with pistols.

Within the NBI there is a special grade structure. A recruit starts out as an agent and advances to special agent, special agent in charge and senior special agent in charge. The two top positions are assistant director and director, the latter post being filled by the president. Pay for NBI agents is somewhat higher than for the police, and officers assigned to the executive mansion receive a 20% bonus.

Recruitment, Education & Training

Police training is provided at the Police Academy, established in 1961 with U.S. aid. All men entering the service receive formal basic training at the academy. The school conducts two six-month courses annually for prospective policemen. The school buildings are among the finest government buildings in the country, on a 100-acre tract.

The Penal System

The Penal Law serves as the formal criminal code and, in fact, replaced earlier legislation known as the Criminal Code. Two categories of offenses are recognized: felonies and misdemeanors. Some of the most grave felonies, including murder, treason, slave trading, arson, rape and robbery are further classed as infamous crimes. The Penal Law also establishes broad categories of offenses, such as crimes against the state, crimes against person and crimes against property. In matters of punishment, the courts are given some degree of latitude, but types of punishment and maximum sentences are strictly defined, ranging from the death penalty and imprisonment for life to small fines. Flogging is permitted under the Aborigines Law. The application of the Penal Law is limited to nonaboriginals.

The Liberian Code of Laws of 1956 acknowledges rehabilitation as the goal of prison administration. There are 20 institutions classified as prisons: three in Monrovia, including the Central Prison, the Municipal Jail and the Belle Yella Camp; and 17 county, district and magisterial jails dispersed throughout the country. Control and direction of these institutions are marked by a lack of uniformity and central guidance. There are no general regulations for prison administration, and records are poorly kept, if at all. Some are run by military personnel, some by the Department of Justice and some by the police.

There is no classification or segregation of different types of prisoners. Persons charged with felonies and misdemeanors, sentenced and unsentenced, male and female, juvenile and adult, often are placed in the same institution and, in some cases, in the same cell or dormitory. Escapes are reported to be fairly frequent, particularly from labor gangs in the rural areas, and no statistics are maintained on them. The only record kept on prisoners is the ledger of commitment, and no records show the number of inmates at any given time or their dates of release. Most prisons are old and in a state of disrepair. They range from concrete structures to mud huts with thatched roofs. Nearly all are overcrowded and insanitary. Only the Central Prison and one other jail have plumbing, and in most others the floors are used for toilet purposes as well as for sleeping. In some jails prisoners sleep on two-by-five-foot spaces on cement floors. Illumination and ventilation are also bad, with only the door as an opening.

The treatment of prisoners varies, although the brutalities of the past have been curbed. There are no teachers, social workers, vocational training programs or medical personnel. Only a bare subsistence diet is provided, usually a cup of rice per day, occasionally supplemented by some dried fish. In rural prisons prisoners raise their own food and in others depend on the kindness of friends and relatives.

There are no uniform regulations governing prison labor. Some work on public projects, others for private contractors. No penal institution has workshops or handicraft facilities.

There are no comprehensive crime statistics. Petty larceny and simple assault appear to be the most prevalent types of offenses. Crimes of violence are rare. There is no organized banditry, and life and property are generally secure. The most serious law enforcement problem is reported to be juvenile delinquency.

LIBYA

BASIC FACT SHEET

Official Name: Socialist People's Libyan Arab Jamahiriya
Area: 1,759,540 sq km
Population: 3,306,825 (1987)
Capital: Tripoli
Nature of Government: Civilian dictatorship
Language: Arabic
Currency: Dinar
GNP: $27 billion (1985)
Territorial Divisions: 46 municipalities
Population per Police Officer: N.A.
Police Expenditures per 1,000: $26,667

History & Background

Shortly after the 1969 coup that brought Muammar Qadhafi to power, military officers were integrated into key police positions. Between 1970 and 1973 a series of ministerial decrees was passed, completely reorganizing the police (or the *shurtah,* as it is known in Arabic). In 1970 the regional police forces were integrated into one unified organization under the Ministry of the Interior. The police were stripped of their historical paramilitary status and realigned as a civilian function.

A decree of the ruling Revolutionary Command Council (RCC) on March 22, 1970, established the General Directorate of Administration, the General Inspection Department, the Public Affairs Directorate and the Central Security Bureau. Law 11 of March 10, 1971, provided new, separate agencies to handle civil defense and fire fighting. Other units, including the Police Supply Department, Wireless and Emergency Department, Identity Investigation Department, Central Traffic Department, Central Department for Criminal Investigation, Arab International Criminal Police Bureau, Ports Security Department, Police Training Department, and Electronic Computer Section were established by separate ministerial decrees between 1970 and 1973.

Structure & Organization

By far the most important piece of legislation during the 1970–73 period was the special police law promulgated by the RCC on January 5, 1972, spelling out the new functions and structure of the police force, formally redesignated the Police at the Service of the People and the Revolution. The statute placed the primary responsibility for law enforcement on the minister of the interior and his deputy. Individual police units were set under the jurisdiction of the regional police directorates throughout the country. The law also established a Police Affairs Council, composed of the deputy minister of the interior as chairman, the directors of the central Police Department, the chiefs of the regional police directorates, and a legal adviser with authority to issue decrees on police matters. In addition, there are specialized departments dealing with criminal research, "morals crimes," juvenile delinquency and police dogs. A camel corps polices desert areas.

There are two civilian organizations associated with the police: the Police Friends System and the Police Children Program. The former is a kind of voluntary neighborhood crime watch program; the latter, a program for boys between eight and 12 years of age to assist in directing traffic in urban areas.

Police rank structure follows closely that of the armed forces. Salary levels are determined in accordance with civil service scales. The uniform is khaki in summer and dark blue in winter. A blue peaked cap is worn throughout the year, with a white cover in summer. All ranks carry pistols or rifles.

Recruitment, Education & Training

No current information is available.

The Penal System

The Libyan Criminal Code was first promulgated in 1954, but it is being progressively amended to bring it into conformity with the Sharia (which embodies

Muslim law). Efforts to align the three categories of offenses in the criminal code—crimes, delits and contraventions—with the five classifications embodied in the Sharia—mandatory, commendable, permissible, reprehensible and forbidden—have involved Libyan legal and religious scholars in a drawn-out process of reconciliation that has not, as yet, been fully resolved.

Little information is available on penal institutions. Three institutions—the central prisons at Tripoli and Benghazi and the Jdeida Prison outside Tripoli—are known to exist, and smaller centers in less populated centers may be assumed to exist. Possibly there are two new prisons, at Tripoli and Darnah. All prisons are administered by the police.

Law 47 of 1975 called for a shift in penal policy from punishment to rehabilitation. Under this law, religious instruction, vocational training, and secondary and university-level education were introduced into prisons. A placement agency also was established to help rehabilitated prisoners find employment after their release from prison.

Although no firm statistics are available, Qadhafi periodically deplores the rise in crimes of all kinds, including "crimes against freedom, honor and the public," a vague category. Another area of criminal activity that has evoked major concern by the regime is corruption and bribery, which are punishable by up to 10 years in prison.

CRIME STATISTICS (1983)

		Number Reported	Attempts %	Cases Solved %	Crime per 100,000	Offenders	Females %	Juveniles %	Strangers %
1.	Murder	48	68.8	4.1	1.60	74	0.6	0.6	0.3
2.	Sex offenses, including rape	591		13.4	19.70	826	10.5	2.8	4.6
3.	Rape	316		11.4	10.53	496		8.8	2.3
4.	Serious assault	35		17.0	1.17	40		0.5	0.5
5.	All theft	8,102		18.5	270.07	4,162	63.0	81.2	20.9
6.	Aggravated theft	1,440		17.9	48.00	841	7.2	20.0	
7.	Robbery and violent theft	127		10.0	4.23	133		0.8	
8.	Breaking and entering	1,313		18.7	43.77	708	7.2	19.1	
9.	Auto theft	2,166		18.6	72.20	400		7.8	
10.	Other thefts	4,347		18.5	144.90	2,776	53.6	51.0	
11.	Fraud	68		23.5	2.27				0.9
12.	Counterfeiting	1			0.03	1			0.0
13.	Drug offenses	126			4.20	277	1.7	0.15	1.01
14.	Total offenses	30		8.9	1,022.27	33,916	7.3	13.6	8.43

Note: Information for some categories is not available.
Criteria of juveniles: aged from 14 to 18 years.

MADAGASCAR

BASIC FACT SHEET

Official Name: Democratic Republic of Madagascar
Area: 592,900 sq km
Population: 10,730,754 (1987)
Capital: Antananarivo
Nature of Government: Military dictatorship
Languages: French and Malagasy
Currency: Malagasy franc
GNP: $2.51 billion (1985)
Territorial Divisions: 6 provinces
Population per Police Officer: 2,900
Police Expenditures per 1,000: N.A.

Structure & Organization

There are four police agencies in Madagascar: the National Gendarmerie, the Republican Security Force, the Civil Police and the Civic Service.

Developed from colonial origins, the National Gendarmerie is the principal organization for the maintenance of public order. It provides police services outside the municipalities. Its equipment inventory includes automatic weapons, armored cars and aircraft, and its units are connected with command centers by a modern system of radio communications. The National Gendarmerie is part of the defense establishment, but its command structure is entirely separate from that of the Army.

The Republican Security Force was originally established as a presidential bodyguard and antiriot unit. It is reportedly less disciplined and less trained than the National Gendarmerie.

The Civil Police maintains order in towns and urban areas. The head of each prefecture has at least a small contingent under his control. They are less trained and less equipped than the National Gendarmerie.

The Civic Service is a paramilitary force. It is a reserve element of the defense forces, and its commanders are military officers in uniform, although its operations are nonmilitary in nature. It participates in rural economic and social development programs.

Recruitment, Education & Training

Potential draftees serve in the Civic Service as an alternative to regular military duty.

The Penal System

The Malagasy Penal Code has developed primarily from French penal codes and procedures, although it is somewhat influenced by Malagasy customary law. The 1962 code provides the accused most of the rights and protections afforded by French and Western codes of law. The highest punishments are death and forced labor for life. The code also shifts control over investigations and prosecutions to the magistrates.

Each province has a central prison for inmates serving sentences of less than five years. There are also 25 lesser prisons for persons awaiting trial and those sentenced to less than two years. Courts at the subprefecture level also have jails where prisoners serve sentences of up to six months. Women serving long sentences are kept at the Central Prison at Antananarivo. Hardened criminals and those serving sentences of over five years are sent to one of the prisons on small coastal islands, such as Nosy Lava or Nosy Be.

MALAWI

```
BASIC FACT SHEET

Official Name: Republic of Malawi
Area: 118,484 sq km
Population: 7,437,911 (1987)
Capital: Lilongwe
Nature of Government: Partial democracy
Languages: English and Chichewa
Currency: Kwacha
GNP: $1.16 billion (1985)
Territorial Divisions: 3 administrative regions, 24 districts
Population per Police Officer: 1,670
Police Expenditures per 1,000: N.A.
```

Structure & Organization

The Malawi Police Force operates under the Ministry of Justice. The force traces its origins to 1921, when it was established during the British colonial regime. It was reorganized in 1947, and its structure and functions were defined by the laws of Nyasaland.

Below the top ranks, administrative and policy matters are handled by the Police Service Commis-

sion. The national headquarters is at Zomba, and there are regional headquarters at each of the three regional capitals. There also are stations in each of the country's 24 districts, plus approximately 37 substations and police posts throughout the country.

All constables, as patrolmen are called, are under the central administration. There are no separate community or local police. Special branches include the

CRIME STATISTICS (1983)

		Number Reported	Attempts %	Cases Solved %	Crime per 100,000	Offenders	Females %	Juveniles %	Strangers %
1.	Murder	176		30.11	2.93	57	7.01	3.50	
2.	Sex offenses, including rape	424		44.33	7.07	197		9.13	
3.	Rape	163		33.74	2.72	65		4.61	
4.	Serious assault	8,089		49.21	134.82	4,230	7.42	1.74	
5.	All theft	41,070		23.27	684.50	10,418	1.79	2.03	
6.	Aggravated theft	15,470		12.13	257.83	2,076	0.38	3.66	
7.	Robbery and violent theft	968		13.42	16.13	178		2.24	
8.	Breaking and entering	1,627		16.47	27.12	337		4.74	
9.	Auto theft	26		3.84	0.43	2			
10.	Other thefts	25,574		30.03	426.23	8,340	2.14	1.63	
11.	Fraud	470		30.85	7.83	150	0.66	1.33	
12.	Counterfeiting								
13.	Drug offenses	824		66.14	13.73	557	0.35	0.71	
14.	Total offenses	63,311		31.47	1,055.18	21,856	5.59	1.81	

Note: Information for some categories is not available.
Criteria of juveniles: aged from 7 to 17 years.

Criminal Investigation Division, the Special Branch for Intelligence and the Immigration Service.

The Police Mobile Force is designed as a quick-reaction force to quell sudden riots and uprisings. PMF members are equipped with rifles, light machine guns and riot gear and move in trucks as well as lighter vehicles such as Land-Rovers and motorcycles. Mobile units are stationed at the Zomba national headquarters and at each of the three regional headquarters, connected by a radio network.

Police strength is about 6,000. The force, once heavily British in its upper echelons, is now almost completely Africanized. Major ethnic groups, as the Chewa, Lomwe and Nyanja, are strongly represented in police ranks. The Ngoni, who constitute only 1.2% of the population, are disproportionately represented, as are Southerners in general.

Recruitment, Education & Training

After an initial four-year enlistment, members of the force can sign up for continuing service until they qualify for a lump-sum payment at age 45 or extend their service further to qualify for retirement benefits. Recruits are trained at Kanjedza, near Blantyre, where the basic police course lasts six months. Selected police officers are given special training at the Zomba national headquarters. Women were permitted to join the force in 1971 and are trained at the Police Training School at Limbe.

The Penal System

The Malawi Penal Code combines British and customary African systems and is based on what is termed "received law" and customary law. Customary law applies to Traditional Court proceedings.

The country has about 20 prisons, mostly small. A central prison is in Zomba, and other prisons are in Lilongwe, Kanjedza and Mzuzu. The government also runs an open prison farm for first offenders and a small school for juvenile offenders. All prisoners are expected to work.

The level of crime is relatively low, although it experienced a slight rise after the 1960s. Traditional attitudes and customs tend to hold down the level of petty crime; in rural areas everyone is under the watchful eye of everyone else. Crimes of violence are very rare, probably because of extremely severe sentences meted out by the courts for such crimes.

MALAYSIA

Patrick Edobor Igbinovia

BASIC FACT SHEET

Official Name: Malaysia
Area: 329,749 sq km
Population: 16,068,516 (1987)
Capital: Kuala Lumpur
Nature of Government: Constitutional monarchy
Languages: Malay and English
Currency: Ringgit
GNP: $31.93 billion (1985)
Territorial Divisions: 14 states
Population per Police Officer: 760
Police Expenditures per 1,000: N.A.

History & Background

The modern Malaysian police force dates from 1806, when the British formed a police force in Penang. In 1824 a similar unit was established in Malacca. The Perak Armed Police was established in 1867, followed by similar organizations in Negeri Sembilan, Selangor and Pahang. These forces operated separately until 1896, when the British amalgamated them into the Federated Malay States Police. These police units were trained by noncommissioned officers of the British Army.

Events in the latter part of the 19th century and the early part of the 20th century in present-day peninsular Malaysia also dictated the development of the police along paramilitary lines. During that period the peninsula was a land of almost continuous disorder punctuated by insurrections and rebellions in various states. Many local territorial chiefs employed armed retainers, who often terrorized the countryside. The problem of maintaining public order, therefore, consisted largely of dispatching armed patrols along the trails and paths between towns and settlements.

By 1920 all states in the peninsula had police forces. Increased immigration by Chinese and Indians early in the 20th century brought new problems, including those associated with increased urbanization. Law-enforcement agencies had to cope with urban criminal gangs as well as with banditry and terrorism in outlying areas, and particularly with the problem of suppressing the Chinese secret societies responsible for these new forms of crime. As a result the police, while retaining a strong paramilitary capability, began to develop larger and more sophisti-

cated facilities for criminal investigation, detection and apprehension; for example, a fingerprint registry was established in 1904.

When the Japanese occupied Malaya in 1942, they used the Malayan police to support Japanese operations against MPAJA (Malayan People's Anti Japanese Army) guerrillas and their suspected supporters. With the surrender of the Japanese in 1945, the organization and operations of the police were disrupted, and much of the police force itself was no longer trusted by the people. The British found on their return that there was a need for extensive investigation and retraining of the entire force. In 1946 the police forces of the Federated Malay States Police and the independent forces of the other states were integrated into the Malay Union Police, renamed the Federation of Malaya Police in 1948.

Law enforcement in Sarawak before the arrival of the first white raja in 1841 was rudimentary and dealt largely with tax collection. People living in outlying areas were not subject to any significant central control. Under the white rajas a police force initially took the form of troops led by the raja himself; subsequently a separate group was formed to perform more conventional duties in the towns. In 1932 these two elements were merged to form the small Sarawak Constabulary. When the last of the white rajas ceded Sarawak to the British in 1946, the British made a major effort to improve the quality and efficiency of these forces instead of merely reorganizing them. The emphasis within the Sarawak Constabulary had been on paramilitary training and procedures; the British put increasing emphasis on regular police work. The

British organized the Sarawak Constabulary into the Regular Police with responsibility for civil police duties, the Field Force to patrol the jungle and rural areas, and the Special Force to deal with investigation and control of subversion. In Sabah the British created an organization similar to that in Sarawak after Sabah was ceded by the British North Borneo Company in 1946.

Immediately after the liberation of Malaya from the Japanese, there were several militant Communist activities throughout the country in the form of labor unrest, murders on innocent civilians and police personnel, and the destruction of millions of dollars' worth of rubber plantations and other property. This resulted in an emergency situation from 1948 to 1960. During this period the police force expanded almost sevenfold, to 75,341 (31,164 regulars and 44,177 special constables); they were given greater authority under centralized state control and directed to increase attention to recruiting, training and equipping police personnel. The police were required not only to fight the Communist terrorists as a paramilitary adjunct to regular armed forces but also to develop a role in gathering specialized intelligence. A confrontation by Indonesia under the Sukarno regime lasted from 1963 to 1965.

The amalgamation of Sabah, Sarawak and the Federation of Malaya into Malaysia in 1963 was the occasion for developing final plans to unify their separate police organizations into a single national police force, to be called the Royal Malaysian Police (RMP). The name change was authorized, the constabularies of Sabah and Sarawak were subordinated to federal authority for policy and supervision, and the RMP in essentially its present form was established.

Structure & Organization

The total strength of the Royal Malaysian Police was estimated at 42,000 in 1976. The 1982 strength was as follows:

ROYAL MALAYSIAN POLICE PERSONNEL, 1982

Departments	Officers	Rank and File
Administration/General Duties	739	21,888
Traffic Duties	55	1,024
Logistics	305	6,264
Training/Training Reserve	287	3,967
Crime	1,150	2,376
Special Branch	1,534	2,187
Internal Security/Public Order	1,041	23,269
	5,111	61,975

The major operating elements of the RMP are the Police Field Force (PFF), the Federal Reserve Units (FRU), the CID, the Special Branch and the Marine Police. Other police units perform support or conventional police tasks, such as directing traffic and ensuring maintenance of communications. The RMP also has a women's contingent, which principally deals with crimes and problems related to women or young children. The police also maintain various kinds of volunteer units, the largest of which is the People's Volunteer Reserve, which supplements the regular force, particularly in time of national emergency.

The Police Act of 1967 established the office of inspector general, who commands the Police Force and is responsible to the minister of home affairs for the direction and control of the organization. The inspector general is assisted by a deputy inspector general.

The inspector general headquarters has four departments, each headed by a director with the rank of commissioner of police. These directors are the principal staff officers of the Inspector General of Police and have executive authority in their respective departments. They are responsible for the criminal investigation, management, Special Branch, and internal security/public order, respectively. They are senior to all commanding officers in the field so as to be able to implement policy decisively.

The Management Branch has four main divisions and services the other departments of the police in day-to-day operations.

Internal Security and Public Order (IS/PO)

The police are primarily responsible for all public order situations involving the suppression of riots and disturbances. In this respect the Army supports the police.

In internal security matters, the police undertake operations in conjunction with the armed forces and actively support them. To facilitate this process, the inspector general is cochairman with the chief of the armed forces staff of the Operational Planning Committee at the national level.

The IS/PO director commands two divisions at his headquarters. One is headed by a senior assistant commissioner of police as deputy director administration/logistics, involved with the administration of the police's field force as a whole. The finance and logistics director and a deputy director for operations are involved in all operational matters and also are responsible for supervision of the commander of the Federal Reserve Units.

Police Field Force (PFF)

The Royal Malaysia Police has always been faced with the need to undertake punitive operations to suppress armed uprisings and widespread subversion as well as to seek out and destroy other criminal elements who operate from bases in the jungle and to patrol the frontiers and sparsely populated areas of the nation. To meet this need, the Police Field Force was formed. The PFF is organized into brigades, battalions and companies that can be deployed on long-term deep-jungle operations either independently or in conjunction with the armed forces. The PFF is also utilized in support of the General Duties Police in crime prevention measures, disasters and public order situations. Units are supplied with scout cars equipped with machine guns and radios.

The force also has organized a platoon of women police trained in jungle warfare to be part of the PFF organization. They are equipped to perform jungle operations along with their male counterparts whenever required.

Federal Reserve Units (FRU)

The Federal Reserve Units are self-contained and highly mobile units of specially trained policemen for the suppression of riots, dispersal of unlawful assemblies and crowd control. They also assist in rescue work during national or local disasters and may be deployed on special tasks in aid of the District Police, the CID or the Special Branch.

Criminal Investigation Department (CID)

The CID was created in 1970. Its director is responsible for the prevention and detection of crime and the apprehension and prosecution of criminals. He has under him:

- Deputy director, Administration/Prevention. This division deals with all matters pertaining to administration, criminal records, fingerprints and CID Railways.
- Deputy director, Planning/Operations. This division deals with the analysis of crime at both national and international levels and maintains links with Interpol, and handles special investigations in various and complicated crimes, technical aids to investigation involving the Dog Unit, the detective establishment, secret societies, and antivice and antinarcotics measures.

Special Branch

The Special Branch is responsible for the acquisition, collation and dissemination of security intelligence with suggested lines of action to government. This department is the intelligence organization of the nation and is structured to facilitate this process down to the district level.

Until 1970 responsibility for finance, supply, works and buildings were structured within ''C'' Department. At that time it was decided to integrate finance and supply with the Ministry of Home Affairs. How-

ever, there has been no physical movement, and this organization still is in the headquarters serving the needs of the police.

The police have fleets of mobile patrol vehicles equipped with radio communications deployed in all districts, major towns and urban areas for round-the-clock, intermittent or special patrols, depending on the coverage required to provide effective crime prevention measures. In addition, highway patrols are deployed.

The country is divided into 13 contingents/components headed by the commissioners of police of Sabah and Sarawak in the Borneo states and the chief police officers of the states of Kedah/Perlis, Pinang, Kuala Lumpur (federal territory), Selangor, Negeri Sembilan, Malacca, Johore, Kelantan, Terengganu and Pahang.

The commissioners of Sabah and Sarawak and the chief police officers of the states in peninsular Malaysia are commanding officers responsible to the inspector general for the control and direction of the state police and all persons appointed for or engaged in police duties. Each of these commanders has a headquarters staffed somewhat comparably to the IGP headquarters but modified according to the areas of importance of the component or the state. There are three categories of commanding officers in terms of rank, which reflect the importance of area of command:

- The commissioners in Sabah and Sarawak and the chief police officers in Kuala Lumpur, Perak and Kedah/Perlis have the rank of deputy commissioner of police.
- The chief police officers of Pinang, Pahang, Kelantan, Johore and Negeri Sembilan have the rank of senior assistant commissioner of police.
- The chief police officers of Malacca and Terengganu have the rank of assistant commissioner of police.

The next level of command is that of the officer in charge of a police district (OCPD), who is responsible to the commissioner/chief police officer for the command and control of his district. The policy is that as far as possible, a police district should comprise an administrative district; however, this is not always possible. There are 74 police districts in the Kuala Lumpur federal territory. The lowest rank is that of an assistant superintendent of police (ASP), in small or rural districts. However, the rank may go up to that of an assistant commissioner of police for the more important, urban, industrialized or busy districts, such as Ipoh or Petaling Jaya.

The next level of command is that of an officer in charge of a police station (OCS). Each police district is divided into a number of station areas under a junior police officer. There are over 500 such police stations, which crisscross the nation. The station area is divided into a number of beat and patrol areas.

Police officers normally wear a full khaki uniform with a bush jacket. Depending on the duties or branches in which they serve, members of the force wear colors such as: Police Field Force, jungle green; Federal Reserve Unit, dark blue; Marine Police, white; Traffic Police, dark blue trousers or white shorts; Women Police, light blue-gray uniform.

Recruitment, Education & Training

No racial or ethnic restrictions are placed on eligibility for membership in any of the police forces; nevertheless, police composition reflects the ethnic makeup of the nation. Most of the police in peninsular Malaysia are Malay because a police career has long been popular with the Muslim Malay. In Sabah and Sarawak, most of the lower ranks come from the native ethnic groups. Indians and Chinese are present in all branches but more visibly in the CID or Special Branch. Ethnic problems do not, however, appear to affect the quality and effectiveness of the police forces. The force is adequately trained, and pay and morale are high.

Given minor variations dictated by local conditions, there are three methods of joining the police services. Candidates with at least six years of primary school are recruited as constables; those holding the Malaysia Certificate of Education are recruited as probationary

inspectors; and university graduates are recruited as probationary assistant superintendents.

The Police Training School in Kuala Lumpur offers basic training for constable recruits and refresher courses for junior officers. Higher-level courses are given at the Police College in Kuala Kubu Baharu. There are separate schools for CID and Special Branch personnel, and paramilitary training for the Police Field Force is given at Ulu Kinta in Perak. Unit training also is given when appropriate. A number of police officers from other countries in Southeast Asia attend the Police College.

The Penal System

The criminal system of Malaysia is defined in the Penal Code that was written by the British for the Straits Settlements. In 1948 it was amended to cover all the peninsular states. Other amendments followed until the code was consolidated in 1970. In mid-1975 the code was extended to cover Sabah and Sarawak, although some elements of the former penal codes in these states have been retained.

The code lists three categories of offenses: against property, against the person, and against the state and public tranquillity. Among authorized punishments are death, imprisonment, fines and whipping, although the number of offenses for which whipping could be imposed are restricted to a few. Imprison-

CRIME STATISTICS (1984)

		Number Reported	Attempts %	Cases Solved %	Crime per 100,000	Offenders	Females %	Juveniles %	Strangers %
1.	Murder	293	22	57	1.97	287	3	1	23
2.	Sex offense, including rape	745		48	5.02	405		10	13
3.	Rape	470		50	3.17	276		11	13
4.	Serious assault	2,163		38	14.57	1,056	3	5	12
5.	All theft								
6.	Aggravated theft								
7.	Robbery and violent theft	5,991		10	40.36	987		10	10
8.	Breaking and entering	22,908		7	154.33	1,946		18	5
9.	Auto theft	2,271		7	15.30	125		2	
10.	Other thefts	43,780		14	294.94	6,881	1	14	6
11.	Fraud	3,477		12	23.42	467	1		2
12.	Counterfeiting	985		8	6.64	110	1		21
13.	Drug offenses	7,080			47.70	10,606	2	5	1
14.	Total offenses	90,163	0.1	11	607.41	23,146	1	9	5

Note: Information for some categories is not available.
Criteria of juveniles: aged from 7 to 18 years.

ment with hard labor and solitary confinement were abolished in 1952.

The death sentence is mandatory for murder or attempt to murder a head of state, and in cases in which firearms are used for purpose of extortion, robbery, resisting arrest, or escaping from custody. Persons convicted of trafficking in dangerous drugs, successfully inciting mutiny in the armed forces or possessing firearms illegally may be punished by death or life imprisonment.

In general the Penal Code permits the judge considerable freedom in passing sentence. Criminal court procedures are based on those of Great Britain.

The corrections system is administered by the Malaysian Prisons Service under the Ministry of Home Affairs. There are separate prison departments for peninsular Malaysia, Sarawak and Sabah, but all of them report to the director general of the Prisons Service. There are 17 facilities in peninsular Malaysia (including the Prison Officers' Training Depot), seven in Sabah and six in Sarawak. Penal institutions range from conventional walled compounds to open farms and detention camps.

In peninsular Malaysia first offenders and well-behaved prisoners are sent to the Central Training Prison at Taiping. Regional training prisons at Pinang, Alor Setar, Kuala Lumpur and Johor Baharu house recidivists. Young male offenders are sent to reform schools in Telok Mas, Ayer Keroh and Malacca; girls are sent to a school in Batu Gajah. The Pulau Jerejak Rehabilitation Center and the detention camps at Taiping and Muar hold detainees awaiting trial. The Special Prison at Seremban receives all classes of prisoners. Local prisons for offenders charged with lesser crimes are maintained at Sungei Petani for young males; Kuantan for adult males; and Kuala Lumpur, Georgetown, Alor Setar and Pengkalan for females.

Sarawak has a central prison and a women's prison at Kuching, regional prisons at Simanggang, Sibu, Miri and Limbang, and detention camps for men and women at Kuching. Sabah has a central prison, a women's prison and a detention camp at Kota Kinabalu, regional prisons at Sandakan and Tawau, a minimum security prison at Keningau and a reform school.

MAURITANIA

BASIC FACT SHEET

Official Name: Islamic Republic of Mauritania
Area: 1,030,700 sq km
Population: 1,863,208 (1987)
Capital: Nouakchott
Nature of Government: Military dictatorship
Languages: French and Arabic
Currency: Ouguiya
GNP: $700 million (1985)
Territorial Divisions: 12 regions and a capital district
Population per Police Officer: 710
Police Expenditures per 1,000: N.A.

History & Background

In the French tradition, the Mauritanian Gendarmerie is a paramilitary force concerned only with the maintenance of internal order. It is organized on a national basis with a military command hierarchy and equipped with military weapons.

Structure & Organization

Originally organized into two companies, one for the East and another for the West, the Mauritanian Gendarmerie was organized in 1963 into two companies in the capital and brigades (of few members each) in each *département*. The police headquarters is attached to the Army headquarters in Nouakchott. One of the two companies in Nouakchott is, in effect, a presidential guard, officially called the Escort and Security Squadron. The total strength of the Gendarmerie is less than 1,000.

The Mauritanian Police is a national organization under the Ministry of the Interior that exercises ultimate command through the governors of the 13 regions. This follows the French Continental model of a centralized system of tightly coordinated units under a unified command structure. The civil police force is organized hierarchically in three main ranks: policeman *(agent de police),* inspector *(inspecteur de police)* and commissioner *(commissaire de police).* Each prefect and town mayor has a certain amount of authority and discretion in using the police under his jurisdiction.

Recruitment, Education & Training

Training is provided at the National Police School.

The Penal System

No current information is available.

MEXICO

BASIC FACT SHEET

Official Name: United Mexican States
Area: 1,972,547 sq km
Population: 81,860,566 (1987)
Capital: Mexico City
Nature of Government: Limited democracy
Languages: Spanish
Currency: Peso
GNP: $163.79 billion (1985)
Territorial Divisions: 31 states and the Federal District
Population per Police Officer: N.A.
Police Expenditures per 1,000: N.A.

Structure & Organization

Mexican police forces exist at the federal, state and municipal levels through many overlapping layers of authority. The main federal police is called the General Directorate of Police and Traffic (Dirección General de Policia y Transito), which is part of the Ministry of Government. The General Directorate is divided into several divisions: Preventive, Riot, Auxiliary, Traffic and Investigation, the last of which was formerly called the Secret Service. The total strength of the General Directorate in the mid-1980s was close to 30,000, including 1,000 policewomen.

Also on the federal level are the Judicial Police, under the command of the Public Ministry, which is empowered to give orders to other police, such as the traffic police. The Federal Highway Police, numbering about 2,000, patrol the federally designated highways and investigate auto accidents. Other governmental agencies and ministries maintain small police forces; these include the Ministry of Public Health, the National Railway of Mexico, the Ministry of Hydraulic Reserves, and Mexican Petroleum.

Each of the states and the Federal District (DF) has its own police force. The state police enforce state laws within their jurisdiction and assist the federal police in enforcing federal laws. Large cities have special units, such as the Park Police and the Foreign Language Police. At the level of the small municipality, the work is less intricate and the pace generally slower except on weekends, when the rural folks come to town for church, marketing and drinking (not necessarily in that order), which may lead to fighting and violence. Municipal police forces in state capitals are under the command of state governors.

In large urban areas there are many precincts, called

police delegations; a typical delegation has between 200 and 250 preventive police assigned to it. The delegation is under the command of a *comandante,* usually an officer with the rank of a first captain. (All police ranks correspond to military ranks.) Lesser officers, usually lieutenants, are in charge of each eight-hour shift and are assisted by first sergeants, second sergeants and corporals. Most of the men operate out of the command headquarters called a *comandancia,* but part of the company is stationed at fixed points throughout the police delegation, usually at small two-man kiosks, accessible to the public. Assisting the preventive police are auxiliary police who patrol the streets on the night shift only. Agents of the Public Ministry assigned to the *delegation* have their offices at the *comandancias.* Many of the *comandancias* also have a first aid post on the premises with a doctor or medical technician in attendance. Many of the *comandancias* have two kinds of cells: large communal cells, usually without bunks, holding numerous persons sentenced for misdemeanors (with separate cells for men and women), and small cells with bunks to confine persons under arrest for felonies during preliminary investigation. The *comandancias* are numbered from one to 23.

Organized along military lines, the force comprises 33 battalions *(batalliónes),* 31 of which are numbered. The second is the Preventive Police; the fourth, fifth, sixth, ninth, 12th, 14th, and 22nd are Auxiliary Police; the 31st is the Auxiliary Private Police; the 18th is administrative; and the 28th is the Women's Police. The unnumbered battalions are the Grenadiers, a riot control force which includes a motorized brigade, and the Transport Battalion.

The Federal Police has its own rescue elements:

the Urban Services and Air Rescue Squadron, equipped with motor vehicles, boats and aircraft.

The Secret Service (Servicio Secreto) is also part of the federal police. It comprises a patrol group and 10 numbered field groups.

Criminal investigation is the responsibility of the Federal Judicial Police, a plainclothes force that represents Interpol in Mexico.

Currency and banking offenses are investigated by the Special Investigation Department of the Bank of Mexico. The Bank and Industrial Police is a separate organization that protects banking institutions and includes two specialized units, the Mounted Police and the Patrol Squadron.

Police units in all jurisdictions tend to be short of funds and equipment and to be undermanned.

The newspapers report regularly on police corruption, immorality and incompetence. Bribes are commonplace and even required for the performance of some tasks; according to published reports, there is a close relationship between the police and the criminal elements in the country. Corruption is not limited to the lower ranks; the former chief of police of Mexico City is in prison in the mid-1980s for organized graft on a massive scale.

There are numerous small private police forces employed by banks, department stores, hotels and similar institutions but assigned to them by the commercial police branch of the police force. The police assigned to department stores have the right to arrest debtors and keep them locked up in the stores until the debt is paid.

Recruitment, Education & Training

Recruitment has been a long-standing problem for the Mexican police. The General Directorate of Police and Traffic operates a Police Academy, where intensive courses of from four to six months are given to selected new recruits. The Federal Highway Police runs a small training school for its personnel. The Technical Institute of the Public Ministry was authorized by the Ministry of Public Education in 1974 to offer graduate-level courses in criminology. A few states have academies for state police; the best are those in the states of Nuevo León, Jalisco and Mexico. Courses at these academies usually last for four months. In cities and other localities where no formal academies exist, policemen are appointed by political bosses.

The Penal System

There are separate criminal codes and codes of criminal procedure for the Federal District and the individual states. The laws for the Federal District are also applicable to territories. Codes for the Federal District are sometimes referred to as federal codes, because they are applicable nationwide in some circumstances.

The Federal Criminal Code dates from 1931, with later amendments. It modernized the previous laws; singled out juvenile delinquency for special attention; and made new provisions for controlling traffic in narcotics and dealing with corruption, pandering and espionage. Crimes are broadly categorized as those against persons, those against property, those against the state, those against public morals and those against public health. Capital punishment was prohibited by the Federal Penal Code of 1931, and although the Constitution permits it for parricide, abduction and highway robbery, it does not require the penalty to be imposed. The next highest punishment is thirty years in prison, which may be imposed for kidnapping. Individual rights may not ordinarily be suspended but may, under special circumstances, be set aside temporarily. These circumstances are contained in Article 29 of the Constitution and are detailed in the Law of Social Dissolution, enacted in 1941. Amendments to the Federal Penal Code have dealt with sophisticated crimes, such as fraud or embezzlement. Mexico grants political and diplomatic asylum.

The most distinctive feature of the Mexican legal system is the writ of *amparo,* which has no exact English equivalent, although it is similar to a writ of habeas corpus. Considered Mexico's contribution to jurisprudence, it has been adopted in part by several other Latin American countries, and some of its provisions are included in Article 8 of the Universal Declaration of Human Rights.

The *amparo* doctrine stems from the Yucatán Constitution of 1841 and was incorporated in the 1847 Reform Act and amplified in the 1857 Constitution and the 1917 Constitution. An *amparo* may be sought by any citizen for the redress of an infringement of his or her civil rights, or against the act of any official, tribunal, police officer, legislature or bureaucrat. A writ of *amparo* is issued only by a federal judge except in emergencies, when a state judge is empowered to issue it. Writs of *amparo* take one of three forms: direct, indirect or constitutional. A direct *amparo* is brought against a judgment of any court or administrative tribunal and seeks a reversal of the decision based upon a denial of due process or a misapplication of the law to the facts in the particular case. Indirect *amparos* are used either against actions of, or to force actions by, nonjudicial authorities, such as the police. Such *amparos* closely resemble the writ of habeas corpus, a writ of mandamus or an injunction. Constitutional *amparo*, or *amparo* against the laws, permits individuals to enjoin the enforcement of a law against them on the grounds of a defect in the law. It does not attack the basic constitutionality of the law itself, and a decision favorable to the plaintiff is applicable only to the parties to the suit.

No class action suits are permissible, and each person aggrieved by a law must file a separate *amparo* for redress, as the defective law remains on the statute books until rescinded by the legislature. Judicial precedent may be established by a decision of the Supreme Court of Justice and becomes binding upon all lower courts and administrative tribunals.

Another distinctive feature of the Mexican penal system dating back to the 19th century is the Public Ministry, which exists at the federal, state and municipal levels. At the federal level, the Public Ministry is headed by an attorney general and performs both investigative and accusative functions. Agents of the Public Ministry, called *fiscales,* are charged with suppressing crime and initiating proceedings in criminal cases. Usually they are assigned to police stations to determine the facts of a given case. They turn over their findings to a central office, which determines whether to initiate prosecution in a criminal case. Public prosecutors are independent of the courts and may not be censured or guided by the judiciary. Since the Public Ministry represents the public, the office may not be sued by defendants if found innocent. Other functions of the Public Ministry are to serve as legal adviser to the executive branch and to command the Federal Judicial Police.

Except where the offender has been apprehended *in flagrante delicto,* when anyone can make an arrest, arrest and detention must be preceded by a warrant issued by a competent judicial authority. The accused is entitled to counsel from the moment of arrest, and detention cannot exceed three days without a formal order of commitment with the specification of charges. Except in cases of offenses that carry a prison term of more than five years as a penalty, bail is permitted. Detention awaiting trial may not exceed the maximum prison term applicable to the crime.

The Constitution requires federal and state governments to organize penal systems on the basis of rehabilitation and social readjustment of the prisoner through education and training. Prisons are divided into federal, state and municipal. Most states have an agreement by which state prisoners may serve in federal institutions.

The largest of the federal prisons are the Penitentiary for the Sentenced; the Lecumberri Penitentiary, or the Preventive Jail of the City where detainees and those under trial are housed; and the Women's Jail. The Federal District also contains four centers of reclusion; three small jails; and 13 jails in the various *comandancias.* There are two federal penal colonies, where the most dangerous criminals and those serving long sentences are placed. The most infamous of these is in the Maria Islands, about 70 miles offshore, in the Pacific Ocean. Married prisoners are permitted to have their families with them and are provided with thatched houses. Unmarried prisoners live in dormitories. All can move freely on the main island but must attend roll call twice daily. Prisoners work to develop the island's resources and work in lime quarries, salt fields, lumber mills, on sisal plantations and in workshops, or engage in agricultural pursuits and cattle raising.

All states have state penitentiaries. Some are old and overcrowded, while others are modern and fairly large. Among the best are those in Sonora, Durango, Michoacán, Jalisco and Mexico. Many of them have large staffs, including psychologists, psychiatrists and other doctors. Every prisoner either works in the shops or on the prison farm or goes to school. Municipal prisons numbered over 2,500 in the mid-1980s. While some are fairly large and have separate sections for women and children, others are primitive, have little or no rehabilitative activities, and lack toilet and water facilities. In some villages, the prisoners work on such public projects as street cleaning and gardening.

Life in Mexican prisons and jails generally is less grim than in other countries. Little friction exists between prisoners and guards, and the guards themselves perform small services for the prisoners in return for tips. Prisoners with skills are permitted to make items and sell them, while others engage in such services as barbering and shoe repairing. Prisoners who can afford it furnish their own quarters and have their own personal servants. Some prisons permit commercial workshops to operate on their premises.

Prisoners usually are on their own during the day to work, loaf or engage in sports or games, as most penal institutions do not have full-time organized activities. There are intramural leagues for baseball or soccer, with daily games. Idle inmates frequently fight among themselves. Families and other relatives usually are permitted to visit twice a week, Sunday being one of the days set aside for such visits. In women's prisons and in women's sections of state prisons, mothers are permitted to have their small children with them at all times.

Male inmates have the right to conjugal visits. Wives usually are permitted to spend up to two hours every two weeks alone with their husbands. Some prisons permit wives to spend the entire night with their husbands, and in others girlfriends or prostitutes are allowed to visit single inmates. No conjugal visits, however, are permitted women inmates. Only fathers or brothers may be alone with them. Prisoners nearing the end of their sentences are permitted to spend weekends with their families.

Although the media are full of lurid crime stories, complete statistical data are not available on the incidence of crime. Data on minor infractions are not compiled, and many crimes do not go through formal judicial procedures, such as those dealt with by the private police. The leading crimes are assault and battery against persons, accounting for 32% of the total; robbery, 25%; homicides, 15%, sex-related crimes, 6%; property damage, 3%; fraud, 2%; and embezzlement, under 2%. Cattle rustling still is reported in the countryside. Kidnappings are reportedly on the increase, partly by dissident political groups and partly by common criminals. Drug abuse and narcotics traffic emerged in the 1970s as the nation's leading crime problem, involving both domestic use and smuggling into the United States. Mexican police and Army elements annually destroy thousands of acres of marijuana and opium poppies, but farmers still manage to grow them in isolated mountain areas or even scattered throughout their cornfields. Shootouts between the police and narcotics pushers are frequently reported in the press.

Crimes committed by juveniles generally occur in urban areas, and there is little juvenile crime reported in rural areas or small towns. There are many youth gangs in Mexico City and other urban areas, and almost every secondary school has one. Professional thieves specialize in house burglary and in picking pockets, usually during the numerous fiestas.

In rural areas, the most prevalent crimes are injuries or homicides, usually as a result of drunkenness. Violent crimes by peasants are related to land disputes, water rights, family feuds and insults to women. The weapon usually is a machete, knife or dagger. Few rural crimes occur during daytime; most take place during nights or on weekends and holidays.

Automobile accidents are classified as crimes in the Penal Code, and drivers usually are held by the police. However, the automobile accident rate in Mexico is the second lowest in the Western Hemisphere, and the death rate from motor vehicle accidents is also extremely low: only two per 1,000 vehicles per year.

Males make up 92% of criminals, leading in every category of crime. Prostitution is not illegal in Mexico, but soliciting clients is. Prostitutes must be registered and periodically examined, and sent to hospitals for treatment if found diseased. Most prostitutes, however, do not register and choose to practice their trade illegally.

Two areas of the country with the highest incidence of crime are the state of Guerrero and the city of Netzahualcoyotl, which is part of the metropolitan area of the Federal District. Acapulco is in Guerrero.

MONGOLIA

BASIC FACT SHEET

Official Name: Mongolian People's Republic
Area: 1,564,619 sq km
Population: 2,011,066 (1987)
Capital: Ulan Baatar
Nature of Government: Communist dictatorship
Language: Mongolian
Currency: Tugrik
GNP: $1.2 billion (1985)
Territorial Divisions: 18 provinces
Population per Police Officer: 120
Police Expenditures per 1,000: N.A.

Structure & Organization

The Mongolian police system comprises the Militia and auxiliary law enforcement groups, all under the Ministry of Public Security. The ministry, a successor to the old Office of State Security, is responsible for a broad range of functions, including the issuance of internal passports (necessary for traveling within the country), fire fighting, traffic control and police administration.

The Militia has a department in each *aimak* (province) and an office in each district. The Militia also conducts criminal investigation under the supervision of procurators. Militia organs, together with local *khurrals* (councils, equivalent to soviets), administer compulsory labor sentences of convicted criminals. The Central Militia Office has a Motor Vehicle Inspection Bureau. Militiamen direct motor traffic and are stationed along railroads.

The Militia includes four battalions of security police and five battalions of frontier guards.

In a number of towns, police brigades exist as auxiliaries to help the Militia in crime detection and prevention. These activist public group personnel also function as deputy sheriffs and special policemen. The most important of these bodies are the Crime Fighting and Crime Prevention Councils, which are voluntary and informal party organizations operating without paid staff. These councils are strictly advisory bodies set up to implement the anticrime decisions of the Politburo. The councils study the problem of crime, work closely with local *khurrals* and public officials fighting crime, and conduct anticrime propaganda through the local media.

The Ulan Baatar Railway Administration has a mounted police patrolling the tracks for roaming livestock.

Recruitment, Education & Training

No information is available on recruitment, education and training.

Penal System

The legal basis for the criminal justice system is the 1961 Criminal Code. According to the code, crimes committed against the state are considered more serious than crimes against persons. Close attention is given in the code to equal rights for women.

The death penalty may be imposed for treason, espionage, public subversion, murder and armed banditry. Prison sentences generally are limited to terms from six months to 10 years, but repeated criminal acts may be punished by prison terms as high as 15 years, the maximum. Probation is permissible, and pardons often are granted. There are statutes of limitations for most crimes.

Mongolia maintains both prison camps and "correctional" or "educational" colonies. There are also detention camps for minor offenders, designed to rehabilitate them by "socially useful labor." Those performing such labor receive neither wages nor food; they must purchase their food or depend on their families to provide it. Local jails exist for brief detentions (24 hours or less) of intoxicated persons or those awaiting indictment.

Antisocialist crimes dominate the police blotters in the country. These crimes include sloth and lack of responsibility toward the protection and conservation of public property, mismanagement of public enterprises, misappropriating, stealing and embezzling public property, negligence, loose work discipline, abuse of authority, racketeering, inefficiency, and speculation.

Mongolians have traditionally considered heavy drinking (especially of the fermented mare's milk brewed by all herdsmen) as at best an amiable failing, but the regime has long waged a losing war against its prevalence. The state is concerned about the criminal fallout of alcoholism and public displays of intoxication, which are embarrassing for a socialist society. Violations of public order while drunk are dealt with severely in the Penal Code.

According to a Communist Party statement, "the rate of crime and offenses among juveniles is considerable." Vandalism and hooliganism are among the crimes most frequently attributed to juveniles. Juvenile criminal activity is believed to stem from a loosening of marriage and family relationships and a consequent increase in the number of broken homes.

MOROCCO

Structure & Organization

Primary responsibility for the maintenance of law and order and for conducting internal security operations is exercised jointly by the country's three separate police organizations: the Sûreté Nationale, the Royal Gendarmerie and the Auxiliary Forces. The Royal Moroccan Army (Forces Armées Royales, FAR) backs up the police in quelling internal disorders. All the three police organizations are modeled on their French counterparts, and all are regarded as paramilitary organizations.

The Royal Gendarmerie is under the operational control of the FAR, and the Auxiliary Forces are attached to the Ministry of the Interior. The Sûreté, under the command and control of a director general, is an autonomous unit with its own responsibility for administrative, operational and financial matters. Although all three are supervised from the top by the prime minister, they are nonetheless directly responsible to the monarch. The commanders of these organizations are personally appointed by the king, who has to approve all major policy decisions. The overlapping of operational functions among the three is maintained deliberately to preclude any possible threat to the throne from any one element.

The Sûreté Nationale, with headquarters in Rabat, exercises primary police authority in the principal urban centers and in certain towns. It shares the patrolling of highways with the Royal Gendarmerie and responsibility for frontier security with the FAR, the Gendarmerie and the Auxiliary Forces. As the national agency for countersubversion, it conducts overt and clandestine operations nationwide. Because of this responsibility, it maintains careful surveillance of foreigners in the country and assists in certain aspects of immigration and emigration control and customs.

The Sûreté Nationale was established by a royal *dahir* (decree) in 1956. It was subordinate to the Ministry of the Interior and commanded by a director general. Its structure, procedures and operational concepts are more French than Moroccan. Except for two reorganizations, the Sûreté has existed without any major modification of its structure and responsibilities. During the period after the disastrous Casablanca riots of 1965, the Sûreté was removed from the Ministry of the Interior and made autonomous, answerable only to the king.

For administrative purposes, the Sûreté Nationale has six subdirectorates: Administration, Public Safety, National Security, Documentation and Regulatory Control, Judicial Police, and Inspectorate and Training. It employs four basic police units: the Urban Corps, the Mobile Intervention Companies, the Judiciary Police and the International Security Service. The country is divided into 10 regions (confusingly, each is called a *sûreté*), each under the command of a commissioner.

The uniformed Urban Corps, the largest of the Sûreté elements, provides most of the police services in the cities and major towns. Routinely armed with automatic pistols and rubber billy clubs, the Urban Corps policemen perform foot, bicycle, motorcycle and automobile patrols. They work in pairs in foot beats and when patrolling in automobiles. They man traffic control stations and provide crowd control. In some cases the Mobile Intervention Companies augment the Urban Corps, and the Urban Corps augment

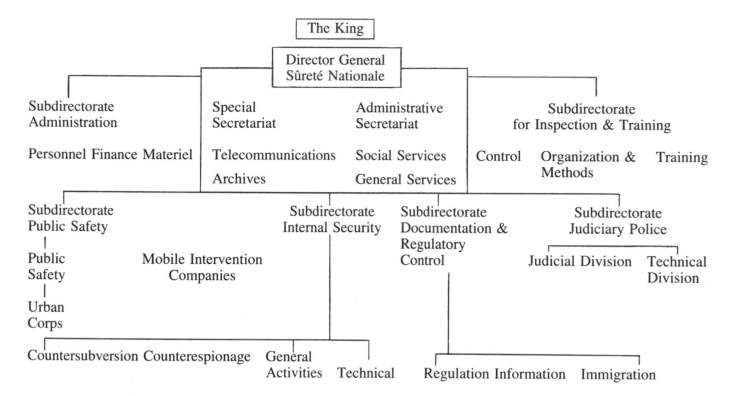

The King

Director General
Sûreté Nationale

| Subdirectorate Administration | Special Secretariat | Administrative Secretariat | Subdirectorate for Inspection & Training |

Personnel Finance Materiel   Telecommunications   Social Services   Control   Organization & Methods   Training

Archives   General Services

| Subdirectorate Public Safety | Subdirectorate Internal Security | Subdirectorate Documentation & Regulatory Control | Subdirectorate Judiciary Police |

Public Safety   Mobile Intervention Companies   Judicial Division   Technical Division

Urban Corps

Countersubversion Counterespionage   General Activities   Technical   Regulation Information   Immigration

the Judicial Police. In time of riots the Urban Corps is provided with steel and plastic helmets, service pistols, submachine guns, rifles and tear gas grenades.

The Mobile Intervention Companies (Compagnies Mobiles pour l'Intervention, CMI) is a uniformed and motorized police unit. Its major mission includes riot control, policing public functions and providing emergency services in times of civil disasters or natural catastrophes. With the Royal Gendarmerie, it patrols the major highways. Motorcycle CMI companies serve as guard of honor for dignitaries. The CMI is deployed in Rabat, Casablanca, Fez, Marrakech, Meknès, Oujda and Tétouan. The force is armed with rifles, submachine guns, automatic rifles, tear gas grenades and water-pump trucks.

Criminal investigation is the responsibility of the Judicial Police. All nonuniformed employees of the Sûreté are certified to act as Judicial Police officials. Its range of operations covers the entire range of criminal offenses and includes arrest. It acts in criminal cases under the technical direction of the prosecutor and his deputies. In such cases it functions as an arm of the court system.

The least publicized element of the Sûreté is the Subdirectorate for Internal Security, which is the police intelligence service. It is under the direct supervision of the director general, and most of its operations are clandestine. It does not make arrests, but it passes on its information to the Judicial Police for follow-up, arrest and prosecution.

The Countersubversion Section of Subdirectorate for Internal Security is organized to deal with Com-

munist, labor union and political party affairs. The Counterespionage Section is concerned with the activities of foreign embassies, trade missions, and commercial enterprises and associations. All other matters of internal security concerns are assigned to the General Activities Section. The three investigative sections are supported by the Technical Section, which provides communications and technological capabilities. The section uses boats, light aircraft and helicopters.

The Sûreté plays an important role in immigration and emigration control, through the Immigration Division of the Subdirectorate for General Documentation and Regulatory Control. The division issues bulletins concerning the arrivals and departures of certain categories of aliens; maintains lists of persons denied entry; monitors movements of foreign vessels and aircraft in Moroccan air and sea space; expels undesirable aliens; scrutinizes requests for visas and work permits; and keeps records of foreigners who die in Morocco, children born of foreign parents and marriages between Moroccans and foreigners. The Customs Service is a separate department operated by the Ministry of the Interior, but the Sûreté works in close cooperation with it.

The Royal Gendarmerie is the main rural police unit. Its commander and many, if not most, of its upper- and middle-level leaders are Army officers. The remainder of its personnel are volunteers who have elected to serve five-year tours of duty. Total personnel strength was estimated in the mid-1980s at 15,000. Technically, the Gendarmerie is under the operational control of the FAR, but in practice it is supervised personally by the king.

In addition to its general mission of enforcing public order, the Gendarmerie provides assistance and support to other government agencies: It serves as the FAR military police, as the Ministry of Education by checking on truant children in rural areas, as the Ministry of Finance by collecting unpaid taxes in rural areas and as the Ministry of Transportation by collecting highway and automobile statistics.

With national headquarters in Rabat, the Gendarmerie is organized into companies that are deployed throughout the country. The companies are in turn subdivided into sections and brigades, the latter being its basic operating unit. The motorcycle brigades share responsibility for highway traffic control with the CMI. Jeep-mounted brigades are employed in patrolling segments of rural territory, and dismounted brigades man police posts in the small villages. The centrally located Mobile Group of the Gendarmerie is maintained for rapid response deployment to assist in riot control and other special emergencies.

After coup attempts by elements of the Army and Air Force in 1971 and 1972, King Hassan began to build up the Gendarmerie as a counterpoise to the FAR. The Mobile Group was expanded by two new companies, and the regular force was expanded by five new territorial brigades, one additional brigade to assist the Judicial Police, one parachute squadron, air and maritime units, and four new armories.

The Auxiliary Forces consist of provincial and municipal guards—collectively referred to as the Administrative Maghzani and a contingent known as the Mobile Maghzani. In some other countries this force would be termed the national guard. They operate under civil administrative authorities at local levels, and by an inspector general of the Ministry of the Interior at the national level.

Military in character, the nonuniformed Administrative Maghzani are recruited from local areas to which they are assigned. Many of its members are Army or Gendarmerie retirees who have some military experience but little, if any, instruction in law enforcement duties. When assigned to a province, they are under the command of a governor. Their responsibilities include guarding buildings, bridges, patrolling *souks* or markets, serving as arbitrators in the frequent water and grazing disputes, and assisting the uniformed police forces whenever needed.

To the extent that it is armed, the Administrative Maghzani is equipped with sidearms, rifles of World War II vintage, and rubber billy clubs. It has a limited number of motor vehicles, but some units still use camels for patrolling desert areas.

The larger Mobile Maghzani is a well-equipped paramilitary force. Its companies, each about 150 officers and men, are motorized and are specifically trained to control riots and put down disorders. These company-size units are deployed throughout the country, at least one in each of the provinces, and others near major population centers. Its two principal missions are patrolling the key border areas and rapid intervention in situations beyond the capabilities of the other branches of the police. The companies are controlled operationally by the provincial and prefectural governors, but when employed in intervention forces, they are under the operational control of the Sûreté chief in urban areas and the Gendarmerie commander in rural areas. Both in armament and transport, they are far superior to their Administrative Maghzani counterparts.

Except for the plainclothes investigation police, others enjoy a relative degree of public confidence. Tourists in Morocco speak favorably of the efficiency and courtesy of the policemen they encounter. Nevertheless, there are confirmed reports of the use of torture by the Judicial Police during interrogation of suspects at police detention centers.

Recruitment, Education & Training

Entrance into the Sûreté is through competitive examinations. Recruits must be fluent in Arabic or French, be of good moral character free from police record, be between the ages of 21 and 35 and have at least primary-school education.

Until about 1970 the uniformed police were mostly illiterate and untrained because of poor pay, poor service conditions, long working hours and limited opportunities for advancement. Following the military-inspired coups of 1971 and 1972, the king initiated a number of reforms to bring the police forces to a level comparable to that of the FAR in pay, fringe benefits and quality of personnel. In addition to a salary commensurate with those paid to other civil servants, the police receive subsidized housing, a family allowance, a hazardous-duty allowance and overtime. In addition, there are medical centers for police personnel and their families and hospital insurance, pension plan and disability coverage.

Initially, police personnel were trained either on the job or in French, West German, British or U.S. police academies. With French assistance, training facilities were established at two sites in Morocco: Sidi Otmane, near Casablanca; and Salé, on the outskirts of Rabat. The former is the general training school; the latter, a specialized training school. In 1965 the National Police Academy was established near Meknès.

Officer training is conducted at the Royal Military Academy near Meknès and the Royal Gendarmerie School for Professional Training in Marrakech. There are regional training centers for specialized training of NCO's.

The Penal System

The Moroccan Penal Code consists of three books containing 600 articles. Not surprisingly, the document reflects strongly the legal traditions of France as well as Morocco's Islamic heritage. Offenses against the law are divided into four categories: *crimes, délits, délits de police,* and *contraventions,* corresponding to felonies, correctional misdemeanors, less serious misdemeanors, and minor violations, respectively, in English law. Offenses are grouped as those against state security; those interfering with the rights and liberties of other citizens; forgery and counterfeiting; acts against public order; and violations against public security, persons, property, the family and public morality. The code differentiates specifically between violations against public order committed by civil servants and those committed by other citizens. Somewhat unique in French-derived criminal law, however, are the sections of the code designed to protect the monarchy and the Islamic religious system, in Articles 163 throught 180. Articles 201 through 212 relate to the national security of the state and provide very harsh penalties by Western standards. The death penalty is prescribed for a number of offenses, mostly political.

Rounding out the statutory basis of the Moroccan criminal justice system is the 1959 Code of Criminal Procedure, consisting of seven books with 772 articles. The accused is granted the right to legal counsel and is not to be held in policy custody longer than 48 hours without indictment, with a possible extension of another 48 hours.

On independence the reponsibility for prisons was transferred from the police to the Ministry of Justice. The ministry's Department of Penitentiary Administration operates 34 prisons and correctional institutions, including central prisons at Rabat, Meknès, Fez, Settat, Oujda, Marrakech, Kenitra, Casablanca, and Tagounite. Prison Ain Borja and Prison Civile in Casablanca and Prison Centrale in Kenitra are maximum-security institutions; the remainder are medium-security institutions. There is one juvenile correctional institution, at Kenitra.

According to Amnesty International, political prisoners are held incommunicado in special detention centers for periods ranging from six months to two years while undergoing interrogation. Amnesty International identifies the location of seven large detention centers: two in the vicinity of Casablanca; one in the Mulay Cherif area; another in the old workshops that serve domestic flights in Anfa Airport; one at Dar el Mokri near Rabat; one south of Kenitra on the road to Rabat; and one near Oujda, in the far northeastern area, near the Algerian border. French sources cite the existence of similar detention facilities at police villages in Agudal, on the Romani Road near the capital; and on Imam Malik Street in Marrakech. Further, they report prison camps at Assa near the Draa River in the southwest and at phosphate quarries in the central part of the country.

Published statistics indicate that the actual prison population is five to 10 times its designed capacity. As a result, sanitary and medical facilities are poor, and bedding and other amenities are in short supply.

Inmates of central prisons are permitted visits from their lawyers and families, who are allowed to bring food to supplement skimpy rations. Letters and books also are permitted, although subject to censorship. Students are permitted to continue their academic studies while serving sentences. Largely because of overcrowding, inmates usually are given only one hour each morning and afternoon for exercise in the prison yard. There are reports of periodic hunger strikes by prisoners, some of them lasting over a month, in protest against prison conditions. Again, according to Amnesty International, a number of prisoners have died from torture, and others have been physically and mentally disabled through abuse by jailers.

In the absence of official statistics, the scope of crime in Morocco is a matter of conjecture. Unlike in most Western nations, there is no distinction between political crimes and "ordinary crimes," as both are violations of the Penal Code. Further, the reporting system on crime is, perhaps deliberately, incomplete, and designed to make the incidence of crime appear less than it really is.

The crime rate varies from city to city. Most reported crimes consist of offenses against persons, property and public morals. A relatively low number of homicides are reported, and a high percentage are cleared by arrest. Crimes against property have increased, but only a small portion are cleared by arrest. Possibly many crimes against property are not reported to the police.

There are other kinds of crimes—prostitution, vagrancy and drug abuse—that are not reported to the police as a rule but nevertheless tax police capabilities. Prostitution is illegal, although certain brothels are permitted to operate. Begging also is illegal, and thousands of beggars are arrested each year. Drug abuse—particularly traffic in *kif* or hashish—is a growing and intractable problem. Much of it is cultivated openly in the Rif area. Police permissiveness soon gave rise to hashish trafficking on a scale that came to be known as the Moroccan Drug Ring. By 1975 the ring had reached England, where Scotland Yard is reported to have broken up one group. Moroccan police permitted tourists and others to leave the country with large amounts of hashish, thus transferring the responsibility for control of the illegal substance to officials at the foreign ports of entry. The drug traffic also generates a system of payoffs—called *bakshish* in Arabic—involving officials up to the royal court.

One factor that keeps serious crime in the country at an acceptable level is the strict gun control law, which is enforced conscientiously. The law permits only the police and the uniformed armed forces to possess pistols, revolvers, rifles, automatic weapons and military ordnance. The Penal Code prohibits the sale and possession by private individuals of firearms with rifled barrels and the ammunition used in such weapons. Shotguns of 12, 16 and 20 gauges are permitted for sportsmen, but owners must register them with the police and obtain a permit for carrying them.

CRIME STATISTICS (1983)

		Number Reported	Attempts %	Cases Solved %	Crime per 100,000	Offenders	Females %	Juveniles %	Strangers %
1.	Murder	156		96.15	0.78	282	6.73	6.38	
2.	Sex offenses, including rape	5,214		100.00	26.07	6,599	92.31	0.02	
3.	Rape	683		106.88	3.41	888	4.16	1.23	
4.	Serious assault	34,084		88.53	170.42	53,300	27.87	3.86	
5.	All theft	43,337		72.47	216.69	46,040	3.84	2.67	
6.	Aggravated theft	17,580		68.49	87.90	3,381	2.89	0.11	
7.	Robbery and violent theft	12,022		43.94	60.11	534	11.61	5.05	
8.	Breaking and entering								
9.	Auto theft								
10.	Other thefts	25,757		51.88	128.78	13,367	8.88	7.58	
11.	Fraud	1,243		91.39	6.21	1,088	5.42	0.27	
12.	Counterfeiting	140		11.42	0.70	126			
13.	Drug offenses	4,973		100.00	24.86	6,661	2.14	0.09	
14.	Total offenses	143,747		82.82	718.73	150,029	22.34	3.74	

Note: Information for some categories is not available.
Criteria of juveniles: aged from 12 to 18 years.

MOZAMBIQUE

BASIC FACT SHEET

Official Name: People's Republic of Mozambique
Area: 783,030 sq km
Population: 14,535,805 (1987)
Capital: Maputo
Nature of Government: Communist dictatorship
Language: Portuguese
Currency: Metical
GNP: $2 billion (1985)
Territorial Divisions: 10 provinces, 112 districts
Population per Police Officer: N.A.
Police Expenditures per 1,000: N.A.

History & Background

Lawlessness was a standard feature of life in Mozambique as it was evacuated by Portuguese before independence. Initially, FRELIMO (Frente de Libertaçao de Mocambique) troops were allowed to make arrests, a right that most of these troops abused. According to some reports, the country became a police state. In 1975 thousands were arrested in a series of police sweeps aimed not only at suspected alcoholics, prostitutes, vagrants and common criminals but also at religious leaders. Those arrested were sent to five reeducation camps. The Public Security Force, the nation's first national police force, was formed in February 1975. Eight months later, it was transformed into the National Service of Popular Security (Servico Nacional de Seguranca Popular, SNASP). It was responsible only to the president of the republic. A parallel organization was set up, the Mozambique Police Corps (Corps Policial de Mocambique, CPM), supplemented by the Criminal Investigation Police (Policia de Investigaçao Criminal, PIC) and the Fiscal Guards, which comprised customs, immigration and port police.

Structure & Organization

President Machel promulgated new regulations for the police in 1976. To reduce the abuse of police powers, only those caught in the act of committing a crime could be arrested, and it could be made only by the proper authorities. Suspects could be held only for 24 hours without trial. Most persons arrested for minor crimes were sent to reeducation camps, officially known as Mental Decolonization Centers (Centros de Descolonizaçao Mental). Vigilance groups under SNASP control keep an eye on counterrevolutionary activities in urban areas.

Recruitment, Education & Training

No current information is available.

The Penal System

No current information is available.

NEPAL

BASIC FACT SHEET

Official Name: Kingdom of Nepal
Area: 140,791 sq km
Population: 17,814,294 (1987)
Capital: Katmandu
Nature of Government: Absolute monarchy
Language: Nepali
Currency: Rupee
GNP: $2.61 billion (1985)
Territorial Divisions: 75 districts, 14 zones
Population per Police Officer: 1,000
Police Expenditures per 1,000: $497

History & Background

Until the middle of the 19th century, police and judicial functions in many areas of Nepal were in the hands of the local princes *(rajas),* who were virtual autocrats. In the villages, headmen and village councils maintained order, but the scope of their police activities varied with local customs. Generally, justice was capricious and punishments harsh. For certain crimes, the plaintiff could summarily execute the offender. Torture by fire, water or mutilation was not abolished until 1851. Court sentences and police powers were influenced by the caste and social standing of the offenders. Brahmins and women were exempted from capital punishment.

Generally, the mountain people resisted attempts by the central government to encroach on their traditional autonomy. In other areas, a few locally recruited policemen were occasionally supplemented by small detachments of the royal police forces.

The Ranas did not establish a nationwide police system, but Prime Minister (Maharaja) Chandra Shamsher Rana, who ruled from 1901 to 1929, partly modernized the police forces in the capital, Katmandu. Villages, however, were expected to police themselves. The militia exercised some police functions, although their main mission was to protect the people from the bands of bandits, known as *dacoits,* common in the Tarai border area.

One result of the 1950–51 revolt against the Ranas was the creation of the Raksha Dal, a paramilitary body of some 5,000 men belonging to the military arm of the Nepali Congress, taken over by the government and invested with police functions. By 1953 approximately 23,500 men were engaged in police functions, divided into five organizations: the Civil Police (2,000), the Raksha Dal (5,000), the Randal or the Katmandu Police (500), the militia (15,000) and military detachments attached to police posts (1,000). In theory, the minister of home affairs had authority over all police forces in the country.

A series of events between 1952 and 1954 shook the fledgling police forces. In 1952, the Raksha Dal supported Kunwar Indrajit Singh in his uprising. A year later, a police-inspired plot to overthrow the government was uncovered. More than 80 police officials were arrested, and the inspector general of police was forced to resign. In the rural areas the police were totally ineffective against better-organized political party activists.

In 1952 the government acted to modernize the police system with Indian assistance. A police training school was founded at Bhimphedi, southwest of Katmandu. The five groups performing police functions were replaced by a single group under central government control. The militia was disbanded and reorganized as a "road army" to help build roads. Military detachments doing police duties were returned to their military units. The Civil Police, Raksha Dal and Randal were merged into a single force of some 7,500 officers and men. The pay and allowances of the force were raised. The 1955 Nepalese Police Act may be said to mark the beginning of the modern police system in Nepal.

Structure & Organization

In accordance with the Nepalese Police Act, the country is divided into three zones (or ranges): eastern, central and western, with headquarters at Biratnagar

(Eastern Tarai), Katmandu (Katmandu Valley), and Nepalganj (Far Western Tarai), respectively. Each zonal headquarters, under a deputy inspector general of police, is responsible for several subsections, composed of four or five police districts operating under a superintendent of police. Each station normally is headed by a head constable. He is in charge of several constables, who perform the basic police functions. Each constable customarily is responsible for three or four villages. The overall system includes 21 district police inspectors, guards for the 32 *bada hakim* (governor) offices, 43 tax collection offices and personnel for 291 outposts. The Central Police headquarters, under an inspector general of police, is under the Ministry of Home Affairs. The headquarters comprises the Criminal Investigation Division, Intelligence, Counterespionage, Traffic and Radio sections, the Traffic Police Company, the Central Training Center and a band.

Recruitment, Education & Training

No current information is available.

The Penal System

The penal system consists of the central prison at Katmandu and at least one jail in the district capitals, all administered by the Ministry of Home Affairs.

In 1953 the prison system was reformed with the introduction of medical treatment, recreational facilities, and visiting permission for relatives. The Cottage Industries Department supervises the operation of workshops.

The highest judicial penalty is the death sentence, which may be imposed only for treason. Less serious crimes include cow slaughter, propagation of atheism and attempting to convert Hindus to Christianity.

NETHERLANDS

F. Perrick

BASIC FACT SHEET

Official Name: Kingdom of the Netherlands
Area: 40,844 sq km
Population: 14,641,554 (1987)
Capital: Amsterdam; The Hague (seat of government)
Nature of Government: Constitutional monarchy
Language: Dutch
Currency: Guilder
GNP: $132.92 billion (1985)
Territorial Divisions: 11 provinces
Population per Police Officer: 410
Police Expenditures per 1,000: $100,727

History & Background

Two foreign occupations of the Netherlands have been of fundamental influence, both positive and negative, in the development of the Dutch police.

First the French occupation (1795–1813), from which the Netherlands rose as a unified state and during which time the modern police system began; and second the German occupation (1940–45), which resulted in the necessity for drastic changes in the system.

Before the French occupation of the United Netherlands, police affairs were a matter for local administration and the courts. After the occupation, during which the police in the Netherlands were a part of the French state police, the city police forces were revived, but their function, though locally performed, was not completely municipal even though the lines of organization were not drawn. This arrangement resulted from the French-inspired judicial organization in which the prosecuting office is attached to the courts under the authority of the minister of justice. As a result, city police forces, so far as the detection of crime is concerned, are responsible to and fall under the authority of the public prosecutor.

Another new force besides the city police, a statewide military force, originated with police authority (at first called the Force Marechaussee, it was later called Wapen der Koninklijke Marechaussee) in Belgium, with which the Netherlands was united. It came into being in 1814 to replace the French Gendarmerie, which had returned to France.

At first these forces worked only in the South, but later they were spread thinly (in the 1930s there were approximately 1,250 personnel) over the Netherlands and were charged with civil police services. As far as organization and management were concerned, the Force Marechaussee fell under the minister of war, and where the police service was concerned, under the minister of justice. In about 1850, the system was overhauled; the result was the anchoring of the city police force in the Municipal Act of 1851, and the creation of a civil police force under the authority of the minister of justice. Called Het Korps Rijkveldwacht, it was started on January 1, 1858, and by the Second World War consisted of 1,260 men.

Several attempts to unify the forces have failed. In fact, until the German invasion in 1940, three kinds of police functioned side by side. The city police, based on the Municipal Act of 1851 and regulated by municipal bylaws, functioned in nearly all communities—in the towns in the form of forces, and in the country villages in the form of one or more police officials *(gemeenteveldwachters)*.

Besides the city police force there were two state police forces of restricted strength—the military Marechaussee and the civil Rijkveldwacht—and in the cities, especially in the years of crisis before World War II, representatives of the police troops (Korps Politietroepen), which had been formed in 1918 to replace the Koninklijke Marechaussee in military duty. This force was an Army unit of never more than 700 men who assisted the police, especially in cases of large disturbances. This situation, in which several kinds of police forces existed, covering the same territory and performing the same functions and competing with each other, though under different management and authority and governed by different regulations, brought forth in the Netherlands the "police question" (politie vraagstuk).

In the meantime, there has been much change, especially since the German occupation. The Germans tried to capitalize on the deep dissatisfaction that existed because of the police question, and they used the situation in an attempt to bring the Dutch police into a unified organization. Formally, however, the German attempt came too late in the occupation and met too much resistence by police personnel to have any influence.

The organizational chaos that the Germans left behind after the liberation forced very serious attention to the problem of the police. This began in 1945 by a royal order of the council (politiebesluit), which was later made into the Police Act of 1957, the first legal regulation of the whole police in the history of the Netherlands.

Although it did not bring the unity that many people had hoped for, this act, which is still in effect, brought many improvements, and it focused on the following main issues:

There were only two kinds of police: the city police forces (gemeentepolitie) appointed by the crown in urban communities (with 25,000 or more inhabitants); and one statewide police force, the State Police (Het Korps Rijkspolitie) in other areas, under the authority of the minister of justice.

Although the city police and the state police are divided as far as organization and functions are concerned, nevertheless they form together the regular Dutch civil police.

The Koninklijke Marechaussee, which has again been revived as a military police unit of the Army, has lost its prewar civil police duties nearly completely and is only mentioned in the act as a body of assistance for "special occasions."

The Police Act, for the first time, gives a general and good description of police duties: to take care of the actual maintenance of law and order and to render assistance to those who need it.

In the leadership of the police a distinction is made between management and authority. Management of the city police forces is based on a partnership between the state and the communities so that daily management falls under the mayor (who appoints, suspends and dismisses all police officials, with the exception of chief commissioners, and commissioners who are appointed by the crown) and a removed management (which handles determination of strength, formation, general legal status, recruiting, education and financing) falls under the minister of the interior.

Authority and management of the state police fall under the minister of justice, but the commanding officers are appointed by the crown.

Especially important is the fact that the postwar police regulations have made a completely unified body. As far as authority is concerned, the police (and in this case there is no difference between city and state police) fall under the authority of the mayor for maintenance of law and order and under the public prosecutor for detection of crimes and execution of sentences.

The Police Act corrected the many shortcomings of the prewar days. But it did not solve the "police question" or dualism—on the one side, the organization and management, and on the other, the question of authority—both of which have continued to resist efforts of reformers.

The tasks the police had to face in the turbulent years of the 1960s revealed a number of failures. In 1969 a preliminary bill for a new Police Act with several improvements for efficiency seemed likely, but this bill was immediately rejected because it maintained the dualism in organization and management. Since that time, Parliament has spent four years studying a government paper. As a result, a new bill for a new Police Act has recently been presented to Parliament.

Structure & Organization

The regular police comprise two main groups: the city police forces, under the authority of the interior administration (the minister of the interior, the mayors, the governors of the queen); and the state police, under the minister of justice. Their total strength, including clerical and technical personnel, is 34,510 people, approximately one official for each 410 subjects. The city police has approximately twice the size of the state police.

The City Police
The city police is the largest and oldest part of the regular police and is spread over 141 more or less autonomous urban communities. The total strength is approximately 22,670 people; the forces vary from 3,200 in Amsterdam to as few as 37 in 12 of the smallest city police force communities. Of the 141 forces, only 12 have a strength of more than 300 and no less than 97 have a strength of less than 100 officials. Present standards for reasonable and independent functioning require a minimal strength of approximately 500 people, and only the five largest cities have forces of that size.

In the communities with city police forces, the population density is 904 persons per square kilometer. The total number of commanding officers in the city police is approximately 650, of whom about 30 have a university degree. The number of women police is 660. Thirty-two women are commanding officers.

General management authority of the city police is formally in the hands of the mayor, who is appointed by the crown for six years. The mayor is the chairman of the council and forms with the aldermen the daily administration of the community. The mayor is in independent charge of the police management, although he is responsible to the council for his actions.

The actual management of the city police is really a partnership between the state and the community; this means that the state regulates the legal position and other administration affairs, determines the strength and pays the cost. The community, on the other hand, and especially the mayor, is in charge of applying central regulations locally. Thus the mayor has a very strong role in the management of personnel and matériel and appoints, promotes and dismisses all police officers with the exception of the commissioners appointed by the crown. The mayor is formally responsible to the council for all his actions.

Daily management and administration of the city police is in the hands of the chief of police. This is always a police officer. In communities of 40,000 or more inhabitants (there are 67 such communities), this person has the rank of commissioner (comparable to a major or lieutenant colonel in the Army). In communities of 125,000 or more inhabitants, the chief of police has the rank of chief commissioner.

Within their jurisdictions, the city police forces are autonomous, which means in principle that they exclusively perform the police duties in their communities. This rule has a few exceptions in emergencies, as declared in the Police Act. Such rules are related to the function of the state police or statewide services and the rendering of assistance when needed.

The city police also have two other groups of officials. The first are the so-called unpaid officials *(onbezoldigde ambtonaron),* who are mostly not police at all but other public functionaries or sometimes civilians. The total number of these officials (no exact data regarding them are known) is approximately 3,500. Also in this group is a growing number of so-called social detectives, who are officials in charge of preventing the misuse of public security measures.

In the second category are the reserve police, an institution that originated in 1948 as a result of the Communist seizure of power in Czechoslovakia. Civilians can be appointed to this force, either in the city police or the state police; and the reserve police, besides other functions, have to assist other legal authorities, especially the regular police, in cases of subversive activities. The members also are meant to assist the regular police in event of war and in all other calamities. Usually the reservists, who are uni-formed and armed in the manner of the regular police, perform under the authority of the regular police. The reservists' duties are mainly simple police duties, but in criminal activities they have the same general authority as their professional colleagues. They are volunteers appointed by the mayor.

Besides the differences in strength, absence of compulsory central regulations characterizes the 141 city police forces.

Formally this organization is administered by the mayor. The duties of the state are really restricted to the establishment of strength; financing; and the appointment of the chief commissioners, which are done only after consultation with the mayor.

Generally speaking, the bigger the force, the more specialization and organizational differentiation take place, and the smaller the force, the less the differentiation.

In a middle-sized force, the city police are divided into three main parts:

1. The Uniformed Division (de Algemene Dienst), consisting of the patrol squad; the traffic squad; and the Bureau of Licenses and Special Bylaws.

2. The Detective Division (de Justitiele Dienst), consisting of the General Detective Bureau; the Juvenile and Vice Squad; and the Technical Investigation and Identification Bureau.

3. The Administrative Division (de administratieve Dienst).

The city police have the following ranks: for commanding officers, head official first, second, and third class; official first, second, and third class and supernumerary, and for others adjutant, brigadier (sergeant), head agent, agent and aspirant. Commanding officer ranks have functional titles also, and a chief commissioner can be appointed in the rank of head official first or second class, a commissioner in the rank of head official second or third class or official first class, a chief inspector in the rank of first or second class, an inspector in the rank of official second or third class and an assistant inspector in the rank of supernumerary.

The State Police

The state police consists of (a) the state police force and (b) special officials of state police. The former is the largest police force in the Netherlands. It is a statewide unit under the minister of justice. He delegates actual direction and administration to the inspector general, who holds the rank of general in the Army. The inspector general has a staff of approximately 330 men. His headquarters is in Voorburg, near The Hague.

The budget of the force has grown in the past four

years more than 15%, making up shortages that now are about 12%. In principle the force performs its duties in those communities where there is no city police force—i.e., in 676 country communities with an average population density of 221 inhabitants per square kilometer.

The force totals 11,840 persons, of whom 1,700 are civilians. There are 276 policewomen on the force, of whom 18 are commanding officers. The total number of commanding officers is 217. All commanding officers are appointed by the crown, and others below that rank by the minister of justice.

By far the largest part of the force is made up of the so-called *landdienst*. It has a total number of 10,286 people, of whom 1,300 are civilians. The *landdienst* is divided into 17 districts. These, in turn, are divided into groups; the groups are in turn divided into posts, the smallest unit.

The Police Act of 1957 tried to organize the state police force into more communitywide forces, and in principle in every state police community there is a group varying in strength from 9 to 53 people.

The state police force has the following ranks for commanding officers: inspector general, directing official first, second, and third class, official first and second class, and for the others, those of adjutant, sergeant, head agent first class, agent and aspirant. The general inspector of the state police force is appointed in the rank of inspector general, and the district commanders in the rank of directing officials of state police first or second class.

In addition to its community duties, the state police force has the following statewide executive services:

1. The Rijkspolitie to Water (the water police of the state police), with a strength of 480 people and a fleet of 64 patrol vessels and 80 speedboats, has its state-wide command in Driebergen, near Utrecht. Under the command the water routes are divided into four districts: Amsterdam, Leeuwarden, Nijmegen and Dordrecht; and these are divided into groups and, where necessary, into posts. The service is in charge of all police duties on all important water routes and along the coasts of the country, including the water routes in the communities with city police forces. (Rotterdam, however, has its own river police, who perform the duties in Rotterdam Harbor.) The function of the water police is aimed especially at shipping, fishing and aquatic sports.

2. De Algemene Verkeeradienst (AVD) the general traffic service, with a strength of approximately 510 people, is also centrally stationed, in Driebergen, and is in charge of all police duties on the highways. However, it is not in charge of the technical control of motor vehicles nor with accidents in city police force communities.

3. De Dienst Luchtvaart (the Aviation Service). This service has a strength of approximately 160 people, and its command is at Schiphol Airport in Amsterdam. It serves also as the base of the Afdeling Vliegdienst, the planes of the force itself. In addition, subdivisions of the service are located at the airports in Rotterdam, Beek and Eelde. It renders assistance from the air to the state police force and to the city police forces. It has five helicopters and five planes.

The state police force has unpaid officials (other officials, members of the semipolice organizations and civilians) numbering about 4,620.

There are a limited number of professional police officers of various ranks and titles (commissioners of the state police appointed by the Crown; the water bailiffs; inspectors of a statewide detective bureau, the Rijkarecherche; and lower officials of the Rijkarecherche appointed by the minister of justice). They all belong to the police but not to the state police force, and they are in charge of special duties.

Statewide services under the Ministry of Justice include:

1. De Rijkarecherche (a statewide detective bureau) has a strength of 54 people and is made up of a combination of personnel under the direction of a commissioner of the state police who is in charge of special duties (e.g., the investigation of complaints against police officers and administrative and judicial authorities) that fall under the authority of the public prosecutors of the Courts of Appeal in the five units into which the Dutch judiciary is divided.

2. De Veiligheidsdienst Koninklijk Houis (the safety of the royal family) has a strength of 73 people, largely special officials of the state police. Because the royal palace is in the center of the country—Soestdijk—the service is stationed there.

3. De Centrale Recherche Informatie Dienst (CRI) (the National Criminal Intelligence Service), with a strength of 256 people, has a mixed composition of police officers (under a chief commissioner and eight commissioners of the state police) and civilians. Its duties are also mixed, being partly executive and partly administrative. The National Criminal Intelligence Service assists the police and the judiciary in criminal matters by supplying information, by coordinating the requested investigations, by assisting the local police, by keeping international contacts and by giving information. The service is also a national center for Interpol. The service, which undoubtedly is the most important of those that fall directly under the minister of justice, is developing very rapidly.

Besides an internal General Administration Department, which is charged with day-to-day operations, the National Criminal Intelligence Service has two external departments as well as executive and information departments. These are the Police Information Department and the Criminal Investigation Department.

The Police Information Department, with a strength of 105 officials, is in charge of the management of large information services in the information section, the circulation section, the central fingerprint section and a number of other police record registrations. The Police Information Department is divided into several subsections, including the Circulation Section, the Central Fingerprint Section and the Police Records Section.

The Criminal Investigation Department consists of nine branches, including the *Special Branch* (charged with statewide duties for the prevention and detection of terrorist crimes); the *Fraud Branch* (which collects, registers and analyzes all information about financial-economic criminality); the *Criminal Intelligence Branch* (which collects and analyzes information of statewide importance about persons who are possibly connected with crimes or who could cause a serious disturbance of law and order); and Interpol.

Other statewide services under the authority of the Ministry of Justice, mainly assisting services, are:

1. De gerechtelijke Laboratoria (judicial laboratories). The personnel of 90 are divided into het Gerechtelijk Natuurwetenschappelijk Laboratorium (the judicial science laboratory) and het Gerechtelijk Geneeskundige Laboratorium (the judicial health laboratory).

2. De Politieverbindingsdienst (PVD) (the Police Communication Service). This service has a strength of 225 civilians and works for the entire Dutch police. It is in charge of telecommunication for the detection of crime and the maintenance of law and order.

3. De Intendance der Rijkspolitie (the service force of the state police). This service, with a strength of 74 people, nearly all of whom are civilians, is stationed in Apeldoorn. Although the name and origin give the impression that it works only for the state police, it now works for the entire Dutch police in procuring uniforms, equipment, armament and repairs, as well as inspection of the firearms used by the police.

4. De Politietechische Dienst der Rijkspolitie (PTD) (the police technical service of the state police). This service, with 114 civilians, is primarily a service of the state police and more generally of the Ministry of Justice. It is in charge of procurement and maintenance of motor vehicles and other technical transportation equipment for the ministry. With headquarters in Delft (near The Hague), the technical service is spread over the country in six workshops.

Other Services with Police Duties

There is no unanimity about whether the Marechaussee, established in 1814, is a police service or one of the special detection services. It distinguishes itself in the meantime from those services because it performs within the Army all police duties for the various Army units, and also because its members are mentioned, though in a very special way, in the Law of Criminal Procedure along with all the other general detection officials.

The special detection services were formed by concerned ministries for the enforcement of laws within their jurisdictions.

Under the central services with a very clear detection character are the following:

1. The Economical Control Service (ECD) (de Economische Controle Dienst). This service, with an executive strength of 215 people, falls under the Ministry of Economics and is mainly in charge of the observance of the economic laws.

2. The General Inspection Service (AID) (de Algemene Inspectiedienst). This service of approximately 970 people, of whom 450 are not paid, falls formally under the Ministry of Agriculture and Fishing and is mainly in charge of regulations for agricultural and fishing products.

3. The Revenue-Taxes Service (de Belastingdienst). One unit of this service is de Dienst Invoerrechten en Accynzen (the services of import and excise duties I and A) and the tax information and detection service (de Fiscale Inlichtingen en Opsporingsdienst, FIOD), together with approximately 5,700 people under the authority of the Ministry of Finance, in charge of the enforcement of the tax laws in the most general sense.

4. The Inspection Service (de Keuringsdiensten). This service inspects goods and meat. With approximately 1,670 people it is formally built up as community- or regionwide state body to guard the quality of meat and other provisions. The service has connections with the Ministry of Agriculture and Fishing as well as with the Department of Health and Environmental Hygiene.

5. The State Traffic Inspection (de Rijksverkeersinspectie). This is a decentralized state service with about 175 people, falls under the Department of Building and Roads and pays special attention to the laws regarding transportation.

   The total number of special detection officials is very difficult to guess. In Dutch legislation there are ample laws as well as general measurements of management (from the queen) for regulation of lower public bodies such as provinces, communities and the jurisdiction of the water boards, and under these regulations special detection officials can be appointed.

   Also in the area of formal laws, because of the development of the welfare state, there are an enormous and growing number of special laws and bylaws that regulate a number of special control services.

   An inventory in 1980 of the Ministry of Justice produced a list of no less than 275 bylaws with punishment sanctions, and all these laws are now in force.

Many such laws originated from the separate ministries, which also created petty regulation.

To get a little more unity, a great number of these laws have been brought together under the Law of Economic Crimes of 1950 (de Wet op de Economische Delicten), which gives uniform regulations for detection, special punishment and special trials.

In the area of the revenue laws, an attempt has been made to get a more uniform system by the General Law for the State Taxes (Algemene Wet Rikjsbelastingen) and the General Law for Customs and Excises (de Algemene Wet Douane en Accijnzen).

6. Private Police Services. Private police services have had a stormy development in the Netherlands. They cause special problems for the official security bodies, stimulate a redefinition of the range of the police function and suggest what can be expected in the area of self-protection by the citizens themselves. According to a recent inventory, there are four groups of private companies that are considered legal: 332 company security services (these guarding services are formed by industrial companies themselves to protect persons and property) with a strength of about 10,000 people; 70 security companies of approximately 4,000 persons who perform various guard and security services for others (contract security); 17 alarm services units; and eight money and valuable goods transportation companies. The total number of persons working this area is at least 20,000.

7. The Railway Police. This force deserves special attention. Though formally a private security service, the state has a dominant share.

Since the 1960s this organization has developed from a company security service to a police force that is equal to the regular police as far as duties are concerned as shown by its change of name in 1978 from the Railway Detective Division.

The main duty of this force when it was established in 1919 was detection of transportation theft. The very strong metamorphosis in 1970 to the present force, which in principle performs the whole police duty in uniform and apart from the duties of the regular police, made the maintenance of law and order and the prevention of crime very important.

This force is closely connected to the state police. The commander is a commissioner of the state police, and all other executive officers are unpaid officials of the state police, with appropriate detection authority and armament.

One commanding officer of the state police is in charge of the supervision of the Railway Police.

The Railway Police force tries to follow the regular police so far as ranks, appointment, promotion and the performance of daily duties are concerned.

The force has a strength of approximately 450 people and is centrally stationed in Utrect, where the railway company has its headquarters (the president-director of the company represents the Railway Police on the Direction Board).

An agent of the city police or agent of the state police (ranks that are given after one year of training and when active service begins) receive a basic monthly salary of 1,827 guilders plus various allowances: 8% to 15% for irregular service and an allowance of 60 guilders for the members of the Mobile Unit to a maximum of 2,920 guilders (an hourly salary of about 10.56 to 16.88 guilders).

An agent will more or less automatically be promoted after five years to head agent (agent first class) with a salary of 2,536 guilders and a final salary at age 36 of 3,215 guilders. An adjutant, the highest rank of the lower officials, earns a minimum of 3,531 and a maximum of 4,321 guilders.

For the commanding officer-ranks the scale is as follows: A starting inspector in the rank of official third class or a commanding officer of the state police second class starts at 3,053 guilders and ends at 4,707 guilders. The highest commanding officer ranks—head official first class of the city police and inspector general of the state police—have a salary (apart from 5% tax-free representation allowance) that runs from 8,793 to 10,844 guilders. The chiefs of police of the city police have a separate scale that runs from 4,405 to 10,844 guilders in the three largest cities.

Officials in administrative and technical ranks have salaries that usually follow the salaries of general civil servants and range from 950 guilders for a typist to 7,590 guilders for a head administrator.

All officials get a vacation allowance of 7½% of yearly salary.

The official age for retirement is 65, but executive police officials get functional age dismissal at age 60. Between 60 and 65 they receive a waiting salary, which lies between the last paid salary and the expected pension.

The maximum pension for all officials is 70% of salary and can be reached only after 40 years of service. The government contributes its part of the pension on account, but the official also pays his part (11.7% at the present time).

The executive official works five days a week for a 40-hour week. Vacation time is connected with salary and varies from 22 to 30 days a year.

Recruitment, Education & Training

To be appointed as an aspirant in the city police or the state police, one has to have the following requirements: Dutch origin; blameless conduct; a height of 1.70 meters (men only); age between 17 and 28 years; and successful completion of health, psychological and psychotechnical examinations. Furthermore, the applicant must possess a diploma of a four-year MAVE (a school that follows the basic school but has a more general formal education) or a diploma equivalent to that of a MAVE and approved by the ministers.

When the applicant has met the requirements, appointment with a probation time of a maximum of three years is possible. During probation, the aspirant must demonstrate theoretical and practical ability—e.g., by earning a supplementary diploma.

For appointment as a commanding officer (inspector of city police third class or official of state police second class) the same regulations apply, with this difference: The required age group is 20 to 28, and in principle, attainment of a higher educational level is required (Dutch high school or junior college training). Also, the applicant must have successfully completed the final examination for inspector of the city police or commanding officer of the state police. This means four years' training at the Police Academy, or for external students, a declaration of ability after they have finished the final academy examination. It is also possible for persons with university degrees (e.g., those with law degrees) to get into the commanding officer ranks of the police. In special cases the ministers can waive possession of the inspectors diploma.

If one has the ability for promotion, in general there is no other requirement other than a certain number of years of service. In principle, an aspirant will be promoted after one year to agent and an agent after five years to head agent (agent first class). For the rank of brigadier (sergeant) there is a special requirement: possession of the so-called B diploma, for which internal preparation in the force is possible. This diploma is mostly based on theoretical knowledge. For promotion in the commanding officer ranks there has been until now no other requirement save a certain minimum service time.

Although the city police personnel, with the exception of the chief commissioners, are appointed by the mayor, this situation is changing. Recruitment of city police personnel under the rank of commanding officer is now centralized in the State Selection Center (Landelijk Selectie Centrum) for the city police in Hilversum.

Over a number of years, the number of appointed officials has been about 10% of applicants for the city police and the state police. Certainly the applications as far as numbers are concerned are adequate, but there are disturbing geographical factors. A total of 50% of the applications for the city police come from the North, East and South of Holland, though the vacancies are more in the western part of the country, in the so-called Randstad.

Training and education of police personnel have been neglected for a long time, a traditionally weak point in the police situation. This was especially true for city police; the prewar state police forces (the Marechaussee and the Rijksveldwacht) had their own internal training facilities. Even when the quality of the police personnel became more important, at about the turn of the century, and the process of professionalization began, the Dutch government left education and training to private initiative. The police unions and a number of privately trained police personnel started to take care of this very neglected matter. Examinations were initiated, and study facilities were provided where possible.

Before the Second World War the government never paid a penny for training. Even when a training program was started, it offered largely legal formal training because at the time the idea that police work should be done in a legal context was generally accepted. After the war this situation changed radically, even though the state and city police went separate ways, in spite of the fact that the police decision of 1945 made the training of all police personnel the responsibility of the minister of justice.

The only institute started by the minister of justice was the Institute for Training Commanding Police Personnel (in 1967 the name was changed to the Dutch Police Academy). It continued the training of the Model Police Vocational School in Hilversum, a school founded in 1919 by the General Dutch Police Union. That school had a one year course for the police diploma and a two-year course for inspector candidates.

Because of its centralized management and the tradition of the state police forces, the state police was the first to start other training institutes, not only for primary training but also for staff officials; traffic police; and other, more specialized work of the police.

Training for the city police came much later. Apart from three large communities, which had primary training in their own day schools, others had to initiate joint training programs. It was not until 1959 that regional training institutions were available for the whole country.

After the Police Act of 1957, which made the ministers of interior and of justice less dependent on each other, developments have been much faster. On the initiative of the Department of the Interior in 1959, the Study Center for the Continuous Education of Commanding Police Officers, for both kinds of police, was started; after that, a statewide traffic school and a school for staff officials of the city police were organized. Also, a detective division school (for both kinds of police), and two centers for the training of the mobile units (one state police and one city police) were formed.

The following police training and education institutes now exist:

- For the Commanding Officers of State and City Police

1. The Dutch Police Academy in Apeldoorn. In this school, training takes four years. The first year is on

an intern basis. After two and one-half years, the training is broken off, and one year of practical work in various forces is given. In the same period, the student prepares a paper, and afterward starts the eighth term, which is concluded with a final report.

The first phase of the two-and-one-half-year program is vocational, while the eighth term is functional. About 150 students are enrolled yearly, and apart from the external students, about 50 students a year are selected from about 2,000 applicants. These students have school training of gymnasium, atheneum, or MAVO (similar to junior college training). Students are exempt from military training.

Students may be admitted on an external basis in one of two ways. A total of 20 to 25% of the students with a diploma are externs. These students have excelled in lower police ranks and have requested school training. However, it is possible for persons with a law degree to be admitted, though these students must already be in the police and will be required to get the Dutch Police Academy diploma. They are, however, given several exemptions.

2. Study Center for Commanding Officers in Warnsveld. This center offers a series of courses of one to three weeks in length. These are aimed at organization and management and at social developments and their effects. The center organizes study conferences, sometimes with representatives from abroad. The capacity is 25 to 30 persons per course, or approximately 500 per year.

A management course for top functionaries is now being organized. The chief of police of the city police and district commanders of the state police must take this course shortly after appointment. For the time being the course capacity is 12 persons, and it is offered for six periods of one week over a period of four months.

- For Other Personnel

1. Primary training for the city police. There are two day schools, one in Rotterdam and the other in The Hague. A foundation for replacing internal training is now in preparation. There are four regional schools with intern training, which lasts one year. Students are exempted from military service, and the training requirements are similar to those of MAVO. The ages are 17 to 28, and the total capacity is 1,600 students. Central selection for the city police has been done in the Selection Institute in Hilversum since 1976.

2. Primary training for the state police. This consists of a training school with intern training of one year in Apeldoorn, and two annexes, in Horn and Harlingen. At the moment 830 students are in training. The total capacity is 950 students.

- Continuous Training and Education

1. Training for the mobile unit for the state police centralized in Neerrijnen and for the city police in Woen-

adrecht. The basic mobile unit training lasts five weeks and is taken immediately following primary training. In addition, there is a four-week staff officers' course and a six-week training program for firearms instructors. The yearly capacity for Neerrijnen is about 2,000 students and for Woenadrecht 1,200 students.

2. Staff training. For the rank of sergeant, students must have ten years of service and have a so-called B diploma (preparation for which is done in the force itself). This training takes place in Apeldoorn for the state police and in Zutphen for the city police. The course lasts eight weeks. Capacity for the state police is 150 and for the city police 500. A course of eight weeks for teachers is given once a year, for six to 12 people. A course for beat officers runs two weeks for 15 persons and is offered eight times a year.

- More Specialized Training Courses

The traffic training program for state police in Bilthoven has about 20 different courses, given to about 350 students each year.

The city police take traffic training in Noordwijkerhout. The basic course lasts three weeks. There are various other courses, of which the most important is a supplementary driving training course of one week for 40 persons; the total capacity is 1,600. The total capacity of the traffic school for city police is 100 students at one time or 4,000 students yearly.

1. Detective training. For state and city police, this training is given in Zutphen. Various courses are offered, the most important of which are: the basic course for detectives, lasting eight weeks with 450 students per year; the primary detective course for commanding officers and members of the prosecution office, lasting six weeks with 30 students per year; and training for technical detection officials, which lasts 12 weeks and has 24 students per year. There are also courses for the juvenile squad, drugs, and fraud and swindling. They last three weeks, and the number of participants is 15 per course. The total capacity is 120 students a day or 700 a year.

2. Sleuth Hounds School. Since 1919 this has been a school of the state police in The Hague. It trains about 30 dog handlers selected from and working in the detection groups of the districts of the state police, and their dogs. The training of the dog lasts one year; that of the handler takes six months, and it is done in groups of four men.

The dog handlers for the sleuth hounds of the state police work in their districts for both the state and city police. The school trains dogs for drug sniffing (a course of four months), not only for the police but also for custom officers.

The sleuth hounds must be distinguished from the patrol dogs, of which the state and city police each have about 130. These dogs are trained in the forces in the dog brigades, and there are about 920 officials working full time in the police training area.

Training and education are also offered internally. For instance, there is training for the B diploma, a requirement for promotion to staff ranks such as sergeant, and the reception and tutoring of young police personnel who have just completed primary training. In tutoring young colleagues, the state police has a uniform practice in which young police officers are accompanied during 13 weeks in their district, followed by an introductory course of six weeks in the district before definite placement in a group. The city police do not have a uniform regulation. Usually the young police officers will be accompanied individually for nine to 26 weeks.

The Penal System

The penal system is based on the following Acts of Parliament and statutory instruments:

- the Criminal Code and the Code of Criminal Procedure
- the Prisons Act and the Prisons Rules
- the Criminal Psychopaths Regulations
- the Aftercare of Discharged Prisoners Regulations

No child under 12 years can be charged with a criminal offense. There is a separate system for those between 12 and 17 years.

When a person has been convicted of an offense, the court may impose a principal sentence with or without an additional sentence or make a special order or both. Penalties for each offense are prescribed in the Criminal Code and practically all acts of Parliament. The principal sentences consist of:

- a term of imprisonment
- detention
- fines varying from five guilders to 1 million guilders

Both the maximum and the minimum penalties are specified by law. Additional sentences may include:

- deprivation of certain rights, such as the right to vote or run for election, to hold public office or to practice certain professions
- confiscation of personal property or stolen goods
- disqualification from driving

Special orders are hospital orders and orders relating to judicial child care and protection.

Criminal Procedure

Suspects may be remanded in custody for a maximum of six days on order of an examining magistrate. The period may be renewed only once. After preliminary examination of the accused, the prosecutor may apply to the court for a warrant to hold him or her in custody for further periods of 30 days. An unrepresented defendant held in custody on a serious charge is assigned an advocate by the president of the court or by the Legal Aid Council. The examining magistrate hears the accused, the witnesses and the experts, such as psychiatrists. A suspect can be placed in the Psychiatric Observation Clinic at Utrecht for some time if necessary. The examining magistrate does not sit on the bench that tries the case. On the conclusion of the preliminary examination the public prosecutor decides whether to prosecute further. The law recognizes the principle of "opportuneness," under which the public prosecutor may decide not to press charges and institute criminal proceedings. On an annual average, only half of the cases registered with the Public Prosecutor's Office are brought before the courts, and of the remaining, 77% are dropped either conditionally or unconditionally.

After serving two-thirds of his or her sentence or spending nine months in custody, whichever is longer, a prisoner may be released on probation (or "license") for a year longer than the remaining period of the sentence. Prisoners so released usually are assisted by one of the probation or aftercare organizations on the basis of a rehabilitation plan drawn up prior to the date of release. Prisoners denied probation may appeal to a special division in the Court of Appeal at Arnhem.

Capital punishment was abolished in the Netherlands in 1870. In addition to the principal penalties for criminal offenses, courts have wide powers under new legislation to impose penalties other than custodial sentences. Provisions regarding the imposition of suspended sentences were incorporated in the Criminal Code in 1915 and in 1929, while in 1925 the courts were empowered to impose fines on a wider scale in lieu of detention and imprisonment. The percentage of unconditional custodial sentences imposed for criminal offenses has declined in recent years from 26% in 1977 to 21% in 1981, while monetary penalties rose from 44% to 53% during the same period. At the same time, the duration of custodial sentences has increased, rising by a third from 1977 to 1981 for terms of one year or more. Short custodial sentences of one month or less, however, still predominated.

Prisons

Equally important changes have taken place in the prison system under the Prisons Act of 1951 and the Prisons Regulation of 1953, which have redefined and reclassified prisons and prisoners, built new prisons and enhanced the education of prison officials. Ultimate responsibility for all penal institutions is vested in the minister of justice, who exercises his authority through the Prisons Department. The director of public prosecutions directs the implementation of prison sentences.

Each prison is administered by a governor, supported by a staff that includes chaplains, counselors, doctors, social workers, psychologists and guards. Supervisory boards oversee all aspects of a prison's treatment of its inmates but have no administrative authority. Prisoners may freely address the board either in writing or in person.

There are two types of penal institutions: house of detention and prisons. Houses of detention are mainly for those remanded to custody awaiting trial and also for those serving prison sentences of less than two weeks. The law requires that there be at least one house of detention per court district, but some districts have more than one. Two-thirds of the average population in these houses of detention are those remanded to custody.

Considerable attention is given in prison legislation to the personality of the prisoner. The Criminal Code stipulates that anyone sentenced to serve a term of sentence in a prison should be committed to the institution best suited to his disposition and background. Section 26 of the Prisons Act states that the prison sentence should be conducive to prepare the prisoner for return to society. To reduce the dangers of isolation and alienation from society, prisoners are brought into frequent contact with the outside world. Prisoners' committees as well as prison newspapers serve as open forums for prisoners. Offenders are allowed to keep their own clothes and personal effects, write letters unsupervised, and visit the outside world for short periods under special circumstances.

Women serve prison sentences in the Women's Prison at Amsterdam, while the houses of detention in Maastricht and Groningen have separate sections for women prisoners.

Prisoners who have not been remanded to custody because their offense is not particularly serious and who have received short terms of imprisonment serve their sentences in a semiopen prison: Bankenbosch Prison in Veenhuizen, Ter Peel in Sevenum, Oostereiland in Hoorn, De Raam in Grave, or Westlinge in Heerhugowaard. Separate quarters are assigned for prisoners serving short-term (less than six months) sentences and those serving long-term (over six months) sentences. Short-term sentences are served in Boschpoort Prison in Breda or in the semiopen Nederheide Penitentiary Training Institute in Doetinchem. Transfer is possible between one institution and another. At Nederheide the prisoner is expected to participate in a social education program. Longer sentences are served in Esserheem and Norgerhaven Prisons in Veenhuizen, Noorderschans in Winschoten, Schutterswei in Alkmaar and in the prison in The Hague. In smaller prisons, inmates are permitted outside employment with normal wages.

Prisoners between 18 and 23 years who have not been remanded to custody are placed in Nieuwe Vesseveld Prison in Vught or De Corridor Penal Training Camp in the village of Zeeland in North Brabant. Long-term prisoners are accommodated in the prison at Zutphen. These prisoners can be transferred to the open prison at Rozenhof.

The Prison Allocation Center, headed by a psychologist, advises the prison authorities on the placement of prisoners. Noorderschans Prison accommodates prisoners who are unable to adjust in a communal establishment.

It is possible for sentences of less than two weeks to be served in installments.

Psychologically disturbed offenders are committed to mental hospitals for a period not exceeding one year. This sanction is known as a hospital order. A number of new provisions incorporated into the Criminal Code of 1925 deal specifically with this group of diminished-responsibility offenders, who are designated by the title of "psychopaths."

The granting of a remission of sentence in respect of a penalty imposed by a court is the prerogative of the crown. A remission may consist of reduction of a sentence or commutation of a sentence to another type. A conditional remission bears some semblance to suspended sentence and release on license.

An organization called the Society for Moral Improvement of Prisoners was set up as early as 1823 to aid offenders both while in prison and after discharge. The introduction of the release-on-license system in 1886, of probation in 1915, and of conditional remissions of sentence in 1976 gave this and similar organizations a role in the criminal justice system by entrusting them with supervision of the fulfillment of special conditions imposed by the court (probation) and by the administration (release on license and remissions). Rehabilitation probation and aftercare remain largely in the hands of religious and voluntary social service organizations officially recognized by the Ministry of Justice.

A recent development is what is known as "early intervention." Since 1974, in nearly all police districts, the Probation and Aftercare Service has been responsible for providing early assistance to suspects in police custody.

NEW ZEALAND

BASIC FACT SHEET

Official Name: New Zealand
Area: 268,676 sq km
Population: 3,307,239 (1987)
Capital: Wellington
Nature of Government: Parliamentary democracy
Language: English
Currency: New Zealand dollar
GNP: $23.72 billion (1985)
Territorial Divisions: 241 territorial units, including 128 boroughs and 90 counties
Population per Police Officer: N.A.
Police Expenditures per 1,000: $38,418

History & Background

The first police presence in New Zealand consisted of a sergeant and four troopers seconded from the New South Wales, Australia, Police Force in the early part of the 19th century. In 1846 a legal basis was created for an armed constabulary under provincial aegis. This gave way to the Armed Constabulary Ordinance of 1867, whereby a national police force consisting of both Maoris and European settlers was established. Provincial police were not abolished but continued to play a limited role. In 1886 the armed constabulary was replaced by a civilian unarmed force on the British model. The last of the Acts of Parliament governing police establishment was passed in 1958.

Structure & Organization

The force is commanded by a commissioner who is responsible to the Ministry of Internal Affairs. At the headquarters he is assisted by two deputy commissioners, two assistant commissioners and six deputy assistant commissioners, and in the field by 14 chief superintendents, 28 superintendents, 54 chief inspectors, 120 inspectors, 279 senior sergeants, 727 sergeants and 3,781 constables. Of the total, 204 are women. There are six headquarters directorates, including one for crime.

For operational purposes, New Zealand is divided into 16 police districts, 10 in the North and six in the South. Only the Auckland district is headed by an assistant commissioner. The others are headed by a chief inspector or a deputy assistant commissioner. District commanders are responsible for all aspects of police work in their areas, including criminal investigation. Each district has its own police barracks.

The first Armed Offenders Squads were formed in 1964. Some 30 specially selected and trained members of this group constitute the Antiterrorist Squad. New Zealand has no separate railway or other transportation police forces; their duties are performed by the regular police.

The uniform is blue jacket and trousers for all ranks, with a large coat of arms over the word "Police" at the top of each sleeve. Sergeants and constables wear British-style white helmets by day and blue helmets at night. Officers wear a blue cap, with a blue/white checkered band for inspectors and superintendents.

Recruitment, Education & Training

Applications for entry into the force undergo rigorous training at the Police College at Trentham, Upper Hutt, where they attend an 18-week training course. Promotions are based on selective examinations followed by further training. Sometimes officers are sent to Australia for specialized training, for which there are no facilities in New Zealand. The Trentham Police College is attended by police officers from the Cook Islands, Fiji, Niue, Tonga, Vanuatu, Hong Kong and Singapore. In 1983 a district training program was initiated by which all police personnel up to and including inspectors participate in a minimum of eight rostered training days a year. A new Police College was established in 1982, at Porirua.

The Penal System

For 1985 a total of 408,484 offenses were reported to the police. The overall clearance rate was 48.4%, compared with 47.8% in 1981. During the year 83 murders were committed nationwide. Drug offenses not involving cannabis increased by 4.6% (mainly in the area of stimulants and depressants), and cannabis by 32%. However, hard drugs such as cocaine, heroin, LSD, opium and morphine showed a strong decline. Fraud rose by 8.3% but had a better clearance rate at 30.1%, compared with 28.6% in 1981. Property worth $125 million was stolen during the year, of which $58 million was recovered, representing a recovery rate of 46.6%. Of the 22,599 motor vehicles stolen, 20,701 were recovered, a recovery rate of 91.6%.

CRIME STATISTICS (1984)

		Number Reported	Attempts %	Cases Solved %	Crime per 100,000	Offenders	Females %	Juveniles %	Strangers %
1.	Murder	83	34.9	89.2	2.54	73	5.5	1.4	
2.	Sex offenses, including rape	3,277	3.3	66.3	100.35	1,972	3.7	33.7	
3.	Rape	471	20.4	74.9	14.42	171	0.6	7.0	
4.	Serious assault	3,597		82.1	110.15	2,716	5.6	8.6	
5.	All theft	236,588		24.1	7,245.08	54,732	21.0	46.5	
6.	Aggravated theft	445		46.9	13.63	283	12.0	32.5	
7.	Robbery and violent theft	487		84.0	14.91	186	16.7	52.2	
8.	Breaking and entering	73,247		20.0	2,243.06	15,598	7.1	53.0	
9.	Auto theft								
10.	Other thefts	163,339		25.8	5,001.96	39,134	26.6	43.9	
11.	Fraud	24,030		51.9	735.88	11,213	29.4	6.6	
12.	Counterfeiting	52		67.3	1.59	11		81.8	
13.	Drug offenses	14,573		91.5	446.27	12,941	15.1	7.1	
14.	Total offenses	408,484		45	12,509.08	156,158	17.1	25.5	

Note: Information for some categories is not available.
Criteria of juveniles: aged from 1 to 16 years.

NICARAGUA

BASIC FACT SHEET

Official Name: Republic of Nicaragua
Area: 130,000 sq km
Population: 3,319,059 (1987)
Capital: Managua
Nature of Government: Marxist dictatorship
Language: Spanish
Currency: Cordoba
GNP: $2.76 billion (1985)
Territorial Divisions: 6 regions, 3 special zones
Population per Police Officer: 90
Police Expenditures per 1,000: N.A.

Structure & Organization

The police are divided into three categories: urban, rural and judicial. Although they are part of the National Guard, they serve the Ministry of the Interior. Like the National Guard, the police are required to be nonpolitical; they may not vote in elections, and they come under military law.

The political administrator of the Police Department, the *jefe político,* is appointed by the president and has overall responsibility for law enforcement throughout his department. He, too, is part of the Ministry of the Interior and is locally in command of the armed forces, including the police. His chief of police, who is a police judge, is the immediate commander of the police forces. Each department has at least one police judge, and two of them, Chinandega and Río San Juan, have two. In addition to the normal complement of the police force in the department, there are about 45 police agents, somewhat above the level of patrolman, on detached duty in various towns throughout the department of Zelaya and in the territory of Cabo Gracias a Dios.

The permanent personnel of the national police force number 5,000 officers and men plus some 1,500 civilian employees. The force is headed by a colonel assisted by subordinate ranks of lieutenant colonels, majors, captains, lieutenants, sublieutenants, sergeants, corporals, and patrolmen. Police uniforms are blue-gray in color, with trousers bloused into boots, and they wear plastic helmets with a triangular-shaped badge with a design of five volcanoes and the cap of Liberty. They normally carry pistols and billy clubs. The police school is part of the Ministry of Defense.

The pay is relatively good by civilian standards. Room, board and clothing are free, as are medical care and other benefits. There are no women in the force.

The Urban Police is concerned with common offenses such as vagrancy, drunkenness, prohibited games, counterfeiting, carrying arms without permission, prostitution, violations of laws concerning health and cleanliness, and maintenance of peace and good order. Peddlers and *curanderos* (native healers) without licenses are the most common problems.

The Rural Police concerns are enforcing the hunting and fishing laws, licensing of guns, railroad rights-of-way and the telegraph system. The Judicial Police run the jails, provide guard services for the courts, and assist in the investigation of crimes and the apprehension of suspects. The security force for the Treasury, also under the National Guard, numbers about 1,000 officers and men.

The secretary of the interior has responsibility for the work of the fire departments and exercises trusteeship over the convict. At the higher jurisdictions there is a public prosecutor *(ministerio público)* who represents the people in criminal cases, and at municipal and lower levels a *síndico* who performs the same functions.

Since the Sandinistas' rise to power, the so-called Shock Brigades have served as the community auxiliary police. Their precise powers and functions are not known.

Recruitment, Education & Training

No current information is available.

The Penal System

Penal Codes were codified in 1837, 1871, 1879, 1891 and 1968. The current Penal Code uses the Chilean Code of 1850 as a model.

Three degrees or kinds of punishment are distinguished: The most serious are the *penas graves,* which cover serious crimes punishable by death, long-term imprisonment, and total or partial deprivation of civil and political rights. The middle level is the *penas menos graves,* and the lowest is *penas leves.* These correspond to the traditional categories of *crimen, delitos* and *faltas,* respectively. In assigning punishment, extenuating and aggravating circumstances are recognized. There are grades of punishment, five within each category, and maximum, medium and minimum sentences within each grade. The highest punishment is death, followed by life imprisonment for 30 years. Banishment is prohibited, and so is confiscation of property.

Prisons are often makeshift in character. The guards are supplied by the Judicial Police. There is a national rehabilitation center called the Centro Penal de Rehabilitation Social, established in 1960.

There are no statistical data on the incidence of crime, and none has been published since the Sandinistas came to power. The majority of the crimes are believed to be against persons. The reported homicide rate, 30 per 100,000 inhabitants, is relatively high for this region, particularly so because possibly not all the homicides are reported.

NIGERIA

Patrick Edobor Igbinovia

BASIC FACT SHEET

Official Name: Federal Republic of Nigeria
Area: 923,768 sq km
Population: 108,579,764 (1987)
Capital: Lagos
Nature of Government: Military dictatorship
Language: English
Currency: Naira
GNP: $75.94 billion (1985)
Territorial Divisions: 19 states
Population per Police Officer: 1,140
Police Expenditures per 1,000: N.A.

History & Background

The national police developed from early constabularies raised to protect British personnel and their administrative and commercial interests after they assumed responsibility for the port of Lagos in 1861. The imposition of British rule in the country triggered protests and demonstrations that threatened law and order in the new colony. To combat the unrest, the Lagos Police Force was formed, from all indications the first modern police force in the territories later designated Nigeria. This early security force grew in size and effectiveness and, as the British expanded operations to the interior, additional constabularies came into being along their route. In the North, the Northern Nigerian Constabulary (the Armed Hausa Police) was formed in 1900, when the British assumed administrative responsibility for the protectorate of Northern Nigeria. The Southern Nigeria Police was created in 1906, six years after the proclamation of the colony and protectorate of Southern Nigeria. The Southern Police Unit absorbed the former Lagos Police Force and Niger Coast Constabulary (the Oil Rivers Irregulars, "Court Messengers"), which had operated in the eastern provinces. In 1930, the Northern Constabulary and the Southern Police Force were merged to form the Nigeria Police Force, which became the federal law-enforcement body.

Prior to the consolidation of the Nigeria Police in 1930, the colonial government had left the development and organization of police establishments to the three political administrations in the country: the Lagos Colony and the Protectorates of Southern and of Northern Nigeria. The main reasons for the decentralized approach to law enforcement was the need at that time to allow each segment of the federation to organize a defense compatible with local conditions and the political climate. As a result, the pattern and extent of development in the three areas differed. Following the amalgamation of all the units of the country into what is now known as Nigeria in 1914, the various departments of the amalgamated protectorates were systematically merged, one after the other. The police were an exception.

Though quite willing to surrender control of other departments, the lieutenant governors of the protectorates were very worried about relinquishing control over maintenance of law and order to the new overall administration in Lagos. They saw no reason for such a surrender of power, since there was nothing really technical in police operations that lay beyond their competence. There is no doubt that these regional government heads appreciated the enormous leverage the control of their regional police establishments could afford them, especially in those days of poor communications between Lagos and the rest of the country. The amalgamation was eventually effected in 1930 because the central government saw the need for a unified "controlling authority over matters of police routine and discipline." The powers that were hitherto exercised by lieutenant governors in the provinces and districts were now vested in the inspector general of police, holding a new position created by the amalgamation of the forces.

Local forces that had any real resemblance to police

organization could be dated back to 1943, when the then northern and western regions of the country established local government police forces. In creating these forces, these two regions capitalized on Section 105(7) of the Nigerian Constitution, which made provision for the maintenance of such a force by local authority, provided men of the forces were employed and deployed only within the area of the jurisdiction of that local authority. These local or provincial forces played a major role in helping police remote areas of the country, where the presence of the Nigerian Police Force would not have been felt.

In 1958, control of the Nigeria Police was put in the hands of the federal government. Appointment of the inspector general of the Nigeria Police and of the regional commissioners of police was strictly safeguarded by special constitutional provisions, and the training and equipment of all police forces were coordinated by a federal police organization.

Sections 98 to 103 of the Nigerian Constitution accordingly provided that:

> The Nigeria Police shall be under the command of the inspector general of the Nigeria Police, and any contingents of the Nigeria Police Force stationed in a region shall, subject to the authority of the inspector general of the Nigeria Police, be under the command of the Commissioner of police of that region. The prime minister may give to the inspector general of the Nigeria Police such directions with respect to the maintaining and securing of public safety and public order as he may consider necessary, and the inspector general shall comply with those directions or cause them to be complied with.
>
> The commissioner of police of a region shall comply with the directions of the premier of a region with respect to the maintaining and securing of public safety and public order within the region or cause them to be complied with, provided that before carrying out any such directions, the commissioner may request that the matter should be referred to the prime minister for his directions.

Despite the constitutional provisions for the Nigeria Police, the then northern and western regional governments refused to amalgamate their forces with the Nigeria Police Force. Amalgamation, however, was accomplished with the sack from the political arena of politicians by the Nigerian Army in January 1966. The study group set up by the military government to examine police matters and make recommendations suggested the gradual integration of the local forces into the Nigeria Police Force. The first group of such men to be absorbed reported for training at the Police College in Lagos in 1968. By March 1969, the process had been completed for all forces in the Western State. The process has now been completed in all of Nigeria.

Structure & Organization

Headquarters of the Nigeria Police is in Lagos and is under the command of the inspector general of police, who is assisted by a deputy inspector general. Its staff operations are supervised by assistant inspectors general.

The duties of the Commissioner of Police at Force Headquarters are split into Departments A, B, C, D and E, each under the command of an assistant inspector general. The functions of these departments are as follows:

Department A. Responsible for general administration of police and for all matters concerning personnel, including assignments, transfers, promotions, leaves and disciplinary action.

Department B. A communications branch that supervises operation of the nationwide police radio system that links all state police commands with force headquarters. It is also responsible for operations and transportation, with the central motor vehicles registry, responsible for traffic control. This branch also monitors government vehicle licensing policy as it affects the police force.

Department C. Responsible for general financial matters and buildings, works and capital development (this formerly included pay and quartermaster services, but these functions are now performed by the accounts/internal audit wing of the administration).

Department D. Responsible for criminal records and investigation. Of the various specialized developments assigned to the national headquarters, the largest is the Criminal Investigation Department (CID), which is responsible for the application of scientific methods to the prevention and detection of crime.

Department E. This is the Special Branch, responsible for internal security and countersubversive activities. It gathers intelligence that could aid police in ensuring peace and order.

Except for special functions that come directly under the national headquarters, control of the force in the field is exercised through a series of state police commands. The 19 headquarters of these commands, each under supervision of a police commissioner, are in the various state capitals. Directly below the state commanders (commissioners) are the provincial police officers and then the district police officers down to the station officers. The police stations usually are commanded by a sergeant or inspector of police.

The size and organizational complexity of the state police commands vary depending on the population density of the state and the need for police authority. Police posts and stations are found in the larger urban centers, mainly along rail lines and major highways.

The largest of the state commands is that in Lagos State. Its headquarters in the capital city's Lion Build-

CHAIN OF POLICE COMMAND IN NIGERIA

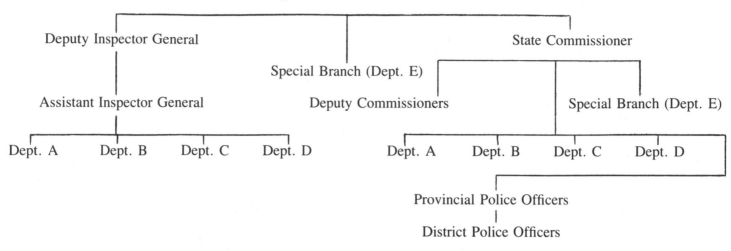

Inspector General of Police

Deputy Inspector General   State Commissioner

Special Branch (Dept. E)

Assistant Inspector General   Deputy Commissioners   Special Branch (Dept. E)

Dept. A   Dept. B   Dept. C   Dept. D   Dept. A   Dept. B   Dept. C   Dept. D

Provincial Police Officers

District Police Officers

Police Station Commander

ing coordinates the activities of a police laboratory, a CID training school, a division responsible for the registration of aliens, and several specialized operational groups. These include a mobile unit and a police dog unit, both at Obalende; a motor traffic division at Ijora; the Nigerian Ports Authority police at Lagos and Apapa; the Nigerian railway police at Ikeja and Shomolu; and a division of policewomen. Because they are better trained and better equipped, the state commands of the Nigerian Police Force usually respond to specialized cases, and all maintain CID capabilities.

Criminal investigations are initially the responsibility of the police station in the area in which the offense is committed. If the initial investigation indicates a serious crime or that the case will be prolonged, the state CID may be called on for assistance. The latter may also call on the force CID in Lagos if inquiries are required in other states of the country or overseas. Generally speaking, however, the force CID is employed to investigate complicated cases of fraud or murder. It also serves as the central agency for the collection, compilation, classification and recording of information concerning criminals and crimes, and the dissemination of such information as required.

The Nigeria Police Criminal Investigations Department (CID)

The force CID investigates cases that either are reported directly by members of the public or referred to the department by other police formations from all parts of the country, government departments, the Central Bank of Nigeria, and commercial banks and firms.

The force CID has several operations sections.

The *Crime Section* is charged with investigating serious cases, such as murder, robbery, boundary disputes and complex fraud cases. The *Missing Persons Section* is part of the Crime Section and deals with cases of missing persons throughout the country. The *Fraud Section* deals mostly with fraud cases, forgery and allied offenses through the country and especially in the capital city of Lagos, where the Central Bank, commercial banks and companies have been fertile grounds for culprits. The *"X" Squad Section* handles various crimes on corrupt practices and related offenses involving police personnel and the public. The *Post and Telecommunication Fraud Section* is attached to the Post and Telecommunication Department (P and T) for crime investigation purposes. This section investigates cases involving not only P and T workers but also other civilians.

The *National Central Bureau, Interpol, Lagos (NCB),* consists of Interpol, narcotics and antiquities units. The activities of each subsection are as follows:

Interpol: Through this section the Nigeria Police Force deals with investigation of crimes that extend to foreign countries. It also conducts inquiries on request of other foreign police organizations, customs, firms and individuals in Nigeria.

Narcotics: The most prevalent cases in this section involve marijuana. The majority of these cases are dealt with by state police commands. Those with international connections are handled by the narcotics section of Interpol. Cases handled internally usually consist of those involving possession, smoking and cultivation, while those treated internationally involve possession, importation and exportation. Lately, illicit drug traffickers have been using post offices. Parcels are sent out in newspaper wrappings, in books used as containers, in wooden carvings, in wearing apparel such as clothes and shoes, and in empty boxes of detergent. Foreign narcotics bureaus have been informed of the addresses used by the offenders. The antiquities branch deals with the theft and smuggling of archaeological artifacts.

Section A22, the police public complaint bureau, is about nine years old and has been very successful. Persons who could not spare the time to visit the police station or those who fear victimization use this service.

The *Ballistic/Counterfeit Investigation Section* deals with classification and identification of forensic ballistics. It also handles cases of counterfeiting, disputed documents, Firearms Registry and the Drawing Office. The counterfeit investigation unit serves as the medium between the Central Bank and various police functions in the country. It also keeps records of all cases of forgeries and counterfeits. Documents from police formations, government offices and individuals are classified by the disputed documents unit. The Firearms Registry deals with registration of firearms throughout the country. The Drawing Office deals with preparation of graphs for the force; prints certificates for graduates of schools of the force CID; writes, designs and paints armorial bearings; repairs damaged chairs and tables; mounts and frames photographs; and stencils.

The *force CID, Kaduna,* is a branch of the force CID, Lagos. It provides specialized services and training facilities to the northern states in fingerprint, photography, criminal records, and detection and prosecution of crimes. It compiles criminal statistics of the northern states and files fingerprints of persons on remand and those seeking employment with banks, the minting company, airways, the fire service, state governments, prisons, and other ministries and departments.

The *Printing Section* prints forms used in the force CID as well as other police forms and literature.

The *Legal Section* generally gives legal advice and prosecutes criminal cases investigated by the force CID. The section also recommends charges to cases that are to be sent to the deputy public prosecutor. The force CID law library also is in this department.

The force CID runs four training schools: Detective Training School, Antifraud Training School, Fingerprint Training School and Photographic Training School. The candidates for the schools were drawn from the force CID; police units throughout Nigeria; the armed forces; and the Customs and Excise and Immigration departments. Each of the training schools conducts four different courses; each course lasts 10 weeks.

The Photographic Training School shows films to students in CID training schools, and photographs police activities for publication and instruction.

The *Statistics and Crime Records Section* of the force CID is solely responsible for supplying criminal statistics data and compiling criminal statistics of the Nigerian states as well as of the force CID and the Railway Police.

Section Units of the Nigeria Police Force

The Mounted Branch was formed in July 1961 in Kaduna as a ceremonial yeomanry troop of 15 men. Between 1880 and 1890 the Royal Higher Company Constabulary had a Mounted Section, "Carroll's Horses," patrolling its installations on the banks of the Niger River.

The Mounted Branch also patrols borders and assists the Customs and Excise Department to combat smuggling.

The Police Dog Section was established in Lagos in 1963 with only six dogs but has been expanded to cover all the states of the country. Police dogs patrol oil installations in addition to routine guard duties and use at crime scenes. The Dog Training School in Lagos also trains dogs for prison service, while police officers are trained as dog handlers.

The Nigeria Railway Police polices all Nigerian Railway premises. Recently, strikes have been common, particularly in the northern and eastern districts. Pickpocketing in railway stations has been reduced to a minimum.

Theft by striking dock workers and others is the prevalent offense in the quays and is combated by the Port Authority Police.

The need for effective communication has made the steady expansion of the Force Signals Section necessary. There are 201 radio stations under this unit. Telex circuits were also commissioned at Abakaliki, Yola, Ijebu-Ode, Onitsha and Aba. These additional installations increased the number in the telex network to 17. A total of 207 patrol cars were equipped with radios.

The Public Relations Branch of Department A (headquarters) has a section in each state command headquarters. The branch is mostly manned by officers trained in journalism and public relations, though assisted by general-duty police officers.

The Central Motor Registry is a branch of the force headquarters and is the principal licensing authority in the country. The functions of the registry are derived from Section 3 of Chapter 184 of Laws of Nigeria of 1958, which provides for the approval of professional driving licenses to qualified applicants, and the issue of international driving permits and international certificates for motor vehicles. The Registry also keeps records of all vehicles registered and licenses issued in Nigeria.

Nigeria Police Force Auxiliaries

The Special Constabulary augments the force in combating crime and maintaining law and order.

There are two categories of supernumerary constables. The first consists of personnel serving at force and area command headquarters. Those in the second category, though enlisted by the force, are hired out to commercial firms on request on the approval of the head of state to protect company property.

The Traffic Warden Service, which started specifically for traffic control in Lagos in 1975, has expanded to state capitals. The wardens support the Motor Traffic divisions to cope with the nation's perennial traffic congestion.

A Police Band with drum, fife, and bugle accompanied British governor H. McCallum on a recruitment tour of Yorubaland in 1897. The present Central Band was formed in 1920 and consisted of drums and fifes. In 1959, pipes were added. The Central Band, made up of the Military Band, Pipe Band and the force School of Music and Piping is a ceremonial arm of the force headquarters based at Ikeja, with branches in six state capitals. With 211 members, it performs at public and private functions and concerts. State bands are in Enugu, Kaduna, Maiduguri, Ibadan, Benin and Jos. The School of Music and Piping has trained many members of state bands.

The Police Medical Service, which was established in 1975, has 12 functioning clinics, five in Lagos and its environs. One is at the staff college in Jos, while three are in police colleges at Kaduna, Enugu and Maiduguri. The remaining three are at Owerri, Umuahia and Aba in Imo State.

Policewomen were first brought into the Nigeria Police Force in 1955. They are concerned mainly with radio dispatch; desk duties; motor traffic control; and investigation of cases involving women, juvenile offenders and missing persons. Nigerian policewomen enjoy good relations with the public and have the same entry standards as their male counterparts except that they have a minimum height requirement of 1.62 meters, no chest measurement and must be unmarried to be eligible for recruitment.

Members of the Nigeria police wear dark blue uniforms and gray shirts with silver buttons for ceremonial occasions and khaki work uniforms of British design with dark blue peaked caps. The cap badge depicts an elephant, two crossed batons, and "The Nigeria Police" in scroll, the whole surmounted by an eagle.

Normally, the Nigerian policeman is unarmed except for a billy club or baton. Many have been trained in the use of light infantry weapons, however, and are armed in emergency situations. In dealing with disturbances he is trained in the use of tear gas and firearms. Antiriot drills and parades are held weekly at police stations.

Particular attention is given to the antiriot drills. For this purpose, the police are formed into units of 50, under command of an officer. These units contain baton sections, a tear gas section, a rifle section, stretcher bearers and buglers. The units are fully mobile, provided with radio communications and can travel over rough terrain. Great emphasis is placed on using only the minimum amount of force to deal with a disturbance, and although one section of seven men in each riot unit is armed with rifles, only rarely are these weapons used.

The size of Nigeria and the scarcity of adequate roads enhance the value of radio communications in police work. The force headquarters in Lagos has a direct link to state headquarters. More than 38 stations maintain subsidiary links within the 12 states. In addition, an expanding VHF teleprinter system links Lagos headquarters with state headquarters and the latter with certain of the more important provinces. Many towns also have VHF stations connecting a control room to patrol cars engaged in traffic control and crime prevention.

A large fleet of motor vehicles designed to carry personnel over rough roads is maintained by the police. A number of motor launches are also used on creeks and the Niger Delta, where many villages and towns are accessible only by water.

Foot Patrols

Foot patrols of uniformed officers have been very effective in preventing crime, facilitating the detection of certain forms of street crime, getting to know the local population and above all for maintaining direct contact between police and public.

Many criteria determine the introduction of foot patrols: the size of the territory to be patrolled, the type of area, the presence of banks and shops, the density of the population, the structure and way of life of the community, the crime rate in the places and the frequency or likelihood of incidents in the streets or area to be patrolled according to the time of day or day of the week.

The same police officers usually are assigned to a particular area in the country. These officers pay particular attention to the protection of public and commercial establishments or deserted premises.

Composition of foot patrols varies, depending on the availability of manpower, the characteristics of the district to be patrolled and the experience acquired by the police. Generally, the patrol has at least two men, who are supported at night by motorized patrols with which they have radio contact. The patrolmen stay on their beat for eight hours a day.

Police officers on foot patrol reach their beat by their own means (usually by bicycles or motorcycles or on foot) or are taken there from an assembly point in a police vehicle. The officers are often in contact with police headquarters, the nearest police station or police cars by means of two-way radio. They usually carry a small stick but sometimes are armed at night or during sensitive assignments. They may also be accompanied by dogs in special circumstances.

Motorized or Car Patrols

There are essentially four methods of car patrol employed by the Nigeria Police Force. These are the so-called roundabout patrol system, antirobbery patrols, the Highway Patrol and the Police Accident Patrol.

The "roundabout" system of patrol was introduced by the Lagos State Police. The system involves assigning policemen to all the important roundabouts (traffic circles) in urban areas on beat duty. Such men usually are equipped with walkie-talkies, with which they call their operational base for reinforcements or to report suspicious activity, while, in turn, instructions are communicated to them through the same medium. The system has made it possible for all the policemen on duty at the roundabout to keep an eye on all movements in the area. Through this means gangs of armed robbers, missing persons roaming the streets and wanted persons have been detected and action taken.

Each police station has antirobbery patrol teams, which are always mobile. Their functions include apprehension of gangs or individuals caught in the act of a robbery, and interception of gangs or individuals suspected to be about to commit a robbery. The antirobbery patrol has been successful in apprehending a number of armed and unarmed robbers, while attempts by several armed gangs have been foiled.

Police Highway Patrol teams are equipped with radios, ambulances, recovery vehicles and a number of motorcycles. Each team has highly sophisticated communications equipment. Their duties include clearing roads to prevent delays and accidents, booking offending drivers and curbing dangerous driving. In addition, they aid accident victims; take the victims to the hospital; and prevent armed robbery on highways.

The reorganized Highway Patrol Unit of the Nigeria Police was introduced during the Third National Development Plan in the first quarter of 1975 with 25 patrol teams. Establishment of this unit has greatly enhanced effective enforcement of traffic laws on the expanding highway system, which had been covered only by conventional police traffic patrol units. The number of patrol units has increased to 36 nationwide, controlled directly from force headquarters in Lagos. At least 60% of the entire federal highway network is effectively patrolled for one eight-hour shift daily. Activities of each patrol team include enforcement of traffic regulations, apprehension of reckless drivers, checking highway robberies, recovering stolen vehicles, rendering first aid to injured victims of road accidents and removal of obstructions.

It has been suggested that efficiency of the Highway Patrol Units could be further enhanced if uniform traffic regulations prevailed throughout the country. There is also need for highway speed limits for all types of vehicles.

The Police Accident Patrol is intended to check instances of and prevent hit-and-run driving and prevent or reduce deaths from lack of immediate medical attention to victims of road accidents.

The Nigeria Police Force has tended to overconcentrate on foot patrol as distinct from motor patrol. As a result, a substantial part of the population and area is virtually unpoliced and unpatrolled, and policemen are also generally frustrated and overworked.

Sometimes horses used for patrols in parts of the northern states. The presence of the tsetse flies has made use of horses impracticable in other parts of the country.

Recruitment, Education & Training

Active recruitment of young policemen is undertaken to provide high-quality personnel. It is as widespread as possible, and a large variety of tribes are represented on the Nigeria Police Force.

Rank in order of seniority, Nigeria Police Force:

1. inspector general
2. deputy inspector general
3. assistant inspector general
4. commissioner of police
5. deputy commissioner
6. assistant commissioner
7. chief superintendent
8. superintendent
9. deputy superintendent
10. assistant superintendent

    Senior Police Officers' Rank

11. chief inspector
12. inspector
13. sergeant major
14. sergeant
15. corporal
16. constable
17. recruit

The requirement that applicants attain a minimum educational qualification standard of Secondary Class IV (a year just short of the full high-school certificate) precipitated initial recruitment problems in the northern states because of the generally lower educational levels there. Recruitment takes place regularly at all divisional police headquarters in every local government area, and at the police colleges at Ikeja, Kaduna, Enugu and Maiduguri. Those who qualify are then required to pass a physical examination, must be of good character and be free from financial embarrassment before they are accepted for training.

The recruit attends a basic six-month course at one of the police colleges. During this training period the young constable is taught basic law and police duties, drill, musketry and first aid. He also undergoes rigorous physical training; participates in a wide variety of sports, such as soccer, field hockey, athletics, boxing and gymnastics; and is taught to be alert and self-reliant. At the same time, he is attached to a particular police command for practical experience in routine matters.

Some candidates are recruited directly into the cadet subinspectorate cadre. This was introduced in 1953 to attract young men with higher-than-average education (usually at least a high-school certificate). In 1925 the first cadet inspectors were recruited by the police, but the scheme was abandoned in 1935. Another group of recruits is admitted directly into the cadet assistant superintendent rank—the lowest senior officer rank in the Nigeria Police and the only one in which direct entry is possible in the upper-officer echelon. Entrants are university graduates.

Both inspector and assistant superintendent ranks are also open to officers of lower rank, who may be promoted to those and other positions depending upon performance in prescribed refresher courses and how well they have applied themselves in their assignments.

There are currently five major police colleges. That at Ikeja was opened in 1948 and is the largest and oldest in the country. It handles basic police training for recruits from the southern states. All police cadet inspectors and senior officers recruited from the civil service or elsewhere are also trained there.

The police college at Kaduna was established in 1949 and is the second-largest basic police training institution in the country. That at Enugu serves the recruitment needs of Anambra, Bendel, Cross River, Imo and Rivers states. It also supplements the police college at Ikeja for police recruit requirements of Lagos, Oyo, Ogun and Ondo states.

Opened in 1973, the police college at Maiduguri started with 120 recruits. This college trains recruits enlisted mainly from Bauchi, Borno, Gongola, Benue and Plateau states.

The police staff college at Jos is exclusively designed to provide police command training for senior police officers. It opened in 1976 with 26 cadet assistant superintendents.

The courses of instruction at these schools include police ordinances and regulations, criminal law, laws of evidence, motor traffic ordinances, police and station duties, fingerprinting, taking statements, and preparation of reports and sketches at the scene of a crime or accident. Interpretation of town ordinances and proper methods of keeping books and records in police stations are also taught. Also covered are theoretical and practical work, including preparation of mock cases for court presentation. An intensive physical training program includes food drill, arms drill, parades, unarmed combat tactics and riot control techniques. Instruction in these colleges can be very advanced, detailed and technical. In addition to specialized training within the force, selected senior members attend courses of instruction in the United Kingdom or the United States. Selected noncommissioned officers and constables are also sent to the United Kingdom to be trained in such specialized areas as fingerprinting, dog handling, handwriting analysis, photography and forensic science.

The Penal System

Nigerian criminal law is entirely statutory and is based largely on two separate criminal codes. The Northern Criminal Code applies to the inhabitants of the six states of the former Northern Region; the Nigerian Criminal Code has universal application in the remaining six states, in the South. Some customary laws dealing with criminal offenses remain in effect, but these have been incorporated into one of the two codes or are supported by separate legislation.

The Nigerian Criminal Code is generally based on the uncodified principles of English criminal law. A crime is punishable only by the state and not by tribal authorities. Offenses are classified as felonies, misdemeanors or simple offenses, each distinguished by a scale of punishments. Felonies are punishable by death or imprisonment for at least three years, while misdemeanors carry imprisonment of from six months to three years. Specified offenses enumerated in the code are categorized as those against persons; those against property and contracts; and those against the state, the last category including offenses against public morals, public health and animals, and the practice of witchcraft.

In addition to the Criminal Code, certain other ordinances apply to the enforcement of criminal law: the Collective Punishment Ordinance, the Preservation of Peace Ordinance and others.

The Northern Criminal Code is based on the Sudan Code, which was derived from the Penal Code of India and ultimately from English common law. It establishes for the northern states a single criminal code compatible with Islam. Unlike the Nigerian Criminal Code, the Northern Criminal Code deviates considerably from Anglo-Saxon legal concepts. Provocation, for example, mitigates the punishment for homicide. Crimes under traditional Muslim law, such as adultery, drinking alcoholic beverages and insults to the modesty of women are preserved in the northern code but are not crimes in the South. The Northern Criminal Code does not contain references to such offenses as treason, sedition, customs violations or counterfeiting. Statutory laws dealing with such activities have been enacted separately and appear as an addendum to the code.

Punishments in both codes are generally harsh and intended as deterrents, although the principle of rehabilitation is acknowledged. The range covers death, imprisonment, whipping, fines and forfeiture of property. A sentence of death may not be passed on any offender who is less than 17 years of age or on a pregnant woman. Before 1966, death sentences were by hanging, but since then convicted death row inmates have been executed by shooting, often in public. Corporal punishment is generally administered in the form of a specified number of strokes by light rod, cane, or whip with a single lash. Islamic law is more severe toward certain offenses, such as consumption of alcoholic beverages and theft, and prescribes draconian punishments such as amputation of the hand and flogging.

Until 1966 the corrections system was under the central as well as the local governments. The federal government controls and operates 51 prisons, at least two prison farms and two reformatories. Four of the facilities are in the North and the rest in the South, mainly in the former Western and Eastern regions and in Lagos. Until 1968 local authorities in the North maintained 64 prisons, and eight penal institutions were run by local governments in the Western State.

The Nigerian correctional system was established during the British colonial era. Originally all federal prisons were operated by the police, but in 1908 a separate Prisons Department was established in southern Nigeria. In 1938 several northern prisons were redesignated federal institutions and placed under the Prisons Department. At independence the federal system was transferred to the central government, while the local prisons continued to operate under local authorities.

Federal prisons are classified as convict, provincial and divisional. Convict prisons are maximum-security institutions that receive all classes of prisoners, while provincial and divisional prisons receive only those whose sentences do not exceed two years.

There are few female prisoners; consequently, there

CRIME STATISTICS (1983)

		Number Reported	Attempts %	Cases Solved %	Crime per 100,000	Offenders	Females %	Juveniles %	Strangers %
1.	Murder	1,687	13.2	53.1	1.69	2,300	0.6	0.1	0.2
2.	Sex offenses, including rape	1,788		48.3	1.79	1,387		0.3	0.2
3.	Rape								
4.	Serious assault	44,958		62.1	44.96	52,628	59.0	2.2	0.05
5.	All theft	63,161		47.0	63.16	71,603	1.7	1.7	0.08
6.	Aggravated theft								
7.	Robbery and violent theft	1,430		25.9	1.43	1,320	0.2	1.0	1.7
8.	Breaking and entering	12,401		39.5	12.40	11,310		0.2	0.5
9.	Auto theft	4,010		31.1	4.01	1,760	0.1	0.5	0.7
10.	Other thefts								
11.	Fraud	223		18.3	0.22	247	0.0	0.8	1.2
12.	Counterfeiting	157		43.9	0.16	116	0.0	2.5	1.7
13.	Drug offenses	118		30.5	0.12	1,428	3.8	0.4	0.1
14.	Total offenses	311,961	0.07	46.4	311.96	177,736	4.7	1.6	0.1

Note: Information for some categories is not available.
Criteria of juveniles: aged from 0 to 17 years.

are no prisons designated for women. Some prisons have segregated sections for women, where they are employed in domestic crafts.

Convicted juveniles between 14 and 18 years are incarcerated in the juvenile section of the Port Harcourt Prison. There are two reformatories for offenders under age 21: the Approved School at Enugu in East-Central State, and the reformatory at Kakuri in North-Central State. In federal prisons male and female prisoners are segregated, and first offenders are separated from hardened criminals. Prison labor is divided into three main categories: industrial labor, domestic labor and unskilled labor.

In 1968 the federal military government federalized all prisons in the country and vested their administration in the Federal Executive Council's commissioner for internal affairs and police. The headquarters is headed by a director of prisons, and each district headquarters by an assistant director of prisons. In 1974 the prisons were reclassified on a functional basis into remand and reception centers, industrial production prisons, industrial training institutions and prison farms.

The Nigerian government does not have a reporting system on crime or corrections, and therefore no statistics are available in these areas. From newspaper accounts, the principal criminal activities appear to be armed robbery, theft, drug trafficking and smuggling. The Robbery and Firearms (Special Provisions) Decree imposes harsh sentences on those convicted of armed robbery. Theft of public property is perhaps the most common criminal activity. Particularly in Lagos ports entire shiploads of machinery and industrial materials disappear overnight. Smuggling, likewise, is so extensive as to defy law-enforcement efforts. Drug trafficking is a more recent problem, placing additional burdens on the limited police capabilities.

NORWAY

BASIC FACT SHEET

Official Name: Kingdom of Norway
Area: 324,219 sq km
Population: 4,178,545 (1987)
Capital: Oslo
Nature of Government: Constitutional monarchy
Language: Norwegian
Currency: Krone
GNP: $57.58 billion (1985)
Territorial Divisions: 19 counties, 407 communes
Population per Police Officer: 560
Police Expenditures per 1,000: $78,262

History & Background

As in other Scandinavian countries, local police existed in Norway from the 12th century. The first chief constable was appointed in Trondheim in 1686 and in Oslo, Bergen and Kristiansand in the 1700s. The nucleus of a national police force was created in 1738, and a full-fledged uniformed police appeared in the 19th century. The force emerged into its modern form with the enactment of the 1936 Police Law, under which the municipal forces were merged with the state police.

Structure & Organization

For operational purposes, the kingdom is divided into 55 districts, each under a *politimester,* appointed by the crown. The *politimester* reports directly to the Ministry of Justice and Police in Oslo. Senior police officers—deputy chiefs, chief superintendents and superintendents—are appointed by royal decree. Junior ranks are appointed by the minister of justice and police or (below inspectors first class) by the Area Board.

Each district has a number of police stations headed by lieutenants first class who have lieutenants and constables under him. The largest police district is Greater Oslo. The urban police forces have at least three branches—Administration, General Duties and Criminal Police—while larger cities have two additional branches—Traffic and Aliens. In Oslo and Bergen there is also a Harbor Police. Other centralized police services include the Intelligence Unit; the Police Security Service; the Central Criminal Police Bureau, which represents Interpol in Norway; the Narcotics Branch; and the Police School.

Some 150 men in the district forces are nominally selected for duty with the Mobile Police Corps, which is raised whenever mobile reinforcements are required in any district. Their nomination lasts for five years. Although originally established to deal with large-scale disorders, the Corps is now mainly used to provide reinforcements for the local police when dealing with heavy summer traffic. There is also a police reserve of 4,500 men, who are conscripted and trained for service in the event of war.

Norway also has a special grade of policeman known as *lensmann,* whose office corresponds to that of sheriff in the United States. He has parapolice duties, such as collection of taxes, execution of distraints, service of civil process and conduct of elections. He may have up to 10 assistants or deputies who, along with him, are subordinate to the *politimester.*

All newly appointed constables spend their probationary period in one of the three large cities—Oslo, Bergen or Trondheim—before being assigned to another district. A number of women are employed in the force and deal mainly with juveniles.

Although major offenses are handled by the state prosecutor, the *politimester* has the authority to prosecute offenders for nonindictable crimes. He may also impose fines on minor offenders, subject to the right of the accused to claim a court hearing.

The uniform is a dark blue jacket and trousers for all ranks and for both men and women. On regular duty, the men wear a peaked cap also in blue but with a white cover in the summer. A type of forage cap is worn when on car patrol and an astrakhan fur hat in the winter. The badge is worn centrally in the front of the hat. For special occasions a black leather Sam

Browne belt is worn, and a similar belt in white is worn when on traffic duty, together with a white baton. Arms usually are not carried, but all constables carry a baton.

Recruitment, Education & Training

Recruits to the force receive a four-week training course before they enter the service. Candidates are required to work one year under the supervision of a senior officer, who submits a personal report on the candidate's performance to the Appointments Board. On the board's recommendation, the candidate is admitted to the Police School, where he or she undergoes a 10-month training course before being appointed as a police constable.

The Penal System

No information is available on this penal system.

CRIME STATISTICS (1983)

		Number Reported	Attempts %	Cases Solved %	Crime per 100,000	Offenders	Females %	Juveniles %	Strangers %
1.	Murder	38		81.6	0.92	33	6.1	27.3	
2.	Sex offenses, including rape	896		45.5	21.73	305	1.6	18.4	
3.	Rape	175		32.0	4.24	65		29.2	
4.	Serious assault	916		52.4	22.22	391	4.9	38.4	
5.	All theft	118,021		15.3	2,862.84	9,260	11.4	58.3	
6.	Aggravated theft	65,888		14.4	1,598.25	5,576	5.5	64.0	
7.	Robbery and violent theft								
8.	Breaking and entering								
9.	Auto theft	11,260		23.1	273.13	723	5.1	61.3	
10.	Other thefts	40,873		14.4	991.46	2,961	24.3	46.9	
11.	Fraud	6,955		53.9	168.71	1,480	17.3	27.4	
12.	Counterfeiting	38		13.2	0.92	5		20.0	
13.	Drug offenses	3,793		83.1	92.01	1,885	16.9	30.2	
14.	Total offenses	159,598		21.1	3,871.38	16,638	11.4	49.4	

Note: Information for some categories is not available.
Criteria of juveniles: aged from 5 to 20 years.

PAKISTAN

BASIC FACT SHEET

Official Name: Islamic Republic of Pakistan
Area: 803,943 sq km
Population: 104,600,799 (1987)
Capital: Islamabad
Nature of Government: Military Dictatorship
Languages: Urdu and English
Currency: Rupee
GNP: $36.23 billion (1985)
Territorial Divisions: 4 provinces, 1 territory
Population per Police Officer: 720
Police Expenditures per 1,000: $1,954

History & Background

For the history of the Pakistani police, see "India."

Structure & Organization

The maintenance of law and order in Pakistan is essentially a provincial function; consequently, the majority of the police are organized under provincial governments. Certain national agencies function under the Ministry of the Interior. These include the small but elite Police Service of Pakistan (PSP), whose members hold the senior positions at national and provincial levels; the Federal Investigation Agency, which investigates corruption in public services; and the Frontier Constabulary, operating against smuggling and tribal feuding. In 1973 a new national-level body, the Federal Security Force, was formed to perform guard duties and as a police reserve. Police services at the provincial and national levels are governed by uniform regulations carried over almost intact from preindependence British India. In general, the police are oppressive and corrupt and much disliked. Several high-level commissions have studied the police system and recommended many changes. The system as a whole, however, is entrenched and has proved resistant to change. They are also subject to partisan political manipulation, sectarian and regional rivalries, and an overburdened bureaucracy. In its role of combating threats to internal security, the police are assisted by regular armed forces.

The provincial forces are not integrated organizationally, but they function under a common system, making them almost identical in operation and administration. Many administrative matters, such as minimum pay, allowances and uniforms, are prescribed at the national level. The basic system is governed by the Police Act of 1861, as amended, subject to the provisions of the 1973 Constitution. The methods and procedures are strongly influenced by British traditions, but the equipment and training reflect U.S. models.

The core of the police establishment is the Police Service of Pakistan, formed at independence with Muslim members of the Police Service of British India as its nucleus. The PSP is not an operational entity. It is a career service from which individual officers are individually assigned to police units. All senior officers both in the national agencies and in the provincial police are members of the PSP.

Two of the principal national-level agencies, both under the Interior Division of the Ministry of the Interior, are the Federal Investigation Agency and the Federal Security Force. The Federal Investigation Agency (FIA) was formed in 1941 as the Anticorruption Agency. This agency has investigative powers and may initiate investigations of its own or respond to requests from other government departments on matters such as embezzlement, bribery, black marketing, and misappropriation of funds. Its director has the rank of inspector general of police, and its strength is estimated at 1,000.

Little information is available on the Federal Security Force, but it appears to have the characteristics of a paramilitary police reserve for control of public disturbances and for important guard duties. It is believed to consist of up to 19 battalions stationed at garrisons in the capital and in key locations throughout the country.

At the national level, the best-known paramilitary police is the long-established Frontier Constabulary, with headquarters in Peshawar under a deputy inspector general of police, who reports to the minister of the interior. Its total strength is estimated at close to 13,000. Constabulary units are stationed in the North-West Frontier Province (NWFP), near the tribal areas inhabited by the fierce Pathans. Their function is to maintain law and order in the traditionally lawless areas bordering Afghanistan. Within the tribal agencies are other paramilitary bodies collectively called the Frontier Corps, which are Army auxiliaries.

At least two other organizations at the national level are involved in tasks relating to law and order, although neither is directly part of the police structure. The Intelligence Bureau, part of the Cabinet Division, reports to the prime minister. The Directorate of Civil Defense under the Interior Division of the Ministry of the Interior is charged with planning and directing civil relief in disasters and other emergency situations.

Because the primary responsibility for the maintenance of law and order rests with the provincial governments, the majority of the police are in the provincial police services. In their respective provinces, the provincial services control the regular police; the other specialized security forces of the special armed reserve; the railway, highway and river police; and the village police. In the mid-1980s, the total strength of these forces was estimated at over 100,000. The largest segment is in the Punjab, followed, in order, by those of Sind, the NWFP and Baluchistan.

Police officers are categorized as gazetted or subordinate, roughly analogous, respectively, to commissioned and noncommissioned officers in the military services. The subordinate grades are further divided into upper and lower categories. The top five grades, in descending order, are those of inspector general, additional inspector general, deputy inspector general, superintendent and assistant superintendent. These grades are invariably filled by PSP officers. In the provincial police services the top grade is deputy superintendent, equivalent to assistant superintendent, the lowest PSP grade. Below these gazetted ranks are the upper subordinate positions, in descending order, of inspector, subinspector and assistant subinspector. Below them are the rank and file, including head constable and constable.

Each province is divided for purposes of police as well as local government administration into a number of divisions, totaling 13 in the four provinces. Corresponding to each division and coterminous with the divisional commissioner's jurisdiction is the territorial police area called a range. Each range, in turn, is divided into districts, which are futher broken down into varying numbers of subdistricts, each of which has a number of police stations called station houses or *thanas*. Some districts do not have subdistricts, and here the station houses report directly to the district headquarters.

In each province the head of the police establishment is the inspector general of police, who reports to the secretary of the home department of the provincial government. The inspector general, who may be aided by an additional inspector general, supervises several deputy inspectors general at the provincial headquarters, each in charge of a certain function, such as criminal investigation, communications, identification, railway security or administrative affairs. Outside the headquarters, the inspector general exercises general supervision over all the police ranges in his province, each under a deputy inspector general.

Within the ranges the districts are the fulcrums of police operations. The district chief is the superintendent, assisted by one or more assistant superintendents and a number of inspectors and other ranks. The subdistrict is supervised by an assistant or deputy superintendent; the station house is commanded by one of the upper subordinate grades and manned by 10 to 20 head constables and constables. In the larger cities, the police are organized on a municipal basis but remain part of the provincial police and answer to the inspector general of that province.

At all levels, the senior police officer is linked to a dual chain of command, that of the police organization and that of designated civil government. This sometimes causes confusion and discord, but the principle of ultimate civilian control was established by the Police Act of 1861 and continued under both civilian and military governments. Thus, at the provincial level, the inspector general reports to the provincial home department; at the division, or police range, level, the deputy inspector general answers to the divisional commissioner; and at the district level, the police superintendent is subordinate to the deputy commissioner—the district officer and magistrate—who is in overall charge of tax collection, law and order, administration of justice, and development. Although the deputy commissioner has no authority to interfere directly in the internal organization and discipline of the police, an important part of his duties is to inspect the police stations of his district at regular intervals. In case the deputy commissioner and the police chief disagree on issues relating to police functions, the deputy commissioner's judgment rules, but he is dependent on police cooperation. In case of serious differences, however, both may refer the disputed matter to higher authorities for reconciliation: the deputy commissioner to his commissioner, and the superintendent to his deputy inspector general.

The provincial police also includes a number of specialized categories. The transportation system is secured by railway, highway and river police. The provincial special force are anticorruption establishments that perform at a lower level functions similar to that of the Federal Investigation Agency. In each province the inspector general also has what is called the Special Armed Police to deal with such critical functions as protection of public installations in times of civil commotion, armed escort for important public officials, peacekeeping during festivals and sports events, relief and rescue work during natural calamities, and the operation of armored cars carrying strategic or other valuable materials.

Assisting the regular police in the rural areas are semiofficial part-time village constables called *chowkidars* or *dafadars,* who report violations to the nearest police station or apprehend offenders on police orders. The village constables are recruited and controlled locally and given some remuneration, clothing for night duty and in some cases small arms. The number of such constables varies with the size of the village and the incidence of crime.

Both national and provincial police forces have their own distinct uniforms, the most common being a gray shirt worn with khaki trousers, or a khaki drill tunic and trousers. A blue cap or beret completes the outfit.

The Pakistani police are one of the most pervasive institutions in society, but they are spread thin, overworked, poorly paid, poorly equipped and trained, and subject to frequent swings in official policy. Attempts have been made periodically to institute radical reforms in the system, but these have fallen by the wayside. The last major effort to do so was the establishment in 1969 of a 12-member Police Commission to study a wide range of law-and-order issues and recommend changes. Their terms of reference included the conduct and efficiency of the police; the working relations between the police and the magistracy; the question of decentralization of authority and the delegation of powers in the police hierarchy; the extent and nature of malpractice and police brutality; recruitment, training and disciplinary procedures; the state of police welfare and remuneration; and the effective utilization of semiofficial rural police organizations. The commission's report, produced in 1970, was given limited circulation among government officials but was not publicly disseminated. By this time, the political unrest in East Pakistan (now Bangladesh) was engaging the primary attention of the government, and nothing resulted from the work of the commission. On the return of civilian government under Z. A. Bhutto in 1972, fresh reforms were proposed in three areas: police pay and remuneration, police communications and mobility, and public relations. With Bhutto's fall, these proposals were shelved and have never been revived. The Zia regime, drawing its strength from the conservative and entrenched elites, was content to coast along and retain the status quo and disinclined to introduce radical changes. Police strikes and public demonstrations against police brutality have been frequent in recent Pakistani history.

Recruitment, Education & Training

PSP officers are selected through comprehensive annual examinations conducted by the Federal Public Service Commission. A ranked list of eligible candidates, based on examination grades, is drawn up annually by the commission, and from this list new officer appointments are made according to vacancies and quotas by the Establishment Division. This division also controls training, assignment, promotion and administrative policy. Typically, only 20 to 30 appointments are made annually. The total strength of the PSP is estimated to be fewer than 1,500.

The successful PSP entrant—or probationer, as he is called—spends the first half of his two-year apprenticeship at the Pakistan Police Academy at Sihala, near Rawalpindi. In his first year, he receives instruction in criminal law, police procedures, forensic medicine and language, among other subjects. The second year customarily is divided between service with a military unit and service at a district police headquarters. Upon completion of the second year, the probationer is given the rank of assistant superintendent of police and assigned either to a national-level agency or, more likely, to one of the provincial police forces, where he will have charge of several police stations. Although he is then likely to remain in the same province for an extended period, the PSP officer, unlike the non-PSP provincial officers and men, always is subject to transfer to any post in the country.

Provincial police officers are recruited and appointed at the provincial level. Constables are recruited at the district level. Each province has a police training center where the constables receive a minimum of six months' training. In the lower subordinate grades, the pay, morale and educational levels are low, and advancement is very slow. Women are eligible for police service, but their number is small, as should be expected in a Muslim society.

The Penal System

Law enforcement and crime and punishment are governed by a number of statutes, some of them inherited from the British raj: the Penal Code of Pakistan, first promulgated in 1860 as the Indian Penal Code; the Police Act of 1861, the Evidence Act of 1872; the Code of Criminal Procedure of 1898; the Criminal Law (Amendment) Act of 1908; and the Official Secrets Act of 1911, as amended. Enacted after independence were the Security of Pakistan Act of 1952;

the Press Publications Ordinance of 1960; the Political Parties Act of 1962; and a host of other laws directed at corruption, espionage and smuggling. In any case, the regular and emergency executive powers of the Constitution, especially in Articles 232 to 235, give the president and the central government more than ample authority to exercise firm control over all segments of society.

The country's most comprehensive penal statute is the Penal Code of Pakistan, which lists major classes of crime, including what are called "offenses against the state." Punishment is divided into five classes: death; banishment, ranging from seven years to 20 or more; imprisonment; forfeiture of property; and fine. The imprisonment may be simple or rigorous, ranging from a minimum of 24 hours for a drunk to a maximum of 14 years at hard labor. Juvenile offenders may be sentenced to detention in reformatory schools for three to seven years; for minor infractions, whipping, not exceeding 15 lashes, may be prescribed as an alternative to detention. With the introduction of Sharia (Muslim law), even more draconian punishments have become commonplace, such as amputation of hands for theft and flogging for adultery.

The Penal Code applies to all citizens except the president, diplomats, provincial governors, and justices of the Supreme Court or a High Court. Tribal areas also are outside the scope of the Penal Code. These areas are administered by centrally appointed political agents and policed by the Frontier Corps and Frontier Constabulary aided by local tribal guards or *khassadars*. The Frontier Crimes Regulation of 1901 and the tribal customary law, adjudicated by the *jirga* or the Council of Mailks (tribal elders), are in force supplemented by governmental regulations. The Penal Code also exempts from liability judicial acts done in good faith, acts of children under seven years of age, acts of persons of unsound mind and acts done in self-defense.

The Security of Pakistan Act of 1952 and its provincial equivalents empower the authorities to indict any person "acting in a manner prejudicial to the defense, external affairs and security of Pakistan, or the maintenance of public order." Preventive detention also may be ordered under Section 107 of the Code of Criminal Procedure when, in the opinion of the authorities, there is a strong likelihood of public disorder. Section 144 of the code, which frequently is invoked by the magistrates, prohibits the assembly of five or more persons, the holding of public meetings and the carrying of firearms. In addition, the Disturbed Areas (Special Powers) Ordinance of 1962 empowers the magistrate or the officer in charge of a police contingent to open fire or use force against any person breaching the peace in disturbed areas and to arrest and search without warrant.

To protect the fundamental rights of a preventive detainee, the authority issuing the order of detention is required by law to inform him or her of the grounds for such action within one month of the date of detention, unless the disclosure of the reason is deemed to affect public interests. The government also is required to grant the detainee the right to counsel within 16 days. As amended in 1974, the act provides that the detention should not exceed three months unless an advisory board finds sufficient cause for extending the period.

A person arrested must be informed of the grounds of his or her arrest, and if detained, the reasons for the detention. The arrested person must be taken before the nearest magistrate within 24 hours and may not be detained in police custody for more than 15 days except as authorized by the magistrate. The arrested or detained person has the right to counsel at once and to be represented by the counsel of his or her choice. Statements made by the arrested person while in police custody are usually inadmissible at the trial, as are confessions obtained under duress. A pretrial inquiry must be conducted by a magistrate if the police investigative report shows reasonable evidence to do so.

The scope of the Security of Pakistan Act extends also to the mass communications media, and it is reinforced by the Press and Publications (Amendment) Ordinance of 1963. A law designed to enforce the political neutrality of public servants is the Government Servants (Conduct) Rules of 1964. Persons charged with espionage are punishable under the Official Secrets Act of 1911, as amended in 1923 and 1968, which prescribes death as the maxmum penalty.

Pretrial proceedings begin with the police investigation. Without a magistrate's warrant, the police may investigate such felonies as rioting; impersonation of a public servant; harboring an offender; counterfeiting; destroying, defiling or damaging a place of worship or sacred object; murder or attempted murder; attempt to commit suicide, abandonment of a child under 12 years of age; serious personal injury; kidnapping; rape; theft; robbery; and dacoity. A warrant from a first- or second-class magistrate is mandatory for investigating offenses against the state, bribery, perjury, causing a miscarriage of justice, inciting enmity between social classes, slave trading, forced labor, extortion, forgery, defamation of character, criminal intimidation, illicit trade by public servants and making a false statement in connection with an election.

Trials are classed in two categories: summons and warrant. In the former, if a finding of guilt is made, the maximum punishment is six months' imprisonment; in the latter, death, or imprisonment exceeding six months. Prosecution is handled by police officers in magistrate courts, by a public prosecutor in a court of sessions and by the provincial advocate general before a High Court. In summons cases, the particulars of the alleged offense are stated orally to the accused, and no formal charge is prepared in writing. In a court of sessions, the judge has the discretionary power to reject the jury decision, even when unanimous, if the judge believes that the verdict is not supported by evidence and hence may constitute a miscarriage of justice. In such cases the judge must refer the case to a High Court as an appeal without recording judgment of acquittal or of conviction.

Under the Penal Code of 1860, the Prisons Act of 1894 and the Prisoners Act of 1900, the custody and rehabilitation of prisoners is a provincial function. The highest provincial official in prison administration is the inspector general of prisons; at the division or police range level, the senior official is called the director of prisons; and at the district or municipal level, the jail superintendent. Below the district jail level are the village police lockups. The central government subsidizes the operations of provincial prisons and operates the Central Jail Training Institute at Lahore.

Even by Third World standards, the prisons are grim and harsh, lacking basic amenities. The poor living conditions and absence of sanitation are attributable in great part to overcrowding, estimated at over 100% over capacity. The Jail Reform Committee of 1972 recommended a number of remedial measures, few of which have been carried out. There is only a single juvenile jail, at Landhi, near Karachi. The greater use of bail, parole and probation since 1972 is reported to have eased the congestion in some jails.

Statistics on crime are collected periodically and consolidated at the provincial and national levels. Available statistics are deficient because they do not take into account the substantial amount of crime not reported to the police. The wide fluctuations in reported crime reflect the fluid quality of the reporting system. Among the rising categories of crime are rape, offenses against property, drug trafficking, illegal possession of firearms, and robbery and burglary among the serious crimes; and illegal gambling, petty theft, harassment by urban hooligans, called *goondas*, the public teasing of women, and traffic offenses among the minor crimes.

PANAMA

BASIC FACT SHEET

Official Name: Republic of Panama
Area: 77,080 sq km
Population: 2,274,833 (1987)
Capital: Panama City
Nature of Government: Quasi-military dictatorship
Language: Spanish
Currency: Balboa
GNP: $4.40 billion (1985)
Territorial Divisions: 9 provinces, 1 intendancy
Population per Police Officer: 180
Police Expenditures per 1,000: N.A.

History & Background

The small Panamanian army that came into being when the country gained its independence in 1903 lasted for only one year before it was demobilized. To replace the disbanded army, the Corps of National Police was formed in December 1904, and for the next 49 years it functioned as the country's only armed force. The government decree establishing the National Police authorized a strength of 700, and the tiny provincial police force that had been operating since independence was incorporated into the new organization. The corps was deployed territorially in the then-existing seven provinces, and by 1908 its overall strength had grown to 1,000. By the 1940s some organizational stability had been achieved, but it was not until the presidency of José Antonio Remon in the early 1950s that the corps was institutionalized and renamed the National Guard, a title it bears today. Its organizations and functions, however, remained substantially the same. The president was designated the supreme chief *(jefe supremo),* and is constitutionally empowered to appoint the commander in chief *(comandante jefe)* of the National Guard, but in practice the real power, both over the organization and the country, is in the hands of the latter.

Structure & Organization

The organization, mission and functions of the National Guard are established by law, and it has evolved over the years to fit its dual role as an army and as the police. The force is divided into three principal segments: the general staff, the military zones and the special units.

The organizational structure of the National Guard is designed to concentrate all power in the *comandancia* (office of the commander). Power below the top is diffused; command lines emanate directly from the *comandancia* to the subordinate units. In 1978 the post of deputy commander was abolished when its incumbent opposed Omar Torrijos, and it was replaced by the newly created post of deputy chief of staff.

The General Staff (Estado Mayor) is structured in approximately the same way as a U.S. Army staff at division level. The basic similarity is in section breakdown: G-1, Personnel; G-2, Intelligence; G-3, Operations; G-4, Logistics; and G-5, Civic Action. The assistant chiefs of staff in charge of the sections are all lieutenant colonels. G-3 also directs the operations of the air and naval arms of the military.

The National Guard is deployed regionally in 10 numbered zones—two (the first and the 10th) in Panama City and one in each of the other eight provinces. By regulation, the headquarters of a zone is in the capital city of the province. A zone is commanded by a lieutenant colonel or a major assisted by an executive officer. The strengths of the zonal personnel are never revealed.

In 1959, following an amphibious invasion by a small group of armed dissidents, the Public Order Company (Compañía de Orden Público) was created as a paramilitary force. Its stated functions were to put down public disturbances; assist in maintaining order on special occasions such as sports events, parades, and festivals; coordinate relief during natural disasters; and furnish raiding parties. The Public Order Force was the precursor of the Company of Infantry that constitutes the true military element and the major combat force of the National Guard. Their only police function is the control of riots, for which they receive special training.

The Cavalry Squadron (Escuadron de Caballeria) is the most colorful unit of the National Guard, and although primarily ceremonial, it is sometimes called upon for crowd-control duties. The squadron is similar to an infantry company commanded by a captain, assisted by lieutenants and sergeants, who lead platoons and squads, respectively. The Presidential Guard is a specially selected unit charged with guarding the president and the presidential palace. On parade, or when mustered to greet foreign dignitaries, the Presidential Guard presents an impressive appearance in khaki uniforms, shiny helmets, boots with white laces, and white belts and rifle slings. Another unit is the Traffic Police (Policía Tránsito), commanded by a lieutenant colonel. Responsibilities of this unit include issuing, renewing and revoking drivers' licenses; vehicle registration; investigation of accidents and infractions of vehicle laws; inspection of vehicles for safety hazards; and development of traffic safety programs. The remaining unit of the National Guard, with a direct command line from the *comandancia*, is the security detachment at the main prison in Panama City.

The Panamanian equivalent of the FBI is the National Department of Investigations (Departmento Nacional de Investigaciónes—DENI), which was established in 1960 as the successor to the National Secret Police, founded in 1941. Unlike the latter, which functioned under the Minister of Government and Justice, DENI is under the attorney general in the Public Ministry. DENI's principal mission is political surveillance. It also maintains an identity and record bureau and a national fingerprint file. Headquarters of DENI is in Panama City, with branch offices in Colón and David. Only the Supreme Court of Justice can remove the director from office. DENI is a member of Interpol, and many of its members are alumni of the International Police Academy in Washington, D.C. After the 1968 coup, DENI was subordinated to G-2 of the General Staff of the National Guard.

The Panamanian National Guard has three officer categories: company grade (second lieutenant through captain), field grade (major through colonel) and general officer—*oficiales, jefes* and *generales,* respectively. The National Guard does not have a military rank higher than brigadier, which is the traditional title of the commander in chief. Noncommissioned officer ranks are corporal, second sergeant and first sergeant.

The most commonly seen National Guard uniforms are either green fatigues or khaki-colored short-sleeved shirts and trousers. Officers sometimes wear short-sleeved khaki shirts with dark green trousers or various (white or dark green) dress uniforms. Headgear varies from helmets or helmet liners to various-colored berets; stiff-sided visored fatigue caps; or visored felt garrison caps similar to those worn by U.S. Army officers. Field grade and general officers wear gold braid on their visored caps. Combat boots are the most common footgear, but officers often wear low-quarter shoes. Officer rank insignia consist of gold bars or stars on an elongated gold oak leaf for a brigadier general. The three NCO ranks are designated by chevrons. Distinctive unit shoulder patches are worn by all ranks on the right shoulder of their uniforms. On the left shoulder all ranks wear the familiar blue, white and red National Guard shield showing crossed rifles bisected by an upright saber.

Recruitment, Education & Training

Recruitment to the National Guard is based on voluntary enlistment. Recruits are trained at the Center for Military Training. Most enlisted men come from rural areas, while most officers come from the urban middle class. The National Guard employs a small number of women, especially as DENI investigators and as traffic police. One woman is reported to hold the rank of major, making her one of the top 20 officers.

Training is provided by both the Center for Military Instruction in the purely military aspects of the National Guardsman's work and by the Police Training Academy in purely police duties. By the early 1980s, the United States had trained over 6,000 Panamanians in its training establishments in the Panama Canal Zone and in the United States. Panamanian institutions also are reported to have trained a number of Sandinista police officers.

The Penal System

The Criminal Code and the Administrative Code, respectively, define felonies *(delitos)* and misdemeanors *(faltas)* as crimes. Sentences are prescribed according to the seriousness of the crime, but in nearly all cases the codes establish upper and lower limits. Capital and corporal punishments are prohibited. The most severe penalty is 20 years' imprisonment, and prison sentences are differentiated as to place of confinement. The most severe sentence, *reclusión* (imprisonment), specifies the place of confinement—Coiba Penal Colony—and the manner of serving—hard labor from 30 days to 20 years. The sentence of *prisión* (also, imprisonment) ranges from 30 days to 18 years. Parole is allowed for the former after three-quarters of the sentence is served and for the latter after two-thirds of the sentence is served. *Arresto* (detention), a penalty assessed for less serious offenses, does not extend beyond 18 months, usually served in a local jail. *Confinamiento* (limit) is a punishment without physical restraint that limits the offender to a specified place of residence. The least punishment is *multa* (fine), which may be combined with a jail sentence. If an offender fails to pay or defaults on payments, *multa* is converted to *arresto*. *Condena condicional* (conditional penalty) is a suspended sentence used at the discretion of a court in sentencing a first offender, except on a major felony charge.

Cases of minors are handled by a special system designed to combat juvenile delinquency and to keep young offenders from contact with hardened criminals. The Guardianship Court for Minors, established in 1951, works closely with the National Guard and various social agencies to handle cases of young offenders and to provide them with guidance. Cases involving persons under age 18 are not revealed to the public.

Although trial by jury is established by Article 197 of the Constitution, in practice most cases are conducted by deposition and the accused is not present during the proceedings, except in the most serious criminal cases. The most frequent complaints against the criminal justice system concern arbitrary arrests and imprisonments; circumvention of the right of habeas corpus and the 24-hour limit on holding an arrestee; and the summary and often arbitrary justice dispensed in the night courts, which sit from 6:00 P.M. to 6:00 A.M.

The penal institutions are governed by Article 27 of the Constitution, which lays down the principle of rehabilitation of prisoners. The Department of Corrections was established in 1940 to administer the prisons for the Ministry of Government and Justice. Operations of the prisons had previously been a direct function of the National Police. Most jails, however, are still staffed by the National Guard. Isla de Coiba is the site of the Coiba Penal Colony, founded in 1919. Although designed for hardened criminals, it also houses a minority of offenders awaiting trial. In the main camp there are facilities for rehabilitation training and a small school, but most inmates live too far away from them. Work without remuneration is required of all prisoners. Some released prisoners have charged the penal colony with brutality, the employment of slave labor, and inadequate food and medical supplies.

The Model Jail (Cárcel Modelo) in Panama City was built in 1920 and has acquired since then a reputation that belies its name. The biggest problem, of course, is overcrowding, with cells designed to hold three holding up to 15. There is a jail in each provincial capital. In contrast to these institutions is the Women's Rehabilitation Center in Panama City run by a Roman Catholic order of nuns. It has acquired a just reputation for being one of the best-organized and cleanest institutions in Central America, with a discipline that is tempered by humaneness and decency.

Of the total number of felonies and misdemeanors, 62% occurred in Panama City, followed by the provinces of Chiriquí and Colón. Crimes against property lead the list of offenses, followed by "crimes against good custom and against family order," which include sex crimes and "disorderly conduct." Other crimes against persons are less numerous.

PAPUA NEW GUINEA

Structure & Organization

The principal police agency is the Papua New Guinea Police Constabulary, under a commissioner of police, who reports to the minister of state for police. The Police Constabulary headquarters is in Port Moresby. This command post comprises four major, functionally organized staff sections, called Police, Training, Special and Criminal Investigation branches. The first coordinates and directs the daily activities of police stations throughout the territory. The second operates the Central Police Training Center at Bomana, near Port Moresby. The third is concerned with internal security and directs the activities of plainclothes policemen. The last maintains the Office of Criminal Records and the Fingerprint Bureau and operates ballistics, photographic and scientific laboratories.

The Police Constabulary is divided into three operating elements. The Regular Constabulary is the major element of full-time professional members, graded and ranked in quasimilitary fashion into commissioners, superintendents, inspectors, noncommissioned officers and constables. The Regular Constabulary is usually unarmed, but rifles are issued in times of emergency. The Field Constabulary patrols rural and remote interior areas where no Regular Constabulary stations have been established. This force is armed with rifles and operates under the general supervision of the local administrative officers of the Department of District Administration. The size of the Field Constabulary is gradually diminishing as central authority over rural areas expands, new permanent police stations are set up, and field personnel are absorbed into the Regular Constabulary.

The Reserve Constabulary is a permanent corps of part-time volunteers appointed by the commissioner in areas where where constabulary strength is less than needed or where additional strength may be required periodically.

Below headquarters level, the constabulary operates through four territorial commands, each headed by a senior police officer. The first division includes Papua and nearby islands; the second, third and fourth are in New Guinea and consist of separate commands for highland, coastal and island areas. Each territorial division is in turn divided into districts and subdistricts. Many interior areas, however, have not been brought under full governmental control, and police presence there is sporadic and minimal. In such places, police functions are discharged by the field staff of the Department of Local Government.

The duty uniforms worn by both officers and men are essentially the same except for the headgear. The uniforms consist of a light blue shirt, dark blue shorts, a black belt and black shoes. Officers were visored caps; other ranks wear berets. Officers and sergeants also have a dress uniform consisting of a light blue shirt, dark blue slacks, a Sam Browne belt, a dark blue tie and a dark blue cap.

Recruitment, Education & Training

The total strength of the constabulary is estimated at 7,000, almost all native personnel recruited by voluntary enlistment. There are no educational requirements, only good character and good health.

Personnel for the ranks are inducted as probationary constables at the Police Training Depot of the Central Police Training Center at Bomana. They undergo six months of training in police procedure, after which they are assigned to regular police stations for two years of training on the job. If at the end of this period they are deemed acceptable, they become full-fledged constables.

Officer cadets are sent to the Police Training College at Bomana for a course of training that lasts four years. Successful cadets are then assigned to police stations for three years of additional on-the-job training. Graduates are commissioned as subinspectors.

The Penal System

The penal system is separate from the police, although it operates directly under the administrator in the executive branch of government. Operational control is vested in the Correctional Institutions Branch of the Department of Law, whose director, called the controller of corrective institutions, has his office at the main facility of the system in Bomana. All jails are called correctional institutions, regardless of size.

The main facility at Bomana is a detention center for prisoners serving sentences of over one year. It is a modern and progressive institution that provides literacy and training programs, workshops, and penal farms. Penal institutions at district headquarters house prisoners sentenced to less than one year. Short-term prisoners and those awaiting trial are placed in jails attached to each patrol post in urban areas.

Organized crime is virtually nonexistent, and serious crimes such as murder and rape are rare.

CRIME STATISTICS (1984)

		Number Reported	Attempts %	Cases Solved %	Crime per 100,000	Offenders	Females %	Juveniles %	Strangers %
1.	Murder	301	27.0	49.5	9.23	168	10.1	7.7	
2.	Sex offenses, including rape	1,023	6.3	47.1	31.36	511	1.4	11.0	
3.	Rape	622	10.3	38.1	19.07	245		2.4	
4.	Serious assault	633		35.1	19.41	258	13.2	2.7	
5.	All theft	10,570		50.1	324.03	5,525	5.9	19.5	
6.	Aggravated theft								
7.	Robbery and violent theft	815	5.0	8.8	24.98	99	2.0	9.0	
8.	Breaking and entering	4,500	5.8	8.0	137.95	437	1.1	17.2	
9.	Auto theft	874		7.1	26.79	82		29.3	
10.	Other thefts								
11.	Fraud	686		38.6	21.03	261	1.1	4.6	
12.	Counterfeiting								
13.	Drug offenses	28		64.3	0.86	18	5.5		11.1
14.	Total offenses	27,196		47.0	833.72	12,931	5.0	15.2	0.5

Note: Information for some categories is not available.
Criteria of juveniles: aged from 8 to 16 years.

PARAGUAY

BASIC FACT SHEET

Official Name: Republic of Paraguay
Area: 406,750 sq km
Population: 4,251,924 (1987)
Capital: Asunción
Nature of Government: Military dictatorship
Language: Spanish
Currency: Guarani
GNP: $3.18 billion (1985)
Territorial Divisions: 19 departments
Population per Police Officer: 310
Police Expenditures per Capita: N.A.

Structure & Organization

The Paraguayan Police, which operates under the provisions of the Police Law of 1951, is a centralized force with two segments: one for the capital and another for the rest of the country.

Asunción's police force, the Policía de la Capital, is divided into 23 borough precincts; three departments—Public Order, Investigations, and Training and Operations—and four main directorates—Surveillance and Offenses, Identification, Alien Registration and Political. The total strength of the force is estimated at 14,000 officers and men.

A special unit in the capital police is the Security Guard, which is called on for emergencies and ceremonies. It consists of two rifle companies, one support company and one headquarters company. Another special unit is the Police of the Presidency, with about 120 men in plain clothes. The Fire Department also is manned by police personnel.

The units of the interior police are under the control of the *delegado* (delegate) of the department to which they are assigned. Operational control of these units rests with the *jefe de policía* (chief of police). The departments are divided into districts headed by an *alcalde* (city judge), under whose jurisdiction are several police conscripts, who usually are not residents of the districts in which they serve.

The internal security organ is the Directorate General of Investigations (Dirección General de Investigaciónes, DGI).

Recruitment, Education & Training

There are four training establishments, all at Asunción: the Police College for basic training, the Higher Police College for specialized training, the NCO School and the Police Training Battalion for in-service training. The Highways Police operates under the Ministry of Public Works.

The Penal System

The Penal Code of 1910, as amended, is in force as of the mid-1980s. The code is in two books, the first of which contains 10 sections of general provisions. The death penalty was abolished in 1967, and the highest punishment is life imprisonment with hard labor. The second book of the code comprises 16 sections, which group offenses into broad categories and specific types of violations. The major categories include crimes against the state, against public order and security, and against persons and property.

Prisons are under the control of the General Directorate of Penal Institutions, which, in turn, is under the Ministry of Justice and Labor. The principal correctional institution is the National Penitentiary at Asunción. Others include the Tacumbu Penitentiary for adult males at Villa Hayes, 32 km (20 mi) north of Asunción, the Women's Correctional Institute under the supervision of the Sisters of the Good Shepherd; and the Correctional Penitentiary for Minors at Emboscada, 40 km (25 mi) northeast of Asunción. In addition, each department has a prison or jail in its capital.

There is no indication of widespread lawlessness, and life and property are, for the most part, safe throughout the country. In some departments, cattle stealing is the major law-and-order problem, followed by alcoholism, vagrancy and rape. The homicide rate is not alarming, but juvenile delinquency has been on the rise for a number of years. Prostitution is not outlawed, although soliciting in the streets is illegal. Drug addiction has not yet assumed serious proportions.

PERU

BASIC FACT SHEET

Official Name: Republic of Peru
Area: 1,285,216 sq km
Population: 20,739,218 (1987)
Capital: Lima
Nature of Government: Representative democracy
Language: Spanish
Currency: Sole
GNP: $17.83 billion (1985)
Territorial Divisions: 24 departments
Population per Police Officer: 730
Police Expenditures per 1,000: N.A.

Structure & Organization

The 1979 Constitution designates the president of the republic as the supreme chief of the national police forces. The specified police forces are the Civil Guard (Guardia Civil), the Peruvian Investigative Police (Policía Investigaciónes Peruana, PIP), and the Republican Guard (Guardia Republicana). Overall direction of police operations is a function of the Ministry of the Interior. Like the armed forces, the police are subject to the Code of Military Justice, and promotions to the rank of general require confirmation by the Senate.

Although the three police forces are subordinate to the same ministry and cooperate with each other in the performance of their duties, they are independent entities, jealous of their separate jurisdictions and prerogatives. The largest of the three, the Civil Guard, was estimated in the mid-1980s at about 30,000; the strength of the others are not revealed, but probably neither totaled more than 5,000. A small number of policewomen are employed in each of the forces. Many cities also maintain municipal police forces, but they are small in number and their functions are limited to minor local affairs. According to Pierre L. van Berghe and George P. Primov, "the municipal police are practically devoid of power, doing little more than running messages and attempting, rather unsuccessfully, to maintain a minimum standard of cleanliness in the market."

The principal police force in the country is the armed and uniformed Civil Guard. It was formed during the early years of the Augusto B. Leguia dictatorship. During the 1920s and 1930s it was reorganized by officers from the Spanish Civil Guard, of which it was a namesake. Leguia designed the Civil Guard to become a counterforce to the Army, and although the Civil Guard grew rapidly as a heavily armed paramilitary force, it never became quite the counterforce to the Army that Leguia hoped it would become, and it has traditionally lacked the Army's political influence. The dictator outfitted the Civil Guard in military uniforms, budgeted substantial amounts of money for weapons and equipment, and gave its officers the same rank, rights and perquisites enjoyed by military officers.

For administrative purposes and operational control, the Civil Guard is organized into 50 or more *comandancias* (commands) and a large number of police stations and posts throughout the country. There are five regional *comandancias,* which provide the major territorial links in the chain of command from the main headquarters in Lima to the other operational *comandancias.* The national headquarters and the principal training center of the Civil Guard are in an area of Lima known as La Campina. The Civil Guard regions reportedly correspond to the five military regions, thus placing major police headquarters in the cities of Piura, Arequipa, Cuzco, Iquitos and Lima. The largest concentration is in the capital; other cities have forces scaled to their requirements. *Comandancias* are in all departmental capitals, and police stations and posts are in every town and village.

Depending on the density of population in an area and on the size of the territory to be patrolled, police detachments range in size from three or four Civil Guardsmen commanded by a sergeant to 30 or 40 commanded by a lieutenant. Some posts in small villages have only a single Civil Guardsman. Prefects and subprefects, the appointed administrative officials at the departmental and provincial levels, exercise some control over Civil Guard units because of their direct political links to Lima. Ultimate command, however, rests with the Civil Guard officer in charge, and the regular chain of command is through police channels. A *comandancia* at departmental level, usually consisting of several hundred officers and Civil Guardsmen, is commanded by a colonel or general. Units in major cities are divided functionally into sections for crime prevention, traffic control, crowd control and other categories of routine police work.

The main headquarters in Lima includes a general staff modeled on military lines. There are sections for operations, training, administration, personnel, logistics, legal affairs, public relations and intelligence. The Civil Guard is an all-volunteer force consisting of career police officers. In the enlisted ranks, a large percentage of the personnel have previously served in the armed forces. The annual turnover rate is low. Although the pay of the Civil Guardsmen is considered to be high compared to that of other public servants, like teachers, they have gone on strike a number of times for higher salaries and fringe benefits.

Within the Civil Guard there is a special service organization of highly trained commando-type, anti-terrorist police. Based in Lima, this organization can operate in any area of the country as a quick-response team. Referred to at times as the State Security Force, it is also known as the Sinchi Battalion. Depending on the terrain, it operates on foot, on horseback or from armored vehicles. Its strength is estimated at 2,000 to 2,500. The commander of the Sinchi Battalion reports directly to the commanding general of the Civil Guard. Detachments of the unit sent out from Lima for operations in other areas usually are supported logistically by the local *comandancia* and subordinated to the ranking Civil Guard official in the area.

Officers wear a normal uniform of gray-green material worn with a beige shirt and a wide black belt with a gray-green cap. The service uniform is the same except combat boots are worn, a set of shoulder straps is added to the belt and a revolver is carried. Other ranks wear a similar uniform except for the cap, which is plain. Forest patrols wear a cowboy-style cap.

The Peruvian Investigative Police is a plainclothes national police force under the minister of the interior, with headquarters at Potao-Rimac in Lima. The PIP is charged specifically with criminal investigation, and through the State Security Branch (Seguridad del Estado) with counterintelligence. For field operations, the PIP has regional headquarters in the same cities as the military and the Civil Guard: Piura, Lima, Arequipa, Cuzco and Iquitos. The force runs the Central Criminal Laboratory and is the national branch of Interpol.

Although a great deal of PIP work is done in plain clothes, uniforms are worn on certain occasions. This consists of an olive green tunic and trousers with a peaked or forage cap. A khaki drill working dress also is worn.

The third national police force is the uniformed and armed Republican Guard, which is concerned primarily with custodial duties rather than with routine police work. Most of its members are employed in guarding the country's penal institutions. Its secondary responsibilities include guarding public buildings and operation of the border patrol.

The uniform of the Republican Guard consists of steel green trousers and an open-necked tunic with two breast pockets. Officers wear a slightly different style of tunic, with four breast pockets. A beige shirt is worn with a tie of the same color as the uniform, and a cap to match with blue edging. Black shoes are worn with street patrol, but for other operations calf-length boots are worn, with a leather belt holding a pistol holster and baton. During military operations, an American-style steel helmet and lightweight beige shirts and trousers are worn.

For normal duties, the Republican Guardsmen carry pistols and batons. During riots, tear gas grenades and other equipment are supplied to them. For frontier patrol duties, carbines and submachine guns are carried.

Recruitment, Education & Training

Civil Guard officers and men are trained in several schools operated under the auspices of the Civil Guard Center of Instruction in Chorrillós. The Officers' School offers a four-year course to police cadets, while another school offers courses to lieutenants preparing for the examinations required of all aspirants for promotion to captain. The center also provides basic police training for recruits and advanced training in technical specialties for corporals and sergeants. High-ranking commissioned police officers also attend courses given by the armed forces.

For the Peruvian Investigative Police, training is provided at the PIP School of Instruction in the Lima suburb of San Isidro, where four-year courses are offered for cadets.

For the Republican Guard, training is provided at the Republican Guard Superior School, founded in 1971.

The Penal System

The Penal Code of 1924, which has been in force since then, consists of four books, dealing with general provisions in the first, description of felonies in the second, description of misdemeanors in the third and the application of punishments in the fourth. Felonies are divided into categories as crimes against the person, against the family, against property, against the state, against public security, against public order and crimes involving moral turpitude.

The maximum sentence is the death penalty, which is administered by a firing squad. Until the 1970s it was rarely used, but with a rash of political killings, kidnappings and terrorism, the list of crimes for which the death penalty could be adjudged was expanded, and summary executions became frequent.

The penal system is administered by the General Directorate of Penal Establishments, a division of the Ministry of the Interior. According to Article 234 of the 1979 Constitution, the goal of the penal system is to rehabilitate and reeducate prisoners and integrate them into society. However, this still remains a distant goal rather than a realized program. Prison conditions remain squalid, overcrowded and primitive. Detention facilities exist in all departments, but the largest are in and around Lima, such as the two Centers of Rehabilitation and Social Adaptation (Center de Rehabilitación y Adaptación Social, CRAS), in Lurigancho and Callao. Both facilities are severely overcrowded, with three times the number of prisoners they were designed for, insanitary, with no adequate drinking water or exercise amenities. The forbidding prison colony at El Fronton, on a small island off the port of Callao, houses the most dangerous convicts. Few escapes have ever been recorded from the island. The island is also the site at which executions by the firing squad are carried out. El Sepa is an agricultural penal colony carved out of the jungle in the Loreto Department, about 430 km east of Lima. The colony is totally inaccessible and all but cut off from the rest of the country by the surrounding jungle. Women prisoners generally are confined in the Women's Prison at Chorrillós.

Annual criminal statistics are not published by the government and can only be estimated on the basis of tangential press reports. Crimes most frequently reported are theft of livestock, assault, rape, public drunkenness and disturbing the peace. The theft of livestock is reported to be an organized criminal activity, especially in the Sierra. Peru is the source of over one-half of the world's supply of cocaine, and reports of trafficking in illegal narcotics fill the newspapers. Efforts to crack down on the drug traffic are hampered by resistance from coca growers in the remote areas and by corruption within the government, the military and the police.

PHILIPPINES

BASIC FACT SHEET

Official Name: Republic of the Philippines
Area: 300,440 sq km
Population: 61,524,761 (1987)
Capital: Manila
Nature of Government: Limited democracy
Languages: English and Pilipino
Currency: Peso
GNP: $32.63 billion (1985)
Territorial Divisions: 74 provinces
Population per Police Officer: 1,160
Police Expenditures per 1,000: $2,423

History & Background

The Philippine national police force was constituted in 1901 when the Constabulary Division in the Philippine Army was converted into a national gendarmerie.

Structure & Organization

The principal law enforcement agencies are the National Intelligence Coordinating Agency, the National Police Commission, the National Bureau of Investigation, the Integrated National Police and the Philippine Constabulary. Other agencies are reportedly active, but their affiliations and operations are not disclosed. Under Marcos, an agency called the Civil Intelligence and Security Agency was known to be active for a while in campaigning against Catholic dissidents and subversives, but it does not seem to have survived his fall.

The National Intelligence Coordinating Agency, under the office of the president, prepares foreign and domestic intelligence estimates for the president. Originally a staff organization, it has some operational responsibility in the control of smuggling.

The National Police Commission was established pursuant to the Police Act of 1966 to improve the administration of local police forces and establish professional standards for them. It functions under the immediate control of five commissioners affiliated with the Department of National Defense.

The National Bureau of Investigation is a subordinate agency of the Department of Justice and is patterned after the FBI in the United States. The organization began as an investigative division in 1936 but was expanded and raised to full bureau status in 1947. It was further reorganized in 1960. The original intent of the NBI was to relieve the constabulary of detective and investigative duties, but since 1960 it has taken on additional service functions, such as providing advanced police training and running crime laboratories.

The bureau is organized into headquarters under a director appointed by the president. It operates through 10 regional offices, in Manila, Batangas, Naga, Dagupan, Ilagan, Vigan, Iloilo, Cebu Island, Zamboanga and Cagayan de Oro. Most have one or more suboffices.

Bureau personnel include agents, laboratory technicians, fingerprint specialists and communications experts. Agents selected for assignment must also possess a degree in law and accounting and meet exacting physical and mental standards. They are generally regarded as the best and most efficient law enforcement personnel in the nation.

The Integrated National Police (INP) is the outcome of a restructuring of the local police forces in 1975. It was created under a mandate written into the 1973 Constitution (Section 12, Article XV). The first phase of the program involved the integration of the forces in the Manila Metropolitan Area.

Under the provisions of Presidential Decree 765, all municipal police, fire and penal institutions were brought under the supervision and control of the chief of the Philippine Constabulary, who was named concurrently director general of the INP. The INP functions directly under the Department of National Defense subject to the general supervision of the president as commander in chief. It consists of 64 city forces and 1,447 municipal forces with a total strength of 60,000 men, with the Philippine Constabulary representing some 37,000 men. As a result of the creation of the INP, provincial governors and municipal mayors have lost most of their effective police control functions to the 13 INP regional commands.

The line of command runs from the director general to four assistant or zonal directors plus the director of the Manila Metropolitan Area. These commands are further broken down into 72 provinces and then into districts. At the provincial level, the force is headed by superintendents and at the district level by district commanders. The Manila Metropolitan Area is divided into a number of districts, each under a district commander. The INP uniform consists of a U.S. police-type eight-point cap, a khaki field service shirt and trousers, black Sam Browne belt on regular duty, and a white shirt and khaki bush jacket for ceremonial occasions. Policewomen wear skirts and a wide-brimmed hat.

As the nuclear organization of the integrated police, the Philippine Constabulary continues to play a central role in law enforcement and domestic security in the broadest sense. The oldest of the four armed forces, the Philippine Constabulary traces its origins to 1901. It was then the constabulary division of the Philippine Army before being constituted as a national police force in 1936. Operating as a national gendarmerie with units dispersed throughout the country, the Philippine Constabulary is concerned primarily with large-scale crime, insurgency, subversion and enforcing law and order in remote areas where local forces are nonexistent or ineffective. Special constabulary units are assigned to missions such as smuggling, piracy, drug traffic, kidnapping and car theft.

Organization of the Philippine Constabulary is similar to that of the Army, corresponding to that of a light infantry force. It is commanded by a major general. Tactical forces operate under a standard military-type headquarters, with battalions consisting of some 450 men each. The total of over 170 companies includes a dog company and a company of horse cavalry. Companies and battalions not in strategic reserve are assigned regionally to one of the five constabulary zones, under which are the provincial commanders, and posts and stations manned by detachments of varying size.

The Philippine Constabulary includes a number of specialized units: the Antinarcotics Unit; the Offshore Anticrime Battalion, with speedboats and patrol craft; the Presidential Security Command, including the Presidential Guards Battalion; and the Highway Patrol Group. The Philippine Constabulary is also involved in civic affairs projects under the Home Defense Program.

The Manila Metropolitan Command, an integral part of the Philippine Constabulary, is a crack unit comprising three sector commands: Northern, Southern and Western. It also includes the Police Intelligence Service, two riot control units and the Bureau of Customs Police Service.

Recruitment, Education & Training

The National Police Commission, created in 1966, is in charge of training and standardization of procedures. A uniform national police manual was adopted in 1969 with the help of the U.S. Agency for International Development. Officers of the Philippine Constabulary are trained at the Philippine Military Academy.

The Penal System

Criminal law is embodied in the Revised Penal Code of 1930, which went into effect January 1, 1932. The code is derived from the Spanish Penal Code of 1887. In the manner of the Spanish legal tradition, common law is not a source of criminal law; there are no punishable acts or penalties other than those expressly stated in the law. The Penal Code applies to Philippine nationals outside the national territory as to certain acts, and crimes against national security and the law of nations. The criminal statutes are to be construed strictly against the state and liberally in favor of the accused.

Criminal law from Spanish times to the present has rested on the classical or juristic school, which considers crime as an objective act with emphasis on punishment. This aspect of law has long been an object of reform effort. The official Code Commission of 1947 recommended a new code of crimes based on the more modern positivist philosophy that criminality is as much rooted in social, environmental and economic factors as on the innate or inherited character of the criminal.

Three principal parts of the Penal Code deal with basic principles affecting criminal liability, provisions for penalties and definition of 14 classes of felonies. The code lists aggravating and mitigating factors; among the latter are age (under 18 or over 70), self-defense, insanity, or acting under uncontrollable impulse or irresistible fear. Penalties are classified as corporal (death), afflictive (six years to life imprisonment), correctional (one month to six years' imprisonment) and light (up to 30 days imprisonment). Sentence of life imprisonment normally entitles the prisoner to pardon after 30 years. The code provides for parole and probation. Death is by electrocution or firing squad; in the former case, the prisoner may request anesthetization before the sentence is carried out.

Penal institutions include national prisons as well as penal farms and provincial and local jails. A reorganization in October 1972 established seven national and regional prisons in which prisoners were segregated according to the length of their sentences. The changes were aimed at relieving overcrowding and promoting rehabilitation by confining prisoners nearer to family and friends. Special prisons for women and children are at Mandaluyong in Rizal Province. Each municipality has its own jail, often only a room or two at the police headquarters building for persons serving short terms. Provincial jails are larger in size but have amenities little better than those of municipal jails. Persons awaiting trial make up as much as 40% of the prison population. All jails and prisons are administered by the police.

The Bilibid Prison in Manila, the largest in the world, is the central national penitentiary for hardened criminals and those sentenced to life or death. Despite its size, it suffers from serious overcrowding and poor living conditions. Conditions in most other prisons are described as inhumane.

There are four penal colonies, at Davao, Zamboanga (San Ramón), Mindoro Island (Sablayon) and Palawan (Iwanig). Prisoners are initially placed on probation for two months, during which they undergo orientation, wear distinctive orange uniforms, work under guard, and are housed in segregated barracks that are locked at night. At the end of this period prisoners join the community of regular colonists, wear civilian clothes and are free to move about without the presence of guards.

Crime is a political as well as a law enforcement problem. The existence of private armies had long been a characteristic of Philippine society until the imposition of martial law by former president Ferdinand Marcos in 1972. Factional rivalries and interfamily feuds often erupt into physical assault, and violence invariably accompanies elections. The widespread possession of unlicensed firearms has engendered a climate in which criminal activities have flourished unchecked. Compounding these are the public's unwillingness to cooperate with police in criminal matters, and the partisanship of police and judicial authorities.

Much of the apparent rise in crime rates is actually a metropolitan rather than a nationwide problem. Greater Manila accounts for 87% of all reported crimes. The notorious Tondo slum district, with about one-sixth of the metropolitan population, accounts for about one-third of the reported crime victims. Juvenile crime, aggravated by the youthfulness of the urban population and by the large number of school-age youths not in school, accounts for much of the theft, robbery and physical assault. Drug trafficking and smuggling are organized criminal activities heavily concentrated in the capital. Less than half of all crimes are reported, and less than half of what are reported are incorporated into the crime statistics published by the government.

CRIME STATISTICS (1984)

		Number Reported	Attempts %	Cases Solved %	Crime per 100,000	Offenders	Females %	Juveniles %	Strangers %
1.	Murder	22,604			42.51				
2.	Sex offenses, including rape								
3.	Rape	1,401			2.63				
4.	Serious assault	29,950			56.33				
5.	All theft	29,531			55.54				
6.	Aggravated theft								
7.	Robbery and violent theft	17,544			33				
8.	Breaking and entering								
9.	Auto theft	1,074			2.02				
10.	Other thefts								
11.	Fraud								
12.	Counterfeiting								
13.	Drug offenses	1,641			3.09				
14.	Total offenses	177,520			333.87				

Note: Information for some categories is not available.
Criteria of juveniles: aged from 15 to 19 years.

POLAND

BASIC FACT SHEET

Official Name: Polish People's Republic
Area: 312,612 sq km
Population: 37,726,699 (1987)
Capital: Warsaw
Nature of Government: Communist dictatorship
Language: Polish
Currency: Zloty
GNP: $78.96 billion (1985)
Territorial Divisions: 49 provinces
Population per Police Officer: 370
Police Expenditures per 1,000: N.A.

History & Background

A national police force existed for a brief period in the Polish Republic from 1918 to 1939, when the country was occupied by German troops. In 1944 a decree of the Polish Committee of National Liberation dissolved the state police and assigned its functions to the internal security forces. Operating under the authority of the Ministry of Internal Affairs (known until 1956 as the Ministry of Public Security), the internal security forces played a central role in suppressing opposition to the Communist regime in the years immediately after the war.

Structure & Organization

The Citizens' Militia (Milicja Obywatelska MO) was established in 1944 as the country's basic police force at the *voivodship* and local levels. According to regulations, the force is charged with safeguarding public order, protecting state and private property, controlling traffic, maintaining identification cards and residence locator information, and countering criminal activities. Although organized on a regional basis, it has a centralized command (Komenda Glowna) in Warsaw. Local units consult and coordinate extensively with local government authorities (*voivods,* mayors, commune heads and local people's councils), but these units are under the sole authority of the Ministry of Internal Affairs.

In the mid-1980s the MO had an estimated strength of about 112,000, or about one policeman for every 300 to 400 Poles. Of these, some 3,000 are affiliated with the Criminal Investigation Sections, and about 4,500 with the Traffic Control Sections. The bulk of the remainder are patrolmen working at local stations. MO officers often are armed. The Citizens' Militia is not directly involved in controlling demonstrations, but it often acts in conjunction with the secret police in such situations. In the spring of 1981, after Solidarity activists were badly beaten by plainclothes police at Bydgoszcz, many policemen sought to form their own union and be disassociated from the security branch. Police union leaders claimed a membership of 40,000 before the union was disbanded after martial law.

As a paramilitary force, the MO is run on army lines, sharing training equipment and facilities with the armed forces. Warsaw, Lodz and Krakow have their own Citizens' Militia commands, controlling a number of commissariats in charge of the city boroughs.

Until 1981 few Poles were aware of its existence, but during the year of martial law an organization known as the Motorized Units of the Citizens' Militia (Zmotoryzowane Oddzialy Milicji Obywatelskiej, ZOMO) established itself as the Jaruzelski regime's most active and least popular enforcer of martial law regulations. ZOMO units were used extensively to control riots and pro-Solidarity demonstrations, to storm factories occupied by workers and to patrol tense areas. In doing so, ZOMO became the target of bitter popular resentment and the object of a number of jokes about the lack of intelligence of its personnel.

ZOMO was established in 1956 after the Poznan riots highlighted the need for troops specially trained in riot control. ZOMO itself was unable to handle the 1970 Gdansk demonstrations, and as a result the force was completely purged, reorganized and retrained. In

1980 ZOMO underwent a major expansion and by 1982 had between 25,000 and 30,000 personnel nationwide. ZOMO is a mobile force with units throughout the country under the control of the Ministry of Internal Affairs, with the capability of being deployed in any trouble spot within a few hours. They are equipped with tear gas, water cannons, and other riot control gear as well as light armored vehicles. In addition to riot control, ZOMO controls public events such as soccer games and coordinates relief efforts during natural disasters.

Although public perception of ZOMO personnel is that of illiterate, half-drunk thugs, most of them are volunteers with at least a secondary education and with no police record. Although the regime acknowledges that some of them are involved in incidents of abuse of power, convicted offenders are severely disciplined. Western observers rate ZOMO members as highly disciplined and effective. However, they are subjected to considerable stress. During riots, they are taunted with epithets of "Gestapo" and "SS," and many are injured by debris hurled by protesters. The force has a large turnover rate, and most members retire early as a result of disability or nervous disorders.

The Volunteer Reserve of the Citizens' Militia (Ochotnicza Rezerwa Milicji Obywatelskiej, ORMO) was formed during the early 1960s, with members drawn from the former People's Guard and various other industrial guard units. As of the mid-1980s it had a manned strength of 465,000, outnumbering all other forces.

ORMO volunteers are unpaid but are compensated for expenses incurred on active duty outside their home areas. Most if not all have other full-time employment and are trained only at odd hours. Their weapons are limited to small arms intended to be used, carried and maintained by the individual volunteer. When on duty, the MO are equipped with armored vehicles. Their uniforms are the identical blue of ZOMO personnel. ORMO units generally are not assigned to handle demonstrations because the government suspects that many of them are Solidarity supporters.

The Security Service (Sluzba Bezpieczenstwa, SB), formerly known as the Security Bureau (Urzad Bezpieczenstwa, UB), is the regime's secret police force. It is a plainclothes force charged with detecting and countering subversive activities. Established in 1944 with help from the KGB, UB was the mainstay of the new Communist regime. By 1953, however, the UB was widely hated by the people, distrusted by the regime and crippled by defections. After Stalin's death the force became internally disorganized and virtually impotent and ineffective. In about 1957 the

force was gradually rebuilt, and in the late 1960s it again attained a certain notoriety under Mieczyslaw Moczar, the powerful minister of internal affairs.

Little is known about SB operations in the mid-1980s. Foreign analysts believe that the SB remains the institution most sympathetic to, and most thoroughly penetrated by, Soviet intelligence. The SB relies heavily on informers and blackmail for its covert operations. Officials credit it with success in countering foreign intelligence activities during the Solidarity period.

Recruitment, Education & Training

The MO is a volunteer force. Militiamen are grouped into NCO (private through sergeant major) and officer (lieutenant through general) categories. NCO candidates spend a year in special training programs after joining the force. Candidates for officer ranks are ordinarily chosen from among those within the forces who have performed well as NCO's. Young persons eligible for military service can also apply for a tour of duty in the MO. Women make up a large proportion of the Citizens' Militia, especially in clerical, traffic control and juvenile sections. The force is relatively well educated, with 70% of the officers possessing a higher education degree and 83% of the NCO's a secondary education. Police personnel could continue their studies at special Ministry of Internal Affairs colleges. Despite a number of privileges, the MO has difficulty recruiting personnel because of large turnover.

The Penal System

The prison system is run by the Main Bureau of Penal Institutions of the Ministry of Justice. Between 1944 and 1955, prisons were administered by the Ministry of Public Security, but serious abuses by prison authorities led to the transfer of its jurisdiction to the Ministry of Justice in 1956. A prison commission in each institution classifies inmates according to their original sentences and conduct in jail. Prisoners are subjected to one of four regimens—mitigated, basic, intense and severe—and are moved from one to another according to their conduct. The severity of the regimen determines a prisoner's privileges, such as correspondence, visitation and exercise.

All penal institutions are considered rehabilitation centers and economically productive units. Most convicts serving a sentence of less than five years are placed in semiopen labor centers. Those serving longer sentences or those convicted of violent crimes are sent to penal institutions. Inmates nearing the end of their sentences are sent to transitional prisons. Special prisons exist for multiple recidivists, prisoners under age 21 and those requiring special medical or psychological attention. Women prisoners are separated from men.

Certain privileges are available to all inmates regardless of the regimen they are in, such as legal assistance and access to prison libraries. Under an agreement with the Roman Catholic Church, prisoners are allowed to observe the religious practices of their choice. In some cases prisoners receive a pass to leave prison for up to five days.

The prison system does not include forced labor camps, as in the Soviet Union, but involuntary supervised labor often is included in a court sentence. Prisoners work in collectivized establishments, business enterprises and public works projects of local people's councils. Prisoners receive standard wages but no Social Security benefits.

PORTUGAL

History & Background

Portugal has one of the oldest police forces in Europe, dating back to the 16th century. By the end of the 19th century, there were three full-fledged forces with police duties: one in charge of general duties, a paramilitary guard and a political or intelligence police. These forces survived the fall of the monarchy in 1910 with only minor changes in titles; for example, the Civil Guard became the National Republican Guard. Under Dictator Antonio de Oliveira Salazar, there were five principal forces: the Maritime or Harbor Police, the Public Security Police, the National Republican Guard, the Fiscal Guard and the Traffic Police (which eventually became the Traffic Brigade of the National Republican Guard). There was also a fascist-inspired state security police, the Surveillance and State Defense Police (PVDE), later renamed International and State Defense Police (PIDE). Under Salazar's successor Marcello Caetano, PIDE because the Directorate General of Security (DGS).

The authority of the police, which was identified with the old regime, was seriously undermined by the April 1974 revolution. Both the Public Security Police and the National Republican Guard were shorn of most of their powers, and the DGS was disbanded. The 1975 countercoup restored the police forces to their effective capacity, although on a more limited scale than under Salazar and Caetano. However, the DGS was not revived. By 1976 control of the police apparatus and responsibility for law enforcement had been returned to civilian authorities in the Ministry of Internal Administration, formerly the Ministry of the Interior.

The Public Security Police (Polícia de Segurança Pública, PSP) was reorganized in 1953 as a paramilitary force under the jurisdiction of the Ministry of the Interior with criminal investigation, protection of property, and public security in urban areas as its principal missions. Before 1953 the urban police had been under the control of the provincial governors. Under Salazar, the PSP was frequently called upon to deploy their mobile assault companies to civil disturbances. During the colonial wars, PSP assault units were sent to Africa to fight guerrilla forces. The PSP was reorganized and retrained in 1975 and its heavy equipment turned over to the Army. Crowd control remains one of the PSP's prime functions.

Structure & Organization

PSP headquarters is in Lisbon under a commander who usually is a senior Army officer, as are all high-ranking personnel. There are divisional headquarters in the main cities and section headquarters in smaller towns. Lisbon has two police divisions, while Oporto has one supported by a section in the suburb of Matosinhos. While operationally centralized, there is some autonomy at the district level. There are 18 districts, divided into three zones: North, Center and South. The North Zone includes Aveiro, Braga, Bragança, Porto, Viana do Castelo and Vila Real; the Center Zone includes Castelo Branco, Coimbra, Guarda, Leiria and Viseu, and the South Zone includes Beja, Évora, Faro, Lisbon, Portalegre, Santarém and Steubal. There are also separate commands for Greater Lisbon and Greater Oporto and a Mobile Company based at the Cruz de Oeiras barracks near Lisbon.

Specialized PSP units include the Traffic Service,

divided into divisions and sections that cooperate with the National Republican Guard's Traffic Brigade in controlling traffic, and a specialized riot control unit called the Intervention Police (Polícia de Intervenção, PI) with mobile sections headquartered at Lisbon, Oporto, Coimbra and Steubal, for ready deployment anywhere in the country.

The Autonomous Regions of the Azores and Madeira are also policed by the PSP. In the Azores there are local commands at Horta on Faial Island, Santa Criz das Flores on Flores Island, Vila do Porto on Santa Maria Island, Calheta on São Jorge Island, Ponta Delgada on São Miguel Island and Angra de Heroismo on Terceira Island, and police stations at Santa Cruz on Graciosa Island and Madalena on Pico Island. In Madeira, the PSP command at Funchal supervises both Madeira and Porto Santo islands. The total strength of the PSP was estimated in the mid-1980s at 17,000.

Minor offenses are handled in police courts known as Tribunals de Polícia. More serious offenses are investigated by the Judicial Police (Polícia Judiciaria, PJ), which handles preparation of cases before the courts and also drug and vice offenses. In each major town, PJ stations are part of the Justice Hall. PJ headquarters has a permanent garrison and a Scientific Police Laboratory. Since the disbandment of the DGS, the PJ also represents Interpol in Portugal. There are PJ inspectorates in the Azores and Madeira.

The National Republican Guard (Guarda Nacional Republicana, GNR) was formed in 1913 as a heavily armed paramilitary constabulary organized in units of up to battalion strength to replace the old Civil Guard, which had functioned under the monarchy. It was designed as a check against the military and was first employed to suppress monarchist revolts within the ranks of the armed forces. Although its initial mission was confined to the countryside, its activities subsequently extended to aiding the urban police in controlling demonstrations and quelling labor unrest. With the increase of motor traffic, the GNR also was assigned to patrolling highways.

In many ways similar to the French Gendarmerie and the Italian Carabinieri, the GNR has mounted units and also a ceremonial Guard of Honor. GNR headquarters is in Lisbon, where three battalions are stationed. The GNR Cavalry Regiment, with three squadrons, is also stationed in Lisbon. Oporto has two battalions and a section, while district capitals have companies and sections. A battalion, with headquarters in Coimbra, covers the central region, supported by a motorized reconnaissance detachment and a cavalry platoon. Another battalion is headquartered at Évora, with jurisdiction over Alentejo and Algarve. GNR personnel are transported in GNR-owned Motor Transport Company vehicles. The Transit Brigade, formerly a separate highway patrol force, was integrated into the GNR in 1974. Headquarters of the Traffic Brigade is in Lisbon, with detachments at provincial and district levels.

Reserve and career officers from all parts of the armed forces are regularly seconded to tours of duty in the GNR. As a result, they receive only specialized, advanced or refresher training. Higher ranks usually are held by senior Army officers. The total strength of the GNR was estimated in the mid-1980s at 16,000.

The City Council of Lisbon operates its own police force, separate from the national police. The Municipal Police of Lisbon (Polícia Municipal de Lisboa) has an Army officer as commandant. There is also a smaller police force responsible to the administrator general of Lisbon.

The Fiscal Guard is a customs and tax service charged with investigating smuggling, tax evasion, currency manipulations, illegal financial transactions, customs inspection and collection of duty. The national headquarters, in Lisbon, includes one battalion (with four companies), a mobile patrol, a maritime detachment and a training camp. Oporto has one battalion with two sections and a maritime detachment. All coastal and frontier towns as well as the Azores and Madeira have Fiscal Guard units.

The Maritime Police (Polícia Marítima, PM) is in charge of harbor patrol duties, with headquarters in Lisbon and a unit near Oporto.

Portugal does not have a state security or secret police.

Recruitment, Education & Training

PSP manpower is drawn from former servicemen, and since the 1970s women have been recruited for plain-clothes investigation and traffic control duties.

The Penal System

The Portuguese Legal Code, grounded in Roman law, has been heavily revised in the 19th and 20th centuries and is now one of the most humane and liberal codes in Europe. The death penalty was abolished in 1867, well before it was in most other states. The most severe punishment is a prison sentence of 16 to 20 years, usually passed for premeditated homicide. Statutory sentences may be increased, however, for particularly heinous crimes, such as murder committed during robbery. Larceny, arson and willful destruction of crops and business establishments are the most common forms of crime against property. Theft of property valued at more than 1 million escudos draws a sentence of eight to 12 years in prison. Laws covering so-called economic crimes were enacted during the Salazar regime. They included certain categories of speculation, hoarding, falsification of contents, adulteration and dilution of food products, and fraudulent export of goods. Many political and economic crimes added to the statute book under Salazar were voided after the 1974 revolution.

The 1976 Constitution emphasized the commitment of the revolution to creating a just society and reinforced the earlier proscriptions against economic crimes. To protect civil rights, guidelines for criminal investigation and treatment of suspects were laid down. No person could be held without trial or imprisoned without a definite judicial sentence. Individuals could not be deprived of citizenship for political reasons. The principle of habeas corpus was restated as applicable without exceptions. Torture, inhumane detention and confessions obtained under duress were declared illegal, and the inviolability of the home, personal correspondence and telephone communications was guaranteed.

The prison system is under the control of the minister of justice. There are local jails in each judicial district, supervised by the deputy attorney general in each district who is, in turn, responsible to the Directorate General of Prison Services. The kind of prison regime to which an offender is sentenced is specified by the court. Youthful offenders are given the opportunity to learn trades. Individuals convicted three times for the same crime are not eligible for parole and may be kept in a strict prison regime. All prisoners earn money for work while in prison.

Persons apprehended in the commission of a crime

are held in preventive detention and are not eligible for conditional liberty. Others are usually allowed bail (except in cases involving homicide, serious assault or grand larceny) on presentation of a fianca (bond). A suspect taken into custody cannot be held for more than 48 hours without being brought before an inquiring magistrate. A person accused of a crime has to be tried within three months. An indigent defendant has an attorney appointed by the court. Verdicts of innocent or guilty are the only ones permitted. Juvenile delinquents under 18 come under the purview of the juvenile supervision courts, in which the state is represented by a special officer from the attorney general's office called the children's guardian. Children under 16 are not considered legally responsible for their actions. Delinquent minors are assigned to special public or private institutions or to a family guardian. There are special reformatories for those between 16 and 18.

Trials are public except in morals cases, where the judge may close the proceedings. Constitutional provisions prohibit the use of improperly obtained evidence. A particularly significant innovation of the 1976 Constitution was the provision for a jury system, consisting of a panel of judges or lay jurors, to be used when requested by the defense or the prosecution in serious cases.

In general, the Portuguese are a law-abiding people. Violent crimes are rare. Generally, murders are crimes of passion. Most persons convicted of either violent

CRIME STATISTICS (1984)

		Number Reported	Attempts %	Cases Solved %	Crime per 100,000	Offenders	Females %	Juveniles %	Strangers %
1.	Murder	461	33.8		4.60	247	10.1		
2.	Sex offenses, including rape	258			2.57	250	10.0		
3.	Rape	198			1.97	163	1.8		
4.	Serious assault	136			1.36	128	14.1		
5.	All theft	35,299			351.93	7,208	13.5		
6.	Aggravated theft	16,204			161.56	3,199	8.8		
7.	Robbery and violent theft	2,162			21.56	633	5.4		
8.	Breaking and entering	9,997			99.67	1,617	7.2		
9.	Auto theft	6,152			61.34	876	2.3		
10.	Other thefts	639			6.37	278	7.6		
11.	Fraud	20,182			201.22	6,060	65.4		
12.	Counterfeiting	1,561			15.56	1,029	12.4		
13.	Drug offenses	1,154			11.51	1,616	8.2		
14.	Total offenses	77,677			774.45	48,585	16.1		

Note: Information for some categories is not available.
Criteria of juveniles: aged from 14 to 16 years.

crimes or crimes against property are not professional criminals but manual and farm workers. Recidivism is not a major problem. Various categories of theft are the most common crimes, but other forms of crime, such as commercial fraud, reckless driving and drug trafficking are increasing. So also is prostitution, which was legally tolerated in Portugal until the 1960s. Large numbers of teenagers turn to prostitution as their sole source of livelihood. Begging is illegal, but beggars are highly visible in Lisbon, less so in Oporto. Juvenile delinquency is also growing, and juvenile courts are handling a record number of cases each year, and many children are placed in state institutions because of parental neglect. Statistics show that only a small percentage of those arrested are eventually brought to trial. A substantial number of such cases are resolved by the municipal council or special tribunals.

PUERTO RICO

BASIC FACT SHEET

Official Name: Commonwealth of Puerto Rico
Area: 9,104 sq. km
Population (1986): 3,300,660
Capital: San Juan
Nature of Government: Representative democracy
Languages: Spanish and English
Currency: U.S. dollar
GNP 1985: $14.03 billion
Territorial Divisions: 28 municipalities
Population per Police Officer: 380
Police Expenditures per 1,000: N.A.

History & Background

The earliest Puerto Rican police force was the Civil Guard, established in 1868 by the Spanish authorities and invested with quasi-military powers. This force was abolished by the U.S. government in 1899, but the larger towns were authorized to set up municipal forces in its stead. In 1901, a centralized police force was created to supplement the municipal forces. Called the Insular Police, this force was an urban force but covered rural areas when needed.

In 1956 the Insular Police underwent considerable reforms. These reforms created two separate entities: the Insular Police Commission, concerned with enlistment, recruitment and enforcing internal regulations and rules; and the office of the chief of police, who directed all police operations. Further reforms were implemented in 1966–67, shaping the police organization as it exists today.

Structure & Organization

The police force is headed by a superintendent and comprises four divisions and four departments. The divisions are Fiscal Affairs, Intelligence, Juvenile Affairs and Planning. The departments are Administration, Field Operations, Inspectorate and Technical Services. The Field Operations Department comprises the Criminal Investigation Corps, the Special Reserve Unit, the Highway Patrol and the Air Unit.

Territorially, the island is divided for purposes of police operations into five areas, each with its *comandancia:*

Metropolitan: Bayamón, Carolina, San Juan

East: Caguas, Humacao

North: Arecibo, Vega Baja

South: Coamo, Guayama, Pone

West: Aguadilla, Mayagüez

Each area comprises two or three zones, subdivided into districts.

The Insular Police Commission is headed by a commanding officer who also is the chief of police. It has two other members, both appointed by the governor. The commission determines the distribution of police services, establishes rules and regulations for police on-the-job conduct, administers recruitment, appoints all members of the force and removes them when necessary, authorizes all expenditures, and reviews salary scales and other perquisites.

The normal workday is eight hours and the workweek 40 hours. Members receive annual vacation leave, sick leave and medical care. Privates may be promoted to corporal if they pass a competitive examination, and corporals may be promoted to sergeant on the recommendation of the chief of police. All grades above second lieutenant are filled at the discretion of the governor.

The police uniform consists of navy blue shirts, trousers and peaked caps. They carry .38-caliber revolvers and a baton. Mounted patrols are used in the Condado Beach area.

The FBI, the U.S. Customs Service and the Marshals Service maintain bureaus in San Juan.

Recruitment, Education & Training

Training is provided by the Police Academy, which all recruits must attend for six months. Initially, candidates who meet all requirements are admitted to the force for a two-year probationary period. Officers are commissioned by the governor.

The Penal System

No information is available on the penal system.

ROMANIA

BASIC FACT SHEET

Official Name: Socialist Republic of Romania
Area: 237,499 sq km
Population (1987): 22,936,503
Capital: Bucharest
Nature of Government: Communist dictatorship
Language: Romanian
Currency: Lei
GNP: $117.6 billion
Territorial Divisions: 40 counties
Population Per Police Officer: 40
Police Expenditures Per 1020: N.A.

History & Background

Before the Communist takeover of Romania in 1944, the police system was modeled on that of France, with a Sûreté Nationale, a rural Gendarmerie and a Security Police. The Communists disbanded the Sûreté Nationale and the Gendarmerie and invested their combined powers in a newly created Militia set up under the Ministry of Internal Affairs, which, in turn, was responsible to the State Security Council.

Structure & Organization

The chain of command in the Romanian Militia runs through the inspector general through the 39 *judet* (county) inspectorates and the Bucharest inspectorate. Local police units and inspectorates are subordinate not only to the Militia command but also to the locally elected people's councils, and, of course, are further subordinate to the Communist Party's ubiquitous officials.

There is at least one police station in every town, commune or enterprise, and others are established at airports, ports, railroad stations and large construction sites. An increasing proportion of routine police work is consumed in traffic control. The Militia may also be called upon to assist in relief work during emergencies or disasters.

Militia regulations require the police to respect individual rights and the inviolability of the home in normal circumstances but permit them to commandeer vehicles or enter private homes and search them without warrant in special circumstances. Provisions authorizing the formation of auxiliary police groups are established in law.

Militia personnel are drawn from those selected annually for compulsory military service. Officers, experts and noncommissioned officers are recruited from graduates of schools operated within the regular military establishments. The Militia's personnel strength of 700,000 yields a ratio of one policeman for every 40 inhabitants.

The Securitate, the national security force, is organized along military lines and most if not all of its men have military ranks. In the mid-1980s it numbered roughly 25,000 men. Administratively it is under the State Security Council through the Ministry of Internal Affairs. The role of the Securitate is diminishing because of reduced domestic tensions and threats.

Recruitment, Education & Training

No information is available on recruitment, education and training.

The Penal Code

The Penal Code in effect before 1968 was one of the most severe in Europe. The Penal Code and the Code of Criminal Procedure that have replaced it make some concessions to civil rights and even speak of the "rights of accused persons." The maximum prison sentence for the first offense is 20 years and for a repeated offense is 25 years. The death sentence also is authorized but usually is commuted to life imprisonment. If the death sentence is carried out, execution is by a firing squad. The most severe sentences are reserved for crimes against the state, and only in exceptional cases are crimes against person and property accorded equal punishment.

The new codes attempt to reduce the court time spent on minor offenses. Those that constitute no significant danger to society have been removed from the list of crimes and relegated to the judicial commissions. In other cases, where such acts are still classified as crimes, an offender may elect to plead guilty without a trial. If the offender does, he or she is charged with one-half the minimum fine for the offense and the case is closed.

Pretrial preventive detention is authorized to protect the individual, to assure that the person will not evade trial or to prevent his or her committing further criminal acts. Detention ordinarily is limited to five days for investigation of a crime or to 30 days if the person has been arrested and is awaiting trial. Extensions of up to 90 days are authorized if requested by the prosecutor.

The prison system consists of correction camps, labor colonies, prisons and military disciplinary units. Prisons include penitentiaries, prison factories, town jails and detention facilities. Increased use of judicial commissions for petty crimes has reduced the prison population and eliminated the need for separate categories of correctional institutions.

Maximum-security prisons house those convicted of crimes against state security, serious economic crimes, homicides and recidivists. All convicted persons are obliged to perform useful work, and all facilities except town jails have labor and educational programs.

A convict is paid according to the standard pay scales. He or she receives 10% of earned wages, and the balance goes to the state treasury. The maximum workday is 12 hours. Inmates are segregated according to category. Women are segregated from men, minors from adults, recidivists and those convicted of serious crimes from those serving short terms. Drug addicts and alcoholics are isolated wherever possible. Persons held in preventive arrest not yet convicted of a crime are separated from convicted persons. Convict privileges include visits, packages and correspondence. Privileges vary with the severity of the original sentence and may be increased, reduced or done away with altogether. Consistently good conduct may earn parole, and an exceptional inmate may be pardoned. Disciplinary measures include reprimand, simple isolation, severe isolation and transfer to a facility with a more strict regimen. All convict mail is censored. Conversations during visits is limited to Romanian unless a translator is present.

Criminal statistics are collected but not published. Reliable data are hard to come by, especially because minor infractions of the law are not treated as crimes and are tried before judicial commissions.

A rough assessment of the overall crime situation can, however, be made from the concern expressed in many speeches and articles published by government and party spokesmen. It is apparent that certain types of crime are considered to be under control adequately and are found to be tolerable. Other categories are proving intractable, such as economic crimes and antisocial crimes. Among the latter are begging, vagrancy, prostitution, black-marketing and currency speculation. Growth in these areas of crime is compounded by the noncooperation of the public in Militia efforts.

RWANDA

BASIC FACT SHEET

Official Name: Republic of Rwanda
Area: 26,338 sq km
Population (1987): 6,811,336
Capital: Kigali
Nature of Government: Military dictatorship
Language: Kinyarwanda and French
Currency: Franc
GNP (1986): $1.86 billion
Territorial Divisions: 10 prefectures; 143 communes
Population per Police Officer: 4,650
Police Expenditures per 1,000: N.A.

Structure & Organization

The National Police (Police Nationale) replaced the Belgian Force Publique on independence. It is commanded by a director general under the authority of the minister of police and the National Guard. Most of the 1,500-man force is assigned to the 10 prefectural administrations. Although responsible to the police headquarters in matters of discipline, promotion, training and general policy, the prefectural detachments receive their operating instructions from the prefect and his assistants.

Police weapons are mostly of Belgian origin. Communications facilities and equipment are very inadequate. Uniforms are of gray twill. Headwear includes

CRIME STATISTICS (1984)

		Number Reported	Attempts %	Cases Solved %	Crime per 100,000	Offenders	Females %	Juveniles %	Strangers %
1.	Murder	349		86	6.71	870	9.2		
2.	Sex offenses, including rape	562		50.4	10.81	757	2.5	6.4	
3.	Rape								
4.	Serious assault	4,564		80.4	87.77	8,702	3.7		1
5.	All theft	5,232		55.0	100.62				
6.	Aggravated theft	1,753		60.4	33.71	3,072	1.4		
7.	Robbery and violent theft	394		31.0	7.58	852	2.0		1
8.	Breaking and entering								
9.	Auto theft	11		79.0	0.21				
10.	Other thefts								
11.	Fraud	186		82.0	3.58	357	1.4		2
12.	Counterfeiting	4		17.0	0.08	5			
13.	Drug offenses	357		78.0	6.87	614	3.2	3.5	1
14.	Total offenses								

Note: Information for some categories is not available.
Criteria of juveniles: aged from 14 to 18 years.

an overseas-style cap, a dress cap with a wide brim and a helmet liner.

Each commune has its own police force commanded by a brigadier, who is appointed by the mayor. The communal police are responsible for implementing communal laws, regulations and ordinances, safeguarding public property, overseeing the public market area and executing court judgments. The maximum size of the communal police is fixed at one per every 1,000 inhabitants. Under conditions of widespread public disorder, the mayor can appeal to the prefect for additional units of the National Police. The Central Information Service (Service Central de Renseignements, SCR) is in charge of criminal investigation and represents Interpol in Rwanda.

Recruitment, Education & Training

The National Police School is in a former Belgian medical training center at Ruhengeri. It provides six-month courses for both enlisted men and officers based on Belgian and French training programs.

The Penal System

Few criminal statistics are collected and published in the country.

SAUDI ARABIA

BASIC FACT SHEET

Official Name: Kingdom of Saudi Arabia
Area: 2,149,690 sq km
Population (1987): 14,904,794
Capital: Riyadh
Nature of Government: Absolute monarchy
Language: Arabic
Currency: Riyal
GNP (1986): $83.27 billion
Territorial Divisions: 14 provinces
Population per Police Officer: 280
Police Expenditures per 1,000: $131,140

History & Background

The organization of a modern public security system in Saudi Arabia was one of the notable achievements of Abd al Aziz. Previously, the country had known law enforcement only on a limited, local level. But even as it evolved, the police system has remained partly entrenched in the tribal social order under which the sheikhs remain the primary guarantors of public order within their bailiwicks. Only when local efforts fail is the National Guard brought in. In this sense, the law enforcement agencies complement but do not intrude on tribal authority.

Structure & Organization

The principal agencies charged with the maintenance of internal security are the National Guard, the Public Security Police, the Frontier Force and the Coast Guard, all within the Ministry of the Interior. The core element is the Public Security Police, the equivalent of a national police force. It is organized at two levels: provincial police directorates and local police directorates. Over 28,000 strong, its units are scattered all over the country and in every province. The provincial governors probably exercise direct control over the police within their administrative divisions. In addition, the governors and the sheikhs usually have their own personal guards, who may be deployed on public duties on occasion.

Police uniforms are similar to those of the Royal Saudi Army except for the distinctive red beret, but there are no paramilitary police units.

The deputy minister of the interior has responsibility for most of the other public security forces in the country, including the Frontier Force and the Coast Guard. In 1960 the government established the Police College at Mecca to train its officers. A secondary-school certificate is required for entrance. Training is provided at the college in the use of sophisticated equipment such as radar and helicopters. Units of all these forces are deployed during the haj season to control the pilgrims who flock into Mecca from various parts of the world.

Another public security police is the autonomous religious police *(mutawwiun),* organized by the authority of the king. The *mutawwiun* serve on the quasi-judicial public morality committees charged with ensuring strict compliance with the puritanical tenets of Wahhabism. Local committees in every town report to two central royal offices, one that covers the western provinces and another that covers the Nejd and Eastern provinces. They are notorious for their rigorous enforcement of such Islamic requirements as the five daily prayers, fasting during Ramadan, modesty in female attire and proscriptions against the use of alcohol and liquor.

These police agencies can call upon, in times of emergency, the paramilitary National Guard or the armed forces and often work in conjunction with them. The National Guard is a highly mobile force recruited primarily from the noble Bedouin tribes. Its authority over the people and its allegiance to the royal family are both unquestioned and have been demonstrated a number of times in recent history.

Recruitment, Education & Training

A separate college, the Internal Security Forces College at Riyadh, provides training for officers belonging to all services.

The Penal System

The Saudi penal system is based on the Sharia, as Koranic law is called. Sharia encompasses two categories of crime: those that are carefully defined and for which there are specific penalties, and those that are only implicit in the Koran and for which penalties may be set at the discretion of the judge *(qadi)*. In addition, a third category of crime has been established since the end of World War II. It consists of governmental decrees and regulations prohibiting certain types of activities. The first two categories are tried in Sharia courts and the third in administrative courts.

For numerous crimes, penalties under the Sharia are extremely severe. The government, however, has directed that these punishments be used only as a last resort. Even though carried out infrequently, the occasional beheading or stoning in public serve as a reminder that these penalties are still in force.

The Sharia carefully defines homicide and personal injury, fornication and adultery, theft and highway robbery and specifies a penalty *(hadd)* for each. Various degrees of culpability for homicide and bodily injury are recognized according to intent, the kind of weapon used and the circumstances. In Islamic law, homicide is not considered a crime against society in which the state moves against the criminal. Sharia recognizes only the right of the victim or the victim's family to bring charges against the accused for the right to retaliation or to blood money. Retaliation actually is permitted to the victim's next of kin, who may kill the criminal or inflict the same bodily injury on him. In practice, however, blood money is preferred. In serious cases, the accused usually is detained by the police until trial. The right of habeas corpus is not recognized. The granting of bond is entirely within the discretion of the local chief of police.

On arraignment, the judge hears the complaints, the defense and the testimonies of witnesses. Under Islamic law the testimony of one man equals that of two women. All cases are heard in public by a single judge. Trial by jury is unknown. After determining guilt or innocence and the right to compensation, the judge arrives at a fair assessment of reparations acceptable to both parties. The judge does not pass sentence. All papers are sent to the district or provincial governor who, with the advice of the local Koranic legal scholars *(ulema),* pronounces the sentence.

In case of a traffic death or injury, the driver at fault is subject not only to the jurisdiction of the Sharia court as regards the rights of the victim's family to indemnity but also to a penalty (generally imprisonment) under the vehicle code. The lack of distinction between simple and criminal negligence makes imprisonment virtually mandatory for even relatively minor violations.

Fornication and adultery are considered to be serious crimes punishable by flogging. However, the law requires rigorous proof, usually four reliable witnesses

CRIME STATISTICS (1984)

		Number Reported	Attempts %	Cases Solved %	Crime per 100,000	Offenders	Females %	Juveniles %	Strangers %
1.	Murder	115			1.15	125	2.40		26.40
2.	Sex offenses, including rape	1,928			19.28	2,669	17.01		26.41
3.	Rape								
4.	Serious assault	3,625			36.25	5,126	2.20		35.90
5.	All theft	5,490			54.90	1,981	2.47		58.25
6.	Aggravated theft								
7.	Robbery and violent theft	16			0.16	(1)			
8.	Breaking and entering								
9.	Auto theft	765			7.65				
10.	Other thefts								
11.	Fraud	92			0.92	115	2.61		52.17
12.	Counterfeiting	75			0.75	75	1.33		93.33
13.	Drug offenses	3,562			35.62	5,971	1.66		33.06
14.	Total offenses								

Note: Information for some categories is not available.
Criteria of juveniles: aged from 7 to 15 years.

to the act. It is extremely unlikely that anyone would commit adultery or fornication in front of four hostile witnesses. If their accusation does not hold up, the witnesses are liable to punishment themselves.

Theft is punished by cutting off the right hand of the thief, but petty larceny and theft from relatives are excluded. If the thief repents before the case is brought to the judge, the punishment may be reduced. Highway robbery is punished more severely, by having alternate hands and feet cut off. In robbery involving murder, the criminal is liable to execution by crucifixion. Penalties for the so-called crimes against public morality, such as drinking, gambling, and not fasting during the Ramadan, are set by the judge at his discretion and may vary from flogging to fines.

No information is available on penal institutions, but the prison population is believed to be very small.

The incidence of crime is not disclosed by the government but is reported to be low. The harsh nature of the laws has helped to deter large-scale crime. Tribal loyalties, religion and the strength of tradition have combined to produce an orderly society at all levels.

SENEGAL

BASIC FACT SHEET

Official Name: Republic of Senegal
Area: 196,192 sq km
Population (1987): 7,064,025
Capital: Dakar
Nature of Government: Authoritarian
Language: French
Currency: CFA franc
GNP (1986): $2.84 billion
Territorial Divisions: 10 regions, 28 departments, 95 arrondissements
Population per Police Officer: 730
Police Expenditures per 1,000: N.A.

Structure & Organization

The Senegalese police system consists of a National Gendarmerie and a National Police Force (Sûreté Nationale, SN). The National Gendarmerie is a paramilitary force controlled by the president through the minister of state for armed forces. It was created in 1843. In 1928 a Mobile Gendarmerie or Emergency Mobile Reserve was added, along with a mounted squadron. In 1949 it was reorganized on a territorial basis and again reorganized as part of the armed forces in 1968. The force is commanded by a high commander who is concurrently the chief of the general staff and commander in chief of the armed forces. Units known as legions are maintained in each of the 10 administrative regions. Legions are divided into smaller units called brigades—some consisting of only a few men—stationed at key positions throughout the country. They constitute a rural police force but have other duties and responsibilities. They have well-trained and well-equipped rapid reaction companies available for antiriot operations. They also guard the presidential palace, government buildings, airports, harbors and key border points.

The Mobile Gendarmerie consists of five squadrons, all based at Dakar. The Territorial Gendarmerie consists of seven companies, each with its own reserve squad. The most picturesque unit is the Mounted Squadron, which inherits the colorful traditions of the Mamelukes and the Spahis.

The regular uniform is a military-type khaki drill tunic or bush shirt with matching trousers. For ceremonial occasions there is an exotic uniform of wide, baggy trousers with a large pattern up the side and tucked into the tops of calf-length boots, a tunic, and an unusual tall cloth cap shaped like a large paper bag. The Mounted Squadron also has a flowing cloak or burnoose.

The National Police, SN, is a centrally directed force under the minister of interior in Dakar. Its strength was estimated in the mid-1980s at 5,000. It is primarily an urban law enforcement agency, and it retains more or less the same functions it had when formed in 1878. The SN is composed of seven central directorates, of which the largest is the Public Safety Directorate (PSD). The PSD comprises two main divisions: the Mobile Support Group and the Regional Public Safety Services. The former consists of a number of self-supporting mobile companies of riot police. Each of the 10 administrative divisions has a police headquarters responsible for the town police stations in the region. Each town has at least one police station or commissariat; larger towns have *commissariats d'arrondissement* or precinct stations. In the smaller towns there is no SN presence, and policing is entrusted to the Gendarmerie. The former Republican Guard (Garde Républicaine) was absorbed into the SN in 1970 and now forms one of its units.

There are five separate rank structures in the SN: *commissaires; officiers de police; officiers de paix; inspecteurs de police;* and *gardiens,* the lowest rank. All personnel are normally unarmed. The regular uniform is of lightweight khaki and consists of a tunic and/or shirt worn with matching trousers and cap. Dark blue epaulettes on the shoulders bear the badge of the force and the badges of rank. For general duties, the lower ranks wear a Sam Browne belt, and for certain duties, such as crowd control, a black beret replaces the usual peaked cap.

Recruitment, Education & Training

No current information is available.

The Penal System

The Penal Code of metropolitan France was applied during the colonial period to French citizens in French West Africa and to gallicized Africans called *évolués*. The criminal courts and the police continued to function under the French code until 1966, when the current Penal Code and the Code of Penal Procedure were promulgated. The new code was based almost entirely on the French one and caused little change in established legal norms, police powers or court procedures. Suspects or defendants have most of the same protections available to persons in similar circumstances under the French legal system. Children receive preferential treatment in the children's court attached to each court of first instance. Trial by jury is common for serious crimes. Death is the most serious punishment, but it is relatively rare. Life imprisonment with hard labor usually is imposed for the most serious crimes, including crimes against the security of the state.

There are 26 penal centers with a capacity to hold about 3,000 prisoners, but actually holding closer to 5,000.

Most crimes occur in the urban centers, especially in Dakar and other towns in the Cap Vert region, which account for more than half of all the prisoners sentenced and jailed.

CRIME STATISTICS (1983)

		Number Reported	Attempts %	Cases Solved %	Crime per 100,000	Offenders	Females %	Juveniles %	Strangers %
1.	Murder	100			1.67	93	7.52	5.37	10.75
2.	Sex offenses, including rape	293			4.88	227	17.62	7.04	6.60
3.	Rape	81			1.35	76	0	14.47	6.57
4.	Serious assault	2,018			33.64	1,735	4.43	1.61	5.70
5.	All theft	5,521			92.05	5,204	0.71	4.23	10.01
6.	Aggravated theft	1,109			18.49	1,229	1.13	4.23	4.39
7.	Robbery and violent theft	344			5.74	495	0.40	1.61	24.24
8.	Breaking and entering								
9.	Auto theft	223			3.72	240	0.41	2.08	12.08
10.	Other thefts	4,068			67.82	3,240	0.61	4.78	9.81
11.	Fraud	798			13.30	682	4.39	1.61	9.23
12.	Counterfeiting	106			1.77	75	6.66	0	16
13.	Drug offenses	901			15.02	1,071	0.37	0.18	9.71
14.	Total offenses	14,113			235.30	11,462	9.30	6.79	17.09

Note: Information for some categories is not available.
Criteria of juveniles: aged from 1 to 18 years.

SIERRA LEONE

BASIC FACT SHEET

Official Name: Republic of Sierra Leone
Area: 71,740 sq km
Population (1987): 3,754,088
Capital: Freetown
Nature of Government: Authoritarian
Language: English
Currency: Leone
GNP (1986): $1.17 billion
Territorial Divisions: 3 provinces, 12 districts, 146 chiefdoms
Population per Police Officer: 600
Police Expenditures per 1,000: N.A.

History & Background

The beginnings of what is known as the Sierra Leone Police Force date back to 1829, when 26 constables, half of whom kept order by day and half by night, were appointed in Freetown. By 1836 the nucleus of a proper police force had come into existence, consisting of a police inspector, three subinspectors and 60 constables. Each was issued one pair of shoes a year but no uniform. Senior officers usually had no prior police experience but were retired noncommissioned Army officers or civilians.

When the British annexed Koya and Sherbro Island in 1861, the police role was expanded to cover the entire colony, not just Freetown and the surrounding villages. Some military structure and training were introduced into the force; the commander became the inspector general; the force was installed in barracks, armed with carbines and given uniforms of white tunics and slacks with broad leather belts. By this time the force numbered 200 men.

In 1891 the Frontier Police was formed to guard the borders. In 1894 the civil force was designated the Sierra Leone Police Force in a government gazette. The first police band was formed in 1900, when the total strength was increased to 600. In September 1909 Superintendent Brook became the first commissioner of police. Under Brook a special riot squad was formed to deal with civil disturbances. Brook also started the Police Training School at Port Loko. The school was later transferred to the naval base at Hastings, where it is still located.

In 1948 the force was again enlarged, this time to 1,000, and the first African was promoted to the rank of assistant superintendent. The riot squad was disbanded, and every police officer began to receive instructions in riot control. In 1954 the force was extended to the main towns of the protectorate, replacing the disbanded court messenger forces. The first policewoman was recruited in January 1947. In 1963 the first native Sierra Leonean was appointed commissioner of police, and the last expatriate officer left the force in 1968. In 1967 and 1968 the police were affected by the political unrest that spread throughout the country, and in 1968 all senior police officers were arrested by the junior ranks of the service.

Structure & Organization

The 4,000-man police force is commanded by a commissioner who, like the military force commander, is a minister of state without portfolio. It is organized into five geographic divisions, including one for the special protection of the diamond industry. Each regional division is subdivided into a number of formations, which include the Criminal Investigations Department (CID), the Special Branch and the Traffic Division. The Special Branch is concerned with counterinsurgency and countersubversive activities. The Traffic Division is also concerned with issuing firearms and ammunition licenses. There are separate men's and women's police bands and a Dog Division.

Constables are issued shoes and uniforms and are housed in barracks. Those not housed in barracks are given special housing allowances. All policemen from constable up are entitled to a pension. The constable's uniform consists of a gray shirt with chrome buttons and serial numbers, a blue cummerbund, khaki shorts, blue hosetops, short puttees, black belt and boots, and a navy blue peaked cap. While on street patrol constables carry a billy club. Rifles are issued only during riots.

There are 15 grades in the service, as follows:

Commissioner of police

Deputy commissioner

Senior assistant commissioner

Assistant commissioner

Chief superintendent

Superintendent

Deputy superintendent

Assistant superintendent

Chief inspector

Inspector

Subinspector

Sergeant major

Sergeant

Corporal

Constable

In addition, there are a number of special police groups, including two internal security units, ISU-1 and ISU-2. Although their precise functions and operations have not been revealed, it is believed that ISU-1 guards important government installations and also constitutes the presidential guard. ISU-2 sometimes is referred to as the Active Security Unit or Militia. It was built up by Cuban advisers in the mid-1970s, and although loyal to APC (All People's Congress, the ruling party) leadership, is poorly-disciplined and poorly equipped.

The Court Messenger Force is a quasi-police force employed by district commissioners to carry warrants and subpoenas. When the police force was extended to the protectorate in 1954, the Court Messenger Force was disbanded, but each local authority was permitted to retain its local unit.

In 1953 a permanent police force was established in the mining district of Kono to counter illegal diamond mining activities. The force has over 100 specially trained uniformed constables.

Sierra Leone's police force has been described by independent observers as one of the best in black Africa. It survived the political turbulence of the late 1960s relatively unscathed. British traditions have been successfully preserved in fairness and integrity.

Recruitment, Education & Training

Direct entry into the force is possible for those who have completed secondary education. Others are sent to the Police Training School in Hastings for a six-month training course, at the end of which they are appointed constables.

The Penal System

Criminal law in Sierra Leone is not contained in a comprehensive code. It is made up of a series of local ordinances substantially similar to English statues. Specifically, by the enactment of the Criminal Procedures Ordinance and the Criminal Law Adoption Ordinance, many English statutes have become part of the criminal law of Sierra Leone.

There are 16 prisons in the country; the major ones are at Bo, Makeni, Kabala and Kailahun, each of which is designed to accommodate 200 prisoners. Masanki Prison accommodates 500 prisoners. Mafanta Prison has an agricultural colony. Freetown Central Prison is the only one with a woman's wing. For juvenile prisoners there are five remand homes—at Wellington, Bo, Kenema, Makeni and Sefadu. All prisons are administered by the Ministry of Social Welfare.

Statistics on the incidence of crime are sketchy. Apart from periodic ethnic conflicts, the most prevalent category of crime is diamond smuggling. Government statistics reveal that the most frequent offenses, in order of the number of occurrences, are burglary, larceny, housebreaking and allied offenses, closely followed by murder, assault and other violent offenses. Sexual offenses are relatively infrequent. There is some indication that offenses by the young—those between 17 and 25—are increasing. The incidence of armed robbery and robbery with violence was apparently high enough for the House of Representatives to approve in 1971 the death sentence for both crimes. Published reports reveal the existence of gangs, such as Black September and Black December. There is also much concern over drug use by the young, particularly the smoking of *djamba*, a form of cannabis. Another kind of crime is ritual murder by secret societies, such as the Kieh, in which children are killed and their blood sold.

SINGAPORE

Patrick Edobor Igbinovia

BASIC FACT SHEET

Official Name: Republic of Singapore
Area: 618 sq km
Population (1987): 2,616,236
Capital: Singapore
Nature of Government: Authoritarian
Languages: Chinese, Malay, Tamil and English
Currency: Singapore dollar
GNP (1976): $19.16 billion
Territorial Divisions: —
Population per Police Officer: 200
Police Expenditures per 1,000: $474,409

History & Background

The major events in the history of the Singapore Police Force are as follows:

1827: Sir Thomas Stamford Raffles sets up a small peacekeeping force consisting of one sergeant and 12 constables.

1857: The Police Act is passed, establishing a regular police force.

1863: The first police uniforms are introduced.

1884: The Criminal Investigation Department is founded.

1901: The Criminal Records Office is founded.

1916: Marine patrols are started to combat piracy.

1923: The Police Force Training Depot is started.

1929: The first Mobile Squad of the Traffic Police begins work.

1946: The police are reorganized under R. E. Foulger following the end of the Japanese occupation.

1948: The Radio Division begins operation.

1949: A female police unit is founded with the first women recruits.

1950: Riot squads are established to deal with street violence.

1955: The Police Dog Unit is founded.

1959: The Police Training School is upgraded as the Police Academy.

1969: Old khaki uniforms are replaced by blue ones.

1972: The Lee Soo Ann Report recommends increased pay and better training for police.

1975: The National Service is introduced for police recruitment.

1981: Police headquarters are reorganized, with four commands.

Structure & Organization

The Singapore Police Force is headed by the commissioner of police assisted by four deputy commissioners, each in charge of a command. Two departments come directly under the commissioner's charge: the Public Relations Department and the Staff Inspectorate. Each of these departments is headed by a deputy assistant commissioner. Together these departments help to keep the commissioner informed of developments in the environment as well as the internal health of the force. The Public Relations Department centralizes control over all dealings between the force and the community. Among other things, it handles relations with the mass media. It plans major campaigns directed at the public as well as its own members. It produces a number of in-house publications and audiovisual education programs, and it organizes exhibitions and community functions to foster stronger ties between police officers and their fellow citizens. The Staff Inspectorate constitutes the eyes and ears of the force. It constantly monitors and assesses the performance of the force and provides feedback to the commissioner.

The deputy commissioner for administration is assisted by three directors—in charge of the Manpower and Administration, Logistics, and Training departments. The Manpower and Administration Department oversees all matters pertaining to force personnel, finances and records. It is also in charge of discipline and of the welfare of all force members. Its welfare program, which has expanded considerably over the past few years, includes the provision of recreational facilities, the organization of social events and budget holidays for members and their families, and the purchase of consumer products on low-cost terms. The Logistics Department administers workshops in the Marine Division and in the Transportation, Communications and Armaments Division and also handles the Store and Supplies Division. In addition, it evaluates new equipment and manages building projects for the force. The Training Department runs the Police Academy, where all force training is centralized. It maintains a Training Development Division, which develops course materials and formulates force doctrine. Moreover, it supervises the National Police Cadet Corps, a school-level organization designed to familiarize children with police activities.

The Planning Command is entrusted with the task of preparing the force for challenges in the coming years. The deputy commissioner of planning is assisted by three directors—in charge of the Operational Planning, Strategic Planning, and Systems and Research departments. The director of the Operational Planning Department supervises two divisions: the Security Planning Division and the Contingency Planning Division. The Security Planning Division formulates policy and doctrine relating to public order and domestic security. It is also responsible for airport security and all entrances and exits into and out of the republic. The Contingency Planning Division prepares for situations such as major disasters and crises and acts of terrorisms such as hijackings. In addition, it looks after the security of visiting VIP's. The Strategic Planning Department is composed of two divisions: the Development Projects Division and the Conceptual Planning Division. The Development Projects Division initiates large development projects and handles the formulation of all building plans until funds are approved. This calls for the presentation of cost-benefit studies from time to time. The Conceptual Planning Division is concerned mainly with five-year rolling plans and annual work plans. This involves data collection and analysis, coordination or planning activities among the various units, and work plan seminars. It also reviews from time to time the broad strategy adopted by the force. The director of the Systems and Research Department supervises three divisions: the Organization and Method Division, the Doctrine Division and the Computer Systems Divi-

sion. The Organization and Method Division reviews and revises work procedures and the organizational structure of various units. It undertakes the research required for demarcation of patrol sectors and adjustment of patrol shifts. It can be required to come up with feasibility studies on recommended new systems and procedures. The Doctrine Division reviews, amends and issues force policies, doctrines, police general orders, force directives and headquarters circulars. It can also collect proposed amendments to legislation and prepare answers to parliamentary questions. The Computer Systems Division is responsible for the maintenance and development of police computer systems. It translates the requirements of the police into the language of systems analysis and design.

The Operation Command forms the front line of the force. This is where the bulk of the force is deployed and where the greatest interactions with the public take place. Five departments come under this complex command: Areas, Detachment, the Criminal Investigation Department or CID, Traffic and Crime Prevention. The commander for areas, assisted by a deputy commander for areas, is responsible for eight land divisions, the Radio Division and the Airport Police. Each land division is headed by a superintendent and carries out regular duties in the field of crime prevention, patrol, investigation, enforcement and other related activities. The Radio Division is the mobile response force, and its primary function is to attend to emergency calls. Headed by a deputy superintendent, it is composed of a large patrol force and a radio communications center; during major crises the latter serves as a combined police military operations room.

The Airport Police have a special role to play. Their duties are basically the same as their counterparts in the other divisions but differ in routine and special task. The Detachment Department serves as an umbrella for a number of security units, mainly the Police Task Force, the Marine Police Division, the Security Branch, the Gurkha Contingent and the Police Dog Unit.

The Police Task Force consists of three units, which serve many functions. In normal times they are deployed to provide security at the airport and to control crowds at large public events such as displays, festivals and sports events. In times of unrest and public disorder, however, their main function is to control riots.

The Marine Police Division is a large one, and its duties involve patrolling territorial water. It ensures that rules and regulations governing the operation of all marine vessels are adhered to, and it checks regarding the entry of all unauthorized aliens and the shipping of contraband goods. The Security Branch guards all VIPs visiting the country. The Gurkha

Contingent acts as backup force to three task forces and is trained for similar functions. The Police Dog Unit trains dogs for guard and security work. It performs a useful function at the immigration counter, where dogs are used to detect heroin and other drugs being brought into the country.

The Criminal Investigation Department (CID) had four divisions. It handles major crimes and provides specialized backup services. Each of these divisions is headed by a superintendent. The Administrative and Specialist Division provides support for investigations into murder, kidnapping and organized crime involving gambling and vice syndicates. The Commercial Crime Division handles sophisticated white-collar crimes. The division takes over from the Land Division cases that involve large sums of money or those considered too complex for the Land Division. The Criminal Intelligence Unit collects information on crime trends and provides essential information to investigators. The Secret Society Division is responsible for the suppression of secret society activities. It also keeps track of known society members and has successfully prevented a resurgence of secret society violence, which was common three decades ago. The Traffic Police is made up of the Operation Division and the Administrative Division. The operation Division oversees traffic control and management, including patrol and enforcement. It investigates traffic accidents and processes violation reports. It also has a research branch, which undertakes data collection, production of management information and dissemination of road safety information. The Administrative Division of the Traffic Police oversees testing and licensing of drivers and also administers the points demerit system. In addition, it provides administrative training and financial support for the entire department. The Crime Prevention Department has a two-fold task. It must persuade the general public and business to play a greater part in protecting their own property, and it educates them on the right measures to adopt. Much of its work involves campaigns through the mass media and direct liaison with community groups and commercial organizations. The Crime Prevention Department is made up of three divisions. The Operation Division leads and supervises crime prevention programs in the land divisions. The Liaison and Exhibition Division speaks directly to the community through neighborhood gatherings and mobile exhibitions. The Collation and Research Division keeps track of criminal activities and trends. The Civil Defense Command is made up of two components: the Civil Defense Corps itself and the Construction Brigade. The Civil Defense Corps is geared to fire fighting, first aid and rescue operations and is composed mainly of police reservists.

Recruitment, Education & Training

Singapore's only police training institution is the Policy Academy.

The Penal System

Singapore has one of the most severe penal codes in the world. The Penal Code, as amended in 1973, makes caning mandatory for crimes of theft or robbery, in addition to imprisonment. The death penalty is prescribed for trafficking in firearms and for kidnapping; 30 years in prison, a S$5,000 fine and 15 strokes of the cane are imposed for drug trafficking; and life imprisonment plus caning is prescribed for robbery with a gun. The Criminal Law (Temporary Provisions) Ordinance of 1958 authorizes 12-month detention without trial for suspected gangsters.

The Prisons Department of the Ministry of Home Affairs is under the immediate control of the director of prisons. He is assisted by a deputy and five superintendents. Females are kept in the Female Prison, a minimum-security institution. The Queenstown Remand Prison, a short-term, maximum-security facility, receives and classifies newly convicted adult male offenders, and it holds persons awaiting trial or sentencing. Changi Prison, a maximum-security facility, houses prisoners sentenced to more than three years and those detained indefinitely. There are two medium-security institutions for first and second offenders and those judged to be rehabilitatable—a prison at Moon Crescent in Changi and the Khasa Crescent Center.

The corrections system also has a prerelease camp, a minimum-security prison for long-term prisoners serving the last six months of their sentence. Young people under 16 are not sent to prisons but to approved homes (for girls) and approved schools (for boys). The Reformative Training Center houses young offenders between 16 and 21.

Because of the harsh laws in the statute books, crime is not a serious problem in this city-state. Offenses are reported in six categories: offenses against property with violence; offenses against property without violence; malicious injury to property; forgery and other offenses against currency; offenses against the Penal Code; and offenses against other laws. The overwhelming majority of the offenses are against property, with housebreaking and theft being the most frequently reported crimes in this category.

One aspect of public order that is rooted in Singapore's history is the presence of Chinese secret societies, which evolve into organized Mafia-type crime groups. Some success was achieved in containing these societies through the 1958 ordinance against gangsters.

CRIME STATISTICS (1984)

		Number Reported	Attempts %	Cases Solved %	Crime per 100,000	Offenders	Females %	Juveniles %	Strangers %
1.	Murder	69	7.2	78.3	2.73	60		0	
2.	Sex offenses, including rape	582		46.0	23.01	278		7.91	
3.	Rape	105		50.5	4.15	71		5.63	
4.	Serious assault	95		38.9	3.76	47		0	
5.	All theft	22,702		18.7	897.63	4,730		12.77	
6.	Aggravated theft								
7.	Robbery and violent theft	1,620	3.5	20.5	64.05	432		9.49	
8.	Breaking and entering	3,134	2.5	16.3	123.92	500		13.80	
9.	Auto theft	542		13.5	21.43	74			
10.	Other thefts	22,160		18.9	876.20	4,656			
11.	Fraud	1,878		28.0	74.26	555		0.90	
12.	Counterfeiting	344		52.0	13.60	6			
13.	Drug offenses								
14.	Total offenses	35,728		23.0	1,412.68	9,446		10.33	

Note: Information for some categories is not available.
Criteria of juveniles: aged from 7 to 15 years.

SOMALIA

BASIC FACT SHEET

Official Name: Somali Democratic Republic
Area: 637,657 sq km
Population (1987): 7,741,859
Capital: Mogadishu
Nature of Government: Military dictatorship
Language: Somali
Currency: Shilling
GNP (1986): $1.56 billion
Territorial Divisions: 18 regions, 16 districts
Population per Police Officer: 540
Police Expenditures per 1,000: N.A.

History & Background

The Somali Police Force grew out of police forces employed by the British and Italians in British Somaliland and Italian Somalia, respectively. Although there were organizational distinctions between armed and police forces, both used to perform the same general functions. The Somali staffed the lower ranks in both forces. Most of those who eventually became senior officers and commanders in the police and the Army began their careers in the Somalia Gendarmerie under British military administration during World War II. By the time of the 1969 military coup, the police had grown from about 3,700 at independence to 6,000. After independence much aid was received from the West, notably the United States, West Germany and Italy, up to 1970.

The earliest Somali law enforcement agency was an armed constabulary of about 15 men established in 1884 to police the northern coast. In 1910 the British formed the Somaliland Coastal Police, and in 1912 they formed the British Somaliland Camel Constabulary to police the interior. The Camel Constabulary took part in the operations against Sayyid Mohamed ibn Abdullah Hassan but were ambushed in 1913, losing their leader and most of their 150-man force. They were later reformed, and they continued to operate until 1920.

In 1926 the British formed the first properly constituted police force in their colony, the Somaliland Police Force. Led by British officers, the force included Somalis in the lower ranks. They were aided by uniformed and armed rural constabulary (illalo) who brought offenders to court, guarded prisoners, patrolled local townships and accompanied nomadic tribesmen over grazing areas.

The Italians used military forces to maintain public order in their colony until 1914, when they developed a small coastal police and a rural constabulary (gogle) to assist Italian residents. By 1930 this force comprised some 300 men.

When the Fascists took over Italy, Italian administrators reconstituted the former Somali Police Corps into a more efficient force called the Corpo Zaptie. The ranks of the older police corps were purged, and Somali, Eritrean and Arab troops were recruited to bring the strength of the Corpo Zaptie to about 800. Italian carabinieri officers trained and supervised the new corps, and new barracks were built to house them. When the Corpo Zaptie proved ineffectual against the nomadic population of Benadir, Obbya and Mijerteyn askaris or policemen were recruited from local clans to disarm the unruly tribes. During the Ethiopian War the Corpo Zaptie expanded to about 6,000 men.

In 1941, after an initial defeat and expulsion from the Horn of Africa, the British returned to crush the Italians and recover the area. The British then established a British Military Administration (BMA) over both protectorates. The Italian colony's police force was disbanded and replaced by the hastily recruited Somalia Gendarmerie, under British officers. By 1943 this force had expanded to more than 3,000 men, led by 120 British officers. In 1948 the Somalia Gendarmerie was renamed the Somalia Police Force. However, the British let the Italian colony's rural police force survive without major alteration, since it resembled their own.

A school was opened for training Somali officers and noncommissioned men. By 1949 a few of the Somali who attended this school had reached the rank of chief inspector, the highest noncommissioned rank.

When in 1950 the southern area became the trust territory of Somaliland under Italian administration, Italian *carabinieri* officers and Somali personnel from the Somalia Police Force formed the Police Corps of Somalia (Corpo di Polizia della Somalia), commanded by Italian officers. In 1958, two years before independence, the force was completely Somalized and redesignated the Police Force of Somalia (Forze di Polizia della Somalia). Similar progress was not made in British Somaliland. Somalia did not receive high command until just before independence, and British officers were not withdrawn until 1960. At that time, the northern and southern forces were integrated.

Of the 3,700 men and officers in the police force at independence, 1,000 belonged to the Mobile Group (Darawishta Poliska or simply Darawishta). This force was used to keep peace in the interior, where frequent disputes over water and grazing rights often led to fighting between rival clans or lineages. The most serious crisis of this sort happened in 1965, when the police had to declare an emergency and resort to infantry tactics to restore order.

A police air wing with Cessna light aircraft and one Douglas DC-3 was formed in 1961 to provide assistance to field police units and to the Darawishta through airlift of supplies, reconnaissance and transport of aircraft. A small unit of policewomen was formed, also in 1961, for interrogation of female prisoners and in cases involving female juvenile delinquents, abandoned girls, prostitutes and child beggars.

From 1959 to 1969 the Somali Police Force, commanded by General Mohammad Abshir Musa, acquired a reputation for professionalism and excellence and also grew to 6,000 in strength. They were able to remain above internal political struggles and to preserve order during elections and shifts in governments.

Structure & Organization

Public order is the legal responsibility of the minister of the interior, regional governors and district commissioners. The Ministry of the Interior controls the police force at the highest levels. Local authorities control the regional and district police commands.

Organizationally the police is part of the armed forces, but the police commandant is under the Ministry of Justice. The force is divided into various departments known as divisions, with branches in all jurisdictions. Each region has a regional commandant and each district a commissioned officer. Outside Mogadishu, the chain of command runs through group commands, divisional commands (corresponding to the regions), subdivisional commands (corresponding to the districts), station commands and police posts. The responsibilities of commanding officers in villages and districts vary with the individual jurisdiction.

The Mobile Police comprises the Darawishta and the Riot Unit (Birmadka Poliska). The former operates in remote areas and the frontier, and the latter operates as a crack emergency unit and also provides honor guards for ceremonial functions.

Technical and specialized units include the Tributary Division, the Criminal Investigation Division (CID), the Traffic Division, the Communications Unit and the Training Unit. The CID handles investigations, fingerprinting, criminal records, immigration and passports, and operates in both urban and rural areas. It has modern equipment and is described as the mainstay of the force. Its communications network enables it to communicate with any station in the country.

Service units include the Transport Department (Gadidka Poliska), Central Stores and the Health Service. The Transport Department has a fleet of motor vehicles with radiotelephones, including Land-Rovers, and motorcycles. The Police Custodial Corps consists of prison guards.

Police ranks are divided into five major groups: senior officers, junior officers, inspectors, noncommissioned officers and *askaris*. Inspectors are equivalent to warrant officers in the Army. Pay and allowances are the same as for members of the Somali armed forces.

There are occasional reports of police brutality, especially in situations where the police attempt to defuse potentially violent situations on the street or involving political dissenters.

In 1972 the government organized a revolutionary group known as the Victory Pioneers. Although a paramilitary force, their primary and most visible function is law enforcement. They have powers of arrest independent of the police, and they constantly scrutinize contacts between Somalis and foreigners. In rural areas they constitute a vigilance corps performing police and guard duties. Dressed in green, they are highly visible in towns and are much feared.

Over the centuries, Somalis have evolved a unique system of handling disputes or acts of violence, including homicide, as wrongs involving not only the parties immediately concerned but also the groups (tribes or lineages) of which they were members. The offending party and his group would pay *dia* (blood compensation, often in the form of livestock) to the injured party and his group. After independence, there was no attempt to develop a system of criminal law uniquely Somali. Court procedures mirrored a synthesis of codes introduced by Great Britain and Italy, but *dia*-paying arrangements continue to play an important role in the actual administration of justice. The military government changed remarkably little of the criminal justice system it inherited. Despite its talk of expunging foreign neocolonial influences, the government concentrated on increasing and extending the influence of Western-type laws introduced by the former colonial masters. A major campaign was directed against *dia* and the concept of collective responsibility for crimes. Thus the government was able to expand its control over an important area of jurisprudence over which it previously had no control.

Recruitment, Education & Training

Recruits to the police force have to be between 17 and 25 years of age, of high moral caliber and physically fit. After joining, they receive six months' training at the National Police Academy in Mogadishu. Once this training is complete, recruits take an examination, and if they pass, they serve two years on the force. When this service is complete the policeman is offered a renewal of his contract. Officers undergo a stiff training course for nine months. Darawishta receive special training in a six-month tactical training course. Some officers are trained in Italy.

The Penal System

The Somali Penal Code, enacted early in 1962, became effective nationwide on April 3, 1964. The essential basis of the code was the constitutional premise of the supremacy of the law over the state and its citizens. The code placed responsibility for determining offenses and punishments exclusively on the written law and excluded all penal sanctions formerly observed in unwritten customary law. However, the code incorporated some authority expressed by customary law and the Sharia. Penal responsibility was declared to be personal and not collective. Judicial action under the code, however, did not rule out the possibility of additional redress in the form of *dia* (customary blood money) through civil action in the courts. The military government that came to power in 1969 forbade this provision entirely.

To be liable criminally a person must have committed an act of omission that causes harm or danger to another's person or property or to the state. Further, the offenses must be committed wilfully, or as a result of negligence, imprudence or illegal behavior. As a result, persons of unsound mind, those suffering from deafness, or total intoxication from alcohol or narcotic drugs, and children under 14 are exempt from criminal liability. The accused is assumed to be innocent until proven guilty beyond all reasonable doubt. The burden of proof rests with the state.

The Penal Code classes offenses as either crimes or contraventions. The latter are legal violations without criminal intent. Death by shooting is the only sentence for the most serious crimes, such as those against the state and murder. The Penal Code usually prescribes a maximum and a minimum punishment but leaves the actual sentence to the discretion of the judge.

The Penal Code comprises three books. The first deals with general principles of jurisprudence; the second defines criminal offenses and prescribes specified punishments; and the third contains 61 particles regulating contraventions of public order, safety, morality and health. The Penal Code recognizes the social character of punishment and its role in restoring the offender to a useful place in society. Some of the major provisions of the Penal Code are rooted in either Somali customary law or the Sharia, especially those that deal with drunkenness.

Matters relating to arrest and trial are governed by the Criminal Procedure Code, adopted by legislative decree in June 1963 and made effective in April 1964. Conforming to Anglo-Saxon law, the code prescribes the kinds and jurisdictions of criminal courts, spells out the functions and responsibilities of judicial officials, outlines the rules of evidence and regulates the conduct of trials. Ordinarily a person can be arrested only if caught in the act of committing an offense or upon issuance of a warrant by the proper judicial authority. The code recognizes the writ of habeas corpus. When a person is arrested, all personal possessions are confiscated and returned only upon his or her release. Those arrested have the right to be taken before a judge within 24 hours. A prison does not accept a person directly from a police station without a judge's order. The prosecutor general handles all cases for the government, controls investigations, and draws up charges and presents them to the court.

Somalia inherited a primitive penal system from the colonial administration, and it deteriorated further during the transition to independence. Under UN auspices, the system was overhauled. The Constitution includes a special provision on penal institutions, emphasizing prisoner rehabilitation. The Penal Code incorporates a provision for payment of wages to prisoners for work done while incarcerated and prohibits placing juveniles with adult offenders.

There are 49 correctional institutions in the country, of which the Mogadishu Central prison is the largest. All inmates at the Central Prison receive literacy training and the services of qualified medical personnel. There is a youth reformatory at Afgoi, on the outskirts of the capital.

The major law-enforcement problems are drunkenness, possession of firearms and livestock theft. Such felonies as armed robbery, rape and other crimes involving violence are not widespread, and there is no indication of a general trend toward lawlessness. The only organized criminal activities are smuggling and illegal traffic in contraband by armed gangs. One form of crime that has shown no signs of decreasing is corruption among public officials, which is reported to be widespread. Public officials and their wives are believed to be engaged in both black-marketing and smuggling. The government's continued efforts to stem the tide of corruption only suggest that the problem is as acute as ever.

SOUTH AFRICA

BASIC FACT SHEET

Official Name: Republic of South Africa
Area: 1,221,037 sq km
Population (1987): 34,313,356
Capital: Pretoria (administrative); Cape Town (legislative); Bloemfontein (judicial)
Nature of Government: White-dominated limited democracy
Languages: English and Afrikaans
Currency: Rand
GNP (1986): $59.91 billion
Territorial Divisions: 4 provinces, 10 homelands
Population per Police Officer: 870
Police Expenditures per Capita: N.A.

History & Background

South Africa had an extensive police system even in the 19th century. The Boer republics had tough, paramilitary mounted police forces, and Cape Colony had an efficient modern force, known as the Cape Constabulary, modeled after London's Metropolitan Police Force. It was aided by the Water Police, who were responsible for patrolling the waterfront and combating smuggling. In rural districts, law and order were maintained by a few constables known as *land-drosts,* who could call upon the assistance of local volunteers when needed. The Natal Mounted Police undertook law enforcement in the neighboring British colony and provided effective support during the Zulu War in 1879.

After the Anglo-Boer War ended in British victory, the new British administration reorganized the mounted police in the Transvaal and Orange Free State. The police forces of the four provinces were consolidated soon after the Act of Union of 1910, and from this amalgamation two law-enforcement agencies emerged. The Mounted Riflemen were detailed to rural areas and to border patrol, and the South African Police (SAP) to urban areas. When the Mounted Riflemen were conscripted during World War I, the SAP assumed law-enforcement duties throughout the nation, although this jurisdiction became statutory only in 1936, when the SAP absorbed the Mounted Riflemen. In 1939, the SAP's responsibilities were extended to South-West Africa. Later amendments to the Police Act of 1912 permitted the SAP to operate outside the republic when requested by friendly governments or when deemed necessary for national security.

Structure & Organization

The South African Police (SAP) is a paramilitary law-enforcement agency centrally organized as a state service and as the primary instrument for maintaining internal security. Operating under the minister of police, it is adminstered by the commissioner of police, who holds the rank of general.

The numerical strength of the SAP in 1984 was 44,696, excluding 16,576 active Reserve Police Force members and 3,810 active Police Reserve Force members. The force is 55% white, 40% black, and 5% Coloured and Asian. However, of the 2,500 commissioned officers, only 4.5% were black, and there were no nonwhite officers above the rank of lieutenant colonel. Assignment policies precluded assigning white policemen in subordinate capacities to nonwhite officers or senior constables. Senior officers are promoted from the ranks, and there is no direct entry into the commissioned ranks.

The police uniform consists of a blue-gray belted jacket worn with lighter gray trousers and a peaked cap. Constables and NCOs add a black Sam Browne belt. In summer police wear blue-gray bush jackets and shorts. All constables on patrol duty have batons and handguns, the latter restricted to white policemen before 1972.

After the passage of the Group Areas Act of 1950, which enforced the resettlement of urban black and colored communities, nonwhite police personnel were given the responsibility for maintaining law and order in the racially segregated townships. Black police were stationed in districts to which they were not native, where they were less likely to feel sympathy for the locals. Blacks are in sole charge of 39 police stations, Coloureds of 14 and Asians of one.

In addition to its primary internal security role, the SAP also discharges routine peacekeeping and crime-prevention police duties. A large part of its work involves implementing apartheid laws. Amendments to the Defense Act allow military reservists and commandos to be mobilized on short notice to assist the police in emergency situations. This is particularly applicable to South-West Africa (Namibia) and other sparsely populated areas.

Traffic control is not a function of the SAP. Most larger municipalities maintain local traffic police, and enforcement of traffic laws on the major highways is exercised by provincial highway patrols. Similarly, policing of railways, airports and harbors is handled by the South African Railways and Harbors Administration.

The SAP is controlled from a central headquarters in Pretoria under a commissioner of police. He has 19 police divisions under his control, each under the command of a divisional commissioner holding the rank of brigadier. Each division is divided into a number of police districts, each headed by a divisional commandant holding the rank of brigadier, colonel, lieutenant colonel or major. The 84 police districts are further subdivided into station areas, each under the command of a station commander, with the rank of captain or lieutenant. There are 843 police stations and 39 border control posts, the last level.

Operationally the SAP was divided into three branches: the Uniformed Branch, the Detective Branch and the Security Branch.

The Uniformed Branch
The bulk of the force is employed in the Uniformed Branch, to which all police recruits are initially assigned. As part of the Uniformed Branch the SAP quartermaster is responsible for the supply and maintenance of police equipment and transportation. The Uniformed Branch makes extensive use of police dogs in investigation of criminal activity, pursuit of suspects, crowd control and constabulary patrols. Dogs and their handlers are trained at Kwaggaspoort Dog Training School in Pretoria. Most of the animals are German shepherds trained for tracking and detecting *dagga (Cannabis sativa)* and sniffing out land mines. They are also given parachute training so they can be dropped from the air into areas inaccessible to motorized police. The Radio Patrol Service, also known as the Flying Squad, works in tandem with the SAP air wing.

The Detective Branch
The Detective Branch is a specialized branch that operates out of the headquarters. Operational units include the Criminal Investigation Division, with district commands, and the Special Branch, concerned with intelligence gathering and surveillance. The Criminal Bureau serves as a clearinghouse for fingerprints and as an archive for criminal records. The Narcotics Squad investigates drug trafficking. The SAP Forensic Science Laboratory is one of the best-equipped facilities of its kind in the world.

The Security Branch
The Security Branch is responsible for border patrol in internal security operations. It is composed of hard-hitting mobile units trained in counterinsurgency tactics and riot control that are ready for deployment anywhere in the country at short notice. The Security Branch's black units are particularly feared by the black community. All units are self-sufficient in weaponry, communications and transportation equipment, and logistical support. In operational situations they are provided with camouflaged battle dress, gas masks, body armor and helmets and are armed with assault rifles, automatic weapons, shotguns and tear gas canister launchers. Units are transported in armored personnel carriers and specially designed riot trucks.

After the Soweto riots of 1978, the Security Branch was upgraded as an antiguerrilla force. In addition to an array of lethal ordnance, units also rely on rubber bullets, electric prods, Plexiglass shields and the "sneeze machine" to control urban disorders. Riot control is undertaken by platoon-size units that move quickly into assigned areas in Hippos. They are required by law to defuse potentially violent situations gradually before resorting to force. But more often than not, they tend to disregard the officially prescribed sequence and resort to an indiscriminate use of firearms, especially shotguns. Frequently, police combine with Army and commando forces in large-scale sweeps of black townships. They surround these areas, usually at midnight, and for the next 24 hours conduct house-to-house searches.

As enforcers of myriad apartheid laws, the police deal daily with a state of endemic resistance by the black community. Even criminal offenses by black people are viewed as subversive acts, and the SAP devotes much of its energy to dragnet information through a network of white and black informers. The organization of black political and social movements is viewed as endangering internal security (i.e., white supremacy), and police monitor their activities and suppress them whenever possible. There are continuing reports of the systematic use of torture and intimidation by the police, resulting in the deaths of detainees, the best-known instance being that of Steve Biko in 1977. Often these deaths are listed as suicides or attributed to bizarre accidents. Legislation guarantees immunity to police for acts committed in the line of duty and in designated operational areas. Under a 1979 amendment to the Police Act, the press is restrained from hostile investigations of police actions. Nevertheless, allegations of brutality sometimes result in temporary suspensions or immediate transfer of the police involved. Also, indemnities sometimes are paid in cases of assault by police and false arrests. Despite their hostility to black political movements, the police behavior is generally humane and responsive to human needs, irrespective of color.

The Police Reserve

The Police Reserve, established in 1961, is composed of civilian volunteers who are organized to perform ordinary police duties when members of the regular force are diverted to more urgent tasks. In 1985 it numbered some 24,000, about one-fourth of them black, consisting of four separate personnel categories:

Group A: Reservists who are regarded as full-time police in times of emergency. They receive paramilitary training and are issued firearms. Inclusion in this category is limited to whites.

Group B: Home guards who perform part-time police duties in their own neighborhoods. Open to all racial groups.

Group C: Typically employees of local authorities and key industries who may be called upon to protect their employers' property in an emergency.

Group D: Reservists who are drawn from rural areas and constitute a civilian restraining force, willing to carry out police duties in the initial stages of an emergency until regular police arrive in sufficient strength.

In the late 1960s black police reservists were trained for part-time service in Soweto and were placed under the supervision of regular police officers in the township. The apparent success of this experiment led to the recruiting of more black contingents for reserve police duty in the townships. Before this time, real police power in the crime-ridden townships belonged to unofficial local vigilantes, the *makgotla,* who acted ostensibly to control crime and punish malefactors according to tribal law. Eventually the *makgotla* became a political force within the community and often wielded arbitrary power through their racketeering and strong-arm tactics. The Community Councils Act of 1977 provided for the establishment of community guards, supplementing the police, as an alternative to the *makgotla,* who were subsequently banned.

Recruitment, Education & Training

The SAP places great emphasis on training, and the broad scope of technical and academic instruction given members of the force, coupled with drill and combat training, have led to a high level of professional competence. Of the four training institutions, the largest is the South African Police College in Pretoria where all-white recruits receive basic training and where other white personnel attend advanced courses in specialized subjects. Black recruits and reservists are trained at Hammanskraal, north of Pretoria; Coloureds at the Bishop Lavis Police Depot near Cape Town; and Asians at Wentworth, near Durban. Recruits in all schools undergo an identical six-month training course and white candidates an additional six-month academic course before assignment to duty.

Recruit training includes both practical and theoretical instruction in physical conditioning, self-defense, first aid, use of firearms, crowd and riot control, close order drill, and infantry tactics. Instruction also is given in various laws police are called on to enforce. All trainees attend lectures on race relations and on social problems such as alcoholism and drug abuse. White recruits are required to have completed secondary school and to be bilingual in Afrikaans and English. For nonwhites the minimum educational qualifications are primary school education and proficiency in either Afrikaans or English. After completing basic training, recruits are promoted to the rank of constable and assigned for two months of duty with a metropolitan police station before receiving a permanent station assignment.

In addition to recruit training, SAP schools provide instruction for police specialists, advanced courses in criminology and law-enforcement techniques for senior personnel, and refresher training in the use of firearms and riot control procedures. Security Branch forces receive intensive training in counterinsurgency tactics. Other courses include crime laboratory work, the use of electronic devices, computer technology, radio operation and repair, motor vehicle operation and maintenance, horsemanship and veterinary science. A three-year course of study leading to a degree is offered at the University of South Africa.

Applicants to the SAP must be between 18 and 35 years with specified physical standards. Women have been admitted to the force since 1972, but female applicants must be either single or widowed.

The Penal System

The South African legal system has its roots in Roman-Dutch and English law, reflecting the legal traditions of the two major components of the white population. Although the former was the first to reach the country, later assimilation of English law after the British rose to power in Cape Colony in 1806 resulted in substantial modifications both in principle and in practice. Court procedures, the jury system and rules of evidence are all patterned on the English rather than the Roman-Dutch model. In contemporary South Africa, the primary source of law is legislation rather than judicial precedent. Acts of parliament, provincial ordinances, municipal bylaws and adminstrative regulations govern all legal relationships.

The national penal system is administered by the Department of Prisons organized into regional commands, each responsible for the operation of prisons within its area. Ultimate authority is vested in the minister in charge, who holds the portfolio for justice and police. The senior officer within the department is the commissioner of prisons, who is the head of the Prison Service, which is staffed by civil servants. The authorized personnel strength of the Prison Service is 15,800, of whom 9,000 are white, 5,200 black and 1,600 Asian or Coloured. Of the total, 1,200 are women. Most of the white personnel are Afrikaners. Of the officers all but a handful are white; the highest-ranking black is a captain. Pay rates for prison personnel, although lower than those of the police, are considered generally satisfactory, especially for blacks, who have lower income expectations. Staff personnel receive full medical benefits, housing, and generous government pension on retirement at age 60. Despite such benefits, there is a high turnover of 15 to 20% annually, resulting from the resignation of trained prison warders, who frequently accept security jobs with private industrial concerns. Community pressure on black recruits has also tended to depress personnel strength and morale. White recruits for the Prison Service are trained at Kroonstad; Coloureds at Pollsmoor; Asians at Durban; and blacks at Baviaanspoort Prison, near Pretoria. Warders are armed with billy clubs, but those assigned to minimum- or maximum-security prisons are authorized to carry firearms. The prisons also employ trained dogs.

The majority of the more than 250 prisons under the Department of Prisons are local or district prisons used as reception centers for newly convicted prisoners and for persons remanded into custody while awaiting trial. The remainder comprises maximum-security prison farms and large, maximum-security central prisons. Although local prisons are classified as medium-security facilities, maximum security is maintained in them because of the potential for violence among remanded prisoners, who make up 40% of the prison population. Reformatories for juvenile offenders are not part of the penal system but are administered by the separate departments responsible for segregated education.

Although some prisons built during the colonial period are still in use, most of them have been extensively modernized since the end of World War II. Newer prisons are consolidated complexes, each containing a reception center, a maximum-security section and a prison farm. This concept permitted advancement from closed to open prison conditions without the need for transfers and readjustment to new surroundings as prisoners progressed toward the completion of their confinement. Typical of the modern prisons built on this model are those at Pretoria; Pietermaritzburg; and Paarl, in western Cape Province.

Although physical facilities, such as floor space, cubic air space, ventilation, lighting and sanitary facilities are subject to local health regulations, sharp discrepancies exist between living conditions for white and for nonwhite prisoners. Standards of hygiene also are reduced by severe overcrowding.

The oldest prison is located off Cape Town, on Robben Island in Table Bay. An impenetrable maximum-security prison, it houses black and Coloured inmates convicted under security legislation as well as prisoners serving life sentences. These prisoners work a typical nine-hour day at hard physical labor. Each of the black homelands operates its own separate penal system and has full jursidiction over its prisons.

South Africa has one of the largest prison populations in the world per capita among any advanced non-Communist country. The average annual prison population is estimated at over half a million, of whom nearly half are sentenced prisoners, with the reamining those remanded while awaiting trial. Nearly 80% of this total is black, and about 10% are women. About 80% of all prisoners are sentenced to terms of six months or less and 40% to terms of one month or less. About 40% of the black prisoners are convicted of pass law offenses. Prisons are segregated according to race and gender, and nonwhite warders are not assigned to white prisoners.

Prisoners are classified according to their offenses, past records and length of sentence, taking also into consideration their psychological condition and prospect of rehabilitation. About 10% are designated Class A and serve in prison farms under minimum security. About 80% are placed in medium-security institutions as Class B prisoners. The remainder, assigned to Class C and Class D, are assigned to maximum-security units.

Solitary confinement usually is imposed on prisoners guilty of disciplinary violations, with a reduced diet for a period not exceeding six days. For more serious violations, such a period may be extended up to one month. Corporal punishment is authorized for the most truculent offenders. Officially, whipping is permitted only after a medical officer certifies that the prisoner is fit to undergo such punishment.

The Prisons Act of 1959 prohibits criticisms of prison administration and imposes a blackout of information on prison conditions. However, charges of prison brutality and ill treatment of prisoners by prison personnel often are made by the UN, Amnesty International and other organizations.

SPAIN

BASIC FACT SHEET

Official Name: Spanish State
Area: 504,782 sq km
Population (1987): 39,000,084
Capital: Madrid
Nature of Government: Constitutional monarchy
Languages: Spanish
Currency: Peseta
GNP (1986): $188.03 billion
Territorial Divisions: 50 provinces; 17 autonomous regions
Population per Police Officer: 580
Police Expenditures per Capita: N.A.

History & Background

Police forces have existed in Spain from about the 12th century, mainly in the major cities. However, the earliest police forces in the modern sense were the Carabineros, formed in 1829, and the Guardia Civil, formed in 1844. At this time, the municipal forces were also reorganized and consolidated. When the Civil War broke out in 1936, it was rebuilt by the Nationalist government to absorb the Carabineros. Modern Spain has three major law-enforcement systems: the Guardia Civil; the Municipal Police; and the Policía Nacional (or Policía Gubernativa), which comprises a uniformed section, the Policía Armada, and a plainclothes section, the Cuerpo General de Policía.

The Cuerpo General de Policía, the plainclothes criminal investigation branch, was established by the Criminal Justice Act of 1882 as the Policía de Seguridad. The force was restructured in 1908, when it became responsible for scientific and technical police work, and a General Police School was established to train its personnel.

In 1870 all uniformed police units in towns and cities were brought together into the Public Order Corps. In 1941 this body was restyled as the Policía Armada y de Tráfico, but when the responsibility for traffic control passed to the Guardia Civil, it became the Cuerpo de Policía Armada. Also in 1941 the first National Police Academy was founded to train Policía Armada personnel.

Structure & Organization

The National Police are headed by a director general assisted by subdirectors general for the Cuerpo de Policía Armada and the Cuerpo General de Policía. He is also responsible for the special services, such as records, identification and Interpol, as well as the police in the Balearic and the Canary islands.

The Policía Armada is headed by an inspector general, with two subinspectorates based at Seville and Zaragoza, each of which covers five territorial divisions. The regional police chiefs have a large measure of autonomy, as have the heads of the provincial stations (comisarías provinciales) and the local stations (comisarías locales). Lower down the scale, the Policía Armada are organized in companies and standards.

Personnel of the Policía Armada wear a gray tunic and trousers with red piping on the trouser seams, cuffs and epaulettes. A gray cap with a red band is worn by all ranks. All buttons and badges are gold. Both the Policía Armada and the Cuerpo General de Policía are issued 9mm short-barrel pistols, although the latter sometimes use .38 revolvers.

When formed in 1844 the Guardia Civil was patterned after the French rural Gendarmerie, and it has been responsible for the maintenance of public order in rural Spain ever since. They have had the added responsibility of highway patrols since 1941. They work in pairs, whether on foot or in a vehicle. It also has responsibility for the borders, serves as the military police and does judicial police work.

The Guardia Civil is headed by a director general, who holds the rank of an Army lieutenant general. Operationally, the force is broken down into inspectorates (under inspectors general), territories (under colonels), command units (under majors), sectors (under captains), lines (under lieutenants) and posts (under corporals). The functional units are detachments,

347

platoons, companies, *comandancías* and regiments. Regiments normally are based in provincial capitals. There are 12 numbered regiments, based in Guadalajara, Badajoz, Las Palmas, Málaga, Cádiz, Granada, Barcelona, Bilbao, Pamplona, Valladolid, Salamanaca and La Coruña.

Each regiment comprises up to six *comandancías,* one of which always is attached to the headquarters. Specialized sections within each regiment include the Traffic Group, Rural Patrols and the Mobile Reserves. Customs duties are handled by the Customs Specialists Company. Helicopter squadrons are attached to most regiments.

The Guardia Civil uniform consists of a gray-green tunic and trousers worn with black tricorn hats. For ceremonial occasions, a blue uniform is worn with a black felt tricorn.

The Municipal Police (Policía Municipal, PM) are separate from the National Police and come under the city governments. Recruited locally, most PM members have served in the Army. Sometimes they carry sidearms but more often are unarmed. Uniforms vary from city to city, but the letters PM usually are imprinted on their caps.

The largest of the PM are the Security and Municipal Police Delegation of Madrid. It includes two specialized units, the Citizens' Protection Patrol and the Ecological Patrol.

The internal security agency is the Directorate General of State Security (Dirección General de Seguridad del Estado, DGSE, commonly referred to as Seguridad). It is an intelligence-gathering organization with powers of arrest, and it is active against Basque terrorists.

The Royal Guard (Guardia Real) provides guards of honor and escorts for the royal family. It is housed in two barracks near the royal palace.

Recruitment, Education & Training

Most of the Guardia Civil officers are graduates of the army's General Military Academy who have completed a two-year course at the Civil Guard Academy. Enlisted personnel are recruited from volunteers who usually have completed their compulsory military service.

The Penal System

The criminal justice system is based on Roman law, and the jury system is not used. The usual procedural safeguards are available to the accused in nonmilitary courts unless a state of emergency is in effect. Crimes involving the security of the state have been handled outside the regular court system ever since the end of the Civil War. The death sentence can be imposed for various crimes of violence but usually is reserved for acts of terrorism. An antiterrorist decree issued in 1975 made the death sentence mandatory for those

CRIME STATISTICS (1984)

		Number Reported	Attempts %	Cases Solved %	Crime per 100,000	Offenders	Females %	Juveniles %	Strangers %
1.	Murder	813		85.24	2.16	866	8.31	1.61	4.04
2.	Sex offenses, including rape	4,719		65.35	12.52	2,932		8.39	
3.	Rape	1,343		58.22	3.56	811			
4.	Serious assault	10,048		60.28	26.65	3,775	4.39	7.65	8.42
5.	All theft	612,378		19.49	1,624.34	88,513	6.08		4.06
6.	Aggravated theft	458,908		12.90	1,217.26	67,496	4.64	19.68	3.10
7.	Robbery and violent theft	55,542		19.99	147.33	12,420	6.97	17.81	3.38
8.	Breaking and entering	403,366		11.90	1,069.94	55,076	4.95		3.60
9.	Auto theft	112,417		11.90	298.19	13,562	2.80		1.85
10.	Other thefts	41,053		20.47	108.89	7,455	18.85		11.22
11.	Fraud	12,127		56.08	32.17	3,377	10.48		16.34
12.	Counterfeiting	75		100	0.20	147			
13.	Drug offenses	9,871		100	26.18	15,740	16.19	5.19	21.91
14.	Total offenses	970,121		28.67	2,573.27	166,893			

Note: Information for some categories is not available.
Criteria of juveniles: aged from 0 to 18 years.

convicted of attacks on the police or the military. However, death sentences usually are commuted to life sentences.

The Penal Code provides a list of crimes and the various penalties that can be imposed by the courts. Many crimes call for specific penalties, with no substitutions permitted. Prosecution is the task of the attorney general's staff, and the attorney general himself is the chief prosecutor of the Supreme Court.

The official prison population is under 20,000, of which less than half are serving sentences; the rest are awaiting trial. Relative to the population, the crime rate is one of the lowest in Europe. Many factors are cited for this phenomenon: the prevailing religious and social climate, the homogeneous nature of the society, close family ties, and the public discipline enforced during the many years of Franco's rule.

SRI LANKA

BASIC FACT SHEET

Official Name: Democratic Socialist Republic of Sri Lanka
Area: 65,610 sq km
Population (1987): 16,406,576
Capital: Colombo
Nature of Government: Parliamentary democracy
Languages: Sinhala, Tamil and English
Currency: Rupee
GNP (1986): $6.46 billion
Territorial Divisions: 9 provinces, 24 administrative districts
Population per Police Officer: 860
Police Expenditures per Capita: N.A.

History & Background

An unpaid rural police force, the Vidanes, was formed by the British in 1806. It comprised one or two headmen in each village, who received a percentage of property recovered from thieves as their reward. In 1833 a Colombo metropolitan police force was formed, and in 1843 a separate police was organized for the maritime provinces. All these forces were united in 1865 as the Ceylon Police Force under the Police Ordinance of that year.

Structure & Organization

The Police Department is headed by an inspector general of police (generally known by the initials IG), who reports to the minister of home affairs. It had a strength in the mid-1980s of 20,000, compared to 5,000 at independence in 1948. These men are assigned to over 300 stations under three range commands: the Northern Range, the Central Range and the Southern Range. The Central Range includes the Colombo Metropolitan Division and the Police Training School. Below the range commands, the operational territory is divided into provinces, divisions, districts and stations. The more densely populated Western, Central and Southern provinces each have more than two subdivisions, while the thinly populated Eastern and North-Central provinces are designated as divisions. As a rule, provinces and divisions are each headed by a superintendent, districts by assistant superintendents and stations by inspectors.

The police establishment includes a special unit called the Criminal Investigation Department (CID) under a deputy inspector general. The CID has three operating divisions: the Special Branch, the Investigation Branch and the Technical Unit.

Police stations in 34 major provincial towns are linked through a system of radio communications that is operated from the radio control room in the police headquarters at Colombo. The radio control room also monitors the police emergency system, under which a person in distress can dial for assistance.

Emergency duties are performed by a specially trained task force of about 450 men called the Depot Police. Located at Bambalapitiya, a suburb of Colombo, the Depot Police is capable or reacting rapidly to trouble anywhere on the island. In addition, they escort important public officials, provide honor guards at ceremonial state functions and enforce law and order during communal disturbances.

The Police Department maintains in various subdivisions an auxiliary force called the Special Police Reserve, with an authorized strength of 3,000. Reservists are provided with uniforms, living allowances and free rail transportation when called into service. Colombo Harbor security is under the Colombo Harbor Division, whose chief, an assistant superintendent, reports directly to the superintendent of the Colombo Division.

Recruitment, Education & Training

Applicants for a police service career must have completed at least high school and usually undergo a four-stage screening process, of which three are interviews and one is a written examination. New recruits are sent to the Police Training School for six months of resident instruction. Transferred to Colombo from

Kalutara in 1967, the school is headed by a director with the rank of superintendent. Classes are held in three languages: English, Sinhala and Tamil. The school maintains eight training stations, where students receive practical experience. Outstanding officers are sent abroad for advanced instruction.

The Penal System

The penal system is governed by the Penal Code of 1883, patterned after the Indian Penal Code of 1860, which was retained after independence with few modifications. Offenses are listed in general categories, and each category is in turn subdivided into specific violations. The scale of punishments ranges from death by hanging, to imprisonment, whipping, forfeiture of property and fines. In meting out the sentence of imprisonment the court has a degree of latitude in deciding whether it should be accompanied by ordinary or hard labor. Female convicts, persons sentenced to death and those sentenced to imprisonment for more than five years may not be punished by whipping. Whipping is restricted to 24 lashes inflicted in the presence of a medical officer. Minors are punished with a light cane or rattan switch, the maximum number of strokes being six.

All correctional institutions are administered by the Department of Prisons under the Ministry of Justice and regulated by the Prisons Ordinance of 1878. The operational head of the department holds the rank of commissioner.

There are 14 major prisons, four open prison camps and two training schools (commonly abbreviated as TYSO) for youthful offenders. The Welikada Prison, the largest, holds nearly 2,500 inmates, about 23% of the total prison population.

Of the daily average prison population, nearly 70% are convicted prisoners; the balance are awaiting trial. According to the Annual Administration Report of the commissioner of prisons, nearly 30% of convicted prisoners are charged with excise offenses. The next largest category is theft, with about 14%. the third category is causing grievous hurt, with 4%. First offenders make up 62%. By districts, Colombo accounts for nearly 34%; Kalutara, in the Western Province, is a distant second, with 9% of the total. Nearly 75% are Sinhalese, 16% Tamils and the balance is distributed among the other ethnic groups. By occupation, farmers are most represented, with 26%, followed by unskilled workers, 24%; skilled workers, 10%; and unemployed, 8%. Based on the length of confinement, 33% serve less than one month, 31% one to three months, 17% three to six months and 8% six months to a year. Only 1% serve more than 10 years.

The Department maintains an open-type correctional house for juvenile convicts at Wathapitiwela, called the Training School for Youthful Offenders. It is patterned after a residential school and divided into a number of houses, each house in the charge of a housemaster. There is another TYSO at Negombo, a closed-type school reserved for more troublesome juveniles requiring strict supervision.

The department also runs four prison camps, at Pallekelle, Anuradhapura, Kipay and Taldena, where facilities are provided for agricultural training.

The six most common crimes are, in descending order of frequency, theft, injury by knife, burglary, grievous hurt, robbery and theft of bicycles. Together they account for an average annual of 85% of the total. Crimes against property are more numerous, with 63%, and crimes against persons the minority, with 57%. In the commission of crimes against persons, the most common weapon is the knife, the use of firearms being negligible. As a result, carrying a knife is controlled under the Dangerous Knives Ordinance of 1906. According to official reports, juvenile crime is becoming a serious problem, the highest rise in offenses being found in crimes by those under 13.

SUDAN

BASIC FACT SHEET

Official Name: Republic of the Sudan
Area: 2,505,813 sq km
Population (1987): 22,524,622
Capital: Khartoum
Nature of Government: Limited democracy
Language: Arabic
Currency: Sudanese pound
GNP (1986): $7.29 billion
Territorial Divisions: 9 provinces
Population per Police Officer: 860
Police Expenditures per Capita: N.A.

History & Background

The Sudan Police Force had its beginning in 1898, when a British Army captain was placed in the central administration for police duties with 30 British Army officers under him to organize provincial police establishments. From 1901 to 1908 police administration was completely decentralized, but in the latter year the central government at Khartoum took over its direction. In 1924 Sir John Ewert of the Indian Police was invited to make a study, and his recommendations resulted in the drafting of a new police ordinance. A police school was opened in Omdurman in 1925 for both officers and noncommissioned ranks. The force was transferred with few changes to the national government on independence in 1955.

At that time, the force consisted of 169 officers and 7,500 men.

Structure & Organization

With a strength of over 30,000 men and officers, the Sudan Police Force is headed by a commissioner, who reports to the Ministry of the Interior. Police headquarters in Khartoum is organized under guidelines initiated by the British during the Anglo-Egyptian condominium. The headquarters division includes those responsible for criminal investigation, administration and training. Separate departments handle passports and immigration and prisons. The department for security investigation reports directly to the minister of the interior.

The police establishment is distributed throughout the nine provinces and along the Sudan Railways, with special reinforcements in areas of potential trou-

ble. Within each province the police are under the control of a commandant. The provincial police have both mounted and foot branches. The mounted police, mainly motorized, are still furnished with camels, mules and horses for special assignments. In addition to the regular force, there are a number of reserve companies completely motorized and organized along semimilitary lines. A separate unit, the Railway Police, guards trains and rail installations.

All policemen are volunteers, with recruits drawn from all groups, but especiallly from the Nuba, who seem to excel in this work. Pay is comparable to that of the armed forces. The police uniform consists of a light olive green shirt and trousers worn with a dark blue cap for the officers and olive green for the other ranks. Belts and badges of rank also are in dark blue. Traffic policemen wear white uniforms.

Below the commissioner, the grades descend through deputy commissioner, assistant commissioner, commandant, superintendent, assistant superintendent, chief inspector and inspector among the officer ranks. The lower ranks consist of soul, sergeant major, sergeant, corporal and nafar.

Other police units include the Border Guards, with a strength of 2,500; the Republican Guard; and the Customs Guards, under the Ministry of Finance and Economy. The Office of State Security was established in 1971 under the Ministry of the Interior. Its functions are primarily political, and its central files are maintained in the office of the president.

Recruitment, Education & Training

The Police College, which took over the former Police School in 1959, is the principal police academy.

Senior officers sometimes are sent abroad for advanced training, mostly to Egypt or East Germany.

The Penal System

Until the introduction of the Sharia as the governing penal code of the country in the late 1970s, Sudan's Penal Code was a synthesis of the penal codes of Egypt, the United Kingdom and India. The imposition of the Sharia is opposed by the non-Muslim peoples of the South where, in large areas, near-anarchy prevails.

The general supervision of the Sudan Prison Service is the responsibility of the Ministry of the Interior acting through the commissioner of prisons. The central prisons at Khartoum North, Port Sudan and Sawakin are directly administered by the commissioner, who also is responsible for the five reformatories, the Kober Institution for the Insane, the Port Sudan Local Prison and the Prison Service Training School at Khartoum North. All provincial detention camps and jails are under the control of provincial authorities. Provincial prisons are classified as Local Class I and Local Class II according to their size. More than 140 local prisons and detention camps are reported by the Sudan Prison Service.

Prison guards are trained at the Prison Guard School in Khartoum. The treatment of prisoners is reported to be generally humane. They are quartered in large barracks or dormitory rooms. First offenders and trusted prisoners are given a 15-day annual vacation with their families. Vocational and literacy training is compulsory. Within the prisons small industries are being developed, and prisoners are paid a small sum for their labor, which is held in escrow until their release. After completing their sentences—which often are shortened by amnesty or probation—prisoners receive discharges that rate them according to their behavior in prison. The recidivism rate is less than 20%. Few Sudanese women commit serious crimes, so there are few female prisoners. Reform schools handle offenders under 15 years of age, giving them regular schooling in detention.

The most common crime is theft, usually of animals. Killings in tribal fights also are common, but they receive less severe sentences than murders committed outside the tribal setting.

CRIME STATISTICS (1984)

		Number Reported	Attempts %	Cases Solved %	Crime per 100,000	Offenders	Females %	Juveniles %	Strangers %
1.	Murder	920	10.5	71.7	4.46				
2.	Sex offenses, including rape	2,394			11.62				
3.	Rape	830		86.6	4.03				
4.	Serious assault	5,861		82.9	28.44				
5.	All theft	51,475			249.82				
6.	Aggravated theft	1,942			9.42				
7.	Robbery and violent theft	144			0.70				
8.	Breaking and entering	162			0.79				
9.	Auto theft								
10.	Other thefts	49,227			238.91				
11.	Fraud	26,439			128.31				
12.	Counterfeiting								
13.	Drug offenses	2,121		46.2	10.29				
14.	Total offenses	364,899		79.8	1,770.94	209,439	19.6	9.1	

Note: Information for some categories is not available.
Criteria of juveniles: aged from 0 to 16 years.

SWAZILAND

Patrick Edobor Igbinovia

BASIC FACT SHEET

Official Name: Kingdom of Swaziland
Area: 17,363 sq km
Population (1987): 715,160
Capital: Mbabane (administrative); Lobamba (legislative)
Nature of Government: Absolute monarchy
Languages: English and SiSwati
Currency: Lilangeni
GNP (1986): $470 million
Territorial Divisions: 4 administrative districts
Population per Police Officer: 610
Police Expenditures per 1,000: $21,249

History & Background

The first policing operations in Swaziland were carried out more than 100 years ago, by the Swazi regiments. The regimental system, based on age groups, was started by King Sobhuza I and greatly expanded by his son, King Mswati. The regiments, each under the command of an *induna,* did not have a purely military role, as they were also used to make arrests for breaches of tribal law.

In 1895, when South Africa took over the administration of Swaziland, Chris Botha, brother of Gen. Louis Botha, who became the first prime minister of the Union of South Africa, was given the task of establishing a police force in the country. Little is known about the arrangements he made, and the force had a very short life as the Republican administration was withdrawn in 1899 soon after the start of the Boer War.

When the war ended in 1902, a victorious Britain assumed control of Swaziland, and that same year a special commissioner with a force of 150 South African Constabulary personnel, both European and African, were sent into the country to establish a provisional administration, with headquarters at Mbabane. The police detachment was under the commissioner's local control but subject to the administration of the South African constabulary headquarters based at Carolina, in the Transvaal.

On February 22, 1907, the Swaziland Administration Proclamation was signed by Lord Selborne, the high commissioner for South Africa. This legislation made provision for the formation of the Swaziland

Police Force, and on April 8, 1907, Capt. C. H. Gilson was appointed assistant commissioner of police for Swaziland, with headquarters at Mbabane. Twenty-one European officers were transferred from the South African Constabulary to the Swaziland Police, and 125 other ranks (Africans), mainly Zulus from Natal, were recruited to complete the establishment of 146 officers and men.

The Training School was established in about 1927. In addition, in May 1965, the Police College at Matsapa was opened. The Swaziland Police provided, up to 1933, staff for the Prisons Department. From 1963 to 1966 the force was reorganized and retrained and the establishment steadily increased until it numbered 644 of all ranks in 1967.

The Swaziland Police was a mounted force until 1953. It was renamed the Royal Swaziland Police in 1969, and a process of Africanization of the force began, with over half the expatriate senior officers being replaced by local officers. The posts of commissioner and deputy commissioner have been filled by local officers since 1972, and the force has no difficulty getting local recruits.

Structure & Organization

The Royal Swaziland Police is constituted under Police and Public Order Act 29/57 and is employed throughout the kingdom to preserve the peace, prevent and detect crime and apprehend offenders. The force combines the functions of a civil police force with those of an armed constabulary. It is commanded by the commissioner of police, who is assisted at headquarters in Mbabane by a deputy commissioner, an assistant commissioner and staff officers.

The country is divided into four police districts: District headquarters are at Mabane, Manzini, Siteki and Nhlangano. There are 18 police stations and eight police posts distributed among the districts.

All ranks wear a winter uniform of blue serge and a blue cap. In the summer lower ranks wear a gray shirt, khaki shorts, blue hosetops and puttees, while inspectors and above wear khaki. On ceremonial occasions khaki tunics and trousers are worn with a khaki cap. Steps are being taken to standardize the summer uniform, with all ranks wearing khaki tunic and shorts with a khaki cap. The force performs its duty armed only with a baton or nightstick but may be armed in emergencies and for certain other duties.

Operational Branches

1. Criminal Investigation Branch. Includes the Dog Squad, the Fraud and Vice Squad, the Drug Squad and the Firearms Registry. Forensic, ballistics and handwriting examinations are carried out by the South African Police Criminal Bureau.

2. Fingerprint Bureau

3. Photographic and Printing sections

4. Traffic and Transport Branch

5. Intelligence Branch

6. Police Mobile Unit, commanded by a superintendent of police, with four platoons. This unit maintains the Permanent Security Guard for the king.

7. Communications Branch

Recruitment, Education & Training

The Police College is at Matsapa, near Manzini. The college's Training Wing is responsible for basic training of recruits and advanced training of officers.

For recruitment as constables, candidates must meet certain minimum physical and educational standards. Men must be between 20 and 30 years of age and women between 18 and 25 years, and they must hold at least a Junior Certificate of Education. Gazetted police officers and inspectors are appointed by the Civil Services Board, while subinspectors and constables are appointed by the commissioner of police. All vacancies above the constable level are filled by promotion.

Penal System

No current information is available.

SWEDEN

```
BASIC FACT SHEET

Official Name: Kingdom of Sweden
Area: 449,964 sq km
Population (1987): 8,383,026
Capital: Stockholm
Nature of Government: Constitutional monarchy
Language: Swedish
Currency: Krona
GNP (1986): $109.95 bllion
Territorial Divisions: 24 counties
Population per Police Officer: 330
Police Expenditure per 1,000: $176,110
```

History & Background

Until 1965, Sweden had only local police forces, who functioned in over 500 very small police districts. Police work was hampered by restrictions on police movements from one district to another and by the combination of the functions of district attorney and public distrainer in the local police chief. In the 1930s, a mobile auxiliary was created as a national police force with limited powers, primarily in the areas of traffic and serious crimes.

In 1964 the Riksdag approved a plan to reorganize the Swedish police system and create a new national force. On January 1, 1965, the Swedish Police (Rikspolis) was born. The law that created it reduced the number of police districts from 554 to 119 and the number of police posts from 989 to 510. The average strength of a police department was raised correspondingly, from 10 to between 20 and 50. The chief of police was also shorn of his functions as district prosecutor and public distrainer, thus enabling him to concentrate on police work proper. The public prosecutor's office was created, with 90 local districts, and the distrainer's office, with 81 local districts.

Structure & Organization

The Rikspolis operates on three levels: national, regional and local.

The highest police authority in the kingdom is the National Swedish Police Board, which is answerable to the Ministry of Justice. The board is headed by the national police commissioner as chairman with the rank of director general, a deputy national police commissioner as vice chairman and six members of the Swedish Parliament representing different political parties. The board is responsible for the administration of the National Police Organization, the State Police College, the Police Council, the State Forensic Laboratory and police training programs.

National Police headquarters in Stockholm is divided into four departments (avdelnings): A (Operations), B (Technical Services), C (Administration) and D (Security), the last of which reports directly to the commissioner's office.

Department A comprises Police Bureaus I and II. The former deals with the work of uniformed policemen, including traffic control and surveillance. The Surveillance Section is assigned the task of allocating personnel to various police districts. Police Bureau II is concerned with detection and investigation work. This bureau is divided into four sections: Planning, Local Records, Intrapolice Coordination and Preliminary Investigations. It also deals with traffic accidents and investigation statistics.

The National Criminal Investigation Department is part of Police Bureau II. It has four squads: Squad A deals with murder and violent crimes, Squad B with narcotics, Squad C with larceny and theft, and Squad D with fraud.

Department B is divided into the Technical Bureau and the Training Bureau. The Technical Bureau has four sections: Equipment, Transport, Telecommunications and Building. The Training Bureau is responsible for both training and recruitment.

Department C is divided into three bureaus, dealing with administration, records and staff. The Administration Bureau has sections dealing with budgeting and planning, purchasing, legal affairs, organization, service and automatic data processing. The Records Bureau, established in 1970, keeps national criminal records, such as fingerprints and records for wanted persons, passports and stolen vehicles. The Staff Bureau is the personnel division of the police and handles collective bargaining, contracts, appointments, dismissals, old age pensions, vacations and salary classifications.

Department D has two bureaus dealing with national security. Bureau A deals with protection and control and Bureau B with detection and investigation.

The National Forensic Science Laboratory is attached to Police Bureau II of Department A but is independent in technical matters. Bureau II of Department A also is the Swedish liaison for Interpol. There is an Intervention Police (Omradespolis) for crowd control and emergencies. There is an Aviation Unit with helicopters for the same purpose.

Territorial organization starts with the county, each of which, except for the county of Gotland, has its own commissioner. The county government board can assume command of local police districts in emergencies. The county government also is in direct command of special county traffic surveillance groups, which are responsible for traffic surveillance across police district limits.

At the local end of police administration are the 118 police districts, most with 20 to 50 policemen. These are usually made up of both uniformed patrolmen and criminal investigation squads. The police authority in each district is the police board, headed by the police chief with the title of police commissioner. The local district has a constabulary or a Surveillance Department and a Criminal Department. The uniformed police of the constabulary carries out routine law enforcement and maintains communication links with national headquarters. In larger districts there are sections for the control of traffic which in the smaller districts is the province of the Surveillance Department.

The local Criminal Department is divided into squads for investigation, general investigation, larceny, fraud and violence. A technical squad handles technical investigations. Working units of at least three men working in areas away from the central headquarters are empowered to make on-the-spot decisions.

A special local body of municipal representatives called the Police Committee acts as an advisory body in the local police commissioner's office.

The 1965 separation of the functions of police chief and public prosecutor led to a redefinition of police duties vis-à-vis the public prosecutor. A preliminary examination is the duty of either the police or the prosecutor, but where it is being carried out by the police, the prosecutor may also issue instructions.

Normal working dress consists of a dark blue jacket and trousers worn with a white-topped peak cap. A similar uniform worn with a skirt and knee-length boots and an Afrika Korps cap is worn by the women police. For car patrol, a hip-length overblouse is worn instead of a jacket, and trousers are worn by women as well as men. Both wear the Scandinavian-type forage cap (batmossa). In summer the normal jacket may be replaced by a gray-blue short-sleeved tunic shirt and, in winter, a heavy overcoat may be worn over the uniform, together with an astrakhan cap. A Sam Browne belt is worn over all types of uniform except that for car patrol and from this is suspended a baton and a pistol holster. In all cases, a large patch is worn over the upper left arm showing the national crest surmounted by the word "Polis." Badges of rank may appear on this patch or on the bottom of the jacket sleeve.

Recruitment, Education & Training

Cadets are recruited by the Training and Recruitment Bureau of Department B. The district police chief accepts applications and conducts preliminary investigations, after which he forwards the application to the Swedish National Police Board. If the board accepts the application, the recruit is sent to one of several training schools, such as the National Institute of Technical Police or the Police high schools at Stockholm or Lund. Basic police training takes place over a 43-week period, including Constable's Course I for 32 weeks, practical work for eight weeks and Constable's Course II for three weeks. Three to five years after completion of the basic course, candidates enter the Higher Police course for 10 weeks.

Police training for the higher ranks is conducted at the Police College at Solna. After promotion to sergeant, the police officer takes a 12-week sergeant's course. An eight-week inspector's course is offered to those who need to learn about police organization. There is a 15-week superintendent's course and a 56-week commissioner's course at the Police College at Solna. Specialized courses are offered at the Swedish Army Driving School for traffic controllers and at the Armed Forces Dog Training Center for dog handlers.

Police commissioners are recruited from law schools, but all other promotions are made from within the ranks of the force. Police in Sweden are allowed to hold public office and to belong to trade unions.

The Penal System

The Swedish criminal justice system is governed by Riksdag legislation. The principal legislative enactments are the Code of Judicial Procedure and the Penal Code. However, all crimes are not listed in the Penal Code. A number of offenses are described in separate statutes, including traffic offenses and narcotics violations. Because Swedish law is not entirely codified, there is latitude for judicial interpretation. Thus, although Swedish criminal law belongs to the Romano-Germanic family, it shares with common-law systems a binding respect for judicial precedent.

The Penal Code, the most important source of criminal law, was promulgated in 1965 and has been revised many times since. The code is divided into three parts: Part I contains general provisions on the applications of the law. Part II contains a list of the major crimes and specific elements that constitute each offense and the actions that may be imposed in each case. The code divides offenses into four major categories: crimes against the person, crimes against property, crimes against the public and crimes against the state. Since Sweden does not have a separate military criminal code, crimes committed by members of the military are treated as crimes against the state. Part III of the code is concerned with principles for assessing sanctions. Articles in this part exempt juveniles under 15 years and persons of unsound mind from criminal responsibility and also provide for milder punishments for offenders below 21 years.

The pretrial process begins with a preliminary investigation. Following the commencement of the preliminary investigation, detention orders are issued by the court for the accused, who could be imprisoned for up to two years if he or she may reasonably be expected to flee, obstruct justice or remove evidence or has no permanent address. Arrests are permitted without a detention order when a person is apprehended in the act of committing a crime. The Code of Judicial Procedure gives police authorities, the prosecutors and the courts the right to search and seize. Within the Constitution there is no right to be released on bail. When there is some risk that the defendant might attempt to flee the area, the code permits prohibition of travel as a substitute for detention. A travel prohibition means that the person cannot leave the area without permission. Other restrictions might be placed on the defendant, such as reporting periodically to the police or being present at his or her residence or place of work at specific hours of the day.

Sweden's correctional system has served as a model for other Western countries. Since the 1940s Sweden has led the way in reducing the number of actions classified as crimes and offenses by decriminalizing victimless crimes and morally deviant behavior. The nature of the sanctions also has changed. Tax offenses, minor frauds and minor property offenses are penalized by a fine rather than imprisonment. Certain offenses such as drunkenness have been consigned to medical and social workers. At the same time, because Sweden has experienced a dramatic rise in serious crime over the past decade, the full force of

the law has been directed against certain other types of crime, such as narcotics trafficking; armed robbery; illegal possession of weapons; and certain types of nonviolent crimes, such as those against the environment. The use of imprisonment as a deterrent and punishment is being restricted and increasingly replaced with fines. Youth imprisonment was abolished in 1979 and internment in 1981. Finally, greater attention is being paid to crime prevention under the auspices of the National Council for Crime Prevention.

The Swedish corrections system is administered by the National Prison and Probation Administration Board, a unit of the Ministry of Justice. It is composed of laypeople appointed by the minister of justice and headed by a director general of adminstration. Parole decisions are handled by the Correctional Service Board, chaired by a Supreme Court justice. This board also hears inmate appeals from decisions made by the local supervisory boards. There are 50 such local supervisory boards, and they are responsible for parole and probation decisions in their respective districts. Each board is composed of five members and is chaired by a lawyer.

Since 1978 Sweden has been divided into 13 correctional care regions. Each region is administered by a regional director, who is a professional probation officer. The regional director determines where an offender sentenced by a court within his or her region would serve the sentence.

The principal correctional institutions are local and national facilities; some are open and some are closed. The largest, at Kumla, can accommodate 224 inmates, while the smaller ones hold between 20 and 60 inmates. Swedish prisons are noted for their cleanliness and maximum living amenities. There is virtually no overcrowding, and each prisoner has his or her own cell.

There are three types of correctional facilities: remand prisons, local facilities and national facilities. Each is designed for a specific purpose and for a specific type of offender. There are 21 remand prisons serving the entire country. They are primarily designed to hold people awaiting trial. Because of the limited number of remand prisons, some of the other correctional institutions have a remand wing attached to them.

Local facilities, numbering 50, are used primarily to house offenders sentenced to less than one year of imprisonment as well as inmates serving longer sentences who are approaching the end of their term. Security measures are minimal at these centers. The primary purpose of local institutions is to keep the inmates as close to their families as possible.

Finally, there are 19 national facilities, administered directly by the National Prison and Probation

Administration, and housing people sentenced to more than one year in prison. Most of them are closed, and some are high-security.

The legal basis of the correctional system is found in the 1974 Act on Correctional Treatment in Institutions, which defines the purpose of corrections as "to promote the adjustment of the inmate in society and to counteract the detrimental effects of deprivation of liberty. Insofar as this can be achieved without detriment to the need to protect the public, treatment should be directed from the outset toward measures that prepare the inmate for conditions outside the institution." The act further declares that "inmates shall be treated with respect for their human dignity. They shall be treated with understanding for the special difficulties connected with a stay in an institution."

The 1974 Correctional Treatment Act requires all inmates to be involved in some form of work, study or training and provides for remuneration for such activities. Even the disabled are given a remuneration for purchasing personal items. Solitary confinement is used rarely and under exceptional circumstances. Inmates who violate prison rules or who are simply recalcitrant may be warned or cited for a specific period of time that does not count toward the sentence. Inmates have also the right to form councils to negotiate grievances with prison authorities. The act also empowers prison authorities to grant furloughs to inmates for work, study and leisure-time activities. The furlough scheme has been considerably expanded over the past decade and is designed to facilitate the prisoner's eventual return to society. Medical furloughs are granted if a person can receive better treatment in an outside hospital or clinic. Short-term and release furloughs are also regular features of the scheme. Short-term furloughs may be granted for a number of hours or a number of days, primarily to enable the inmate to maintain ties with his or her family. Release furloughs are available for inmates eligible for parole. Inmates are allowed conjugal visits. Although correspondence may be scrutinized, it is not censored, with the exception of high-security risks. Telephones are readily available, and inmates have access to a wide range of reading matter, including legal books and periodicals, and may borrow books from local public libraries. In fact, those within prison walls have the same rights to general social services as those outside.

The largest high-security prison is at Kumla. Built in 1965, this prison holds 224 inmates and has a staff of 280. (The high ratio of staff to inmates is typical of Sweden's correctional system.) Kumla has a 21-foot wall around it, and its security is reinforced by an extensive television and radar monitoring system. In addition to living blocks for regular prisoners,

Kumla has two special blocks: one containing a hospital, psychiatric ward, temporary detention unit and a disciplinary section, and the other for more dangerous inmates and security risks. Inmates are employed in one of the traditional prison workshops, or they can participate in one of the full-time educational programs. Generally, inmates are granted furloughs and conjugal visits as well as sojourns to local cultural and sports events.

Tillberga is an open national prison where inmates are employed in the construction of prefabricated homes that are sold by a state-owned company. All the workers are members of the construction union and are paid free-market wages negotiated by the union. However, they receive only 70% of the wages (because they are not subject to the national income tax). Of this amount, inmates actually receive only 25%; the rest is used to support the inmate's family and pay the cost of his or her food. The remaining sum is placed in a savings account, which the inmate receives on release.

Under Sweden's privacy laws, newspapers cannot publish the names of people accused or convicted of crimes. Similarly, employers cannot ask a potential employee if he or she has served a prison term.

Parole is granted by the Correctional Service Board for inmates serving more than a year of imprisonment in a national institution and by local supervisory boards for others, and it is never granted before at least three months have been served. A probation officer is assigned to the inmate upon eligibility for parole. A parolee is expected to maintain contact with the probation officer during the term of parole and is expected to maintain a residence and find employment. The parolee may be subject to special directives, such as residing at a specific place, joining a job training program, or seeking medical or psychiatric care.

Sweden utilizes a number of noninstitutional programs in an effort to minimize the imposition of prison sentences. These include conditional sentences, probation orders and fines. A conditional sentence is a form of probation for a period of up to two years, but the offender is not supervised by a probation officer. The sanction is a conditional warning to refrain from criminal activity. A probation order is imposed on offenders who have committed an imprisonable offense and may be imposed for up to three years. It differs from the conditional sentence in that the offender is placed under supervision and may be sentenced to a short-term imprisonment (not exceeding three months) as well. Although the offender retains liberty while under supervision, he or she may be enjoined to pay fines or make compensation for damages, and the local supervisory board may issue other directives with which the probationer must comply.

These directives usually include reporting periodically to the probation officer in any one of the 63 probation districts, and notifying the officer of place of residence, employment or schooling. Fines are extensively used in Sweden as a penal sanction. Fines are of three types: standardized, fixed and day fines. Day fines are determined by the per diem income of the offender and thus vary according to the economic resources of the offender. A person who fails to pay a day fine may have the fine converted to a sentence of imprisonment.

Despite its affluence and welfare-state programs, Sweden has been plagued since the end of World War II with rising juvenile crime, which has grown by 400% during the past 40 years. The crime rate among young people between 18 and 20 years has risen 500% and that among those between 15 and 17 years by 700%. Sweden's 14- to 16-year-olds have been identified as the most criminally active age group. Much of juvenile criminal activity is linked with drug abuse.

Despite the ever-rising juvenile crime rate, Sweden's juvenile justice system is committed to social and medical treatment rather than traditional institutionalization. The age of criminal responsibility is fixed by the Code of Judicial Procedure at 15 years. Persons below this age cannot be subject to criminal prosecution or penal sanction. The police, however, may interrogate a person under 15 if the child's parents or guardians are present. Juveniles between 15 and 20 may be prosecuted and sentenced, but this is rarely done, especially if the suspect is under 18. If the prosecutor decides to bring charges against a person under 18, he usually turns the matter over to the Child Welfare Board. Sweden does not have a separate juvenile court, and the Child Welfare Board functions as its closest parallel. Each municipality has such a board, which is composed of five members elected by the municipal council for four-year terms. The board usually includes a minister, a lawyer, a schoolteacher and a child specialist. Board members are not paid a salary. The Board has both civil and criminal jurisdiction for juveniles under 21 years of age. The civil jurisdiction involves care proceedings where the child is neglected or is delinquent. In criminal cases it is not concerned with establishing the offender's guilt but rather with determining the appropriate treatment. The Social Services Act of 1982 requires that the board's decision to place a child in custody be reviewed by an administrative court of appeal. In cases where criminal charges are pressed, fines, probation or suspended sentences are generally handed down. In exceptional cases a person under 18 can be imprisoned but never can be sentenced to life imprisonment. The Penal Code further provides a milder sanction for persons under 21 than for adults who commit the same offense.

Probably the best-known Swedish innovation in juvenile justice is the social police. Young people are

CRIME STATISTICS (1984)

		Number Reported	Attempts %	Cases Solved %	Crime per 100,000	Offenders	Females %	Juveniles %	Strangers %
1.	Murder	479	76	68	5.74	246		4.07	
2.	Sex offenses, including rape	3,846		45	46.10	1,389		7.78	
3.	Rape	995	37	47	11.93	315		12.70	
4.	Serious assault	2,141		57	25.66	1,023		5.57	
5.	All theft	578,214		17	6,930.99	96,825		26.56	
6.	Aggravated theft	146,236		12	1,752.92	26,890		27.74	
7.	Robbery and violent theft	3,681		29	44.12	982		10.79	
8.	Breaking and entering	142,555		12	1,708.79	25,908		28.39	
9.	Auto theft	38,378	29	20	460.03	9,701		94.34	
10.	Other thefts	393,600		19	4,718.04	60,234		23.17	
11.	Fraud	91,080		83	1,091.77	66,264		3.38	
12.	Counterfeiting	125		30	1.50	12		0	
13.	Drug offenses	40,130		100	481.03	38,453		11.98	
14.	Total offenses	983,175		38	11,785.22	340,663		13.42	

Note: Information for some categories is not available.
Criteria of juveniles: aged from 15 to 17 years.

the primary focus of the social police, although their efforts are not solely directed at juveniles. Introduced in the 1950s, the social police are plainclothes police officers who patrol the streets with social workers.

The purpose of this mixed patrol is to identify potential delinquents and offer them assistance. The social police keep the Child Welfare Board informed of incidents that may need their intervention.

SWITZERLAND

Structure & Organization

As a federal republic, Switzerland has a decentralized police force, with most police powers being delegated to the cantons. Each self-governing canton has its own police force and, in addition, most cities have their own municipal police. Together these forces number over 70. However, some police powers are retained and exercised by the federal government, mainly in the area of criminal justice legislation. The centralized Federal Police is responsible for the enforcement of certain laws against treason, counterfeiting, forgery and election fraud.

At the federal level there are three police organizations, all under the Ministry of Justice: the Federal Police Division, the Aliens Police and the Federal Division of the Public Prosecutor. The Federal Police Division, formed in 1935, coordinates national police activities, including border patrol and traffic control. The Aliens Police enforces laws governing entry, exit and residence of foreigners. Many Aliens Police officers are recruited from cantonal and municipal police forces but operate in civilian clothes. The Federal Division of the Public Prosecutor comprises five sections: Criminal Police, Political Police, Central Police Records Office, Swiss Interpol secretariat and Central Office, the last concerned with vice, drug abuse and currency offenses.

The Cantonal Police and the Municipal Police in the larger cities perform all police functions outside the jurisdiction of the federal agencies. Cantonal forces are headed by a commandant (or *commissaire,* as in Geneva), who reports to the director of police, a member of the cantonal government.

Although each cantonal or municipal police is slightly different from the other, there are a number of common features. Each has a central and regional headquarters, variously known as Polizeidirektion, Polizeikommando, Polizeiamt, Commissariat or Commissariato, which includes administrative and records departments. The most common operational branches are the Gendarmerie or the uniformed police; the plainclothes security force, variously known as Sicherhietsdienst, Service de la Sûreté or Pubblica Sicurezza; the Criminal Police, variously known as Kriminalpolizei, Police Judiciare or Polizia Giudiziaria; the Frontier Police, variously known as Grenspolizei, Police de Frontière or Polizia della Frontiera; and the Lake Police or Gewässerschutz Polizei in Zurich. Traffic and Highway Police are part of the Gendarmerie.

Cooperation is very close at every level among the municipal, cantonal and federal law-enforcement agencies. Police chiefs meet at regular intervals to coordinate their activities. Police units commonly are located at stations and barracks.

Each canton provides training for its policemen in its own schools. The duration of the training course varies from four months to a year.

Cantonal Police

Vaud, Geneva and Berne are three of the largest and most typical of the Swiss cantons, and some details of their police forces are as follows:

Vaud The Vaud Gendarmerie traces its origins to 1741, when a constabulary was formed to hunt for vagabonds. Following the French occupation of the canton under Napoleon, the Gendarmerie was formed on the French model in 1803. Seventy-four years later, the Sûreté was formed also on the French model, but it functioned under the Department of Justice and police, whereas the Gendarmerie came under the Department of Military affairs. In 1943 the two agencies were combined.

The Gendarmerie Vaudoise is divided into four territorial divisions and a Traffic Division. The latter as well as one of the territorial divisions are headquartered in Lausanne. Each territorial division is commanded by a lieutenant or first lieutenant and is divided into two brigades (three in the case of Lausanne). Altogether there are 59 police posts, ranging from one with about 20 men to a one-man rural office. The Gendarmerie also man a number of powerboats, which patrol the lakes of Geneva, Neuchâtel and Morat. The uniform is gray with colored facings. Normally, a French-style képi is worn, but motorcyle policemen wear a forage cap. The Sûreté is divided into a Lausanne Town Section and four territorial sections.

Geneva The gendarmes were introduced into Geneva by Napoleon, who placed them under police magistrates *(commissaires)*. The system was retained after Napoleon's fall. In 1853 a new corps of Agents de Police was formed, with a strength of 27 men. By 1918 the force had grown to 250 gendarmes and 76 agents.

Both the Gendarmerie and the agents now come under a joint control of a chief of police assisted by a general staff, two *commissaires* and five senior judicial police officers. The uniform is gray-green with a képi of the same color.

Berne The Berne cantonal police goes back to Napoleonic days in 1804, when a force of 100 men was formed, divided into four geographical areas. A fifth was added in 1815. The force comprises four main departments: Headquarters, Traffic, Crime Investigation and Public Safety. Territorially, the canton is divided into 30 districts with 74 stations.

The uniform is a dark military-style tunic and trousers with a matching képi. A leather belt and pistol holster are worn over the tunic. The traffic police have a white belt and holster and a white top over the képi. Fur caps and warm overtrousers and jacket are worn when on winter duty in the mountains.

Although there is no national police in Switzerland and no central coordination of police operations, there are several avenues of collaboration and cooperation among the 23 cantonal and over 100 municipal police corps, particularly in cases of serious crime extending beyond cantonal borders. Such cooperation is institutionalized through three agencies: the Conference of Swiss Police Commanders, the Swiss Association of Police Chiefs and the Swiss Police Technical Com-

Attorney General of the Swiss Confederation	Executive Secretary

- *Legal Service*
  Prosecutorial Tasks
  for Federal Offenses

- *Police Service (Federal Police)*
  State Security

- *Swiss Central Police Bureau*
  Central Offices
  Identification Service
  Interpol Service
  Register of Convictions

- Security Service of the Federal Administration
  (Buildings, Persons, Informations)

- EDP-Section

- Administrative / Personnel Matters

mission. The latter is in charge of standardization of police equipment and procedures and provision of information on technical advances in communications and electronics. A further step in this direction of cooperation is the 1974 intercantonal agreement on a system of alert and search in serious crime cases, as murder, armed robbery and terrorism. Another important channel of intercantonal cooperation is the federal attorney general's office under the Federal Justice and Police Department. The attorney general's office has three divisions: Legal Service; Police Service, or Federal Police; and Central Police Bureau. The Legal Service deals with questions of law, such as penal law and procedure, delegation of federal penal cases to cantonal courts, prosecution of political offenses, penal cases involving federal officers, etc. The Police Service, commonly known as the Federal Police, is in charge of the security of the state. It is also the national central bureau of Interpol in Switzerland. The Central Police Bureau was created on

October 26, 1903 at the request of the majority of the cantons in order to facilitate the suppression of crime by means of a coordinated central police office. It is composed of four sections: Identification Section, Central Criminal Records Section, Interpol Section (NCB Interpol Switzerland), and Central Offices.

The duties of the Identification Service are the registration, use and delivery of identification material (fingerprint sheets, palm prints, photographs and personal descriptions) to national and foreign police services. Single and 10-finger prints as well as prints taken at the place of crime are compared in the central automated fingerprint collection. In this way it is possible to identify unknown persons, unidentified bodies and criminals. This technical activity is complemented by an extensive exchange of information. The Identification Service has an international phototelegraphy center and the Automatic Fingerprints Identification System. With the AFIS, all prints secured at locations of crime can be automatically compared with the collection of the Identification Service.

The activity of the Central Criminal Record Office is based on a decree of the Federal Council, last reviewed in 1982. With the help of a computer all persons who have been convicted by a Swiss court for crimes, offenses or violations of prison sentences or given fines of more than 500 Swiss francs for criminal acts are registered. Also registered are all Swiss citizens convicted by a foreign court if the crime is also a punishable offense under Swiss law. On request and in special cases ex officio, excerpts from the criminal records are delivered to courts, police and other authorities. Also, a private person is entitled to request and receive an excerpt concerning his own person. There is also an exchange of information with foreign countries, insofar as a bilateral treaty exists or the concerned country guarantees reciprocity. The tasks of the registrar also include the supervision of the periods of probation in cases of suspended prison sentences as well as the issuance of probation and recidivism notifications. Finally, the Central Criminal Record Office supplies the Federal Office for Statistics with the data for the annual report on the convictions pronounced in Switzerland.

The Interpol Service serves exclusively for the exchange of information between the federal and cantonal police authorities on the one hand and the National Central Bureaus of the ICPO-Interpol (International Criminal Police Organization) and the Interpol General Secretariat on the other hand. In the daily work, the Interpol-Service deals with many different police requests, e.g. the location of a person, the transmission of information concerning a criminal, the search for stolen property, the identification of seized objects, the distribution of warning notices, etc. The working languages are German, French, Italian, English and Spanish.

The Central Offices concentrate on four areas:

CRIME STATISTICS (1984)

		Number Reported	Attempts %	Cases Solved %	Crime per 100,000	Offenders	Females %	Juveniles %	Strangers %
1.	Murder	144	50.7		2.24	133	11.3	11.3	33.1
2.	Sex offenses, including rape	3,711	7.7		57.65	1,765		17.8	23.6
3.	Rape	374	44.7		5.81	222		10.3	43.2
4.	Serious assault	3,064			47.60	2,664	8	10.6	29.5
5.	All theft	295,193	4.8		4,585.66	35,707	17.1	38.7	27
6.	Aggravated theft								
7.	Robbery and violent theft	1,555	18.1		24.16	855	6.3	26.7	35.2
8.	Breaking and entering	62,879	16.3		976.79	9,674	6.8	34.1	27.7
9.	Auto theft	105,160	1.1		1,633.60	7,272	4.3	58.7	19.3
10.	Other thefts	1,616	5.5		25.10	327	4.9	53.8	21.1
11.	Fraud	7,230	6.8		112.31	5,437	15.7	5.9	24.2
12.	Counterfeiting								
13.	Drug offenses	13,689			212.65	13,689	19.3	13.0	23.8
14.	Total offenses	330,492			5,134.02	64,445		26.6	26.2

Note: Information for some categories is not available.
Criteria of juveniles: aged from 0 to 20 years.

counterfeit money, drug trafficking, illegal traffic in women and children, and illegal traffic in war material. The Central Offices are in contact with the cantonal police and judicial authorities, with other federal offices (the Mint, the National Bank, the Office of Public Health, the Custom Service), as well as with central offices in other countries.

Since 1982 the Central Police Bureau is responsible for the compilation and publication of the *Criminal Statistics of the Police*.

Recruitment, Education & Training

Training for federal and cantonal police is provided by the Swiss Police Institute, founded in 1946. The Institute conducts 30 courses, including a three-month basic school course for police candidates and a three-year course as preparatory training for a police career.

The Penal System

No information is available on the penal system.

SYRIA

BASIC FACT SHEET

Official Name: Syrian Arab Republic
Area: 185,180 sq km
Population (1987): 11,147,763
Capital: Damascus
Nature of Government: Civilian dictatorship
Language: Arabic
Currency: Syrian pound
GNP (1986): $16.98 billion
Territorial Divisions: 13 provinces
Population per Police Officer: 1,970
Police Expenditures per Capita: N.A.

History & Background

Less is known about the Syrian police than about that of any other major Middle Eastern country. The reason is that the law enforcement system as inherited from the French underwent drastic changes after President Hafiz al Assad came to power in the early 1970s. Like the military, the police forces were highly politicized and became a domain of the Alawaite community. With the development of a powerful internal security apparatus outside the police agencies, their importance to the regime diminished, although they continue to play a major role in riot and crowd control.

Structure & Organization

The core police agency, the Syrian Public Security Police, operates under the Ministry of the Interior, is headed by a director general and is organized by administrative districts. Damascus has a metropolitan police under the jurisdiction of the director general. The headquarters is divided into four main branches: Administration, Criminal Investigation, Public Order and Traffic.

The police are supplemented by two paramilitary forces: the 10,000-man Gendarmerie and the Desert Guard. The Gendarmerie had originally been formed under the French mandate to police the rural areas. The 2,000-man Desert Guard is responsible for guarding the country's border regions, especially those near hostile Iraq. The 15,000-man People's Militia and the 5,000-man Detachments for the Defense of the Regime are more military and political than police organizations, but they have increasingly encroached on police functions in recent years.

The internal security apparatus is known to consist of myriad organizations with overlapping missions. Each organization is directly responsible to the president or his closest advisers (among whom is his brother); there is no coordination among them or knowledge of each other's activities. The largest of these organizations is the National Security Directorate, directly under the president's office.

Recruitment, Education & Training

No information is available on recruitment, education and training.

The Penal System

Although criminal data are published in the government's *Statistical Abstract*, they do not reveal much about the nature of crime. Nearly three-fourths of all convictions are said to result from "crimes and contraventions not mentioned in the Penal Code." Of the other convictions, the largest category is for "crimes against religion and the family." There are 19 other classifications of crime. Discussions of crime in Syria in Western media are limited to state security crimes, such as assassinations and bombings, and to crimes such as bribery and embezzlement uncovered by the Committee for the Investigation of Illegal Profits, set up by the government in 1977.

Criminal and judicial procedures are modeled after those of France. After the police make an arrest, they present their evidence to a public prosecutor, who conducts his own investigation. If he decides to proceed, he refers the case to the appropriate court, where decisions are made by a majority of the three judges. There are no juries. About 90% of all criminal court cases result in conviction. Penalties are severe and range from death by hanging or firing squad to fines, loss of civil rights, life imprisonment, forced labor and exile. Public hangings of convinced thieves, murderers, assassins and spies are commonplace. Nevertheless, the Syrian judicial system is generally fair, except in political and security cases.

The penal system is geared toward punishment rather than rehabilitation. Prison conditions are tolerable in terms of health care, food and family access. Interrogations, however, sometimes are harsh, and Amnesty International suggests that torture is regularly used to cow prisoners.

CRIME STATISTICS (1984)

		Number Reported	Attempts %	Cases Solved %	Crime per 100,000	Offenders	Females %	Juveniles %	Strangers %
1.	Murder	221	4	87	2.25	75	24	51	
2.	Sex offenses, including rape	608	11	99	6.18	538	366	178	
3.	Rape	97	2	98	0.99	46	24	22	
4.	Serious assault	29	0.5	100	0.29	5		5	
5.	All theft	3,703	69	58	37.63	836	120	716	
6.	Aggravated theft	2,069	38.6	54	21.03	535	100	435	
7.	Robbery and violent theft	6	0.1	83	0.06				
8.	Breaking and entering	2,063	38.5	54	20.97	535	100	435	
9.	Auto theft	448	8	47	4.55	17	1	16	
10.	Other thefts	1,186	22	68	12.05	284	19	265	
11.	Fraud	302	6	93	3.07	28	10	18	
12.	Counterfeiting	69	1	90	0.70	7	5	2	
13.	Drug offenses	324	6	99.7	3.29	57	21	36	
14.	Total offenses	5,353	92	70	54.40	1,592	564	1,028	

Note: Information for some categories is not available.
Criteria of juveniles: aged from 8 to 18 years.

TAIWAN

BASIC FACT SHEET

Official Name: Republic of China
Area: 32,260 sg km
Population (1987): 19,768,035
Capital: Taipei
Nature of Government: Civilian dictatorship
Language: Mandarin Chinese
Currency: New Taiwan dollar
GNP (1985): $56.6 billion
Territorial Divisions: 16 counties
Population per Police Officer: 720
Police Expenditures per Capita: N.A.

Structure & Organization

The Taiwanese police system is made up of three broad categories of forces: the regular police organization; the Peace Preservation Corps, concerned with the detection and suppression of Communist subversive activities; and a number of other security agencies primarily engaged in counterespionage activities.

The Taiwan regime is traditionally reluctant to release information about its police because the police, like the armed forces, are vital elements in national security in a nation that still is in a state of siege. According to the best available estimates, the regular forces number about 25,000, including specialized units. According to the Taiwan Police Law, the basic police mission is to preserve public order by enforcing criminal and civil codes and routine police regulations. They are also charged with issuing police orders; punishing contraventions of police regulations; assisting in the investigation of crimes; searching, detaining and arresting suspects; and executing administrative orders. Their responsibility also extends to regulation of traffic, protection of public health, protection of public and private property, census enumeration and regulation of social vices. Except for infractions of police regulations, they have no punitive powers, and even then are limited to imposition of fines and detention not exceeding 14 days. Criminal offenders apprehended by the police must be turned over to the appropriate law court within 24 hours of arrest. Enforcement of various antinarcotics laws are the prime functions of the police and an area where they are very effective.

Generally speaking, the General Police appear to be well trained and well disciplined. They display high morale and a professional sense of duty. Although stern and dispassionate, they are considerate and avoid undue interference in the daily lives of citizens. There is some evidence of graft and corruption, especially in cases involving gamblers and prostitutes, but it is not widespread. The Chinese are traditionally law-abiding people and have a deeply ingrained respect for constituted authority.

A special security force, the Peace Preservation Corps, operates under the Ministry of National Defense. The Peace Preservation Corps was established in 1949 and incorporated with other agencies into a combined Taiwan Garrison Command to deal with the problem of Communist subversion. The governor of Taiwan Province is the ex officio commander of the PPC, but its actual operation is directed by a deputy commander, who always is a military officer.

Among PPC functions are issuance of entry and exit permits, protection of public utility installations, prevention of smuggling and control of shipping. Its major task, however, is counterespionage. The PPC also helps persons who escape from mainland China to settle in Taiwan. Units of the PPC are organized in companies and stationed at strategic points. Entrances to the mountain areas of the aboriginal tribes are guarded to prevent the infiltration of Communist agents.

A number of other security agencies, such as the Files Office, attached to the president's household, are also charged with counterespionage activities.

Recruitment, Education & Training

The principal training schools for the police are the Senior Police Officers Training School for officers and the Taiwan Police Academy for enlisted men.

Applicants to the former must be graduates of an institution of higher learning, and those of the latter at least high-school graduates. Courses for officers vary from two to four years and those for enlisted men from six months to a year.

The Penal System

The Criminal Code was first enacted on the island in 1928 but was revised and put into effect in 1935. The revised form was declared in effect for Taiwan when the island was returned to Chinese sovereignty after World War II and has been in force ever since. Its provisions are based on the Continental rather than the Anglo-Saxon legal system. It does not acknowledge collective responsibility for criminal acts and expressly states that no person shall be held guilty of an offense not spelled out in the code. Unpremeditated or negligent acts as well as criminal acts done by minors and the insane are exempt from criminal liability.

The code recognizes that the prevention of crime is more important than its punishment, and the penalties are accordingly directed more toward reformation than retaliation. The same humane goal informs its provisions, granting suspension of punishment and conditional release on fairly easy terms. The code also directs judges to pay special attention to extenuating circumstances in every crime, such as motive, provocation, the character of the offender, and his or her conduct after the offense.

The Republic of China (Taiwan) is a participating member of the UN Conference on the Prevention of Crime and the Treatment of Prisoners. The administration of penal institutions conforms to the guidelines of that body.

The penal system, administered by the Ministry of Justice, consists of three types of custodial institutions: prisons, detention houses and reformatories. Prisons are used to confine criminals whose sentences run longer than one year. Detention houses are used to house persons awaiting trial in temporary custody and to accommodate offenders sentenced to terms of less than one year. Reformatories are institutions holding juvenile criminals between 14 and 18 years of age, who, under the law, may not be jailed with adults.

Each district court has an associated prison and a detention house. Figures on prison population are not released by the government. Prisons and detention houses are usually though not always located in or near the city of the district court they support. The Taipei Prison, for example, is at Taoyuan, about 16 km west of the capital. There are three reformatories: Taoyuan, Changhua and Kaohsiung, serving northern central and southern Taiwan, respectively.

Administratively, each prison is headed by a warden and consists of five divisions: Education and Reform, Work, Health, Guard and General Affairs. Facilities are quite extensive and include well-staffed medical sections and dispensaries, workshops, classrooms and recreational areas. Each has one or more farms as well as full-scale factories. Under law 25% of the profits from these enterprises is distributed to the convicts, 40% is set aside for working capital, 10% is put into the National Treasury and the balance is set aside to improve prison conditions.

There are no exclusive prison facilities for women, but each regular prison is segregated by sex. Convict mothers are permitted to bring their children under three years of age to live with them, and kindergarten amenities are provided for these children.

Upon entering the system, each prisoner is given a thorough physical and psychiatric examination and is categorized into one of four grades. Grade Four is the lowest, reserved for dangerous criminals who are subject to strict, often solitary, confinement with no privileges. Grade Three prisoners have better quarters, with four persons to a room, a double-decked iron cot, a stool and a desk-table for each. They are required to attend classes in academic subjects as well as political indoctrination, trained in the prison shops to develop useful skills and permitted a limited amount of free time to engage in sports or other recreational activities.

Grade Two prisoners are housed in better quarters and have more privileges. They are allowed to mix with one another during daytime and to participate in the full range of recreational activities. Grade One convicts are comparable to what are commonly called "trusties" in the West. They have single rooms for quarters; their free time is their own; there are no locks on the doors of their cells; and they may move within the confines of the prison wearing ordinary clothes without restriction. Convicts of the first and second grades are permitted to receive visitors in special rooms. From time to time prison officials schedule family reunion parties, during which prisoners get together with their whole families. Prisoners may move up or down the grades on the basis of their performance. Convicts also are given the opportunity to practice self-government, to elect a slate of officers and representatives to act as intermediaries before prison officials and to form a council that administers a program of self-discipline among inmates.

The incidence of crime is classified information, and the data are never revealed to the public. Based on newspaper reports, the most common crimes appear to be theft, fraud, forgery, assault and battery and homicide, roughly in that order. Smuggling and traffic in narcotics are the most reported organized crime. Juvenile crime has not yet reached alarming proportions.

The low rate of criminal activity may be attributed

to the popular Chinese concepts of law. Chinese stress reasonableness in law, administration and criminal justice. They believe that common sense rather than technicalities should govern these transactions. They also are not litigious or contentious, disliking the complexity and tardiness of legal procedures. Family quarrels or money disputes rarely are brought into the open. In towns and villages, people prefer the mediation of their disputes by elders to adjudication in the courts.

TANZANIA

BASIC FACT SHEET

Official Name: United Republic of Tanzania
Area: 942,623 sq km
Population (1987): 23,502,472
Capital: Dar es Salaam
Nature of Government: Authoritarian
Languages: Swahili, Bantu, Arabic and English
Currency: Shilling
GNP (1986): $5.37 billion
Territorial Divisions: 25 regions (20 on mainland and 5 in Zanzibar)
Population per Police Officer: 1,336
Police Expenditures per 1,000: 1,953

History & Background

Before the arrival of the Europeans, the native peoples policed themselves through tribal traditions and institutions. During the German colonial period there was no regular police force, and police work was done by the Army. The first police system was set up by the British in 1919 by extending the British East Africa Police to the new territory. The police and the prisons were administered as a combined service until 1931. The top ranks were filled by the British, the middle ranks by Asians and the lower ranks by Africans.

The recruitment of native police was biased in favor of the "fierce and tough tribes," such as the Wanyamwazi and the Wayao. The native policemen were subjected to harsh treatment as the best means of creating a loyal and disciplined force. Police operations were largely confined to townships. Policing of rural areas was largely left to the native chiefs, except in the case of white-settler farms and plantations, which were given extra protection through periodic visits by provincial police chiefs.

At independence, the postcolonial state inherited the British structure intact. A colonial police officer continued to head the force until 1963, when the first Tanzanian was appointed to head it. It was not until 1969 that the entire headquarters was Africanized.

Structure & Organization

Up to 1964 the police force was headed by a commissioner of police. But following the union between Tanganyika and Zanzibar in April 1964 and the creation of a single force for the union, the commissioner was replaced by an inspector general of police. Below him are three commissioners: one in charge of Zanzibar, one in charge of the mainland and the last in charge of the Criminal Investigation Department. There are two major divisions at the headquarters: Administration, and Operations and Training. Field units such as Traffic, Air Wing, Marine, Signals, Railways and Harbors are under the latter. Below the headquarters the force is organized on regional and district levels. The regional level is headed by the regional police commander, while the regional crime officer is in charge of criminal investigations. The officer in charge of the district and the officer in charge of criminal investigation perform similar functions in the district. The noncommissioned ranks (formerly known as the rank and file) include sergeants, corporals and constables.

The administrative wing at the national headquarters is under a senior assistant commissioner, who reports directly to the deputy commissioner.

As part of President Julius Nyerere's socialization policies, the police force is now considerably politicized. Under the doctrine of party supremacy, all policemen must be party members, and there are party cells at each level in the force, from district to headquarters.

To give a more specific socialist orientation to law enforcement, Nyerere created the People's Militia (Jeshi la Mgambo). Every member of the militia has powers to arrest similar to those of a constable. With over 40,000 members, the People's Militia functions as a parallel law-enforcement organization in the country. There is also the Field Force Unit, a heavily armed and highly mobile paramilitary unit, elements of which are strategically placed at regional and district capitals. The strength of this unit is estimated at over 2,000.

Constitutionally, police force and police work are governmental matters and technically are under the jurisdiction of the central government. In practice, however, it appears that the Zanzibar police force, even though centrally funded, is a separate force operating under the direct control of the Zanzibari government.

Recruitment, Education & Training

Recruits for the various branches of the police force are selected from the ranks of the National Service, and standards of selection are relatively high. Recruits are required to be fluent in both Swahili and English and must be members of the CCM Party or the Youth League. All enlistments are voluntary.

Initial training is for 15 months. It may take place at the Police Training School at Moslin or the Police College at Dar es Salaam. Tanzania has the distinction of having one of the highest numbers of university-trained policemen in black Africa. A large number of police officers are also trained abroad. Tanzania also helps to train police officers of neighboring countries, such as Uganda.

The Penal System

The penal code that was introduced into British Africa was based on the Indian Penal Code, which earlier British colonial authorities had developed for the Indian subcontinent. Some modifications were made by the British in Africa but, more often than not, these were based on English common law rather than local customary law. In effect, the code was quite alien to the people who were subject to its provisions. In Tanzania the code was not substantially revised except for the innovation of minimum sentencing, which was legislated in 1963 and again in 1972.

Two major categories of offenses covered by the code are felonies and misdemeanors. The former are serious crimes punishable by death or imprisonment; misdemeanors are less serious ones punishable by imprisonment or fines. Murder, manslaughter, treason, offenses against public order, rape, arson, theft (particularly of cattle), aggravated assault, causing bodily harm and official corruption are all felonies; petty theft, common assault, minor disturbances of the peace and various traffic violations are misdemeanors.

In 1963 a minimum sentencing act made flogging a mandatory sentence for a variety of crimes and seriously curtailed the discretion of judges and magistrates in sentencing. Flogging had been a common punishment in German East Africa, and it was retained under British rule after World War I, in deference to local sentiments. To many jurists it seemed incongruous that an independent nation would endorse a form of punishment that had been considered a brutal and degrading legacy of the past.

The Preventive Detention Act of 1962 authorizes the president to arrest and detain any person who threatens the security of the republic or who is per-

CRIME STATISTICS (1983)

		Number Reported	Attempts %	Cases Solved %	Crime per 100,000	Offenders	Females %	Juveniles %	Strangers %
1.	Murder	1,734		13.17	8.67	1,135			
2.	Sex offenses, including rape	91		0.39	0.46	65			
3.	Rape	60		0.32	0.30	56			
4.	Serious assault								
5.	All theft					1,504			
6.	Aggravated theft	3,796		0.19	18.98	995			
7.	Robbery and violent theft	1,029		5.37	5.15	381			
8.	Breaking and entering	2,767		13.98	13.84	614			
9.	Auto theft	138		0.78	0.69	29			
10.	Other thefts								
11.	Fraud	56		0.35	0.28	21			
12.	Counterfeiting								
13.	Drug offenses	114		0.70	0.57	128	0.16		
14.	Total offenses	12,779		46.44	63.90	4,923	0.16		

Note: Information for some categories is not available.
Criteria of juveniles: aged from 0 to 16 years.

ceived as a threat to public order. The detainee may be held for 15 days without hearing or charge; Amnesty International has alleged that political detainees have been incarcerated for as long as 10 years without trial.

Until the coming of the Europeans, prisons were unknown in East Africa. Malefactors were punished according to the custom of the local group to which they belonged. Punishment of the offender, however, was considered less important than compensation to the offended.

The first prisons in mainland Tanzania were built by the Germans. Corporal punishment by beheading, flogging and hard labor were widely used under the Germans. The British, who succeeded the Germans as colonial masters, built more prisons but curtailed some of the more brutal methods used before their takeover.

Prisons were administered by the commissioner of prisons under the Ministry of Home Affairs. Very few new prisons have been built since independence, and conditions in existing prisons are deplorable by internationally accepted standards. Even at Ukonga Prison in Dar es Salaam, food, living conditions and medical facilities are grossly inadequate. Visits are rarely allowed. All prisons suffer from severe overcrowding.

Crime statistics are not officially reported or published. But newspaper reports suggest serious crime problems, including smuggling, black-marketing in price-controlled goods, and cattle stealing. Violent crimes are less frequent, although street muggings and daylight holdups of retail stores are almost daily reported in the press. As in other developing societies, economic crimes appear to cause the most official concern.

THAILAND

BASIC FACT SHEET

Official Name: Kingdom of Thailand
Area: 514,820 sq km
Population (1987): 53,645,823
Capital: Bangkok
Nature of Government: Constitutional monarchy (de jure); military dictatorship (defacto)
Language: Thai
Currency: Baht
GNP (1986): $42.44 billion
Territorial Divisions: 72 provinces
Population per Police Officer: 530
Police Expenditures per 1,000: 4,262

History & Background

Thailand has had organized police forces since the 16th century, but the first Western-type police was created with the help of British advisers in 1861. A Railway Police was established in 1894 followed by a Provincial Police Force in 1897. The latter became the Gendarmerie and the Patrol Department in 1915, and it was reorganized as the Royal Thai Police Department in 1932.

Structure & Organization

The Thai National Police Department is a division of the Ministry of the Interior and is charged with the enforcement of law and order throughout the kingdom. It is a unitary agency whose power and influence in politics have at times rivaled those of the Army.

The formal functions of the TNPD cover more than the mere enforcement of laws; they play an important role in counterinsurgency operations. The police personnel could, in the event of a war, be mobilized under the Ministry of Defense.

Originally based on the Japanese model, the TNPD was reorganized under U.S. aid programs and has adopted many American practices and concepts. All components of the force are administered by the central headquarters in Bangkok, which also provides a centralized array of technical functions. The major organizational units are the Provincial Police; the Border Patrol Police; the Metropolitan Police; and smaller, specialized units under the Central Investigation Bureau. The total strength of the force, including administrative and support personnel, is estimated at 100,000. Of this number, half are assigned to the

Provincial Police and some 14,000 to the Border Patrol Police. More than 15,000 serve in the Metropolitan Police Force. Quasi-military in character, the TNPD is headed by a director general who holds the rank of police general. He is assisted by three deputy directors general and five assistant directors general, all of whom have the rank of police lieutenant general. Throughout the system, all ranks, except that of the lowest (constable), correspond to those of the Army. Ninety-five of the senior positions are occupied by officers who hold one of the three grades of police general.

The Provincial Police

Largest of the TNPD segments in terms of both manpower and territorial jurisdiction is the Provincial Police. With the exception of metropolitan Bangkok and the territory contiguous to the national land borders, the Provincial Police provides police services in every town and village throughout the kingdom. The Provincial Police is headed by a commander who reports directly to the director general of the TNPD. For operational and administrative purposes, the Provincial Police is divided into seven regions, as follows: Region I, Korat; Region II, Udon Thani; Region III, Chiang Mai; Region IV, Phitsanu Lok; Region V, Nakhom Pathom; Region VI, Nakhom Sithammarat; and Region VII, Pattani.

Since 1977, the regional commissioners who head the regional forces have been granted considerable initiative and authority and also have been given responsibility over the railway, highway, marine and forestry police operating within their jurisdictions. Under the commissioner there are provincial headquarters in each of the country's 72 provincial capitals.

The Border Patrol Police

The paramilitary Border Patrol Police is an elite unit that enjoys considerable autonomy in its field operations, although it is technically part of the TNPD. Enjoying the direct patronage of the royal family, the BPP also has direct links to the Royal Thai Army, and many of its commanders are former military officers.

Charged with border security along some 4,800 km of land frontiers, the BPP has to deal with a variety of opponents: smugglers, bandits, illegal immigrants, infiltrators and insurgents. As part of its mission, it maintains an extensive surveillance and intelligence network in the border districts. Despite its modest size in relation to the other units, the BPP has become the country's primary and most effective counterinsurgency force. The basic operating units are line platoons of 32 men each, which function as security teams. Each platoon is supported by one or more heavy weapons platoons stationed at each regional police headquarters as a mobile reserve support force. A special police aerial reinforcement unit airlifts BPP platoons to trouble areas during emergencies. Because of its superior skills and equipment, the BPP has been employed even to quell popular disturbances in the interior and in Bangkok.

In the border areas, the BPP works closely with villagers and hill tribes, primarily to gain their goodwill, but also to obtain information and to deprive the insurgents of potential bases of support. The BPP is involved in numerous civil action projects designed to secure the confidence and loyalty of rural peoples. During the 1970s, the BPP built over 200 schools in remote areas in addition to medical aid stations, airstrips and agricultural stations.

The BPP was instrumental in developing a local law-enforcement adjunct known as the Volunteer Defense Corps (VDC). Founded in 1954, the corps was established as a civilian militia to protect local inhabitants from guerrillas and infiltrators by denying them food and other supplies and by passing along to the BPP information on the modus operandi and movements of antigovernment groups.

The Metropolitan Police

Probably the most visible of TNPD components is the Metropolitan Police of Bangkok. It operates under the command of a commissioner who holds the rank of a police major general, assisted by six deputy commissioners of the same rank. Organizationally the force is divided into three divisions: Northern Bangkok, Southern Bangkok and Thon Puri. Together, there are 40 police precincts in the three divisions, which are patrolled around the clock. In addition to foot patrolmen the Metropolitan Police maintains motorized units, a canine corps, building guards, traffic control specialists and juvenile specialists. The Traffic Police Division also provides mounted escorts and guards of honor for the king and visiting dignitaries and serves as a riot control force to disperse unruly crowds.

The Central Investigation Bureau

With jurisdiction over the entire country, the Central Investigation Bureau (CIB) assists both the Provincial Police and the Metropolitan Police in their investigative duties. The CIB has specialized units including the Railway Police, the Marine Police, the Highway Police and the Forestry Police. In addition to directing these special units, the CIB has five other divisions: the Crime Suppression Bureau, the Special Branch, the Criminal Record Office, The Scientific Crime Detection Laboratory and the Licenses Division. The Crime Suppression Division—the bureau's largest—is responsible for technical investigation of criminal offenses such as counterfeiting, fraud, illegal gambling, narcotics trafficking, secret societies and organized crime. The Special Branch is the nation's principal intelligence-gathering organization and thus engages in clandestine and covert operations against subversive political groups.

Recruitment, Education & Training

The Education Bureau at the TNPD headquarters is responsible for education and training of police personnel. It runs the Police Officers' Academy at Sam Phran; the Detective Training School at Bang Khen; the Metropolitan Police Training School at Bang Khen; and the Provincial Police Training Centers at Nakhon Pathom, Lampang, Nakhon Ratchasima and Yala. The BPP has its own schools for training line platoons in counterinsurgency operations, particularly the national school at Hua Hin and smaller schools at Udon Thani, Ubon Ratchathani, Chiang Mai and Songkhla.

The Penal System

Thai criminal law is embodied in the Criminal Code of 1956. It incorporates features borrowed from French, Italian, Japanese, English and Indian models but retains some traces of traditional Thai jurisprudence. The explicitness and details of its provisions suggest that its authors were consciously preparing it for judges and lawyers who have only a superficial acquaintance with the Western legal concepts that predominate in the document. The code begins by defining numerous terms such as ''assault,'' ''fraudulent'' and ''official documents,'' and then provides instructions for the application of criminal law, including explanations regarding penalties, criminal liability, principals, accessories and judgments. Twelve kinds of offenses are characterized as felonies:

1. crimes against the security of the kingdom, including those against the royal family, treason, espionage and acts that damage friendly relations with foreign countries.

2. crimes relating to public administration, such as corruption and offenses against public officials

3. crimes relating to justice, such as perjury

4. crimes against the Buddhist religion

5. acts against public order and safety

6. offenses relating to counterfeiting

7. crimes against trade, including use of false weights and measures and misrepresentation of goods

8. sexual offenses

9. crimes against the person

10. crimes against liberty and reputation, such as kidnapping and libel

11. crimes against property

12. offenses such as receipt of stolen property and misappropriation

The code also lists a wide assortment of petty offenses classed as misdemeanors. These acts are defined officially as violations punishable by imprisonment of not more than one month, a modest fine or both.

Five penalties are stipulated for contravention of the code: death, imprisonment, detention, fines and forfeiture of property. The death sentence is mandatory for murder or attempted murder of a member of the royal family; a public official; father or mother; premeditated murder; or murder accompanied by torture. Execution is carried out by a firing squad. The maximum prison term is 20 years.

Children under eight years are not subject to criminal penalties. Juveniles between ages seven and 15 are not fined or imprisoned but may be restricted to their homes, placed on probation or sent to a vocational training school. Offenses committed by minors between ages 15 and 17 may result in fines or periods of confinement, the length of which is one-half of that prescribed for adults committing the same acts.

The criminal justice system suffers from the problem of sentence disparity. Judges have a list of standard sentences measures by past practices, but these guidelines are not compulsory. Even so, criminal courts have shown a tendency to pass down cruel and arbitrary sentences.

The corrections system is administered by the Department of Corrections within the Ministry of the Interior. The system consists of 48 regular penal institutions, including seven central prisons, five regional prisons, 23 prison camps, seven correctional institutions, three reformatories and one detention home. In addition, all metropolitan, provincial and district police stations have jails used to confine offenders sentenced to terms less than one year.

The seven central and five regional prisons house the bulk of long-term prisoners. The Khlong Prem Central Prison in Bangkok is the largest and oldest, with a capacity of 6,000 inmates. The Nakhon Pathom Prison is a maximum-security institution for habitual criminals. One of the 23 prison camps is on Ko Tarutao, an island in the Strait of Malacca, and is administered separately.

Among the seven correctional institutions, one at Ayutthaya and one at Bangkok house primarily youthful offenders of 18 to 25 years of age serving terms of up to five years. The Women's Correctional Institution, also is in Bangkok, while the Specialized Medical Correctional Institution for drug addicts and prisoners requiring medical attention is in Pathum Thani Province, northwest of the capital. Two minimum-security correctional centers are in Rayong and Phitsanulok.

Of the three reformatories, the Ban Lat Yao (sometimes called Lardyao) facility, just north of Bangkok, receives the majority of the more recalcitrant juvenile delinquents and has a capacity of about 2,000. Limited rehabilitation activities are undertaken there; those who fail to respond are sent to a second reformatory, near Rayong, which is operated as a prison farm. A third reformatory, at Prachuap Khiri Khan, about 200 km southwest of Bangkok, is used to accommodate the overflow from the other two institutions.

Additional special facilities for juvenile offenders, called observation and protection centers, are administered by the Central Juvenile Court and the Central Observation and Protection Center of the Ministry of Justice. Three of these centers are in Bangkok, Songkhla and Nakhon Ratchasima. A center is attached to each juvenile court and assists it in supervising delinquent children charged with criminal offenses both before and after trial. Probation officers, social workers and teachers are assigned to these centers.

Prisoners are classified into six classes, according to conduct. Those in the first three classes are considered eligible for parole and may be released when they have completed two-thirds, three-fourths and four-fifths, respectively, of their terms.

As most prisoners are relatively uneducated, each facility runs special literacy classes. Some prisons also have vocational training programs and workshops. Products from prison labor are sold, and 35% of the net profit is returned to the individual prisoner. A small portion of this amount is credited outright to the prisoner for his or her pocket expenses, but the greater part is put into a savings fund to afford the prisoner funds for a new start upon release.

There are no official crime statistics, although the Thailand National Police Department occasionally releases some figures on certain classes of crime. According to these figures, the overall crime rate has been steadily rising, which is not surprising in a developing society. A major share of these criminal activities take place in Bangkok and some of the larger towns. In general, organized crime appears to be rare, except for illicit trade in opium and heroin, a problem that has not only serious domestic implications but international repercussions as well. The problem has its origins in the growing of poppies as a primary cash crop, a traditional practice of the hill peoples who inhabit Thailand's portion of the Golden Triangle—a mountainous interborder territory shared with Burma and Laos. For many decades, peasant cultivators in this region have produced a major share of the world's opium. According to official estimates, the average annual crop yields up to 1,000 tons of opium which, when processed, produces about 100 tons of pure heroin. About half of this annual crop finds its way to Europe and North America, and the other half to Southeast Asia. It is believed that Thailand alone has close to 1 million addicts, most of them in Bangkok. In the Golden Triangle alone some 16% of all inhabitants over age 10 are addicts. Although grown by the hill tribes, opium is transported by Burmese insurgents and exported by the Chaozhou Chinese. Thus there are ethnic as well as economic equations in this historic trade.

The Chaozhou Chinese, with roots in drug trafficking since the days of the Opium Wars, operate a maze of syndicates from Hong Kong. They have a virtual monopoly in the illicit opium and heroin trade, and they operate their own laboratories. The syndicates have an army of international couriers who ship the drug to their worldwide customers.

The efforts of the Thai government to stem the flow of drugs have been largely ineffective because of corrupt officials in the Thai Army, police and bureaucracy. During the 1960s and 1970s, the drug trade was protected by one of the highest officials in the Thai government—Field Marshal Praphat Charusathian, deputy prime minister, commander in chief, national master of the Boy Scouts and director of the government's tourist association as well as director of over 100 business enterprises. He received tribute and a cut of the profits from the drug traffickers. After his fall, the Thai government mounted more effective efforts to suppress the drug trade, including the establishment of the Narcotics Suppression Center within the Police Department. Tough amendments have been added to the Criminal Code as deterrents.

TRINIDAD AND TOBAGO

BASIC FACT SHEET

Official Name: Republic of Trinidad and Tobago
Area: 5,128 sq km
Population (1987): 1,250,839
Capital: Port-of-Spain
Nature of Government: Parliamentary democracy
Language: English
Currency: Trinidad and Tobago dollar
GNP (1986): $6.17 billion
Territorial Divisions: 8 counties
Population per Police Officer: 280
Police Expenditures per 1,000: $142,083

History & Background

Organized as the Trinidad Constabulary Force in the early decades of the 20th century, the Trinidad and Tobago Police Service was known as the Trinidad and Tobago Police Force from 1938 to 1965. It assumed its present form under the Police Service Act of 1965, which provides the legal basis for the mission, staffing, pay and allowances, retirement system and other related matters.

Structure & Organization

The Police Service Act established two schedules of police officers: commissioned officers who are the commissioner of police, deputy commissioners, assistant commissioners, senior superintendents, superintendents and assistant superintendents; and noncommissioned ranks, which include inspectors, sergeants, corporals and constables. Of the total force of about 4,800, approximately 70% are constables.

The Police Service is centralized at the national level, with headquarters at Port-of-Spain. It is headed by the commissioner of police assisted by three deputy commissioners, all of whom are appointed by the president on the advice of the prime minister. The deputy commissioner for administration supervises finance, personnel, training, the highway patrol in the northern part of the country, transport, telecommunications and the mounted branch. The deputy commissioner for operations is responsible for police units throughout the country and the prevention and detection of crime. He is assisted by an assistant commissioner for crime, who supervises the Criminal Records Office and the Criminal Investigation Department.

The third deputy commissioner is in charge of the Special Branch, concerned with security and intelligence.

The country is divided for police operational purposes into nine divisions under two branches: a northern branch, operating from the central headquarters in Port-of-Spain; and a southern branch, headquartered in San Fernando. Headquarters of local stations are changed from time to time. Government quarters are provided for married commissioned and noncommissioned personnel in major stations. A Traffic Branch is in Port-of-Spain and a training school is in St. James Barracks, St. James, the former headquarters of the British troops in Trinidad. Special units include a larceny mobile patrol charged with the control of theft from landed estates; an estate police unit called the Antisquatting Brigade, assigned to prevent illegal settling on private lands; and the police band.

A volunteer reserve police force, called the Special Reserve Police, was organized in 1939. Its members, estimated at over 1,000, are attached to divisions of the regular police throughout the islands. The Special Reserve Police are under the jurisdiction of the commissioner of police and are commanded by a senior superintendent.

In addition to the national Police Service there is a small municipal police force in Port-of-Spain. Their functions are limited to the protection of buildings, parks and government installations is the city.

In spite of the large East Indian population, the Police Service is predominantly black. Blacks are reported to constitute over 90% of the officers and men. Various reasons have been cited for this racial imbalance. Both qualifications and selection procedures favor blacks. East Indians, because of their smaller stature, generally do not measure up to the physical requirements for recruits. East Indians are also largely rural people who historically have been excluded from the service or have not actively sought participation in it.

The Trinidad and Tobago (Constitution) Order in Council of 1962 established the Police Service Commission, whose chairman is concurrently the chairman of the Public Service Commission. The other four members of the commission are appointed by the president on the advice of the prime minister.

The Police Service Act authorizes the formation of a police association empowered to function as a police union and represent policemen in discussions with the commissioner on matters relating to pay and grievances.

The police uniform consists of a gray shirt and khaki shorts or a white tunic and blue slacks topped by a white helmet in daytime, and a blue tunic and blue peaked cap at night. Weapons are not carried during normal patrol, but rifles and bayonets are carried on ceremonial parades.

Recruitment, Education & Training

Police recruits are assigned to St. James Barracks for an initial training program. Training programs at the advanced level also are provided, and some officers are sent abroad for specialized training.

The Penal System

The Criminal Code is based on the British models that prevailed before independence. All common law, doctrines of equity and general statutes that were in force in England on March 1, 1848, became applicable to Trinidad. English common law and doctrines of equity originating between 1848 and 1962 are generally accepted by Trinidad and Tobago courts but are not necessarily binding. Penalties for crime include fines, imprisonment, corporal punishment and death. Corporal punishment is rarely used because of strong public opposition. Prison sentences tend to be short.

The Prison Service Act of 1965 provides the legal basis for the correctional system. The service is headed by a commissioner of prisons and staffed, in order of rank, by a deputy commissioner, senior superintendents, assistant superintendents, supervisors, welfare officers and prison officers class I and II.

The country has three prisons: the Royal Gaol in Port-of-Spain, the island prison on Carrera Island in the Chaguaramas area and the Golden Grove Prison near Arouca. The first two are maximum-security prisons, while the third is an open prison designed for first offenders of minor crimes and others ame-

CRIME STATISTICS (1984)

		Number Reported	Attempts %	Cases Solved %	Crime per 100,000	Offenders	Females %	Juveniles %	Strangers %
1.	Murder	98	24.48	69.38	6.76	80	6.25		
2.	Sex offenses, including rape	148	4.72	57.43	10.21	91			
3.	Rape	133	5.26	56.39	9.17	80			
4.	Serious assault	1,577		67.27	108.76	1,167	1.71	0.86	0.12
5.	All theft	19,522	0.25	12.61	1,346.34	3,058	0.49	0.65	0.16
6.	Aggravated theft	9,097	0.65	12.10	627.38	1,571	0.76	2.54	0.06
7.	Robbery and violent theft	1,651	4.23	20.59	113.86	553	0.90	1.98	0.36
8.	Breaking and entering	7,446	0.33	10.22	513.52	1,018	1.08	1.17	
9.	Auto theft								
10.	Other thefts	10,425	0.57	12.69	718.97	1,487	1.68	1.41	0.26
11.	Fraud	245	3.25	93.46	16.90	235	10.92		2.18
12.	Counterfeiting	9		100	0.62	9			
13.	Drug offenses	2,867		99.68	197.72	2,816	4.26	0.16	0.19
14.	Total offenses	43,735	0.27	29.71	3,016.21	14,247	2.17	0.36	1.11

Note: Information for some categories is not available.
Criteria of juveniles: aged from 0 to 16 years.

nable to rehabilitation. Women constitute less than 5% of the prison population. Offenders under age 16 are classified as juveniles and are not processed through the prison system but committed to an orphanage or industrial school.

Crime statistics are regularly published in the *Annual Statistical Digest* published by the government.

Crimes are classified into three categories: serious crimes, minor crimes and minor offenses. Most of the crimes are against property, and murder and manslaughter are relatively rare. Only about 10% of the serious crimes reported result in convictions. Among rising crime categories are drug trafficking and traffic violations.

TUNISIA

BASIC FACT SHEET

Official Name: Republic of Tunisia
Area: 163,610 sq km
Population (1987): 7,561,641
Capital: Tunis
Nature of Government: Authoritarian
Languages: Arabic and French
Currency: Dinar
GNP (1986): $8.34 billion
Territorial Divisions: 18 governorates
Population per Police Officer: 340
Police Expenditures per Capita: N.A.

History & Background

At independence there were two law-enforcement agencies in Tunisia: the Sûreté Nationale (SN), an outgrowth of the administrative branch of its French counterpart in the protectorate era, and the newly established Garde Nationale. The Sûreté was an urban police and the Garde a rural police after the manner of the Gendarmerie that served in Tunisia until 1956. Until 1967 the two organizations operated autonomously, but the Garde had a closer relationship to the Tunisian National Army (TNA), especially in its training philosophy, interchange of personnel and types of equipment used. Nonetheless, both forces were under the jurisdiction of the Ministry of the Interior. Following the anti-Jewish riots that took place in the wake of the Arab-Israeli War of 1967, the Ministry of the Interior took stronger control of domestic police functions. The two police forces were as a result amalgamated to form the Directorate of National Security Forces, under whom the director of Sûreté and the Garde were placed. Both forces have the same pay scales and conditions of service.

Structure & Organization

The Sûreté Nationale is the effective national police force in principal cities and urban centers. It is charged with the maintenance of public order in these areas, including investigation of crimes and traffic control. Its strength is estimated at 12,000.

The Sûreté is organized generally along the lines of its French counterpart, with operational and investigative branches and supporting services. The section best known to the public is made up of the uniformed urban police, segments of which are assigned to each of the 18 governorates. These elements are under the supervision of the director general of the Directorate of National Security Forces in Tunis. A separate section of the Sûreté handles functions that include border control, immigration, political intelligence, security of the president and general information. Other components are responsible for criminal files and for the Judiciary Police, crime research laboratories, the Licensing Bureau and the prison system

The Traffic Police, a branch of the Sûreté, is limited to the very large cities and includes a number of women. Generally, the Traffic Police are the most visible and the friendliest of the police units.

In the late 1960s, particularly after the ineffectual performance of the Sûreté against the anti-Jewish rioters of 1967, the government established a special Sûreté unit known as the Brigade of Public Order (Brigade de l'Ordre Publique, BOP) with U.S. assistance. With six battalions recruited largely from the Army's growing pool of reservists, the BOP specializes in controlling riots, crowds, strikes and other demonstrations.

A special section of the Sûreté known as the Directorate of Territorial Surveillance is responsible for intelligence and counterespionage operations and constitutes the equivalent of a secret service. The directorate has drawn much criticism for its regular use of torture and other repressive tactics in the course of its investigations.

The Garde Nationale was formed at independence to carry out police operations in rural areas, formerly the responsibility of the colonial Gendarmerie. Its strength is estimated at over 10,000, of which the bulk served in rural areas and the balance served as highway patrol and as presidential bodyguards and ceremonial troops. Because of its size, training, equipment, and tactical deployment capability, the Garde is a versatile paramilitary force. It is also responsible for aiding the army in counterinsurgency tasks when needed and in assisting in civic action projects and in emergency relief during disasters.

Recruitment, Education & Training

Sûreté personnel are public servants recruited in accordance with civil service regulations. The force has six categories of personnel divided into several classes based on seniority and achievement. The highest is that of police superintendents, who are also authorized to exercise the powers of magistrates in administrative, judicial or municipal capacities. Most of them are recruited by means of a competitive examination; the rest are selected from among officers of the Garde Nationale, the Army and the regional administrations. Frequent transfers tend to keep them under the influence of the central government and out of local politics.

The second-highest rank, known as police officials, assist the superintendents in the performance of their duties and perform additional investigative and administrative tasks. The majority of them are recruited by a special competitive examination and the rest from the Garde Nationale.

Police secretaries, the third rank, assist in investigation and administration. They are recruited on the basis of tests from applicants with at least six years of secondary education. Technical police detectives, who make up the fourth rank, are charged with identification, documentation and other technical and scientific tasks required in police work. Their recruitment is on the same basis as secretaries. Inspectors, the fifth-ranking group, work under the direction of superintendents and officials. Most inspectors are recruited by tests for civil service applicants with a high-school diploma, and the rest by application, or personnel with 18 months' experience. The last category is the uniformed urban police corps, known as police constables. Of these, some are recruited from students at the Police Academy and others by competitive examinations.

Applicants accepted by the Sûreté are trained at its academy at Bir bu Ruqbah. The duration of their courses varies with the service in which they are enrolled. Members of the force may be called upon at any time to attend special training courses at the academy, and all except those in the grade of superintendent are required to participate in sports and physical education training.

Garde personnel are recruited in accordance with civil service regulations and consist mostly of former enlisted men and junior NCOs. Selected applicants are trained at the Garde training academy at Bir bu Fishah for at least six months.

The Penal System

Tunisian jurisprudence has undergone radical change during the past century, particularly since 1956 as the government has sought to adjust the legal system to modern needs. The whole body of Tunisian law is now codified. The Penal Code was first enacted by beylical decree in 1913 and was amended after independence in 1956. Similarly, the Code of Criminal Procedure was introduced in 1921 but was amended extensively by the Bourguiba government in 1968. Not surprisingly, both codes reflect strongly the legal traditions of France.

Although the Penal Code is the basic collection of criminal law, many other codified legal sources, such as the Press Code and the Code of Personal Status, also impinge on the administration of criminal law. The Penal Code consists of three sections: General Provisions; Various Offenses; and Punishments and Violations. The first defines basic principles, such as that an act is not deemed to be an offense unless its commission is prohibited by temporal law at the time it occurs. This provision precludes the application of the Sharia to criminal cases.

Following French tradition, offenses are divided into three classes: *crimes, délits* and *contraventions.* The first, equivalent to felonies in Anglo-Saxon law, are serious acts punishable by death or prison sentences exceeding five years. *Délits,* equivalent to misdemeanors in Anglo-Saxon law, are acts punishable by 16 days to five years in prison, or by a fine of more than 60 Tunisian dinars. *Contraventions* are minor violations for which punishments are less than 15 days in prison or a fine of less than 60 Tunisian dinars.

The code's last two sections deal categorically with various offenses and prescribes their penalties. Punishments are classified as principal and accessory. Accessory punishments include such measures as forbidding a convicted person to be in a certain place for up to 20 years, denial of voting rights, prohibition from carrying arms, confiscation of property or restrictions against the practice of specified professions. Recidivists are particularly subject to accessory punishments. First offenders are in many cases required to perform work regarded by the courts as rehabilitating. Principal punishments include death by hanging (or by firing squad in serious offenses against state security), hard labor for life, hard labor for specified terms, imprisonment and a variety of fines.

Death sentences are reserved for those convicted of such *crimes* as treason, attempts against the life of the president, certain acts that threaten national security, premeditated homicide, and arson that results in death. The court grants the president the power to pardon anyone against whom the death sentence is imposed, and President Bourguiba has exercised it on several occasions.

Offenses against the state include a wide variety of acts, such as treason, corruption by a public official, insulting the president, unauthorized assembly or association, inciting illegal strikes and defaming the Tunisian National Army. At the same time, the code contains none of the provisions dealing with economic offenses that are heavily stressed in other authoritarian states. It also contains few of the Islamic restrictions commonly found in the laws of Muslim countries.

The revised Code of Criminal Procedure is characterized by emphasis on two major areas: simplification of procedures and protection of the rights of the accused. Its five books outline the course to be followed from investigation to execution of the sentence. Under the code, two legal actions can result from each detected offense: a public action by the state and a private action for damages, both of which may be tried simultaneously. Juveniles under 13 years and insane persons are exempt from criminal liability. The public prosecutor is a key figure in criminal procedure. He supervises all criminal investigations through the Judiciary Police of the Sûreté. Arraignment is conducted before a judge of instruction, who performs the functions of a grand jury. The jury system was abolished in 1966; since then, all trials have been conducted by a judge or judges, who must decide questions of fact as well as questions of law. Proof of intent is required in a *crime* or *délit* but not in a *contravention*. Sentences other than death are executed immediately, despite the possibility of appeal.

Article 12 of the Constitution states that the accused is considered innocent until proved guilty in court, where he or she is guaranteed the necessary conditions for self-defense. The defendant has the right to legal representation even if indigent. The right to bail also exists except in cases of serious felonies. Confessions made under duress are not admissible in court.

Preventive detention while awaiting judgment is limited to specified circumstances. It must not exceed five days after an interrogation if the prior record of the accused shows less than a year of imprisonment. In all cases of the death penalty, appeal to the Court of Cassation is automatic.

The penal system is the responsibility of the Ministry of the Interior and is administered by a department of the Sûreté. It includes central prisons at Tunis, Bajah, Bizerte, Qabis, Qafsah, Al Qayrawan, Al Kaf, Safaqis, Susah and Bardo and smaller facilities at less populated centers. Habitual criminals usually are sentenced to hard labor at the agricultural penitentiary at Jabal Faqirin. All these prisons were originally established by the French in the colonial era.

Wherever possible, juvenile offenders are segregated from adults, and women prisoners from men. Selected prisoners serving less than five years are placed in open camps called reeducation centers for rehabilitation. Here they perform useful work, for which they receive a token wage.

Prison conditions during French rule were generally grim, and prisons were looked upon as sources for cheap labor for roadbuilding and other heavy construction jobs. Reforms have proceeded slowly since independence, but some improvements have been reported. All cells are equipped with beds and mattresses, and all have radio and television amenities. Health care, literacy classes and vocational training are some of the improvements introduced since independence. Food rations still are meager, and visits by families and friends are permitted only for a short duration.

There is considerable social stigma attached to prisoners and ex-prisoners, as a result of which former prisoners find it difficult to secure gainful employment or to be reabsorbed into society. Large-scale general unemployment also makes it harder for ex-prisoners to be hired.

Based on official statistics, the incidence of crime is low compared to many other developing countries. Generally, crime is more of a probem in urban areas than in rural areas. Moreover, the scope and pattern of criminal activity is more complex and varied in proportion to the size of the population. Homicide, forgery, abortion, libel, failure to pay debts, fraud, intoxication and disturbing the peace are more common in urban areas, while theft and related acts are more common in the rural ones.

Social, or victimless crimes, such as prostitution, vagrancy and drug abuse take up more police time than others. Prostitution is illegal, and periodic, if unsuccessful, efforts are made to stem its practice. Begging is illegal, although almsgiving is one of the traditional virtues required of good Muslims. Intoxication is prohibited in the Koran as well as in the Penal Code. However, the consumption of alcohol as a criminal problem has been overshadowed in recent years by the use of drugs, such as *kif*, which is fairly widespread throughout North Africa. Both drug users and drug pushers are equally liable to penalties, which may range up to fines of 10,000 Tunisian dinars and a maximum of five years' imprisonment.

Two other criminal problems, neither peculiar to Tunisia, have been engaging official attention for some time. Graft and corruption by public officials, endemic features of Third World societies, are attested to by periodic and well-publicized trials. Official denunciations of corrupt practices have had little impact on the higher and middle echelons of public servants, who look upon them as perquisites of office. Juvenile delinquency is the other problem that has assumed serious proportions since independence. Lack of employment opportunities and vocational training, the adverse effects of urbanization and the gradual erosion of traditional values are cited as the most common reasons for this phenomenon. Reeducation centers at Gammarth and Safaqis allow juvenile offenders to be rehabilitated without contact with adult criminals. These centers provide vocational training in a variety of trades and in agriculture. Inmates also receive psychological counseling from trained social workers.

TURKEY

BASIC FACT SHEET

Official Name: Republic of Turkey
Area: 780,576 sq km
Population (1987): 52,987,778
Capital: Ankara
Nature of Government: limited democracy
Languages: Turkish
Currency: Lira
GNP (1986): $57.12 billion
Territorial Divisions: 67 provinces
Population per Police Officer: 1,570
Police Expenditures per Capita: N.A.

History & Background

The principal agencies devoted to law enforcement are the National Police and the Gendarmerie (Jandarma). Both trace their origins to 1845, when the first European-style police force was established. However, police regulations were not codified until 1907, when the three branches of service were introduced: Judicial, Administrative and Executive. In 1913 the Police Code was further revised. After the Kemalist republic was established, the Directorate of Public Security was set up in 1923. A further reorganization, in 1932, divided the police into two branches: uniformed, and plainclothes detectives. The last revision of police regulations took effect in 1937 and remains in force today.

Structure & Organization

Both the National Police and the Gendarmerie are administered by the Ministry of the Interior, but the two services have separate operational commands, the first under the General Directorate of Security and the second under the Gendarmerie General Command. Auxiliary police units include the National Intelligence Organization (Milh Istihbarat Teskilati, MIT), which operates under the office of the prime minister, and two other security organizations, one devoted to the protection of banks, factories and public installations against terrorist attacks and the other a rapid-response mobile intelligence and countersubversion agency under the Ministry of the Interior.

The territorial organization of the National Police corresponds to the administrative subdivisions. Below the General Directorate are 67 provincial directorates and district commands in most of the 572 administrative districts. Despite wide territorial distribution, a vast majority of the police are clustered in the larger cities, with Istanbul alone claiming 70%. The total strength of the force was estimated in the mid-1980s at 70,000.

A chart organization of the General Directorate shows six assistant directors general under the director general responsible for political policy, security, personnel, finance, traffic and technical matters, respectively. In the provincial directorates there are three categories of functions: administrative, judicial and political. Provincial directorates are headed by commissioners and district commands by superintendents. Sometimes municipalities provide all or part of the funding in support of the administrative police in their jurisdictions. Administrative police carry out routine police functions, such as prevention of smuggling, quelling disorders, fingerprinting, photographing, regulation of public licensing, censorship of films and press, traffic control, motor vehicle inspection, apprehension of criminals, location of missing persons, providing travel information and keeping track of foreigners traveling through the country. The Judicial Police are detective forces working closely with the judicial administration and attached to the offices of public prosecutors. The Judicial Police investigate crimes, prepare and issue arrest warrants and assist the public prosecutor in organizing evidence for trials. The political police combat subversion. Specialized squads focusing on particular problems, such as narcotics traffic, are in the larger commands. At the other end of the scale, the police used unskilled auxiliaries in many towns as unarmed watchmen.

Official documents also refer to two other branches of police: criminal police, who appear to be technical personnel working in laboratories and technical bureaus; and financial police, concerned with countering smuggling. Another relatively specialized group, variously referred to as mob control police or riot police, was organized in 1965. In 1971 they were given the additional duties of safeguarding public officials, and emergency relief during the frequent earthquakes in the country.

A major area of police administration is transportation, which is placed under the jurisdiction of a number of units, such as Harbor Police, Bosporus Bridge Security Police, Airport Security Police and Regional Traffic Police.

In 1979 the chain of police command was slightly altered. Replacing the single hierarchy in such cities as Istanbul, Ankara, Izmir and Adana was a set of regional chains manned by teams responding to incidents in their specific regions and called into action by a sophisticated communications system.

Police ranks range from constable through sergeant, lieutenant, captain, superintendents first and second class and several grades of police chiefs. Occasionally the chief of police in a town is referred to as a commissioner. The normal uniform is a dark blue, open-neck tunic and trousers worn with a light gray shirt and an American-style peaked cap. A large metal badge with the national star and crescent device is worn on the left breast. Badges of rank are worn on the right breast and consist of stars and leaf-shaped disks. All personnel carry a pistol and a rubber billy club.

New regulations that came into effect in 1978 prohibit police unionization, political partisanship, participation in political assemblies, strikes and work slowdowns. Police performance came under much criticism during the premartial law trubulence of the 1970s. In personnel, training and numbers, the police proved themselves inadequate to cope with Turkey's mounting law-enforcement problems.

Organized in 1930 as a paramilitary force the Gendarmerie retains its military character. New career junior officers are obtained by quota from the graduating classes of the Turkish Military Academy, and junior reserve officers are allocated from university graduates for their period of required service. Training is conducted in the Gendarmerie school under armed forces General Staff supervision. Conscripts who volunteer to remain on duty after required service are sent for extended training.

Uniforms, ranks and pay are the same as those for the Army. Uniforms are of dark olive-brown color, with different-colored patches on the collars of the uniform to show rank and specialization. In addition to pay, gendarmes receive free transportation on public facilities, reduced prices at places of public accommodation and entertainment, and membership in commissaries, clubs and recreation camps. Gendarmes usually are armed with light infantry weapons. A company of gendarmes is attached to each Army division as military police.

The Gendarmerie's headquarters in Ankara is headed by a four-star general, and the General Staff is directed by a major general. Under the chief of staff are typical military staff sections, such as personnel, intelligence, operations and logistics, and the headquarters commandment. Other units include the Legal Advisory Office, the Gendarmerie Officer School and the Basic Training Command.

The field operational units include the Aegean District Command and 12 other commands, headquartered at Erzurum, Bitlis, Diyabakir, Trabzon, Malatya, Tokat, Adana, Ankara, Konya, Istanbul, Bursa and Aydin. These 13 district commands encompass all 67 provinces. In each province the provincial Gendarmerie commander, a colonel or lieutenant colonel, advises the governor in matters of security and has direct charge of the country Gendarmerie commands, usually headed by captains. Below them are the Gendarmerie commanders in administrative districts, each of whom controls the fixed posts in his area, which usually are located at intervals of 15 to 20 km along the main roads and are manned by a sergeant and six to 12 gendarmes. To foster detachment from local groups, gendarmes usually are assigned away from their home areas.

The main administrative functions of the Gendarmerie correspond roughly to those of the National Police but also include enforcing hunting and fishing laws, fighting forest fires and patrolling borders. Their judicial tasks include guarding prisons, escorting and transporting convicts, and assisting the Judicial Police in investigation. They also have military duties in apprehending deserters and working in military courts.

The main intervention elements in the Gendarmerie consist of three mobile infantry brigades, the personnel of which are called commandos or ''blue berets,'' and their units as commando regiments or battalions. The mobile brigades are reported to be deployed mainly in the Second and Third Army areas. There is an Air Wing equipped with helicopters.

The total strength of the Gendarmerie was estimated in the mid-1980s at over 150,000, almost double their 1970 strength. This growth was partly in response to the government decision to introduce gendarmes into towns where the police had proved incapable of meeting mass violence.

Recruitment, Education & Training

There are four police academies: two founded in 1967 and 1971, the latter known as Kemalettin Eroge, at Istanbul; one founded in 1960 at Izmir; and one known as Yusuf Kahraman, founded in 1971 at Ankara. Candidates for officer rank are sent to Police College and then to the Police Institute. Those who graduate after three years at the institute are appointed assistant chiefs. Turkey has received aid from the United States, the United Kingdom and West Germany in building up its training facilities and courses.

The Penal System

The current Penal Code was enacted in September 1971. It provides more serious penalties for some offenses and expands others. The penalty for kidnapping, for example, was raised from five to 15 years to 15 to 20 years. Hijacking was explicitly added to the list as well as manufacture and possession of explosives.

Punishments for felonies are death, strict imprisonment, ordinary imprisonment and heavy fines. Conviction for certain crimes against the state or for premeditated murder carries the death penalty. Strict imprisonment entails labor for one year to life and may begin, in the case of a recidivist convicted of multiple offenses, with a period of solitary confinement. Ordinary imprisonment may range from three days to 20 years and also require labor. Conviction for a felony that leads to a sentence of five years or more also disqualifies a person for life from holding public office. Conviction for a serious misdemeanor

may entail disqualification from practicing a profession or trade.

The Penal Code does not permit indeterminate sentences except for drug addicts and alcoholics. A sentence for an offense must fall between the maximum and minimum penalties specified for that offense. First offenders sentenced to a term of one year or less may have that sentence conditionally suspended.

A warrant is required for arrest, but a person may be held without a warrant for as long as one month. The Code of Criminal Procedure, however, provides for release on bail even of individuals charged with serious offenses unless the charge is one of crime against the state or carries the penalty of death or life imprisonment. Bail may also be refused an accused with a record of past convictions.

The penal system is administered by the General Directorate of Prisons and Houses of Detention in the Ministry of Justice. There is a prison or jail in almost every town. The older penal institutions include most of the town and district jails and the larger provincial prisons used in Ottoman times. These have been supplemented by new "penitentiary labor establishments," where there are facilities for rehabilitative labor. Prison labor is compulsory for all in old and new prisons. The choice of work is never left to the prisoner, although aptitudes are taken into account in assigning work. Pay rates are determined by the minister of justice. Prisoners may send monthly payments

CRIME STATISTICS (1984)

		Number Reported	Attempts %	Cases Solved %	Crime per 100,000	Offenders	Females %	Juveniles %	Strangers %
1.	Murder	677			1.41	877			
2.	Sex offenses, including rape								
3.	Rape	91			0.19	134			
4.	Serious assault	7,836			16.33	11,537			
5.	All theft	37,015			77.11	34,079			
6.	Aggravated theft								
7.	Robbery and violent theft	729			1.52	703			
8.	Breaking and entering								
9.	Auto theft	3,187			6.64	1,772			
10.	Other thefts	32,952			68.65	31,424			
11.	Fraud	2,306			4.80	2,717			
12.	Counterfeiting	141			0.29				
13.	Drug offenses	792			1.65	2,156	3.1	1.7	2.82
14.	Total offenses	85,726			178.60	85,399	3.1	1.7	2.85

Note: Information for some categories is not available.
Criteria of juveniles: aged from 1 to 15 years.

of up to one-half their earnings to a dependent; part is withheld for rations and the remainder is paid to the prisoner upon discharge.

The Turks, like all Muslims, look upon punishment as divinely willed and do not favor rehabilitation or reeducation. Penal practice, therefore, is heavily weighted on more, rather than less, punishment. However, severe punishments such as solitary confinement on bread and water may be imposed by a warden only with the approval of the prison's disciplinary board. Chains may be prescribed only by order of a judge with the approval of the minister of justice.

The incidence of ordinary crimes, as distinguished from political crimes, is low compared to other Middle Eastern or West European countries. However, it is possible that because of the deficiencies of the statistical reporting system, most crimes are not officially registered. Perhaps the most common of serious offenses in the urban areas are crimes of personal violence and crimes against property. Many offenses contain both elements. Specifically, homicide, beating and fighting appear to occur fairly frequently. In the more isolated rural communities, affronts to honor and personal wrongs are still dealt with without recourse to law-enforcement agencies. It was the obligation of male kin to avenge breaches of family honor involving illicit sexual behavior of the women under their control by killing the woman, her male accomplice or both. Similarly, close kin are expected to avenge the death of a man or a woman.

Another major source of law-enforcement concern is smuggling and black-marketing. The southeastern borders are particularly sensitive in this respect. Narcotics traffic engenders criminal problems of a different kind, often with international repercussions. Although the Turkish connection has been supplanted in size by that of Latin America and other Asian countries, it still remains a headache to narcotics control officials in the United States and Western Europe.

Juvenile crime is increasing in urban areas, where children in squatter communities are exploited by organized criminals. The most common crimes committed by juveniles are theft, assault, sex crimes and homicide.

UGANDA

BASIC FACT SHEET

Official Name: Republic of Uganda
Area: 235,385 sq km
Population (1987): 15,908,896
Capital: Kampala
Nature of Government: Military dictatorship
Language: English
Currency: Uganda shilling
GNP (1985): $5.9 billion
Territorial Divisions: 10 provinces, 34 districts
Population per Police Officer: 1,090
Police Expenditures per 1,000: 1,173

History Background

The forerunner of the Uganda Police Force was the Armed Constabulary, formed in 1900 with 1,450 Africans under the command of British district officers. In 1906 an inspector general was appointed as the commanding officer of all police detachments. Although established as a civil force, the police from the outset were frequently assigned military duties. During World War I the constabulary detachments patrolled the border between Uganda and East Africa. In addition, police units were regularly assigned to peacekeeping patrols in Karamoja District to suppress cattle raiding and tribal skirmishes.

During the protectorate period and for the first few years after independence the semiautonomous federal states maintained their own police forces. The forces in Ankola, Bunyoro and Toro were small, but the Uganda Police Force was a large, well-organized corps. The 1962 Constitution provided that these forces were subordinate to the Uganda inspector general of police, but in fact he was able to exercise only nominal control. The 1967 Constitution abolished the federal states, and the police forces in those states were either merged into the Uganda Police Force or became local constabularies responsible to the district commissioners but under the overall control of the inspector general.

Structure & Organization

The Uganda Police Force is a multitribal, nonpolitical armed constabulary of 12,000 to 15,000 officers and men who in addition to regular police work perform intensive paramilitary duties, provide large guard of honor detachments for visiting dignitaries and perform most of the public prosecution in criminal courts.

The ratio of policemen to the population is 1 for every 1,090 inhabitants, one of the smallest in Africa. A significant imbalance exists in the assignment of police among the districts, ranging from one to 100 in Kampala to one to 5,000 in Tezo District and one to 8,000 in Kigezi District. The heavy burden of law enforcement in the historically lawless outlying areas is placed on a relatively small force.

The police force is commanded by an inspector general of police appointed by the president on the advice of the Public Service Commission. The actions of the inspector general of police are exempt from judicial inquiry or review, and he reports directly to the minister of internal affairs and the president.

The inspector general of police is directly assisted by four regional commanders, who manage police operations within their regions. A Police Council composed of the inspector general, the permanent secretary of the Ministry of Internal Affairs, and four other members appointed by the minister oversees all aspects of recruitment and service. Senior police officers are appointed by the Public Service Commission after consultation with the inspector general of police.

The force is divided into several branches or units: the Uniform Branch, assigned mainly to urban duties; the Special Branch and the Criminal Investigation Department; the Special Constabulary; the Special Force Unit; the Signals Branch; the Railway Police; the Air Wing; the Police Tracker Force; the Police Band; and the Dog Section. The Public Safety Unit was formed in 1971 to combat armed robbery.

The cream of the corps is the Special Force Unit,

formerly the Internal Security Unit. The Special Force is a paramilitary organization trained in riot control and border patrol by Israeli instructors. Each unit consists of 50 men. The Police Tracker Force, the successor to the Karamoja Constabulary, also is organized along military lines. Their special assignment is the suppression of cattle-raiding. The detective branch of the force is the Criminal Investigation Department, which maintains fingerprint, identification and criminal records and operates the Photographic and Scientific Aids Section. Communications are handled by the Signals Branch.

Recruitment, Education & Training

New recruits are assigned for initial training to the Police Training School in Kampala. Noncommissioned officers and constables are sent for promotion and refresher courses to the Police College at Naguru. Selected officers are also sent abroad, particularly to Australia, Israel, the United Kingdom and the United States.

The Penal System

Criminal justice is governed by the Penal Code of 1930, as amended in 1968. The list of punishments includes death by hanging, imprisonment, whipping and fines. The sentence of whipping was incorporated in the Penal Code from English law, but it has strong historical local precedents; thief-beating by the community is a frequent police entry.

In June 1968 Parliament amended the Penal Code to provide for a mandatory death penalty for persons convicted of armed robbery; of threatening to use deadly weapons before, during or after a robbery; or for inflicting grievous bodily harm. Parliament also amended the Criminal Procedure Code to provide that convicted thieves or burglars shall, when released from prison, be issued a card that identifies them as convicts. This card is to be carried at all times and must be presented for examination at police stations at frequent, fixed intervals.

In securing the passage of these amendments, the government admitted that organized violent crime had increased significantly after independence. The reported figures, however, do not present the complete story. In areas without police stations crimes are never reported, and the crime rate is directly proportionate to the ratio of policemen to the population.

The law governing police interrogation, evidence rules (statements to police officers) is drawn from English and Indian law. The rules stipulate that a policeman in the course of an investigation of a reported crime may question any person, but if there is an intent to charge the person, he must be cautioned that his statement may be used against him. A confession to a policeman of or above the rank of corporal is admissible in court.

The Constitution provides for the Presidential Advisory Committee on the Prerogative of Mercy, chaired by the attorney general, which reviews all death sentences and may review sentences for life imprisonment or whipping. The president, who is not required to act on the advice of the commission, has unlimited power to pardon, postpone or reduce a sentence for any offense.

The Prison Service is a part of Public Service, under the command of the commissioner of prisons. The commissioner is appointed by the president acting on the recommendations of the Public Service Commission and is responsible to the minister of internal affairs.

The Prison Service operates 30 prisons, many of which are industrial and agricultural prisons. There are special prisons for long-term prisoners and those placed in preventive detention as "habitual criminals"—those convicted of a serious crime more than four times. Prisoners under the death sentence are confined in the Upper Prison at Murchison Bay in Kampala, where all executions are carried out.

In addition, there are local prisons or jails administered by the District Council administrations. Figures on the number of local prisons and their population are not available. Prison Service personnel are trained at the Prisons Training School.

UNION OF SOVIET SOCIALIST REPUBLICS

BASIC FACT SHEET

Official Name: Union of Soviet Socialist Republics
Area: 22,402,200 sq km
Population (1987): 284,008,160
Capital: Moscow
Nature of Government: Communist dictatorship
Languages: Russian and more than 200 other recognized languages
Currency: Ruble
GNP (1985): $1.96 trillion
Territorial Divisions: 15 union republics, 20 autonomous republics, 6 krays, 123 oblasts, 8 autonomous oblasts, 10 autonomous okrugs
Population per Police Officer: 1,050
Police Expenditures per Capita: N.A.

History & Background

The Soviet Union is a police state in the classical sense of the term. The police are entrenched in law as well as in the totalitarian philosophy of the Bolshevik regime. There are cycles of repression and thaw, but the underlying premise of Soviet law enforcement has not changed in the past 70 years: Law exists for the benefit of the state. No nation in modern times—including Nazi Germany—has perfected this theory and held on to it so successfully as the Soviet Union.

There are two agencies at the central government level responsible for internal security: the Ministry for Internal Affairs (Ministerstvo Vnutrennikh Del, MVD) and the Committee for State Security (Komitet Gosudarstvennoy Bezopasnosti, KGB). Both have ministerial status within the Council of Ministers. Although they are government agencies, they are under the direct and undisputed control of the Politburo of the Central Committee of the Communist Party of the Soviet Union.

The MVD appears to have had the major portion of the internal security mission and most of the routine functions related to a national police force. Since the KGB is the more powerful organization, it retains some specific internal security tasks, such as the investigation of major crimes and, particularly, those considered to be crimes against the state. In addition, all party and governmental institutions are infiltrated by the KGB.

Between the October Revolution of 1917 and World War II, internal security was maintained by the same police agencies that had responsibility for state security. After World War II, however, separate internal and state security ministries were created. The Soviet leaders have demanded not only an orderly but also a submissive social climate as the *sine qua non* of a socialist society in which they could perpetuate themselves in power. Police agencies are considered the key to the achievement of such a climate, and the leadership is continuously refining and fine-tuning the apparatus of terror that the security agencies represent. By all external standards the Soviets have by the mid-1980s managed to achieve an Orwellian society with little or no overt dissidence. The bulk of the population appears to be totally docile, and public manifestations of unrest are limited to juvenile delinquency, alcoholism and hooliganism—problems that the police are entirely capable of dealing with.

A third police agency is the Militia, corresponding to city and rural police forces in other countries. The Militia is subordinate to the MVD but is generally administered by local governments, whereas the MVD and the KGB are responsible through their own channels to the top-level authorities in Moscow. The Militia are concerned with local crimes, whereas the MVD and the KGB are interested in the preservation of the Bolshevik order.

In an effort to curb the worst abuses of the Stalinist era, numerous reforms were initiated by Stalin's successors. Extrajudicial police powers were curbed. Economic agencies under the MVD were transferred to other governmental ministries. Labor colony regimes were made less severe. The average Soviet citizen in the mid-1980s had less to fear from a sinister and unpredictable police system than had been the case in any period of modern Soviet history.

The Special Commission for the Fight Against Counterrevolution was established on December 4, 1917, less than four weeks after the Bolshevik Revolution. On December 20, 1917, it became the All-Russian Extraordinary Commission to Fight Counterrevolution, Sabotage and Speculation, but this long title was usually shortened to the Extraordinary Commission (Chrezvychaynaya Kommisiya, or Cheka). The Cheka's informal founding decree directed it to carry out preliminary investigations and to hand over saboteurs and counterrevolutionaries for trial by revolutionary tribunals. The Cheka was established by a decision of the Council of People's Commissars, but the council never agreed to a formal decree, and no legislative authority existed for it until 1924, two years after it was abolished. It had its forerunner in the secret police dating from Ivan the Terrible's 16th-century private Oprichnina and the secret police organization of the Romanovs, the Okhrana, which operated between 1881 and 1917. Cheka's stated mission was to punish "spies, traitors, plotters, bandits, speculators, profiteers, counterfeiters, arsonists, hooligans, agitators, saboteurs, class enemies and other parasites"—in short, anyone who was not a Bolshevik.

The Cheka rapidly became bolder in its operations. In February 1918 it performed its first execution without trial. It established its own courts in April and was then able to arrest, try and sentence without restraint. By August of that year, after Lenin had been seriously wounded by a would-be assassin, the Cheka no longer confined its actions to legitimate suspects. The nearly 400 provincial and district Chekas were directed to take hostages from the bourgeoisie and former Army officers and execute them. This initiated the period known as the Red Terror. The Cheka also could send suspects to concentration camps by simple administrative decisions without trial. When trials were conducted, decisions were reached without any reference to the laws; the accused were not necessarily present and probably had already been executed. There was no defense and no appeal.

The terror that the Cheka struck into the people caused many to calculate that it had executed hundreds of thousands. The actual figure was more likely about 50,000. The figures usually quoted of 1 million or more deaths attributed to the Cheka included civilian casualties in the 1917–22 civil war.

Revulsion against the excess of the Red Terror caused the Cheka to be abolished in February 1922. The State Political Administration (Gosudarstvennoye Politicheskoye Upravleniye, GPU), which succeeded the Cheka, was placed under the People's Commissariat of Internal Affairs (Narodnyy Komisariat Vnutrennikh Del, NKVD). With the formation of the Union of Soviet Socialist Republics, the GPU was removed from subordination to the NKVD, made a separate people's commissariat and renamed the Unified State Political Administration (Ob'edinyonnoye Gosudarstvennoye Politicheskoye Upravleniye, OGPU). These changes were purely cosmetic, since Felix Dzerzhinsky, the notorious head and founder of the Cheka, also was the head of the NKVD, the GPU and the OGPU. As such, until his death in 1926, he headed both the police apparatus and the ministry-level agency that controlled it.

The 1922–28 period was a time of consolidation, with some respite from the earlier horrors. The OGPU was as much an extralegal organization as the Cheka, but its efforts were directed mainly at criminals and active political deviationists rather than ordinary citizens. Prisons were filled to their capacity of some 300,000, but the labor camp population probably was as low as 30,000.

Lenin died in 1924. With Stalin in power the OGPU began a sweep of the nobility, clergy, bourgeoisie, landowners, former White Army officers and White Guards, peasants who withheld produce, Mensheviks and others. With the Five-Year Plan, the OGPU became responsible for the confiscation and nationalization of over 400,000 privately owned shops and small business enterprises that had been allowed to exist until then. Owners who resisted or stalled were imprisoned and deported to labor camps. In 1929 the OGPU became the chief agency for enforcing the collectivization of agricultural lands. The approximately 1 million independent farmers, or *kulaki*, were uprooted en masse. The OGPU readopted Cheka practices of meting out long terms of imprisonment and death sentences without trial. During the late 1920s and early 1930s, a more general purge was directed toward the intelligentsia, managers and engineers in the industrial sector. Managers were particularly vulnerable because they could be held responsible for the failings of their subordinates. Political crimes were expanded to include not only the commission of punishable acts but also the failure to prevent or report them. Punishment was meted out to those accused of contemplating crime or political deviation.

In 1934 the OGPU suffered the fate of the Cheka and the GPU and was absorbed into the NKVD. In the legislation surrounding this transfer it appeared that the NKVD was subject to more legal restraint than its predecessors. Administrative deportation, exiles and sentences to labor camps were restricted to five years. Death sentences were restricted to military tribunals. Furthermore, in 1933 the office of the procurator general had been established; it was charged with monitoring the legality of security police actions. The NKVD began to assume more administrative functions, such as maintaining population statistics, and administering roads, automobile transport, survey and cartographic work, forest conservation, and weights and measures. These tasks expanded the scope of NKVD control over the population.

Having destroyed the dangerous elements in the industrial sector, among the intelligentsia and in the rural population, Stalin now turned his attention to the party, seeking to remove all potential challengers to his power. The repression culminated between 1936 and 1938 in the period known as the Great Purge or the Great Terror.

The purge was sparked initially by the assassination of Sergei Kirov, a Politburo member, head of the Leningrad Communist Party organization and a Stalin henchman. There is conjecture as to whether Stalin himself had instigated the murder, in which case Kirov was the first of the purged. In the first phase of the purge, the party rolls were screened and membership reduced from 2.8 million to about 2 million. The worst of the purge occurred between September 1936 and July 1938 when N. I. Yezhov, who had replaced G. Yagoda, was head of the NKVD. Known as Yezhovshchina (the Yezhov Period), it eliminated as much as 90% of the senior military officers and a majority of the Central Committee. The purge of Communist Party members was so thorough that less than 2% of the delegates to the 18th Congress, held in 1939, had attended the 17th Congress five years earlier.

Having achieved his goals, Stalin disavowed the destruction of the party and turned the purge on the purgers. Yezhov followed Yagoda to the executioner. Prisoners were joined in their cells by NKVD agents who had arrested and interrogated them earlier.

The purge had eliminated all of the active Bolshevik Old Guard and finally those purgers who knew the planning behind, and the extent of, the carnage. The population was reduced to obedience, apathy and silence. The labor camp population continued to increase, the new arrivals being Polish, Volga Germans, Chechens, Balkars, Crimean Tartars, Kalmyks, Karachy, ethnic groups from Baltic states and German prisoners of war. The last large group of deportees consisted of nearly 600,000 rural Baltic peoples who resisted the collectivization of their farmlands in the 1948–49 period.

The People's Commissariat of State Security (Narodnyy Komisariat Gosudarstvennoy Bezopasnosti, NKGB) was created in 1941, and state security was for the first time divorced from the NKVD. With the German attack on the Soviet Union in June 1941, the old organization was temporarily reinstated, but the separation was again made in 1943. In 1946 the NKVD was redesignated the MVD in the reorganization of the government in which former people's commissariats became ministries. The MVD almost immediately went into decline. In 1949 the state security agency that had been created during World War II and redesignated the Ministry of State Security (Ministerstvo Gosudarstvennoy Bezopasnosti, MGB) in 1946 had taken over all of the more important MVD functions.

The MGB remained dominant until about 1953. In the power struggle that followed Stalin's death, Lavrenti P. Beria used the MVD as a power base. As a result, the MVD absorbed the MGB and for a short time again became the only agency exercising both internal and state security functions. After Beria's execution, the state security organization emerged in March 1954 as the KGB and rapidly regained its pre-1953 position relative to the MVD. The MVD was gradually reduced in status until, in 1960, the central MVD was abolished and all of its functions were delegated to the union republic governments. From

EVOLUTION OF THE SOVIET POLICE SYSTEM

Date	State Security	Combined	Internal Security
1917–22		Cheka	
1922–23		GPU	
1923–34		OGPU	
1934–41		NKVD	
1941	NKGB		NKVD
1942–43		NKVD	
1946–53	MGB		MVD
1953		MVD	
1954–60	KGB		MVD
1960–68		KGB	
1966–68	KGB		MOOP
1968–	KGB		MVD

1962 to 1968 the MVD's were known as Ministries for the Preservation of Public Order (MOOP).

Considered in relation to the size of the Soviet population and the length of near total police control, the Soviet police system has not had a parallel in modern history. The major innovations of Lenin and Stalin and their main contributions to police science are the deliberate use of terror as an instrument of law enforcement and the branding of any deviation from Bolshevik principles as a heinous crime.

Under both Lenin and Stalin extrajudicial police tribunals had the authority to sentence political suspects without the nuisance of a legal proceeding. After the Cheka period the two most nefarious police courts were the military tribunals and the Special Board. The military tribunals, despite their name, handled civilian offenses as well, especially those arising from disclosure of state secrets, evasion of conscription and noncompliance with martial law regulations. During peacetime, these tribunals were used in areas under martial law or where large-scale police activities, such as mass deportations, were under way.

The Special Board was established in 1934. No defense was admitted, nor was the accused necessarily present during the trial. The sentence was based on police recommendation forwarded with the evidence. The Special Board was dissolved in September 1953 as one of the most hated relics of the Stalinist regime.

To control population mobility, a system of internal passports was introduced in 1932, and it greatly enhanced the power of the security agencies. Collective and state farmers did not receive passports and thus were barred from cities except on permitted visits, when they were required to register with the Militia and to carry certificates showing the purpose of their visits. The system also made it possible to exile any individual forcibly to another area, to prevent prisoners from returning to their homes after their release and to compile statistics. Labor booklets were issued to workers in state industries. These booklets were retained by the management and returned only when the employment was terminated. Until 1956 a worker could not quit without his employer's permission.

There was a renewed emphasis on police control of internal travel in the 1960s.

Beginning with Cheka, all security organizations have been structurally built into the governmental system. They are separate from the Party, although subject to the Party's policy decisions. At the highest organizational level, both the MVD and the KGB are responsible to the Council of Ministers and, technically, to the Supreme Soviet. Each union republic has a KGB and an MVD, responsible, at least administratively, to the Council of Ministers of that republic. The KGB, with more of its functions relating to national concerns, has little if any substantive subordination to local governments. The opposite is perhaps true of the MVD. MVD operations are also more restricted by law to the procedural controls of the procuracy. Such constraints are less effective in the case of the KGB. Thus, despite some overlapping of functions between the two, the KGB is the more powerful of the Soviet security agencies.

Structure & Organization

The Committee for State Security (KGB)

The KGB is a state committee, which is a ministry equivalent, under the Council of Ministers of the USSR. The chairman of the KGB is one of the core members of the Council of Ministers. All KGB heads since 1958 have been party functionaries and members of the Central Committee of the Communist Party. Yuri Andropov, who took over the KGB in 1967, became the first to reach the General Secretaryship of the Party.

The organizational structure of the KGB is subject to change; new sections are constanty being created and old ones are either abolished or given new titles. In any case, details about its operations or personnel are never made public and must be pieced together from unofficial sources.

The KGB's major subdivisions are called administrations or directorates. There are four chief directorates, four directorates and six independent departments:

First Chief Directorate	Foreign Operations. Divided into 10 regional departments:
	First: U.S.A. and Canada
	Second: Latin America
	Third: United Kingdom, Australia, New Zealand and Scandinavia
	Fourth: West Germany and Austria
	Fifth: Benelux, Ireland, Italy, Portugal and Spain
	Sixth: China, Vietnam and South Korea
	Seventh: India, Indonesia, Japan and Philippines
	Eighth: Albania, Greece, Yugoslavia, Turkey and the Middle East
	Ninth: English-speaking African countries
	10th: French-speaking African countries

Second Chief Directorate	Internal security; 12 departments
Fifth Chief Directorate	Dissident activity
Chief Directorate of Border Guards	
Third Directorate	Armed forces; 12 departments
Seventh Directorate	Surveillance
Eighth Directorate	Communications and intelligence
Ninth Directorate	Physical protection of government and party leader

Departments include Finance, Operational Experience Processing, Physical Security, Registry and Archives, Special Investigations, and State Communications. Other administrations include collection of economic data. The administration of special sections operates with Soviet troops abroad. The Mobile Group for Special Operations handles sensitive and clandestine projects. This group maintains a vast Central Index of Biographical Data, containing dossiers of all major Soviet and foreign personalities. The KGB is especially active in East European and Third World countries, locating vulnerable areas to infiltrate.

There are local KGB's in each of the union republic governments and smaller ones at lower government levels—in the armed forces; in industrial, economic, trade and scientific organizations; in government administrative branches; in Communist Party organs; and in labor camps, prisons and local militia. All KGB units report directly to Moscow. In the Army, for example, KGB personnel have communications channels to which the military commander has no access. The personnel strength of KGB is never divulged and is difficult even to estimate because many of its members are in clandestine operations.

Less known of the KGB functional units are the Economic Administration, the State Construction Trust, the Secret Political Administration, the Road and Transport Administration, and the Main Administration of Prisons. The Economic Administration maintains surveillance over the management of government industrial enterprises. The State Construction Trust uses manpower in the Corrective Labor Colonies. The Main Administration of Prisons has its own special places of detention and interrogation.

The Ministry of Internal Affairs (MVD)

Except for the three or four years before 1953 and approximately 10 years after about 1957, the MVD has had most of the responsibility for internal security. Its principal elements include the security police, the Internal Troops, special units in the regular armed forces, the labor camps, a portion of the prisons and certain courts. Operational directorates comprise Internal Troops, Militia, Economy, Corrective Labor Colonies, Places of Detention, Local Air Defense, Fire Protection, Geodesy and Cartography, and State Archives. Guard Troops, Railway Troops and Convey Troops sometimes are considered part of Internal Troops and other times as separate units.

The largest MVD organization is Internal Troops, with main administration headquarters in Moscow and local agencies in the union republics and possibly in smaller territorial divisions. The other directorates not only have branches in the union republic and lower-level governments but also perform most of their operations at those levels and are subordinate in varying degrees to local authorities.

Internal Troops were first identified as a separate entity in 1923, when they were part of the OGPU. Before that time there were Cheka units of Special Purpose and GPU Guard Troops dating back to 1920. These units probably were small and attached within the regular Red Army establishment. MVD Troops are uniquely subordinate both to the Moscow headquarters and to the local authorities. Units are stationed in or near large towns. They are divided into Guard Troops, Railway Troops, Convoy Troops and Troops of Special Purpose. The last are fully equipped units of up to division size. In addition, there are forces variously known as Units of Special Designation, Special Troops or Troops of Special Purpose who are elite units guarding the Kremlin and the more important civil and military installations. They operate normally in small groups but can assemble into sizable military formations.

Internal Troops are recruited during the annual military conscription. Screening at induction ensures the political reliability of the recruits. Persons skilled in communications and mechanics are preferred. The tour of duty is two years, as in the armed forces.

The Border Troops

The Border Troops, an administrative unit of the KGB, is responsible for guarding the Soviet Union's 37,000-mile-long frontier. The frontier zones are of unspecified depth, varying with the topography and the degree of hostility or friendliness of the neighboring state. Admittance into this area is restricted and controlled by local militia, which share authority with the Border Troops within the zone. There are additional and stricter controls in the narrower frontier strip where the Border Troops have complete control.

The frontier strip is up to 1.5 miles wide and, along the borders where crossings are prohibited, contains special barriers. Inside the border fence there is a strip that is kept freshly plowed so that footprints would be readily noticeable. A second strip is patrolled by armed guards with dogs. It is kept floodlighted and equipped with rows of barbed wire, traps, automatically firing weapons or land mines. Observation posts may be visible or concealed.

The Border Troops control the entry and exit of people, currency, literature and goods in border zones. They enforce quarantine in case of an epidemic disease, man guard posts, construct and maintain barriers and lights on the border strip, and conduct raids, checks and searches. Along the land frontier they are responsible for collecting topographical and military information from a zone extending 30 miles from the border either with the help of clandestine agents or through electronic devices. The majority of the Border Troops are ground forces, referred to as the Land Border Troops. There are smaller Aviation Border Regiments and units of the Maritime Border Troops. In normal peacetime situations, border units try to foster good relations with the local population, assisting them in harvests, local construction projects, transportation services and emergency situations.

Although border patrol is a hardship post, the Border Troops receive the best food rations in the Army and pay that exceeds that of the regular services. Leave accrues at two days per month, but normally long absences are not permitted. The daily schedule comprises three hours of work. However, during emergencies duty hours may reach 16 hours a day, as most units are frequently below authorized personnel strength. The frontier is guarded 24 hours a day, every day of the year, regardless of the weather.

Noncommissioned officers usually are selected from those who appear most promising during basic training. They receive up to 10 months of additional training and then are required to serve an additional year of mandatory duty. Officers ordinarily are the products of the regular military cadet academies and officers' candidate schools. They have 25-year service obligations, which may be discharged either entirely within the Border Troops or rotating among the other services. The Frunze Military Academy, which is a command and staff college equivalent, offers a special one-year extension to Border Troops at the end of its three-year midcareer course. The Higher Border Officers School is part of the Border Troops organization and offers a variety of courses, most of them tactical. Rank designations in the Border Troops are the same as in the Soviet Army. With proper career progression an officer is promoted from junior lieutenant to colonel in 17 years. The normal retirement age is 55. Outstanding Border Troops officers are given a number of awards and decorations, including the Badge of the Honorable Chekist, Combat Services Award and the Order of Lenin.

The Militia

The Soviet Militia (Militsiya) corresponds approximately to the uniformed police organizations of other countries. Originally subordinated to the NKVD, it later was made subordinate to the republic governments and local soviets as well. Except for a short period between 1949 and 1953, when it was brought under state security, control of the Militia always has been vested in the internal security organization. Administratively, the commander of the Militia reports to the MVD.

The Militia is concerned solely with local law enforcement. It has powers of search, arrest, detention and pursuit. Although it has authority to conduct criminal investigations, those relegated to the militia probably are the least important. Militia members are armed, but the circumstances in which they can use their weapons are specified. It has wide controls over traffic and motor vehicle operation, and it administers the internal passport or visa system. Its other miscellaneous functions are varied; it enforces a variety of regulations concerning firearms, printing appliances, poisons, radioactive materials, photography, and licenses and permits. It maintains address information and traces missing persons and draft evaders. It maintains contacts with resident aliens and foreigners. It supervises crowds in public places and during parades.

A large portion of the officers and noncommissioned officers are products of the Militia schools. Salaries are not large, but privileges such as guaranteed housing at reduced rents increase the attraction of Militia work.

The uniform jacket, trousers, cap and tie are navy blue; the shirt is blue poplin and the trousers have red piping; cap insignia and banding also are red. For winter there is a heavy overcoat or cloak, and for extreme weather a sheepskin coat.

In the villages and some rural areas, the entire population over 18 years of age is required to assist the Militia for three months each year. Other such groups are formed on collective farms and in industrial plants and educational institutions. They are variously referred to as People's Voluntary Militia, Public Order Detachments and People's Squads. Their subordination usually is to the local Party organization, indicating that their purpose is primarily political rather than strictly law enforcement. The organizations are collectively referred to as local volunteer forces, although participation is anything but voluntary.

These groups augment the Militia on occasions when it needs more manpower. They also act as police informers. Much of their work is intended to be of a preventive or persuasive nature. Estimates of the number of people who are members of these groups run as high as 6 million.

Recruitment, Education & Training

The KGB

KGB agents are carefully selected and trained in the 200 Chekist, or security police, schools. Komsomol and Party members are preferred, but all candidates are subject to continuous surveillance. Some 20 schools train agents for work abroad. The basic curriculum is two to four years and includes police work, indoctrination and physical conditioning, such as wrestling, judo and boxing. Technical subjects include photography, chemistry and laboratory work. Specialized training involves languages, interrogation and investigation techniques, crowd control, insurgency and propaganda. Whereas individuals with no family attachments are preferred for internal security work, married men are preferred as foreign agents, since wife and children can be held as virtual hostages for their good conduct abroad. Foreign agents receive only living expenses and allowances, and the bulk of their salary is withheld in Moscow. A substantial number of KGB agents are recruited abroad through various Communist or front organizations. KGB personnel also constitute a sizable portion of Soviet embassy personnel at every post. These include technical and economic specialists who are trained to gather vital information on energy programs, military installations and new industrial techniques.

The MVD

Recruitment of agents and operatives is done individually through recruiters placed in universities, trade schools, military units, government offices, trade unions, factories, cooperatives, and state and collective farms. After the recruiters recommend an individual, a preliminary check is made for family and political background. Individuals with no family ties receive favorable consideration. If the initial check is positive, the individual is kept under careful observation for a period, then called before a selection committee. If approved by this committee, he is sent to one of 200 Chekist schools for a training program running from two to four years.

Basic training features individual combat techniques and small-unit tactical exercises. These cover counterinsurgency tactics, riot control, techniques for conducting raids and area searches, inspection of documents, investigation and arresting procedures, and methods for safeguarding sensitive and large installations. In subsequent training it is usual for Troops of Special Purpose to engage in large-scale division-size maneuvers and for Convoy and Guard troops to participate in battalion- and regiment-size exercises. Political indoctrination is not left out, and still claims 25% of training time. Noncommissioned officers usually are selected at induction or during early basic training. These men receive up to a year of added training and are required to serve a year longer than the usual mandatory tour of duty. Officers usually are Army career men who could rotate in and out of the Internal Troops or serve within them for their entire careers.

Border Troops

The Border Troops are recruited from those called annually for compulsory military service. Since they are required to serve alone or in small groups and use sound judgment in the review of passports, identification papers and credentials, they are generally selected more carefully from among the better-educated candidates.

Early training is similar to that in the Army. If the conscript has had premilitary training he gets two to four months of basic training with his unit. He also receives special training equipping him to work in remote areas. This training includes medical and veterinary instruction, disease control, care of frostbite, quarantine, personal hygiene, radioactivity decontamination, maintenance of equipment, map-reading, cooking, baking, tailoring, shoe repairing, vehicle operating and dog handling. A typical monthly program may include 64 hours of training, of which political instruction accounts for nearly a third.

The Militia

Militiamen are volunteers who agree to serve a minimum two-year tour of duty. The rank and file include a high percentage of men released from the armed forces or security forces.

The Penal System

The Soviet Penal Code was enacted in 1922, soon after the establishment of the Union of Soviet Socialist Republics. Among its major innovations was the introduction of crime by analogy. According to this principle, a judge who considered an individual socially dangerous could convict him or her of a crime even though the accused had violated no specific provision of the Criminal Code. It was sufficient for a judge to find that the act of the accused closely resembled a crime specified in the code. The doctrine was also applicable vice versa: the perpetrator of an act specifically defined as a crime in the code may not be punished if the judge found him or her not socially dangerous. This provision opened the door wide to abuse of judicial power until it was materially amended in 1958.

A crime is defined in the Soviet Union as a "socially dangerous act," and a punishment as "a measure taken in social defense." Soviet jurisprudence considers crime as a protest against the social system. Since the Communist system is the ultimate political ideal in Soviet thinking, there is a continuing effort to gloss away crime as inspired by foreign agents or as a residue of the old society that requires time to be eradicated. Soviet jurisprudence, however, does make a distinction between political and criminal offenses. Between 1936 and 1950 politicals outnumbered criminals in the labor camps by a ratio of five to one. This ratio has probably been reversed.

The death sentence has become rare since the 1950s. Besides imprisonment and fines, there are three types of unusual sentences: corrective labor, banishment and exile. Corrective labor sentences are handed down most frequently in cases where an individual's work, working habits or attitudes are unsatisfactory. The sentence involves mandatory performance of "socially useful work" under close supervision and in the convicted person's usual place of work. Such work is not recorded on labor records, does not apply toward pay raises and does not add to vacation time.

Under a sentence of banishment, a person is sent away from his or her place of residence for a specified time. The court determines the size of the local banishment area and adds other prohibited places. The typical sentence is "USSR minus six," meaning exclusion from home area and the six largest Soviet cities. The person may also be restricted from places where work and housing are scarce. Other than as prohibited, the person chooses his or her new residence. Local soviets in the area assist the person to find employment.

Exile is banishment *to* a specified area. This is as severe a punishment as imprisonment at a labor colony, because in most cases the place of exile is a labor colony in Siberia. In all exile sentences, regulations prescribe socially useful work in the job provided by the local soviet in the district to which a person is exiled. Generally, those banished or exiled fall into the category of persons officially described as "parasites."

Soviet penal institutions fall into three categories: prisons, corrective labor colonies and educational labor colonies. Most prisons are designed to detain arrested persons for interrogation before trial rather than to house inmates. Total prison capacity is estimated at 300,000, but during the great Stalinist purges the prison population considerably exceeded that figure. Conditions in prisons vary. A few in Moscow are as clean as first-class hotels and often are shown

on conducted tours for visiting penologists. In the better ones convicts get a bath with soap every 10 days. Others, particularly in the rural areas, are much less satisfactory. As a general rule, however, prisoners get good medical attention, and epidemics of communicable diseases are rare. To prevent suicides, stairwells have nets, shaving is done with clippers and hunger strikers are force-fed. Food is plain and uninteresting and is given out in bare subsistence quantities. Prisoners generally emerge from prison emaciated, but lack of exercise and insufficient exposure to sunlight generally contribute more to their deterioration than does inadequate food.

Generally, prisoners are segregated by categories: men from women, juveniles from adults, first offenders from recidivists. Dangerous criminals and those awaiting death sentences are isolated from other inmates.

Prison mail is censored, and packages, cells and persons are searched. Until a prisoner has demonstrated good behavior, he or she can receive no parcels and is limited to two visits of up to four hours each per year. The prisoner may receive an unlimited amount of mail and may send one letter per month. Complaints to prosecutors and other specified government officials are not included in the limitations on correspondence.

A stricter regimen is provided for second offenders and as a punitive measure short of solitary confinement for uncooperative inmates. This regimen is so rigorous that it is limited to two to six months at a time. Exercise periods are cut from one hour to one-half hour per day, no visitors are allowed, and only one letter may be sent out every two months. Prisoners in disciplinary cells or solitary confinement are deprived of their warmer clothing and have no furniture or beds. Exercise periods are reduced by half, and the food ration is cut between one-half and two-thirds of the standard. Persons held in preventive detention must be released within 72 hours, although this period can be extended to 30 days in extreme cases.

Labor colonies are the invention of Felix Dzerzhinsky, the first Cheka head. The earliest camps frequently were referred to in official publications as forced labor, concentration, or corrective labor camps or corrective labor colonies. After the 1930s it became customary to call them corrective labor camps or colonies only. After 1957 the term "camp" was dropped altogether. The existing colonies were divided into five categories, their regimes varying in severity. Those with the most severe regimes were called punitive colonies.

Between 1930 and 1950 the labor camps were an important element in the national economy. Dzerzhinsky almost certainly had had little in mind beyond trying to get something useful from his prisoners to apply against the cost of keeping them alive. By Stalin's time, with a labor camp population of 7 to 10 million, many of them competent managers and engineers, it became obvious that they represented a sizable and effective labor force in its own right. From that time until nearly the end of the Stalin era, camps played an important role in the building of canals, railways and hydroelectric plants as well as in mining and forestry. After Stalin's death, a number of factors caused penal policymakers to discontinue the use of forced labor. A succession of amnesties between 1954 and 1957 reduced camp populations from the high World War II totals to a fraction. Soviet penal philosophy also changed to rehabilitation of prisoners and their return to society as useful members. According to new legislation enacted in 1969, adults go to corrective labor colonies and minors under 18 to educational labor colonies, where they undergo political indoctrination and vocational training.

Corrective labor colonies for adults fall into five categories: standard, intensified, strict, special and colony settlements. The court sentence specifies the appropriate regime for each convict. A regime change can occur as the sentence is being served, either as a reward or as a punishment. One camp complex usually contains colonies with several different regimes. In all regimes except the colony settlements, prisoners are segregated according to the same principles that apply to prisons.

Ordinarily, the standard regime is for first offenders charged with less serious crimes. Prisoners work an eight-hour day with six days in a workweek, except on holidays. There are no vacations and no other privileges. Vocational and general educational training are scheduled in addition to the regular workday. Pay and work conditions conform to national norms. By regulation, 10% of earned wages after various deductions goes into the prisoner's account, from which he or she may spend up to 15 rubles per month. The prisoner may have five visits a year, including three short visits of up to four hours each and two long visits of up to 72 hours each. Long visits may be made by close relatives only and include the right of cohabitation with a spouse. A prisoner can have unlimited correspondence but cannot receive parcels until he or she has served one-half of the sentence. The limit then is three per year. All mail is censored except complaints or official requests that a prisoner may send to his court or other authorities.

Good behavior is rewarded by a variety of incentives, ranging from permission to have extra visitors to pay bonuses, transfer to a colony with an easier regime or commutation of part of the sentence. After a portion of a sentence has been served, a cooperative prisoner may work outside the colony unguarded.

First offenders convicted of grave crimes go to colonies with intensified regimes. Second offenders and those guilty of dangerous state crimes are sent to colonies with strict regimes. Women are sentenced to colonies with standard and strict regimes only. Special regime colonies are for dangerous recidivists and those serving commuted death sentences. Living conditions deteriorate progressively as the regime grades become more severe. For example, correspondence is unrestricted in the standard regime, limited to three letters a month in the intensified, two a month in the strict and one a month in the special. Visiting privileges decrease similarly to one short visit and one long visit annually in the special regime.

Colony settlements constitute a halfway house program for prisoners who have completed a required portion of the sentence and have demonstrated good behavior and a cooperative attitude. Supervision is minimal, and movement within the compound is unrestricted in daytime. Prisoners may work outside unsupervised, wear civilian clothes and retain money, valuables and personal possessions. They have unrestricted visiting and correspondence privileges, and if facilities are available they may live with their families in the colony.

Living conditions in the camps have improved considerably since the Stalinist era, when the annual average camp death rates reached a high of 30%. Nevertheless, even during the worst years, treatment of prisoners, although deplorable by Western standards, seldom if ever was sadistic. Shortages of food, shelter and fuel took a heavy toll of camp inmates, but few former prisoners complain of brutal or inhumane treatment at the hands of the camp guards.

Educational labor colonies for minors under 18 feature more tolerable regimes, additional privileges, and considerably greater emphasis on rehabilitation and education. General education is programmed to continue from the level reached by the inmate in his or her earlier schooling in addition to vocational courses intended to give the inmate a usable technical skill upon release. The penal regime comprises five parts: socially useful labor, general education, technical or vocational training, political and social indoctrination, and a penal regime. There are only two categories of educational labor colonies—standard and intensified—and girls are committed to the former only, where they are separated from boys. All inmates who turn 18 in the middle of their sentence may stay for up to two more years in the colony but must transfer to adult colonies at 20. Labor is performed under general labor legislation codes, and 45% of wages go into the personal accounts of the inmates.

Conditions in the two regimes generally parallel those of the same names in corrective labor colonies, but each has somewhat more privileges than its adult colony counterpart. In the standard regime, for example, youths may receive about twice as many parcels and may have more than double the visits. Correspondence is unlimited, except that inmates must have permission to write persons other than their relatives. All mail, except outgoing correspondence to court and governmental authorities, is censored. After six months of good behavior, the young people may work unguarded outside the colony and may go and come unescorted.

The intensified regime for boys who have committed grave crimes, or who are second offenders, allows fewer privileges and has a more severe penal regime, except for unrestricted correspondence and a lenient parcels privilege.

Good behavior is rewarded with extra privileges. On the other hand, uncooperative inmates are put into isolation rooms with no visitors or parcels, and a reduced food ration that cannot be supplemented with purchases from prisoner accounts.

UNITED KINGDOM

T. G. Lamford

BASIC FACT SHEET

Official Name: United Kingdom of Great Britain and Northern Ireland
Area: 243,977 sq km
Population (1987): 56,845,195
Capital: London
Nature of Government: Constitutional monarchy
Language: English
Currency: Pound sterling
GNP (1986): $504.85 billion
Territorial Divisions: 54 counties in England and Wales; 12 regions in Scotland; 26 districts in Northern Ireland
Population per Police Officer: 414
Police Expenditures per 1,000: $79,281

History & Background

The development of the "New Police"—that is, the modern common law police as an industrial-urban phenomenon—can be claimed, with some justification, to have taken place in London in 1829. The real catalyst was the industrial revolution. The introduction of a professional police force in London was important not only for Britain; it was followed elsewhere: Philadelphia in 1833, Boston in 1838 and New York in 1844. Today it forms the basis of much modern policing, worldwide.

There are two main stages in the history of the police in England and Wales between the Anglo-Saxon period and the 19th century, when the first statutory police forces were created. From very early times, and certainly from the time of Alfred the Great (A.D. 871–99), the primary responsibility for maintaining the king's peace fell upon each locality under a system of collective security. The most serious problem in those days was to discover and punish those evildoers whose deeds struck at the roots of an orderly society. Every freeman (a term that encompassed every male over 12 years), unless excused by high social position or property, was enrolled for police purposes in a group of about 10 families, known as a "tything," headed by a tything man. If a member of the group committed a crime, the others had to produce him for trial; if they failed, they could be fined or had to make compensation. In essence the system relied on the principle that all members of the community accepted an obligation for the good be-havior of each other. Groups of tythings formed "hundreds," and overall the shire reeve or sheriff had a general responsibility under the king for preserving the peace in the shire. He was able to muster the *posse comitatus,* the whole available civil force of the shire, in case of emergency. All members of the community were also obliged to join in pursuit of a felon by means of "hue and cry."

These simple arrangements were taken over by the Normans (the Norman French word "county" being the equivalent of the Anglo-Saxon "shire") and modified and systematized under the designation "Frankpledge," the most important police institution of the Middle Ages, "a system of compulsory collective bail fixed for individuals, not after their arrest for crime, but as a safeguard in anticipation of it."

Under the feudalism of the Normans, the unit of responsibility became not the tything but the manor, and about a century after the Norman Conquest we find a person designated by the title "constable" taking over the tythingman's duties. The English parish constable of the Middle Ages emerges as the direct lineal descendant of the ancient tythingman.

The next important development was the Statute of Winchester in 1285. This was a consolidating measure codifying and preserving the well-tried features of local responsibility for policing a district, and embodying three features of the greatest importance:

1. It introduced a system of town watchmen—watch and ward—to support the traditional duties of the consta-

ble, and there emerges for the first time a distinction between town and rural policing.

2. The system of hue and cry was revived as a means of dealing with strangers who resisted arrest by the watchmen. In effect, the fugitive was to be pursued by the whole population—work had to be laid aside if the offender was not caught red-handed, and anyone who failed to respond to the call was deemed to be siding with the felon and was himself hunted down.

3. Everyone was obliged to keep arms with which to follow the cry when required, the extent of his commitment being in accordance with his station in life, a brilliant anticipator of the classical taxation theory that, to be nonregressive, there should be equality of sacrifice rather than the equality of contribution.

The first stage lasted until the 14th century; during that time the constable, as the executive agent and representative of the village or township, was the local keeper of the peace, exercising his powers under common law as a person paid to perform, as a matter of duty, acts that if he were so minded he might have done voluntarily.

During the second stage, from the 14th until the early 19th centuries, the constable was subordinate to the justice of the peace. The justices, who were technically officers under the crown but who were not wholly subordinate to it, were given local responsibility for exercising the ancient prerogative of maintaining the king's peace. Thus they became the superior, while the constables became the inferior, conservators of law and order. In Scotland, the principle that each locality should be responsible for its own good order probably was established as long ago as it was in England and Wales. The office of constable, however, is neither so old nor so deeply rooted in tradition there. The office of justice of the peace also was imported from England, but the most important local judge in Scotland always has been the sheriff, who retained his powers to give orders to the police. Before the 19th century, then, Britain had no organized police system, and the Statute of Winchester in 1285 was the only general public measure of any consequence passed to regulate the policing of the country from the Norman Conquest in 1066 until the Metropolitan Police Act in 1829.

In Wales and in England outside London, the local manorial courts, and subsequently the justices, appointed a constable or constables for each town and rural parish, and these constables invariably appointed a deputy of low degree to act for them. Wealthy merchants and farmers were unwilling to engage in the time-consuming and dangerous policing activities, so they paid others to take their place. Any man who could afford to bought a substitute, and policing came to be left on a more or less permanent basis to those "of inferior origin, that is, those whose antecedents and qualifications preclude them from more lucrative or reputable employment. These . . . were for the most part infirm from age and starvation, drunken. . . . They were the subject of considerable amusement, but for the prevention of crime, they were worse than useless.''

In London, the appointment of the police in the boroughs was vested in a variety of municipal, parish and ad hoc authorities, and the forces thus formed took their orders from the bodies that appointed them. In individual cases, magistrates themselves organized and paid full-time bands of constables. Among these special forces were the famous Bow Street Runners, for which the home secretary eventually became responsible, but which were first established by Henry Fielding and his blind half brother, John, when they were known as ''Mr. Fielding's men.'' These arrangements, which worked reasonably well in predominantly rural communities, proved inadequate when it came to dealing with the consequences of the industrial revolution in the 18th and 19th centuries. However, successive governments tried to combat the increasing lawlessness that resulted from the rapid growth of population, and the equally rapid and unregulated growth of towns, mainly by increasing the severity of the Penal Code. The Royal Commission on the Police in 1962 commented, ''Parliament seems to have feared less the visible dangers of insecurity . . . than the threat to liberty which it saw in an effective police force.'' Public sentiment was strongly opposed to the idea of a police, ''for across the Channel there were well-patrolled, secure cities, epitomized in the Paris of the *ancien régime:* But to the 18th-century Englishman it seemed that the price of such security was too high, involving arbitrary arrest, imprisonment without trial, the compilation of dossiers by police spies and the existence of numerous armed forces on which the government could rely.'' Even after the French Revolution, the Committee of Public Safety, succeeded by the sinister shadow cast by Fouché, minister of police, certainly did nothing to allay British fears. The gendarme and the spy were not for England.

However, mob violence increased, as did the use of the Army to control it. This was shown to be entirely inappropriate in an incident at Manchester that became known as the ''Peterloo'' massacre. (Peterloo in a scurrilous, and satirical comparison with Waterloo, the great military victory over Napoleon.) This occurred in 1819, when troops charged a peaceful crowd gathered to hear a speech in St. Peter's Fields. Eleven persons were killed and hundreds injured. ''For the first time, popular reaction against the exclusive use of troops for dealing with disorder was voiced by all classes. . . . Other means of enforcing the law must be found. Police were the only alternative.'' But by 1822, another of the interminable parliamentary committees that looked into the problems of the time found it possible to report, ''It is difficult to reconcile an effective system of police with that perfect freedom of action and exemption from interference which are the great privileges and blessings of society in this country.''

By 1829, however, the duke of Wellington, who was prime minister, was unsure how far he could rely on potentially mutinous troops to deal with public disorder, so he lent his immense prestige to his home secretary's efforts to get the Metropolitan Police Act through Parliament. The home secretary was the extremely able politician Robert Peel, who, with consummate skill, established the world's first modern common law police force. The threat of unbridled public disorder, rather than the level of crime, was the catalyst for change.

The claim that today's British police constable is a direct descendant of the medievcl constable who held independent office, not subject to superior control, has been severely castigated by Professor Goodhart in a dissent to the Royal Commission on the Police Report in 1962. This view ignores, says Goodhart, the revolutionary character of the 1829 legislation, and the claim to have the honor of having the parish constable as an ancestor seems an odd ambition, since his contemporaries had nothing but evil to speak of him. Goodhart quotes Blackstone that ''Of the extent of which powers, considering what manner of men are for the most part put upon these offices, it is perhaps very well that they are generally kept in ignorance.'' It is fortunate, says Goodhart, that the police constable today can claim a more distinguished ancestry, for he finds his origin in the courageous men of 1829.

When the Metropolitan Police Act became law in 1829, Peel appointed two commissioners to implement the provisions: one an able ex-soldier who had commanded the most disciplined regiment in the British Army, Colonel Charles Rowan; the other an able young Irish barrister named Richard Mayne. The partnership of Rowan and Mayne became famous. They immediately set about recruting the 3,000 men required; regulations provided that the men should be under 35 years of age, of good physique, at least five feet, seven inches in height, literate and of good character. From the outset it was a deliberate policy to recruit men ''who had NOT the rank, habits or station of gentlemen.'' There was to be no caste system of officers and other ranks, and when vacancies occurred in supervising ranks they were to be filled from within the force. The original supervisers were recruited mainly from former Army warrant officers and noncommissioned officers.

The limits of the force area was a radius of up to seven miles from Charing Cross in London. There were to be 17 divisions, each under a superintendent, under each of whom were to be four inspectors and 16 sergeants. Each sergeant controlled nine constables. Though the organization was paramilitary, the men were clothed in nonmilitary uniforms of blue tailed coat, blue trousers (white trousers was optional in summer) and a peculiar glazed black top hat strengthened with a thick leather crown ''which was just homely enough to save the situation.'' Clearly the force was to be ''of the people,'' working class to a man.

The original instructions for the new force were calculated to gain and reinforce public acceptability; the force had to rely on public cooperation and good will.

The principles embodied in the 1829 instructions to the police have become enshrined in the philosophy of British policing and are generally regarded to be as valid today as when they were drafted:

> It should be understood at the outset that the object to be attained is the prevention of crime.
>
> To this great end every effort of the police is to be directed. The security of person and property and the preservation of a police establishment will thus be better effected than by the detection and punishment of the offender after he has succeeded in committing crime. . . .
>
> He [the constable] will be civil and obliging to all people of every rank and class.
>
> He must be particularly cautious not to interfere idly or unnecessarily in order to make a display of his authority; when required to act he will do so with decision and boldness; on all occasions he may expect to receive the fullest support in the proper exercise of his authority.
>
> He must remember that there is no qualification so indispensable to a police officer as a perfect command of temper, never suffering himself to be moved in the slightest degree by any language or threats that may be used; if he does his duty in a quiet and determined manner, such conduct will probably excite the well disposed of the bystanders to assist him, if he requires them.
>
> In the novelty of the present establishment, particular care is to be taken that the constables of the police do not form false notions of their duties and powers.

One could interject here that the exclusively working-class background of the force, the thrust for general acceptability, and the military background of the first commissioner, necessary though they were at the time, have had a pervasive effect on the development of professionalism in police forces ever since. In the latter half of the 20th century the service has had to tackle a very professional task, yet it is still saddled with a paramilitary organisation—some would claim an ossified 19th-century paramilitary structure! It is a very rigid pyramid in organizational terms, with the professional skills being exercised at the bottom level of the pyramid, and much of the work being generated at that level, too, and occurring in "an area of very low visibility." There has been much concern expressed in recent years at the quality of policing at the all-important contact point with the public. Too often the person who deals with the public is a very young recruit or a disillusioned older man. There are calls for a return to the primacy of the contact point, to ensure that the bright young men and women who join the service are deployed at the sharp end of policing rather than being whisked into the hierarchical pyramid of administration, or into specialized departments. In addition, the *overall* intellectual and academic level of recruits is still low, and the recruit-

ment base, in social terms, is still predominantly working class. "Many recruits, when they join, are possessed of a fairly simplistic and conservative view of the world. They tend to see the society they live in through the lens of limited experience, meager education, and in terms of 'people like themselves.' They have little knowledge and less understanding of contrasting life-styles; there is a tendency therefore to revere authority, and mistrust anything new, strange, different, intellectual, or "arty." Though this analysis is about police in the United States, it is profoundly accurate in the British context. Much of the British police is still recruited with pathetically low educational standards; and good though the training is at certain levels, there is a need to cultivate greater intellectualism, planning and the development of skills.

The London Police of 1829 were a success, soon overcoming the expected opposition to an organized and trained police force—showing, in general, that

POLICE FORCE STRENGTHS

	1976	1977	1978	1979	1980	1981	1982
England and Wales							
Regular police							
Authorized establishment	116,880	116,980	117,668	118,322	118,930	120,008	120,125
Strength:							
Men	101,042	98,935	99,134	102,360	105,563	107,379	108,517
Women	6,997	7,789	8,477	9,394	10,355	10,702	10,935
Seconded:							
Men	1,368	1,400	1,386	1,477	1,430	1,424	1,419
Women	69	77	78	78	75	70	80
Additional constables:							
Men	144	97	85	114	96	90	89
Women	—	—	1	2	1	1	1
Scotland							
Regular police							
Authorized establishment:							
Men	13,163	13,144	13,162	13,148	13,187	13,195	13,205
Strength:							
Men	11,442	11,069	11,477	12,280	12,419	12,379	12,433
Women	737	763	746	786	771	749	719
Central service:							
Men	55	52	51	56	60	54	55
Women	2	3	4	4	5	2	2
Seconded:							
Men	99	78	72	72	69	78	73
Women	7	8	5	3	2	5	4
Additional regular police:							
Authorized establishment	157	174	179	126	72	67	62
Strength	138	174	176	148	71	66	62
Northern Ireland							
Royal Ulster Constabulary							
Strength:							
Men	4,811	5,140	5,495	5,938	6,224	6,622	7,017
Women	442	552	615	676	711	712	701

they were honest, impartial and efficient. Within six years, legislation was enacted to provide for the police in other towns. Later this was extended to the more rural areas. Apart from the powers of the home secretary in relation to the Metropolitan Police, where he is to this day the police authority, the central government was not at first concerned with the new police forces. However, in the 1850s (1857 for Scotland), legislation provided for the appointment by the crown of inspectors of constabulary to inspect all police forces and to report to the home secretary, and the secretary of state for Scotland, respectively, whether or not they were efficient. It was also stipulated that any force certified as efficient should receive an annual grant from the Exchequer. This was at first limited to a contribution toward the cost of pay and clothing but later was extended to one-half of the approved expenditure for the force. (The City of London—a square mile that is the financial center of the country and with its own police force—has always had special arrangements, and even today the grant from the Exchequer is only one-third of approved total expenditure.)

However, central government, though having few statutory powers, was able to exercise considerable influence to encourage high standards and the development of progressive ideas and techniques through the inspectorate, for the threat of withholding the grant was a powerful weapon. In 1919 ministers were given statutory power to make regulations dealing with a wide range of matters such as national rates of pay, pensions and other conditions of service; every police authority was required to comply. The central government also provided the main thrust for a process of amalgamation of forces to ensure that the operating units be near the optimum size for the tasks involved in an ever more complex society. In the 1960s a royal commission reviewed the constitutional position of the police and the arrangements for their administration and control. After considering the arguments in favor of a national police force, the commission concluded that there was much to be gained in continuing a system of local police forces, but a number of measures were suggested to improve central control. Their recommendations were accepted, and enacted in the main, in the Police Act 1964, which replaced all previous general police legislation in England and Wales. The home secretary was given a new duty to promote the efficiency of the police and given new powers to discharge that duty. The main functions of each police authority (now composed of two-thirds elected councillors and one-third magistrates) were defined as the maintenance of an adequate and efficient force, property housed and equipped; and the appointment, and if necessary removal, of the chief constable. A police authority, like

the home secretary, has the powers to call for reports from its chief constable, but each force was explicitly placed under the control and direction of its chief constable.

Structure & Organization

Today there are 43 regular police forces in England and Wales and eight in Scotland. The police service in Northern Ireland is organized as a single force. Outside London most counties (regions or islands in Scotland) have their own forces, although where there are advantages in terms of operational efficiency, a number have combined forces. In London, the Metropolitan Police, with headquarters at New Scotland Yard, now police an area within a radius of 15 miles from Charing Cross (but still excluding the square mile of the City of London). The ratio of police to the population varies from 347 per officer in Merseyside to 523 in Derbyshire. In the Metropolitan Police area it is 278 per officer, and the average ratio throughout the country is 414 per officer. Besides the regular police, there are a number of bodies (principally docks, airports, harbors and some islands) that have their own police forces.

In addition to the police forces listed, there are a large number of private security organizations. Those that are members of the British Security Association Ltd.—a kind of self-regulating professional body—employ about 33,000 people, and it is estimated that over 6,000 are employed by the several hundred very small companies that are not members of the association.

Although successive governments have discussed regulatory provisions for the industry and have even published discussions and consultative proposals for formal regulation, there are at present no regulatory or inspectoral provisions in existence. However, the private security industry is, of course, subject to the law of the land and does not enjoy any dispensation whatsoever. Its members are not allowed to carry firearms or any other offensive weapon.

The relationship between police and government, including the vexed question of who polices the police, is as old as history. It is related to an assumed conflict between order and liberty. Dr. Johnson, the major literary moralist of the 18th century, is frequently quoted as having said: "The danger of unbounded liberty and the danger of bounding it have produced a problem in the science of government which human understanding seems hitherto unable to solve."

It is clearly in the public good that the police should be strong and effective in preserving law and order and preventing crime; but it is equally to the public good that police power be controlled. A balance must be struck between the danger of a strong, professionally controlled police, albeit subject to law, becoming a threat to personal liberty, and the predicament that weak, fragmented, police forces will be too pusillanimous to deal with the problem of urban terrorism, subversion, and the challenge of serious and organized crime. To quote Critchley, "There is no freedom without order" (indeed, without order it is hardly possible to conceive of any society at all); "a strong, respected police is therefore a condition, not a denial, of liberty, subject to the constraints of law. The compromise has to ensure that the police are efficient without being officious, they must form an impartial force and yet be subject to a degree of control by persons who are not required to be impartial, and who themselves are liable to police supervision."

The position in Britain is that every constable—which means every police officer, from chief constable or commissioner down to the newest recruit—personally has to justify every act or omission in the performance of his duties, by positive law. This is not an empty platitude, but a very real constraint on police action. The police are in no different position in that regard from any other citizen, although they have been given additional (but still meager) powers. The police are subject to the Discipline Code for police and the Independent Complaints Procedure, but these are in addition to the ordinary law of the land. If a constable arrests a person, he must show that this is supported by a relevant legal provision; if he commits even a technical assault in carrying out the arrest, he must justify the arrest as being lawful, to avoid the consequences of a civil action for trespass to the person, or even false imprisonment.

Back in the 19th century, one of England's most distinguished constitutional lawyers, when examining French legal provisions, castigated the French Droit Administratif as a substitution for "regular law" in determining the procedure by which rights and liabilities of private individuals are enforced against the representatives of the state in that country.

If a person claims to have been assaulted by a constable, the person does not have to rely on the complaints procedure (although that is available), but has access to the courts and can claim assault so the matter can be tested in the courts. On the other hand, if a person claims to have been illegally arrested, the action for false imprisonment lies in the civil courts. Furthermore, though the police officer concerned may be of limited means, and therefore not worth the expense of suing him, the Police Act of 1964 has rectified the matter, for although the relationship of master and servant does not exist between the chief constable and his officers (nor between the police authority and their police officers), yet the chief constable is put in the position of "master" for purposes of vicarious liability, and the police authority is required to meet any damages awarded against him or her by the courts.

When, therefore, it is claimed that the police are judges in their own cause (claims that sometimes are made), they are judges of conduct that is below the level of criminality and that is not tortious. Nevertheless, a new complaints procedure has been introduced in recent years; the main provisions are as follows:

A new and independent Police Complaints Board, on which no police officer past or present can sit, has been established for England and Wales. Whenever a complaint is made against a police officer, the chief officer of police must cause it to be recorded and investigated. (In practice, because the chief constable may well be later involved in the matter as the disciplinary authority, the chief constable invariably delegates his or her responsibilities regarding complaints to the deputy chief constable). In the vast majority of cases in England and Wales the police decide whether to bring criminal proceedings against a person, but where a complaint against a police officer involves allegations of crime, at the conclusion of the inquiry the deputy chief constable is required to submit the file to the director of public prosecutions—an independent legal officer. It is for the director to decide in all instances where a complaint alleges that a police officer has committed any criminal act, whether the officer should be prosecuted. Where the decision is to prosecute, the matter proceeds. But if the decision is not to prosecute, the deputy chief constable decides whether to bring disciplinary proceedings, as this person has to do in all other complaints that do *not* involve an allegation of crime. If the deputy chief constable decides that no disciplinary proceedings are to occur, the reports of the investigation and of the original complaint must first be referred to the Police Complaints Board—unless the complaint has been withdrawn. The board has authority to overrule the deputy chief constable and to recommend which charges should be made. If all else fails, the board may *direct* that certain charges be made.

The chief constable is normally the disciplinary authority and hears the charges alone. However, in exceptional cases a chief constable from another force may hear and determine the issue, although punishment is still normally a matter for the chief constable of the force. The Police Complaints Board, where they *direct* that specific charges are to be preferred, and also where they consider it desirable due to exceptionable circumstances in a particular case, may also direct that the hearing of the issue should be by special tribunal consisting of the chief constable of the force as chairman, and two members of the Police

Complaints Board. This tribunal may find the accused officer guilty or not guilty by majority vote—i.e., the chief constable can be outvoted.

The determination of punishment, however, is a matter for the chairman (chief constable) after consultation with the other members of the tribunal. (There are certain minor variations—in the case of the Metropolitan Police, and also when the chief constable who chairs the hearing is not the chief constable of the force concerned.) There is a right of appeal against both finding and punishment to the secretary of state. Regulations have been made to exclude certain trivial, vexatious, and withdrawn complaints from these provisions.

The Police Complaints Board is required to make annual and special reports to the home secretary. It has consistently reported that it is generally satisfied with the way complaints are dealt with by the police but has commented on the time it takes to complete investigations. Recently it has drawn attention to the incidence of allegations of assault by police officers. It has recommended setting up a special investigation unit made up of seconded officers from police forces, to deal with such investigations.

The central government, through the home secretary and the secretary of state for Scotland, have great responsibilities for promoting the efficiency of the police. They must approve the appointment of chief and assistant chief constables; may require a police authority to retire a chief constable in the interests of efficiency; may call for a report from a chief constable on any matter relating to the policing of his area; or may cause a local inquiry to be held. They also have the power to make, and do make, regulations with which all police authorities must comply, concerning such matters as rank; qualifications for appointment, promotion and retirement; discipline; hours of duty; leave, pay and allowances; and uniforms and equipment. Some of these matters are first negotiable, and the secretary of state is required to take them to the negotiating body before making the regulations. Other matters are discussed though not negotiated. All forces in Great Britain (except the Metropolitan Police, for which the home secretary is the police authority and therefore directly responsible) are subject to government inspection.

Her Majesty's inspectors of constabulary, under a chief inspector for England and Wales, and a separate chief inspector for Scotland, carry out a formal inspection of the forces in their regions, when they visit and inquire into the state and efficiency of the forces and report to the respective secretaries of state. Annual reports are published and cover a whole range of police matters. The inspectors have a more abiding influence, however, for they keep in close touch with the forces for which they are responsible. They have a special responsibility to examine how complaints against the police are dealt with, and also any allegations of corruption in public life; they have to be satisfied that senior officers in the force who have been given special responsibility for supervising the recording and investigation of public sector corruption have properly carried out this important task.

The financing of the police forces is a partnership between the central and the local government, the central government making a grant of one-half the total approved expenditure; payment of this is conditional on the home secretary (or the Secretary of State for Scotland) being satisfied that a force is being maintained and administered effectively.

The local police authority—which consists of two-thirds elected local government councillors and one-third magistrates—is responsible for maintaining the police force. The Metropolitan Police is in a different category, the home secretary being the police authority. The square mile of the City of London, with its own police force, comes under the Court of Common Council. In Scotland the police authority is the Regional or Island Council. Where there are combined forces in England and Wales there is a combined police authority, which is generally a corporate body in its own right; otherwise the police authority is notionally, at least, a committee of the relevant county council.

The primary duty of the police authority is the maintenance of an adequate and efficient force, properly housed and equipped, and the appointment, and if necessary the removal, of the chief and assistant chief constables; fixing the establishment of the force and the number of officers in each rank; appointing traffic wardens; and providing and maintaining police buildings and equipment. Their discretion in some of these matters is not unfettered, however, because government grants are paid on *approved* expenditures; therefore for an expenditure to qualify for a grant, the approval of the secretary of state is a prerequisite.

It is now well settled that, notwithstanding the enormous responsibilities of the central government ministers and of the local police authority, the sole responsibility for the control and direction of the force is with the chief constable. This interpretation has been confirmed both by ministerial statement in Parliament and by the Court of Appeal.

Accountability and control of police can be summed up as follows (because there are clearly different issues between an ordinary constable and a chief constable or a metropolitan police commissioner, they have to be looked at separately):

Constables: In relation to the performance of his duties, every constable is accountable to the law. He can be sued (e.g., for wrongful arrest or malicious prosecution) or prosecuted (e.g., for assault). He is accountable to his chief constable under the Police Discipline Code for the performance of his duties and can be disciplined by the chief constable for disobedience to orders, misconduct, neglect of duty, corruption, etc. The ultimate sanction is dismissal from the force. *He is not accountable to any other body.*

A constable is under the control and direction of his chief constable and is obliged to carry out the lawful orders of his superiors on the force, including the policy of the force. This does not mean that he can only act under orders. His powers are vested in him by virtue of his tenure of office as constable. He has a wide measure of discretion and may have to make difficult decisions entirely on his own initiative. He is not subject to the control of his police authority; he is not their servant, and this lack of control ensures that he is free from any risk of political or other interference from outside bodies.

Chief constables or a metropolitan police commissioner: Chief constables, like other constables, are not in law the servant of anyone. They are accountable in that they can be sued or prosecuted if they personally infringe the law in performing their duties; they are also vicariously liable in law for the torts of their constables, and they are subject, in addition, to the Police Disciplinary Code and procedures. (There are slight differences in that the disciplinary body for chief, deputy and assistant chief constables is the police authority, acting on a report of a tribunal of enquiry; independent persons appointed by it and meeting under a qualified lawyer). It may be that in strict constitutional terms, the home secretary, as police authority, has slightly greater powers of control over the commissioner of police of the metropolis than an ordinary police authority has over a particular chief constable. While there is some ambiguity as to whether and how much the home secretary can interfere with the operations and policy of the Metropolitan Police, in practice he does not do so. The commissioner can, however, be removed by the queen on the advice of the home secretary. Questions regarding the operations of the Metropolitan Police can be asked of the home secretary in Parliament, but although he has potentially wide accountability to Parliament for policing generally, the home secretary takes a restrictive view of his obligation to answer questions regarding other forces, certainly on law enforcement and operational matters.

Chief constables and the commissioner are not accountable to the ombudsman.

With regard to a chief constable and his police authority, the authority is only able to require information from him. It is entitled to receive annual reports regarding policing in the area and to require him to give other reports from time to time, but in relation to these he may, with the home secretary's concurrence, decline to supply information if its disclosure would be contrary to the public interest or unnecessary for the discharge of the authority's functions. It is clear that the authority can hold the chief constable accountable on questions of administration, equipment, etc.; and accountable in a *general* way for the *general* conduct of the force but not for particular matters of policy and law enforcement. A police authority can only give instructions to a chief constable when the instructions relate to purely administrative matters and cannot interfere in police operations and policy by giving the chief constable directions on these matters, nor can it give directions concerning particular enforcement measures or incidents.

The Police Complaints Board can order the commissioner or the chief constable to bring disciplinary proceedings against a constable against whom a complaint has been made, even though the commissioner or chief constable does not think this necessary.

Whereas in many police forces in the world, the policeman's image is that of a very tough person, that of the British policeman—and it is a deliberately cultivated one—is of a peaceful, mature person, slow to anger, not easily provoked. Slightly ponderous perhaps, but solidly dependable. It is precisely because of this self-image, that police officers have hitherto (with few exceptions) dealt with public disorder situations without any special equipment. It was felt that if they were trying to cool a worsening public order situation, the very act of suddenly producing special equipment would be calculated to escalate the confrontation. Until quite recently, therefore, public order situations were always dealt with by officers dressed in their normal uniform. However, on a few occasions in the past few years, protective shields have been used, and to a lesser extent plastic visors. Police casualties were at an unacceptable level. Policing, however, necessarily reflects the society it serves, and if society challenges the police to react more aggressively in the future, then there will probably be an irrevocable step toward tougher policing. Chief officers of the day are, however, particularly anxious not to sacrifice the basic strategy of mild British policing for immediate tactical advantage. In dealing with particular cases of public disorder and mass demonstrations, a police force can call on "mutual aid" schemes that are well developed between forces. Each force has a tactical reserve of officers generally known as Police Support Units or Tactical Aid Groups. In the main these are generally young and physically fit ordinary officers who normally perform routine outside police duty. However, they can be brought together quickly to form a tactical reserve force for deployment either within their own force area or in support of a neighboring force. The Metropolitan Police, because of its size and the incidence of demonstrations within a capital city, has a permanently established tactical reserve known as the Special Patrol Group. This, and the other units mentioned are in no way a riot police, or a "third force" between the police and the Army. It is universally accepted in Great Britain that below the level of armed insurrection, there is no role for the Army to play in public order situations. In industrial disputes the government of the day has deployed troops on very rare occasions, but only in a logistical sense and to maintain essential services, not to maintain public order. Specialized Army units such as the SAS are available in support of civil authority in such instances as terrorist activities and hijackings. Although they had hitherto maintained a very low profile, their spectacular rescue of hostages from the Iranian embassy in London in the full glare of television cameras has underlined their availability and expertise.

There is a Home Office-serviced comprehensive communications system throughout the United Kingdom. The main VHF system joins adjoining force headquarters and is the main base-to-car system. Different forces have a number of frequencies allocated to them. Each force has its own control room with one or more satellite controls as well, from which it deploys its vehicles. Officers on foot patrol are equipped with "personal radios" (transceivers) on UHF. Generally these interface with car transceivers so that if the officer is out of the car and is out of range of the UHF system, it is still possible to remain in contact.

There has been considerable capital expenditure in recent years in computerized tactical response systems, known generally as command and control systems, which are vital management tools in the allocation of resources. There is also a well-developed police national computer (PNC) installed at Hendon, just outside London, with on-line terminals at all police forces in England and Wales. Terminals are generally visual display units (VDU's), but facilities for hard copy are also available. The command and control systems of some of the larger forces can access the police national computer directly. Although there is no interfacing as such, there is duplication of much of the vehicle licensing records from the National Licensing Center, carried on the PNC.

A large number of functions have already been assumed by the PNC. These include stolen vehicles (and suspected vehicles) index; vehicle engine and chassis numbers; plant/marine engine index; criminal records; criminal name index; wanted/missing persons index; disqualified drivers; the PNC broadcast system (an instantaneous dissemination of messages such as express messages and port warnings); and a Cross-reference index (an index showing which regional record office holds the latest file). The entire fingerprint index also is being put on the PNC. The computer language is BASIC.

Although the national fingerprint collection is being computerised, facsimile transmission of fingerprints into the Records Office is not being contemplated, certainly not at this stage. Fingerprint forms still will have to be submitted manually to the Records Office for subsequent fingerprint search.

There is a computerized criminal intelligence system being tried on an experimental basis by one force, with Home Office technical backing. This has been a sensitive development and has been more controversial than the other projects.

There is no public right of access to crime data banks, or to police information generally.

The various police forces in the United Kingdom do not have a uniform policy as to the particular vehicles they use for police work. Because of the wide disparity in the nature of the areas policed, this is unremarkable. High-powered, domestically produced cars such as British Leyland Rovers and Jaguars, and Ford Granadas, as well as imported performance cars such as BMW's are used for highway patrol. Smaller cars are used for beat patrols and general patrol duties, where their economy and maneuverability make them particularly suitable. In recent years, the motorcycles used have tended to be BMW's. Only the Metropolitan Police and the Devon and Cornwall police have their own helicopter facility, and these are very recent acquisitions; other forces rely on hired helicopters for special-occasion work, because of the heavy backup expenditure.

With regard to police response time, there is a particularly well-developed "999" emergency telephone call system, and the response time, though varying widely from town center to isolated rural area, is good. However, in recent years the allocation of resources to meet quick response times has been questioned. It is claimed they are inadequate, that building up facilities for quick response causes policing to degenerate into a "fire brigade" activity, and that the quality of the response can be sacrificed for speed. Furthermore, in the fight against crime and disorder, the heavy resources necessary to effect a quick response, could, it is claimed, be more effectively deployed by anticipating and taking the initiative rather than merely reacting to criminal activity.

There is no separate traffic bureau in the United Kingdom. All traffic departments come under the police force of the area concerned, although some highway patrol units are made up of personnel and vehicles from more than one force area.

In many forces traffic patrol constitutes a separate division with its own command structure; in some other areas the whole policing function—Criminal Investigation Department (CID) as well as traffic—comes under the aegis of the particular territorial division. The chief superintendent of the division is therefore responsible for all aspects of crime and traffic, and at force headquarters there is only a small staff to deal with the forcewide aspects of these activities.

All forces wear basically the same uniform, with only minor differences in detail. It consists of an open-necked dark blue belted tunic with four pockets and with matching trousers. In most forces constables and sergeants wear a light blue shirt, but in some forces all ranks wear a white shirt and a black tie. Most constables and sergeants wear the well-known British bobby's helmet—now somewhat strengthened—but there are minor variations in style. When not on foot patrol, a peaked cap with a blue and white diced band is worn. Inspectors and above always wear a peaked cap with black braid on the peak for inspectors, silver braid for superintendents and chief superintendents, and more elaborate silver thread workings for higher ranks.

In summer, shirtsleeves are allowed (sometimes without ties), and the badges of rank are then worn on blue epaulettes fitted to the shoulders of the shirt. In general the British Police Service is unarmed, although officers on special assignment (such as security duties outside embassies) are armed. Rifles and handguns are, however, available for issue; generally this can be done only by order of an inspector and above, in appropriate cases. A substantial proportion of the force receives regular firearms training. Some forces (e.g., in Lancashire, West Yorkshire and the Metropolitan Police) have developed very sophisticated firearms training systems.

Recruitment, Education & Training

Police Training is organized under three main heads: probationer training; specialized training; and higher training, to prepare officers for the middle and higher ranks in the service.

Single-tier entry has been the standard for the British police for the past 150 years, and this is reflected in the arrangements for education and training. All entrants to the service, even those who join directly from a university, join as probationary constables. They are on probation for two years, and during that time training is continuous, though most of it is on the job. A probationer receives one or more weeks of induction training in the force he has joined, then normally attends a ten-week initial training course at a district training center, of which there are now eight in Great Britain. These are run by the Home Office as a central service. The Metropolitan Police is large

enough to run its own training complex for recruits and specialized training at Peel Center, Hendon, London. They also give a considerably longer initial training course of 15 weeks.

The curricula at district training centers have been extensively modified in recent years and have moved away from being cramming courses on law and police procedures to having a greater emphasis on the sociological problems that confront a young probationary constable. An attempt is made to inculcate a greater awareness of the policeman's role in society today.

After the initial course, the probationer returns to his force for two or more weeks' instruction on local procedures that could not practically be taught on a district basis. He is also made aware of the backup resources available to him within the force. Then he is attached to a senior constable for up to two months (sometimes there are constables designated as tutor constables), when he learns his craft on routine outside police patrol, both on foot and in a beat patrol vehicle. During the next 18 months he will return at least once to the district training center, and in addition will attend on a day-release basis a continuation course at his force training center. There will be a series of attachments (generally three) each of about one month, to the Criminal Investigation Department, the Traffic Department and Administration. (There is total interchangeability of personnel among uniformed police work, the Criminal Investigation Department and the Traffic Department.)

If the probationer performs satisfactorily, his appointment will be confirmed after two years; otherwise his services can be dispensed with at any time up to that stage if it is thought that he is unlikely to make an efficient officer.

Specialized trianing courses are held in a vast array of subjects, mostly on an in-house basis within the force. However, driver training and courses on criminal investigation are generally held at a number of centers; normally a large force runs such courses and places are allocated to other forces. Instructors are normally assigned temporarily from the various forces concerned.

Higher police training, to prepare officers for the middle and higher ranks in the service, is mainly concentrated at the Police Staff College, Bramshill, Hampshire, England. A somewhat similar institution for Scotland is at Tulliallan Castle, Kincardine, but because of the smaller geographical area involved it is not possible to conduct the most senior courses there.

The Police Staff College provides higher training for future leaders of the service and offers a comprehensive pattern of courses at each level of command. The basic aim of the college is to develop the students' potential for higher responsibility by broadening their outlook, building up their professional knowledge and increasing their understanding of the community they serve. The college also gives police officers an appreciation of the liberal and humane values central to the society. Bramshill has acquired an international status, which is regularly enhanced by the attendance of a considerable numbers of students from all parts of the world.

Five courses are conducted concurrently at the Police Staff College. They are:

The special course. This trains young officers of outstanding promise who have been selected by extended interview (a civil service-type selection process spread over about three days and involving a battery of tests and interviews). This course is for young officers, and admission to it can be gained before the end of an officer's third year of service. Successful completion of the course entitles the officer to be promoted to sergeant, and after a year's satisfactory service in that rank, to inspector. The course is also linked to a scheme whereby about 20 graduates each year are recruited from their final year at a university, and after going through a somewhat similar extended interview selection procedure can join the police service with an almost certain guarantee of being accepted for the special course. They must, however, pass their promotion examination—constable to sergeant—between joining the force and starting the course. The syllabus of the course consists of professional, academic and management studies. The professional component includes police duties, the criminal law and the courts, road traffic and community relations. The academic content is primarily concerned with social and political studies; it also includes work in economics, psychology, history, international affairs and the academic study of police. Management studies include organization, administration and management science. The course is designed to further the student's professional knowledge and skill and in so doing to develop wider interests and intellectual ability. The course lasts 12 months.

The junior command course. This course trains selected inspectors and some recently promoted chief inspectors for the responsibilities of the middle ranks of the police service, especially subdivisional command. The course lasts six months. The syllabus embodies both professional and academic material, which are integrated to provide three themes of police studies:

1. operational responsibilities of first independent command: crime, traffic and public order

2. police organization: resource allocation, organization and personnel

3. police responsibilities and accountability: police and government; law and society

Smaller groups of students pursue specialized subjects in addition to the core syllabus. The course lasts six months.

Intermediate command course. This course is designed to equip superintendents with the knowledge and skills necessary for that rank and for the later responsibilities of divisional command. The course lasts three months. The syllabus embraces the four main aspects of British policing:

1. common law and civilian origin

2. increasing community involvement and responsibilities

3. operational function of police in the fields of crime, traffic and public order

4. organizational structure and managerial styles

The senior command course. This course is designed to equip officers for the highest posts in the service. Competition for places is intense, and final acceptance for the course is by extended interview. A number of senior police officers from overseas also attend the course, which lasts six months. The material is structured on a thematic basis and examines:

1. command responsibilities in operational situations

2. police powers and accountability

3. scientific and technological aids to police operations

4. finance, budgeting and government

5. responsibilities and relationships of command

6. police organisation: design, monitoring and evaluation

The themes are examined not only within the Police Staff College but also in exercises and research studies with police forces in the United Kingdom, Western Europe and the United States.

Recruitment is carried out on a force basis. Forces with vacancies have in the past advertised regularly, but recently (due no doubt to the economic recession) recruiting has been very buoyant, and vacancies are shrinking rapidly. Forces recruit as vacancies occur and there is some national advertising by the Home Office. There is a national entrance test, but forces that had substantial vacancies in the past accepted a lower passing mark than those that were near their quota. The entrance examination is always supplemented by a thorough interview, culminating in either the chief constable or one of his assistants giving the final approval. Prior to final acceptance, an exhaustive screening procedure examines the applicant's entire suitability for police work. This includes a search of crime and security indices. Strenuous efforts are made to recruit persons from ethnic minorities, but they have to meet the same educational and physical standards as all other applicants. There is no quota system to ensure that the percentage of a particular ethnic group in the police is similar to the relative numbers of that group in the general community. Neither is there a system of accepting a particular group of people who may be slightly below educational entry standards, with a view to bringing them up to that standard before final acceptance.

The Penal System

The primary sources of English law are common law, legislation and equity, but only the first two form the basis of criminal law. The earliest common law offenses were felonies (such as murder, arson, rape and larceny) punishable by death, mutilation or the forfeiture of property. Other, less serious offenses were called misdemeanors. Most common law crimes were codified and defined by statutes. The historical distinction between felonies and misdemeanors was abolished by the Criminal Law Act of 1967 and was replaced by a new classification scheme in which offenses were divided into arrestable and nonarrestable. Arrestable offenses are defined as "offenses for which the sentence is fixed by law or for which a person may be sentenced for a term of five years." The power to arrest without a warrant was extended to all arrestable offenses. All offenses are tried either summarily in a magistrate's court or on indictment in a crown court, depending on the classification of the offense. Summary offenses are tried without a jury

and include the vast majority of offenses, such as traffic violations, disorderly conduct and soliciting.

There are criminal procedure pretrial processes and trial processes. The first define the power to arrest, the power to search and seize, the power to stop and question, and the power to interrogate. Bail is governed by the Bail Act of 1976. In general, this act grants the right of bail to all persons accused of crimes except fugitives, those who have been previously convicted for the same offense, those arrested for breach of bail and those accused of crimes for which the punishment is imprisonment. If bail is granted, it can be either conditional or unconditional.

Since the 19th century, the correctional system has functioned under the authority of the home secretary. At the top of the administrative hierarchy that manages prisons is the Prison Board, which is composed of a chairman (who is a civil servant) and five additional board members who are responsible for the formulation and implementation of penal policy. In addition, there are four regional headquarters.

Boards of Visitors exist for all correctional institutions. Members of these boards are appointed by the home secretary for three-year renewable terms. Over half of all board members are magistrates. By statute, boards have the power to adjudicate alleged breaches of prison discipline, and they also exercise general oversight over the physical condition and administration of penal facilities.

British prisons generally belong to one of four categories: local, short-term, medium-term and long-

CRIME STATISTICS, ENGLAND AND WALES (1983)

		Number Reported	Attempts %	Cases Solved %	Crime per 100,000	Offenders	Females %	Juveniles %	Strangers %
1.	Murder	678	19	93	1.37				
2.	Sex offenses, including rape	20,410		73	41.14				
3.	Rape	1,334		67	2.69				
4.	Serious assault	108,980		75	219.69				
5.	All theft	2,541,429		35	5,123.15				
6.	Aggravated theft	835,505		30	1,684.25				
7.	Robbery and violent theft	22,119		24	44.59				
8.	Breaking and entering	813,386		30	1,639.67				
9.	Auto theft	325,699		26	656.56				
10.	Other thefts	1,380,225		40	2,782.33				
11.	Fraud	121,791		69	245.51				
12.	Counterfeiting								
13.	Drug offenses	4,994		95	10.07				
14.	Total offenses	3,247,030		35	6,545.53				

Note: Information for some categories is not available.

term. Each is designed to serve a specific purpose and for a specific type of inmate. Local prisons hold those who have been remanded in custody until their trial or sentence. They also serve as distribution centers for the rest of the prison system and house inmates serving very short sentences.

Since 1948, the Home Office has attempted to transform prisons into corrective training centers. This has led to the establishment of three types of prisons: short-term prisons for those serving up to 18 months; medium-term prisons for those serving between 18 months and four years; and long-term prisons for those serving longer than four years. About one-third of these facilities are open institutions without walls or fences. All facilities emphasize rehabilitation and have trained psychotherapists and counselors on their staff. Work is considered an integral part of rehabilitation, and all prisoners are required to work.

The chief prison official is known as the governor, who has the same responsibility as a warden in a U.S. facility. Governors are traditionally recruited outside the prison service. Below the governor are two categories of staff: uniformed civil servants; and professional and technical cadre, including chaplains, medical personnel, psychiatrists, social workers, teachers and prison industries instructors.

The 1967 Criminal Justice Act introduced the parole system, providing for early release from correctional institutions. Inmates are eligible for parole after they have served one year or one-third of their sentence (whichever is longer). The parole process consists of four stages. First a four-member committee headed by the prison governor examines the inmate's case. The case is then referred to the Home Office for the second stage, where expert opinion is given. At the third stage the Parole Board makes its recommendations. At the fourth stage the home secretary grants his decision.

Noninstitutional treatment of prisoners is handled by the Probation and Aftercare Department, another unit within the Home Office. Although linked administratively to the Home Office, the 56 local probation committees exercise a great deal of local control and also operate such facilities as hostels and training centers. Probation orders contain some standard conditions, such as good behavior, keeping in touch with the probation officer and notifying the officer of a change in address. The court may impose additional requirements, such as specifying the place of residence, seeking medical or psychiatric treatment and prohibiting association with certain people or frequenting specific places.

In the early 1970s the British experimented with a new noncustodial sentence, the community service order, which requires the offender to provide 40 to 240 hours of unpaid community service, generally within a year. Many offenders sentenced to this form of service are recidivists between ages 17 and 21.

Like many other European countries, Britain widely uses the fine as a penal sanction. Magistrate courts

CRIME STATISTICS, NORTHERN IRELAND (1983)

		Number Reported	Attempts %	Cases Solved %	Crime per 100,000	Offenders	Females %	Juveniles %	Strangers %
1.	Murder	310	80	47	19.78	41	9		
2.	Sex offenses, including rape	396	4	73	25.26	140		3	
3.	Rape	79	21	78	5.04	22			
4.	Serious assault	2,052		52	130.92	1,183	2	2	
5.	All theft	53,802		26	3,432.56	6,992	17	13	
6.	Aggravated theft	23,197		24	1,479.97	2,727	2	20	
7.	Robbery and violent theft	1,870		30	119.31	309	1	8	
8.	Breaking and entering	21,327	5	23	1,360.66	2,418	2	21	
9.	Auto theft	1,665		5	106.23	43			
10.	Other thefts								
11.	Fraud	2,855		60	182.15	599	24	2	
12.	Counterfeiting	186		17	11.87	14	28		
13.	Drug offenses	139		111	8.87	95	9	2	
14.	Total offenses	63,984		27	4,082.17	14,603	17	11	

Note: Information for some categories is not available.
Criteria of juveniles: aged from 10 to 17 years.

(but not crown courts) are limited in the amounts they can impose as a fine. Generally, fines are imposed in addition to custodial sentences.

The suspended sentence was first introduced by the Criminal Justice Act of 1967. The Criminal Justice Act of 1977 introduced a variant in which sentences ranging from six months to two years can be partially served and partially suspended. Finally, the Criminal Justice Act of 1972 provides for deferred sentencing in which a court may defer imposing a sanction on the offender for up to six months.

The major impetus in the development of community-based corrections has come from a voluntary nonofficial organization called the National Association for the Care and Resettlement of Offenders (NA-CRO), founded in 1966. Among its projects are the Whitechapel Day Center, which helps homeless offenders and ex-offenders by providing food, medical care, counseling, placement and job training; the NA-CRO Education Project; the Onward Workshop Project, which provides job training; the Lifeline Project, which provides counsel to drug users; and the Lance Project, which runs hostels for homeless ex-offenders.

Despite the high percentage of offenders receiving noncustodial sentencing, Britain's prisons are overcrowded. Few new institutions have been built since the end of World War II, although the prison population has grown since then from 16,000 to 45,000. Most of the prisons are antiquated structures dating to the 19th century. Many cells are without sinks or toilets, and slop buckets still are used. Ventilation is poor, and bathing facilities are inadequate. According to Peter Evans' *Prison Crisis,* "the system is now in such a state of decay and the backlog of replacing obsolete prisons so great that even if it were possible to replace one every two years beginning in 1980, the last Victorian prison would not be phased out until 2060."

Until the mid-19th century, juveniles were treated as adults in the British criminal justice system. They were tried in the same manner as adults and sentenced to the same sanctions, although, in practice, juveniles were accorded much leniency by juries and judges. Children were sentenced to transportation and imprisonment for minor offenses and served their terms of imprisonment in adult prisons.

With the passage of the Youthful Offenders Act of 1854, juveniles were for the first time separated from adults in the administration of criminal justice. It also established the first reformatory schools for juvenile offenders. In 1887, the Probation of First Offenders Act created the suspended sentence; in 1907 it was followed by the Probation of Offenders Act, which established probation. Finally, the Children's Act of 1908 created the juvenile court. This court is not a separate tribunal, as in the United States, but rather a special session of a magistrate court to handle juvenile matters. These courts adjudicate all offenses (except murder) committed by juveniles between ages seven and 16 and issues involving care of children before

CRIME STATISTICS, SCOTLAND (1984)

		Number Reported	Attempts %	Cases Solved %	Crime per 100,000	Offenders	Females %	Juveniles %	Strangers %
1.	Murder	71		95.8	1.38	33	0	0	
2.	Sex offenses, including rape	5,710		66.4	111.97	1,764	63.7	0.3	
3.	Rape	224		79.9	4.35	20	5	0	
4.	Serious assault	4,740		65.4	92.12	1,310	5	0.5	
5.	All theft	330,320		26	6,419.31	32,127	11.8	0.7	
6.	Aggravated theft								
7.	Robbery and violent theft	4,471		24.6	86.89	578	3.3	2.2	
8.	Breaking and entering	112,104		18.1	2,178.59	9,403	1.9	1.1	
9.	Auto theft	32,557		23.7	632.70	3,408	1.5	1.8	
10.	Other thefts	181,188		26.4	3,521.14	18,738	19	0.2	
11.	Fraud	19,577		73.1	380.45	3,301	17.1	0.1	
12.	Counterfeiting	7,439		71.6	144.57	428	22.2	0.2	
13.	Drug offenses	4,404		99.4	85.59	2,270	9.2	0	
14.	Total offenses	809,450		57.6	15,730.54	189,299	10.6	1.5	

Note: Information for some categories is not available.
Criteria of juveniles: aged from 8 to 15 years.

age 14. Further changes were introduced in juvenile justice by the Children and Young Persons Act of 1933 and its companion statute of the same name of 1969.

Imprisonment was abolished as a punishment for juveniles between 14 and 16 in 1908. The minimum age for sentencing has since been raised to 17. Prior to sentencing anyone under 21, the courts are mandated to consider alternative types of custodial care, of which there are now four types: Borstal training centers; detention centers; community, voluntary or foster homes supervised by local authorities; and attendance centers. Borstals, developed at the turn of the century, are designed for juvenile offenders between ages 15 and 21 who have been convicted on indictment of an offense that is punishable by imprisonment. Only crown courts may impose such a sentence, which may vary in length from six months to two years. The Borstal regime comes closest to that of an adult prison. Upon release, the juvenile offender is subject to a two-year period of supervision. The term of custody in a detention center usually is three to six months. Attendance centers usually are run by the local police or social service workers and are open only on weekends. These centers teach juveniles how to utilize their free time constructively.

UNITED STATES

BASIC FACT SHEET

Official Name: United States of America
Area: 9,372,614 sq km
Population (1987): 243,084,000
Capital: Washington, D.C.
Nature of Government: Parliamentary democracy
Language: English
Currency: Dollar
GNP (1986): $4.22 trillion
Territorial Divisions: 50 states
Population per Police Officer: 460
Police Expenditures per 1,000: $73,687

History & Background

When the 13 original Colonies broke with the English crown and declared themselves independent in 1776, they already had a century or more of criminal justice history behind them. The criminal laws themselves changed little in the decades that followed independence. The English common law that had prevailed in the Colonies continued to hold sway. But in one important aspect the new country developed something unique: Unlike most other advanced nations of its time, the United States did not legislate a national criminal code. Each of the original states maintained full sovereignty in criminal matters, as did the states that subsequently joined the Union. The only exception was jurisdiction over the originally quite limited number of federal crimes, which were prosecuted in federal courts.

Consequently, each state had to rely on its own resources to maintain its criminal justice system—the lockups, the courts, the prison buildings—and to pay for its law officers, sheriffs, magistrates, judges and prison wardens. Each state system was only as good as its human and financial resources.

Developments in law enforcement and criminal justice in the early years were as rowdy and robust as any in the world. The republic grew from the rawest possible beginnings. Most of the North American continent was still virgin wilderness. Only the most primitive types of communication linked the widely scattered communities. Even the more established cities on the Eastern Seaboard were primitive compared to their European counterparts.

In such a society, crime flourished; it was violent and commonplace. Newspapers of the era reported offenses of every kind, including "counterfeiting, petty thievery, housebreaking, burglaries of every description, highway robbery, rape, assault and murder." The *Newport Mercury* reported on January 18, 1773: "Our City is filled with Play-Actors, and Horse-riders, W——s, and Thieves. . . . Three of our Philadelphia Bucks in the Night, lately attacked one of our Watchmen with swords, reprimanding them for breaking of Windows: and before he got relief they wounded him, of which Wounds he died."

A Philadelphia paper reported that "wonton Frolicks of sundry intoxicated Bucks and Blades of the City" stole brass knockers from the doors of fashionable homes. The problem was such that Daniel King invented a knocker "the Construction of which is peculiarly singular, and which will stand Proof against the United Attacks of those nocturnal Sons of Violence." In 1767 the *Newport Mercury* advised, "The Public would do well to keep a Look-out at their Shops, Houses, &c, as there are at present a Number of Loitering Persons, of the infamous Sort, lurking about Town—Some thieves narrowly made their escape in their Attempt one Morning Last Week, being discovered in their Attempt to rob a Store belonging to Mr. Bird."

In 1762 the New York printer John Holt wrote of "such various attempts to rob, and so many Robberies actually committed, having of late been very frequent within the circuits of this City, both Day and Night; it is become hazardous for any person to walk in the latter."

In the Colonies trained police forces did not exist, and peacekeeping methods were ineffective. In New York, policing was undertaken by "night watchmen, constables, sheriffs, jailkeepers, and justices of the peace.'' The forces were small and often ill-trained and poorly managed. Some were paid, others were members of the community obligated to take their turns at the watch. The work was hazardous. Strangers sometimes assaulted officers standing duty on the streets. Many citizens prudently refused to take their turns at the watch, preferring fines to risking their lives.

The watchmen's weapons did not offer them much protection. Some carried muskets. Others had to carry a long wooden stick, which could be tapped on the cobblestones, or a wooden whistle to attract attention.

The court system was also based on English common law, under which there were 160 offenses punishable by death, including high or petty treason, piracy, murder, arson, burglary, housebreaking, ''putting in fear,'' highway robbery, horse stealing, stealing from a person to the value of one shilling and all robberies.

There were many problems in the early American judicial system. Many judges were illiterate. Courts were closed during the winter. Witnesses and arresting officers often failed to appear in court. Suspects were more often released than punished. Those who were convicted faced three kinds of punishment. Minor offenders were whipped, dunked, pilloried or maimed. The sentences were carried out in public in a carnival atmosphere. Counterfeiters and larcenists were hanged. Others were banished, imprisoned or executed. Conditions in the early jails were intolerable. Overcrowding was the norm. The Rev. Charles Woodmason described the conditions in Charles Town's prison in 1767 as follows: ''A Person would be in a better Situation in the French Kings Gallies or the Prison of Turkey or Barbary than in this dismal place—Which is a small House hir'd by the Provost Marshal containing 5 or 6 Rooms, about 12 feet square each and in one of these Rooms have 16 Debtors been crowded. . . . They often have no Room to lye at length, but succeed each other to lye down—One was suffocated by the Heat of the Weather of this Summer—and when a Coffin was sent for the Corps, there was no room to admit it, till some Wretches lay down and made their wretched Carcasses a Table to lay the Coffin on. . . .''

Adults and children were treated alike. Under English common law a judge could consider children between seven and 14 as adults regarding criminal actions. There was only one punishment from which children were exempt: public whipping.

The early Colonial policing system followed that of the mother country and was based on the parish constable. Colonial sheriffs and constables were large landowners appointed by the governors. The Chesapeake sheriff of early Maryland settlements, for example, not only policed the counties, but also was the chief financial officer who collected the taxes and fees and kept 10% of the proceeds.

As the population grew, violence and crime kept pace. Even in the 17th century, America was gaining a reputation for lawlessness and wanton violence, a reputation not entirely unearned, although the English conception of the New World as a hotbed of criminal activity was greatly exaggerated. Town officials therefore adopted the English system of having night watchmen in addition to constables. The first night watch in U.S. police history was instituted in Boston in the 1630s. It was formed at sunset and initially consisted of an officer and six men. Other cities, such as Philadelphia and New Amsterdam (New York), followed Boston's lead. In New Amsterdam, the ''rattlewatch,'' as the group was called, consisted of citizens equipped with rattles to warn the populace of their presence. The group consisted of unpaid volunteers.

In 1658 eight paid watchmen replaced the citizen volunteers. When the British took over New Amsterdam and renamed it New York, the police were placed under a high constable. This situation remained unchanged until 1693, when the first uniformed police officer was appointed and the mayor selected a 12-man watch. In 1731 the first precinct station or ''watch house'' was erected.

Policing on the backwoods frontier sometimes was assumed by self-appointed vigilantes such as Charles Lynch, who led a band of men who tracked down wrongdoers as well as wayward Indians and British sympathizers. His notoriety was such that his surname has entered the American language as a word for nonjudicial summary execution.

The move toward formal metropolitan civilian law enforcement was sidetracked by the American Revolution as the military forces assumed public safety duties previously handled by watchmen. The Army, however, tended to ignore petty crime and vice. Civilian police control resumed after the war, but crimes against persons and property rose dramatically during this period. Law enforcement remained haphazard and capricious. Following the Revolution, one important change occurred: Patronage gradually disappeared, giving way to the popular election of constables and sheriffs.

On the national level Congress created the first federal law-enforcement official—the U.S. marshal—in 1789. In 1829 the Postal Act was passed, and police powers were endowed for the first time on a federal agency.

The 19th century was the formative period of the American police. Boston became the first city to require by statute the maintenance of a permanent night watch; pay for the watchmen was 50 cents a night. The first police districts were established in 1807, and in 1823 the city named its first marshal, James Pollard, a Harvard graduate and practicing attorney. Cincinnati required all male citizens over age 21 to serve in rotation without pay on its night watch. Each night 12 men would gather at the watch house, choose an officer for the night and patrol the streets, equipped with a rattle and a lantern. In New Orleans the military police were replaced by a civilian patrol unit *(garde de ville)* in the early part of the 19th century. In 1818 this force was disbanded and a professional force of paid watchmen was hired.

Although England had already made a transition to a modern police force as a result of the passage of Sir Robert Peel's Metropolitan Police Bill in Parliament, the night-watch system continued to flourish in the United States well into the mid-1800s. In the 1830s, Philadelphia's crime problem was such that a wealthy philanthropist, Stephen Girard, left a large sum of money to the city to finance a competent police force. The city established a day force of 24 policemen and a night force of 120 watchmen and thus became the first U.S. city to have a 24-hour organized metropolitan police service. The force, however, was short-lived.

Boston was in a period of tumult at this time. William Lloyd Garrison, publisher of *The Liberator,* was assaulted in his offices by a crowd infuriated by his antislavery writings. The Broad Street Riot of 1837—as this incident came to be known in history— pitted voluntary firemen against mourners in an Irish funeral procession, and for the first time in the city's history the military had to be called out to quell a disturbance. These events led to the hiring of Marshal Francis Tukey, who built up a competent and efficient force. However, when his night force of 22 men captured more criminals than the day force of 200 volunteer watchmen, the public was antagonized. Tukey was later discharged for malfeasance, but the idea of police reform became one whose time had come.

Police divisions were created in the Tukey table of organization, and eight precinct stations were opened. The city created the country's first police department detective division in 1851 and the first harbor patrol in 1853. In 1855 the separate Boston watch and police were reorganized and united to form the Boston Police Department. In 1870, when the city aldermen fired the chief of police, the police nominated one of their own to replace him. Their recommendation was followed, and Edward Hartwell Savage, one of the first reform-minded police administrators, was appointed. In his time, officers' pay was increased, and assignment of manpower was made more equitable.

New York during the same period had a police force with three separate components. Rivalries existed among the units, and each force was supervised by a separate authority. In 1844 these forces were merged into a unified police department. In 1854 Boston consolidated its forces, and by the 1870s most large American cities had unified police forces.

Nevertheless, mob riots continued to occur, and organized bands of ruffians terrorized large areas. Police officers were badly paid, untrained and ill-equipped. The police had a generally bad public image and were said "to inspire no respect." Complaints of slovenly police dress lead to prescribed uniforms supplied by police departments. News accounts of the day tell of policemen leaving scenes of trouble. Sometimes they were beaten up for sport. Corruption was rampant.

The system of state control was introduced in New York in 1857, when the legislature declared the city too politically corrupt to govern itself and took over the police department. The Metropolitan Police Bill, modeled after Peel's, called for police officers to be regulated by a board appointed by the governor. New York City's major, Fernando Wood, immediately appointed a force loyal to him, in defiance of the state. The two sets of police forces patrolled the streets, and there were more clashes between them than between the police and the criminals. In time the Mets, as the state unit came to be known, assumed full control and held it for the next 13 years. Baltimore, St. Louis, Chicago, Kansas City, Detroit and Cleveland followed New York's lead in imposing state control over municipal forces. State-controlled forces lasted for a year or two in some states and for decades or more in others.

Police reform was slowed by the Civil War and Reconstruction. Probably the most devastating effects were on the police departments of the South. For example, when New Orleans was captured in 1861, civil government was disbanded, martial law was imposed and the military assumed the policing. A professional police force was not reestablished until 1898.

The westward expansion of the country posed special law-enforcement problems. Formal policing was not available, and citizens banded together to protect life and property. Four types of law enforcement evolved at this point: extralegal citizen police, formal police, legal citizen police and parapolice. Vigilante committees were first organized in California by citizen volunteers to patrol towns. Most were not lynch mobs but honest men who were forced to collective action to protect their communities. Settlements in Arizona, Colorado, Montana and Nevada utilized this form of policing.

Formal policing in the West provides a colorful historical footnote to American history. The exploits of the western law-enforcement officials became the stuff of legends, embroidered with fanciful feats. The names of such men as Wyatt Earp, Bat Masterson, ''Wild Bill'' Hickok and Pat Garrett are part of this era.

Out of the cow-town atmosphere and from the work of such early lawmen the Wichita Police system evolved into a competent police agency. In 1897 the city established a significant precedent by electing the first black town marshal in the United States.

At the end of the 19th century police officials began to come together to solve their common problems. In 1871 a total of 112 police officials gathered to discuss crime. Twenty-one years later, in a meeting called by a Nebraska police chief, the National Chiefs of Police Union was begun. In 1902 the group changed its name to the International Association of Chiefs of Police (IACP), a name it bears even today. Its first major contribution was establishment of a central clearinghouse for criminal identification records. Later it was converted into a fingerprint repository, which a city could use by paying a fee.

In 1870 the corrupt influences of William Marcy Tweed, a political patronage dispenser in New York, prompted officials there to look at the city's police administration. ''Boss'' Tweed had a good portion of the city's criminal justice system on his payroll or afraid to defy him. There was a subsequent trial-and-error period as New York and other cities experimented with various police administration systems. The bipartisan board, the commission government plan and unified administrative leadership were tried. The bipartisan board, with Republican and Democratic representatives, was an admission that politics would never be completely eliminated from police management. In reality political influence was compounded, and both parties frequently teamed to thwart aggressive law enforcement.

Various police administration systems were tried in the late 1800s. The commission government system integrated the legislative and executive powers in a small commission elected by popular vote. The concept entailed the designation of one member to serve as a commissioner of public safety with authority over police and fire operations, enforcement of building codes, and health and welfare services.

These efforts were followed by a system of single executive control. One person was appointed by the city's ruling body to run the police department in a system of unified administrative leadership.

The drive for municipal police administrative reform was furthered by the federal government's passage of the Pendleton Act of 1883. This civil service law ended 75 years of the spoils system by classifying a number of federal jobs open to applicants chosen through competitive examinations. Although the law did not specifically apply to municipalities, it did set a precedent for civil service standards. Many communities incorporated this law into their own systems.

The police profession was also changed by the invention of the telephone and the telegraph, the first of many communication technologies directly impinging on police patrol and crime control. The advent of the automobile ended the horse and buggy days of law enforcement and enabled the police to respond with speed to calls for help. The invention of photography was another milestone in the interaction of police work and technology, and it introduced new avenues of fingerprinting and criminal identification.

During three years as police commissioner in New York City, Theodore Roosevelt gained national acclaim for his reforms. He pioneered a bicycle squad, a telephonic communications system, and training for new recruits. He routed out corrupt elements in the police department and instituted a promotion system based entirely on merit. Later he was an enthusiastic supporter of the Pennsylvania State Constabulary, which became the model for modern state police organizations. In 1908, as president, he organized the Bureau of Investigation in the Department of Justice, the forerunner of the FBI.

The growth of trade unionism in the early 1900s affected the police rank and file. The Boston Social Club, a police fraternal organization, petitioned the American Federation of Labor for a union charter in 1919. Ired by the police commissioner's order forbidding union membership, 19 patrolmen refused to disband and were brought up on departmental charges, tried and convicted. Sentencing was postponed as the union patrolmen demanded leniency. Ultimately they were suspended, and this action precipitated a strike. The strikers were subsequently fired and a new force was hired. In other cities, the drive to organize continued. In 1915, in Pittsburgh, two patrolmen founded the Fraternal Order of Police, which became a national organization with a membership encompassing both the ranks and the chiefs. However, unlike unions, it did not favor strikes.

Two other developments were notable during this period. State police began to emerge as major components of law enforcement, particularly in Texas, Massachusetts and Pennsylvania. These forces were responsible only to the state governors. Second, women began to serve on the force in increasing numbers. Women had served as police matrons since 1845, but it was not until 1893 that the first woman—Marie Owens—was appointed to perform police duties in Chicago. In 1910 the Los Angeles Police Department appointed Alice Stebbins Wells as the first full-time paid policewoman in the United States. By 1915 a total of 25 cities had paid policewomen on their staffs. In the same year the International Association of Policewomen (IAP) was formed in Baltimore. In 1918 Ellen O'Grady was appointed deputy police commissioner in New York City, and in 1919 the Bureau of Policewomen was created in Indianapolis.

On another front, U.S. police training systems lagged behind those of Europe. It was not until 1915, when Raymond B. Fosdick published his *European Police Systems,* that serious attention began to be paid to this area. The first formal training school for policemen was established in Berkeley, Calif., in 1908. The New York, Detroit and Philadelphia police departments created academies and training schools during the next few years. In 1916 the University of California at Berkeley established the first university-level training school under the direction of August Vollmer, one of the pioneers in professional police education.

The biggest law-enforcement problem of the post-World War I era was Prohibition. Policemen had a difficult time trying to enforce what was essentially an unenforceable law. Many worked under politicians who themselves were under the thumbs of mobsters. Prohibition accelerated the rise in organized crime, and underworld empires were built on bootlegging.

As the problems multiplied, so did the search for remedies. Many communities created ad hoc commissions to study the interrelated problems of crime, police and justice. More than 100 such surveys were conducted during the 1920s. One in Cleveland found waste, inefficiency, corruption, overburdened courts, crowded jails and poor police management. Another, in Illinois, found corrupt politicians hand in glove with corrupt policemen.

In 1929 President Herbert Hoover named an 11-member National Commission on Law Observance and Enforcement, whose chairman was a former U.S. attorney general, George W. Wickersham. In 1931 the commission concluded a comprehensive study, which made major recommendations about police administration. Among them: Police department commanders should be selected according to their competence. Patrolmen should rate at least a "B" on the Alpha intelligence tests. Salaries should support a decent standard of living. State police forces should be established in all states along with state bureaus of investigation and information. Training, communications and record-keeping systems should be expanded.

Although no massive wave of reform followed the Wickersham Report, there were gradual changes. For example, the Chicago Police Department established flying squads that rushed to the scenes of crimes and launched immediate investigations. The police departments also moved to minimize political pressure. Modern crime laboratories were developed, and the two-way radio was adopted for law-enforcement use. August Vollmer's *The Police and Modern Society,* published in 1936, was a seminal work that provided much of the basis for innovation during the New Deal era. As every state organized a police force, the need for training institutions led to the establishment of several new ones: the FBI's National Academy in 1935; San Jose State College's police program in 1931; the cadet program of the Wichita, Kansas, Police Department under Chief O. W. Wilson; and the four-year program at Michigan State College.

The Depression actually helped to augment the ranks of police forces with persons who otherwise would not have considered policing as a career. The Works Progress Administration helped to build new police stations, jails and police academies without unduly burdening police budgets. Although World War II was a disruptive interregnum in police history, returning veterans proved to be a welcome source of hardy manpower.

In 1950 the Senate Special Committee to investigate Organized Crime in Interstate Commerce, chaired by Senator Estes Kefauver, heard hundreds of witnesses allude to the existence of crime syndicates and of covert police collusion in underworld crime activities. Sheriffs, police chiefs and command officers were found on syndicate payrolls.

Serious reform initiatives were begun in the Los Angeles Police Department during this period. Under Chief William H. Parker, the department's emphasis was on superior personnel. Chief Parker formed an internal affairs division to investigate citizens' complaints of police misconduct. He coauthored a City Board of Regents procedure guaranteeing the separation of police discipline from politics. Community relations programs were started. The Bureau of Administration with two new features—an intelligence division and a planning and research division—were added. It is believed that under Chief Parker, California police officers were among the best trained in the nation.

The Eisenhower lull in new developments in police history was followed by two turbulent decades filled with the spread of drugs, sit-ins, boycotts, rent strikes and terrorism, all of which tested police mettle in a way it had never been tried before. There was yet another factor that had not existed earlier. Through a series of decisions, the U.S. Supreme Court under Chief Justice Earl Warren debilitated the police vis-à-vis the criminal. The Court reaffirmed the right to counsel, the right against unconstitutional searches and seizures, and the right against self-incrimination. One of the most important benchmark cases was *Miranda* v. *Arizona* 384 U.S. 436 of 1966, which required the police to inform a suspect of his or her rights at the time of arrest, including the right to remain silent, and of the potential trial use of any statements he or she makes. Another decision required states to appoint counsel for indigent defendants.

The social turbulence of the 1960s prompted the

federal government to launch official inquiries into the causes and prevention of crime. Chief among these was the President's Commission on Law Enforcement and Administration of Justice, whose chairman was the then attorney general, Nicholas deB. Katzenbach. Its report, *The Challenge of Crime in a Free Society,* was published in 1967 and was followed by task force reports on specific components of the report. The report found that police were isolated from the communities they served, that city officials had given all responsibility for running police agencies to their chiefs and that police executives had not assumed roles as major policymakers. The report cited the urgent need to improve relations with three segments of society: the poor, minorities and juveniles.

In the 1970s, when the waves of violence and unrest had peaked, the Law Enforcement Assistance Administration (see later in this chapter) helped set up the National Advisory Commission on Criminal Justice Standards and Goals to formulate models for the reduction and prevention of crime at state and local levels. The commission's police task force report was issued in 1973. It recommended specific guidelines for evaluating existing practices or setting up new programs. The report's standards and goals are being successfully adopted by state and municipal agencies.

Structure & Organization

Federal Law Enforcement

The U.S. Department of Justice, a cabinet-level department, presides over federal law enforcement, although many agencies are outside its jurisdiction. Established through congressional legislation on June 22, 1870, it was placed under the control of the attorney general, whose office had been created by the Judiciary Act of 1789. In 1871, again by congressional legislation, the federal prison and correctional system was added to the jurisdiction of the attorney general. In 1879 he was authorized to investigate and prosecute violations of federal laws. This authority eventually led to the formation of the FBI.

The Department of Justice (DOJ) performs both civil and criminal prosecution duties on behalf of all federal agencies. It represents federal agencies in civil suits and is the only avenue of prosecution for federal offenses. In the mid-1980s, the DOJ consisted of 15 offices, seven divisions, five bureaus and three boards or commissions. The attorney general's office has direct responsibility over the Office of Public Affairs, the Office of the Solicitor General, the Office of the Legal Counsel, the Office of Legal Policy, the Office of Intelligence Policy and Review, the Office of Professional Responsibility, the FBI, the Drug Enforcement Administration and the Justice Management Division. The chain of command runs through the deputy attorney general, who also is an appointed official, to the associate attorney general, who is in charge of agencies and bureaus.

The Criminal Division of the DOJ is under an assistant attorney general, assisted by four deputies. The office supervises all federal criminal prosecutions except those relating to civil rights, antitrust, land and natural resources, and taxes. The first deputy assistant attorney general for enforcement manages the Organized Crime and Racketeering Section; the Public Integrity Section, which coordinates federal efforts against corrupt public officials; and the Office of Policy and Management Analysis. The second deputy assistant attorney general is responsible for the Fraud Section; the Appellate Section; and the Office of International Affairs, which handles extraditions. The third deputy assistant attorney general heads general and international litigation, which consists of the Internal Security Division, the General Litigation and Legal Advice Section, and the Office of Special Investigations. The fourth deputy assistant attorney general manages the Narcotics and Dangerous Drugs Section, the Office of Legislation, the Office of Administration, the Office of Enforcement Operations and the Office of Asset Forfeiture.

The next major DOJ office is the U.S. National Central Bureau (USNCB) of Interpol. It is managed by a chief assisted by a deputy chief and is composed of three sections: Investigation, Administration and Operations. Officers are temporarily assigned to the USNCB from various agencies, and the posts of chief and deputy chief are filled by Treasury and Justice Department officials on a two-year rotating basis.

The Bureau of Alcohol, Tobacco and Firearms (BATF) is the only law-enforcement agency under the Department of the Treasury. Originally a unit of the IRS, it later became a division of the IRS as the Alcohol, Tobacco and Firearms Division, until 1972, when it was transferred to the Treasury Department. The ATF's golden age was the Prohibition era, when it had to enforce the Volstead Act.

The BATF is headed by a director appointed by the president with congressional approval. There are eight offices under the director, including that of the comptroller, who is in charge of the two laboratories, at San Francisco and Atlanta. The BATF National Firearms Tracing Center was initiated in 1972. The BATF also prepares firearms certifications and performs serial number searches as part of the National Firearms Registration and Transfer Record Act. There are five regional criminal enforcement offices, with smaller resident agency offices in every state and in all major cities.

The Compliance and Investigations Group (CIG), an investigative office under the Office of Personnel Management (OPM), was established by the Civil

Service Reform Act of 1978. It administers federal civilian personnel laws and regulations. The CIG is headed by an associate director assisted by a deputy associate director. There are 10 Office of Personnel Management divisions, each under a director. OPM investigators are involved primarily in conducting background investigations to determine a person's suitability for a government position through three types of security clearances: National Agency Check (NAC), NAC with Inquiries (NACI) and full-field background investigation (PSI).

Criminal Investigation Command (USACIDIC), Department of the Army. USACIDIC controls and conducts all Army investigations of serious crimes and other offenses, including offenses involving controlled substances and protective services for the Department of Defense, and provides forensic science support to Department of Defense criminal justice agencies. The agency was formed as the Criminal Investigation Division (CID) under General John J. Pershing, commanding the U.S. Army Expeditionary Forces in France, for detecting and preventing crime in territories occupied by the U.S. Army. The unit was deactivated at the end of World War I and revived in 1944. However, CID operations were fragmented and decentralized in field commands. The CID remained in operation after World War II as the investigative arm of the Army. In 1969 the provost marshal established the U.S. Army Criminal Investigation Agency. Two years later, the USACIDC was established under a commanding general. (The letter D is retained as an historical reminder of the first CID). The command reports directly to the Army chief of staff.

The USACIDC is located at Falls Church, Virginia, and is commanded by a major general assisted by a deputy commander and a chief of staff. The headquarters comprises six directorates, five regions, three crime laboratories and the Crime Records Center. Several units report directly to the commanding general, including the Office of the Inspector General.

The six directorates are Personnel and Administration, Resource Management, Logistics, Policy, Plans and Training, Communications and Operations. The last is the nucleus of the USACIDC and comprises the Administrative Support Division; the General Crime Division; the Economic Crime Division; and the Protective Services Agency, which provides security to selected senior officials of the Department of Defense. The Crime Records Center, composed of four divisions, administers the polygraph program. The three crime laboratories are in Atlanta; Frankfurt, West Germany; and Camp Zama, Japan.

The USACIDC is divided into five regions, with an additional Washington district headquarters at Fort Myer, Va. The five regions are headquartered at Fort George G. Mead in Maryland; Heidelberg, West Germany; Fort Gillem, Georgia; the Presidio in San Francisco; and Seoul, South Korea.

The Criminal Investigation Division (CID), Internal Revenue Service, investigates possible criminal violations of tax laws and recommends appropriate civil and criminal sanctions where warranted. Formed in 1919 under IRS commissioner Daniel C. Roper, the CID has an impressive track record against tax evasion by criminal elements. The CID is headed by the IRS commissioner, who supervises seven regional offices, at Cincinnati, Philadelphia, Chicago, New York, Atlanta, Dallas and San Francisco, each under a regional commissioner, and 63 district offices. The assistant commissioner for operations is in charge of the CID's Examination, Collection and Employee Plans and Exempt Organizations.

The Defense Investigative Service (DIS), Department of Defense (DOD), conducts background and other investigations, oversees programs involving industrial security and manages the Defense Department's Central Index of Investigations. The DIS also performs security checks for the National Security Agency. The DIS headquarters staff consists of a director, an inspector general, two deputy directors and three assistant directors. DIS personnel who perform investigative functions are known as special agents, and most are DOD civilians. They wear civilian clothes, drive unmarked cars and are issued badges and credentials. The Industrial Security Program comprises the Industrial Facilities Protection Program, the Defense Industrial Security Program and the Survey Program for Contractors. DIS security clearance information is stored in the Defense Central Index of Investigations in Baltimore, Md.

The Division of Law Enforcement Services (DLES), Bureau of Indian Affairs (BIA), Department of the Interior, is charged with the prevention and deterrence of crime in tribal areas, and enforcement of tribal laws and federal statutes. The DLES was founded in 1878 as the Indian Police Service. BIA enforcement programs are supervised by the commissioner for Indian Affairs, who reports to the assistant secretary for Indian affairs in the Department of the Interior. The DLES functions under a chief, who manages the three separate offices of Special Operations Services; the Criminal Justice Data Unit in Bingham City, Utah; and the Inspection Unit. There are 10 area offices, each under a special officer, at Aberdeen, S.D.; Albuquerque, N.M.; Billings, Mont.; Anardarko, Okla.; Washington, D.C.; Minneapolis; Window Rock, Ariz.; Phoenix; Portland, Ore.; and Sacramento.

The Division of Probation (DOP), Administrative Office of the U.S. Courts, Department of Justice, completes probation reports, presentence investigations and other duties for the federal court system. It also performs parole office duties for the U.S. Parole Commission, which is under the attorney general. The DOP is under an assistant director for program management. It is headed by a chief assisted by a deputy chief and five regional probation administrators. There are 94 federal court districts, each of which has a probation officer.

The Division of Ranger Activities and Protection (DRAP), National Park Service (NPS), Department of the Interior, provides law-enforcement services in national parks, performs rescue missions and provides emergency medical services. The DRAP is one of the five divisions of the NPS under an assistant director who reports to the associate director of management and operations. There are 10 regional offices, at Boston; Philadelphia; Santa Fe; San Francisco; Washington, D.C.; Atlanta; Omaha; Seattle; Denver; and Harpers Ferry, W. Va. Rangers become involved in a wide range of law-enforcement operations. Most of these are minor offenses, such as camping without a permit, theft of property and setting illegal campfires.

The Drug Enforcement Administration (DEA), Department of Justice, is the primary agency responsible for drug and narcotics enforcement, sharing this authority with the FBI. The enforcement of laws against narcotics was the task of the Bureau of Revenue from 1914 to 1930, when the Bureau of Narcotics was established under the Department of the Treasury. This latter bureau was charged with the enforcement of the Harrison Narcotics Act of 1914 which imposed a tax on all narcotics. In 1968 the Bureau of Narcotics was transferred to the Department of Justice and merged with the Bureau of Drug Abuse Control to form the Bureau of Narcotics and Dangerous Drugs (BNDD). In 1973 the BNDD was renamed the DEA and combined with the Office of Drug Abuse Law Enforcement and the Office of National Narcotics Intelligence.

The DEA is under an administrator appointed by the president. Nineteen divisional field offices and three foreign offices report to the headquarters: Atlanta; Boston; Chicago; Dallas; Denver; Detroit; Houston; Los Angeles; Miami; Newark, N.J.; New Orleans; New York; Philadelphia; Phoenix; San Diego; Seattle; St. Louis; New Orleans; and Washington, D.C., in the United States and Bangkok, Mexico City and Paris abroad. The DEA has task forces with the New York, Chicago and Los Angeles police departments and in 13 other cities, where it supplies the matériel. The Office of Diversion Control is responsible for regulating the distribution of legal narcotics and drugs. About half of the DEA's personnel are special agents; the remainder are compliance investigators, chemists, intelligence specialists and clerical workers. The DEA operates a fleet of over 45 airplanes, including helicopters.

The Federal Aviation Administration Police (FAAP), Department of Transportation, enforces rules, regulations and federal statutes at Washington National and Dulles International airports. Originally called the Washington National Airport Police, the FAAP was established on June 29, 1940, by congressional legislation. It is part of the FAA's Public Safety Division and is under a chief of police.

The Federal Bureau of Investigation (FBI), Department of Justice. The best-known and most powerful law-enforcement agency in the United States, the FBI is the principal investigative arm of the Department of Justice. Although its functions and objectives are defined by law, there are few criminal areas beyond its purview, and it also represents the standard of excellence to which all other agencies aspire. Under Edgar Hoover and his successors, the agency has carefully built up a reputation for competence and integrity, which is its most enduring contribution to American public life.

Founded as the Bureau of Investigation in July 1908 under Attorney General Charles J. Bonaparte, the FBI's earliest task was the enforcement of the 1910 Mann Act, which prohibited the transportation of females across state lines for purposes of prostitution. Its powers were expanded with the 1919 Dyer Act, prohibiting transportation of stolen vehicles across state lines, and laws relating to espionage and Selective Service (military draft) violations. The FBI's early history was characterized by corruption, inefficiency and brutality. Consequently, there were suggestions that the bureau be disbanded. The turning point in its history was the appointment of 29-year-old J. Edgar Hoover as director in 1924. When Attorney General Harlan F. Stone offered him the job, Hoover set certain conditions: The bureau would be free from politics, and all appointments and promotions would be based on merit. Hoover's conditions were accepted, and he immediately set to work reorganizing the bureau, establishing new procedures, firing incompetent men and establishing austere rules of personal conduct. In 1935 Congress changed the name of the agency to the Federal Bureau of Investigation. In the same year the FBI Academy was founded, becoming in time the premier police training institution in the country. The Identification Division was formed as a national depository for fingerprints.

The FBI's reputation has been built on many sensational arrests, as that of George "Machine Gun" Kelly in 1933, John Dillinger in 1934, Charles "Pretty Boy" Floyd in 1934 and other Prohibition era criminals. In 1939 President Roosevelt placed internal security matters within FBI purview, leading to the arrest of several German spies during World War II and Soviet and other Communist spies after the war. An ardent foe of communism, Hoover pursued Communists and fellow travelers relentlessly. Civil rights activists and student dissidents consumed much of Hoover's attention until his death in 1972.

The FBI is headed by a director who is appointed by the president and confirmed by Congress for a term not to exceed 10 years. (This provision did not apply to Hoover.) Organizationally, there are 10 divisions at the headquarters, which coordinate the activities of 59 field offices. Three major bureau functions are the responsibility of executive assistant directors who report to the director: Law Enforcement Services, Investigations and Administration.

The first major component, the Law Enforcement Services Section (LESS), is divided into three divisions: Identification, Training and Laboratory. The first maintains over 200 million fingerprints; the second runs the National Academy at Quantico, Va.; and the Laboratory Division works through several units, such as: Instrumental Analysis Unit, Chemistry and Toxicology Unit, Serology Unit, Minerology Unit, Metallurgy Unit, Microscopic Analysis Unit, National Fraudulent Check File, Firearms Toolmark Unit, Explosives Unit, Elemental Analysis Unit, and Document and Cryptanalysis Section. The Investigations Section is composed of the Domestic Intelligence Division, the General Investigative Division and the Special Investigative Division.

The FBI also publishes national crime data statistics through *Uniform Crime Reports,* published annually. It also operates the National Crime Information Center (NCIC), a nationwide criminal justice information teleprocessing network that checks for stolen articles, wanted persons, warrant information, criminal history data and missing children. The network operates in all 50 states, Puerto Rico and Canada. It compiles the periodic "Ten Most Wanted Criminals" list familiar to Americans. The FBI also maintains foreign liaison offices in U.S. embassies abroad.

The Federal Communications Commission (FCC) monitors and investigates violations of federal regulations of broadcasting. The FCC enforcement arm is within the Field Operations Bureau. The Complaints and Compliance Division also conducts inquiries and investigations. The FCC has six regional offices and 13 monitoring stations and a district office in Anchorage.

The Federal Maritime Commission (FMC) monitors and investigates violations of federal laws by common carriers by water through its Bureau of Investigations and its Office of Investigations. The FMC has five district field offices and two suboffices nationwide.

The Federal Protective Service (FPS), General Services Administration (GSA), is charged with the preservation of peace, protection of life and property, prevention and detection of crime, apprehension of criminals and trespassers, and enforcement of rules and regulations on all properties owned by the General Services Administration (GSA). FPS personnel supervise the activities of contract guards at GSA buildings and installations, with the exception of the U.S. Capitol and the U.S. Supreme Court.

The Federal Trade Commission (FTC) is an independent federal regulatory agency exercising law-enforcement functions through its Bureau of Competition and its Bureau of Consumer Protection. The former is concerned with antitrust actions. It can investigate and prosecute unfair methods of competition and price fixing. The latter attempts to keep the marketplace free of deception, fraud and unfair practices, especially in advertising, warranties, credit and sales gimmicks.

The Fish and Wildlife Service (FWS), Department of the Interior, investigates and prosecutes violations of federal statutes relating to the environment in general and endangered species in particular through its special agents and game inspectors. The FWS does not always pursue criminal prosecutions in wildlife violations but often obtains civil judgments for actions detrimental to the environment.

The Forest Service (FS), Department of Agriculture, enforces a variety of statutes in national forest lands through special agents and investigators. The FS is a decentralized agency that manages 154 national forests, 19 national grasslands and 653 ranger districts. The law-enforcement functions of the regional foresters and administrators include fire or disease prevention and control; protection of property, roads and trails; protection of endangered species of flora or fauna; public safety; and enforcement of federal statutes.

The Immigration and Naturalization Service Border Patrol (INS-BP), Department of Justice, is the law-enforcement arm of the INS established in 1924. Originally it patrolled the Mexican and Canadian land borders; the Gulf Coast border was added in 1925. Nonuniformed criminal investigators were added in 1947 to replace immigration inspectors. The BP is directed by the Office of Enforcement within the INS, and its programs include investigation, detention, deportation, antismuggling and intelligence. The Investigations Division locates and apprehends illegal aliens residing in the United States as well as those who conspire to gain illegal entry for aliens. The Intelligence Program involves the use of strategy as well as sophisticated electronic equipment and sensors as well as more traditional means, such as dogs.

Four regional commissioners are responsible to the headquarters. Within each region, a chief BP agent has field responsibility for patrol operations within its patrol sectors. The regions are composed of 35 districts and 20 BP sectors: five in the North, three in the East, seven in the South and five in the West.

The Inspection Service (IS), Internal Revenue Service, Department of the Treasury, investigates allegations of criminal and serious administrative violations against IRS employees, bribery attempts against IRS personnel and conducts background checks of IRS employees. The IRS functions through two segments: the Inspection Service and the Criminal Investigation Division, both jointly responsible to the under secretary of the Treasury for Enforcement. The IS is divided into two primary components: the Internal Audit Division and the Internal Security Division. Internal Security inspectors are criminal investigators, although many of their cases involve noncriminal activity.

The Intelligence and Law Enforcement Branch (ILEB), U.S. Coast Guard, Department of Transportation, is the investigative arm of the Coast Guard. Operationally the ILEB is a segment of the Coast Guard headquarters staff under the commandant. It enforces U.S. laws within territorial waters and fishery zones, interdicts narcotics and illegal aliens en route to the United States and prevents illegal goods from entering the country.

The Intelligence and Security Command (INSCOM), Department of the Army, conducts intelligence-related investigations for the U.S. Army, including counterintelligence, photographic image interpretation and electronic interception. Founded in 1977, the INSCOM is a separate branch of the Army located at Fort George G. Meade, Md., and Baltimore, and is commanded by a major general. There are 10 main field stations, four single-discipline intelligence groups and six multidiscipline intelligence groups in addition to other undisclosed elements.

The International Trade Administration (ITA), Department of Commerce, has investigative powers derived from the Tariff Act of 1930, the Trade Act of 1974 and the Antidumping Act of 1921. The assistant secretary for trade administration is in charge of two offices having law-enforcement functions: Export Enforcement and Import Administration. The former investigates suspected violations of antiboycott regulations; the latter enforces regulations regarding antidumping.

The Interstate Commerce Commission (ICC) investigates and prosecutes violations of tariff rules as well as federal statutes relating to interstate rail, land and water shipments and foreign transportation. The Office of Compliance and Consumer Assistance is the primary enforcement arm of the ICC. The ICC is headed by a director, who presides over four boards: the Revocation Board, the Motor Carrier Licensing Board, the Insurance Board and the Railroad Service Board. In addition, there are two sections, one for operations and the other for enforcement. The ICC has six regional offices, at Boston, Philadelphia, Atlanta, Chicago, Fort Worth and San Francisco.

The Metropolitan Police Department, Washington, D.C. (MPD-WDC). Since Washington, D.C., is a federal enclave, all criminal violations within the city are federal crimes. However, MPD policemen are not federal but municipal employees. The MPD was formed as a night watch early in the 19th century and was given the legal status of a police force by act of Congress in 1861. It evolved slowly and did not obtain badges until 1961. The MPD functions like other municipal forces, under a chief of police. There are four main bureaus reporting to him: Field Operations Bureau, Administrative Services Bureau, Technical Services Bureau and Inspectional Services Bureau. Each of the seven districts under the Field Operations Bureau is supervised by a commander, who holds the rank of deputy chief. Also under the Field Operations Bureau are the Youth Division, the Special Operations Division and the Criminal Investigation Division, each headed by a deputy chief.

The Military Police Corps (MPC), Department of the Army, performs uniformed traffic, law-enforcement and public safety duties on Army posts and installations, conducts preliminary criminal investigations involving Army personnel and guards Army correctional facilities.

One of the oldest law-enforcement agencies, the MPC's progenitor was the Provost Corps, established in 1778 by Congress to enforce rules and regulations in the Continental Army. It reappeared briefly in 1919 as World War I was drawing to a close and was reactivated in 1941. This time, however, the MPC became part of the peacetime military structure.

The MPC has units operating at the local base level responsible to a base commander. The ultimate control lies with the Office of Army Law Enforcement under the deputy chief of staff for personnel. Like civilian police, MPC personnel work around the clock, in three shifts.

The National Marine Fisheries Service (NMFS), National Oceanic and Atmospheric Administration (NOAA), Department of Commerce, enforces domestic fishing regulations, particularly those pertaining to foreign vessels operating within 200 miles of the coast. The Enforcement Division is under the Regional Fisheries Management Center.

The National Zoological Park Police (NZPP), Smithsonian Institution, performs police functions within the National Zoological Park in Washington, D.C., under Public Law 206 of October 24, 1951.

The Naval Investigative Service (NIS), Department of the Navy, is the naval counterpart of the Army

CID. The NIS is a field activity of the Naval Intelligence Command and consists of a headquarters in Washington, D.C., and 150 field components throughout the world. The NIS director, a Navy captain, is responsible to the chief of naval operations. The director is assisted by a civilian deputy director, and five assistant directors in charge of internal security, criminal investigations, career services, technical services and administration, respectively. There are 10 regional offices, 65 smaller resident units, 16 agent afloat locations and four regional forensic laboratories. Agents afloat are assigned to naval combat vessels. About 70% of all NIS cases involve criminal investigations and 30% foreign counterintelligence operations.

The Office of the Inspector General (OIG), Department of Agriculture (USDA), is the primary law-enforcement arm of the USDA and was established in 1962, abolished in 1974 and reestablished in 1977. There are six OIG regional offices, at Kansas City; Chicago; Hyattsville, Md.; New York; Atlanta; and Temple, Tex. Its major areas of jurisdiction are the Food Stamp Program, child nutrition programs, the Federal Grain Inspection Service and the Farmers Home Administration. Its meat and stockyard inspection programs ensure compliance with federal standards and regulations.

The Office of the Inspector General (OIG), Department of Commerce (DOC), is the primary law-enforcement arm of DOC and was established in 1978. The OIG is composed of five district offices, of which the Office of Investigations conducts actual operations through its Investigative Operations Division and the Fraud Intelligence Division.

The Office of the Inspector General (OIG), Department of Defense (DOD), is the principal investigative arm of the DOD. The OIG is a relatively new organization, established in 1982 by amendments to the Inspector General Act of 1978. It did not replace other existing military investigative agencies. The inspector general is an appointed official who reports to the secretary of defense. Under the inspector general are seven main offices: Auditing, Investigations, Management, Criminal Investigations, Audit Follow-Up, Audit Oversight and Policy, and Inspections and Management. The Office of Investigations is generally referred to as the Defense Criminal Investigations Service (DCIS) and functions under an assistant inspector general. It is a civilian force of special agents who investigate criminal and other serious allegations against DOD employees and contractors. There are 10 field offices, 16 resident agencies and one sub-office.

The Office of the Inspector General (OIG), Department of Education (USDE), is the principal law-enforcement agency of the USDE and was established in 1978. The inspector general, an appointed official, is assisted by the director of fraud control. OIG investigations are handled by the Office of Investigations, with the Division of Headquarters Investigations, the Division of Field Operations and regional investigative offices.

The Office of the Inspector General (OIG), Department of Health and Human Services (HHS), is the principal law-enforcement arm of HHS and was established in 1976. The inspector general, who is appointed by the president, reports directly to the HHS secretary. The primary offices within the OIG are Audit, Investigations, Program Inspections and Health Financing Integrity. The Office of Investigations is composed of five distinct segments: the Criminal Investigations Division; the Social Security Program Integrity Division; the Civil Fraud Division; the State Fraud Division; and the Security and Protection Division. The first has line authority over 11 field offices, each under a special agent-in-charge; the second has 10 field units; the third has three units, including a Hot Line unit; and the fourth has three branches. The 10 regional offices are in Boston; New York; Philadelphia; Dallas; Kansas City, Mo.; Denver; Atlanta; Chicago; San Francisco; and Seattle.

The Office of Inspector General (OIG), Department of Housing and Urban Development (HUD), is the primary law-enforcement arm of HUD and was established in 1972. The inspector general is appointed by the president and presides over three offices: Audit, Fraud Control and Management Operations, and Investigation. The last has 10 regional offices. The OIG participates in the Target Cities Program to eliminate fraud and corruption in HUD programs.

The Office of the Inspector General (OIG), Department of the Interior (DINT), is the principal law-enforcement arm of the DINT and was established in 1978. The inspector general is appointed by the president and is responsible to the secretary of the interior. The Office of Investigations is the operational branch of the OIG and includes a Special Investigations Branch with three regional offices.

The Office of the Inspector General (OIG), Department of Labor (DOL), is the principal law-enforcement arm of the DOL and was established in 1969. The inspector general is appointed by the president and reports to the secretary of labor. Under him are six offices: Internal Affairs Staff, Administrative Management, Audit, Loss Analysis and Prevention, Organized Crime and Racketeering, and Investigations. The Organized Crime and Racketeering Office participates in the Organized Crime Strike Force groups nationwide.

The Office of the Inspector General (OIG), Department of Transportation (DOT), is the primary law-enforcement arm of the DOT and was established in 1978. Among the DOT agencies that the OIG services are the Federal Aviation Administration, the Federal Highway Administration, the National Highway Traffic Safety Administration, the Maritime Administration, the U.S. Coast Guard, the Federal Railroad Administration, the Urban Mass Transportation Agency, the Regional and Special Programs Administration and the Office of the Secretary of Transportation.

The inspector general is appointed by the president. OIG investigations are handled by the Office of Investigations, composed of the Office of Special Assignments, the Office of Investigative Operations, five regional offices and seven resident agency offices.

The Office of the Inspector General (OIG), Department of the Treasury (USDT), is one of the law-enforcement agencies of the USDT and coordinates internal affairs investigations, including fraud by contractors. The inspector general reports directly to the secretary of the Treasury. There are three discrete offices within the OIG: Audit, Investigations and Operations. The OIG conducts investigations of official misconduct in the Office of the Secretary and in the five USDT bureaus that have no investigative components. The OIG also conducts, controls and supervises investigations of senior-level officials regardless of bureau.

The Office of the Inspector General (OIG), Environmental Protection Agency (EPA), is the principal law-enforcement agency of the EPA and investigates all violations of statutes relating to environment, except air pollution. The inspector general is appointed by the president and reports directly to the EPA administrator. Investigations are conducted by the Office of Investigations. There are five regional offices, in New York, Philadelphia, Chicago, Atlanta and San Francisco.

The Office of the Inspector General (OIG), General Services Administration (GSA), is the principal law-enforcement arm of the GSA. The OIG is under an inspector general appointed by the president and cannot be removed for political reasons. The Office of Investigations within the OIG is composed of the Investigative Operations Division and the Investigative Support, Programs and Projects Staff. Investigative field offices are in Boston; New York; Philadelphia; Atlanta; Chicago; Kansas City, Mo.; Fort Worth; Denver; San Francisco; Auburn, Wash.; Arlington, Va.; and St. Louis.

The Office of the Inspector General (OIG), National Aeronautics and Space Administration (NASA), is the primary law-enforcement arm of NASA. The inspector general is appointed by the president. The Investigations Division is one of the three principal

components of the OIG and oversees eight regional offices, at Moffett Field, Calif.; Greenbelt, Md.; Pasadena, Calif.; Houston; JFK Space Center, Fla.; Hampton, Va.; Cleveland; and Center, Ala.

The Office of the Inspector General (OIG), Office of Personnel Management (OPM), is the principal law-enforcement arm of the OPM. The inspector general reports to the OPM director. The OPM has no regional field offices.

The Office of the Inspector General (OIG), Office of the Public Printer, Government Printing Office (GPO), is the primary law-enforcement arm of the GPO. The inspector general reports directly to the public printer concerning audits and investigations of GPO operations. Operations are conducted by the Office of Investigations and Security.

The Office of the Inspector General (OIG), Veterans Administration (VA), is the principal law-enforcement arm of the VA and was established in 1978. The inspector general is appointed by the president and reports directly to the administrator. The Office of Investigations within the OIG consists of the Investigative Operations Division with eight regional offices, and the Special Operations Division. Special agents also coordinate medical investigations with the medical inspector under the Department of Medicine and Surgery.

The Office of Legal and Enforcement Counsel (OLEC), Environmental Protection Agency (EPA), investigates all violations involving air, water and land pollution by both private and governmental bodies. It uses administrative, civil and criminal enforcement methods to enforce pollution laws. Operationally, there are two discrete units within the OLEC: The first, the Office of Deputy General Counsel, oversees the Air, Noise and Radiation Division; the Pesticides and Toxic Substances Division; the Water Division; the Solid Waste and Emergency Response Division; and the Grants, Contracts and General Administration Division. The second, the Office of Enforcement Counsel, manages the Civil Enforcement Divisions of Air, Waste, Water, and Pesticides and Toxic Substances, and the Criminal Enforcement Division. The OLEC has five regional investigative offices, in Philadelphia, Atlanta, Chicago, Seattle and Denver.

The Office of Security (OS), Department of State (DOS), is a relatively small law-enforcement force that protects foreign diplomats and official visitors (but not heads of state) in the United States, and protects DOS employees and embassies from terrorist activities, and investigates passport and visa violations. The OS is headed by a deputy assistant for security assisted by a deputy director of security. The major OS components are Protective Security; Personnel Security and Investigations; Policy, Training and Information; Operations; and Security. In addition, there are a 24-hour Command Center and a Special Assignments Staff. The Foreign Operations Division of the Office of Operations has grown in importance and size in recent years in the wake of terrorist attacks against U.S. embassies and diplomats. Security engineering officers, members of the Technical Security Division, are assigned to foreign service posts.

The Office of Security Police (OSP), Department of the Air Force (USAF), is the principal law-enforcement arm of the Air Force. The OSP protects USAF installations, provides traffic enforcement services, investigates vehicular accidents, guards Air Force personnel incarcerated in stockades and provides security for nuclear or missile sites. The OSP is commanded by a chief of security police and comprises three primary directorates: Operations; Plans and Programs; and Information Security. OSP headquarters is at Kirkland Air Force Base, N.M. The main Security Clearance Office is in Washington, D.C. The OSP use canine patrols extensively in guarding Air Force bases and nuclear installations and missile sites. The dogs are trained at the Military Working Dog Studies Branch at the OSP Academy, Lackland Air Force Base, Tex.

The Office of Special Investigations (OSI), Department of the Air Force, investigates serious allegations involving USAF military and civilian employees. Established in 1947, the OSI is under a commander responsible to the inspector general. Six primary directorates report to the OSI commander: Criminal Investigations, Fraud Investigations, Counterintelligence, Special Techniques, Technical Services and Training. OSI district offices are at USAF bases, and there are smaller field offices in New York; Bolling Air Force Base and Anacostia Naval Air Station, Washington, D.C.; and Los Angeles. There are 13 overseas offices. OSI headquarters are at Bolling Air Force Base, which also is the location of the OSI Academy.

The Postal Inspection Service (PIS), U.S. Postal Service (USPS), is the principal law-enforcement arm of the USPS and was established in 1737. It investigates violations involving approximately 85 federal statutes relating to USPS PIS functions under a chief postal inspector, assisted by three assistant chief inspectors in charge of Criminal Investigations, Audit and Administration, respectively. The Investigations Division comprises three branches, which specialize in external crimes, internal crimes, and fraud and prohibited mailings, and the crime laboratory. There are five regional offices, each of which is divided into divisional offices and smaller field offices. The five regional laboratories are in Chicago; Memphis; New York; San Bruno, Calif.; and Washington, D.C.

The Public Safety Service (PSS), Tennessee Valley Authority (TVA), is the principal law-enforcement arm of the TVA and was established in 1933. The PSS headquarters are at the TVA main offices in Knoxville, Tenn. The PSS chief reports to the general manager.

The Securities and Exchange Commission Division of Enforcement (SECDE). The SECDE is the principal law-enforcement arm of the Securities and Exchange Commission. It investigates complaints by investors and the public, makes surprise inspections to ensure that dealers and brokers are complying with the law, and initiates inquiries when market fluctuations in particular stocks appear to be manipulated by crooks, such as Ivan Boesky in 1986. It also investigates reports of missing, lost, counterfeited or stolen securities and ensures compliance of gas and electric utilities with federal statutes.

The Security Service (SS), Department of Medicine and Surgery (DMS), Veterans Administration (VA), investigates criminal activities at DMS facilities, conducts preemployment screening, and conducts compliance checks and inspections. The SS-DMS is operationally under a director. SS-DMS personnel are responsible not only to the local director of the medical center but also to the regional security officer. There are three regional SS offices, at Indianapolis; Little Rock; and Livermore, Calif.

The Treasury Police Force (TPF), U.S. Secret Service, Department of the Treasury, polices the main Treasury Building in Washington, D.C. The TPF is commanded by a chief who manages three separate shifts, each managed by a lieutenant.

The U.S. Capitol Police (USCP) maintains law and order within the 190 acres of the Capitol grounds in Washington, D.C., three House office buildings, two House office building annexes, the Senate office buildings, five Senate office building annexes and the Capitol power plant. It was established in 1851. Commanded by a chief, the USCP is divided along traditional line and staff functions. The main divisions are field operations, Investigations, and Staff and Auxiliary Services, each under a deputy chief. Field operations are divided into four details: House, Senate, Capitol and Patrol. Investigations comprise criminal investigations, protective services and special investigations.

The U.S. Customs Service (USCS), Department of the Treasury (USDT), is the principal law-enforcement arm responsible for collection of customs, excise duties, fees and penalties on imported or exported merchandise as well as interdiction and seizure of contraband entering the country. It also administers certain navigation laws; apprehends individuals engaged in revenue fraud; enforces regulations and statutes relating to antidumping, copyright, patent and trademark provisions; and collects international trade statistics. Both civil and criminal avenues are used in gaining compliance with federal customs laws.

The USCS is headed by a commissioner appointed by the president, under whom are five major components: Office of the Comptroller, Commercial Operations; Enforcement; Inspection and Control; and Internal Affairs.

The USCS employs a wide range of techniques to apprehend violators: dogs, high-resolution X-ray machines, ground sensors, television systems, electronic tracking transmitters, night-vision scopes and computers. USCS computers are interfaced with the FBI's National Crime Information Center.

There are three categories of USCS personnel: uniformed inspectors, nonuniformed special agents, and customs patrol officers (CPO). The USCS has seven regional offices, at Boston, New York, Miami, New Orleans, Houston, Los Angeles and Chicago, over 300 district offices in the United States and nine overseas offices.

The U.S. Marshals Service (USMS), Department of Justice (DOJ), is one of the oldest federal law-enforcement agencies. The Office of the U.S. Marshal was established by the Judiciary Act of 1789, and the first 13 marshals—one for each of the original states— were appointed by George Washington himself. The marshal's legendary image was established during the period of the early West by such lawmen as Wyatt Earp. Often the marshal was the only symbol of law and order in the West, and it was a lonely and dangerous position. The USMS was established in 1969 and subsequently became a bureau in 1974. There are now 94 judicial districts and 93 marshals, including at least one marshal for each state, the District of Columbia, the Virgin Islands and the Northern Marianas.

U.S. marshals and deputy marshals act as court officers enforcing edicts from the U.S. Supreme Court and the federal district courts; transport prisoners; provide security to federal judges, prosecutors and jurors; arrest defendants indicted by federal grand juries; manage the Witness Protection Program; put down riots on federal lands and reservations; serve subpoenas and arrest warrants; and secure judgments.

The USMS headquarters is at McLean, Va., under a director who reports directly to the attorney general. A deputy director supervises the assistant directors for operations and administration and the 93 USMS districts.

The U.S. Park Police (USPP), National Park Service (NPS), Department of the Interior (DINT), is a specialized, uniformed agency that performs police functions in national parks. Named as the Park Watch from 1802 to 1919, the USPS was placed under the National Park Service in 1934. Outside the headquarters in Washington, D.C., there are two field offices, in Brooklyn, N.Y., and San Francisco. Commanded by a chief, the USPP is composed of an Office of Inspectional Services, the Services Division, the Operations Division and the Field Offices Division.

The U.S. Secret Service (USSS), Department of the Treasury (USDT), is composed of two branches: The first consists of special agents who protect the president and family, former presidents and families, the vice president and family, the president-elect and vice president-elect, major presidential candidates in an election year and heads of state of foreign countries visiting the United States. The also investigate counterfeiting of all U.S. currency and coins and forged government checks, bonds and other obligations. The second, or uniformed branch, protects the White House and other buildings, including foreign embassies.

Founded as the Secret Service Division (SSD) in 1870, the agency was originally responsible only for anticounterfeiting activities. After the assassination of President William McKinley in 1901, it was given responsibility for protecting the president, and this protection was extended to the president's immediate family in 1917. After the assassination of President John F. Kennedy in 1963, the SSD was reorganized as the USSS. In 1968, after the assassination of Robert F. Kennedy, major presidential candidates began to receive USSS protection.

USSS headquarters is in Washington, D.C. The James J. Rawley Training Center is in Beltsville, Md. Commanded by a director, the USSS has three major staff offices and five main components, including the Office of Inspection, the Office of Protective Operations, the Office of Protective Research, the Office of Investigations and the Office of Administration.

The U.S. Supreme Court Police (USSCP) the primary law-enforcement arm of the Supreme Court of the United States, is operationally under a captain responsible to the marshal of the Supreme Court.

State, County, Municipal & Local Police Agencies

Each state within the United States has a Department of Justice headed by an attorney general, either appointed or elected. This person is rarely, however, the head of a unified state organization of public prosecutors, and his or her activities usually are confined to rendering legal advice to the governor and representing the state in civil suits to which the state is a party.

State Police The responsibility of ensuring compliance to state laws is vested in the governor. Until the 20th century, this gubernatorial function was discharged through sheriffs, municipal police or the state militia. However, with the breakdown of the traditional sheriff-constable structure, the states have ventured directly into criminal justice operations. Texas was the first state to establish a statewide police, the Texas Rangers, in 1835. By 1905, Massachusetts, Connecticut and Pennsylvania had followed suit, and by the end of World War I almost all states had established some form of state police agency.

State police usually are organized within the state's Department of Public Safety. In some states this department has general policing powers, while in others its jurisdiction is confined to the enforcement of highway traffic laws. In most states, the state police have been granted general criminal jurisdiction, authorizing them to act anywhere within the state where state laws are violated. They may also be requested by the governor to assist other state agencies. However, they are prohibited by law from interfering in local cases unless specifically invited to do so, from taking action in labor disputes and from serving civil processes.

Each state has a number of other regulatory and administrative agencies with police powers and agents. State identification units sometimes are part of the state police and sometimes separate. They compile statistics and serve as a centralized records collection and maintenance agency. Many states have their own crime laboratories whose work impinges on law enforcement. Many state departments have investigation and enforcement agencies, such as those connected with state parks, state forests, and state fish and game agencies. There are also specialized units for enforcing narcotics laws and the regulation and licensing of alcoholic beverages. Many states employ a state fire marshal, and in some states the Public Health departments are responsible for enforcement of and investigation into violations of state health laws.

County Police Each state is divided into a number of counties. The majority of criminal prosecutions are handled by county or district attorneys, elected for a term of two to five years. They also advise the state attorney general on local matters.

The principal county police position is that of sheriff, perhaps the oldest law-enforcement office in Anglo-American history. A sheriff usually is elected for a two- or a four-year term. A sheriff's qualifications are defined by state law and his or her salary is fixed by the state legislature. In the majority of counties, the sheriff's income is based on services rendered, but he or she receives food and lodging expenses. The sheriff has the authority to choose anyone as a deputy, whether on an auxiliary or an honorary basis. The sheriff has broad powers covering the entire spectrum of criminal justice, including detection and apprehension of offenders, administration of county jails, execution of court orders and collection of taxes.

County constables perform similar functions and, like sheriffs, are not full-time employees. They are elected for short terms, and their functions include executing civil processes, collecting taxes, attending local courts and issuing election notices. They are assisted by deputy constables.

Rural and unincorporated areas of most counties generally are served by the county sheriff or constable through request or contract.

In most counties there are specialized police forces in charge of harbors, bridges, freeways, tunnels and parks.

Municipal Police All urban settlements in the United States have municipal police forces under the control of the municipal government. They are commanded by officers variously known as commissioners in large cities and chiefs of police in others. In Baltimore, St. Louis and Kansas City, Mo., the head of the police department is directly subordinate to the state governor, and in other cities to the mayor.

All city police duties fall under one of two categories: line or staff. Line functions are defined as operational and special activities; staff functions relate to administration and inspection.

Line functions common to most municipalities consist of patrol beats, including surveillance, investigation of crimes, enforcement of minor laws, crowd control and arrest of offenders; investigation, including investigation of reported crimes, recovery of stolen property, arrest of criminals and case preparation; vice or victimless crime activities; traffic control, juvenile activities and crime prevention activities. In some towns and cities the police are vested with additional responsibilities, including ambulance and rescue service, civil defense, regulation of animals, youth service, guard service and licensing.

Staff functions comprise personnel and training, human resource management, planning and research, finance and budgeting, public relations and community relations. Auxiliary staff services cover crime laboratories, prisons and jails, central records and identification files, communication networks, transportation vehicles and maintenance. Inspectional services are concerned with the elimination of corruption, graft and what is broadly termed police brutality.

Each police precinct has a dispatch center that controls the police telephone center and radio network keeping in touch with the policemen on the beat equipped with a personal portable two-way radio. Each patrol cruiser also is equipped with a camera, red lights, loudspeakers, a siren and a double-barreled shotgun as well as a first-aid kit and a resuscitator.

Smaller communities in the United States, defined as towns, villages, townships or boroughs, have law-enforcement officers called constables, marshals or policemen. Constables serve in towns or townships and marshals in small, incorporated places. Constables usually are elected for two- or four-year terms and are unpaid. During emergencies they call on the municipal, county or state police for aid.

Organizational units in a typical local police department are divided into three broad areas: functional, geographical and chronological.

Functional units consist in descending order of bureau, division, section and unit or office. The bureau is the largest unit, usually under a deputy or assistant chief. A division is the primary subdivision of a bureau commanded by a captain or lieutenant— e.g., the Investigation Division. A section is a subdivision of a division and usually is commanded by a lieutenant—e.g., the Homicide Section. A unit is a component of a section—e.g., an accident investigation unit within the Traffic Section.

The geographical units are, in ascending order, post, route, beat, sector, precinct and area. A post is the fixed point or place where a police officer is assigned—e.g., an intersection. A route is a stretch of a street patrolled by, e.g., a foot patrolman. Beat is the fundamental unit of patrol and is a marked area assigned to an officer or team. A sector consists of several beats, usually under a sergeant or line supervisor. A precinct is a group of sectors and is the term most familiar to the public because it is the divisional headquarters. An area is an administrative subdivision of a city.

The chronological units are shift and platoon. A shift (or watch in some cities) is a time division of the workday to which personnel are assigned. A shift usually is eight hours in duration, with three shifts in a day. Platoon refers to the men assigned to a specific shift, normally commanded by a lieutenant.

A major landmark in the development of American police systems was the creation in 1965 of the Law Enforcement Assistance Administration (LEAA) under the Omnibus Crime Control and Safe Streets Act. This act made federal funds available to states and municipalities and nonprofit organizations for improving methods of law enforcement, court administration and prison operations, improving the training of criminal justice personnel, and preventing and controlling crime. The LEAA was terminated in 1982 and was succeeded by the Office of Justice Assistance, Research and Statistics (OJARS), which was created by the Justice System Improvement Act of 1979. The OJARS coordinates the work of the National Institute of Justice (NIJ), the Bureau of Justice Statistics (BJS) and the Office of Juvenile Justice and Delinquency Prevention (OJJDP). It also operates the "Sting," Treatment Alternatives to Street Crime, Regional Information Sharing Systems, Public Safety Officers' Benefit, National Crime Prevention and Law Enforcement Accreditation programs. The National Institute of Justice conducts basic and applied research into crime, criminal behavior and crime prevention. The BJS is the national repository of statistical information on crime and criminal justice, which is made available to the public through the National Criminal Justice Reference Service. The OJJDP operates programs to deter juvenile delinquency and improve state and local juvenile justice programs.

Law enforcement in the United States is served by a number of major professional organizations, including:

- International Association of Chiefs of Police, the largest and the best-known association, with a membership limited to police chiefs and managers.
- Police Executive Research Forum, founded in 1976 with a membership limited to police chiefs of cities with a population of over 100,000.
- National Organization of Black Law Enforcement Executives, established in 1976.
- Academy of Criminal Justice Sciences, founded in 1963 as the International Association of Police Professors.

FULL-TIME AND PART-TIME EMPLOYMENT FOR POLICE PROTECTION AND CORRECTIONS ACTIVITIES, BY LEVEL OF GOVERNMENT, UNITED STATES, OCTOBER 1980 AND 1981

Level of Government	October 1980			October 1981			Percent Increase or Decrease (−) from 1980 to 1981		
	Total	Police Protection	Corrections	Total	Police Protection	Corrections	Total	Police Protection	Corrections
Total	985,307	714,660	270,647	997,193	716,600	280,593	1.2	0.2	3.6
Federal	66,397	56,472	9,925	65,141	55,505	9,636	−1.8	−1.7	−2.9
State-local, total	918,910	658,188	260,722	932,052	661,095	270,957	1.4	0.4	3.9
State	239,566	75,896	163,670	246,790	76,477	170,313	3.0	0.7	4.0
Local, total	679,344	582,292	97,052	685,262	584,618	100,644	0.8	0.3	3.7
Counties	209,096	131,645	77,451	215,925	135,919	80,006	3.2	3.2	3.2
Municipalities	470,248	450,647	19,601	469,337	448,699	20,638	−0.1	−0.4	5.2

Source: U.S. Department of Justice, Bureau of Justice Statistics, Justice Expenditure and Employment Extracts: 1980 and 1981 Data from the Annual General Finance and Employment Surveys (Washington, D.C.: U.S. Government Printing Office, 1984), Table B.

EMPLOYMENT AND PAYROLL FOR STATE AND LOCAL POLICE PROTECTION AND CORRECTIONS ACTIVITIES, BY STATE AND LEVEL OF GOVERNMENT, OCTOBER 1981

NOTE: October payroll data may not add due to rounding.

(— represents zero or rounds to zero).

State and Level of Government[a]	Police Protection					Corrections				
	Employment			October Payroll (in Thousands)	Average October Earnings, Full-Time Employees	Employment			October Payroll (in Thousands)	Average October Earnings, Full-Time Employees
	Total	Full-Time Only	Full-Time Equivalent			Total	Full-Time Only	Full-Time Equivalent		
State-local, total	661,095	576,225	594,982	$977,698	$1,655	270,957	258,900	262,862	$380,467	$1,447
States	76,477	75,439	75,837	129,035	1,704	170,313	165,647	167,518	241,899	1,442
Local, total	584,618	500,786	519,145	848,663	1,648	100,644	93,253	95,344	138,568	1,455
Counties	135,919	122,446	125,237	192,988	1,547	80,006	73,177	75,152	104,845	1,396
Municipalities	448,699	378,340	393,908	655,675	1,680	20,638	20,076	20,192	33,723	1,671
Alabama	9,580	8,739	8,905	11,672	1,312	3,222	3,176	3,203	3,913	1,225
State	1,270	1,269	1,269	1,910	1,505	2,129	2,125	2,125	2,786	1,310
Local, total	8,310	7,470	7,636	9,762	1,278	1,093	1,051	1,078	1,126	1,053
Counties	1,593	1,505	4,523	1,929	1,265	943	907	933	981	1,063
Municipalities	6,717	5,965	6,113	7,832	1,282	150	144	145	145	995
Alaska	1,310	1,269	1,279	3,939	3,086	686	639	643	1,556	2,419
State	429	413	417	1,379	3,321	609	605	607	1,482	2,441
Local, total	881	856	862	2,559	2,972	77	34	36	73	2,029
Boroughs	62	62	62	229	3,701	—	—	—	—	—
Municipalities	819	794	800	2,330	2,916	77	34	36	73	2,029
Arizona	8,994	8,481	8,504	14,904	1,753	4,034	3,823	3,889	5,928	1,525
State	1,601	1,598	1,598	2,676	1,674	2,722	2,556	2,613	3,863	1,478
Local, total	7,393	6,883	6,906	12,227	1,771	1,312	1,267	1,276	2,065	1,619
Counties	1,714	1,685	1,692	2,782	1,647	1,265	1,222	1,231	1,998	1,624
Municipalities	5,679	5,198	5,214	9,444	1,812	47	45	45	67	1,467
Arkansas	4,673	4,394	4,422	4,861	1,095	1,502	1,450	1,464	1,421	971
State	751	749	750	1,025	1,368	1,097	1,084	1,089	1,117	1,026
Local, total	3,922	3,645	3,672	3,835	1,039	405	366	375	303	809
Counties	1,100	1,019	1,019	983	952	382	343	352	280	797
Municipalities	2,822	2,626	2,653	2,852	1,072	23	23	23	22	994
California	70,777	64,001	65,417	142,111	2,186	34,214	30,580	31,789	58,070	1,825
State	8,872	8,672	8,722	19,697	2,261	13,714	12,197	12,784	25,138	1,964
Local, total	61,905	55,329	56,695	122,414	2,174	20,500	18,383	19,005	32,932	1,741
Counties	19,557	17,650	17,826	38,499	2,161	19,726	17,611	18,232	31,515	1,729
Municipalities	42,348	37,679	38,869	83,915	2,180	774	772	773	1,417	1,835
Colorado	8,452	7,857	8,001	12,969	1,627	3,215	3,113	3,140	5,082	1,618
State	739	737	738	1,266	1,717	1,961	1,919	1,936	33,423	1,769
Local, total	7,713	7,120	7,263	11,702	1,618	1,254	1,194	1,204	1,659	1,375
Counties	1,777	1,643	1,677	2,288	1,369	826	776	786	993	1,262
Municipalities	5,936	5,477	5,586	9,413	1,693	428	418	418	665	1,586
Connecticut	9,712	7,723	8,201	12,546	1,552	3,276	3,220	3,253	4,609	1,417
State	1,421	1,416	1,418	1,932	1,363	3,276	3,220	3,253	4,609	1,417
Local, total	8,291	6,307	6,783	10,613	1,594	—	—	—	—	—
Counties	—	—	—	—	—	—	—	—	—	—
Municipalities	8,291	6,307	6,783	10,613	1,594	—	—	—	—	—
Delaware	1,754	1,504	1,575	2,699	1,725	1,149	1,088	1,095	1,552	1,417
State	604	602	603	1,065	1,767	1,146	1,088	1,095	1,552	1,417
Local, total	1,150	902	972	1,634	1,697	3	—	—	—	—
Counties	513	358	397	776	1,980	—	—	—	—	—
Municipalities	637	544	575	857	1,511	3	—	—	—	—
District of Columbia	4,324	4,099	4,181	8,345	2,003	2,911[b]	2,911	2,911	4,372	1,502
Local, total	4,324	4,099	4,181	8,345	2,003	2,911[b]	2,911	2,911	4,372	1,502
Municipalities	4,324	4,099	4,181	8,345	2,003	2,911[b]	2,911	2,911	4,372	1,502
Florida	31,994	29,549	30,118	45,426	1,514	14,548	14,152	14,307	17,110	1,196
State	2,468	2,459	2,461	3,750	1,524	11,247	10,874	11,027	12,783	1,159
Local, total	29,526	27,090	27,651	41,676	1,513	3,301	3,278	3,280	4,327	1,318
Counties	12,781	11,860	12,099	17,650	1,464	2,831	2,809	2,811	3,724	1,324
Municipalities	16,745	15,230	15,558	24,026	1,552	470	469	469	603	1,286
Georgia	15,456	13,768	14,110	17,305	1,230	7,974	7,808	7,855	8,920	1,136
State	1,927	1,927	1,927	2,770	1,438	5,928	5,917	5,920	6,887	1,163
Local, total	13,529	11,841	12,183	14,535	1,196	2,046	1,891	1,935	2,033	1,053
Counties	5,303	4,746	4,869	5,561	1,146	1,777	1,631	1,673	1,699	1,019
Municipalities	8,226	7,095	7,314	8,974	1,229	269	260	262	333	1,272

See footnotes at end of table.

NOTE: October payroll data may not add due to rounding.

(— represents zero or rounds to zero).

	Police Protection					Corrections				
	Employment			October Payroll (in Thousands)	Average October Earnings, Full-Time Employees	Employment			October Payroll (in Thousands)	Average October Earnings, Full-Time Employees
State and Level of Government[a]	Total	Full-Time Only	Full-Time Equivalent			Total	Full-Time Only	Full-Time Equivalent		
Hawaii	2,625	2,582	2,594	$4,707	$1,818	731	718	728	$940	$1,292
State	28	28	28	31	1,115	731	718	728	940	1,292
Local, total	2,597	2,554	2,566	4,676	1,825	—	—	—	—	—
Counties	731	691	703	1,320	1,891	—	—	—	—	—
Municipalities	1,866	1,863	1,863	3,355	1,801	—	—	—	—	—
Idaho	2,472	2,262	2,303	3,003	1,305	693	670	676	848	1,253
State	412	401	405	560	1,384	531	529	530	672	1,268
Local, total	2,060	1,861	1,898	2,443	1,287	162	141	146	175	1,193
Counties	911	812	838	940	1,126	161	140	145	174	1,192
Municipalities	1,149	1,049	1,060	1,503	1,413	1	1	1	1	1,290
Illinois	42,782	36,090	37,395	66,583	1,790	11,333	11,075	11,186	16,303	1,458
State	3,405	3,405	3,405	6,248	1,835	7,785	7,711	7,767	11,758	1,513
Local, total	39,377	32,685	33,990	60,335	1,786	3,548	3,364	3,419	4,544	1,331
Counties	5,996	5,264	5,383	7,268	1,353	3,533	3,356	3,411	4,533	1,331
Municipalities	33,381	27,421	28,607	53,065	1,869	15	8	8	11	1,295
Indiana	13,011	11,368	11,702	14,416	1,236	4,563	4,419	4,461	5,525	1,240
State	1,803	1,793	1,797	2,623	1,461	2,881	2,868	2,874	4,068	1,415
Local, total	11,208	9,575	9,905	11,793	1,194	1,682	1,551	1,587	1,457	915
Counties	2,162	2,045	2,074	2,303	1,111	1,341	1,210	1,246	1,169	935
Municipalities	9,046	7,530	7,831	9,490	1,217	341	341	341	288	845
Iowa	6,114	5,490	5,592	8,342	1,498	2,482	2,341	2,371	3,363	1,420
State	787	778	780	1,613	2,067	1,609	1,578	1,585	2,468	1,557
Local, total	5,327	4,712	4,812	6,729	1,404	873	763	786	895	1,138
Counties	1,456	1,263	1,308	1,700	1,307	873	763	786	895	1,138
Municipalities	3,871	3,449	3,504	5,029	1,439	—	—	—	—	—
Kansas	6,397	5,580	5,751	7,392	1,292	2,232	2,127	2,153	2,738	1,270
State	681	680	680	1,073	1,576	1,650	1,599	1,616	2,175	1,345
Local, total	5,716	4,900	5,071	6,319	1,252	582	528	537	563	1,041
Counties	1,699	1,392	1,475	1,608	1,111	571	527	536	560	1,041
Municipalities	4,017	3,508	3,596	4,711	1,308	11	1	1	2	1,000
Kentucky	7,675	6,628	6,839	9,350	1,375	2,963	2,883	2,904	3,392	1,169
State	1,520	1,519	1,519	2,463	1,621	2,306	2,297	2,300	2,771	1,204
Local, total	6,155	5,109	5,350	6,887	1,301	657	586	604	620	1,032
Counties	1,887	1,457	1,530	1,997	1,317	568	497	515	518	1,010
Municipalities	4,268	3,652	3,790	4,890	1,296	89	89	89	102	1,156
Louisiana	11,716	10,381	10,650	12,798	1,202	6,154	6,066	6,084	7,981	1,313
State	1,295	1,295	1,295	2,083	1,608	4,949	4,916	4,919	6,677	1,357
Local, total	10,421	9,086	9,355	10,715	1,144	1,205	1,150	1,165	1,304	1,121
Counties	3,598	2,922	3,044	3,440	1,129	340	285	300	296	986
Municipalities	6,823	6,164	6,311	7,275	1,151	865	865	865	1,008	1,165
Maine	2,899	2,026	2,134	2,714	1,268	1,082	958	986	1,210	1,236
State	333	333	333	548	1,647	773	766	769	1,017	1,324
Local, total	2,566	1,693	1,801	2,166	1,193	309	192	217	192	887
Counties	397	223	245	261	1,054	302	185	210	185	883
Municipalities	2,169	1,470	1,556	1,904	1,214	7	7	7	6	998
Maryland	13,248	12,242	12,462	21,432	1,724	7,080	6,920	6,987	10,491	1,502
State	2,090	2,090	2,090	3,494	1,671	5,713	5,594	5,648	8,341	1,476
Local, total	11,158	10,152	10,372	17,938	1,735	1,367	1,326	1,339	2,150	1,610
Counties	6,136	5,277	5,453	10,441	1,924	813	775	788	1,230	1,568
Municipalities	5,022	4,875	4,919	7,497	1,529	554	551	551	920	1,670
Massachusetts	19,538	15,801	16,632	26,855	1,635	4,620	4,540	4,562	6,087	1,334
State	1,622	1,567	1,590	2,386	1,507	3,445	3,423	3,431	4,578	1,334
Local, total	17,916	14,234	15,042	24,469	1,649	1,175	1,117	1,131	1,508	1,332
Counties	53	45	46	66	1,455	830	773	787	1,098	1,395
Municipalities	17,863	14,189	14,996	24,403	1,649	345	344	344	410	1,192
Michigan	23,752	20,552	20,988	42,615	2,038	9,858	9,359	9,513	17,422	1,834
State	2,991	2,919	2,947	6,611	2,247	6,449	6,324	6,384	12,295	1,926
Local, total	20,761	17,633	18,041	36,004	2,003	3,409	3,035	3,129	5,127	1,642
Counties	3,588	3,410	3,446	5,710	1,659	3,216	2,862	2,953	4,779	1,622
Municipalities	17,173	14,223	14,595	30,294	2,083	193	173	176	348	1,987

See footnotes at end of table.

EMPLOYMENT AND PAYROLL FOR STATE AND LOCAL POLICE PROTECTION AND CORRECTIONS ACTIVITIES, BY STATE AND LEVEL OF GOVERNMENT, OCTOBER 1981

NOTE: October payroll data may not add due to rounding.

(— represents zero or rounds to zero).

State and Level of Government[a]	Police Protection					Corrections				
	Employment			October Payroll (in Thousands)	Average October Earnings, Full-Time Employees	Employment			October Payroll (in Thousands)	Average October Earnings, Full-Time Employees
	Total	Full-Time Only	Full-Time Equivalent			Total	Full-Time Only	Full-Time Equivalent		
Minnesota	8,891	7,865	8,004	$14,226	$1,780	3,631	3,157	3,283	$5,697	$1,738
State	858	825	836	1,567	1,879	1,610	1,480	1,505	2,623	1,743
Local, total	8,033	7,040	7,168	12,659	1,768	2,021	1,677	1,778	3,074	1,733
Counties	2,188	1,992	2,042	3,327	1,639	2,021	1,677	1,778	3,074	1,733
Municipalities	5,845	5,048	5,126	9,331	1,819	—	—	—	—	—
Mississippi	5,509	4,631	4,828	5,136	1,068	2,062	1,990	2,002	1,884	941
State	896	855	876	1,265	1,454	1,695	1,659	1,663	1,612	969
Local, total	4,613	3,776	3,952	3,871	980	367	331	339	271	797
Counties	1,169	994	1,023	951	923	321	289	296	225	757
Municipalities	3,444	2,782	2,929	2,919	1,001	46	42	43	46	1,075
Missouri	15,542	13,566	13,912	19,771	1,422	4,738	4,570	4,623	5,141	1,096
State	1,704	1,704	1,704	2,402	1,410	2,975	2,923	2,943	3,140	1,067
Local, total	13,838	11,862	12,208	17,369	1,424	1,763	1,647	1,680	2,001	1,196
Counties	2,680	2,430	2,512	3,007	1,208	1,151	1,040	1,072	1,207	1,132
Municipalities	11,158	9,432	9,696	14,362	1,479	612	607	608	794	1,305
Montana	2,226	1,884	1,942	2,647	1,368	812	682	718	990	1,382
State	292	284	285	466	1,636	584	547	566	791	1,399
Local, total	1,934	1,600	1,657	2,180	1,320	228	135	152	198	1,315
Counties	1,035	808	856	1,033	1,224	202	110	127	167	1,332
Municipalities	899	792	801	1,147	1,418	26	25	25	31	1,241
Nebraska	4,288	3,385	3,462	5,142	1,484	1,978	1,804	1,857	2,127	1,148
State	520	515	516	805	1,562	1,415	1,372	1,388	1,610	1,160
Local, total	3,768	2,870	2,946	4,337	1,470	563	432	469	516	1,113
Counties	894	789	817	952	1,169	563	432	469	516	1,113
Municipalities	2,874	2,081	2,129	3,384	1,583	—	—	—	—	—
Nevada	3,366	3,122	3,168	5,531	1,745	1,513	1,482	1,490	2,357	1,582
State	308	307	308	579	1,883	948	934	939	1,358	1,446
Local, total	3,058	2,815	2,860	4,952	1,730	565	548	551	999	1,813
Counties	2,138	1,959	1,991	3,416	1,712	513	496	499	923	1,851
Municipalities	920	856	869	1,535	1,771	52	52	52	75	1,456
New Hampshire	2,953	1,946	2,104	2,950	1,404	686	626	644	833	1,291
State	282	280	281	375	1,339	436	394	409	536	1,310
Local, total	2,671	1,666	1,823	2,575	1,415	250	232	235	296	1,260
Counties	161	132	137	166	1,214	220	204	207	256	1,238
Municipalities	2,510	1,534	1,686	2,407	1,432	30	28	28	39	1,393
New Jersey	34,259	26,356	28,236	44,665	1,612	10,245	9,969	10,078	13,795	1,370
State	4,551	4,379	4,436	6,624	1,497	4,356	4,273	4,305	6,501	1,510
Local, total	29,708	21,977	23,800	38,041	1,636	5,889	5,696	5,773	7,294	1,265
Counties	2,430	2,300	2,332	3,366	1,447	5,880	5,695	5,770	7,291	1,265
Municipalities	27,278	19,677	21,468	34,675	1,658	9	1	3	2	797
New Mexico	3,686	3,527	3,570	4,321	1,212	1,823	1,802	1,807	1,789	988
State	618	618	618	737	1,193	1,386	1,385	1,385	1,386	1,000
Local, total	3,068	2,909	2,952	3,584	1,217	437	417	422	402	945
Counties	777	720	732	858	1,171	260	253	253	252	987
Municipalities	2,291	2,189	2,220	2,726	1,231	177	164	169	149	879
New York	64,165	56,209	59,302	111,895	1,928	29,552	28,801	29,022	48,818	1,684
State	4,999	4,910	4,928	8,611	1,749	16,301	16,174	16,221	25,468	1,570
Local, total	59,166	51,299	54,374	103,284	1,945	13,251	12,627	12,801	23,350	1,830
Counties	11,769	10,517	10,964	20,930	1,940	6,032	5,535	5,680	8,197	1,450
Municipalities	47,397	40,782	43,410	82,354	1,947	7,219	7,092	7,121	15,153	2,128
North Carolina	14,866	13,691	13,907	17,502	1,259	8,381	8,262	8,289	10,139	1,223
State	2,910	2,895	2,898	4,091	1,412	7,295	7,279	7,282	9,136	1,254
Local, total	11,956	10,796	11,009	13,410	1,218	1,086	983	1,007	1,003	994
Counties	3,628	3,369	3,423	3,900	1,140	1,083	980	1,004	1,001	995
Municipalities	8,328	7,427	7,586	9,509	1,253	3	3	3	2	751

See footnotes at end of table.

NOTE: October payroll data may not add due to rounding.

(— represents zero or rounds to zero).

State and Level of Government[a]	Police Protection					Corrections				
	Employment			October Payroll (in Thousands)	Average October Earnings, Full-Time Employees	Employment			October Payroll (in Thousands)	Average October Earnings, Full-Time Employees
	Total	Full-Time Only	Full-Time Equivalent			Total	Full-Time Only	Full-Time Equivalent		
North Dakota	1,447	1,223	1,240	$1,841	$1,465	410	340	351	$466	$1,336
State	173	172	172	305	1,773	290	258	259	359	1,387
Local, total	1,274	1,051	1,068	1,536	1,415	120	82	92	107	1,175
Counties	407	322	332	436	1,295	120	82	92	107	1,175
Municipalities	867	729	736	1,099	1,466	—	—	—	—	—
Ohio	27,199	22,498	23,473	36,005	1,546	10,315	9,817	9,945	12,071	1,215
State	1,967	1,947	1,952	2,835	1,452	6,552	6,380	6,419	8,044	1,253
Local, total	25,232	20,551	21,521	33,170	1,555	3,763	3,437	3,526	4,027	1,144
Counties	4,228	3,940	4,009	5,026	1,257	3,319	3,061	3,142	3,490	1,114
Municipalities	21,004	16,611	17,512	28,144	1,625	444	376	384	537	1,388
Oklahoma	7,276	6,842	6,961	8,709	1,253	3,813	3,596	3,721	4,467	1,199
State	962	949	951	1,678	1,764	3,429	3,251	3,372	4,072	1,207
Local, total	6,314	5,893	6,010	7,031	1,170	384	345	349	395	1,116
Counties	972	904	924	926	1,000	287	256	260	287	1,097
Municipalities	5,342	4,989	5,086	6,104	1,201	97	89	89	108	1,180
Oregon	6,813	6,367	6,400	11,006	1,714	3,214	3,023	3,082	4,638	1,505
State	1,061	1,056	1,058	2,135	2,019	1,889	1,863	1,877	2,830	1,507
Local, total	5,752	5,311	5,342	8,870	1,653	1,325	1,160	1,205	1,808	1,501
Counties	2,059	1,907	1,926	3,075	1,596	1,315	1,150	1,195	1,795	1,503
Municipalities	3,693	3,404	3,416	5,794	1,685	10	10	10	12	1,239
Pennsylvania	35,170	26,981	28,655	47,487	1,678	10,398	9,901	10,075	14,707	1,462
State	4,644	4,643	4,644	8,561	1,843	4,302	4,215	4,256	6,805	1,598
Local, total	30,526	22,338	24,011	38,926	1,644	6,096	5,686	5,819	7,902	1,360
Counties	2,047	1,804	1,866	2,358	1,262	4,358	4,007	4,131	4,806	1,163
Municipalities	28,479	20,534	22,145	36,568	1,677	1,738	1,679	1,688	3,096	1,832
Rhode Island	2,893	2,533	2,611	3,946	1,525	950	940	945	1,591	1,683
State	239	239	239	507	2,121	950	940	945	1,591	1,683
Local, total	2,654	2,294	2,372	3,439	1,462	—	—	—	—	—
Counties	—	—	—	—	—	—	—	—	—	—
Municipalities	2,654	2,294	2,372	3,439	1,462	—	—	—	—	—
South Carolina	7,125	6,334	6,493	7,758	1,198	3,898	3,872	3,882	4,691	1,208
State	1,253	1,246	1,248	1,890	1,514	3,312	3,292	3,302	4,133	1,251
Local, total	5,872	5,088	5,245	5,867	1,120	586	580	580	558	959
Counties	2,495	2,080	2,170	2,499	1,157	551	547	547	524	956
Municipalities	3,377	3,008	3,075	3,367	1,093	35	33	33	33	1,007
South Dakota	1,714	1,339	1,405	1,804	1,283	482	375	417	492	1,186
State	272	257	262	393	1,501	341	278	307	386	1,262
Local, total	1,442	1,082	1,143	1,411	1,231	141	97	110	105	967
Counties	456	347	362	406	1,101	140	97	110	105	967
Municipalities	986	735	781	1,003	1,291	1	—	—	—	—
Tennessee	11,301	10,281	10,498	12,942	1,204	5,539	5,484	5,507	5,987	1,088
State	962	959	961	1,262	1,313	3,978	3,974	3,975	4,357	1,096
Local, total	10,339	9,322	9,537	11,680	1,192	1,561	1,510	1,532	1,630	1,068
Counties	2,604	2,374	2,429	2,643	1,092	1,092	1,041	1,063	1,098	1,038
Municipalities	7,735	6,948	7,108	9,037	1,274	469	469	469	532	1,134
Texas	35,621	32,949	33,629	49,353	1,472	12,279	12,027	12,115	16,521	1,365
State	3,930	3,852	3,942	4,750	1,209	6,770	6,754	6,759	9,817	1,452
Local, total	31,691	29,097	29,687	44,603	1,507	5,509	5,273	5,356	6,704	1,253
Counties	6,315	6,100	6,136	7,839	1,269	5,393	5,159	5,242	6,577	1,255
Municipalities	25,376	22,997	23,551	36,764	1,570	116	114	114	133	1,158
Utah	3,458	2,924	3,031	4,860	1,616	1,272	1,156	1,195	1,912	1,600
State	513	508	514	892	1,743	943	885	911	1,551	1,704
Local, total	2,945	2,416	2,517	3,968	1,589	329	271	284	361	1,266
Counties	1,037	866	895	1,381	1,551	329	271	284	361	1,266
Municipalities	1,908	1,550	1,622	2,587	1,608	—	—	—	—	—
Vermont	1,371	1,044	1,089	1,500	1,371	437	373	406	531	1,302
State	440	415	422	682	1,624	437	373	406	531	1,302
Local, total	931	629	667	817	1,203	—	—	—	—	—
Counties	51	20	22	20	850	—	—	—	—	—
Municipalities	880	609	645	797	1,212	—	—	—	—	—

See footnotes at end of table.

EMPLOYMENT AND PAYROLL FOR STATE AND LOCAL POLICE PROTECTION AND CORRECTIONS ACTIVITIES, BY STATE AND LEVEL OF GOVERNMENT, OCTOBER 1981

NOTE: October payroll data may not add due to rounding.

(— represents zero or rounds to zero).

	Police Protection					Corrections				
	Employment			October Payroll (in Thousands)	Average October Earnings, Full-Time Employees	Employment			October Payroll (in Thousands)	Average October Earnings, Full-Time Employees
State and Level of Government[a]	Total	Full-Time Only	Full-Time Equivalent			Total	Full-Time Only	Full-Time Equivalent		
Virginia	12,748	11,978	12,078	$17,231	$1,434	10,341	9,880	10,078	$12,734	$1,263
State	2,086	2,005	2,036	3,027	1,492	7,177	6,945	7,067	9,218	1,304
Local, total	10,662	9,793	10,042	14,203	1,422	3,164	2,935	3,011	3,515	1,165
Counties	4,436	4,061	4,162	6,310	1,522	1,273	1,184	1,209	1,456	1,200
Municipalities	6,226	5,732	5,880	7,893	1,351	1,891	1,751	1,802	2,058	1,142
Washington	8,820	8,277	8,411	16,360	1,956	5,683	5,416	5,509	8,816	1,602
State	1,273	1,272	1,272	2,696	2,119	3,848	3,718	3,772	6,092	1,615
Local, total	7,547	7,005	7,139	13,663	1,926	1,835	1,698	1,737	2,724	1,572
Counties	2,570	2,408	2,438	4,521	1,858	1,755	1,622	1,660	2,603	1,572
Municipalities	4,977	4,597	4,701	9,141	1,961	80	76	77	121	1,566
West Virginia	3,696	3,284	3,383	4,193	1,244	1,076	1,052	1,059	1,061	997
State	861	844	853	1,217	1,431	772	756	763	791	1,037
Local, total	2,835	2,440	2,530	2,976	1,179	304	296	296	269	894
Counties	750	740	742	818	1,099	304	296	296	269	894
Municipalities	2,085	1,700	1,788	2,158	1,213	—	—	—	—	—
Wisconsin	13,719	11,506	11,936	19,579	1,648	4,349	3,934	4,064	6,572	1,620
State	675	674	674	1,144	1,698	3,245	3,024	3,107	5,103	1,642
Local, total	13,044	10,832	11,262	18,434	1,645	1,104	910	957	1,468	1,548
Counties	3,170	2,836	2,883	4,510	1,565	1,104	910	957	1,468	1,548
Municipalities	9,874	7,996	8,379	13,923	1,673	—	—	—	—	—
Wyoming	1,718	1,477	1,499	2,356	1,555	558	533	538	816	1,521
State	179	179	179	336	1,882	426	413	415	658	1,588
Local, total	1,539	1,298	1,320	2,019	1,510	132	120	123	157	1,289
Counties	439	398	403	563	1,394	122	111	114	147	1,300
Municipalities	1,100	900	917	1,455	1,561	10	9	9	10	1,152

a. Local government data and the state-local totals are estimates subject to sampling variation.
b. Data are for October 1979.
Source: U.S. Department of Justice, Bureau of Justice Statistics, Justice Expenditure and Employment Extracts: 1980 and 1981 Data from the Annual General Finance and Employment Surveys (Washington, D.C.: U.S. Government Printing Office, 1984), Table 4.

EXPENDITURES FOR STATE AND LOCAL POLICE PROTECTION AND CORRECTIONS ACTIVITIES, BY TYPE OF EXPENDITURE, STATE AND LEVEL OF GOVERNMENT, FISCAL YEAR 1981

(Dollar amounts in thousands; — represents zero or rounds to zero.)

	Police Protection					Corrections				
		Direct Expenditure			Intergovernmental Expenditure[b]		Direct Expenditure			Intergovernmental Expenditure[b]
State and Level of Government[a]	Total[b]	Total	Direct Current	Capital Outlay		Total[b]	Total	Direct Current	Capital Outlay	
State-local, total	$14,918,094	$14,918,094	$14,227,996	$690,098	—	$7,458,133	$7,455,822	$6,524,984	$930,838	$2,311
States	2,479,905	2,240,908	2,078,686	162,217	$239,002	5,179,448	4,843,857	4,203,970	639,887	335,591
Local, total	12,678,955	12,677,191	12,149,310	527,881	1,764	2,636,064	2,611,965	2,321,014	290,951	24,099
Counties	3,091,038	3,084,570	2,926,920	157,650	6,468	2,066,269	2,022,857	1,768,648	254,209	43,412
Municipalities	9,678,462	9,592,621	9,222,390	370,231	85,841	602,148	589,108	552,366	36,742	13,040
Alabama	178,602	178,602	168,306	10,296	—	85,745	85,745	73,228	12,517	—
State	31,240	31,240	27,827	3,413	—	66,088	63,025	54,584	8,441	3,063
Local, total	147,362	147,362	140,479	6,883	—	22,720	22,720	18,644	4,076	—
Counties	33,315	33,315	31,398	1,917	—	19,887	19,887	15,891	3,996	—
Municipalities	114,048	114,047	109,081	4,966	1	2,935	2,833	2,753	80	102
Alaska	70,841	70,841	65,207	5,634	—	40,632	38,321	27,175	11,146	2,311
State	28,559	28,315	27,178	1,137	244	40,117	37,153	26,033	11,120	2,964[c]
Local, total	42,526	42,526	38,029	4,497	—	1,168	1,168	1,142	26	—
Boroughs	6,914	6,914	3,077	3,837	—	—	—	—	—	—
Municipalities	35,612	35,612	34,952	660	—	1,168	1,168	1,142	26	—

See footnotes at end of table.

(Dollar amounts in thousands; — represents zero or rounds to zero.)

State and Level of Government[a]	Police Protection Total[b]	Police Protection Direct Expenditure Total	Police Protection Direct Current	Police Protection Capital Outlay	Police Protection Intergovernmental Expenditure[b]	Corrections Total[b]	Corrections Direct Expenditure Total	Corrections Direct Current	Corrections Capital Outlay	Corrections Intergovernmental Expenditure[b]
Arizona	262,345	262,345	238,347	23,998	—	133,986	133,986	95,472	38,514	—
State	60,401	60,401	53,412	6,989	—	88,395	87,770	57,964	29,806	$625
Local, total	201,944	201,944	184,935	17,009	—	46,216	46,216	37,508	8,708	—
Counties	46,439	46,439	43,511	2,928	—	45,240	45,240	36,536	8,704	—
Municipalities	155,609	155,505	141,424	14,081	104	2,428	976	972	4	1,452
Arkansas	77,358	77,358	73,045	4,313	—	36,988	36,988	33,108	3,880	—
State	19,167	19,167	17,601	1,566	—	28,808	28,808	27,108	1,700	—
Local, total	58,191	58,191	55,444	2,747	—	8,180	8,180	6,000	2,180	—
Counties	16,915	16,915	16,082	833	—	5,845	5,822	5,175	647	23
Municipalities	41,298	41,276	39,362	1,914	22	2,386	2,358	825	1,533	28
California	2,139,115	2,139,115	2,049,235	89,880	—	1,121,857	1,121,857	1,071,471	50,386	—
State	334,637	317,892	300,164	17,728	16,745	576,972	502,396	482,283	20,113	74,576
Local, total	1,822,098	1,821,223	1,749,071	72,152	875	621,344	619,461	589,188	30,273	1,883
Counties	554,601	553,709	534,760	18,949	892	593,358	590,919	560,787	30,132	2,439
Municipalities	1,310,818	1,267,514	1,214,311	53,203	43,304	29,067	28,542	28,401	141	525
Colorado	198,843	198,843	190,462	8,381	—	84,710	84,710	76,637	8,073	—
State	32,480	32,379	31,019	1,360	101	58,731	58,731	52,777	5,954	—
Local, total	166,464	166,464	159,443	7,021	—	25,979	25,979	23,860	2,119	—
Counties	35,748	35,748	33,673	2,075	—	18,712	18,712	17,126	1,586	—
Municipalities	130,716	130,716	125,770	4,946	—	7,277	7,267	6,734	533	10
Connecticut	190,833	190,833	183,113	7,720	—	80,024	80,024	69,767	10,257	—
State	34,866	34,866	34,196	670	—	80,024	80,024	69,767	10,257	—
Local, total	156,054	155,967	148,917	7,050	87	—	—	—	—	—
Counties	—	—	—	—	—	—	—	—	—	—
Municipalities	156,447	155,967	148,917	7,050	480	—	—	—	—	—
Delaware	42,499	42,499	40,953	1,546	—	36,717	36,717	23,819	12,898	—
State	14,925	14,305	13,580	725	620	36,717	36,717	23,819	12,898	—
Local, total	28,235	28,194	27,373	821	41	—	—	—	—	—
Counties	12,365	12,324	12,308	16	41	—	—	—	—	—
Municipalities	15,870	15,870	15,065	805	—	—	—	—	—	—
District of Columbia	115,311	115,311	113,530	1,781	—	89,407	89,407	88,722	685	—
Local, total	115,311	115,311	113,530	1,781	—	89,407	89,407	88,722	685	—
Municipalities	115,311	115,311	113,530	1,781	—	89,407	89,407	88,722	685	—
Florida	711,321	711,321	675,226	36,095	—	298,051	298,051	254,378	43,473	—
State	77,091	74,960	66,808	8,152	2,131	224,485	224,485	201,792	22,693	—
Local, total	636,534	636,361	608,418	27,943	173	73,566	73,566	52,786	20,780	—
Counties	287,666	287,199	269,915	17,284	467	62,698	62,698	41,950	20,748	—
Municipalities	349,162	349,162	338,503	10,659	—	10,868	10,868	10,836	32	—
Georgia	267,625	267,625	253,034	14,591	—	210,861	210,861	154,483	56,378	—
State	43,361	42,018	39,832	2,186	1,343	162,303	156,852	112,872	43,980	5,451
Local, total	225,609	225,607	213,202	12,405	2	54,028	54,009	41,611	12,398	19
Counties	93,501	93,491	89,105	4,386	10	41,285	41,142	36,538	4,604	143
Municipalities	132,391	132,116	124,097	8,019	275	12,998	12,867	5,073	7,794	131
Hawaii	64,429	64,429	62,875	1,554	—	25,167	25,167	20,931	4,236	—
State	1,036	421	421	—	615	25,167	25,167	20,931	4,236	—
Local, total	64,008	64,008	62,454	1,554	—	—	—	—	—	—
Counties	17,769	17,769	17,176	593	—	—	—	—	—	—
Municipalities	46,239	46,239	45,278	961	—	—	—	—	—	—
Idaho	44,523	44,523	42,415	2,108	—	19,018	19,018	15,402	3,616	—
State	8,072	8,072	7,740	332	—	16,741	16,741	13,388	3,353	—
Local, total	36,451	36,451	34,675	1,776	—	2,277	2,277	2,014	263	—
Counties	14,704	14,697	13,742	955	7	2,277	2,277	2,014	263	—
Municipalities	21,912	21,754	20,933	821	158	6	—	—	—	6
Illinois	921,015	921,015	875,113	45,902	—	342,782	342,782	286,869	55,913	—
State	100,636	96,191	90,457	5,734	4,445	268,933	262,801	214,768	48,033	6,132
Local, total	824,825	824,824	784,656	40,168	1	79,981	79,981	72,101	7,880	—
Counties	89,847	89,841	82,810	7,031	6	83,390	79,702	71,822	7,880	3,688
Municipalities	735,636	734,983	701,846	33,137	653	287	279	279	—	8
Indiana	228,670	228,670	212,388	16,282	—	136,930	136,930	111,120	25,810	—
State	52,410	52,410	42,843	9,567	—	104,937	104,937	85,157	19,780	—
Local, total	176,266	176,260	169,545	6,715	6	33,051	31,993	25,963	6,030	1,058
Counties	37,380	37,374	35,093	2,281	6	22,705	22,173	16,737	5,436	532
Municipalities	138,942	138,886	134,452	4,434	56	10,403	9,820	9,226	594	583

See footnotes at end of table.

EXPENDITURES FOR STATE AND LOCAL POLICE PROTECTION AND CORRECTIONS ACTIVITIES, BY TYPE OF EXPENDITURE, STATE AND LEVEL OF GOVERNMENT, FISCAL YEAR 1981

(Dollar amounts in thousands; — represents zero or rounds to zero.)

State and Level of Government [a]	Police Protection					Corrections				
		Direct Expenditure			Intergov-ernmental Expenditure [b]		Direct Expenditure			Intergov-ernmental Expenditure [b]
	Total [b]	Total	Direct Current	Capital Outlay		Total [b]	Total	Direct Current	Capital Outlay	
Iowa	130,358	139,358	125,308	5,050	—	60,463	60,463	55,398	5,065	—
State	21,239	21,239	20,728	511	—	51,831	42,345	40,424	1,921	$9,486
Local, total	109,119	109,119	104,580	4,539	—	18,118	18,118	14,974	3,144	—
Counties	28,068	28,023	26,291	1,732	45	17,827	17,796	14,652	3,144	31
Municipalities	81,279	81,096	78,289	2,807	183	519	322	322	—	197
Kansas	109,284	109,284	103,135	6,149	—	47,249	47,249	43,433	3,816	—
State	14,028	14,028	13,189	839	—	39,731	39,489	36,829	2,660	242
Local, total	95,273	95,256	89,946	5,310	17	7,760	7,760	6,604	1,156	—
Counties	27,066	27,065	25,502	1,563	1	7,572	7,572	6,420	1,152	—
Municipalities	68,512	68,191	64,444	3,747	321	197	188	184	4	9
Kentucky	161,710	161,710	151,270	10,440	—	94,172	94,172	78,237	15,935	—
State	66,038	59,523	54,262	5,261	6,515	83,124	73,680	62,691	10,989	9,444
Local, total	102,187	102,187	97,008	5,179	—	20,492	20,492	15,546	4,946	—
Counties	21,625	21,590	21,027	563	35	16,037	16,037	12,512	3,525	—
Municipalities	80,597	80,597	75,981	4,616	—	4,462	4,455	3,034	1,421	7
Louisiana	284,681	284,681	266,462	18,219	—	140,662	140,662	131,831	8,831	—
State	82,959	57,179	53,727	3,452	25,780	114,830	103,614	98,114	5,500	11,216
Local, total	227,502	227,502	212,735	14,767	—	37,048	37,048	33,717	3,331	—
Parishes	107,384	107,372	99,533	7,839	12	14,389	14,274	11,784	2,490	115
Municipalities	120,904	120,130	113,202	6,928	774	22,890	22,774	21,933	841	116
Maine	45,845	45,845	43,368	2,477	—	22,073	22,073	21,399	674	—
State	13,252	13,231	11,974	1,257	21	18,273	18,273	17,852	421	—
Local, total	32,614	32,614	31,394	1,220	—	3,800	3,800	3,547	253	—
Counties	4,369	4,369	4,106	263	—	3,800	3,800	3,547	253	—
Municipalities	28,624	28,245	27,288	957	379	—	—	—	—	—
Maryland	316,944	316,944	308,343	8,601	—	207,571	207,571	178,544	29,027	—
State	144,245	69,952	68,249	1,703	74,293	174,207	165,793	145,777	20,016	8,414
Local, total	247,002	246,992	240,094	6,898	10	41,778	41,778	32,767	9,011	—
Counties	140,330	140,250	135,083	5,167	80	25,496	25,496	18,823	6,673	—
Municipalities	106,802	106,742	105,011	1,731	60	16,282	16,282	13,944	2,338	—
Massachusetts	406,315	406,315	388,658	17,657	—	1,166,858	166,858	155,605	11,253	—
State	38,926	35,526	31,834	3,692	3,400	133,352	133,333	123,975	9,358	19
Local, total	370,789	370,789	356,824	13,965	—	33,525	33,525	31,630	1,895	—
Counties	1,971	1,971	1,945	26	—	24,346	24,346	22,771	1,575	—
Municipalities	368,851	368,818	354,879	13,939	33	9,179	9,179	8,859	320	—
Michigan	709,593	709,593	690,796	18,797	—	328,404	328,404	295,390	33,014	—
State	106,059	91,658	89,952	1,706	14,401	212,355	209,245	202,578	6,667	3,110
Local, total	617,935	617,935	600,844	17,091	—	121,770	119,159	92,812	26,347	2,611
Counties	115,186	115,185	108,890	6,295	1	120,933	111,465	85,335	26,130	9,468
Municipalities	507,621	502,750	491,954	10,796	4,871	9,175	7,694	7,477	217	1,481
Minnesota	233,751	233,751	213,440	10,311	—	118,466	118,466	98,398	20,068	—
State	41,736	28,660	26,422	2,238	13,076	77,794	64,988	49,716	15,272	12,806
Local, total	195,166	195,091	187,018	8,073	75	53,506	53,478	48,682	4,796	28
Counties	57,479	57,276	54,528	2,748	203	53,575	53,262	48,466	4,796	313
Municipalities	140,281	137,815	132,490	5,325	2,466	845	216	216	—	629
Mississippi	96,448	96,448	90,341	6,107	—	44,240	44,240	34,573	9,667	—
State	26,953	26,953	24,650	2,303	—	37,964	34,638	27,274	7,364	3,326
Local, total	69,495	69,495	65,691	3,804	—	9,602	9,602	7,299	2,303	—
Counties	19,966	19,951	18,895	1,056	15	8,523	8,522	6,229	2,293	1
Municipalities	49,592	49,544	46,796	2,748	48	1,081	1,080	1,070	10	1
Missouri	299,345	299,345	284,842	14,503	—	105,467	105,467	86,949	18,518	—
State	47,496	44,745	41,870	2,875	2,751	73,662	73,452	55,452	18,000	210
Local, total	254,600	254,600	242,972	11,628	—	32,015	32,015	31,497	518	—
Counties	46,729	46,726	44,914	1,812	3	19,725	19,725	19,361	364	—
Municipalities	207,985	207,874	198,058	9,816	111	12,290	12,290	12,136	154	—

See footnotes at end of table.

(Dollar amounts in thousands; — represents zero or rounds to zero.)

State and Level of Government[a]	Police Protection Total[b]	Police Protection Direct Expenditure Total	Police Protection Direct Expenditure Direct Current	Police Protection Direct Expenditure Capital Outlay	Police Protection Intergovernmental Expenditure[b]	Corrections Total[b]	Corrections Direct Expenditure Total	Corrections Direct Expenditure Direct Current	Corrections Direct Expenditure Capital Outlay	Corrections Intergovernmental Expenditure[b]
Montana	40,598	40,598	38,133	2,465	—	18,400	18,400	17,059	1,341	—
State	10,412	7,561	6,929	632	2,851	14,856	14,856	13,764	1,092	—
Local, total	33,093	33,037	31,204	1,833	56	3,544	3,544	3,295	249	—
Counties	16,004	15,953	14,414	1,539	51	3,368	3,347	3,100	247	$21
Municipalities	17,663	17,084	16,790	294	579	229	197	195	2	32
Nebraska	73,455	73,455	69,353	4,102	—	45,360	45,360	30,322	15,038	—
State	14,533	14,533	12,817	1,716	—	36,445	36,163	22,074	14,089	282
Local, total	58,922	58,922	56,536	2,386	—	9,197	9,197	8,248	949	—
Counties	13,921	13,921	13,320	601	—	8,321	8,321	7,492	829	—
Municipalities	45,017	45,001	43,216	1,785	16	922	876	756	120	46
Nevada	87,875	87,875	84,732	3,143	—	75,036	75,036	51,317	23,719	—
State	8,866	8,866	8,290	576	—	49,505	48,410	26,761	21,649	1,095
Local, total	79,009	79,009	76,442	2,567	—	26,629	26,626	24,556	2,070	3
Counties	52,203	52,203	5,125	978	—	25,313	25,310	23,312	1,998	3
Municipalities	45,755	26,806	25,217	1,589	18,949	1,316	1,316	1,244	72	—
New Hampshire	46,301	46,301	43,749	2,552	—	19,940	19,940	16,538	3,402	—
State	10,301	10,301	8,926	1,375	—	12,490	12,490	11,967	523	—
Local, total	36,029	36,000	34,823	1,177	29	7,450	7,450	4,571	2,879	—
Counties	2,821	2,806	2,706	100	15	7,367	7,367	4,488	2,879	—
Municipalities	33,231	33,194	32,117	1,077	37	83	83	83	—	—
New Jersey	581,331	581,331	566,356	14,975	—	221,622	221,622	199,948	21,674	—
State	92,613	81,111	75,275	5,836	11,502	124,184	122,186	102,481	19,705	1,998
Local, total	500,220	500,220	491,081	9,139	—	99,481	99,436	97,467	1,969	45
Counties	40,135	40,135	39,830	305	—	99,137	99,092	97,343	1,749	45
Municipalities	460,085	460,085	451,251	8,834	—	344	344	124	220	—
New Mexico	78,045	78,045	73,901	4,144	—	49,460	49,460	36,616	12,844	—
State	17,433	17,113	15,556	1,557	320	40,681	40,105	28,306	11,799	576
Local, total	60,932	60,932	58,345	2,587	—	9,355	9,355	8,310	1,045	—
Counties	13,004	13,004	12,487	517	—	6,053	4,521	3,882	639	1,532
Municipalities	48,083	47,928	45,858	2,070	155	4,976	4,834	4,428	406	142
New York	1,626,432	1,626,432	1,582,857	43,575	—	767,950	767,950	731,652	36,298	—
State	137,817	137,817	137,817	—	—	516,191	431,400	405,017	26,383	84,791
Local, total	1,488,615	1,488,615	1,445,040	43,575	—	346,808	336,550	326,635	9,915	10,258
Counties	396,610	396,610	377,917	18,693	—	144,202	133,944	132,831	1,113	10,258
Municipalities	1,092,030	1,092,005	1,067,123	24,882	25	202,606	202,606	193,804	8,802	—
North Carolina	282,329	282,329	260,204	22,125	—	228,492	228,492	184,013	44,479	—
State	66,594	66,490	57,780	8,710	104	215,546	211,228	167,798	4,340	4,318
Local, total	215,839	215,839	202,424	13,415	—	17,264	17,264	16,215	1,049	—
Counties	72,089	72,089	67,183	4,906	—	17,259	17,259	16,210	1,049	—
Municipalities	143,794	143,750	135,241	8,509	44	5	5	5	—	—
North Dakota	27,104	27,104	25,604	1,500	—	9,378	9,378	9,046	332	—
State	4,978	4,978	4,220	758	—	7,561[d]	7,561	7,229	332	—
Local, total	22,126	22,126	21,384	742	—	1,817	1,817	1,817	—	—
Counties	7,054	7,054	6,871	183	—	1,800	1,712	1,712	—	88
Municipalities	15,155	15,072	14,513	559	83	138	105	105	—	33
Ohio	582,796	582,796	561,626	21,170	—	207,618	207,618	195,479	12,139	—
State	47,830	47,830	44,500	3,330	—	156,302	139,043	134,428	4,615	17,259
Local, total	534,971	534,966	517,126	17,840	5	68,575	68,575	61,051	7,524	—
Counties	88,932	87,199	83,437	3,762	1,733	61,046	5,369	46,401	7,248	7,397
Municipalities	450,500	447,767	433,689	14,078	2,733	16,345	14,926	14,650	276	1,419
Oklahoma	145,491	145,491	133,492	11,999	—	83,534	83,534	71,921	11,613	—
State	38,732	38,672	32,629	6,043	60	77,297[d]	76,195	65,766	10,429	1,102
Counties	15,243	15,243	14,522	721	—	4,400	4,400	4,016	384	—
Municipalities	91,580	91,576	86,341	5,235	4	2,939	2,939	2,139	800	—
Oregon	176,190	176,190	170,615	5,575	—	99,813	99,813	95,414	4,399	—
State	34,350	33,504	32,978	526	846	64,262	56,244	55,020	1,224	8,018
Local, total	142,700	142,686	137,637	5,049	14	43,569	43,569	40,394	3,175	—
Counties	46,709	46,174	44,565	1,609	535	43,337	43,320	40,153	3,167	17
Municipalities	100,068	96,512	93,072	3,440	3,556	310	249	241	8	61

See footnotes at end of table.

EXPENDITURES FOR STATE AND LOCAL POLICE PROTECTION AND CORRECTIONS ACTIVITIES, BY TYPE OF EXPENDITURE, STATE AND LEVEL OF GOVERNMENT, FISCAL YEAR 1981

(Dollar amounts in thousands; — represents zero or rounds to zero.)

State and Level of Government[a]	Police Protection					Corrections				
		Direct Expenditure			Intergov-ernmental Expenditure[b]		Direct Expenditure			Intergov-ernmental Expenditure[b]
	Total[b]	Total	Direct Current	Capital Outlay		Total[b]	Total	Direct Current	Capital Outlay	
Pennsylvania	645,861	645,861	628,422	17,439	—	306,454	306,454	289,970	16,484	—
State	142,457	140,125	133,852	6,273	2,332	139,647	135,928	134,721	1,207	$3,719
Local, total	505,737	505,736	494,570	11,166	1	178,716	170,526	155,249	15,277	8,190
Counties	13,771	13,771	13,501	270	—	104,610	98,217	89,528	8,689	6,393
Municipalities	492,266	491,965	481,069	10,896	301	74,631	72,309	65,721	6,588	2,322
Rhode Island	58,253	58,253	57,103	1,150	—	23,391	23,391	22,309	1,082	—
State	11,726	8,929	8,856	73	2,797	23,391	23,391	22,309	1,082	—
Local, total	49,324	49,324	48,247	1,077	—	—	—	—	—	—
Counties	—	—	—	—	—	—	—	—	—	—
Municipalities	49,324	49,324	48,247	1,077	—	—	—	—	—	—
South Carolina	135,821	135,821	125,203	10,618	—	83,152	83,152	80,533	2,619	—
State	37,176	37,176	33,438	3,738	—	71,314	71,314	70,722	592	—
Local, total	98,647	98,645	91,765	6,880	2	11,838	11,838	9,811	2,027	—
Counties	42,501	42,399	38,491	3,908	102	11,105	11,105	9,098	2,007	—
Municipalities	56,251	56,246	53,274	2,972	5	786	733	713	20	53
South Dakota	29,494	29,494	27,720	1,774	—	11,421	11,421	11,264	157	—
State	7,271	7,271	6,862	409	—	9,622	9,622	9,491	131	—
Local, total	22,223	22,223	20,858	1,365	—	1,799	1,799	1,773	26	—
Counties	7,136	7,136	6,083	1,053	—	1,772	1,755	1,729	26	17
Municipalities	15,242	15,087	14,775	312	155	58	44	44	—	14
Tennessee	212,094	212,094	197,696	14,398	—	122,666	122,666	107,040	15,626	—
State	25,823	25,823	22,089	3,734	—	99,407	89,717	80,097	9,620	9,690
Local, total	186,600	186,271	175,607	10,664	329	32,949	32,949	26,943	6,006	—
Counties	38,644	38,315	36,730	1,585	329	26,011	26,000	20,257	5,743	11
Municipalities	148,001	147,956	138,877	9,079	45	6,949	6,949	6,686	263	—
Texas	724,134	724,134	671,625	52,509	—	341,302	341,302	243,834	97,468	—
State	99,726	99,726	86,275	13,451	—	207,918	188,983	149,522	39,461	18,935
Local, total	624,447	624,408	585,350	39,058	39	152,323	152,319	94,312	58,007	4
Counties	99,928	99,863	93,837	6,026	65	148,931	148,903	91,156	57,747	28
Municipalities	525,234	524,545	491,513	33,032	689	4,791	3,416	3,156	260	1,375
Utah	83,586	83,586	78,323	5,263	—	34,236	34,236	30,965	3,271	—
State	22,455	21,108	18,092	3,016	1,347	24,363	23,739	23,105	634	624
Local, total	62,478	62,478	60,231	2,247	—	10,497	10,497	7,860	2,637	—
Counties	20,675	20,675	19,865	810	—	10,464	10,464	7,827	2,637	—
Municipalities	41,860	41,803	40,366	1,437	57	33	33	33	—	—
Vermont	20,772	20,772	19,786	986	—	13,677	13,677	10,803	2,874	—
State	9,579	9,579	9,008	571	—	13,630	13,630	10,761	2,869	—
Local, total	11,193	11,193	10,778	415	—	47	47	42	5	—
Counties	184	184	171	13	—	41	41	36	5	—
Municipalities	11,009	11,009	10,607	402	—	6	6	6	—	—
Virginia	288,333	288,333	271,789	16,544	—	227,307	227,307	193,252	34,055	—
State	101,929	56,957	50,834	6,123	44,972	189,667	161,292	137,002	24,290	28,375
Local, total	231,376	231,376	220,955	10,421	—	66,015	66,015	56,250	9,765	—
Counties	98,912	98,852	93,477	5,375	60	34,658	34,596	26,035	8,561	62
Municipalities	132,754	132,524	127,478	5,046	230	31,821	31,419	30,215	1,204	402
Washington	250,986	250,986	240,207	10,779	—	209,748	209,748	158,937	50,811	—
State	47,313	44,237	39,452	4,785	3,076	148,525	144,800	101,147	43,653	3,725
Local, total	206,749	206,749	200,755	5,994	—	64,948	64,948	57,790	7,158	—
Counties	75,950	74,247	71,090	3,157	1,703	62,167	61,384	54,259	7,125	783
Municipalities	135,976	132,502	129,665	2,837	3,474	5,207	3,564	3,531	33	1,643
West Virginia	64,207	64,207	60,181	4,026	—	24,093	24,093	22,884	1,209	—
State	20,770	20,770	18,795	1,975	—	16,404	16,404	16,278	126	—
Local, total	43,437	43,437	41,386	2,051	—	7,689	7,689	6,606	1,083	—
Counties	12,158	12,158	11,243	915	—	7,478	7,474	6,391	1,083	4
Municipalities	31,279	31,279	30,143	1,136	—	305	215	215	—	90

See footnotes at end of table.

(Dollar amounts in thousands; — represents zero or rounds to zero.)

State and Level of Government[a]	Police Protection					Corrections				
		Direct Expenditure			Intergov-ernmental Expenditure[b]		Direct Expenditure			Intergov-ernmental Expenditure[b]
	Total[b]	Total	Direct Current	Capital Outlay		Total[b]	Total	Direct Current	Capital Outlay	
Wisconsin	316,698	316,698	292,867	23,831	—	133,564	133,564	119,562	14,002	—
State	17,825	15,511	15,214	297	2,314	106,378	106,378	95,256	11,122	—
Local, total	301,187	301,187	277,653	23,534	—	27,186	27,186	24,306	2,880	—
Counties	88,203	88,152	80,370	7,782	51	27,153	27,153	24,273	2,880	—
Municipalities	213,366	213,035	197,283	15,752	331	79	33	33	—	$46
Wyoming	42,304	42,304	37,240	5,064	—	22,019	22,019	11,767	10,252	—
State	9,584	9,584	8,267	1,317	—	18,321	18,321	9,023	9,298	—
Local, total	32,720	32,720	28,973	3,747	—	3,698	3,698	2,744	954	—
Counties	10,914	10,914	10,221	693	—	2,656	2,656	2,643	13	—
Municipalities	21,880	21,806	18,752	3,054	74	1,119	1,042	101	941	77

a. Local government data and the state-local totals are estimates subject to sampling variation.
b. For each state and the U.S. summary, the expenditure figures shown on the "Local, total" lines and the combined State-local total lines (opposite each state's name) exclude duplicative intergovernmental transactions. Thus the "Local, total" lines include intergovernmental payments only to the state government, and the combined state-local total lines include intergovernmental payments only to the federal government. This was done to avoid the artificial inflation that would result if an intergovernmental expenditure of a government were tabulated and then counted again when the recipient government or governments expended that amount.
c. Includes payment to the federal government.
d. Partially includes data for fiscal year 1979.
Source: U.S. Department of Justice, Bureau of the Justice Statistics, Justice Expenditure and Employment Extracts: 1980 and 1981 Data from the Annual General Finance and Employment Surveys (Washington, D.C.: U.S. Government Printing Office, 1984), Table 2.

- Fraternal Order of Police, whose membership consists primarily of patrolmen.
- Lambda Alpha Epsilon, whose membership is limited to police officers enrolled in college law-enforcement programs.

Recruitment, Education & Training

Most federal law-enforcement agencies maintain their own training facilities. However, there are two facilities that provide general and specialized training to any agency personnel: the Federal Law Enforcement Training Center (FLETC) at Glynco, Ga., and the FBI Academy at Quantico, Va.

The basic FBI special agent course lasts 15 weeks or 600 hours. The FLETC is operated under the authority of the secretary of the Treasury and is the successor to the Treasury Law Enforcement School, founded in 1946. The basic FLETC law-enforcement course lasts from five to 17 weeks, the criminal investigator course lasts 300 hours and the firearms instructor training program lasts 10 days.

The oldest federal law-enforcement school is the Coast Guard Academy, founded in 1877 at New Bedford, Conn. Ten years later the school moved to New London, Conn. The academy is under the direction of a commandant of the Coast Guard, who delegates the actual operation to a superintendent. The academic curriculum lasts four years and leads to a bachelor of science degree.

The Penal System

British colonists brought to the New World an ancient institution: the jail. Early in the 19th century the young country itself invented another type of institution that was to have a profound influence on correction throughout the world: the penitentiary. Also in the 19th and 20th centuries, the United States originated or further developed noninstitutional methods of correction, such as parole, probation, diversion, work-study release and other methods designed either to keep offenders out of institutions altogether or shorten their terms of incarceration or permit them to serve part of their time under supervision.

Jails in the Colonies, as in Europe, were not primarily institutions for the punishment of those who broke the law. Rather than imprisonment, convicted persons faced death or corporal punishment—the gallows or the whipping post, the branding iron or the stocks, and other methods of inflicting pain or public humiliation. A lawbreaker who did not live in the locality might be whipped and sent on his way with all dispatch. The major functions of the jail were to hold convicted persons until the sentence and punishment had been meted out and to detain persons accused of crime until trial.

However, the insane, the ill, vagrants, deserted wives or children, the aged and the poor were more numerous than lawbreakers in the country's early jails. Typically, the Colonies provided housing and other care for the sick, the aged and the poor. Larger cities had almshouses, and relief for the poor was a traditional function of government. Workhouses were set up where vagrants could be introduced to the virtues of work. But where none of these arrangements was available, these people were placed in jails.

In addition to being crowded into filthy quarters, inmates had to pay for their keep. The poorest among them begged passersby for food or money to buy it, and instances are on record of starvation in jails. On the other hand, those who had money could acquire liquor as well as food, privacy and privilege. Inmates who had no such resources but were strong enough were used in heavy manual labor on public works. Clad in conspicuous uniforms and encumbered with ball and chain, they were under constant surveillance by armed guards.

The beginnings of reform came in Philadelphia in the latter part of the 18th century, owing in part to a group of Quakers called The Philadelphia Society to Alleviate the Miseries of Public Prisons, an organization that still functions today as The Philadelphia Prison Society. The society urged that hardened criminals be separated from lesser offenders, that the sexes be segregated, and that the sale and consumption of liquor be prohibited.

In 1790 the Pennsylvania legislature ordered the renovation of the Walnut Street Jail in Philadelphia to segregate hardened offenders. They were housed in single cells in a separate building in almost total isolation. Other prisoners worked together and spent their off-hours and nights in larger rooms. Women and debtors had their own buildings. Children were removed from the jail entirely. Food and clothing were supplied at public expense, and no liquor was allowed. Thus, with a rudimentary system of classification and the provision of free essential services, the fundamentals of modern correctional management were introduced.

For a time, the Walnut Street Jail seemed to offer hope for more effective and more humane corrections. But serious problems soon arose. The planners had miscalculated the expected number of inmates, and the workrooms became so crowded that work became impossible. Fifteen years after the jail's founding, the cells held four times the number originally anticipated. Two visiting Frenchmen, Gustave de Beaumont and Alexis de Tocqueville, wrote that "[the Walnut Street Jail] corrupted by contamination those who worked together and it corrupted by indolence those who were plunged into solitude."

As the Walnut Street system became unpopular, Pennsylvania turned to the "silent system," under which no inmate could speak to another. The Eastern State Penitentiary at Cherry Hill, which opened in 1829, was designed with seven cellblocks radiating from a central rotunda like the spokes of a wheel. Each prisoner occupied a cell about eight by 12 feet in dimension, with running water and toilet facilities. Each prisoner also had his own exercise yard, about eight by 20 feet, surrounded by a high brick wall. Walls between cells were thick and virtually impenetrable to sound. The prisoner, therefore, neither saw nor heard anyone else except the keepers (who in-

spected prisons three times daily) and occasional pious people (who came to pray and offer spiritual guidance). Meals were delivered through a hole in the otherwise solid door. In his cell, the prisoner worked at weaving, carpentry, shoemaking, sewing and other hand manufactures. When he was not at work or exercising, he was to read the Scriptures and meditate upon his sins.

Another "silent system" operated at the Auburn Prison in New York. This, too, provided for the solitary and silent confinement of prisoners, but only at night. During the day they worked together under surveillance, and even then they could not speak to one another. The prisoners marched in lockstep, one hand on the shoulder of the man ahead, with all heads turned in the direction of the guard. Arriving at their worksite in the prison, they marked time until commanded to stop.

The Auburn system was a brutal one, with silence enforced by lashes and other punishments. But it was attractive to the legislatures because the sale of prison-made goods produced almost enough money to cover prison expenses. Prison labor emerged as the guiding philosophy of succeeding prison administrators. While different forms and types of prison labor have been used, three types have predominated. The first was the contract system, under which prisoners were let out to an outside contractor, who furnished machinery and raw material and supervised their work. The second was the lease system, under which contractors assumed entire control of the prisoners, including their maintenance and discipline, subject to regulations fixed by statute. The third was the state system, under which the states operated the prison industries and bought all their products for state use. In 1887 New York became the first state to mandate the state-use system, and in the same year the U.S. Congress passed a law forbidding contracting federal prisoners, who were then being housed in state institutions.

However profitable their production, penitentiaries were expensive to construct. Eastern State was estimated to have cost $500,000 for 250 prisoners, an enormous sum for the time. In fact, it was the most expensive public building built until that time in the New World, and it was the first public building to have flush toilets and hot air heating. Most of the 19th-century prisons were built for maximum security. They were forbidding structures and were called bastilles for good reasons. Even the reformatories built for young felons were built on the maximum-security model of Elmira in New York. Not until the 20th century did medium- and minimum-security institutions come into being as well as institutions for juveniles.

Corrections outside the penitentiary originated in the 1840s. The basic concept was that not all offenders need be incarcerated and that, indeed, many will become law-abiding citizens more quickly and permanently if they are not shut up out of contact with the community. It was realized, too, that institutions are expensive to operate.

The oldest form of noninstitutional corrections in the United States is probation. In 1841, John Augustus, a Boston bootmaker, asked the court to release to him certain misdemeanants he thought he could assist. Methods used by Augustus as a volunteer worker still are used by probation officers: investigation and screening, interviewing, supervision, vocational training and education. Augustus was so successful that in 1878 the Massachusetts legislature established the first state probation agency, with a paid staff. Another step in the development of noninstitutional corrections was the indeterminate sentence, which allowed prison authorities to release the offender before his time if he showed signs of genuine reformation. The first indeterminate sentence was passed in 1876.

During this period federal prisoners were assigned to state and local institutions to serve their sentences. In 1825 the federal government authorized hard labor but abolished whipping and the pillory for federal prisoners. In 1870 Congress established the Justice Department. A general agent within the department was placed in charge of all federal prisoners in state and local facilities. Later the general agent became the superintendent of prisons.

Serious overcrowding in prisons following the Civil War made many states reluctant to take federal prisoners in their facilities. Consequently, in 1891 the U.S. Congress authorized the construction of three federal penitentiaries. The first was on the Fort Leavenworth, Kan., reservation; it was first occupied in 1906, and final construction was completed in 1928. The second was the U.S. Penitentiary at Atlanta; it was first occupied in 1902, and construction was completed in 1921. The third was a territorial jail on McNeil Island, Wash., designated as a federal penitentiary in 1907. All these facilities were fortresses in the Auburn style, and they followed the Auburn regime as well except for the lockstep and the striped clothes. Wardens and prison employees were political appointees; the former were chosen by the U.S. senator from the state where the facility was located.

Between 1900 and 1935 U.S. prisons were primarily custodial, punitive and industrial. Overcrowding left few resources for anything but custodial care. Standards of administration and correctional theory were set by progressive states rather than the federal government.

Nonetheless, there were significant developments during this period that shaped the evolution of the U.S. penal system. The most important among these was the passage of good-time and parole laws by the U.S. Congress in 1910, partly as an attempt to reduce overcrowding.

The parole mechanism authorized the release of prisoners upon completion of one-third of their sentence. The parole power was vested in a committee of three: the superintendent of prisons in the Department of Justice, the institutional warden and the institutional physician. A parole officer was assigned to each institution to compile information for the parole board, which met quarterly. The supervision of parolees was entrusted to the U.S. Marshals Service. From 1913, even those serving life terms were eligible for parole after 15 years in prison.

Between 1910 and 1925 the federal prison population swelled as a result of the expansion of federal criminal jurisdiction in the wake of the passage of the White Slave Act of 1910, the Harrison Narcotics Act of 1914, the Volstead Act of 1918 and the Dyer Act of 1919. In 1925 Congress authorized a reformatory for male prisoners between ages 17 and 30 on a 1,300-acre tract, once a World War I cantonment, near Chillicothe, Ohio. In 1927 a new 500-inmate institution for women was opened at Alderson, W. Va. It included an industrial institution built on the cottage plan. In 1929, when overcrowding reached a critical stage in New York prisons, state and local authorities ordered the removal of all federal prisoners from the Tombs and the Raymond Street Jail. In response, a new federal detention center in New York City was established, called Federal Detention Headquarters.

In response to growing national concern over the state of the prisons, the 70th Congress in 1928 appointed a Special Committee on Federal Penal and Reformatory Institutions under John G. Cooper of Ohio. The Cooper Committee Report of 1929 recommended among other things the establishment of a centralized administration for federal prisons at the bureau level. This recommendation was implemented by President Hoover in 1930 by creation within the Department of Justice of the U.S. Bureau of Prisons, with Sanford Bates as its first director. With the appointment of Bates, penal administration in the federal government changed from one of political patronage to professional management.

One of the first acts of the Bureau of Prisons was to open eight new prisons, in abandoned Army camps at Camp Bragg, N.C.; Petersburg, Va.; Camp Riley, Kan.; Camp Meade, Md.; Fort Lewis, Wash.; Camp Dix, N.J.; Fort Wadsworth, N.Y.; and Montgomery, Ala. In 1930 the old New Orleans Mint was transformed into a jail. In 1932 a new regional jail was opened at La Tuna, Texas, primarily to house the influx of immigration violators, and in 1933 a similar institution was opened in Milan, near Detroit. In Lewisburg, Pa., a new penitentiary was added that represented some of the most innovative ideas in prison architecture. The need for a men's reformatory west of the Mississippi River resulted in the establishment of a new institution at El Reno, Okla., in 1933. In that same year a hospital for mentally ill prisoners and those with chronic medical ailments was opened at Springfield, Mo.

The early 1930s witnessed a spate of anticrime legislation directed at organized criminal groups. These included the Kidnaping Act and the Threatening Communications Act of 1932, and the National Bank Robber, Anti-Racketeering, Fugitive, Felon, National Firearms and National Stolen Property acts of 1934. To house the dangerous criminals netted by these acts, the government brought the old military prison on Alcatraz Island near San Francisco under the control of the Department of Justice in 1934.

Developed and implemented in 1934, the Bureau of Prisons classification system provided the single most dramatic departure from the state systems. Federal facilities were divided into penitentiaries, reformatories, prison camps and hospital facilities. Within each type of facility, further classification was done by age, offense, sex, etc. Classification was devised as a means of evaluation and rehabilitation. For the first four weeks following commitment, the inmate lived in a separate unit. With information from interviews and other sources, a caseworker wrote a summary of the offender's life. Inmates were examined by a doctor and in some institutions also by a psychiatrist. The educational and vocational supervisor and the chaplain also visited to determine participation in their respective programs. The findings of these officials were compiled into a classification summary on which the warden could plan his program of rehabilitation. Prison discipline was designed to generate a sense of social responsibility and to help the inmate acquire new interpersonal values. Hired on a full-time basis, chaplains regularly conducted services and classes and programs of individual and group counseling.

Prison industries were totally overhauled during the New Deal. In 1934 President Roosevelt created a corporation called Federal Prison Industries that oversaw the operation of all federal prison industries except farming, road construction and forestry work. Parole and probation also were extensively reorganized at this time. Legislation was passed creating an independent Parole Board within the Department of Justice and transferring the supervision of parolees from the U.S. Marshals Service to the probation offices of the federal courts. Five regional training centers were established for training Bureau of Prisons employees, and these centers were brought under the jurisdiction of the Civil Service Commission by 1937.

In 1950 the Congress passed the Youth Corrections Act, which provided a broad range of correctional alternatives not previously available. It was the first of several initiatives that endorsed and reinforced the Bureau's philosophy of rehabilitation. The statute provided for the commitment of federal offenders under age 22 to the custody of the attorney general for a six-year indeterminate term or for as long as the maximum sentence provided by law for the offense. Youth sentenced under this procedure could be paroled at any time but not later than two years before expiration of the sentence. Youth who made a particularly good parole adjustment could be discharged from supervision and their conviction set aside by the Board of Parole. The law was implemented in 1954, a Youth Division was established in the U.S. Board of Parole and four facilities—at Ashland, Ky.; Englewood, Colo.; Petersburg, Va.; and Lompoc, Calif., were designated as youth institutions.

In 1961 the bureau established two prerelease guidance centers for youthful offenders, in New York and Chicago, and an additional two centers in 1963. With the passage of the Prisoner Rehabilitation Act of 1965, these centers were expanded to include adults. Called community treatment centers, they were halfway houses between prisons and total release.

The 1970s provided the Bureau of Prisons with more new facilities than at any time since the 1930s. The new institutions resemble college campuses and are more manageable and more flexible than earlier prisons. Some of the older penitentiaries were closed. There was also a significant shift in the bureau's philosophy to accommodate the new voices on the right. The bureau publicly acknowledged that prisons exist for purposes other than rehabilitation, and incorporated retribution, deterrence and incapacitation among the goals of the penal system.

Among the administrative innovations of the 1970s was the Administrative Remedy Procedure, which allows inmates to file formal grievances concerning treatment, custody or regulations. Another key development was the establishment of the Commission on Accreditation for Corrections. A total of 37 federal facilities had been accredited by 1985.

The population of the federal prisons reached an all-time high of 35,042 in 1985. This number was 41% more than the combined rate capacity of the 46 institutions. A former seminary in Loretto, Pa., was purchased in 1984 for use as a federal correctional institution.

The Bureau of Prisons

The Bureau of Prisons has a headquarters office in Washington, D.C., and five regional offices. The headquarters comprises four divisions: Correctional Programs; Administration; Medical and Services; and Industries, Education and Vocational Training. Each

FEDERAL CORRECTIONAL SYSTEM

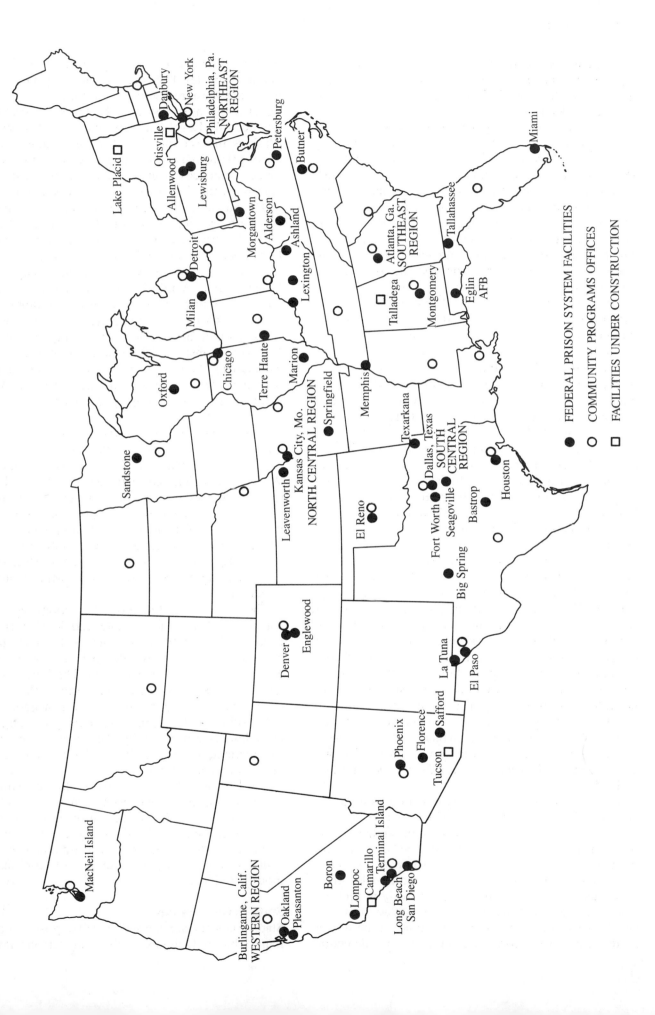

FEDERAL PRISON SYSTEM FACILITIES ●

COMMUNITY PROGRAMS OFFICES ○

FACILITIES UNDER CONSTRUCTION □

division is headed by an assistant director. The five regions are headed by regional directors, with headquarters at Atlanta; Dallas; Philadelphia; Belmont, Calif.; and Kansas City.

To alleviate prison population pressures, the bureau has expanded use of contract confinement and halfway houses. In 1985 approximately 80% of eligible offenders released to the community were released through Community Treatment Centers. These centers are also used for offenders serving short sentences, for unsentenced offenders participating in the Pretrial Service Program and for offenders under community supervision. SENTRY, the Bureau of Prisons' computer-based inmate information system, covers all 46 federal facilities. The system monitors inmates in federal institutions and federal inmates in contract facilities, plays an integral part in the inmate designation process and also has a sentence designation capability.

The Federal Prison Industries, Inc., with the corporate trade name UNICOR, employs 40% of all eligible inmates in the federal system. The gross sales of the 75 industrial operations in 40 facilities were $250 million in 1985. The corporation also conducts vocational training programs and apprenticeship programs. Inmate industrial wages rose to $16.2 million in 1985, and payments to inmates who work in nonindustrial assignments involving institutional operations and maintenance rose to $6 million.

The Bureau of Prisons also provides academic and occupational training programs to prepare inmates for employment upon release. Although enrollment is voluntary, program options are extensive, ranging from Adult Basic Education (ABE) through college courses. Occupational training programs include accredited vocational training and apprenticeship programs as well as prevocational and world-of-work courses, and work and study release. A mandatory literacy policy was implemented in 1983, requiring all federal prisoners with less than a sixth-grade education to enroll in the ABE program for a minimum of 90 days. In 1985 there were 9,000 enrollments and over 5,000 completions for which certificates were awarded. The education program is staffed by 500 employees and had an annual budget of $23 million in 1985.

The Bureau of Prisons' classification system has been in effect since 1977. Variables such as severity of the offense, history of escapes or violence, expected length of incarceration and type of prior commitments are used to determine an inmate's security level. This system also eliminates traditional correctional terms such as minimum- or medium-security institutions and groups the 46 federal facilities into six security levels based on the type of perimeter security, number of towers, external patrols, detection devices, security of housing areas, type of living quarters and level of staffing. Security Level 1 provides the least restrictive environment and Security Level 6 the most secure. The bureau operates only one Security Level 6 facility, the U.S. Penitentiary at Marion, Ill. Security Level 1 institutions house inmates primarily serving short sentences or completing longer sentences begun elsewhere and account for approximately 23% of the prison population.

The bureau's staff training network is composed of the Staff Training Operations Office at the Washington, D.C., headquarters; a Training Academy at Glynco, Ga.; a Management and Specialty Training Center at Denver; and a Food Service and Commissary Training Center at Fort Worth, Texas. All new employees are required to undergo four weeks of training during their first 45 days in the service, and all employees receive a minimum of 40 hours of training each year. Minorities constituted 25% of all employees in 1985, as compared to 8% in 1971, when the Bureau started implementing a minority recruitment program. Women made up 21% of the employees in 1985 compared to 11% in 1971.

The bureau provides a variety of services and programs for women. It operates four cocorrectional facilities and one all-female institution, in Alderson, W. Va. The federal correctional institution at Lexington, Ky., serves as the medical and psychiatric referral center for women with acute physical or emotional problems. The Bureau also offers a range of medical, dental and psychological services, with five primary medical referral centers, at Springfield, Mo.; Butner, N.C.; Lexington, Ky.; Rochester, Minn.; and Terminal Island, Calif.

The National Institute of Corrections was established in 1974 to assist state and local corrections agencies. The institute is governed by a 16-member advisory board and is administered by a director appointed by the attorney general. The National Academy of Corrections, the training arm of the institute, offers training programs for prison managers.

Outside of federal prison systems, jails and prisons are administered either by the states, as in Alaska, Connecticut, Delaware, Rhode Island and Vermont, or by counties and cities.

During the 1960s and 1970s, the constitutional rights of prisoners have been increasingly acknowledged by prison officials and enforced by the courts. These rights include legal assistance; medical treatment; educational facilities; correspondence; family visits; segregation by age, sex and offense; and religious activities.

State Prison Systems

State prisoners are housed in jails, prisons or community-based facilities. Jails hold persons awaiting

PERCENTAGE OF POPULATION CONFINED IN INSTITUTIONS BY OFFENSE

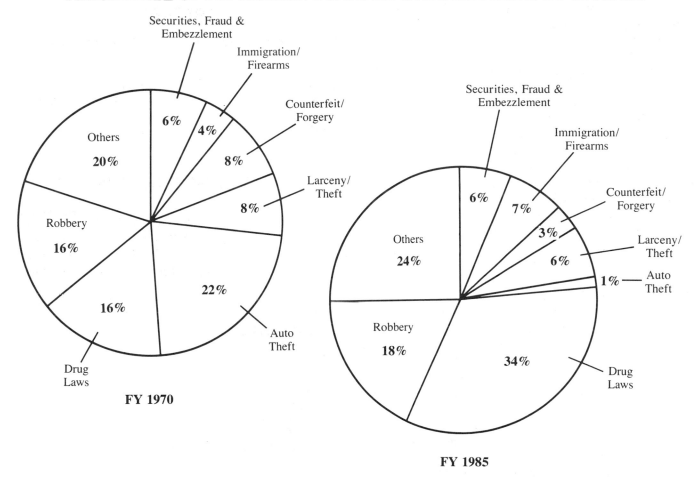

FY 1970

FY 1985

trial or those sentenced to confinement for less than a year. Prisons hold persons sentenced to confinement of more than one year. Community-based facilities are operated publicly or privately (under contract) to hold persons for less than 24 hours a day to permit the offender limited opportunities for work or education. Such facilities may include drug or alcohol treatment.

There are 3,493 local jails in the United States, a decline of 544 from 1970. Of the total, 65% reported in 1978 an average daily population of less than 21 inmates. By contrast, 4% (130) of the jails each housed more than 250 inmates. About half the total number of jails are in the South, housing about 43% of the national jail inmate population. Although only three of 10 jails in the Northeast house an average of less than 21 inmates on a given day, nearly eight out of 10 jails in the north-central states are of this size.

Rapid population turnover occurs in all jails. Nationally, the average population is about 10% greater on weekends than on average weekdays. In some states such as Iowa, North Dakota, South Dakota, Nebraska, West Virginia, Kentucky, Arkansas, Oklahoma, Montana, Idaho, New Mexico and Alaska the

relative percentage is 20%, while in Massachusetts, New York, New Jersey, Pennsylvania, Illinois, Maryland and the District of Columbia it is less than 5%. It is estimated that in 1982 a total of 57% of all jail inmates were not convicted.

Only 4% of the population of state prison systems are housed in the 223 community-based facilities. Of these, 54% are in the southern states. Nearly half of these facilities have an average daily population of between 21 and 60 inmates, but about half of all inmates live in a facility housing 41 to 100 inmates.

Prisons hold a somewhat less diverse population than do local jails. A large proportion of prisons are old and lack the facilities of modern ones. Nearly 44% are more than 30 years old, and they house about 61% of the inmates. More than 11% of the prison population resides in facilities built before 1875, and eight of 10 inmates in the oldest prisons are in facilities that house more than 1,000 prisoners.

Prisons are classified by level of security as maximum- or close-security, medium-security and minimum-security. Maximum-security prisons are typically surrounded by a double fence or wall (usually 18 to 25 feet high) with armed guards in observation towers. Such facilities usually have large interior cellblocks for inmate housing. About 41% of these prisons were built before 1925.

Medium-security prisons typically have double fences topped with barbed wire to enclose the facility. Housing architecture is quite varied, consisting of outside cellblocks in units of 150 cells or less, dormitories or cubicles. More than 87% of these prisons were built after 1925.

Minimum-security prisons typically do not have armed posts and may or may not have fences to enclose the institution. To a large degree, housing consists of open dormitories. More than 80% of these prisons were built after 1950.

In 1979 a total of 52% of all prison inmates were held in maximum-security prisons, 37% in medium-security prisons and 11% in minimum-security prisons. The percentages, however, varied greatly among states. The percentage in maximum-security prisons ranged from 94% in Texas to 10% in New Hampshire, North Carolina and Wyoming. In 14 states more than half of all prisoners are confined in maximum-security institutions. Of the 150 prisons built between 1970 and 1978 a total of 85% hold an average daily population of less than 500 inmates, and three-quarters are designed for medium security or minimum security.

Crowding and conditions of confinement pose difficult problems in most states. As of 1983, the courts had declared unconstitutional the entire prison systems of Alabama, Florida, Mississippi, Oklahoma, Rhode Island, Tennessee, Texas and all male penal facilities in Michigan. One or more facilities in 21 states were operating under a court order or consent decree as a result of inmate crowding and conditions of confinement. Seven states were involved in litigation relating to the same problem. In eight states courts had appointed receivers to operate the correctional systems or facilities, had ordered emergency release of inmates as a result of crowding or had ordered the closing of specific institutions.

The total population of state and federal prisons increased by an average of more than 16,000 per year between 1977 and 1981. In 1981 alone the net annual gain was 37,309 inmates.

Over the period 1970–82, the one-day count of jail residents increased from 160,863 to 209,582, a growth of 30%. Over the same period, the rate of confinement (the rate of inmates per 100,000 general inhabitants) increased from 80 to 90, or by about 12.5%. These data suggest that jail populations generally have not been increasing at the rate experienced by prisons (85% between 1970 and 1981).

Over the period 1974–79 total admissions to juvenile institutions declined by about 9.5%. Admissions to public juvenile facilities declined by nearly 13%

U.S. PRISON POPULATION, 1977–81

Year	Total Admissions	Total Releases	Net Gain
1977	163,203	147,895	15,308
1978	162,574	154,484	8,090
1979	172,753	166,132	6,621
1980	182,617	169,826	12,791
1981	212,254	174,955	37,309

INCARCERATION

Offense	Average (Median) Sentence Length in Years		Percent of Inmates Sentenced to Death or Prison
	Minimum	Maximum	
All crimes	4.3	8.6	10.6
Violent	5.6	13.3	15.3
Murder/attempted murder	10.5	21.9	33.3
Rape	5.8	14.9	13.4
Robbery	5.4	12.8	6.7
Property	2.7	5.6	2.2
Burglary	2.9	5.7	2.9
Larceny/auto theft	2.4	5.2	0.5
Forgery/fraud	2.6	5.4	1.4
Drug	3.0	5.7	13.1
Public order	2.3	4.5	3.7

WHAT ARE THE CHARACTERISTICS OF JAILS?

Number of jails	3,493
Facilities with populations of—	
Less than 10	1,538
10–249	1,825
250+	130
Year built	
Before 1875	156
1875–1924	732
1925–1949	768
1950–1969	1,182
1970–1978	655
Employees	70,517
% administration	25
% custodial	53
% service	9
% other	13

Source: American Prisons and Jails, *vol. III, 1980.*

NUMBER OF JAILS, NUMBER OF JAIL INMATES AND RATE OF INMATES (PER 100,000 POPULATION) BY LEGAL STATUS OF INMATES, REGION AND STATE ON FEBRUARY 15, 1978, AND JUNE 30, 1983

NOTE: The 1983 National Jail Census was conducted by the U.S. Bureau of the Census for the U.S. Department of Justice, Bureau of Justice Statistics. Questionnaires were mailed to all (N=3,358) locally administered jails in the nation in January 1983. Through the use of various follow-up procedures a response rate of 99% was achieved.

A jail was defined as "a locally administered confinement facility, intended primarily for adults but sometimes also detaining juveniles, that holds persons pending adjudication and/or persons committed after adjudication for sentences, usually of a year or less." (Source, p. 1).

Connecticut, Delaware, Hawaii, Rhode Island and Vermont had integrated jail-prison systems and therefore were excluded from the analysis. Alaska, which had five locally operated jails in addition to an integrated jail-prison system, was included.

Region and State	Jails			Jail Inmates									Rate of Inmates per 100,000 Population		
				Total			Adults			Juveniles					
	1978	1983	Percent Change	1978	1983	Percent Change	1978	1983	Percent Change	1978	1983	Percent Change	1978	1983	Percent Change
United States	3,493	3,338	−4	158,394	223,551	41	156,783	221,815	42	1,611	1,736	8	76	98	29
Northeast	207	223	8	24,228	36,634	52	24,129	36,315	51	99	319	222	54	82	52
Maine	13	14	8	325	560	72	319	542	70	6	18	300	30	49	63
Massachusetts	15	17	13	2,317	3,304	43	2,317	3,304	43	0	0	0	40	57	43
New Hampshire	11	11	0	370	475	28	362	469	30	8	6	−25	43	50	16
New Jersey	28	32	14	3,873	5,971	54	3,873	5,956	54	0	15	X	53	80	51
New York	72	72	0	10,936	16,154	48	10,852	15,877	46	84	277	230	61	91	49
Pennsylvania	68	77	13	6,407	10,170	59	6,406	10,167	59	1	3	200	54	85	57
North Central	1,042	972	−7	28,452	39,538	39	27,937	39,200	40	515	338	−34	49	67	37
Illinois	100	98	−2	5,781	8,849	53	5,758	8,819	53	23	30	30	52	77	48
Indiana	90	93	3	2,453	3,599	47	2,301	3,466	51	152	133	−13	46	66	44
Iowa	91	90	−1	664	839	26	654	828	27	10	11	10	23	29	26
Kansas	86	86	0	998	1,328	33	934	1,305	40	64	23	−64	43	55	28
Michigan	93	87	−7	5,729	7,637	33	5,708	7,627	34	21	10	−52	63	84	33
Minnesota	65	67	3	1,517	1,954	29	1,504	1,941	29	13	13	0	38	47	24
Missouri	137	129	−6	2,849	3,783	33	2,829	3,761	33	20	22	10	60	76	27
Nebraska	77	67	−13	676	844	25	638	817	28	38	27	−29	44	53	21
North Dakota	39	31	−21	118	243	106	117	236	102	1	7	600	18	36	100
Ohio	150	121	−19	5,465	7,116	30	5,377	7,087	32	88	29	−67	51	66	29
South Dakota	44	31	−30	276	316	15	253	310	23	23	6	−74	40	45	13
Wisconsin	70	72	3	1,926	3,030	57	1,864	3,003	61	62	27	−57	41	64	56
South	1,678	1,607	−4	67,444	89,479	33	66,775	88,639	33	669	840	26	98	113	15
Alabama	108	108	0	5,049	4,464	−12	5,027	4,452	11	22	12	−46	137	113	−18
Arkansas	92	89	3	1,334	1,602	20	1,277	1,540	21	57	62	9	62	69	11
District of Columbia	2	2	0	1,407	2,843	102	1,407	2,820	100	0	23	X	208	456	119
Florida	112	103	−8	10,305	14,668	42	10,263	14,313	40	42	355	745	122	137	12
Georgia	223	203	−9	8,278	10,214	23	8,269	10,213	24	9	1	−89	165	178	8
Kentucky	111	96	−14	2,149	3,711	73	2,089	3,652	75	60	59	−2	62	100	61
Louisiana	93	94	1	5,232	8,507	63	5,217	8,501	62	15	6	−60	134	192	43
Maryland	25	30	20	3,553	4,608	30	3,553	4,572	29	0	36	X	86	107	24
Mississippi	94	91	−3	2,427	2,498	3	2,359	2,482	6	68	16	−77	102	97	−5
North Dakota	95	99	4	2,798	3,496	25	2,766	3,474	26	32	22	−35	51	57	12
Oklahoma	102	104	2	1,704	2,215	30	1,676	2,164	29	28	51	82	61	67	10
South Carolina	68	58	−15	2,362	2,690	14	2,328	2,674	15	34	16	−53	84	82	−2
Tennessee	111	108	−3	4,553	6,005	40	4,492	5,975	33	61	30	−51	106	128	21
Texas	296	273	−8	10,995	15,224	39	10,931	15,176	39	64	48	−25	86	97	13
Virginia	92	95	3	4,232	5,719	35	4,077	5,616	38	155	103	−34	84	103	23
West Virginia	54	54	0	1,066	1,015	−5	1,044	1,015	3	22	0	−100	57	52	−9
West	566	536	−5	38,270	57,900	51	37,942	57,661	52	328	239	−27	100	129	29
Alaska	6	5	−17	44	37	−16	43	34	21	1	3	200	11	8	−27
Arizona	39	31	−21	2,501	2,940	18	2,484	2,906	17	17	34	100	108	99	−8
California	135	142	5	26,206	41,720	59	26,093	41,656	60	113	64	−58	120	166	38
Colorado	61	60	−2	1,681	2,747	63	1,658	2,739	65	23	8	−65	65	88	35
Idaho	45	36	−20	539	604	12	498	566	14	41	38	−7	62	61	−2
Montana	58	50	−14	324	405	25	304	394	30	20	11	−45	43	50	16
Nevada	22	23	5	912	940	3	896	928	4	16	12	−25	144	105	−27
New Mexico	38	35	−8	794	1,346	70	755	1,324	75	39	22	−44	67	96	43
Oregon	48	39	−19	1,872	2,304	23	1,855	2,304	24	17	0	−100	78	87	12
Utah	24	24	0	676	906	34	675	906	34	1	0	−100	53	56	6
Washington	59	65	10	2,453	3,610	47	2,437	3,595	48	16	15	−6	68	84	24
Wyoming	31	26	−16	268	341	27	244	309	27	24	32	33	66	66	0

Source: U.S. Department of Justice, Bureau of Justice Statistics, The 1983 Jail Census, Bulletin NCJ-95536 (Washington, D.C.: U.S. Department of Justice, November 1984), p. 2.

MORE PRISONERS ARE HOUSED IN CELLS THAN IN DORMITORIES AND IN MULTIPLE- THAN SINGLE-OCCUPANCY UNITS; MOST UNITS PROVIDE LESS THAN 60 SQUARE FEET OF FLOOR SPACE PER PERSON

	U.S. Total	Federal	State
Number of In- mates	256,676	28,124	228,552
Type of housing			
Cells	61.7%	48.3%	63.4%
Dormitories	38.3	51.7	36.6
Occupancy			
Single	40.9	38.4	41.2
Multiple	59.1	61.6	58.8
Density (sq. ft.)			
Less than 60	64.6	61.2	65.0
60–79	22.8	29.2	22.0
80 or more	12.6	9.6	13.0
Inmate/staff ratios			
Total	2.8	3.3	2.7
Administrative	125.9	147.2	123.7
Custodial	4.6	7.7	4.4
Service	16.8	14.2	17.2
Other	13.7	10.1	14.4

Source: American Prisons and Jails, *vol. III, 1980.*

while those to private ones increased by more than 29% during the same period.

Juvenile Crime & Delinquency

Juvenile delinquency, as it is known today, did not exist in the Colonies. Most Puritan children joined the labor force by age 12, and some were apprenticed and indentured outside the home. In 1619 the Virginia Company began to import children from London under an English law that permitted the deportation of children. Upon arrival in the New World, the children were apprenticed until they reached 21, when they were freed and given public lands with cattle and corn.

Punishable offenses for youths in Colonial days were running away from masters, incorrigibility, lying, swearing, fighting, stealing and cheating—offenses for the most part not punishable if committed by adults. Until the Revolution, Americans lived under English common law, which held a child accountable for its acts after the seventh birthday. Prior to that age a child was considered incapable of possessing the ability to understand the nature of criminal behavior. Judges determined the culpability of children

between ages seven and 14. But the maximum sentence—death by hanging—was the same as for adults. Capital punishment was common for children in 17th-century England, where there were 33 offenses for which the sentence applied. In the Colonies, it was less frequently imposed. Instead, corporal punishment or incarceration was often used, although one eight-year-old was convicted and hanged for burning a barn with "malice, revenge, craft and cunning." From the 17th century to the early part of the 18th century, children were sentenced to public whippings and to long-term prison sentences. Prisons held men, women and children under the same roof.

The first call for reform came in the beginning of the 19th century, in New York City, from the Society for the Prevention of Pauperism, established in 1817. It called attention to the condition of "those unfortunate children from 10 to 18 years of age, who from neglect of parents, from idleness and misfortune have . . . contravened some penal statute without reflecting on the consequences, and for hasty violations, been doomed to the penitentiary by the condemnation of the law."

The House of Refuge opened its doors in 1825 in

WHAT ARE THE CHARACTERISTICS OF PRISONS?

	Federal	State
Number of Prisons	38	521
Security level		
Maximum	13	140
Medium	17	207
Minimum	8	174
Inmate population		
Less than 500	10	366
500–999	18	80
1,000 or more	10	75
Year built		
Before 1875	0	25
1875–1924	3	76
1925–1949	16	125
1950–1969	8	156
1970–1978	11	139
Prisoners housed		
Males	31	460
Females	2	40
Coed	5	21
Prison employees		
Number	8,626	83,535
% administrative	2.2	2.2
% custodial	42.4	62.9
% service	23.0	15.9
% other	32.4	19.0

Source: *"Prison Facility Characteristics, March 1978,"* American Prisons and Jails, *vol. III, 1980.*

New York City as a result of the society's efforts. It was funded by private donations. It admitted two types of children: those convicted of a crime and sentenced to incarceration, and those who were destitute and neglected and in imminent danger of becoming delinquent. Superintendent Joseph Curtis devised a system of rewards and deprivations to reform his young wards. Infractions were tried by a jury composed of peers, with Curtis as the judge. Whipping, solitary confinement, reduction in food supply and the "silent treatment" were common. For serious offenses, the children were placed in irons. The boys made salable goods, and the girls did domestic work. Some were apprenticed and released in the custody of masters. The house was given the right to act as a legal parent.

Before long, Houses of Refuge were established in Philadelphia and Boston, the latter by state funds. Corporal punishment was prohibited in these houses.

In the privately funded Philadelphia House, each child had his or her own small cell, well lighted and well ventilated, and with a bed and a shelf. Black children were not accepted in these houses initially, but in 1834 the New York House established a "colored section." Destitute immigrant children began swelling the population of these houses and by 1829 made up 58% of the total.

The 1827 Report of the Boston Prison Discipline Society showed that children constituted between 15 and 33% of the prison population in New England. The report added that many of the children were under 12 years of age and that some incarcerated in the Massachusetts House of Corrections were as young as six.

The pace of reform increased after Massachusetts opened its first institution for the reform of juveniles in 1847. The Massachusetts State Reform School was patterned after the Houses of Refuge. It accepted any boy under age 16 convicted of an offense and who was thought to be capable of change. They could be bound out as servants or apprentices after living in the school for one year.

Concern for female juvenile offenders led to the founding of the Massachusetts State Industrial School for Girls in 1856. Reform schools for girls were different in that girls were believed to need a strong mothering environment and also to be taught high moral values. The school adopted the cottage plan, which departed from the traditional dormitory style.

Other states followed. The Chicago institution adopted the cottage plan to create "a family life for children." The Ohio Reform School, founded in 1857, also followed the cottage plan and was located in the country. Prevailing theory held that cities were evil environments that bred most juvenile problems. Cities had temptations such as bars and theaters, while the countryside had few corrupting influences but encouraged hard work and close family ties. In 1853 the New York Children's Aid Society was founded, providing placement service in the country rather than institutionalization. Some children were sent West to start new lives.

The beginning of the 1860s witnessed yet another kind of experiment: the ship schools, where boys were accepted until age 16. These schools did not flourish long because of disciplinary problems, heavy operating expenses, and economic depressions that put adult seamen out of work. The last of the new reformatories was the Catholic Protectory, founded in New York in 1863. It was the largest institution of its kind at that time.

Discrimination against blacks, Hispanics, Native Americans and poor whites remained a problem in all types of reformatories from their inception. Sexual abuse and physical attacks by peers and sometimes

IN ALL STATES, A MAJORITY OF OFFENDERS ARE UNDER COMMUNITY SUPERVISION RATHER THAN CONFINEMENT

	Confined		Under Supervision	
	Adults*	Juveniles*	Adults*	Juveniles*
Alabama	12,468	770	15,382	5,476
Alaska	1,062	373	1,454	892
Arizona	7,695	1,218	15,608	3,944
Arkansas	4,560	901	6,718	4,546
California	57,453*	14,859	166,677	57,225
Colorado	4,430	1,191	13,871	3,868
Connecticut	4,647	614	26,962	2,296
Delaware	1,716	206	4,517	800
Florida	33,501	2,740	51,582	16,372
Georgia	22,299	1,419	66,202	10,259
Hawaii	1,202	145	5,465	1,245
Idaho	1,492	307	2,462	2,531
Illinois	19,257	1,691	74,196	10,376
Indiana	10,355	2,048	24,255	11,662
Iowa	3,367	814	10,635	5,387
Kansas	3,746	1,425	14,162	5,152
Kentucky	6,082	925	22,300	5,085
Louisiana	14,622	1,424	17,793	5,672
Maine	1,185	466	3,182	976
Maryland	12,888	1,547	54,200	7,019
Massachusetts	6,096	804	30,618	15,222
Michigan	20,700	2,714	32,135	18,701
Minnesota	3,528	1,450	33,633	8,179
Mississippi	6,983	442	8,402	3,991
Missouri	8,983	1,516	22,140	12,383
Montana	1,102	291	3,011	2,097
Nebraska	2,271	745	8,025	2,227
Nevada	3,037	452	6,843	3,464
New Hampshire	746	400	2,337	1,196
New Jersey	10,831	1,815	45,032	12,045
New Mexico	2,279	572	4,624	1,655
New York	36,510	4,716	88,551	11,963
North Carolina	18,557	1,201	45,247	7,244
North Dakota	425	193	1,227	1,403
Ohio	20,345	3,734	36,471	21,669
Oklahoma	6,924	1,265	17,400	4,197
Oregon	5,137	1,239	15,943	7,317
Pennsylvania	15,763	3,272	63,361	16,975
Rhode Island	962	207	5,959	2,194
South Carolina	10,855	767	22,476	7,136
South Dakota	946	382	5,259	1,359
Tennessee	12,375	1,546	13,510	7,672
Texas	42,433	3,118	173,473	15,728
Utah	1,815	438	8,119	1,683
Vermont	534	142	3,671	332
Virginia	13,465	1,613	18,316	8,215
Washington	7,773	1,631	29,050	9,557
West Virginia	2,356	286	3,335	3,240

	Confined		Under Supervision	
	Adults*	Juveniles*	Adults*	Juveniles*
Wisconsin	6,242	1,273	22,920	9,103
Wyoming**	802		1,335	
Federal	28,133		65,293	
U.S. total	526,408	71,792	1,445,798	381,194

*Includes estimated 2,093 adult inmates under the jurisdiction of the California Youth Authority.
**Juvenile data from Wyoming excluded to protect confidentiality guarantees.
Sources: Prisoners in 1981, BJS bulletin, May 1982. Census of Jails and Survey of Jail Inmates: Preliminary Report, NPS bulletin SD-NPS-J-6P (Washington, D.C.: U.S. Department of Justice, February 1979). Children in Custody 1979 (Washington, D.C.: U.S. Bureau of the Census, forthcoming). Probation and Parole, BJS bulletin, August 1982. State and Local Probation and Parole Systems, February 1978.

the staff were also universal problems—ones that have not been quite overcome even today.

In the 1870s and 1880s, a group of genteel women in Chicago began what came to be known as the "child-saving" movement, which agitated for separate juvenile courts. As a result of their efforts, Illinois established the nation's first juvenile court system in 1899. In that same year, the city of Denver and the state of Rhode Island passed juvenile court legislation.

The first federal effort in this direction was the establishment of the Children's Bureau in 1912 and the passage of the first federal Child Labor Law in 1916. Subsequent youth programs at the federal level included the National Youth Administration during the Depression, the congressional Interdepartmental Committee on Children and Youth in 1948 and the Midcentury White House Conference on Children and Youth in 1950.

The 1950s brought new approaches to aiding troubled juveniles. The teachings of John Dewey, Karen Horney, Carl Rogers and Erich Fromm, among others, gained prominence. There was a greater acceptance in criminal justice work of professionals from the psychological disciplines. Several outstanding local programs were created to deal with the psychological roots of juvenile problems. Among these was the guided group interaction therapy utilized at Highlands, N.J., in 1950. It was an approach copied across the country during the next two decades.

In 1950 the federal Youth Correction Act established a Youth Correction Authority to improve techniques for the treatment and rehabilitation of youthful offenders. The U.S. Department of Health, Education and Welfare, established in 1953, included a Children's Bureau with a Juvenile Delinquency Division.

Beginning in 1966, five landmark Supreme Court decisions helped to define juvenile rights: Kent v. United States, 383 U.S. 541 (1966); In re Gault, 387 U.S. 1 (1967); In re Winship, 397 U.S. 358 (1970); McKeiver v. Pennsylvania, 403 U.S. 528 (1971); and Breed v. Jones, 95 S. Ct. 1779 (1975). These cases

and others gave juveniles the right to proper hearings, the right to counsel, the right to confront the accuser, the right to cross-examine witnesses and the right to protection against double jeopardy. The one right denied was the right to a jury trial. These rulings ushered in a new era for juvenile justice.

In 1972 the state of Massachusetts closed its juvenile reformatories and placed the children in community-based work and education programs. Many other states followed suit.

However, juvenile crime continued to rise, confounding the social scientists and penologists. Between 1960 and 1973 the arrests of juveniles for acts of violence and other crimes increased by 144%. Persons 18 years of age or younger accounted for 45% of the arrests for serious crime and 23% of the arrests for violent crime. Burglaries and auto thefts were found to be committed overwhelmingly by youths. The peak age for arrests for violent crime was 18, followed by 17, 16 and 19 years of age. The peak age for arrest for major property crime was 16, followed 15 and 17 years of age.

At the same time, many youths were incarcerated for so-called status offenses, which are acts that could not be considered criminal if committed by an adult. These offenses include running away from home, truancy, promiscuity, drinking beer, curfew violations and incorrigibility. Worse, there was no agreement among states on what constitutes juvenile delinquency or even on what age constitutes majority.

These conditions prompted 1974 congressional hearings on the subject. These hearings led to the passage of the historic Juvenile Justice and Delinquency Prevention Act of 1974. This act created the Office of Juvenile Justice and Delinquency Prevention (OJJDP) and, within that office, the National Institute for Juvenile Justice and Delinquency Prevention. The key elements of the program are the coordination of federal delinquency programs, formula grants to states, technical assistance, research, training, standards and the dissemination of information. The National Ad-

CURRENT SENTENCING ALTERNATIVES

Death penalty: In some states for certain crimes such as murder, the courts may sentence an offender to death by electrocution, exposure to lethal gas, hanging, lethal injection or other method specified by state law.

- As of 1982, 36 states had death penalty provisions in law.
- Most death penalty sentences have been for murder.
- As of year-end 1982, six persons had been executed since 1977, and 1,050 inmates in 31 states were under sentence of death.

Incarceration: The confinement of a convicted criminal in a federal or state prison or a local jail to serve a court-imposed sentence. Custody usually is within a jail, administered locally, or a prison operated by the state or the federal government. In many states, offenders sentenced to less than one year are held in a jail; those sentenced to longer terms are committed to the state prison.

- More than 4,300 correctional facilities are maintained by federal, state or local governments, including 43 federal facilities; 791 state-operated adult confinement and community-based correctional facilities; and 3,500 local jails, which usually are county-operated.
- On a given day in 1982, approximately 412,000 persons were confined in state and federal prisons and approximately 210,000 persons were confined in local jails.

Probation: The sentencing of an offender to community supervision by a probation agency, often as a result of suspending a sentence to confinement. Such supervision normally entails the provision of specific rules of conduct while in the community. If the rules are violated, a sentencing judge may impose a sentence of confinement. It is the most widely used correctional disposition in the United States.

- State or local governments operate more than 2,000 probation agencies. These agencies supervise nearly 1.6 million adults and juveniles on probation.

Split sentences and shock probation: A penalty that explicitly requires the convicted person to serve a period of confinement in a local, state or federal facility (the "shock") followed by a period of probation. This penalty attempts to combine the use of community supervision with a short incarceration experience.

- 1977 and 1978 California data reveal that by far the most common disposition in felony cases was a combined sentence of jail and probation.

Restitution: The requirement that the offender provide financial remuneration for the losses incurred by the victim.

Community service: The requirement that the offender provide a specified number of hours of public service work, such as collecting trash in parks or other public facilities.

- By 1979 nearly all states had statutory provisions for the collection and disbursement of restitution funds. In late 1982 a restitution law was enacted at the federal level.
- By 1979 nearly a third of the states authorized community service work orders. Community service often is imposed as a specific condition of probation.

Fines: An economic penalty that requires the offender to pay a specific sum of money within the limit set by law. Fines are often imposd in addition to probation or as an alternative to incarceration.

- Many laws that govern the imposition of fines are undergoing revision. These revisions often provide for more flexible means of ensuring equality in the imposition of fines, flexible fine schedules, "day fines" geared to the offender's daily wage, installment payment of fines and a restriction on confinement to situations that amount to intentional refusal to pay.

visory Committee for Juvenile Justice and Delinquency Prevention advises the administrator of the OJJDP.

The disposition of juveniles adjudicated to be delinquent extends until the juvenile legally becomes an adult or until the offending behavior has been corrected, whichever is sooner.

Of the 45 states that authorize indeterminate periods of confinement, 34 grant releasing authority to the state juvenile corrections agency, five place such authority with the committing judge and six delegate it to the juvenile paroling agencies.

Certain states, such as Georgia, Illinois and New York, have new laws that mandate minimum periods of confinement when juveniles are adjudicated delinquent for having committed designated felonies. Ohio,

Washington and California also have set or variable minimum periods of confinement.

Juvenile courts cannot order death sentences or life sentences. Yet juvenile courts may go farther than criminal courts in determining the life-styles of juvenile offenders who are placed in the community under probation or supervision. For example, the court may order them to live in certain locations, to attend school and to participate in reformatory programs. The National Center for Juvenile Justice estimates that 70% of the juveniles whose cases are not waived or dismissed are put on probation and about 10% are committed to an institution.

Of the 72,000 juveniles in custody in 1979, about half lived in detention centers, training schools or other institutions and the other half in shelters, group homes or other open settings with minimal control. Slightly more than two-thirds of the juveniles in custody were classified as delinquent, the other third were held for other reasons (status offenders, 13%; voluntary admissions, 9%; dependent, neglected or abused juveniles, 8%; and emotionally disturbed or mentally retarded youth, 2%). More than a third of all the juveniles in custody were held in privately operated facilities.

A total of 2,576 public and private juvenile custody facilities are in operation nationwide. These facilities include detention centers, training schools, diagnostic centers, shelters, ranches and group homes. Four of five public facilities are secure residences where residents are controlled through staff monitoring or hardware restraints. Virtually all group homes and most ranch-type facilities are nonsecure. A third of the juveniles in custody are held for reasons other than a criminal charge.

The language used in juvenile courts is less harsh. For example, juvenile courts:

- accept "petitions of delinquency" rather than criminal complaints
- conduct "hearings," not trials
- "adjudicate" juveniles to be delinquent rather than find them guilty of a crime
- order one of a number of "dispositions" rather than sentences

Despite such wide discretion and informality, juveniles are protected by most of the due process safeguards associated with adult criminal trials. For example:

- Prosecution and defense attorneys are present at such hearings
- The state must prove its case beyond a reasonable doubt
- Juveniles have the right to appeal juvenile court decisions
- In more than a dozen states, juries are permitted in juvenile courts

While adults begin criminal justice processing only through arrest, summons or citation, juveniles may be referred to court by parents, schools or other sources. Although 84% of the cases are referrals from law-enforcement agencies, 3% are from parents or relatives, 3% are from schools, 2% are from probation officers, 2% are from other courts and 5% are from other sources.

The first step in the processing of juveniles is called "intake," which frequently is performed by the juvenile court or prosecutors. Intake units handle a case with or without a petition to the court. Relatively few juveniles are detained prior to court appearance. All states allow juveniles to be treated as adults in criminal courts in one of three ways: judicial waiver, concurrent jurisdiction and through excluded offenses provision. Under judicial waiver, the juvenile court waives its jurisdiction and transfers the case to the criminal court. Under concurrent jurisdiction, prosecutors have the discretion to file charges for certain offenses in either juvenile or criminal courts. Under excluded offenses provision, the legislature may exclude certain offenses, either very minor (such as traffic or fishing violations) or very serious (such as murder or rape). Juveniles tried as adults have a very high conviction rate.

The age of juvenile criminal responsibility is 16 in Connecticut, New York, North Carolina and Vermont, 17 in Georgia, Illinois, Louisiana, Massachusetts, Michigan, Missouri, South Carolina and Texas and 18 in all other states.

Of the referrals to juvenile courts, 11% are for crimes against persons, 49% for crimes against property, 6% for drug offenses, 15% for offenses against public order and 20% for status offenses.

U.S. National Central Bureau—Interpol (Interpol-USNCB)

The International Criminal Police Organization (Interpol) was founded to promote mutual assistance among international law enforcement authorities in the prevention and suppression of international crime. Established in 1923 and reorganized in 1946, Interpol's membership today numbers 138 countries, the most recent additions being the nations of Kiribati and St. Vincent and the Grenadines.

U.S. participation in the organization began in 1938, when Congress authorized the attorney general to accept membership on behalf of the U.S. government. World War II intervened, however, and Interpol operations were temporarily terminated. The organization was reestablished in 1946, and a year later the United States resumed membership under the jurisdiction of the Federal Bureau of Investigation (FBI).

Stating various reasons, the FBI withdrew from Interpol in 1950. The Department of the Treasury, however, seeking to maintain international contacts because of its enforcement responsibilities in criminal narcotics and currency violations, continued an informal liaison with Interpol until 1958, at which time the U.S. attorney general officially designated the Department of the Treasury as the U.S. representative to Interpol, placing complete responsibility for maintaining U.S. membership in the organization under Treasury's purview. In 1969 Treasury established the U.S. National Central Bureau (USNCB) to carry out the Interpol functions. Then, on January 18, 1977, a memorandum of understanding between officials of the two departments established their dual authority in administering the USNCB.

In 1979 the memorandum was amended, designating the attorney general as the permanent representative to Interpol and the secretary of the Treasury as the alternate representative, and the USNCB became one of several components of the Office of the Deputy Attorney General. The USNCB continued to develop and expand, and in 1981 it was officially removed from the Office of the Deputy Attorney General and established as a separate organization of the Department of Justice.

The memorandum of understanding was again amended in April 1983, designating that the position of chief of the USNCB was to be occupied by a career professional law-enforcement employee of the Department of Justice or the Department of the Treasury for a term not to exceed four years, and that the position of deputy chief for investigations was to be occupied by a professional law-enforcement employee of the Departments of Justice, Treasury or other law-enforcement agency participating at the Interpol-USNCB, for a four-year term. The commencement of service of the chief and deputy chief for investigations could not occur simultaneously. In addition, to ensure management and leadership continuity of the USNCB, the position of deputy chief for operations and administration was established and was to be held by a permanent Justice Department employee.

The goals of Interpol, and hence of the USNCB, are to promote and ensure mutual assistance among all police authorities within the limits of the laws existing in the different member countries and in the spirit of the Universal Declaration of Human Rights. The National Central Bureau (NCB) of each Interpol member country likewise operates within the framework and guidelines of the Interpol Constitution. Article 3 of the Constitution prohibits intervention in, or activities or investigations of, matters of a military, religious, racial or political character.

To guard against misuse of investigative information contained in Interpol files, the Interpol General Secretariat specifies that information provided by any member country should not be released to a nonlaw-enforcement organization without the express permission of the country providing the information. Furthermore, written guidelines concerning the relaying of law-enforcement information, drafted by the General Secretariat, have been approved by the Interpol General Assembly and are followed by each Interpol participant.

A 1982 headquarters agreement with the French government grants Interpol the authority to develop and implement regulations regarding the security and maintenance of the General Secretariat archives. And to ensure the internal control and data protection of Interpol archives, the organization is currently establishing a Supervisory Board whose purpose is to review cases brought to their attention by the Executive Committee or by other means. Composed of five international judges, the board will verify that personal and investigative information contained in the General Secretariat archives is: (1) obtained and processed in accordance with the provisions of the Interpol Constitution; (2) recorded for specific law-enforcement purposes and not used in any way incompatible with those purposes; (3) accurate; and (4) maintained in accordance with the criteria established by the General Secretariat. The Supervisory Board will also notify the Interpol Executive Committee of the results of any investigations it conducts and any modifications that must be made to the appropriate components of the organization.

As U.S. liaison to Interpol, the USNCB functions as the primary conduit for maintaining law-enforcement communications among this country, other Interpol member countries and the Interpol General Secretariat. Through the National Law Enforcement Telecommunications System (NLETS), the USNCB also serves as the communications link among the more than 20,000 U.S. federal, state and local police agencies and the NCB's of other Interpol member countries. Requests for investigative information received by the USNCB include those pertaining to crimes of violence, including terrorism, murder, robbery, large-scale narcotics, fraud and counterfeiting violations. Such cases often involve arrests and extraditions to the countries where the crimes were committed. Requests for information are also made regarding criminal history backgrounds, license checks, and information of a humanitarian nature. In addition, Interpol and the USNCB can assist foreign and domestic police organizations in tracing weapons and stolen works of art and/or locating witnesses to interview for investigative purposes. These activities represent the primary but not the complete range of activities undertaken by the USNCB.

The USNCB Quality Control Unit reviews all incoming requests for compliance with Interpol and USNCB regulations prior to opening a case. All requests must: (1) come from a legitimate domestic law-enforcement agency or an Interpol member country; (2) be an international investigation; (3) be a violation of U.S. federal or state law, as well as a crime in the country involved; (4) be in compliance with the Interpol Constitution; (5) show a link between the crime and the subject of the case; and (6) contain a clear reason indicating the type of investigation and the fullest possible identifying details of the subject. If this information is not stated, the requester is contacted for additional information before an investigative case in initiated by the USNCB.

In addition, before any information can be released, a written verification of the request is required. Senior investigative agents coordinate the release of information in accordance with carefully established policies and guidelines. Before a case is closed, it must be reviewed by an assistant chief to ensure that the case was handled appropriately and within the guidelines and procedures delineated in the USNCB investigations manual.

For operational, analytical and administrative matters, the staff of the USNCB consists of 41 permanent, detailed and temporary employees. In addition, the USNCB functions through the collaborative efforts of the 13 participating federal law-enforcement agencies, which include the Federal Bureau of Investigation; the Drug Enforcement Administration; the Immigration and Naturalization Service; the Criminal Division; the U.S. Customs Service; the U.S. Secret Service; the Internal Revenue Service; the Bureau of Alcohol, Tobacco and Firearms; the Office of the Comptroller of the Currency; the Federal Law Enforcement Training Center in Glynco, Ga.; the Department of Agriculture's Office of the Inspector General; the U.S. Postal Inspection Service; and the U.S. Marshals Service.

A critical element of the structure and success of Interpol is its network of communications between member countries and the General Secretariat. Currently there are 72 Interpol member countries, including the General Secretariat, on the Interpol radio network; the remaining member countries may be reached via international telex or cable. In an effort to maintain the most efficient communications among all member countries, a Standing Committee on Information Technology was created in June 1984 to upgrade equipment and expand the Interpol communications network. Satellite communications is being studied as an effective alternative to the existing system. Additionally, an automatic message switching system at the General Secretariat is scheduled to begin operation in July 1986; this will greatly enhance the transmission of the more than 500,000 international messages currently being relayed each year. To ensure secure communications, five European countries have encrypted their systems, and it is anticipated that the other countries on the radio network will be secured by January 1987.

The number of new cases opened during fiscal year 1985 was 11,100, an increase of 31% over the fiscal year 1984 total of 8,492. In addition, further implementation of the Interpol Case Tracking System (ICTS) enabled the USNCB to close 10,424 cases during fiscal year 1985, an increase of 258% over the previous year's total of 2,910. Investigative matters not resulting in case openings numbered 667, with an additional 341 being declined because they did not meet USNCB criteria or were deferred pending receipt of additional information.

These figures only partially reflect the full range of activities conducted at the USNCB. The Administrative and Special Projects Unit handled approximately 1,200 noninvestigative matters in fiscal year 1985. These included requests for information about Interpol and the USNCB from both foreign and domestic law-enforcement agencies, the media and the general public; requests from Interpol member countries for information about various law-enforcement topics; the processing of administrative requirements pertaining to budgetary justifications and financial operations; personnel actions; property and procurement requirements; and the preparation and processing of all special and routine reports required by the Department of Justice, the Office of Management and Budget and Congress. Of this number, more than 150 represented Freedom of Information and Privacy Act requests.

The detailee from the Federal Law Enforcement Training Center (FLETC) is also assigned to the Administrative and Special Projects Unit and is presently developing a training curriculum on the Interpol-USNCB and Interpol programs to be used at the FLETC, primarily for the state and local law-enforcement communities. In addition, a working relationship has been established with representatives from seven Interpol member countries and initial contact made with representatives from five others to explore opportunities for exchanging training information. The FLETC detailee has also coordinated attendance at more than 30 conferences and symposia, handling all necessary arrangements for foreign law-enforcement officials as well as U.S. officials abroad.

In early fiscal year 1985, a task group was formed to plan and execute the activities involved in the United States hosting the 54th General Assembly meeting of Interpol member countries. This event, scheduled for October 1–8, 1985, was particularly significant for the United States and the USNCB since this marked the first time in 25 years that the United States had hosted the event and, for the first time in the organization's history, an American serves as president. The task group consisted of 31 full-time employees detailed from federal agencies plus approximately 75 detailees who were brought on board during the final two weeks. As the result of a major fund-raising effort conducted by the task group, approximately $485,000 in private sector contributions were received to assist in keeping the government's financial contribution to a minimum. Attorney General Edwin Meese was official host for many of the activities, and Deputy Attorney General D. Lowell Jensen served as head of the U.S. delegation.

The public-relations requirements for the General Assembly were handled by the USNCB, another significant "first" for the United States in light of the fact that previous General Assembly host countries had never prepared documentation for distribution to members of the media and the general public. These tasks were an extension of the public-relations function implemented at the USNCB in 1984 to deal with the publicity generated by the election of the first American as president of Interpol. Documentation included articles for journals and magazines dealing with previous General Assembly sessions and Interpol's position on terrorism, press releases, position

papers on Interpol's program areas, the history of Interpol and a summary of the Interpol function. Also included was a publication prepared with the assistance of the Office of Justice Assistance, Research and Statistics.

During 1985 the USNCB pursued plans to install automated translation equipment. Fully implemented in 1986, the equipment enhances the USNCB's translation capabilities by providing rapid rough-draft translations of incoming and outgoing messages relating to criminal investigative reports and analyses. This equipment also enables the rapid translation of all Interpol-USNCB case-related documents both from and into the official Interpol languages, French and Spanish, as well as translation of working papers and statements expressing the United States' position at conferences, regional working party meetings and future General Assembly meetings.

The international stolen artworks program continues to circulate information on stolen works of art and, since January 1985, the USNCB has been recording statistics showing thefts as well as the recovery of stolen art. Figures for 1985 indicate an increase

HOW DO THE UCR AND THE NCS COMPARE?

	Uniform Crime Reports	National Crime Survey
Offenses measured:	Homicide Rape Robbery (personal and commercial) Assault (aggravated) Burglary (commercial and household) Larceny (commercial and household) Motor vehicle theft Arson	Rape Robbery (personal) Assault (aggravated and simple) Household burglary Larceny (personal and household) Motor vehicle theft
Scope:	Crimes reported to the police in most jurisdictions; considerable flexibility in developing small-area data	Crimes both reported and not reported to police; all data are for the nation as a whole; some data are available for a few large geographic areas
Collection method:	Police department reports to FBI	Survey interviews; periodically measures the total number of crimes committed by asking a national sample of 60,000 households representing 135,000 persons over age 12 about their experiences as victims of crime during a specified period
Kinds of information:	In addition to offense counts, provide information on crime clearances, persons arrested, persons charged, law-enforcement officers killed and assaulted, and characteristics of homicide victims	Provides details about victims (such as age, race, sex, education, income, and whether the victim and offender were related to each other) and about crimes (such as time and place of occurrence, whether or not reported to police, use of weapons, occurrence of injury, and economic consequences)
Sponsor:	Department of Justice, Federal Bureau of Investigation	Department of Justice, Bureau of Justice Statistics

METROPOLITAN AREAS HAVE THE HIGHEST RATES OF REPORTED CRIME

	UCR Index Crime Rates per 100,000 Population			
	Violent Crimes	% Change 1973–81	Property Crimes	% Change* 1973–81
Standard Metropolitan Statistical Areas (SMSA's) Urbanized areas that generally include at least one central city of 50,000 or more inhabitants, the county in which it is located, and contiguous counties that satisfy certain criteria of population and integration with the central city.	691	+37%	5,913	+37%
Non-SMSA cities Cities that do not qualify as SMSA central cities and are not included in other SMSA's.	330	+49%	4,834	+55%
Suburban areas Suburban cities other than central cities and counties within metropolitan areas.	373	+50%	4,503	+36%
Rural areas	173	+17%	2,004	+51%

This period was chosen for comparison, as 1973 was the first year for which the current crime classification was used in FBI tabulations of UCR Index crimes.
Source: FBI Uniform Crime Reports, 1981.

WHAT ARE THE CHARACTERISTICS OF OFFENDERS?

	U.S. Population 1980	1981				
		Index Crime Arrestees		Convicted Jail Inmates	State Prison Inmates	Federal Prison Inmates
		Violent	Property			
	226,545,805	464,826	1,828,928	91,411	340,639	28,133
Sex						
Male	49%	90%	79%	94%	96%	94%
Female	51	10	21	6	4	6
Race						
White	86	53	67	58	52	63
Black	12	46	31	40	47	35
Other	2	1	2	2	1	2
Ethnic origin						
Hispanic	6	12	10	10	9	16
Non-Hispanic	94	88	90	90	91	84
Age						
Under 15	23	5	14	*	0	0
15–19	9	25	36	14	7	0
20–29	18	42	31	53	56	34
30–39	14	17	11	19	25	40
40–49	10	7	4	9	8	17
50–59	10	3	2	4	3	7
60+	16	1	2	1	1	2

Less than 0.5%.
Sources: Statistical Abstract of the United States, 1981. Crime in the United States, 1981, 1982. Profile of Inmates of Local Jails, 1980. Prisoners in State and Federal Institutions on December 31, 1981, 1983. Unpublished revised U.S. Census data. Unpublished age data for state and federal prisoners.

UCR SHOW INCREASES IN ALL INDEX CRIMES REPORTED BY POLICE DURING THE 1970s

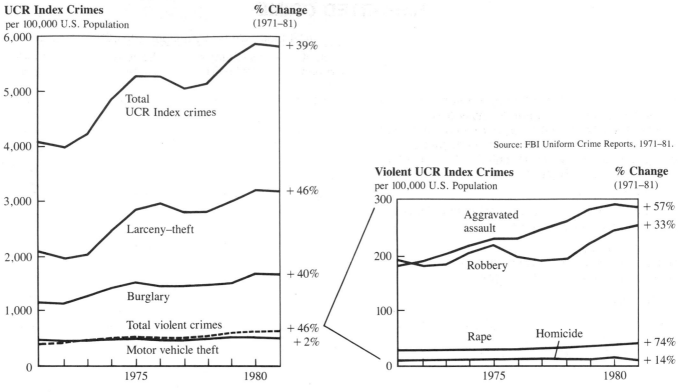

UCR Index Crimes
per 100,000 U.S. Population

% Change
(1971–81)

Total UCR Index crimes +39%

Larceny–theft +46%

Burglary +40%

Total violent crimes +46%

Motor vehicle theft +2%

Source: FBI Uniform Crime Reports, 1971–81.

Violent UCR Index Crimes
per 100,000 U.S. Population

% Change
(1971–81)

Aggravated assault +57%

Robbery +33%

Rape +74%

Homicide +14%

THE NATIONAL CRIME SURVEY SHOWS RELATIVELY LITTLE CHANGE IN VICTIMIZATION RATES BETWEEN 1973 AND 1981

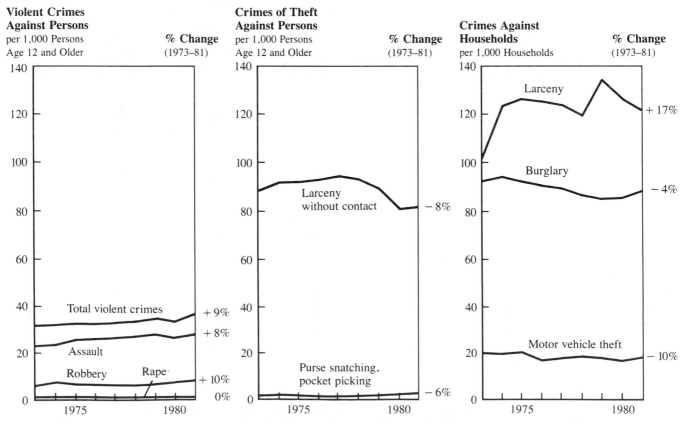

Violent Crimes Against Persons
per 1,000 Persons Age 12 and Older

% Change
(1973–81)

Total violent crimes +9%

Assault +8%

Robbery   Rape +10%

0%

Crimes of Theft Against Persons
per 1,000 Persons Age 12 and Older

% Change
(1973–81)

Larceny without contact −8%

Purse snatching, pocket picking −6%

Crimes Against Households
per 1,000 Households

% Change
(1973–81)

Larceny +17%

Burglary −4%

Motor vehicle theft −10%

Source: BJS National Crime Survey, 1973–81.

WHILE MOST ARRESTS ARE OF MALES, THE SHARE OF ARRESTS THAT ARE OF FEMALES IS HIGHEST FOR LARCENY-THEFT

UCR Index Crimes	Males	Females
Murder	87%	13%
Rape	99%	
Robbery	93%	7%
Aggravated assault	87%	13%
Burglary	94%	6%
Larceny-theft	71%	29%
Motor vehicle theft	91%	9%
Arson	89%	11%

Source: FBI Uniform Crime Reports, *1981.*

	White	Black
I Index crimes	64%	34%
Violent crimes	53	46
Murder	50	49
Rape	50	48
Robbery	39	60
Assault	61	37
Property crimes	67	31
Burglary	69	30
Larceny-theft	66	32
Motor vehicle theft	68	30
Arson	78	21

Note: Percentages do not add to 100% because arrests of persons of other races are not shown.
Source: FBI Unform Crime Reports, *1981.*

in the number of items recovered, which had been reported through Interpol channels. Interpol recently established an international committee to research and recommend a standardized system of computerization for the international tracing of stolen art objects. Various systems already in existence are being studied in an effort to develop a comprehensive system that will be most compatible to all. In addition, preparations have been made for the installation of a laser disk system at the USNCB that will provide an image of the artwork to coincide with the computerized data.

The USNCB's international terrorism and organized crime program, established in 1983, has as-sumed greater significance as a result of increases in these areas of international criminal activity. Resolutions approved at the Interpol General Assembly in 1984 categorized international terrorist activity as a law-enforcement rather than a political matter and established parameters enabling the member countries, for the first time, to exchange information regarding terrorist matters. Furthermore, an August 1985 meeting of experts, coordinated by the Interpol General Secretariat, developed a proposal to establish a separate Antiterrorist Unit at the General Secretariat to coordinate international interest in this growing concern. Further resolutions passed during the 54th

PERCENT CHANGE IN RATES (PER 1,000 UNITS OF EACH RESPECTIVE CATEGORY) OF PERSONAL AND HOUSEHOLD VICTIMIZATION BETWEEN 1973 AND 1982, BY TYPE OF VICTIMIZATION, UNITED STATES

	Percent Change in Victimization Rate								
Type of Victimization	1973–82	1974–82	1975–82	1976–82	1977–82	1978–82	1979–82	1980–82	1981–82
Personal victimization:									
Crimes of violence	5.3[a]	3.9	4.4	5.2[a]	1.1	1.6	−0.8	3.0	−3.0
Rape	−14.7	−17.4	−11.0	−3.6	−9.0	−16.5	−25.0[b]	−13.8	−14.7
Robbery	5.0	−1.4	4.7	9.6	13.8[b]	20.2[b]	13.1[a]	7.9	−4.5
Assault	6.1[a]	6.2[b]	4.8	4.4	−1.5	−1.8	−3.1	2.5	−2.2
Aggravated assault	−7.6[a]	−10.4[b]	−3.1	−5.6	−6.7	−3.9	−6.2	0.5	−3.4
Simple assault	15.4[b]	18.3[b]	9.8[b]	10.8[b]	1.6	−0.5	−1.2	3.6	−1.4
Crimes of theft	−9.4[b]	−13.3[b]	−14.1[b]	−14.1[b]	−15.2[b]	−14.7[b]	−10.2[b]	−0.6	−3.1[b]
Personal larceny with contact	−0.3	−1.6	−1.0	5.9	15.5	−1.9	6.6	1.0	−5.8
Personal larceny without contact	−9.7[b]	−13.6[b]	−14.5[b]	−14.8[b]	−16.0[b]	−15.2[b]	−10.8[b]	−0.7	−3.0[a]
Household victimization:									
Household burglary	−14.7[b]	−16.0[b]	−14.7[b]	−12.1[b]	−11.7[b]	−9.1[b]	−7.0[b]	−7.2[b]	−11.1[b]
Household larceny	6.4[b]	−8.0[b]	−9.2[b]	−8.2[b]	−7.6[b]	−5.0[b]	−14.8[b]	−10.0[b]	−5.9[b]
Motor vehicle theft	−15.3[b]	−14.1[b]	−17.0[b]	−1.9	−4.8	−7.7	−7.8	−3.2	−5.6

a. The difference is statistically significant at the 0.10 level.
b. The difference is statistically significant at the 0.05 level.
Source: U.S. Department of Justice, Bureau of Justice Statistics, Criminal Victimization in the United States, Special Report NCJ-90541 (Washington, D.C.: U.S. Department of Justice, September 1983), p. 3, Table 3.

ESTIMATED NUMBER OF PERSONAL AND HOUSEHOLD VICTIMIZATIONS AND PERCENT NOT REPORTED TO POLICE, 1973–82 AND ESTIMATED NUMBER OF BUSINESS VICTIMIZATIONS AND PERCENT NOT REPORTED TO POLICE, 1973–76, BY TYPE OF VICTIMIZATION, UNITED STATES[a]

Type of Victimization	1973 Estimated Number	1973 Percent Not Reported	1974 Estimated Number	1974 Percent Not Reported	1975 Estimated Number	1975 Percent Not Reported	1976 Estimated Number	1976 Percent Not Reported	1977 Estimated Number	1977 Percent Not Reported
Personal victimizations										
Rape and attempted rape	152,740	51	161,160	47	151,055	44	145,193	47	154,237	42
Robbery	1,086,700	46	1,173,980	46	1,121,374	46	1,110,639	46	1,082,936	44
Robbery and attempted robbery										
with injury	376,000	35	383,470	37	353,493	34	360,700	36	386,405	33
Serious assault	208,800	28	215,000	32	207,114	33	175,660	32	214,670	24
Minor assault	167,200	42	168,460	44	146,380	37	185,041	39	171,735	45
Robbery without injury	396,740	43	466,400	41	467,595	41	453,867	40	412,505	35
Attempted robbery without injury	313,960	64	324,120	63	300,285	69	296,071	67	284,026	70
Assault	4,001,820	55	4,063,680	54	4,176,056	54	4,343,261	52	4,663,827	55
Aggravated assault	1,616,700	47	1,695,440	46	1,590,080	44	1,694,941	41	1,737,774	47
With injury	496,960	39	545,990	39	543,175	34	588,672	37	541,411	37
Attempted assault with weapon	1,197,740	51	1,149,450	49	1,046,905	49	1,106,269	43	1,196,363	51
Simple assault	2,385,120	61	2,368,240	61	2,585,976	60	2,648,320	59	2,926,053	60
With injury	603,500	51	582,190	54	687,352	51	691,534	53	755,780	51
Attempted assault without weapon	1,781,610	64	1,786,050	63	1,898,624	63	1,956,786	60	2,170,273	63
Personal larceny with contact	495,590	66	511,480	65	513,952	65	497,056	63	461,014	62
Purse snatching	103,280	51	90,230	36	119,096	36	91,595	32	87,937	36
Attempted purse snatching	71,260	B	62,830	B	60,912	B	55,535	B	46,687	B
Pocket picking	321,050	68	358,410	71	333,943	72	349,926	70	326,390	66
Personal larceny without contact	14,635,655	77	15,098,118	75	15,455,660	73	16,021,110	73	16,469,154	74
Household victimizations										
Burglary	6,432,350	52	6,655,070	51	6,688,964	51	6,663,422	51	6,766,010	50
Forcible entry	2,070,950	29	2,190,330	28	2,251,869	27	2,277,063	29	2,300,292	27
Unlawful entry without force	2,956,830	62	3,031,080	62	2,959,734	62	2,826,599	60	2,962,705	60
Attempted forcible entry	1,404,560	68	1,433,660	64	1,477,361	67	1,559,760	66	1,503,013	67
Larceny	7,506,490	74	8,866,060	74	9,156,711	72	9,300,854	72	9,415,533	74
Under $50	4,824,900	84	5,641,160	84	5,615,914	84	5,601,954	84	5,443,697	85
$50 or more	1,884,280	47	2,351,490	51	2,707,605	46	2,745,097	47	2,851,831	52
Amount not ascertained	263,750	77	296,000	77	277,922	81	299,350	78	410,196	82
Attempted	533,560	80	577,410	75	555,270	76	654,454	73	709,808	73
Vehicle theft	1,335,410	31	1,341,890	32	1,418,725	28	1,234,644	30	1,296,759	31
Completed	884,710	13	855,680	11	910,253	8	759,816	11	797,671	11
Attempted	450,710	67	486,210	68	508,472	63	474,828	61	499,089	63
Business victimizations										
Robbery	264,113	14	266,624	10	261,725	9	297,516	12	X	X
Burglary	1,384,998	21	1,555,304	19	1,518,339	18	1,576,242	25	X	X

a. Subcategories may not sum to total because of rounding.

General Assembly Meeting in Washington, D.C., were addressed in the annual report for fiscal year 1986.

The Economic and Financial Crime Unit, created at the USNCB in 1984, has been expanded to include an additional detailee from the Customs Service and additional analytic support for the collection, analysis and dissemination of financial information to address this area of international criminal activity more effectively. Investigative and analytic work includes counterfeiting, computer fraud and concealment of assets, to mention just a few. In this regard, the USNCB was instrumental in forming the American Regional Working Party, which has met twice to address the problems of offshore banking and money-laundering schemes taking place in the Americas. Model legislation drafted by the working party and scheduled for presentation to the 54th General Assembly session would permit police access to bank records on accounts derived from criminal activity and seizure of their proceeds. Some Interpol member countries are already beginning to draft legislation based on this prototype.

The Fugitive Unit, established in 1983, has been expanded and renamed the Alien/Fugitive Enforcement Unit. In conjunction with other federal, state and local law-enforcement agencies, this unit not only coordinates the identification, location and return of internationally wanted fugitives but also strengthens existing measures that permit the arrest of fugitives or the exclusion of undesirable aliens at border points before actual entry into the country. Specifically, the unit is working with the State Department's AVLOS system to incorporate information about internationally convicted criminals as well as fugitives. This would further improve the screening process for grant-

1978		1979		1980		1981		1982	
Estimated Number	Percent Not Reported	Estimated Number	Percent Not Reported	Estimated Number	Percent Not Reported	Estimated Number	Percent Not Reported	Estimated Number	Percent Not Reported
171,145	49	191,739	48	173,770	57	177,541	42	152,570	45
1,038,074	49	1,115,870	42	1,209,039	41	1,380,962	43	1,333,620	42
330,843	33	381,245	35	415,615	28	440,075	31	414,353	29
179,905	29	203,300	32	210,410	22	215,204	23	212,725	24
150,939	37	177,946	38	205,205	34	224,871	39	201,629	35
408,833	44	470,846	34	478,035	38	595,194	39	584,781	38
298,398	72	263,778	67	315,388	64	345,693	66	334,486	62
4,730,097	56	4,845,822	54	4,747,256	52	5,023,806	53	4,972,832	51
1,707,883	46	1,768,683	44	1,706,745	43	1,795,702	44	1,754,184	39
576,731	36	599,136	36	587,530	36	590,542	33	586,718	29
1,131,152	51	1,169,547	49	1,119,215	46	1,205,160	50	1,167,466	44
3,022,214	62	3,077,139	59	3,040,511	57	3,228,104	58	3,218,648	58
755,125	51	795,483	46	849,984	49	842,949	46	858,958	47
2,267,089	66	2,281,656	64	2,190,527	60	2,385,154	62	2,359,690	62
549,967	64	510,790	64	557,760	63	604,875	58	577,125	66
111,475	44	119,548	40	143,626	40	146,330	38	131,429	40
65,568	B	46,707	B	55,168	B	48,975	B	46,467	B
372,924	66	344,535	70	358,966	69	409,571	62	399,229	71
16,492,446	74	15,861,378	74	14,758,069	71	15,273,714	72	14,975,908	71
6,698,581	52	6,684,018	51	6,973,932	48	7,392,603	47	6,662,843	49
2,199,925	29	2,154,639	27	2,462,080	26	2,587,098	23	2,104,087	24
2,911,696	61	3,109,280	60	3,033,163	57	3,078,168	59	2,932,122	59
1,586,959	67	1,420,099	67	1,478,690	64	1,727,337	64	1,626,634	65
9,344,239	75	10,631,289	74	10,466,874	72	10,174,660	73	9,704,598	72
5,177,916	87	5,726,441	86	5,060,050	86	4,903,484	86	4,613,488	87
3,125,604	54	3,666,796	55	4,150,033	55	4,032,487	56	3,963,988	55
395,943	77	562,414	77	500,321	70	507,655	75	443,905	75
644,776	77	675,639	75	756,469	72	731,033	73	683,217	75
1,364,549	33	1,392,837	30	1,380,796	29	1,438,980	33	1,376,866	26
860,016	11	920,158	13	936,593	12	890,898	12	946,887	10
504,533	71	472,679	36	444,203	64	548,082	65	429,979	63

ing or denying U.S. visa requests. In addition, the Federal Bureau of Investigation's NCIC system will be adding information on international fugitives for the first time. This will augment efforts to locate international fugitives who have entered the United States and will assist the federal, state and local police agencies who utilize the NCIC. Fugitive investigations as well as financial/fraud crimes are frequently related to international drug trafficking. Improving these law-enforcement programs will contribute to a more effective international antidrug trafficking program.

The USNCB's international antidrug trafficking program currently provides the DEA with information on U.S. nationals arrested abroad who have not yet been entered into the DEA's NADDIS, as well as information on drug seizures made *outside* the United States but destined *for* this country. This type of information is gleaned from operational reports received from other NCB's and from the General Secretariat's computerized system, which can provide a wide variety of data, such as types of concealment, routing, nationality and frequency of particular modus operandi. The USNCB can be a valuable tool for the domestic law-enforcement community since it is the only channel through which they can obtain drug trafficking information compiled from reports submitted by Interpol's member countries and maintained in the records and files of the General Secretariat.

Crime
The definition of crime varies among federal, state and local jurisdictions but is always specified in their written laws. Criminal offenses are classified according to how they are handled by their criminal justice systems. Most jurisdictions recognize two classes of

CRIME CLOCK, 1985

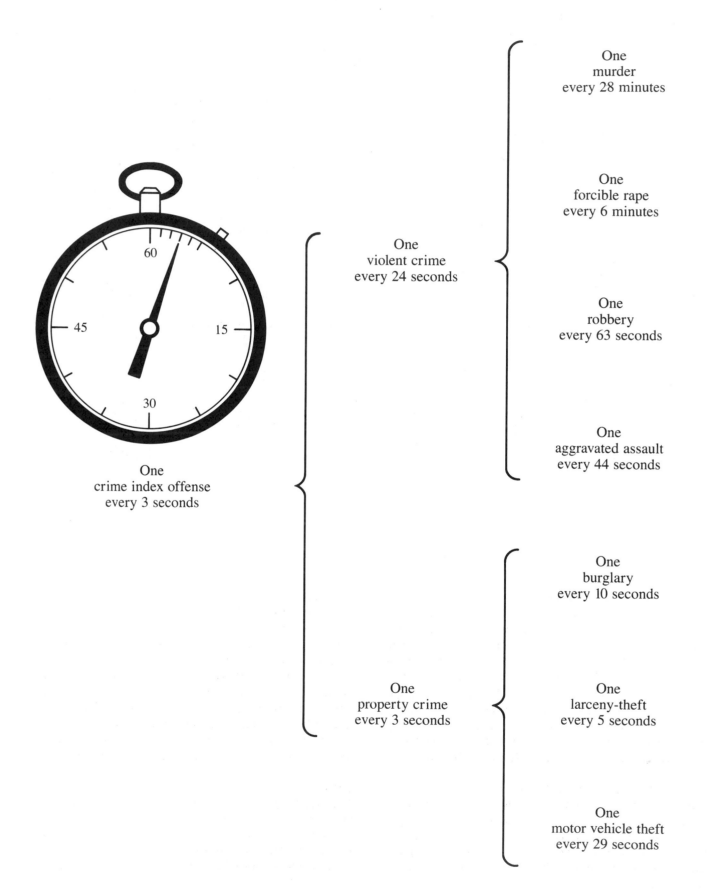

One
murder
every 28 minutes

One
forcible rape
every 6 minutes

One
violent crime
every 24 seconds

One
robbery
every 63 seconds

One
aggravated assault
every 44 seconds

One
crime index offense
every 3 seconds

One
burglary
every 10 seconds

One
property crime
every 3 seconds

One
larceny-theft
every 5 seconds

One
motor vehicle theft
every 29 seconds

ESTIMATED NUMBER AND RATE (PER 100,000 INHABITANTS) OF OFFENSES KNOWN TO POLICE, BY OFFENSE, UNITED STATES, 1960–83

NOTE: These data were compiled by the Federal Bureau of Investigation through the Uniform Crime Reporting Program. On a monthly basis, law-enforcement agencies (police, sheriffs and state police) report the number of offenses that become known to them in the following crime categories: murder and nonnegligent manslaughter, manslaughter by negligence, forcible rape, robbery, asault, burglary, larceny-theft and motor vehicle theft. A count of these crimes, which are known as Part I offenses, is taken from records of all complaints of crime received by law-enforcement agencies from victims or other sources and/or from officers who discovered the offenses. Whenever complaints of crime are determined through investigation to be unfounded or false, they are eliminated from the actual count (Source, p. 2).

The Uniform Crime Reporting Program uses seven crime categories to establish a "crime index" to measure the trend and distribution of crime in the United States. Crime index offenses include murder and nonnegligent manslaughter, forcible rape, robbery, aggravated assault, burglary, larceny-theft and motor vehicle theft; the "total crime index" is a simple sum of the index offenses. Arson was designated as a Part I index offense in October 1978; data collection was begun in 1979. However, due to the incompleteness of arson reporting by police in 1979–83, arson data are not displayed, nor are they included in the total crime index of the offenses known to the police.

The figures in this table are subject to updating by the Uniform Crime Reporting Program. The number of agencies reporting and populations represented may vary from year to year. This table presents estimates for the United States or particular areas based on agencies reporting.

Population[a]	Total Crime Index[b]	Violent Crime[c]	Property Crime[c]	Murder and Nonnegligent Manslaughter	Forcible Rape	Robbery	Aggravated Assault	Burglary	Larceny-Theft	Motor Vehicle Theft
Number of offenses:										
1960—179,323,175	3,384,200	288,460	3,095,700	9,110	17,190	107,840	154,320	912,100	1,855,400	328,200
1961—182,992,000	3,488,000	289,390	3,198,600	8,740	17,220	106,670	156,760	949,600	1,913,000	336,000
1962—185,771,000	3,752,200	301,510	3,450,700	8,530	17,550	110,860	164,570	994,300	2,089,600	366,800
1963—188,483,000	4,109,500	316,970	3,792,500	8,640	17,650	116,470	174,210	1,086,400	2,297,800	408,300
1964—191,141,000	4,564,600	364,220	4,200,400	9,360	21,420	130,390	203,050	1,213,200	2,514,400	472,800
1965—193,526,000	4,739,400	387,390	4,352,000	9,960	23,410	138,690	215,330	1,282,500	2,572,600	496,900
1966—195,576,000	5,223,500	430,180	4,793,300	11,040	25,820	157,990	235,330	1,410,100	2,822,000	561,200
1967—197,457,000	5,903,400	499,930	5,403,500	12,240	27,620	202,910	257,160	1,632,100	3,111,600	659,800
1968—199,399,000	6,720,200	595,010	6,125,300	13,800	31,670	262,840	286,700	1,858,900	3,482,700	783,600
1969—201,385,000	7,410,900	661,870	6,749,000	14,760	37,170	298,850	311,090	1,981,900	3,888,600	878,500
1970—203,235,298	8,098,000	738,820	7,359,200	16,000	37,990	349,860	334,970	2,205,000	4,225,800	928,400
1971—206,212,000	8,588,200	816,500	7,771,700	17,780	42,260	387,700	368,760	2,399,300	4,424,200	948,200
1972—208,230,000	8,248,800	834,900	7,413,900	18,670	46,850	376,290	393,090	2,375,500	4,151,200	887,200
1973—209,851,000	8,718,100	875,910	7,842,200	19,640	51,400	384,220	420,650	2,565,500	4,347,900	928,800
1974—211,392,000	10,253,400	974,720	9,278,700	20,710	55,400	442,400	456,210	3,039,200	5,262,500	977,100
1975—213,124,000	11,256,600	1,026,280	10,230,300	20,510	56,090	464,970	484,710	3,252,100	5,977,700	1,000,500
1976—214,659,000	11,304,800	986,580	10,318,200	18,780	56,730	420,210	490,850	3,089,800	6,270,800	957,600
1977—216,332,000	10,935,800	1,009,500	9,926,300	19,120	63,020	404,850	522,510	3,052,200	5,905,700	968,400
1978—218,059,000	11,141,300	1,061,930	10,079,500	19,560	67,130	417,040	558,100	3,104,500	5,983,400	991,600
1979—220,099,000	12,152,700	1,178,540	10,974,200	21,460	75,990	466,880	614,210	3,299,500	6,577,500	1,097,200
1980—225,349,264	13,295,400	1,308,900	11,986,500	23,040	82,090	548,810	654,960	3,759,200	7,112,700	1,114,700
1981—229,146,000	13,290,300	1,321,900	11,968,400	22,520	81,540	574,130	643,720	3,739,800	7,154,500	1,074,000
1982—231,534,000	12,857,200	1,285,710	11,571,500	21,010	77,760	536,890	650,040	3,415,500	7,107,700	1,048,300
1983—233,981,000	12,070,200	1,237,980	10,832,200	19,310	78,920	500,220	639,530	3,120,800	6,707,000	1,004,400
Rate per 100,000 Inhabitants:[d]										
1960	1,887.2	160.9	1,726.3	5.1	9.6	60.1	86.1	508.6	1,034.7	183.0
1961	1,906.1	158.1	1,747.9	4.8	9.4	58.3	85.7	518.9	1,045.4	183.6
1962	2,019.8	162.3	1,857.5	4.6	9.4	59.7	88.6	535.2	1,124.8	197.4
1963	2,180.3	168.2	2,012.1	4.6	9.4	61.8	92.4	576.4	1,219.1	216.6
1964	2,388.1	190.6	2,197.5	4.9	11.2	68.2	106.2	634.7	1,315.5	247.4
1965	2,449.0	200.2	2,248.8	5.1	12.1	71.7	111.3	662.7	1,329.3	256.8
1966	2,670.8	220.0	2,450.9	5.6	13.2	80.8	120.3	721.0	1,442.9	286.9
1967	2,989.7	253.2	2,736.5	6.2	14.0	102.8	130.2	826.6	1,575.8	334.1
1968	3,370.2	298.4	3,071.8	6.9	15.9	131.8	143.8	932.3	1,746.6	393.0
1969	3,680.0	328.7	3,351.3	7.3	18.5	148.4	154.5	984.1	1,930.9	436.2
1970	3,984.5	363.5	3,621.0	7.9	18.7	172.1	164.8	1,084.9	2,079.3	456.8
1971	4,164.7	396.0	3,768.8	8.6	20.5	188.0	178.8	1,163.5	2,145.5	459.8
1972	3,961.4	401.0	3,560.4	9.0	22.5	180.7	188.8	1,140.8	1,993.6	426.1
1973	4,154.4	417.4	3,737.0	9.4	24.5	183.1	200.5	1,222.5	2,071.9	442.6
1974	4,850.4	461.1	4,389.3	9.8	26.2	209.3	215.8	1,437.7	2,489.5	462.2
1975	5,281.7	481.5	4,800.2	9.6	26.3	218.2	227.4	1,525.9	2,804.8	469.4
1976	5,266.4	459.8	4,806.8	8.8	26.4	195.8	228.7	1,439.4	2,921.3	446.1
1977	5,055.1	466.6	4,588.4	8.8	29.1	187.1	241.5	1,410.9	2,729.9	447.6
1978	5,109.3	486.9	4,622.4	9.0	30.8	191.3	255.9	1,423.7	2,743.9	454.7
1979	5,521.5	535.5	4,986.0	9.7	34.5	212.1	279.1	1,499.1	2,988.4	498.5
1980	5,899.9	580.8	5,319.1	10.2	36.4	243.5	290.6	1,668.2	3,156.3	494.6
1981	5,799.9	576.9	5,223.0	9.8	35.6	250.6	280.9	1,632.1	3,122.3	468.7
1982	5,553.1	555.3	4,997.8	9.1	33.6	231.9	280.8	1,475.2	3,069.8	452.8
1983	5,158.6	529.1	4,629.5	8.3	33.7	213.8	273.3	1,333.8	2,866.5	429.3

a. Populations are U.S. Bureau of the Census provisional estimates as of July 1, except for the April 1, 1960, 1970 and 1980 preliminary census counts, and are subject to change.

b. Due to rounding, the offenses may not add to totals.

c. Violent crimes are offenses of murder, forcible rape, robbery and aggravated assault. Property crimes are offenses of burglary, larceny-theft and motor vehicle theft. Data are not included for the property crime of arson.

d. Crime rates calculated prior to rounding number of offenses.

Source: U.S. Department of Justice, Federal Bureau of Investigation, Crime in the United States, 1975, p. 49, Table 2; 1982, p. 43, Table 2; 1983, p. 43, Table 2 (Washington, D.C.: U.S. Government Printing Office).

ARRESTS BY OFFENSE CHARGED AND SEX, UNITED STATES, 1983

(10,827 agencies; 1983 estimated population, 200,692,000)

Offense Charged	Persons Arrested					Percent Distribution of Offense Charged[a]		
	Total Number	Male		Female		Total	Male	Female
		Number	Percent	Number	Percent			
Total	10,287,309	8,581,823	83.4	1,705,486	16.6	100.0	100.0	100.0
Murder and nonnegligent manslaughter	18,064	15,653	86.7	2,411	13.3	0.2	0.2	0.1
Forcible rape	30,183	29,883	99.0	300	1.0	0.3	0.3	(b)
Robbery	134,018	124,159	92.6	9,859	7.4	1.3	1.4	0.6
Aggravated assault	261,421	226,088	86.5	35,333	13.5	2.5	2.6	2.1
Burglary	415,651	387,504	93.2	28,147	6.8	4.0	4.5	1.7
Larceny-theft	1,169,066	823,817	70.5	345,249	29.5	11.4	9.6	20.2
Motor vehicle theft	105,514	96,108	91.1	9,406	8.9	1.0	1.1	0.6
Arson	17,203	15,099	87.8	2,104	12.2	0.2	0.2	0.1
Violent crime[c]	443,686	395,783	89.2	47,903	10.8	4.3	4.6	2.8
Property crime[d]	1,707,434	1,322,528	77.5	384,906	22.5	16.6	15.4	22.6
Total Crime Index[e]	2,151,120	1,718,311	79.9	432,809	20.1	20.9	20.0	25.4
Other assaults	481,615	410,971	85.3	70,644	14.7	4.7	4.8	4.1
Forgery and counterfeiting	74,508	49,588	66.6	24,920	33.4	0.7	0.6	1.5
Fraud	261,844	156,511	59.8	105,333	40.2	2.5	1.8	6.2
Embezzlement	7,604	5,141	67.6	2,463	32.4	0.1	0.1	0.1
Stolen property; buying, receiving, possessing	112,424	99,580	88.6	12,844	11.4	1.1	1.2	0.8
Vandalism	212,629	192,174	90.4	20,455	9.6	2.1	2.2	1.2
Weapons; carrying, possessing, etc.	160,534	148,002	92.2	12,532	7.8	1.6	1.7	0.7
Prostitution and commercialized vice	119,262	35,485	29.8	83,777	70.2	1.2	0.4	4.9
Sex offenses (except forcible rape and prostitution)	77,119	71,369	92.5	5,750	7.5	0.7	0.8	0.3
Drug abuse violations	616,936	530,677	86.0	86,259	14.0	6.0	6.2	5.1
Gambling	38,403	34,209	89.1	4,194	10.9	0.4	0.4	0.2
Offenses against family and children	46,111	40,999	88.9	5,112	11.1	0.4	0.5	0.3
Driving under the influence	1,613,184	1,432,154	88.8	181,030	11.2	15.7	16.7	10.6
Liquor laws	427,230	357,338	83.6	69,892	16.4	4.2	4.2	4.1
Drunkenness	977,924	892,642	91.3	85,282	8.7	9.5	10.4	5.0
Disorderly conduct	678,917	569,069	83.8	109,848	16.2	6.6	6.6	6.4
Vagrancy	31,262	28,081	89.8	3,181	10.2	0.3	0.3	0.2
All other offenses (except traffic)	2,005,797	1,699,605	84.7	306,192	15.3	19.5	19.8	18.0
Suspicion	12,262	10,464	85.3	1,798	14.7	0.1	0.1	0.1
Curfew and loitering law violations	68,148	52,099	76.4	16,049	23.6	0.7	0.6	0.9
Runaways	112,476	47,354	42.1	65,122	57.9	1.1	0.6	3.8

a. Because of rounding, percents may not add to total.
b. Less than one-tenth of 1 percent.
c. Violent crimes are offenses of murder, forcible rape, robbery and aggravated assault.
d. Property crimes are offenses of burglary, larceny-theft, motor vehicle theft and arson.
e. Includes arson.
Sources: U.S. Department of Justice, Federal Bureau of Investigation, Crime in the United States, 1983 (Washington, D.C.: U.S. Government Printing Office, 1984), p. 186.

offenses: felonies and misdemeanors. Most states define felonies as offenses punishable by a year or more in state prisons. While the same act may be classified as a felony in one jurisdiction and as a misdemeanor in another, the most serious crimes are never misdemeanors and the most minor offenses are never felonies.

The Uniform Crime Reports (UCR) and the National Crime Survey (NCR) are the main sources of national crime statistics. Both concentrate on measuring a limited number of well-defined crimes. They do not cover all possible criminal events. Both sources use commonly accepted definitions rather than legal definitions of crime. The UCR cover the eight most serious crimes (called "index crimes"), while NCS covers six (excluding homicide and arson). Both the UCR and the NCS count attempted as well as completed crimes.

In 1984 a total of 26% of U.S. households were touched by at least one crime. This is only slightly lower than the 32% reported in 1975. This small overall drop resulted in a decrease (from 16 to 13%) in the percentage of households touched by personal larceny without contact. The NCS shows relatively little change in victimization rates between 1973 and 1981, while the UCR show increases in all UCR Index crimes reported by police during the 1970s. According to the National Center for Health Statistics, the homicide rate reached its highest level in this century in 1980.

Areas with the highest crime rates tend to be very urban or resorts, while those with the lowest rates tend to be very rural. Resort areas such as Atlantic County in New Jersey, Nantucket in Massachusetts and Summit County in Colorado, with a high number of transients, have the highest crime rates. Crime rates also tend to be higher in the Pacific and mountain regions (except for Idaho, Montana and Wyoming). Violent and property crime rates are consistently higher for Standard Metropolitan Statistical Areas (SMSA's) and consistently lower for rural areas. The typical crime victim is young, black, urban, divorced or never married, with low income. Men are victimized by violent strangers at an annual rate almost triple that of women (29 vs. 11 per 1,000), and blacks are more than twice as likely as whites to be robbed by strangers.

NCS data indicate that in 1980 direct cash and property losses from personal robberies, personal and household larcenies, household burglaries and privately owned motor vehicle theft approached $9.5 billion, of which the amount recovered through insurance was less than $3.6 billion. In addition, almost $600 million worth of damage was done to personal and household property. UCR data show that reported commercial robberies, nonresidential burglaries and shoplifting surpassed $1 billion in 1980. Computer-related fraud, arson for profit, embezzlement and underground economic crimes also lead to staggering losses, but their impact is difficult to measure. The cost of crime is borne by all segments of society, but as a proportion of reported annual family income, it was five times greater in 1980 on families with incomes of less than $6,000 than on those with incomes of $25,000 or more. UCR data also show that in 1980 more than 2 million injuries resulted from violent crimes other than homicide and that 30% of all rape, robbery and violent assault victims were injured. Some 15% of the victims of violent crime required some kind of medical attention, while 8% required hospital care.

Only about a third of all crimes are reported to the police. The reporting rate varies by type of crime (higher for violent crimes), sex (higher for female than male victims) and age of victim (higher for older than for younger victims).

In 1965 California launched the first statewide program of victim compensation, and since then more than half of all states have started similar programs. Most programs provide for recovery of medical expenses and some lost earnings. To pay for these programs, 14 states rely on penalty assessments against convicted offenders, another 14 states rely on legislative appropriations and the remaining states rely on a combination of the two.

Half of all persons arrested for UCR Index crimes are youths under age 20, and four-fifths are males. By far the highest rate of offending occurs among black males aged 18 to 20. Like their victims, offenders are predominantly male, young, black and unmarried and typically from low-income families. Except for a minority of offenders, the intensity of criminal activity slackens after the mid-20s. When repeat offenders are apprehended, they serve increasingly longer sentences, thus incapacitating them for long periods as they grow older. The success of habitual offenders in avoiding apprehension also tends to decline as their criminal careers progress.

A majority of the crimes are committed by a small group of career criminals described as chronic offenders, with five or more arrests. In contrast, 67% of American males and 86% of American females have never been arrested, 14% of the males and 8% of the females have been arrested once, and 11% of the males and 5% of the females have been arrested two to four times. These percentages are much higher for black men and women. Although chronic offenders make up only 7% of the U.S. population, they commit 61% of all homicides, 76% of all rapes, 73% of all robberies and 65% of all aggravated assaults. Studies have established that chronic violent offenders usually start out their careers as such and remain so throughout their lifetime. Relatively few offenders in all categories of crime are female, but the female rate of arrest has grown much faster in recent years.

Blacks are victimized by crime, especially violent crime, at a higher rate than whites. Black males sustain the highest victimization rates of any race or sex group. Blacks, who constitute 12% of the U.S. population, also constitute a highly disproportionate segment of criminals. In 1981 they accounted for 26% of arrests, 34% of all UCR Index crime arrests and 46% of all arrests for violent crimes. Blacks make up 40% of local jail populations and 46% of state prison populations. According to the NCS, 44% of all robbers are black. The lifetime probability of incarceration is three times higher for blacks. Hispanics, too, fare badly on crime data. They make up 6% of the U.S. population but account for 12% of all arrests and constitute 11% of the jail population.

URUGUAY

BASIC FACT SHEET

Official Name: Oriental Republic of Uruguay
Area: 176,215 sq km
Population (1987): 2,964,052
Capital: Montevideo
Nature of Government: Limited democracy
Language: Spanish
Currency: Peso
GNP (1986): $5.63 billion
Territorial Divisions: 19 departments
Population per Police Officer: 170
Police Expenditures per Capita: N.A.

Structure & Organization

The National Police of Uruguay was established in December 1829, a year after the country gained its independence. Article 168 of the Constitution of 1967 gives the president, acting through the minister of the interior, the responsibility for the preservation of public order. Article 173 authorizes him to appoint a chief of police for each of the departments, whom he may remove at will. These officers must have the same qualifications as senators. The responsibility for law enforcement in coastal areas and shores of navigable rivers and lakes is vested in the Maritime Police under the Ministry of National Defense.

The National Police is organized into four operating agencies: three staff units and a nationwide communications network. The operating agencies are the Montevideo Police, the Interior Police, the Highway Police and the National Corps of Firemen. The total strength of these units is estimated at 20,000, a ratio of about seven policemen for each 1,000 inhabitants. The annual police budget is about 5% of the national budget. Approximately 40% of the police force is assigned to urban areas, and the remainder to rural settlements. The chief of police of Montevideo controls three paramilitary organizations as well: the Republican Guard, the Metropolitan Guard and the National Corps of Firemen.

The Republican Guard is a mounted unit with a strength of about 500 men and officers and commanded by an Army officer. It is organized into a headquarters and service squadron of about 120 men, and two cavalry squadrons of about 190 men each. Its personnel are armed with sabers. The cavalry units are used for guard duty at police headquarters, for parades and ceremonial occasions, and for riot duty as a backup for the National Police.

The Metropolitan Guard is a special elite force, with about 1,000 men in infantry-type units. Its equipment consists of machine guns, gas weapons and fire hoses, all designed for riot situations and controlling crowds. Its members are distinguished by special training, good height and impressive physical appearance, and they are assigned as guards at public buildings such as the presidential palace and the General Assembly buildings and as escorts for important foreign visitors. The commander and deputy commander of the Metropolitan Guard are Army officers.

The Technical Police is a branch of the Montevideo Police and has been in operation since 1945. Working in three shifts, it is on duty 24 hours a day. Technical operations include laboratory work, criminal identification, fingerprinting and photography. The patronymic file contains details of all individuals charged with a crime in the past.

The Montevideo Police also includes a small woman's unit, the Feminine Police Corps. Formed in 1966, the unit provides assistance to tourists, interrogates and guards female delinquents, and transports them from police custody to the courts or prisons. Another branch is the Quick Action Unit, which undertakes operations against dissidents and guerrillas.

The Maritime Police, organized in 1925 under the Ministry of National Defense, is commanded by a director general who usually is the second-ranking officer of the Navy and is staffed by active naval officers. The Maritime Police performs traditional coast guard functions.

The principal state security agency is the National

Directorate of Information and Intelligence (Dirección Nacional de Información y Inteligencia, DNII), which consists of a number of specialized departments. It works in cooperation with the military intelligence agency, Antisubversive Operations Coordination Organ (Organismo Coordinador de Operaciónes Antisuversivas, OCOA).

Recruitment, Education & Training

Police training is provided at the Police Training Academy, established in 1943. The training is conducted at two schools, one for cadets and officers and the other for enlisted men. The course for agents is for three months, that for noncommissioned officers one year, the cadet program is for two years and the in-service qualification courses for promotion for both commissioned and noncommissioned officers are three months. In 1967 regional courses for training were inaugurated.

The Penal System

The criminal justice system is governed by the Penal Code of 1889 as revised in 1934 by Law 9155. It consists of three books containing a total of 366 articles. Book I is concerned with general principles and the definition of offenses. Offenses are divided according to gravity into felonies and misdemeanors. Book I also lists the various punishments, of which the death penalty is not one. The maximum punishment is 30 years in a penitentiary.

Book II describes crimes against the sovereignty of the state and against persons and property. Book III is concerned with crimes against public order and morals.

A code for minors was enacted in 1934 and revised in 1938. It created the Juvenile Court in Montevideo with jurisdiction over offenders under 18, or in some cases 21. It is also responsible for the inspection of institutions concerned with child welfare, the committal of children to foster homes and the determination of the suitability of adoptive parents. Hearings of the Juvenile Court are not public, but parents and social workers may be present.

The Ministry of Culture runs three federal prisons and a work colony. Each of the 19 departments has jails for the temporary detention of prisoners, but after sentencing, prisoners are transported as soon as possible to one of the federal institutions, all of which are in the vicinity of Montevideo. Two of the prisons—known as Prison 1 and Prison 2—are for men; the third, known as the Establishment for the Correction and Detention of Women, is for female prisoners. The other federal facility is known as the Educational Colony for Work.

Article 70 of the Penal Code provides that inmates of rural minimum-security institutions may be employed in roadbuilding, quarrying, draining and clearing of land, and similar projects. Work is mandatory for all prisoners. Prisons are committed by basic regulations to provide training programs in crafts and trades. New prisoners are examined by members of the Criminological Institute, which was created in 1942; the members recommend suitable work or training for them. All inmates are paid wages in accordance with Articles 72 and 73 of the Penal Code. Payments are not made until the prisoner is released except for small amounts that may be sent to dependents. The remunerations cannot be attached for any reason, and they are payable to the prisoner's heirs if he or she dies during incarceration.

The Educational Colony for Work is in San José de Mayo, the capital of San José Department and about 50 miles from Montevideo. It has maximum-, medium- and minimum-security units in an area of 1,800 acres of arable land. There is a prerelease pavilion for prisoners about to complete their terms. Prisoners themselves are in charge of this facility, where inmates may bring their families to live with them. The colony buildings are surrounded by two moats 60 feet wide, with a 30-foot embankment between them and enclosed by a 10-foot wire fence carrying low-tension electric current. Visits to minimum-security inmates take place in the open; medium-security inmates are separated from visitors by a glass partition; and maximum-security inmates are separated from visitors by a reinforced glass partition, with telephones for communication. The prerelease pavilion is outside the moats.

The incidence of crime is relatively low. The annual average for homicides is only about 100. Theft and assaults are more numerous, averaging 15,000 annually. Except for assault, only a small proportion of the reported crimes are cleared by the courts, suggesting a low conviction rate. The police, however, have wide latitude in making arrests on suspicion. The majority of the minor offenders are exonerated.

VENEZUELA

BASIC FACT SHEET

Official Name: Republic of Venezuela
Area: 912,050 sq km
Population (1987): 18,291,134
Capital: Caracas
Nature of Government: Parliamentary democracy
Language: Spanish
Currency: Bolivar
GNP (1986): $51.94 billion
Territorial Divisions: 20 states, 1 federal district, 2 federal territories, 72 island dependencies
Population per Police Officer: 320
Police Expenditures per Capita: N.A.

Structure & Organization

Venezuela has four police agencies with nationwide jurisdiction, each under the control of a different ministry of the federal government. State governments control some 450 state, metropolitan and municipal police agencies. Normally these agencies operate as independent entities, and only in emergency situations, such as during elections and serious civil unrest, do they coordinate their activities under the Unified Police Command. The multiplicity of agencies creates considerable problems, including interagency rivalries resulting from overlapping jurisdictions.

The core police force is the Armed Forces of Cooperation, commonly known as the National Guard, created in 1937 as part of the Ministry of the Interior. In 1954, when the Ministry of National Defense was formed, the National Guard was incorporated as one of its four armed services. With over 15,000 men, the National Guard is the largest, the best-trained, the best-equipped and the most effective and respected law-enforcement agency in the country.

The National Guard is organized along military lines and is similar in structure to the other branches of the armed forces. The general commander, who usually holds the rank of general, reports to the minister of national defense. In addition to general command headquarters in Caracas, there are three regional commands, in San Antonio de Tachira, Maracaibo and Caracas. The basic unit is the detachment, which corresponds in size to a battalion. Detachments are composed of a various number of companies, which are subdivided into platoons and squads deployed throughout the country.

The National Guard's principal functions are to protect the national resources such as mines and oil fields, patrol frontiers, guard prisons and public buildings, and assist local police in times of emergency. The National Guard also is the sole police in rural areas outside incorporated municipalities. It also assists in the development of state and local police forces.

The Directorate of Intelligence and Prevention Services (Dirección de Seguridad e Inteligencia Policíal, DISIP) is a nonuniformed force of about 2,000 men under the Ministry of the Interior. Described as a political police force, the DISIP is responsible for the investigation of subversive groups and crimes against national security as well as cases involving narcotics and illegal arms.

The DISIP is headed by a director. Personnel work in all principal cities, but nearly 50% are concentrated in Caracas. New employees take an intensive eight-week course in criminal investigation at DISIP headquarters.

The third force is the Technical and Judicial Police (Policía Técnica y Judicial, PTJ), established in 1948 as part of the Ministry of Justice. A corps of about 2,000 plainclothesmen, the PTJ is in charge of nonpolitical investigative police work, including investigation of common crimes, apprehension of criminals, gathering evidence, and preparing cases for courts in cooperation with instruction judges. The Criminal Identification Division maintains criminal records.

The PTJ is headed by a director who is appointed by the president on the recommendation of the minister of justice. By regulation, the director must be a lawyer. Operations are conducted from the Caracas headquarters, where the majority of the PTJ personnel are stationed, and in 43 delegations and subdelegations throughout the country. Chiefs of delegations enjoy considerable autonomy in operational matters. New recruits are trained at the National Academy in Caracas.

The Traffic Police are a uniformed corps of 2,000 men under the Ministry of Communications, with responsibility for nationwide traffic control and enforcement. Stationed in major cities, Traffic Police issue drivers' licenses, inspect motor vehicles, control traffic and determine public transportation routes.

Although not a police agency, the Division of Identification and Immigration, under the Ministry of the Interior, plays an important role in criminal identification and also keeps immigration records on resident aliens. It has headquarters in Caracas and branch offices in principal cities.

In addition to federal police agencies, Venezuela has some 450 state, metropolitan and municipal police forces, with a total strength of some 15,000 men. They are budgeted under the Ministry of the Interior but controlled by the state governments. These forces vary greatly in size and effectiveness. The majority are characterized by low-caliber personnel who frequently are appointed through political patronage. Only four states have statewide forces; the rest are administered on a local level.

The largest of the municipal police agencies is the 10,000-man Metropolitan Police of Caracas, formed in 1969 through the merger of the Caracas Police and the police of several smaller outlying areas. The city is divided into police zones, which are divided into detachments.

Smaller agencies include the Tourism Police; the Custodial Police, in charge of prisons; a female brigade; a helicopter section; and a mounted squadron.

All uniformed personnel carry a Smith & Wesson .38. For special duties, revolvers, rifles and submachine guns are issued.

Recruitment, Education & Training

The National Guard is a completely volunteer force. A citizen may satisfy his military obligation by serving in the National Guard rather than in the Army, although less than half the applicants screened are accepted. Enlistment is for two years; the first year is dedicated to basic training at the Ramo Verde School near Los Teques. Officer candidates must have completed three years of secondary school and are trained at the Officers Training School in Caracas. Cadets who graduate receive a bachelor's degree and the rank of second lieutenant. Additional officer training for advancement to higher rank is provided by the Advanced Officers School in Caricuao, near Caracas. Selective recruitment and excellent training facilities are credited as the major reasons for the superiority of the National Guard personnel. For provincial police, training is provided at the Police Academy at El Junquito, near Caracas.

CRIME STATISTICS (1984)

		Number Reported	Attempts %	Cases Solved %	Crime per 100,000	Offenders	Females %	Juveniles %	Strangers %
1.	Murder	1,673		100	9.93	2,320			
2.	Sex offenses, including rape	7,505		100	44.54	5,629			
3.	Rape	2,928	10.17	80.25	17.38	2,452			
4.	Serious assault	22,466		92.75	133.32	14,396			
5.	All theft	94,496		39.81	560.77	36,005			
6.	Aggravated theft								
7.	Robbery and violent theft	27,122		36.52	160.95	10,644			
8.	Breaking and entering								
9.	Auto theft	14,482		40.87	85.94	4,295			
10.	Other thefts	52,892		41.20	313.88	21,066			
11.	Fraud	7,279		79.88	43.20	2,875			
12.	Counterfeiting	25		88	0.15	33			
13.	Drug offenses	5,212		100	30.93	9,009			
14.	Total offenses	141,090		60.52	837.27	77,782			

Note: Information for some categories is not available.
Criteria of juveniles: aged from 0 to 18 years.

The Penal System

The criminal justice system is governed by the Penal Code of 1964, which replaced the Penal Code of 1915. Article I states that no one can be punished for any crime not expressly prohibited in the code and that all punishable crimes are divided into felonies and misdemeanors. Article VIII states that all punishments are divided into corporal and noncorporal. There are six corporal punishments: penitentiary term, prison term, arrest, relegation to a penal colony, confinement to a specific place and expulsion from the country. Those sentenced to a penitentiary are subject to maximum security and mandatory labor. For each crime, an appropriate maximum and minimum punishment are prescribed.

The maximum sentence is 31 years in a penitentiary, for homicide. The death penalty has not existed in Venezuela in the 20th century and is expressly forbidden in the 1961 Constitution. Under the Penal Code, minors under 12 years are exempt from punishment for criminal acts, and those between 12 and 18 years are exempted from between one-third and one-half of the punishment. Severe penalties are prescribed in the Penal Code for repeat offenders.

The prison system consists of 25 institutions, of which 17 are judicial detainment centers; seven are national jails and penitentiaries; and the last is the National Institute of Female Orientation, in Los Teques. Prisons are staffed by civilian employees of the Ministry of Justice but guarded by the National Guard.

Venezuelan prisons are notoriously overcrowded, housing four times their designed capacity. Nearly 80% of the prisoners are awaiting trial. Poor living conditions have led to periodic hunger strikes by inmates as well as occasional riots. Although prisoners are required to work by law, few prisons have meaningful work facilities. As a result, corruption, drug abuse and homosexuality are growing problems within the system. One large Caracas prison has an entire wing exclusively for homosexuals.

Conditional liberty is granted any prisoner who has served at least three-fourths of his or her sentence and has a favorable conduct record. Several organizations exist to help prisoners find jobs and readjust to society on their release, but their work is hampered by the social stigma attached to ex-convicts.

Rapid social change triggered by the influx of oil wealth has generated a considerable increase in the incidence of crime, particularly in metropolitan Caracas. Although Caracas accounts for only one-fifth of the national population, it accounts for one-half of the nation's crime. White-collar crime and juvenile delinquency are two areas that have experienced the highest growth rates. An interesting phenomenon is the low rate of crime among women, estimated at less than 3% of the total. An increasing incidence of alcohol-related crime has led to the passage of a series of laws against selling liquor in certain places and at certain times.

VIETNAM

BASIC FACT SHEET

Official Name: Socialist Republic of Vietnam
Area: 329,707 sq km
Population (1987): 63,585,121
Capital: Hanoi
Nature of Government: Communist dictatorship
Language: Vietnamese
Currency: Dong
GNP (1985): $18.1 billion
Territorial Divisions: 40 provinces
Population per Police Officer: N.A.
Police Expenditures per Capita: N.A.

History & Background

During French rule in Indochina, public order functions and organizations were patterned after those of metropolitan France. For administrative purposes the region was divided into five areas: Tonkin (north Vietnam), Annam (central Vietnam), Cochin China (south Vietnam), Cambodia and Laos. Control was exercised from the headquarters of the French governor general in Hanoi by a French director general of police and general security.

Overall responsibility for public order and safety in each region was in the hands of the Sûreté, directed by a regional chief of police who was responsible to the director general for technical and operational matters and to the regional governor for disposition of the police forces. Ordinary police duties, such as patrol work, were performed by local policemen. All important command and administrative positions were held by French nationals. The French Sûreté Nationale supervised recruitment and training.

At the beginning of World War II large cities, such as Saigon, had municipal police departments administered by the mayor. After the Japanese occupied Vietnam in 1941 they permitted the old French police organization to continue to function under the Vichy French Administration. After the fall of Vichy France in 1945, a short-lived nationalist regime was formed under former emperor Bao Dai, who retained the existing police organizations. This regime was tolerated by the Japanese, but as Japan's position in the area deteriorated, Communist Viet Minh forces in the North, led by Ho Chi Minh, increasingly took control. In 1945 Bao Dai abdicated in favor of a Viet Minh

government. Meanwhile, the British, who at the Potsdam Conference in 1945 had been designated to accept the Japanese surrender of Vietnam, arrived in the area and exercised police powers until the French Expeditionary Force arrived. During this interregnum, the country witnessed much disorder. Most criminal files were lost or destroyed. Moreover, Communists infiltrated key positions in the military and police.

French efforts to reestablish police control over their colony were unsuccessful and were constantly thwarted by the Viet Minh. By June 1954, when the Indochina War ended with the partition of the country along the demarcation line, the police had ceased to be effective even in the cities. In Saigon, control of both the Municipal Police and the Security Police had been turned over by Bao Dai to the Binh Xuyen, a racketeering organization that was given a monopoly of police functions along with the right to run gambling, opium traffic and prostitution in the metropolitan areas. The group also collected fees for visas and licenses and controlled the import and sale of rice, fish and pork. Two large politico-religious sects, the Cao Dai and the Hoa Hao, controlled large areas of the countryside, maintaining their own police and security forces.

With the election of Ngo Dinh Diem as president, the state of near-anarchy began to mend. By April 1956 the Binh Xuyen had been defeated as an organized armed insurgent force, and the dissident remnants of the Cao Dai and Hoa Hao were crushed or forced into exile. Meanwhile, arrangements were made to acquire the services of a police advisory group from Michigan State University to replace the French advisers. In 1959 this group was replaced by personnel operating under the Public Safety Division of the U.S. AID.

In 1962 President Diem signed a decree integrating all the existing police forces into a single police agency, called the Directorate General of National Police, under the direction of the director general of the National Police under the Department of the Interior. The directorate general was composed of the headquarters proper; six regional directorates; and a municipal directorate, which included the Saigon Metropolitan Police and the surrounding province of Gia Dinh. The regional directorate headquarters were at Hue, Nha Trang, Ban Me Thuot, Bien Hoa, My Tho and Can Tho. They were charged with the supervision of the police units located within the provinces making up the region, as well as the municipal police forces in the larger towns such as Hue, Da Nang, Nha Trang, Cam Ranh, Da Lat and Vung Tau. Each province was under a police chief.

The headquarters of the director general was in Saigon, where he was assisted by a staff consisting of a deputy director and four assistant directors, one each for administration, intelligence, telecommunications and operations. Also at the assistant director level were the chiefs of the two major counterinsurgency organizations: the National Police Field Forces and the Resources Control Service. Directly under the director general were the Internal Activities Division and the Internal Affairs Branch, the latter concerned with irregularities within the police departments.

The assistant director for operations was responsible for supervision of the activities of the Judicial Police; Administrative Police; Rehabilitation Service; Immigration Service; Uniform and Traffic Police Service; and Order Police, formerly Combat Police.

Each of the six regional directorates was a scaled-down version of the Directorate General and was headed by a director whose immediate assistants were a deputy director, a chief for administration, a chief of uniformed police and a chief of special police. The Saigon Municipal Directorate enjoyed a special position within the system as the largest—with about 10,000 uniformed men—and as dealing with the most severe law-enforcement problems. It was organized into a headquarters, eight precincts, the Harbor Police, the Airport Police, the Traffic Police and the Gia Dinh Provincial Police.

In the North, the People's Police Force took over the law-enforcement functions from the French. The centrally controlled force, known as Bo Cong An, was organized under the minister of public security, Tran Quoc Hoan. According to the fragmentary accounts available, the force was organized hierarchically, with the chain of command running down to the smaller territorial units—provinces, cities, districts and villages. Larger cities such as Hanoi and Haiphong were divided into wards, stations and posts. After the conquest of the South in 1975, the northern police system was extended to the former Republic of Vietnam.

Structure & Organization

Details of the police structure and operations are never released to the public and are pieced together from scattered accounts in the press. At the provincial level, there is a police force branch organized into several sections to deal with matters pertaining to political conformity, internal security, passports and identity cards, counterintelligence and administration. Smaller groups having similar responsibilities are maintained at the district level. A group of special agents, subdivided into cells, is concerned with counterrevolutionary activities. Each village administrative committee has a security section composed of trusted Party members concerned with the surveillance of suspects. The security sections receive considerable information through complaints and denunciations made by local people—a practice encouraged by the Constitution as one of the duties of a good citizen. Villages also maintain their own local watchmen for patrol and guard duties.

The rank structure for officers and noncommissioned officers of the police force is prescribed in the decree law of July 16, 1962. It indicates a strong military influence on the service. The structure comprises three ranks for officers: general's rank with two additional grades (lieutenant general and major general); field rank with four grades (senior colonel, colonel, lieutenant colonel and major); and company rank with four grades (senior captain, captain, senior lieutenant and lieutenant). Noncommissioned officers are provided with three ranks: senior sergeant, sergeant and corporal. A temporary rank called aspirant is provided for those who are preparing for promotion to officer rank. The equivalent of a military private is referred to as a policeman.

Included in the commissioned ranks are Army officers who are graduates of the Officers School and are transferred to the police force; Party cadres or specialists, and cadres in various branches of government who are transferred to the police force; graduates from police cadres' training schools of the Ministry of Public Security; reserve police officers who are recalled to active duty; and policemen and police noncommissioned officers who have distinguished themselves through outstanding courage or skill or have accomplished some notable feat while carrying out their duties.

The 1962 decree stipulates that the nomination of officers and men is based as much on their political records as their professional skills and on the "services rendered to the revolution." Nominations to aspirant and company ranks are made by the minister of public security and to noncommissioned officers' ranks by the Council of Ministers. Nominees for lieutenant must be graduates of a police cadre training school or noncommissioned officers or soldiers with a distinguished record for valor, skill and proficiency in combat.

Promotions are based on the needs of the police force, political records, achievement records and the length of service in grade. The service normally required in each grade is two years for corporal up to lieutenant, three years for lieutenant to captain, four years for captain to lieutenant colonel and five years for lieutenant colonel and higher grades. The same authorities who are authorized to nominate are also authorized to promote and demote. In emergency cases, a police unit commander with the rank of a senior captain or higher may dismiss a subordinate two ranks below him and nominate another officer as replacement. Age limits for different ranks are 38 to 48 for lieutenant and senior lieutenant, 43 to 53 for captain and senior captain, 48 to 58 for major, 53 to 63 for lieutenant colonel and colonel, 55 to 63 for senior colonel and 58 to 65 for major general.

The 1962 decree accorded broad powers to the police force for enforcing state political, military and economic policies. Their political duties include the defense of the socialist regime and the destruction of counterrevolutionaries. Their specialized duties include apprehension of hooligans, bandits, thieves, embezzlers, speculators and other criminals; control and reform of counterrevolutionaries; safeguarding of public property; ensuring security of land, river, air and sea transport; census enumeration; issuing of passports and travel permits; control of production, sale and use of radio and television sets; control of hotel, printing, engraving and other trades; and control of weapons, explosives and poisons. Periodically, policemen and officers receive awards for exceptional performance of any of these duties.

The Armed Public Security Force, founded on March 3, 1959, is a second police agency functioning under Army control. Although its responsibilities overlap those of the regular police in some areas, the Armed Public Security Force is charged with more specific and specialized functions, such as protecting ports and coastal areas, borders, factories, construction sites, communication and transportation centers, public utility installations, mines and cooperatives. It also is the training agency for the district police and the militia.

The Armed Public Security Force also engages in public works and civic projects. It helps farmers during planting and harvesting seasons; combats floods and drought; constructs communication routes and irrigation works; conducts rescue missions; clears jungles; builds canals, camps and access roads; and even helps to deliver babies. These ostensibly public-spirited missions in fact help to reinforce its main task of maintaining constant surveillance over the population.

The Armed Public Security Force is organized along military lines into sections, platoons, companies, battalions and larger formations, depending on the availability of personnel and the security requirements of the region.

Armament and equipment are limited to those items commonly found in infantry units. The principal weapons are submachine guns, automatic rifles, rifles, pistols and hand grenades. Training is carried out under the supervision of Army officers. The courses are limited mainly to basic subjects commonly given to infantry rifle units, such as marksmanship, grenade throwing, reconnaissance and tactics. Pervading all types of training is political indoctrination and ideological awareness-raising.

The rank structure, promotion system and uniform are patterned after those of the Army. Collar tab insignia for officers and noncommissioned officers have a green base instead of the red base found on Army uniforms. Shoulder boards also have a green base instead of the brown base used for Army officers and the gray base used for Army noncommissioned officers.

Recruitment, Education & Training

All men of military age are eligible to join the force if they can pass basic literacy, intelligence and health tests and if their loyalty is vouched for by a Party official. Former soldiers who become reservists at the expiration of their service terms and soldiers discharged upon reaching age 45 form the core of the force. Officers are obtained mainly from the Army either by direct transfer or by granting commissions to graduates of Army officers training schools. A majority of the enlisted men have some previous military training.

The Penal System

The Penal Code consists of a body of decrees, legislation and court rulings, some of which date from the colonial period. Juridical concepts and practices combine Vietnamese, Chinese, French and Soviet elements. In the absence of a uniform code of criminal law, sentences vary greatly for the same offense, and political considerations often intrude on judicial decisions. As in other socialist countries, crimes against the state are dealt with more seriously than the other three classes of crimes: petty offenses, misdemeanors and felonies.

The basic concept of penal practice is that the

salvageable violator should not so much be punished as isolated from society until he or she has reformed. In accordance with this concept, a new prisoner usually undergoes a course of instruction designed to expose the prisoner to his or her previous erroneous attitudes toward society in general and toward political matters in particular. After the prisoner has advanced to the stage of ''self-criticism and self-denunciation,'' he or she begins to receive intensive indoctrination in Communist theories. The prisoner's progress in this phase largely determines the nature of treatment in prison and prospects for probation or parole.

Corporal punishment does not appear to be among the penalties that the courts are legally authorized to impose. The pillory and the more severe forms of torture used in the 1950s in the public trials of landowners and other class enemies have been discontinued.

Information on the prison system is scanty. Prison installations and facilities, with only a few newer additions, consist almost entirely of those formerly inherited from the French. The major prisons are the Chi Hoa in Ho Chi Minh City (formerly Saigon); and in Hanoi; Haiphong; Nam Dinh; and the prison island of Con San, 140 miles south of Ho Chi Minh City. Each provincial and district capital has a detention room and, in some instances, a jail to confine prisoners during interrogation. There are indications that some labor camps after the Soviet model have been established in outlying areas.

Crime statistics are not made public, and most official statements on crime are self-serving and unreliable. Officials periodically report decreases in crime as compared to the preceding year but without giving hard data. However, there is no evidence that crime is a major problem because Vietnamese are by nature submissive and have been further reduced to a state of total fear of the police agencies.

YEMEN ARAB REPUBLIC

BASIC FACT SHEET

Official Name: Yemen Arab Republic
Area: 194,250 sq km
Population (1987): 6,533,265
Capital: Sanaa
Nature of Government: Military dictatorship
Language: Arabic
Currency: Rial
GNP (1986): $4.51 billion
Territorial Divisions: 11 provinces
Population per Police Officer: 1,440
Police Expenditures per Capita: N.A.

Structure & Organization

Policing in Yemen is limited to the southern part of the country. In the northern and central Zaydi areas, public order is maintained by tribal sheikhs. Neither the Army nor the police is welcome in these tribal areas, where the authority of the central government is historically weak. The government is making cautious efforts to extend its police power to the northern tribes.

The national police is divided into three zones: Central, with headquarters at Sana'a; Southern, with headquarters at Ta'izz; and Western, with headquarters at Al Hudaydah. Total strength is estimated at 18,000. Control of the force is vested in the minister of the interior. In the 1970s radio networks were established linking all police stations with governorate headquarters and national police headquarters. Officers are trained at the Police Academy in Sana'a and enlisted men at special training units at Sana'a, Ta'izz and Al Hudaydah. Radio-equipped mobile units in Sana'a and Al Hudaydah respond to public requests for medical and other assistance.

Recruitment, Education & Training

No current information is available.

The Penal System

There are four main prisons: at Sana'a, Al Hudaydah, Ibb and Dhammar. Prison conditions have greatly improved since the overthrow of the imamate. Most prisons have attached dispensaries for medical care, and prisoners are permitted radios and newspapers. The prison population is not large.

The incidence of crime has steadily diminished after peaking immediately after the civil war. This decline is significant because of the heavily armed nature of this tribal society—it is estimated that there are enough small arms in the country to arm every man, woman and child twice over. The low incidence of violent crime may be due partly to the tribal attitude that violence is not criminal and thus not reportable.

YEMEN (SOUTH)

History & Background

The first police force in the British protectorate of Aden (as South Yemen was known until independence in 1967) was the Aden Police Force, formed in 1937. After the Marxist takeover of the country, all traces of British influence were purged from this force, and a new Public Security Force was set up in its place.

Structure & Organization

The three main divisions of the Public Security Force are the Armed Police, the Riot and Security Police, and the Rural Police. The total strength of the force is not known but is believed to rival that of the Army or the militia. The Armed Police and the Riot and Security Police are quasi-military units armed with light weapons and small arms. The Rural Police are assigned to more than 100 police posts scattered throughout the provinces. All units include gun-carrying members of the National Front, the country's sole political party.

According to unofficial accounts, there are two other police elements. One is the police of the first governorate of Aden, simply known as the Aden Police; the second is the Revolutionary Security Service. The Public Security Force and the Aden Police are believed to be under the Ministry of the Interior, while the Revolutionary Security Service is under the Ministry of State Security. As in other Communist countries, all police agencies are under the firm control of the National Front. Police forces were reorganized in the 1970s with East German assistance and reflect East German operational patterns and philosophy.

Recruitment, Education & Training

No current information is available.

The Penal System

South Yemen has been described as the worst police state in the Middle East. In addition to the jailing of thousands of the regime's opponents, an undetermined number has simply disappeared. Trials are held in secret, and arrests are not announced. Many prisoners are subjected to torture and degrading treatment, and some are summarily executed.

The prison population is estimated at over 10,000, almost all of them political prisoners. Many prisoners are held incommunicado for months and when released are subject to constant surveillance. Prison conditions at Al Mansura Prison are reported to be relatively good, but conditions elsewhere are harsh and inhuman.

YUGOSLAVIA

BASIC FACT SHEET

Official Name: Socialist Federal Republic of Yugoslavia
Area: 255,804 sq km
Population (1987): 23,430,830
Capital: Belgrade
Nature of Government: Communist dictatorship
Languages: Serbo-Croatian, Slovene and Macedonian
Currency: Dinar
GNP (1986): $53.59 billion
Territorial Divisions: 6 republics
Population per Police Officer: 140
Police Expenditures per Capita: N.A.

Structure & Organization

The enforcement of law and order is vested two interlocking nationwide police organizations: the State Security Service (Sluzba Drzavne Bezbednosti, SDB); and a conventional People's Militia, known as the Public Security Service (Sluzba Javne Bezbednosti, SJB). The SJB is charged primarily with the customary duties of preserving law and order, but it also cooperates with the SDB in the suppression of political nonconformity or antiregime activity. The two organizations represent modified versions of the earlier security forces created as part of the Partisan forces by Tito and used by him to assist in the establishment and consolidation of Communist authority. Although they ostensibly operate under a decentralized, self-management system at federal, republic and local levels, under the 1966 Basic Law on Internal Affairs, the Federal Secretariat for Internal Affairs exercises close and direct control over the operations of both agencies and is empowered to issue binding instructions to their personnel. At the same time, the independent attitudes of many of the constituent nationalities within the republic continue to hamper the enforcement of law and order and the application of uniform procedures and regulations. By law, internal security is no longer an area under exclusive federal jurisdiction.

The SDB is organized as a decentralized agency, with units at each level operating under a chief of state security, who is responsible to the respective organs of internal security at the federal, republic or provincial, district and commune levels.

All SDB units have a common mission specified in Article 39 of the 1966 Basic Law as "the gathering of data and other information for the purpose of discovering organized and secret activities aimed at undermining or subverting the constitutionally established order." The Federal Secretariat for Internal Affairs coordinates rather than directs these activities.

The Federal Secretariat for Internal Affairs also is responsible for the supervision and coordination of the SJB, which also is organized on a decentralized basis, with units operating at all governmental levels. In addition to carrying out ordinary police functions, the SJB also is charged with enforcing traffic regulations, fire fighting, the conduct of criminal investigations, the control of the movement of personnel across borders and the security of penitentiaries and prisons.

The basic SJB unit is the local or commune police, with its varying number of police stations and substations. Posts also are maintained at borders to control smuggling and illegal migration and to assist in customs collection. The SJB is organized and uniformed along military lines. Although militiamen usually patrol in groups of two to four men, units of up to company size are available for emergencies. Generally, weapons are limited to sidearms, but in the case of serious disorders billy clubs, rifles, submachine guns, tear gas equipment and protective helmets are available for issue.

In early 1967 all insignia of rank were abolished within the SJB and substituted by insignia of function or service. Such insignia are displayed on shoulder boards or on the upper left arm and indicate functions such as penitentiary guard, traffic policeman or frontier guard.

479

Recruitment, Education & Training

All SJB recruits receive a minimum of three months of basic training, supplemented by periodic refresher courses at police schools. Generally, militia officers are recruited from among Army officers and reserve officers.

The Penal System

The Yugoslavs are in the main free from arbitrary arrest and enjoy, compared to other Communist countries, a broad range of judicial protection. According to the Penal Code, a defendant must appear before a judge within 24 hours of arrest. As a rule, arraignment quickly follows an arrest. The law also stipulates that an indictment be brought within three months, although this period may be extended. Federal statutes contain detailed provisions for conducting searches, including the requirement for a court order, except under certain limited conditions. The Constitution states that illegal entry is ''prohibited and punishable.'' Some of these provisions are not strictly applied to political dissidents.

Overall control and supervision of the prison system are the responsibility of the Federal Secretariat for Internal Affairs, except for military prisons, which are administered by the Federal Secretariat for National Defense. By delegation of authority, the penal institutions in the various republics are administered by the respective republic secretariats for internal affairs. Penal institutions comprise penitentiaries, reformatories and jails, in all of which men and women are segregated. Special wards or sections are maintained for special categories of prisoners, such as alcoholics, pregnant women, juvenile offenders and political prisoners.

All prisoners sentenced to strict imprisonment are required to work, if physically able, and the work schedule is prescribed as eight hours per day, six days a week. Prisoners are allowed to work outside the prison on a supervised basis but receive reduced wages. Prisoners are authorized to keep only part of their pay, one portion being withheld until discharge, with the remainder going toward the support of dependents or relatives.

Living conditions in Yugoslav prisons are strict and harsh but not inhumane. By law, prison inmates are entitled to free medical care, the right to correspond, and the privilege of receiving visitors and parcels. Conditions, however, vary considerably among the republics.

ZAIRE

BASIC FACT SHEET

Official Name: Republic of Zaire
Area: 2,345,409 sq km
Population (1987): 32,342,947
Capital: Kinshasa
Nature of Government: Military dictatorship
Language: French
Currency: Zaire
GNP (1986): $5.07 billion
Territorial Divisions: 8 regions
Population per Police Officer: 910
Police Expenditures per Capita: N.A.

History & Background

Under its original organization, the colonial Force Publique combined the functions of a police force and an army, and this dual role was retained unchanged until shortly after World War I. At that time the Belgians reorganized the force and created a mixed organization composed of Garrison Troops for general military purposes and Territorial Service Troops for police duties. Although they remained an integral part of the Force Publique and could revert to the direct control of the commander of the force when needed, primarily the Territorial Service Troops were deployed throughout the colony and, under the command of the provincial governors, performed a constabulary function.

The Territorial Service Troops became the Gendarmerie in 1959 and, a year later, after independence, were incorporated into the Armée Nationale Congolaise (ANC). The strength of the Gendarmerie at independence was about 3,000, but almost all of the officers and many of the NCO's were Belgians. Virtually all the Belgians in the Gendarmerie left the country in the wake of ANC mutinies and the general European exodus, and the Gendarmerie found itself, almost overnight, entirely Africanized. In addition to the Gendarmerie, two other police forces existed under colonial rule and were carried over into postindependence Congo: the Chief's Police and the Territorial Police. The former were rural police forces used to maintain order as well as to fulfill the functions of messengers, jailers and court attendants. Although these small police units were uniformed, they did not carry firearms, their pay was low and they received practically no training.

The Territorial Police was a more formal organization and at independence numbered over 6,000 stationed throughout the country. Each province supported and administered its own force which, in most instances, were officered by Belgian former policemen. In addition to the conventional mission of maintaining law and order, the Territorial Police operated prisons, guarded public buildings, and reinforced the Chief's Police if needed. Detachments of the Territorial Police were permanently located in the provincial capitals and performed all the civil police functions of a municipal force. Territorial Police personnel were uniformed and armed, and recruits received six months' training before being assigned. In the mining areas of Katanga, a special police force recruited, financed and controlled by the Union Minière du Haut-Katanga (UMHK) policed mines and the camps, but were agents of the company rather than the colonial administration.

After the departure of the Belgians, the Territorial Police all but disintegrated. Many policemen deserted to join the rebels. The police system had to be rebuilt over the next four years with the help of the United Nations, Nigeria, Belgium and the United States. Nigeria and Belgium sent in experienced police advisers, and the United States undertook a broad assistance program to provide specialized training as well as necessary arms and equipment.

The task of restoring an effective police system was exacerbated by the continuing disorders in the mid-1960s and also by the increase in the number of provinces from six to 21. Each new province hastened to form its own police force, and the shortage of trained personnel led to serious problems. After the

481

Mobutu coup the number of provinces was cut from 21 to eight, thus reducing the size of the police bureaucracy and allowing the concentration of trained personnel in fewer establishments. The most noteworthy development, however, was the enactment of laws in 1966 that nationalized all existing police forces, standardized police organization and equipment, and centralized control under what was then called the Ministry of the Interior. Ministries are now called state commissions.

The 1966 laws that established the National Police gave it responsibility for all police functions in both urban and rural areas. The force soon had a strength of 22,000 and was charged with the prevention and detection of crime, the apprehension and prosecution of offenders, and the maintenance of public order. By 1970 the authorized strength of the National Police was set at 20,000.

Operating forces of the National Police were divided into nine detachments, one for each province and one for the capital. Although a central authority was maintained in Kinshasa, the detachments stationed in the various cities were under the command of a police commissioner, who was immediately responsible to the mayor. In cases of major breaches of the peace, such as riots, the mayor had the authority to request Gendarmerie units to supplement the police.

The laws established a system of ranks comparable to that of the armed forces. The personnel authorization provided for 1,400 officers and 6,600 NCO's. The top police rank of inspector general was equivalent to a brigadier general in the Army. Enlistment was voluntary, and women were admitted in small numbers. Training, mostly by Belgian instructors, was conducted at Kinshasa and Lubumbashi.

On August 1, 1972, President Mobutu dissolved the National Police and transferred its functions to the National Gendarmerie. By two edict-laws—Number 72-031 of July 31, 1972, and Number 72-041 of August 30, 1972—Mobutu decreed the makeup of the National Gendarmerie as it assumed the role of the National Police. The change was not merely cosmetic, as was the case with many of Mobutu's other administrative changes. The police jurisdiction was taken away from the Ministry of the Interior and restored to the Ministry of Defense, in a return to the concept of the colonial Force Publique.

While the end result of the change was a concentration of power in the hands of the president, maintenance of law and order became more difficult at the lower levels. Whereas before the merger the mayor had direct authority over a police detachment, this was not the case with the Gendarmerie. Instead of issuing an order, the mayor had to send in a request to the local commander that, more often than not, went unanswered. As a result, urban authorities turned to the local disciplinary brigade of the Youth of the Popular Movement of the Revolution (Jeunesse du Mouvement Populaire de la Revolution, JMPR), which was not intended to act as general police but which had been formed to maintain discipline in the party. In many cases the disciplinary brigades usurped the regular police functions of the Gendarmerie.

Structure & Organization

The commander of the Gendarmerie is the chief of staff, who reports to the captain general of the armed forces and the commissioner of state for defense, both of which positions are held by Mobutu.

Apart from the Gendarmerie, there exists a small, little-known organization titled Centre National de Documentation (CND), which inherited the role of the former Sûreté Nationale, an investigative unit originally established by the Belgians. During the first few years after independence, the Sûreté became a semiautonomous agency under the Ministry of the Interior, but after Mobutu became president in 1965, he brought the agency into the office of the president and transformed it into a virtual secret police. Possessing the power of arrest without warrant and maintaining its own independent communications network, the agency, renamed CND in 1969, did all the dirty work to ensure that no political opponent gathered enough support to oppose Mobutu. It also has foreign agents working in Europe to infiltrate anti-Mobutu exile groups.

Recruitment, Training & Education

No current information is available.

The Penal Code

The basis of Zairean criminal law is the penal code developed by the Belgians. The Penal Code of 1888 enacted by the Congo Free State, proscribed the cruel and barbarous punishments meted out under customary law. It continued in force until World War II, when it was abrogated and replaced by the Penal Code of 1940. The latter code, amended in places after independence, remains in force today.

The code prescribes severe penalties for crimes of violence as well as crimes against the state. The death penalty is permitted and is used liberally by the Mobutu regime to get rid of its enemies. Judges can both reduce and increase sentences: They have been reduced in cases of youth, the influence of custom or superstition, extreme provocation, or drunkenness, and increased in cases of habitual offenders or crimes committed while on parole.

The administration of prisons is the responsibility

of the commissioner of justice. The system includes separate facilities for juvenile and adult offenders. The major penitentiaries are in the regional capitals; smaller prisons and detention centers are in other large towns. Prison conditions are deplorable, bedeviled by a shortage of funds, lack of qualified personnel and overcrowding. Corruption is endemic in every walk of Zairean life, and prison administration is no exception. In 1977 the commissioner of justice was impeached for diverting prison food into the black market while prisoners were dying of malnutrition. Not much has changed since then.

Zairean law is very liberal in its treatment of juvenile offenders, though in 1961 the age of criminal responsibility was reduced from 18 to 16. Juveniles are housed in separate rehabilitation centers, and where such facilities are not available, segregated from adult prisoners in regular prisons. Very often, juveniles are released into the custody of their parents with a warning.

No statistics are collected or published by Zaire on any aspect of crime or criminal justice. From newspaper reports it appears that violent crimes have increased in all provinces since independence.

ZAMBIA

BASIC FACT SHEET

Official Name: Republic of Zambia
Area: 752,614 sq km
Population (1987): 7,281,738
Capital: Lusaka
Nature of Government: Authoritarian
Language: English
Currency: Kwacha
GNP (1986): $2.06 billion
Territorial Divisions: 9 provinces
Population per Police Officer: 540
Police Expenditures per 1,000: $3,960

History & Background

Like the military services, the Zambian police has evolved from its colonial predecessor. Before independence, the Native Authorities were responsible for maintaining law and order in rural areas. The forces and means available to them for this purpose, however, were limited and consisted only of unarmed policemen, who usually were little more than messengers serving court summonses. In serious situations, the Native Authorities called on the Northern Rhodesia Police through the district commissioners. At the time of independence, this latter force had reached a strength of 6,000.

In 1964 the Northern Rhodesia Police were tranferred to Zambia and became the Zambia Police. Most European and Asian officers remained with the force for a period of many years after independence, allowing an orderly transfer of functions to native Zambians.

Structure & Organization

The first Zambian Constitution established the Zambia Police Force as one of the public (civil) services administered by the Public Service Commission. The 1973 Constitution removed the police and prison services from the jurisdiction of the Public Service Commission and established the Police and Prison Service Commission, consisting of a chairman and not more than six and not less than three members. In 1979 the Police and Prison Service Commission was combined with three other commissions under the title of Civil Service under the supervision of a minister of state in the office of the prime minister. The actual line of command flows through an inspector general of police, whose staff includes a commissioner, a deputy commissioner and a senior assistant commissioner. Administrative control of the force is vested in the Ministry of Home Affairs.

The Zambia Police is the sole national force, with jurisdiction over the entire republic. Its strength is believed to be close to 12,000, augmented by 2,000 men of the Zambia Police Reserve. The main headquarters is in Lusaka. It has five functional departments: Administration, Staff, Criminal Investigation, Communications and Training. Operationally, the force is broken down into nine territorial divisions, coterminous with the provinces. There are also four special divisions: The Mobile Unit, headquartered at Kamfinsa (near Ndola); the paramilitary battalion, headquartered at Lilayi (near Lusaka); the Police Training School, also at Lilayi; and the Tazara Police, headquartered at Lusaka. The latter is a special security force that protects the Tanzania–Zambia Railway.

Subordinate units include divisional police, district police, and police posts established in towns and villages. Grade structures conform to the British pattern and are grouped into three basic categories: superior officers, subordinate officers and other ranks. In the larger towns, subordinate officers supervise the activities of sergeants and constables and manage the so-called charge offices, where public complaints are received and police records are maintained. Subordinate officers, sergeants and constables participate in beat duty and operate motorized patrols.

The Zambian Police are authorized to carry weapons in the performance of their duties, but the law places explicit restrictions on the use of firearms. The uniform of the lower ranks consists of a gray shirt and khaki shorts worn with a black fez. The officers wear shirts and trousers of khaki with a blue peaked cap. Sergeants and corporals wear chevrons on the upper arms.

In dealing with major unrest, the police are assisted by the Mobile Unit or the Paramilitary Battalion (PMB). The PMB is divided into four operational companies, each of which consists of four platoons with a total strength of a 1,000. The Mobile Unit has a similar structure.

The Mounted Section often is visible on ceremonial occasions, when it escorts the president. In addition to ceremonial assignments, it also combats cattle rustlers. The Marine Service operates a variety of small boats and launches in antismuggling patrols along Lake Tanganyika and Lake Mweru in the northeastern part of the country and anti-infiltration patrols on Lake Kariba in the South.

A rather unusual feature of the Zambian Police is the Prosecutions Branch. Almost all criminal prosecutions in magistrate courts are conducted by police prosecutors under the general supervision of the director of public prosecutions (DPP). Police officers above the rank of subinspector are appointed as public prosecutors after a nine-month course, at the end of which they must pass an examination in criminal law and procedures and rules of evidence. The Prosecutions Branch is headed by a senior superintendent who is part of the Lusaka headquarters.

Recruitment, Education & Training

The Police Training School provides initial training for new police recruits and also offers promotion courses, refresher training, motor vehicle and motorcycle courses, traffic courses and instructor training for all ranks. The school is commanded by a senior superintendent. Basic training for recruits lasts 26 weeks, and the curriculum includes a course in Kaunda's philosophy of humanism. To be accepted as a recruit, a candidate must be between 18 and 25, at least five feet, six inches tall (five feet, two inches for women) and have a Form III school certificate. The Training School includes a dog training school with a large kennel, including trained German shepherds.

The Penal System

The basic source of Zambian criminal law is the Penal Code, which is divided into two parts: General Provisions and Crimes. The code states that the "principles of English law" apply in Zambia's courts. For example, the burden of proof in a criminal trial rests on the government, proof beyond any reasonable doubt is required and an accused person may not be placed in double jeopardy. Children under age eight cannot be charged with a crime, and those between eight and eighteen receive less severe punishment if convicted.

CRIME STATISTICS (1984)

		Number Reported	Attempts %	Cases Solved %	Crime per 100,000	Offenders	Females %	Juveniles %	Strangers %
1.	Murder	569	18.28	9.72	9.73	616			
2.	Sex offenses, including rape	456		7.79	7.79	240		5.83	
3.	Rape	341	11.14	40.76	5.83	144		13.88	
4.	Serious assault	23,056		53.36	394.11	9,013	3.55	3.61	
5.	All theft	58,864		30.65	1,006.19	15,120	39.25	6.60	
6.	Aggravated theft								
7.	Robbery and violent theft	3,567		17.69	60.97	602		3.32	
8.	Breaking and entering	25,226		20.59	431.20	4,685	0.11	8.90	
9.	Auto theft	1,173		33.42	20.05	269		1.11	
10.	Other thefts	28,898		37.74	493.97	9,564	0.36	5.83	
11.	Fraud	651		38.86	11.13	330	30.90	1.21	
12.	Counterfeiting	96		47.92	1.64	47	2.13		
13.	Drug offenses	358		82.96	6.12	311	2.57	2.57	
14.	Total offenses	150,311	0.06	58.50	2,569.33	85,241	14.07	4.83	

Note: Information for some categories is not available.
Criteria of juveniles: aged from 8 to 19 years.

The range of punishments is carefully defined, although the courts generally have some latitude in sentencing. Penalties start with death by hanging, followed by imprisonment with or without hard labor, corporal punishment (with a rod or a cane), fine, forfeiture of property, payment of compensation and deportation. Conviction for murder carries a mandatory death sentence. Corporal punishment is treated in detail and consists of whipping with a rod or a cane. The number of strokes cannot exceed 12 for a person under 19 years of age, 24 for older persons and only less than 12 if no medical officer is present. The code prohibits the caning of females, males over 45 and males sentenced to death.

Responsibility for the prisons is vested in the Prison Service of the Ministry of Home Affairs. The minister is advised by the constitutionally appointed Police and Prison Service Commission. There are 52 penal institutions under the control of the Prison Service. By law adult males are segregated from juveniles, males from females, and first offenders from recidivists. Twelve prisons distributed among the provincial capitals are designed to house male convicts only. Kabwe Maximum Security Prison is designed for hardened criminals, Kasama Prison in Northern Province for female convicts whose sentence exceeds three months and Katambora Reformatory near Livingstone for juvenile offenders. Prison staff are trained at the Training School in Kabwe.

Prison conditions are reported to be generally unsanitary because of overcrowding. There is, however, no evidence of systematic maltreatment or torture.

Official criminal statistics are presented under eight categories: offenses against public order; offenses against lawful authority; offenses injurious to the public in general; offenses against the person; offenses against property; forgery, coining and impersonation; malicious injury to property; and offenses relating to corrupt practices. With the deterioration of the Zambian economy in the 1980s, crime has increased in all these categories. Over 96% of all arrests are for drunkenness, which is a national problem of serious proportions. Public corruption is not a major problem, and according to the periodical *Africa,* corrupt practices are the exception rather than the rule in Zambia. The homicide rate also is low relative to the size of the population. One of the particularly serious crimes is poaching in wildlife areas, even though the laws against poaching are reportedly among the toughest. Game wardens and park rangers are at a disadvantage because of their small number and lack of suitable transportation. Most Zambians blame the "crime wave" on the presence of illegal alien residents in the country.

ZIMBABWE

BASIC FACT SHEET

Official Name: Republic of Zimbabwe
Area: 391,090 sq km
Population (1987): 9,371,972
Capital: Harare
Nature of Government: Authoritarian
Language: English
Currency: Zimbabwean dollar
GNP (1986): $5.41 billion
Territorial Divisions: 8 provinces
Population per Police Officer: 750
Police Expenditures per 1,000: $12,457

History & Background

When the British South Africa Company settled in and eventually annexed Mashonaland, it organized a private police force, the British South Africa Company Police. In 1896 it became independent of the company as the British South African Police (BSAP), which was both an unarmed constabulary and a standing army. When an army was finally created in 1939, the BSAP gave up its military duties, but it retained its paramilitary functions until the creation of Rhodesia and Nyasaland in 1953. At the time the federation was dissolved in 1963, the BSAP had an approximate strength of 8,000. It included a reserve of 35,000 partially trained policemen, of whom three-fourths were white. The BSAP was divided into rural and urban units. Most of the African recruits were

CRIME STATISTICS (1984)

		Number Reported	Attempts %	Cases Solved %	Crime per 100,000	Offenders	Females %	Juveniles %	Strangers %
1.	Murder	1,690		51.1	21.22	520	17.88		4.21
2.	Sex offenses, including rape	2,657		87.06	33.35	1,416		5.56	
3.	Rape	2,309		55.3	28.99	1,132		3.45	2.65
4.	Serious assault	10,188		73.3	127.89	7,810	20.08	1.35	2.98
5.	All theft								
6.	Aggravated theft								
7.	Robbery and violent theft	6,488		72.48	81.45	4,931	1.95	1.59	4.68
8.	Breaking and entering	26,312		66.5	330.30	11,361	11.14	6.70	4.06
9.	Auto theft	1,655		65.1	20.78	1,166			1.29
10.	Other thefts	55,334		63	694.63	23,889	10.60	6.25	3.87
11.	Fraud	3,935		80.33	49.40	545	5.22		2.38
12.	Counterfeiting	168		98.21	2.11	133	1.84		1.50
13.	Drug offenses	5,096		86.51	63.97	4,525	2.08	2.70	4.49
14.	Total offenses	113,528		70.37	1,425.16	56,219			

Note: Information for some categories is not available.
Criteria of juveniles: aged from 7 to 18 years.

from the minority Ndebele, who had strong military traditions. They wore military-style uniforms and made considerable use of the authority accorded them by their European bosses. They also had the opportunity to increase their income by extracting bribes, by playing confidence games on the gullible and by outright theft. A large stick or *sjambok* (whip) was the policeman's symbol of authority, and it was freely used.

Structure & Organization

On independence in 1980, the BSAP became the Zimbabwe Police Force. Central headquarters is at Harare (formerly Salisbury), where also are based the headquarters of the Criminal Investigation Department and the Traffic Branch, three provincial headquarters (Harare North, Harare South and Mashonaland South), three district headquarters (Harare Central, Harare South and Harare Rural) and the Police Forensics Laboratory.

Bulawayo, the capital of Matabeleland, houses the Matabeleland provincial headquarters, three district headquarters (Bulawayo Central, Bulawayo Western and Bulawayo Rural), a CID branch, and a provincial training and reserve headquarters. Other district headquarters are at Gweu (formerly Gwelo), Kwekwe (formerly Queque) and Umtali. The Police Reserve headquarters is at Morris Depot, Harare. The main training units are the Willowvale Police Training Center, the Morris Police Training Depot and the Tomlinson Police Training Depot, all at Harare. Police camps exist at Gweu and Umtali.

Internal security duties are performed by two Harare-based units, both mainly staffed by former ZANU guerrillas: the Machipisa Crime Prevention Unit and the Chirukubi Support Unit, attached to the Chirukubi political prison. The secret service is the Central Intelligence Organization.

Recruitment, Education & Training

No current information is available.

Penal System

No current information is available.

SMALLER COUNTRIES AND MICROSTATES

ANDORRA

The Andorran Police was established in 1931 and now consists of 42 members divided into a criminal investigation team, a motorcycle traffic branch and a mountain rescue team. The uniform is beige in summer and green in winter. All uniformed personnel carry arms.

ANGUILLA

The Anguillan Police was established in 1972 on the departure of a detachment of the London Metropolitan Force that had been stationed on the island since 1969. Since Anguilla has no defense, the police also function as a military force. However, the force is not armed.

The police is headed by a chief of police, who reports to the minister of home affairs. The island is divided into five police districts. There is a small traffic police and a Criminal Investigation Department attached to the headquarters.

Officers and inspectors wear khaki trousers with either a khaki bush shirt or a khaki tunic over a white shirt, both worn with a blue cap and a Sam Browne belt. Ceremonial dress consists of white tunic and blue trousers or overalls worn with a sword and a blue cap for officers and a white helmet for inspectors.

ANTIGUA AND BARBUDA

BASIC FACT SHEET

Official Name: Antigua and Barbuda
Area: 280 sq km
Population (1987): 69,280
Capital: St. John's
Nature of Government: Parliamentary democracy
Language: English
Currency: East Caribbean dollar
GNP (1986): $190 million
Territorial Divisions: 6 parishes, 2 dependencies
Population per Police Officer: 120
Police Expenditures per 1,000: $41,624

The Antigua and Barbuda Police dates to 1886, when Antigua Island was the headquarters of the Leeward Islands. In 1965 the police force was granted the prefix Royal; on independence in 1981 it became the Antigua and Barbuda Police.

Part of the Judicial and Legal Services Commission, the Antigua Police is headed by a commissioner with divisional headquarters at St. John's and subdivisional headquarters at All Saints, Barbuda, Bolans, Parham and St. John's. Personnel strength is about 700. The police force is also in charge of the fire service and prisons.

The working dress for the junior ranks is a gray, short-sleeved shirt, navy blue serge trousers with a white stripe on the seams (a similar skirt for women) and a peaked cap. Officers from the rank of inspector up wear a khaki bush tunic with shorts or trousers and a blue peaked cap. For ceremonial occasions all ranks wear a white tunic and blue trousers with a white stripe (buff stripe for officers). Lower ranks wear white spiked helmets, while the senior ranks wear caps.

BAHAMAS

BASIC FACT SHEET

Official Name: The Commonwealth of the Bahamas
Area: 13,934 sq km
Population (1987): 238,817
Capital: Nassau
Nature of Government: Parliamentary democracy
Language: English
Currency: Bahamian dollar
GNP (1986): $1.7 billion
Territorial Divisions: —
Population per Police Officer: 166
Police Expenditures per Capita: N.A.

The Royal Bahamas Police Force has a long history. It goes back to 1840, when 16 volunteers were appointed to patrol the town of Nassau. In the 1850s similar guards, known as privates, were appointed to the other islands. Toward the end of the 19th century a second force, the Bahamas Constabulary, was formed to undertake guard and fire-fighting duties. In 1909 the two forces were amalgamated into the Bahamas Police Force, elevated with the prefix "Royal" in 1966.

The headquarters of the force is at Nassau, on New Providence Island. The headquarters comprises eight sections: Administration, Criminal Investigation, Security and Intelligence, Fire Service, Training, Marine Operations, Communications and the police band. Operationally, there are two districts, one on New Providence and the other on Grand Bahamas, each under an assistant commissioner. Each division includes, in addition to routine police sections, a prosecution branch, a CID, a traffic section, and a radio and communications section. Police auxiliaries include police reserve units on the two main islands and parapolice local constables on the other islands.

Higher officers wear dark blue uniforms in winter and, on formal occasions in summer, a khaki bush jacket and trousers. The rank and file wear trousers with a red stripe with a white tunic on formal or ceremonial occasions and a white bush jacket for normal duty in the summer. The trousers are blue in winter and khaki in summer. A dark blue tunic is worn at night the year-round. All ranks wear a blue cap with a red band, but in summer sergeants and below wear a white helmet during the day. The headgear is a tricorn hat.

Normally, policemen are unarmed. However, the Police Force is a quasi-military body, and all members are trained in the use of rifles. Officers and members of the CID are also trained in the use of handguns.

CRIME STATISTICS (1984)

		Number Reported	Attempts %	Cases Solved %	Crime per 100,000	Offenders	Females %	Juveniles %	Strangers %
1.	Murder	58	63.79	56.90	25.66	51	5.88	3.92	
2.	Sex offenses, including rape	150	2.67	54	66.37	71		11.27	7.04
3.	Rape	88	4.55	57.95	38.94	39		7.69	
4.	Serious assault	183		77.60	80.97	150	10	10	9.33
5.	All theft	4,102		25.21	1,815.04	779	14.63	12.45	2.18
6.	Aggravated theft								
7.	Robbery and violent theft	805	6.34	31.68	356.19	171	2.92	7.60	1.17
8.	Breaking and entering	4,767	1.51	16.68	2,109.29	474	4.85	23.63	
9.	Auto theft								
10.	Other thefts								
11.	Fraud	497	5.03	59.76	219.91	104	13.46	0.96	17.31
12.	Counterfeiting								
13.	Drug offenses	1,126		100	498.23	1,501	12.79	7.33	24.72
14.	Total offenses	13,099	1.16	36.47	5,706.02	4,079	10.15	10.27	12.50

Note: Information for some categories is not available.
Criteria of juveniles: aged from 7 to 17 years.

BAHRAIN

BASIC FACT SHEET

Official Name: State of Bahrain
Area: 676 sq km
Population (1987): 464,102
Capital: Manama
Nature of Government: Autocratic monarchy
Language: Arabic
Currency: Bahrain dinar
GNP (1986): $3.67 billion
Territorial Divisions: —
Population per Police Officer: 180
Police Expenditures per Capita: N.A.

The Bahrain Police and Public Security Department was founded in 1926. It is commanded by a director general assisted by a deputy director general and a director of security and intelligence services. The Administrative Branch is the first of many headquarters divisions, which include Immigration, Prosecutions, Traffic, Criminal Investigations, Women Police, Education and Sport, Mounted Police, Public Security and the Flying Wing. The Public Security Division also controls the Directorate of Coast Guard and the Bahrain Fire Service. Territorially, the sheikhdom is divided into five divisions: Manama, Bahrain Airport, Mina Sulman, Rural North and Rural South. There are police training centers at Muharraq and Safra. Bahrain's Women Police Division was a major innovation in the Middle East when formed in the 1970s.

The Emergency Squad is a police reserve for special situations, such as natural disasters. The Initial Training Depot also provides a reserve facility.

The uniforms are khaki in summer and dark blue in winter. A dark blue cap is worn throughout the year.

BARBADOS

BASIC FACT SHEET

Official Name: Barbados
Area: 430 sq km
Population (1987): 323,839
Capital: Bridgetown
Nature of Government: Parliamentary democracy
Language: English
Currency: Barbados dollar
GNP (1986): $1.31 billion (1984)
Territorial Divisions: 11 parishes
Population per Police Officer: 280
Police Expenditures per Capita: N.A.

The Barbados Police Force was established under British auspices in 1835, and it became the Royal Barbados Police Force in 1966. Headed by a commissioner, it consists of three territorial divisions—Northern, Southern and Mobile; the Headquarters Division; a CID; and a band. Junior ranks are housed in barracks and work on a day/night double-shift system. There is a mounted detachment for ceremonial and rural patrol duties.

The Royal Barbados Police Force Regional Police Training Center at Grantley Adams International Airport at Seawell provides training not only for Barbadians but also for the police forces of the Cayman Islands, Grenada, Montserrat, St. Lucia, St. Vincent,

Turks and Caicos, and the British Virgin Islands.

Officers wear a working dress of khaki trousers; an open-neck, short-sleeved bush tunic with a belt; and a blue forage cap with a red band. On formal occasions a long-sleeved tunic is worn with a white shirt and tie. Rank and file wear a gray shirt or open-neck short-sleeved tunic with blue serge trousers with a two-inch-wide red stripe on the seam. A white helmet, black boots and a brown leather belt complete the uniform. On ceremonial occasions officers wear a white tropical helmet and other ranks wear a white spiked helmet. Generally, police patrols, other than sentries are unarmed.

CRIME STATISTICS (1984)

		Number Reported	Attempts %	Cases Solved %	Crime per 100,000	Offenders	Females %	Juveniles %	Strangers %
1.	Murder	15		86.67	6.14	18	16.67		
2.	Sex offenses, including rape	126		37.30	51.59	46	2.17	2.17	
3.	Rape	62		27.42	25.39	17			
4.	Serious assault	195		53.85	79.84	100	12	1	
5.	All theft	4,497		13.88	1,841.31	684	9.94	4.33	
6.	Aggravated theft	1,171		7.43	479.47	91	1.11	8.06	
7.	Robbery and violent theft	165		16.36	67.56	33	3.03		
8.	Breaking and entering	679		7.22	278.02	76	1.32	8.33	
9.	Auto theft	35		20	14.33	7			
10.	Other thefts	2,447		18.55	1,001.93	477	13.63	3.14	
11.	Fraud	333		76.28	136.35	236	16.95		
12.	Counterfeiting								
13.	Drug offenses	248		100	101.54	256	9.77	0.78	
14.	Total offenses	8,147		34.33	3,335.82	2,696	11.28	2	

Note: Information for some categories is not available.
Criteria of juveniles: aged from 7 to 16 years.

BELIZE

BASIC FACT SHEET

Official Name: Belize
Area: 22,963 sq km
Population (1987): 168,204
Capital: Belmopan
Nature of Government: Constitutional democracy
Language: English
Currency: Belize dollar
GNP (1986): $200 million
Territorial Divisions: 6 districts
Population per Police Officer: 290
Police Expenditures per Capita: N.A.

The first constabulary force in British Honduras (as Belize was known until 1973) was formed in 1885. It became the British Honduras Police Force in 1902 and the Belize Police Force in 1973. Directly subordinate to the Ministry of Home Affairs, the Belize Police Force is headed by a commissioner. It is divided territorially into Eastern (including Belmopan and Belize City urban areas), Central and Western. Police headquarters is in the former capital of Belize City, but the commissioner resides in Belmopan. The uniformed strength of the force is estimated at 600.

There are three operations branches in the headquarters: General Duties, Criminal Investigation and Special. The Special Branch is the internal security organ.

Officers in the force still wear British police uniforms. For sergeants and lower ranks the uniform consists of khaki shirts, blue serge trousers with a green seam on both sides, a brown leather belt and a dark blue peaked cap. The ceremonial uniform includes a white tunic with a white buff belt. Helmets have been discontinued.

BENIN

BASIC FACT SHEET

Official Name: People's Republic of Benin
Area: 112,622 sq km
Population (1987): 4,339,096
Capital: Porto Novo (de jure); Cotonou (de facto)
Nature of Government: Dictatorship
Language: French
Currency: CFA franc
GNP (1986): $1.14 billion
Territorial Divisions: 6 provinces, 84 districts
Population per Police Officer: 3,250
Police Expenditures per 1,000: $1,138

As in other francophone countries, there are three main branches of the police in Benin: the Gendarmerie, the Sûreté and the Judicial Police. The Gendarmerie is primarily concerned with law and order. Though it is by law a regular branch of the armed forces under the minister of defense, it has a separate command hierarchy. Its total strength of about 1,800 is divided into nine companies. The Sûreté is more concerned with criminal investigation. Its strength is estimated at 1,500.

BERMUDA

BASIC FACT SHEET

Official Name: Bermuda
Area: 533 sq km
Population (1987): 58,033
Capital: Hamilton
Nature of Government: Parliamentary democracy
Language: English
Currency: Bermuda dollar
GNP (1986): $1.14 billion
Territorial Divisions: 9 parishes
Population per Police Officer: 370
Police Expenditures per 1,000: $290,191

A proper islandwide police force was first instituted in Bermuda in 1879. Its strength has never exceeded 500 officers and men. Governed by the 1974 Police Act, the force is divided into five divisions, two administrative and three territorial. The administrative divisions are under chief inspectors and the territorial ones under inspectors. All of them report to the commissioner. There is a reserve constabulary of 200. In addition, the Marine Section, with four patrol boats, patrols Bermuda Harbor. Training is provided by the Training School.

There are two basic uniforms, one for summer and the other for winter. The summer uniform consists of a light blue (white for officers) short-sleeved open-neck shirt, a black webbed belt, navy blue shorts, navy blue long hose and black shoes. The winter uniform is the same as the British police uniform. Plain flat black caps are worn by all ranks, with the exception of beat personnel, who wear British-type helmets. Police personnel usually are unarmed.

CRIME STATISTICS (1984)

		Number Reported	Attempts %	Cases Solved %	Crime per 100,000	Offenders	Females %	Juveniles %	Strangers %
1.	Murder	6	66.6	100	10.79	6			
2.	Sex offenses, including rape	49		34.69	88.08	30			
3.	Rape	9		88.88	16.18	8			
4.	Serious assault	86		90.69	154.59	83	7.22	1.20	
5.	All theft	2,492		20.14	4,479.44	307	15.63	11.72	
6.	Aggravated theft								
7.	Robbery and violent theft	30		30	53.93	5			
8.	Breaking and entering	1,164		23.19	2,092.32	88	4.54	15.90	

CRIME STATISTICS (1984)

		Attempts %	Cases Solved %	Crime per 100,000	Offenders	Females %	Juveniles %	Strangers %
	Number Reported							
9.	Auto theft							
10.	Other thefts	1,298		29.04	2,333.19	214	20.56	10.28
11.	Fraud	483		67.90	868.21	199	37.18	1.50
12.	Counterfeiting							
13.	Drug offenses	445		100	799.90	428	7.71	0.46
14.	Total offenses	4,124		48.9	7,413	604	14.90	4.61

Note: Information for some categories is not available.
Criteria of juveniles: aged from 14 to 16 years.

BHUTAN

BASIC FACT SHEET

Official Name: Kingdom of Bhutan
Area: 16,620 sq km
Population (1987): 1,472,911
Capital: Thimphu; Paro (administrative capital)
Nature of Government: Absolute monarchy
Language: Dzongkha
Currency: Ngultrum
GNP (1986): $200 million
Territorial Divisions: 4 regions, 18 districts
Population per Police Officer: N.A.
Police Expenditures per Capita: N.A.

Bhutan has a small paramilitary police force stationed in the capital, Thimphu. No other information is available on this force.

BRUNEI

BASIC FACT SHEET

Official Name: State of Brunei Darussalam
Area: 5,788 sq km
Population (1987): 249,961
Capital: Bandar Seri Begawan
Nature of Government: Absolute monarchy
Language: Malay
Currency: Brunei dollar
GNP (1986): $3.57 billion
Territorial Divisions: 4 districts
Population per Police Officer: 100
Police Expenditures per 1,000: $126,103

The uniformed police force was formed in Brunei following the appointment of a British resident in 1905. The nucleus of the force was a small detachment of the Straits Settlement Police. In 1921 this force received the formal designation of Brunei State Police, to which the title ''Royal'' was added in 1965. The sultan also is the inspector general of Royal Brunei State Police.

Directly under the sultan is the commissioner of police, who is the operational head of the force. Territorially, the country is divided into two police districts: Brunei, with headquarters at Bandar Seri Begawan; and Belait, with headquarters at Kuala Belait. The current personnel strength is over 2,200.

The force is divided into three functional branches: A (Operational), B (Administration) and C (Criminal Investigation), the last of which includes the internal security unit, known simply as the Special Branch. Specialized units include the Marine Police, the Airport Police and the Royal Guard. A volunteer police unit guards the oilfields. Training is provided by the Police Training Center at Manggis. There is a Police Reserve Force with two companies.

The uniform is typically tropical: silver-gray shirt and khaki slacks and a blue peaked cap. Officers wear bush jackets instead of shirts for normal duties.

CRIME STATISTICS (1984)

	Number Reported	Attempts %	Cases Solved %	Crime per 100,000	Offenders	Females %	Juveniles %	Strangers %
1. Murder	2			0.95				
2. Sex offenses, including rape								
3. Rape	6	33	67	2.86	17			33.33
4. Serious assault								
5. All theft	590	2	42.12	280.95	139	2.8	12	21
6. Aggravated theft								
7. Robbery and violent theft	8		13	3.81	3			67
8. Breaking and entering	261	1	52	124.29	15	27	13	44
9. Auto theft								
10. Other thefts								
11. Fraud								
12. Counterfeiting	25		66	11.90	14			100

CRIME STATISTICS (1984)

		Number Reported	Attempts %	Cases Solved %	Crime per 100,000	Offenders	Females %	Juveniles %	Strangers %
13.	Drug offenses	92		42.4	43.81	46	5		22
14.	Total offenses	984		28.6	468.57	234	11.6	4.3	48

Note: Information for some categories is not available.
Criteria of juveniles: aged from 7 to 18 years.

BURKINA FASO

BASIC FACT SHEET

Official Name: Burkina Faso
Area: 240,200 sq km
Population (1987): 8,276,272
Capital: Ouagadougou
Nature of Government: Military dictatorship
Language: French
Currency: CFA franc
GNP (1986): $1.24 billion (1983)
Territorial Divisions: 30 provinces, 250 departments
Population per Police Officer: N.A.
Police Expenditures per Capita: N.A.

Burkina Faso's police force, inherited from colonial days, is French in organizational structure, equipment and nomenclature. Its principal units are the Gendarmerie, the Sûreté and the Compagnies Républicaines de Sécurité (CRS). The paramilitary Gendarmerie and the largely ceremonial Garde Nationale are under the Ministry of Armed Forces.

CAPE VERDE

BASIC FACT SHEET

Official Name: Republic of Cape Verde
Area: 4,040 sq km
Population (1987): 344,282
Capital: Praia
Nature of Government: Civilian dictatorship
Languages: Portuguese and Crioulo
Currency: Escudo
GNP (1986): $150 million
Territorial Divisions: 14 administrative districts
Population per Police Officer: 460
Police Expenditures per Capita: N.A.

The principal law-enforcement organ is the Public Order Police (Polícia de Ordem Pública), under the National Directorate of Security and Public Order within the Ministry of the Interior. It encompasses not only regular uniformed police and the plainclothes criminal investigation police (the Judiciary Police), but also the Economic and Fiscal Police, who combat smuggling.

Internal security functions are carried out by the National Security Department, which is closely tied to the Central Committee of the ruling PAICV Party.

CAYMAN ISLANDS

BASIC FACT SHEET

Official Name: Cayman Islands
Area: 260 sq km
Population (1987): 23,192
Capital: George Town
Nature of Government: British dependent territory
Language: English
Currency: Cayman dollar
GNP (1985): $225 million
Territorial Divisions: 8 electoral districts
Population per Police Officer: 110
Police Expenditure per Capita: $33

The Royal Cayman Islands Police Force is a characteristically British force and follows British organizational structure. The RCIP headquarters is at George Town; in addition there are five police stations at Bodden Town, East End, North Side and West Bay, all linked to headquarters by an efficient radio-communications system. Of the uniformed strength of 160, a total of 151 are stationed at Grand Cayman and nine in Cayman Brac.

The RCIP has three main departments, each under

a superintendent: General Duties, Criminal Investigation and Traffic. Specialized units include the Marine Section and the Airport Guard and Police Section. The police also run the island's only prison.

CRIME STATISTICS (1984)

	Number Reported	Attempts %	Cases Solved %	Crime per 100,000	Offenders	Females %	Juveniles %	Strangers %
1. Murder	1		100	5	1	1		
2. Sex offenses, including rape	17		88.24	85	15			
3. Rape	5		80	25	4			1
4. Serious assault	71		98.59	355	17	3	3	
5. All theft	611		24.88	3,055	106	9	14	
6. Aggravated theft	323		16.10	1,615	52			
7. Robbery and violent theft	7		28.57	35	2			
8. Breaking and entering	316		15.82	1,580	50			
9. Auto theft								
10. Other thefts	288		35.07	1,440	54			
11. Fraud	40		100	200	40	6		
12. Counterfeiting	1		100	5	1			
13. Drug offenses	108		100	540	108	10		
14. Total offenses	1,367			6,835				

Note: Information for some categories is not available.
Criteria of juveniles: aged from 10 to 16 years.

CENTRAL AFRICAN REPUBLIC

BASIC FACT SHEET

Official Name: Central African Republic
Area: 622,984 sq km
Population (1987): 2,669,293
Capital: Bangui
Nature of Government: Civilian dictatorship
Language: French
Currency: CFA franc
GNP (1986): $770 million
Territorial Divisions: 14 prefectures, 47 subprefectures
Population per Police Officer: 2,740
Police Expenditures per 1,000: N.A.

The three police organs of former French Equatorial Africa have been preserved in the Central African Republic: the Sûreté, which polices urban areas; the paramilitary Gendarmerie, which polices rural areas; and the Judiciary Police, which performs criminal investigation functions.

COMOROS

BASIC FACT SHEET

Official Name: Federal Islamic Republic of the Comoros
Area: 2,171 sq km
Population (1987): 415,220
Capital: Moroni
Nature of Government: Civilian dictatorship
Languages: French, Shaafi Islam (a Swahili dialect)
Currency: CFA franc
GNP (1986): $130 million
Territorial Divisions: 3 islands, 7 regions
Population per Police Officer: 960
Police Expenditures per Capita: N.A.

The national police force is the Force de Police Nationale, headquartered at Moroni, with detachments in the other islands. The total strength of the force is estimated at 500.

COOK ISLANDS

BASIC FACT SHEET

Official Name: Cook Islands
Area: 230 sq km
Population: 17,898 (1987)
Capital: Avarua
Nature of Government: Self-governing territory in free association with New Zealand
Language: English
Currency: New Zealand Dollar
GDP: $21 million (1985)
Territorial Divisions: islands
Population per Police Officer: N.A.
Police Expenditure per 1,000: N.A.

The Cook Islands is a self-governing territory under the protection of New Zealand, with the seat of government at Avarua on the island of Rarotonga.

Under the supervision of the prime minister, the minister of police is responsible for the maintenance of law and order. He is assisted by the chief of police, who presides over the police headquarters at Avarua. The strength of the force is only about 100 officers and men, and most of them are on Rarotonga, so that many outlying islands have no police presence at all or, at best, are served by only a single constable. All policemen are recruited in the islands. The policemen wear short-sleeved shorts and slacks of khaki cotton drill, a red tie, brown shoes, and a peaked cap of matching khaki color. They are not armed with either firearms or batons, but each man is issued a pair of handcuffs.

Recruitment, Education & Training

Selected members of the force are sent to New Zealand for training and upon their return are assigned to conduct in-service training of their fellows at a small school established at police headquarters. Courses last about one week and gain additional impact by the distribution of copies of all lectures to police in outer areas. Mobile training teams also tour the islands periodically. In addition, some members of the force are brought to Rarotonga each year for refresher training.

The traditional practice of controlling public behavior through social sanctions imposed by the family and local village councils reduces the necessity for formal penal institutions. In fact, there is only one correctional facility: a plantation at Arorangi that produces commerical crops. Prisoners fulfill their sentences by working on the plantation.

The incidence of crime is limited to about 1,000 cases a year. The number of violations handled in village councils is not known, because no records are kept. The most frequent offenses are drunkenness, illegal production of beer, traffic violations, thefts, assaults and illegal trespass.

DJIBOUTI

BASIC FACT SHEET

Official Name: Republic of Djibouti
Area: 22,000 sq km
Population (1987): 312,405
Capital: Djibouti
Nature of Government: Civilian dictatorship
Language: French
Currency: Djibouti franc
GNP (1985): $369 million
Territorial Divisions: 5 *cercles*
Population per Police Officer: N.A.
Police Expenditures per Capita: N.A.

As in other former French colonies, there are two law-enforcement organs: the Sûreté Nationale in urban areas and the Gendarmerie in rural areas. The current strength of these forces is estimated at over 1,000.

DOMINICA

BASIC FACT SHEET

Official Name: Commonwealth of Dominica
Area: 752 sq km
Population (1987): 94,191
Capital: Roseau
Nature of Government: Parliamentary democracy
Language: English
Currency: East Caribbean dollar
GNP (1986): $100 million
Territorial Divisions: 21 districts
Population per Police Officer: 300
Police Expenditures per 1,000: $29,740

The Dominica Police Force is an agency inherited from the British. It is headed by a chief of police who also is the traffic commissioner. Its total personnel strength is estimated at 400, distributed among 20 police stations. Training is provided by the Police Training School at Morne Bruce, northeast of Roseau.

CRIME STATISTICS (1984)

		Number Reported	Attempts %	Cases Solved %	Crime per 100,000	Offenders	Females %	Juveniles %	Strangers %
1.	Murder	2		100	2.67	2		100	
2.	Sex offenses, including rape	15	46.67	53.33	20	8		100	
3.	Rape	8		100	10.67	8		100	
4.	Serious assault	21		100	28	21	28.57	71.43	
5.	All theft	1,174	3.40	96.60	1,565.33	1,134	22.92	77.08	
6.	Aggravated theft	577	12.30	87.70	769.33	506	27.66	72.34	
7.	Robbery and violent theft	31	67.74	32.26	41.33	10		100	
8.	Breaking and entering	546	36.64	63.36	728	346		100	
9.	Auto theft	17	23.52	76.48	22.67	13		100	
10.	Other thefts								
11.	Fraud	19		100	25.33	19	5.26	94.74	
12.	Counterfeiting	1		100	1.33	1		100	
13.	Drug offenses	251		100	334.67	293	7.84	92.16	2.04
14.	Total offenses	13,746	42.84	57.16	18,328	5,890	4.69	92.12	1.61

Note: Information for some categories is not available.
Criteria of juveniles: aged from 12 to 18 years.

EQUATORIAL GUINEA

BASIC FACT SHEET

Official Name: Republic of Equatorial Guinea
Area: 28,051 sq km
Population (1987): 340,434
Capital: Malabo
Nature of Government: Civilian dictatorship
Language: Spanish
Currency: Ekuele
GNP (1985): $75 million
Territorial Divisions: 6 provinces
Population per Police Officer: 190
Police Expenditures per Capita: N.A.

The Equatorial Guinean police force is a legacy of Spanish rule and is called the Guardia Civil after its Spanish counterpart. It functions under the Ministry of State Security, with headquarters in Malabo. No other details are available.

FALKLAND ISLANDS

BASIC FACT SHEET

Official Name: Falkland Islands
Area: 12,710 sq km
Population (1987): 1821
Capital: Stanley
Nature of Government: British dependent territory
Language: English
Currency: Falkland Island pound
GNP (1985): N.A.
Territorial Divisions: 3
Population per Police Officer: 330
Police Expenditure per Capita: $38

The Falkland Islands police force is organized on British lines and consists of one sergeant and five constables under a superintendent. The force is unarmed. The uniforms and badges are the same as those of the British police. Most of the police personnel are stationed in Port Stanley, with a small detachment in South Georgia.

FRENCH GUIANA

BASIC FACT SHEET

Official Name: Department of French Guiana
Area: 91,000 sq km
Population (1987): 92,038
Capital: Cayenne
Nature of Government: Overseas department and region of France
Language: French
Currency: Franc
GNP (1985): $180 million
Territorial Divisions: 2 arrondissements and 19 communes
Population per Police Officer: N.A.
Police Expenditure per Capita: N.A.

The police force in French Guiana, a French overseas department, is controlled by the French government.

There is a Préfecture de Police at Cayenne and a Gendarmerie unit for rural policing.

GABON

BASIC FACT SHEET

Official Name: Gabonese Republic
Area: 267,667 sq km
Population (1987): 1,039,006
Capital: Libreville
Nature of Government: Civilian dictatorship
Language: French
Currency: CFA franc
GNP (1986): $3.15 billion
Territorial Divisions: 9 provinces, 36 prefectures
Population per Police Officer: 1,290
Police Expenditures per capita: N.A.

Organized along French lines, the police forces of Gabon comprise the National Police Forces (Forces Nationale de Police) and the paramilitary Gendarmerie Nationale Gabonaise, with about 1,000 and 1,800 men, respectively. The National Police Forces are commanded by a high commissioner; the Gendarmerie, by a commander in chief. The former has two operational units: the National Security Police or the Sûreté, and the Judiciary Police (Police Judiciare).

The Gendarmerie consists of three brigades subdivided into companies: the Mouanda Company in the East, the Libreville, Makokou and Oyem companies in the North; and the Lambarene, Mouila, Port Gentil and Tchibanga companies in the South. Gendarmes are trained at the Gendarmerie School in Owendo.

CRIME STATISTICS (1984)

		Number Reported	Attempts %	Cases Solved %	Crime per 100,000	Offenders	Females %	Juveniles %	Strangers %
1.	Murder	14		14	1.12				
2.	Sex offenses, including rape	6		4	0.48				
3.	Rape	4		3	0.32				
4.	Serious assault	20		22	1.60				
5.	All theft	603	41	99	48.24				
6.	Aggravated theft	300		44	24				
7.	Robbery and violent theft	41		26	3.28				
8.	Breaking and entering	251	10	14	20.08				
9.	Auto theft	73		14	5.84				
10.	Other thefts	202	57	41	16.16				
11.	Fraud	83		76	6.64				
12.	Counterfeiting	7		7	0.56				
13.	Drug offenses	55		16	4.40				
14.	Total offenses					720	54		414

Note: Information for some categories is not available.
Criteria of juveniles: aged from 13 to 18 years.

GAMBIA

BASIC FACT SHEET

Official Name: Republic of The Gambia
Area: 11,295 sq km
Population (1987): 760,362
Capital: Banjul
Nature of Government: Limited democracy
Language: English
Currency: Dalasi
GNP (1986): $180 million
Territorial Divisions: 5 divisions
Population per Police Officer: 3,310
Police Expenditures per Capita: N.A.

Gambia's first organized police force was the River Police, formed in 1855 for the prevention of smuggling along the Gambia River. In 1866 it was supplemented by an armed constabulary of 40 men. In 1870 the constabulary force was raised to 100. On the eve of independence, its strength had grown to 284 officers and men. When the Gambia Regiment was deactivated in 1958, the force, by now known as the Gambia Police Force, took over the defense role, under an inspector general as commander.

Territorially, the country is divided into four operational divisions, including one division covering the capital city of Banjul. The functional divisions include a CID, a licensing office and a traffic division. The police also supervise the fire brigade.

The uniform is a khaki drill, short-sleeved, open-necked tunic worn with matching trousers or black trousers and a gray bush shirt. For night duty, a black, close-neck tunic is worn with matching trousers. A black peaked cap and a black leather belt complete with uniform. The police are generally not armed.

GIBRALTAR

BASIC FACT SHEET

Official Name: Gibraltar
Area: 6.5 sq km
Population (1987): 29,048
Capital: Gibraltar
Nature of Government: British dependent territory
Language: English
Currency: Gibraltar pound
GNP (1985): $130 million
Territorial Divisions: —
Population per Police Officer: 170
Police Expenditures per Capita: N.A.

The Gibraltar Police is the British Police in miniature. Formed in 1830, it is headed by a commissioner of police. Of its two divisions, the Territorial Division is charged with general policing, including the dockyard. The Headquarters Division is charged with administration, training, immigration, criminal investigation, prosecution and other specialized sections, such as traffic, marine operations and police dogs. The police wear British-type uniforms and are not armed.

GRENADA

BASIC FACT SHEET

Official Name: Grenada
Area: 344 sq km
Population (1987): 84,748
Capital: St. George's
Nature of Government: Parliamentary democracy
Language: English
Currency: East Caribbean dollar
GNP (1986): $120 million
Territorial Divisions: 6 parishes
Population per Police Officer: 230
Police Expenditures per 1,000: $15,202

The Grenada Police was established in 1783 as the Militia and later evolved into the Grenada Constabulary. There are three police divisions on the island: Central and Western, with headquarters at St. George's;

and Eastern, with headquarters at Grenville. There are a number of functional departments within the headquarters. Most personnel are trained at the Barbados Training Center. The uniform consists of blue serge trousers and a cotton shirt worn with a dark blue peaked cap.

GUADELOUPE

BASIC FACT SHEET

Official Name: Department of Guadeloupe
Area: 1,779 sq km
Population (1987): 336,354
Capital: Basse-Terre
Nature of Government: Overseas department of the French Republic
Language: French
Currency: Franc
GNP (1985): $1.18 billion
Territorial Divisions: 3 *arrondissements,* 34 communes
Population per Police Officer: N.A.
Police Expenditures per Capita: N.A.

The police force in Guadeloupe is a branch of the French Gendarmerie (Gendarmerie d'Outemer). It has two *compagnies* based at Basse-Terre and Pointe-a-Pitre.

GUINEA-BISSAU

BASIC FACT SHEET

Official Name: Republic of Guinea-Bissau
Area: 36,260 sq km
Population (1987): 928,425
Capital: Bissau
Nature of Government: Civilian dictatorship
Language: Portuguese
Currency: Guinea-Bissauan peso
GNP (1986): $150 million
Territorial Divisions: 9 regions, 3 circumscriptions
Population per Police Officer: N.A.
Police Expenditures per Capita: N.A.

The national law-enforcement force is the Polícia da Segurança Pública under the State Commissariat for National Security and Public Order. The structure of the force is a carryover from colonial days, but other details are lacking.

ICELAND

BASIC FACT SHEET

Official Name: Republic of Iceland
Area: 102,845 sq km
Population (1987): 244,676
Capital: Reykjavik
Nature of Government: Parliamentary democracy
Language: Icelandic
Currency: Krona
GNP (1986): $3.26 billion
Territorial Divisions: 23 counties, 200 parishes
Population per Police Officer: 940
Police Expenditures per Capita: N.A.

Iceland was policed by the Danes until 1944, when the police duties were delegated to municipal forces. In 1972 a national police force was established.

For operational purposes, the country is divided into 26 police districts, each under a police chief, who enjoys considerable local autonomy. In the capital city of Reykjavik, police functions are divided between the chief judge of the Criminal Court, who is the head of the CID, and the chief of police, who is in charge of all other areas. Chiefs of police generally are trained lawyers who perform other civil functions as well, such as tax collection.

There is no army in Iceland, and the police are organized along civilian lines. In addition to regular duties, they are vested with considerable administrative tasks, such as granting commercial licenses, dance and public meeting permits, driving licenses and issuing passports. The national police force, despite its name, is very much decentralized and does not have a single administrative head. All the district chiefs answer directly to the minister of justice.

A typical police district has four branches: Uniformed Patrol, Traffic, Mobile and Narcotics Surveillance. The Reykjavik police chief is also the head of the Police College. The Icelandic National Central Bureau of Interpol is a division of the Ministry of Justice.

The uniform consists of black trousers and a black jacket with brass buttons and insignia, a white peaked cap, a white shirt for inspectors and higher ranks and a light blue shirt for lower ranks. Ranks are indicated by brass numbers in the case of sergeants and constables and by brass plates, stars and badges for higher ranks. The force includes only a small number of women. The force is unarmed except for a small baton or nightstick.

KIRIBATI

BASIC FACT SHEET

Official Name: Republic of Kiribati
Area: 719 sq km
Population (1987): 66,441
Capital: Tarawa
Nature of Government: Representative democracy
Languages: English and Gilbertese
Currency: Australian dollar
GNP (1985): $25 million
Territorial Divisions: —
Population per Police Officer: 290
Police Expenditures per Capita: N.A.

On achieving independence as Kiribati, the former Gilbert Islands group of the Gilbert and Ellice Islands colony of Great Britain, the police structure was left intact. The police force is divided into a Constabulary and a District Police. The Constabulary is headed by a chief of police, who presides over a system of superintendents/inspectors, NCO's and constables. The District Police is a decentralized unit consisting of part-time policemen and is established on every island with a separate administrative authority. It operates under the administrative officer of the area with no set strength but with as many temporary men as are needed in any given situation. Small islands have only one constable.

Headquarters of the regular Constabulary is at Betio. Below the headquarters level there are three stations, at Betio, Bairiki and Bikenibeu on Tarawa and 15 on other islands of the district. Recruits receive training at a school run by the Constabulary at Betio.

Until 1968 the country had five prisons, in major population centers, but in that year all outlying prisons were closed and merged with the Central Prison on Tarawa Island. It accommodates all prisoners sentenced to two months or more; those given shorter terms are not confined but serve their sentences in their homes.

Prison conditions are not onerous; the quarters and the diet are good, and discipline is not harsh. Prisoners are expected to work on public projects, such as roadmaking and seawall repairs for men and light handicrafts for women. Prisoners usually have their sentences reduced by as much as one-third for good behavior. There is no provision for aid to prisoners after their release, nor is such assistance necessary. Imprisonment carries no social stigma, and released offenders are accepted back into their homes as though they had simply been on a voyage.

The incidence of reported crime has increased slightly since independence, although juvenile delinquency has declined during the same period.

LIECHTENSTEIN

BASIC FACT SHEET

Official Name: Principality of Liechtenstein
Area: 160 sq km
Population (1987): 27,074
Capital: Vaduz
Nature of Government: Constitutional monarchy
Language: German
Currency: Swiss franc
GNP (1985): $420 million
Territorial Divisions: 11 communes
Population per Police Officer: 660
Police Expenditures per Capita: N.A.

The Princely Liechtenstein Security Corps, perhaps one of the smallest police forces in the world with a strength of 40 officers and ranks, was formed in 1933, when it replaced the historic Landweibel. An auxiliary part-time force was formed in 1937. The corps is divided into three sections—General, Criminal Investigation and Traffic—each headed by a *Feldwebel* or sergeant major. Basic training is carried out alternatively in Austria and Switzerland, but the auxiliaries are trained locally.

The uniform is an olive-green open-neck jacket and trousers or breeches with a green shirt and tie and a peaked cap. On ceremonial occasions, black trousers, white shirt and gloves are worn.

LUXEMBOURG

BASIC FACT SHEET

Official Name: Grand Duchy of Luxembourg
Area: 2,586 sq km
Population (1987): 366,127
Capital: Luxembourg City
Nature of Government: Constitutional monarchy
Languages: German, French and Luxembourgish
Currency: Franc
GNP (1986): $5.83 billion
Territorial Divisions: 3 districts
Population per Police Officer: 730
Police Expenditures per 1,000: 15,067

Luxembourg shares it police history with that of France rather than Germany, although German traditions are strong in other areas. The Marechaussee, a military police, was created in the 17th century on the lines of the French and Belgian Gendarmerie and given limited powers. In the Napoleonic era, a new Police Corps (Corps de Police) was formed to patrol urban areas, and the Gendarmerie was vested with rural patrol, border guard and traffic duties. The police organization has remained substantially unchanged since then.

The Corps de Police is responsible for law enforcement in urban settlements. The former regional commands were replaced by a centralized national command in 1930, with headquarters in Luxembourg City. The chief of police reports to the Ministry of the Interior but is administratively under the control of the Ministry of the Armed Forces.

With a personnel strength of 800, the Corps de Police is organized in urban brigades and borough *commissariats*. The *commissaires* are, except in disciplinary matters, responsible to the town mayors. Villages have police posts. Traffic duties are assigned to the Traffic Police.

The Gendarmerie is a military force under the minister of defense. Its jurisdiction extends throughout the grand duchy. The Sûreté, unlike in most other French countries, is a branch of the Gendarmerie rather than a separate organization but conducts all criminal investigations through its own cadres.

The headquarters of the Gendarmerie in Luxembourg City is headed by a colonel. It has three main branches, each under a lieutenant colonel or major: Uniformed Gendarmerie, Sûreté Publique and General Services. The uniformed Gendarmerie conducts routine police work in three *arrondissements*, based in Luxembourg City, Diekirch and Esch. Each *arrondissement* is commanded by an officer with a warrant officer (*adjudant-chef*) as deputy and is divided into 10 to 13 brigades, each commanded by a brigadier.

The uniform is basically French, with a dark blue jacket and trousers worn with a blue kepi. On ceremonial occasions a shako cap is worn with aiguillettes from the left shoulder. The Gendarmerie grenade symbol is worn on the lapels of all ranks. Members of the Sûreté work in plain clothes. All police personnel carry 9mm and 7.65mm pistols. Belgian FAL rifles and Uzi submachine guns are issued during emergencies.

Gendarmes are recruited from the corporals of the Army, but receive two years' training at the National Gendarmerie School before appointment to the force.

CRIME STATISTICS (1984)

		Number Reported	Attempts %	Cases Solved %	Crime per 100,000	Offenders	Females %	Juveniles %	Strangers %
1.	Murder	21		90.47	5.25	19	11.76	0	47.05
2.	Sex offenses, including rape	106		63.83	26.50	79	11.39	10.12	37.97
3.	Rape	11		72.72	2.75	8			50
4.	Serious assault	155		98.69	38.75	190	9.47	2.10	40.52
5.	All theft	8,263	13.92	16.85	2,065.75	1,618	11.92	21.87	39.98
6.	Aggravated theft	2,202		17.89	550.50	451	6.87	22.83	42.35
7.	Robbery and violent theft	163		26.99	40.75	52	5.76	5.76	65.38
8.	Breaking and entering	2,039		17.16	509.75	399	7.01	25.81	39.34
9.	Auto theft	437		27.68	109.25	189		8.46	50.79
10.	Other thefts	2,603		18.67	650.75	540	16.66	21.48	28.88
11.	Fraud	80		80	20	68	23.52	5.88	35.29
12.	Counterfeiting	2			0.50				
13.	Drug offenses	518		100	129.50	551	17.42	10.16	33.57
14.	Total offenses	15,787		34.38	3,946.75	6,027	10.05	8.42	37.18

Note: Information for some categories is not available.
Criteria of juveniles: aged from 0 to 18 years.

MACAU

```
BASIC FACT SHEET

Official Name: Macau
Area: 15.5 sq km
Population (1987): 437,822
Capital: Lisbon (Portugal)
Nature of Government: Portuguese dependent territory
Languages: Chinese and Portuguese
Currency: Pataca
GNP (1985): $1.03 billion
Territorial Divisions:—
Population per Police Officer: N.A.
Police Expenditures per Capita: N.A.
```

There are three police forces in Macau: the Policia de Seguranca Publica, a subdirectorate of the Policia Judiciaria, and a combined Policia Maritima e Fiscal. The Policia de Seguranca Publica includes seven services: Administration, Communications, Identification, Immigration, Information, Public Security and Traffic.

MALDIVES

```
BASIC FACT SHEET

Official Name: Republic of Maldives
Area: 298 sq km
Population (1987): 195,837
Capital: Male
Nature of Government: Authoritarian
Language: Divehi
Currency: Rufiya
GNP (1986): $60 million
Territorial Divisions: 19 administrative districts
Population per Police Officer: 35,710
Police Expenditures per 1,000: $2,003
```

The national police is the National Security Guard, which combines the roles of a militia, gendarmerie and army. It is administered by the Ministry of Public Safety.

CRIME STATISTICS (1984)

	Number Reported	Attempts %	Cases Solved %	Crime per 100,000	Offenders	Females %	Juveniles %	Strangers %
1. Murder	3		66.66	1.76	5	40		
2. Sex offenses, including rape	275		95.27	161.29	791	39.82	1.64	1.01
3. Rape	19		100	11.14	16	39.82		25
4. Serious assault	3		100	1.76	3		66.66	
5. All theft	1,676		96.30	982.99	532	0.56	10.33	0.93
6. Aggravated theft								
7. Robbery and violent theft								
8. Breaking and entering								
9. Auto theft								
10. Other thefts								
11. Fraud	238		100	139.59	19	5.26		5.26
12. Counterfeiting								
13. Drug offenses	52		92.30	30.50	382	2.35		9.16
14. Total offenses	6,801		97.67	3,988.86	4,476	24.84	5.49	6.52

Note: Information for some categories is not available.
Criteria of juveniles: aged from 0 to 16 years.

MALI

BASIC FACT SHEET

Official Name: Republic of Mali
Area: 1,240,000 sq km
Population (1987): 8,422,810
Capital: Bamako
Nature of Government: Military dictatorship
Language: French
Currency: CFA franc
GNP (1986): $1.33 billion
Territorial Divisions: 8 administrative regions
Population per Police Officer: 160
Police Expenditures per 1,000: N.A.

The Malian police is organized on French lines into two forces: the Security Service equivalent to the Sûreté and a paramilitary Gendarmerie. Total strength of these two forces is about 2,000.

MALTA

BASIC FACT SHEET

Official Name: Republic of Malta
Area: 313 sq km
Population (1987): 361,704
Capital: Valletta
Nature of Government: Parliamentary democracy
Languages: Maltese and English
Currency: Lira
GNP (1986): $1.24 billion
Territorial Divisions: 2 islands
Population per Police Officer: 236
Police Expenditures per 1,000: $34,223

The Malta Police Force was formed in 1814, when Malta was annexed to the British crown. The force underwent considerable reorganization following independence in 1964.

The force is commanded by a commissioner assisted by three assistant commissioners, one of whom is responsible for administration, one for operations and the third for criminal investigation. The general headquarters in Floriana also houses the Traffic Branch and the Security Branch. The CID is commanded by a senior superintendent and is composed of the uniformed Detection Section, the Dog Section, the Immigration Section, the Security Section, the Specialized Services Division, the Weapons Office, the Criminal Records Office and the Planning and Research Section.

Territorially, the force is deployed over 77 police stations, including 57 in Malta, 19 in Gozo and one on Comino. These stations are consolidated into divisions and districts. Each of the five divisions is in charge of a senior superintendent, and each of the divisions is under an inspector.

The winter uniform consists of a dark blue tunic and slacks, a dark blue peaked cap, black boots, a light blue shirt and a black tie. The summer uniform consists of khaki slacks and tunic, the winter cap with a khaki cover, khaki shirt and black tie. During very hot summer days, the police may wear half-sleeved shirts. The force is unarmed, but patrolmen carry wooden billy clubs.

CRIME STATISTICS (1984)

		Number Reported	Attempts %	Cases Solved %	Crime per 100,000	Offenders	Females %	Juveniles %	Strangers %
1.	Murder	14	78.57	64.28	4.24	8	12.5		
2.	Sex offenses, including rape	31	6.45	51.61	9.39	12	16.66		25
3.	Rape	4	50	50	1.21	2			
4.	Serious assault	104	4.80	29.80	31.52	33	9.09	9.09	15.15
5.	All theft	4,710	4.92	3.48	1,427.27	200	1.50	13	2
6.	Aggravated theft	1,358		6.48	411.52	67	4.47	16.41	4.47
7.	Robbery and violent theft	38	10.52	13.15	11.52	17		29.41	
8.	Breaking and entering	300			90.91				
9.	Auto theft	654		1.98	198.18	20		35	

CRIME STATISTICS (1984)

		Number Reported	Attempts %	Cases Solved %	Crime per 100,000	Offenders	Females %	Juveniles %	Strangers %
10.	Other thefts	2,698		2.33	817.18	65		12.30	1.53
11.	Fraud	94		100	28.48	68	5.88		
12.	Counterfeiting	9		44.44	2.73	4			100
13.	Drug offenses	201		100	60.90	201	2.98	8.95	2.48
14.	Total offenses	6,291		13.01	1,906.36	634	3.94	7.88	4.25

Note: Information for some categories is not available.
Criteria of juveniles: aged from 10 to 18 years.

MAURITIUS

BASIC FACT SHEET

Official Name: Mauritius
Area: 1,860 sq km
Population (1987): 1,079,627
Capital: Port Louis
Nature of Government: Parliamentary democracy
Language: English
Currency: Mauritian rupee
GNP (1986): $1.24 billion
Territorial Divisions: 5 municipalities and island dependencies
Population per Police Officer: 240
Police Expenditure per Capita: N.A.

A national police force was created in 1859 (with a separate unit for Port Louis) and modified by the Police Ordinance of 1893 as the Mauritius Police Force under an inspector general of police and, (from 1934) a police commissioner. It is under the jurisdiction of the Ministry of Internal Security.

The Mauritius Police Force comprises a regular armed police, a special constabulary, and a special mobile force. The regular police, with an authorized strength of 4,500 is deployed in 51 outstations. At the headquarters the force is divided into a number of specialized units, such as riot control, criminal investigation, traffic control, immigration and water police.

Since Mauritius has no armed forces, the special mobile force functions as a paramilitary service.

CRIME STATISTICS (1984)

		Number Reported	Attempts %	Cases Solved %	Crime per 100,000	Offenders	Females %	Juveniles %	Strangers %
1.	Murder	23		13	2.33	33	3	3	
2.	Sex offenses, including rape	68	38.28	79	6.88	70		8.57	
3.	Rape	24		45.8	2.43	26			
4.	Serious assault	170		88.2	17.19	100	3	2	
5.	All theft	9,922		20.05	1,003.46	2,089	3	4.55	

CRIME STATISTICS (1984)

	Number Reported	Attempts %	Cases Solved %	Crime per 100,000	Offenders	Females %	Juveniles %	Strangers %
6. Aggravated theft	1,560		22.65	157.77	613	3.42	5.7	
7. Robbery and violent theft	441		35.6	44.60	157	2.5	1.7	
8. Breaking and entering	536		18	54.21	144		0.69	
9. Auto theft								
10. Other thefts	8,362		18.48	845.69	1,476	3.65	4.9	
11. Fraud	869		53.27	87.89	515	6.4	0.19	
12. Counterfeiting	26		19.23	2.63	10	20		
13. Drug offenses	1,392		68.46	140.78	575	6	0.58	0.34
14. Total offenses	23,393	1.60	25.4	2,365.84	5,782	3.73	3.77	0.03

Note: Information for some categories is not available.
Criteria of juveniles: aged from 13 to 17 years.

MONACO

BASIC FACT SHEET

Official Name: Principality of Monaco
Area: 1.9 sq km
Population (1987): 28,641
Capital: Monaco
Nature of Government: Constitutional monarchy
Language: French
Currency: Franc
GNP: —
Territorial Divisions: 1 commune, 4 communal sectors
Population per Police Officer: N.A.
Police Expenditures per Capita: N.A.

A rudimentary police force was established by the Prince of Monaco in 1867 under the control of a *commissaire* of police, who was answerable to the mayor for general duties and to the governor general for criminal matters. Eight years later the post of a director of police was established, with three *commissaires* under him. In 1902 the force became the Direction de la Sûreté Publique and, in 1929, it was placed under the government counselor for the interior.

The organization of the Sûreté follows guidelines laid down in 1875. Under the director, there are three principal services, each under a *commissaire:* The

Urban Police, or the uniformed branch, is headed by a principal commandant assisted by *officiers de paix,* chief brigadiers, brigadiers and agents. The Urban Police is divided into four operational sections, one of which is the Motorcycle Squad.

The Police Judiciare is in charge of criminal investigation, criminal records and Interpol liaison. The third branch is the Administrative Police, responsible for all non-criminal police functions.

The director is in immediate charge of the Maritime Police, the Women Police, the Communications Section and the prison.

The uniforms of the Monaco Police are very elaborate and colorful. The ceremonial dress of the director and *commissaires* consists of a black peaked hat around which are rows of silver acanthus leaves—two for the director and deputy director and one for the *commissaires*. A straight-cut open-neck tunic in black bears rows of leaves on the cuff. Black trousers and a white shirt and tie complete the uniform. The director usually wears a silk-covered belt. Commandants wear a black peaked cap bearing four rows of silver braid to indicate their rank. In winter a black, open-neck tunic is worn with a white shirt and a black tie. Stiff epaulettes on the tunic carry four rows of silver braid. The trousers are dark blue with a wide black stripe.

Officiers de paix wear the same uniform as the commandant but fewer rows of braid on the cap and epaulettes. In summer they wear sky-blue, long-sleeved, open-neck shirts with air force blue trousers striped with red on the seams. The shirt has stiff air force blue epaulettes and a shoulder patch on the left arm. A white cover is worn on the cap in summer.

The uniform for the lower-ranking brigadiers and agents is similar to that of the officers, with the royal cipher in place of the badges of rank on the epaulettes.

The Riot Squad wear a special uniform consisting of a padded waistcoat worn under a dark blue blouse made of fire-resistant material and matching trousers, gathered at the ankles, worn with a black plastic helmet. The Maritime Police wear navy blue trousers and a double-breasted naval-type tunic worn with the same type of cap as the foot police. A distinctive anchor badge is worn on the cap, the epaulettes and the overcoat. In summer navy blue trousers are worn with a navy blue, open-neck, long-sleeved shirt, with the usual shoulder patch. Light blue overalls are worn on board together with yellow rubber boots.

Women Police wear belted tunics, dark blue in winter and light blue in summer, with matching skirts and Robin Hood-style caps.

All uniformed personnel carry a Smith & Wesson .38 revolver in a black (white ceremonial occasions) holster on the right side. Submachine guns are used during road checks.

CRIME STATISTICS (1984)

		Number Reported	Attempts %	Cases Solved %	Crime per 100,000	Offenders	Females %	Juveniles %	Strangers %
1.	Murder								
2.	Sex offenses, including rape	4		100	14.39	4			100
3.	Rape								
4.	Serious assault	3		100	10.79	3			66.66
5.	All theft	614	4.72	12.21	2,208.63	100	9	13	99
6.	Aggravated theft	151	13.90	9.93	543.17	16	12.50	6.25	100
7.	Robbery and violent theft	12	33.33	16.66	43.17	4	25		100
8.	Breaking and entering	139	12.23	9.35	500	12	8.33	8.33	100
9.	Auto theft	49	2.04	12.24	176.26	11		9.09	100
10.	Other thefts	414	1.69	13.04	1,489.21	73	9.50	15.06	98.63
11.	Fraud	148		90.54	532.37	125	19.20	1.60	94.40
12.	Counterfeiting	11		81.81	39.57	12		8.33	100
13.	Drug offenses	22		100	79.14	40	20	42.50	80
14.	Total offenses	943	3.07	36.26	3,392.09	391	13.04	8.95	94.11

Note: Information for some categories is not available.
Criteria of juveniles: aged from 0 to 18 years.

MONTSERRAT

BASIC FACT SHEET

Official Name: Monserrat
Area: 102 sq km
Population (1987): 12,076
Capital: Plymouth
Nature of Government: British dependent territory
Language: English
Currency: East Caribbean dollar
GNP (1985): $32.4 million
Territorial Divisions: 7 districts
Population per Police Officer: 110
Police Expenditures per 1,000: $16,901

The British colony of Montserrat has a police force of about 150 under a commissioner of police. There are three territorial divisions and a number of operational ones, including the CID and the Marine Division. There are police stations at Cudjie Head, Harris, St. Patrick and Salem.

NAURU

BASIC FACT SHEET

Official Name: Republic of Nauru
Area: 20.7 sq km
Population (1987): 8,748
Capital: Nauru
Nature of Government: Representative democracy
Languages: Nauruan and English
Currency: Australian dollar
GNP (1985): $160 million
Territorial Divisions: —
Population per Police Officer: 110
Police Expenditures per Capita: N.A.

Nauru has a police force of around 100 men, administered by the director of police.

NETHERLANDS ANTILLES

BASIC FACT SHEET

Official Name: Netherlands Antilles
Area: 1,821 sq km
Population (1987): 182,218
Capital: Willemstad
Nature of Government: Dutch dependent territory
Language: Dutch
Currency: Netherlands Antilles florin
GNP (1985): $860 million
Territorial Divisions: 3 island territories
Population per Police Officer: 330
Police Expenditures per Capita: N.A.

The Netherlands Antilles Police is organized along the lines of the Dutch State Police (Rijkspolitie). Headquarters is at Willemstad, with regional posts on each island. Total personnel strength is estimated at 900.

NIGER

BASIC FACT SHEET

Official Name: Republic of Niger
Area: 1,267,000 sq km
Population (1987): 6,988,540
Capital: Niamey
Nature of Government: Military dictatorship
Language: French
Currency: CFA franc
GNP (1986): $1.69 billion
Territorial Divisions: 7 departments, 32 *arrondissements*
Population per Police Officer: 2,350
Police Expenditures per Capita: N.A.

The police of Niger is composed of two forces: the Sûreté Nationale (National Security Police) and the Gendarmerie Nationale, both organized on French lines. The Sûreté is headed by a director and organized in brigades, one of which is stationed in each departmental capital. Niamey has a separate Sûreté command.

The 1,800-man Gendarmerie Nationale is a para-military force headquartered in Niamey, with four regional *groupements,* based at Niamey, Agadès, Marach and Zinder. The Gendarmerie patrols rural areas.

Auxiliary police forces include the Republican Guard and the Presidential Guard. The former carries out mainly ceremonial duties.

CRIME STATISTICS (1983)

		Number Reported	Attempts %	Cases Solved %	Crime per 100,000	Offenders	Females %	Juveniles %	Strangers %
1.	Murder	13	7.69	100	0.21	15	46.66		13.33
2.	Sex offenses, including rape	88	10.22	98.86	1.44	101	5.94	6.93	16.83
3.	Rape	28	25	85.71	0.46	30	3.33	10	
4.	Serious assault	152		94.07	2.49	166	12.65	3.01	4.81
5.	All theft	622	7.23	79.09	10.20	615	1.78	7.64	10.73
6.	Aggravated theft	140	7.14	55	2.30	101		0.99	7.92
7.	Robbery and violent theft	9		66.66	0.15	7			28.57
8.	Breaking and entering	63	30.15	68.25	1.03	53		5.66	9.43
9.	Auto theft	4		25	0.07	1			
10.	Other thefts	448	11.16	86.38	7.34	436	3.44	5.27	12.84
11.	Fraud	183	1.09	91.25	3	220	5.90	7.27	5
12.	Counterfeiting	15		85.66	0.25	17	5.88	5.88	35.29
13.	Drug offenses	218		100	3.57	344	2.03	2.90	3.19
14.	Total offenses	1,983	7.21	84.26	32.51	2,106	3.89	5.50	9.11

Note: Information for some categories is not available.
Criteria of juveniles: aged from 13 to 18 years.

OMAN

BASIC FACT SHEET

Official Name: Sultanate of Oman
Area: 212,380 sq km
Population (1987): 1,226,923
Capital: Muscat
Nature of Government: Absolute monarchy
Language: Arabic
Currency: Rial
GNP (1986): $6.44 billion
Territorial Divisions: 1 province, 2 governorates
Population per Police Officer: 430
Police Expenditures per Capita: N.A.

The Royal Omani Police is the descendant of the tribal police composed of *askars,* or traditional guards, as well as the more organized Oman Gendarmerie and the Muscat Police Force, the latter formed in 1931.

Created and staffed by the British until recently, the Royal Oman Police is built up on British lines. The commander is the inspector general of police and customs, who reports to the minister of the interior. Specialized headquarters functions include traffic and criminal investigation, and units include the Marine Division, the Fire Service and the Police Air Wing. Training is provided by the Police Academy at Nizwa. Personnel strength is about 4,000.

Working dress for all ranks consists of khaki shirts and trousers with black belt and black shoulder epaulettes bearing rank badges. A British-style blue peaked cap with a checkered cap band also is worn. On occasions, an open-neck khaki tunic is worn instead of the shirt. The ceremonial uniform is a white tunic and blue trousers with a broad stripe on the seams.

QATAR

BASIC FACT SHEET

Official Name: State of Qatar
Area: 11,000 sq km
Population (1987): 315,741
Capital: Doha
Nature of Government: Absolute monarchy
Language: Arabic
Currency: Riyal
GNP (1986): $4.18 billion
Territorial Divisions: —
Population per Police Officer: N.A.
Police Expenditures per Capita: N.A.

The Qatar Police, established as an organized force in 1948 for law enforcement in the capital town of Doha, has made considerable progress since the end of Britain's protectorate in 1971.

The force is commanded by a commandant who is a senior military officer. For operational purposes, the sheikhdom is divided into four departments: Airport, Doha, North and Umm Said. Training is provided at the Police Training School in Doha. Internal security functions are performed by the Emergency Police Force, stationed at Rayman Palace. Specialized sections include the Fire Brigade, the Coast Guard, the Doha Seaport and Marine Section, the Mounted Section and the Police Air Wing.

CRIME STATISTICS (1984)

		Number Reported	Attempts %	Cases Solved %	Crime per 100,000	Offenders	Females %	Juveniles %	Strangers %
1.	Murder	6	0	16.6	1.71	8	25	12.5	12.5
2.	Sex offenses, including rape	105	6.6	82.8	30	165	13.3	17	63
3.	Rape	4	50	100	1.14	8	12.5	0	75
4.	Serious assault	37	0	78.3	10.57	58	1.7	13.7	62
5.	All theft	461			131.71	288			
6.	Aggravated theft	214	30		61.14	116	0.88	51.3	23
7.	Robbery and violent theft	0	0	0	0	0	0	0	0
8.	Breaking and entering	214	0	30	61.14	116	0.88	51.3	23
9.	Auto theft	24	0	45.8	6.86	18	0	22.2	11
10.	Other thefts	223	0	42.6	63.71	154	0.64	35	31
11.	Fraud	41	0	100	11.71	54	3.7	3.7	48
12.	Counterfeiting	0			0				
13.	Drug offenses	94	0	100	26.86	152	0.65	0	72
14.	Total offenses	744	9.6	87.6	212.57	725	2	4.6	55.6

Note: Information for some categories is not available.
Criteria of juveniles: aged from 8 to 18 years.

ST. HELENA

BASIC FACT SHEET

Official Name: St. Helena
Area: 122 sq km
Population (1987): 8,524
Capital: Jamestown
Nature of Government: British dependent territory
Language: English
Currency: Pound sterling
GNP: —
Territorial Divisions: 2 dependencies (Ascension and Tristan da Cunha)
Population per Police Officer: 170
Police Expenditures per 1,000: $8,368

A property of the English East India Company from 1659 to 1834, St. Helena has been a British crown colony since 1834. Within four years of the beginning of crown rule, the first police ordinance was passed, and in 1865 the first constabulary force was organized, along British lines. In 1975 a new police ordinance was enacted, defining police duties and powers. The chief of police also serves as registrar of the Supreme Court, clerk of the peace, jail superintendent, fire officer, and inspector of weights and measures. The current strength of the force is about 40.

A detachment of force, under an assistant superintendent, serves on Ascension Island.

St. Helena Police wear British-type uniforms.

ST. KITTS-NEVIS

BASIC FACT SHEET

Official Name: Federation of St. Christopher & Nevis
Area: 261 sq km
Population (1987): 54,775
Capital: Basseterre
Nature of Government: Parliamentary democracy
Language: English
Currency: East Caribbean dollar
GNP (1986): $70 million
Territorial Divisions: 11 districts
Population per Police Officer: 300
Police Expenditures per Capita: N.A.

The St. Kitts-Nevis Police is a force of about 150 men supported by a paramilitary tactical unit at Springfield. Training is provided by the Police Training School at Pond's Pasture on Kitts Island.

ST. LUCIA

BASIC FACT SHEET

Official Name: St. Lucia
Area: 619 sq km
Population (1987): 152,305
Capital: Castries
Nature of Government: Parliamentary democracy
Language: English
Currency: East Caribbean dollar
GNP (1986): $180 million
Territorial Divisions: 16 parishes
Population per Police Officer: 430
Police Expenditures per Capita: N.A.

The St. Lucia Police was established in 1834 but took its present form following legislation enacted in 1965.

Headed by a commissioner who is responsible to the premier, the force comprises the regular force and three auxiliary forces: the Port Authority Constabulary, the Special Reserve Police and the Rural Constabulary. The Administrative Division handles finance and also includes the Special Branch, CID, Telecommunications, Traffic and Licensing, Passports and Immigration, Transport and Stores, the police band and the Services Unit for emergencies.

Territorially, the force is divided into two divisions: the northern division with six police stations and the southern division with five police stations. Total personnel strength is over 300.

There are four uniforms for gazetted officers and inspectors: working dress, undress, mess dress and full dress. The working dress is a khaki short-sleeved bush tunic with matching trousers, worn with either a Sam Browne belt or a cloth belt. The full dress is white close-neck tunic, waist sash, sword, blue overalls with wide white stripes on seams and Wellington boots. There is a blue peaked cap with both types of uniforms, with silver oak leaves or silver braid on the peak according to rank. There are four uniforms for other ranks. The working dress is a white, short-sleeved, open neck tunic with blue trousers and a blue peaked cap. Ceremonial dress is the same as that for officers except that a white or black leather belt is worn instead of a sash, and trousers are blue with a white stripe. Headgear is either a blue cap or a white helmet. Generally, all ranks are unarmed.

ST. VINCENT AND THE GRENADINES

```
BASIC FACT SHEET

Official Name: St. Vincent and the Grenadines
Area: 389 sq km
Population (1987): 131,215
Capital: Kingstown
Nature of Government: Parliamentary democracy
Language: English
Currency: East Caribbean dollar
GNP (1986): $110 million
Territorial Divisions: —
Population per Police Officer: 250
Police Expenditures per 1,000: $18,008
```

The St. Vincent and the Grenadines Police is a 520-man force administered by a commissioner. The Fire Brigade is part of the police.

SAN MARINO

```
BASIC FACT SHEET

Official Name: Republic of San Marino
Area: 62 sq km
Population (1987): 22,791
Capital: San Marino
Nature of Government: Parliamentary democracy
Language: Italian
Currency: Lira
GNP: —
Territorial Divisions: 9 "castles"
Population per Police Officer: N.A.
Police Expenditures per Capita: N.A.
```

San Marino has two police organizations: the older Corps of Gendarmerie (Corpo Gendarmeria), whose personnel are Italian citizens and members of the Italian Carabinieri; and the Corps of Urban Police, formed in 1947, whose personnel are San Marino citizens.

The Gendarmeria comprises the City Unit for the town of San Marino and seven brigades. In accordance with the law, all gendarmes, as well as inspectors and judges, must be foreigners to ensure that no citizen of San Marino will receive more favorable treatment at the hands of the police than any other San Marino citizen.

The Corps of Urban Police is concerned with enforcement of traffic laws and municipal parking as well as collection of customs duties.

The corps has two uniforms. The winter uniform is blue, complete with helmet and white shirt, gloves, white armlets and black socks, ties and shoes. The summer uniform is all aquamarine.

SÃO TOMÉ AND PRÍNCIPE

BASIC FACT SHEET

Official Name: Democratic Republic of São Tomé and Príncipe
Area: 963 sq km
Population (1987): 114,025
Capital: São Tomé
Nature of Government: Authoritarian
Language: Portuguese
Currency: Dobra
GNP (1986): $40 million
Territorial Divisions: 7 counties
Population per Police Officer: 400
Police Expenditures per Capita: N.A.

The regular police in São Tomé and Príncipe is the Public Order Police, with a strength of over 300, under the Ministry of National Security. The Public Order Police works mainly in the towns. Rural areas are policed by the National Guard.

SEYCHELLES

BASIC FACT SHEET

Official Name: Republic of Seychelles
Area: 280 sq km
Population (1987): 67,522
Capital: Victoria
Nature of Government: Limited democracy
Languages: English and French
Currency: Rupee
GNP (1985): $175 million
Territorial Divisions: —
Population per Police Officer: 120
Police Expenditures per Capita: N.A.

History & Background

Seychelles was first policed in 1775, when as a dependency of Île de France (Mauritius), 15 soldiers were sent to Seychelles to perform security duties. This system continued until 1802, when a small police force was established under the command of a Citizen Savy. Seychelles was ceded to Britain in 1814, and between 1822 and 1840 various combinations of policemen and soldiers formed the security forces of the country.

The police station at Victoria, which is the capital of Mahé, the main island, was destroyed together with all local records in a landslide in 1862, leaving a gap in the history of the force. By 1879 the strength of the force had increased to 45 and outstations had been established at Port Glaud, Anse Aux Pins and Takamaka in addition to Victoria.

In 1903 the Mahé group and Corallines became the separate Colony of Seychelles, by which time the force had grown to 79 men, with 12 outstations in operation.

The Special Force unit of 45 men, paramilitary in character, was established in 1964 to assist the regular police in dealing with civil unrest and disturbance. During 1967 and 1968 radio communication facilities were obtained by police, and women police officers also were appointed. A criminal record office based on fingerprint identification was set up in the same period.

Seychelles Airport was inaugurated in 1971, and the Airport Police Section established. The Police Dog Unit was established in 1973, and preparations were laid to establish on the island of Praslin the Police Training School; it was opened in 1974.

The Marine Section, established in 1976, provides coastal and interisland policing for the inner islands of Seychelles.

When the Colony of Seychelles became independent on June 28, 1976, the force's structure and organization were not affected. The number of expatriate officers at the time of independence was 10, functioning as heads of departments and as advisers.

The force in general was significantly affected by the coup d'état of June 5, 1977. The police armories were the prime foci for attack to acquire the necessary weapons to consolidate the success of the coup. In this incident only one police officer was killed in the line of duty.

Structure & Organization

The Seychelles Police Force is subject to the Police Force Act and consists of such number of police officers as may from time to time be approved by the president and enrolled in the force. The police are under the direction of officers appointed by the commissioner of police. These officers carry out orders of the commissioner regarding discipline, internal administration and training of the police under them.

The Seychelles Police Force is administered from force headquarters in Victoria. For operational and administrative purposes the country is divided into the Central Police Division, comprising the capital, Victoria; the North Police Division; the South Police Division; and the Praslin/La Digue Police Division.

Each of these police formations is under the command of a senior police officer. There is a total of 17 police stations in all the divisions. The Police Training School and the Police Mobile Unit are each under the command of an assistant superintendent; each is directly responsible to the deputy commissioner. The force departments are staffed by police officers or civil staff, and in some cases a combination of both. The organization of the force and distribution of work to departments is divided as follows:

1. Headquarters: Administration and Support Services (including Prosecution, Marine, Dogs, Training and Traffic sections, and Interpol/NCB)

2. Criminal Investigation Department

3. Special Force (Police Mobile Unit)

4. General Duties

5. Special Branch

Practically all local crime is investigated by uniformed and CID officers in districts, while headquarters CID is concerned with the investigation of certain serious crimes within districts, the compilation of fingerprints and criminal records, photography and other specialized duties. In addition to the officers' work in the CID, they also supply intelligence information to other police stations, and their knowledge of the criminal activities of chronic thieves has reportedly resulted in apprehension in several cases.

The Police Mobile Unit, under the command of a superintendent, is responsible for the preservation of public order, and its restoration in the event of civil unrest or uprising. This unit also has the responsibility for providing personnel for parades.

The Special Branch, which is under the direct control of the commissioner of police, is responsible for the maintenance and operation of security and intelligence services and the prevention and detection of activities detrimental to the security of the country.

The Seychelles Police Special Constabulary is a permanent volunteer force appointed under the Police Force Act, which empowers the president, through the commissioner of police, to make regulations as to its government, administration and conditions of service. Special constables have all the powers and privileges of a regular constable.

Other departments include:

1. Traffic Department
2. Marine Section
3. Finance Department
4. Radio and Telephone Communication
5. New Port Police
6. Airport Police
7. Security Guards—Tracking Station, La Misère

Other special branches of the Seychelles Police Force include the Police Transport Branch, the Rescue Unit, the Police Band (formed in early 1978), the Excise Section, the Canine Section and the Police Women Branch.

Regular police inspectors and above wear a white open-necked shirt with royal blue shorts or trousers. Junior ranks wear a blue shirt with royal blue shorts. Personnel in the Special Force (Police Mobile Unit) wear khaki shirts and shorts. Headgear consists of a dark blue cap with a white checkered band. Members of the force are normally unarmed, but the Police Mobile Unit is equipped with the latest weaponry, including 7-62 SLR rifles.

The police Training School at Praslin is under a commandant and is responsible for recruit and refresher course training (15 weeks' duration), supervisory officers' courses (two weeks), the promotion course (two weeks) and basic courses (taught in Creole; four weeks). Field training, under field training officers, is conducted weekly on a district basis. Prepromotion classes, under a course director, are held to prepare candidates for future promotion examinations.

The Police Training staff establishment consisted in 1979 of an assistant superintendent (commandant); one inspector and two sergeants as instructors; and one civilian clerk/typist.

Instruction given to recruits at the school includes law, general police duties and procedures, first aid, foot and arm drill, physical training, and general knowledge. After passing, they are assigned to general duties. Normally, after at least three months, they are assigned specialized branches for continued training.

CRIME STATISTICS (1984)

		Number Reported	Attempts %	Cases Solved %	Crime per 100,000	Offenders	Females %	Juveniles %	Strangers %
1.	Murder	5		80	7.69	2			
2.	Sex offenses, including rape	33		27.27	50.74	14		35.71	
3.	Rape								
4.	Serious assault	532		49.06	818.06	324	17.90	3.09	
5.	All theft	1,026		16.67		219	9.13	9.13	
6.	Aggravated theft								
7.	Robbery and violent theft	3		33.31	4.61	3			
8.	Breaking and entering	426		13.61	655.06	109	2.75	16.51	
9.	Auto theft								
10.	Other thefts	33		45.45	50.74	19	5.26	15.79	
11.	Fraud	57		59.65	87.65	39	12.82		
12.	Counterfeiting								
13.	Drug offenses	45		77.78	69.20	28			3.57
14.	Total offenses	4,142			6,369.17				

Note: Information for some categories is not available.
Criteria of juveniles: aged from 7 to 18 years.

SOLOMON ISLANDS

BASIC FACT SHEET

Official Name: Solomon Islands
Area: 29,785 sq km
Population (1987): 301,180
Capital: Honiara
Nature of Government: Representative democracy
Language: English
Currency: Australian dollar
GNP (1986): $150 million
Territorial Divisions: 4 administrative districts
Population per Police Officer: 620
Police Expenditures per 1,000: $5,112

The Solomon Islands Police Force is a relatively small establishment. Its functions, in additional to maintenance of law and order, include immigration control, firefighting and administration of prisons. The force also is called upon to participate in ceremonial functions, and it maintains a small band for that purpose.

Operationally, the force is controlled centrally by the chief of police from headquarters in Honiara. Administratively, the force is divided into four police districts, which correspond to similar divisions in the civil administration. Each police district is commanded by a police inspector and is assigned operating forces in accordance with geographic and population needs. The Western District covers Choiseul Island and the Shortland and New Georgia Island groups from its headquarters on Gizo Island in the New Georgia group. The Central District includes Santa Isabel, Guadalcanal, Bellona, Rennell, and the Russell and Florida islands clusters. Its headquarters is contiguous to that of the overall force in Honiara. The Malaita District embraces Malaita Island, Sikaiana and the Ontong Java atoll. Its headquarters is at Auki on Malaita. The Eastern District directs police activities on San Cristóbal and Santa Cruz from headquarters at Kirakira on San Cristóbal.

Training for all ranks is provided by headquarters at Honiara through the Police Training School. The courses include two in basic police activities and one refresher course for constables.

Members of the force wear two uniforms: one for duty and the other for ceremonial occasions. The working uniform consists of a khaki shirt and shorts, a blue beret and black sandals; the dress has a white tunic, a blue sulu or short sarong and black sandals. Both are worn with a black belt superimposed on a red sash.

The chief of police is also the superintendent of prisons and runs the country's four major prisons. The Central Prison at Honiara, the largest, is used to house prisoners guilty of serious crimes. Smaller prisons, called district prisons, are at the headquarters of the other police divisions. Two-thirds of the prisoners are serving sentences of three months or less. All prisons are oriented to rehabilitation and provide vocational and adult education classes.

The incidence of crime is relatively low, although, because of better detection and reporting, the crime rate is gradually increasing. More than half the crimes are offenses against the person.

SURINAME

BASIC FACT SHEET

Official Name: Republic of Suriname
Area: 163,265 sq km
Population (1987): 388,636
Capital: Paramaribo
Nature of Government: Military dictatorship
Language: Dutch
Currency: Suriname guilder
GNP (1986): $1.01 billion
Territorial Divisions: 9 districts
Population per Police Officer: 740
Police Expenditures per 1,000: $12,049

The Armed Police Corps (Het Korps Gewapende Politie) was founded during Dutch rule in 1865, and it has evolved over the years into a paramilitary force. It is headed by a commissioner of police who reports to the attorney general, but for operational purposes it is under the Ministry of Army and Police. Training is provided by the Police Training School at Paramaribo.

TOGO

BASIC FACT SHEET

Official Name: Republic of Togo
Area: 56,980 sq km
Population (1987): 3,228,635
Capital: Lomé
Nature of Government: Military dictatorship
Language: French
Currency: CFA franc
GNP (1986): $780 million
Territorial Divisions: 21 prefectures
Population per Police Officer: 1,970
Police Expenditures per Capita: N.A.

The Togolese police comprise three branches: the Corps de Police Urbaine de Lomé, the National Police (formerly the Sûreté Nationale) and the Gendarmerie Nationale.

The Corps de Police Urbaine de Lomé is a municipal force under joint municipal and police control and organized in four commissariats, one for each *arrondissement*. A criminal investigation unit known as Brigade Criminelle is part of the corps.

The National Police, commanded by a director, has many sections, including Administration, Judiciary (the Judicial Police), Intelligence (Special Service), the Harbor Police and the Railway Police. The National Police also is in charge of the Fire Service and the National Police School.

The Gendarmerie Nationale has a strength of 1,800 men deployed in one operational unit and five brigades: Air, Criminal Investigation, Harbor, Traffic and Territorial. The Gendarmerie also is in charge of the Central Criminal Archives and provides the presidential bodyguard.

TONGA

BASIC FACT SHEET

Official Name: Kingdom of Tonga
Area: 997 sq km
Population (1987): 98,689
Capital: Nuku'alofa
Nature of Government: Constitutional monarchy
Languages: Tongan and English
Currency: Pa'anga
GNP (1986): $70 million
Territorial Divisions: 3 island groups
Population per Police Officer: 330
Police Expenditures per 1,000: $7,139

The Tonga Police Force is a national agency with jurisdiction throughout the kingdom. There are no separate local or municipal police forces. It is commanded by a commissioner of police with about 300 men and officers from the central headquarters in the capital city of Nuku'alofa on Tongatapu Island. Below this command post the force is deployed in three territorial districts, for the Tongatapu, Haapai and Vava'u island groups.

Most of the police forces are permanently stationed on Tongatapu Island. Many of the other small islands do not have any force stationed on them because they are too remote. The island of Niuatoputapu, for example, is so far to the north that it is visited by a government vessel only once every two months. Peace and order are maintained on such islands only through the authority of the local chiefs.

Tongan police on regular duty wear uniforms consisting of khaki shirts and sarongs, a blue cummerbund fitted with a black belt, a navy blue slouch hat and black sandals. For ceremonial occasions a white jacket is worn over the shirt, and the khaki sarong is replaced by one of white material. The force is unarmed, but batons are held in reserve and issued when required.

The mission of the regular police includes monitoring sales in local retail shops, issuing licenses to fishermen, registering bicycles and apprehending truants in the school system. They also regulate all matters having to do with Tongan custom and tradition.

There are no police schools, and recruits undergo no formalized training. Duty personnel usually devote about one hour a week to foot and arms drill and are required to attend lectures on practical police work delivered by their superiors. In outer areas, these lectures are provided by mobile teams sent from headquarters.

Tonga's penal institutions include the main prison at Hu'atolitoli, near Nuku'alofa, and three smaller ones, at Haapai, Vava'u and Niuatoputapu. Persons sentenced to terms of six months or more are incarcerated at the main prison. All sentences of more than one month may be remitted by as much as one-fourth for good behavior. This reduction is automatically granted at the time the prisoner enters the facility and can be revoked only if the prisoner fails to live up to disciplinary standards.

Living conditions in all penal institutions are relatively good. Food and quarters are sanitary and adequate; discipline is lightly applied, and security measures are neither harsh nor burdensome. Prisoners are required to perform labor on public works or on copra plantations owned by the government.

The incidence of crime is not significantly high.

Most of the 4,000 or so cases a year are misdemeanors. The most common violations are adultery, offenses against property, cruelty to animals, simple assault, fighting, theft, trespassing and traffic violations.

TURKS AND CAICOS

BASIC FACT SHEET

Official Name: Turks and Caicos Islands
Area: 430 sq km
Population (1987): 9,052
Capital: Grand Turk
Nature of Government: British dependent territory
Language: English
Currency: U.S. dollar
GNP (1985): $15 million
Territorial Divisions: 3 districts
Population per Police Officer: 100
Police Expenditures per Capita: $20.60

The Royal Turks and Caicos Islands Police is a force of 90 men under a chief of police. Headquarters is in Grand Turk, and there are police outposts in Providenciales and South Caicos islands. Training is provided by the Police Training Center at Grand Turk.

TUVALU

BASIC FACT SHEET

Official Name: Tuvalu
Area: 26 sq km
Population (1987): 8,329
Capital: Funafuti
Nature of Government: Parliamentary democracy
Languages: Tuvaluan and English
Currency: Australian dollar
GNP (1985): $4 million
Territorial Divisions: 8 islands
Population per Police Officer: 290
Police Expenditures per 1,000: $13,059

Tuvalu shares its history until independence in 1975 with Kiribati, which together were known as the Gilbert and Ellice Islands. The Gilbert and Ellice Islands Armed Constabulary, founded in 1892, was split into two forces: the Kiribati Police and the Tuvalu Police. At independence the Tuvalu Police had a strength of only 10, of whom half were women.

UNITED ARAB EMIRATES

BASIC FACT SHEET

Official Name: United Arab Emirates
Area: 83,600 sq km
Population (1987): 1,846,373
Capital: Abu Dhabi
Nature of Government: Absolute monarchy
Language: Arabic
Currency: Dirham
GNP (1986): $20.59 billion
Territorial Divisions: 7 member states
Population per Police Officer: 140
Police Expenditures per Capita: N.A.

Federal police and security guard forces in the United Arab Emirates are authorized under the 1971 Constitution and were established by decree law on April 24, 1974.

The Federal Police are subordinate to and part of the Ministry of the Interior. For a number of years following the federation, many of the personnel were British and Jordanian. There is some local police autonomy in each member emirate.

The Federal Police headquarters includes Administrative, Criminal Investigation, Public Security and Traffic branches. There is also a Federal Air Wing, with about a dozen helicopters.

CRIME STATISTICS (1984)

		Number Reported	Attempts %	Cases Solved %	Crime per 100,000	Offenders	Females %	Juveniles %	Strangers %
1.	Murder	27		2	1.79				
2.	Sex offenses, including rape	40		2	2.65				
3.	Rape								
4.	Serious assault	78		8	5.17				
5.	All theft								
6.	Aggravated theft	2,574		187	170.87				
7.	Robbery and violent theft								
8.	Breaking and entering								
9.	Auto theft								
10.	Other thefts								
11.	Fraud	207		22	13.74				
12.	Counterfeiting	7			0.46				
13.	Drug offenses	228		18	15.13				
14.	Total offenses	19,538		1,185	1,297				

Note: Information for some categories is not available.
Criteria of juveniles: aged from 10 to 18 years.

VANUATU

BASIC FACT SHEET

Official Name: Republic of Vanuatu
Area: 14,763 sq km
Population (1987): 149,652
Capital: Port-Vila
Nature of Government: Parliamentary democracy
Languages: English and French
Currency: Australian dollar
GNP (1986): $79 million
Territorial Divisions: 4 administrative districts
Population per Police Officer: 450
Police Expenditures per Capita: N.A.

The Vanuatu Police Force comprises the combined police forces of the former French and British police forces of the Anglo-French Condominium of New Hebrides, as Vanuatu was called until independence. The force is under a commandant, who supervises four ranks of officers and men: superintendent of police, inspector, noncommissioned officers and un-rated constables, in addition to administrative personnel.

Below headquarters, there are four operating territorial units, whose headquarters are at Vila, on Efate Island, Santo (Luganville) on Espiritu Santo Island, Lakotoro on Malekula Island, and the major settlement on Tana Island. There are no facilities for training, and trainees sometimes are sent to police schools in Fiji.

There are four prisons and one rehabilitation center in Vanuatu: at Vila, and at each of the district headquarters. Few inmates are confined for long terms. Most serve sentences of a month or less for drunkenness. All sentences are automatically remitted by one-third for good behavior. The prisons, though small, are well run and adequate. All convicted prisoners undergo some form of vocational training.

The rehabilitation center, located at Pialulub, is a minimum-security facility where prisoners are permitted to have families and, after a training period, are paid wages and permitted to participate in a savings program.

VATICAN CITY

BASIC FACT SHEET

Official Name: Vatican City
Area: 0.44 sq km
Population (1987): 738
Capital: Vatican City
Nature of Government: Theocracy
Languages: Italian and Latin
Currency: Lira
GNP: —
Territorial Divisions: —
Population per Police Officer: N.A.
Police Expenditures per Capita: N.A.

The world's most colorful and unusual police is the Swiss Guard, which protects the pope, the papal palace and Vatican City. Formed in 1506 by Pope Julius II, it is also among the oldest. The guard is headed by a colonel commandant. It retains its picturesque, centuries-old uniform.

In 1970 Pope Paul VI abolished three additional guard forces employed by the Vatican: the Noble Guard, the Palatine Guard and the Papal Gendarmerie.

WESTERN SAMOA

BASIC FACT SHEET

Official Name: Independent State of Western Samoa
Area: 2,934 sq km
Population (1987): 175,048
Capital: Apia
Nature of Government: Constitutional monarchy
Languages: Samoan and English
Currency: Tala
GNP (1986): $110 million
Territorial Divisions: —
Population per Police Officer: N.A.
Police Expenditures per 1,000: $6,997

The Western Samoan Police was first organized by the Germans during their colonial administration from 1900 to 1914. In the latter year, the New Zealand forces arrived and redesignated the force as Military Controlled Police. In 1921 the Samoan Constabulary was established, and it became the Western Samoan Police on independence in 1962.

The police and the penal systems are organized as the Department of Police and Prisons under a commissioner of police, who reports to the prime minister. There are no operating or territorial divisions. Elements of the police are assigned as required to stations on Upolu and Savai'i islands. There are three stations on Upolu and three on Savai'i. Subordinate agencies under the commissioner of police include the Firearms Registry; a public-relations office; the Special Branch, concerned with internal security; and five divisions: Crime, Technical, Administration, Training and Mobile.

The daily working uniform is a light gray, short-sleeved shirt worn with a light gray *lava-lava* or wraparound skirt. A white British-style helmet is worn. Officers wear the same uniform with a dark blue peaked cap. Traffic officers wear long trousers instead of the *lava-lava*. All policemen are unarmed.

The Prison Service is headed by a police sergeant, who administers two penal institutions: a conventional prison at Tafa'igata near Apia, and a prison farm at Vaia'ata on Savai'i Island. Both are minimum-security prisons where inmates receive vocational training.

APPENDIX I: INTERPOL

Interpol is the world association of national police forces established for mutual assistance in the detection and deterrence of international crimes and criminals. Its aim is to facilitate cooperation for those purposes among the police of member countries, despite differences of language, culture and systems of criminal justice.

Legal Status

Interpol is something of a legal curiosity. It conducts intergovernmental activities, but it is not based on an international treaty, convention or similar legal instrument. It is founded on a constitution written by a group of police officers who did not submit it for diplomatic signatures nor have they ever submitted it for ratification by governments.

Nevertheless, the organization received almost instant official recognition. Governments began applying for membership immediately after its formation, appointing delegates, appropriating funds for dues and otherwise acting in accordance with the organization's rules and regulations. The League of Nations, while it was in existence, gave it de facto official recognition by mandating to it the administration of the 1929 League of Nations Convention on the Suppression of Counterfeiting. A number of international official bodies have affiliated with Interpol, such as the Council of Europe, the Customs Cooperation Council and the International Narcotics Control Council. The United Nations Economic and Social Council has granted it official status as an intergovernmental agency.

A significant aspect of Interpol's legal status is that member governments have not delegated to it any powers or authority. For this reason, it must function wholly within the limits of the laws of each member country as well as within the provisions of its own constitution. That explains why Interpol itself has no powers of arrest, nor of search and seizure, nor authority to conduct criminal investigations. These powers are exercised by the police of member nations themselves.

Moreover, in its function of facilitating cooperation among member police agencies, Interpol must deal exclusively with "common law" crimes; its constitutional mandate rigorously excludes involvement with political, military, racial or religious matters.

Origins

One of the most striking features of 20th-century crime is its international nature. Criminals have become increasingly mobile as restrictions on international travel have been gradually lifted and means of communication and transport have improved. At the same time, economic and social activities have expanded and increased in complexity at both national and international levels, and this phenomenon has provided offenders with more and more opportunities for their illicit activities.

Although "international crime" has never been clearly defined in legal terms, the offenses covered by this phrase are clearly recognizable in practice, either because they are the subject of international conventions such as the 1929 Convention on the Suppression of Counterfeiting, the 1949 Convention on Traffic in Persons and Exploitation of Prostitution, the 1961 Single Convention on Narcotic Drugs and the 1971 Convention on Psychotropic Substances, or because of other international aspects of a purely circumstantial nature. Such aspects may include the fact that an offense was prepared and carried out in different countries, the revelation that a single offender has committed a number of crimes in different countries, or that an offender has absconded to another country or transferred the proceeds of his or her offense to another country; finally, offenders, victims or witnesses may be foreigners in the country where the offense was committed.

When international offenses such as those described above are committed, the police and judicial authorities in the countries concerned need to exchange information rapidly to obtain evidence and to identify, locate and arrest offenders with a view to extradition. The need for international cooperation in these circumstances first made itself felt at the beginning of this century and gradually became more pressing until it led to the establishment of Interpol as an instrument of cooperation.

While these factors make life easier for criminals, they

hinder the police, whose actions are subject to various legitimate constraints, such as territorial limitations on jurisdiction, respect for the law and limited resources. Consequently, although these factors make for a higher standard of living, they also mean that society is more vulnerable to criminal activities.

In 1914 the First International Criminal Police Congress met in Monaco, where legal experts and police officers from 14 different countries discussed the possibility of establishing an international criminal records office and of harmonizing extradition procedures.

The outbreak of the First World War prevented further progress until 1923, when the Second International Criminal Police Congress met in Vienna to continue the work that had begun in Monaco. The Congress set up the International Criminal Police Commission (ICPC), with its official headquarters in Vienna and its own statutes. The ICPC was essentially European in character, and it operated until the outbreak of World War Two.

The third "new start" for international police cooperation was in 1946, when a conference was held in Brussels. The milestones in the Organization's existence from that date onwards are given later in this appendix.

With the growth in membership from 50 in 1955 to 100 in 1967 and 138 at the time of writing, Interpol's worldwide mission has naturally become more apparent. Article 4 of its Constitution states that "any country may delegate as a member to the organization any official police body whose functions come within the framework of activities of the organization." In practice, the appropriate governmental department submits an application for membership, which must be approved by Interpol's General Assembly.

Aims and Basic Principles of Cooperation Within Interpol

Aims
The organization's aims are summarized in Article 2 of its Constitution, as follows:

- "to ensure and promote the widest possible mutual assistance between all criminal police authorities within the limits of the laws existing in the different countries and in the spirit of the Universal Declaration of Human Rights
- "to establish and develop all institutions likely to contribute effectively to the prevention and suppression of ordinary law crimes."

Having thus defined Interpol's aims, the Constitution states in Article 3 that "it is strictly forbidden for the organization to undertake any intervention or activities of a political, military, religious or racial character."

This article is interpreted to mean that Interpol may not intervene in connection with offenses which, because of

circumstances and factors particular to the case, are predominantly political, military, religious or racial in character. This interpretation was given in a resolution adopted by the General Assembly in 1951 and redefined in two further resolutions the General Assembly adopted in 1984.

Basic Principles
The organization conducts its activities on the basis of the following fundamental principles:

- respect for national sovereignty
- application of the provisions of Article 3 of the Constitution in Interpol's crime-prevention and law-enforcement activities
- universality: Any member state may cooperate with any other, and cooperation must not be impeded by geographic or linguistic factors.
- equality of all member states: All the member states are provided with the same services and have the same rights, irrespective of their financial contributions to the organization.
- cooperation with other agencies: Cooperation is extended, through the National Central Bureaus, to any governmental agency concerned with combating ordinary criminal offenses.
- flexibility of working methods, which are governed by principles designed to ensure regularity and continuity but to keep formalities to a minimum and to take account of the wide variety of structures and situations in different countries

Respect for these principles in day-to-day operation obviously means that Interpol cannot have teams of detectives with supranational powers who travel around investigating cases in different countries. International police cooperation has to depend on coordinated action on the part of the member states' police forces, all of which may supply or request information or services on different occasions.

Interpol's Structure

Interpol's activities are based on two types of institution: its deliberative bodies—the General Assembly and Executive Committee—and its permanent departments—the General Secretariat and National Central Bureaus.

The Deliberative Bodies
The *General Assembly* is the organization's supreme governing body. It is composed of delegates appointed by the appropriate governmental authorities in their countries, and it meets once a year.

The General Assembly makes all the major policy decisions affecting the organization as well as decisions on working methods, finances and budgeting, means of cooperation and the program of activities; it elects persons to hold office and approves applications for membership.

The *Executive Committee* usually meets three times a year. It ensures that General Assembly decisions are implemented, prepares the agenda for General Assembly sessions, approves the program of activities and the draft budget before they are submitted to the General Assembly and supervises the secretary general's administration and work. The committee has 13 members (a president elected for a four-year term of office, three vice presidents and nine delegates elected for three-year terms of office), and the seats are shared equitably among the different continents.

The Permanent Departments

The *General Secretariat* is the permanent administrative and technical institution through which Interpol operates. It implements the decisions made by the General Assembly and the Executive Committee, supervises and coordinates the fight against international crime, centralizes information in crime and criminals, and maintains contact with national and international authorities. The General Secretariat is administered by the secretary general, who is elected by the General Assembly for a five-year term of office. The General Secretariat has three divisions and one department, each responsible for specific tasks:

- The Organization and Development Department is directly attached to the secretary general and is responsible for rationalizing working methods and structures.
- Division I (General Administration) has five subdivisions and a unit. This division deals with finance and accounts, personnel, supplies and internal services, and logistics (telecommunications, translation, typing, printing and security). It also organizes conferences and some symposia and meetings, including the sessions of the General Assembly and the Executive Committee.
- Division II (Police Division) centralizes information on criminal cases under investigation in member states. It processes the information, writes reports on cases, and drafts and issues international notices. This division also makes arrangements for specialized meetings and symposia. In addition to the criminal records, identification, fingerprinting and international notices sections, the Police Division has three subdivisions, each of which deals with one sector of crime: general offenses against persons and property (including international terrorism); economic and financial crime (including currency counterfeiting); and illicit drug traffic. The division also edits the review *Counterfeits and Forgeries*.
- Division III has three subdivisions and includes the organization's Legal Department. It also provides a legal and technical reference service (police, crime prevention, criminal law and procedure, and criminology) both for member states and for the General Secretariat's own departments. Within the context of its overall mission, it conducts surveys, analyzes documents, organizes certain Interpol symposia, and shares in the work of various other international agencies in connection with legal and criminological subjects. It also publishes the *International Criminal Police Review*.

The General Secretariat's staff can be divided into two categories: police officers or civil servants who are either assigned temporarily or detached by member states, and staff employed directly by the organization. The total staffing level was 95 persons in 1966, 170 in 1976, and 250 persons of about 40 different nationalities in 1986.

In each of the organization's member states the *National Central Bureau* is the focal point of cooperation. In most cases the department chosen to act as the NCB is a high-level one with wide powers, a choice that helps to reduce the difficulties inherent in international cooperation. There are a number of advantages to the system: each member state has a single Interpol "contact," whatever the type of criminal case involved; linguistic difficulties are reduced, as it is easier to ensure that a single national department is staffed by persons familiar with Interpol's working languages than to appoint similarly qualified persons to a number of different national police departments; and finally, a department that specializes in international cooperation acquires experience in this field with relative rapidity and ease. Furthermore, each NCB should be empowered to initiate, at the request of any other NCB, large-scale operations that may involve other police or government departments.

The NCBs' activities can be summarized as follows:

- From sources in their own countries they collect documents and information relating to international law enforcement, and they pass this material on to the other NCBs and the General Secretariat.
- They ensure that police inquiries and operations requested through Interpol channels are carried out in their own countries and that the results are communicated to the requesting party.
- They transmit to NCBs in other countries requests for international cooperation made by their own judicial authorities or other governmental departments.

International cooperation also enables investigators from one member state to travel to another member state to investigate offenses with international aspects. Permission for this type of operation may be given rapidly where circumstances require, and foreign police officers are thus able to establish links with the police forces in the country they visit and be present at police and judicial operations such as evidence gathering, arrests, interviews and searches. The NCBs are responsible for organizing these missions or for authorizing them with the consent of the appropriate judicial authorities (on the basis of rogatory commissions, for example). In 1985 a total of 23 NCBs provided statistics on this aspect of cooperation and a total of 709 missions were carried out on the national territories of those countries.

The heads of NCBs attend Interpol General Assembly sessions as members of their countries' delegations and subsequently ensure that the Assembly's resolutions are implemented.

NCBs may communicate directly among themselves. However, they are expected to send copies of their corre-

ICPO ORGANIZATION CHART

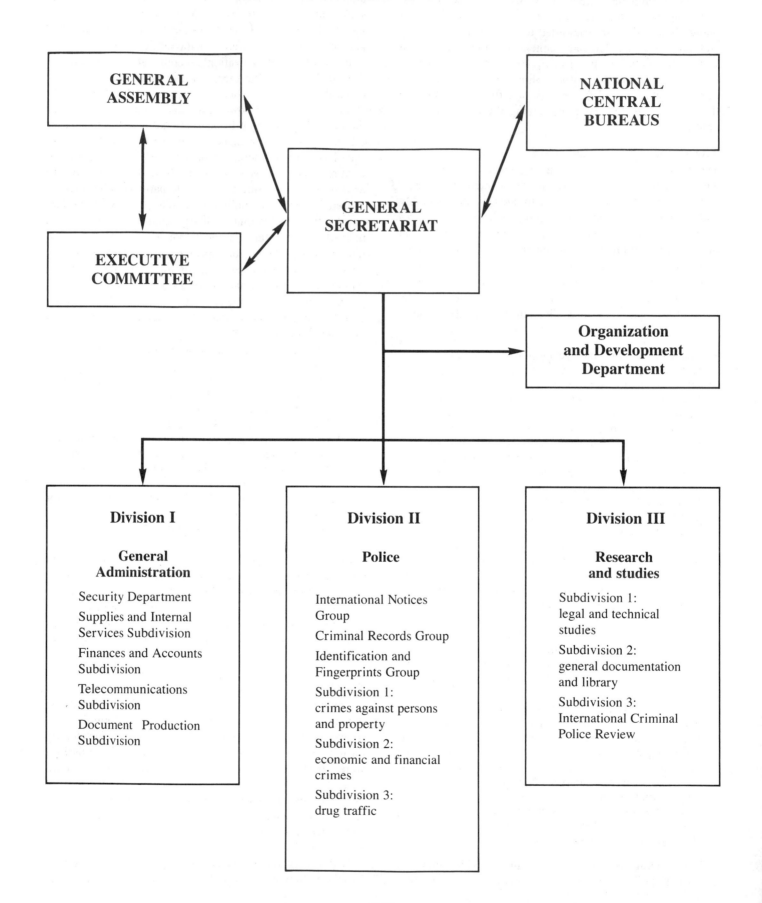

spondence to the General Secretariat so the latter can perform its task of centralizing information and coordinating cooperation.

The organization's *advisers* are highly qualified experts with worldwide reputations who are appointed by the Executive Committee for three-year terms to assist Interpol with scientific and technical problems.

Resources and Instruments for International Police Cooperation

Budget

Interpol's activities are financed by the annual budget contributions of the member states. These contributions are expressed in "budget units" and countries are divided into 12 groups, paying from one to 80 units a year. The General Assembly sets the value of the budget unit. The secretary general is responsible for implementing the budget and is answerable to the deliberative bodies. An external audit is conducted by an outside body appointed by the General Assembly.

Telecommunications

Rapid and reliable communications are vital to the success of international cooperation, and consequently the importance of the telecommunications network cannot be exaggerated. More than half of the organization's member states have joined the independent International Police Telecommunications Network, which links them with the other NCBs and the General Secretariat. The national stations in a particular geographical area are grouped around regional stations, which are linked directly to the central station in France. The system allows a message to be transmitted simultaneously to several Interpol radio stations, to all the stations in one or more zones or to all the NCBs on the network. Moreover, approximately 25 national central bureaus and the General Secretariat now have phototelegraphy equipment for transmission and reception of photographs and fingerprints. About 100 national central bureaus and the General Secretariat are telex subscribers. Radio traffic, which is increasing by about 10% every year, is now such that the General Secretariat is to be provided with automatic message-switching equipment in a few months.

Criminal Records

Criminal records are of fundamental importance to an organization that centralizes and supervises international cooperation. The General Secretariat has two records groups:

- The *General Records Group* has indexes of the names of people connected with international police investigations as well as indexes of offenses and indexes of missing documents and objects.
- The *Special Records Group* has fingerprint (ten-print and single-print) files, as well as a photograph file for specialized offenders.

International Notices

The General Secretariat issues several types of notices to circulate items of information to member states.

Individual notices may be circulated for different reasons. "Wanted" notices are circulated to ask for someone's arrest with a view to extradition and are issued at the request of judicial authorities in member states. "Inquiry" notices are designed to identify or collect information about individuals (e.g. those suspected of international criminal activities, missing persons or unidentified persons). "Warning" notices give information about professional offenders liable to operate in several countries. "Unidentified body" notices are issued in an attempt to identify dead bodies. In 1983 a total of 322 "wanted" notices were canceled and 550 new ones were published.

Stolen-property notices are published with photographs wherever possible, as these are of vital importance when the notices concern property (such as works of art) that could be difficult to describe.

Modus operandi sheets give details of new or unusual modus operandi used by international offenders and likely to spread to several countries.

Circular letters, summary reports and *brochures* provide factual, up-to-date information on certain types of crime and criminals.

To assist the national police forces in member states with their daily identification tasks, the General Secretariat has conducted a number of technical studies on specific subjects and has produced a report on Chinese names and their transcription, a typewriter identification index with specimens of the typing produced by different makes of typewriter, a brochure on the vehicle registration plates used in various countries, brochures on the identification of cartridges, a manual on disaster victim identification, etc.

Training Police Personnel and Technical Cooperation

The organization also participates in the training of member countries' personnel. The following are some of the activities that have been conducted in this area:

- symposia for heads of police training colleges
- training courses for personnel involved in combating counterfeit currency
- training seminars for NCB officers
- training courses for personnel involved in combating traffic in psychotropic substances

Interpol has also produced a number of training aids, including a film on currency counterfeiting, a guide for law-enforcement officers on illicit drug traffic, an inventory of police training films produced in member countries, a slide teaching program on drugs and a teaching program on illicit drug traffic for use in police training colleges.

Travel and maintenance grants are awarded every year to police officers from member states to enable them to attend training courses at the General Secretariat or symposia on specific subjects. In 1983 and 1984 a total of 40 grants were awarded to participants at the training seminars for NCB officers.

Meetings and Conferences

Representatives of member states meet to discuss cooperation matters specific to a particular continent or region, or to discuss certain types of crime, at continental and other meetings, regional conferences, regional meetings of heads of national drug services, etc.

Experiences and technical information are shared at symposia organized by Interpol on specific subjects (training, forensic science, drugs, electronic data processing, organized crime, crime prevention, hostage-taking, international fraud, theft of cultural property, etc.). Police officers and experts on the subject under discussion participate in these symposia.

Interpol's Priorities

Cooperation in Combating International Crime

Certain types of international crime require special attention by Interpol.

- *Crimes of violence* against persons may, if particularly serious, lead the offenders concerned to try to take refuge by fleeing to a different country; they may also be committed by international criminal organizations (e.g., kidnappings for ransom and bombings).
- *Unlawful interference with international civil aviation* is defined in the 1970 Hague Convention and the 1971 Montreal Convention. In 1970, 1977, 1978 and 1982, the Interpol General Assembly adopted resolutions recommending measures designed to prevent offenses against civil aviation and to ensure that offenders could be brought to justice. The organization has shared and circulated information about security measures, detection devices and procedures designed to afford better protection to aircraft and ground installations.
- *Many thefts are committed to supply international traffickers dealing with cultural property, freight, vehicles, airline tickets,* etc. This type of offense often involves expert criminals belonging to gangs with worldwide structures. Interpol has a special index devoted to stolen works of art, and the General Secretariat issues, *inter alia,* a special bulletin on the "12 most wanted works of art," which is intended for the appropriate national departments and designed to draw the attention of the general public and the art world (antiques dealers, art galleries, etc.) to the problem. A working party is currently studying ways of computerizing data on stolen works of art and will make proposals to member states when its work is completed.
- *White-collar crime* is a very complex international problem that can result in enormous losses. The offenders involved in this type of crime often have an extensive knowledge of both national and international laws and regulations on economic and financial matters and are familiar with sophisticated techniques such as electronic data processing.
- *Criminals engage in financial operations* either to commit a further offense (e.g., a drug deal) or to invest the proceeds of their illegal activities. Interpol and a number of other international organizations (the United Nations, the Customs Cooperation Council, the Council of Europe, etc.) have been concentrating on this line of approach as a means of combating organized crime (with particular reference to large-scale trafficking operations). In particular, Interpol's General Assembly adopted a resolution in 1983 setting up a special group to concentrate on questions relating to illicitly obtained financial assets (the FOPAC Group).

In addition to analyzing information for operational purposes to identify money-laundering operations, the group is also responsible for studying techniques that can then be made available to police forces in member states to assist them in identifying, freezing and confiscating illegally obtained financial assets. In particular, the group has:

- published the *Financial Assets Encyclopaedia,* giving details of national laws, allowing the police access to financial information and describing the procedures to be followed for requesting and obtaining such information
- drafted and circulated model legislation that, if enacted, would give the police an optimal legal instrument to assist in detecting, tracing and seizing illicitly obtained funds
- developed a training course on financial investigations

Currency counterfeiting is a typical example of crime with international ramifications. The General Secretariat is the central international information office under terms of Article 15 of the 1929 Convention on the Suppression of Counterfeiting. It has a laboratory that examines suspect banknotes submitted by member states and that studied 748 notes as well as 29 checks in 1985.

In application of the 1929 Convention, Interpol organizes international conferences on counterfeit currency at which all aspects of prevention and detection can be discussed.

Also under the provisions of the 1929 Convention on the Suppression of Counterfeiting, Interpol publishes the review *Counterfeits and Forgeries,* edited by the secretary general. This professional journal appears every month and is available to NCBs, law-enforcement services, banks and other official institutions combating currency counterfeiting. It is published in Arabic, English, French, German and Spanish and appears in two parts. Part One contains particulars of the different types of counterfeiting, while Part Two contains descriptions of genuine currency and travelers checks. Subscriptions to Part One, which contains confidential information, must be authorized by the secretary general.

Other types of counterfeit and forged documents, such as various means of payment and identity and travel documents, are also examined at the General Secretariat.

There can be no doubt about the international ramifications of *illicit drug trafficking*. The many different operations, between the harvesting of the basic crop and the final retailing to addicts, may each take place in a different country, and it is not unusual for five to 10 Interpol member states to be involved in a single investigation.

International cooperation on illicit drug trafficking cases can achieve results in two spheres. In the first place it can lead to the pinpointing of trafficking routes, to the collation of information about types and quantities of drugs seized and the circumstances in which the seizures occurred and to the identification of the people concerned. Second, such cooperation can build up a body of reference material on the processes used in the clandestine manufacture of drugs, on traffickers' modus operandi and on new drugs that have appeared on the market.

The Drugs Subdivision at the General Secretariat has a number of liaison officers who maintain close contact with national drug-enforcement services. Their activities are financed by a system of special contributions to the organization's budget. The liaison officers also organize meetings to enable police officers from different member states involved in the same investigation to share information and to decide on a common strategy when necessary. The subdivision prepares and circulates documents to NCBs, including a weekly drugs intelligence message giving details of the latest international cases reported to the General Secretariat, a statistical analysis monthly and annual reports. The studies and documents on drug-related problems that have been published include: ''The Use of Drugs and Psychotropic Substances Among Young People''; ''Use of Dogs to Detect Drugs''; ''Powers and Attitudes of Police with Regard to Young Drug Users''; ''Clandestine Drug Laboratories—Chemicals and Equipment''; and ''Liquid Hashish.''

International exploitation of prostitution is a general term that encompasses a variety of illicit practices covered by international conventions (e.g., traffic in human beings).

The International Terrorism Group

The International Terrorism Group came into being in January 1986 and serves as the focal point for all information concerning terrorist activity, compiling and analyzing data as available.

As one of its first tasks, the group developed a manual outlining what can be done using existing organizational methods, such as publication of:

- international lookouts
- wanted notices
- information of property, such as passports, vehicles and weapons
- other identifying information

In addition, the group organizes symposia on the subject and develops various means to enhance cooperation among other international groups and organizations.

Research and Studies

In addition to assistance with crime investigations, the organization also makes available to member states a whole range of legal and technical reference material. This material often is based on information supplied by the member states themselves, thus enabling all the countries to benefit from each other's experiences. Reference material and documentation are the responsibility of the Research and Studies Division, which has three subdivisions handling the various duties described below.

Reports are prepared, both in application of the program of activities approved by the General Assembly and to meet specific needs. Such reports may be legal studies on certain aspects of Interpol's operations or on specific types of crime discussed at working party meetings, examinations of Interpol's position in respect of legal and technical problems raised in the context of the work of other international organizations, replies to requests from NCBs, etc.

General reference material is selected, acquired and circulated. The division's international library comprises 5,000 volumes as well as various collections of studies, monographs, reports, records of meetings of international organizations, texts of national laws (especially those on extradition) and journals specializing in subjects of interest to the police, including 160 periodicals from 25 countries. The division publishes documents designed to assist national police forces with their research and also publishes volumes of international crime statistics based on information supplied by NCBs on standardized forms.

In 1985 the division responded to some 350 requests for information or material from departments or research workers in 65 member countries or from General Secretariat departments.

The *International Criminal Police Review,* a monthly professional journal that began life under the title *Sûreté publique internationale* in 1925 and that has existed in its current form since 1946, is published in the organization's four working languages (Arabic, English, French and Spanish). The secretary general is the editor of the *Review,* and the Research and Studies Division oversees its production. It specializes in articles on the legal and technical aspects of police work. Because of the confidential nature of its material, circulation of the *Review* is restricted to 6,000 copies supplied essentially to law-enforcement agents, members of the judiciary and legal experts.

Scope of Interpol's Activities

The papers, reports and international symposia prepared and organized by Interpol can be classified under various headings:

- *National and international aspects of crime:* These include organized crime, hostage-taking, large-scale trafficking, international fraud, interference with civil aviation, international exploitation of prostitution, etc.
- *Crime prevention:* Certain types of crime lend them-

VOLUME OF INTERPOL RADIO TRAFFIC
(in number of messages)

635,000

246,233

112,765

43,726

1956   1966   1976   1985

POLICE CASES AND INFORMATION HANDLED BY THE GENERAL SECRETARIAT

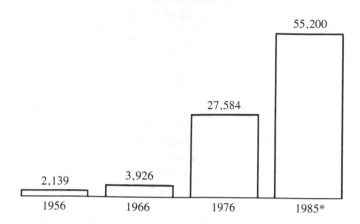

55,200

27,584

2,139   3,926

1956   1966   1976   1985*

The true figure for 1985 is in fact higher than the one given as, for the offenses against persons and property (other than economic and financial crime and drug trafficking), the 1985 figure includes only cases and information that were "new" in relation to the previous years.

CRIMINAL RECORDS AT THE GENERAL SECRETARIAT
(number of index cards)

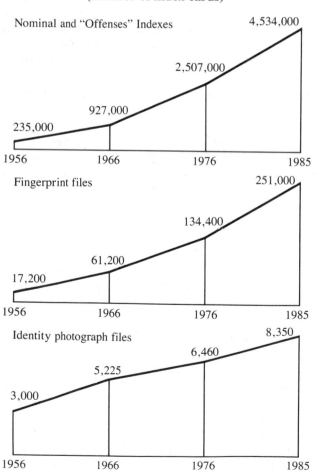

Nominal and "Offenses" Indexes

4,534,000

2,507,000

927,000

235,000

1956   1966   1976   1985

Fingerprint files

251,000

134,400

61,200

17,200

1956   1966   1976   1985

Identity photograph files

8,350

6,460

5,225

3,000

1956   1966   1976   1985

IDENTIFICATION AND NOTICES

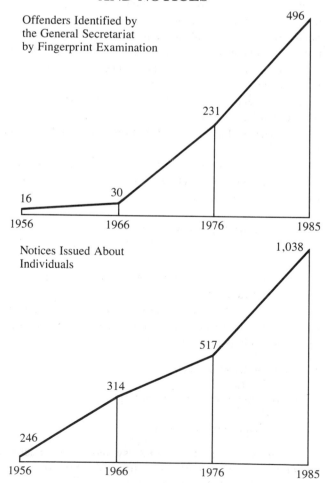

Offenders Identified by the General Secretariat by Fingerprint Examination

496

231

16   30

1956   1966   1976   1985

Notices Issued About Individuals

1,038

517

314

246

1956   1966   1976   1985

selves more easily than others to prevention programs and consequently have been the subject of detailed studies and concrete recommendations on such subjects as juvenile delinquency, aircraft hijacking and traffic in human beings. Detailed technical studies have also been produced (e.g., on the protection of taxi drivers from attack, safeguarding museums, theft of cultural property and vehicles, and protection of banks and financial establishments, cash transporters, pharmacies, etc.).

- *Human rights:* Interpol has collaborated with the United Nations in this area. In 1965, a document titled *Standard Minimum Rules for the Treatment of Prisoners* and in 1980 a *Code of Conduct for Law-Enforcement Officials* were distributed to all the NCBs. Furthermore, in 1982 the General Assembly approved the establishment of a Supervisory Board, as provided for in the "Rules on International Police Co-operation and on the Internal Control of Interpol's Archives" and in the exchange of letters appended to the headquarters agreement between the organization and the French government. The board's tasks have been laid down as follows: "The Supervisory Board shall verify that personal information contained in the archives is: (a) obtained and processed in accordance with the provisions of the organization's Constitution and the interpretation thereof given by the appropriate organs of the organization; (b) recorded for specific purposes and not used in any way that is incompatible with those purposes; (c) accurate; (d) kept for a limited period in accordance with the conditions laid down by the organization." The board has five members: one appointed by Interpol, one appointed by the headquarters country and a chairman chosen jointly by these two, plus a member of the organization's Executive Committee and an electronic data processing expert. The establishment of the Supervisory Board is an innovation in the field of international law, and it provides further evidence of the organization's desire to conduct its operations in accordance with Article 2 of its Constitution and in conformity with the Universal Declaration of Human Rights.
- *Criminal law and procedure:* As Interpol is one of the vital links in international judicial cooperation, it is naturally interested in these matters and has published a number of papers on such subjects as the powers and duties of the police, specific legislation covering certain offenses and the legal aspects of deportation and refusal of entry. Interpol also has a part to play in the preparatory phase of extradition; in fact, the European Convention on Extradition (1957) specifically provides for the use of Interpol channels to transmit requests for provisional detention with a view to subsequent extradition. In this connection, Interpol suggests amendments to national laws and provides member states with specific background material (e.g., the EXTRA/600 circulars, which describe the laws under which national police forces operate, and the texts of national extradition laws that are circulated to all NCBs).
- *Technical aids for the use of the police* (e.g., computers, aircraft, data safeguards): International symposia on forensic science and on ways of identifying persons and collecting evidence have been held since 1963. In addition, the organization has produced a number of publications for member states (such as an inventory of reference collections compiled by forensic science laboratories, an inventory of the research projects in progress in forensic science laboratories and an inventory of mass spectrograms).

Interpol in the International Community

As a truly international organization, Interpol has many contacts with various authorities and international institutions likely to be of assistance with any of its tasks.

Its long-standing relationship with the United Nations was formally recognized in 1971 with the adoption of a "Special Arrangement on Cooperation" between the U.N. Economic and Social Council and Interpol. Contacts are closest with three United Nations institutions: the Commission on Narcotic Drugs, the Center for Human Rights, and the Crime Prevention and Criminal Justice Branch.

Interpol cooperates on specific problems with other international bodies, such as the International Civil Aviation Organization (ICAO), the International Telecommunications Union (ITU), the United Nations Educational, Scientific and Cultural Organization (UNESCO) and the World Intellectual Property Organization (WIPO). In addition, Interpol has had observer status with the United Nations Commission for Trade and Development (UNCTAD) since 1984.

The organization also maintains close contact with the Customs Co-operation Council to make sure that police and customs officers can work together in spheres where such cooperation is essential (e.g., on preventing and combating illicit traffic of all types).

Interpol signed a cooperation agreement with the Council of Europe in 1959; since then it has worked with the council on crime problems and on the preparation of European conventions, many of which contain provisions stating that the signatories may use Interpol channels to forward judicial documents.

Interpol also cooperates with a number of other international bodies, including the Commonwealth Secretariat, the Panarab Organization for Social Defense and the Colombo Plan Bureau, and it participates in the activities of a number of nongovernmental organizations (e.g., the International Air Transport Association and the International Society of Criminology).

Relations with the headquarters country are governed by the headquarters agreement that came into force on February 14, 1984, having previously been approved by the organization's General Assembly in October 1982 and ratified by the French Parliament in 1983. This agreement replaces the 1972 headquarters agreement and widens the scope of the privileges and immunities granted to the organization so it can continue to develop smoothly.

Development of the Interpol Organization

1914: At the invitation of Prince Albert I of Monaco, jurists, lawyers and police officials from 14 nations and territories met in Monaco at the First International Criminal Police Congress to discuss improvements in arrest procedures; perfection of identification techniques; establishment of central international criminal records; and unification of extradition proceedings. The meeting was so successful that the attendees agreed to meet in Bucharest in 1916, but World War I erupted, so the meeting never took place.

1919: Colonel M. C. Van Houten, Royal Netherlands Police, unsuccessfully tried to convene a conference on police cooperation.

1920: French professor Donnedieu de Vabres voiced renewed interest in international police effort.

1923: Dr. Johannes Schober, president of the Vienna Police, convened the Second International Criminal Police Congress in Vienna, with 19 attendees. The meeting agreed to establish the International Criminal Police Commission, drew up a Constitution of 10 articles and agreed to carry on the goals of the Monaco Congress.

Vienna was selected as the site for the headquarters because:

1.   Austria agreed to house and finance.
2.   Vienna police were leaders in maintaining central records on international criminals.

From this came the Austrian influence during the early years. Austrian police chief Schober became president of the Executive Committee, and D. O. Dressler, a lawyer and chief of the Austrian Federal Police, was elected secretary general.

Dues were set at one Swiss franc for every 10,000 inhabitants. It was also established that a General Assembly would convene once a year.

1925: The Third General Assembly, held in Berlin, suggested that each country establish a central point of contact within their police structure. This was the forerunner of the National Central Bureau.

1927: Adopted resolution to establish NCBs.

1930: The General Assembly, held in Antwerp, began organizational independence by voting to elect ICPC Executive Committee members by majority vote rather than the automatic appointment of Austrian police officials.

Specialized departments were also established at headquarters:

1.   Central International Bureau—concerned with counterfeiting
2.   International Criminal Records Office
3.   Passport Forgery Bureau

1932: Dr. Schober died and was replaced by Austrian police commissioner Skubl.

1935: The International Radio Network was initiated.

1937: A total of 34 member countries.

1938: The last recorded General Assembly before World War II, in Bucharest.

In 1938 the Nazis deposed Skubl and replaced him with a Nazi, Steinhausl, who was taken from a German penitentiary and made chief of the Austrian police and thus president of the ICPC. Also in 1938 the free world countries stopped participating, and the ICPC ceased to exist.

1946: A group of individuals still interested in continuing the idea of international police cooperation met to reorganize the organization. Lt. Col. Floren E. Louwage, inspector general of Belgium State Security and former ICPC Executive Committee member, met with Harry Soderman, Swedish Criminal Institute; Werner Muller, Chief of the Swiss Federal Police; Louis Ducloux, director of the French Judicial Police; and Ronald Howe, assistant commissioner of Scotland Yard. Their efforts resulted in the 15th General Assembly session in Brussels, where 17 nations were represented.

France was chosen as the most suitable location to headquarter the organization because it provided:

1.   central location
2.   superior communications facilities
3.   pivotal location for international criminals
4.   French acceptance of financial and other obligations as host nation

Also, in reorganizing, the ICPC established the presidency as an elective office and an Executive Committee consisting of a president, the secretary general and three vice presidents. Ducloux, as host country representative, was named secretary general. Louwage was elected president, with Howe, Muller and Soderman as vice presidents.

1948: ''Interpol'' was adopted as the official designation by the commission.

1949: The U.N. gave the ICPC consultative status.

1953: A total of 27 member countries.

1955: A total of 50 member countries.

1955: The U.N. Commission on Narcotic Drugs encouraged use of ICPC channels for exchange of information on illicit drug traffic.

1956: The 25th General Assembly session, in Vienna. The name was changed to ICPO-Interpol to give permanence and recognition.

1956: NCBs were officially recognized by Constitution Articles 32 and 33.

The organization became autonomous by assessing dues from member countries and relying on investments as the main means of support.

A total of 57 member countries.

1959: Council of Europe recognized Interpol as having constitutive status equal to a U.N. specialized agency, thus allowing cooperation and information exchange.

1960: The General Assembly met for first time outside Europe, in Washington, D.C.

1961: The Counterfeit Currency Group, formerly in The Hague, was moved to the General Secretariat.

1963: The first regional conference was held in Monrovia, Liberia.

1965: The General Assembly set forth the policies for operation of the NCBs.

1966: ICPO headquarters were moved from Paris to St. Cloud.

1967: A total of 100 member countries.

1971: The U.N. Economic and Social Council replaced Interpol's consultative status by granting it status as an intergovernmental organization, which, in essence, clarified Interpol's legal status as an international organization and allowed two-way exchange of information, documentation, consultation, technical cooperation, representations at General Assembly Sessions by U.S. official observers, and written statements and proposals to both groups' agendas.

1972: A Headquarters agreement with the French Parliament recognized the ICPO as an international organization.

1975: A total of 120 member nations.

1977: A total of 126 member nations.

1982: A headquarters agreement with the French government granted security and maintenance of archives.

1984: The first U.S. president was elected: John R. Simpson.

1985: The first non-French secretary general was appointed since reorganization in 1946: Raymond E. Kendall, appointed as acting secretary general in February 1985.

1985: A total of 138 member nations.

1985: The organization decided to transfer the General Secretariat from St. Cloud to Lyons, planning to complete the operation by 1988.

1986: The Supervisory Board for the Internal Control of Interpol's Archives held its first meeting in January.

List of Interpol Members

Algeria	China	Guinea*	Lebanon
Angola	Colombia	Guyana	Lesotho
Argentina	Congo	Haiti	Liberia
Australia	Costa Rica	Honduras	Libya
Austria	Cuba*	Hungary	Liechtenstein
Bahamas	Cyprus	Iceland	Luxembourg
Bahrain	Denmark	India	Madagascar
Bangladesh	Djibouti	Indonesia	Malawi
Barbados	Dominica	Iran	Malaysia
Belgium	Dominican Republic	Iraq	Maldives
Benin	Ecuador	Ireland	Mali
Bolivia	Egypt	Israel	Malta
Botswana	Equatorial Guinea	Italy	Mauritania
Brunei	Ethiopia	Ivory Coast	Mauritius
Burkina Faso	Fiji	Jamaica	Mexico
Burma	Finland	Japan	Monaco
Burundi	France	Jordan	Morocco
Cameroon	Gabon	Kampuchea*	Nauru
Canada	Germany, West	Kenya	Nepal
Central African Republic	Ghana	Korea, South	Netherlands
Chad	Greece	Kuwait	Netherlands Antilles
Chile	Guatemala	Laos*	New Zealand

*Countries that have ceased to be functioning members.

List of Interpol Members (*continued*)

Nicaragua	Rwanda	Switzerland	Venezuela
Niger	Saint Lucia	Syria	Yemen, Arab Republic of
Nigeria	Saudi Arabia	Tanzania	Yugoslavia
Norway	Senegal	Thailand	Zaire
Oman	Seychelles	Togo	Zambia
Pakistan	Sierra Leone	Tonga	Zimbabwe
Panama	Singapore	Trinidad and Tobago	
Papua New Guinea	Somalia	Tunisia	
Paraguay	Spain	Turkey	*United Kingdom NCB*
Peru	Sri Lanka	Uganda	*Subbureaus:*
Philippines	Sudan	United Arab Emirates	Bermuda
Portugal	Suriname	United Kingdom	Cayman Islands
Qatar	Swaziland	United States	Gibraltar
Romania	Sweden	Uruguay	Hong Kong

*Countries that have ceased to be functioning members.

APPENDIX II: WORLD POLICE DIRECTORY

Algeria

Direction Générale de la Sûreté Nationale, Place Mohammed Ouanouri, Alger

Commandement da la Gendarmerie, Alger

Argentina

Jefatura de Policía Federal, Moreno 1550, Buenos Aires (37-8844)

Policía de la Provincia de Buenos Aires, A Sabattini 56, Caseros, Buenos Aires (750-0948)

Escuela Superior de Policía "General de Brigada Cesario A Cardozo," Buenos Aires (99-1685)

Escuela de Suboficiales de Policía "Comisario General Alberto Villar," Cavia 3302, Buenos Aires (72-5475)

Escuela de Cadetes de Policía "Coronel Ramon L Falcon," Corvalan 3698, Buenos Aires (601-1308)

Comisaria de Vigilancia y Custodia de la Residencia Presidencial, Libertador San Martin, Buenos Aires (791-8494)

Dirección General de Proteccion Federal, Belgrano 1547, Buenos Aires, (38-1046)

Dirección General de Inteligencia, Bartolome Mitre 2815, Buenos Aires (89-0933)

Australia

Australian Capital Territory

AFP Headquarters, London Crescent, Canberra, ACT (49 7444)

Regional offices:

Campbell Street, Sydney, NSW (2-0966)

21 MacLachlan Road, Fortitude Valley, Brisbane, QLD (52-8144)

214 Greenhill Road, Eastwood, Adelaide, SA (272-2377)

Magnet Court, Sandy Bay, Hobart, Tasmania (23-6508)

43 Mackenzie Road, Melbourne, VIC (662-2400)

214 St George Terrace, Perth, WA (22-4788)

New South Wales

Commissioner's Office, 14 College Street, Sydney (2-0966)

Criminal Investigation Branch, Campbell Street, Sydney (2-0966)

Traffic Branch, 52 Rothschild Avenue, Rosebery, Sydney (2-0966)

NSW Police Academy, 749 Bourke Road, Redfern, Sydney (2-0966)

Northern Territory

Divisional Headquarters, 18 Mitchell Street, Darwin (81-5555)

District Headquarters, Parsons Street, Alice Springs (52-2777)

Queensland

QLD Police Headquarters, 43 Makerston Road, Brisbane (32-0431)

Criminal Investigation Branch, 366 Upper Roma Street, Brisbane (32-0431)

Traffic Branch, 2 Herschel Road, Brisbane (32-0431)

South Australia

SA Police Headquarters, 1 Angas Road, Adelaide (87-0333)

Criminal Investigation Branch, 1 Angas Road, Adelaide (87-0333)

SA Police Barracks, Thebarton, Adelaide (87-0333)

SA Police Academy, Fort Largs, Adelaide (248-1111)

Tasmania

Burnie Headquarters, Wilson Street, Burnie (31-1444)

Hobart Headquarters, Liverpool Street, Hobart (38-1101)

Launceston Headquarters, 381 Main Road, Glenorchy (72-6633)

Rokeby Police Training Academy, Hobart (47-7100)

Victoria

Police Headquarters, Russell Street, Melbourne (662-0911)
Traffic Control Branch, 20 Dawson Street, Brunswick
City Traffic Police, Elizabeth Street, Melbourne Mounted Branch, St. Hilda Road, Melbourne (62-3078)
Police Academy, View Mount Road, Glen Waverley (566-9566)
Detective Training School, 193 Spring Street, Melbourne
Police Cadet Academy, Spencer Street, Melbourne
Police Officers' College, 260 Domain Road, Sunbury (26-5684)

Western Australia

WA Police Headquarters, East Perth (25-0121)

Austria

Generalinspektorat der Sicherheitswache, Schottenring 7–9, 1010 Wien (31-31-0)
Kriminalbeamteninspektorat, Schottenring 7–9, Wien (31-31-0)
Bundespolizeidirektion Wien, Schottenring 7–9, Wien (31-31-0)
Bundespolizeidirektion Wien-Schwechat, Wienerstrasse 13, Schwechat (covers Vienna Airport) (77-76-55)

Bahamas

Police Headquarters, P.O. Box N458, Nassau (2-4444)
Criminal Investigation Department, P.O. Box N3020, Nassau (2-2311)
Police Marine Division Headquarters, Nassau (2-2383)
Royal Bahamas Police College, Nassau (5-8851)

Bahrain

Public Security Headquarters, P.O. Box 13, Manama (253281)
Directorate of Criminal Investigation, Manama (254021)

Bangladesh

Bangladesh Police Directorate, Dacca (404003)
Department of National Security Intelligence, Dacca (402203)
Department of Anticorruption, Dacca (244868)

Barbados

Police Department Headquarters, Bridgetown (426-0800)
Regional Police Training Center, Seawell (428-7125)

Belgium

Commissariat de Police, 30 rue du Marché au Charbon, Bruxelles (517 96 11)
Police Judiciaire, 6 boulevard Anspach, Bruxelles (517 98 33)
Service Technique de la Circulation, 30 rue du Marché au Charbon, Bruxelles (517 98 33)

Centre d'Instruction de la Police, 30 rue du Marché au Charbon, Bruxelles (517 98 51)
Commandement et État-Major de la Gendarmerie, 47 rue Fritz Toussaint, Bruxelles (649 00 00)
Légion Mobile, 292 boulevard Général Jacques, Bruxelles (762 31 50)
Détachement Judiciaire Interpol, Palais de Justice, Bruxelles (512 58 20)
Centre Logistique de la Gendarmerie, 31 rue Baron G van Hamme, Bruxelles (376 51 70)
École Royale de la Gendarmerie, avenue 2ème Régiment de Lanciers, Bruxelles (762 31 50)

Belize

Police Headquarters, Queen Street, Belize City (2222)

Benin

Direction de la Sûreté Nationale, Cotonou

Bermuda

Police Headquarters, Prospect Dev, Hamilton (5-0011)
Police Training School, Hamilton (5-0011)

Botswana

Police Headquarters, Post Bag 0012, Gaborone (55232)
Criminal Investigation Department, P.O. Box 1082, Gaborone (53215)
Special Support Group, P.O. Box 10017, Gaborone (56476)
Police Training College, P.O. Box 516, Gaborone (56297)

Brazil

Centro de Policia Especializada, SAI/Sudoeste L-02, Brasília, DF (233-1500)
Comando Geral da Policia Militar do Distrito Federal, Brasília, DF (243-5816)
Policia Rodoviaria Federal, Rua 24 de Maio 208-10°, São Paulo, SP (37-4460)
Policia do Cais do Porto, Rua Sacadura Cabral 120, Rio de Janeiro, RJ (243-3971)

Brunei

Ibu Pejabat Polis Gadong (Police HQ Gadong), Bandar Seri Begawan (3901)
Pusat Latehan Polis (Police Training Center), Manggis (271)

Burma

Director General of the People's Police, Old Secretariat, Rangoon

Burundi

Police Nationale, Boîte Postale 417, Bujumbura
Gendarmerie du Burundi, Bujumbura

Cameroon

Delegation Générale de la Sûreté Nationale, Boîte Postale 530, Yaoundé

École Nationale de Police, Yaoundé

Canada

RCMP HQ Division, 1200 Alta Vista Drive, Ottawa, Ont. (993-1928)

RCMP Depot Division, Box 6500, Regina, Sask. (569-5760)

Ontario Provincial Police, Eagleson Side Road, Ottawa, Ont. (828-9171)

Quebec Police Force/Force de Police du Québec, 4225 Dorchester Ouest, Montréal, Qué. (283-6000)

Cape Verde

Comando da Policia, Rua Guerra Mendes, Praia (395)

Departmento de Seguranca Nacional, Rua Guerra Mendes, Praia (393)

Cayman Islands

Police Headquarters, P.O. Box 909, George Town (94222)

Central African Republic

Direction des Services de Sûreté Nationale, Bangui

Direction des Services de Police Judiciaire, Bangui

Chad

Direction de la Sûreté Nationale, Boîte Postale 446, N'djaména

Chile

Dirección General de los Carabineros de Chile, Plaza Bulnes 1196, Santiago (8-2761)

Centro de Especialidades de Instrucción de los Carabineros, Avenida Pedro Aguirre Cerda 6655, Santiago (57-6171)

Escuela de Carabineros, Avenida Antonio Varas 1842, Santiago (225-7814)

Escuela de Suboficiales de Carabineros, Rodrigo de Araya 2601, Santiago (46-2007)

Instituto Superior de Carabineros, Charles Hamilton 9308, Santiago (220-1585)

Dirección General de Investigaciones de Chile, General Mackenna 1314, Santiago (8-2211)

Escuela de Investigaciones, Sargento Candelaria 1966, Santiago (225-4314)

Dirección General de la Gendarmeria de Chile, Rosas 1274, Santiago (8-2155)

Escuela de Gendarmeria, Artemio Gutierrez 1153, Santiago (5-3438)

China

Ministry of Public Security, Dong Changan Jie, Beijing 55-3871

Colombia

Dirección General de la Policía Nacional, Carrera 146-05, Bogotá (43-69-34)

Policía Judicial, Carrera 15-10-41, Bogotá (43-95-22)

Escuela de Suboficiales de Policía "Jimenez de Quesada," El Muna Carretera a Sibate, Bogotá (66-41-94)

Escuela de Cadetes de Policía "General Santander," Autopista Sur CL 42, Bogotá (70-31-11)

Congo

Direction de la Sûreté Nationale, Boîte Postale 2004, Brazzaville

Costa Rica

Dirección de Inteligencia y Seguridad, Apartado Postal 5/203, Zapote, San José

Cuba

Policía Nacional Revolucionaria, Calle de Dragones y Zulueta, La Habana

Cyprus

Cyprus Police Headquarters, Nicosia (403535)

Police Training School, Nicosia (403351)

Denmark

Rigspolitichefen, Københavns Vej 14, 2500 København (14-14-48)

Direktoratet for Kriminalforsorgen, Klarebodgade 1, København (13-57-83)

Kriminalforsorgens Personaleskole, Faengselsvej 1, Albertslund, København (64-43-00)

Dominica

Police Headquarters, King George V Street, Roseau (2222)

Police Training School, Morne Bruce (2050)

Dominican Republic

Cuartel General de la Policía Nacional, Palacio de la Policía Nacional, L Navarro, Santo Domingo (682-2151)

Departamento de Investigaciones Criminales, Santo Domingo (689-9241)

Escuadron contra Homicidios, P Henriquez Urena, Santo Domingo (682-2151)

Departamento de Ametralladoras, Santo Domingo (689-9355)

Escuadron de Caballeria, Independencia, Santo Domingo (533-1762)

Servicio Secreto, Santo Domingo (682-0274)

Ecuador

Comandancia General de la Policía Nacional, Cuenca y Mideros, Quito (21-00-52)

Policía Municipal, Pereira 103, Quito (51-15-87)

Policía Militar Ministerial, Exposicion 208, Quito (21-10-70)

Instituto Nacional de Policía, Avenida de la Prensa, Quito (24-00-45)

Escuela de Formacion de Oficiales de Policía, Avenida de la Prensa, Quito (24-05-45)

Escuela de Formacion de Tropa de Policía, Pusunqui (53-28-04)

El Salvador

Dirección General de la Policía Nacional, 6a Calle Oeste, San Salvador (22-44-22)

Dirección de la Policía Municipal, 91 Calle Oriente 320, San Salvador (26-24-52)

Dirección General de la Guardia Nacional, Carretera Troncal del Norte, San Salvador (25-32-77)

Dirección General de la Policiia de la Hacienda, Calle Concepcion, San Salvador (26-85-86)

Escuela de Policía Nacional, Nueva San Salvador (28-12-42)

Ethiopia

Police Headquarters, P.O. Box 199, Addis Ababa

Police School, Addis Ababa

Falkland Islands

Falkland Islands Police Office, Port Stanley (95)

Fiji

Royal Fiji Police Headquarters, MacArthur Street, Suva (312-999)

Finland

Poliisilaitos Helsingin, Kasarmikatu 25, Helsinki (176831)

Keskusrikospoliisi, Box 152, 00121 Helsinki (16271)

France

Direction Générale de la Police Nationale, 11 rue des Saussaies, 75800 Paris (266-28-30)

Cantonnement des CRS, Bois de Vincennes, 75012 Paris (368-80-78)

École Nationale Supérieure de Police, 8 avenue Gambetta, St-Cyr-au-Mont-d'Or (Lyon) (864-02-88)

École Nationale de Police, chemin Calquet, Toulouse (49-36-65)

Centre de Formation des Personnels de Police, Fort Montluc, rue Jeanne Hachette, Lyon 3 (853-34-51)

Sécretariat National de la Police de l'Air et des Frontières, rue Commandant Becker, Marseille (91-90-40)

Préfecture de Police de la Ville de Paris, 9 boulevard des Palais, 75195 Paris (260-33-22)

Direction Nationale de la Gendarmerie Nationale, 35 rue Saint-Didier, 95016 Paris (505-14-47)

École des Officiers de la Gendarmerie Nationale, Quartier Augereau, Mélun (452-22-90)

École Préparatoire de Gendarmerie, Caserne Damremont, avenue de la République, Chaumont (15-00)

Gabon

Direction de la Sûreté Nationale, Boîte Postale 2233, Libreville

Gambia

Police Force Headquarters, Banjul (210)

Germany, West

Bundeskriminalamt, Thaerstrasse 11, Wiesbaden (55-1)

Grenzschutzkommando West, 1 Willemombler 80, Bonn (6-18-1)

Ghana

Police Headquarters, P.O. Box 116, Accra (28112)

Special Branch, P.O. Box 4368, Accra (75561)

Police Depot and Officers' Training College, P.O. Box 740, Accra (28744)

Forensic Science Laboratory, Accra (76647)

Greece

Dieythynsis Astynomias, Athine (35 7401)

Guatemala

Cuerpo de Detectives, 14 Calle 6-77 Zona 1, Ciudad de Guatemala

Guinea

Direction des Services de Sécurité, Conakry

Haiti

Département de Police de Port-au-Prince, Champ de Mars, Port-au-Prince (2-5555)

Poste de Police des Volontaires de la Sécurité Nationale Thomassin, Port-au-Prince (7-1324)

Honduras

Jefatura de la Policía Nacional, Tegucigalpa Cuerpo Especial de Seguridad, Cuartel General Casamata, Tegucigalpa

Hungary

Belugyminiszterium, 2-4 Jozsef Attila utca, Budapest V

Iceland

Logreglustod, Huerfisgata 115, Reykjavik

India

Superintendent of Security Police, Delhi (387390)

Security Police Barracks, Ashoka, Delhi (43131)

Central Bureau of Investigation, Sadar Patel Bhavan, Parliament Street, Delhi (225470)

Directorate General of Central Reserve Police Force, R K Puram, Delhi (226575)

President's Police Guard, Delhi (375321)

Delhi Armed Police, Kingsway Camp, Delhi (375321)

Directorate General of Border Security Forces, Delhi (386785)

Bureau of Police Research and Development, Curzon Road Barracks, Kasturba Gandhi MRG, New Delhi (372050)

Indonesia

Korps Perairan & Udara Kepolisian, Jin Senjaya 1/1, Jakarta (74183)

Iraq

Directorate General of Police, Baghdad

Ireland

Garda Siochana Headquarters, Phoenix Road, Dublin 8 (77-11-56)

Metropolitan Area HQ, Lower Castle Yard, Dublin 2 (78-11-22)

Garda Training Centre, Templemore, Co. Tipperary (3-13-83)

Israel

Israel Police Headquarters, Sheikh Jerah Quarter, Jerusalem (28-17-11)

Central Training Depot, Shefar'am, Haifa (72-57-44)

Investigation of Nazi Crimes Department, 14 Havakevet Street, Tel Aviv (62-52-11)

Institute for Forensic Medicine, Yagur, Haifa (93-35-34)

Italy

Comando Raggruppamento PS, 30 via Statilia, Roma (77-62-92)

Accademia della Polizia de Stato, 3 via Piero della Francesca, Roma (39-47-41)

Battaglione Allievi Agenti di PS, 6 via dell'Ospedale, Reggio nell'Emilia (3-92-34)

Scuola Allievi Agenti di PS, 402 corso Acqui, Allessandria (34-21-35)

Scuola Allievi Agenti di PS, 46 viale Druso, Bolzano 4 54 90 Scuola Allievi Agenti di PS, 8 via Eleuterio Ruggiero, Caserta (30-10-60)

Scuola Allievi Agenti di PS, 11 viale Malta, Piacenza (2-12-36)

Scuola Allievi Agenti di PS, 11 via della Chiesa, Trieste (5-55-31)

Scuola di Polizia Giudiziaria, 3 via Vittorio Veneto, Brescia (5-10-04)

Scuola Tecnica di Polizia, 3 via Castro Pretorio, Roma (495-19-71)

Centro Addestramento Polfer, 12 via del Chiu, Bologna (38-24-81)

Centro Addestramento Formazione Conducenti Automotoveicoli, 2 piazzale d'Italia, Foggia (2-21-24)

Comando VV UU, 4 via della Consolazione, Roma (678-07-41)

Scuola Allievi Vigili Urbani, via Fedro, Milano (846-33-53)

Comando Generale dell'Arma di Carabinieri, 45 viale Romania, Roma (8-52-91)

Comando Carabinieri per l'Aeronautica Militare, 4 viale dell'Universita, Roma (49-86)

Comando Carabinieri per la Marina Militare, piazza della Marina, Roma (36-80)

Battaglione Paracadutisti CC, 133 via dell'Ardenza, Livorno (50-23-93)

Scuola Allievi Carabinieri, 80 via Colle delle Api, Campobasso (6-22-44)

Scuola Allievi Carabinieri, 3 via Legnano, Roma (38-61-42)

Scuola Sottufficiali Carabinieri, Caserma G Mamelli, 1 piazza della Stazione, Firenze (29-83-51)

Scuola Ufficiali Carabinieri, 511 via Aurelia, Roma (62-00-31)

Comando Generale della GdiF, 178 via Sicilia, Roma (4-73-71)

Comando Scuole della GdiF, 51 via XXI Aprile, Roma (42-07-82)

Accademia della GdiF, 20 piazza Armellini, Roma (42-19-11)

Scuola Sottufficiali GdiF, 18 via Fiamme Gialle, Roma (562-38-00)

Scuola Alpina GdiF, via Fiamme Gialle, Predazzo (5-16-61)

Scuola Nautica GdiF, 216 lungomare Caboto, Gaeta (47-00-05)

I Battaglione Allievi GdiF, 6 via Battisti, Cuneo (5-59-15)

II Battaglione Allievi GdiF, via Manzoni, Portoferraio (9-23-82)

III Battaglione Allievi GdiF, via Giolitti, Mondovi (4-74-24)

Ivory Coast

Direction Générale de la Sûreté Nationale, Boîte Postale 1384, Abidjan (32-00-22)

Préfecture de Police, Abidjan (32-17-13)
École Nationale de Police, Abidjan (44-17-51)
Gendarmerie Nationale, Abidjan (32-02-88)
École de Gendarmerie, Abidjan (44-34-46)

Jamaica

Police Headquarters, 105 Old Hope Road, Kingston 6 (937-5611)
Police Marine Division, Newport (933-9728)
Police Training School, Port Royal (938-7345)
Detective Training School, 16 Lower Ellerton Road, Kingston 16 (928-1108)
Forensic Laboratory, 19 West Avenue, Kingston 4 (932-6979)

Japan

National Police Agency, 1–2 Kasumigaseki 2-chome, Chiyoda-ku, Tokyo (581-0141)
Imperial Guard HQ (Kougu Keisatsu Honbu), 3 Chiyoda 1-chome, Chiyoda-ku, Tokyo (231-3115)
Tokyo Metropolitan Police Department Headquarters (Honbu), 2–9 Nishi Shinbashi 1-chome, Minato-ku, Tokyo (581-4321)
National Research Institute of Police Science, 6 Sanbancho, Chiyoda-ku, Tokyo (261-9986)
National Police Academy, 1–2 Kasumigaseki 2-chome, Chiyoda ku, Tokyo (581-0141)

Jordan

Directorate of Public Security, P.O. Box 935, Amman

Kenya

Police Headquarters, P.O. Box 30083, Nairobi (33-51-24)
Police Training School, Nairobi (82-22-33)

Kiribati

Police Headquarters, Betio, Tarawa

Korea, South

National Police Headquarters, C.P.O. Box 8948, Seoul

Kuwait

Kuwait Public Security Department, Kuwait (817772)
Police Academy, Kuwait (811811)
State Security Department, Kuwait (439011)

Laos

Directorate General of the National Police, Vientiane

Lesotho

Police Headquarters, Box MS 13, Maseru (23061)
Police Training College, Box MS 659, Maseru (22396)
National Security Service, Maseru (23061)

Liberia

Liberian National Police Force, Capitol Hill, Monrovia

Libya

Security Affairs Department, P.O. Box 2322, Tripoli

Liechtenstein

Fürstlich Liechtensteinisches Sicherheitkorps, Vadus (2-17-71)

Luxembourg

Commandement Central de Police, 60 rue Glesener, Luxembourg (49-49-49)
Commandement de la Gendarmerie, 11 rue Auguste Lumière, Luxembourg (48-80-11)

Malawi

Police Headquarters, Post Bag 305, Lilongwe (733-999)
Police College and Reserve Company, Lilongwe (522-439)
Police Training School, Box 5299, Limbe (650-314)

Malaysia

Polis Jabatan Diraja Malaysia, Jalan Bukit Aman, Kuala Lumpur (03-87-771; telex MA30469)
Biro Siasatan Negara, Kuala Lumpur (03-442-906)

Mali

Direction des Services des Sécurité, Boîte Postale 234, Bamako

Malta

General Headquarters, Floriana (24002)
Criminal Investigation Department, Valletta (23241)
Traffic Branch, Floriana (24002)
Water Police, New Port, Marsa (27105)

Mauritania

Direction de la Sûreté Nationale, BP 107, Nouakchott

Mauritius

Mauritius Police Force HQ, Port Louis

Mexico

Dirección General de Policía y Transito del Distrito Federal, Chimalpopoca y 20 de Noviembre, Mexico, DF (5-88-51-00)
Policía Judicial Federal, Niños Héroes y Dr. Liceaga, Mexico, DF (7-61-06-48)
Batallón de Granaderos C. Robelo y Sur 103, Mexico, DF (5-42-62-19)

Policía Auxiliar Privada, Avenida Insurgentes Norte 202, Mexico, DF (5-47-84-39)

Dirección de la Academia de Policía, C. Robelo y Sur 113, Mexico, DF (5-42-61-81)

Policía Bancaria y Industrial, Cruz Verde y Avenida del Canal, Mexico, DF (5-68-45-99)

Monaco

Direction de la Sûreté Publique, rue Raymond Suffren, Monaco-Ville

Montserrat

Police Headquarters, Plymouth (2555)

Morocco

Direction Générale de la Sûreté Nationale, Cité Mabella 38 Rabat (55765)

Préfecture de Police de Rabat-Salé, Rabat (71631)

Gendarmerie Royale Marocaine, avenue Kennedy, Rabat (55432)

Nepal

Police Headquarters, Post Box 407, Kathmandu

Netherlands

Rijkspolitie Districtsbureau, Sarphatistraat 110, Amsterdam (22-63-22)

Opleidingsschool Rijkspolitie, Arnhemseweg 348, Apeldoorn (33-09-03)

Kaderschool Rijkspolitie, Arnhemseweg 346, Apeldoorn (33 09 59)

Gemeentepolitie Bureau, Elandsgracht 117, Amsterdam (559-91-11)

Gemeentepolitie Bureau, Haagseveer 23, Rotterdam (14-31-44)

Kon Marechaussee Brigade Amsterdam, R Kochplantsoen 35, Amsterdam (94-28-33)

Kon Marechaussee Brigade Schiphol, Lindberghstraat 34, Schiphol (94-28-33)

Kon Marechaussee Opleidingscentrum Koning Willem III, Frankenlaan 70, Apeldoorn (77-54-33)

Netherlands Antilles

Politie Curaçao, Fort Amsterdam, Willemstad (611222)

New Zealand

New Zealand Police Headquarters, Waring Taylor Street, Wellington 1 (723000; telex 3550)

Wellington District HQ, Johnston Street, Wellington 1 (723000)

Police College, Trentham, Upper Hutt (87755)

SAR Coordination Center, Dunedin (75716)

Niger

Direction de la Sûreté Nationale, Boîte Posatle 133, Niamey

Nigeria

Police Headquarters, Obalende, Lagos (664911)

Police College, Ikeja, Lagos (900561)

Norway

Oslo Politikammer, Gronlandsleiret 44, Oslo (66-90-50; telex 71428)

Politiets Overvakingstjeneste, Gronlandsleiret 44, Oslo (66-90-50)

Kriminalpolitisentralen, Stromsvegan 106, Oslo (66-40-00)

Utrykningspolitiet, Chr Krohgs Gaten 2, Oslo (11-02-55)

Politiskolen, Slemdalsvegen 5, Oslo (46-18-60)

Oman

Sultan of Oman's Police Headquarters, P.O. Box 2, Muscat, Qurum Roundabout (60-0009; telex 3377)

Pakistan

Central Police Office, Sind, Karachi (22-33-88)

Federal Investigation Agency, Isa Moulni Tamizuddin Khan Road, Karachi (55-12-85)

Recruit Training Center, Karachi (7-14-36)

Panama

Comandancia de la Guardia Nacional, Avenida 8a Sur, 23–61, Panama (22-1703)

Jefatura de Policía, Apartado Postal 1299, Panama (22-6990)

Academia de Policía, Panama (67-5985)

Academia de Capacitación Policial, Panama (22-9390)

There is a U.S. police division in the Panama Canal Zone. It comprises two districts (Balboa and Cristóbal) and three services (General Police, Detective and Traffic).

Papua New Guinea

PNG Constabulary Headquarters, P.O. Box 2085, Konedobu, Port Moresby (25-9222; telex 22113)

Criminal Investigation Branch, P.O. Box 6001, Boroko, Port Moresby (25-5555)

Police Training College, Bomana, Port Moresby (28-1022)

Police Barracks, Gordons Estate, Port Moresby (25-4044)

Paraguay

Policía de la Capital, El Paraguayo Independiente y Chile, Asunción (43-1125)

Colegio de Policía, Villa Policía, Nu Guazu (66-008)

Colegio Superior de Policía, 14 de Julio y Chile, Asunción (49-344)

Escuela de Sub-Oficiales de Policía, El Paraguayo Independiente y Chile, Asunción (49-008)

Batallon de Instruccion Policial, Yegros y 24 Portada, Asunción (72-956)

Jefatura de Policía Caminera, Oliva y Alberdi, Asunción (45-204)

Peru

Guardia Civil del Peru, Los Sauces 34, Lima

Guardia Republicana del Peru, Los Cibeles 150, Lima

Philippines

Philippine Constabulary HQ, Camp Crame, Quezon City (78-79-61)

PC Metropolitan Command HQ, 80 Lovely Road, Las Pinas, Manila (83-80-21)

PC Intelligence Service, Camp Crame, Quezon City (79-94-66)

PC Crime Laboratory, Manila (78-34-33)

Poland

Milicja Obywatelska — Komenda Glowna, 148–50 Pulawska, Warszawa (43-02-21)

Portugal

Comando Geral da PSP, Largo da Penha de Franca, Lisboa 1 (84-97-36)

Comando Geral do Servico de Transito da PSP, Rua de Santa Marta 61, Lisboa 2 (55-37-33)

Escola Pratica de Policia, Rua 1 de Maio 3, Lisboa 3 (64-09-26)

Comando Geral da PJ, Rua Gomes Freire, Lisboa 1 (53-31-31)

Servico Interpol, Rua Gomes Friere, Lisboa 1 (57-44-30)

Laboratorio da Policia Cientifica, Rua Joaquim Bonifacio 9, Lisboa 1 (53-11-12)

Comando Geral da GNR, Largo do Carmo, Lisboa 2 (36-86-51)

Comando da Brigada de Transito da GNR, Rua Presidente Arriaga 13, Lisboa 3 (67-00-22)

Centro de Instrucão da GNR, Calcada da Ajuda, Lisboa 3 (63-72-52)

Comando Geral da GF, Cruz de Santa Apolonia, Lisboa 2 (84-93-63)

Destacamento Maritimo da GF, Travessa do Cais da Lingueta, Lisboa 2 (86-52-29)

Comando da PM, Alcantara-Mar Norte, Lisboa 3 (60-81-01)

Puerto Rico

Superintendencia de Policía, San Juan, PR (766-6000)

Qatar

Qatar Police Headquarters, P.O. Box 920, Doha (33-0000)

Capital Police Department, Doha (32-1122)

Police Training School, Doha (80-3445)

Rumania

Inspectoratul General al Militiei, Soseaua Stefan cel Mare 13, Sectorul 2, Bucuresti

Rwanda

Police Nationale, Boîte Postale 125, Kigali, Rwanda

St. Kitts-Nevis

Police Headquarters, Cayon Street, Basseterre (2241)

Police Training Complex, Pond's Pasture, Basseterre (2660)

St. Lucia

Police Headquarters, Bridge Street, Castries (22855)

Port Police, Jeremie Street, Castries (22371)

Training Division, La Toc (22443)

St. Vincent and the Grenadines

Police Headquarters, Kingstown (71211)

San Marino

Corpo di Polizia Civile, Piazza Titano, San Marino (99-10-00)

Comando Gendarmeria, Piazza Titano, San Marino (99-13-38)

Saudi Arabia

Department of Public Security, Riyadh (4036510)

Border Guards Security, Riyadh (4035755)

Senegal

Commandement de la Police, 27 rue du Dr Thèze, Dakar (222-01)

École Nationale de Police, avenue Bourguiba, Dakar (333-77)

Commandement de la Gendarmerie, Camp Pol Lapeyre, Ouakam (323-32)

École de Gendarmerie, Camp Pol Lapeyre, Ouakam (323-32)

Seychelles

Seychelles Police Headquarters, Box 46, Revolution Avenue, Victoria (22011; telex 2298)

Singapore

Police Headquarters, Phoenix Park, Tanglin Road, Singapore (235-9111)

Police Academy, Singapore (256-4466)
Police Training Center, Singapore (255-4656)
Central Narcotics Bureau, Eu Tong Sen Street, Singapore (91-3344)

Solomon Islands

Solomon Islands Police Force Headquarters, Honiara
Police Training School, Honiara

Somalia

Police Headquarters, P.O. Box 960, Mogadiscio

South Africa

Police Headquarters, John Vorsterplein, Johannesburg (838-7455)
Security Branch Headquarters, John Vorsterplein, Johannesburg (834-6318)
Medico-Legal Laboratory, 10 Joubert Street North, Johannesburg (724-7211)

Spain

Inspección General de la Policía Nacional, Fernando e Santo 9, Madrid (419-8370)
Comisaria General de Seguridad Ciudadana, R Calvo 25–27, Madrid (410-5950)
Delegación de Seguridad y Policía Municipal, Conde Duque 9, Madrid (242-0807)
Comisaria General de Policía Judicial, R Calvo 25–27, Madrid (410-5551)
Dirección General de la Guardia Civil, Guzman el Bueno 110, Madrid (234-0200)
Dirección General de la Seguridad del Estado, Puerta del Sol, Madrid (221-6516)
Guardia Real, Acuartelamiento de El Pardo, Madrid (736-0000)

Sri Lanka

Police Department Headquarters, P.O. Box 534, Colombo (21111)
Police Cadet Corps, Colombo (83908)
Intelligence Services Division, Colombo (23388)

Sudan

Sudanese Police Headquarters, P.O. Box 288, Khartoum

Suriname

Het Korps Gewapende Politie, Paramaribo

Swaziland

Police Headquarters, P.O. Box 49, Mbabane (42501)
Police College, Manzini (84229)

Sweden

Rikspolisstyrelsen, Polhelmsgatan 30 Box 12256, S-102 26 Stockholm (769-70-00)
Stockholms Polisdistrikt, Agnegatan 33–37, S-102 29 Stockholm (764-30-00)
Polishogskolan, Ulriksdal 1, S-171 92 Solna (85-00-40)

Switzerland

Polizeikommando des Kantons Aargau, Poststrasse 17, Aarau (22-14-01)
Polizeikommando des Kantons Appenzell-inner-Rhoden, Gaiser Strasse 8, Appenzell (87-34-20)
Polizeikommando Basel-Stadt, Spiegelgasse 6, Basel (21-71-71)
Polizeikommando des Kantons Bern, Sternengasschen 5, Bern (40-40-11)
Police Cantonale, Central, Fribourg (21-17-17)
Gendarmerie Cantonale, boulevard Carl Vogt 17, Genève (27-51-11)
Polizeikommando des Kantons Glarus, Glarus (63-11-11)
Polizeikommando des Kantons Graubunden, Ringstrasse 2, Chur (21-71-11)
Gendarmerie Cantonale du Jura, route de Bâle 23, Delemont (21-53-53)
Polizeikommando des Kantons Luzern, Kasimir Pfyfferstrasse 26, Luzern (28-11-17)
Police Cantonale de Neuchâtel, rue de la Balance 4, Neuchâtel (24-24-24)
Polizeikommando des Kantons Nidwalden, Kreuzstrasse, Stans (63-11-66)
Polizeikommando des Kantons Obwalden, Foribachstrasse, Sarnen (66-43-44)
Polizeikommando des Kantons St. Gallen, Klosterhof 12, St. Gallen, (23-11-51)
Polizeikommando des Kantons Schaffhausen, Klosterstrasse 9, Schaffhausen (4-24-24)
Polizeikommando des Kantons Schwyz, Bahnhofstrasse 7, Schwyz (23-11-23)
Polizeikommando des Kantons Solothurn, Ambassadorenhof, Solothurn (21-51-21)
Polizeikommando des Kantons Thurgau, Grabenstrasse 11, Frauenfeld (22-18-33)
Comando Polizia Cantonale di Ticino, via Bossi 2b, Lugano (22-83-21)
Polizeikommando des Kantons Uri, Tellsgasse 5, Altdorf (2-45-45)
Police Cantonale Valaisanne, avenue de France 69, Sion (22-56-56)
Police Cantonale Vaudienne, rue Cité-Derrière 28, Lausanne (44-44-44)
Polizeikommando des Kantons Zug, Aabachstrasse 1, Zug (23-31-31)
Polizeikommando des Kantons Zürich, Kasernenstrasse 29, Zürich (247-22-11)
Polizei Stadtischer, Rathausgasse 1, Aarau (25-11-55)

Polizeidirektion Stadtische, Tenghausgasse 16, Bern (64-61-11)

Polizeidirektion der Stadt Chur, Klostergasse 2, Chur (21-43-23)

Police Locale, rue du 23 Juin 1944, Delemont (22-44-22)

Stadtpolizei, Rathaus, Frauenfeld (24-52-46)

Commissariat de Police, boulevard Carl Vogt 17, Genève (27-51-11)

Police' Municipale, chaussée des Pêcheurs 11, Lausanne (27-42-54)

Polizeidirektion der Stadt Luzern, Stadthausstrasse 6, Luzern (21-81-11)

Police de la Ville, faubourg de l'Hôpital 6, Neuchâtel (25-10-17)

Polizei Stadtischer, Neugasse 3, St. Gallen (21-51-21)

Polizei Stadtischer, Stadthausgasse 10, Schaffhausen (5-40-17)

Police Municipale, avenue de France 69, Sion (21-21-91)

Polizei Stadtische, Barfussergasse 17, Solothurn (22-99-91)

Polizia Comunale, Palazzo Civico, Ticino (23-23-72)

Polizeiwesen der Stadt Zug, Zug (25-15-15)

Stadtpolizei, Bahnhofquai 3, Zürich (216-71-11)

École de Formation de Police, 18 rue Fontenette, Carouge (Genève) (42-12-80)

Polizeischule, Lutschenstrasse, Ittigen (Bern) (58-36-66)

École d'Apprentis de Gendarmerie, 18 rue Fontenette, Carouge (Genève) (43-70-00)

Syria

Directorate General of Public Security, Damascus

Taiwan

National Security Council, Chiehshou Hall, Chungking South Road, Taipei (311-5687)

Taipei Municipal Police Headquarters, 96 Yenping South Road, Taipei (311-3165)

Tanzania

Police Headquarters, Box 9492, Dar es Salaam (27291)

Criminal Investigation Dept, Box 9093, Dar es Salaam (21266)

Police Barracks, Kilwa Road, Dar es Salaam (50031)

Police College, Box 2503, Dar es Salaam (50016)

Thailand

Police Headquarters, Parusakawan Palace, Bangkok (281-9141)

Central Investigation Bureau, Bangkok (251-6995)

Detective Training School, Bangkok (281-5480)

Togo

Commandement Central de Police de Lomé, Lomé (28-71)

Direction de la Sûreté Nationale, BP 352, Lomé (37-87)

Commandement da la Gendarmerie Nationale, Lomé (26-01)

École Nationale de Police, Lomé (23-54)

Tonga

Police Headquarters, P.O. Box 8, Nuku'alofa

Trinidad and Tobago

Police Divisional Headquarters, St. Vincent, Port of Spain (62-36552)

Tunisia

Police Municipale Headquarters, Tunis (255-145)

Direction de la Sûreté Nationale, avenue Habib Bourguiba, Tunis (255-145)

Commandement de la Gendarmerie Nationale, Tunis (255-145)

Turkey

Polis, Gayrett Telsiz Kumanda Merkezi, Istanbul (66-66-66)

Jandarma, Ev Lal Fethibey S9, Istanbul (22-56-14)

Turks and Caicos

Police Headquarters, Grand Turk (2299)

Police Training Center, Grand Turk (2299)

Uganda

Uganda Police Headquarters, Parliamentary Buildings, P.O. Box 7055, Kampala (54033)

Uganda Police College, P.O. Box 7163, Naguru (65511)

Police Training School, Nsambya (33548)

USSR

KGB, Dzerzhinski Square, Moscow

GRU, Znamensky Street, Moscow

United Arab Emirates

Directorate General of Police, P.O. Box 253, Abu Dhabi (330830)

Dubai Police Headquarters, P.O. Box 1493, Dubai (225111)

United Kingdom

Police Department, 50 Queen Anne's Gate, London SW1H 9AT (01-213-3000)

Police Staff College, Bramshill RG27 0JW (0734-2931)

National Identification Bureau, New Scotland Yard, Broadway, London SW1H 0BG (01-230-3247)

Police National Computer Unit, Horseferry House, Dean Ryle Street, London SW1P 2AW (01-211-5812)

British Transport Police, P.O. Box 25, Coronation Road, London NW10 7QP (01-965-2441)

Avon and Somerset Constabulary, P.O. Box 188, Bristol BS99 7BH (0272-290721)

Bedfordshire Police, Woburn Road, Kempston, Bedford MK43 9AX (0234—855222)

Cambridgeshire Constabulary, Hinchingbrooke Park, Huntingdon PE18 8NP (0480-56111)

Central Scotland Police, Randolphfield, Stirling FK8 2HD (0786-3616)

Cheshire Constabulary, Castle Esplanade, Chester CH1 2PP (0244-315432)

City of London Police, 26 Old Jewry, London EC2R 8DJ (01-606-8866)

Cleveland Constabulary, P.O. Box 70, Dunning Road, Middlesbrough TS1 2AR (0642-248184)

Cumbria Constabulary, Carleton Hall, Penrith CA10 2AU (0768-64411)

Derbyshire Constabulary, Butterley Hall, Ripley, Derby DE5 3RS (0773-43551)

Devon and Cornwall Constabulary, Middlemoor, Exeter EX2 7HQ (0392-52101)

Dorset Police, Winfrith, Dorchester DT2 8DZ (0305-462727)

Dumfries and Galloway Constabulary, Loreburn Street, Dumfries DG1 1HP (0387-2112)

Durham Constabulary, Aykley Heads, Durham DH1 5TT (0385-64929)

Dyfed and Powys Police, Friar's Park, Carmarthen SA31 3AW (0267-6444)

Essex Police, P.O. Box 2, Springfield, Chelmsford CM2 6DA (0245-67267)

Fife Constabulary, Wemyss Road, Dysart, Kirkcaldy KY1 2YA (0592-52611)

Gloucestershire Constabulary, Holland House, Lansdown Road, Cheltenham GL51 6QH (0242-23121)

Grampian Police, Queen Street, Aberdeen AB9 1BA (0224-29933)

Greater Manchester Police, P.O. Box 22 (SW PDO), Chester House, Boyer Street, Manchester M16 0RE (061-872-5050)

Guernsey Island Police Force, Amherst, St. Peter Port (25111)

Gwent Constabulary, Croesyceiliog, Cwmbran NP44 2XJ (063-33-2011)

Hampshire Constabulary, West Hill, Winchester SO22 5DB (0962-68133)

Hertfordshire Constabulary, Stanborough Road, Welwyn Garden City AL8 6XF (96-3117)

Humberside Police, Queen's Garden, Kingston-upon-Hull HU1 3DJ (0482-26111)

Isle of Man Police, Douglas, IOM (0624-26222)

States of Jersey Police, Rouge Bouillon, St. Helier (75511)

Kent Constabulary, Sutton Road, Maidstone ME15 9BZ (0622-65432)

Lancashire Constabulary, Hutton, nr. Preston PR4 5SB (0772-614444)

Leicestershire Constabulary, 420 London Road, Leicester LE2 2PT (0533-700911)

Lincolnshire Police, Church Lane, Lincoln LN5 7PH (0522-29911)

Lothian and Borders Police, Fettes Avenue, Edinburgh EH4 1RB (031-311-3131)

Merseyside Police, P.O. Box 59, Liverpool L69 1JD (051-709-6010)

Metropolitan Police, New Scotland Yard, Broadway, London SW1H 0BG (01-230-1212)

Norfolk Constabulary, Martineau Lane, Norwich NR1 2DJ (0603-21234)

Northamptonshire Police, Wootton Hall, Northampton NN4 0JQ (0604-63111)

Northern Constabulary, Perth Road, Inverness IV2 3SY (0463-39191)

Northumbria Police, Morpeth Road, Ashington NE63 8PU (0670-814511)

North Wales Police, Glan-y-Don, Colwyn Bay LL29 8AW (0492-57171)

North Yorkshire Police, Newby Wiske Hall, Northallerton DL7 9HA (0609-3131)

Nottinghamshire Police, Sherwood Lodge, Arnold, Nottingham NG5 8PP (0602-269700)

Royal Ulster Constabulary, Knock Road, Belfast BT5 6LE (0232-650222)

South Wales Constabulary, Bridgend CF31 3SR (0656-55555)

South Yorkshire Police, Snig Hill, Sheffield S3 8LY (0742-78522)

Staffordshire Police, Cannock Road, Stafford ST17 0QG (0785-57717)

Strathclyde Police, 173 Pitt Street, Glasgow G2 4JS (041-204-2626)

Suffolk Constabulary, Marthlesham Heath, Ipswich IP5 7QS (0473-624848)

Surrey Constabulary, Mount Browne, Sandy Lane, Guildford GU3 1HG (0483-71212)

Sussex Police, Malling House, Lewes BN7 2DZ (079-16-5432)

Tayside Police, P.O. Box 59, West Bell Street, Dundee DD1 9JU (0382-23200)

Thames Valley Police, Kidlington, nr. Oxford OX5 2NX (086-75-4343)

Warwickshire Constabulary, P.O. Box 4, Leek Wootton, Warwick CV35 7QB (0926-45431)

West Mercia Constabulary, Hindlip Hall, Hindlip, Worcester WR3 8SP (0905-27188)

West Midlands Police, P.O. Box 52, Lloyd House, Colmore Circus Queensway, Birmingham B4 6NQ (021-236-5000)

West Yorkshire Police, P.O. Box 9, Wakefield WF1 3QP (0924-75222)

Wiltshire Constabulary, London Road, Devizes SN10 2DN (0380-2341)

Uruguay

Estado Mayor de la Policía de Montevideo, Yi 1310, Montevideo (98-60-46)
Jefatura de Policía, Yi 1310, Montevideo (8-95-11)
Policía Nacional de Transito, 8 Octubre 3247, Montevideo (58-55-33)
Guardia Metropolitana, Magallanes 1620, Montevideo (4-53-12)
Guardia Republicana, Sierra 3140, Montevideo (58-07-43)
Escuela de Tropa de Policía, Millan 3976, Montevideo (3-69-77)

Vanuatu

Police Station/Commissariat de Police, Vila (2252, 2333)

Venezuela

Policía Nacional Venezolana, Caracas
Guardia Nacional, Calle 6 con Avenida 1, Caracas

Western Samoa

Commissioner of Police, Apia (228)

Yugoslavia

Criminal Service Department, P.O. Box 565, Belgrade

Zaire

Police Judiciaire des Parquets, Building du 20 Mai, boulevard du 30 Juin, Kinshasa 1

Zambia

Police Headquarters, Box RW 50103, Ridgeway, Lusaka (214466)
Police Paramilitary Unit, Lilayi, Lusaka (214340)
Police Training School, Lilayi, Lusaka (214340)

Zimbabwe

Central Headquarters, Kenneth Kaunda Avenue, Harare (700101)
Police Reserve, Morris Depot, Harare (791323)
Criminal Investigation Department, Harare (700171)
Traffic Branch Headquarters, Harare (700101)
Willowvale Police Training Centre, Harare (65501)
Morris Police Training Depot, Montagu Avenue, Harare (700171)
Tomlinson Police Training Depot, P.O. Box 8331, Harare (700171)
Provincial Training and Reserve Headquarters, Khami Road, Bulawayo (74335)
Police Forensic Laboratory, Harare (707978)

APPENDIX III: BIBLIOGRAPHY

Ames, W.L. *Police and Community in Japan*. Berkeley, Calif., 1981.

Andrade, John. *World Police and Paramilitary Forces*. London, 1986.

Bayley, D.H. *Patterns of Policing: A Comparative International Analysis*. New Brunswick, N.J., 1985.

Becker, Harold K. *Police Systems of Europe*. Springfield, Ill., 1980.

———. *Handbook of World Police*. Metuchen, N.J., 1986.

Beckman, Erik. *Law Enforcement in a Democratic Society*. Chicago, 1980.

Biles, David. *Crime and Justice in Australia*. Melbourne, 1977.

Chaturvedi, S.K. *Metropolitan Police Administration in India*. Delhi, 1985.

Cole, George F. *Major Criminal Justice Systems*. Berkeley, Calif., 1981.

Cooper, John L. *You Can Hear Them Knocking: A Study in the Policing of America*. Port Washington, N.Y., 1981.

Cox, Steven, and Fitzgerald, Jack D. *Police in Community Relations: Critical Issues*. Dubuque, 1983.

Cramer, James. *Uniforms of the World Police*. Springfield, Ill., 1968.

Danns, George. *Domination and the Power in Guyana: A Study of the Police in Third World Context*. New Brunswick, N.J., 1982.

Dorey, Marcia A., and Swidler, George J. *World Police Systems*. Boston, 1975.

Folley, Vern L. *American Law Enforcement: Police, Courts, and Corrections*. Boston, 1980.

Fowles, N. *After the Riots: Police in Europe*. London, 1979.

Gupta, A. *The Police in British India, 1861–1947*. New Delhi, 1980.

Holdaway, Simon. *British Police*. London, 1983.

Hurt, Jenifer M. *British Police*. London, 1951.

Ingleton, Roy. *Police of the World*. New York, 1979.

Kelly, William, and Kelly, Nora. *Police in Canada*. Agincourt, Ont., 1975.

Lee, W.L.M. *History of the Police in England*. Montclair, N.J., 1901.

McDowell, Charles P. *Criminal Justice: A Community Relations Approach*. Cincinnati, 1984.

Mosse, George L. *Police Forces in History*. Ann Arbor, Mich., 1980.

Ostrom, Elinor; Parks, Roger B.; and Whitaker, Gordon P. *Patterns of Metropolitan Policing*. Cambridge, Mass., 1974.

Parker, L.C., Jr. *Japanese Police System Today: An American Perspective*. New York, 1984.

Reith, Charles. *The Blind Eye of History: A Study of the Origins of the Present Police Era.* Montclair, N.J., 1975.

Richardson, James F. *Urban Police in the United States.* Port Washington, N.Y., 1981.

Roach, John, and Thomaneck, Jurgen. *Police and Public Order in Western Europe.* London, 1985.

Stead, P.J. *The Police of France.* London, 1983.

Stratton, John G. *Police Passages.* Manhattan Beach, Calif., 1984.

Terrill, R.J. *World Criminal Justice Systems: A Survey* (of England, France, Sweden, the Soviet Union and Japan). Cincinnati, 1984.

Torres, Donald A. *Handbook of Federal Police and Investigative Sources.* Westport, Conn., 1985.

Whitaker, Ben. *The Police.* Harmondsworth, England, 1964.

APPENDIX IV: COMPARATIVE STATISTICS ON POLICE PROTECTION

COMPARATIVE STATISTICS ON POLICE PROTECTION, 1984–85

	Population per Police Officer	Public Expenditures per 1,000 Inhabitants, in Dollars
Andorra	1,125	—
Anguilla	—	24,233
Antigua and Barbuda	—	25,133
Australia	461.9	16,132
Austria	466.3	—
Bahamas	164.8	—
Bahrain	183.3	—
Belgium	585.5	—
Benin	—	1,138
Bermuda	182.9	—
Botswana	176.9	—
Brunei	117.3	126,103
Burma	645.3	—
Cameroon	1,173.1	—
Canada	358.0	—
Chile	375.8	6,459
China	1,363.5	—
Colombia	418.2	—
Costa Rica	969.1	—
Cuba	150.0	2,503
Cyprus	177.7	35,383
Denmark	594.1	67,601
Dominica	446.1	3,924
Dominican Republic	464.4	—
Egypt	446.7	—
Equatorial Guinea	135.0	—
Ethiopia	956.4	—
Falkland Islands	326.2	38,723
Fiji	408.9	3,629
Finland	643.0	44,927

COMPARATIVE STATISTICS ON POLICE PROTECTION, 1984–85

	Population per Police Officer	Public Expenditures per 1,000 Inhabitants, in Dollars
France	632.0	—
Gambia	812.0	—
Ghana	624.0	—
Gibraltar	167.2	—
Greece	303.3	—
Grenada	218.4	15,202
Guatemala	673.1	—
Guinea	1,143.9	—
Honduras	1,040.0	—
Hong Kong	219.3	—
India	820.0	—
Indonesia	1,319.3	768
Iran	—	21,088
Iraq	193.5	—
Ireland	489.1	58,654
Israel	191.1	23,099
Italy	285.7	—
Jamaica	659.7	24,259
Japan	555.5	55,594
Jordan	277.8	27,536
Kampuchea	1,976.6	—
Kiribati	425.1	—
Korea	441.4	—
Laos	275.2	—
Liberia	1,570.0	—
Libya	—	26,667
Luxembourg	434.6	15,067
Madagascar	2,904.7	—
Malawi	1,666.7	—
Malaysia	292.9	—
Maldives	35,703	2,003
Mali	157.0	—
Malta	276.9	34,223
Mauritania	1,170.0	—
Mauritius	243.6	—
Mongolia	116.7	—
Montserrat	153.6	16,901
Nauru	106.2	—
Nepal	1,000.0	497
Netherlands	552.7	100,727
New Zealand	642.1	38,418
Nicaragua	93.0	—
Niger	2,352.9	—
Nigeria	1,142.1	—
Norway	661.2	78,262
Oman	131.7	—
Pakistan	722.2	1,954
Papua New Guinea	721.4	—
Paraguay	312.5	—
Peru	508.6	—
Philippines	1,158.0	2,423
Poland	350.0	—
Portugal	624.0	—

	Population per Police Officer	Public Expenditures per 1,000 Inhabitants, in Dollars
Puerto Rico	380.6	—
Réunion	216.7	—
St. Helena	321.7	8,368
St. Lucia	240.3	—
St. Vincent and the Grenadines	204.5	13,198
São Tomé and Príncipe	500.0	—
Saudi Arabia	280.0	131,140
Senegal	732.7	—
Seychelles	142.9	—
Sierra Leone	782.1	—
Singapore	234.8	—
Solomon Islands	614.3	5,112
Somalia	537.5	—
South Africa	867.1	28,460
Spain	861.6	—
Sri Lanka	740.7	12,049
Swaziland	609.8	21,249
Sweden	327.7	176,110
Switzerland	—	135,820
Syria	1,150.0	—
Tanzania	1,333.3	1,953
Thailand	527.8	4,262
Tonga	409.5	7,139
Trinidad and Tobago	284.2	—
Tunisia	337.8	—
Turkey	1,571.4	—
Turks and Caicos	113.1	20,611
Tuvalu	294.0	13,069
Uganda	1,093.3	1,173
USSR	1,045.4	—
United Arab Emirates	138.0	—
United Kingdom	400.0	79,281
United States	458.5	73,687
Uruguay	176.5	—
Vanuatu	445.0	—
Venezuela	324.3	—
Western Samoa	—	6,997
Yemen, Arab Republic of	500.0	1,905
Yemen, Southern,	1,440.0	—
Zaire	1,409.1	—
Zambia	538.1	7,141
Zimbabwe	750.0	12,457

Index

Abdur Rahman Shah, 1
Aden. *See* Yemen (South)
Afghanistan, **1-2**
Agriculture, Department of
  (U.S.), 426
Air Force, Department of
  (U.S.), 428
Albania, **3**
Alcohol
    Bolivia, 32
    Bulgaria, 42
    Cuba, 88
    Czechoslovakia, 93
    Finland, 118
    Hungary, 170
    Mongolia, 263
    Somalia, 341, 342
    Venezuela, 472
    Zambia, 486
Alcohol, Tobacco and Firearms,
  Bureau of (U.S.), 421
Algeria, **4-5**
Amnesty International
    Cuba, 87
    Czechoslovakia, 92
    Ethiopia, 112
    Iran, 189
    Morocco, 267
    South Africa, 346
    Syria, 367
    Tanzania, 373
amparo (Mexican legal
  doctrine), 259-60
Amputation (punishment)
    Iran, 186
    Pakistan, 300
    Saudi Arabia, 330
Andorra, **491**
Andropov, Yuri, 394
Angola, **6-7**
Anguilla, **491**
Antigua and Barbuda, **492**
Argentina, **8-10**
  foreign aid and influence:
    Columbia, 69
Army, Department of (U.S.),
  422, 425
Assad, Hafiz al, 366
Australia, **11-19**
Austria, **20-24**

Bahamas, **492-93**
Bahrain, **493**
Bail
    Afghanistan, 2
    Dominican Republic, 98
    France, 133

    Israel, 195
    Mexico, 260
    Portugal, 320
    Sweden, 358
    United Kingdom, 412
Bakhtiar, Teimur, 185
Balmain, Pierre, 130
Banishment (punishment)
    USSR, 398
Bangladesh, **25-26**
Barbados, **494-95**
Bates, Sanford, 443
Beheading (punishment)
    Saudi Arabia, 329
Belgium, **27-29**
    foreign aid and influence:
      Rwanda, 327
      Zaire, 481
Belize, **496**
Benin, **496-97**
Beria, Lavrenti P., 393
Bermuda, **497-98**
Bhutan, **498**
Bhutto, Zulfikar Ali, 299
Biko, Steve, 344
Black Law Enforcement
  Executives, National
  Organization (U.S.), 431
Bolivia, **30-32**
Bonaparte, Charles J., 423
Bootlegging, 420
Border police
    Germany (West), 141
    Guatemala, 156
    Guinea, 157, 158
    Hungary, 169
    Israel, 192, 194
    USSR, 395-96, 397
    see also Customs
      Service (U.S.)
Botha, Chris, 354
Botswana, **33-36**
Brazil, **37-39**
Britain. *See* United Kingdom
Broad Street Riot (1837), 418
Brook, Superintendent (Sierra
  Leone), 333
Brunei, **499-500**
Brutality. *See* Police
  brutality
Burgaria, **40-42**
Bureau of Alcohol, Tobacco and
  Firearms (U.S.), 421
Burglary. *See* Theft and
  burglary
Burkina Faso, **500**
Burma, **43-44**
Burundi, **45-46**

Caetano, Marcello, 318
Calvert, W.A., 208
Cambodia. *See* Kampuchea
Cameroon, **47-48**
Canada, **49-58**
Caning (punishment)
    Singapore, 337
    Sri Lanka, 351
    Zambia, 486
       see also Whipping
       and flogging
Cape Verde, **501**
Capital punishment
    Afghanistan, 1, 2
    Algeria, 5
    Australia, 17
    Austria, 24
    Bangladesh, 26
    Belgium, 28
    Bolivia, 31
    Brazil, 38
    Bulgaria, 41
    Cameroon, 47
    China, 67
    Colombia, 77
    Cuba, 88
    Cyprus, 89-90
    Czechoslovakia, 92
    Denmark, 96
    Dominican Republic, 98
    Ethiopia, 111
    France, 133
    Germany (East), 137
    Germany (West), 144
    Ghana, 150
    Greece, 154
    Haiti, 161
    India, 177
    Iran, 187-88
    Israel, 195
    Italy, 202
    Jordan, 222
    Kenya, 228
    Korea (South), 235
    Liberia, 245
    Madagascar, 249
    Malaysia, 255
    Mexico, 259
    Mongolia, 262
    Nepal, 271
    Netherlands, 280
    Nicaragua, 285
    Nigeria, 292, 293
    Pakistan, 300
    Panama, 303
    Paraguay, 307
    Peru, 310
    Philippines, 313
    Portugal, 319
    Romania, 324
    Saudi Arabia, 330
    Senegal, 332
    Singapore, 337
    Somalia, 341
    Spain, 348-49
    Sri Lanka, 351
    Syria, 367
    Tanzania, 372
    Thailand, 376

    Trinidad and Tobago,
      379
    Tunisia, 382, 383
    Turkey, 387
    Uganda, 390
    USSR, 398
    United States, 417,
      441, 450
    Uruguay, 469
    Venezuela, 472
    Yemen (South), 478
    Zaire, 482
    Zambia, 486
Capitol Police (U.S.), 428
Castro, Fidel, 86
Castro, Raúl, 86
Cayman Islands, **501-502**
Central African Republic, **502**
Central Intelligence Agency
  (U.S.), 221
Centralized police systems
    Austria, 21-22
    Belgium, 27
    Brazil, 37
    China, 64
    Colombia, 69-70
    Congo, 79
    Costa Rica, 81
    Cuba, 85
    Cyprus, 89
    Ecuador, 99
    Egypt, 103
    El Salvador, 109
    France, 128, 129
    Germany (East), 136
    Italy, 197, 199
    Japan, 211
    Liberia, 244
    Malawi, 250
    Nepal, 270
    Panama, 302
    Sri Lanka, 350
    Sudan, 352
    Sweden, 356
    Syria, 366
    Thailand, 374
    Turkey, 385-86
    Uganda, 389
    Vietnam, 474
    Yemen (South), 478
    Zaire, 482
    Zambia, 484
    Zimbabwe, 488
Chad, **59-60**
Charter 77 (Czechoslovakia), 92
Charusathian, Praphat, 377
Cheka (USSR), 392, 394, 395,
  398
Chiefs of Police, International
  Association of
  (IACP; U.S.), 419, 431
Chile, **61-63**
  foreign aid and influence:
    Nicaragua, 285
China, **64-68**
  foreign aid and influence:
    Vietnam, 475
CIA. *See* Central Intelligence
  Agency

City police (U.S.), 430
Civilian role in police
    Australia, 13
    Bolivia, 31
    France, 129
    Netherlands, 274
    USSR, 396-97
    United States, 417
Civil liberties
    Afghanistan, 2
    Algeria, 5
    Bulgaria, 41
    Canada, 56, 57
    China, 65, 67
    Colombia, 74-75, 76
    Czechoslovakia, 92-93
    Finland, 119
    France, 133
    Germany (East), 137
    Ghana, 148, 150
    Greece, 154
    India, 177
    Iran, 187
    Israel, 195
    Italy, 200, 202
    Japan, 212-13
    Jordan, 222
    Mexico, 259-60
    Mozambique, 269
    Pakistan, 300
    Portugal, 320
    Romania, 324
    Senegal, 332
    Somalia, 341
    Sweden, 358
    Tunisia, 383
    Turkey, 387
    Uganda, 390
    United States, 420
    Yugoslavia, 480
    Zambia, 485
    Zimbabwe, 488
Clearance of cases
    India, 178
    New Zealand, 282
Coast and waterways police
    Canada, 51
    Hong Kong, 163-64, 166
    Hungary, 168
    Israel, 194
    Korea (South), 232-33
    Netherlands, 275
    Singapore, 335, 336
    United States, 424,
        425, 441
    Uruguay, 468
Coast Guard (U.S.), 425
Coast Guard Academy (U.S.),
  441
Cocaine
    Colombia, 78
    Peru, 311
Colombia, **69-78**
Commerce, Department of
  (U.S.), 426
Communications, police
    Botswana, 34
    Colombia, 74
    India, 173

    Japan, 215
    Kenya, 227
    Netherlands, 276
    Nigeria, 289, 290
    Singapore, 336
    Sri Lanka, 350
    United Kingdon, 409
    United States, 456
Comoros, **503**
Compliance and Investigations
  Group (U.S.), 421-22
Computers, police
    Germany (West), 140,
      141
    Hong Kong, 164
    India, 173, 178
    Italy, 200
    Japan, 215
    Switzerland, 364
    United Kingdom, 409
Congo, **79-80**
Convict labor. *See* Labor
  camps; Prison - work
Cook Islands, **503-504**
Cooper, John G., 443
Corruption
    Afghanistan, 2
    Algeria, 5
    Australia, 18
    Bangladesh, 26
    Czechoslovakia, 93
    Jamaica, 209
    Mexico, 259
    Peru, 311
    Somalia, 342
    Thailand, 377
    Tunisia, 384
Costa Rica, **81-84**
Countersubversion
    Algeria, 5
    Argentina, 9
    Guatemala, 156
    Guinea, 157
    Indonesia, 181
    South Africa, 344
    Taiwan, 368
    Thailand, 374, 375
County police (U.S.), 430
Coups, police. *See* Mutinies
  and coups, police
Court proceedings. *See* Trials
Crime statistics tables. *See*
  country names
Criminal Justice Sciences,
  Academy of (U.S.), 431
Crucifixion (punishment)
    Saudi Arabia, 330
Cuba, **85-88**
  foreign aid and influence:
    Angola, 7
    Congo, 79
    Sierra Leone, 334
Curtis, Joseph, 451
Customs Service (U.S.), 322,
  428-29
Cyprus, **89-90**
Czechoslovakia, **91-93**
  foreign aid and influence:
    Guinea, 158

Dacoity, 178
Death penalty. *See* Capital
Punishment
Decapitation (punishment)
Saudi Arabia, 329
Defense, Department of (U.S.),
422, 426
Deng Xiaoping, 65, 68
Denmark, **94-96**
foreign aid and influence:
Iceland, 511
Diamonds
Botswana, 36
Sierra Leone, 333, 334
Diem, Ngo Dinh, 473, 474
Disciplining of police
Colombia, 71-72
Denmark, 95
Finland, 118
France, 129
India, 172
Israel, 194
Japan, 212-13
United Kingdon, 406-408
Djibouti, **504**
Dominica, **505**
Dominican Republic, **97-98**
Drug Enforcement Adminis-
tration (DEA) (U.S.), 421,
423, 463
Drug traffic. *See* Drug
Enforcement Administration;
Narcotics; specific drugs
Dubcek, Alexander, 92
Durham, Lord, 49
Duvalier, François, 161
Dyer Act (U.S.), 423
Dzerzhinsky, Felix, 392, 398

Earp, Wyatt, 419
Ecuador, **99-101**
Education, Department of
(U.S.), 426
Education, police. *See*
country names
Eqypt, **102-106**
foreign aid and influence:
Sudan, 353
Eichmann, Adolf, 195
El Salvador, **107-108**
England. *See* United Kingdon
Environmental Protection
Agency (U.S.), 427
Equatorial Guinea, **506**
Espionage
China, 66
Ethiopia, **109-112**
Ethnic divisions, police
Cyprus, 89
Fiji, 114
Ghana, 146
Ivory Coast, 204, 205
Kenya, 227
Malawi, 251
South Africa, 343-44
Swaziland, 354
Tanzania, 371
Trinidad and Tobago, 378-79
European Police Systems
(book), 420

Ewert, Sir John, 352
Execution. *See* Capital
punishment
Exile (punishment)
USSR, 398

Falkland Islands, **506**
FBI. *See* Federal Bureau of
Investigation
FBI Academy (U.S.), 441
FCC. *See* Federal
Communications Commission
Federal Aviation Admin-
istration Police (U.S.),
423
Federal Bureau of
Investigation (FBI) (U.S.)
and Canada, 51
forerunner, 419
formation, 421
and international
fugitives, 463
and Interpol, 455
and the Philippines, 312
profile of, 423-24
and Puerto Rico, 322
Federal Communications
Commission (U.S.), 424
Federal Law Enforcement
Training Center (U.S.),
441, 457
Federal Maritime Commission
(U.S.), 424
Federal Prison Industries
(UNICORP) (U.S.), 444, 446
Federal Protective Service
(U.S.), 424
Federal Trade Commission
(U.S.), 424
Female police. *See* Women
police
Fielding, Henry, 402
Fielding, John, 402
Fiji, **113-14**
Fish and Wildlife Service
(U.S.), 424
Flogging. *See* Whipping and
flogging
Forced labor. *See* Labor camps
and forced labor
Foreign aid. *See* names of
donor countries
Forest Service (U.S.), 424
Fosdick, Raymond B., 420
Foulger, R.E., 335
France, **127-35**
foreign aid and influence:
Algeria, 4, 5
Benin, 497
Burkina Faso, 500
Central African
Republic, 502
China, 66
Colombia, 69
Djibouti, 504
French Guiana, 507
Gabon, 507
Guadeloupe, 510
Guinea, 157, 158
Italy, 197

Ivory Coast, 204, 205
Japan, 217
Jordan, 222
Kampuchea, 224
Laos, 237
Luxembourg, 513
Madagascar, 249
Mauritania, 257
Morocco, 266
Netherlands, 272
Niger, 522
Romania, 324
Rwanda, 327
Senegal, 332
Seychelles, 529
Spain, 347
Switzerland, 362, 363
Syria, 366
Thailand, 376
Tunisia, 381, 382
Vanuatu, 536
Vietnam, 473, 475
Francis Joseph I, Emperor
  (Austria), 20
French Guiana, **507**
Frontiers. *See* Border police

Gabon, **507-508**
Gambia, **508-509**
Garrett, Pat, 419
Garrison, William Lloyd, 418
General Services
  Administration
  (U.S.), 427
Germany (East), **136-37**
  foreign aid and influence:
    Angola, 6
    Ethiopia, 110
    Yemen (South), 478
Germany (West), **138-45**
  foreign aid and influence:
    Afghanistan, 1
    Ethiopia, 109
    Japan, 218
    Somalia, 339
    Tanzania, 372, 373
Gestapo (Germany), 138
Ghana, **146-51**
Gibraltar, **509**
Gilson, C.H., 354
Girard, Stephen, 418
Glubb Pasha, 220
Goodhart, Professor, 403
Government Printing Office
  (U.S.), 427
Gragier, François, 152
Great Britain. *See* United
  Kingdom
Greece, **152-54**
Grenada, **509-510**
Griffiths, Charles, 241
Guadeloupe, **510**
Guatemala, **155-56**
Guerrillas. *See*
  Countersubversion
Guinea, **157-58**
Guinea-Bissau, **510**
Guma, Sharawi Muhammad, 102
Gun control
  Algeria, 5

Greece, 154
Japan, 219
Morocco, 268
United States, 421
Guyana, **159-60**

Habeas corpus
  Jordan, 222
  Kenya, 228
  Mexico, 259
  Panama, 304
  Portugal, 320
  Saudi Arabia, 329
  Somalia, 341
Haile-Mariam Mengistu, 110
Haile Selassie, Emperor
  (Ethiopia), 111
Haiti, **161**
Handgun control. *See* Gun
  control
Hanging
  Kenya, 228
  Korea (South), 235
  Nigeria, 293
  Sri Lanka, 351
  Syria, 367
  Tunisia, 382
  Uganda, 390
  United States, 441
  Zambia, 486
Harbors. *See* Coast and
  waterways police
Hashish
  Cyprus, 90
  Morocco, 267-68
Health and Human Services,
  Department of (U.S.), 426
Heroin
  Cyprus, 90
  Thailand, 377
Heureaux, Ulises, 98
Hickock, "Wild Bill," 419
Hoffmann, Heinz, 136
Holliday, Frederick, 152
Homosexuality
  Australia, 18
  Cuba, 87, 88
  Germany (West), 144
  Venezuela, 472
Honduras, **162**
Hong Kong, **163-67**
Hoover, Herbert, 420, 443
Hoover, J. Edgar, 423, 424
Housing and Urban Development,
  Department of (U.S.), 426
Hua Guofeng, 64
Human Rights, Universal
  Declaration of, 259, 456
Hungary, **168-70**
Husák, Gustav, 92
Hussein, King (Jordan), 220

IACP. *See* International
  Association of Police
Iceland, **511**
Identificaion cards
  Cuba, 86
  Hungary, 168
  Korea (North), 230
  Poland, 315

Immigration and Naturalization
Service Border Patrol
(U.S.), 424-25
India, **171-78**
foreign aid and influence:
Nigeria, 293
Sudan, 353
Thailand, 375
Uganda, 390
Indian Affairs Bureau of
(U.S.), 422
Indonesia, **179-83**
Infanticide
China, 68
Insurgency. *See*
Countersubversive
Inter-American Human Rights
Commission, 87
Interior, Department of the
(U.S.), 426, 429
Internal Revenue Service
(U.S.), 422, 425
International Association of
Police (IACP) (U.S.), 419
International Criminal Police
Organization. *See* Interpol
International Police Academy,
303
International Police
Association, 241
International Trade
Administration (U.S.), 425
Interpol, 457-58, 461, **539-50**
Austria, 20
Belgium, 28
China, 66
Denmark, 95
Ecuador, 100
Finland, 116, 122
France, 129
Germany (West), 141
Ghana, 148
Italy, 200
Kenya, 227
Lesotho, 245
Mexico, 259
Nigeria, 288
Norway, 295
Panama, 303
Peru, 310
Portugal, 319
Switzerland, 363
United States, 421, 455-58, 461-63
Interstate Commerce Commission
(U.S.), 425
Iran, **184-87**
Iraq, **188-89**
Ireland, **190-91**
Islamic law
Afghanistan, 1
Iran, 186-87
Libya, 247-48
Morocco, 267
Nigeria, 293
Pakistan, 300
Saudi Arabia, 328-29
Somalia, 341
Sudan, 353
Tunisia, 382, 383

Israel, **192-96**
foreign aid and influence:
Ethiopia, 109
Uganda, 390
Italy, **197-203**
foreign aid and influence:
Iran, 184
Thailand, 375
Ivan the Terrible (Russia),
392
Ivory Coast, **204-207**

Jails. *See* Prison headings
Japan, **211-19**
foreign aid and influence:
Thailand, 374, 375
Jamaica, **208-210**
Jensen, D. Lowell, 456
Job conditions, police
Australia, 15
France, 132
India, 173
Ireland, 191
Japan, 213, 214
Malawi, 251
Morocco, 266
Netherlands, 277
Puerto Rico, 322
South Africa, 346
USSR, 396
Vietnam, 475
Johnson, Samuel, 405
Jordan, **220-23**
Josefine Code of 1787, 24
Joseph II (Austria), 24
Julius II, Pope, 537
Justice Assistance, Research
and Statistics, Office of
(U.S.), 431
Justice, Department of (U.S.),
421, 423, 429
see also Federal Bureau
of Investigation
Juvenile Justice and
Delinquency Protection Act
(U.S.), 453
Juvenile offenders
Afghanistan, 2
Argentina, 10
Australia, 17
Canada, 56, 57
Chile, 63
China, 68
Colombia, 77-78
Cuba, 88
France, 135
Germany (West), 144
Ghana, 150
Greece, 154
Hong Kong, 167
Israel, 194
Jamaica, 209, 210
Japan, 218, 219
Kenya, 229
Liberia, 246
Mexico, 261
Mongolia, 263
Panama, 304

Portugal, 320, 321
Senegal, 332
Somalia, 341
Sweden, 358, 360
Thailand, 376
Turkey, 388
USSR, 399-400
United Kingdom, 414-15
United States, 444,
    448, 450-51, 453-55
Uruguay, 469
Venezuela, 472
Zaire, 483
Zambia, 485

Kampuchea, **224**
Katzenbach, Nicholas B., 421
Kefauver, Estes, 420
Kennedy, John F., 429
Kennedy, Robert F., 429
Kenya, **225-29**
KGB (USSR), 316, 391, 393-96,
    397
KHAD (Afghanistan), 2
Khomeini, Ayatollah Ruhollah,
    187
Kiribati, **512**
Kirov, Sergei, 393
Knives, restrictions on
    Sri Lanka, 351
Korea (North), **230-31**
Korea (South), **232-35**
Kuwait, **236-37**

Labor camps and forced labor
    China, 66, 67
    Haiti, 161
    Hungary, 170
    India, 177
    Jordan, 222
    Madagascar, 249
    Malaysia, 255
    Panama, 303
    Paraguay, 307
    Poland, 317
    Romania, 325
    Senegal, 332
    Syria, 367
    Tunisia, 382
    Turkey, 387
    USSR, 392, 398-400
    United States, 442, 443
    Vietnam, 476
    see also Prison work
Labor, Department of (U.S.),
    426
Lambda Alpha Epsilon (U.S.),
    441
Laos, **238**
Law Enforcement Assistance
    Administration (U.S.), 431
Lawyer's Committee for Human
    Rights, 224
Lebanon, **239-40**
Lenin, Vladimir, 392, 394
Lesotho, **241-43**
Liberia, **244-46**
Libya, **247-48**
Liechtenstein, **513**

Lie detectors, 422
London Metropolitan Police
    System, 163, 171, 208, 407,
    408, 409, 410
Lo Wei-chin, 64
Luxembourg, **513-14**
Lynch, Charles, 417

Macau, **515**
Machel, Samora, 269
Madagascar, **249**
Madjitey, E.R.T., 146
Mafia, 198, 202
Malawi, **250-51**
Malaysia, **252-56**
Maldives, **515-16**
Mali, **516**
Malta, **517-18**
Mao Zedong, 64, 66
Marcos, Ferdinand, 312, 314
Maria Theresa, Empress
    (Austria), 24
Marijuana
    Argentina, 10
    Botswana, 36
    Colombia, 78
    Costa Rica, 83
    Ghana, 151
    Jamaica, 209, 210
    Kenya, 229
    Mexico, 261
    Nigeria, 288
    Sierra Leone, 334
Maritime police. *See* Coast
    and waterways police
Marshals Service (U.S.), 322,
    429
Masterson, Bat, 419
Mauritania, **257**
Mauritius, **518-19**
Mayne, Richard, 403
McKinley, William, 429
Meese, Edwin, 458
Mengistu, Haile-Meriam. *See*
    Haile-Mariam Mengistu
Mentally ill offenders
    Netherlands, 281
    United States, 444, 453
Mexico, **258-61**
Military and paramilitary
    forces
    Afghanistan, 1, 2
    Algeria, 4
    Angola, 6
    Austria, 25
    Belgium, 27
    Bolivia, 30
    Brazil, 37-38
    Bulgaria, 41
    Burma, 43
    Cameroon, 47
    China, 64
    Colombia, 70
    Egypt, 103
    Ethiopia, 109
    France, 128
    Greece, 152
    Guatemala, 155
    Guinea, 157, 158

Guyana, 159
Haiti, 161
Indonesia, 179
Iran, 184, 185
Iraq, 188
Italy, 197
Korea (South), 232
Lebanon, 239
Madagascar, 249
Mauritania, 257
Nepal, 270
Netherlands, 272
Pakistan, 297
Panama, 302
Peru, 309
Poland, 315
Romania, 324
Saudi Arabia, 328
Seychelles, 529
Somalia, 340
Syria, 366
Tanzania, 371
Thailand, 375
Tunisia, 382
Uganda, 390
United Kingdom, 403, 404
United States, 422, 425
Uruguay, 468
Venezuela, 470
Vietnam, 475
Yemen (South), 478
Military Police Corps (U.S.), 425
Miranda v. *Arizona*, 420
Mobutu Sese Seko, 482
Moczar, Mieczyslaw, 316
Monaco, **519-20**
Mongolia, **262-63**
Montserrat, **521**
Morocco, **264-68**
Mounties. *See* Royal Canadian Mounted Police
Mozambique, **269**
Mswati, King, (Swaziland), 354
Muburak, Hosni, 103, 104
Municipal police (U.S.), 430
Musa, Mohammad Abshir, 340
Mutinies and coups, police
Egypt, 104
Ghana, 146-47
Sierra Leone, 333
MVD (USSR), 391-92, 393-94, 395, 397

Napier, Sir Charles, 171
Napoleon Bonaparte, 362, 363
Narcotics
Australia, 17, 18
Bolivia, 30
China, 68
Cuba, 88
Czechoslovakia, 93
Jamaica, 210
Nigeria, 289
Singapore, 337
Somalia, 342
see also specific drugs
NASA. *See* National Aeronautics and Space Administration

Nasser, Gamal Abdal, 102, 103
National Aeronautics and Space Administration (NASA) (U.S.), 427
National Central Bureau - Interpol (U.S.), 455-58, 461-63
National Crime Survey (U.S.), 466-67; 458 *t.*
National Marine Fisheries Service (U.S.), 425
Nauru, **521**
Naval Investigative Service (U.S.), 425-26
Navy, Department of (U.S.), 425-26
Nepal, **270-71**
Netherlands, **272-81**
foreign aid and influence:
Netherlands Antilles, 522
South Africa, 345-46
Suriname, 532
Netherlands Antilles, **522**
New Zealand, **282-83**
foreign aid and influence:
Cook Islands, 503-504
Nicaragua, **284-85**
Niger, **522-23**
Nigeria, **286-94**
foreign aid and influence:
Zaire, 481
Nkrumah, Kwame, 146-47
Norway, **295-96**
Nyerere, Julius, 371

Office of Personnel Management (U.S.), 421-22
O'Grady, Ellen, 419
Oman, 523
Opium
Mexico, 261
Thailand, 377
Organized crime
Australia, 18
Colombia, 78
Interpol, 461
United States, 420
Vietnam, 473
see also Mafia; Secret societies; *Yakuza*
Otto, King, (Greece), 154
Owens, Marie, 419

Pahlevi, Shah Mohammed Riza, 184
Pakistan, **297-301**
Panama, **302-304**
foreign aid and influence:
Nicaragua, 303
Papua New Guinea, **305-306**
Paraguay, **307-308**
Parker, William H., 420
Park Police (U.S.), 429
Parole
Australia, 17
Ecuador, 100
France, 134
Germany (East), 137
Germany (West), 144

Israel, 196
Kenya, 228
Romania, 325
Sweden, 359
United Kingdom, 413
United States, 423, 444
Parole Board (U.S.), 444
Paul VI, Pope, 537
Peel, Robert, 403
Penal system. *See* Prison
headings
Pendleton Act (U.S.), 419
Pershing, John J., 422
Personnel Management, Office
of (U.S.), 421-22, 427
Peru, **309-311**
"Peterloo" massacre (1819)
(United Kingdom), 402
Philadelphia Prison Society
(U.S.), 442
Philippines, **312-14**
Poland, **315-17**
Police and Modern Society, The
(Vollmer), 420
Police brutality
Colombia, 71
Jamaica, 209
Somalia, 340
see also Torture
Police communications. *See*
Communications, police
Police, disciplining of. *See*
Disciplining of police
Police ethnic divisions. *See*
Ethnic divisions, police
Police Executive Research
Forum (U.S.), 431
Police, Fraternal Order of
(U.S.), 441
Police job conditions. *See*
Job conditions, police
Police mutinies and coups.
See Mutinies and
coups, police
Police ranks. *See* Ranks,
police
Police uniforms. *See*
Uniforms, police
Police unions. *See* Unions,
police
Police vehicles. *See*
Vehicles, police
Police weapons. *See* Weapons,
police
Political prisoners
Cuba, 87
Ethiopia, 111
Yemen (South), 478
Pollard, James, 418
Polygraphs, 422
Portugal, **318-21**
Postal Service (U.S.), 428
Prison conditions
Algeria, 5
Angola, 7
Argentina, 9-10
Bangladesh, 26
Belgium, 28
Bolivia, 32

Brazil, 39
Burma, 44
Burundi, 46
Cameroon, 47
Costa Rica, 83
Cuba, 87
Czechoslovakia, 92
Ecuador, 100
Egypt, 105
El Salvador, 108
Ethiopia, 111-12
Ghana, 151
Haiti, 161
India, 178
Indonesia, 181
Iran, 187
Israel, 196
Italy, 203
Jamaica, 209
Liberia, 246
Mexico, 260
Morocco, 267
Pakistan, 301
Panama, 304
Peru, 311
Philippines, 314
South Africa, 346
Sweden, 358
Syria, 367
Taiwan, 369
Tanzania, 373
Tunisia, 383
USSR, 398
United Kingdom, 414
United States, 443
Venezuela, 472
Yemen Arab Republic,
477
Yemen (South), 478
Yugoslavia, 480
Zaire, 483
Zambia, 486
Prisoner classification
(U.S.), 444, 447-48
Prison reform
France, 133
Iran, 187
Jordan, 223
United States, 442
Prisons, Bureau of (U.S.),
443, 444-45
Prisoners, rehabilitation of.
See Rehabilitation of
prisoners
Prison work
Chile, 62-63
Colombia, 78
Czechoslovakia, 92
Dominican Republic, 98
Ecuador, 100
Egypt, 105
Ethiopia, 112
Germany (West), 145
Greece, 154
Guinea, 158
Haiti, 161
Romania, 325
Sweden, 359
Taiwan, 369
Thailand, 376

United States, 446
Yugoslavia, 480
Private police
    Netherlands, 277
    United Kingdom, 405
Probation, Division of (U.S.),
    422-23
Prohibition, 420
Psychological treatment of
    offenders
    Netherlands, 281
    United States, 444, 453
Puerto Rico, **322-23**
Punishments. *See* specific
    punishments
Pushtunwali (Afghan tribal
    law), 1

Qadhafi, Muammar, 247, 248
Qatar, **524**

Racial divisions, police. *See*
    Ethnic divisions, police
Radio. *See* Communications
Raffles, Sir Thomas Stamford,
    335
Ranger Activities and
    Protection, Division of
    (U.S.), 423
Ranks, police
    Austria, 23
    Bangladesh, 25
    Belgium, 27, 28
    Bolivia, 31
    Botswana, 34
    Burma, 43
    Canada, 53
    China, 66
    Colombia, 73-74
    Costa Rica, 82
    Egypt, 103
    El Salvador, 108
    France, 131, 132
    Guatemala, 156
    Guinea, 157, 158
    India, 174-76, 175 *t.*
    Indonesia, 180
    Israel, 194-95
    Ivory Coast, 205, 206
    Korea (South), 233
    Kuwait, 237
    Liberia, 244-45
    Malaysia, 254
    Mauritania, 257
    Netherlands, 274, 275,
      277
    Nigeria, 291
    Pakistan, 298
    Panama, 303
    Senegal, 331
    Sierra Leone, 334
    Somalia, 340
    Sudan, 352
    Tanzania, 371
    Trinidad and Tobago,
      378
    Tunisia, 382
    Turkey, 386
    Vietnam, 474

Zaire, 482
Zambia, 484
Ray, James Earl, 51
RCMP. *See* Royal Canadian
    Mounted Police
Recruitment, police. *See*
    country names
Reform, prison. *See* Prison
    reform
Regimentation of citizenry
    Cuba, 86-87
    Iran, 184, 186
    Korea (North), 230
Rehabilitation of prisoners
    Cuba, 87-88
    Greece, 154
    Guinea, 158
    Guyana, 160
    Indonesia, 181
    Israel, 196
    Jamaica, 209
    Jordan, 223
    Kenya, 228
    Liberia, 245
    Netherlands, 281
    Peru, 311
    Poland, 316
    Somalia, 341
    South Africa, 346
    Sweden, 359
    Taiwan, 369
    Tunisia, 382
    United Kindgom, 413
    United States, 444
    Vietnam, 476
Remon, José Antonio, 302
Reschke, Erich, 136
Reza Pahlavi (Shah of Iran),
    184, 187
Riot control
    India, 173-74
    Japan, 215
    Malawi, 251
    Nigeria, 290
    Poland, 316
    Singapore, 335
    South Africa, 344
    Tunisia, 381
    United Kingdom, 408-409
    Uruguay, 468
Ritual murder
    Sierra Leone, 334
Rivers. *See* Coast and
    waterways police
Romania, **324-25**
Roosevelt, Franklin D., 423,
    444
Roosevelt, Theodore, 419
Roper, Daniel C., 422
Roushdi, Ahmed, 104
Rowan, Charles, 403
Royal Canadian Mounted Police
    (RCMP) (Mounties), 50-51,
    53-56
Rural law enforcement
    Algeria, 4
    Argentina, 9
    Australia, 13
    Belgium, 28

Chile, 61
Cyprus, 89
Ecuador, 99
Ethiopia, 110
Finland, 116, 123, 124
Guatemala, 155
Guinea, 157
Hong Kong, 164
India, 171, 172
Kenya, 226
Morocco, 265
Nicaragua, 284
Papua New Guinea, 305
Spain, 347
Tunisia, 381-82
Rwanda, 326-27

Sadat, Anwar el-, 103
Saharf, Sami, 102
St. Helena, 525
St. Kitts-Nevis, 525
St. Lucia, 526
St. Vincent and the
Grenadines, 527
Salazar, Antonio de Oliveria,
318, 320
Salim, Mamduh, 103
San Marino, 527-28
São Tomé and Príncipe, 528
Saudi Arabia, 328-30
Savage, Edward Hartwell, 418
SAVAK (Iran), 184, 185-86
Secret police
Bulgaria, 40
Hungary, 168-69
Indonesia, 181
Iran, 184, 185-86
Korea (South), 233
Poland, 316
Tunisia, 381
Zaire, 482
Secret Service (U.S.), 428,
429
Secret societies
Singapore, 337
Securities and Exchange
Commission (SEC) (U.S.),
428
Selborne, Lord, 354
Senegal, 331-32
Sentencing and sentencing
alternatives
Belgium, 28
France, 134-35
Germany (East), 137
Germany (West), 144
Iran, 187
Japan, 218
Netherlands, 281
Saudi Arabia, 329
Spain, 349
Sweden, 359-60
Tanzania, 373
Thailand, 376
United Kingdom, 414
United States, 443, 454
Zaire, 482
Seychelles, 528-30
Shah of Iran, 184, 187

Sharia. See Islamic law
Sierra Leone, 333-34
Sigurimi (Albania), 3
Singapore, 335-38
Smuggling. See individual
goods
Sobhuza I, King, 354
sokaiya (Japanese stock
extortion), 219
Solidarity (Polish labor
movement), 315, 316
Solomon Islands, 531
Somalia, 339-42
South Africa, 343-46
foreign aid and influence:
on Swaziland, 354
Soviet Union. See Union of
Soviet Socialist Republics
Spain, 347-49
foreign aid and influence:
Colombia, 59
Equatorial Guinea, 506
Peru, 309
Special Weapons and Tactics
teams. See SWAT
Sri Lanka, 350-51
Stalin, Joseph, 392-93, 394,
399
State, Department of (U.S.),
427
State police (U.S.), 429-30
Statute of Winchester (1285)
(United Kingdom), 401-402
Stone, Harlan F., 423
Stoning (punishment)
Iran, 189
Saudi Arabia, 329
Strauber, Johann, 20
Sudan, 352-53
Suharto, 181
Sun Yat-sen, 64
Suriname, 532
SWAT (Special Weapons And
Tactics teams)
Greece, 153
Swaziland, 354-55
Sweden, 356-61
foreign aid and influence:
Ethiopia, 110
Iran, 184
Swiss Guard, the (Vatican
City), 537
Switzerland, 362-65
Syria, 366-67

Taiwan, 368-70
Tanzania, 371-73
Tennessee Valley Authority
(TVA) (U.S.), 428
Terrorism
France, 129
Greece, 153
Interpol, 461
Italy, 201
Japan, 215
Peru, 310
Spain, 348

Texas Rangers (U.S.), 430
Thailand, **374-77**
Tito (Josip Broz), 479
Togo, **532-33**
Tonga, **533-34**
Torture
    Afghanistan, 2
    Austria, 24
    China, 65
    Colombia, 71
    Cuba, 87
    Ethiopia, 111
    Iraq, 189
    Kampuchea, 224
    Korea (South), 233
    Portugal, 320
    South Africa, 344
    Syria, 367
    Tunisia, 381
    Vietnam, 476
    Yemen (South), 478
    see also Police
      brutality
Touré, Sékou, 157, 158
Traffic police
    China, 66
    Ecuador, 99
    Finland, 123
    Germany (West), 139-40,
      143
    India, 174
    Indonesia, 180
    Israel, 194
    Japan, 215
    Netherlands, 275
    Panama, 303
    Saudi Arabia, 329
    Singapore, 335
    South Africa, 344
    Tunisia, 381
    United Kingdom, 409-10
    Venezuela, 471
Training, police. *See* country
  names
Transportation, Department of
  (U.S.), 426-27
Treasury, Department of
  (U.S.), 421, 427, 428, 429,
  455-56
Trials
    Colombia, 77
    India, 177
    Japan, 217-218
    Pakistan, 300-301
    Panama, 304
    Portugal, 320
    Romania, 325
    Saudi Arabia, 329
    Senegal, 332
    Somalia, 341
    Spain, 348
    Syria, 366
    United States, 455
Trinidad and Tobago, **378-80**
Tukey, Francis, 418
Tunisia, **381-84**
Turkey, **385-88**
Turks and Caicos, **534**
Tuvalu, **534**
Tweed, William Marcy, 419

Uganda, **389-90**
UNICORP (Federal Prison
  Industries) (U.S.), 446
Uniform Crime Reports (U.S.),
  466-67, 458 *t.*
Uniforms, police
    Argentina, 9
    Australia, 14
    Austria, 23
    Belgium, 27, 28
    Brazil, 38
    Burma, 43-44
    Cameroon, 47
    Canada, 53, 54
    Colombia, 72-73
    Costa Rica, 82
    Czechoslovakia, 91
    Denmark, 95
    El Salvador, 107
    Ethiopia, 110
    Fiji, 114
    Finland, 125
    France, 130, 131
    Ghana, 148
    Greece, 153
    Guatemala, 156
    Guyana, 159
    Hong Kong, 165
    Hungary, 168, 169
    Iran, 185
    Iraq, 188
    Ireland, 190-91
    Israel, 194
    Ivory Coast, 205
    Japan, 213
    Jordan, 221
    Kenya, 227
    Korea (South), 233
    Kuwait, 237
    Lesotho, 242-43
    Liberia, 245
    Libya, 247
    Malaysia, 255
    New Zealand, 282
    Nicaragua, 284
    Norway, 295-96
    Pakistan, 299
    Panama, 303
    Papua New Guinea, 305
    Peru, 310
    Philippines, 313
    Poland, 316
    Puerto Rico, 322
    Saudi Arabia, 328
    Senegal, 331
    Sierra Leone, 333-34
    Singapore, 335
    South Africa, 343
    Spain, 347, 348
    Sudan, 352
    Swaziland, 355
    Sweden, 357
    Switzerland, 363
    Trinidad and Tobago,
      379
    Turkey, 386
    USSR, 396
    United Kingdom, 403,
      410
    Vietnam, 475

Yugoslavia, 479
Zambia, 485
Union of Soviet Socialist
Republics, **391-400**
   foreign aid and influence:
     Germany (East), 136
     Korea (North), 231
     Vietnam, 475, 476
Unions, police
   United States, 419
United Arab Emirates, **535**
United Kingdom, **401-415**
   foreign aid and influence:
     Anguilla, 491
     Brunei, 499
     Cayman Islands, 501
     Dominica, 505
     Falklands, 506
     Gibraltar, 509
     Greece, 152
     India, 171
     Jamaica, 208, 209
     Kenya, 225, 227
     Kiribati, 512
     Malawi, 251
     Malaysia, 252
     Montserrat, 521
     New Zealand, 282
     Nigeria, 286, 292, 293
     Pakistan, 297, 299
     St. Helena, 525
     Seychelles, 529
     Sierra Leone, 334
     Somalia, 339-40, 341
     Sri Lanka, 350
     Sudan, 352, 353
     Swaziland, 354
     Tanzania, 371-73
     Thailand, 374, 375
     Trinidad and Tobago, 379
     Uganda, 389, 390
     Vanuatu, 536
     Zambia, 484, 485
United Nations (UN)
   Lesotho, 241
   Somalia, 341
   South Africa, 346
   Zaire, 481
United States, **416-67**
   foreign aid and influence:
     Afghanistan, 1
     Bolivia, 30
     Costa Rica, 81-82
     Guatemala, 155
     Iran, 184, 185
     Japan, 211, 218
     Jordan, 221
     Korea (South), 232
     Laos, 238
     Lesotho, 241
     Liberia, 244, 245
     Pakistan, 297
     Panama, 302, 303
     Philippines, 312, 313
     Somalia, 339
     Thailand, 374, 375
     Vietnam, 473, 474
     Zaire, 481
Universal Declaration of Human
   Rights, 259, 456

Urban law enforcement
   Algeria, 4
   Argentina, 9
   Australia, 13
   Cyprus, 89
   Ecuador, 99
   Ethiopia, 110
   Finland, 116
   India, 171, 172
   Iran, 185
   Morocco, 264
   Netherlands, 273-74
   Nicaragua, 284
   Portugal, 318
   Tunisia, 381
   United States, 430
Uruguay, **468-69**
USNCB. *See* National Central
   Bureau - Interpol (U.S.)

Vanuatu, **536**
Vatican City, **537**
Vehicles, police
   India, 173
   Japan, 214
   Jordan, 220
   Kenya, 226
   Netherlands, 275
   Somalia, 340
   United Kingdom, 409
Venezuela, **470-72**
Veterans Administration
   (U.S.), 427, 428
Vietnam, **473-76**
Vigilantes
   United States, 417, 418
Vollmer, August, 420

Warren, Earl, 420
Washington, George, 429
Waterways. *See* Coast and
   waterways police
Weapons, police
   Argentina, 9
   Australia, 14
   Austria, 22
   Belgium, 27, 28
   Brazil, 38
   Burma, 44
   Cameroon, 47
   Canada, 53, 54
   Chad, 59
   Colombia, 72-73
   Congo, 79
   Denmark, 95
   Ethiopia, 110
   Fiji, 114
   Finland, 118
   Greece, 152
   Guatemala, 156
   Guyana, 159
   Hong Kong, 165
   India, 172
   Indonesia, 181
   Iraq, 188
   Ireland, 191
   Israel, 194
   Jordan, 220, 221
   Kenya, 227
   Kuwait, 237

Liberia, 245
Libya, 247
Malawi, 251
Morocco, 264-65, 266
Nicaragua, 284
Nigeria, 290
Norway, 296
Papua New Guinea, 305
Peru, 310
Puerto Rico, 322
Rwanda, 326-27
Senegal, 331
Sierra Leone, 334
South Africa, 343, 344
Spain, 347, 348
Swaziland, 355
Sweden, 357
Trinidad and Tobago, 379
Turkey, 386
United Kingdom, 410
United States, 430
Uruguay, 468
Venezuela, 471
Vietnam, 475
Yemen (South), 478
Yugoslavia, 479
Zambia, 484
Weapons, restrictions on
Algeria, 5
Greece, 154
Japan, 219
Mexico, 268
Sri Lanka, 351
Wellington, Duke of, 403
Wells, Alice Stebbins, 419
Western Samoa, **537-38**
Whipping and flogging
(punishment)
Cyprus, 89-90
Kenya, 228
Liberia, 245
Malaysia, 255
Pakistan, 300
Saudi Arabis, 329
Singapore, 337
South Africa, 346
Sri Lanka, 351
Tanzania, 372, 373
Uganda, 390
United States, 417,
441, 443, 450
Zambia, 486
White-collar crime
Australia, 19
China, 68
Japan, 219
see also Securities and
Exchange Commission
Wickersham, George W., 420
Winchester, Statute of (1282)
(United Kingdom), 401-402

Witchcraft
Nigeria, 292
Witness Protection Program (U.S.), 429
Women police
Australia, 13-14
Botswana, 34
Canada, 55
China, 65
Colombia, 71
Ethiopia, 110
Finland, 123
Germany (West), 140
Ghana, 148
Greece, 152
Hong Kong, 166
Hungary, 168
India, 172
Indonesia, 180
Ireland, 190, 191
Italy, 199
Jamaica, 208
Japan, 212
Jordan, 220
Korea (South), 233
Lesotho, 242, 243
Malawi, 251
Malaysia, 254
Netherlands, 275
Nicaragua, 284
Nigeria, 290
Norway, 295
Pakistan, 299
Panama, 303
Peru, 309
Philippines, 313
Poland, 316
Seychelles, 529
Sierra Leone, 333
Singapore, 335
Somalia, 340
South Africa, 345
Swaziland, 355
Tunisia, 381
United States, 419
Uruguay, 468
Work. *See* Labor camps; Prison work

Yagoda, G., 393
Yakuza, 219
Yemen Arab Republic, **477**
Yemen (South), **478**
Yezhov, N.I., 393
Youth. *See* Juvenile offenders
Youth Corrections Act (U.S.),
444
Yugoslavia, **479-80**

Zaire, **481-83**
Zaisser, Wilhelm, 136
Zambia, **484-86**
Zimbabwe, **487-88**